D1474304

JAMES H. CHARLESWORTH is
George L. Collord Professor of New
Testament Language and Literature,
and director and editor of the Princeton
Dead Sea Scrolls Project, Princeton
Theological Seminary. He is the author
or editor of more than sixty-five books
and four hundred articles.

THE GOOD AND
EVIL SERPENT

THE ANCHOR YALE BIBLE REFERENCE LIBRARY

THE GOOD AND EVIL *S*ERPENT

How a Universal Symbol Became Christianized

JAMES H. CHARLESWORTH

YALE
Yale UNIVERSITY PRESS
AYBRL New Haven and London

The Anchor Yale logo is a trademark of Yale University.

Copyright © 2010 by James H. Charlesworth.

Designed by Leslie Phillips.
Set in Sabon type by dix!

Printed in the United States of America by Sheridan Books, Inc.

Library of Congress Cataloging-in-Publication Data

Charlesworth, James H.
     The good and evil serpent : how a universal symbol became christianized /
James H. Charlesworth.
          p.   cm.—(The Anchor Yale Bible reference library)
     Includes bibliographical references and index.
     ISBN 978-0-300-14082-8 (alk. paper)
     1. Devil—Christianity. 2. Symbolism. 3. Snakes—Religious aspects—Christianity.
4. Good and evil.   5. Good and evil—Religious aspects—Christianity.   I. Title.
BT982.C43   2009

220.6'4—dc22   2008036207

A catalogue record for this book is available from the British Library.

This paper meets the requirements of ANSI/NISO Z39.48-1992 (Permanence of Paper).

10 9 8 7 6 5 4 3 2 1

For faithful *viātōrēs* and biblical colleagues
who have shared parts of two millennia with me:

Savas Agourides   Jim Armstrong   Peder and Inge Borgen

Frank Cross   Archbishop Damianos   Tom Gillespie

Martin and Mariana Hengel   Doron and Michal Mendels

Pat Miller   Petr and Věra Porkorný   Jim Roberts

James Sanders   Moody and Jane Smith

Walter Weaver   Orval Wintermute

and those especially close who passed over:

Hugh and Jean Anderson

Pierre Benoit

Ray Brown

Roland de Vaux

Noel Freedman

John Priest

William Stinespring

—indeed, all who helped me intermittently enjoy
the wise serpent's *viāticum*

Contents

Preface

Writing this book has been a journey. I have been searching for spiritual insights. For six years of research, I have attempted to discover what the serpent may have symbolized for the ancients as they explored the perennial questions that define the human. During this period, I tried to keep in mind all who question boldly and freely. Since before attending seminary I have admired the great minds who with apparent Promethean arrogance focus on the Scriptures, boldly searching for the original meaning(s) of some perplexing passages. Thus, I am writing not so much for scholars, preachers, or rabbis as for those who are searching for answers in a culture shaped and influenced by the church and synagogue. I am writing for those who are no longer afraid of freely studying the books canonized as the Bible. Such free inquiry was often condemned in the past, especially after the Palestinian Jesus Movement became an institution. The leading thinkers in this organization, the church, had to fight for its survival against many powerful ideologies and mythologies. In the following pages, I will clarify how the Asclepius story threatened the "Jesus Gospel."

Did the Fourth Evangelist inherit an ophidian Christology; that is, was the Evangelist's conception of Jesus influenced by the symbolism of a serpent? Did this genius imagine Jesus in terms of the serpent symbolism that had developed for millennia prior to his masterpiece? Did he formulate his presentation of Jesus, whom he hailed as God's Son and the Christ, in some way with images obtained from the mythology of the serpent?

I have found that the commentators on the Fourth Gospel have missed the full meaning of John 3:13–16. It is evident that some of them were afraid to boldly and freely raise fresh questions. Far too many did not wrestle with the original meaning of this passage. Perhaps now, at the beginning of the third millennium, it is possible for all of us to think faithfully and creatively. Is that not the freedom Jesus shared with his earliest followers?

I see my task as a professor of New Testament at Princeton Theological Seminary rather simply. All of us who are interested in hearing the truth need to cleanse our ears of the disturbances in Western society. Then we may hear the authors who speak to us from the ancient canonical and extra-canonical texts. There is a vast amount to learn from those who lived long ago in the Near East. Some authors of biblical books and works contemporaneous with them were geniuses. Sometimes they understood aspects of life better than any of us today. This is especially clear when we examine carefully and afresh the thoughts and language of the authors of Genesis 3 and John 3.

If I can help some to appreciate the creativity of the biblical authors and to read the Bible free from dogmas that deafen our ears to eternal truths, then my joy in writing will be complete. I am not eager for all to agree with my attempt to understand the biblical texts, but I do urge all attracted by the Bible to attend personally to the words in our texts. The Scriptures are our main source for inspiration. As those in the synagogue and church have endeavored to teach, despite some of their administrators, the ancient writings contain echoes of the still small voice that resonates within our hearts.

Finally, it might be of interest to some readers to know why I have been attracted to this subject. Why would a scholar at Princeton spend six years studying the images and symbols of serpents? Rather than consider me nuts, virtually all who have heard about my forays into ancient folklore stop, listen, and then utter words like: "Wow, that is fascinating."

What then is my answer to this question? I grew up on the eastern fringes of the Everglades. Rumors about dangerous snakes would circulate around Delray Beach, Coconut Grove, and Coral Gables—the places in which I lived in the 1950s and 1960s. Some of these stories were about snakes finding their way into homes. There were reports of a woman entering the bathroom only to find a moccasin in the bathtub. I also recall the account of a woman who sat down on a toilet and looked down, between her legs, at a poisonous snake in the water below.

I heard about coral snakes and feared these small reptiles that hide threateningly under Palmetto palms. The attractively colored snakes have venom more deadly than cobras. My encounter with a gigantic serpent, however, was unusual. This frozen moment in time may have shaped my fascination with snakes far more than I may realize.

Thinking back to 1953, when I was thirteen, I remember a golden-domed figure rising before me. He was massive in size and weight. The creature reflected the sun that poured down on us from the right. I remember that his eyes were on the level of my own, and I was then roughly 5 feet, 5 inches (1.65 meters) tall. He swayed before me. I was simultaneously frightened and awestruck at this wonder of creation. He stood erect, and the sun transformed him into blinding gold. For years I dismissed from memory the height of this monster, and how time and eternity stopped as we looked deep into each other's eyes. You, the reader, will think I have succumbed to mythology.

But the encounter transcends the normal, and it happened. The place was the Serpentarium in Miami, Florida. Dr. William E. Haast, the head of the Serpentarium, was beginning to milk a king cobra. He was assisted by two young men. The monster shook loose and slithered toward me over the recently cut green grass. Then he chose me from about one hundred spectators. He swiftly rose up and stared at me. I felt him towering over me, and the sun flashing off his golden hood, which was now fully expanded. The only words Haast spoke were, "Don't move, son." Obviously, I didn't.

Almost fifty years later I talked with Dr. Haast for the first time. We spoke over the phone on March 9, 2001. He said something like, "It is odd that you would remember that event so long ago." I thought to myself, "It would be odd not to remember a life-threatening confrontation with a king cobra." Dr. Haast informed me that the cobra weighed about 20 pounds (less than 10 kilograms) and was about 15 feet (4.6 meters) long. I had imagined it was over 20 feet (6 meters) long and well over 300 pounds (100 kilograms). Had I also imagined how high this wondrous creature could "stand"? Can a king cobra raise itself to 5 feet (1.5 meters)?

Long after the encounter, I learned that a serpent can raise itself one-third of its length. This gigantic king cobra could have raised itself to about 5 feet. I was not imagining or embellishing the encounter when I remembered how he faced me, eyes to eyes.

I cannot assume that you have "enjoyed" a similar experience. Still, I am convinced that we have all encountered the exceptional creature we call the snake. Biblical scholars who attended the meeting of a New Testament congress at Duke University in 1976 were alarmed when they heard about a poisonous snake found dead in the basement of my newly constructed house in Durham, North Carolina. They spoke as if such occurrences were conceivable only in the wilderness. Thus, for most of us living in Western societies, the snake is not a friend but a sinister and feared monster that symbolically is associated with sin. Jews, Christians, and Muslims have informed me for over six years that the snake is the symbol of the Devil, Satan.

My research will take the reader back in time, especially into the cultures that shaped the Holy Land from about 2000 BCE to about 400 CE. The ancients also portrayed the serpent as sinister; the animal could symbolize Satan. But primarily, they used the serpent to symbolize numerous human ideals, as we shall soon see. Thus, it is impossible for me to agree with F. S. Bodenheimer, who claimed that in antiquity serpents "must have been held in abhorrence in general." Bodenheimer's use of "must" indicates a failure to dig deeply into the question concerning the symbolic meaning of the serpent in ancient cultures. The present book raises many questions; these are united by one: What did the serpent symbolize in antiquity?

My investigations of the symbolic meaning of the serpent led me to explore serpent images from approximately 40,000 BCE to the present. I endeavored to read ancient documents in search of the symbolic meaning of the serpent. Such research was then supported by a study of ancient art as well as by an exploration of archaeological data. It became obvious that the serpent was often held in esteem, adored, and even worshipped. From studying images and texts, I was surprised by one discovery: almost all gods and goddesses in the first century CE were accompanied by serpents or were perceived as serpents.

Such discoveries became possible because I kept two lines of inquiry in central focus. First, I sought to discern what the serpent symbolized to the ancients (while keeping an eye on what was happening recently, especially in India, Africa, Australia, and the southern states in the United States). This task took me into diverse disciplines (viz., the philology of all ancient Near Eastern languages, archaeology, anthropology, sociology, iconography, and symbology). Second, simultaneously observing the various meanings of serpent symbolism, I periodically refined criteria for discerning which of the possible meanings was probably intended by the artist or author (authorial intent) and what additional meanings might have been added by those who saw the object or read the text (readers' response).

No book has been more difficult for me to write. None has taken so long. Yet the joys of discovery have been exceptional. I feel we have lost the oneness with nature that shaped the spiritual journeys of our ancestors. I know we habitually fail to hear the subtleties in symbols that alone make life full of excitement. May you share this joy as you rediscover yourself in the texts and the images. May you obtain the poetic vision of the Yahwist and the Fourth Evangelist.

Do the biblical narratives not indicate that the first humans and Jesus knew the wisdom of the serpent? Can one wisely claim to be perceptive and remain in ignorance?

JHC
Princeton Theological Seminary, Universität Tübingen,
Ecole Biblique de Jérusalem,
Università degli Studi di Napoli Federico II,
Albright Institute in Jerusalem,
and Hebrew University, Jerusalem

Acknowledgments

I intend this book for all those who approach the Bible with the freedom to raise challenging questions. Those who say that they believe "everything" in the Bible probably have never read everything in the Bible. The Bible is full of passages that are replete with meaning, but the symbolic and deeply theological meaning of a passage has far too often been missed by many, including biblical experts. The present work reveals that the symbolic meaning of a passage in my favorite biblical book, the Fourth Gospel, has been missed by modern commentators. And many of these experts have written two or three volumes on the twenty-one chapters in the Fourth Gospel. Yet the meaning of John 3:14 was perceived, if only in nuances, by such luminaries as Justin Martyr, Irenaeus, Augustine, and Calvin.

If my research enables others to appreciate the biblical record, then it has been worthwhile. If my labors help others to puzzle over obtuse or confusing passages and to discover a hidden gem of wisdom, then I will have been richly rewarded.

I am grateful to so many who have helped me in this study. Joe Zias of the Rockeller Museum, Jerusalem, helped me study the artifacts in that famous museum. Zaher Barakat, a specialist in antiquities, helped me obtain serpent objects from ancient Israel. Dr. Johnny Awwad, now of the Near East School of Theology in Beirut, helped me find and obtain many of the books and articles cited. Michael Davis, Shane A. Berg, Joseph M. Eason, and Brian D. Rhea have also assisted me in locating sources and books in Princeton, and Enno Popkos has aided me with this task in Tübingen. I appreciate Susan Laity's editorial skills; she found some errors and helped me improve this work. Professor Hermann Lichtenberger has been of inestimable assistance as I continued my work in the Institut für antikes Judentum und hellenistische Religionsgeschichte in the Eberhard-Karls Universität Tübingen. Richard C. Miller, Scott J. Pearson, and James J. Foster helped me with digitizing and cropping images. Alice Y. Yafeh helped me complete the work on the Selected Bibliography. Ross Voss assisted me in the study of serpent images in Ashkelon. Khader Baidun, an antiquities dealer in Jerusalem's Old City who has provided artifacts for Moshe Dayan, Nelson Glueck, and others, as well as a friend for over thirty years, worked with me to obtain ancient ophidian objects. Dr. Shimon Gibson drew my attention to the "Bezetha Vase," which is now in the Palestine Exploration Fund office in London, and helped me study this vase and contextualize it in ancient Jerusalem. Professor O. Keel spent days with me in Freiburg, helping me to comprehend the subtleties of symbology. Professor A. Biran shared with me his discoveries at Dan. Professors McGrath, Mann, and Ryan of the Warburg Institute in London helped me peruse the vast amount of images of the serpent in antiquity and more recently. Dr. Mikhail Piotrovsky, Director of the State Hermitage Museum in St. Petersburg, was most gracious and helped me study the priceless treasures in that museum. Professors Del Verme and De Simone of the Università degli Studi di Napoli Federico II helped with my work in the Archaeological Museum in Naples and in Pompeii. Lara Guglielmo was a devoted and gifted research assistant when I was a visiting professor in Naples. Dr. Michal Dayagi-Mendels and Professor Doron Mendels continue to be special dialogue partners. I express appreciations to the Research Council of Princeton Theological Seminary, the Alexander von Humboldt Stiftung, the American Schools of Oriental Research (Annual Professor), and the Hebrew University, Jerusalem (Lady Davis Professor), for financial assistance. Grants from the Foundation on Christian Origins and the Edith C. Blum Foundation helped me cover some expenses for research.

Numerous libraries and museums have offered exceptional assistance and provided some essential photographs or images. I cannot list them all, but I am especially indebted for such help and images to the State Hermitage Museum in St. Petersburg, the British Museum in London, the Palestine Exploration Fund in London, the Università degli Studi di Napoli Federico II and Archaeological Museum in Naples, the National Library and National Museum in Athens, the Archaeological Museum at Epidaurus, the Archaeological Museums on Crete at Herakleion and Chania, the Metropolitan Museum of Art in New York, the Brooklyn Museum of Art, the Skirball Museum in Jerusalem, and the Israel Museum in Jerusalem. The initials JHC at the end of an illustration's caption indicate the photograph was taken by the author. My colleagues, old and new, at the Ecole Biblique generously supported me during the last year in which I worked in the famous library in the Ecole. The late Noel Freedman discussed each chapter with me, making valuable suggestions for improving the clarity of presentation; he again proved to be a super editor. Additional appreciations and indebtedness will be noted in the following pages.

Abbreviations

Ancient Sources

1 Apol.	Justin Martyr, *1 Apology*
1 En	*1 Enoch*
2 Bar	*2 Baruch*
3 Bar	*3 Baruch*
4 Mac	4 Maccabees
1QH	Thanksgiving Hymns from Qumran
1QM	War Scroll from Qumran
11QT	Temple Scroll from Qumran
AcJn	*Acts of John*
AcThom	*Acts of Thomas*
Adv. Haer.	Irenaeus, *Against Heresies*
Agr.	Philo, *De agricultura*
Alex.	Lucian, *Alexander the False Prophet*
Ant	Josephus, *Jewish Antiquities*
ApEl	*Apocalypse of Elijah*
ApMos	*Apocalypse of Moses*
ApVir	*Apocalypse of the Virgin*
b.	Babylonian Talmud
B. Bat.	*Baba Batra*
Barn.	*Barnabas*
Ber.	*Berakot*
Cels.	Origen, *Contra Celsum*
Cyn.	Xenophon, *Cynegeticus*
Descr.	Pausanias, *Descriptio Graeciae*
Dial.	Justin Martyr, *Dialogue with Trypho*
GosThom	*Gospel of Thomas*
Haer.	Hippolytus, *Refutation of All Heresies*
HE	Eusebius, *History of the Church*
HelSynPr	*Hellenistic Synagogal Prayers*
Hist.	Herodotus, *Histories;* Tacitus, *Histories*
Hist. an.	Aristotle, *Historia Animalium*
j.	Jerusalem Talmud
Leg.	Philo, *Legum allegoriae*
Ling.	Varro, *On the Latin Language*
LivPro	*Lives of the Prophets*

m.	Mishnah
Metam.	Ovid, *Metamorphoses*
Nat.	Pliny, *Natural History*
Nat. an.	Aelian, *De natura animalium*
Nat. d.	Cicero, *De natura deorum*
OdesSol	*Odes of Solomon*
Pan.	Epiphanius, *Panarion*
Part. an.	Aristotle, *Parts of Animals*
PG	Eusebius, *Preparation for the Gospel*
PssSol	*Psalms of Solomon*
QG	Philo, *Questions and Answers on Genesis*
Rosh Hash.	*Rosh Hashanah*
Sanh.	*Sanhedrin*
Sat.	Juvenal, *Satires*
t.	Tosephta
Ta'an.	*Ta'anit*
Vita	*Vita Adae et Evae*
Wis	Wisdom of Solomon

Modern Sources

AA	*Archäologischer Anzeiger*
AcOr	*Acta orientalia*
AfO	*Archiv für Orientforschung*
AJA	*American Journal of Archaeology*
AJSL	*American Journal of Semitic Languages and Literatures*
ANEP	*Ancient Near East in Pictures Relating to the Old Testament.* Edited by J. B. Pritchard. 3rd ed. Princeton, 1954.
ANET	*Ancient Near Eastern Texts Relating to the Old Testament.* Edited by J. B. Pritchard. 3rd ed. Princeton, 1954.
ANF	*Ante-Nicene Fathers*
ANRW	*Aufstieg und Niedergang der römischen Welt*
AntW	*Antike Welt. Zeitschrift für Archäologie und Kulturgeschichte*
ASOR	American Schools of Oriental Research
AYBD	*Anchor Yale Bible Dictionary.* Edited by D. N. Freedman. 6 vols. New York, 1992.
BAR	*Biblical Archaeology Review*
BASOR	*Bulletin of the American Schools of Oriental Research*
BBR	*Bulletin for Biblical Research*
BeO	*Bibbia e oriente*
BHH	*Biblisch-historisches Handwörterbuch: Landeskunde, Geschichte, Religion, Kultur.* Edited by B. Reicke and L. Rost. 4 vols. Göttingen, 1962–1966.
BN	*Biblische Notizen*
BRev	*Bible Review*
BZ	*Biblische Zeitschrift*
CBQ	*Catholic Biblical Quarterly*
ChrEg	*Chronique d'Egypte*

Context	*The Context of Scripture: Canonical Compositions, Monumental Inscriptions and Archival Documents from the Biblical World*. Edited by William W. Hallo and K. Lawson Younger, Jr. 3 vols. Leiden, 1997, 2000, 2002.
CRAI	*Comptes rendus de l'Académie des inscriptions et belles-lettres*
CUL	*A Concordance of the Ugaritic Literature*. R. E. Whitaker. Cambridge, Mass., 1972.
DACL	*Dictionnaire d'archéologie chrétienne et de liturgie*. Edited by F. Cabrol. 15 vols. Paris, 1907–1953.
DCA	*A Dictionary of Christian Antiquities*. Edited by William Smith and Samuel Cheetham. Vol. 1: Boston, 1875. Vol. 2: London, 1880.
DCH	*Dictionary of Classical Hebrew*. Edited by D. J. A. Clines. Sheffield, 1993–.
DDD	*Dictionary of Deities and Demons in the Bible*. Edited by K. vander Toorn, B. Becking, and P. W. van der Horst. Leiden, 1995.
Di	*Dialog*
DJD	Discoveries in the Judaean Desert. Oxford, 1955–.
DNP	*Der neue Pauly: Enzyklopädie der Antike*. Edited by H. Cancik and H. Schneider. Stuttgart, 1996–.
EAA	*Enciclopedia dell'arte antica, classica e orientale* (Rome, 1958–1984)
EncJud	*Encyclopaedia Judaica*. 16 vols. Jerusalem, 1972.
EPRO	Études préliminairies aux religions orientales dans l'Empire romain
ER	*The Encyclopedia of Religion*. Edited by M. Eliade. 16 vols. New York, 1987.
ERE	*Encyclopedia of Religion and Ethics*. Edited by J. Hastings. 13 vols. New York, 1908–1927. Reprint, 7 vols., 1951.
ErIsr	*Eretz-Israel*
EstBib	*Estudios bíblicos*
ETL	*Ephemerides theologicae lovanienses*
ExpTim	*Expository Times*
FF	*Forschungen und Fortschritte*
GCDS	*Graphic Concordance to the Dead Sea Scrolls*. Edited by J. H. Charlesworth et al. Tübingen, 1991.
GKC	*Gesenius' Hebrew Grammar*. Edited by E. Kautzsch. Translated by A. E. Cowley. 2nd ed. Oxford, 1910.
Hen	*Henoch*
HR	*History of Religions*
HTR	*Harvard Theological Review*
HUCA	*Hebrew Union College Annual*
IDB	*The Interpreter's Dictionary of the Bible*. Edited by G. A. Buttrick. 4 vols. Nashville, 1962.
IMJ	*Israel Museum Journal*
IntJPsycholRelig	*International Journal for the Psychology of Religion*

ISBE	*The International Standard Bible Encyclopedia.* Edited by G. W. Bromiley. 4 vols. Grand Rapids, 1979–1988.
JAOS	*Journal of the American Oriental Society*
JBL	*Journal of Biblical Literature*
JdI	*Jahrbuch des deutschen archäologischen Instituts*
JNES	*Journal of Near Eastern Studies*
JRA	*Journal of Roman Archaeology*
JRS	*Journal of Roman Studies*
JSJ	*Journal for the Study of Judaism in the Persian, Hellenistic, and Roman Periods*
JTS	*Journal of Theological Studies*
JWI	*Journal of the Warburg Institute*
KBL	Koehler, L., W. Baumgartner, and J. J. Stamm. *The Hebrew and Aramaic Lexicon of the Old Testament.* Translated and edited under the supervision of M. E. J. Richardson. 4 vols. Leiden, 1994–1999.
KJV	King James Version
KTU	*Die keilalphabetischen Texte aus Ugarit.* Edited by M. Dietrich, O. Loretz, and J. Sanmartín. AOAT 24/1. Neukirchen-Vluyn, 1976.
LexSyr	C. Brockelmann. *Lexicon Syriacum.* 2nd ed. Halle, 1928.
LCL	Loeb Classical Library
LIMC	*Lexicon Iconographicum Mythologiae Classicae*
LSJM	Henry George Liddell, Robert Scott, Henry Stuart Jones, and Roderick McKenzie. *A Greek-English Lexicon.* 9th rev. ed. Oxford, 1996.
LTK	*Lexicon für Theologie und Kirche*
LXX	Septuagint [the Greek translation of the Old Testament]
MDAI	*Mitteilungen des Deutschen archäologischen Instituts*
NEAEHL	*The New Encyclopedia of Archaeological Excavations in the Holy Land.* Edited by E. Stern. 4 vols. Jerusalem, 1993.
NEB	New English Bible
NKJV	New King James Version
NPNF1 (2)	*Nicene and Post-Nicene Fathers,* Series 1 (Series 2)
NRSV	New Revised Standard Version
NTS	*New Testament Studies*
OBO	Orbis biblicus et orientalis
OCD	*Oxford Classical Dictionary.* Edited by S. Hornblower and A. Spawforth. 3rd ed. Oxford, 1996.
OEANE	*The Oxford Encyclopedia of Archaeology in the Near East.* Edited by E. M. Meyers. New York, 1997.
OTP	*Old Testament Pseudepigrapha.* Edited by J. H. Charlesworth. 2 vols. New York, 1983.
Pauly-Wissowa	*Paulys Realencyclopädie der classischen Altertumswissenschaft.* Munich, 1914–72.
Payne Smith	*Thesaurus syriacus.* Edited by R. Payne Smith. Oxford, 1879–1901.
PEF	*Palestine Exploration Fund*
Per	*Perspectives*

PGL	*Patristic Greek Lexicon.* Edited by G. W. H. Lampe. Oxford, 1968.
RA	*Revue d'assyriologie et d'archéologie orientale*
RAr	*Revue archéologique*
RB	*Revue biblique*
RE	*Realencyklopädie für protestantische Theologie und Kirche*
RevQ	*Revue de Qumran*
RHR	*Revue de l'histoire des religions*
RS	Ras Shamra
RSO	*Rivista degli studi orientali*
RSR	*Recherches de science religieuse*
RSV	Revised Standard Version
SJOT	*Scandinavian Journal of the Old Testament*
SJT	*Scottish Journal of Theology*
SPap	*Studia papyrologica*
TANAKH	*JPS Hebrew-English TANAKH.* Philadelphia: The Jewish Publication Society, 1999.
TBT	*The Bible Today*
TDNT	*Theological Dictionary of the New Testament.* Edited by G. Kittel and G. Friedrich. Translated by G. W. Bromiley. 10 vols. Grand Rapids, 1964–1976.
TDOT	*Theological Dictionary of the Old Testament*
TLL	*Thesaurus linguae latinae*
TWNT	*Theologisches Wörterbuch zum Neuen Testament*
TynBul	*Tyndale Bulletin*
UF	*Ugarit-Forschungen*
VT	*Vetus Testamentum*
VTSup	Supplements to Vetus Testamentum
WO	*Die Welt des Orients*
WUNT	Wissenschaftliche Untersuchungen zum Neuen Testament
ZAW	*Zeitschrift für die alttestamentliche Wissenschaft*
ZNW	*Zeitschrift für die neutestamentliche Wissenschaft und die Kunde der älteren Kirche*

Other Abbreviations

BHS	*Biblia Hebraica Stuttgartensia*
LB	Late Bronze
MB	Middle Bronze
MT	Masoretic Text
N.F.	Neue Folge [= New Series]
N.V.	Non Videre [a publication not seen]

THE GOOD AND
EVIL SERPENT

1 Introduction

STARTING POINT: THE PERPLEXING NATURE OF JOHN 3:14

The present search began in a PhD seminar in Princeton. I was bothered by a passage and asked the members of the seminar to assist me in obtaining some insight into what it could mean. The passage is John 3:14–15:

> And as Moses lifted up the serpent in the wilderness,
> So it is necessary for the Son of Man to be lifted up,
> In order that all who are believing in him may have eternal life.[1]

In the Christian Bible no passage is so misunderstood and yet equally full of symbolism as these two verses.

What is the symbolic meaning of these two verses? They reflect the author's refined thoughts because they are placed at a crucial point in the discussion between Jesus and Nicodemus. They come at the climax of Jesus' words to this "ruler of the Judean leaders." The significance of these words is also obvious because they have been carefully couched by the Fourth Evangelist in some of his common technical terms *(termini technici)*, specifically "lifted up," "Son of Man," "all who are believing," and "eternal life."

Virtually any student of the Fourth Gospel will readily grasp the major point the Evangelist is making. It is clear that the author is foreshadowing Jesus' crucifixion. The key verb is "to lift up,"[2] which obtains singularly important Christological meaning in the Fourth Gospel. This well-known Greek verb attains a new meaning here; it signifies that Jesus' crucifixion was not a failure but an exaltation; note especially 12:32–33, " 'And I, when I am lifted up from the earth, shall draw all to myself.' He said this to signify by what death he was about to die."

1

The major problem remains: Why does the author mention the serpent? Another problem is the meaning of the simile. Does "as" denote only the action of lifting up—Jesus was lifted up as the serpent was lifted up—or does it also intimate an association of what is lifted up: the serpent and then Jesus? That is, has the Fourth Evangelist inherited a typos for Jesus, the serpent? Is the author suggesting that Jesus is being compared to the serpent raised up by Moses? Initially it seems obvious that the author of the Fourth Gospel cannot be claiming that Jesus is a serpent. Such a thought repels us as being abhorrent, since the serpent, as snake, is a pejorative image in Western cultures (especially among Jews, Christians, and Muslims).

New Testament scholars habitually fail to raise the crucial question: Did the Fourth Evangelist, or those in the Johannine community, imagine that Jesus could be portrayed symbolically as a serpent? Most New Testament experts tend to assume prima facie that those possibilities are nil, taking for granted that serpents symbolically denote evil and demons. These scholars presuppose that such a suggestion cannot be contemplated as appropriate for Jesus. They reject, out of hand, that such an allusion is possible for the sophisticated and refined theology of the Fourth Evangelist. In one sense they are right. Of course, the Fourth Evangelist surely cannot be associated with the Ophites, those "heretical" so-called Christians who worshipped Jesus as the serpent, according to Epiphanius of Salamis.[3]

In our Western culture the snake has become only a pejorative symbol (as portrayed in the movies about Indiana Jones). The first and last books in the Christian Bible leave most readers with a foreboding fear of snakes. We think about "the wild animal," the snake, that deceived Eve and Adam and introduced sin and death into creation. We obtain such symbolism from Genesis 3, and we inherit from Revelation many symbols that have shaped our Western culture. Surely one of these is the snake or dragon that comes to the cosmic woman and futilely attempts to devour her child (Rev 12:1–6). Then Michael and his hosts fight and defeat the dragon, the ancient serpent, who is the Devil and Satan (12:7–9).

The conception of the snake as the embodiment of evil has permeated our Western culture. Young people who have had no means of learning about the myths that explain the snake as evil nevertheless have dreams that mysteriously seem to be mirror images of those myths. Carl Gustav Jung refers to a dream that was difficult for him to understand. It was unique. It was the first in a series of dreams an eight-year-old experienced. She so cherished them that she compiled them into a booklet that she gave to her father for a Christmas present when she was ten. Although he was a psychiatrist, Jung was baffled by them. The first of the twelve dreams had what he called the following "relevant motifs":

"The evil animal," a serpent-like monster with many horns, kills and devours all other animals. But God comes from the four corners, being in fact four separate gods, and gives rebirth to all the dead animals.[4]

The serpent-like monster is clearly a feared "evil animal."

It is apparent, therefore, that many will think it scandalous, sacrilegious, and an aspect of anti-Christian polemic to suggest that Jesus may be like a snake or serpent. It will probably seem even more blasphemous to claim that such a thought was in the mind of the Fourth Evangelist and was an aspect of the mythology and lore in the Johannine community or school. But should we lack the courage to explore whether the Evangelist might have held something like an ophidian Christology? Did the Fourth Evangelist, or some in his community, contemplate—perhaps even conceptualize—that Jesus Christ had the attributes of a serpent?

Would not my colleagues lose respect for me and perhaps ostracize me for contemplating what may be to them heretical—even corrupt—thoughts? Surely, no scholar should be swayed by what some revered colleagues might think about the conclusions of careful work that seeks to obtain answers to obscure passages that have been ignored by experts. Thanks to hundreds of years of struggles by Wycliffe, Luther, Pascal, Kierkegaard, Nietzsche, Bultmann, Bonhoeffer, Tillich, J. A. T. Robinson, and so many others, we are finally free from ecclesiastical controls to explore the full range of the words and intentions in our sacred Scriptures. We now have the freedom to proceed with every conceivable question without fear of reprisal or condemnation.

This thought—that Jesus may be represented as a serpent—has sounded so incredible to many with whom I have shared it that it deserves exposition. I am astounded that a scholar would imagine it was not an insightful question to ponder. One leading scholar, during the sessions of the Society for New Testament Studies in South Africa, asked me what I was now focusing upon in my research. When I told him I was striving to comprehend the symbolic meaning of the serpent, he replied, "I hate snakes."

Often those who are attracted to biblical studies assume that scholars are in some ways constrained by the questions they might raise or the conclusions that are permitted. They assume that because I am a Methodist minister and teaching at Princeton Theological Seminary that some issues and conclusions are not allowed. Nonsense! I spent over a year at New College in the University of Edinburgh, at the Universität Tübingen and at Hebrew University in Jerusalem, and twenty-three years at Duke University. I feel as free here at Princeton Seminary as I did in those universities to pursue my creative reflections, without any person or institution dictating what might be considered proper. This freedom for research is absolutely necessary if the major seminaries can be considered "academic" institutions in which free inquiry and advanced research are fostered.

It is imperative to share openly that this freedom to pursue research has been a hallmark of Protestant seminaries for approximately two centuries, with an improvement in raising questions and discerning answers over the past century. In 1787, J. P. Gabler, for example, emphasized that we must "establish some distinction between biblical and dogmatic theology," and also "distinguish among each of the periods in the Old and New Testaments, each of the authors, and each of the manners of speaking which each used as a reflection of time and place, whether these matters are historical or didactic or poetic." [5] Particularly important for all who are offended, if only initially, by the suggestion that the Fourth Evangelist thought of Jesus as a serpent is Gabler's ageless advice that we must discern what symbol an evangelist might have employed "as an accommodation to the ideas or the needs of the first Christians" (pp. 142–43).

The *dicta classica* must not be a list of texts isolated from their literary or sociological contexts. Nothing other than the texts themselves, understood in terms of the original meaning of the authors of long ago, should inform us of Scripture; that is, to say with Gabler, "everything must be accomplished by exegetical observation only" (p. 143). The thrust of what Gabler argued seems to be the axiom followed today in every leading Jewish or Christian seminary: that dogmatic theology must not dictate agendas and methods to biblical scholars but, instead, must be informed by biblical theology, which is shaped by careful exegesis not marred by our own wishes or desires.[6] Most of the readers of this search for the original meaning of the Fourth Gospel will agree with Gabler that the Bible does contain revealed truths and that the task of biblical theology is to discover these and distinguish them from the mythology used in antiquity.

In consequent developments of the insights advanced by Gabler at the end of the eighteenth century are thoughts echoed today in many seminaries. W. Wrede argued that our work as New Testament scholars must not deal with the "New Testament" because the collection called the canonical New Testament postdates the period in which these twenty-seven writings were formed, shaped, and edited. The canon of the New Testament was given to the church by bishops and theologians. No specialist, who is a scholar, can accept limiting questions to a closed canon without severely compromising free inquiry and the ability to learn something strikingly new and fresh (even if such a "revelation" was common knowledge for the ancients).[7] A. Schlatter wisely urged us to have a perspective that seems essential in our search for the intended meaning of John 3:14–15: "Our work has a historical purpose when it is not concerned with the interests which emerge from the course of our own life, but directs its attention quite deliberately away from ourselves and our own contemporary interests, back to the past."[8] Our search will thus focus on what the Fourth Evangelist intended when he wrote that "the Son of Man"—Jesus to him—must be lifted up as the serpent was raised up by Moses.

Many vehemently resist thinking of Jesus as a serpent or snake precisely because they assume this creature symbolically has only a negative connotation. To demonstrate the hypothesis, or thesis, that the Fourth Evangelist in John 3:14 contends that Jesus is like the serpent raised up by Moses in the wilderness depends on establishing that:

1. The serpent is sometimes a good symbol in world cultures.
2. The serpent was admired in Old Testament times and within Early Judaism.
3. The serpent was appreciated in the Greek and Roman periods.
4. The serpent was a positive symbol in the Judaism of the Fourth Evangelist.
5. John 3:14 means more than a parallel between the lifting up of the serpent and of Jesus.
6. John 3:14 is a poetic statement in parallel thought so that "the serpent" is synonymous with "the Son of Man."
7. We can find an exegesis of Numbers 21 by a Jew contemporaneous with the Evangelist, and that the Jewish expositor stresses the positive symbolism of the copper (or bronze) serpent.
8. The Fourth Evangelist does not cavalierly treat the symbolism of the serpent he inherits from Numbers 21, but appreciates it and develops it in significantly positive ways.

These are formidable criteria to fulfill. The possibility that John 3:14–15 mirrors something like an anguine Christology will be essentially established if these criteria, or some of them, are validated.[9] Thus, our central question: Did the Fourth Evangelist or perhaps some members in his community imagine that Jesus could be symbolized as a serpent?

The tasks before us are daunting but promising. If the Fourth Evangelist was a Jew and his community essentially Jewish, and if we can discover positive images of the serpent in the Judaism of his time, then a presupposition against considering the possibility of a positive meaning of ophidian symbolism is diminished. Does the serpent ever represent something positive in the Jewish literature anterior to or roughly contemporaneous with the Fourth Evangelist? The words in John 3:14 are attributed to Jesus; is there evidence that he mentioned the serpent in other passages, and are these symbolic of positive meanings?

If some members in the Johannine community were Greeks or Romans (as seems evident from Jn 12:20–26), did some bring with them a posi-

Figure 1. Asclepius. Roman Period.
Courtesy of the Hermitage. JHC

tive ophidian or anguine symbolism? Did some converts come from a cult
of Asclepius, and would they perhaps have portrayed Jesus as the divine
healer, "the Savior," who is "like a serpent"? Given Jesus' heroic exploits,
did members of the Johannine community link him with Hercules who
took the apple signifying immortality from a tree—guarded by a serpent—
in the Hesperides? [10] In the Catacomb of Via Latina, in Cubiculum N, is
a depiction of Hercules in the Garden of the Hesperides, with a large serpent.[11] The art seems shaped by Christian interpretations, perhaps like
the one found recently in Lower Galilee (see Fig. 2). Is there a possible
link between Johannine symbolism and the pervasive ancient understanding that the serpent alone has the secret to immortality and wins back its
youth yearly?

Raising such intriguing questions leads us to an ancient body of twenty-
seven documents that are now labeled "the New Testament." What are
these texts, and how should one study them in search of a better grasp of
ancient ophidian iconography? Before digging into the Fourth Gospel, we
should pause and consider the problems confronted in the so-called New
Testament.

Figure 2. Christ as Hercules, Defeating the Serpent. From the ruins of a church in Lower Galilee. JHC

BEING HONEST ABOUT HOW THE NEW TESTAMENT TOOK SHAPE

Why is there such confusion regarding the study of the New Testament? Why have New Testament experts explored the deep symbolisms in the Fourth Gospel but shown little or no interest in the history of symbology generally and the study of ophidian symbolism specifically? The first question is raised because of claims found in the New Testament and the highly charged methods with which these texts are studied. They are not simply ancient texts according to Christians; they have a contemporary authority and message. The second question is raised because the New Testament texts demand so much intensive labor that sometimes broad issues, such as symbology, are left to be considered later, which often means never.

How did the New Testament take shape? For more than two centuries, at least, scholars in all Western societies have come to a consensus on how the New Testament writings were composed. Attempts to communicate academic discoveries to the church and synagogue—and to the wider public—have not been as successful as sharing the fruits of other scientific explorations. Seminary students study for three years at the major seminaries such as Princeton Theological Seminary. They are taught what scholars have learned about the composition of the books selected as "the Bible"; they often do extremely well in our classes, and then they leave us to serve a local church. Within a few years, their interest has shifted to the needs of the congregation, and often as young pastors they are no longer dedicated to struggling against the ignorance of those who pick up the Bible and read it as if it were this morning's newspaper. Fearing that the local church leaders may not be supportive, they frequently forget our teachings and proceed to preach and teach, far too often, as if the uneducated have the final word on the composition of the biblical books. For example,

1 Timothy, which is a work by someone influenced by Paul, is placarded as Paul's own composition.

It is no wonder then that most people in the highways and byways of our culture assume that the Gospel of Matthew and the Gospel of John were composed by the disciples of Jesus who are called "Matthew" and "John, the son of Zebedee." The assumption is that these works are by eyewitnesses—Matthew and John heard what Jesus said and saw what he did. Furthermore, it is presupposed that we have exactly what they wrote and that no changes have been made by the Greek scribes who copied what had been written. We are assured that the Gospels we have are identical to the compositions that left the desks of Jesus' disciples.

Now, let us be honest. All of this is incorrect. It is false, and the truth about the origins of our Gospels has been known for about two hundred years.

The Gospel attributed to Matthew cannot have been written by an eye-witness of Jesus and his first disciples. All New Testament scholars would be pleased if this assumption could prove to be the father of a valid conclusion. But, alas, the First Gospel was written over fifty years after Jesus' crucifixion, and—most important—the author, who is anonymous and unknown, based his story of Jesus on the Gospel of Mark, which was written first. And Mark never met Jesus. Attempts to prove that the Gospel of Matthew is either early or not literarily dependent on Mark are usually fired by Christian apologetics, in the sad attempt to "shore up the faith." Moreover, the author of the First Gospel is understandably more interested in serving the needs of his community than in giving us a factual, objective, and uninterpretive account of what Jesus said and did.

The identity of the Fourth Evangelist is also unknown. The attempts to prove that he must be John the son of Zebedee have failed, and the two major commentaries on the Fourth Gospel, written by Roman Catholics, have shown that the Beloved Disciple is probably not the Apostle John.[12] The Fourth Gospel, the focus of our attention, reached its present form (with 7:53–8:11) sometime in the second century CE. An earlier form, the second edition, appeared in the late nineties, and the first edition—which we cannot date with precision—was composed, I am convinced, probably in the mid-sixties. The author inherited earlier sources, as I shall try to clarify later.

Another point needs to be clarified. We do not have even one fragment of the Gospels from the first century. We must work on second century, and even much later, copies of the Gospels to discern what the author may have written. I have announced the discovery of a copy of Mark that dates from the sixth century CE, and scholars around the world are eagerly waiting to hear what variant readings it might contain.[13] We text critics of the New

Testament have grudgingly been forced to admit that many times scribes, who were copying the books of the New Testament, deliberately altered the text. Sometimes the alterations were for doctrinal reasons, sometimes they were caused by what seems to have been an embarrassing saying or episode. Often it was to "correct" the text in light of more recent theologies and Christologies.

Do these discoveries prove that the Gospels cannot preserve the inviolate word of God? Is it not clear that the Gospels can no longer be used authoritatively for salvation and for Christian living and thinking? Such conclusions usually result when members of a congregation learn that they cannot believe what they had been told. They lose faith in the preaching and integrity of preachers and teachers. What can be said to correct this error?

Obviously, Christian salvation and teaching cannot be based on what is false. The discovery of the truth can transport us back into the time of the evangelists, and, to a certain extent, even further. Sometimes, thanks to critical research, we are taken back into the time of Jesus, perhaps even into his presence. Scholarship has not deafened us to the word of God; it has helped scholars, who are often professors and preachers, to hear more clearly God's word within the words of Scripture. The result is not a dependence on historians—it is an awakening of spirituality. I think we can hear the voices of those who are being freed from the dogmatism of literalism to spiritualism in some of the songs by Sting and Enya.

In the attempt to be honest—to clear the air—so that the present search can be understood, I have chosen to present seventeen succinct points on being honest about the shaping of the New Testament, with special attention to the Gospels, especially the Fourth Gospel, since that masterpiece is the focal point of the present investigation. Each of these seventeen points results from over two hundred years of intense and focused research on Early Judaism and Christian origins; not one is idiosyncratic.

1. Jesus was born during the reign of Herod the Great, who was king from 37 to 4 BCE. Most likely Jesus was born sometime before 6 BCE, since Matthew reports that King Herod sought to kill Jesus in Bethlehem. Herod ordered his troops to massacre all boys up to two years of age in and near Bethlehem (Mt 2:16).

2. Jesus was crucified by Roman soldiers in 30 CE, during the prefecture of Pontius Pilate (26–36 CE) whose name and title have been located on a stone found in Caesarea Maritima.

3. Jesus' ministry was from approximately 26 to 30 CE.

4. Jesus wrote nothing, but he was able to write if we take literally John 7:53–8:11.

5. Jesus focused his thoughts into well-crafted speech, designed to be

heard and not read. His words were shaped by intensive and thoughtful preparation.

6. His words were often deeply metaphorical and pictorial. Rather than warning that piety should not be ostentatious, he stated that it was easier for a camel to pass through the eye of a needle than for a rich person to enter heaven (Lk 18:25).

7. There is absolutely no record that anyone who heard his speeches copied them; and—of course—there were no video or tape recorders two thousand years ago.

8. Jesus spoke Aramaic, and he knew Hebrew, some Greek (if he spoke to Pilate), and a little Latin (since he is shown to have related to Roman soldiers).

9. None of his disciples wrote a Gospel. Not one of the Gospels was written by or based on what a disciple had written. The titles to the Gospels may be second-century additions, and the earliest extant fragments of the Gospels date from the second century CE.

10. After Jesus' death his message was remembered, and often by people with incredible memories, but those who passed on what he had said and done shaped their records based on the needs of communities different from those Jesus had known. His message was shaped by itinerant preachers, teachers, and prophets who carried his message to the East and the West. The most famous of these Jewish itinerant teachers was Paul, a recognized genius, who probably died in Rome, where Jesus' message preceded him.

11. Within fifteen years of Jesus' death a collection of his sayings was apparently put into written form. This Sayings Source, called Q, was quoted in an edited form by both Matthew and Luke. About the same time a Signs Source was composed and it was used by the Fourth Evangelist who retained some of the numbers of the signs (see Jn 2:11, 4:54). These are well-accepted "facts" that are taught in the leading seminaries and universities in the United States and abroad. Less well established is a probability to which I subscribe: The *Gospel of Thomas* seems to be another Sayings Source, but it was shaped by later Christians.

12. Mark, conceivably Peter's secretary, most likely wrote the First Gospel. It was completed either just before or after the burning of Jerusalem by the Roman armies in 70 CE, since chapter 13 knows either that this epochal event has already happened or is a foregone conclusion.

13. Matthew and Luke were probably composed in the eighties. They depended on Mark's outline of Jesus' life, as well as on the otherwise lost Sayings Source (Q), in addition to traditions that they alone inherited and shaped.

14. The Fourth Gospel also took shape very early. The author probably did not depend on Mark and utilized sources independent of the

other intra-canonical gospels. A first edition may have appeared in the mid-sixties and a second edition in the late nineties. Some of the Fourth Evangelist's sources derive ultimately from the forties, thirties, and, when freed from the Evangelist's own theology, into the twenties when Jesus was teaching. Thus, behind the sayings of Jesus in the Fourth Gospel may be reworked sayings of Jesus or valid summaries of what he had intended to communicate to his fellow Jews.

15. All four Gospels are shaped by the Easter faith, the proclamation that Jesus did not end his life on the cross but was resurrected by God during the Passover festival in Jerusalem in 30 CE. Thus, the Gospels are not so much histories as they are proclamations of the good news that God was present in Jesus, who is the Messiah (the Christ) promised to God's people and the One who as Christ will return in glory, triumphantly bringing to fruition all the promises associated with the Messiah or Christ.

16. The Fourth Evangelist wrote his Gospel as his theological affirmation of Jesus. He was not interested in producing the first biography of Jesus. He shaped Jesus' life and message for a time and a community that was appreciably different from the ones experienced by Jesus.

17. Each evangelist shaped Jesus' message in terms of his own theology. The evangelists' own thoughts are often subtly couched in their narratives, which reflect the myths and symbols that shaped first-century culture. If we want to know what the Fourth Evangelist intended to say to his own community and others who might have read his work, then we must immerse ourselves in the symbolisms of his time. That is indeed the task of the present work.

THE PROBLEM WITH COMMENTARIES ON JOHN 3:14

Brilliant and gifted commentators on the Fourth Gospel often tell the reader what any seminary student of this gospel knows: that "to raise up" is the Evangelist's way of celebrating Jesus' crucifixion as a triumph rather than a failure (see Jn 8:28, 12:32–34). This emphasis, most likely, is one of the major differences between the Synoptic gospels (Mt, Mk, and Lk, which relate Jesus' life synoptically) and the Johannine Gospel. As J. Ashton states, "Where John differs from the Synoptics is chiefly in his reluctance to see the crucifixion as demeaning or degrading." [14] Ashton then goes on to point to the Fourth Evangelist's unique meaning given to *hupsoō*, which he takes to denote not only "to exalt" but "to lift up" on the cross. Actually, if it were not for the Fourth Evangelist's peculiar use of *hupsoō*, we would assume that it meant, as it does prior to the Fourth Gospel, only "to exalt."

Note how the commentators avoid any discussion of the Evangelist's typological use of the symbol of a serpent for Jesus and their preoccupation with the verb "to lift up." Note these representative samples, which are characteristically erudite and insightful for exegesis and exposition of John 3:14:

> The central idea of this verse is that of the lifting up of the Messiah. . . . to the very fact of His suspension on the cross. [Godet, 1886, reprinted in 1978][15]

> The allusion to the serpent in the wilderness (Num. xxi, 8.9) is very clear, and John never employs this word [i.e., ὑψωθῆναι] except to signify the exaltation of the Passion (viii, 28; xii, 32.34). [Lagrange, 1925][16]

> . . . . and for those who are in the secret the "elevation" of the Son of man in iii.14–15 suggests the thought of the cross; but the suggestion is left undeveloped. [Dodd, 1960][17]

> The event which is necessary in order that faith may receive eternal life is the exaltation of the "Son of Man.". . . V. 14 mentions only the exaltation; this is the fulfillment of the Son's mission, and by this alone is it made effective (cf. 13.31f.), for it is the exalted, glorified Lord who is the object of Christian faith. [Bultmann, 1964 (German), ET in 1971][18]

> John exploits three points which he sees as intrinsically connected: the "exaltation," its salvific power and the divine plan behind all. [Schnackenburg, 1965 (German), ET in 1987][19]

> The phrase "to be lifted up" refers to Jesus' death on the cross. This is clear not only from the comparison with the serpent on the pole in vs. 14, but also from the explanation in xii 33. . . . [I]n John "being lifted up" refers to one continuous action of ascent: Jesus begins his return to his Father as he approaches death (xiii 1) and completes it only with his ascension (xx 17). [Brown, 1966][20]

> The Lord clearly viewed His death as being in line with the purpose of God as foreshadowed in the Old Testament, wherein the sacrifice for sin takes on the character of sin and thereby provides the antidote to the death-bearing malady (cf. Jn 3:14 and Num. 21:6–9). [Cook, 1979][21]

> The Son of Man must be "exalted," crucified, "that whoever believes in him may have eternal life." [Haenchen, 1980 (German), ET in 1984][22]

Moses' serpent of bronze, if looked upon with trust in God, preserved the Israelites from death (cf. Num. 21:9). The exalted Jesus, looked on believingly, gives the life of the final eon ("eternal life") to those who believe (v. 15; cf. Dan. 12:2). [Sloyan, 1988][23]

. . . . the deepest point of connection between the bronze snake and Jesus was in the act of being "lifted up." [Carson, 1991][24]

And, just as that serpent was "lifted up" in the wilderness, so, Jesus says, "the Son of Man must be lifted up." This must refer to his being "lifted up" on the cross. [Morris, 1995][25]

The consensus is that the Greek of John 3:14–15 means that the simile refers to Jesus, as the Son of Man, being lifted up (little is made of the simile of the serpent). None of these commentators discusses the symbology of Jesus as the serpent. In fact, they mention the serpent almost routinely and usually only when Numbers is quoted. The experts on John merely suggest that Jesus is like the serpent only in the parallel of being raised up. They fail to observe the symbolism and misrepresent the symbolic meaning of John 3:14–15. Perhaps they have been too influenced by previous commentators and have also resisted, or been oblivious of, any implication that Jesus may be like a serpent, which often symbolized life.

Far too often biblical experts harbor the presupposition that the serpent symbolized only evil in antiquity and, sad to report, this assumption continues unexamined. One may find a nuance of this penchant in T. L. Brodie's work. He writes as if the narrative in Numbers 21 implies that the copper serpent is the same as the venomous ones: "It is by facing the thing which most terrifies—by putting the fiery serpent on a standard and looking straight at it (Num 21:8–9)—that greater life is achieved."[26] The fiery serpent is not put on a standard; Moses makes a metal serpent and places it on a stake.

Do any of the New Testament commentators consider the possibility that the serpent symbolically represents Jesus or that it is a typos of Jesus? Yes, in addition to the previous quotation from Schnackenburg, note his following comment: "The point of the comparison is neither the stake nor the serpent, but the 'exaltation.' "[27] At least Schnackenburg pondered the possibility. Earlier, Bultmann noted in his masterful commentary on the Fourth Gospel the opinion that the Fourth Evangelist placed "no emphasis on the identification of Jesus with the serpent" (p. 152). This is correct, but Bultmann apparently perceived that John, without emphasis, identified Jesus with the serpent. Thus, it is worth exploring how and in what ways, if at all, the Fourth Evangelist thought of Moses' upraised serpent as a typos of Jesus.

Some commentators come closer than Bultmann in seeing—as did Justin, Irenaeus, Augustine, and Calvin—that the Fourth Evangelist compared Christ, as the Son of Man, to the copper serpent. E. Ruckstuhl suggested that the actual comparison between the serpent and the Son of Man is to emphasize the lifting up of the Christ not only on the cross but up into heaven and to the right hand of God. But he also states that "as the serpent was lifted and placed on a standard, so (must be raised) the Son of Man on the cross."[28] The thought is not developed or expanded and is perhaps no more than a paraphrase of John 3:14. The commentators who seem closest to perceiving the simile of Jesus as a serpent are P. W. Comfort and W. C. Hawley. In their *Opening the Gospel of John,* they conclude that "Jesus was not comparing himself directly to the serpent—although the indirect simile cannot be excluded."[29] Does this statement not beg the question and prompt deep exploration into the symbology in the Fourth Gospel, especially a possible ophidian Christology?

The phenomena that plague the New Testament field are also reflected in works that point to the cultural setting of the New Testament documents. The valuable *Hellenistic Commentary to the New Testament* presents a history-of-religions parallel to help the exegete understand John 3:14,[30] but the reader is told only of the importance of Pseudo-Callisthenes' *Life and Deeds of Alexander of Macedonia* 2.21:7–11. The sole use of the long citation is to point up the double meaning of some words, especially "to lift up." The reference is simply in line with that found in the commentaries; no information is provided to help the reader of the New Testament understand the possible portrayal of Jesus as a serpent.

C. R. Koester's *Symbolism in the Fourth Gospel*[31] does not discuss the concept of the serpent in the Fourth Gospel; but he does correctly stress, as we shall demonstrate, the prerequisite for understanding the symbolism that shaped it: "Johannine symbolism cannot be treated adequately within the confines of one discipline; it demands consideration of the literary, the socio-historical, and the theological aspects of the text" (p. xi).

Why have New Testament commentators missed the possible ophidian symbolism of John 3:14–15? Why have they avoided the apparent implications of this passage and circumvented the conclusion that Jesus is being compared to a serpent? The most important reason is the contemporary loss of the ancient symbolic language; as H. Bayley demonstrated, long ago in 1912, in his *The Lost Language of Symbolism,* we have lost touch with the origins of our language and its grounding in nature and the world that sustains us.

More should be suggested on why New Testament experts miss the in-depth meaning of symbols. On the one hand, these scholars have seldom been trained in symbolism; and, unlike many of their Old Testament colleagues, they have not been intimately involved in the archaeology and iconography of the Near East. On the other hand—and indeed more important—their biblical exegesis is perhaps too influenced by hermeneutics and theology, coupled, perhaps, with fears of condemnation from church leaders, dogmatic theologians, and administrators who issue salary checks and control raises and promotions. No New Testament scholar would want to be branded as one who thought of Jesus as a snake. Hence, the potential resistance to my present research might be considerable.

As we shall soon see, New Testament commentators receive rather low marks in interpreting the rich symbolism of John 3:14–15, but Old Testament commentators earn praise for their exegesis of Numbers 21:8–9, exactly the passage cited by the Fourth Evangelist. Perhaps this discrepancy within the biblical field results because Old Testament experts, in contrast to their New Testament colleagues, are forced to include archaeology and to study the myths and symbols that have shaped the biblical narratives.

It is surprising that some of the best insights regarding the symbolic meaning of John 3:14 appear not in commentaries on the Fourth Gospel but in commentaries on Numbers. For example, D. T. Olson in his *Numbers* offers the following insights:

> The serpent is a potent symbol of both life and death. . . . The bronze serpent in Numbers 21 is one of the best-known images of the book of Numbers for Christians because of its use by Jesus in the Gospel of John. . . . The words of Jesus emphasize God's desire to give eternal life to all those who look to and believe in Jesus.[32]

We now turn to what commentators report about the symbolic meaning of the serpent in Numbers 21, which is the intertext of John 3:14.

THE ATTRACTIVENESS OF COMMENTARIES ON NUMBERS 21:8–9

According to Numbers 13–14, the loss of faith in Yahweh threatens the existence of the Exodus generation. Fortunately, the Hebrews confess their sins. After hearing about the death of Aaron (20:22–29), the reader is told the story of the last in a series of complaints by the Hebrews, and it is the most devastating because the complaint is directly against God and Moses (21:5).[33] God thus sends poisonous snakes among the people, and these kill many of them. The people come to Moses and confess their sin; they ask him to pray for them. He fulfills their request. Here is the text that is crucial for us (Num 21:8–9):

> And the Lord said to Moses, "Make a poisonous serpent,[34] and set it on a pole; and everyone who is bitten shall look at it and live." So

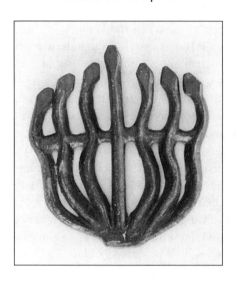

Figure 3. Bronze Menorah with Seven Serpents. Roman Period (?). Courtesy Shlomo Moussaieff. JHC

Moses made a serpent of bronze, and put it on a pole; and whenever a serpent bit someone, that person would look at the serpent of bronze and live. [NRSV]

Two points are significant: the symbol of a serpent that gives life and the requisite action of trusting and looking up to the symbol of a serpent for healing. As Olson states, "The serpent was a symbol of evil power and chaos from the underworld as well as a symbol of fertility, life, and healing. The copper (or bronze) serpent in Numbers 21 bears some relationship to a healing ritual known as sympathetic magic, common in the ancient Near East." [35]

This section of Numbers is thoughtfully composed. The "poisonous" snakes are actually "fiery" snakes, signifying at once two ideas: the burning sensation when venom attacks the human body, and the fiery anger of God when the people earlier complained to Yahweh (Num 11:1–2).[36] Moses makes the serpent *(neḥaš)* of copper or bronze *(neḥōšet).*

The exegesis of Numbers 21:8–9 has been improved by two related archaeological discoveries. First, the image of a winged serpent placed on a rod is engraved on a bronze bowl found in the royal palace in Nineveh; it dates from the later part of the eighth century BCE. Moreover, on the bowl can be seen inscribed a Hebrew name. Many scholars suggest insightfully that this bowl was booty taken from ancient Palestine by Tiglath-pileser III (745–727) or Sennacherib (in 701 he besieged Jerusalem), and that it once was displayed in the Temple cult in Jerusalem. If this advice is sound, we have palpable evidence today of the positive symbol of a serpent in ancient Israel. Perhaps the bowl symbolized the story about the fiery serpents and the copper serpent made by Moses, according to Numbers.[37]

Second, a 12.5-centimeter-long copper serpent was found at Timnaʿ (north of the Gulf of Aqabah); it dates from the period 1200–900 BCE.[38] Milgrom offers the learned opinion that this discovery indicates "the snake story was inserted" into the narrative in Numbers "precisely when Israel was in the vicinity of the Timnaʿ copper mines."[39]

The play on words (paronomasia) in Numbers 21 has most likely helped to shape the careful crafting of words in John 3:14. In Numbers, the "serpent" *(nᵉḥaš)* is made of "copper" *(nᵉḥōšet),* which as S. R. Hirsch stressed, brings out the purpose of the figure;[40] that is, the word for "copper" in Hebrew sounds like "serpent" and thereby draws the reader's attention to the serpent. The narrator chose his words carefully to indicate why Moses made the "copper serpent" and placed it on a pole.

Is it possible that a similar paronomasia may be found in the Fourth Gospel? Does the twofold meaning of the Greek verb in John 3:14—"to lift up" and "to exalt"—contain the Fourth Evangelist's Christological perspective? It is conceivable that the Fourth Evangelist couched his words artistically to indicate the following: Jesus did not die on the cross; he was exalted on it. Hence he gives life, like the serpent. To all who look up to him, who is from above, he imparts life. Later, in the chapter devoted to the exegesis of John 3:14, we shall explore these exegetical possibilities.

The thrust of the passage in Numbers is that as the poisonous snake brought death, so the upraised copper serpent on the pole shall give life to all who look up to it. To demonstrate this idea, the commentators on Numbers 21:8–9 must first bring out the concept of the serpent as good.[41] They frequently do so; note these representative examples:[42]

> In the present story the widespread religio-historical concept of the serpent as the representation or symbol of a god of healing to which one must turn might also play a part. [Noth, 1966 (German), ET in 1968][43]

> In Egypt the Pharaoh had a replica of a cobra fixed to his crown for protection. [Maarsingh, 1985 (Dutch), ET in 1987][44]

> In the ancient Near East, "the snake was rightly seen as a symbol of life and fruitfulness." [Jagersma, 1988][45]

> The homeopathic use of snakes is a distinctive feature of ancient Egypt. . . . The association of snakes with healing is attested elsewhere in the Near East. [Milgrom, 1990][46]

> . . . . copper was employed widely for making snakes used in cult worship by the ancient Near Eastern peoples. [Harrison, 1990][47]

> The serpent was a symbol . . . of fertility, life and healing. [Olson, 1996][48]

The commentators on Numbers must also stress that the good serpent, "the copper (or bronze) serpent," brings "life" for all who look up to it. Note how these scholars successfully bring out this meaning of the story.

> . . . release from the fatal effects of the serpent bites is linked to a test of obedience set by Yahweh in his free judgment. [Noth, 1966 (German), ET in 1968][49]

> . . . . all who were afflicted with the deadly poison were directed to fix their gaze upon this objectified evil lifted up in the air; those who did so would be healed. [Maarsingh, 1985 (Dutch), ET in 1987][50]

> Hence the raising of the copper snake on a standard is a sign of salvation in the wilderness. [Jagersma, 1988][51]

> Those who looked at the snake recovered. [Milgrom, 1990][52]

> One who looks at it shall be healed of the snake bite. [Scharbert, 1992][53]

> The Lord's response was somewhat homeopathic in nature, consisting of a bronze serpent erected upon a pole that mediated God's healing power to any sufferer who looked upward at it. [Harrison, 1990][54]

> In both the command (v. 8) and its fulfillment (v. 9), healing must be accompanied by an act of obedience to Yahweh: looking at the image of the snake. . . . a definite act of the will—if one wanted to be healed. [Ashley, 1993][55]

> . . . . the pole with the bronze serpent stood between the dead who were not willing to look to God's chosen instrument of healing and the living who were willing and were healed (21:9). [Olson, 1996][56]

For the first time in the history of salvation, God commands some action from the Hebrews. This point was emphasized by J. G. Frazer in his *Folklore in the Old Testament*[57] and by K. R. Joines in her *Serpent Symbolism in the Old Testament*.[58] We have succeeded in establishing the second criterion: that the serpent was admired in Old Testament times.

Old Testament experts have accurately understood the full symbolism of Numbers 21:8–9. They have emphasized that serpents were symbols of good as well as evil. They have explicated the life-giving symbolism of the copper (or bronze) serpent, and they demonstrate the importance of the positive meaning of ophidian symbolism for understanding Numbers 21. These scholars have been trained in symbolism and in the iconography of the Near East. Since many of these scholars are not Christians, they are not in any way concerned about Christian dogmatics.

MOSES' IMAGE AND THE SECOND COMMANDMENT

There is a problem exegetes have confronted in interpreting Numbers 21:8, "Then the LORD said to Moses, 'Make a seraph figure and mount it on a standard. And if anyone who is bitten looks at it, he shall recover' " [TANAKH]. The problem was noted long ago in the second century CE by Justin Martyr in his *Dialogue with Trypho* (94). Has not God broken one of God's own commandments?

According to Scripture, God revealed the Ten Commandments, and he said: "You shall not make for yourself a sculptured image, or any likeness of what is in the heavens above, or on the earth below, or in the waters under the earth. You shall not bow down to them or serve them" (Exod 20:4–5; cf. Deut 5:7–10; TANAKH). Hence, did not God break the second commandment when God instructed Moses to make an image of a serpent? Obviously, the "likeness" of a serpent is an image of what is "on the earth below" and also "in the waters under the earth."

The author of the *Epistle of Barnabas,* perhaps composed a little earlier than Justin Martyr's work, explains away the problem. Moses, following God's word, commanded Israel not to make an image to worship, yet "makes one himself to show a type of Jesus." [59]

How did ancient Jews justify making images if they had been prohibited by God from crafting them? In light of the vast amount of iconographic images now available from Second Temple Judaism, it is wise to ponder how Jews—and even Israelites before the Exile—interpreted the second commandment. Perhaps some Jews began to understand the second commandment not as anti-iconic (a prohibition against making an image) but anti-idolic (a prohibition against making an image as an idol). [60] That is, the command was not one long prohibition; it consisted of two parts. Those who obeyed God's commandments could make images (whether sculptures or paintings), but they must not worship them. [61] Hence, according to this reasoning, God does not break God's commandment. God instructs Moses to make an image, but God never intended anyone to "bow down" to it "or serve" it. Rather, in looking up to the serpent on a stake, the Israelites were affirming their dependence on God.

Figure 4. A Demon with a Phallic Serpent in an Early Church, Northern Spain. Before fourth century CE. JHC

THE PRESUPPOSITION THAT THE SERPENT DENOTES ONLY EVIL OR SATAN

An Unexamined Presupposition

The commentators on the Fourth Gospel tend to assume—without investigation—that the "serpent" is only a pejorative symbol. This point is illustrated by a comment found in D. Simpson's *Judas Iscariot: The Man of Mystery, History, and Prophecy.*[62] His exegesis of Genesis 3:15, where God curses the serpent, and of John 13:21, which narrates the entry of Satan into Judas, is typical of popular exegesis: "By the possession, Judas becomes the seed of the serpent, Satan, the son of perdition; at all events, he is then revealed as such by our Lord Himself" (p. 48).

What can be dismissed as emotionalism or uninformed exegesis appears pervasively in scholarly works. Those who assume that the snake is always a negative symbol can mine the biblical text to prove their point. According to Leviticus 11:41–43, the serpent cannot be eaten because it is an abomination and would make one unclean.

The Apocrypha also may be mined—which is not acceptable methodology—to prove that the snake is evil. The author of the Wisdom of Solomon seems to be alluding to Numbers 21 when he refers to God's wrath that was meted out by "the stings of crooked snakes" (Wis 16:5). According to the second-century Jewish scholar Sirach, the snake is evil. He instructs his "son" to flee from sin as "from the face of a snake" (Sir 21:2). Later, he warns that as there is no wrath greater than the wrath of an enemy, so there is "no head above the head of a snake" (Sir 25:15). According to the author of 4 Maccabees 18:8, who is roughly contemporaneous with the Fourth Evangelist, the righteous mother of the seven sons reports that "the destructive, deceitful snake (ὄφις)" did not spoil her virginity. This verse is surely an example of the snake as a pejorative symbol of the phallus.

The authors of publications on the history of evil or on Satan customarily do not ask if the serpent can signify positive as well as negative concepts; they presuppose that the serpent is a symbol of evil and denotes Satan. Note these examples (in chronological order):

> . . . . the serpent, of old the "seer," was, in its Semitic adaptation, the tempter to forbidden knowledge. Satan played this part to our ancestors in the Garden of Eden. [Rudwin, 1931][63]

> Both the Hebrew and the Persian Devil are associated with the serpent. [Russell, 1977][64]

> Justin Martyr "established the connection between the Devil and the serpent of Eden forever after." [Russell, 1988][65]

> Next, the angel-dragon-beast was linked with "that serpent of old" responsible for the fall of Adam and Eve from Eden. [Turner, 1993][66]

> Satan, Lucifer, Beelzebub, Belial . . . [is] the serpent who tempts Eve in the Garden of Eden. [Stanford, 1996][67]

There are often many brilliant and significant ideas in these books, yet a search for the various meanings of serpent symbolism is not one of them;[68] this is essential if one is to talk about the literature in which the serpent is mentioned. Evil appears iconographically as the snake in many interpretations of Genesis, as Naga who is the chief among Krishna's enemies, as the snakes that torment Laocoon and Hercules, and as the snake-worm that kills Sigmund, the Nordic hero.[69] Questions should guide the scholar and the nonscholar, as in G. Messadié's *The History of the Devil*, "Yet we must wonder if it was really our Devil who in the guise of the 'subtle serpent' of Genesis told Eve that she and Adam would never die if they ate the fruit from 'the tree in the midst of the garden.' "[70] In fact, the author or compiler of Genesis 3 does not envision the serpent as Satan, and that equation does not appear in the Old Testament.[71] It must not be assumed that the serpent represents only, or primarily, evil or Satan in antiquity or modernity; moreover, Satan appears in Christian literature as every animal that had been represented by "pagans" as a god (ape, bat, bear, bee, bull, cat, crocodile, eagle, even fish).[72] According to Tyndale's vision, Satan appeared "blacker than a crow."[73] And one should recall Ben Jonson's comedy called *The Devil Is an Ass*.

Negative symbolic use of the snake is too well known or presumed to need much further illustration. In the New Testament Apocrypha and Pseudepigrapha, the examples are numerous. One example alone must suffice. In the "Hymn of the Pearl," we find this confession by "the snake" or Satan in the *Acts of Thomas:* "I am a reptile of reptile nature . . . I am he who hurled the angels down from above . . . I am he who kindled Judas and bribed him to betray Christ to death" (*AcThom* 109:31). As we all know, the issue is not whether the serpent could mean something negative. The question is: What did the serpent symbolize, and did it often represent something positive?

The Ambiguity of Genesis 3

In Genesis 3 the "serpent" appears in a role that often is assumed by critics today to represent Satan and evil. A thoughtful reading of the text, however, prohibits one from categorizing this creation as "evil." The animal has been created by God and is not dumb.

What does the serpent inform the woman (Eve)? It is that she, the mother of all life, will have knowledge of good and evil if she eats from the tree in the middle of the garden (Gen 3:5). The woman and Adam eat the forbidden fruit, and God confirms the insight of "the serpent" by stating: "The man has become like one of us, knowing good and evil" (3:22 [NRSV]). Thus, knowledge, which is certainly desirable—according to the biblical view expressed especially in Proverbs—is what results first from eating the forbidden fruit. Did the serpent not speak the truth? Was this not consequently confirmed by God? What is the meaning of Genesis 3:1? Is the serpent deceitfully clever or cleverly wise? Rather than assuming that the serpent is evil, we need to examine what seems to be a confusing portrayal of the serpent in Genesis 3.

The presentation of the Genesis serpent as Satan and evil has rightly been resisted by many authors from antiquity (see the following discussion of *ApMos*) to modernity. For example, Lord Byron (1788–1824), the Romantic poet whose compositions are frequently autobiographical, wrote in "Cain: A Mystery" about the characteristics of the serpent. The drama is based on an imaginative exegesis of Genesis 3:1 that is parallel in startling ways to many legends that had developed among the early Jews. Lord Byron said Lucifer did not tempt Eve "in the shape of a serpent." Byron read Genesis 3 carefully. He correctly pointed out in his preface to "Cain" that "the book of Genesis has not the most distant allusion to anything of the kind, but merely to the Serpent in his serpentine capacity." [74] By attending so carefully to the biblical narrative and not being persuaded by what a scholar had published, Byron discloses that he would have been a fine biblical exegete.

In Byron's drama, Lucifer—the "Master of Spirits"—appears to Cain as a serpent, denies that he ever tempted Adam and Eve, and stresses that the serpent who appeared to them in the Garden of Eden, before the fall, was neither a spirit nor a demon. Note Scene I:

> The snake *was* the snake—
> No more; and yet not less than those he tempted,
> In nature being earth also—*more* in *wisdom,*
> Since he could overcome them, and foreknow
> The knowledge fatal to their narrow joys.[75]

Here in this drama is an imaginative recreation of human origins, according to the Bible, with often brilliant attention to the details of Genesis 3. Lord Byron removes from the serpent the condemning cloak of evil. The portrayal of the serpent in Genesis 3 as wise and clever—and not Satanic—appears in many other compositions that antedate or are roughly contemporaneous with the composition of the Fourth Gospel. It is no longer prudent to assume that the serpent is evil in Genesis. Likewise, we dare not fail to heed the full symbolic thrust of the Fourth Gospel in 3:14–15. Calvin, a genius in interpreting Scripture, may provide some insights.

OVERCOMING THEOLOGICAL PRESUPPOSITIONS: CALVIN AND JESUS THE SERPENT

Calvin (1509–1564) does indeed make the equation clear between Jesus and the serpent. We should expect Calvin to grasp the symbolism of John 3:14, since he was a focused, logical, and systematic thinker; he also mastered both Greek and Latin grammar. His commentary on the Fourth Gospel was completed in 1552, three years before he controlled Geneva. The second edition of his commentary appeared in that year, 1555. Although Calvin is more interested in engaging exposition (preaching the gospel to his followers) than historical exegesis (exploring the original meaning intended by the Evangelist), he does state clearly that in 3:14 "Christ compares Himself to the serpent."[76]

Moreover, for Calvin the "similitude is not inappropriate or far-fetched" (p. 72). He shuns the idea regnant among ancient and especially modern commentators that the comparison is to Jesus' being lifted up on the cross; for him, the verb refers to "the preaching of the Gospel" (p. 72). He is adamant: "The explanation which some give of it as referring to the cross does not agree with the context and is foreign to His [the Evangelist's] argument" (p. 72).

What does Calvin think the Evangelist meant by comparing Christ to the serpent? He provides two logical options: a resemblance between Christ and the serpent or a sacrament like manna. Calvin is clear that it is the latter, although his language is opaque. He intends, with Paul who referred to the manna as a mystery (1 Cor 10:3), to think of the serpent in the same way. Here Calvin has substituted one simile (the serpent and Christ) with another (the manna and the serpent). His words, "I think it was the same with the serpent" (p. 73), are far from lucid.

Calvin does not include any mention of the positive portrayal of the serpent nor does he suggest that the serpent symbolizes life, healing, wisdom, or resurrection. Nevertheless, Calvin correctly perceives that the Fourth Evangelist presented Christ comparing himself "to the serpent" (p. 73). These preliminary observations disclose that it is imperative and fruitful to explore what the "serpent" symbolizes in the Fourth Gospel and what ophidian symbology the Fourth Evangelist might inherit. How shall we continue?

PUBLICATIONS THAT GROUND THE SEARCH

We have clarified the question that launched this research: What is the symbolic meaning of John 3:14? It is now imperative to move beyond the Fourth Gospel and even the canonical texts. We need to focus on the underlying question: What did the serpent symbolize in antiquity? If we intend to learn about the possible symbolic meaning of John 3:14, we should attend also to broader questions: What did the serpent symbolize in the ancient world, in the Near East, in Assyria, Babylon, and Persia, in Egypt and Africa, in Greece and Rome, and especially in the place where the Fourth Gospel may have been composed or the areas from which it received its symbolism? Jerusalem and ancient Palestine, Egypt (especially Alexandria), Antioch and eastern Syria, and in or near Ephesus should be included in our research. Fortunately, many gifted scholars have already contributed to the search for answers to these questions.

After six years of examining the meaning of serpent symbolism in antiquity, I am impressed by the vast number of books ostensibly devoted to this concern.[77] Reviewing them briefly, I am struck by three insights.[78] First, none of the authors who have worked on ophidian iconography knows the astronomical number of publications in this field of inquiry.[79] Second, the biblical experts who have studied the concept or symbol of the serpent in key biblical passages—notably Genesis 3, Numbers 21, John 3, and Revelation 12—are ignorant of the plethora of publications dedicated to the concept of the serpent. Almost all tend to err in assuming that the serpent symbolized evil and Satan. Third, no scholar who has published on serpent symbolism seems to have worked in the museums and libraries that have priceless collections of ophidian iconography, visited the sites in which there were serpent cults, collected ophidian realia, or studied herpetology, especially ophiology, and the taxonomic uniqueness of the 2,900 species of snakes.

Far too many authors assume, without examining the evidence, that the serpent simply signifies, or is an archetype of, the phallus. It is ludicrous to think that "we have, in the Mosaic account of the 'fall,' a phallic legend," as was claimed in 1875 in *Ancient Symbol Worship*.[80] Many gifted thinkers have vitiated their own research by keeping one eye, perhaps both, on Freud or Jung. Here is a sample of myopic perusals of the meaning of the serpent:

W. H. Fischle, *Das Geheimnis der Schlange* (1983; 1989 [2nd ed.])
G. Sauer, *Traumbild Schlange* (1986; 1992 [3rd ed.])
E. Ghazal, *Schlangenkult und Tempelliebe* (1995)
B. A. Mertz, *Dein archetypisches Tier* (1997)

Despite their lack of historical criticism and failure to explore the ancient (or primordial) mind that invented serpent images, these publications are often full of penetrating insights, especially into human psychology.[81] Unfortunately, none of these authors apparently knows that in the Indian Tantric cult a goddess is depicted with a serpent-phallus emerging from the vulva,[82] that some "gods" in antiquity are depicted with an erect phallus that is a serpent (see the following chapters), or that the Egyptian fertility god named Min is depicted as ithyphallic and also with an upraised hand (see the relief on the temple of Chon in Karnak).[83]

Equally devoid of an open investigation of the varied symbolical meanings of the serpent in antiquity and world culture are the numerous books that are theocentric or Christocentric. Such authors are content to explain how God or Christ has conquered the serpent. Here are some examples:

W. Kramp, *Protest der Schlange* (1970)
E. W. Lutzer, *The Serpent of Paradise* (1996)

H. Fritsche's *Die Erhöhung der Schlange* (1994 [4th ed.]) is a mixture of psychology and theology. One will not find in his book a search for the meaning of ophidian iconography.

I now list in chronological order the books and monographs on ophidian iconography and symbology that I have found during my research in many countries (and from most of which I have learned something):[84]

H. Clarke and C. S. Wake, *Serpent and Siva Worship* (1877)
W. Boelsche, *Drachen* (1929)

P. Lum, *Fabulous Beasts* (1951)

A. Rosenberg, *Michael und der Drache* (1956)

J. Fontenrose, *Python: A Study of Delphic Myth and Its Origins* (1959)

J. L. Henderson and M. Oakes, *The Wisdom of the Serpent* (1963, 1990)

D. Krekoukias, *Gli animali nella meterorologia popolare degli antichi Greci* (1970)

L. Bodson, *Contribution à l'étude de la place de l'animal dans la religion grecque ancienne* (1978)

M. Burkolter-Trachsel, *Der Drache* (1981)

H. Egli, *Das Schlangensymbol* (1982)

K. Zimniok, *Die Schlange das unbekannte Wesen: In der Kulturgeschichte, freien Natur und im Terrarium* (1984)

B. Johnson, *Lady of the Beasts: Ancient Images of the Goddess and Her Sacred Animals* (1988, 1990)

H. M. Lins, *Tiere in der Mythologie und ihre religiöse Symbolkraft* (1990, 1994 [2nd ed.])

G. A. Samonà, *Il sole, la terra, il serpente* (1991)

F. Huxley, *The Dragon* (1992)

A. de Pury, *Homme et animal Dieu les créa* (1993)

J. A. West, *Serpent in the Sky* (1993)

S. Golowin, *Drache, Einhorn, Oster-Hase* (1994)

M. Nissenson and S. Jonas, *Snake Charm* (1995)

J. Cherry, *Mythical Beasts* (1995)

K. Shuker, *Dragons* (1995; 1997 [German edition])

P. Bandini, *Drachenwelt* (1996; a translation of *Mondo Drago*)

P. Busch, *Der gefallene Drache* (1996)

C. Paul-Stengel, *Schlangenspuren* (1996)

B. Young, *The Snake of God* (1996)

Worthy of special attention, because of its breath, quality, and perception (if dated), is M. O. Howey's *The Encircled Serpent: A Study of Serpent Symbolism in All Countries and Ages* (1926). In his *The Bosom Serpent* (1988), H. Schechter illustrates that folklore reveals the fictive imagination of humans. And K. Lapatin—in his *Mysteries of the Snake Goddess* (2002)—demonstrates the problems with forging history and then exploring ophidian symbology in light of fakes.[85]

Many significant books examine the snake handlers who take the appendix to Mark literally;[86] here is a selection:

J. B. Collins, *Tennessee Snake Handlers* (1947)

W. La Barre, *They Shall Take Up Serpents* (1962)

R. W. Pelton and K. W. Carden, *Snake Handlers* (1974)

S. M. Kane, *Snake Handlers of Southern Appalachia* (1979)

T. Burton, *Serpent-Handling Believers* (1993)

D. L. Kimbrough, *Taking Up Serpents* (1995)

Still valuable are such classics as E. R. Goodenough's *Jewish Symbols in the Greco-Roman Period* and L. Ginzberg's *The Legends of the Jews*. Outstanding books on the meaning of the serpent in the ancient Near East, the Bible, Judaism, and Christianity have appeared over the past two decades (although none of the authors has really studied most of the books already cited or closely examined ophidian realia). The following works add significantly to K. R. Joines' *Serpent Symbolism in the Old Testament:*[87]

M. Avi-Yonah, *Art in Ancient Palestine* (1981)

R. Hachlili, *Ancient Jewish Art and Archaeology in the Land of Israel* (1988)

E. Pagels, *Adam, Eve, and the Serpent* (1988)

R. Milburn, *Early Christian Art and Architecture* (1988, 1989)

A. Golan, *Myth and Symbol: Symbolism in Prehistoric Religions* (1991)

P. Prigent, *L'Image dans le Judaïsme du IIe au VIe Siècles* (1991)

H. Schreckenberg and K. Schubert, *Jewish Historiography and Iconography in Early and Medieval Christianity* (1992)

S. Koh, *An Archaeological Investigation of the Snake Cult in the Southern Levant* (1994)

F. Tristan, *Les premières images chrétiennes* (1996)

H. de Borchgrave, *A Journey into Christian Art* (1999, 2000)

J. G. Westenholz, ed., *Images of Inspiration: The Old Testament in Early Christian Art* (2000)

L. S. Wilson, *The Serpent Symbol in the Ancient Near East* (2001)

Reading and studying these publications can be enriched by additional examinations of some fairly recent publications devoted to Greek and Roman art and symbolism, especially these:

J. Hirschen, ed., *La grammaire des formes et des styles: Antiquité* (1981)

J. J. Pollitt, *Art in the Hellenistic Age* (1986, 1999)

P. Zanker, *The Power of Images in the Age of Augustus* (1988, 2000)

L. Burn, *The British Museum Book of Greek and Roman Art* (1991, 1999)

R. Turcan, *The Cults of the Roman Empire* (1996; French of 1992)

J. Elsner, *Imperial Rome and Christian Triumph: The Art of the Roman Empire AD 100–450* (1998)

J. Onians, *Classical Art and the Cultures of Greece and Rome* (1999)

W. Ball, *Rome in the East: The Transformation of an Empire* (2000)

Research into any form of symbolism is enhanced if one obtains a panoramic view of ancient symbology by examining the most important lexicons on the subject, such as the following:

E. Kirschbaum, *Lexikon der christlichen Ikonographie* (1968, 1990)

J. Chevalier and A. Gheerbrant, *A Dictionary of Symbols* (1969, 1996)

N. G. L. Hammond and H. H. Scullard, *The Oxford Classical Dictionary* (1970 [2nd ed.])

G. Heinz-Mohr, *Lexikon der Symbole* (1971, 1983 [7th ed.], 1998)

M. Lurker, *Lexikon der Götter und Symbole der alten Ägypter* (1974, 1987; reprinted in 1998)

P. Grimal, *The Dictionary of Classical Mythology* (1986, 1996; French of 1951)

G. J. Bellinger, *Lexikon der Mythologie* (1989, 1997)

G. de Champeaux and Dom S. Sterckx, *Einfürung in die Welt der Symbole* (1990; French of 1989)

M. Lurker, *Die Botschaft der Symbole: In Mythen, Kulturen und Religionen* (1990)

M. Girard, *Les symboles dans le Bible* (1991)

M. Lurker, ed., *Wörterbuch der Symbolik* (1991 [5th ed.])

H. Biedermann, *Dictionary of Symbolism* (1992)

J.-P. Ronecker, *Le symbolisme animal* (1994)

M. Cazenave, ed., *Encyclopédie des symboles* (1996; German of 1989)

G. Löwe and H. A. Stoll, *Lexikon der Antike: Griechenland und das römische Weltreich* (1997)

F. Glunk, *Das große Lexikon der Symbole* (1997)

P. Preston, *Metzler Lexikon antiker Bildmotive* (1997; English of 1983)

W. Bauer, I. Dümotz, and S. Golowin, *Lexikon der Symbole* (1998 [17th ed.])

M. Ferber, *A Dictionary of Literary Symbols* (1999)

J. C. Cooper, *Illustriertes Lexikon der traditionellen Symbole* (n.d.)

No publication can compare in depth and sophistication to the richly illustrated, multivolumed *Lexicon Iconographicum Mythologiae Classicae*. It has been my source of inspiration and has helped me refine my thoughts and reflections, but, unfortunately, it is limited to Greek and Roman iconography.

As one examines these lexicons, one should also consult the data amassed in Stith Thompson's *Motif-Index of Folk-Literature* and contemplate the language of art. Although Joseph Campbell's work is not appreciated by many scholars, I have found his books to be often stimulating. Scholarly and informative are the insights by Mircea Eliade.[88] I have found astute the many publications by Erwin Panofsky, especially the following:

E. Panofsky, *Studies in Iconology* (1939, 1962, 1972)
E. Panofsky, *Meaning in the Visual Arts* (1955, 1982)
E. Panofsky, *Perspective as Symbolic Form* (1991; original German of 1927)

Also extremely helpful in studying Panofsky's method and perspectives are M. A. Holly's *Panofsky and the Foundation of Art History* (1984) and J. Elkins' *The Poetics of Perspective* (1994).

The most sophisticated methodology for studying ancient iconography has been developed by O. Keel. He rightly stresses that images must not be read in terms of some mythology that has influenced us; they must be examined meditatively so that their silent language begins to speak. I have refined my research by visiting and talking with Keel in Freiburg and examining his numerous publications (cited in the following pages), especially the following:

O. Keel, *Die Welt der altorientalischen Bildsymbolik und das Alte Testament* (1972)
O. Keel, *Deine Blicke sind Tauben* (1984)
O. Keel and S. Schroer, *Studien zu den Stempelsiegeln aus Palästina/Israel*, vol. 1 (1985)
O. Keel et al., *Studien zu den Stempelsiegeln aus Palästina/Israel*, vol. 2 (1989)
O. Keel et al., *Studien zu den Stempelsiegeln aus Palästina/Israel*, vol. 3 (1990)
O. Keel, *Das Recht der Bilder Gesehen zu Werden* (1992)
O. Keel, *Studien zu den Stempelsiegeln aus Palästina/Israel*, vol. 4 (1994)
O. Keel and C. Uehlinger, *Gods, Goddesses, and Images of Gods in Ancient Israel*, trans. T. H. Trapp (1998).

Also extremely important are books published in Keel's series, especially U. Winter's *Frau und Göttin*, H. Brunner's *Das Hörende Herz*, and A. Berlejung's *Die Theologie der Bilder.*[89]

If we really want to hear the symbol "speak," and if we seek to proceed so as not to read into the image our own presuppositions, we should study each detail on an image, observe the whole composition, and imagine the historical and sociological setting in which it was given and received meaning. Most important, we should seek to enter into the world of meaning in which the artist and his or her viewers lived. That means not merely to

Figure 5. Hermes. Jerusalem. Early Roman Period. Bronze. Note the caduceus on his staff. JHC Collection

visit the places in which the symbol or similar images were employed, and perhaps revered. It demands more: sitting, for example, in Epidaurus and imagining how and why the devotees of Asclepius chose his symbol. It is the depiction of the serpent curled around his staff. Such informed imagination is supported if one holds in one's hand a bronze image of Hermes, from Jerusalem at the time of the Fourth Evangelist. Especially stimulating for a perception of ophidian iconography would be evidence that he held in his left hand a caduceus (two serpents facing each other). As J. Milgrom urges us to engage "handmade midrash," or visual theology,[90] as I have elsewhere endeavored to show, exegetes need to join those like Michelangelo who tried "to imagine and live within the biblical scenes."[91]

When we immerse ourselves in antiquity, the sights we see are often astounding. We see gods that are part serpents; some have serpents as legs and feet (anguipedes). The Seraphim have wings and feet—but are they not also serpents? Some lions have serpents for tails. Serpents appear with beards and crowns. An odd serpent, Ouroboros, is shown in a full circle so as to swallow his own tail. Dragons appear in art and iconography, almost everywhere and in almost every century. Serpents as gods or accompanying gods appear in images or are described in literature among the Assyrians, Babylonians, Canaanites, Hebrews, Israelites, Egyptians, Greeks, Etruscans, and Romans. Athena appears with serpents on her garments or around her neck. Marble sculptures, made by artisans who seem almost as skilled as the incomparable Michelangelo, have created living masterpieces out of marble: Asclepius with a serpent around his staff and Hygieia holding a serpent that drinks out of a cup. In European art alone we see a human with an elephant's head, gigantic serpents struggling against elephants, and one trying to swallow a pachyderm (enacting a report found in Pliny, *Nat.* 8). We also see imagined worlds filled with indescribable beasts including reptiles and dragons, snakes devouring a tiger or a gazelle, and a seductive woman enveloped by a dark snake.[92]

What are the limits of the human imagination? What did these pictures and images symbolize? How did those who created them envision our world, the animal kingdom, and our place within it? Having explored almost all our globe, except the ocean's floor, have we lost the poetry of imagination?

SUMMARY

It is certain that we have lost the origin of our language and the subtleties inherent in our words. Some of the lost meanings may be found in Italian, which is rooted in Latin. In Italian, for example, we find numerous words etymologically linked with the serpent.[93] The word *serpènte* signifies the literary and mythological use of "serpent" in good and evil ways.[94] The verb *serpènte* is the present participle of *serpere* and means "to move serpentinely" in a zigzag.[95] The noun *serpeninamènte* denotes not only a perfidious creature but also the possession of great agility.[96] The noun *serpentino* indicates that something or someone has the properties of a snake, can move in a zigzag manner; it also denotes the ability to move elegantly and with agility. It also has the meaning of being astute.[97]

What will be discovered in our search for the meaning of ophidian symbolism? Why is the serpent a universal symbol, appearing in virtually all creation myths, from the Australian Aborigines to the Israelites?[98] If the serpent is primarily a phallic symbol, then why can B. Johnson conclude that "the predominant evidence from early times presents the snake as distinctly feminine, and etymology bears out this primal identification"?[99] Is it true that the serpent is always a pejorative symbol in Christianity, as A. T. Mann and J. Lyle contend when they write that the snake "is always portrayed in Christian teachings as devilish and evil"?[100] What credence should be given to M. Gimbutas' claim that the "snake is life force, a seminal symbol, epitome of the worship of life on this earth. It is not the body of the snake that was sacred, but the energy exuded by this spiraling or coiling creature which transcends its boundaries and influences the surrounding world."[101] Will the conclusions to our research prove what is reported by M. Girard: the serpent is the animal that has given to the world of symbolism the most varied and rich meanings?[102]

2 Physiology Undergirds Symbology: Thirty-two Virtually Unique Characteristics of a Snake

No work on symbolism is well researched if the object featured in art and metaphor is not examined physiologically. Consequently, ophidian symbolism must be grounded by studying and holding snakes. These creatures have no arms or legs, yet they seem to move effortlessly and swiftly.

The books that have informed me about this intriguing animal are the following:

C. Mattison, *Snakes of the World* (1986, rep. 1992)

J. Coborn, *The Atlas of Snakes of the World* (1991)

G. R. Zug, L. J. Vitt, and J. P. Caldwell, *Herpetology* (1993, 2001)

R. Bauchot, ed., *Les Serpents* (1994; *Schlangen*, German of 1994)

C. Mattison, *The Encyclopedia of Snakes* (1995)

H. W. Greene, *Snakes: The Evolution of Mystery in Nature* (1997)

C. Mattison, *Snake* (1999)

THE PSYCHE OF MODERNS: THE SERPENT SYMBOLIZES EVIL AND SATAN

The failure of scholars in the humanities—and not only biblical experts—to appreciate the multivalent meanings of serpent symbolism is understandable. Beginning in the fourth century CE, as we shall see, the leading savants in the church triumphant began to disparage serpent imagery,[1] as M. Martinek demonstrates in his book on how the serpent became equated with the Devil (Satan, Belial, Beliar, Lucifer, Beelzebub, Leviathan [the serpent], Samael).[2]

In 1728, J. J. Kambach published a book on the mystery of Jesus Christ and

Figure 6. Snake Handler, Cobra, Author, and Boys. Marrakech.

the upraised serpent. His text was John 3:14. His method was to approach the Old Testament in light of the New Testament. He was convinced that the serpent in John 3:14 did not denote Jesus Christ; it signified Satan. This ex-egesis reflects the unexamined presupposition that the serpent is Satan.[3]

In the *Evangelisches Gesangbuch,* we find reference to the serpent. The image is always negative. In "Erschienen ist der herrlich Tag," we find the following second verse:

> The old serpent, [as well as] sin and death,
> [With] Hell, all misery, dread and distress
> Is overcome by Jesus Christ,
> Who today has risen from the dead. [my translation][4]

The old serpent is the sin and death that have been destroyed by Jesus Christ, as Paul states in Romans. There should be little wonder that New Testament experts who memorize such hymns find it impossible to ponder the positive symbolism of ophidian iconography, simile, and metaphor.

The symbolism of the serpent as the embodiment of sin and death reaches far beyond the walls of the church. For example, in F. Nietzsche's *Also sprach Zarathustra (Thus Spake Zarathustra: On the Other Side of Good and Evil),* Zarathustra enters a region of death. Here there is neither grass nor tree. One does not hear the sound of a bird singing. "It was like a valley, which all the animals, even the predators, avoid. There is one exception. One hateful species comes here: a thick green serpent, but only when it is old in order to die. Thus, the shepherds call this valley 'the Serpents' Grave' (Schlangen-Tod)."[5] The German denotes "the Serpents' Death."

The symbolic meaning of the serpent to denote sin permeates secular

Figure 7. Christ Shown
Spearing a Basilisk and
Trampling on Asps and
Snakes. North Africa. Lamp.
Circa fifth century. JHC
Collection. Compare Psalm
91. See the photograph and
discussion of a similar lamp
in J. G. Westenholz, *Images
of Inspiration: The Old
Testament in Early Christian
Art* (Jerusalem, 2000) p. 149.

paintings. In 1893, Franz von Stuck visualized the concept of woman as seductress, which was a fin-de-siècle pervasive concept, especially in Germany before 1900. He captured the mood in his *Die Sünde* (The Sins). A seductively attractive nude woman, with long black hair, seems to beckon to the observer. She looks askance, as Kierkegaard portrayed his seducer in his *Either-Or*. Alas, over the shoulder of this heavenly endowed woman stares a threateningly black serpent. It curls over her back and down her left shoulder. Any possible acceptance of her bewitching invitation has dreadful consequences.[6]

Two years earlier, in 1891, using a greater mastery of "symbolismus," Franz von Stuck achieved a superior oil painting of the costly wiles of the seductress. It is a masterpiece in the history of symbolism. It is called *Die Sinnlichkeit* (Voluptuousness) and is now in the Galerie Gunzenhause in Munich. A voluptuous woman, a sexually alluring vamp, looks invitingly at the interested, now captivated, viewer.

Again, there is one massive problem with the seductive invitation. Around her, from below her knee, around her thigh, through her legs and up to her waist, around her back and over her right shoulder curls a massive monster. It is a hideous black serpent. Its mouth is open. Its eyes have chosen any prospective Don Juan for lunch.[7] One is reminded of R. Briffault's claim that we should "speak of the sexual impulse as pervading nature with a yell of cruelty rather than with a hymn of love." [8]

Why is the earlier attempt by Franz von Stuck far more successful? *Die Sinnlichkeit* is much more effective and ingeniously conceived and composed than *Die Sünde*. The titles are well chosen, since *Voluptuousness*

is far more tantalizing than *Sin*. And the earlier painting is much more focused. It is also smaller; *Die Sünde* is 89 × 53 centimeters; *Die Sinnlichkeit*
is 56 × 36 centimeters. But these comments scarcely explain why the earlier
painting is superior.

If von Stuck's purpose was to present a woman who had airs of "superiority" and the demonic, then the 1893 *Die Sünde* is more effective. If he
sought to depict an enticing seductress who comes with the deadly serpent,
then the 1891 *Die Sinnlichkeit* is far more successful. In it, the vamp leans
back invitingly. Her arms are behind her. Her face seems to say, "Warum
Nicht?" The spontaneous answer would be, "Why not, indeed!" Her body
is curvaceous and pulchritudinous. The later painting shows the woman
standing straight up with a standoffish posture. In the earlier painting,
perhaps, von Stuck may have felt he had given too much rein to the positive
and erotic lures of a young woman and he later wanted to accent more the
mature woman as superior and demonic. Perhaps he had also depicted the
serpent too powerfully.

What makes the earlier painting far more effective and emotionally cap-
tivating? It is the depiction of the serpent with the woman. In the earlier
painting, the serpent is much more effectively drawn. Its mouth is open
wider; its teeth and fangs are exposed and too ready for action. Its girth is
equal to the size of the young woman's buttock. In the 1891 painting, the
serpent appears with more powerful symbology. In contrast to the later
painting, the only way to the inviting gate is through the serpent. And in
the earlier painting, the serpent has sufficient coils behind the seductress
so that it can spring forth to action and come out from hiding. The ophidian symbolism is better conceived and presented in the earlier painting.

Clearly, the serpent or dragon was the symbol of the god that needed to
be defeated at creation. One can think of numerous examples, including
the mythological snakes that shape the myths and religions of those in
northern Europe. For example, the primordial serpent lived in the ocean
and, like Leviathan of the Bible, it was the monster of the deep and the
chief enemy of Thor.[9]

I intend to demonstrate, beyond doubt, that the regnant portrayal of
the serpent as demonic and an embodiment of sin and temptation is only a
partial and misleading portrayal of the multifaceted dimensions of ophidian iconography. There is much more to learn about this mysterious creature. What positive symbolic meanings has the serpent generated to be
worshipped by or through by so many? Note the following focused selection of cultural groups:[10]

* the Aborigines in Australia and the Rainbow Serpent
* the Sumerians and Akkadians who worshipped snake gods like Nirah

Figure 8. A God and Associates Slaying the Dragon. Ancient Palestine or Syria. Courtesy of O. Keel [*Die Welt* (1972) No. 48; *Das Recht* No. 245].

- the Pharaohs and other Egyptians with their depictions of Isis and other gods as serpents and their penchant for the uraeus
- the unnamed people of the Indus Valley who depicted on a stone bowl a male figure grasping a serpent in each hand [11]
- the Minoans with their voluptuous serpent goddesses
- the Canaanite serpent cults in Beit Shean and elsewhere
- the Israelites who were associated with Nechushtan
- the Python group at Delphi
- the devotees of Asklepios (the Greek name) with his serpent staff, Hermes with the caduceus, and Athena with her serpents (among other gods) in ancient Greece
- the bards who popularized the Greek myths, especially those concerning Herakles (Hercules)
- those who were devoted to Agathadaimon and employed the Ouroboros
- the Etruscans and Romans who idealized the serpent
- the Ophites who worshipped Christ as the serpent
- the Gnostics who revered the serpent
- the Norsemen who skillfully crafted a serpent ring for a woman around 300 CE [12]
- the Celts with the image of Cernunnos who holds a large serpent [13] and their double-headed guardian snakes [14]
- the Zulus with their Mamba, or the snake hero [15]
- the Aztecs and their feathered serpent, or Quetzalcoatl
- the group in Peru who made the first-century CE drum with Nasca iconography of a rotund figure with a snake "moving" from his chin and with serpent hair [16]
- the serpent gods among the Native Americans, including the Hopi Indians in the United States and their snake dance [17]
- the snake handlers in the Bible Belt in the southern parts of the United States

Figure 9. Viking Serpent Ring. The image is from a replica made by the firm David-Anderson; it was purchased in Oslo. JHC Collection

- the Burmese snake worshippers
- the groups in India that revere the serpent as the guardian, and those who endorse the ancient tradition that Vishnu manifests himself as Shesha, the cosmic snake[18]
- the Dinkas in Africa who revere snake magicians and call snakes their brothers, washing them with milk and anointing them with butter[19]
- the Chinese who revere or worship the dragon[20]
- the cobra-focused religious groups in India

This summary could be easily expanded to include others nations and regions, notably Melanesia,[21] Haiti,[22] and Tanganyika.[23]

Serpent symbolism pervades human culture. When C. F. Oldham, a brigade surgeon in the British army in India, began his study of serpent worship, he thought he could focus on India and the challenging culture he had entered. But when he published his *The Sun and the Serpent: A Contribution to the History of Serpent-Worship*, he admitted that "the worship of the Sun and the Serpent" was "once well-nigh universal."[24]

The list mirrors more than ophidian concerns. It discloses the commonality of the human. Does it reflect the human's reception of meaning from another sphere or dimension? Does it help define human needs? To what extent was Jung tapping into primordial elements inherited by humans at birth? Why has virtually every culture and civilization been enamored of the serpent? Why did the ancients place this creature in accounts of creation (Aborigines, Assyrians, Babylonians, Israelites, Greeks, and others)? Surely, those who cavalierly report that the serpent is a symbol of evil or Satan need to be exposed as uninformed. Yet we have only begun to launch our own investigations.[25]

Figure 10. Consort of Shiva, the Milder Parvatī or Umā. JHC Collection

The bronze statue in Fig. 10 depicts the consort of Shiva (who is often displayed with serpents in his hair [like Medusa]), not the terrible Kālī or Durgā but the milder Parvatī or Umā. Her tongue and mouth do not drip with blood; she has a bewitchingly attractive smile. The statue was purchased in Jerusalem in the late 1990s and is not more than one hundred years old.

As almost always, the goddess is shown dancing (but here not on the body of her lord). Note the serpents: one in the hair (with a head at each extremity), one in a left hand (reminiscent of one of the Minoan serpent goddesses), and one as an upraised cobra at her feet (with eyes and mouth depicted). Another serpent curls behind her right foot. She is the Mother Goddess in Hinduism. As R. C. Zaehner surmised, Shiva's consort is "terrifying in her beauty, and her loveliness lies precisely in her frightfulness." [26] Shiva creates, sustains, and destroys through his "power," his consort. Since these serpents appear within an image of a goddess, it would be unthinkable that the artist and those who saw the statue were to imagine that they denoted evil. As Ninian Smart reminds us, the depictions of Shiva and his consort symbolize the "awe-inspiring and frightening" aspect of a deity; god "in some sense (so the Hindu tradition claims)" is "beyond good and evil." [27]

THE DOUBLE ENTENDRE OF EXISTENCE AND
OPHIDIAN SYMBOLOGY

Why are these two paintings so important for our present quest? They each, especially the earlier *Die Sinnlichkeit,* embody the "both–and" of the phenomena that permeate our very existence and were perennially captured in ophidian symbolism. Both paintings are phenomenal and unforgettable examples of the double entendre, of symbolism that is possible, or most creatively present, in the language of iconography. That is, the alluring invitation is wedded with the venomous curse.

Thus, in this sense the language of art has an advantage over the art of music. Like Kierkegaard's "either–or," music can present only one or the other. It is the "either" or it is the "or." If one chooses the "either" and grounds a concerto on G major, then one is limited by such structure and will scarcely achieve the heights of Mozart's Konzert für Flöte, Harfe und Orchestra C-Dur. If one chooses the "or" and grounds one's work on C major, then one will be constricted by that key and eventually become depressed by the inability to achieve what Mozart did in his Konzert für Flöte und Orchester G-Dur.

While music is bounded by such an "either–or," art is free to present to the reader the "both–and." That is, the good and evil can both be seen in a painting—and felt simultaneously in a somatic double entendre.

We in the West trifurcate time; thus we are too dependent on Greek and Latin grammar, failing to appreciate the subtleties of "fulfilled" or "unfulfilled" time represented by Semitic languages (as in Hebrew, Aramaic, Syriac, and Arabic). We know from our own life, and reflections on it, that the past, present, and future are not hermetically sealed categories. Existential time transcends such trifurcation. Thus, art, as in the Celtic figure with three faces,[28] can in a blink confront us with past, present, and future. Michelangelo clearly had the gift to present to the viewer the Creator who reaches out to the created and, by the touch of a finger, brings both into a "both–and."

In the history of symbolism, as in art, the serpent seems to be the quintessential image for representing life's double entendre. We will soon see that this iconographical message extends from the present back to circa 40,000 BCE; that is, far back into the prehistorical period. In human existence the serpent is such a multivalent symbol that it can at once symbolize opposites. It can represent, in its bite, "death," and in its molting "new life." That is symbolically present in the caduceus (two serpents facing each other), which signifies, sometimes, apotropaism (an object to avert evil).[29] The caduceus is not only reminiscent of Numbers 21, as we shall see, but also placed by physicians and pharmacists on our prescriptions

Figure 11. Marble Votive Relief, Dedicated to Zeus Meilichios (Who Conflates with Asclepius). Found in Piraeus. Fourth century BCE. Athens NAM No. 1434. The image is taken from a professionally made replica in the JHC Collection.

and placarded on buildings for health or health insurance in many places, notably in Amman and Jerusalem. J. B. Russell incorrectly reported that the Ouroboros is "a mythological motif of ambivalence common to the most diverse cultures." [30] The Ouroboros was not an ambivalent symbol—it showcases the dual symbolic power of the serpent. [31]

The curled serpent found on Zea Island in the Cyclades probably dates from the fourth century BCE, but its identification has been disputed. [32] The serpent reminds one of the numerous reliefs depicting Asclepius as a snake—especially the relief found at Piraeus and dating from the fourth century BCE. B. Johnson too readily announces that the serpent is Zeus Meilichios. [33] Such an identification may seem beyond question because the Greek above the figure identifies the relief as ΔΙΙ ΜΕΙΛΙΧΙΩΙ. That would mean, perhaps, Zeus Milik, [34] or "Zeus, King (of the universe)." It may not be wise to declare that the figure is simply Zeus. Those who made the image and perhaps those who revered the figure many centuries later may well have imagined that the figure represented Zeus Asclepius. It is imperative to remember that by the time of the Fourth Evangelist Asclepius was equated with Zeus.

Thus, the relief is not to be identified as either Asclepius or Zeus, as too many authors and scholars have struggled to prove. It is both, as Hunger has seen, [35] and the image was made at a time when Asclepius was being perceived as Zeus. Both represent iconographically and mythologically "the king of the universe."

Another example of the language of symbolism brings forward the problems of deciding between an "either–or" and even whether such a distinction might be meaningful. In 1562, Jacopo Tintoretto painted for the citizens of Venice the recovery of the corpse of St. Mark. He depicted the Alexandrians as fleeing, except for one Egyptian. At the Egyptian's side is depicted a man who is behind an aged Venetian holding a camel, which will transport the corpse. The man from Alexandria lifts up his left hand. In it is apparently an asp that is about to bite the elder statesman in his buttock.[36]

Is the serpent a good or bad symbol? For the Alexandrian man, the serpent is the means chosen to achieve an end, so the serpent is a positive image. Does the serpent depict immortality? And how is the serpent image related to St. Mark's corpse?

Perhaps the paradigm of good or bad is not the appropriate one suggested by this picture. The proper approach may be to think about the asp in the history of Egypt. It both administers death and transports one into eternity. Is not St. Mark also then seen as the one who symbolizes the promise of eternity—of resurrection with Christ?

Ophidian iconography is often a double entendre; that is, there is an intentional paronomasia linking at least two concepts at the same time. The artist thereby brings together concepts that are related but often separated by distinguishing categories with too rigid boundaries.

There is no greater iconographical symbol than the serpent for presenting the undulating vagaries of human existence. The serpent can embody both evil and good, not only sickness but also health; and—most important—the selfsame iconographical representation. The serpents often depicted beside Anat (a fierce goddess warrior worshipped in the Middle East as early as 2500 BCE) may signify in one image her role as both creator and destroyer. As with Ouroboros, one is all and all is one. In the fifteenth-century manuscripts of *Aurora consurgens* we are shown, inter alia, an Ouroboros dragon boiling in a flask. Above the monster, sitting on its tail, is an eagle above which is a dove.[37] The Ouroboros can be an androgynous symbol, with the tail as the phallus and the mouth as the womb. Also, with Ouroboros, our two conceptual philosophical paradigms meet: cosmos and chronos. Not only these two concepts, but also many others, are present in one symbol: the serpent.

THE LOST LANGUAGE OF SYMBOLISM AND OUR DISTANCE FROM NATURE

Pondering the symbols of the ancients, we enter an "inner world" and begin to grasp, as D. Fontana states in *The Secret Language of Symbols,* that "a symbol can represent some deep intuitive wisdom that eludes direct expression." [38] In writing this book, and while discussing the meaning of ophidian symbolism with established experts, I periodically reflected on how far removed we now are from nature and our earth. The snake once represented the earth and water. The dragon came to symbolize the four cardinal elements according to the Greeks: earth, air, fire, and water.

Except in special locations,[39] as in the Snake Temple in Malaya where numerous venomous snakes are fed by monks, or in rare ceremonies, as in the cult of San Domenico at Cocullo,[40] the snake is now feared and avoided. In seeking to recover the lost language of symbolism, we might remember that "language is fossil poetry" and that a "close and intimate relation exists between symbolism and philology."[41]

Most of the images we examine will challenge interpretation. While many are clearly positive, the exact meaning of the symbol is shrouded in opaqueness. Fortunately, we now may employ more than "author-criticism," which is the search for what the one who made an image may have intended to denote to his or her viewers. We also may utilize "audience-criticism," which opens new possibilities for seeking to comprehend what those viewing the image might think. As an example of the difficulty in interpreting ophidian symbolism, I cite the fourth-century BCE golden headstall of a horse's bridle that was found south of St. Petersburg and north of the Black Sea (near Cimbalka). A serpent goddess is clearly depicted. Her head, arms, and body are those of a woman, but the feet are two bearded serpents. One is reminded of the anguipede giants depicted on the Pergamum altar (now on public display in Berlin)[42] and the Etruscan depictions of sea demons with snake heads for legs.[43] The serpents—and the whole image—clearly denote positive meanings, perhaps royalty, power, beauty, invincibility, magic, and mystery. The interpretation of the image should not be limited to its elements (she is holding two lions); it was placed on the forehead of a horse, probably a majestic stallion, and it is crafted in gold. One is reminded of the uraeus on the gold mask of Tutankhamen.

What could the snake symbolize to the observant human in antiquity? This is a complex question, and we need to be aware of two factors. First, the ancients were more in tune with the environment than we are today. They knew themselves as a part of nature. Most important, unlike most of us, they lived within nature. While we often are far removed from nature by asphalt, concrete, automobiles, and so-called music blaring in our ears, the ancients heard the sounds of animals—birds and donkeys—when they awoke. We see snakes only in zoos; they saw them in gardens and even in houses.

Far too often I hear confused, clearly unreflective comments. Those who say, "I hate snakes" are often afraid of them, but also fascinated by them.

Figure 12. Serpent Goddess. Courtesy of the Hermitage. JHC

Those who claim to detest snakes may stand for a few minutes before gi-raffes, camels, lions, and elephants; but they are mesmerized for hours at a serpentarium in a zoo. The herpetologist at the Smithsonian, J. A. Peters, estimates that over 3,344,000 specimens of reptiles were imported to the United States in 1968–1969, and probably about one million were snakes.[44] That means people in the United States are fascinated by and at-tracted to snakes. As J. Coborn states in *The Atlas of Snakes of the World,* the human is naturally curious about most things and wants "to know a little more about those things that frighten him or that he does not fully understand. Because snakes are imagined to come under the categories of evil, dangerous, slimy, devious, and unknown, people like to know more about them."[45]

Before the advent of civilization and the move into villages and then cit-ies, the ancients were hunters and gatherers, moving in and with the flow of other animals. We civilized humans, who for approximately the past five thousand years have lived within cities, have been consecutively losing our physical abilities—especially to hear and see—and have forfeited a close relation with nature that is necessary to appreciate such animals as snakes. The snake shares our earth and belongs to our natural heritage.[46] So, it behooves us to listen to the ancients who could, and did, observe snakes from the beginnings of human existence, perhaps over three million years ago.[47]

THE MYSTERY OF THE SNAKE:
THIRTY-TWO VIRTUALLY UNIQUE FEATURES

At the outset, we should pause and imagine how we should ground ophidian symbolism in reality. Most promising would be to study the snake and compare it with other creatures.[48] The snake represents about 2,900 species that belong to the class Reptilia, the order Squamata (scaly creatures that include lizards), and the suborder Serpentes or Ophidia; thus, both Latin and Greek have contributed to the name of its suborder. The size of snakes is not certain, but ranges from 11.5 centimeters to nearly 10 meters. The weight of a South American anaconda can exceed 150 kilograms.[49]

One hears from eighteenth- and nineteenth-century explorers about how they encountered a snake over 12 meters long. Snakes can grow to enormous lengths, but careful scholars experience the sometimes threatening dimensions of nature without excessive exaggeration. For example, during his expedition in 1799–1800 to South America, Alexander von Humboldt reported seeing in one glance six 6-meter alligators, and being "accompanied by occasional 7-meter-long anacondas swimming alongside."[50]

Thirty-two features tend to make the snake distinct or unique, compared to other creatures the ancients met, such as the lion, bear, tiger, dog, camel, donkey, and cat. As C. Mattison states in *Snake,* "There has always been something of a mystery about snakes. How can they move so quickly without legs? How can they kill prey with only a single bite, delivered at the speed of an eye-blink? And how do they swallow prey whole when it may be several times bigger than their jaws?"[51]

First, the snake has neither arms nor legs.[52] Although a fossil snake with legs has been recovered, it is ninety-five million years old.[53] The present creature called a snake is a "limbless tetrapod" (Greek for "four feet"); it remains on the earth when it moves. It does not pound the earth as a horse or a human does. This could signify that the snake is earthy in the sense that it is attuned to and sensitive to Mother Earth, from which we come and to which we shall all return.

The movement of the snake is also unusual.[54] Its locomotion is varied, but it often leaves a "serpentine" trail in the sands of the desert; that is,

Figure 13. Cobra. Marrakech. JHC

it moves forward by moving left to right and often moving backward to move forward. There is a quasi-circular rhythm to the movement. This serpentine movement can easily be seen as symbolic of time, as it also goes forward but also frequently is repetitious in its main features; thus, human history is not from war to peace, or from sickness to health, but a repetition of these in some forward hopeful progression. The snake thus becomes a symbol of time, especially in Ouroboros (the presentation of the serpent with tail in its mouth).

Second, the snake has no ears. It has lost the eardrum (tympanum), outer and middle ears, and also the Eustachian tube. Only the uninformed believe that a cobra can hear the airborne sounds of a snake charmer who plays a musical instrument and sways to the sounds. Yet, very well-informed experts are influenced by such "authoritative" reports as the one by J. A. MacCulloch in the otherwise perspicacious entry in the *Encyclopaedia of Religion and Ethics:* "As certain snakes are susceptible to musical, rhythmical sounds or movements, these are used by snake-charmers to exhibit their power over them." [55] One who has handled and studied snakes would know better than to be misled by such a claim. The snake can only "respond to low-frequency waves," [56] so a cobra is simply following the movements of the snake charmer's flute. [57] The deafness of a snake could signify to the imaginative that it is attuned to otherworldly voices, since it is deaf to earthly noise. It thus can become a symbol for wisdom.

Third, the snake is voiceless. It can hiss, but it cannot bark like a dog, sing like a bird, purr like a cat, or whinny like a horse. Thus, the snake has no vocal way of communicating with humans. That could imply that it lives in the world of silence in which the word of God alone can be heard.

Even more profound thoughts could be generated by reflections that communication is impossible where there is no silence, and that silence is the essence of language.

Fourth, whether possessing a round or slit eye, the snake has no eyelids; only a scale, the brille, covers the eyes of most snakes. And some snakes have no vision.[58] That could denote the open-eyed quality of the snake. It can see and is not blinded by blinks and disrupted vision. The eyes of some snakes—notably the Boomslang of South Africa and the nocturnal Yellow Blunt-headed Vine Snake of Costa Rica—are enormous.[59] Again, along with its state of being earless, this creature might appear to some ancients to be a symbol of special wisdom. Noticeably, most images of a snake in antiquity depict the eyes in special ways.

Fifth, the snake has not only a limbless body but is elongated. That could symbolize unity and oneness. It is also symbolic of simplicity, and that can be imagined as attuned to wisdom and purity (as in: purity of heart is to will only one thing).

Sixth, the snake moves rapidly and without making a sound. That attribute could symbolize swiftness and dexterity. It can also connote elusiveness, which is a characteristic of deities imagined or experienced. Its elusiveness, as well as fear of it, may have given rise to the following limerick by Edward Lear:

> There was an old man with a flute,
> A sarpint ran into his boot;
> But he played day and night,
> Till the sarpint took flight,
> And avoided the man with a flute.[60]

Seventh, the male snake has two "penises" (the term is "hemipenes") that are solely used for copulation, and either may be so utilized.[61] That unique somatic quality could enable the snake to symbolize not only the erotic but also fertility. The female also should be included now; she produces so many offspring that an observer would imagine that the creature was an ideal symbol for fertility.

Eighth, the snake has a split tongue that can exit its mouth through a hole; that is, the snake does not have to open its mouth to send forth its tongue.[62] The bifid tongue, along with the two penises, can symbolize duality. It can also denote duplicity and the ability to say two things at the same time. Thus, the snake can symbolize lying. This symbolic meaning of the snake has misled some commentators on Genesis 3.

Ninth, the snake eats in a vicious manner, and all snakes are carnivores.[63] This "degenerate quadruped"[64] can ingest an animal that outweighs it.[65] The scene can be revolting to humans when one sees a reptile swallow whole a beautiful bird, an impala, pet dog, or other creature.[66] All snakes swallow animals whole, and anacondas along with the aptly named boa constrictor crush the life out of helpless creatures. In zoos, animal specialists will frequently show the public a lion eating supper, but never a king cobra swallowing a live fawn whole.[67] This characteristic of the snake could cause fear, wonder, astonishment, and awe. Folklore associates the pigeon with the serpent, whose bodies are similar, not because they are monsters, but because they are wonders.[68]

Frequently, artists use the serpent to create in their viewers the feeling of fear and dread. For example, Kubin Otakar (1883–1969), an Eastern European who was influenced by Impressionism and Neoclassicism (especially works by van Gogh and Gauguin), painted in 1908–1909 *Der Schlangenbeschwörer*, which is now in the Saarlandmuseum.[69] The title of the painting means *The Serpent Exorcist*. The dark painting is riveting, depicting an easterner, perhaps an Indian, playing a flute before which four cobras—four times his size and twice his height—not only rise far above him but encircle him. He is also alone and in an abandoned subterranean chamber. He appears peacefully playing away on his musical instrument, and perhaps with eyes closed. He seems unperturbed, and even unaware, of the monsters swaying above him. The painting is impressionistic, but it inspires subjective reflections regarding fear and anguish. One is struck with questions about deadly power. The cobras do not threaten, but their sheer massiveness and immediate presence awaken primordial fears. Such reflections raise other questions. For example, why do the depictions of extraterrestrials look like snakes with large eyes?[70]

Tenth, massive snakes can sometimes go for months without eating. This phenomenon could denote that this creature is different from others: it does not experience the need to eat as do other animals. Observing a snake that has no need to forage for food could suggest that it might be divine or at least godlike. It is easy to imagine the ancients pondering this question: Is not this creature, so unique and awesome or "awe-full," blessed by the gods or fed by the gods?

Eleventh, the snake is socially independent. It is usually seen in groups only at birth or at the culmination of hibernation. It is not gregarious as are dogs, and does not live in groups like lions. It does not hunt in packs, like wolves and hyenas; it hunts alone. There are no reports of seeing examples of cooperative hunting. The snake stays in a place alone. The only social behavior—with the exception of some sea snakes that swim in groups—is the grouping of snakes in a den to hibernate and mate; neither of these activities is what sociologists classify as social behavior. Both are things that have to be done, and there is no dialogue or social interchange involved. Unlike the ant, snakes have no hierarchies, no dominance, and no territoriality. All these seemingly unique features of the snake could represent its elite nature. It can thus easily symbolize mystery and wonder.

Twelfth, the snake is cold blooded and needs to obtain its warmth from its surroundings. That might strengthen its association with the earth. It lives off Mother Earth and from the Sun, also often seen as a god. A golden cobra, especially when aroused, becomes like the sun on earth, blazing forth radiance.[71] It is easy to imagine why the ancient Egyptians chose the cobra in making the uraeus and placing it on the crowns or heads of the pharaohs.

Thirteenth, the snake is almost invisible when it is resting because its color is usually similar to its surroundings.[72] This attribute of the snake might add to its elusiveness and invisibility. It can signify the being that is there, but cannot be perceived. Thus, the snake may symbolize the mysterious elusiveness of a god.

Fourteenth, the snake can hide in an abundance of places: in trees, caves, under rocks and fallen trees, in the water, in holes, in cactus bunches, in tunnels, and in nests. It can also hide itself in the sand. Thus, the Horn-viper is imperceptible in the beige desert sand.[73] This ability would add to its power to symbolize the hidden one: a god or the God.

Fifteenth, the snake does not show fear, as do dogs and even lions. When confronted by danger it does not slink away or lower its neck, in obedience and submission.[74] It either relies on passive strategies or rises and faces the danger.[75] It seems fearless and strikingly independent. This phenomenon is especially notable in the python, since the Asian Netpython grows to well over 10 meters.[76]

Such fearlessness would make the snake more admired and revered. The king cobra, lightning fast and deadly, may be revered because it is feared. It can kill an elephant.[77]

Sixteenth, the snake is amphibious. The ability to move rapidly over land, into the earth, up a tree, or through water would symbolize the ability to go virtually everywhere. It is the creature that can go where it wants. It is no wonder that some ancients added to ophidian symbolism the feathered or winged snake, which was especially strong among the Aztecs, who worshipped the Feathered God, Quetzalcoatl, an incarnation of the "Serpent Sun," Tonacatocoatl. This feathered serpent symbolized many good things: healing, learning, and the art of poetry. The feathered serpent is the lord of healing and the lord of the Morning Star (the god who brings back the sun to the heavens).[78] It now becomes clear what the artists intended in the depictions on Greek vases (especially those in the Hermitage) and on sarcophagi (notably in Basel and Berlin) of chariots drawn by large snakes with wings, especially in the Medea symbolism (see Chap. 4).[79] The snake can go everywhere: under the earth, over the earth, under and through the water, and even, with wings, into the heavens.

Seventeenth, the snake sheds its skin (called ecdysis), as many as four times a year.[80] Ecdysis would symbolize the snake's ability to rejuvenate itself and to gain a new, better, and larger body and existence. The ancient would assume that old age and death were signaled by wrinkles, which would be lost if we could shed our old skin, like the snake.

It is no wonder so many ancient tales and fables,[81] like the story of Gilgamesh, relate how the snake alone knows (and has) the power of rebirth, rejuvenation, reincarnation, and immortality. It is also no wonder that the Asclepian cult chose the snake as the symbol of medicine and health since the physician gives new life to one who is about to die from some disease. The snake curled around a staff in statues of Asclepius signifies the power to give health and new life. Similarly, the monuments placed above graves, for example, at Rhodes, depict large curled serpents; most likely these denoted the symbol of immortality.[82]

While many scholars err in presupposing that the snake is to be dreaded and is a symbol of evil, some experts on snake symbolism exaggerate the positive symbolism of a serpent, often concluding that this creature symbolizes only, or primarily, immortality. Note the words of R. Briffault, who points his reader to "an animal which plays a larger part in religious and mythological conceptions than any totem or any of the creatures that have become connected with the gods, namely, the serpent. The serpent is in all primitive thought, as well as in later symbolism, the emblem of immortality."[83]

The symbolism is worldwide; for example, the Aztecs considered the rattlesnake the "yellow lord" of all serpents. For them, this serpent symbolized lightning, cycles of rebirth, and renewal. Images, such as a gold double-headed serpent in the triangular form holding in its mouth a frog, are Aztec images. This image dates from 1000 to 1530 and probably antedates 1520. The conquering Spaniards were horrified by live rattlesnakes considered sacred by Aztecs and revered in their temples.[84]

Often today the serpent appears in unusual places. The image of a serpent drinking from a bowl, a modern depiction inspired by the images of Asclepius or Hygieia, is found on the doors of an institute for the study of ancient Judaism. Why? Is it because of the importance of ophidian symbolism within Judaism? No; the building was formerly a hospital.

Eighteenth, the snake can disappear into the earth. Thus, it is chthonic; that is, it enters into the lower world that is unknown to humans. The snake can also plunge into the sea, in which some ancients thought the gates to the netherworld were placed. It is able to penetrate the source of the life that pours into the grasses, bushes, and trees through their roots. It

Figure 14. Close-up of Serpent Drinking. Tübingen; Institutum Iudaicum. JHC

knows and even enters the underworld. It is also symbolic of the agitation that creates new growth from the earth.

Nineteenth, the snake can be astonishingly beautiful. It needs no cosmetics. Nothing in nature can be so bewitchingly lovely as a gigantic cobra raised fully before you with the hood extended and its gold glistening scales blinding one from the sharp rays of the sun. The Green Mamba can also bewitch; if it is large, it can "easily look a human in the face!"[85] The beauty may be considered demonically attractive. It should also be astonishingly divine. Such attributes of the snake were reasons the ancient Egyptians chose the snake to symbolize divinity, beauty, wisdom, royalty, and power; all these attributes were symbolized by the uraeus.

Too many interpretations of Genesis 3 assume, without exploring the issue, that the serpent is male. The serpent may have been depicted as innocent and good and perhaps very attractive so that "the woman" would want to converse with it.

Though the noun *nāḥāš* (*nᵉḥaš*; Gen 3:1) in biblical Hebrew is masculine, the gender of a noun does not necessarily indicate the gender of the one being depicted. Thus, one cannot use grammar alone to determine the sex of a creature. Sometimes the "serpent" of Genesis 3 is imagined to be a female. In Muenster, in the Westfälisches Landesmuseum für Kunst und Kulturgeschichte, is Johann Brabender's *Sündenfall*. He depicts a serpent curled around the tree of life. The serpent is a she, and has exposed breasts like "the woman." She is attractive, innocent, even angelic. Likewise, the serpent depicted so attractively in the Brancacci Chapel in Florence is feminine.[86]

In 1860, the serpent was found so attractive that an elegant set of glasses with a pitcher was made with serpents prominently depicted. Between 1899 and 1908, a blue jeweled cigarette case was crafted; on the cover is a gold serpent with inlaid diamonds. It is 9.4 centimeters in length and stunning. A sun umbrella of 1899 bears a ruby that is held by gold serpents in a

Figure 15. Black African Cobra. Marrakech. JHC

spiral form. A jeweled pen with a ruby and diamonds is artistically formed into two serpents.[87] This and other serpent-ornamented jewelry belonged to the czars.

Twentieth, the snake often possesses deadly venom. That makes it the giver of death. The Boomslang can deliver venom that kills an adult human rapidly.[88] The power of snakes to administer death rapidly, mysteriously, and unexpectedly would empower the snake as a symbol of death, life, and power. Thus, envenomation could symbolize a god that can bring the end even to those who are mighty, young, and full of health. And such demise appears instantaneously.

The serpent as the one who brings death is well represented in antiquity. For example, almost all in Western society today know about the Trojan War, and if they do not remember the details, many are aware of the fate of Laocoon (G. Laokoon) and his two sons. He was the priest of Poseidon, and he tried to warn the Trojans that the horse left by the Greeks was a danger. Two large serpents ascend from the sea. They strangle his two young sons and then Laocoon. Finally, they slither under the altar of Athena, probably symbolizing that a Greek god had sent them to kill Laocoon and his sons. A marble aesthetically depicting the two serpents killing Laocoon and his two sons dates from about 150 BCE and is on public display in the Vatican.[89]

The episode is immortalized by memorable portrayals of the mythical event. The *Laocoon* created by El Greco is now in the National Gallery in Washington. El Greco depicted one son as already dead. The other futilely holds one serpent at a distance. Laocoon wrestles with a larger serpent that is about to bite him on the right eye.[90]

The use of the serpent to denote danger is found virtually everywhere. It is well known on flags, especially on the Revolutionary War serpent flag and on an early flag of Texas. Both flags have the motto, "Don't tread on me."

Twenty-first, the snake can show no facial emotion. It cannot smile or grimace; it can only open its mouth partly or fully. Any putative smile usually becomes perceived as a grimace. It is a deadly threat or promise, as the horrific fangs become visible.[91] The expressionlessness of the snake could symbolize its superiority. It is above emotions. It is from another realm or world. It does not act like earthly creatures. Sometimes, to accentuate a serpent's benign or even inviting quality, the animal is depicted with a smile, and it looks like a placid duck (see, e.g., the sculpture of Hygieia in the Hermitage).

Twenty-second, the raised snake can resemble an engorged phallus. That could signify its sexual powers. Despite the fact that snakes sometimes copulate only after hibernation, this factor along with its two penises would add to its ability to symbolize the phallus, eroticism, sexuality, and fertility. It is no wonder that the snake is deemed an aphrodisiac in some countries, even today. It is obvious why the Greeks and Romans depicted Priapus as grossly ithyphallic and some deities with a lingam that was a serpent.[92]

Twenty-third, the snake is physiologically and definitively unlike humans. It is thus something that can be seen as inhuman, subhuman, or superhuman. The snake cannot wink, laugh, or talk, but it can rapidly deliver a deadly dose of venom. Not only fear but also loathing often accompany thoughts related to the snake. The symbolisms here are numerous. They move within the world of folktales, legends, myths, and into the heart of religion and spirituality.

Twenty-fourth, the snake hibernates. That is, it enters into the earth for long periods. Where does it go? What is it doing? What is it learning? All these and many more reflections might spring to the mind of our primordial—certainly not primitive—ancestors. They did not simply assume that the snake was sleeping in its hibernaculum, as we dismiss through categorization of this rare phenomenon (it is not unique in the animal kingdom, but it is still a remarkable aspect of the snake's life). This chthonic dimension of the snake would add to anguine symbolism the dimension of wisdom. It is clear, then, from this and previous observations, why the Egyptians, early Jews, and Jesus used the snake to symbolize wisdom.

Twenty-fifth, the snake appears slimy and cold. It is not warm and fluffy like a puppy; it is often disturbing to the touch. This feature adds to its demonic or diabolical features or symbolism. Thus, it is evident why the Babylonians[93] and many early Christians stressed that the snake was an embodiment of evil.

In Persian (or Iranian) thought there are two gods. Ahura Mazda is the Wise Lord, the Creator. Angra Mainyu (later called Ahriman) is the arch-demon, the one who causes destruction and woes. He lives in dark-

Figure 16. *Left.* Bronze Dragons. Early Hellenistic Period. Found near Jerusalem. JHC Collection.

Figure 17. *Right.* Medusa. The fence of the Summer Palace in St. Petersburg. JHC

ness and can appear as a youth, lizard, or snake. The hero Thraetaona can cure some sicknesses, like Asclepius, and struggles "against the evil done by the serpent." [94] Ahura Mazda creates Mithra (Mithras), "the ruler of all countries," who apparently conflates with Thraetaona and Vima ("the good shepherd" [*Vendidad* 11.21], and the great hero within Persian mythology)—perhaps as "Manly Valor"—to slay "the horse-devouring, poisonous, yellowish-horned Serpent." [95] In the Tauroctony, found virtually everywhere but not yet in Pompeii, Herculaneum,[96] or Iran, Mithra is depicted slaying the bull. A serpent is usually shown. Sometimes it is only on the ground, but at other times it is depicted biting the bull (or perhaps drinking its blood).[97] F. Cumont, the father of the modern study of Mithraism, read the Tauroctony in terms of Zoroastrian dualism, concluding that the snake is an evil creature.[98] This interpretation does not do justice to the vast and complex examples of the Tauroctony; sometimes the serpent helps Mithra.[99] Along with R. Merkelbach, I take the serpent to be a positive symbol in Mithraism.[100] The bronze object in Fig. 16 seems to be from the East or Luristan;[101] it may depict the two deities known to the Persians.[102]

Twenty-sixth, the snake digs in and around a garden, providing stimulus and growth. It also kills rodents and mice. Hence, it would be seen as the one who helps provide for the fertility of the soil. It is thus no wonder that the Greeks and Romans frequently used anguine symbolism to denote fruitfulness. It is also clear why the Rabbis advised Jews to have snakes in their gardens.

Twenty-seventh, the snake kills animals that are dangerous to humans, including mice and other rodents. Thus, the snake would most likely be-come perceived as the great guardian. This continues, for example, in the illustrated poem by Mechtilde Lichnowsky entitled "Die Dackeln und die Schlange." Two puppies disobey their mother and dig an inviting hole in the garden, seeking to find something exciting there. They unearth a large ser-pent. The two puppies beg for mercy from this apparent monster who surely is about to devour them. The boa wraps herself around the babies. And, to the puppies' surprise and delight, the boa brings them home to their mother (*Marbacher Magazin* 64 [1993]). Perhaps this attribute of the snake as the protector or guardian helps to explain the presence of snakes on ancient jars and the ophidian symbolism of Medusa, as well as the stories and myths in which the snake is the guardian of treasure, most notably in the influential Syriac composition *Hymn of the Pearl* (second to fourth centuries CE).

In Dante's masterpiece, in Canto Nono 41, Medusa and others appear with "asps and vipers have they for hair" *(Serpentelli e ceraste avean per crine)*.[103] Figure 17 is a photograph of Medusa on the iron fence surround-ing the Summer Palace in St. Petersburg.

To dismiss the perception that the serpent symbolizes "the guardian" only in ancient lore, literature, and iconography, I bring forward a rather recent poem. The poem is entitled "Die Schlange" and was composed by Friedrich Georg Jünger (1898–1977).[104] Here is the German and my trans-lation:

> Deine Schlange ist bei dir,
> Die stille, die stumme.
> Die alle Kammern des
>   Hauses kennt,
> Deine Schlange ist bei dir.
>
> Kehre wieder, was mag,
> Die dich hütet im Umlauf.
>
> [Your serpent is by you,
> The silent one, the mute one.
> Who knows every recess
>   in the house,
> Your serpent is by you.
>
> Come again, what may,
> She guards you in life's circles.]

This theme—"Your serpent is by you"—makes it clear that the serpent as the one who "guards you in life's circles" is not an archaic thought or symbol.

Twenty-eighth, the snake can illustrate grandeur and majesty. No creature can be so awesomely regal as the upraised cobra with its hood extended.[105] Before such majestic power one feels total awe. Perhaps it can be categorized partly as divinity and partly as royalty. It is thus no wonder that Isaiah used this imagery in his throne vision and that the Egyptians used the uraeus to symbolize their belief that the pharaohs were divine kings.

Twenty-ninth, the snake does not smell. It cannot be discerned by smell, like the horse, dog, cat, lion, hyena, and especially the pig. That quality might add to its symbolic nature of being imperceptible and elusive. The *nāḥāš* (Nachash) in Genesis 3 appears suddenly, without introduction; this "serpent" is not heard, seen, or smelled. No animal can compete with the snake for appearing unexpectedly and almost instantaneously. This characteristic of the snake would make it a good symbol for the appearance of the Spirit or God.

Thirtieth, some snakes look as if they are two-headed; that is, the head and tail are virtually indistinguishable.[106] This phenomenon would lead to numerous symbolic meanings. The snake may symbolize two opposites at once. The symbol most appropriate would be the caduceus.

As a complete circle, this two-headed snake could symbolize perfection, completeness, and the unity of time and the cosmos. It is no wonder that bracelets, especially in the Greek and Roman world, are intricately carved with snake heads at each end. The origin of the Ouoboros lies in this characteristic of the snake.

Also, some snakes do have two heads.[107] This may be caused by some genetic alteration or defect, but when ancients saw such a snake they would probably reflect about the symbolism it evoked. Anguine symbolism can thus denote duplicity, double-mindedness, the oneness of all duality, and other related concepts and ideas. Symbolizing sickness and health, the cause of evil or good fortune, the snake is behind the creation of the caduceus that appears often with Hermes and is placed on the coins of King Herod, as elsewhere.

Thirty-first, the snake is mysterious and unknown. Even today, much is still unknown.[108] Seeing a one-eyed snake, as a mutated *viper xanthina,*[109] can be an alarming experience. It evokes the mythology associated with Cyclops. The so-called combat dance or sex dance of the snake is often not between a male and female; it is now often recognized as a struggle between two male snakes that are competing for a mate. Sometimes herpetologists consider that the dance is a homosexual attempt of two males attempting to copulate. We are insufficiently informed about the longevity of snakes and about their potential length (since, unlike humans, snakes grow each year of their lives). Little is known today about the physiological changes that occur during hibernation, especially in the tropics. It is debated whether snakes swim or simply float and use their terrestrial means of locomotion to move them forward in the water. Thus, the snake is well chosen to symbolize the mystery that surrounds and accompanies human lives. Even as late as 1557, a French poet, probably inspired by ancient Greek tales, perhaps those well known and associated with Herodotus, could believe the following words: "Dangereuse est du serpente la nature, Qu'on voit voler près le Mont Sinai" ("Dangerous is the serpent by nature, which one observes flying near Mount Sinai").[110]

Finally, perhaps repeating some previous reflections, the snake is antisocial in the sense that a human cannot communicate with it and develop a relation with it. One can live together with a snake, but it is an odd companion whether in a prehistoric cave setting or in a modern garden. Stories abound of individuals who have pet boas that are treated royally for years and then swallow a child beloved by the owner. In Marrakech, I observed that snake handlers were constantly jumping back to avoid their pet, who was striking out at them. When they "kissed" the cobra, it was when the cobra had struck and was fully extended; moreover, it was held up and at a distance by the handler. There is no way to communicate with or develop something like "love" or "respect" with a snake. One cannot enjoy a relationship with a snake as one can with a dog.

SUMMARY

In seeking the physiological basis for the ophidian symbolism we shall be exploring, we have learned a vast amount about a remarkable creature. The snake has no arms, no legs, no ears, no eyelids, and only one functional lung. It cannot speak. It must swallow its food whole and is consigned to being carnivorous. When it falls asleep and hibernates, it cannot wake itself. It is totally dependent on its environment for heat. It cannot migrate, like the elephant, lion, or wildebeest to find food or water. Humans who have the physical limitations of a snake are immediately institutionalized;[111] but the snake is fearless, independent, must hunt only by ambush, and has survived from the time of the dinosaurs. Should we not recognize something special in this creature that we have been taught to hate (since such behavior has to be learned)?

In his *Patterns in Comparative Religion*, M. Eliade concluded that the "symbolism of the snake is somewhat confusing, but all the symbols are directed to the same central idea: it is immortal because it is continually reborn, and therefore it is a moon force, and as such can bestow fecundity, knowledge (that is, prophecy), and even immortality."[112] Eliade may be

Figure 18. Snake Stickpin, Vienna 1830. Gold with emerald, rubies, and a pearl. The person who made this jewelry and the one who wore it took the serpent to symbolize something good, such as beauty. It is clear that the serpent was admired, and not only in antiquity. This photograph is from a replica made at the Metropolitan Museum of Art, New York. JHC Collection

commended for his focus, but he failed to represent all the various meanings of the symbol of the serpent.[113]

It is now becoming clear that the ancients, the great artists, and even many people today, think of the snake as a symbol of many diverse ideas, concepts, and feelings. Humans in their early history, and perhaps in prehistory especially, did not categorize the snake, as do most westerners and Americans today, as a symbol of horror and fear. They eventually observed what we now know: snakes kill only out of hunger or fear.[114] Virtually no snake is interested in eating us, and we are the reason the snake is afraid.

We have become aware of how physiology lies behind symbology; as the ancients carefully studied the physical characteristics of snakes, they developed and evolved ophidian symbolic and mythical language in art and writing. As K. Sälzle stated in his book on animals and humans, the rational thought of modern humans is in sharp contrast to the intuition of the early humans.[115] They developed not only symbolism but also poetry; their imaginations were more fertile than ours.[116] With these observations of snakes in mind, we can now explore what is available from antiquity to help us comprehend the full meaning of the ophidian symbols so obvious in many places. Surely, such exploration will help us in the exegesis of major, influential texts, especially John 3:14.

3

Realia and Iconography: The Symbolism of the Serpent in the Ancient Near East (and the Religion of Israel)

ARCHAEOLOGY AND THE SYMBOLISM OF THE SERPENT

Having introduced the subject of serpent iconography and symbology in antiquity, how do we continue? Do we go directly to the ancient texts? Or do we begin with realia (the objects) and iconography?

In the past, scholars began with the texts, often at an early age, in the synagogue, church, or grammar school. The result was that they examined realia and images only later. This textual myopia left its errors. Images were read in light of the biblical text, perceived literally, and the ancient myths were usually misunderstood. We have seen, in detail, how the presupposition that the serpent denotes evil, the demonic, and even Satan is deaf to the voice of the images. As O. Keel points out in his book on the right of the pictures to be seen, from 1847 to the present experts have tended to study ancient iconography in light of what was known about Mithra, Gilgamesh, Enkidu, Tammuz, and others.[1] Now, we must pause, look long and sensitively at a work of art (or artifact), and ponder such questions as the following: What did ancient authors imagine? What did they intend to encapsulate in imagery? How did their culture help them choose the details and the constellation of images? How did those who used and saw the image add to the alleged intended meaning?

How do we comprehend the subtleties of the language of iconography and symbology? One might agree with Coleridge that the creative imagination is "a repetition in the finite mind of the eternal act of creation in the infinite I Am."[2] One might want to ponder the point, yet most readers would agree that, without informed imagination, images remain mute. To help them speak to us today we need to seek to dwell in their own time (even if they appear timeless) and approach with sensitivity the one who fashioned them.

It has been claimed that "we are ultimately responsible [for] and alone with the anxiety of structuring meaning in a world that has no inherent meaning." [3] While such reflections have some import and clarify the need for assigning meaning to a reality that does not come with labels and values, I tend to disagree with the basic thought. I am rather convinced that we are born into a world of meaning. We grow up in a linguistic culture. It comes to us, daily, with images and symbols that have been interpreted and invested with meaning. We inherit over three thousand years of iconographical explorations into our universe. It is our task, now, to explore what meaning was "poured into" what we have inherited or rediscovered.

As E. Panofsky pointed out, we need to apprehend form, subject matter, meaning, and psychological nuances, and familiarize ourselves with the times, customs, and culture in which realia were fashioned and in which they were given (sometimes different) meanings. A warning by Panofsky bears highlighting: "It is just as impossible for us to give a correct *iconographical analysis* by indiscriminately applying our literary knowledge to the motifs, as it is for us to give a correct *pre-iconographical description* by indiscriminately applying our practical experience to the forms." [4] In my own continued study, what I now perceive to be "indiscriminate" will be removed. With these reflections, and caveats, let us proceed with a presentation and appreciation of ancient ophidian images. (Due to the thousands I have collected, the selection must be focused.)

PREHISTORIC FINDS

The earliest cave art, especially at Lascaux (ante 20,000 BCE), represents numerous animals. [5] Most notable are the images of bison and early deer, cows, and horses; no animal depicted is clearly a serpent. [6] This may be explained by the fact that the serpent is cold-blooded and would not have been present in the European Ice Age. The earliest known image that could be a serpent appears to have been found in a cave at La Baume-Latrone, France. It has been dated somewhere between 40,000 and 26,000 BCE. Imagination is required to obtain a grasp of its form and meaning. The art is a line drawing. [7] A large serpent seems evident; the fangs and forked tongue are discernible. It appears that the serpent is depicted to evoke thoughts about a woman. The contrast is striking: the serpent seems threatening, the woman inviting. Perhaps B. Johnson is correct to imagine that we are faced with "a visual pun. The pun continues from the serpent as woman to the serpent as goddess. The play of images is enlivened by the mammoths that literally and figuratively support the snake-woman-deity. She is often called Our Lady of the Mammoths." [8]

A cave found in 1970 at the southern tip of Italy at Porto Badisco nel Salento, between Brindisi and Lecce, boasts of paintings that are dated by carbon analysis (C-14) to about 39,000 BCE. Some specialists are convinced that the drawings in this cave are the most important and numerous examples of post-Paleolithic art. There are no clear depictions of a serpent, but there are lines and drawings that are serpentine forms ("serpentiformi e zig-zig").[9] I am convinced that someone, long ago, intended to depict serpents. One end of the drawing is wider and the other elongated; that could indicate a head and tail. All images are impressionistic depictions of human life in an agricultural setting. In all, there appear to be twenty-four serpentine drawings.[10] It is far from clear what these drawings mean; perhaps the one who made them tried to illustrate that the meaning of life includes appreciation of serpents.

ARCHAEOLOGICAL DISCOVERIES IN ANCIENT PALESTINE

Numerous and significant studies have been written on serpent symbolism in Egypt,[11] Babylonia,[12] Greece,[13] and Rome.[14] As of the present, no survey has been published of serpent symbolism in ancient Palestine from Dan to Beer-sheba with special focus on controlled archaeological excavations.[15] The purpose of this chapter is to fill this gap, thus providing objective foundations for discerning what the ancients might have intended when they made, or used, images of serpents.

Where has serpent iconography been found in ancient Palestine from Dan to Beer-sheba, in the centuries before the Byzantine Period when there was a major cultural change and a shift in the perception of the serpent? In 1943, J. B. Pritchard, thinking of goddesses depicted with serpents, listed only four examples of serpent iconography: two were from Beth Shan, one from Tell Beit Mirsim, and one from Shechem.[16] Today the evidence of serpent iconography in ancient Palestine is far more extensive, even when we presently focus only on the obvious, or relatively certain, examples. The following summary is selective; for a detailed examination see my *Serpent Iconography and the Archaeology of the Land from Dan to Beersheba* (in press).

For convenience, here is a synopsis of the ages and periods used in the following discussion: [17]

PN[18]   c. 6000–4500 BCE
Chalcolithic   c. 4500–3300 BCE

EB I	c. 3300–3000 BCE
EBII–III	c. 3000–2250 BCE
EBIV	c. 2250–2000 BCE
MBI	= EBIV
MBIIA	c. 2000–1800 BCE
MBIIB–C	c. 1800–1550 BCE
LBI	c. 1550–1400 BCE
LBIIA	c. 1400–1300 BCE
LBIIB	c. 1300–1200 BCE
Iron I	c. 1200–925 BCE
Iron II	925–586 BCE
Persian	539–332 BCE
Hellenistic	332–63 BCE
Early Roman	63 BCE–135 CE [Herodian c. 40 BCE–70 CE]
Late Roman	135–325 CE
Byzantine	325–640 CE

Munhata

The earliest evidence of serpent iconography has been found at Munhata and antedates 4000 BCE. Munhata is situated about 13 kilometers south of the Sea of Galilee (Kinneret Yam) in the Jordan Rift Valley. It is about equidistant between Beth Shan in the south and the Sea of Galilee in the north. Six occupation levels have been discerned, beginning with Levels 6 to 3B that date from the Pre-Pottery Neolithic B culture (i.e., c. 8300–5500 BCE, a culture also found in Jericho).[19] Near the end of the fourth millennium BCE, Munhata was deserted. It lay abandoned until recent times.

Level 2A, the Wadi Rabbah Stage, probably dates to Pottery-Neolithic A or 4800–4000 BCE and reflects the Halafian culture of Syria. Excavators found two serpent objects in this level.[20] Each is a plastic decoration; that is, before firing, an image of a serpent in clay strips was fastened to the outer surface of a vessel. One curled serpent was attached to the side of a hole-mouth pithos. Its body is curled around, with the tail on top of the body.[21] The serpent's head reaches over the top of the rim of the pithos, and the mouth seems to be open.[22] I do not think the serpent is seeking water—it is more likely placed on the vessel to bless or guard the contents. That interpretation fits well with what we found about the widespread meaning of the serpent, including its meaning in this area of the world.

Ein Samiya

A cemetery covering about 3 kilometers is located near Ramallah on the border of the Samaritan mountain range and the Jordan Rift Valley. It is between Bethel and Shiloh and west of Wadi ed-Daliyeh. The graves date to the period from the Early Bronze Age to the Byzantine Period.

Figure 19. Ein Samiya Silver Cup. 2250–2000 BCE. Courtesy of the Israel Museum.

A sheet-silver cup was found in an Early Bronze Age tomb at Ein Samiya. It shows two fat serpents with large eyes, nostrils, and closed mouths.[23] One serpent with odd markings around its mouth and with circular markings on its body looks left and rises up in an undulating form to a strange plant held in the left hand of a Janus-headed figure with bull's hindquarters. The other serpent, with diagonal markings, looks right and crouches with its tail curled beneath it; the serpent is below two human figures who hold a crescent-shaped object within which is a rosette with a human face in the center. The iconography is unique, but individual features link it with Mesopotamia.[24]

Y. Yadin rightly saw a connection between the mythological scene in this cup and the Enuma Elish ("The Creation Epic"). The text mentions monstrous serpents or dragons whose bodies are filled with venom and that rear up. Yadin suggested that the cup's left scene shows a deity neutralizing "the poison of the monsters with plants grasped in his outstretched hands."[25] The right scene could be one of triumph. The serpents seem to have been chosen to evoke fear and wonder before an awesome god. Most likely the cup was made in Mesopotamia or elsewhere and imported into Canaan.

Ancient Palestinian culture was influenced by Babylonian art. The Sumerians and the Akkadians revered, even worshipped, snake gods. Sometimes the god is represented with anguipedes (serpent legs and feet) and sometimes as a dragon-serpent.[26] The mythical animal may be a beast with seven serpent heads.[27] As E. Douglas Van Buren stated, "from prehistoric days until the Seleucid era there is no evidence to show that the dragon was inimical to the gods or malevolent towards mankind. It inspired awe because it possessed supernatural qualities." Indeed, in Sumer and Akkad, the symbol of the serpent or dragon-serpent was "always regarded as a talisman which averted drought and consequent famine." Serpent symbolism was "a happy omen of abundance and blessing."[28]

Jericho

Jericho, in the Jordan Valley east of Jerusalem, may be the oldest continuing city in the world. One of the monumental structures there is a Pre-Pottery Neolithic tower that seems to antedate 8000 BCE. Debates continue on the intended use of this structure. The city (Tel es-Sultan) is about 10 kilometers north of the Dead Sea and 230 meters below sea level, on the Great African Rift Valley. Jericho was a major city on the caravan route from the East to the West, and famous primarily because of the biblical account of the entrance into the "Promised Land" by the Hebrews under the leadership of Joshua (Josh 2–6). Early historians, in particular Strabo, Pliny, and Josephus, emphasized Jericho's strategic location, both economically and militarily.

Although the archaeological evidence at Jericho stretches back before the ninth millennium BCE, serpents do not appear as symbols until long after the development of culture and civilization.[29] In an MBIIB stratum of Jericho dated to circa 1700 BCE, in a chamber that apparently stored temple objects of unusual quality, were found fragments of a ceramic vessel bearing a serpent with its mouth open.[30] It was recovered from seventy-three pieces and laboriously put back together. It is imperative to observe that this vessel with ophidian symbolism belonged with a group of vessels reserved for sacred use. Hence, J. Garstang, the excavator, opined that the "snake was in fact a terrestrial emblem of the Mother-goddess, symbolizing Life within the Earth."[31]

In a Middle Bronze Age tomb at Jericho was found a ceramic vessel with two serpents. Here is K. M. Kenyon's description of the pottery vessel in zoomorphic form:

> The filling aperture is a cup on the bird's back, up which climbs a snake to drink. The pouring aperture is the bird's mouth. Another snake, partially broken away, is curled round the bird's neck and along the top of the head. Feathers of wings and tail are indicated by incisions. Found in scattered sherds, but nearly complete.[32]

Each serpent has numerous dots to signify skin, and the eyes are prominently featured. The serpent on the neck, looking down into the vessel, has three curves. The object should not be designated "Bird Vase," but "Elegant Bird Vase with Two Serpents."

The serpents are clearly positive symbols and nonthreatening. Their mouths appear to be directed to the opening from which water would pour out. The ophidian iconography probably symbolizes the protection of the

Figure 20. Large Shard with Serpent, with Dots to Designate Skin. MB. From Jericho. Courtesy of the Weingreen Museum of Biblical Antiquities, Trinity College, Dublin, Accession No. WM 104.

contents that embody health and life. Water and milk that would probably have been contained in such vessels can provide not only health but also sickness, and before the invention of refrigeration the ancients could only appeal to serpents for protection.

Ashkelon

Ashkelon is on the Mediterranean coast in the south of ancient Palestine. The beginnings of Ashkelon can be dated to about 2000 BCE; thus, the name Ashkelon is a pre-Philistine name and is Canaanite or Amorite. The tell is massive; it covers a little over 100 hectares. Ekron and Dan extend only to about 20 hectares each.[33] At Ashkelon archaeologists found a red-clay pottery Canaanite storage jar with two serpents on its shoulder, one on each side and near the handles. The jar was discovered in Grid 50, Square 48, Feature (= Locus) 487, and comes from a tomb. It dates from MBIIB or about 1800 BCE. The jar was found in 1996 and is unpublished until now.[34] Each serpent is incised with prominent eyes. Most unusual in early art, but found in the Hellenistic depictions of serpents,[35] are the three short spreading lines coming out of the mouth of the serpent. These lines may indicate the forked (bifid) tongue that informs the serpent about its surroundings and, perhaps, also symbolizes the powerful venom.[36] They are strikingly similar to the ophidian image found at Arad that dates from the Early Bronze Age.

One serpent is carefully incised and has eight curves, probably to indicate it is in motion. A horizontal line is deeply etched in front of its head. The other serpent is less sophisticated, and has no clear undulations and no horizontal strokes before the mouth. Unique, as far as I can detect, are the incisions to denote serpents and the discovery of them on a Canaanite storage jar. These are locally produced ophidian images, since there is little or no Egyptian pottery at Ashkelon, and typological analysis indicates that the objects were most likely made in or near this site. The ophidian iconography probably symbolized the protector of the contents of the jar, usually wine or oil.

Shechem (Tell Balatah)

Shechem lies on the main road that leads northward from Jerusalem. It is situated at the eastern end of a pass that continues between two famous mountains, Ebal to the north and Gerizim to the south. Shechem is also located between Jacob's Well and New Testament Sychar, just as described in the fourth century by Eusebius (in his *Onomasticon*) and by the Bordeaux Pilgrim and in the sixth century on the Madaba map.

In 1927, E. Sellin and his team found the remains of a clay vessel at Shechem. It has a serpent attached to it. Dark circles are painted on its body, which is mostly straight.[37] The vessel with a serpent dates from the Middle Bronze Age and was found in the temple. That provenance clearly indicates positive meanings for the serpent and reveals that there was probably a serpent cult there.

In 1934, H. Steckeweh found a small limestone plaque at Shechem with iconography that seems to denote a serpent. The large serpent moves from the earth to the pudenda of a goddess. F. M. Th. Böhl judged it to be from the Middle Bronze Age.[38] Both Albright and J. B. Pritchard concurred with this approximate date.[39] Albright opined that the plaque represented the serpent goddess.[40]

The evidence of ophidian iconography at Shechem has increased with more recent research.[41] Two MBIIB pottery sherds with serpent motifs were found in Strata 18s and 20.[42] The shards were unearthed during the excavations from 1956 to 1973. It is a pity that the evidence of serpent imagery at Shechem is now in such a fragmented state that little may be discerned about the meaning of serpent symbolism there.

Megiddo

Clearly one of the most impressive mounds representing the remains of ancient cities is Megiddo, which is situated on the *via maris* (the way of the sea), as it continues northward from the Sharon Plain into the Jezreel Valley. It is about thirty-two kilometers south of Haifa. The strata at Megiddo run from Chalcolithic (somewhat before 3300 BCE) to Iron II (600–350), according to the field director, Gordon Loud, in 1948.[43]

Two bronze serpents were found at Megiddo. One was discovered in Stratum X, which dates to 1650–1550 BCE.[44] It is elongated with an upraised head and is 18 centimeters long. The serpent has no details. The other bronze serpent is also elongated and straighter; it is 10 centimeters long. It has a rounded but triangular head and no markings. It was found in a later stratum (LBIIB or Iron I).

Archaeologists noted serpent symbolism at Megiddo on a pottery bowl that was found in Stratum XIIIA or XII that dates to the eighteenth century BCE.[45] The well-crafted bowl is associated with the cult and has an image of four bull heads; these are separated by four serpents. The serpents are elongated with upraised heads, and two dots in vertical rows are neatly arranged, perhaps to signify the skin. The line of dots is visible in Plate 26. The bulls, but not the serpents, are given eyes. The zoomorphic animals are applied pottery. Since the serpents are associated with the bulls and the latter were symbols of divinity, power, and sexuality in antiquity, then the serpents most likely also were assigned some, or all, of these features;[46] snakes clearly represent these concepts in other contexts.

In a Middle Bronze or Late Bronze Age tomb, numbered 1100C,[47] at Megiddo excavators found a vase with a long serpent.[48] The serpent curls artistically around the base of the long spout and lies on the upper section of the body of the bowl. The serpent is not near the rim, as in many other examples. In another tomb at Megiddo, dated to MBII, were found three jugs bearing serpent motifs on the handles.[49] In each case the serpent is more stylized than detailed; no dots, eyes, or tongue are depicted, and the serpent's tail recedes into the jug. One handle is connected to the rim, as is usual, and the serpent does not reach to the rim (P 3060). Two other features are distinguished. The handle is attached only to the bowl and the neck is more truncated. No heads are shown; the slanting "head" of one serpent clearly ends on the handle (P 3083); the other's "head" reaches over from the handle to the rim and rests on the outside of the rim (P 3061).[50]

Other ophidian iconography seems to be among the archaeological discoveries, but went undetected. Perhaps three bronze bracelets are ophidian-shaped (Plate 87:7, 8, 9).[51] One seems to have a well-defined serpent head and tail (Plate 87:9 [M 937]).[52] It was found in Locus 310 of Stratum IV or circa 1000 to 800 BCE, according to the excavators of 1925–1934.[53] Also, in Strata I–IV eight scarabs with a uraeus or uraei were found at Megiddo.[54] Scarabs with images of serpents, with one or more uraei, are found all over ancient Palestine.[55] Scarabs and amulets are not mentioned in this survey, unless they are in stratified layers, since they usually are Egyptian and not local.[56]

Some possibly undetected ophidian objects may have been recovered in the tombs. A bracelet has two animal heads facing one another; these are oxidized but look like triangularly pointed serpent heads.[57] A ring looks as if it might be a base with a raised serpent on it, but it also is too oxidized for us to be certain.[58]

Gezer

Rising prominently above the Coastal Plain is a high hill or tell that commands virtually a 360-degree sweep of the area from Ashdod in the southwest to nearly Mount Carmel in the northwest and the Judean hills to the east. It is about 11 kilometers southeast of Ramleh. Gezer is thus a strategic lookout and ideally suited to guard the main route that leads up to and from Jerusalem and Jericho (and other more eastern parts of the world) from the via maris that connected Egypt and Babylon, passing below Megiddo. The site is also blessed by the fertility of the region, along with abundant springs near its base.

A small bronze serpent, perhaps a cobra, was found at Gezer in the high place. The body is wavy, but without any detail, and the head is raised, but no eyes are marked. It is about 18 centimeters long.[59] The object is dated to the Late Bronze Age.[60] R. A. S. Macalister suggested that, despite the "wild words that have been written about serpent worship," there was certainly some worship of the serpent in the Jerusalem Temple, as 2 Kings 18:4 demonstrates. Macalister opined that the "bronze serpent from Gezer may well be a votive model of some such image."[61] These informed reflections should be kept in mind when we study the biblical texts.

A second ophidian object was found at Gezer in Cave 15 IV. It is a curved ornament in the form of a serpent. The head is especially prominent and triangular, but no eyes or skin are indicated. The cave and its contents date to the "Second Semitic Period" that is from the thirteenth to the eighteenth Egyptian Dynasty, or sometime before 1400 BCE.[62] Macalister suggested that this object "may have been a sympathetic prophylactic against the bite of these creatures."[63]

At Gezer in 1969–1971, archaeologists, under the direction of W. G. Dever, discovered another impressive example of serpent iconography. It is a copper/bronze serpent found in LBII Stratum 9, which is a mixed fill also containing material from MBIIC and MBIIC/LBI.[64] It is a crude object, showing little detail; there are no eyes indicated and no dots. It may have been intended as a cobra.[65] The nose is excessively elongated; perhaps the artist wanted the observer (or worshipper) to think about the cobra's deadly tongue. As with the uraeus, the serpent has an upraised head. The body has one main semicircular curve.[66] If this stratum was looted in antiquity, it is possible that more impressive serpent objects had once been present.

Six of the Cypriot Base Ring I jugs found at Gezer in Field I Caves may contain an artist's attempt at a stylized serpent.[67] Each of the jars, in various stages of preservation, has an image that is formed from the bottom left and continues in a clockwise fashion until it circles back and ends well beyond the right side of the circle created. No decoration is added to the image to help the observer discern that it is a serpent. Yet the "raised molding" is serpentine and may be an idealized ophidian image. These bibil jugs date from the Late Bronze Period and are imported probably from Cyprus.[68]

Archaeologists have found additional examples of ophidian symbolism at Gezer, and these date from the Iron Age. One, a Qadesh type,[69] depicts erect serpents on a clay plaque that can be dated to 1000–550 BCE. They seem to be celebrating the fertility goddess Asherah. Upraised serpents with faces turned toward the goddess are depicted on each side of Asherah.[70] A second clay plaque that may represent serpents was found at Gezer. It shows a goddess with serpentine artwork ascending from her shoulders and over her head.[71] These serpentine features may denote serpents since similar iconography was found at Hazor. It is difficult to date the second ophidian object because it was found in nonstratified waste. Since some serpents rise up before Asherah, it is apparent that they may well denote the phallus, a symbol of fertility, sex, and regeneration.

Hazor (Tel el-Qedah)

Hazor is located north of the Sea of Galilee in Upper Galilee and in the Huleh Valley. It was clearly not only one of the major Canaanite cities but also a prominent trade center in the Fertile Crescent. Hazor is massive. The mound proper occupies 12 hectares, while the lower settled areas extend over 70 hectares. The upper city of Hazor was settled in the Early Bronze Age. The lower city was occupied sometime near the beginning of the second millennium BCE.[72]

Two small incised bronze serpents were found at Hazor in the "holy of holies" in the temple of Area H (Locus 2113), and in Strata 2 and 1A,[73] which are dated to LBIIA and B, or 1400–1200 BCE.[74] One, 7 centimeters long, is rather straight (339:5 [H179]); it may have been a pendant for wearing around the neck since it has a hole in it. Five straight lines are found on the head and four angular ones on the body. The other, 11.2 centimeters long (339:6 [H1350]), has eyes indicated and is curved in a serpentine fashion, with perhaps four curves, probably to suggest motion.[75]

A third object that appears to be a bronze serpent was found at Hazor. It has six curves and the head is upraised.[76] It has virtually no decorations that would prove it to be a serpent—that is, it has no tongue, eyes, or dots. The object was found in Area A in Phase 9A or LBI. The object—probably a serpent—was thus found in the temple area of the upper city. This temple may have been where the upper echelon of Hazor worshiped; a monumental building (L. 389) was discovered near the Area A Temple.

A fourth example of ophidian iconography was found on a pottery sherd

Figure 21. Cult Standard. Hazor. Fourteenth to thirteenth century BCE. Courtesy of the Israel Museum.

(A6119); it is dated to MBII.[77] The serpent is relatively small and has dots to indicate skin. Its body stretches semihorizontally, and its head is beside a handle on the top of the rim, as if the serpent were blessing or guarding the contents. It was also found in Area A.

A fifth object that is probably a serpent appears to be indicated on the handle of a clay jug (F1454/6); it was found in Area F, Locus 8187, which dates from MBII.[78]

A sixth ophidian object was found on the remains of a small bowl (H1004/1). An example of ophidian iconography was applied to the body of a "sherd of a very unusual vessel."[79] The object is a clay-sculptured serpent. The serpent has two large dots where the eyes would be located. A small slit indicates its mouth.[80] The serpent appears to be looking over the lip of a bowl, perhaps guarding the contents within. It was found in Area H.

A seventh example of ophidian iconography was discovered at Hazor. It proves what has probably already entered the mind of the reader: Hazor was the center of a Canaanite serpent cult. This serpent object is the most important found at Hazor. Yadin's team found a silver-plated bronze cult stand in Locus 6211. Silver-plated bronze was often the most elegant way to fashion a mirror, but this is a cult stand, and it dates from the Late Bronze Age II, or the fourteenth and thirteenth centuries BCE.[81]

The tang was not plated with silver because it was most likely intended

to be hidden by a pole on which the cult stand would be erected. Only a minuscule part of the silver plate can be seen by the naked eye. The object has
been on public display in the Israel Museum (Room 307, Case 4, Item 3).

Two serpents in relief are shown rising on each side of, and even above,
a woman; she is incised in the center of the sliver-plated bronze object.
The serpents have no decorations to indicate skin, eyes, or tongues. The
serpent on the left has four curves, and the one on the right has two; these
most likely symbolize the serpent's dynamic quality. The woman's hair
falls downward beside each cheek, ending in curls. A crescent is indicated
in relief above the woman; perhaps some connection with the moon is
indicated.[82] She is most likely a goddess. It is possible, as Yadin imagined,
that she is holding the serpents and wearing a necklace (this interpretation
is reinforced by minute examination of other iconography, especially that
on the scarabs and seals).[83]

Since the object is constructed of expensive material, though poorly
crafted, and since it is a cult standard and found among other cult objects,
I have no doubt that the woman is a serpent goddess and like the Qudshu
models. The object is similar to the images of a woman holding serpents in
both hands;[84] this motif may have been intended, but not actually achieved
or made less clear, by the silver plating. In the official report of the excavation we read: "This standard of the snake goddess is so far unique among
archaeological discoveries. It may be conjectured that it was used in cult
processions such as we see on the monuments of Egypt and Mesopotamia."[85] There can be no doubt that when the people with Joshua entered
Palestine, goddesses were symbolized as serpents. It is now certain that
there were numerous serpent cults in Palestine before Joshua's time.

The images depicted on the cult stand are clearly serpents.[86] I can see no
reason why these serpents, or any ophidian iconography found at Hazor,
should be associated with an iconography of bulls. Yet Yadin speculated
that the temple in Area H was a Canaanite one dedicated to the storm god
Baal, Hadad.[87]

An eighth and a ninth example of ophidian iconography were found
at Hazor. Archaeologists discovered two examples of what they judge to
be a "snake house." Similar objects were found at Ugarit and Dan. One
"house-shaped vessel," found in 1957, was well preserved.[88] The vessel
is spherical, but its small opening is rectangular. It most likely had a door
that closed it, since a socket for one appears on the left side. Perhaps the
vessel needed to be closed, so as to hinder poisonous snakes from wandering. It is conceivable that the door would have been made of some fabric
or basket-weaved plant so that the serpent could breathe. Above the vessel
rises a vertical façade, and the front has a horizontal lip below the opening.
The design seems cultic and is reminiscent of a temple. A similar vessel at

Ugarit (Ras Shamra), dating from 1500 to 1400 BCE, has an elegant door that is also rectangular, but extended vertically and not horizontally as are those at Hazor and Dan.[89]

Perhaps the serpent houses were designed for transporting the serpent to a ceremony since we have iconographical evidence that a serpent cult flourished at Ugarit and Hazor.[90] The two serpent houses found at Ugarit are the most elegantly crafted I have studied.

The Hazor snake house was found in the temple of Area H (Locus 2113).[91] This is the area in which the bronze serpents were discovered; hence, there is reason to posit that what Yadin called the "house-shaped vessel" should be identified as a "snake house." Perhaps sacred snakes or serpents were kept in the tiny house that appears too small for a cat.

Another "unique vessel" was found in LBII and in Area C (Locus 6211). The vessel has "a circular aperture in its side" and, although the upper section is lost, the vessel was most likely originally closed.[92] In it was found the silver-plated bronze cult standard described earlier (and shown in Fig. 21). This connection suggests that the strange vessel is a snake house, and should be so understood in the light of the examples found at Ugarit and elsewhere.

It is clear that the ophidian iconography found at Hazor has deep symbolic meanings. For example, the pendant serpent, like the later so-called gnostic amulets, might serve to symbolize the one who can protect the bearer from misfortune, especially through sympathetic magic, from a deadly snakebite. Like most amulets, it was most likely prophylactic and apotropaic—that is, used to ward off evil.

Timnaʿ (Tel Matash)

Timnaʿ is a valley about 30 kilometers north of the Gulf of Aqabah. Copper smelting installations were active at Timnaʿ from the Chalcolithic Period to the Byzantine Period.

A Midianite votive offering was found in the Hathor Temple at Timnaʿ.[93] It is a serpent from the thirteenth century BCE.[94] The serpent is primarily copper, but its head is gilded and the eyes highlighted. The gold that remains around the face and the way it ends behind the eyes suggest that the whole serpent originally was covered with gold. Its skin is artistically represented. The head is pointed and its eyes clearly marked with recessed circles in the gilded copper. It has seven well-defined undulations, and the tail curves. It is less than 13 centimeters long. Since it was found in the Egyptian Temple to Hathor, it probably symbolized divinity and protection. Also, since Hathor is the goddess of mining, it most likely also signified success and prosperity in mining.[95]

Also found at Timnaᶜ was another ophidian object. It is a snake crawling

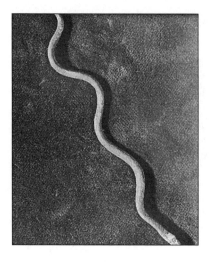

Figure 22. Timnaᶜ. Gilded Serpent. 1550–1200 BCE.
Courtesy of the Israel Museum.

along the rim of a votive altar.[96] It should be evident that these examples of snake iconography denoted something positive; the gilded serpent was found in a temple and should be interpreted in terms of the goddess of the temple, Hathor. In Canaanite religion this goddess was associated with vegetation;[97] in Egypt she was a cow and the serpent who ruled the world. The Timnaᶜ gilded serpent probably denotes Hathor's divinity. As is well known, the serpent was a god and the assistant of gods in ancient Egypt. One papyrus of about 990 BCE depicted four cobra gods and a gigantic serpent guiding the boat of the sun god.[98]

Beth Shan (Beth-shan, Beth Shean, Beisan)

The site in which the most abundant and impressive ophidian iconography has been discovered in Palestine is Beth Shan, a prominent tell (Tel el-Hosn) in the valley of the Harod, a stream that flows into the Jordan River.[99] The site was apparently deserted from 700 BCE until the time of Alexander the Great; then it was renamed Scythopolis. On the tell, archaeologists have found abundant evidence of Egyptian influence, which is understandable since an Egyptian garrison was stationed there in the period from Seti I to Rameses III, or from circa 1318 to circa 1166/67 BCE.

Quite confusing are the dates given to the numerous strata of the tell, and these are often debated.[100] I have thus decided to treat them together, with asides about the dates assigned to them by Alan Rowe, the field director of the excavations in the 1920s and the author of the two volumes that reported and assessed the discoveries. Serpent iconography is dated long after the period of Hyksos control, or beginning in MBIIB and C; this information may strengthen the thesis that the Hyksos brought ophidian symbolism into Palestine if one adds to it the increase of such symbolism under Egyptian domination.

Here is an inventory of ophidian iconography excavated at Beth Shan.[101]

1. A fragmented cylindrical cult stand with four serpents (14:1 [1021A]). There appear to be four apertures: one rectangular-like aperture on opposite sides.[102] The top is crowned. Large serpents with dots indicating the skin are depicted moving upward and into the apertures (photo on 58A:1–2, drawing on 58A:3).[103] Doves clearly sit above each handle. Rowe assigned this stand to the time of Rameses III (1183–1152 BCE). It was found in the southern temple.

2. A fragment of a second cylindrical cult object with a serpent and the top of an oval aperture (16:4 [1021]). Rowe dated it to the southern temple of Rameses III.

3. A third fragmented cylindrical cult stand showing serpents with dots and along with doves (14: 3, 4, 5 [1027, 1029]).[104] Around the cylinder, with a sloping top, portions of doves are depicted in eight (perhaps)[105] triangular-shaped apertures. Originally a dove was in each hole. Four serpents curled around the doves, but did not enter the openings (photo on 57A:3; drawing on 57A:4).[106] Doves most likely also originally sat on each handle.

What did this serpent iconography symbolize? The scene is peaceful and the serpents are not heading for the doves. It seems unlikely that the ancients imagined the serpents were seeking the doves for food. Perhaps the doves and the serpents represented the beginning of spring, with the doves symbolizing heaven and the serpents the earth and beneath it. Rowe dated the serpent cult stand to Rameses III. It was found in the southern temple.

4. A fourth fragmented cylindrical cult stand with serpents and doves. It has two triangular openings (base below) with a dove in each and two serpents with heads facing the doves (16:3 [1080]). Rowe dated it to Rameses III. Like items one, two, and three, it was also found in the southern temple.

5. A fifth very fragmented cylindrical cult stand, with doves and serpents (16:1 [1024]).[107] Each of the two oval apertures probably originally held a dove. A serpent faced each dove. The cult stand was found under the plaster floor of the northern temple from the time of Rameses III.

6. A fragmented base of a sixth cylindrical cult stand with serpents at the bottom, not to be confused with the previous five items. The cult stand shows serpents with tiny dots and semirectangular windows or apertures. Thus, the archaeologists found at least six cylindrical serpent cult stands at Beth Shan.

Rowe reported that seven cylindrical cult stands with serpents were found at Beth Shan.[108] Only the six previously reported are clear in the plates.[109]

None of these cylindrical cult stands is as ornate as the one found at Byblos that has bulls below the rim and serpents near square windows.[110]

7. A cult object; a serpent curled up in a U-shape (19:1). Rowe reported that this artifact is the only cult object that was found in the "Pre-Amenophis III Level." [111] By analogy with passages in the Pyramid Texts and ophidian symbolism found in Egypt, it is likely that this object was set up at the entrance to a temple as a guardian.[112]

8. Another serpent with dots; it is lying in a serpentine line (19:8).

9. A pottery serpent in a serpentine line (20:2).

10. A pottery cult object; serpent coiled back on itself, head broken off. Rowe dated it to Amenophis III or 1386–1349 BCE (20:3; see the photo on 44A:5).[113]

11. A pottery cult object; an undulating serpent on a base with head missing, dated by Rowe to Seti I or 1313–1292 BCE (21:15; see the photo on 42A:5).

12. Small pieces of ivory that are perhaps the remains of serpents (30:21–31).

13. Tiny bronze pieces that are probably the remains of serpents (31:25 especially).

14. A faience Egyptian-like pendant that is an upraised serpent or uraeus with a human face like a sphinx (33:7).[114]

15., 16., 17. Three faience pendants that look like Egyptian cobras (34:42, 61, 62).[115]

18. A serpent cult object with head broken off, which Rowe dated before Amenophis III or prior to 1447 BCE (41A:2, 21:5).

19. A pottery cult object, an upraised serpent, like a cobra,[116] with female breasts indicated by two circular deposits of clay. The head is lost. Rowe dated it also before 1447 (42A:2).[117]

20., 21. Two clay cult objects, serpents most likely. One is with a cup; perhaps the cup was intended to catch lacteal fluid from the two breasts, as Rowe thought, both with a vertical slip of clay (to denote cleavage?; 42A:5).[118] Each seems to be an upraised serpent, perhaps a cobra like the uraeus, and each appears related to the cult at Beth Shan that reveals strong Egyptian influence. These ophidian symbols, and the preceding one, probably denoted a goddess or symbolized one of her attributes.

22. A pottery cult object; a serpent—probably a cobra—depicted with female breasts and a receptacle beneath them, most likely to capture lacteal fluid. Rowe dated it to the time of Amenophis III or 1447–1412 BCE (45A:4; cf. 42A:5).[119] Found with Ashtoreth figurine, whose hands cup naked female breasts (45A:5). This cult serpent also represented a goddess or her attributes.

23. Numerous fragments of a rectangularly shaped cult shrine house

with a serpent on the front moving up to rest beneath a man's feet and near the feet of a dove. Above the gracefully curved serpent are two men, reaching over to touch the head of the other.[120] A nude woman sits above them with her legs separated to show her exaggerated mons veneris. On the right is a walking lion. Most of the appliquéd clay for the serpent has broken off. Rowe dated this shrine to Rameses (56A:1–3, 17:1–3, 57A:1–2; cf. 17:2, 17A:1–2). It is on display in the Israel Museum. This rectangular serpent cult stand is not be confused with the six cylindrical ones.

24–27+. In 1973, E. D. Oren published for the first time the report on the 1920 to 1931 excavations of the northern cemetery of Beth Shan. In this northern cemetery were found the following ophidian objects: (a) in Tomb 7, from EBIV, four uraei carnelian pendants,[121] (b) in Tomb 27, contents from the Late Bronze Age, a white steatite scarab with two uraei whose bodies contain a crisscross design, facing in opposite directions, with a cartouche with *Aa-kheperw-Ra,* the prenomen of Amenophis II,[122] (c) and in Tomb 219, EBIV, one faience scarab with a single uraeus facing a reed sign.[123] These are not to be confused with numbers 14–17 that are faience pendants with ophidian imagery.

One notable feature seems impressive. Most of the serpent objects have their heads broken off. Is this intentional? The broken heads do seem to distinguish the serpent objects from others found at Beth Shan. Note the following examples: cracked pottery with a serpent whose head is partly missing (20:2), serpent base with head missing (20:3 = 44A:4), a pottery cult object showing a serpent head missing (21:15), a serpent cult object with head missing (41A:2), serpent cult object with female breasts and head broken off (42A:2), two serpents, cult objects, with heads missing (42A:5), serpent cult object with breasts and a cup for lacteal fluid (45A:4). Infrequently, other objects also appear as if someone has broken them or smashed the head; note especially the Ashtoreth (45A:5). Also, recall that the six cylindrical and one rectangular cult stands with serpents are fragmented. Are these broken serpent objects related to Hezekiah's reform? He did banish the worshippers of Nechushtan (the serpent idol) from the Jerusalem Temple.

It seems relatively certain that Beth Shan, beginning in the second millennium BCE, was the center of a serpent cult.[124] The worship of the serpent there may have given rise to the name; for example, N. H. Snaith was convinced that "Beth-shan means 'house of the snake.' "[125]

In fact, so many serpent objects were found at Beth Shan that the categories are often shaped by serpent iconography. For example, the so-called Beth Shan sacred boxes are divided into those with serpents, those with serpents and doves, and those without serpents and doves.[126] There can be no doubt that before Beth Shan fell to the Israelites it was the center of a cult in which serpents and doves represented a fertility goddess. Serpent iconography thus most likely symbolized power, health, rejuvenation, and life.[127] There can also be no doubt that the deity worshipped at Beth Shan was symbolized as a serpent, and since the ophidian iconography often has breasts, we should conclude that a serpent goddess was worshipped there. The association of the serpent and the dove indicates that both may well have been related to the celebration of spring and the return of vegetation. To what extent is Jesus' statement about serpents and doves informed, and once understood, in terms of the ancient association of serpents and doves: "Be wise as serpents and innocent as doves" (Mt 10:16; NRSV)?

Dan

Dan (Laish, Tell el-Qadi) sits beneath Mount Hermon in northern Galilee. The huge spring nearby provides the major source of the River Jordan, and the water that pours out of the earth here, from the Anti-Lebanon range, is often breathtaking and always refreshing in this semi-arid land.[128] Excavations at Dan most likely reveal evidence of the revolution led by Jeroboam I, the son of Nebat, who, after the death of Solomon in 928 BCE, set up shrines at Dan and Bethel to rival the cult in Jerusalem (Judg 18:30, 1 Kgs 12:29–30).[129] Both these "new" shrines were built at old traditional cult centers linked respectively with Jacob and the first settlements of the tribe of Dan that conquered this area (assuming there is historical meaning in the Bible regarding this site).

At Dan "two complete pithoi with a snake decoration" were uncovered;[130] in fact, three pithoi with ophidian iconography were recovered, although one was found in fragments.[131] They were discovered "under a thick layer of crushed travertine," along with an incense stand; hence, A. Biran can conclude that "we were digging within the sacred precinct of the city of Dan of the 10th and beginning of the 9th centuries B.C.E."[132] That is precisely the time of Jeroboam I.

The two well-preserved pithoi (large vessels) could contain over 300 liters each. They were found with a Phoenician juglet, and Phoenician influence appears also on some shallow bowls or plates.[133] On one pithos is an impression of a man, perhaps a god, who holds two ibexes. The serpents on each pithos are in relief and appear just above the middle horizontal triple line. The head of each serpent is raised, and the bodies are displayed so that the serpents appear to be writhing.[134] One rises at about a 45-degree angle, the other at almost a 90-degree angle. No dots indicate skin, and no eyes or tongues are depicted. These are certainly serpents since the bodies appear in a serpentine fashion and the heads are larger, especially on one of the pithos, but the tails are much thinner. It is not clear what the symbolic meaning could be; perhaps the raised head symbolized power and thus the serpents protected the contents. A positive meaning is assured since the ophidian imagery was found in a cultic setting.

Also, at Dan a "serpent house" was found in Stratum V of the twelfth century BCE (in room 7082), which is immediately after the conquest of Laish (the Canaanite name of Dan; Judg 18:29). I agree with Biran who thinks that the "snake house may well have been modeled after a temple."[135] The intended use of this vessel becomes clear when one studies it in light of what has been learned after examining the similar objects found at Ugarit (Ras Shamra), Hazor, and especially at Enkomi and Athienou on Cyprus.[136] Since no holes are provided for the sacred serpent to breathe, it is unlikely that the serpent lived in the house. If it did, the opening could not have been closed, or it would have been closed with cloth that would allow air to enter the house. Perhaps the serpent house at Dan had a door and the object was used for temporarily transporting the serpent from its home to the ceremonial room of a temple.

What would the serpent have symbolized? In light of the veneration of serpents in antiquity and in ancient Palestine, most likely the images represented a divinity and perhaps a god. The god would be the protector of the city and the provider of human wants, including fertility, beauty, and regeneration.

Jerusalem

An examination of all the archaeological reports of Jerusalem would tend to reveal that no ophidian iconography has been found in the numerous and varied excavations there.[137] This fact needs to be reassessed in light of two major observations. First, the continuous building programs in Jerusalem have required taking the restorations down to bedrock, thus destroying the evidence of former levels and their contents. Second, the "Holy City" was purified of ophidian imagery by the successive reforms to stress the worship of Yahweh according to the Deuteronomist, so that the worship in the Temple and Holy City would meet such standards. One is reminded especially of the reforms by Hezekiah. He removed the images of the serpent and their worshippers from the Temple (Nechushtan; we shall discuss this in a subsequent chapter).

Yet one would think that, as at other ancient archaeological sites, some ophidian imagery would be discovered, perhaps in a cistern (that has proved to be the case, as we shall explain). No ophidian iconography has been found in what seems to be left of the Jebusite city. Today, it seems appropriate to repeat the comment P. H. Vincent of the Ecole Biblique made in 1912: to make any sweeping conclusions regarding the Jebusite city "would be for the moment premature."[138]

How extensive was the image of the serpent in Jerusalem, especially in the period from 1000 BCE until 135 CE? Four observations help answer this question. First, prior to the United Kingdom or at least dating from its earliest days is a place known as the "Zohelet Stone" (הזחלת) or "Serpent Stone." It is beside Ain Rogel, and it was to this spring and the Serpent Stone that Prince Adonijah went to be crowned king while his father lay dying on his bed (1 Kgs 1:9). B. Mazar wisely suggested that this "site and the Serpent's Stone seem to echo past traditions of a 'holy place' hallowed by traditions held dear by the natives and their ancestors."[139] What was the Serpent's Stone? It was by a spring; was the spring home to serpents? Did it have snake houses with serpents that protected the spring?

Second, at night Nehemiah exits Jerusalem by the Valley Gate, which he identifies as near the "Dragon Well," or Fountain, or Spring (Neh 2:13). The Hebrew word used is *tnyn* (תנין), which has a variety of meanings, most of them negative. It basically means a dragon. Was Nehemiah referring to the same area as designated by the Serpent Stone?

Third, in his *War of the Jews,* Josephus mentions a "Pool of Serpents" (*War* 5.108).[140] What was it? Where was it? Most nineteenth- and twentieth-century scholars assume that the Serpents' Pool, which according to Josephus is near Herod's Monument, is to be identified with the Sultan's Pool. They are thus indebted to C. Schick who first made this identification and announced it in a letter dated November 1891.[141] In his informed study of Jerusalem, D. Bahat places the Serpents' Pool where Schick had thought it to be.[142]

More recently, M. Broshi, building on the discoveries of E. Netzer and S. Ben Arieh,[143] reached a different conclusion. He argued, quite persuasively, that the Pool of Serpents and Herod's Monument must be located north and slightly west of the Damascus Gate.[144] This hypothesis has archaeological, literary, and topographical support. There is an aqueduct dating from the Hasmonean Period about 4 meters southwest of the southern tower of the Damascus Gate, as D. Bahat has shown.[145] It must lead to some pool to the north of the city, and the most likely place is northwest where there used to be a natural depression for runoff water. During the period of the Crusades a pool was located there called *lacus legerii*.[146] The area was once called "Ard el-Birkeh" (Neighborhood of the Pool). Situated nearby and northwest of the pool are the remains of a monumental building with impressive *opus reticulatum* (a refined form of construction). The building is Herodian and constructed similarly to monuments in Rome and Herodian Jericho.[147] This monument, probably a tomb for Herod's family, was on a major thoroughfare to Jerusalem.[148]

It is not imperative to discern where the Serpents' Pool and Dragon Well were located in or near Jerusalem. In our search for the meaning of serpent iconography in ancient Palestine, it suffices to know that serpents provided names to the areas in and near Jerusalem.

Fourth, there can be no doubt that serpent imagery and symbolism were prevalent in Jerusalem before 70 CE, and especially before Hezekiah's reform, since ancient serpent iconography is abundant in the antiquities market in or near the Old City. Surely some of it comes from the environs of Jerusalem, usually from caves or tombs.

These assumptions and suggestions are proved by archaeological research. First, an impressive vessel with a serpent was found long ago in or near what is called the *via dolorosa*. The object will be discussed in the second portion of this chapter, when we examine a possible Asklepieion in Jerusalem.

Ekron (Tel Miqne, Khirbet el-Muqanna')

Ekron is 35 kilometers southwest of Jerusalem, on the edge of the coastal plain by the northeast corridor that ran from Ashdod to Gezer in antiquity.[149] It was one of the capitals of the Philistine Pentapolis and considered part of "the land that remains" (Jos 15:11). According to 2 Kings 1:2, King Ahaziah in the ninth century sent messengers to consult "Baal Zebub" (which means "Lord of the Fly or Swarm," a deliberate corruption of the better-known epithet "Baal Zebul," which denoted the Royal Baal),[150] who was probably the major god at Ekron. Excavations at Ekron reveal cities in the Middle Bronze, Late Bronze, and Iron Ages.

In the wealthy and elite Lower City of the Iron Age, which indicates the new culture of the Philistines, archaeologists discovered a golden cobra. The ophidian object was found in the palace at Ekron and dates from the time when Egypt controlled the area. The palace was destroyed in 603 BCE during Nebuchadnezzar's campaign, so the cobra most likely dates from the seventh century BCE. The cobra is elegantly crafted and rises up realistically. It is hammered out of fine gold and fashioned in the Egyptian style.[151] The hood is expanded, like the uraeus, and horizontal strokes mark its center.

Tell Beer-sheba

Tell Beer-sheba is located at the northern end of the southern desert, the Negev, and was the southernmost part of "the Land" in the famous formula "from Dan to Beer-sheba."

A large horned altar intended for animal sacrifices was found at Tell Beer-sheba in the summer of 1973. It is the first such object ever uncovered. All four horns of the altar were found and the stones are beautiful ashlars.[152] Blackened portions of the altar attest to the fact that it was used in antiquity. The altar is a cube: 1.6 × 1.6 × 1.6 meters.[153] The altar was discovered in a wall of a storehouse that was destroyed near the end of the eighth century BCE, about the time that some artist depicted a large serpent in the middle of an alabaster relief from Khorsabad, dated to the time of Sargon II (721–705 BCE).[154] The altar thus antedates Sargon's reign. Because of similarities with other horned altars found in the land, one may suggest that it was constructed sometime between the eleventh and ninth centuries BCE.

On the ashlar beneath one of the horned altars is an engraved image of a serpent.[155] The serpent's head is clear and the body is twisting back upon itself so that its head is parallel with its tail. The serpent's head points downward to the earth, perhaps to signify its chthonic character. Y. Aharoni, who directed the expedition that found the altar, prefers to emphasize the fertility of serpent iconography: "One stone has a deeply engraved decoration of a twisting snake . . . , an ancient symbol of fertility widely dispersed throughout the Near East." He continues, "The symbol of a snake was venerated in Israel from Moses' times (Num. 2:8–9) and the bronze serpent was worshipped in the Jerusalem temple until the days of Hezekiah (2 Kings 18:4)."[156] Keel rightly stresses the numinous character of this ophidian symbol.[157] Aharoni correctly conjectures that since the horned altar was dismantled prior to the end of the eighth century, it may have been destroyed because of the edict of King Hezekiah (2 Kgs 18:22).[158]

Mareshah (Tel Sandahanna)

Mareshah is a site in Judah about halfway between Beer-sheba and Ramleh, just north of Gezer. The town seems to have originated in the Iron Age; it was conquered in 701 BCE by Sennacherib.

In the third and second centuries BCE, Idumeans, Sidonians, and Greeks buried their dead in the necropolis at Mareshah. Tombs I and II are rich with paintings. One scene shows a serpent rising up before a bull.[159] The exact meaning of the ophidian symbolism is far from clear. Is it conceivable that the artist was thinking about Mithraic mythology that has a serpent helping Mithra slay a bull? While this answer is possible, bulls and serpents were linked in non-Mithraic myths. A search for answers may be aided by iconography found elsewhere. For example, one should consider the vase in the form of a bull found in Luristan with a serpent looking out from a circular hole above the bull's two front legs and another serpent gazing from behind the head.[160]

Carmel

Mount Carmel is a long mountain range running southeast to northwest. At its southern end is Megiddo, and at its northern promontory that overlooks the Mediterranean Sea sits Shiqmona. Mount Carmel is thus the

Figure 23. The Carmel Aphrodite. Courtesy of the Israel Museum.

northwestern continuation of the Samaritan hills. Impressive prehistoric caves are found, especially on its southern flank, including Abu Usba, Skhul, Jamal, Sefunim, Tabun, Kebara, and el-Wad.[161] Mount Carmel is most famous because it is the site on which Elijah confronted Ahab and the prophets of Baal (1 Kgs 18:17–46). In the first century BCE, Alexander Jannaeus captured Mount Carmel (*Ant.* 13.396), but Pompey took it from the Hasmoneans and linked it with Acco (*War* 3.35). In the Hellenistic and Roman periods, a temple to Zeus and an altar were situated there.[162]

In 1929, fragments of a statuette were found on this famous mountain, recovered from the large cave named Magharat el Wad. The portrayal of Aphrodite (Venus) is unlike her embodiment in the famous Venus de Milo now prominently displayed in the Louvre in Paris[163] or her depictions on the Parthenon.[164] She is also dissimilar to the depiction of bare-breasted Aphrodite being born from the sea fully mature. That is, she is shown entirely nude, as in the following: the mirror in the Louvre that depicts her with Eros, the crouching Aphrodite in the Museo Nazionale Romano, the bathing Aphrodite from Rhodes, the Aphrodite from Cyrene in the Museo Nazionale Romano, the Aphrodite from Delos in the National Archaeological Museum in Athens, and especially the Aphrodite created by the sculptor Praxiteles now in the Vatican.[165] In the Mount Carmel statuette, her weight is on her left leg, and her right leg is inclined forward.

The terra-cotta statuette was originally dated to the "late fourth or third century B.C.," [166] but has been redated to the first century CE. While the statuette was rightly associated with Praxiteles (c. 370–c. 330 BCE) because he was the first Greek to display the female body in full nudity, it is nevertheless a copy or an imitation from a later period.[167] Praxiteles' statues were widely copied, and his style became internationally famous and influential. The Roman style, languid body, and elongated form place the statuette within the art of the first century CE or maybe slightly earlier.[168]

The iconography does not indicate that the figure is a serpent goddess. She is clearly Aphrodite. Her weight is on her left foot. Her left hand seems to rest on something to her left, now worn away. What is unique and highly significant for us about this statuette of Aphrodite? This is the only representation of Aphrodite, as far as I know, that has a snake on her body.

On her right leg she wears an anklet. On this leg, above the knee, and on the thigh is carved a serpent. The serpent appears from behind the right thigh and curls upward. The serpent's head is well shaped. The artist placed no features on the serpent; there are no dots to signify skin or eyes. One cannot be certain how the head of the snake originally looked since it is badly worn. Are we to imagine something like a serpent garter? [169]

What is the meaning of the serpent symbolism? The "serpent garter" probably meant to denote the sexual attractiveness of the female, but it could also evoke images of beauty, as well as the erect phallus, fertility, and power. We have already seen that the rampant tendency to interpret the serpent, only and always, as phallic or a symbol meaning only or primarily eroticism (as, e.g., in the publications by P. Diel)[170] is misleading and not perceptive of the extensive meanings of snake symbolism in antiquity.[171] Of course, one of the meanings of the serpent is the phallus or eroticism.[172]

The sculpture is on public display in the Israel Museum. It is very similar to the figurine of Aphrodite found at Dardanos and dated to the second century BCE.[173] This figurine also has a serpent as a garter belt, but it is on the left thigh. Once again, the head of the serpent is not directed to the pubic area; in fact, it is turned away from the woman. Another serpent is depicted as coiled rings on the upper left arm.[174] The statuette of Aphrodite at Dardanos with the serpent's head turned away from the attractive body should warn those seeking to discern the meaning of serpent symbolism that the Freudian approach is often not suggested by the iconography, which may resist such sexual interpretations.

Another marble statue is similar to the Carmel Aphrodite. Again Aphrodite is completely nude. She has a snake bracelet on her right hand. No eyes, mouth, or skin are depicted. The head faces downward, following the fall of the arm, which covers her pubic area. The finish of the surface and the modeling of the pierced ears indicate, perhaps, the late Hellenistic Period or the early Roman Period.[175]

Aphrodite was also revered in Akko, only a little north of Carmel. We know this from a passage in the Mishnah. Rabbi Gamaliel II (late first century CE) was ostensibly asked by a non-Jew in the baths at Akko (Acre) how he could explain entering a bath with pagan idols. Gamaliel replied, "I came not within her limits: she came within mine! They do not say, 'Let us make a bath for Aphrodite,' but 'Let us make an Aphrodite as an adornment for the bath.'. . . thus what is treated as a god is forbidden, but what is not treated as a god is permitted" (*Avodah Zarah* 3:4, Danby). This passage is quite remarkable. It not only specifies that in the first century CE there was a statue of Aphrodite at Akko, but that the intention of an author is not to be confused with the meaning supplied by an observer. In this case, the two perspectives are antithetical. The author depicted a statue of the goddess Aphrodite, but Gamaliel dismissed the sculpture as merely a decoration.

It is clear that Aphrodite did not primarily represent sex and eroticism. She was the embodiment of beauty. L. Kreuz has explored the genesis of the conception of beauty by focusing on Aphrodite in antiquity.[176] The statuette discovered on Mount Carmel depicts Aphrodite as the one who symbolizes beauty and aesthetics, especially as contemplated by some at the beginning of the Common Era. The serpent is thus a positive symbol, perhaps of goodness, life, and beauty.

Summary

This survey of snake objects found in controlled excavations grounds our reflections on serpent symbology. Since many of the snake objects or images were discovered in or near temples or cult settings, it is certain that the serpent denoted a god, a divinity; it also denoted other human aspirations, needs, and appreciations, including—but not limited to—beauty, power, fertility, rejuvenation, royalty, the cosmos, and life. Since the serpent is often carved on the top of vessels that would have contained water, milk, or wine, it symbolized the divine protector. I have not found what will become so obvious when we study ophidian symbolism in the Asclepian cult; that is, I have not found clear evidence from controlled excavations that the serpent denoted, or connoted, rejuvenation and immortality. Perhaps rejuvenation and new life are reflected on the snake stands and altars found in the Canaanite sites, especially at Beth Shan.

EGYPTIAN SERPENT ICONOGRAPHY:
ARCHAEOLOGICAL AND LITERARY EVIDENCE

Early ophidian symbolism takes stunning form among the Egyptians sometime around 3000 BCE. Even their language is influenced by serpent iconography; hieroglyphs evolved from pictorial art. In the Middle Egyptian language of 2240 to 1740 BCE, which continued on monuments and in some texts into the Roman Period, two of the twenty-four phonograms are the symbol of a snake: the sound *f* is represented by a line drawing of a horned viper and *d* by a snake in the form of a uraeus.[177]

The study of Egyptian serpent iconography is too well known today, throughout the world, to warrant anything but a summary. Serpents are featured on monuments, on thrones, in stelae, and just about everywhere in ancient Egypt.[178] As E. A. Wallis Budge of the British Museum stated in 1911: "The serpent was either a power for good or the incarnation of diabolical cunning and wickedness." [179] Perhaps Egyptian serpent iconography is well known not only because of the vast number of tomes, scholarly and popular, but because of the pervasive image of the gold mask of Tutankhamen with the noticeably raised cobra. The cobra was an ideal choice for the creature who would guard the pharaoh. The Egyptians observed that the cobra had no eyelids and thus would always be awake to guard the pharaoh, a god on earth. The uraeus probably signified kingship, power, royalty, and divinity.[180]

Figures 24 and 25 are two striking examples of the uraeus, with the cobra upraised and placed on the head of Tutankhamen and later depicted as a bronze figure. The latter example was found in or near Jerusalem, dating from the Roman Period. What did the uraeus symbolize? In the Strasbourg Musée Archéologique we are told, "The uraeus personifies the eye of Re which destroys enemies by fire. The royal crown with the uraeus should be identified with the eye of Re." [181]

One of the most impressive, but little known, examples of ophidian iconography is found in the catacombs of Kom el-Shuqafa in Alexandria. They date from the first century CE. The doorway to the burial chamber is filled with serpent symbolism. Note the words of Jean-Yves Empereur in *Alexandria Rediscovered:* [182]

> To enter the burial chamber, one has to pass through a doorway above which there is a winged disk under a *frieze of cobras*. On either side of it are circular shields covered with scales and with a *Medusa* head in the center (to "petrify" tomb-robbers), and *two snakes (representing the Agathodaimon, the benevolent deity),* wearing the double crown of Egypt and coiled around *the caduceus of Hermes* and beribboned

Figure 24. *Left.* The Mask of Tutankhamen, Showing the Uraeus. JHC Collection

Figure 25. *Right.* Raised Serpent, Similar to the Egyptian Uraeus. Probably Roman Period. Provenance unknown, but perhaps Judaea. JHC Collection

thyrsus of Dionysus, both Greek symbols. [Italics added to stress the ophidian symbology.]

Most impressively, each massive Agathadaimon on the sides of the entrance to the burial chamber holds a caduceus of Hermes Psychopompos (the god who leads the dead into the next world). Above each large serpent is a Medusa with snakes in her hair.[183] Here in one scene we have a collage of serpent imagery, and one point is central: the serpent is chthonic and symbolizes immortality.

Some comment should be focused on Cleopatra VII's association with the snake. Cleopatra usually appears in art and lore with an asp biting or about to bite her breast.[184] Probably under the influence of Simonetta Vespuccis' Cleopatra, Michelangelo drew a Cleopatra who is virtually encircled by a large snake that bites her right breast.[185] Such well-known art helps explain why this Egyptian queen is celebrated for taking her own life by letting an asp bite her.[186] While there is abundant evidence for this belief, it is less fact and more myth. As Dio Cassius stated in his *Roman History* (second or third cent.): "No one knew for sure how she died. They only found small pricks on her arm. Some said she brought an asp to her." [187]

The myth has created history. Note this unreliable report by the Roman

Figure 26. Ceramic Ophidian Object under Egyptian Influence or Maybe Egyptian. Date and provenance unknown. JHC Collection

historian Suetonius in his *The Twelve Caesars:* "Antony sued for peace, but Augustus forced him to commit suicide—and inspected the corpse. He was so anxious to save Cleopatra as an ornament for his triumph that he actually summoned Psyllian snake-charmers to suck the poison from her self-inflicted wound, supposedly the bite of an asp." [188] As would be expected for a Roman who was politically one of the friends of the emperor *(amici principis)*, Suetonius is lauding Augustus, who forced Antony to commit suicide, and defaming Cleopatra, whom Augustus was "anxious to save." As A. Wallace-Hadrill indicated, Suetonius belonged to the equestrian rank and served the emperor, and his report reflects "the views of the courts" at which he served.[189] Such self-serving tendencies are transparent and reveal the fact that objective history was not the only goal for Suetonius' writing. What interests us is the anguine symbology: Cleopatra and the asp.

An asp's bite could be extremely painful, and a pin dipped with poison may have sufficed. The bite of an asp, however, provides a myth that explains how the famous queen was introduced to immortality. It is this symbolical meaning that is in focus: the asp is the purveyor of immortality. Unfortunately, many busts and sculptures of Aphrodite were altered by restorers who added a snake to make the figure the famous queen of Egypt, so one has to dismiss these as fabrications based on myth.[190] So powerful were the legends of Cleopatra's death that history blends with myth and makes her almost indistinguishable from Dido, an earlier African (Carthaginian) queen whose suicide is recounted in Virgil's *Aeneid*.

Long before her death at thirty-nine, Cleopatra was associated with serpent symbolism. A first-century BCE blue glass intaglio shows her por-

Figure 27. Serpent with Two Legs. "Papyrus." Egyptian. Late Dynastic Period–Ptolemaic Period. H: 12.4 cm. L: 76.3 cm. Courtesy of the Brooklyn Museum of Art 47.218.136.

trait with a triple uraeus as headdress. The snakes are crowned with sun discs.[191] The royal bearing, hairstyle, diadem, and especially the serpents clarify that this woman is Cleopatra. For most people, myth is more attractive than history, as we have been seeing; thus, Cleopatra will continue to be portrayed with an asp about to bite her naked breast. The imagery, as is now evident to the reader, is both ancient and primordially psychic. The asp in the Cleopatra saga represents not only immortality but also mortality; we are again confronted, as we saw in the introduction, by the double entendre of anguine iconography. The venom produces the anti-venom. We shall see, in a subsequent chapter, how all this plays out in the study of Numbers 21 and John 3.

The ceramic ophidian object, shown in Fig. 26, is clearly under Egyptian influence and may be Egyptian. It was purchased from an antiquities dealer in Jerusalem[192] who brought artifacts from Egypt to Israel. The object's date and provenance are unknown. It is perhaps three thousand years old. The serpent appears with a bovine figure, and the piece is rather crudely fashioned. What is the symbolic meaning of this piece? It is introduced now for discussion.

Sometimes biblical and classical scholars assume that the serpent does not have legs and so some literary descriptions of fantastic animals with legs cannot be a serpent. The classical example occurs in the exegesis of Isaiah 6. Each of the Seraphim covers "his legs" (רגליו) with wings (Isa 6:2).

We should not doubt that the Seraphim are serpents. We have seen that fossil snakes have legs. We have also perceived that modern snakes often have truncated legs. Now, it should be clarified that in antiquity snakes are often depicted with legs. In some serpent iconography and literature a serpent has five feet.[193]

One of the most stunning examples is found in a papyrus now preserved in the Brooklyn Museum. The artist depicted a serpent with two strong legs with feet and two hands. Serpents clearly were assumed to have had legs in antiquity. As we shall see, the serpent according to the Genesis myth probably had feet and could walk. Otherwise God's curse that he will henceforth be condemned to crawl on his belly makes no sense. In legends and iconographically, the serpent tends to regain its legs sometime in the Middle Ages.[194] Yet, most people—and scholars—presuppose today that the serpent is, and has always, been without legs or feet.

ARCHAEOLOGICAL EVIDENCE FROM CRETE: OPHIDIAN OBJECTS AND THE MINOAN SERPENT "GODDESSES"

Serpent iconography and symbology appear on Crete. One impressive example is the burnished terra-cotta snake goddess recovered from Kato Chorio, which is near Ierapetra.[195] This Neolithic (6500–3500 BCE) symbol depicts a woman seated, with her lower torso that of a snake (we announce the discovery of a ceramic Isis with an anguine body when we discuss the Greek and Roman data). Numerous jugs and vessels from Minoan culture bear serpents.[196] A jug with two serpents on it was found on Cyprus in Dhenia. The serpents are not clearly depicted; there is no head or tail. Twelve circles with white paint indicate the animal's scales. Other objects in the Pierides Museum display snakes and snake motifs.

Since this serpent vessel was recovered from a cultic area and a temple, it clearly had religious significance. What did the devotees of the serpent cult imagine the creature to symbolize? One may imagine that they assumed it was a god or had divine features, providing protection and a good life. Perhaps it was celebrated to assure the fertility of the earth, especially the gardens that were plentiful on Crete.[197]

As the reader might expect, we now come to the famous "serpent goddesses" of Crete.[198] Fragments of at least five faience serpent goddesses (if they are not cultic priestesses) can be seen in the Herakleion Archaeological Museum.[199] Two have been considerably restored and are the most famous ophidian realia from ancient Crete. One is a mother figure, and the other may be her daughter. They can be seen on public display in the Archaeological Museum in Herakleion.

The serpent goddesses date from the New Temple Period (1700–1400)[200] or about 1600 BCE. This period is the pinnacle in Minoan art; the finest frescoes and elegant buildings are contemporaneous with these faience treasures.

The tall goddess with the serpent on top has two serpents that curl down each arm and are held by the goddess in her hands (No. 63 on Crete). The

Figure 28. Two Serpent "Goddesses" from Knossos. Circa 1600 BCE. JHC Collection from professional replicas

mouths of the snakes are turned outward. The serpent on the right arm has markings for the mouth and eyes. A serpent is laced around each breast. A bodice, or girdle, rises from the hips to the bottom of the breasts. A leather thong pulls the bodice tight, lifting the breasts and making the waist small. The breasts are exposed with pointed nipples. The interest of the artist is on the torso, which is better crafted and detailed.

On the back of the goddess, the hair hangs straight down and rests on her back, just below the shoulder; it is cut horizontally. The garment hangs on her shoulders, leaving the back as exposed as the front. The serpents on the arms continue to just below the lower buttock on the back. The leather strap spirals from the bodice to the back and was probably attached behind the neck and under the carefully cut hair.

She stands erect with her head tilted slightly forward, balanced over her legs, which are of no interest to the artist, since he hides them behind her skirt. She looks forward and downward at about a 55–degree angle. Her eyes are wide open, her ears large, and a gentle smile graces the face. The breasts now are slightly whiter than the rest of the statuette.

The large lower garment flows downward to form a strong base similar to a pyramid. One receives a feeling of strength, firmness, and being well grounded. The light horizontal lines on the skirt modify the otherwise too forceful downward movement of the head, gaze, and slanting arms. The overall effect is a sense of grace, beauty, charm, nourishment, comfort, a mild sensual efficaciousness, and awesome femininity. The symbolic force evokes feelings of motherhood, life, and sexual energy.

The smaller goddess, or younger woman, is perhaps in her twenties

(No. 65 on Crete). Her youthful face is not nearly as attractive as the older woman's. The gentle smile of the older woman is gone in place of a mouth, with full lips, that suggests some concern. This may add to the wonder or fear instilled in the viewer, who is immediately drawn to the uplifted serpents. These are held high with arms outstretched.

The head of each serpent is below the hands. An impression of concern, or alertness, is carried forth by the painted, wide-open eyes. The ears are small and more realistic than those of the older woman. As with the former, no feet or legs are visible.

Two exposed full breasts explode outward from a bodice pulled tight, making the breasts rise and protrude. The nipples crown the exposed breasts that are whiter than the rest of the body, and, like the exposed sections of the arms, are clear of any decoration. On the back, the hair flows downward to the upper buttock.

The serpents in the younger woman's hands are medium sized. They almost reach from her fingertips to her shoulders. These smaller snakes are in contrast to the larger snakes on the older figure.

The young woman seems more naïve and less experienced than the older one. The young woman does not appear as comfortable with the snakes as the older woman. Both women stand erect, with their weight over their feet and breasts thrust forward.

As impressive as these goddesses or priestesses appear, they should be understood within Minoan art. Neither has received the skill and attention of the rhyton (drinking vessel) in the shape of a bull from the Little Palace at Knossos. The goddesses are made of faience and have not been decorated with gold, silver, or gems. The bull libation vase is of steatite. The eyes are made of rock-crystal with red iris. The mouth is white shell. The horns (now restored) are gilded wood.[201] The bull rhyton reveals the Minoans' inherent love of nature. Yet there is a power generated and felt when one examines the serpent goddesses; surely, it is because of the serpent symbolism.

What could be the symbolic meaning of these serpents held by the full-breasted women? To obtain insights for a perceptive answer to this question we should immerse ourselves in Minoan culture. We must divorce ourselves from the old methodology that provides answers to questions that have not been astutely evaluated; we need to avoid wish-fulfillment conclusions and aim toward those that are well founded.

The palace of Minos in Knossos is almost ultramodern, with running water and a cool lower area. The king and queen's chambers are sumptuously decorated. The Minoans seem to have lived peacefully together in a common society; something like a corporate personality developed. The setting is ideal. It is most restful in Knossos, when one is sitting by the high palace and looking at the surrounding hills that seem to hug and nourish this spot.[202]

The Minoans loved nature; they focused their art on depicting marvelously beautiful animals and attractively verdant gardens. An elegant fruit stand with molded flowers was found on Phaistos;[203] it dates from the Proto-palatial Period. Focusing only on art and flower appreciation can be misleading, and such blind methodology would lead one to assume that the plantation owners in Mississippi, with their paintings of flowers and flower-decorated cups, lived in a peaceful democratic society in which all were flower lovers.[204] Yet Cretan archaeology does support the conclusion that the Minoans were nature lovers. As R. Castleden states: "Minoan art . . . focuses on themes from nature—crocuses, sailing nautiluses, dolphins, octopuses, swallows, ibexes among them—rather than themes from contemporary events."[205] Due to the evidence of trade with other countries, the Minoans were influenced by Egyptian and Anatolian art, but they developed their own art in dynamic and creative ways. Hence, the ancient Minoans were not only the first artists within European society. They remain among the most surprisingly skilled in art and iconography.

Life in Bronze Age Crete was robust, dynamic, and prosperous. The youth were well fed and muscular; they enjoyed the challenging sport of bull jumping as is stunningly revealed in the "Bull-leaping" fresco in the Palace of Knossos.[206] During the history of Christianity, the human body was not always admired and often perceived as the source of sex, which was deemed sinful. The Minoans, however, like the Israelites, had a healthy attitude toward the body. The serpent goddesses and other bare-breasted women like the one depicted in terra-cotta and found in the shrine at Hagia Triada (its Minoan name is still unknown) are impressively well made.[207] Not only the goddesses or priestesses, but the average women, if we can depend on the art left for us to study, were often bare breasted.[208] They were "elegant, graceful, poised, well-mannered and sexually alluring, with their breasts displayed and their lips and eyes accentuated by make-up."[209] S. Alexiou concludes that the snake goddesses are attired in the "dress fashionable in the Minoan court round 1600 BC: a skirt with flounces, an apron and an open bodice leaving the breasts bare."[210] On Crete, and within Minoan society, the feminine was not feared or marginalized; the female dominated in the most attractive ways.[211] During the New Temple Period, women most likely became dominant, especially in religious ceremonies.

Is the date of the serpent goddesses significant? Yes, archaeologists have uncovered a vast amount of evidence that the Old Temple Period or Proto-palatial Period (2000–1700) ended abruptly and with a cataclysm that destroyed Monastiraki, Phaistos, and Knossos. Archaeologists found not only evidence of fire, but also leveled buildings and crushed pottery mingled with lime, especially at Phaistos.[212] One event need not be sought to explain the widespread destruction, and the catastrophic fires may not have happened on the same day, yet it is evident that an earthquake caused some of the destruction.[213] Earthquakes also devastated Crete in 1450 BCE, 1650 CE, and 1956 CE.[214] An "earthquake storm" seems to have struck the entire eastern Mediterranean world from about 1225 to 1175 BCE.[215] It is certain that earthquakes have shaped human history; Khirbet Qumran shows signs of the earthquake in 31 BCE, and at Sussita the columns of a church lie in parallel lines due to the earthquake of 749 CE.

The snake goddesses were made shortly after the earthquake in 1700 BCE, the event that probably brought to an end the first Palatial Period.[216] Their meaning may well be connected with this horrible event and the attempt by the Minoans to comprehend it.

One can imagine the Minoans bemoaning their fate and calling on the gods for assistance. What gods would be implored? Surely, the Minoans would appeal to the gods who controlled the ground, the ones who were causing the earth to move. What chthonic symbol would be most appropriate?

The answer is the serpent, the animal that was seen habitually burrowing into the earth.[217] These observations and insights are corroborated by the recognition that Potnia, most likely the name given to the mother serpent goddess, is the Earth Mother.[218] A tablet recovered from the archives at Knossos mentions an offering offered to "da-pu-ri-to-jo po-ti-ni-ja" which means "Potnia of the Labyrinth."[219] Since the offering is honey and since it is offered to Potnia, it seems evident that the goddess was represented by a living serpent housed beneath the surface in one of the subterranean labyrinths at Knossos.

One is reminded of a legend about Homer, who dug a trench in the earth and offered libations of milk, honey, sweet wine, and water for the dead. While it is not certain that Homer was thinking about serpent symbolism, his actions take us back to a time when such liquids were offered to snakes. Their chthonic nature becomes apparent.

Snakes were revered on ancient Crete. Their relation with honey is also grounded. Archaeologists recovered a terra-cotta snake that is crawling above a honeycomb. The figure also dates from the New Palace Period.[220] Vases for use in the worship of domestic snakes are on view in the Herakleion Archaeological Museum.

The dove was associated with goddesses on Crete. Most likely the dove signified fertility, procreation, and perhaps love.[221] We know that the Minoans traded with nations in the east, including Palestine. We also know that their art was influential on the Canaanites. Were the cult stands at

Beth Shan, with the clay serpents and doves, influenced by Minoan iconography and symbolism? That discovery would not be surprising.

The exposed breasts of the women could also be a key to the meaning of the ophidian symbology of the goddesses—fertility, power, beauty,
motherhood, and the desirable all come to mind. If the creator of these
masterpieces, who represented the naturalism of the new period that began after 1700 BCE,[222] did not have all these ideas and concepts in mind,
surely many of those who viewed them in ancient Knossos would have
these, and similar ideas, brought to consciousness. Other realia show that
the Minoans depicted women, priestesses probably, dancing. Perhaps one
is reminded of the poetry of the tenth Muse, the poetess Sappho of about
600 BCE. Recall Sappho's words:

> And their feet move
> rhythmically, as tender
> feet of Cretan girls
> danced once around an
> altar of love, crushing
> a circle in the soft
> smooth flowering grass.[223]

A gold ring, dating about one hundred years after the faience snake goddesses, was found near Knossos, in the tomb of Isopata; it is elegant and
shows "a religious scene which may represent an ecstatic ritual dance and an
'epiphany' of a goddess." [224] The snake also appears on a gold amulet.[225]

The artworks on Crete, in contrast to those on the southern plantations,
were not merely decorative; they served the spiritual dimensions of Minoan
culture. The women, after all, are goddesses. Their long triangular skirts,
like the Egyptian pyramids, anchor them with the earth and draw one's
eyes eventually downward. The older woman points downward with the
serpents on her arms. From the waist of both goddesses hangs a garment
that directs one's attention to the earth. Surely, we should finally conclude
that among the many meanings of the serpent represented by these faience
objects is the worship and adoration of the serpent, the god of the world
beneath the earth. When one is reminded that in ancient cosmology that is
also the place of the "underworld," then one can connect with these images
the concept of the serpent as the one who knows the secret of immortality.

Finally, let me reflect on the type of serpents held by the goddesses. Three
types of snakes are native to Crete: the Balkan Whip Snake *(Coluber ge-
monensis),* the Leopard Snake *(Elaphe situla),* and the Dice Snake *(Na-
trixz tessellate).* None is poisonous. The goddesses do not hold poisonous
snakes, since neither ancient fossils nor modern species on Crete are poisonous.[226] The markings of the snakes are not realistic; judging by length,

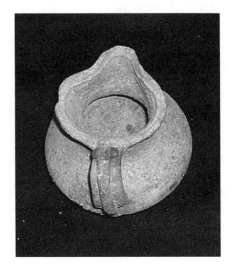

Figure 29. *Left.* Canaanite Bowl with Serpent on Handle. From Jerusalem or the environs of Jericho. JHC Collection

Figure 30. *Right.* Canaanite Serpent Pitcher. From Jerusalem or the environs of Jericho. JHC Collection

the older woman may be holding Dice Snakes or Leopard Snakes and the younger one two Balkan Whip Snakes.

ARCHAEOLOGICAL EVIDENCE OF MINOAN INFLUENCE AMONG THE ANCIENT CANAANITES: THE SERPENT BOWLS FROM ANCIENT PALESTINE

Four new discoveries must suffice to conclude our study of serpent iconography among the Canaanites in ancient Palestine, which, as we have indicated, was significantly influenced by Minoan art and culture. These objects were not previously known.

The ceramic vessel in Fig. 29 is 14.1 centimeters high and 8.9 centimeters wide.[227] It is most likely an example of Canaanite art of the Middle Bronze Age. It is rounded on the bottom and may have been intended to stand upright in sand. The aspect of interest for us is the appliquéd clay on the handle. In light of our previous research and the following study, it is evident that a serpent is intended in a stylized shape. There is no tail, no head. In light of the insights already obtained, it is apparent that a serpent was placed on the vessel, perhaps to protect the contents and not merely to provide decoration. It is conceivable that in a snake cult the serpent would be offered water or milk that could be inside the vessel.

The second ceramic vessel (Fig. 30) is 7.2 centimeters high and 6.3 cen-

Figure 31. *Left.* Clay Vase with Snake Images on Body. Allegedly from a cave northwest of Jericho. Bronze Age. Courtesy of Tom Cousins.

Figure 32. *Right.* Clay Vase with Two Serpent Images on Handle. Allegedly from a cave northwest of Jericho. Bronze Age. Courtesy of Tom Cousins.

timeters wide at the middle (not counting the single handle). It seems to be dated a little later than the larger vessel. Although cracked, it is in one piece and has not been restored. The bottom has a pedestal that is 3 centimeters in diameter; the fast wheel is evident.

It is an elegantly made pitcher with an attractive lip. Perhaps it was used on a table in a prosperous house for the pouring of some liquid, perhaps oil, milk, wine, or honey. What is of keen interest for us is the snake depicted on the handle. It has no tail and no curves. The nose becomes one with the body of the vessel. It does have two pieces of appliquéd clay, above the body that is also made of appliquéd clay; they indicate the eyes of the serpent. As we shall clarify, the eyes are usually the aspect of the snake that receives most of an artist's attention. Are the eyes detailed because the serpent symbolized keen awareness (it does not blink) and wisdom? Perhaps the serpent was placed with its head on the lip of the vessel to guard the contents, and perhaps also within a Canaanite serpent cult to offer the deity something to drink.

Two vases appeared within the storeroom of an antiquities dealer in Jerusalem. Both allegedly come from a cave northwest of Jericho. They each date from the Middle Bronze Age.[228]

The more crude clay vessel is in good shape, although the handle was repaired in modern times (Fig. 31). It is an example of bichrome ware, with light brown on beige-white. On the body, one finds the crude drawing of an animal with four legs, two horns, a beard, and a tail; perhaps a goat is depicted. On the other side of the vessel is a drawing of a bird or rooster. The images were applied after the clay had dried in the sun. The images seem to have been made with a small, crude brush, as was often the practice in antiquity when applying paint to pottery.[229]

Is the vessel ancient and authentic? I took both vessels to Dr. B. J. Bortolot, head of Daybreak/Archaeometric Laboratory Services in Guilford, CT. He drilled a minuscule hole at the base of the first vessel, applied thermoluminescence authenticity dating to it, and concluded that "the material of this sample was last fired 3060 ±650 years before the present time."[230] Thus, the object is ancient. It probably dates before 1060 BCE since thermoluminescence only ascertains the authenticity of an object.

Around the body are two bands with a wavy line inside. There are decorations on the neck and five wavy lines on the body. The handle has a crisscross pattern, with wavy lines going up to the top. The neck has three wavy lines that depict water or serpents. These two images are often indistinguishable in ancient artwork; perhaps stylized serpents seem more probable if this vessel is associated with the one that follows.

The second ceramic vessel is more elegantly crafted. The preparation of the pot is more refined and the art more careful or advanced (but not necessarily dated differently) than the previous example. The light clay was probably burnished before painting. This bichrome ware has brown on white (or light beige).

Is the object ancient? Dr. Bortolot drilled a small hole in the base. He then applied thermoluminescence authenticity dating to the vessel. He reported that "the material of this sample was last fired 1760 ±400 years before the present date."[231] Thus, this vessel is also ancient. Since, as just mentioned, thermoluminescence can only suggest that the vessel is ancient, the date of manufacture is open for debate. The object is not similar to the vessels made about 240 CE. One should heed Dr. Bortolot's words, added as "special comment" to this vessel (an identically worded caution accompanies the other vessel): "This area has clays prone to anomalous fading where part of the TL signal is not stable, leading to underestimates of age by TL. This appears to be the case here." At this stage, all that can be assured is that each vessel is ancient. We can also assume that the date of each vessel has been underestimated; that will prove to be the case.

The iconography is interesting. Probably more than one utensil was used to apply the paint to the clay; one was probably a small brush, and another might have been a reed or stick.

On the body are horizontal and vertical lines. On the bottom are two horizontal and two vertical ones that form a cross as in tic-tac-toe. There is a circle in each quadrant. On the neck are three sets of four concentric lines, then a wavy line at the tip of the jug. On the handle are four wavy lines with pronounced flat "heads." In the center of the handle (see Fig. 32) are two wavy lines. They probably depict serpents, since each wavy line ends in a flat end that looks like the head of a serpent. A circle in each "head" probably designates an eye. The serpent depicted on the left seems to have a straight line coming out of its mouth. In the Late Bronze Age, serpents are often depicted with elongated heads, prominent eyes, and sometimes with straight lines protruding from the mouth.[232] The snake images, even though more stylistic than real, appear to be Canaanite and are paralleled by the evidence of serpent worship at Hazor, which is well known through the silver-plated bronze cult stand. Both this serpent cult stand, which was probably held high by a priest, and the two clay vessels introduced here date from about the fourteenth or thirteenth century BCE.[233]

It is not clear what was contained in such vessels. Perhaps it is wise to avoid specifics. Various foodstuffs (even opium) could have been stored inside; the vessels could have held water, wine, milk, and conceivably honey. Without refrigeration, milk sours quickly and can cause illness. I am convinced that the images of serpents were often placed on vessels to protect the contents, especially milk, from souring and causing sickness. In the world of symbology, as is abundantly clear from texts and objects, the serpent is the quintessential guardian. As Edward Topsell stated in 1658, in his *The History of the Serpent,* the serpents are "the watchful keepers of Treasures."

What is the probable date of these two vessels? While pottery first appears around 7000 BCE,[234] these examples are clearly much later. But how much later should we date them? The shape and decoration of these objects implies some date in the Middle Bronze Age or Late Bronze Age. We will need to study these vessels in terms of what can be known from ceramic ethno-archaeology.[235]

We may now explore how and in what ways, if at all, these vessels are similar to ones already dated. The ceramic jars are dissimilar to the imported ware from Egypt, Mycenae,[236] Minoa, and Cyprus found in ancient Palestine.[237] They are also unlike the decorated Philistine pottery. The latter, in contrast, are sophisticated.[238] The objects remind me of a jar in the Moshe Dayan Collection.[239] This "chocolate-on-white" jar, with creamy white burnished slip, was "found in Jericho"; it is dated between 1700 and 1400 BCE. The Moshe Dayan jar may be significant for comparison with the two newly found vessels, since it is claimed that each was discovered in a cave northwest of Jericho.

The excellent state of preservation of each vessel reveals that they were found in tombs or perhaps sealed caves. Among the ceramic juglets found by K. Kenyon in tombs at Jericho, the closest parallel to either of these two vessels seems to be a piriform juglet with one shoulder handle and a long neck.[240] Neither vessel is to be confused with the Middle Bronze Age single-handled cylindrical juglets,[241] the shoulder-handled juglets, or the piriform juglets found in the Jericho tombs. The data for comparison from Jericho need to be evaluated in light of the fact that while many examples of ceramic ware from the Middle Bronze Age were recovered, no examples exist from the Late Bronze Age. The city had ceased to exist by that time. By the Early Bronze and Middle Bronze Ages, Jericho was no longer an urban center. Thus, the jars buried to the north and northwest of Tel es-Sultan, where Kenyon found them, represent the life of nomads.[242]

Both jars now introduced were produced on a wheel. Both vessels are noticeably different; yet, within pottery typology, they represent a similar type. Both, especially the second vessel with the typical tilted look, seem to be examples of the wheel-made Base Ring Jug called a *bilbil*. The origin and meaning of the name *bilbil* are not clear. It may be onomatopoeic to denote the sound made when liquid was poured from it: *bl, bl* (Yadin's suggestion).[243] The name could also derive from the Hebrew and Arabic word *bulbul* that denotes a type of thrush-like songbird (J. Seger's speculation).[244] The latter explanation may be denoted by the long neck of the second vessel, and such a bird might be depicted on the first one.

Rather than Cypriot imports,[245] the two vessels introduced here seem to be examples of the well-known painted ware of Canaan that is a local imitation of the Cypriot imports of Base Ring Ware Bilbils. Compare, for example, how they seem to be modeled after the imported Cypriot jug found at Dan that dates from the Late Bronze Age II.[246] The period for the two vessels thus appears to be the Late Bronze Age or 1550–1200 BCE. The ascertained time of composition also coincides with the final revival in the declining urban culture in Canaan.

Perhaps more can be speculated at this initial stage of research on the two vessels. The first jar appears to be an example of the local Canaanite ware. It is cruder and heavier like the local ware from the end of Late Bronze Age Palestine. The second jar is a classic example of refined Bilbil Ware made locally in Canaan. As W. G. Dever states, "The local wares, while rather poorly made, now feature relatively common painted decoration, with both geometric and naturalistic and animal motifs (e.g., a pair of ibexes and the sacred tree; a palm tree and panel)."[247] To Dever's list of images we seem now able to add ophidian iconography. These comments are only provisional and prolegomenous to an intensive examination by experts in ceramic ethno-archaeology.

Can we find links between the artwork and datable objects from Palestine? The crude drawing on the first vessel shows an animal with four legs, two horns, a beard, and a tail. The artwork is reminiscent of the bronze bull statuette found in or near Samaria (ASOJS 3941).[248] It dates from the early twelfth century BCE. Both the clay drawing and the bronze statuette

Figure 33. Clay Jar with Serpents. Middle
Bronze. Courtesy of the Israel Museum.

show an animal with horns and legs similarly fashioned. The depiction of
each animal has the legs excessively long and the horns curving gently inward.[249] The ceramic vessel, however, appears to be older. Perhaps one can
surmise that both reflect, in differing ways and on different substances, the
late Canaanite stylistic tradition. The combination of reality and stylized
features appears to link these two works of art.

Thus, both of these vessels seem to be Canaanite jars. They are probably
luxury items made by Canaanite potters and artists. Most important, they
provide significant new data for assessing the veneration of the serpent by
Canaanites, ostensibly near Jericho, before the "Conquest."

The date (1550–1200 BCE) and alleged provenance (near Jericho) of
both vessels seem especially significant. At the end of the thirteenth century, Canaanite culture was determined by four momentous events. The
Hittite empire to the north collapsed, Egypt's control of Canaan was
weakened, the "Sea Peoples" began infiltrating from the West, and the
Israelite tribes probably began incursions from the East.[250] Perhaps there
were also local revolts and disruptions; we have previously surmised that
these events may have been accompanied by, and even aided by, earthquakes.

This research has been informed by a study of the vast amount of vessels with serpents on the rim or handles in museums, antiquities dealers,
and private collections. One vessel is so special for this study that I will
conclude with it.

This "chocolate on white ware" ceramic serpent vessel is one of the most
elegant ever found in ancient Palestine; unfortunately, its precise provenance is unknown.[251] The 32-centimeter red-clay vessel is late Canaanite

(Middle Bronze Age) and dates from the middle of the second millennium BCE. As indicated previously, the zenith of pottery-making in ancient Canaanite culture corresponded with the time of this object.

The serpent was certainly a popular "decoration" on Canaanite vessels. They are rarely so ornately depicted as in the present example; here they are realistic and obviously snakes. They appear to curl upward as if moving. The bodies are punctuated by tiny holes to signify skin (as in most examples). The eyes are detailed, and again it is wise to recall that usually the eyes receive the attention of the ancient artist or worker. On other vessels the snakes are merely appliquéd round pieces of clay without any indications of a mouth, eyes, or scales. It would be counterintuitive to imagine that such snakes are only decorations.

What did the two serpents symbolize to the maker of this vessel and to those who used it? The placing of the serpents is crucial. One could imagine that the owner wanted the serpents to obtain a drink of water or milk. That makes sense in a serpent cult civilization as in ancient Canaan. But they could be placed there to protect and guard the contents, probably wine, milk, or water. Clearly, the serpents add to the beauty of the vessel, so beauty and aesthetics also come into play as we ponder serpent iconography.

ARCHAEOLOGICAL EVIDENCE OF THE INFLUENCE OF GRECO-ROMAN OPHIDIAN ICONOGRAPHY IN ANCIENT PALESTINE: THE JEWELRY OF POMPEII AND JERUSALEM

Anguine jewelry has been found in the ruins of Pompeii. As is well known, this city south of Rome was destroyed in 79 CE when the volcano Vesuvius erupted. Here are the words of Pliny the Younger, who witnessed the horrifying event:

> Ashes were already falling, not as yet very thickly. I looked round: a dense black cloud was coming up behind us, spreading over the earth like a flood. . . . We had scarcely sat down to rest when darkness fell, not the dark of a moonless or cloudy night, but as if the lamp had been put out in a closed room. You could hear the shrieks of women, the wailing of infants, the shouting of men; some were calling their parents, others their children or their wives, trying to recognize them by their voices. . . . Many besought the aid of the gods, but still more imagined there were no gods left, and that the universe was plunged into eternal darkness for evermore.[252]

Pliny was with his mother on a high hill north of Pompeii and Vesuvius; he was visiting his uncle, Pliny the Elder. The latter's inquisitive nature not

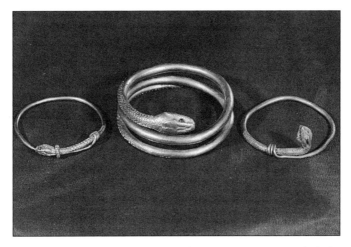

Figure 34. Pompeii. Serpent jewelry. Naples Antiquities Museum. I thank the Soprintendenza Archeologica delle Provincie di Napoli e Caserta and Professor Marcello del Verme for assistance and permission to publish this photograph. JHC

only provides us with valuable information about ancient society, including the Essenes who lived at Qumran; it also led to his death on the shores west of Pompeii as he was seeking to explore the events of 79 CE.

At least four beautiful anguine bracelets have been recovered from the debris in Pompeii. The elegant gold bracelets shown in Figs. 34 and 35 perhaps were crafted within the one hundred years that preceded 79 CE.[253]

Note the detail of the serpents. The eyes are clearly marked, sometimes with a jewel. The head and skin are detailed. These are not stylized serpents; these are snakes. The gold jewelry bracelets from Pompeii and the gold ring from Alexandria (perhaps) are impressive and draw one's attention and admiration. They were crafted and intended to be displayed prominently.

There is ample evidence that wealthy women wanted to be seen with anguine jewelry. Surely, something positive was symbolized by these works of art. It is clear that serpents were admired, even worshipped, at Pompeii. More can be surmised about the symbol of the serpent among the residents at Pompeii.

At Pompeii the Romans apparently worshipped various gods through Agathadaimon (the good serpent or demon). This god of goodness is often represented on gems with the sacred cista (the box in which mysteries were kept) and as a serpent or a human–bird figure with serpents as feet (anguipedes). Agathadaimon was revered in Pompeii and openly. This is certain because a painting of this serpent can still be seen in the House of the Vettii. In this room, the occupants of the house gathered in a sacred place to devote themselves to the household gods (the Lares).

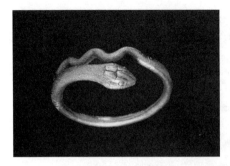

Figure 35. Pompeii. Gold Jewelry; reference no. 1946,7-2,2 (transparency number PS208051). British Museum Ring no. 950. Courtesy of the Trustees of the British Museum.

Gold anguine symbols do not appear only on jewelry. They appear also as serpents. At Herculaneum, in the Palaestra, a massive bronze serpent with five heads spewed water into the swimming pool.[254] This serpent image is unrealistic, but replicas of snakes are often strikingly lifelike and realistic. One example was the pride and joy of Leo Mildenberg. He published many of his serpent realia, including the cornelian snake head attachment (third–second cent. BCE), bronze snake with eight undulations (c. 1320–1200 BCE), gray granite cobra goddess (Greco-Roman), and bronze snake with five undulations (first–second cent. CE).[255] As far as I know, he never published his gold snake, which, as he reported to me, was found in southern Italy and dates from the Roman Period.[256]

Evidence of the popularity of anguine jewelry is present not only in the West, in Pompeii, but also in the East, including Jerusalem.[257] For the Roman Period, there is a vast amount of evidence. I have seen gold, silver, and bronze serpent armbands, earrings, and especially bracelets. Because of their composition and the quality of their artwork some of the jewelry belonged to the upper classes and others to the poorer people.

Figure 38 displays four bronze bracelets and one bronze ring. All are

Figure 36. Pompeii. Agathadaimon. JHC

Figure 37. Leo Mildenberg and Author with Gold Snake Jewelry.

from the early Roman Period and were found in or near Jerusalem.[258] Like so many other illustrations, they appear here for the first time. From left to right: the first and last bracelets show a stylized serpent, the next has the two eyes of the serpent etched in an enlarged manner. Because of the quality of the bronze work, it is likely that these bracelets belonged to rather wealthy persons. The next to last one is crude; the head of the snake, with

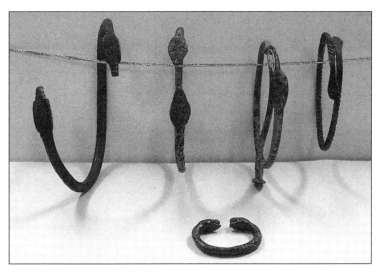

Figure 38. Four Bronze Bracelets and One Silver Ring. Early Roman Period. All from Jerusalem or nearby. JHC Collection

Figure 39. Two Rings from Jerusalem and the Roman Period. The ring on the left is silver and shown previously, the one on the right is bronze. The left serpent ring depicts the eyes and mouths of the serpents. The one on the right is more stylized, but horizontal lines depict the serpent's skin. Most likely the head of the serpent was broken off. JHC Collection

the elongated tongue, is merely wrapped around the bronze; this bracelet probably belonged to one who was not wealthy. The ring below the bracelets is artistically crafted; the mouths of the serpents are open and the eyes and heads are professionally designed. More detail was poured into it than the serpent ring found at Herculaneum.[259]

The bronze earring in Fig. 40 shows a serpent with large eyes. It dates from the Roman Period and was found in or near Jerusalem.[260] Because of its quality, the work probably belonged to a wealthy person. The jewelry or clasp shows dragons.

Figure 40. *Left.* Bronze Earring Showing Serpent with Large Eyes. Early Roman Period. From in or near Jerusalem. JHC Collection

Figure 41. *Right.* Bronze Jewelry. Roman Period. Jerusalem. Probably a Persian dragon with mouth, ears, and eyes. JHC Collection

Figure 42. Bronze Upraised Serpent. JHC Collection

Figure 42 is an anguine symbol found in the environs of Jerusalem, probably dating from the Roman Period. It is an upright bronze serpent. Perhaps it was once part of wooden furniture.

The previous discussion can only represent some selected examples of the abundance of serpent jewelry from antiquity. It is clear that the serpent—perhaps more than any other animal—was chosen to adorn jewelry and make wearers more attractive.[261] Note the following table of gold jewelry with serpents; all date from between 100 BCE and 100 CE (the date for the final editing of the Fourth Gospel, without the latter addition of 7:53–8:11; also see the additions in Appendix III):[262]

Table 1. A Selection of Roman Era Gold Jewelry with Serpents

Type	Number of Snakes	Provenance	Museum*
ring	2 pairs	Alexandria?	BM [Ring 771]
ring	2 pairs	Greece?	Benaki Museum, Athens
ring	one	Alexandria?	BM [Ring 950][263]
ring	snake and hawk	Unknown	BM [EA 15715]
ring	serpent at each end	Pompeii	AMH[264]
ring	detailed serpent	Jerusalem?	JHC collection
2 armlets	one on each	Italy	MNA [24824–25]
bracelets	one on each	unknown	BM GR 1917.6-1.2780–2781
3 bracelets	serpent at one end	Pompeii	MNA[265]
armlet	serpent at one end	Pompeii	MNA[266]
2 bracelets	serpents at each end	Herculaneum	Not clear[267]

* BM = British Museum; AMH =Archaeological Museum in Herculaneum; MNA = Naples' Museo Nazionale Archeologico

One should also recall the earlier discussion and picture of the Greek-Scythian gold serpent goddess image that was made for the forehead of a horse (fourth cent. BCE).[268]

ARCHAEOLOGICAL EVIDENCE OF ROMAN GLASS AND OPHIDIAN ICONOGRAPHY

During the Hellenistic Period, glass flasks, beakers, and goblets appeared with monochrome threads. This artwork is categorized as "snake-thread" decoration. The glass is applied to the outside of the vessel. The snake-thread ornamentation winds like a serpent and often has slanting indentations. Occasionally, these snake-threads are strikingly reminiscent of serpents clearly applied to other vessels.[269] It seems that the technique of decorating glass with snake-thread designs originated sometime in the early first century BCE or CE in the eastern area of the Mediterranean.[270] Most of the examples date from the second or third centuries CE.[271] Although fragments of snake-thread glass were found at Dura-Europos,[272] the provenance of a piece is frequently unknown.[273]

Decoration of another type, which is also evocative of serpents, appears on glassware. It is glass with bifurcated ribs, or pinched ribbed glass (not pinched thread glassware).[274] The parison (preliminary shape) of the vessel is pinched during the earliest stages of blowing. This time the design on the glass is not always easy to distinguish from the caduceus or two serpents that rise, sometimes around a central rod, and almost always face each other.[275] Some of the glass with bifurcated ribs clearly was made in the glass factory at Jalame,[276] a northeast foothill of Mount Carmel,[277] during the first centuries of the Common Era. Examples were found at Dura-Europos.[278] The snake-thread and the pinched-rib decorations on Roman glass are intended to make the glass more attractive.

While these markings reflect knowledge of serpents and perhaps of ophidian iconography, they must not be interpreted as an example of serpent symbolism. Although the "snake-thread" decorations are mere ornamentations, we should allow for the possibility that serpents appeared on glass, yet this assumption is denied in recent publications. We should be open to the possibility that serpents were depicted on glass, if only ideally or impressionistically. We have seen that serpent iconography was ubiquitous in the Hellenistic Period. Giants were depicted having anguipedes. Gods and goddesses—especially Apollo, Asclepius, Hygieia, and Isis—appeared as serpents. Actors, poets, and soldiers were hailed as heroic because of the presence of a serpent on a monument.[279]

Romans originally were not fond of glassware, but, beginning with

Figure 43. Glass Bottle with Serpent Appliqué. Serpents are upraised and eyes are prominent. First century BCE. From Hizma, northeast of Jerusalem. JHC Collection

the new imperial iconography established during the reign of Augustus (37 BCE–14 CE) and the development of slave trade routes, glass became popular in the West as it had been formerly in the East. Glassblowing was discovered (or invented) in the East (Syria, including Judaea), and many of these craftsmen may have migrated to Italy. By the late first century BCE, Horace could refer to a spring on his villa as "more sparkling than glass" *(splendidior vitro).*[280]

Now I will introduce a sensational discovery; it will become certain that serpents were depicted on glass (see Fig. 43).[281] This glass was found allegedly at Hizma, which is less than 8 kilometers northeast of Jerusalem.[282] Two serpents are clearly depicted.[283] This decoration is quite unlike the ornamentations that appear on the necks of beakers or jugs.[284] The serpents are appliquéd glass. While a somewhat similar example is preserved in the Israel Museum,[285] on the present piece of glass two serpents are indisputably depicted. Their heads are obviously those of a serpent; the eye is noticeably present, and the skin is depicted by lines. Both serpents are upright, as if they are aroused cobras. One is reminded of the uraeus and the imagery of Numbers 21 and John 3:14.

ARCHAEOLOGICAL EVIDENCE FOR "PAGAN" CULTS
EMPLOYING SERPENT SYMBOLOGY

An Asclepian Cult in Jerusalem?

We can once again return to the search for ophidian objects in and near Jerusalem. It is becoming clear that there was a temple to Asclepius in Bethesda (Bethzatha) that is just inside Jerusalem and north of the Sheep's Gate (Stephen's Gate, Lion's Gate). There probably also was an Asklepieion with healing baths and a room for incubation.[286] Stones from a temple to Asclepius have been uncovered near the Church of Saint Anne (surely, as Saladin knew, one of the masterpieces of the Crusader Period). To the northeast of it are vaulted rooms, which most likely had columns (stoa as suggested by Jn 5), and a private pool. This pool is neither a cistern nor a mikveh (ritual cleansing bath). Stratigraphy, coins, and pottery indicate that these installations were in place during the time of Aelia Capitolina, Hadrian's name for the city that replaced Jerusalem, or after 135/36 CE. It is probable that the Asclepian cult was active here before 132 and after 70 CE. There were healing groups congregated there for centuries before the destruction of 70 CE, and these would not threaten or be threatened by the sanctity of the Temple and the power of the Sadducees.

The stratification is dated by coins and sherds. The area was occupied prior to 135/36 CE. The best evidence for the presence of a cult of Asclepius comes from the post-135/36 period, but there is reason to think that the healing cult of this god goes back to an earlier period. There were healing cults in this area of Jerusalem long before 70 CE.

After 135/36 there were healing pools (not mikvaoth or baths) in the northeast section of the excavated area. The small pools also had vaulted ceilings that were most likely used for incubation and the dreams that Asclepius was alleged to have given to his devotees who needed healing. Although the excavations at Bethesda were from 1882 to 1964, with long periods of interruptions, I have been told by those involved in preparing future excavations that no reports have been published. I shall thus turn to some realia that indicate Bethesda had an Asklepieion.

Six realia found at Bethesda are important for understanding ophidian symbolism related to the Asklepieion.[287] First, a piece of marble contains the remains of a serpent in relief (catalogue M.S.A. 3). The fragment is 13.7 centimeters at the base, 11.1 centimeters high, and 4.1 centimeters thick. It was found west of the Byzantine Church in a channel that connects the north and south pools.[288] At the left are remains of two columns. To the right of them is a serpent; it is in high relief extending above the marble as much as 1.5 centimeters. The serpent is raised and curled, perhaps to indicate power and the dynamism of life. The serpent's scales are denoted by scale-like carvings.

Second, a lamp was recovered near the Asklepieion (PB0613). In the center of the lamp is shown an enthroned Asclepius with his right hand on the head of a dog. The left side of the lamp is worn away, but one can see what appears to be a raised left hand that may have held a staff. If a serpent was once depicted on the staff, there is no longer a trace of it. This object may also be a votive offering.

Third, a marble fragment was found northeast of the Church of Saint Anne (M.S.A. 4). It is an ex-voto offering that is 14.7 centimeters wide, 13 centimeters high, and 4.7 centimeters thick. The marble shows that the carving was ornate and under the influence of the Hellenistic style. A seashell is shown below a triangular carving. Of special importance are the remains of a sheaf of wheat (perhaps) that may have been carved to celebrate harvest or spring. Kore or Persephone both come to mind. The object dates from the Roman Period, but cannot be dated precisely until we know the date of the stratum in which it was recovered.

Fourth, another ex-voto object was discovered; it is also related to the Asklepieion. The marble fragment is 10 centimeters long, 5.4 centimeters wide, and 4.8 centimeters high. The artist expertly depicted a foot with five toes within a sandal with straps. The object is clearly Roman, but its exact date is unknown. Perhaps someone left this object to thank Asclepius for healing his foot.

Fifth, a second ex-voto foot was recovered near or within the Asklepieion (M.S.A. 7). The marble is 13.3 centimeters high, 14.5 centimeters wide, and the left side is broken diagonally. These ex-voto feet seem to indicate that a devotee wanted to thank the god for healing his feet.

Sixth, a piece of marble was discovered not far from the Asklepieion (M.S.A. 5). It is 13.2 centimeters high, 11.7 centimeters wide, and 4.0 to 1.6 centimeters thick from top to bottom. The object seems to depict a nude woman. Her hair is pulled back in a bun, as she prepares for her time in a healing bath. She may be moving her right hand to remove her garment before entering the healing bath. Taking off clothes was a ritual that could symbolize the removal of impurities. The healing baths are shaped like an "L" so that one inside removing clothes would not been seen by others outside waiting their turn. Above her to the right is shown a hand descending. As in so many other ancient works of art, the hand symbolizes the presence of a god. There is no reason to suggest any god but Asclepius.

We now may introduce a magnificent example of ophidian iconography that was found over one hundred years ago by C. Clermont-Ganneau. He announced the discovery, which he called the "Vase of Bethzatha," in a letter dated May 31, 1874.[289] The object was found during excavations of caves beneath the *via dolorosa* and north of the Temple Mount.[290] Most likely the vase was discarded in a refuse dump along with other unwanted items.[291] The terra-cotta vase was found in pieces, but it was "so nearly complete" that it was "possible to reconstruct it by gumming the pieces together."[292] The pottery is gray and 36 centimeters high. It sits on a low foot. The maximum circumference is 1 meter. Here are selections from Clermont-Ganneau's description (italics are mine):

> It is ornamented by two handles, each formed of a double tress elegantly twisted. On the upper part of each handle is cut a small rectangular cavity, towards which *two large serpents* appear to be turning as if to drink. They are in relief, symmetrically disposed, and climbing along the sides of the vessel; their tails are lost in the base of the handles. Immediately below each handle is sculptured in relief a Gorgon's head.
>
> Further, close to either handle is twice impressed a kind of small medallion, representing a male figure, nude, upright, the left arm raised and leaning on a long lance or thyrsus; the right arm extended and pointed to the ground. The right hand appears to hold an indistinct object over another also indistinct placed upon the ground.
>
> The external moldings of this little figure, of which I shall speak presently, are repeated six times on one vase.
>
> At nearly equal distances from the two handles, and on each side of the vase, is repeated twice a second molded medallion of larger dimensions, representing a nude Mercury, whose body is seen in full, the head turned to the left. He has the petasus, and has his tunic tied across the breast and thrown behind him; he holds the *caduceus* in his left hand, and raises with his right an object which seems to be a purse—the frequent attribute of the Hermes of antiquity.
>
> In the circle which surrounds him are four objects, which appear to be meant for fir-cones.[293] The medallion is encircled by a small border, formed by means of a molded repetition of six points arranged in a circle round a seventh central point. This ornament is reproduced in profusion on the rest of the vase. . . .
>
> I must lastly mention, in concluding this segment of the vase, a large leaf, with its branches in high relief, stamped beside one of *the serpents*. . . .
>
> This great vase, so rich in ornamentation, is nevertheless executed with a certain amount of negligence. Its form is elegant, but it wants symmetry and is not perpendicular; the handles are put on awkwardly; and the details of the moldings show carelessness. All round it may be seen the marks of the fingers which repaired the accidents produced in removing the mould. The arrangement of the figures and the symbols

seems done by chance and without rigorous method. Nevertheless, such as it is, this vessel, with all its imperfections, is most remarkable from an artistic point of view.

The profuseness in detail and the carelessness in execution, lead me to think that it is a kind of specimen, the essay of some artist wishing to make a model, which he might subsequently reproduce with greater care, perhaps in metal.[294]

Two other ceramic fragments were found near this vase. They seem to have been made in the same workshop as the Vase of Bethzatha. A Gorgon mask was detected and a "little male figure leaning on a spear" that was "probably obtained from the same mould."[295] There is no reason to doubt that these objects and the vase indicate a local workshop.

Given what we now know about the wealth and grandeur of Jerusalem before 70 CE, it seems that the "Bethzatha Vase" may antedate 70. It dates from sometime between 63 CE and 325 CE; it is surely closer to the earlier date than the latter. It was conceivably made long before 135/36 CE when Jerusalem became Aelia Capitolina. Clermont-Ganneau was convinced that it belonged to Aelia Capitolina.[296] The object has never received a proper publication and scholarly assessment.[297] In fact, most scholars do not know about this object, the "Bethzatha Vase," that is now stored in London at the Palestine Exploration Fund building.[298]

The serpents on this vase face each other at the top of the rim, just above where the handle joins the body of the vase. The heads are rounded and triangular; thus, they are reminiscent of vipers or cobras. Two small circles indicate the eyes and the skin is depicted by tiny indentations and linear strokes. Each serpent seems to have four curves, perhaps to symbolize its dynamism and elusiveness. Clermont-Ganneau thought that "the four serpents which are proceeding to drink . . . the drops which have escaped from the *simpulum,*[299] appear to represent the *genii loci,* and remind me of the serpentine form of the Ἀγαθοδαίμων, to which in so many ancient monuments libations are offered."[300] It is not clear that the serpents are about to drink. They are also headed to the rim of the vase and may have signified the powers that protect the contents of vessels.

The idea that serpents on vessels indicate that they are seeking water was articulated not only by Clermont-Ganneau, but also by Kenyon and Joines. It is possible that the "water" was a symbol of votive offering for the serpent. The importance of water in the Asclepian cult is clarified by Festus, who wrote that a temple was built on an island in the Tiber by Rome for Asclepius "because sick people are aided by physicians particularly through water [*a medicis aqua maxime sustententur*]."[301]

I am persuaded, however, that the primary symbolic meaning of the

Figure 44. Bethzatha Vase with Many Serpents. Bethzatha Asklepieion. Jerusalem. Early Roman Period. Courtesy of Dr. R. L. Chapman III and the Palestine Exploration Fund. AP 4149. JHC

ophidian iconography is protection. Indeed, one should continue reading Festus, who states in the next sentence that "the serpent is the guardian of this temple because it is a most vigilant beast and this faculty is especially appropriate in safeguarding the health of invalids." Note, furthermore, that in antiquity in the Levant and in Greece and Rome the serpent, often as a dragon, symbolizes the one who guards the water that comes out of the earth or the treasure that the human desires. This is clear from abundant sources, for example, from the story in the *Hymn of the Pearl* in which a large serpent guards the pearl, from a quotation by Artemidorus ("The serpent . . . lies on guard over treasures"),[302] and from another statement by Festus ("serpents . . . lying near treasures to guard [*thesauris custodiae*] them").[303] It is enlightening to read that E. J. Edelstein and L. Edelstein concluded their authoritative and thorough study of the Asclepian cult with the following words:

> To determine the meaning of the serpent in connection with Asclepius is very difficult. That the snake indicated the rejuvenation which the god perfected, or his shrewdness, or his medical knowledge cannot be denied entirely. But it seems more plausible that the animal symbolized the mildness and goodness of Asclepius, his guardianship over men.[304]

Thus, the serpents were placed on the vase probably not to indicate that they needed a drink of water or were seeking water. They were placed there—I am persuaded—to symbolize their protection of the liquid that is vital for human life. The vessel, moreover, may have contained wine. The serpents would thus protect it from turning bad.

Clermont-Ganneau stated that his letter would be accompanied by "two photographs."[305] No photographs appear in the publication of his announcement of this monumental discovery, but see the photography supplied in my illustrations.

It is conceivable that the object was associated with the Asclepian cult that was located just east of where it was discovered—that is, inside Stephen's Gate to the north and where the author of the Gospel of John places the five-porticoed Bethzatha or Bethesda (Jn 5:1–2). There is abundant evidence that Bethzatha was a popular site for healing in the Roman Period.[306] An Asclepian cult, not necessarily an Asklepieion with sleeping quarters, may have been located at the pools of Bethzatha.

If the female figure on the vase is Hygieia, then surely the vase is most likely related to the Jerusalem shrine of Asclepius and Hygieia. One way to advance this argument would be to demonstrate that the woman depicted on the vase should be identified as Hygieia. The iconography favors this possibility. The woman is not nude like a goddess; she is draped like a human or demigoddess.[307] She seems to be holding in her left hand a long ceremonial staff[308] or torch (perhaps to give light to the underworld or to symbolize the knowledge of healing).[309] In her right hand, which points to the ground,[310] is a staff that could be the one associated with her father, Asclepius.[311] The staff denotes, inter alia, support for the weak,[312] and the attention necessary for the physician.[313] Note how Ovid has Asclepius state: "Look upon this serpent which twines about my staff."[314] I know of no other Asclepian cult in or near Jerusalem except the one at Bethzatha (Bethesda), and the "Vase of Bethzatha" was discovered near the two pools of Bethzatha.

Those who wish to claim that such a hypothesis cannot be proved should note that not one "of the Asclepius statues that are extant can be identified with certainty as one of the sacred cult statues of the god."[315] As scientists, we are not governed by claims of proof or the criterion of certainty. We should strive to obtain the closest approximation to the probable or conceivable, and the coins minted in Jerusalem showing Hygieia help ground the conclusion that this vase was associated with the cult of Asclepius and Hygieia that was in Jerusalem, most likely at Bethzatha.

Clermont-Ganneau concluded his assessment of this vase with these words: "The vase, which I propose to call the Vase of Bethzatha, remains one of the most precious archaeological objects that Jerusalem has yet produced; and I do not doubt that the interest it will excite among savants will equal the curiosity that it will excite among the public."[316]

Unfortunately, the object was never published. Its description was hidden in Clermont-Ganneau's words, and the object itself is not on public display. One might consider this object to be a fake, but it was discovered by Clermont-Ganneau and, being retrieved in fragments, was not planted falsely.

Figure 45. Glass Serpent. Courtesy of the Studium Biblicum Franciscanum Museum, Jerusalem. JHC

Why was this object never accurately documented? Only now—over a century later—is the "Vase of Bethzatha" mentioned in something more than a letter or an article about explorations of the Holy Land by the English.[317] Now, we may publish a photograph and preliminary analysis of this intriguing, if rather unattractive anguine object.[318]

A ceramic fragment with an image of a serpent was discovered in Jerusalem or nearby.[319] It probably dates from the early Roman period. Human faces (only five remain) and a large serpent are appliquéd to the outside walls of a vessel. The skin of the serpent is marked by artistic indentations in the clay, and notably, the serpent's mouth is opened wide. Did this feature indicate that the serpent was the symbol of wisdom? This could be the meaning intended by the author or supplied by some who saw it. Numerous legends about serpents whispering insights into the ears of kings and gods are known from antiquity (as we learned in earlier chapters). Most likely the fragment is the remains of a votive offering; perhaps it was part of a vessel used in Jerusalem's Asklepieion. Does its lack of sophistication and almost crudeness help us with the Bethzatha Vase that is strikingly unattractive and may have been a model for a vessel perhaps fashioned in bronze? It is a pity that the Bethzatha Vase and the fragment were not recovered from a controlled archaeological excavation.

The anguine object in Fig. 45 is housed in the Studium Biblicum Franciscanum (SBF) Museum, Jerusalem.[320] It is made of glass and is 7.4 cen-

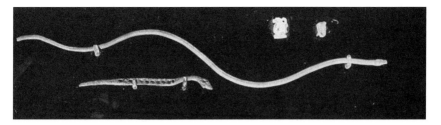

Figure 46. Serpents. Courtesy of the Studium Biblicum Franciscanum Museum, Jerusalem. JHC

timeters long, 3.7 centimeters wide, and .4 centimeter thick. The glass is translucent and green, but black dots signify eyes and skin; the dots are slightly larger for the eyes. I would judge this glass ophidian object to date from the Roman Period. Its high quality points to the early Roman Period. It is similar to numerous glass objects and glassware that clearly antedate 70 CE. Most ancient glass serpents from the area of Jerusalem are dated to the first centuries BCE or CE.[321]

The eyes and skin are impressively marked. The pointed nose is shaped by an area of the glass that is slightly raised. The artistically shaped head is raised 1.4 centimeters above the level for the body. The serpent's body is straight until midway when it is coiled up into three concentric circles.

This ophidian object is unique; I have not seen anything to compare with it. Its beauty and the artisan's skill may suggest that the serpent served in some cultic capacity. The raised head might symbolize, like the uraeus, divinity and power. The attractive translucent glass could evoke thoughts about beauty, health, happiness, and rejuvenation. The coiled and concentric body might represent the unity of time and cosmos; it would thus have the symbolic meaning associated with the Ouroboros.

The two serpents, and the two small uraei, shown in Fig. 46 are also housed in the SBF Museum. The small bronze serpent is 9.2 centimeters long and now dark green. The object was purchased from an antiquities dealer in the Old City of Jerusalem, and thus the site in which it was discovered cannot be examined to ascertain its date. It can be dated only by analogy and a study of the object itself. The glass has circular holes that indicate skin. I would date it to the Roman Period, primarily because of the quality of the glass and workmanship.

The small serpent is elongated and straight, although a curve appears just before the triangular head. Eyes are indicated by clear circles cut into the bronze. Originally there was a piece of glass in each of the eleven holes, but only one round piece of glass (rather clear) remains in place. It is in the second hole from the left.

No hole in the object suggests that the serpent was intended to be worn. It may have been a cultic object because of its intricate details and fine design. The elongation could denote unity, and the triangular head a poisonous serpent that might denote good and evil, as well as life and death. Again, it is important to recall the multivalent nature of serpent symbolism and the power of the serpent to denote both–and (double entendre).

The larger serpent is composed of silver; it is 26 centimeters long (the tail may be broken off). It is copper-colored; in places it is dark. Since the object was also purchased, we cannot rely on what a Bedouin or a dealer might claim, even if they were being as honest as training and experience might allow. The ophidian object must be dated by analogy. I would compare it with the copper and gilded serpent found at Timna'. They are similarly constructed; that is, they depict serpents crawling and are relatively long. It is impossible to date the object; it might date as early as the Late Bronze Age (1550–1200 BCE) or as late as the Roman Period.

The serpent is long; the five curves most likely were crafted to indicate that it is moving. The skin is elegantly denoted with fine markings. The eyes and mouth are barely visible. The head is raised .6 centimeter above the level of the body.

This serpent also may have been a cultic object because of its elegance and fine workmanship. It is similar to the copper serpent with gilding that was found at Timna' in a cultic context. The curves would evoke thoughts about dynamism and speed, as well as the elusive and mysterious quality of the serpent.

It is conceivable that these anguine objects are associated with Bethzatha because of their presence in the SBF Museum just to the west of it. One must not forget, however, that these realia were purchased and placed in the museum. What can be known about Bethzatha? Votive offerings have been found there, as indicated earlier, and they seem associated with an Asklepieion.

Ophidian Cults in Ancient Palestine: The Meaning of the Serpent Images

In her article entitled "The Bronze Serpent in the Israelite Cult," Karen R. Joines explained the meaning of the images as follows: "Apparently, the answer is to be found in its associations with other cultic emblems, most notably with sex and sexual organs, the bull, water, and the dove." [322] This answer is helpful and a good beginning, but ophidian symbolism is much more complex and variegated. Far more representative is Joines' conclusion that the "association of the serpent with water accentuates the intermingling of the serpent symbol with the fertility of the earth, for this reptile was often observed in or near water, the means of life for both animals and vegetation." [323] As we have seen, the serpent symbolized far more than what Joines has suggested.

Archaeological realia show the serpents appearing alone, in pairs, and in various numbers. Serpents are often found iconographically paired with scorpions, bulls, lions, and doves. The scorpion added to the threatening bite of the serpent and may have increased its chthonic symbolism as a source of death as well as life. The bull strengthened the ability of the serpent to symbolize power, protection, and divinity. The lion increased the royal and divine symbolic dimensions of the serpent. The image of the dove with ophidian symbolism added to the serpent's ability to symbolize a transcendence from the earth, an ascension into the heavens where Wisdom seems to dwell, and perhaps the source of new and rejuvenated life. Most likely each, especially the dove,[324] removed the negative symbolic dimension of the serpent and increased its friendliness to humans. Thus, the meanings of ophidian symbolism in the Land, which is decidedly inferior in quality to that found in Egypt to the south and in what is now Turkey to the north,[325] are usually positive and clearly multivalent. Perhaps one of the attractive aspects of ophidian symbolism is its ability to denote and evoke a wide range of possible meanings.

The following categories seem to capture the meaning probably intended by one who used a serpent symbol and the additional meanings supplied by later observers. The categories clearly overlap, and more than one meaning was most likely intended by an author and surely by any observer.

The serpent is often found associated with the cult, and the iconography is often discovered in a stratum linked with the cult. Joines concludes that "the cultic significance of the serpent in the Ancient Near East, whether the symbol be of bronze or pottery, from a sanctuary or a tomb, was that of fertility and the return of life."[326] This conclusion is not necessarily wrong, but it is rather bold and tends to impose too much systematization and harmonization on the archaeological evidence of ophidian symbolism in the Land. In some sites and tells this might be warranted as the primary meaning in some strata, but not all, and surely not in all locations. As we have seen, the archaeological evidence is vast and variegated.

At Gezer the serpent from the Late Bronze Age stratum was discovered in the high place.[327] It is thus probably linked with some positive meaning in the cult.

The two serpents found at Hazor in the "holy of holies" in the temple of Area H clearly denoted some positive symbolism. The silver-plated bronze cult stand,[328] which shows two serpents rising on each side of a woman, probably a serpent goddess, most likely denoted fertility and fruitfulness, along with some dimensions of sexuality. If it was held in ceremonial processions or in cultic celebrations, its symbolic significance would be increased.

The evidence for the cultic dimension of the serpent increases in the Late

Bronze Age. Indicative of the increase of the significance of ophidian imagery are the over twenty-seven examples of serpent objects or iconography found at Beth Shan.[329] The serpent symbolism denoted some positive meaning because of its connection with the cult.[330]

The serpent symbolism on the Beth Shan pottery cult stand, now displayed in the Israel Museum and dated to the eleventh century BCE or Iron Age I, is impressive. The stand is attractive, but it is far less artistically crafted than vessels in contiguous countries.[331] The serpents are well designed, and the dots for their skin are represented by circular depressions in the clay. The mouth of the serpent is open and eyes are depicted, but no forked tongue is shown. The image is clearly a positive one, and probably more than one meaning was intended by the author; additional positive meanings could have been perceived by worshippers. Certainly, we need to imagine that they added to the meaning intended by the author.

It is good to return to the symbolic meaning of serpents and doves, so richly represented at Beth Shan. In such a context, the serpent symbolized the chthonic world, and rejuvenation, as well as fertility. Along with the dove, the serpent most likely symbolized the return of vegetation in the spring.

This interpretation is reinforced by Rowe's suggestion that the rectangular shrine houses and cylindrical serpent cult vessels, which must not be confused with cylindrical incense burners that are devoid of serpent iconography,[332] were, in fact, like the classical writers' "Gardens of Adonis."[333] That is, the vessels were filled with rich soil into which seeds from flowers, wheat, or special vegetables were wisely arranged. Then, with the proper watering and exposure to the sun, the plants would spring to life; but with an inadequate root system they would also wither relatively rapidly. Thus, the vessels with ophidian iconography would signify the cycle between life and death. Serpents with doves herald spring according to passages in the Song of Songs and Jeremiah.[334] Serpents with doves seem to symbolize the yearly cycle. Perhaps together they, through sympathetic magic, were imagined to stimulate or awaken fresh growth in the earth and the return of spring.[335] Moreover, under the possible influence of Assyrian and Babylonian myths,[336] the doves might symbolize the allegorical rebirth of Astoreth (the dove), and Tammuz (the serpent) from the chthonic world.[337] The significance of the dove in the aperture and serpents heading there enhance a fertility (though not a Freudian) interpretation. Finally, the remains of serpents with breasts and sometimes with a cup beneath to catch milk indicate that there was a goddess at Beth Shan who was perceived as a serpent.[338]

The apertures could also signify the female womb and, for some, the serpent the lingam; it is clear that the Beth Shan shrine house with serpents, doves, and a lion shows a female's mons veneris; moreover, these ophidian realia were found alongside of a nude Ashtoreth with exposed breasts.[339] The practice seems to have been widespread and continues much later into the Iron Age. Isaiah seems to have spoken against this practice and its dependence on magic and allegiance to the fertility cults.[340]

The circular dots that represented the serpent's skin probably had more than decorative meaning. They could have evoked in the mind of some worshippers the pervasive meaning of serpent symbolism, specifically the completeness of time and the unity of the cosmos, even though this aspect of ophidian symbolism becomes explicit only in the Hellenistic Period.

The Late Bronze Age Beth Shan pottery sherds that show a serpent with female breasts and perhaps a bowl to catch lacteal fluid are challenging and perhaps revealing. They seem to be unique to Beth Shan and also constitute a coalescence of the cobra and female figurines.[341] These serpent symbols appear to be a Palestinian adaptation of foreign, especially Egyptian, models. If these objects are accurately assessed, then the imagery indicates that the serpent sometimes represented the female principle. That is, the serpent symbolized the life found in a mother's milk.

In the Beth Shan Iron Age ophidian symbolism, depictions of the serpent's mouth as open and with impressive eyes but no forked tongue indicate a positive meaning. Most likely more than one idea was intended by the author, and numerous positive meanings were certainly perceived by the worshippers. Surely, the deity worshipped is intended, and the serpents indicate the power of the deity to provide what worshippers needed, especially their own prosperity, health, fertility, and good life, and similar prayers and desires for the land on which they lived and the animals on it.

Perhaps roughly the same meaning should be applied to the Iron Age I (1000–800 BCE) serpent symbol, found on pottery at Megiddo, and connected with the shrine.[342] Joines, following Albright,[343] rightly stresses that serpent symbolism does not necessarily denote or imply a phallic meaning. As she states, the symbolism "merely sets out the intimate connection between the goddess and the source of life."[344] In many cases, especially at Beth Shan—and most obviously in the Aphrodite sculpture from Roman Carmel—sexuality is implied, but beauty or fertility, not the phallus or eroticism, seems to be the primary meaning. This meaning seems warranted by the presentation of Aphrodite as attractive rather than erotic and the association of the gentle, not aroused, serpent with the body and not the mons veneris.

It is clear that the serpent usually represented a positive meaning. Sometimes it symbolized a god or goddess. At other times, and perhaps simultaneously, it signified a personified concept such as power, divinity, life, beauty, or health. Conceivably, the serpent could evoke a hypostasis of a god or goddess (especially in the Greek and Roman world).

It is not easy to discern the meaning of the serpent iconography at Beth Shan in the mind of the artist. The potter may have wanted also to denote wisdom, knowledge, and truth, since the mouth of the serpent is open, eyes are depicted, and no forked tongue is evident.

The Late Bronze Age ophidian iconography added to the pottery vessels was intended to signify some positive dimension of the serpent. The symbolism appeals to the imagination because only the serpent's body is depicted. The deadly head was not illustrated graphically. If the clay vessel contained cosmetics, the meaning could be some form of sexual attractiveness, perhaps eroticism. If the large ceramic jar contained water, wine, or milk, then the serpent could symbolize the life-giving commodity, as well as the protector of its freshness and taste.

Joines lists numerous examples of ophidian symbolism at Megiddo, Beth Shemesh, Jericho, and Gideon. She opines that these are examples of "the motif of the water-seeking serpent." For example, she mentions the serpent symbolism found in an MBII tomb at Megiddo and comments, "The serpent on one of these vessels rests its head on the rim, apparently searching for water." [345] She thus concludes that the serpents are shown looking for water.

Does a serpent resting its head on a rim denote a serpent searching for water? That would shift the intention of the symbolism to the serpent itself. This makes sense in a cultic setting, but some of the serpent vessels were clearly not linked with a cult. It seems more likely that the serpent was used to symbolize something for the humans who would use the vessel and its contents. The serpents' mouths are close to or directed toward the water or the place from which the water was poured out. The symbolism thus seems not to be a putative category of a "water-seeking serpent"; it appears to be another example of the use of serpent symbolism as a protector of the water or milk that would have been contained inside. Before the discovery of bacteria, it was mysterious why milk and water could both provide both life and death. Without so-called modern scientific knowledge, humans would need a symbol to protect the water and milk so that it would not kill us but provide health and life. These ophidian symbols thus do not seem to indicate some new unknown category; they are further examples of the well-known and pervasive use of serpent symbolism to denote the one who protects health and life.

Another meaning seems also evident. Almost all the examples of ophidian symbolism Joines lists were found in tombs. There are exceptions, such as the serpent iconography found on the temple vessel from MBIIB Jericho and the example from the Shechem temple. Thus, the vast number of ves-

sels with serpents near the rims were found in tombs. Apparently the use of
the serpent was meant to symbolize its role in the restoration and enhance-
ment of life and health. The meaning seems also enhanced by the contents
of the vessel: water or milk. These were also symbols of health and life.
Perhaps the serpent vessels in tombs might also, when the belief is present,
denote immortality, rejuvenation, or renewed life—or the hope of such.

Similar to the symbolism of protector is the meaning of power. The Middle Bronze Age cultic bowl with serpents and bulls found at Megiddo most
likely was intended to symbolize majesty, power, and protection. More
important, these concepts denote or at least connote divinity. The meaning
of the serpent symbolism becomes clear when we read Nebuchadnezzar
II's inscription for the high Ishtar Gate in honor of Marduk: "The gate
of Nana (Ishtar . . . I built) with (blue) enamelled bricks . . . for Marduk
my lord. Lusty bulls of bronze *and mighty figures of serpents* I placed at
their thresholds, . . . , Marduk, exalted lord . . . eternal life . . . give us a
gift." [346] Nebuchadnezzar frequently refers to his practice of erecting monuments with "terrible bronze bulls" and "dreadful" or "terrible serpents
standing erect." [347] Many meanings would be evoked by this practice. Perhaps Nebuchadnezzar's main purpose was to stress the power and protection provided by a god. The serpents thus did not signify the embodiment
of Marduk; they symbolized the presence of his power and protection.

The serpent can also symbolize justice and the one who protects it. One
of the best examples comes from ancient Mesopotamia. A limestone deed-
stone highlights a large serpent that covers the top and circles down to the
bottom. The eyes and nostrils of the serpent are prominent and its scales
are remarkably indicated. It dates from about 1100 BCE. The serpent represents the goddess of justice. [348]

Fertility and positive dimensions of eroticism are a, but not the, dominant meaning of Palestinian ophidian symbolism. The ophidian symbolism found at Beth Shan could also have been intended to denote fertility.
The serpent is displayed crawling upward, and although the figures directly above it are lost, the woman in the upper square window has spread
her legs to expose a prominent mons veneris. More than eroticism and
some forms of phallic meaning are certainly intended. Fertility and fruitfulness seem to be the main meanings of the ophidian iconography found
at Beth Shan.

The Late Bronze Age plaque at Beth Shemesh also seems to denote fertility and eroticism. The serpent is depicted lying on the left shoulder of the
goddess, across the left breast, and resting on the left thigh. The place of
the serpent on the body of the goddess enhances an erotic interpretation.

The LBII serpent artifacts at Beth Shan seem to symbolize fertility and
eroticism. One serpent has human-like breasts. Another serpent is depicted

with a cup placed beneath the nipple. The iconography denotes the life-giving quality of lacteal milk.[349] The breasts symbolize nourishing milk, not sexual allurement.

The erect serpents featured on the Iron Age Gezer plaque, celebrating Hathor and Asherah, probably denoted fertility and some positive aspects of eroticism. This dimension is clear since the serpents are upraised, and depicted on each side of Asherah.[350] A second serpent object was found at Gezer. It shows a goddess with serpentine artwork ascending from the shoulders.[351]

It is certain that these ophidian images, in stone, clay, bronze, silver, copper, and sometimes with gold heads, should not be restricted to Canaanite cults. The story about Moses lifting up of a serpent in the wilderness may be an etiological cult legend developed to support the worship of or through a serpent. Certainly a serpent was worshipped in the Jerusalem Temple before the reforms of Hezekiah. E. Stern rightly claims that "it should be emphasized that the snake cult in the ancient Near East was not, by any means, peculiar to the Canaanite culture alone, but snakes also occur as sacred attributes in other cultic centres of the region." [352]

Summary

The amount of ophidian iconography unearthed by archaeologists is vast and astonishing; its message will be enlightening to those who assume that serpents, serpent cults, and serpent veneration were never a significant aspect of worship in "the Holy Land." Let us summarize what has been collected and discussed in the preceding pages.

All the seven serpents discovered in ancient Palestine, and thus excluding the thirteenth- or twelfth-century gold-plated copper serpent from Timnaʿ, are bronze and date from the Late Bronze Age or earliest years of Iron I. The exception is the gold serpent from Ekron that dates from the seventh century BCE and is explained as an Egyptian importation. Why do all the serpents share this material and time; how do we explain this circumscribed floruit of individual bronze serpents?

While contemplating possible answers to this question, we may examine three further observations. First, the serpent iconography in ancient Palestine is markedly inferior to that found in some contiguous cultures. For example, the most elegant snake boxes are found only in Ugarit. Nowhere in Palestine is there a sophisticated work of ophidian art to compare to the magnificent serpent vase unearthed at Susa in Persia.[353] Likewise, nothing found in Palestine begins to compare with the artistry found so frequently in Egypt. The treasures in Tutankhamen's tomb—many with ophidian iconography[354]—are only examples and not exceptions to the sophisticated serpent iconography so replete in ancient Egypt. Nowhere in ancient Palestine is there anything to compare with Egypt's Sphinx, Nineveh's winged bull, the serpent designs on Boeotian ceramics,[355] or the Phoenicians' glass artwork.[356]

Second, even including the numerous ophidian objects found at Beth Shan, no site in ancient Palestine can be said to rival the vast amount of serpent objects and ophidian symbolism found elsewhere. For example, no one site from Dan to Beer-sheba has produced anything like the vast amount of ophidian iconography recovered from the "Mound of Serpents." This site, which dates from that area's Iron Age (circa 1200 BCE to circa 250 BCE), is in the Arabian Peninsula in Oman and in the small tell near the Al-Qusais graves.[357] Likewise, while a dog cemetery was found at Ashkelon, no serpent burials have been discovered in ancient Palestine like the forty "snake bowls" with skeletons of serpents often curled around a precious gem like a pearl. These were found beneath the floor of the Palace of Uperi at Qal'at Bahrain, which dates from the seventh century BCE.[358] Finally, no ancient place in Palestine has produced the amount and variety of serpent iconography so typical of sites in Italy, Greece, and Egypt.[359]

Third, the ophidian iconography found in ancient Palestine is basic or realistic; that is, the object is clearly a serpent or an idealized serpent. There are no mixed figures, such as we will see in the Greek and Roman world, like chimera, that is, a lion with a ram protruding from his back and with a serpent as a tail, the Giants with anguipedes, or Medusa with serpents protruding from her hair. Furthermore, nothing found in ancient Palestine is similar to the "snake-dragon" and "lion-dragon" so common in the iconography of ancient Mesopotamia.[360]

CONCLUSION

Snakes are not drawn to exercise artists' fingers. The iconography represents a need. Whenever the serpent could be physically present among us and where humans have left traces we find serpent iconography. To make a form of a serpent or to draw one, no matter how primitive, is to express the "I" and the "We." Such drawings of serpents help us connect with each other and with nature, including life and death. The human needs symbols and needs to make them. We pour ourselves into symbols and in so doing express our fears and hopes. In serpent iconography, humans, since 40,000 BCE, have found a way of finding the self.

In its very nature of being able to represent—at once and immediately—two opposites, the serpent signifies the archetypal, primordial, and phenomenological mode of symbology. It articulates for us our presence in this world. We approach truth; that is, the insight sought through the tension symbolized by two opposites: life–death, truth–falsehood, and good–evil. Sometimes truth comes in pairs: father–son, heaven–earth, morning–night, man–woman. From myths that even antedate 40,000 BCE we observe the primordial need of all humans: to express in storied forms the attempt to obtain meaning within a chaotically uncategorical meaningless cascade of phenomena. Human existence and meaning tend to need symbolism.

There should be no doubt now that the vast amount of ophidian jewelry from Greek and Roman times heralds the serpent as a symbol of numerous positive meanings, including beauty, protection, and comfort.[361] For a millennium, and more, the serpent had been associated in Mediterranean cultures with the feminine and goddesses. By the time of the Fourth Evangelist, the serpent had lost most of its evil symbolic meanings. As R. S. Bianchi states, the serpent "was primarily linked with goddesses who were considered protectors of women. It became fashionable to wear golden finger rings and bracelets in the shape of snakes, which would wrap their protective curls around the wearer's finger or wrist." [362] We have reviewed succinctly the evidence of such impressive ophidian jewelry from the West and the East. Some of the most stunning examples are the golden bracelets from Pompeii, which we know were being worn during the life of the Fourth Evangelist who was probably not born after 79 CE, when Pompeii was covered with ash from Vesuvius.

4

The Perception That the Serpent Is a Positive Symbol in Greek and Roman Literature

If we were to proceed chronologically, we would now begin a study of serpent imagery in the Old Testament (Hebrew Bible). It is best, for three reasons, to reserve the examination of biblical passages until the Greek and Roman data have been assessed. First, biblical studies demand the same methodology as all ancient literature, but the issues become very complex and often demand reexamining set presuppositions and cultural animus for or against these texts. Second, the Greek data canvasses many centuries; it does not simply begin after the last book in the Old Testament, Daniel, was composed and compiled about 164 BCE. Hence, a chronological approach would be prima facie impossible. Third, it would be absurd to think that we should attend to the date of an example of serpent iconography as if the symbology appeared only then. The date of an artifact is not a reliable date for iconography. A gold, silver, or bronze serpent can be found in a Roman stratification of a site, but the object may antedate the stratum by many years. Valuable and imperishable objects were used and passed down, and ancient graves were robbed by Romans, as they are today by Bedouin.

GREEK AND ROMAN OPHIDIAN SYMBOLISM AND IRANIAN MYTHOLOGY

In contrast to other ancient cultures, with the exception of the Egyptian religion, the Greeks, followed closely by the Romans, employed serpent symbolism the most. Both the Greeks and the Romans were deeply influenced by Egyptian ophidian symbolism. The unique development of ophidian symbolism within Greek and Roman art and culture becomes clear when one contrasts Greek and Roman myths with Persian myths.

The evil god Angra Mainyu (Ahriman) does sometimes change into a lizard or a serpent. In a second-century CE stone carving he appears with two raised serpents near his left shoulder, and perhaps two serpents protruding from each shoulder.[1] The warrior and physician called Thraetaona is "the most victorious of all victorious men next to Zarathustra" (*Avesta, Yasht* 19.36–37).[2] He cures the evil caused by the serpent, and he battles dragons. According to the early myths in the Shahnameh (*Book of Kings* [c. 1010 CE]), evils and death are caused by black demons called *"divs,"* which are not personifications of Ahriman, Satan, but represent enemy kings.[3] Shahnameh art of the eighteenth century CE shows Rustam and his horse Rakhsh defeating a monstrous dragon. In addition to the pervasive negative meaning of a serpent and dragon, one finds positive meanings for the serpent in Persia. For example, in early Roman times Mithra is depicted in a Tauroctony virtually everywhere from upper Germany to Persia.[4] That is, Mithra (in Latin Arimanius) is shown slaying a bull: he is accompanied by a serpent, a scorpion, and a dog. Aeon (Zrvan Akarana), a lion-faced god in Mithraism, appears with serpent coils surrounding his body; these represent the repetitious nature of time.[5]

Yet the dominant image in such widespread depictions of the Tauroctony is not the serpent; it is Mithra followed by the bull. Sometimes in Rome and the West, Mithra appears with a lion's head and serpent feet (anguipedes).[6] An ambiguous figure in Mithraism is a lion-headed statue with a body that is entwined by a snake. The image may denote Aion, Chronos, or Zurvan, and while some scholars (like S. Insler) think the figure should be associated with the evil god Ahriman, most scholars interpret it to denote some benevolent deity.[7]

Thus, serpent iconography is found in Iranian religion, literature, and art. Most of it dates from Christian times, but there is some from pre-Christian eras. Yet, in contrast to Egyptian and Greek and Roman culture, serpent and dragon images do not abound in Persian culture. Thus, we should distinguish between searching for evidence and the actual evidence.

Greek and Roman Serpent Symbolism: An Overview

In contrast to Persian culture, images of serpents permeate Greek and Roman literature, art, and culture. To grasp the significance of the in-depth exploration that will soon commence, it is wise to get an overview of the area for exploration.

Ophidian or anguine iconography appears on the painted walls of homes in Pompeii, on pithoi (large storage jars), on ornately decorated jars (like

Figure 47. Gorgon with Two Elegant Serpents Highlighted on Head. Royal Tomb at Vergina. Circa 350–336 BCE. Courtesy of the Archaeological Museum of Thessaloniki.

the Athenian red-figured hydria (water jars), on coins, and through words in epics, poems, and official documents.

It is impressive to note how ophidian or anguine symbolism permeates Greek and Roman legends and myths, shaping Hellenistic culture. Demeter and her daughter, Persephone, are often depicted sending Triptolemus to humans with the gift of wheat. He is often shown seated on a chariot drawn by raised serpents (see the final section on serpents and chariots).[8]

Well known on buildings and painted vases, beginning at least in the eighth century BCE, are depictions of Medusa. She and the other Gorgons are shown as women with serpents rising from their hair. Serpents are the ones who reveal to Melampus the languages of animals; he thus becomes the first human with prophetic powers. The serpents had licked his ears when he was sleeping. Scylla had six snaky heads. Basilisk is the king of serpents. Asclepius almost always appears with a staff around which a serpent is coiled, and Hermes is associated with the caduceus (two raised serpents facing each other).

Ovid describes Phaëton's ill-fated ride into the heavens on a chariot. The venture resulted in cosmic disasters; in particular, the Serpent, which had been coiled harmlessly around the North Pole, rises with rage. In order to avoid the advances of Peleus, Thetis changes into fire, monsters, and serpents. When Priam's wife was pregnant with Paris, she dreamed of giving birth to a torch from which streamed hissing serpents. When Laocoon, Poseidon's priest during the Trojan War, warned about the wooden horse the Greeks had left, he and his two sons were strangled by two massive serpents that had been called out of the sea, presumably by the warlike Athena (more will be said about Laocoon).

In the legend of the Golden Fleece, perhaps older than the *Iliad* and the *Odyssey,*[9] Aeetes hangs the fleece in a grove that was guarded by a serpent. Before Jason can obtain the Golden Fleece, he must defeat armed warriors who originate from the teeth of the dreadful serpent, who had guarded Ares' pool but had been defeated by Kadmos. The maenads are women who became ecstatic during the worship of Dionysus; they often are depicted as those who charmed serpents.

The founding of great cities is recorded in legends and myths featuring serpents. The Pythian games celebrated how Apollo founded Delphi by slaying the enormous serpent, Python, with his arrows, and helped bring order out of chaos after the great flood.

Likewise the myths about the founding of Thebes resonate with serpent imagery. Cadmus, in searching for Europa, the daughter of a king of Phoenicia, killed a large dragon or massive serpent that had annihilated his servants. The serpent had been sacred to Mars. The "Sown Men" *(Spartoi)* are brothers who evolve from the dragon's or serpent's teeth that had been planted in the earth. In his *Classical Art and the Cultures of Greece and Rome,* J. Onians astutely stresses the significance of the "Sown Men" who originate from snake's teeth:

> Snake's teeth possess inherently, and more perfectly, many of the properties people sought in stone, and others besides. They are harder, sharper, more regular than even the most carefully finished blocks. They also fulfil a commander's dream. Arrayed in three rows in the snake's jaw those behind move up unbidden when necessary to replace those in front. A phalanx made of men who sprang from snake's teeth was even better than one made of men who sprang from stones.[10]

These reflections help us grasp the original meaning seen in this myth by many reflective Greeks and Romans. The story of Cadmus is tragic; he and his wife, Harmonia (the daughter of Venus), live harassed lives, because of Mars' revenge. How does the story end? Both are turned into serpents.

Ophidian iconography thus not only shaped Greek myths and culture; it saturated them. At this stage in our work, it would be unwise to ask if the iconography and stories represented serpents embodying good or evil symbols. We ought rather to explore what are the many positive and negative meanings represented by the myriad of serpents in art, religion, and literature during the Greek and Roman eras. In this endeavor, we need to be aware of modern methods, or allegorical interpretations, which as R. Martin states, "dampen the rich, symbolic overtones and resonances in the myth."[11]

Since our focus has been the first century CE, before we begin an in-depth study of Greek and Roman ophidian or anguine iconography, we need to observe the major changes that occurred with the rise of the monarchy and the emperors. With the collapse of the Roman Republic, first with the civil war between Julius Caesar and Pompey and then between Octavian and Antony, Rome lost its hold on its own identity. The traditional patriarchal family units closely tied to farmers in Italy, France, Spain, and elsewhere had produced little art or literature.

When Rome militarily conquered Greece, Roman culture was intellectually conquered by Greek culture, especially in the spheres of art and iconography. The words of Horace are worth citing:

Graecia capta ferum	Captive Greece captured
victorem cepit	her untamed victor,
et artes intulit agresti	And brought the arts to
Latio	countrified Latium.
[*Epistles* II, 1.156–57]	[my idiomatic translation]

The word "untamed" also represents wild and savage. The adjective "countrified" intends to evoke thoughts about the rustic, boorish, and agrarian world of the Romans. The noun "Latium" denotes the area near Rome. Both Greece and Rome are portrayed as "captured." What does this signify? As R. Turcan states in *The Cults of the Roman Empire* (p. 2), Horace's vision primarily means that "Greek civilization was a daughter of the East, as Roman civilization was the product of Greek education."

When Octavian defeated Mark Antony and Cleopatra at Actium in 31 BCE, he was faced with a nation and world that had been shattered and lost its powerful symbols. He wisely decided not to call himself "Romulus," which would have brought up the unattractive concept of kingship. "Augustus" was a superb choice, whether it is related to *augere* "to increase," or *augur,* one who interprets omens. As Florus stated, the title "Augustus" seemed to confer "divinity upon him" (2.34.66).[12]

The Augustan Age thus saw the rebuilding of temples and the resurgence in the use of powerful and effective symbols. In the Roman world, Octavian was the son of Apollo and Antony the son of Dionysus. The latter had little chance for success, in the world of Roman symbolism, since prior to 31 BCE there had already developed a strong pro-Apollo culture and polemics against Dionysus. Virgil, under the patronage of Augustus, helped create a new myth: Apollo had fought with Augustus against Antony and empowered him to conquer the world.[13]

As P. Zanker states in *The Power of Images in the Age of Augustus,* scarcely in history has art been "pressed into the service of political power so directly as in the Age of Augustus."[14] Horace had predicted that Rome would remain "sullied with the guilt of your fathers, until you have rebuilt

Figure 48. Bronze Sarcophagus. Two dolphins above and two baskets filled with fruit framing a Medusa with serpents in her hair. Circa third–sixth century CE. JHC Collection

the temples and restored all the ruined sanctuaries" (*Carmen* 3.6). It is thus a paradigmatic shift in the history of Roman iconography and art to hear Augustus claim: "I restored 82 temples of the gods of Rome and did not omit a single one which was at that time in need of renewal" (*Res Gestae* 20).[15] While this claim seems unrealistic, it does place the religious revival under Augustus.

It is this perspective that will inform our research. Some, perhaps many, studies of ancient Roman art and iconography have given insufficient attention to the political power struggle that marred the first century BCE. These historical forces frame the meaning often poured into art, architecture, and iconography. It is in this context and with this perception that Greek and later Roman ophidian iconography will be collected and assessed. Under Augustus in the West and in the East (after 70 CE when Jerusalem was burned) Hellenistic culture could flourish under a world peace, when poetry and art could thrive with imaginings of a better and blessed world ahead. As texts need contexts to reveal their meanings, so iconography is best studied in light of what we can discern about the history behind, and perhaps mirrored within, it.

The educated today, when prompted to think about serpent symbolism in Greek and Roman antiquity, would most likely suggest some images that have been ingrained in our modern consciousness (and the unconscious).[16] The image of Laocoon struggling with large serpents might be suggested because of the monumental sculptures seen in museums and in photographs (as we indicated earlier).[17] The Minoan goddess holding aloft from each hand two writhing serpents would probably come to mind,[18] not least because of her impressive breasts, seductively exposed.[19] The image of Medusa with serpents crawling in her hair is so well known and ubiquitous in modern culture that even the untutored might mention this anguine symbol in a discussion. The contemporary mind might remember also depictions of Hercules wrestling with serpents,[20] perhaps because the image is so well disseminated in our Western culture.[21] For example, in Dresden's Skulpturensammlung is a bronze sculpture of Hercules (probably not Laocoon as some think). It is by Francesco di Giorgio Martini and is dated 1495. In Hercules' uplifted left hand is a captured serpent that curls along his arm.

The amount of anguine iconography from the Greek and Roman world is remarkable.[22] The evidence comes from virtually every part of the world known to the Greeks and Romans. The serpent was not highlighted in ornamental jewelry merely for decoration, as we demonstrated earlier;[23] it had religious and symbolic meanings. Fountains were sometimes decorated not only with nymphs but also water serpents.[24] In the following pages, I will present a selection of these data, now focusing on literary texts. The amount of attention the Greeks and Romans gave to serpent imagery will most likely prove astounding to many scholars.

Before proceeding further with an examination of the meaning of ophidian iconography and symbology in the Greek and Roman worlds, we should bring into focus that there are forty-one names for snake taxonomy in Greek (see Appendix II). The Greeks also had a word for "belonging to serpents." In fact, that same word, *ophiakos*, also denoted "a form of leprosy in which the patient sheds his skin like a snake." The richness of Greek vocabulary in regard to snakes is remarkable. The Greeks had words for "the food of serpents," "serpent-eating," "serpent-chaser," "serpent-killer," "serpent-fighter," "snake charmer." The Greeks were able to denote with one word "serpent-tailed," "serpent-eating," and "serpent-bearing."[25] It is certain that we cannot represent in English the exact meanings of some Greek terms and that the Greeks knew more about serpents than English-speaking people. The Greeks were different from us; they were much closer to our earth than most of us.

Serpents on Vases

Serpent iconography on vases reaches a high level in the second half of the seventh century BCE. It flourished especially in Corinth. Artwork of a certain type is so unusual that it is referred to as the work of the "Snake Painter."[26] The artwork is elegant, often with stunning black figures on white ware. The serpent is usually raised, with a triangular head, and with six curves—probably to indicate power and mobility.[27]

Figure 49. Large Upright Serpent with Harmonia Seated. Greek vase. Metropolitan Museum of Art 07.286.66.

Gods and Goddesses as Part Snake

The veneration of Isis continued into the Greek and Roman periods with some modification. She is portrayed sometimes with a woman's face and a serpent's body. The ceramic serpent images shown in Figs. 50 and 51 probably portray Isis with a serpent's torso. They date from around 100 BCE, most likely, and were obtained in Israel. Reputedly, the one that is not broken was found south of Ashkelon and the broken one in the vicinity of Jerusalem. The broken one depicts an Isis with a serpent's body, a high crown *(polos),* and a torch. Both are similar to the first-century BCE sandstone stele of the snake bodied Isis and Dionysus in the British Museum.[28]

Isis was portrayed not only as partly serpentine, but also holding a cobra,[29] or with two large serpents.[30] Like Asclepius who appears ubiquitously holding a staff[31] around which is curled a serpent,[32] Isis is also imagined as an upraised cobra with its hood extended.[33] It is now clear that the Egyptian Isis cult was active in Rome, especially in the coastal cites, like Venice, ancient Ostia, and particularly Aquileia.[34]

Other gods beside Isis were portrayed as a serpent, and this will be evident later; for now, a short synopsis would help introduce the following summaries. Typhon is conceived with the body of a serpent below the

Figure 50. *Left.* Isis with Serpent's Torso. Circa 100 BCE. Reportedly found south of Ashkelon. JHC Collection

Figure 51. *Above.* Isis with Serpent's Torso. Circa 100 BCE. Reportedly found near Jerusalem. JHC Collection

waist and sometimes with anguipedes (serpents as feet).[35] Serapis (or Sarapis) sometimes appears as a large upraised serpent with a goatee.[36] Amphiaraos is shown as a serpent as he heals Archinos from his sickness.[37]

The imagination of the ancients was not chaotic or without any control. It is precarious to suggest that syncretism was in full force. We should talk about influence from one culture on another or of acculturation and assimilation.[38] Athena, for example, is never portrayed with a uraeus, the upraised cobra that signified divinity in Egypt. This fact seems impressive since Mercury was imagined sometimes with a uraeus[39] as were Hermes (his Greek equivalent)[40] and Isis.[41]

Depictions of Gods and Goddesses with Animals

It is well known that the ancient gods were often portrayed with animals. Neptune is often depicted with a dolphin,[42] and Poseidon with a fish.[43] Prometheus is shown with a vulture.[44] Castores is associated with a horse.[45] Leda is almost always pictured with a swan,[46] sometimes copulating with a large male swan.[47] Hyakinthos is imagined riding on a swan,[48] as is Kamarina,[49] and sometimes Aphrodite.[50] Europa is associated with a bull,[51] and Theseus is frequently conceived as fighting a bull.[52] Selene or Luna (the moon) is sometimes depicted in a chariot pulled by oxen.[53]

Romulus and Remus are imagined with a female fox.[54] In our search for the meaning of serpent symbolism, a brief digression exploring the symbolic meaning of the fox helps frame our quest. Is the fox only a symbol of the founding of Rome? Did it always mean that, or was it merely an ornamentation, as it is today on some shelves and desks? F. Cumont suggested

Figure 52. Athena. Early
Roman Period. Courtesy of the
Hermitage. JHC

that the twins' wolf denotes a type of eternity.[55] If so, then it behooves
us to follow the lead of A. D. Nock and ask if we are intended to contemplate "absolute eternity," whatever that might mean among an array of
options, the eternity of "invincible" Rome or our own personal immortality.[56] With Nock, I am convinced that Cicero was correct to point out
that Rome's eternity was tantamount to the universe's eternity, and that a
person would only be eternal because of his or her quality of being Roman;
that is, as a Roman permanently linked with so-called eternal Rome.[57]

Telephos is shown with a deer.[58] Artemis is depicted with a hunting
dog.[59]

Athena is portrayed with serpents as fringes on her garments.[60] She is
imagined with serpents rising from her shoulders,[61] joined to make a necklace,[62] or coiled on her shawl.[63]

Athena is also one of the war goddesses. She has serpents on her helmet.[64] Serpents are shown, infrequently, on the shields of her warriors,[65]
and sometimes fighting for her.[66] Occasionally, a serpent is portrayed encircling a tree before her.[67] Most important, a serpent is portrayed coiled
upright next to her shield that is held by her left hand and resting on a
surface.[68] This conception seems significant because she was most likely
seen in this fashion by the thousands who visited the Parthenon in Athens.
There stood a colossal statue of Athena, in gold and ivory, made by Pheidias in about 400 BCE and she was represented by serpents.

We can catch a glimpse of Pheidias' masterpiece through the "Varvakeion Athena," a marble copy of the Athena Parthenos he had made for
the Parthenon in about 447 BCE. The copy dates from the second or third

Figure 53. Two Silver Coins. *Above:* Asclepius feeding a snake, courtesy of the Numismatic Museum in Athens. *Below:* Philip I with Salus, in the Charlesworth collection. The serpent depicted the prosperity Rome in the third century CE brought to those in the world. JHC Collection

century CE. It is chryselephantine (made of gold and ivory). It bears thirteen serpents on the chest, with a Gorgon. One serpent appears on each wrist. A large serpent is depicted on the inside of her shield and a Gorgon on the outside. Two serpents are on the belt. The chest garment *(aegis)* is decorated as snake skin, similar to the skin of a large serpent on the lower right. The profusion of serpents is remarkable.[69]

A serpent is often shown along with Minerva and Athena, probably because of the association of these goddesses with the earth. This survey of gods with animals opens a deeper appreciation of the appearance of gods as serpents, as partial serpents, or with serpent images.

Most of the gods were linked with the awesome wonder of the serpent. Jupiter is sometimes shown with a serpent on his right shoulder.[70] Dionysus is depicted fighting with the assistance of one or more serpents.[71] Bacchus,[72] Dioskouroi,[73] Hecate,[74] and Harmonia[75] are imagined on coins with two serpents. Prokles is portrayed with a serpent, or dragon, on her head.[76] Salus, the Roman personification of prosperity, is conceived in ways reminiscent of Hygieia; that is (as we shall see), with a serpent eating out of a bowl in her right hand.[77] Lar or Lares is imagined with a large serpent.[78] Minerva, depicted as either a female or a male, is portrayed with a serpent eating out of a bowl held in her right hand,[79] and with serpents fighting with her.[80] She is also depicted with feminine breasts and with serpents crawling upward,[81] as well as with serpents curled around her neck and chest.[82] In a similar fashion, Sirona is portrayed with a serpent draped around her right arm.[83] Thetis is shown with her human husband Peleus, with serpents, or a serpent, biting him.[84] Common themes are highlighted by a serpent moving into the picture.[85]

Agamemnon, Talthybios, and Epeios, the builder of the wooden horse for the Trojans, are depicted with a large upraised, coiled serpent that bears a crown.[86] Tiberius is portrayed beneath a menacing serpent.[87] And, as one might imagine, Fortuna is portrayed with animals and her cornucopia;[88] sometimes she is imagined holding a serpent in her right hand and feeding it from a bowl, or philiae, in her left hand (as Hygieia is often depicted).[89] Nephthys is associated with a serpent swallowing its own tail (perhaps Ouroboros) and sometimes with one or two upraised cobras.[90] Harpokrates,[91] Strymon,[92] and Heros Equitans[93] are imagined before a large upraised serpent. Perseus[94] and Kreousa[95] frequently, and Cerberus[96] usually, are depicted with a serpent. Peleus is shown with two serpents in his right hand,[97] and Somnus with a serpent in each hand.[98] Pegasus is frequently shown stomping a serpent and a chimera (a lion with a ram protruding from its back and with a serpent for a tail).[99]

Cybele is customarily depicted with a lion, riding a lion (perhaps influenced by the iconography that depicts the Syrian goddess Qadesh),[100] and in a chariot pulled by lions.[101] She is also, notably, shown with a serpent.[102] A stunning example is the depiction of the cosmic triumph of Cybele and Attis that is immortalized on a silver patera from 360–390 CE. Two serpents appear in the scene. One winds majestically up a column. It has seven curls, indicating its cosmic powers.[103]

Cadmus is shown fighting an aroused hydra.[104] The supposition that on the earth there were serpents with more than one head was recorded by Aelian. Presumably drawing upon a work entitled *Concerning Wild Animals* by a certain Pammenes, he claimed that "there are two-headed Snakes (ὄφεις δικεφάλους) which have two feet in the region of the tail."[105]

The Argonauts are portrayed battling the dragon-serpent,[106] and Septem is shown about to kill a serpent.[107] Archemoros is depicted as a child in the coils of a large serpent,[108] and Cadmus before a threatening and large serpent.[109] From the influential and classical myths comes a depiction of Jason being swallowed by a large serpent,[110] befriending a serpent that is in a tree,[111] and fighting a serpent that has a goatee or beard.[112] This description may be odd for us but not for the ancients, since Aelian reported that it is common knowledge that there are serpents with beards (or goatees) beneath their chins.[113] We find another more believable explanation for the serpent's beard in the *Scholia in Nicandrum* (*Ad Theriaca* 438): "The serpent . . . is by nature black, with a yellow pale belly, beautiful in shape . . . and along its chin raised scales give the impression of a beard, yellow like the body."[114]

Aphrodite is depicted with serpents,[115] and Mars between two large upraised serpents.[116] One or more Maenads are shown thrusting forward an aroused serpent,[117] holding a thyrsus (rod) with a coiled serpent[118] or just holding a serpent.[119] Scylla is usually depicted with a dragon's tail or fish tails; she is also shown with anguipedes.[120]

More than a few deities were portrayed anatomically, as we have already seen, with serpent characteristics. Chimaera was depicted as a lion with a ram protruding from his back and with a serpent as a tail.[121] Titeos is portrayed as a "lion" with a serpent as a tail.[122]

Did the Learned Not Reject Serpent Mythology and Symbology?

Did not the educated Greeks and Romans tend to discount these myths? Yes; although many intellectuals recognized their power and utility, they did not take the myths literally. The best example is found in the writings of Cicero. This learned Roman could not tolerate such uninformed mythology. In his work on the nature of the gods (*De natura deorum* 1.101), he claims that the Egyptians foolishly deified animals. Cicero scoffs at the belief that the ibis "protects Egypt from plague, by killing and eating flying serpents (*volucris anguis*) that are brought from the Libyan desert by the southwest wind."[123] Also in the same work he rightly castigates the superstitions of the many and the erroneous portrayal of the gods. Cicero advised his contemporaries to consider such nonsense "old wives'" tales (*De natura deorum* 2.70–72).

Socrates in the pages of Xenophon can claim that if the universe had no soul it would be impossible, or at least difficult, to imagine the source of our own soul. Cicero demurs. He admits that there is "concord and harmony" in nature, but he claims that "coherence and permanence are achieved by the forces not of the gods, but of nature."[124]

Another example of the rejection of serpent iconography is found in the writings of Ovid. After 8 CE, when Ovid was exiled (actually "relegated" [*relegates*]) and Augustus forbade anyone to correspond with him, he wrote that it was more difficult to believe that a dear and loyal friend had not written to him than to believe "that the gorgon Medusa's face was garlanded with serpent hair [*anguineis*], that there is a Chimera, formed of a lioness and serpent held apart by a flame . . . and Giants with serpent feet [*serpentipedesque Gigantes*]." That is, all these are easier for Ovid to believe than to imagine his beloved friend had forsaken his love for him (my translation; *Tristia* 4.7.1–26). It is clear that Ovid did not believe that a Medusa existed with serpents for hair, a Chimera that was part lioness and part serpent, and Giants with serpent feet. Finally, in Virgil the serpent is usually a negative symbol.[125]

The Poetic Imagination of the Greeks and Romans

Rather than proceeding as if only words had been gathered together, we should stop and reflect on the denigration of serpent imagery by some great minds. What did the Greek and Roman iconography symbolize, and what symbolic power did it possess? It was widespread, as we have been seeing, and clearly many of the intelligentsia approved of it.

The serpent images show remarkable imagination. It is arresting to contemplate a Giant with serpents as feet.[126] It is difficult to suppose that the intelligentsia in Greece and Rome took such images literally.[127]

They were symbols for something beyond the literal. The point seems to have been missed by Lucretius, who could not imagine that in primordial times the Chimera had such a form, with "in front a lion, in the rear a serpent, [and] in the middle, as her name shows, a goat [*prima leo, postrema draco, media ipsa, Chimaera*]." [128] We need to remember that symbols point our mind and imagination to that which cannot be stated or explained. We so-called moderns have trouble with what was culturally engrained in the Greeks: the poetics of imagination and the art of perspective. Our perception of the world is incomplete and abstracted since we have no place or canon in which to perceive and appreciate "perspective," as James Elkins reminds us in his *The Poetics of Perspective*.[129] The ancient ophidian iconography is not bizarre; we are presented with symbols that are suggestive of concepts and ideas, many of which have been stressed already. Suffice it to state now that the ordinary lion is so impressive and ferocious that to encapsulate its power the ancients add, for example, a serpent on its back or as a tail.

As we continue to contemplate the meaning of the symbol of the serpent in antiquity, it is essential to attempt to enter into their symbolic universe. How did the ancients comprehend the world; was it not full of wild, mysterious, and wondrously complex animals? The attempt to enter their world is ultimately impossible, but it may be facilitated by imagining that the following account, from Aelian, is accurate:

In Metelis, a town of Egypt, there is a sacred Serpent [δράκων ἐστὶν ἱερός] in a tower, and it receives honours and has ministers and servants, and before it are set a table and a bowl. So every day they pour barley into this bowl and soak it in honey and milk and then depart, returning on the following day to find the bowl empty.[130]

This account by Aelian clarifies and proves our earlier surmises regarding what the ancients offered the sacred serpents to eat and drink. It also indicates that the ancients attributed human characteristics to the serpent. This serpent even has ministers and servants who wait on it as if it were a god or king.

In Greek and Roman mythology the serpent symbolically represents not only the obscure powers that the Greeks and Romans thought tormented gods and humans, but also the positive attributes of numerous gods. As Artemidorus reported in *Onirocritica,* the "serpents [Δράκων] . . . stand for all the gods who are sacred. These are Zeus, Sabazius, Helios, Demeter, Kore, Hecate, Asclepius, [and] the Heroes." [131] In the following pages, we will focus on Zeus, Asclepius, and other gods and goddesses who are more significantly represented by snakes.

THE INDIVIDUAL GODS OR GODDESSES AND SERPENT ICONOGRAPHY

In a focused attempt to understand the symbolism of (or behind) the Fourth Gospel, I will highlight from Hellenic and Hellenistic iconography and Greek and Roman authors the gods and heroes (since the boundaries between them were fluid) who were associated in the Hellenic and Hellenistic mind with the serpent. Thus, the following will be discussed briefly: Hermes (Mercury), Agathos Daimon or Agathadaimon, Giants, Hercules, Cerberus, Laocoon, Glykon, Medusa, Ladon, Aion, Ouroboros, Babli, Chnoubis, Zeus, Apollo, Mithra, Abraxas, Asclepius, and Hygieia. I will then conclude by asking some central questions concerning Greek and Roman serpent symbology and by quoting and assessing the uniquely significant comments about the meaning of the serpent by Philo of Byblos.

Hermes (Mercury)

Hermes (Mercury) is the messenger of the gods; he communicates not only their will to humans but also human prayers to the gods.[132] He is the Greek god who mediates between heaven and earth.

The Greek imagination associated Hermes with the caduceus.[133] He is often depicted with a staff with one, two, or three circles. Above them are two serpents.[134] The caduceus is often only stylized serpents, but sometimes the heads of the caduceus reveal two realistic snakes with mouths open, as in the mosaic "da Porta Portese" now in the Vatican Museum.[135]

Usually, the serpents face each other; sometimes they look in opposite directions.[136]

Hermes is also conceived to be the guide of the dead to the next world that is imagined to be under the earth—that is, the chthonic realm.[137] He is the god who dwells under the earth;[138] thus, his chthonic nature is understandably symbolized by serpents. Sometimes, the circles are stylized serpents.[139] As J. L. Henderson states, an "important and widespread symbol of chthonic transcendence is the motif of the two entwined serpents. These are the famous Naga serpents of ancient India; and we also find them in Greece as the entwined serpents on the end of the staff belonging to the god Hermes."[140]

As we imagined when studying the serpent images found on Crete and in ancient Palestine, so it is clear now that no other creature represents so pervasively the underworld. This fact becomes evident as we study the literature from Greek culture and the myths of the serpent. I am convinced that this symbolism did not originate with the Greeks; it was inherited from the East, perhaps ultimately from India since other ideas from there flowed into the fertile imagination of the Greek mind, particularly into Plato's philosophy.[141]

The ancient Greeks and Romans saw the serpent slither away and disappear perhaps deep into the earth.[142] For them this chthonic region was mysterious and the source of life; after all, plants were seen to spring up out of the earth, especially in the spring, when Persephone returned to the surface of the earth. The cosmos in ancient cosmology was usually conceived to be twofold (cf. Gen 1);[143] above the earth are the heavens, then the earth, and finally the world beneath the surface of the earth. There was no three-tiered universe with the heaven above, the earth beneath, and a separate underworld far below the earth. While there is some debate on this issue, I am convinced that the underworld was part of the earth; "beneath" it meant beneath the earth's surface.

The underworld was not a world devoid of life. It was assumed to be a place to which persons went after death. There were gods of the underworld, and they were important for those living on the earth. Note the following inscription that dates near the century in which the Fourth Gospel received its edited form:

DM	To the gods of the underworld:
AELNOVELAE[144]	Aelia; Novella,
MRI·VIXITN·LXX	her mother, 70 years old;
E·VICTRIAE·FOR[145]	And Victoria,
TIONCONVGI	daughter of Fortionus,
VIXIT·N·XL·ET·	40 years old; and

HERMETIFILIO·146	his son Hermes,
VIXIT·N·XIX·FL·	19 years old;
SERENVS·PISSM147	and Flavius Serenus, in pure love.

The opening, DM, is an abbreviation for D(is) M(anibus), which means "To the gods (or Pluto) of the underworld." The Latin inscription was found near Ulm; it is on display in the Lapidarium in Stuttgart (no. 35). The underworld seems to be part of the earth.

Thus, the serpent, when it disappears mysteriously into the earth, has entered into the region in which the dead reside, not only literally when they are buried in the earth, but also symbolically where they reside forever after death. It is easy to imagine why the ancient Greeks, and possibly those living in or near the Johannine community, thought about and portrayed Hermes with a staff topped by two entwined serpents (the caduceus).

Agathadaimon

Agathadaimon was a snake; the Greek word means "good god (spirit or genius)."[148] According to the *Alexander Romance,* the beneficial deity was killed during the construction of the city. Alexander the Great thus sought to mollify the god by building him a sanctuary in Alexandria. From the time of Alexander III of Macedonia ("the Great" [356–323 BCE]), an annual feast celebrated the sacred snake deity.[149] The serpents that eventually lived in the temple were given a type of porridge made from Egyptian wheat. The anti-Greek *Potter's Oracle* is an Egyptian polemical reply: the snake god has left Alexandria and migrated to Memphis.

As we saw earlier, when studying the gods at Pompeii, Agathadaimon was known elsewhere besides Alexandria.[150] In Athens he seems to have been a minor household god. He was revered throughout most of Greece.[151] Families had snakes not as house pets but as house gods. The snakes were often fed by the family after their main meal. The family left food behind for the serpents such as a mixture of barley and wine. Associated with the fate of cities, as indicated by the *Potter's Oracle,* Agathadaimon became assimilated and indistinguishable in many cities and on many altars with Agatha Tyche. As Fraser indicated, Agathadaimon most likely originated within Greece, perhaps Macedonia, and was brought to Egypt by the Greeks.[152] The earliest indisputable representation of Agathadaimon is from the fourth century BCE.

Following the time of Alexander, the power and importance of Agathadaimon increased. The most important god in the pantheon at Alexandria was Serapis. He is depicted as a snake, but with the head recognizable as Serapis. Scholars have shown that Serapis in this image is clearly Agathadaimon. The identification is confirmed by coins, monuments, figurines, reliefs, lamps, and other realia.[153] For Alexandrians, the three most important gods seemed to have been Serapis, often associated with Isis, Isis herself, and Harpocrates. Each of them is depicted as a serpent.

Agathadaimon is iconographically a serpent. Besides the mural in the House of the Veti at Pompei, shown earlier, the serpent appears in Pompeii in the Temple of Isis.[154] Sometimes he is depicted like an old philosopher,[155] and sometimes apparently as a raised and coiled serpent, as on a slab of white marble found in a private house in Delos and in a mural in the Pistrinum in Pompeii.[156] Numerous reliefs from the Greco-Roman Period, and virtually all from Alexandria, depict an upraised cobra and a large upright serpent; the former is Isis-Thermouthis, the latter Agathadaimon.[157] The deity, Agathadaimon, appears on coins, especially from the second century CE; on one he is with Isis-Thermouthis, and on another he is on a horse and has the head of Serapis.[158] It is notable—especially for a better grasp of the symbolism found in the Fourth Gospel—that the double representation of Isis and Agathadaimon appears for the first time on coins during Hadrian's reign (117–38 CE). A statue from the Roman Period and from Kasr Daoud in Egypt—and now on display in the Louvre (collection Fouquet)—depicts Serapis as Agathadaimon with a human face.[159]

Dunand concluded that Agathadaimon symbolized the protection of the house or home, the grantee of the fertility of the soil, and perhaps as "un génie funéraire"[160]—the one who conducts the corpse to another life or merely protects it.

Focusing on Serapis, Agathadaimon, and Isis-Thermouthis, each of whom is depicted as a serpent, Dunand helped clarify the symbolic meaning of serpent iconography. He perceived three dominant themes of serpent iconography in Alexandria: concern for the fertility of Egyptian soil, an eschatological dimension especially in the use of the caduceus, and the idea of kingship.[161] The serpent thus assured prosperity in this life and in the next. Fraser was dubious that Agathadaimon had any chthonic or eschatological overtones or meaning.[162] Pietrzykowski admits that Fraser is correct for the Hellenistic Period,[163] but that in the Roman Period, especially in the early second century CE, during the reign of Hadrian, Agathadaimon, Serapis, and Isis-Thermouthis were assimilated, portrayed as serpents, and had obtained chthonic and eschatological symbolic meaning.

Giants (and the Monstrous Size of Snakes)

During the Hellenic and Hellenistic periods a myth developed that influenced many;[164] it even influenced Palestinian Jews, who composed a book titled *The Book of the Giants*. The myth relates how in primordial times Giants (which are sometimes similar to the Titans)[165] fought on earth against the gods.[166] The most impressive depiction of this battle is found on the frieze in the Pergamum Temple,[167] which is exceptionally ornate because of the great natural wealth and silver mines found there. Pergamum developed into one of the most majestic and beautiful of the Greek cities. Her library was second only to the incomparable one in Alexandria. The Pergamum frieze featuring the Giants is now prominently and attractively displayed in Berlin in the Humboldt Museum.[168] Not all the Giants were evil; some were good, namely Atlas.

The Greek name for these Giants is instructive, as are the words derived from it. Note the following: [169]

Γίγας	Titan, Giant (usually in plural)
Γιγαντολέτης	Giant-killer (Dionysus and Apollo esp.)
Γιγατομαχία	Titanomachia, battle between the gods and Giants

While the etymology of the Greek word for "Giants" is uncertain, the connection with "Gaia," the Greek word for earth, is possible. According to Hesiod (c. 700 BCE), who along with Homer represent the early Greek epic, the Giants were born from Gaia and the blood of heaven (Ouranos).[170] Also, evidence in favor of some etymological connection between the Giants and Gaia, the Earth, is found in the earliest compendium of this mythology. It is by Pseudo-Apollodorus, who is a mythographer who wrote perhaps shortly before or after the time of the Fourth Evangelist. Apollodorus' account is very long (comprising all of *The Library* 1.6); here is a selection:

> But Earth [Γῆ], vexed on account of the Titans [Τιτάνων], brought forth the Giants, whom she had by Sky [Οὐρρνοῦ]. These were matchless in their bodies' bulk and invincible in their might . . . and with the scales of dragon-serpents [δρακόντων] for feet. . . . Surpassing all the rest were Porphyrion and Alcyoneus, who was even immortal so long as he fought in the land of his birth. . . . Now the gods [θεοῖς] had an oracle that none of the Giants [τῶν Γιγάντων] could perish at the hand of gods, but that with the help of a mortal they would be terminated.[171]

Note that the Giants and Titans are nearly synonymous by the early second century CE. Thus, it is apparent that although some fifth-century BCE texts indicate that the Giants are simply strong men,[172] at least by the first and second centuries CE the Giants are more than beings intermediate between humans and gods; they seem more like the gods. They are born in full armor and size, and they nearly defeat the gods.[173] Indeed, not only the earth but also the entire universe was nearly destroyed. Thus, the Giants are like the gods; at least they seem more like gods than humans.

Unlike the gods, however, they die. They are mortal (and not only according to the opinion of Hesiod [frag. 43a]).[174] In a Greek illustrated manuscript they seem to be depicted with anguiepedes and are being destroyed by serpents.[175]

What concerns us now is the depiction of the Giants. They often have serpents as legs or feet.[176] This iconographic depiction, usually centered on the battle among the Giants and the gods, is found throughout the ancient world. It is even depicted on coins.[177] The Giants have serpent feet that encircle the gods, rise up and bite them, and fight against them in numerous ways.[178] These depictions on the Pergamum altar are monumental and majestic; they are on public display in the Pergamum Museum in the Staatliche Museen in Berlin. The anguipede Giants were also depicted in many other temples and shrines, and on amulets, plates, and especially vase-paintings that date from as early as 600 BCE.[179]

Thinking about "Giants" with serpents as legs may make sense in a world unconquered and unexplored. What is beyond the boundaries? Hence, it is understandable why the ancients imagined the astronomical size of snakes or serpents. The boa does grow to extreme lengths, and Aelian claimed that a certain Alexander, in his *Voyage Round the Red Sea,* reported to have seen snakes "forty cubits long." [180] That would be about 18 meters long.

Strabo (64/3 BCE–c. 21 CE) is far less reserved than Herodotus (484?–c. 420 BCE), and he is no critic like Cicero (106–43 BCE). In his famous *Geography,* Strabo reports on the size of serpents, and his account borders on incredibility. Although Strabo is dubious of the source, he still does not dismiss the possibility that there are serpents that are even 140 cubits in length (15.1.28). An astounding report, to which Strabo seems to subscribe, is found in *Geography* 16.4.16: "Artemidorus also speaks of serpents [δρακόντων] thirty cubits in length which overpower elephants and bulls; and his measurement is moderate, at least for serpents in this part of the world, for the Indian serpents are rather fabulous, as also those of Libya, which are said to grow grass on their backs." [181] Strabo is serious. He has no doubt that one can find in India, as some have reported to him, serpents that swallow oxen and stags (2.1.9).[182]

Why did the ancient Greeks depict the Giants with anguipedes? We can only speculate. They wanted to show how difficult it was for the gods to overcome evil. The serpents were most likely chosen to enhance the perception of the awesome and deadly power of the Giants. They can thus overcome most obstacles, moving over land and sea. They can engage the gods from all directions and administer not only deadly bites, but also entangle the extremities of the gods. Thus, to depict Giants with serpent feet was an apt way to present such ideas.

We need to be careful not to assume that because the Giants usually were perceived as evil and destructive, the serpents consequently were always negative symbols. The symbol of the serpent added positively to the ability of the Giants to engage and almost defeat the gods. Thus, the serpent feet denoted agility, freedom to traverse land and sea, swiftness, power, incredible and deadly ability to wrestle with gods, and elusiveness in combat. Who would want to enter a wrestling ring with an opponent who had cobras for feet?

Perhaps the bizarre and trans-experiential dimension of anguipedes added to the need to contemplate the transcendent otherworldliness of the Giants. It would be rash to suggest the serpents cannot denote evil in any way or that they depicted something symbolically positive in the image of the Giants. Serpents, after all, also denoted evil, sin, and the lie. Thus, the serpents in the depiction of the Giants also signify something evil. Note the informative words on this thought by Ovid. He imagined that the king of the gods who was enthroned majestically, and perhaps above, castigates the gods' savage enemy, "the serpent-footed Giants [anguipedum]." [183]

Hercules

We have already seen that one of the great men who conquered the Giants was Hercules; he was the archetype of the sociological category "the Great Man."

Among the prominent symbolic uses of the serpent in Greek and Roman culture, the legends of Hercules are prominent. Hercules (Herakles), which means in Greek "Glory of Hera," had to strangle two powerful serpents at birth. These were sent to harm Hercules, the son of Zeus (Jupiter) and Alcmene, the human wife of Amphitryon, by the jealous and vindictive wife of Zeus, Hera.

His second labor at the command of Eurystheus (king of Argos or Mycenae) was to kill the Lernaean Hydra, the many-headed water snake. His tenth labor was to obtain the red cattle guarded by Geryon who was aided by the herdsman Eurytion. The latter's dog, Orthos (the brother of Cerberus), was two-headed and had a snake as a tail. Hercules' eleventh labor was to descend into Hades and, with the help of Hermes, to defeat Cerberus, the hound of Hell who had many hissing and poisonous serpents accompanying him and protruding from his body. His twelfth and final labor was to obtain the apples of immortality from the Hesperides. As will become more apparent later, he is successful and obtains immortality (momentarily) despite the serpent that was guarding the tree (cf. Gen 3 and the Gilgamesh legend). Finally, in the Hercules legends and myths, the serpentine wandering river-god Achelous in struggling against the hero transforms himself into a serpent.

While Hercules is never shown with anguipedes, he is often depicted fighting Giants with feet that are serpents. Here is the account in Pseudo-Apollodorus:

> Hercules first shot Alcyoneus (one of the most majestic Giants) with an arrow, but when the Giant fell on the ground he somewhat revived. However, at Athena's advice Hercules dragged him outside Pallene, and so the Giant died. . . . As for the other Giants, Ephialtes was shot by Apollo with an arrow in his left eye and by Hercules in his right. . . . The other Giants Zeus smote and destroyed with thunderbolts and all of them Hercules shot with arrows as they were dying. When the gods [οἱ Θεοὶ] had overcome the Giants [τῶν Γιγάντων], Earth [Γῆ], still more enraged, had intercourse with Tartarus and brought forth Typhon in Cilicia, a hybrid between man and beast. . . . One of his hands reached out to the west and the other to the east, and from them projected a hundred dragon-serpents' [δρακόντων] heads. From the thighs downward he had huge coils of vipers [ἐχιδνῶν], which when drawn out, reached to his very head and emitted a loud hissing. His body was all winged.[184]

Observe the connection again between the Earth (Ge or Gaia) and the Giants. Serpent symbolism plays a major role in depicting Typhon. Note that from his hands projected one hundred dragon-serpent heads.

Continuing with the story, we learn that the gods flee to Egypt to escape Typhon. To hide from him they change themselves into animals. Zeus, however, pursues him, albeit pelting him with thunderbolts from a safe distance, and subsequently felling him with a sickle. The battle ensues again on Mount Casius in Syria:

> There, seeing the monster sore wounded, he [Zeus] grappled with him. But Typhon twined about him and gripped him in his (serpent) coils, and wresting the sickle from him severed the sinews of his hands and feet, and lifting him on his shoulders carried him through the sea to Cilicia and deposited him on arrival in the Corycian cave.[185]

It is quite amazing what Typhon has done to Zeus, and how the description of Zeus is so anthropocentric. Zeus triumphed in the end, but only with the aid of Hermes, Aegipan, and the Fates.

The Greeks and Romans were fond of tales celebrating the heroic exploits of Hercules. According to one of the stories, Hercules falls asleep in the country called Scythia and his mares escape. He later meets a woman who has two forms. Above her buttocks she was a woman; below it a serpent (ὄφιος). She retains Hercules until he enables her to have three sons. Then Hercules departs, taking with him the mares that the woman had sequestered.[186]

Figure 54. *Left.* The Babe Hercules Killing Two Serpents. Courtesy of the trustees of the British Museum.

Figure 55. *Right.* A Standing Sculpture of the Babe Hercules Killing Two Serpents. Courtesy of the Hermitage. JHC. Both sculptures Roman Period.

As one can imagine, Hercules looms large in ancient iconography.[187] For our focus on serpent symbols, it is imperative to note how frequently Hercules is depicted with serpents. A sixth-century BCE bronze statuette, from Doris, Greece, helps us imagine how Hercules was perceived by the Greeks. He wears a lion's skin tied at the chest and waist with its paws. He is brandishing a club at a hydra. It is a serpent with a goatee, and it rises up to about his waist.[188]

According to Pseudo-Apollodorus, when Hercules was only eight months old Hera, incensed by her husband Zeus' "infidelity," tried to kill the baby by sending into his bed two large serpents (δύο δράκοντας ὑπερμεγέθεις). Hercules strangled them with his bare hands.[189] This episode found a life in sculpture, seal impressions, vases, coins, jewelry, clay lamps, and other ceramics. In artwork he is usually depicted as a boy wrestling with one or more serpents, but in some illustrations he is a well-developed man fighting monstrous serpents.[190]

Hercules' last labor was to go to the Garden of the Hesperides to obtain a golden apple, which was the source of immortality. Ironically, the golden apples were a wedding gift from Gaia, the earth god, to Zeus and Hera. The tree was guarded by a large serpent. According to the *Theogony* (lines 333–35), the serpent was the child of Phorkys and Keto.[191] The snake, however, was never given a name (neither was the serpent in Gen 3). It is

Figure 56. Hercules in the Garden of the Hesperides with a Serpent in the Tree [BM 827; Neg. No. VI D 321]. Early Roman Period. Courtesy of the Trustees of the British Museum.

not clear how and in what ways Hercules accomplishes this feat. In passing, it is interesting to compare this legend with the lore that shapes the story of Gilgamesh and Genesis 3. All three legends or myths include the search for immortality and a serpent. Clearly, the serpent was the quintessential symbol for new life and immortality.

Hercules is imagined fighting with serpents[192] or with a hydra.[193] On a Roman sarcophagus an artist has skillfully displayed the sequence of scenes depicting Hercules' exploits; the serpent is featured prominently.[194]

Cerberus

Homer and Hesiod mention a mythological dog that guards the gates to the underworld. Its name is Cerberus. It is depicted in numerous ways. Sometimes it has serpents for tails. At other times it is shown with serpents sprouting from a head or two heads, or with serpents as paws. Cerberus' mandate was to guard the gates so that no one left the underworld. According to one version of the myth, Hercules persuaded it to come out and Orpheus overcame it with music.

Another version of the myth is represented on a Greek amphora from the late sixth century BCE. It envisions Hercules bending down to pet one of the heads of Cerberus. Each head sprouts at least one upraised serpent, and the tail is a serpent. Hercules has bewitched the hound, since after petting its head he will enchain it.[195] Another Greek vase is generic; it depicts Cerberus with serpents on its paws and elsewhere.[196]

Laocoon

We have already mentioned the Greek legend about Laocoon. Now, we can dig deeper into this intriguing legend. Laocoon was a priest of Apollo, but he offended the god by breaking his vow of celibacy. Apollo then sent two massive sea serpents to crush him and his two sons, Antiphas and Thymbraeus (Melanthus), as he, as was his duty, was preparing to sacrifice a bull to Poseidon. The names of the two serpents were either Porces and Chariboea or Curissia and Periboea. Another legend, the one mentioned earlier in this book, indicates that he was killed by a Greek god. Now we can state it was Apollo, because he had warned the Trojans not to accept the Greeks' gift of a wooden horse.[197]

The classic source for the Laocoon legend is in the *Aeneid* by Virgil (70–19 BCE).[198] According to Virgil, Laocoon warned the people of Troy to be wary of the Greek gift:

> Oh, wretched citizens, what wild frenzy is this? Do you believe the foe has sailed away, or do you think any gifts from the Greeks are free from treachery? . . . Either enclosed in this frame lurk Achaeans, or this [wooden horse] has been built as a war engine against our walls [*aut haec in nostros fabricata est machina muros*], to spy into our homes and come down upon the city from above. [2.42–47][199]

Many lines later, Laocoon reappears. Notice how Virgil describes the serpents:

> Laocoon (Laocon), priest of Neptune [Apollo], as drawn by lot, was slaying a great bull at the customary altars; and lo, from Tenedos, over the peaceful depths—I shudder as I tell the tale—a pair of serpents with endless coils [*immensis orbibus angues*] ascend out of the sea, side by side, and make for the shore. Their bosoms rise amidst the surge, and their crests, blood-red, top the waves. The rest of them skims the main behind and their huge backs curve in many a fold; we hear the sound sent from foaming seas. And now they gain the

fields and, with blazing eyes suffused with blood and fire, lick with quivering tongues their hissing mouths. Pale at the sight, we scatter. They in unswerving course speed towards Laocoon; and first each serpent [*serpens*] enfolds in its embrace the youthful bodies of his two sons and with its fangs feed upon the hapless limbs. Then himself too, as he comes to their aid, weapons in hand, they seize and bind in mighty folds; and now, twice encircling his waist, twice winding their scaly backs around his throat, they tower above head and lofty necks. He the while strains his hands to burst the knots, his fillets steeped in gore and black venom; while lifting to heaven hideous cries, like the bellow of a wounded bull that has fled from the altar and shaken from its neck the ill-aimed axe. But, gliding away, the dragon-serpent pair [*gemini . . . dracones*] escape to the lofty shrines, and seek fierce Tritonia's citadel, there to nestle under the goddess' feet and the circle of her shield.[200]

This story was well known by the end of the first century CE, when the Fourth Gospel reached its second edition. The description of the serpents awakens fear in the reader.

The story of Laocoon is also familiar today because it has become a part of Western culture. One reason for the story's popularity is the well-known sculpture seen by millions in the Vatican. It was made probably in the second century BCE by Agesander, Polydorus, and Athenodorus, three Rhodian sculptors. It depicts in living marble Laocoon vainly struggling against monstrous serpents.[201] Another reason Laocoon is well known today is the famous book by Lessing about the limits of painting and poetry, which was entitled *Laokoon: Oder über die Grenzen der Malerei und Poesie*. This monumental work, which dates from 1766, attempted to distinguish between the art of painting and the art of poetry, and concluded, somewhat idiosyncratically, that poetry, unlike painting, had to do, not with description, but with movement.

The depiction of Laocoon being destroyed by serpents was a popular aspect of Hellenic and Hellenistic culture. It appears on the murals at Pompeii in the Casa del Menandro and can be seen in situ. Another example, also with the bull to be sacrificed in the background, comes from the Casa di Laocoonte in Pompeii and is on display in the National Museum in Naples.[202] The symbolism here is rather uncomplicated. The serpents are not necessarily demonic;[203] but they do appear to destroy and kill. Since they do the will of the god, perhaps a double entendre is present: the serpents represent both good and evil.

Glykon

Glykon is a serpent often depicted with a human-like face.[204] He appears on coins as a large upright serpent.[205] Pseudo-Alexander, whom we will meet in the writings of Lucian, claimed that the serpent he saw was Glykon, a reincarnation of Asclepius. Sometimes Glykon appears with Asclepius; he is depicted as the serpent with anthropomorphic features.[206] As the Greek name Glykon implies, he is "the sweet one." He is like the serpent often seen with Asclepius, but, unlike that serpent, Glykon is shown with a separate personality and with human emotions. Glykon, the serpent, is thus a positive symbol. He is the personification or incarnation of the concept of health and healing.

Medusa

We have already seen that the Southern Palace in the Hermitage has images of Medusa on its fence. Who was she, and what is the explanation of the serpent imagery?

According to Greek mythology a group of women—Stheno, Euryale, and Medusa, all daughters of Phorcus—were divine and had serpents as hair or in their hair.[207] Frequently they are shown with wings.[208] They are depicted with the tongue sticking out (and even with beards) and are usually unattractive; sometimes, however, they are bewitchingly lovely. They are called Gorgons because occasionally Gorgo is the name of a daughter of Phorcus. In the *Aeneid,* the goddess tosses a serpent *(anguem)* at Alecto (one of the Furies whose head is covered with serpents). The serpent entwines itself around her, and finally its venom "courses through her whole frame" (7.341–77).

The only mortal, and most famous of the Gorgons, was Medusa. Perseus killed her by cutting off her head. Her head was impaled on Pallas' spear (i.e., Athena's spear), and from her blood came Pegasus, the winged horse.

How was Perseus enabled to behead Medusa? An answer may be found in Ovid's *Metamorphoses*. Perseus beheads Medusa while she and the serpents slept by looking not at her but at the reflection of her in the bright bronze shield in his left hand (*Metam.* 4.782–86).

Why did Medusa have serpents in her hair? Again, an answer is provided by Ovid. Note especially the explanation, by a guest to one of the princes with Perseus:

> She was once most beautiful in form, and the jealous hope of many
> suitors. Of all her beauties, her hair was the most beautiful—for so I
> learned from one who said he had seen her. 'Tis said that in Miner-
> va's temple Neptune, lord of the Ocean, ravished her. Jove's daughter

turned away and hid her chaste eyes behind her aegis. And, that the deed might be punished as was due, she changed the Gorgon's locks to ugly snakes [*turpes mutavit in hydros*]. And now to frighten her fear-numbed foes, she still wears upon her breast the snakes [*angues*] which she has made.[209]

Ovid seems to supply answers to questions that would have arisen in antiquity.

The land of Libya is plagued by snakes. A myth explains why. Libya is full of deadly serpents *(angues)* because as the head of Gorgon was carried over Libya some blood fell to the earth and immediately turned into serpents (*Metam.* 4.615–20).

According to Lucan (39–65 CE), the ancients—at least some of them, probably the masses—believed the following about Medusa:[210]

In her body malignant Nature first bred these cruel plagues; from her throat were born the snakes [*e faucibus angues*] that poured forth shrill hissings with their forked tongues. It pleased Medusa [*Medusae*], when snakes dangled close against her neck; in the way that women dress their hair, the vipers hang loose over her back but rear erect over her brow in front; and their poison wells out when the tresses are combed. These snakes are the only part of ill-fated Medusa that all men look upon and live. For who ever felt fear of the monster's face and open mouth? Who that looked her straight in the face was suffered by Medusa to die? . . . No living creature could endure to look on her, and even her serpents bent backward to escape her face. She turned to stone Atlas, the Titan who supports the Pillars of the West.[211]

Thus, the accomplishment of Perseus, in beheading her, was something astoundingly remarkable. According to Lucan, it was Medusa's look, not the serpents, that killed.

More women than the Gorgons had serpents in their hair. For example, Tisiphone, with snakes covering her face, puts on as a girdle "a writhing snake." Then she, aided by the Furies, hinders the retreat of both Ino (the daughter of Cadmus and Harmonia) and Athamas (king of Thebes and son of Aeolus). Ovid's account is remarkable:

And stretching her arms, wreathed with vipers [*vipereis*], she shook out her locks: disturbed, the serpents hissed horribly. A part lay on her shoulders, part twined round her breast, hissing, vomiting venomous gore, and darting out their tongues. Then she tears away two serpents [*duos . . . angues*] from the midst of her tresses, and with deadly aim hurls them at her victims. The snakes go gliding over the breasts of Ino and of Athamas and breathe upon them their pestilential breath.

No wounds their bodies suffer; 'tis their minds that feel the deadly
stroke.[212]

What could be the symbolism or function of depictions of Gorgon heads,
especially the head of Medusa? They could symbolize power, magic, mystery, and fear of the gods. One of the main uses of the image of the head
of Medusa, or another Gorgon, with its horrifying serpents was for protection, especially of one's home. Thus, someone put numerous faces of
Medusa on the iron fence of the Southern Palace of the Hermitage to keep
unwanted people out and to protect those inside.

This symbolic meaning goes back to the early days of Greek mythology
since Agamemnon had a Gorgon on his shield,[213] and vases often depict
a Gorgon on a shield.[214] Only two examples must suffice here. One is the
bronze relief from Olympia, which dates from around 600 BCE.[215] Another
is a floor mosaic showing the head of a Gorgon with ten menacing serpents
squirming from her head. It was found in Domus delle Gorgoni at Ostia
Antici and dates from the third or fourth century CE.[216] Under the sad face
appear the words *Gorgoni Bita,* perhaps "flee from the Gorgon."[217] The
mosaic is reminiscent of one almost all tourists see at the entrance to a
house in Pompeii: *cave canem,* "Beware of the dog."

Ladon

Ladon (Λάδων) denotes the name of two rivers, one in Bithynia that is often personified, and the other in Daphne near Antioch. The noun, spelled
the same, also denotes a serpent (called in Greek δράκων and ὄφις and
in Latin *draco*). The animal is usually much larger than a human. It frequently has a goatee and more than one head, but in the Imperial Period
it has usually only one head. I have found no iconography to support the
claim by Pherekydes of Athens (fifth cent. BCE) that Ladon had one hundred heads (ἔχων κεφαλὰς ρ).[218]

Ladon is the mythological sleepless serpent *(insopiti quondam tutela
draconis)* [219] that guards the golden apples in the garden of the Hesperides.
It is the creation of Keto and Phorkys, Typhon and Echidna, or Ge; and,
according to many sources, was killed by Hercules.[220]

Ladon is depicted as a large serpent entwined around a tree and protecting the golden apples (see Fig. 56). It is shown sometimes drinking out of a
bowl (a phial) held by a goddess (probably a Hesperid). Frequently it deco-
rates vases, and sometimes appears on coins and in mosaics. It is shown in
paintings preserved from Rome (fourth cent. CE) and Pompeii (first half of
first cent. CE).

What could this serpent symbolize? That it was placed among the stars,
after its fatal encounter with Hercules, would mean it could have astrologi-

cal and heavenly powers.[221] Ladon was able to guard *(tutela draconis)* the golden apples because it never slept. It also emitted "all kind of sounds" (φωνὰς παντοιάς).[222] Hence, it could be seen positively as the ideal guardian; that was as important then as it is now. Its chthonic powers might also be elevated as important for one facing death or the meaning of life, since it derives from the earth (χθόνιος ὄφις).[223]

Aion

This Greek word denotes not only "an indefinitely long period of time" ("eternity" in Platonic thought) but also "life" and "lifetime" and even "age" and "generation." It can denote also one's entire life, one's destiny. Thus, the god Aion is a personification, actually a hypostatization,[224] of all these interrelated concepts, especially "eternity" after Plato's pervasive influence.[225] Note the poetic passage in Euripides' *The Children of Hercules* (898–99):

> For many blessings Fate fleetingly engenders,
> With which Aion, child of Chronos, gives final completeness.[226]

For us the key words are "Aion, child of Chronos" (Αἰών τε Κρόνου).[227] How should one render this noun? The poem signifies that Aion denotes one's own lifetime, one's own destiny, and especially the culmination of it: "eternity" in many post-Platonic circles.

Chronos is sometimes depicted nude with a large serpent wrapped around him, from the bottom to the top, with the head of the serpent resting on the head of Chronos. An excellent example is the statue of Chronos preserved in Merida.[228]

Thus, under the influence of Platonic and speculative Greek philosophy, this noun developed from a concept grounded in this world, "lifetime," to an abstract concept, "eternity." For Plato, Aion denoted "eternity," as is well known from his *Timaeus* 37d.[229]

Thinking about Plato's dialogues awakens thoughts about time and eternity. The very transience of "becoming," in its very nature of always being in the process of tending toward the elusive, is itself a mirror of the eternal, the everlasting.[230] We thus learn that for Greeks and Romans, by the first century CE, Aion meant "Life and Eternity." Moreover, Aion was the offspring of Time (Chronos).

In Alexandria in Greco-Roman times, there was an annual festival honoring Aion. It may have been a New Year's festival. It was a mixture of Greek and Egyptian ideas and myths. The festival's high point seems to have been when Aion's image was brought out from a sanctuary. It appears there was an announcement to the crowds; perhaps a priest proclaimed that the Maiden (Kore) had given birth to Aion.[231]

Aion is frequently depicted in antiquity as a nude male around whom a large serpent is entwined, from ankles to shoulders; from the male's head the large serpent frequently looks down. Occasionally, the large serpent is shown to the side of the god and curled upward around an obelisk. Sometimes Aion has a beastly face, somewhat like that of a lion. Occasionally, Aion is depicted with wings on his back. The art appears on amulets, and in mural paintings in tombs (as in the Isola sacra d'Ostie, tomb 57, from the end of the end of the second cent. BCE).[232]

What is the meaning of the serpent in this inconographic representation of Aion? The variety and different dates of this symbol indicate that Aion reflects a multiplicity of concepts, and I think predominantly good ones. The depiction of Aion with a serpent curled around him, and in the center of a zodiacal circle, indicates that Aion combined with the serpent is a very powerful positive symbol for time and eternity.[233] Surely, any reflection will be enriched by the following discussion of Ouroboros. As that symbol represents completeness, so Aion, as its name clarifies, symbolizes "Eternity." The serpent is thus a positive symbol that denotes the fulfillment of time. It also denotes the cyclical renewal of time and the return to the primordial so-called Golden Age (see esp. the cosmogonic mosaic in Merida, Spain).[234]

Ouroboros

We have already introduced Ouroboros. What more may be said? Ouroboros is a Greek noun that means "devouring its own tail." It is composed of two Greeks words: the noun "tail" (οὐρά) and the verb "to devour" (βοράω). The symbol is a serpent formed into a circle and eating its own tail. This symbol appears in many places in antiquity, especially on seals, drawings, and gems, and often in late magical papyri. One attractive depiction of Ouroboros has the serpent with a dark beginning and white tail with scales; the tail is almost in the serpent's mouth. Some ancient testimonies, namely Horapollon and Olympiodorus,[235] indicate (probably correctly)[236] that the concept of Ouroboros was borrowed by the Greeks from the Egyptians. Within the circle formed are the words "one [is] the whole" (ἓν τὸ πᾶν).[237]

Thus, it is clear what Ouroboros symbolized, at least in essentials. It denoted, and personified, time, continuity, and the cosmos. Because Ouroboros is a serpent with its tail in its mouth, so the symbol seems to indicate the circularity of time and the movement of the cosmos as complete.[238]

The cosmic dimension of Ouroboros is often overlooked, but not by the author of one of the Greek magical papyri, who explains how to make a small ring that will bring "success" (ἐπιτυχίαν):

Taking an air-colored jasper, engrave on it a snake [δρά[κοντα κυ] κλοτερῶς τὴν οὐρὰν ἔχοντα ἐν τῷ στόματι] in a circle with its tail in its mouth, and also in the middle of [the circle formed by] the snake [Selene] having two stars /on the two horns, and above these, Helios, beside whom ABRASAX should be inscribed.[239]

The perception that Ouroboros denoted the completion of time and the cosmos, or at least that the serpent symbolized the cosmos, at times, in Greek and Roman mythology is enhanced by a study of Ovid's *Metamorphoses*. He occasionally mentions the constellation called the serpent. Referring to the cosmic serpent or the constellation of the serpent, Ovid has Titan advise his son, Phaëthon, about driving the celestial chariot so as not to burn up the heavens or the earth and avoid the "writhing Serpent (Anguem)."[240] Subsequently, Ovid explains that "the Serpent (Serpens), which lies nearest to the icy pole, once harmless because it was formerly sluggish with the cold, now grew hot, and conceived great frenzy from that fire."[241]

It thus becomes clearer that Ouroboros did not necessarily denote only repetitiousness or repetitive time. There was movement and progression. While the tail ended up in the mouth, it completed the circle of being because the tail had reached the mouth. The Ouroboros denoted optimism and the return to the best of times. The ancients, Greeks and Semites, seem to have shared the idea that the beginnings were better than the present. Kiss rightly perceives that Ouroboros is "a symbol of the constant cycle and in this sense Eternity."[242] The inscription, "the One [is] the whole," indicates more than that the beginning is the end or the end is the beginning;[243] it denotes the harmony and unity of creation, especially the humans' place within time and space.

Thinking of Aion and Ouroboros, and what they symbolized in the various dimensions, leads to reflections on Henry Vaughan's perception that eternity is a "great ring of pure and endless light."[244] The serpent is thus a profound symbol, and it is a positive one. In all these reflections, we need to be circumspect and not forget the odd sensations we first had when we saw a drawing of a serpent swallowing its own tail.

The Ouroboros may also symbolize something more. The tail can resemble the lingam. The mouth can represent the mons veneris. Hence, the Ouroboros, I am convinced, would symbolize for some Greeks and Romans the completed human: the androgynous one (the harmony of male and female).

Babi

Another serpent god is Babi, Sid. An image of Babi, Sid, was discovered in the Antas Valley in Carthaginia. This image dates from the fifth or sixth

Figure 57. Zeus or Jupiter
Enthroned. Roman Period.
Courtesy of the Hermitage. JHC

centuries BCE and is accompanied by the inscription "To Sid, Babi, I dedi-
cate 94 deniers." The god is to be identified with *Pater Sardus*. The serpent
image symbolizes eternity.[245]

Chnoubis

On magical gems a serpent figure appears; it is named Chnoubis (Χνοῦβις,
Χνοῦφις, Χνοῦμις, or Κνοῦφις).[246] The origin of the myth is Egyptian. In
Elephantine, from which so many Aramaic papyri have been recovered,
Chnoubis was hailed as the king of the first cataract of the Nile. Note
the report in Strabo: Elephantine "is an island in the Nile . . . and a city
therein . . . has a temple of Cnuphis [ἱερὸν Κνούφιδος]." [247] The gems date
from the second to the fourth century CE. One gem with Chnoubis in the
middle has written around its edges the names Gabriel, Ouriel, and Sou-
riel. On the back appears the name Adonai. The first three are the names
of the archangels; the back contains the Hebrew name "Lord," which is
to be pronounced when God's own name (the ineffable Tetragrammaton)
appears in a text, and in place of it.

What does this serpent god symbolize? It is far from clear. Perhaps it is
associated with the Egyptian god Khnoum and has some solar meaning.

Zeus

Zeus, the greatest of the Greek gods, is originally the god of the sky. As
Greeks wondered about the stars and the universe they accorded more

honor to this sky god. In the words of Dion Chrysostomos, Zeus is "the giver of all good things, the Father, the Saviour, the Keeper of mankind."[248]

Zeus is often represented as having the features of a serpent. He is frequently shown with a serpent, as in the sixth-century BCE Laconian vase-painting of an eagle eating Prometheus' liver.[249]

While Hermes is portrayed almost always with a caduceus and Asclepius with a serpent wound around a staff, Zeus in not typically shown with serpents. When humans turned their attention to the earth, themselves, health, healing, and youthful regeneration, they elevated Asclepius until he was virtually the supreme god; then Zeus appears as Zeus-Asclepius.[250]

Apollo

Apollo, the god of music and poetry, is the twin of Artemis, the huntress. He is the son of Leto and Zeus. Like Zeus, Apollo only rarely appears with a serpent. Aelian (actually Aelianus; 170–235 CE) reports a festival in honor of Apollo; it does feature serpents. The account deserves reporting in full:

> The people of Epirus and all strangers sojourning there, beside any other sacrifice to Apollo, on one day in the year hold their chief festival in his honour with solemnity and great pomp. There is a grove dedicated to the god, and round about it a precinct, and in the enclosure are Serpents [δράκοντες], and these self-same Serpents are the pets of the god. Now the priestess, who is a virgin, enters unaccompanied, bringing food for the Serpents. And the people of Epirus maintain that the Serpents are sprung from the Python at Delphi. If, as the priestess approaches, they look graciously upon her and take the food with eagerness, it is agreed that they are indicating a year of prosperity and of freedom from sickness. If however they scare her and refuse the pleasant food she offers, then the Serpents are foretelling the reverse of the above, and that is what the people of Epius expect.[251]

The account by Aelian raises many questions: What if the serpents bite and kill the virgin? What if the serpents have already been fed, or have not eaten in months? Historians and sociologists, as well as others, would like to know if the account was taken literally and believed, or if it is like the humorous watching of the groundhog's shadow in the United States.

Mithra

The worship of Mithra used to be considered only a military religion, but now we know that Mithraites built shrines and thus worshipped in major cities, including ancient Ostia and Rome.[252] Originating in the East, this religion was transformed in the Greek and Roman world and became very popular. Mithra, the all-conquering sun god, is usually depicted slaying a bull.

Sometimes Mithra's struggle against the bull is aided by a dog and a serpent (in other images they are both drinking the blood of the bull).[253] The serpent in Mithraism is thus depicted as passive or active.[254] It is often shown drinking not only the blood but sometimes also the semen of the slaughtered bull.[255] Serpent symbolism in Mithraism contrasts with both the general Old Testament view of the serpent and with Zoroastrianism in which the serpent is an incarnation of the evil Ahriman. The devotees of Mithra perceived the serpent as an assistant of Mithra.

The rejuvenating powers of the serpent would also have been noted and found attractive to the followers of Mithra since they, unlike the Zoroastrians, believed in a cycle of births, as we know from the Avestan accounts and as Porphyrius reported (in *De abstinentia* 4.16). Furthermore, it is certain that the serpent was a positive symbol in Mithraism; it sometimes is associated with the zodiac and curls around the two bears, Ursus major and Ursus minor.[256] As S. Insler has indicated, Mithraism in Italy and the West became primarily associated with astronomy and astrology. These separate concepts in modernity were not usually distinguishable in antiquity; that is, western Mithraism was essentially an astral cult, "with its theology founded upon the mysteries seen in the sky and their effects upon the course of time."[257] The connection with time, chronology, and serpent iconography will be obvious to the reader by now.

That Mithraism was a threat to Christianity needs no demonstration. On the one hand, the triumphant Christians destroyed many of the Mithraea and forced them to cease about the end of the fourth century CE. On the other hand, they co-opted the solar force of Mithraism by assigning the birth of Jesus to December 25, the birthday of Mithra. It is conceivable that another cult, one known as Deus sol invictus—which celebrated the supreme deity the sun, had its zenith during the reign of Emperor Elagabalus (218–222 CE), and celebrated the "rebirth" of the sun on December 25—was even more influential, at least at times and in some places, than Mithraism.[258] One must be careful to focus on the time and place of possible influence from either cult; Mithra, moreover, as Vermaseren shows, was often identified with Saturn.[259]

Abraxas

Abraxas is a demon well known from early Christian texts. It is also often found within Proto-Gnostic works and in Gnosticism. It is pictured with a torso of a man, the head of a rooster, and two serpents as feet.[260]

Asclepius

We now come to the Greek and later Roman god who more than any other god is associated with the serpent. While serpents are customarily shown with Hermes, they form a caduceus and usually the serpents are only stylized. Asclepius (Greek: Asclepios, Latin: Aesculapius)[261] appears as a full serpent and is almost always portrayed with a serpent entwined around his staff.

Asclepius appears first in literature as a human, and then he is elevated to be a god. In Homer's *Iliad* (2.729), which was written sometime before the seventh century BCE,[262] Asclepius is mentioned in the catalogue of the Achaean army as the father of Machaon and Podaleirios (Latin: Podalirius).[263] Homer's portrayal of Asclepius as a human physician is altered by Hesiod, who refers to him as semi-divine, or as a god.[264] In fact, it seems that Hesiod is the first one to refer to Asclepius as a healing god.

By 500 BCE, Greek hymns appeared celebrating a god of healing.[265] Asclepius, however, was not the only god of healing in Greece. In principle, Greeks assumed that every god could perform healings.[266]

According to legends, Asclepius dies when Zeus destroys him with a thunderbolt because he had raised the dead (see Pliny, *Natural History*).[267] In ancient lore antedating even Homer, Asclepius was perhaps originally a deity—an earth deity or earth daimon—who healed the sick. His two means were: first, dreams that informed the one asleep of the proper means and methods for recovery of health; second, incubation.[268] The devotees (the incubants) performed some rituals to purify themselves, then they entered the temple of the god for periods up to more than one year. The object was to sleep in the god's temple and receive information, usually a cure, through a dream. Incubation was especially central to the Asclepian cult. There were Asclepian shrines or temples for incubation at Epidaurus, but also at Cos, Lebene, Pergamum, Rome, and Smyrna. Peloponnesians had a penchant for building an Asklepieion, as we know from a recent survey by S. G. Stauropoulos.[269]

Clearly, the most important Asklepieion was at Epidaurus (see Fig. 59).[270] This temple was magnificent. The setting is also remote and relaxing. It is far from the commercialism of Corinth to the north, close to the sea, and quietly nestled beneath some verdant hills. The temple in Epidaurus was supported by plenteous springs and dense vineyards; hence, Homer could call it *ambeloessa*, "vine-clad."[271] The temple is only one of the many buildings in the vast complex at Epidaurus.[272]

There were also monumental temples at Cos, Pergamum, and Corinth.[273] Devotees, especially when healed, left a votive offering, usually in the form of the part of the body that had been healed, ostensibly, by Asclepius: notably a breast, a phallus, an arm, a leg, a foot. The votive offerings do not come interpreted, and so we need to admit that there is much we do not and cannot know. M. Lang rightly points out this fact: "Although complete and parts of arms are very well represented among the votives at Corinth, there is very little evidence concerning the kinds of infirmity for the cure of which they were given as thank-offerings."[274] H. Avalos corrects the view of the Edelsteins; he is convinced that "doctors" in the Asklepieion did perform surgeries.[275]

Most likely Asclepius was originally a man who, in the dim recesses of history, was remembered as a physician and who became semi-divine and eventually a full deity.[276] As L. R. Farnell stated, this deification of a physician is not so unusual; Im-hotep was once a real Egyptian physician who came to be considered a god.[277] As Pliny, in *Nat.* 29.22, states, the Asclepian serpent *(anguis Aesculapius)* was brought from Epidaurus, where it originated, to Rome. Kerényi summarizes the most likely stages in the evolution of the Asclepian myth:[278]

Before 1000 BCE	Flowering of the myth in Thessaly; Asclepius is a physician and teacher
1000–600 BCE	Time of Homer and Hesiod
600–400 BCE	Flowering of the Asclepian family at Cos [Hippocrates]
500–300 BCE	Beginning of the flowering of the Asclepian cult in Epidauros
291 BCE	The Asclepian cult comes to Rome (the island in the Tiber)

Our concern is not with the origins of the Asclepian myth and cult. It is with the elevation of Asclepius to a full god, equal to Zeus, and the Asclepian serpent iconography and symbology. The evidence for this is abundant; note, for example, the ideas preserved on an Attic stone from the second century CE: "O Asklepios . . . O blessed one, O God of my longing. . . . Thou alone, O divine and blessed one, art mighty."[279] Long before the first century CE, when the Fourth Gospel was composed, Asclepius was depicted with serpents as the god of healing. Not only was Asclepius deified, but physicians, who were unusually successful and thus revered, were deified as Asclepius.[280]

Celsus (fl. c. 14–37 CE), author of *De Medicina,* helps us understand the evolution of the Asclepian myth. He wrote that Asclepius was "celebrated as the most ancient authority" on medicine. He "was numbered among the gods [*in deorum numerum receptus est*]" because "he cultivated this science, as yet rude and vulgar, with a little more than common refinement." His sons, Podalirius and Machaon, were not magicians or physicians who could heal all diseases. As Homer stated, during the Trojan War, they were able to heal battle wounds only "by the knife and medicaments."[281]

Figure 58. A Statue of Asclepius with the Serpent Staff. Greek or Early Roman Period. Courtesy of the Hermitage. JHC

Asclepius appears to the Greeks and Romans as a serpent.[282] He usually is depicted with a staff around which a serpent is entwined.[283] This imaginative portrait of Asclepius dates as early as the fifth century, and perhaps sixth century, BCE. Marcus Aurelius (Roman emperor from 161 to 180 CE), though he was imbued with Stoicism, occasionally thought of himself as Asclepius (actually Aesculapius), and liked to be seen as a god holding a staff like Asclepius' staff. Asclepius is depicted with Telesphoros and with a serpent on a staff; the work dates from the second century CE.[284]

Some guidance in perceiving the meaning of anguine symbols in the Asclepian cult is provided by texts. For example, Q. Ogulnius has a dream in which Asclepius appears; here are the pertinent words of Ovid (43 BCE–17 or 18 CE):[285]

Fear not! I shall come and leave my shrine. Only look upon this serpent which twines about my staff [*hunc modo serpentem, baculum*

Figure 59. The Asklepieion at Epidaurus. The Temple of Asclepius is in the foreground. JHC

qui nexibus ambit], and fix it on your sight that you may know it. I shall change myself to this, but shall be larger [*sed maior ero*] and shall seem as great as celestial bodies should be when they change.[286]

Thus, the god of healing, Asclepius, was envisioned as a serpent by the contemporaries of the Fourth Evangelist.

Originally at Epidaurus in southern Greece and then after he came to Rome in 291 BCE,[287] Asclepius became more and more a dominant god who was needed each day for health and healing. For example, one can think of the ancient retaining wall of Tiber Island. On it is etched the bust of Asclepius with a serpent on a staff.[288] Ancient Greek and Roman iconography and literature habitually portray Asclepius as a serpent.[289]

Tame snakes considered sacred were fed by devotees at the shrines of Asclepius. From Athens comes an inscription that dates from the time of the composition of the Fourth Gospel. Note the words of the inscription: "to Asclepius: the celestial serpent of the gods."[290] The adjective "celestial" is almost as important in the history of serpent iconography as "serpent."

Worship and veneration of Asclepius were widespread in antiquity, especially in the first century CE. The evidence indicates that by the first century CE this "demigod" evolved in Western consciousness from being considered a mortal to a half-god and finally to a full god, perhaps the supreme deity. Clearly, in some centers of Western culture Asclepius was the most revered of all gods. Asclepius was finally identified with Zeus, and this belief seems to have been widespread in antiquity. When one considers how the ancients desired good health and yearned for healing against all forms of rampant illness, it is easy to imagine the worldwide adoration of the god of healing.[291] His shrines and cult celebrations were prevalent in the Greek and Roman world, especially, as we mentioned briefly, in Athens,[292] Epidaurus,[293] Cos,[294] Pergamum,[295] and Rome.[296] Edelstein, in the magisterial volumes on Asclepius, gives us a hint of the veneration of Asclepius:

> Small wonder that the reverence paid him increased steadily, that his worship gradually spread over the entire ancient world, that he acquired a position of preeminence. Asclepius truly was a living deity, near to men's hearts. It was he who now gave shelter to the more ancient gods and supported their failing might; it was his festivals that were still celebrated when those of other deities began to be forgotten.[297]

It seems no exaggeration to think that in antiquity no god was more revered and had more devout followers than Asclepius.[298] That is important since the devotees in his cult elevated the positive meaning of the serpent.[299] The longevity of this cult is also noteworthy. It was influential from about the fifth century BCE to the middle of the fourth century CE.

The Fourth Evangelist lived in a cosmopolitan area and perhaps wrote in one of the major cities (conceivably originally in Jerusalem, and then edited in Ephesus or not far from Antioch). He and the members of the Johannine community may have been influenced by the depiction and adoration of Asclepius as a serpent. Since the Johannine community, while primarily Jewish, included Greeks (see Jn 12), one may ask: Were any members of the Johannine community converts from the Asclepian cult?

Is there any link between the use of "Savior" in the Fourth Gospel and the celebration of Asclepius as "Savior"? This name is frequently used for Asclepius,[300] and "Savior" (Σωτήρ) appears on numerous coins that would have been held by the contemporaries of the Fourth Evangelist.[301]

What then did the serpent and the staff symbolize in antiquity? In *De slangestaf van Asklepios als symbool van de Geneeskunde*, J. Schouten provides some thoughtful reflections. He understands the Asclepian symbolism of the serpent to denote the following:

> Originally it was an independent chthonical symbol of the ever renewing and indestructible life of the earth. As such it was also the symbol of deliverance from disease, in other words: a healing symbol. It should be noted that in the antique view of life it is by no means a symbol in our modern sense, but rather an expression of direct experience of reality. [p. 184]

It is this in-depth indwelling of our phenomenal world that is so essential in perceiving the meaning of serpent symbolism. The serpent is of the earth and crawls on the earth. The snake does not pound the earth as horses or as we do when walking. The snake also often darts into and out of the earth.

What then does the serpent staff symbolize?[302] Again, listen to the reflections of Schouten: "From times immemorial the staff has been the symbol of vegetative growth: it represented the everlasting life of the earth in all its aspects; it therefore symbolized recovery from disease, in other words: deliverance from death" (p. 184). The serpent entwined around the staff symbolized what the human most required: health, healing from sickness and injuries, and protection from death.

In antiquity, artists often showed Asclepius with a serpent around a staff and a dog nearby. About 350 BCE, a silver coin was minted at Epidaurus. It shows Asclepius with his right hand over a large serpent and a dog curled up under his throne.[303] A little earlier, an artist created a relief in Epidaurus that showed Asclepius with a dog between him and his two sons; quite surprisingly no serpent is depicted.[304] This iconography stems from the myth that Asclepius when a child was guarded by a dog and as a god was accompanied by a dog. In Greek mythology, the dog and the serpent were often conceived in similar ways; they both represented the underworld. A dog can represent a serpent.[305]

In an earlier chapter we saw a bronze of Hermes or Mercury. The caduceus was held in his left hand. At his feet sits a dog. Excavations at Jericho proved the supposition that the dog was the first animal to be domesticated. In Egypt, the god Anubis appears as a dog. We have seen that a dog was chosen symbolically to guard the portals of the next world, the afterlife; it is called Cerberus.

In the Bible, dogs appear in a negative light. As R. de Vaux stressed in his lectures on daily life during the monarchy, the dog was the garbage man in Jerusalem and elsewhere.[306] The hunter dogs so familiar in Egyptian scenes and Assyrian lore are singularly absent from the Bible. In the Old Testament we learn about pariah dogs.[307] In the New Testament, we hear Jesus warning about giving what is holy to dogs (Mt 7:6), and a woman telling Jesus that she is willing to lap up crumbs under the table like a dog (Mt 15:26–27). We also learn that Lazarus is visited by dogs (Lk 16:21), that Paul uses the dog negatively (Phil 3:20), and that the author of Revelation has dogs cast out of the blessed city (Rev 22:15).

Although in Arab countries today the dog is shunned as unclean because it is a scavenger, and although in Greek mythology the evil goddess Hecate is accompanied by fierce fighting dogs, the dog is almost always seen as a positive symbol in Greek and Roman mythology.[308] Not only Hermes and

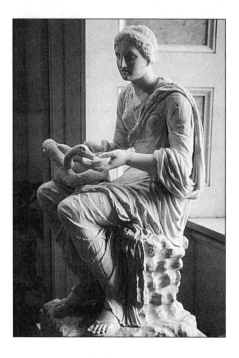

Figure 60. Hygieia. Greek or Early Roman Period. Courtesy of the Hermitage. JHC

Asclepius had companion dogs, but so did the saints, especially Hubert, Eustace, and Roch.[309] Perhaps the dog represented the faithful companion of the human (the *viator* on the eternal *via*).

Asclepius, the son of Apollo, was the quintessential patron of physicians. One of his devotees may have been Hippocrates, the father of modern medicine. Galen was devoted to him. The Hippocratic oath, now sworn to by modern physicians, at least in the West, used to begin as follows: "I swear by Apollo the healer, by Asklepios, by Hygieia, by Panakeia and by all the powers of healing, and call to witness all the gods and goddesses that I may keep his Oath and Promise to the best of my ability and judgement." [310]

Hygieia

Hygieia, the daughter[311] of Asclepius "who is worth as much as all" his other offspring,[312] is often depicted on coins feeding a serpent.[313] She is the goddess of health and hygiene.[314] It is from her name that the word "hygiene" derives. She is often depicted with a serpent eating from her hand or from a bowl that she is holding. This image appears in statues[315] and on coins celebrating her cult.[316] Some of these coins were minted at Tiberias during the time when Trajan was emperor (98–117 CE), at Neapolis (Shechem) during the reign of Antoninus Pius (137–61 CE), and at Aelia Capitolina in the third century CE.[317] Coiled serpents often appear on coins symbolizing the cult of Demeter and of Roman emperors.[318]

Hygieia is depicted in Fig. 60 with a large serpent eating out of a bowl in her hand (as is customary, it is her left hand). This sculpture is superior to the ones I examined in the Metropolitan, British Museum, and at Epidaurus and Athens. Notice the way the artist portrayed the serpent as friendly and attractive. This example in the Hermitage in St. Petersburg[319] dates from the end of the first century BCE.

A marvelously sculptured statue of Asclepius with Hygieia and a large serpent, winding up Asclepius' staff, across his lap, to eat from Hygieia's right hand, is preserved in the Vatican Museum.[320] It dates from the Imperial Empire. A similar one is to be found in Turin, in the Palazzo Reale.[321] It is also from the Imperial Empire. Whether in elegant works, such as the ones just mentioned, or crude etchings on stone, Hygieia almost always appears with a serpent. As *salus* ("health" in Latin) she is found in the famous Fontana di Trevi in Rome.

What is the meaning of this symbolism? Hygieia is not depicted erotically and the serpent does not have phallic features or functions. The serpent appears as gentle and affectionate;[322] and when resting on Hygieia's bosom it is below her breasts and not evoking any sexual overtones.[323] Her gaze is away from the serpent and often upward. Typically, as in the example preserved in the Hermitage, her gaze is pensive and directed to something far off. Her association with Asclepius and her portrayal in literature make it certain that the serpent with her depicts health, the return to health, and one of the main sources for healing. Thus, Hygieia is the goddess of health, and the serpent is her symbol. Because she is an incarnation of health and healing, so the serpent is a symbol of that incarnation. This insight is in line with, but also a significant development beyond, what we contemplated when working on serpent symbolism in ancient Palestine, especially with Jericho's "Elegant Bird Vase with Two Serpents" and the incense shrines at Beth Shan.

THE SIGNIFICANCE OF SNAKES IN THE CLASSICAL WORLD: GENERAL QUESTIONS AND CONSIDERATIONS

Snakes in the Greek and Roman Home

In many Greek homes, snakes were pets. This fact constitutes a category outside of ancient serpent iconography, but it is important for comprehending its setting. The snakes served to protect the house from vermin, rats, and other undesirable small animals.[324] In Roman society, the serpent sometimes represented the paterfamilias ("father of the family," or the head of the house).[325] Serpents are also associated with the tombs of one's parents. Indeed, in Virgil's *Aeneid* 5.83ff, it is a serpent who accepts

Figure 61. Greek Vase Detail. Courtesy of the Hermitage. JHC

the food Aeneas left at the grave of his father. Pliny in his *Natural History* stated that after the Asclepian cult was brought to Rome a snake was "commonly reared even in private houses [*in domibus*]." [326] The ancients played a came called *mehen*, which means "coiled one"; the roundel, or game board, is often carved with the face of a serpent that is coiled up. [327] The game boards have been found especially in Egypt, as early as the fourth millennium BCE, but also in Crete, many Aegean islands, Cyprus, Lebanon, and Syria.

What Is the Meaning of Serpent-drawn Chariots?

An ornate sarcophagus is on display in the Archaeological Museum in Basel, Switzerland. It depicts two large serpents in high relief and with wings pulling a chariot in which a woman is standing. The woman is identified with Medea. [328] This iconography is also found, and in stunning fashion, on the Medea sarcophagi on display in Berlin in the Pergamon Museum, [329] in the Museum in Ostia Antici, [330] and in the Thermen Museum in Rome. [331] It is obvious now why artists often placed depictions of serpents on sarcophagi, [332] but why would one depict serpents pulling chariots? Is this iconography not patently absurd?

The answer is "no"—or at least not for the ancients. In antiquity, others besides Medea were depicted with serpents drawing chariots. These include heroes, gods, and goddesses (but no heroines as far as I have been able to detect). [333] Medea's lover and husband who betrayed her, Jason, also is shown in a chariot that is pulled by two fierce serpents with beards or goatees. [334] Aphrodite often appears in a chariot pulled by powerful serpents. [335] Tellus (a divinity that represented the earth) is depicted in a char-

iot drawn by two serpents.[336] *Paidis iudicium* appears in a chariot pulled
by two serpents with beards or goatees.[337] Amor or Cupid is chiseled on
a sarcophagus; she is shown with two serpents pulling a chariot.[338] Pluto,
with Persephone, appears on two sarcophagi; he is in a chariot pulled by
two serpents.[339] Persephone is shown sitting in a chariot that is pulled by
serpents,[340] and once she is with a caduceus.[341] Ceres is shown with two
serpents drawing a chariot on numerous sarcophagi and on a plate.[342] Ian-
itor Orci appears in a scene with two angry serpents with wings; they are
pulling a chariot.[343] From the Eleusian cult we inherit a depiction of Triptolemus in a chariot being pulled on the Nile by two strong serpents.[344]

A unique example of iconography depicting a god being drawn by a
creature with serpent legs or feet has been found in southern Germany.
The god is none other than Jupiter. The iconography develops out of the
myth of the Giants. Jupiter is sometimes shown on his horse trampling a
Giant. In other stone sculptures Jupiter is depicted being pulled along by
a Giant. Sometimes a Giant elevates the horses of Jupiter with his hands
or his serpentine feet. On occasion, Jupiter's horses and chariot are swept
into the sky by the heads of the serpents.[345] The symbolic meaning of this
iconography is represented by the verbs "elevate" and "swept." The massive stone showing the serpent heads pushing upward on the lower chest of
the horses adds to the impression. Jupiter soars heavenward, employing the
mighty anguiepede Giants, and the power emanates from the serpents.

The same anguine symbolism is celebrated in the Orphic hymns. In particular, note the hymn to the Eleusinian Demeter. While Aphrodite's chariot is drawn by swans (55.20), the hymn to Demeter describes a chariot
drawn by serpents (or dragon-serpents): "You yoke your chariot to bridled
serpents" (40.14).

While the imagery of winged serpents drawing chariots is odd to us, it
was far from uncommon in antiquity, as we have already seen.[346] Herodotus influenced many Greeks and Romans in believing in the reality of such
mythology when he reported the existence of large serpents and serpents
with wings. He wrote that in the western sections of Libya are found monstrous serpents (οἱ ὄφιες οἱ ὑπερμεγάθεες [4.191]).[347] He reports to have
seen in Thebes "sacred serpents" (ἱροὶ ὄφιες). He proceeds to Buto and
then further deep into Arabia to learn about "winged serpents" (περὶ τῶν
πτερωτῶν ὀφίων). His belief in the existence of such creatures was bolstered by what he saw and heard: lots of dead bones and the claims of the
natives.[348] Herodotus also describes "small winged snakes of many colors" (ὄφιες ὑπόπτεροι, μικροὶ τὰ μεγάθεα) in the spice-bearing trees that
only in Arabia produce frankincense and myrrh and other precious spices
(*Hist.* 3.107). Herodotus also believes that vipers and winged serpents are
not plentiful because the female bites off the neck of the male during copu-

lation and then (as in retribution) the young eat their way through their mother's womb, killing her also (*Hist.* 3.109). Perhaps it was easier for the ancients to believe in flying serpents of great size because they, like us, have seen fish rise out of the sea and fly for something like a hundred yards. When scuba diving off the coast of southeast Florida, I remember seeing flying fish shoot out of the water and skim speedily ahead of the boat, about 1.5 meters above the surface.

Herodotus reports that the wings of these flying serpents are like bats', but they are not feathered. They are like water snakes (*Hist.* 2.76). There is no doubt that Herodotus thought that winged serpents could be found in Arabia, because in Book Three he makes the following comment: "The Arabian winged serpents [οἱ δὲ ὑπόπτεροι ὄφιες] do indeed seem to be many"; but whereas there are vipers (ἔχιδναι) in every land, these winged serpents are only in Arabia and are not to be found anywhere else on earth.[349]

Aelian also influenced the masses by his report that serpents did have wings. Like Herodotus, Aelian claims one has to go to Arabia, perhaps deep into the interior, to see the winged serpents. Note his words: "The Black Ibis does not permit the winged serpents [τοὺς πτερωτοὺς ὄφεις] from Arabia to cross into Egypt, but fights to protect the land it loves."[350] When much of our earth was unexplored, myth and legends helped to describe the animals and creatures that roamed the mysterious regions.

What could this anguine iconography symbolize and why are serpents pulling Medea's chariot and not horses (oxen or lions)? Is it mere ornamentation, or did the ancients believe there was truth in such mythological symbolism? If there is meaning to the symbols, is there a deeper meaning and, if so, what is it?

F. Cumont and A. D. Nock explored the meaning of symbolism on sarcophagi.[351] Both of them correctly pointed out, as the attentive reader already grasps, that we cannot answer this question with logic or our own modern presuppositions. Both scholars warned that images and symbols were, and can be, copied without attributing any meaning to them. But both experts chose, with variations of emphasis, to opt for meaning in the symbols.

Yet we must be wary of assuming all iconographic images are to be interpreted from the presupposition that the maker and buyer were both interested primarily, or only, in some deep symbolism. The fact of death, the loss of life, is commemorated in and on sarcophagi; that does not allow us to assume epitaphs must contain a deep allegorical or mythological meaning. The symbols on sarcophagi are silent, and epitaphs may be fundamentally silent philosophically and spiritually. It is we, the living, who bring voice and meaning to them. Hence, we must be careful that we do not attribute our own ideas, or own perceptions about antiquity, to silent monuments. On the one hand, we must be aware that no symbolic meaning may have been intended, and, on the other hand, we need to be sensitive to the possibility that metaphorical and allegorical meanings may be embodied in an image even if we do not seem aware of it at the outset.

It will not be easy to discern the meaning of the serpents pulling a chariot. More than one meaning could and probably was intended. The symbol most likely evoked a range of meanings. A symbol can indeed point to verbal meanings. Perhaps an example of ancient iconography cannot display meanings, but it may evoke reflections that stimulate them. Symbols may even help one endorse meanings and values, at least at times, by the reflective and educated observer. Since the winged and upright serpents are often on sarcophagi, they probably were intended to denote something positive, at least originally by the one who devised the imagery.

The wings would denote the power, otherworldliness, and elusiveness of serpents. Since they were attached to chariots depicted on sarcophagi, and with images of Medea and Persephone, it is apparent that life after death could be intended. Since Medea and Persephone were seeking to travel to a world unknown to humans and by a way unknown to us, a serpent seems the best guide. A serpent, the wisest of all creatures (including the human?), can move over the earth, through the water, and deep into the earth. With wings it can go everywhere an ancient could imagine a postmortem world could be located.

What did the ancient Greeks and Romans think about death? Was it the end of life? Was there life after death? The Greeks and Romans were not guided or limited by some form of orthodox revelation. Thus, the views of most were unsystematic and often contradictory. Some form of belief in existence after death was widely held.[352] The most ancient belief may be that the dead continued some form of existence in the tomb and still felt needs that the family could supply. In the *Odyssey,* Homer gave classic expression to the idea that the dead live together in some subterranean (not in a sphere separate from and beneath the earth) abode sometimes called Hades. The good and bad live the same shadowy existence. Another thought is also found in Homer and Hesiod; there is an Abode (or Isle) of the Blessed Ones. It is situated somewhere mysterious on the earth. For some, Pindar's *Olympian Odes* contain the thought[353]

> that immediately after death, on earth, it is the lawless spirits that suffer punishment . . . while the good, having the sun shining for evermore . . . receive the boon of a life of lightened toil . . . in the presence of the honoured gods, all who were wont to rejoice in keeping their oaths . . . in keeping their souls pure from all deeds of wrong, pass by the highway of Zeus unto the tower of Cronus, where the

ocean-breezes blow around the Islands of the Blest [μακάρων νᾶσος].
[*Olympian Odes* 57–71][354]

Benefiting from the insights of Homer and Hesiod, Pindar (518–438 BCE), whom L. R. Farnell called "the first great master of eschatological poetry,"[355] has given us a glimpse into what seems to be the Orphic theory of postmortem existence.

The Greeks and Romans also held many divergent ideas about postmortem existence. By at least the sixth century BCE, the Eleusinian Mysteries offered to its devotees a blessed, or at least happy, afterlife. Apparently similar ideas were advocated by many Pythagoreans.[356] The mysteries appealed to those who were seeking to experience the sacred, but they did not promise resurrection or even immortality.[357] The first to record the idea that souls after death entered something like a celestial home may have been Phocylides;[358] perhaps this is one of the reasons why we have the Jewish work in the Pseudepigrapha entitled *Pseudo-Phocylides*.

Plato never defined his concept of immortality, but he affirmed it and somehow connected it to his teaching that the advanced (gold) person receives good and is related to God. Aristotle and the Academy rejected this aspect of Platonism; they were skeptical about any form of postmortem existence. Epicurus flatly affirmed that the soul, like the body, is composed of "atoms" (indivisible particles) that dissipate at death. Some Stoics thought that the soul is immortal and partakes of the eternal Divine Fire; others advocated some survival, at least for the wise souls. The mysteries, like Cybele-Attis,[359] Demeter-Persephone, and Isis-Osiris,[360] promised some form of blessed immortal life for their initiates.[361]

Thus, we should avoid talking about a Greek or Roman belief in resurrection,[362] except for some of their gods like Persephone, Cybele, and Aphrodite, but even here I would caution that the term "resurrection" can be misleading, if not defined and carefully qualified. For many Greeks and Romans—like many Jews of that time—there was an afterlife, and another world. It was there that the soul would be taken. The chariot was the means of carrying the soul to its ultimate destination. The serpent—as the wisest creature in the universe—would know how to take the soul to its heavenly abode or postmortem existence. The serpents' wings would provide the means of transportation. Thus, these serpents could travel over land, sea, under the earth, and up into the air.

This interpretation of the sarcophagi depicting chariots drawn by winged serpents receives support from the Greek tragedians. The play *Medea* by Euripides (c. 485–406 BCE) has the sorceress and daughter of King Aeetes appear to Jason after killing her sons by him (lines 1317–22). She is depicted above the palace's roof in a chariot drawn by serpent-dragons; the text refers to her appearance in "such a chariot." She is on her way to Hera's mountain, to Erechtheus' land (*Medea* 1379–84).³⁶³ This episode follows a discovery by the Heroes on the ship *Argo;* they learned that the Golden Fleece was guarded by fire-breathing bulls and a never-sleeping serpent-dragon (the primordial guardian, as we have seen).

Our understanding of the symbology of winged serpents pulling a chariot is enhanced by the observation that they usually appear on sarcophagi. A passage in Ovid is also helpful. Stretching her arms to the stars, and then kneeling on the earth in prayer, she says to the moon (*Luna*), and perhaps also the Night (*Nox*), Earth (*Tellus*), and other celestial deities: "I have need of juices by which aid old age may be renewed and may turn back to the bloom of youth and regain its early years. And you will give them; for not in vain have the stars gleamed in reply, not in vain is my chariot [*currus*] at hand, drawn by winged dragon-serpents [*volucrum tractus cervice draconum*]." ³⁶⁴

The reference to the moon brings to mind the connection between serpent iconography and the moon. The moon, as well as the sun (as is well known), attracted the fascination of the ancients. The moon is conceived in terms of serpent imagery. According to Ennius' *Epicharmus*, as well as the report found in Varro, the moon is called "Proserpina" because it creeps "like a serpent [*serpens*]," moving intermittently to the left and then to the right, and so proceeding forward.³⁶⁵

Having recorded the words of Medea, quoted earlier, Ovid clarifies what happened: "There was the chariot, sent down from the sky. When she had mounted therein and stroked the bridled necks of the dragon-serpent team, shaking the light reins with her hands she was whirled aloft. She looked down on Thessalian Tempe lying below, and turned her dragon-serpents towards regions that she knew." ³⁶⁶

Earlier Ovid had described another dragon-serpent-drawn chariot. In this passage, Ceres, the goddess of fertility, yoked "her two serpents to her chariot [*angues curribus*], and soared into the air that is between heaven and earth [*et medium caeli terraeque*]." ³⁶⁷

As we have seen from the opening chapters, the serpent represented reincarnation. By shedding its skin, it died to live again in a new and stronger body. The scene of chariots drawn by serpents, therefore, might also denote the journey of the soul to another human body.

A search for meaning in anguine symbolism may be assisted by reflections on the second-century BCE funeral stele from Smyrna. Quite unusually, two scenes are depicted. The upper one shows the tearful exit of the departed. The lower scene portrays a woman feeding a serpent from a phial; the serpent is coiled around a tree, which recalls not only the traditions about the Hesperides but also those concerning Genesis 3.³⁶⁸ The lower image suggests the underworld and the chthonic nature of the serpent, since the serpent can burrow down into that region. The context, a funeral stele, indicates that there is some concern, perhaps hope, for some further life after death.

Even more meaning might be represented by the winged serpents pulling a chariot. It suffices for our present purposes to once again stress that the serpent had a positive meaning in the ancient world. It was clearly a polyvalent symbol.

Were Serpents the Quintessential Guardians?

Having discussed the Gorgons and Ladon and perceived how the guardians in Greco-Roman antiquity are almost always serpents, as is clear also in the *Hymn of the Pearl,* we come now to a famous passage in Ovid's *Metamorphoses.* According to the account, Cadmus sends his attendants out to seek a spring of fresh-running water *(vivis libandas fontibus undas)* for libation to Jove. They enter a primeval forest and a cave in which dwells a monstrous serpent sacred to Mars. When the "wayfarers of the Tyrian race" let down their vessels to obtain "fresh-running water," breaking the place's silence, the serpent springs forth. Thus, the "serpent [*serpens*] twines his scaly coils in rolling knots and with a spring curves himself into a huge bow." This account reminds us of Ouroboros, the serpent.

The attendants are all destroyed. The massive serpent, then, "lifted high by more than half his length into the unsubstantial air . . . looks down upon the whole world, as huge, could you see him all, as is that serpent in the sky that lies outstretched between twin bears [*geminas qui separat arctos*]."[369]

Meanwhile, Cadmus, "wondering what had delayed his companions," seeks them out and finds them all killed by the serpent. A ferocious battle ensues. Wounded by Cadmus' javelin, the serpent, coiled in huge spiral folds, "shoots up, straight and tall as a tree; now he moves on with huge rush, like a stream in flood, sweeping down with his breast the trees in his path." The serpent is eventually killed by Cadmus.[370]

The close relation between humans and animals is indicated by the metamorphoses of Cadmus. Later, overcome with age and despondency, he wonders if the serpent he had slain was a sacred serpent *(vipereos;* cf. *Metam.* 4.543). He then asks that if he had been a sacred serpent, the gods turn him into a serpent *(et ut serpens in longam).* He is then turned into a serpent with scales. Note the description: "He fell prone upon his belly, and his legs were gradually folded together into one and drawn out into a slender, pointed tail. His arms yet remained." He calls out in horror to his wife: "Touch me, take my hand, while I have a hand, while still the serpent [*anguis*] does not usurp me quite." His wife bewails: "Where are your feet?" Then, Cadmus, now a snake, curls up into his wife's naked breasts.[371] There is some sexual innuendo here.

Another account, again preserved by Ovid, presents us with an additional example of the motif and symbolism of the guarding serpent. In preparing a feast for Jupiter, Phoebus instructed a raven "to bring a little water from running springs" (*tenuem vivis fontibus adfer aquam* [*Fasti* 2.250]). On this journey, the raven sees a fig tree filled with fruit, but all of it was green. He waits until the fruit ripens and eats his fill. To cover his disobedience, the raven brings a long water snake *(longum . . . hydrum)* in his talons and tells Phoebus, "This snake caused my delay. He blocked the fresh-flowing water *(vivarum obsessor aquarum)*, and kept the spring from flowing and me from doing my duty" (*Fasti* 2.258–60).[372]

It is apparent that the guardian serpents should not be categorized as negative symbols. They provide protection. In his *Theogony*, Hesiod refers to a serpent that guards treasure (line 334: ὄφιν). In the *Hymn of the Pearl*, it is a serpent that guards the precious pearl. From Sparta comes a relief showing two women sitting in an elegant chair; behind them looms a large serpent with a goatee. The serpent seems to be guarding them.[373] I would agree with M. L. West's conclusion that in antiquity it is almost always a serpent that guards treasure, especially in mythology.[374]

What then is the symbolic meaning of the guardian serpent? Far too often it is taken as a negative symbol. The judgment lies in the eyes of the one looking at the serpent. If you are seeking water or some other thing guarded by a serpent, then the serpent would be an impediment and perhaps evil in your eyes. But, if you wanted something guarded, then the serpent is your best option. Note that, in particular, the serpent that Cadmus and his attendants met was sacred to Mars. Later, even Cadmus perceives, unfortunately too late for his fate, that the serpent was "sacred." The serpent that guards the treasure may be sacred and a symbol of what is good and sacred in the cosmos.

Cities did have serpent guardians. Guarding the city from plagues or enemies is one of the functions of the serpent on the Tiber island (Asclepius) and the serpent in Alexandria. Lanuvium, a city near Rome, was imagined to be protected by a serpent. Finally, serpents are depicted in murals at Pompeii as the protectors of the city.[375]

To What Extent Did Serpents Symbolize the Erotic?

The serpent is often employed to indicate or stress eroticism. The depictions of Leda with the swan have already been mentioned. I expected to find Satyrs with a phallus like a serpent. I did not. I did find Priapus depicted with a serpent for a lingam, with two serpents below him swaying to his music.[376] The Silenoi are shown with erect phalluses and kneeling by a tree. Two upraised serpents are portrayed behind them.[377]

It is obvious why too many specialists assume the serpent in antiquity denoted only, or primarily, the phallus and eroticism. They are too uncritically influenced by the psychoanalysts Freud and Jung. While these two geniuses made undeniably perspicacious insights into human psychology and behavior, they did not discover the universal key for discerning ancient symbols. It is impressive how many sophisticated books have been devoted to Greek symbolism from the vantage point of psychology.[378]

Attractive women depicted with serpents are understandably symbols of eroticism in our twentieth-century culture, but they may have had other meanings originally. Clearly, as we have seen, the bare-breasted serpent goddesses, or priestesses, in Minoan culture were not intended primarily to denote the erotic. Most interesting, along these lines of reflection, is the necklace on Simonetta Vespucci by Piero di Cosimo (1462–1521 CE). This famous portrait of 1480 contains an idealized image influenced by allegorical details and with a live serpent entwined around a gold necklace.

I am persuaded that Western culture seems in the post-Enlightenment Era to be especially interested in the serpent as a phallic symbol. For example, the erotic serpent is depicted in fantastic fashion by Franz von Stuck (1863–1928) in his *Die Sünde, um 1912* that is on display in Munich (Stuck-Jugendstil-Verein). It portrays a vamp, partly nude, with a beastly serpent curling around her right shoulder and above her right breast. Equally erotic is Gustav Klimt's (1862–1918) painting titled *Wasserschlangen II*. This picture about "water-serpents" depicts the figures of nude women flowing into serpentine shapes.

One point is necessary to emphasize. Too many specialists who have studied the symbol of the serpent in antiquity begin with the assumption that it is a phallic symbol. This is scarcely an adequate description of the vast amount of data assembled here and extant from antiquity. For example, Hygieia is depicted with Eros-Hypnos in iconography dating from the second century CE, and she has a serpent in her hand.[379] But Hygieia is not a symbol of ancient eroticism. She symbolized healing and health, and she appears in poses that are pensive and reflective, but by no means erotic.

Were the Etruscans Enamored of Serpent Symbolism?

Before leaving an analysis of Greek and Roman serpent iconography, it is imperative to scan the Etruscan evidence for the symbol of the serpent.

The most important examples of Etruscan serpent iconography are the following: a deity or demon, perhaps Gorgo, with anguine feet, is preserved on a Greek bronze krater from the sixth century BCE.[380] Also, protruding from under each arm is a serpent that is upraised and looking ahead. The krater was found in a grave in Vix in Châtillon-sur-Seine.[381] Part of a chariot trapping has been recovered from Castel San Mariano. It seems similar to the fourth-century Scythian gold image of a serpent goddess that was designed for a horse's brow shown earlier; this one appears to depict a large serpent over a woman between two lions that she holds by the throat.[382] The woman is probably Gorgo, the goddess of animals.[383] Quite interesting is the depiction of a sea demon with feet and legs in the form of serpents and with upraised heads with goatees. It was found in Conca (Satricum), near Rome. It dates from the fifth century BCE.[384]

How Did the Celts Employ Serpent Symbolism?

Similarly, the Celtic myths employed the imagery of the serpent to portray danger. Note the following lament by the famous bard Talyessin (Taliesin) who fears the invasion of Britain by the Anglo Saxons (my translation):[385]

Eine sich ringelnde Schlange	A once curled up serpent
Stolz und gnadenlos,	Haughty and merciless,
mit goldenen Schwingen,	With golden wings,
so koomt sie aus Deutschland.	Soars out of Germany.

The Celts took from Roman iconography the figure of Mercury. Several examples of Celtic images of Mercury with the caduceus are seen throughout the world,[386] especially in the Musée Archéologique in Strasbourg. They date from the second century BCE until the second century CE. In the example from the second century BCE, the two serpents are clearly etched with eyes; on the statue are the words: [M]ERCVR[VS].[387] A bronze Celtic Mercury was found in a cemetery at Tongeren in Belgium; the statuette has three phalli, one in the usual place, a second on the head, and one for the nose. These images stress "potent fertility and good-luck."[388] Such meanings would apply also when one saw Mercury with anguine iconography. In her *Dictionary of Celtic Myth and Legend,* Miranda Green rightly points out that the Celts endowed the serpent "with multifarious symbolism," notably, the underworld, water, regeneration, fertility, awe, and fear.[389]

In the fifth century BCE, Europe was torn by massive invasions. In that century, the Celts settled in Gaul, near the Rhine, and eventually reached Britain. This period provides us with one final example of the serpent (or dragon) as the source of misfortune and danger. When Julius Caesar invaded Britain, the ruling person was Cassibellawn. He had succeeded Lud (Lludd) who founded "London." This Lud lived when Britain was plagued by a shriek that occurred each evening in May. It caused men to lose their courage and strength, women their children, and young persons their minds. It is said that animals, trees, and earth were rendered barren. Lud's brother, Llevelys (the king of France), explained to him that the shriek was caused by the Red Dragon of Britain because it was being attacked by the White Dragon of the Saxons. Lud succeeds in subduing both dragons.[390]

Two bronze serpent-shaped clothing clasps, dating from circa 550 BCE, have been discovered. They belonged to the Celts, who left no written records, and were found in a grave unearthed southwest of Hohenasperb by Ludwigsburg. It was excavated in the 1970s.[391] The serpent-shaped clasps are, in fact, brooches that were found on the chest of a prince, or some distinguished person, who received a wagon-burial.[392] The gold serpent brooches were deliberately broken at the time of burial, which was a typical ritualistic custom in wagon-burials. The golden serpent brooches indicate the high status and social rank of the forty-year-old male who was buried. Serpents signified and symbolized the exceptional social rank of the deceased. Perhaps he was a "Great Man," in sociological terms, and one who through hero worship was deemed a demigod. Thus, serpents sometimes did not signify a religious meaning; they denoted the aristocratic status of a person.

What Other Ways Were Snakes Used Symbolically?

From the vicinity of, or perhaps in, Württemberg was unearthed the bronze attachment to a horse's bit; it dates from the pre- or early-Roman Period. The bit is shaped in the form of an Omega with two serpent heads.[393] It is interesting to compare this bit with the Etruscan and Scythian pieces already examined. Two bronze belts with three gold serpents, two still attached, have been recovered; they date from the first or second century CE.[394] Clothing clasps are made, sometimes ornately,[395] in the form of a serpent.

Sometimes two serpents, at each end of a coiled clasp, look in different directions, in a Janus-like pose; other times they face in the same direction.[396] On the right side of the majestic Roman grave monument of L. Poblicius, as one faces it, is a magnificent portrait of Pan. Behind him is a tree around which is wrapped a large serpent, in an iconographic motif virtually identical to that which symbolizes the tree and serpent in the Garden of Eden. The whole monument is impressively displayed to the public in the Römisch-Germanisches Museum in Cologne.[397]

As the toga signaled that the wearer was a Roman citizen, so costly and well-crafted jewelry signified that the bearer, usually a woman, was one of the elite and was to be accorded the requisite honor and respect. Our historical imaginations of what the Egyptians, Greeks, and Romans looked like, especially in public and in official dress, are guided by frescoes, sculptures, mummies, and written descriptions.[398]

Earlier we focused on the gold bracelets found in Pompeii and elsewhere; now we can explore how serpent iconography and symbology revealed one's high status. Elegant gold bracelets were discovered beside the skeleton of a woman who was felled by the volcanic eruption of Vesuvius in 79 CE. She was found with something cherished beside her: two intricately crafted gold bracelets; perhaps she had chosen these as prized possessions to take with her into the frightful and fateful night.[399] Each bracelet or armband ends with a serpent's mouth; it is uniquely open and the teeth are exposed. Each serpent's eye is also highlighted.

Most likely she customarily wore one of the gold serpents on each arm. They would have accorded her status. Perhaps the serpent jewelry would have been her only proof of status later, if she had succeeded in escaping the inferno. Serpent-shaped jewelry, especially a ring or a bracelet, was often worn by the upper classes in Greek and Roman times.

Silver serpent rings were also found in Pompeii dating from the early or middle decades of the first century CE.[400] A less elaborate serpent ring was found, for example, in Backworth in Northumberland, and refined serpent jewelry was found at Llandovery. All are from the Roman Period, and not far in date from the composition of the Gospel of John.[401]

The third-century CE Roman bath in Kreuznach contains a mosaic of the ocean. In it there is a large dragon-serpent. Serpents often appear in mosaics depicting the world of the gods.

Did Some Deities Lack Serpent Iconography?

Not all Greek, Roman, Etruscan, and Celtic gods are associated with the serpent or shown anatomically with serpent features. For example, I have failed to find a depiction of Venus with a serpent. Beginning with the end of the second century BCE, there were twelve gods in Rome.[402] According to a distich attributed to Ennius (second cent. BCE), they are the following: Juno, Vesta, Minerva, Ceres, Diana, Venus, Mars, Mercury, Jupiter, Neptune, Vulcan, and Apollo.[403] Many of these, but not all of them, as we have seen, were associated with serpents or were creatively portrayed in anguine form. For example, allegedly from the Diana Temple in Ephesus comes a bronze figure. Diana's deer is shown with a lamb about to suckle from her. Coiled around the neck of the sheep is a serpent with a triangular head (see Fig. 81).[404]

Again, while there is abundant evidence that the serpent symbolized something good in ancient culture, one needs to examine all the evidence and seek to be balanced. The serpent also represented a negative symbol. Aelian, for example, records the folklore that assumes a serpent originates from the spine of a wicked man when dead (*Nat. an.* I.51).[405]

Were Venomous Snakes Milked in Antiquity?

The information assembled draws attention to the suggestion by Farnell that the data frequently reveal "the bias of mystic symbolism towards theriomorphism"[406]—that is, becoming like a god. Since the god or goddess was conceived to be in the form of an animal, often a serpent, the votary, seeking to be one with the deity, either emotionally or entirely, sought to be one with the god imagined or experienced. As the god or goddess became a serpent, so the devotee became the god, or sought to become one with the god. As one became one with Bacchus by becoming intoxicated, so one became one with Asclepius by descending into the subterranean chambers in which live snakes would be "bosom companions."

Yet the search for the meaning and symbolism of the serpent in the first century is not yet complete. Were snakes milked in antiquity for their venom? And, if so, how was the venom used? Venomous snakes were indeed milked in antiquity, as they are today. The ancients obtained the serum necessary to heal various diseases and to provide an antidote to a venomous snake bite.

In *De natura animalium,* Aelian reports the legends about the so-called purple snake of India. It has no fangs, but can be deadly when it "vomits," even causing entire limbs to putrify (4.36). When the extract from such a snake is properly selected and prepared, it prolongs the lives of many for up to two years (4.36).[407]

Flavius Philostratus (c. 170–c. 248 CE) in his *Life of Apollonius,* which was composed about 220 CE, describes how physicians learned from Asclepius. This son of Apollo taught them to extract venom from serpents in order to cure many diseases. Note the following section:

> And who [he said] can deprive the art of divination of the credit for discovering serums which heal the bites of venomous creatures and in particular of using the venom itself as a cure for many diseases? For I do not think that humans without the assistance of prophetic wisdom would ever have ventured to mix with medicines that save life these most deadly venoms.[408]

This insightful account surely represents what many people, from the highly educated to the rustic peasant, believed and experienced during the first century CE. There is no reason to doubt that the members of the Johannine community knew about the use of venom to heal diseases. This insight adds another significant dimension to the mythology and ideology that surrounded the symbol of the serpent in antiquity. It is imperative that the exegesis of the New Testament be informed by such discoveries and insights.

SANCHUNIATHON: THE HOLIEST BEING IS THE SERPENT

Philo of Byblos, who wrote at the end of the first century or the beginning of the second century CE, claims to translate from a work by a certain Sanchuniathon. This author may have been a historical person or he may be only a creation of Philo of Byblos.[409] For us the issue is not relevant. What is important is his symbolism and his ideology. Philo of Byblos wrote a long work devoted to snakes or serpents.[410] It is a major source to study as we seek to comprehend the culture in which the symbolism of the Fourth Gospel was fashioned.[411] Reference is made to the "divine nature of the serpent and snakes; this animal is 'fiery and the most filled with breath of all crawling things.' The creature has matchless swiftness by means of its breath [*sic*]."[412] Note how important for an understanding of serpent symbolism the following excerpt from Philo of Byblos is (814.23–815.13):

> The nature there of the snake [τοῦ δράκοντος] and of serpents [τῶν ὄφεων], Taautos himself regarded as divine, and after him, again, the Phoenicians and Egyptians [did so]. For he presented the animal as that of all the reptiles which contained most spirit and as being [of the nature] of fire. Besides which he also attributes to it unsurpassable swiftness on account of the spirit, since it lacks feet and arms or any other limbs by means of which the other animals move. . . . And it is most long lived, for it not only sheds its old skin and becomes young but also it is increased [by the process] and becomes bigger. And when it has filled out the established measure [of age] it consumes itself, just as Taautos himself described in the sacred writings. Therefore, too, this animal is taken into the temples and mysteries. It has been discussed by us more fully in the treatise entitled Ethothion, in which it is established that the snake is immortal [ὅτι ἀθάνατον εἴη] and that it is resolved into itself as was said above. For the nature of this animal is such that it does not die unless it is struck by some violent force. The Phoenicians call it Agathos Daimon.[413]

These comments have been reserved until this point in the presentation of our discoveries. Many of our earlier insights and suggestions were judiciously informed and based on such clear insight into the complex meaning of ancient serpent symbolism. Here we have proof, in clear prose, that the snake contained the most spirit and fire of all reptiles, lacks feet (contrast some depictions of snakes with feet), lives the longest of all reptiles, and regains its youth each time it sheds its skin. In fact, the snake is immortal; it does not die unless it is hit the way Hercules pounded it.

Philo of Byblos continues by quoting Epeeis, who claims that the "first and holiest being is the serpent which has the form of a falcon and is very pleasing" (815.18).

SUMMARY

We have now been able to establish the first three criteria specified in the introductory chapters: (1) The serpent or snake is clearly often a good symbol in world cultures. (2) The serpent was admired in antiquity especially in Old Testament times and the Second Temple Period. (3) The serpent was appreciated in the Greek and Roman periods, especially before and during the time that the Fourth Gospel was composed and edited.

What is the most important or prevalent meaning of the serpent in the Greek and Roman periods? Any answer would depend on when and where one focused one's attention. Throughout "the known world" (and even elsewhere, in Mexico and South America, as well as among the Native Americans at that time, for example) the serpent frequently denoted health, healing, and the hope of a new and better life. The supreme example is in the pervasive Asclepian cult.

A thorough survey of serpent symbolism needs to move behind the symbolic and religious categories and seek to penetrate the world in which such symbols and religious motifs were given life. Perceiving how important religious symbolism was in antiquity, we need to grasp that the serpent was also a friend, like the dog in American homes today. As Pliny states in his *Natural History,* the Greeks and Romans often had serpents as household pets: "And a snake is commonly kept as a pet even in our homes." [414]

It has become clear that ophidian or anguine symbolism was prevalent in the ancient Greek and Roman world. These symbols were on statues and friezes in public buildings and temples and even in private homes. They circulated throughout the Levant and elsewhere and were often worn as jewelry. For example, in the fourth century BCE the two dominant armies and cultures were Persian and Greek, yet each stressed the symbolism of the serpent. Two silver bracelets have been recovered, but not published until now. [415] One is Persian and shows two serpents, with triangular heads, looking at each other at the point at which the circle would have been completed. Another silver bracelet is Greek. It is more delicate and refined, but again the circle is open so that two serpents, with protruding eyes, can look at each other. Both bracelets are from the fourth century BCE and before the defeat of the Persians by Alexander the Great, with the Persian one conceivably slightly earlier. As one studies the two bracelets with ophidian images, one is impressed at the common culture shared by Persians and Greeks.

The bracelet on the left in Fig. 62 is Greek; the one on the right is Per-

Figure 62. Two Silver Serpent Bracelets. JHC Collection

sian. Observe that in each ophidian object the eyes of the animal are highlighted. It is significant that two artists, one each from two warring cultures, chose the serpent for a symbol. Both pieces of jewelry indicate snakes or dragons at the end of each circle. What do the animals signify? We now know the serpents are not merely decorations. They may symbolize or evoke thoughts about Ouroboros, the caduceus, and perhaps something more.

The bronze ladle in Fig. 63 was found in the Levant.[416] It most likely dates from the early Roman Period. Numerous examples of this type of ladle are found in world-class museums. Large bowls of wine mixed with

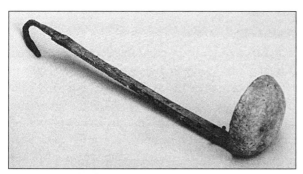

Figure 63. Bronze Ladle (and detail at left). Roman Period. Levant. JHC Collection

water were served by the host or an attractive slave. The ladle was used to convey the drinks to the guests. No ladle that I have seen has a serpent on the curved upper part. The animals on the handle are usually ducks or deer. The present example clearly shows a serpent. No ears are indicated, and the eyes and face are those we have already seen numerous times.

An approximation of what the symbol of the serpent might have denoted, at least to some ancient Greeks and Romans, and at least sometime during their lives, might be surmised by looking at the features given to the serpents in the virtual myriad of realia from antiquity. The wings denote the serpents' swiftness, mobility, and elusiveness. As W. Burkert claims, the serpents symbolize what is "ubiquitous and unassailable."[417] The serpent sometimes has a large mouth, pricking the fear of humans who in primordial times lived with the anguish that they might be swallowed whole (like Jonah) or devoured by a dragon-serpent beast. The goatee or beard probably denoted that the serpent was wise and cunning. The anguine-pedes of the Giants and other creatures denote their ability to be elusive as well as to skim over all surfaces, earth and water. Reflection on this symbolic meaning is enhanced by Cicero's remark in *De natura deorum*. He asserts that serpents born on land immediately take to the water, like sea turtles (2.124).[418]

Symbolism can be abused, especially when it is within the realm of religion or spirituality, as it was surely in the Hellenic and Hellenistic Period. There were charlatans who made a profit from the odd mixture of gods and serpents.

Alexander of Abonuteichos (fl. c. 150–70 CE) is little known, except in the emotionally distorting satire of Lucian. According to Lucian, he "became the most perfect rascal of all those who have been notorious far and wide for villainy."[419] Lucian thus names the arch villains, but each pales in comparison with Alexander. This false priest of Asclepius played on the fears of the masses. He manipulated their need to believe in myths. He provided what they wanted (but not what they needed). For a meager sum, Alexander purchased a serpent from Pella where there were many "immense serpents" (δράκοντας παμμεγέθεις) that were tame and gentle. He had a devious plan.

With another charlatan, Alexander would masquerade under the guise of representing the two great tyrants of humans: hope and fear. They founded "a prophetic shrine and oracle." They schemed to become prosperous and rich. In the temple of Apollo in Chalcedon they buried bronze tablets "which said that very soon Asclepius, with his father Apollo," would live in Abonuteichos. Before his companion died, perhaps from the bite of a viper, he and Alexander had constructed "a serpent's head of linen, which had something of a human look, was all painted up, and appeared very lifelike. It would open and close its mouth by means of horsehairs, and a forked black tongue like a snake's, also controlled by horsehairs, would dart out."

Subsequently, Alexander secretes a goose egg in which he had hidden a newly born snake in the foundation of a temple being built in expectation of the appearance of Asclepius and Apollo. Naturally, the next day he causes a disturbance and exposes the egg and the serpent. He then proclaims that he held Asclepius in his hand. He takes the god to his home, before the watchful eyes of the crowds. When, some days later, the crowds come to his home, he lets them see him sitting with the immense snake from Pella, hiding only the head. The head that the crowd saw was the one made of linen. The crowds believed in a miracle, since in so short a time a tiny serpent became an immense serpent "with a human face." Not only the ancients who read Lucian would have denounced the pseudo-prophet of Asclepius. Most would have known he was an imposter. Thus, they would have continued to honor, adore, and worship Asclepius and his "true prophets."

CONCLUSION

This survey has highlighted serpent symbolism in numerous cultures, from Minoan Crete to Asclepian Epidaurus. We have learned that the serpent appears to have been the most complex and pervasive symbol in antiquity. It not only denoted evil but also, and primarily, symbolized good. It dominated especially in the Asclepian cult.

When Christianity became the dominant political force, beginning in the early fourth century CE, it was empowered to relegate other religions. Then, many former positive symbols were demoted to a negative connotation and denotation.[420] Constantine the Great banned most magicians because "paganism" was still deep in his court and army. He thus forbade maleficent magic, but permitted medical and agricultural magic.[421] His edict against pagan sacrifice on 17 December 321 was a prolegomenon to the universally observed Theodosian Code of 438, which proscribed any sacrifices to pagan deities.[422]

Although, there were some intellectuals, like Porphyry (232/33–305 CE), who perceived the *daimones* to be evil,[423] "the demon" was usually considered good in Hellenic, Hellenistic, and Roman society. Socrates (469–399 BCE) claimed that a good "demon" played a major role in his life. He contended that the voice that had guided him since his youth was a divine demon (θεῖόν τι καὶ δαιμόνιον).[424] Plato, Xenophon, and Aristophanes attested that Socrates was under the power of "a demon"; that is, a good spirit. K. Kleve examines the evidence and concludes that Socrates thus should be seen not as an intellectual but a religious figure.[425]

Tertullian (c. 160–c. 240 CE), as a Christian, could abide by none of this. He thus declared that Socrates did have a demon, and that it was evil.[426] This kind of damnation is what one might expect when a religion moves from a Jewish, prophetic, charismatic Jesus, to a Carthaginian lawyer who has mastered every rhetorical device, castigates his adversaries relentlessly, and writes works that usually begin with the prefix "Anti." With Tertullian's lead, Christians "baptized" the demon as only "demonic." The sad and misrepresentative claim that only through Christ can one reach God, or know anything about God, so typical of Tertullian (*Cui deus cognitus sine Christo?* [*De Anima* I.4), has fortunately been left behind as archaic in modern missiology.

In Greek and Roman antiquity, Orpheus is often seen with harp and with all the animals, including the serpent.[427] When the Christians copied this image, they frequently omitted the serpent from the picture.[428] Likewise, the serpent became eventually portrayed as evil and as Satan, as we saw at the outset.

Before the birth of Christianity, the lion and the serpent both represented kingship, power, and divinity. After 325 CE the iconography was reinterpreted. The serpent denoted evil, and the lion was there to kill it. As E. R. Goodenough stated in his *Jewish Symbols in the Greco-Roman Period,* when a woman appears with a serpent or as a serpent on amulets,

> her association with a snake, or the fact that a snake can take her place altogether, indicates that the design may have represented, at least for some people, the warfare of spirit versus flesh, since for both Philo and many early Christians the snake of Eden, Eve, and woman in general, interchangeably symbolized sexual pleasure, and thereby fleshly pleasure par excellence. That the destruction of this, or victory over it, is the essence of salvation and the chief work of the Christian savior is an idea which, while not "official," was always, as it still is, widely current. From this point of view it is indifferent whether the cavalier, or St. George, kills a woman, a snake, or both.[429]

In summary, we have explored how ophidian or anguine symbolism was pervasive in the Greek and Roman world. The serpent as symbol was also widely appreciated in Persia, Egypt, and elsewhere. The serpent denoted not only evil and death but also, and more prevalently, good and life, as well as other positive meanings, especially, health, healing, and rejuvenation.

It is not easy to ascertain the various meanings of an ophidian or anguine symbol. We have acknowledged the need not to delimit the possible meanings of serpent symbolism and not to read our own concepts into it. A serpent might represent a threat or danger, but it also—more likely—denoted a goddess or some concept such as divinity, life, health, healing, beauty, and new life. The artist might have chosen one or several meanings. The one who purchased the symbol, or those who saw it, were free to add additional meanings to the iconography. The symbol might have meant at the same time something evil and something good. Serpent iconography, as indicated previously, often confronts us with a possible double entendre.

One final word needs to be said regarding serpent symbolism and ancient culture. By the time of Socrates, the masses yearned for any god; their need for a relationship with a god did not wane when the gods of Olympus failed to meet their needs. The one remaining god of influence was the one whom they had experienced and who provided health, healing, and a promise of a renewed life.[430] That god was Asclepius, who was symbolized with or as a serpent. Did not the intellectuals, even some skeptics, feel his gravitational pull? What about the great philosophers? Recall the last words of Socrates, as his body lost its warmth: "Crito, I owe a cock to Asclepius; will you remember to pay the debt?"[431]

5 The Full Spectrum of the Meaning of Serpent Symbolism in the Fertile Crescent

The study of the symbolic meaning of John 3:14—and other biblical texts with ophidian symbolism—benefits from reflections on serpent symbolism. This perspective must be extended to include all world cultures and encompass all images and texts from prehistoric times.[1] The preceding analysis proves that the snake, serpent, and dragon constitute one complex symbology that is a prevalent and pervasive theme. We have traced serpent symbolism from at least 40,000 BCE and in mythologies on all continents.[2]

Recently, carvings of snakes on rocks near Mitzpeh Ramon and the Adid mountain (or Karkom) in southern Israel have been found. They are clearly ancient works of art, maybe tens of thousands of years old, but the meaning of the serpent images is presently unknown.[3]

A fascination with the serpent is a common dimension of human consciousness and expression. This commonality is most likely not so much due to influences of one culture on another or to some unfathomed and primordial structuralism. It results from the shared commonality of all humans. Recently, a group of hikers in Zion National Park, Utah, confronted by a large and rather handsome rattlesnake, tended to concur with a timeless and boundless sentiment: "That is so cool! I've never seen one of these things outside a zoo before."[4]

We have seen the image of the serpent often mixed with human features or with those of other animals. Despite the claims of misinformed professors,[5] some snakes have legs, physically and iconographically (see Fig. 27). A serpent may be imagined with ears and a bird's beak.[6] The serpent appears as the tail of a dog or a lion, and as part of a lion or bull. The snake, realistically or with mythic features, also appears as a monster. Men and Giants are widely shown with anguipedes. An Egyptian god, Bes, appears ithyphallically; and the phallus is sometimes a snake. The serpent is up-raised to form the uraeus, shaped into a circle to make the Ouroboros, and depicted face-to-face with another snake to constitute the caduceus.[7] The serpent can become a staff, be part of a branch or a tree, or encircle a branch or a tree.

When did serpent images first appear in the Levant? Sha'ar Hagolan covers 30 hectares. It is thus the largest settlement in the Middle East in the Neolithic Period.[8] The eight-thousand-year-old site preserves the largest collection of prehistoric art in the world. Well-planned streets and large courtyard houses define the Yarmukian village; this is the beginning of settlement planning in the Holy Land.

The site is significant not only because of the impressive evidence of organized village life, but also for its abundant and arresting artwork. One building covers 400 square meters, and one exposed street is 3 meters wide. The Yarmukians apparently originated pottery in this area. More than three hundred art objects (usually anthropomorphic and zoological figurines) found at Sha'ar Hagolan reveal the importance of art, iconography, and symbolism when village life first began. Most of the objects are anthropomorphic and zoological, but not one serpent image has been discovered.

Quite different from Sha'ar Hagolan is Göbekli Tepe. This site in Upper Mesopotamia, now southeastern Turkey, is monumental but enigmatic. It also dates from the Neolithic Period and covers approximately 9 hectares with about 15 meters of deposit.[9] The site is not a city since no traces of daily life have been found. It is a central cultic settlement that is surrounded by small villages. No occupation has been found that postdates the Pre-Pottery Neolithic Period (it became an agricultural site from Roman to modern times). Why is this site important for us?[10]

One building, in Layer III, is labeled "the Snake Pillar House." Why? It is an enclosure (Enclosure A) that has snake reliefs on freestanding monolithic pillars. Another area of Layer III, discovered in 2002, boasts eleven pillars discovered in situ. Many reliefs depict animals, including lions, bulls, foxes, boars, cranes, quadruped reptiles, and snakes. Images of snakes were also found in the Crane Pillar Building. The archaeologists found a green stone plaquette in Layer I that derived from Layer III; it is decorated with images of an arrow, a bird perhaps, and a snake. It is clear that this Neolithic site was a cultic setting on a mountain (a high limestone ridge) in which serpents symbolized something positive, perhaps fertility, life, and divinity. The massive and numerous columns, which demanded expenditure of time and assets, signify that the serpents were chosen to symbolize what was needed when the ancients gathered there for exchanges of goods and words.

Caveat

One caveat seems necessary before proceeding further. It is imperative to continue seeking to observe a coherent and clear methodology. Similarities must be judged and differences observed. Lines that denote water or a mountain range can be wrongly interpreted to signify a snake, or they can be misinterpreted as only one of these, missing a possible double entendre. Serpentine appliqué on glass can be mere decoration and have nothing to do with serpents, or such appliqué may appear to constitute a rule that serpents never appear on glass—which is a widely held opinion that we have demonstrated is a fallacy (see Figs. 43 and 71). It is easy to confuse, as some great scholars have, the image of a snake coming out of the ground and wrapping itself around a goddess with the furls on the long garment of a human.[11]

One site must suffice now as an example. At Sha'ar Hagolan, just north of the River Yarmuk and west of the Jordan River, hundreds of art objects have been found, which is highly significant since this site bore witness to a major change in human history: after over two million years humans began to settle into villages and turn from hunting to agriculture. The anthropological and zoomorphic figures are highly symbolic, but other objects are probably not. The basalt stones with slits are not images of a female fertility goddess; they are for sharpening stones.[12] The basalt stones with images of numerous lines, sometimes crisscrossing in parallel lines, are designed for neither games nor a calendar;[13] they are probably designed to brand animals. While it is not always easy to separate realia into symbolic objects and practical tools, some images are symbolic. The cross, with both lines of equal length, is most likely carved to denote harmony, a central point, or some other symbol. It is clear that a line may be for utilitarian purposes or invested with some unknown deep symbolic meaning.[14]

Sometimes the study of symbology can lead to statements that seem absurd. For example, in *The Penguin Dictionary of Symbols*, J. Chevalier and A. Gheerbrant state under the entry "Serpent" the following: "Lines have neither beginning nor end and, once they come alive, they become capable of depicting whatever you like or of changing into any shape."[15] When focused on how pygmies depict snakes on the ground as a line, this statement has some stimulating meaning; taken literally, it is patently absurd. If lines had neither beginning nor end, we could never measure them, as we do constantly. Also, a line can never come alive; as a symbol it can take on life, provided that is what its creator intended or what a putative viewer might have perceived. Thus, the study of symbology must be grounded. The interpreter must strive to indwell the sphere of meaning in which an author created or crafted a meaningful symbol. Virtually none of the images studied so far and to be assessed now can be categorized as "art for art's sake" or "mere decoration." [16]

Dreams

As we seek to discern the origin and meaning of serpent symbolism, it is imperative to add to a study of the physiological characteristics of snakes the importance of serpents in human dreams. Human imagination and dreams help explain the often fantastic elements in ophidian iconography and symbology.

It is in dreams that many, perhaps most, of our symbols are fashioned. No one helped us to understand dreams as much as Carl Gustav Jung. In *Man and His Symbols,* which we cited at the beginning of this work, Jung rightly stressed that "the images and ideas" that appear in dreams "cannot possibly be explained solely in terms of memory" (p. 26). Jung correctly observed: "Elements often occur in a dream that are not individual and that cannot be derived from the dreamer's personal experience" (pp. 56–57). These archaic remnants, to use Jung's word, appear to be primordial and inherited by all humans, regardless of place or time.

I can agree with Jung that dreams, like the one by the eight-year-old,[17] which depict the primordial evilness of a serpent, are not easily attributable to memory.[18] I must beg to differ with him, however, when he explains them too cavalierly as "sudden pictorial 'revelations' from the unconscious," [19] which "cannot be derived from the dreamer's personal experience." [20] Are dreams nothing less than the "aboriginal, innate, and inherited shapes of the human mind"? [21]

Human Commonality

I am persuaded that the shared thread observable in so many different cultures is the result of the commonality of human experiences and reflections on serpents.[22] Culture may be ten thousand years old, but the human has been on this earth for over three million years. Much of our art and symbolism are shaped, in various ways, by these "earlier years."

In impressive prose, D. Newton explains how the human was once the insignificant one in creation. Indeed, there was a long period of time when "the puny population of the human race could have been trampled out of existence under the advance of a single great herd of bison or reindeer." The first humans, and most succeeding generations, knew "that the animals were stronger, fiercer, cleverer than themselves, and certainly more beautiful." We can recapture some of this perspective by studying ancient art. The human desired to acquire what the animals possessed. Depictions of animals sometimes represent them, but more often represent their attributes, qualities, or characteristics that were so lacking and desirable to humans.[23]

All peoples who have myths or theologies that feature the snake, serpent, or dragon live where venomous snakes are present (or imagined present), are prevalent, and mysteriously appear and disappear. Snakes bring fear and the threat of death. The snake is odd because of its habit of scurrying away from humans, while many animals are eventually drawn to humans.

For millennia, humans have observed that the snake has an odd means of moving and eating. It burrows into the earth, which was revered by the ancients not only as *magna mater* (the Great Mother who nourishes all life) but also as the realm of life, water, wisdom, and mystery.

The serpent is widely seen as representing a resurgence of life because it sheds its old skin. The shed skin may be all we see of the elusive creature that we know keeps on living, leaving the old skin behind and moving ahead with a younger and larger body. This feature of the snake evoked thoughts about immortality, a "fountain of youth," rejuvenation, and eventually resurrection.

This common element in human culture explains the prevalence and similarity of serpent symbolism in the earth's diverse cultures. We need no theories of some distant place of origin. J. Fergusson was misinformed when he claimed that the serpent cult originated in the lower Euphrates.[24]

G. E. Smith claimed that the serpent cult originated in Egypt around 800 BCE.[25] We know this is impossible for numerous reasons; only four now suffice.[26] First, the Minoan serpent goddesses (or priestesses)[27] date to about 1600 BCE, and the serpent cults at Beth Shan and Hazor,[28] and elsewhere, are also from the second millennium BCE.[29] Second, in his *Histoires de serpents dans l'Égypte ancienne et moderne,* L. Keimer wisely drew attention to a prehistoric pictograph from Aswan. On the left is a woman in adoration with her two hands raised; before her rises a cobra.[30] This may be the earliest depiction of the *Naja haje* as the divine uraeus. Third, serpent symbolism was highly developed in Assyrian thought and iconography. Fourth, the serpent is a symbol in many cultures, including among Aborigines in Australia and the prehistoric cave dwellers who experienced snakes, beginning after the Ice Age in which no reptile could exist.

The Language of Art and Symbolism

If under the influence of Aristotle we can speak about the essence of the serpent, then the symbol of the serpent does not reside in its physicality *(natura sua).* Serpent symbolism derives from what the human imaginatively adds to the concept of the animal: the form. The symbol of the serpent thus represents what cannot be reduced to the formal essence of a snake. The symbol and symbology are what the human perspective adds to nature, creating a meaningful world out of chaotic phenomenology.[31]

The Greeks did not pour time, thought, money, and effort into a sculpture of a god for merely aesthetic purposes (see Appendix II). Their artwork is a language that results from careful symbolic reflections. A moving work of art is full of symbolism. Without such symbolism, life is artless—it remains hollow or devoid of meaning. According to Eusebius' *Preparation for the Gospel,* Porphyry pointed out that the nature of Zeus cannot be represented because he is the whole world, "god of gods," and mind. What has the Greek thus represented in an image of Zeus? Note Eusebius' report:

> [The Greek] made the representation of Zeus in human form, because mind was that according to which he wrought, and by generative laws brought all things to completion; and he is seated, as indicating the steadfastness of his power: and his upper parts are bare, because he is manifested in the intellectual and the heavenly parts of the world; but his feet are clothed, because he is invisible in the things that lie hidden below. And he holds his sceptre in his left hand, because most close to that side of the body dwells the heart.[32]

Porphyry's insight into the symbology of Zeus is helpful when we see a sculpture of him seated in majesty, as in the monumental Zeus on public display in the Hermitage (see Fig. 57).

Hercules' labors defined superhuman efforts for all time: such actions were and are "Herculean." They were well known in antiquity, featured almost everywhere in song as well as bronze and marble statues. They were on public display. For example, in the Augustan-age Palaestra's large (35 meter) cross-shaped swimming pool at Herculaneum, there was a bronze image of a snake with five heads. It served as a fountain from which water gushed into the pool. The serpent is coiled around a tree. What is the meaning of this prominent symbol? It depicts the many-headed Hydra slain by Hercules.[33] Nearby frescoes of Hercules and a miniature altar that is dedicated to him provide further evidence of the legends from which the citizens of this city chose the name, Herculaneum.[34]

What is meant by the appearance of the serpent in so many tales of Hercules and his twelve labors? What could these symbolize? According to Eusebius, Porphyry explains that each of the twelve labors is "the symbol of the division of the signs of the zodiac in heaven." What then are the symbolic meanings of his club and lion's skin? Porphyry, through Eusebius, explains that Hercules is arrayed "with a club and a lion's skin" because the club is "an indication of his uneven motion," and the lion's skin is a "representation of his strength in 'Leo' the sign of the zodiac."[35]

What about Asclepius (or Aesculapius [the Latin] or Asklepios [the

Greek]) and ophidian symbolism? According to Eusebius, Porphyry offered the following explanation of Asclepian symbolism:

> Of the sun's healing power Asclepius is the symbol, and to him they have given the staff as a sign of the support and rest of the sick, and the serpent is wound round it, as significant of his preservation of body and soul: for the animal is most full of spirit, and shuffles off the weakness of the body. It seems also to have a great faculty for healing: for it found the remedy for giving clear sight, and is said in a legend to know a certain plant which restores life.[36]

Porphyry's comments surely represent more than his view of serpent iconography and symbology.[37] The image of the serpent is a language unto itself. It is now beyond doubt that the art of the Greeks—and the later Romans—is evocative and the artists' details often represent a world of symbolic thought.

Ophiology and Mythic Lore

Greek and Roman thinkers mixed keen observations with mythic lore, and they often showed ignorance of ophiology. In his study of animals *(De natura animalium)*, Claudius Aelianus (or Aelian, 165/70–230/35 CE) makes numerous rather absurd comments about snakes.[38] He gives some credence to the lore that the snake is born from "the putrefying marrow" in the spine of an evil person's corpse (I.51).

In his polemic against Celsus, Origen, citing a letter from Pliny the Elder, reported: "[A]t the present time a snake might be formed out of a dead man, growing, as the multitude affirm, out of the marrow of the back."[39] Such reports are invaluable insights into the folklore of the average person in the first century.

Aelian baldly states that snakes, when coupling, produce "a most offensive odor" (9.44). The keen sight of the snake is due to molting (9.16). Along with others who exaggerate the size and characteristics of snakes in India, Aelian, under the influence of Megasthenes, thinks that in India snakes (ὄφεις, *serpentes*) have wings (πτηνούς, *volucres;* 16.41; cf. 2.38). Aelian announces that the snake emits urine (οὖρον, *urinum*) that produces "a festering wound on any body on which it may happen to drop" (16.41). This comment is significant, since, as pointed out previously, snakes do not urinate. Aelian can be surprisingly misinformed, as when he claims that Egypt is "the moistest of all countries" (2.38).

Snakes are exceedingly fast. In fact, according to Aelian, one snake called Acontias (ἀκοντίας, *acontiae;* the Javelin-snake) can shoot forth as fast as a javelin (6.18).[40] The ability of snakes to rise up is exaggerated: they can "rise upright and stand upon the tip of their tail" (6.18).

Snakes can foretell the future (11.2). In Epidaurus and in a grove sacred to Apollo are snakes that are "the pets of the god" (11.2). In a sacred grove in Lavinium are snakes in a deep cavern (11.16). Blinded "holy maidens" can walk as if seeing due to the "divine inspiration" received from the snakes. The snakes can even determine "their impurity." Clearly, snakes are considered divine (11.17).

Aelian seems to accept a certain Alexander's report that snakes can grow to 40 cubits, and are sacred to Poseidon (17.1; cf. 17.1–4). While frequently warning of the dangerous bite of a snake, Aelian accepts Phylarchus' report that in Egypt asps (ἀσπίς, *aspides*) are "extremely gentle and tame." This mild behavior is because the asps are treated with such respect, being fed with the children, and creeping out of their lairs when called. How? They obey when one snaps one's fingers (17.5).

The following account helps us comprehend the context of ancient serpent symbolism, the penchant for depicting serpents upraised (as in Num 21 and Jn 3), and the seeming ubiquity of asps in Egypt, even in the bedroom:

> Then the Egyptians give them presents in the way of friendship, for when they have finished their meal they soak barley in wine and honey and place it on the table off which they happen to have dined. Then they snap their fingers and summon "the guests," so to call them. And the Asps as at a signal assemble, creeping out from different quarters, and as they encircle the table, while the rest of their coils remain on the floor, they rear their heads up [ἄρασαι δὲ τὴν κεφαλὴν, *caput allevantes*] and lick the food; gently and by degrees they take their fill of the barley and eat it up. And if some need causes the Egyptians to rise during the night, they again snap their fingers: this is a signal for the Asps to make way for them and to withdraw. . . . Accordingly the man who has got out of bed neither treads upon nor encounters any of them. [17.5]

I cannot imagine a clearer example that illustrates the vast differences between the ancient Egyptian culture and our own.[41] Perhaps this quotation signals why an appreciation of serpents and their symbology has eroded. The shift is paradigmatic.

Aelian serves as an example of the ancient and continuing ignorance of snakes. In the Babylonian Talmud we find additional examples. In *Avodah Zarah* (30b) we receive the misinformation that a snake (נחש) grows stronger as it ages, but in aging the venom loses its potency (זיהריה קליש). Of course, we should not expect the ancients to know about pure toxin, which was isolated for the first time in the 1960s, or comprehend that 0.3 micrograms of the neurotoxin from a *naja naja* is lethal.[42]

A brief summary of the common theme of the symbolic meaning of the serpent in world cultures follows. I have ordered the shared concepts and symbols according to their importance for a better understanding of ancient perceptions of the serpent and the relevance of such insight for an improved exegesis of biblical passages, especially John 3:14–15.

THE SYMBOL OF THE SERPENT IN ANCIENT NEAR EASTERN ICONOGRAPHY, ARCHAEOLOGY, AND MYTHOLOGY

Many biblical exegetes have assumed that the symbol of the serpent means something primarily evil. We have seen abundant reasons why this assumption is wrong. Learned experts in psychology have assumed that the serpent symbolically always denotes the phallus. We have perceived why this conclusion is invalid and misrepresentative. We have also observed how and why serpent symbology is fundamentally multivalent. It denotes and connotes a bewildering variety of concepts and ideas that we have organized into sixteen negative and twenty-nine positive typologies. It is understandable why M. Eliade opined that serpent symbolism is "confusing." [43]

Serpent imagery and symbology were used in antiquity to signify the triumphant power of a political regime. Two examples must suffice: First, with W. von Soden[44] and M. Görg,[45] K. Holter sees a hidden polemic against Solomon's foreign policy in the serpent imagery of Genesis 3. He claims more than Egypt is in view, since *nachash* in the Old Testament symbolizes Egypt as well as other nations. Because the Yahwist perceived Israel as a blessing for all nations (Gen 12:3: "and whoever curses you I will curse"), some scholars claim that this tradition preserves a critique of Solomon's alliances with other nations that had cursed Israel.[46] Second, H. P. Laubscher argues, persuasively, that the depictions of baby Hercules strangling the two snakes sent to him by the jealous Hera had political significance; it was used especially to legitimize the new power of the Ptolemies.[47]

As we continue, and try to summarize what has been learned, it is prudent to recognize that the study of snakes in ancient Palestine should not be guided by the presence of snakes in Israel or Palestine today.[48] Many species of Irano-Turanian origin have entered this area only in the past three hundred years, as F. S. Bodenheimer, a professor of zoology at the Hebrew University, stated in *Animal Life in Palestine* in 1935.[49] A large reticulated python *(python reticulatus)* can be seen at Hamat Gader and in the reptile "farm" on the way from Jerusalem to Eilat, but these were brought to the area for the purpose of entrapping tourists or so that people might see these large snakes.

Figure 64. Bronze Cobra Lamp. Herodian Period. Jerusalem. JHC Collection

In the following review, we shall try to avoid redundancy with the preceding pages by citing publications that have not yet been noted. The summaries will tend to move from the global meanings of serpent symbolism to the eastern Mediterranean world, and from prehistoric images and then from more modern perspectives, to the late first century CE; that is, our goal continues as it was from the outset: to seek a deeper meaning of John 3:14–15, wondering what this passage might have symbolized to its author and to its readers. The ordering of all the variegated data amassed so far is essential so that we might have a perspective on the meaning of ophidian and anguine iconography in the Levant by the end of the first century CE.[50] With this summary and a perception of a continuity or development in serpent symbolism,[51] we may then obtain a coherent perspective that will guide us in the interpretation of such crucial biblical passages as Genesis 3, Numbers 21, 2 Kings 18—and, of course John 3.[52] References will be made to the illustrations included; it will become clear that only seldom can we with confidence obtain negative denotations from serpent iconography. Those who created serpent images almost always worked with the understanding that they were making something helpful to them and their associates. By the first century CE, Jews realized the importance of art and ornamentation, as we know from archaeological discoveries in the Upper City of Jerusalem, Masada, and elsewhere. Assimilated Jews probably saw no problem with having a human statue in their homes.[53] In parentheses I have drawn the reader's attention to what was learned about the thirty-two virtually unique physical characteristics of a snake; thus, "cf. 2.1," e.g., means as follows: consult Chapter 2, the first characteristic of a snake.

NEGATIVE SYMBOLIC MEANING

Sixteen negative meanings of serpent symbolism may be discerned in the data already collected. Thus, we shall now discuss succinctly the following meanings:

Death-Giver	Friendless One
Destroyer (Impure One)	Battler (or Enemy)
Chaos and Darkness	God's Antagonist
Bearer of Corruptible Knowledge	Devil
Liar	Evil
Duality	Evil Eye
Self-made One	Fear
Tempter	Symbol of Corrupted Sex (the Phallus)

Death-Giver

The snake can administer almost instant death with only one bite (cf. 2.20), but the lion must maul its prey. The snake is forced to swallow another animal whole, and usually when it is still alive (cf. 2.9). Thus, the serpent symbolizes the Death-Giver. Examining serpent images from the Megalithic world of western Europe as well as southern Russia, J. Maringer concludes: "The serpent was closely related with the Goddess of Death." [54]

The usual nouns in Ugaritic for "snake" are *bathnu* and *nahshu;* [55] four Ugaritic texts are devoted to liturgies or incantations against venomous snakebites, indicating that venomous snakes terrorized horses and humans. [56] In medieval etchings and paintings, the snake is often shown with a skeleton, sometimes sliding down the Devil's throat. [57] It was common knowledge in antiquity, as today, that venomous serpents had the ability to cause death. It seems to be used by the author of Ecclesiastes to indicate that death will come to any who breaks the hedge, probably the boundaries of the Torah:

> He who digs a pit shall fall into it;
> And who breaks a hedge, a serpent [נחש] will bite him.
> [Eccl 10:8; [58] cf. Amos 5:19]

Much earlier, in an inscription of Sefire (southeast of Aleppo) that antedates the conquest of Arpad by Tiglath-pileser III, the king of Arpad will be cursed if he violates the treaty; among the animals that will devour Arpad is the snake. [59]

Many Hellenistic and early Roman literary accounts and artistic depictions celebrate Hercules, the son of Zeus and Alcmene, for successfully, as a baby, strangling the two serpents sent by Hera to kill him. [60] A real baby, perhaps a depiction of Caracalla or Marcus Aurelius' son, Annius Verus, shapes the body in a portrayal of Hercules as he strangles a snake; this sculpture is on display in the Capitoline Museum. [61] The boy with two large black snakes, with red mouths and white fangs, is graphically real in the mosaic in "the House of the Evil Eye" in Antioch. [62] The serpents sent to kill Hercules indicate that this animal is the quintessential Death-Giver (see Figs. 54 and 55).

The same iconography and symbology apply to the large serpents sent to kill Laocoon and his sons. Sometimes Laocoon's wife is depicted with upraised axe trying to slay the large and death-dealing snakes.[63] Artists who render Cleopatra's death almost always evoke the legend that the asp is the one who brought the kiss of death. According to the Jewish author who wrote the *Testament of Abraham* (shorter text; 14 and 17), Death is a being, and one of his heads is a snake.

According to the compiler of the *Lives of the Prophets*, Jeremiah prayed "and the asps left" the Egyptians. Moreover, "to this very day" (reports the author), God's faithful take the dust from the place where Jeremiah performed this miracle. Then these people remove the fear brought by snakes, since the dust heals "asps' bites."[64]

The author of the book of Revelation imagined that a large portion of humankind would be killed (9:20), and reported a vision of wild horses. The tails of these horses are "like serpents" (9:19). According to Jewish lore, when Hadrian inspected the corpse of Bar Kokhba he discovered his *petuma* (body or phallus) was encircled by a snake and was responsible for his death (*j. Ta'an* 4.69a). The author of the *Acts of Andrew* relates how a large snake (50 cubits long) threatens a family and kills a child, but Andrew slays the beast (cf. *AcJn* 69–77).

Aulus Cornelius Celsus (fl. 14–37 CE), famous for his book on medicine, offered cures for bites from various types of poisonous snakes.[65] His remedies for snakebite are scarcely insightful or efficacious. He tells the afflicted to apply a cup, plaster, or salt on the wound (5.27.1). Experience or practice *(usus)* reveals that when an asp strikes one *(quem aspis percussit)*, the victim should drink vinegar *(acetum;* 5.27.4). Elsewhere, Celsus instructs the victim to place goat's dung *(stercus caprinum)* over the bite *(super vulnus;* 5.27.8). I would rather follow his preceding advice and drink some wine.[66]

According to the author of the *Testament of Abraham,* Death shows Abraham "venomous wild beasts—asps and cobras and leopards and lions and lion cubs and bears and vipers." Then Death tells him: "and in a word I showed you the face of every wild beast." The reason these dangerous creatures were shown to Abraham is because many humans "being breathed on by venomous snakes—[dragons and asps and horned serpents and cobras] and vipers—depart life."[67] The serpent is the Death-Giver.

The Gemara in the Babylonian Talmud relates an incident that saved Rabbi Eleazar from danger and perhaps death. While Rabbi Eleazar was in a latrine, a nondescript Roman rudely pushed him aside. After Rabbi Eleazar left the latrine, a dragon-snake (דרקונא) killed the Roman (Berachot 62b). The snake also serves as the executioner, according to a saying attributed to Shimon ben Shetach in the Babylonian Talmud (b. Sanh. 37b). In early times, Jews were afraid of drinking water that may have been contaminated with the poison of a snake.[68] Why? They perceived the snake as the Death-Giver.

The depiction of Christ defeating the serpent signifies that the serpent is the agent of death (see Fig. 2). At the Last Judgment, Christ is holding the snake, and that might signify the judgment on the one who brought death. According to a Coptic amulet, Christ descended to earth on December 25 (Choiak) to pass "judgment on all the poisonous snakes."[69] That is, Christ brings death to the Death-Giver.

The snake as the Death-Giver is epitomized in Aesop's fable, "A Countryman and a Snake." The countryman found a snake under a hedge in a very cold winter. It was virtually frozen to death. The man picked it up and placed it on his warm chest. As soon as the snake revived, he bit and killed the man who had saved his life. The man's last words were a question: Is the "Venemous Ill Nature of thine" to be satisfied "with nothing less then [sic] the Ruine of thy Preserver?"[70]

According to the Gospel of Bartholomew, Death with his six sons comes to the tomb of Jesus. They appear in the form of serpents. Death asks Jesus: "Who are you?" Jesus, removing the napkin from his face, looks into the face of Death and laughs. The serpent gods flee.

The image of the snake as the Death-Giver appears throughout Western culture. In one of Shakespeare's most polished works, A Midsummer Night's Dream, Hermia elopes to marry Lysander. At one point she feels he is lost—even dead. With passion she hisses at Demetrius and accuses him of killing her lover:

> And hast thou kild him, sleeping? O braue tutch!
> Could not a worme, an Adder do so much?
> An Adder did it: For with doubler tongue
> Then thyne (thou serpent) neuer Adder stung.[71]

At this point, some readers may be satisfied that we have adequately summarized serpent symbolism. They knew all along that the snake is the one who causes death.[72] The snake is the bloodthirsty creature. After all, three hundred to four hundred snakebites are reported each year in modern Israel.[73] Such a conclusion is not only unthinkable in light of the insights obtained in the preceding pages, but it fails to perceive the true bloodthirsty creature on this planet.

The mosquito bites more than five hundred million people each year. This little monster, whose wings flap at the rate of six hundred times a minute, causes plagues, including yellow fever, which killed twenty thousand during the French attempt to dig the Panama Canal. It is well known for delivering the deadly malaria. This creature never—or barely—made it into the elite animal world of mythology. The lion devours the human (GosThom), the serpent is the venomous Devil, but the mosquito is unperceived to be the little vampire. It is actually more misperception than perception that categorizes the snake as the Death-Giver. Ophiologists agree that poisonous snakes are usually reclusive and reluctant to attack and bite someone; perhaps they conserve their venom for use in life-threatening circumstances or to obtain life-sustaining food.

One of the symbolic meanings of the serpent is the Death-Giver. Unfortunately, too many people today end with this mere beginning in the study of serpent symbolism.

Destroyer (Impure One)

The unparalleled ability of a snake to force its mouth open to five times its diameter and to swallow whole, and alive, a heavier (but not longer) animal elicited reflections on the serpent as the ideal symbol of the Destroyer (cf. 2.9). In Egyptian iconography the serpent god Apophis (Apep) is the "Destroyer." [74] Not many humans would relish the task of taking apart their own skeleton to eat; thus, the snake came to symbolize the Destroyer.

Today, especially in the desert and wilderness, Bedouin believe in demons called *jinn*. These beings can intermittently take human forms, but they are often perceived to be serpents with real bodies; they are not phantasms.[75] These *jinn* when disturbed will protect or avenge themselves. They can spew forth sickness and madness. According to many accounts, Muhammed ed-Dib, who found Qumran Cave I, fled, initially, when he heard the sound of his rock careening off ceramics; he feared that *jinn* inhabited the cave.

The one who expanded the sayings of the prophet Isaiah with 65:25 caught a vision of the future perfect time when no longer will there be a destroyer in Zion. The wolf will no longer kill the lamb: "They will feed together." The lion shall no more devour the ox; both "shall eat straw." But the author, knowing that God had ordered the serpent to eat dust (עפר) forever (Gen 3:14), could only foresee that "dust [עפר] shall be the serpent's food." Yet, God did not say the serpent must continue as the destroyer. He (or she) will henceforth eat only dust. Why? The answer is because no creature "shall hurt or destroy in all my holy mountain."

Some Jews may have eventually imagined that the serpent had not been eternally cursed. Perhaps some of the compilers or readers of *Perek Shirah* imagined the snake, along with other creatures, could quote Scripture and praise God: "The snake is saying: 'God supports all the fallen, and straightens all the bent' (Psalms 145:14)." [76]

The author of *3 Baruch*, in the Greek recension, records a tradition that depicts the serpent's belly as Hades. The Slavonic recension has these words: "As great as its [the serpent's] stomach, so great is Hades."[77] The author of 4 Maccabees called the serpent "the deceitful serpent" and "the destroyer" (18:8). Perhaps the bronze dragons from east of Jerusalem denoted or connoted the destroyer (Fig. 16).

Reviewing the portrayal of the serpent or snake as the destroyer reveals that this meaning is carried along with the opposite: the serpent as the protector. A good example is found in *Tanhuma*, which reached its present form after the compilation of the Babylonian Talmud in the sixth century:

> There is a story about a certain snake who came hissing from the field. He entered someone's house on the Sabbath eve at nightfall, and saw a bowl of crushed garlic placed on the table. He put his mouth over it to eat the garlic. After he had eaten it, he vomited it into [the bowl]. Then he covered the bowl just as it had been at first. Another house snake saw it. What did he do? He went and uncovered the bowl. When they found it uncovered, they emptied it out. Who caused this householder not to die? The snake who uncovered [the bowl].[78]

From this parable we learn either that some Jews had pet or household snakes or that Jews could relate positively to a story about house snakes.

As with Numbers 21, and in light of our comments earlier, the snake can represent opposites (the caduceus and the double entendre of serpent symbology).[79] As mentioned earlier, the caduceus was esteemed—and perhaps intermittently conceptualized—by first-century Palestinian Jews, since it appears on coins minted by Herod the Great (73–4 BCE [reign: 37–4]) in Jerusalem, Archelaus (4 BCE–6 CE), and Valerius Gratus (15–26 CE).[80]

As G. St. Clair points out, the "serpent bites, and the serpent heals. . . . People worship the serpent, or they worship Apollo for destroying it. It is the serpent who tempts Eve, yet Eve herself is the serpent." Is the final sentence an example of rhetorical language living on itself? St. Clair never again mentions Eve or substantiates his claim.[81] Yet there is linguistic evidence that suggests the author of Genesis 3, or some of his readers, thought of Eve as, or in light of, the snake, who may have been female (see Appendix I).

About 1600 BCE the Minoans created models and gems of women with snakes. We have already seen the early Roman depictions of Venus or Aphrodite with a serpent on her thigh (see Fig. 23). Not all images of women with snakes are positive. For example, in the Middle Ages women were imagined with serpents sucking their breasts. The *femme-aux-serpens* may denote lust or, more likely, as A. Luyster has suggested recently, bad mothers.[82] The author of the *Vision of St. Paul (Apocalypse of St. Paul)* envisioned in Hell the women who killed their infants and were bad mothers (cf. *ApVir* [Greek]). These were tortured by "dragons and fire and serpents and vipers."[83] The juxtaposition of images of these bad mothers in chiseled porches of churches opposite Mary, the perfect mother, supports Luyster's argument. It is further bolstered by the study of the *"virgin ecclesia"* contrasted on the opposite side of a church porch by the wayward *"female synagogue."*[84]

In Leviticus 11:29–38 numerous "creeping things" are judged to cause impurity. While none of the eighteen nouns for "snake" in the Hebrew Bible (Appendix I) appears in these verses, some snakes are included in the list of creeping things mentioned in verses 29–30. These "creeping things" bring danger and make one impure. Snakes are found in caves whose floors are piles of bat dung, and caves can be perceived as the entrance to the world beneath: Sheol and the abode of the dead. The snake frequents graves and tombs, bearing the pollution of death and danger. Thus, the snake can denote impurity.

Chaos and Darkness

The snake sometimes has a tail that is indistinguishable from its head; this characteristic suggests undifferentiated chaos (cf. 2.30). The snake's deafness (cf. 2.2) to God's creative word and its ability to scale barriers (cf. 2.16) helped stimulate perceptions, especially among Jews and Christians, that the serpent symbolized chaos.

In *Purity and Danger,* Mary Douglas rightly points out that negative valence is assigned to whatever animal escapes space or place.[85] The creature, par excellence, that is the great barrier breaker is the snake (as we indicated at the outset). Thus, the serpent, which disappears beneath the horizon of the water and below the earth (a chthonic creature), and leaves its skin behind, is dangerous because it seems to have no assigned place, as do, for example, dogs, horses, cattle, and sheep. The snake invades our dwellings and habitually comes through apertures we cannot use. The snake has the uncanny ability to slide over or around barriers and remain undetected. This habit helps explain why the serpent was chosen by many to symbolize monsters that represent or reflect chaos and the rebellious one in creation.

The Hittite text known in second-millennium Anatolia called "The Storm-God and the Serpent" relates how "the serpent smote the Storm-god."[86] The Ein Samiya cup depicts serpent monsters that seem to denote the chaos defeated by the gods or god at creation (see Fig. 19). The mythical monsters, the Tanninim, personify chaos in Isaiah and the Psalms (see Appendix I). Note, especially, Psalm 74:13 (14 in English):

> You divided the sea by your strength;
> You broke the heads of the dragons [תנינים] upon the water.

Note that the dragons may have more than one head (as in Ugaritic, Babylonian, Persian, and Greek mythology). The serpent symbolizes chaos in most world cultures and myths; he is Azĭ-Dahaka in Persia, Tiâmat and Labbu in Babylon, Apophis in Egypt, and the Python in Greece.[87]

The Old Testament Apocrypha contains an expansion of Daniel called *Bel and the Dragon*. In it, a large dragon-serpent is described; it is worshipped by the Babylonians. Daniel feeds it its final meal: a mixture of pitch, fat, and hair. The idolatrous dragon-serpent devours the meal and bursts asunder. Such rhetoric is polemical and reduces an enemy's religiosity to falsehood; far too many scholars are thereby misled to imagine that serpents are demonic.[88]

In *From Chaos to Enemy: Encounters with Monsters in Early Irish Texts*, J. Borsje discussed the serpent monsters that are prevalent in early Ireland.[89] The serpent monsters include Apophis, Behemoth, Cerberus, and Leviathan.[90]

In a Ugaritic text, Baal claims to have "crushed Tannin," and "shattered the wounded snake," which had "seven heads."[91] The text is reminiscent of Isaiah 27:1 in which "the twisted serpent" appears as a monster of chaos.

In 1817, chaos was created by the alleged sightings of a sea-dragon. General David Humphreys, formerly on George Washington's staff, interviewed "eyewitnesses" who believed it was over 18 meters long. A research committee claimed to have discovered evidence of a new genus dubbed *Scoliophis Atlanticus*. In the South, William Crafts, a Charleston playwright, composed a play that lampooned the monster; the play was entitled *The Sea Serpent; or, Gloucester Hoax: A Dramatic Jeu d'Esprit in Three Acts*.[92] Accounts of seeing a sea serpent appear intermittently in the United States, beginning in 1641 and continuing until the present.[93] The monster symbolizes great confusion (which to the ancients meant chaos).

From the third century BCE until the second century CE, the Jewish apocalyptists talk about the order of creation. One repetitive note in their symphony of perceptions is that all that is created runs according to its assigned task. The lone exception is the moon, which, failing to rule only the night because it wanders into the light of day, periodically suffers by losing some of its light and wanes each month. The authors of the Jewish apocryphal works never could describe the snake as one who follows the order of creation; it was sometimes a symbol of chaos.[94]

As one might imagine, the image of a snake that is so closely linked with chaos serves as a symbol of darkness. The snake can burrow deep into the earth or delve into the depths of the sea—each of these, in contrast to the heavens, is perceived as the realm of darkness. The snake is the only animal damned to eat dust (perhaps a symbol of chaos and darkness). As

Figure 65. Bronze Stamp, a Serpent with Bifid Tongue. Jerusalem. JHC Collection

J. Chevalier and A. Gheerbrant state in *The Penguin Dictionary of Symbols*: "Throughout the world . . . [the] great god of darkness . . . is a serpent."[95]

A good example of the serpent as a symbol of darkness is found in Egypt, after the Eighteenth Dynasty. The god Horus is portrayed as an eagle, representing good and light, and is set over temples. He has defeated Set, the monster who symbolizes evil and darkness—and who is represented by a snake (often as two uraei).[96] We shall see that the uraeus symbolized not only evil and darkness but also power, royalty, life, and divinity—especially on the crowns of the pharaohs.

Bearer of Corruptible Knowledge

The snake's bifid tongue (cf. 2.8)[97] and deafness (cf. 2.2) lie behind the serpent's ability to symbolize the one who brings corruptible knowledge. Since it represents duplicity and cannot hear the Word, it symbolizes corruptible knowledge. Many Ugaritic incantation texts mention serpents, and even sorcerers being attacked by them.[98] In the Garden of Eden, the serpent was depicted as intelligent and clever; he (or she) could talk with the woman. The serpent was not a liar; he (or she) did point the way to knowledge, but it was a knowledge that ultimately separated the created from the Creator. What the human pair received was not wisdom; it was corruptible knowledge.

A Baraita preserved in the Babylonian Talmud (*b. B. Bat.* 17a) warns of the evil knowledge one can derive from a snake. According to this text, Rabbis taught that four people died "because of the counsel (or advice) of the serpent" (בעטיושל נחש).

Ignorant of ophiology and eager to stress that the snake is the bearer of damnable knowledge, the fifth-century Spanish poet Prudentius claimed that the female snake was impregnated by "oral union." This culminated with her devouring her "lover." Proceeding uninformed about biology, Prudentius claims that human sin is like the offspring of a viper:

> For because there is no passage to give them birth, the belly is tortured and gnawed by the young as they struggle into light, till a way is opened through the torn sides . . . and the young creep about licking the corpse that bore them, a family of orphans at their very birth. [*The Origin of Sin*, 584–608][99]

Intent on explaining the origin of sin, Prudentius reveals the hatred and ignorance he has of vipers that, he assumes, transmit knowledge to humans that damns them.

Liar

The bifid tongue of the snake symbolized duplicity, and thus lying (cf. 2.8). Many early Jewish texts interpret Genesis 3 so that the serpent is the liar and the source of lies. Paul interprets Genesis 3 by placing the blame on the serpent's lying: "The serpent [ὁ ὄφις] deceived [ἐξηπάτησεν] Eve by his cunning [ἐν τῇ πανουργίᾳ αὐτοῦ]" (2 Cor 11:3). Thus, Paul perceived the serpent to be the Deceiver or Liar. The same interpretation of serpent symbolism was expressed in the early first century CE by Philo of Alexandria. He claimed that the serpent "deceives by trickery and artfulness." [100] Sometime before 70 CE, the author of 4 Maccabees called the serpent "deceitful" (18:8). One can readily understand why many scholars, especially E. Williams-Forte, are convinced that in Genesis 3 the serpent symbolizes evil and cunning, and that the serpent is primarily the Deceiver or Liar.[101]

Geryon, the Monster of Falsehood, is imagined to resemble a serpent. His face may be that of a pious man, his feet those of a bear, but his body is a serpent with a long poisonous tail. Virgil spoke of him. Dante put him in the eighth circle of Hell. This scene appears in vivid colors in a fifteenth-century manuscript preserved in the Biblioteca Nazionale Marciana in Venice (Cod. It. IX, 276 [= 6902]).[102]

Often the symbol of the serpent as the "Liar" appears when one castigates an adversary. A good example is found in *The Genuine Acts of Peter*. The author labels Arius a snake. Note this excerpt: "Nearly about the same time Arius, armed with a viper's craft, as if deserting the party of Meletius, fled for refuge to Peter, who at the request of the bishops raised him to the honours of the diaconate, being ignorant of his exceeding hypocrisy. For he was even as a snake suffused with deadly poison." [103]

In *To the Bishops of Egypt*, Athanasius also likened the teaching of Arius and those with him to the poison of a snake. He urged the bishops in Egypt to "condemn them as hypocrites, who hide the poison of their opinions, and like the serpent flatter with the words of their lips. For, though they thus write, they have associated with them those who were formerly rejected with Arius, such as Secundus of Pentapolis, and the clergy who were convicted at Alexandria." [104]

Much earlier, but sometime after 135/36 CE, the author of the *Apocalypse of Elijah* records a tradition that "the son of lawlessness . . . will perish like a serpent which has no breath in it." [105] In both Judaism and Christianity, the tradition that the serpent denotes lying escalates after the time of Bar Kokhba (132–35/36). One example must suffice. A sage teaching is recorded in a Baraita in the Babylonian Talmud: "They said to him, 'It is not possible for a man to dwell (safely) with a snake (נחש) in a basket' " (*Ketubot* 72a). This use of serpent symbolism was directed against a woman who habitually breaks her marriage vows. The meaning is not in doubt; a man who continues to live with a wife (like that) is like a snake. It cannot be trusted with true behavior, since it will eventually bite and kill.[106] The Arabic saying "The serpent does not bring forth [anything] except a little serpent" is used to denote someone who purveys mischievous or malignant information.[107] In his *Finitude et culpabilité: Le symbolique du mal*, Paul Ricoeur explains why the serpent is the symbol of lying and distortion.[108]

Duality

The two penises (hemipenes; cf. 2.7) and the bifid tongue (cf. 2.8) helped the snake to symbolize duality. This concept is reflected in the caduceus (two serpents facing each other, sometimes in opposite ways). We have seen the amazing ability of the serpent to symbolize two things at once (cf. the discussion of double entendre in Chap. 2). In Euripides' *Ion*, two drops of the Gorgon's blood—equal to the viper's poison—can either bring death (θανάσιμον) or heal sicknesses (νόσων).[109] The snake in *The Shipwrecked Sailor* is, on the one hand, frightening; but, on the other hand, it is kind.[110]

Duality, not dualism, can be a negative concept, as in the duplicity or the uncanny ability of politicians to be like a snake. When one labels politicians snakes, one means that such persons are guilty of duplicity. They have been speaking words that appease or mollify a constituent; they have not been seeking to report objectively and with integrity the true situation or possibilities.[111] In antiquity and modernity, the serpent symbolized such duplicity.

Self-made One

The deafness (cf. 2.2) and social independence of the snake (cf. 2.8 and 2.32) helped placard the serpent as the self-made one. The evil serpent

cannot hear God because it can only detect earthborne low-frequency vibrations, and so will not (and cannot) acknowledge that it was created by
God. Its rebellion alters its memory, at least from the perspective of the
biblical writers. The classic passage in which the serpent is depicted as the
self-made one is Ezekiel 29:3,

> Thus declares the Lord God:
> "Behold, I am against you,
> O Pharaoh, king of Egypt,
> O great dragon [התנים] who dwells in the midst of his rivers,[112]
> Who has said, 'My river is my own;
> And I made [it] for myself.' "

We should expect reference to the serpent within the Hebrew Bible, since
the uraeus of Pharaoh's sun casts shadows on it and within it.[113]

Tempter

The snake's bifid tongue helped make the serpent the symbol of the tempter
(cf. 2.8). In the Garden of Eden the serpent tempts the woman to disobey
God. The author of *Pseudo-Philo,* in a review of the Fall, stated that the
serpent "deceived" the first man's wife (13:8). According to the author of
Jubilees 3:23, God cursed the serpent and remained forever angry with
the creature. In the Middle Ages, and especially in art beginning in many
circles in the late nineteenth century, the snake is the tempter. Often it is
shown with the dark, bewitching temptress.

Friendless One

The social independence of the snake (cf. 2.11), its inability to wink, laugh,
or talk (cf. 2.23), and above all its antisocial nature (cf. 2.32) helped make
it a symbol of the Friendless One. The snake does not seem capable of
any type of affection, not even paternal love. The parents abandon their
offspring. Some ophiologists claim that the Eastern Diamondback Rattlesnake stays with its hatch to protect and mother the offspring. I would
think that perhaps she remains with her hatch because she is too ex-
hausted to move, after suffering through nine hours of labor. Since the
mother snake shows no affection for her young (as do most animals), she
seems unfriendly to them, and is perhaps the most unmotherly of creatures.

The Cincinnati Art Museum has a nude figure of a man with two fish
hanging from a neck ring that fits below his beard. His arms are bound by
four snakes that come from behind him. Two snakes curl to face his beard,
and the heads of two more appear above his waist. A. Perrot was convinced
that the piece was genuine and stolen from the excavations at Tello.[114] The

meaning of this image is far from clear, but since the man is bound by the serpents, they may symbolize the animal that is unfriendly.[115]

According to Japanese myths, the wild god, Susanoh, was exiled from heaven. On "Izumo" he learned that every year a serpent with eight heads devoured a girl from the village. Surely, many Japanese imagined the serpent as even worse than the Friendless One.

According to Josephus, the serpent in the Garden of Eden showed "an envious disposition" and a "malicious intention." God thus deprived him of speech and made him an enemy to humans (*Ant.* 1.1.4). Josephus thinks that the serpent has a cruel mind (*Ant.* 17.5.5). Most of the rabbinic references to the serpent are negative; for example: "No one can live with a serpent in the same basket" (*m. Ketubot* 72a). As we saw when reviewing the physiological characteristics of a snake, the snake cannot become a friend of the human; there is no possibility of developing a trustworthy relationship, as humans habitually do with dogs, horses, and some cats.

The snake as the Friendless One is adumbrated in God's cursing the serpent at the end of Genesis 3. It is found in Aesop's fable of "A Countryman and a Snake":

> There was a *Snake* that Bedded himself under the Threshold of a Country-House: A *Child* of the Family happen'd to set his Foot upon't; The *Snake* bit him, and he Dy'd on't. The *Father* of the *Child* made a Blow at the *Snake*, but Miss'd his Aim, and only left a Mark behind him upon the Stone where he Struck. The *Countryman* Offer'd the *Snake*, some time after *This*, to be Friends again. No, says the *Snake*, so long as you have this Flaw upon the Stone in Your Eye, and the Death of the *Child* in your Thought, there's No Trusting of ye.[116]

The serpent as the Friendless One often appears in the other fifteen negative symbolic meanings of ophidian iconography and symbology.

Battler (or Enemy)

The snake has horrifyingly deadly venom (cf. 2.20). Its ability to conquer larger foes is evident (cf. 2.9)—a king cobra can kill a large elephant with one bite. These facts lie behind the serpent as symbolizing the Battler or Enemy.

In the Akkadian *Enuma Elish,* we learn about the serpent as the great warrior or battler at creation.[117] Gods are depicted slaying serpent-dragons (Fig. 8). God's malediction to the snake in the Garden of Eden, which was never rescinded, proclaims the snake in many Jewish and Christian symbols and texts as "l'ennemi insidieux et irréconciliable." [118] The *Hymn of the Pearl,* written sometime between the second and fourth centuries CE, describes the search of a young man for the priceless pearl. The youth discovers that the pearl is in the depths of the sea surrounded by a serpent; he must battle against this opponent.

A vast amount of art as well as serpent iconography depicts Michael slaying the dragon, the one whom the gods and angels must confront in battle. Amulets and texts are extant in which one calls on God for protection against enemies, like the snake.[119] Coptic and Arabic art abound with illustrations of the serpent as the symbol of hostile power.[120] Constantine developed the symbol of the serpent so that he, the Emperor, would be seen as the one who had slain the dragon or serpent with the lance (Labarum).[121] Medals were circulated to announce the new symbolic meaning of the serpent, and Eusebius heralded the proclamation in his Vita Constantin 3.3. A considerable amount of early Christian art depicts the serpent or dragon as the enemy defeated by Christ; sometimes the snake appears at the foot of the cross.[122]

God's Antagonist

The deafness of the snake (cf. 2.2) helped make it a symbol of one who could not hear God's word and was thus rebellious and disobedient to God. Succinctly put, the serpent was God's antagonist. Although powerful now in this age, it will be judged in the coming age. Many murals in churches feature this judgment, including the modern mural in the monastery of the Greek Orthodox Church in Capernaum.

The leading word for "snake" in Assyrian is $ṣēru$[123] or $ṣerru(m)$,[124] which is very similar, and perhaps cognate, to $ṣerru$. The latter noun denotes not only a door-pivot that is an entryway for "demons," but also "enemy" or "adversary." The worship of the serpent was an aspect of the Canaanite cult at Timnaʿ (Fig. 22), Beth Shan, Hazor (Fig. 21), and elsewhere (Figs. 29–33). While the snake often denoted to the Israelites, in contrast, the antagonist of God, it is clear that at biblical Dan the snake house, which was probably modeled after a temple, and the three pithoi (large vessels) with serpent decorations from the time of Jeroboam I, found only in the sanctuary area, indicate the importance of snakes to the cult at Dan.[125]

In Euripides' Ion, the son of Zeus, during the gigantomachia (battle of the gods with the Giants), slays Zeus' adversary. The latter is the snake of Lerna (Λερναῖον ὕδραν).[126] According to Pseudo-Apollodorus' Library, Periclymenus turned himself into various forms, including a snake (ὄφις), but he was eventually slain by Hercules (I.9.9).[127]

Recognizing that Canaan provided much of the iconography and symbology for ancient Israel, F. Hvidberg concluded that, according to Genesis 3, the serpent brought death and not life. He was the deceiver who is not synonymous with Satan but with Baal, Yahweh's old adversary.[128]

Devil

The snake is perceived to be slimy. He is not warm and fluffy like a puppy (cf. 2.25); thus, the apparently disgusting feel and behavior of the serpent (e.g., swallowing another animal whole and sometimes while it is still alive) caused the creature to become a symbol of the Devil. The snake's elusiveness (cf. 2.6), deafness (cf. 2.2), and fearlessness (cf. 2.15), as well as its cold-bloodedness (cf. 2.12), made him an ideal symbol for the Devil, Satan.[129]

In Second Temple Judaism, the serpent is most often identified with the Devil or equated with the Devil, Satan. In the first-century CE *Lives of the Prophets,* Habakkuk is reputed to have forewarned the faithful that they will be pursued "by the serpent in darkness as from the beginning."[130] Sometime at the end of the first century CE, the author of the *Vita Adae et Evae* presented an expansion or Midrash on Genesis. In his retelling the story of the Fall, the serpent is replaced by the Devil, the adversary. Hear the words placed in the mouth of Adam: "The Lord God appointed two angels to guard us. The hour came when the angels ascended to worship in the presence of God. Immediately the adversary, the devil, found opportunity while the angels were away and deceived your mother so that she ate of the illicit and forbidden tree. And she ate and gave to me."[131]

In the Greek recension of this Pseudepigraphon, the serpent is not the Devil. They become one in the dastardly act of Genesis 3. Note the following excerpt:

> And the devil spoke to the serpent, saying "Rise and come to me, and I will tell you something to your advantage." Then the serpent came to him, and the devil said to him, "I hear that you are wiser than all the beasts; so I came to observe you. I found you greater than all the beasts, and they associate with you; but you are prostrate to the very least. Why do you eat of the weeds of Adam and not of the fruit of Paradise? Rise and come let us make him to be cast out of Paradise through his wife, just as we were cast out through him." The serpent said to him, "I fear lest the LORD be wrathful to me." The devil said to him, "Do not fear; only become my vessel, and I will speak a word through your mouth by which you will be able to deceive him."[132]

The author is more interested in expanding and obtaining moral lessons from Genesis 3 than in understanding it (as we shall see);[133] he does not grasp that the serpent in the beginning had feet and did not have to eat "weeds" or dust. He does, however, portray the serpent as the vessel into which the Devil entered. The serpent and the Devil are then one and the same.

In the New Testament, two authors equate, indirectly or directly, the serpent with the Devil. Luke associates Satan and the serpent. Alone among the Evangelists, he has Jesus state to the Seventy when they return joyful: "I saw Satan fall like lightning from heaven. Behold, I have given you authority to tread on serpents" (Lk 10:18–19). Within the New Testament clearly, and within Early Judaism (300 BCE–200 CE) probably, the clearest equation of the dragon, the serpent, the Devil, and Satan is in Revelation 12:9. The passage is thus singularly important to warrant a full citation: "And he was cast down—the great dragon, the ancient serpent, the one called Devil and the Satan, the one deceiving the whole world. He was thrown down to the earth, and his angels with him were cast down." Sadly missed in modern translations is the intricately crafted *inclusio*: "He was cast down," "they were cast down." The completed action of the thrice-used Aorist passive is also impressive. Yet no translator could miss the equation: The dragon is the serpent; he is the Devil, the Deceiver, and Satan. Later, the author of Revelation sees another vision in which an angel, holding a key and a great chain, seizes the dragon, that ancient serpent, the Devil and Satan, and binds him within the bottomless pit for a thousand years (20:1–3). The equation is so clear,[134] graphic, and pictorial that it has influenced almost all biblical scholars,[135] who—without hesitation—have told me for six years that I was wasting my time because the serpent is simply Satan. A symbol clearly defined, and in a canonical book that completes a perceived climax to revelatory literature, should not determine how the selfsame symbol was understood by others.

In the Apocrypha and Pseudepigrapha of the New Testament, Satan appears as a snake. Only two examples must suffice. According to the *Arabic Gospel of the Infancy of the Savior* 16, Satan takes the form of a serpent. According to the *First Gospel of the Infancy of Jesus Christ* 23, Satan appears as a dragon.

By the time of the Quran, the equation between the serpent and Satan is so ingrained in consciousness that it influences Muhammad. Note his words in "the Heights": "Children of Adam, do not let Satan tempt you just as he turned your two ancestors out of the Garden, stripping them of their clothing in order to show them their private parts." [136]

Evil

The fierce independence (cf. 2.11), cold-bloodedness (cf. 2.12), and sudden appearance of a snake (cf. 2.6) made it a good symbol for evil. Among the Semites, especially those in the south, the serpent tended to symbolize demons in the desert,[137] a tradition that clearly appears in the *Books of Enoch*. The Arabic *jinn* denotes both a desert evil spirit and a snake.

The serpent often symbolizes the source of evil. In Sumerian and Akkadian mythology, the serpent often symbolized evil.[138] In ancient Egyptian religion, Apophis, the serpent, was perceived as the archenemy of the Sun God Re. In Indian religion, Kaliya, who is the prince of serpents, symbolizes evil; he is conquered by Krishna.[139] In Native American lore, the dark of winter is perceived according to the myth about the beginnings of time: then the sun was covered by the powers of darkness, which are controlled by Sisiul, the serpent.

In biblical lore, the snake sometimes symbolized evil. A passage in the Psalms that is well known announces that no evil will befall those who make the Most High their dwelling place; indeed, note what they will be able to do:

> You will tread upon the lion and the cobra [ופתן],
> The young lion and the dragon [ותנין] you shall trample under foot. [Ps 91:33]

We have seen how this biblical image was represented on clay by Christians in North Africa sometime after the fourth century CE (Fig. 7). According to Revelation 12:1–6, evil in the form of "a great red dragon" pursues a "woman" who is depicted in terms of astrology and may well symbolically represent the Church (and perhaps at the same time Mary [double entendre]).

In the *Song of Moses* (Deut 32:1–43), the enemies of God and the Hebrews are depicted as the poison of serpents and the venom of asps. This passage is quoted by the author of the *Damascus Document* who employs it to denote his hatred of kings (cf. also *1 En 37–71*) and "the head of the kings of Greece" that render vengeance on God's people:

> And each chose according to the wantonness of his heart, and did not remove himself from (the) people. And they arrogantly became unruly, walking in the way of the wicked ones, of whom God said, "The poison of serpents (is) their wine and the head of asps (is) cruel." "The serpents" are the kings of the peoples and "their wine" is their ways, and "the head of the asps" is the head of the kings of Greece, who will come to do vengeance among them. [CD MS A 8.8–12a] [140]

It is clear that the metaphor of the serpent and asp was chosen by the author of the *Damascus Document* to stress the evil among the leaders on earth: kings and the head of kings.

We have examined ophidian and anguine golden jewelry.[141] The women of Pompeii were especially fond of these ornaments; many examples are preserved in the world's museums, including the Benaki Museum in Athens,[142] and the Archaeological Museum in Naples (see Appendix III).[143] A stunning confirmation of our search for the serpent as a symbol of evil and the evil one is found in *The Instructor* by Clement of Alexandria (c. 150–215 CE) of whose biography very little is known. He castigates women who wear golden serpentine jewelry:

> But now women are not ashamed to wear the most manifest badges of the evil one. For as the serpent [ὁ ὄφις] deceived Eve, so also has ornament of gold maddened other women to vicious practices, using as a bait the form of the serpent, and by fashioning lampreys and serpents as decoration. Accordingly the comic poet Nicostratus says, "chains, collars, rings, bracelets, serpents [ὄφεις], anklets, earrings." [*Paedagogos* 2.13][144]

Notably, Aphraate also uses the serpent to symbolize evil.[145] According to the compiler of the *Lives of the Prophets*, the serpent is evil and pursues people in darkness (as we mentioned earlier).[146]

The Rabbis tended to attribute sin to the snake in Eden. We even hear that the snake shook the tree of knowledge and its fruit fell to the ground. Then "he pushed" the woman and "she touched the tree." The serpent becomes the source of evil.[147] Again, in an impressive fashion, the Genesis story has been read with eisegesis and impressionistically.

Although the Gnostic who composed the *Teaching of Silvanus* refers twice to the "intelligence of the snake," according to the Gnostic who gave us the *Apocryphon of John* (the long version), Sophia of the Epinoia gave birth to an evil monster named Yaltabaoth. This monster is "ignorant darkness" and has a form different from her. He has the shape of a lion-faced serpent.

Literary evidence that the serpent symbolizes evil comes from an unexpected source. In *The Acts of the Disputation with the Heresiarch Manes*, Archelaus claims that while the serpent symbolizes evil now, he originally was not evil, but "willed" himself to be evil when he encountered the human. Note this excerpt:

> Even that great serpent himself was not evil previous to man, but only after man, in whom he displayed the fruit of his wickedness, because he willed it himself. If, then, the father of wickedness makes his appearance to us after man has come into being, according to the Scriptures, how can he be unbegotten who has thus been constituted evil subsequently to man, who is himself a production? But, again, why should he exhibit himself as evil just from the period when, on your supposition, he did himself create man? What did he desire in him?[148]

This is a rather odd and novel interpretation of Genesis 3.

Lions and snakes are joined iconographically in the ancient world. For example, a fourth-century BCE funerary monument shows a lion with a snake on its right hip.[149] Lions and snakes appear in more recent iconography. At St. Quenin, in southeastern France, one can see a capital with two asps facing each other. Just below St. Quenin and at St. Christol in the apse of a church is a capital with the depiction of a lion biting a serpent.[150] The lion seems to symbolize God and resurrection, and the serpent death and the earth. If that is the meaning, then the symbol of the serpent has been altered by Christian ideas.

St. Patrick did not drive snakes out of Ireland. They ceased to exist there after the Ice Age. This well-known myth developed because Patrick became a saint, and he drove evil out of Ireland. The best symbol to represent this belief is the serpent.

Evil Eye

The lack of movable eyelids and the inability to blink make the snake a perfect symbol for the evil eye (cf. 2.4).[151] One of the Greek words for "snake" means the blind one (τυφλώψ). In many late Jewish and Christian amulets, the snake appears to represent the evil eye.

It is not clear what the two snakes that end as ribbons on the lintel stone of the School of Rabbi Eliezar ha-Kappar at Dabara mean. But, given their time period and the fact that the snakes' heads are in eagles' mouths, they suggest that the serpent imagery may denote the evil eye.

The meaning of serpent imagery has come full circle. In Babylon, the serpent symbolized the protection of the palace, but at Dabara the snakes had to be killed by the ever-protective eagle. The geographical setting is also important. I have seen eagles soaring around Gamla and other places in the Golan. These birds of prey search out and eat snakes.

In the late 1930s, R. Wittkower drew attention to the universal use of iconography that showed the serpent and eagle together. Such images are found in Sumer and Babylonia (c. 3000 BCE),[152] India (c. 3000 BCE), Scythia (sixth–fifth cent. BCE), Turkestan (fourth–ninth cent. CE), Java (eleventh cent. CE). Today images of the serpent and eagle are seen in Mexico and Costa Rica.[153] The snake appears with the eagle in iconography found in many cities, including Alexandria, Athens, Rome, Canterbury, and Constantinople.

The image of an eagle holding a snake continues into the modern era; the symbol appears on medals, engravings, etchings, paintings, doorknockers, mirrors, and sculptures.[154] A good example of this imagery appears in Blake's *Marriage of Heaven and Hell*. The reactionary forces in France chose the eagle, so the revolutionary forces and Napoleon adopted the snake as their symbol.

Throughout the lore and myths of the ancient Near East are tales about harmful and fearful monsters that are snakes. Sometimes they have names like Behemoth, Leviathan, and Rahab (see Appendix I). The human imagination and lack of knowledge of antiquity and of the earth and its oceans led to dreams and speculations on the ferocity and size of these ancient serpent monsters. This recognition helps us comprehend why serpents appear with seven heads and other oddities. MacCulloch stated so perceptively the relation between the snake and the evil eye:

> Although the serpent is frequently worshipped, its harmful character and the repulsion which it arouses, its frequent large size and strength, and the mystery of its movements have often caused a sinister character to be given it, and made it an embodiment of demoniac powers. Because of the brightness of its eye and its power of fascination over animals the serpent was commonly supposed to have the evil eye.[155]

The Jewish, Christian, and Gnostic amulets with serpents often reveal the evil-eye power of the serpent (Fig. 87). Perhaps the same attribute was embodied in the wooden and bronze images of serpents shown earlier (Fig. 85).

Fear

The soundless swiftness of the snake, and its ability to appear unexpectedly, helped to make the snake a symbol of fear (cf. 2.6).[156] The need for a snake to swallow its victim whole, at once, and often while alive also stimulated fear (cf. 2.9). The sheer size of snakes can cause fear; the anaconda and reticulated python can grow to at least 9 meters, the king cobra to over 5 meters, and the Diamondback Rattlesnake can weigh over 15 kilograms.[157] No creature seems to strike fear in the heart of the human as much as the snake.

This fear aroused by the deadly snake is obvious to most humans, especially when one is suddenly aware that one is too close to a rattler whose unexpected warning sends shivers up and down the spine. I remember a harrowing moment near dusk one summer in the mountains of North Carolina. Without warning, and with shocking suddenness, I had confronted at least five large rattlesnakes. I could not imagine how I had become so unlucky. The whole area seemed unexpectedly alive with the sound of rattlers. As my eyes became accustomed to the dusk of the evening, I realized that in the darkness—only 2 meters in front of me—were five large rattlesnakes. Fortunately, they were housed in cages. They had been collected from various areas of the mountains by the camp manager.

The snake is often a symbol of fear in Rabbinics. For example, Rabbi Ben Azzai is reputed to have said, "Lie on anything but on the ground for fear of serpents" (m. Ber. 62b).

Symbol of Corrupted Sex (the Phallus)

The elongated nature of the snake and its imagined phallic shape, especially when aroused, stimulated reflections on sex (cf. 2.5 and 2.22). Also, the male serpent has two penises (hemipenes); thus, the serpent symbolizes, sometimes, the phallus and sex (cf. 2.7). Plutarch relates how Philip, the father of Alexander the Great, lost the sight of his eye, which had been "applied to the chink in the door when he espied the god, in the form of a serpent, sharing the couch of his wife." [158] The association of the snake with the penis is widespread; it may be mirrored in the early fear of Jews that in the privy a snake might curl around one's penis (*j. Taʿan* 4.69a). The serpent often symbolizes sex in dance and art.[159]

Due to the snake's ability to represent opposites, as in the caduceus, it can also symbolize the womb. From very ancient times, serpent iconography appears with circles. This symbol is present in pre-70 Judaism, as in the Herodian serpent pendant with circles. These circles are called lozenges and signify the vulva. The serpent with lozenges might symbolize the gates to the chthonic world.[160]

Sex can be violent, and sex crimes are as old as humankind. Today we baptize them with less odious terms like "crimes of passion." The wild orgies of antiquity degenerated into corrupted sex. The gods with a serpent as a phallus, especially Priapus,[161] displayed the erotic power of the lingam, but also connoted violent and corrupt sex (if sex is defined as a caring and physical dialogue between two lovers).

We have seen significant evidence that the serpent is often a negative symbol. The author of 4 Maccabees refers to "the seducing and beguiling serpent" that defiles young women.[162] In 2 Corinthians 11:2–3 Paul expresses a similar thought. Metaphorically, he compares his converts to "a pure bride" who may be deceived, as Eve, by a serpent.[163]

Should we agree with R. H. Isaacs: "The biblical snake is continually used to represent temptation and power of evil"?[164] Was P. Haupt correct to conclude that in "the Story of Paradise the serpent symbolizes carnal desire, sexual appetite, concupiscence"?[165] Should we concur with H.-G. Buchholz, who contended that in biblical lore the serpent plays a negative role and is an unclean animal?[166]

That should now be unthinkable to the reader. Such conclusions would create a biblical text from our own misperceptions. The serpent is not necessarily an evil creature in Genesis 3, as we shall see. In Numbers 21 two serpent symbols appear and one is clearly good and salvific. Dan is likened to a serpent that guards Israel: "Dan shall be a snake by the roadside" (Gen 49:17 [NRSV]).

Another fallacy needs to be clarified, exposed, and rejected. First, some thinkers imagine that the serpent is primarily a negative symbol. Second, others imagine that the snake symbolizes one of the sixteen meanings previously described. Third, other thinkers imagine that many of the images appear in a complex collage. All represent misleading and misinformed positions. The snake can symbolize one or more of these negative images, but it also can symbolize one or more of the following positive concepts or images. Emphatically clear is the perception that while the taxonomy of serpent symbology divides into sixteen negative symbolic meanings, it also continues into no fewer than twenty-nine positive symbolic meanings, as we shall see. Moreover, some serpent symbols, like the caduceus, are clearly a double entendre, and the paronomasia is most likely intentional; that is, the serpent symbolizes both light and goodness as well as darkness and evil. Let us now turn to examine how the biblical authors, and others, saw the snake as a positive symbol.

POSITIVE SYMBOLIC MEANING

Twenty-nine positive meanings of serpent symbolism may be discerned in the data already collected. Unfortunately, scholars and nonspecialists have missed the positive symbolic meaning of the serpent, myopically taking medicine without seeing that it is almost always administered with a symbol: the caduceus or a snake curled around a lance or staff.[167]

In ancient Greece, we noticed the preponderance of ophidian imagery; some of it is clearly negative. Hercules is constantly confronted with serpents. As a baby, he must struggle against two snakes. Later he fights the Hydra, meets the snake in the tree in the Hesperides, and is confronted by the serpent-dog Cerberus. Laocoon and his sons are strangled to death by snakes. The Scylla often is depicted with a dragon as a torso. Jason can obtain the Golden Fleece only when Medea diverts the attention of the snake-dragon.[168] Orpheus descends into Hades, searching for his beloved wife, a beautiful nymph, who had been fatally bitten by a snake. At "the navel of the earth," Delphi, Apollo defeats the python.[169]

Despite these depictions of the snake as evil or harmful, ophidian iconography in Greek mythology and theology was emphatically and pervasively positive. Zeus, Apollo,[170] Asclepius, Athena—virtually all the Greek gods and goddesses—are presented as snakes or accompanied and identified by snakes or serpents.[171] The "Good-Spirit" (Agathadaimon) appears as a large upraised snake; it was later identified with the god Aion.[172] Galen found amulets with Agathadaimon helpful, advising that, when worn on the throat and chest, they benefit the internal organs: "Some, indeed, set the stone in a ring and engrave upon it a serpent with his head crowned

Figure 66. *Left.* Agrippa's Temple. *Right.* Giants with anguipedes (close-up). Athens Agora. JHC

with rays, according as is prescribed by King Nechepsos in his thirteenth book." [173] And at Delphi, a large column with three serpents (the Tripod of Plataea) was erected near the temple of Apollo.[174] A candelabrum with a serpent with beard, eyes, and open mouth with its tongue visible was found; [175] archaeologists have also uncovered the Fountain of Asclepius and a sanctuary of Asclepius.[176] In Athens, three gods were revered with ophidian iconography: Athena, Hermes, and a giant snake.[177] In the agora in Athens, the temple of Agrippa boasted columns that featured Giants having anguipedes.

Similar positive use of the serpent may be found in Jewish sources. For example, according to the compiler of the *Hellenistic Synagogal Prayers,* God has filled the world with, inter alia, the "hissings of serpents" and "many-colored birds." [178]

While sixteen negative symbolic meanings of the serpent have been illustrated, at least twenty-nine positive symbolic meanings may be ascertained. Thus, we shall now succinctly discuss the following positive meanings of serpent symbolism:

Phallus, Procreation, Fertility, and Good Sex	Magic
	Mystery, Wonder, and Awe
Fruitfulness	Wisdom
Energy and Power	God's Messenger
Beauty	(Judgment and Revelation)
Goodness	Life
Guardian	Water
Creation and Light	Soul (and Personal Names)
Cosmos	Health and Healing
Chronos	Purifying
Kingship	Transcendence
Divinity	Rejuvenation
Unity (Oneness)	Immortaility, Reincarnation,
Ancestor Worship	and Resurrection
Earth-Lover	Purely Decorative
Chthonic	Riches and Wealth

Most examples of positive serpent symbolism come from the Levant, even the land of Israel. We have seen that in antiquity positive serpent symbolism was much more prevalent in the ancient Near East (although not in the religion of Israel, especially after Hezekiah).[179] The examples of positive serpent symbolism markedly outnumber those of negative symbolism.

The Seraphim most likely were serpents with six wings (see Appendix I). In ancient Christian illuminated manuscripts, paintings, and frescoes, they appear with six wings (two over the genitals) and with human faces, but they are not depicted with features of a serpent. This is especially true in the monasteries of Meteora,[180] near Thessaly, the birthplace of Asclepius.[181] Today, in virtually all parts of the world the serpent symbolizes medical research and pharmacies. The serpent is placed on medicines and prescription drugs. Note the signs in Fig. 67 seen in Greece, West Jerusalem, and East Jerusalem.

While the snake is almost always regarded as a symbol of Satan or evil today, the positive meaning of ophidian symbolism frequently remains unperceived. The serpent is highlighted in the signs of pharmacies and medical colleges (as just intimated). Quite surprisingly, a drawing of three intertwined snakes (like the Tripod of Plataea) appears as an embellishment of the first word in "T" in numerous chapters in Sister Theotekni's

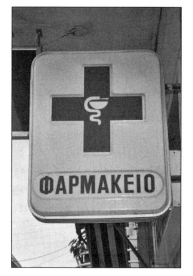

Figure 67. Serpent Signs in Greece (*top left*), West Jerusalem (Israel Medical Association, *top right*), East Jerusalem (*bottom*). JHC

Meteora: The Rocky Forest of Greece.[182] On Mount Nebo, the cross almost always is shown with a serpent draped over it—clearly an interpretation of John 3 in light of Numbers 21.

While some of the data we have collected as serpent symbolism cannot be neatly arranged under only one of these categories, most are easily placed in one, or two, of the forty-five categories. There is now no basis to doubt that the snake, above all animals, has provided the human with the most varied and complex symbology. As mentioned in Chapter 2, we need to recall that at the same time the serpent may symbolize opposites (double entendre) as with the uraeus and caduceus. The bearer of evil is neutralized (and perhaps superseded) by the bearer of good. Each is symbolized as a serpent. Perhaps the first is an evil snake, the second a benevolent serpent.

Phallus, Procreation, Fertility, and Good Sex

The male serpent has two phalli (each is a hemipenes). The female produces an abundant number of offspring, as Aristotle knew (but he may not have known that the reticulated python can produce a clutch of one hundred eggs).[183] These two characteristics—the male's two penises and the female's fecundity—make the snake an ideal symbol of sex and fertility (cf. 2.7). We have previously mentioned that the physical appearance of the snake, especially when aroused, is reminiscent of the engorged phallus (cf. 2.5). As many have observed, and the Freudians popularized myopically, the serpent can remind the viewer of the lingam. Additional symbolic meanings of the serpent, therefore, are procreation, fertility, good sex, and power.

In the ancient Near East, the serpent played a part in sacred marriages.[184] According to Eusebius in his *Preparation for the Gospel,* Porphyry wrote: "[The] phallic Hermes represents vigour, but also indicates the generative law that pervades all things." [185]

The bronze serpent pendant found in or near Jerusalem is also strikingly reminiscent of the phallus. I have seen many images of the hand and the phallus as amulets that were worn by soldiers who lived in the first century; some of these images seem to be Jewish because the marks of circumcision are clear. I have not found an amulet with the depiction of a hand, a phallus, and a serpent. Such an amulet would strikingly denote serpent symbolism as representing power. Perhaps someday one will show up in the antiquities shops of Old Jerusalem, but it might be a gifted forger's attempt to supply such an amulet.

Dionysus was symbolized as both a snake and a phallus.[186] Sometimes it is far from clear what the *cysta mystica* ("the mystical chest") contained. What was inside? Did it include a snake or a phallus? Were both symbols conflated? [187] On coins the *cysta mystica* often appears with one or more snakes.[188] Generally, but not always, the Greeks and Romans considered the snake, among other things, a phallic symbol.[189] According to Clement of Alexandria, as quoted by Eusebius in his *Preparation for the Gospel,* the "mystic chests" contained not "holy things," but various common items such as a "sesame-cake, and pyramids, and balls, and flat cakes full of knobs, and lumps of salt." What else was in the box? It included "a serpent also, mystic symbol of Dionysus Bassarus." [190] Post-second-century Christians, like Clement, were offended by serpent symbolism: "The mysteries of the serpent are a kind of fraud devoutly observed by men who, with spurious piety, promote their abominable initiations and profane orgiastic rites." [191]

With an awareness of Clement's own disdain for serpents, we should read his report about the bacchanals with some skepticism. Clement reported that they

> hold their orgies in honour of the frenzied Dionysus, celebrating their sacred frenzy by the eating of raw flesh, and go through the distribution of the parts of butchered victims, crowned with snakes, shrieking out the name of that Eva by whom error came into the world. The symbol of the Bacchic orgies is a consecrated serpent. Moreover, according to the strict interpretation of the Hebrew term, the name Hevia, aspirated, signifies a female serpent. [192]

There may be some historical truth in Clement's account, but he is striving to denigrate the worship of Dionysus.

No one should doubt that the serpent was used to symbolize illicit sex. We should recall the iconography of the Greek and Roman erotic gods whose phallus was upraised and sometimes resembled a serpent. [193] For example, Bes is frequently shown ithyphallically, and sometimes his exaggerated protrusion is a snake.

Numerous gods or heroes were also believed to be Ophiogenae; that is, they were born from mothers who had been impregnated by a god that had appeared to them as a serpent in a dream or often as beings in the temple of Apollo. Thus, the ancients linked the birth of great men with a serpent. Such luminaries were Aristomenes, Alexander the Great, Aratos of Sikyon, Scipio Africanus, Caesar Augustus, the twins Commodus and Antoninus, Alexander Severus, and Galerius. [194] Was Jesus' birth celebrated in myth only by a virgin birth, as many of these other "Great Men," to use a sociological term, or was Mary also visited by an Agathadaimon? An apocryphal story recorded in Aelian's *De natura animalium*, seems to indicate that the Jewish girl visited by a serpent during the time of King Herod was none other than Mary, the mother of Jesus. [195]

A singularly important passage for comprehending serpent symbology and procreation appears in another section of Aelian's *De natura animalium*. Halia, the daughter of Sybaris, entered a sacred grove of Artemis in Phrygia. [196] A "divine serpent" (δράκων ἐπεφάνη θεῖος, *draco quidam sacer*) appeared to her; he was of "immense size." He lay (ὡμίλησεν, *et cum ea coivit*) with the young girl, "and from this union sprang the *Ophiogenis* [snake-born (Ὀφιογενεῖς)] of the first generation" (12.39). While different interpretations seem possible, it is not clear what the symbolic meaning is of the two serpents tied around the waist with upraised heads on a god, dated to 580 BCE, in the Temple of Artemis at Korfu. [197]

The faience Minoan serpent goddesses or priestesses symbolized many things desired by human; we have suggested fertility and the need to protect the earth from destructive earthquakes. Their ample hips, small waists, and full exposed breasts indicate they also connoted good sex and fertility (see Fig. 28). The stunning artwork showing Aphrodite with a serpent on her thigh, found on Mount Carmel, clearly signifies good sex, power, and fertility (Fig. 23). The same interpretation applies to the Aphrodite with a serpent curled around her right arm; the figure found at Agrigento dates from the second or first century BCE.[198]

The symbol of Diana or Artemis as a deer with a serpent around its neck brings to mind many positive perspectives. Perhaps the snake and the deer symbolized the fertility of the earth for humans.

In Peru, scholars have been impressed with figures having human and serpent features. They date from approximately 200 BCE to 700 CE and convey ideas preserved in sixteenth- and seventeenth-century Spanish lexicons that are still evident today. According to A. M. Hocquenghem, these images embody symbolically immortal power.[199]

In 1999, in the Museum of Ethnology at Rotterdam, the Netherlands, African art was featured. One modern work was striking. It depicted a woman with a pink serpent, with two large eyes, placed on her chest.

Fruitfulness

The snake digs in a garden and aerates and irrigates it. The snake also kills rodents that destroy vegetation (cf. 2.26). The serpent, consequently, may symbolize fruitfulness. Sometimes this symbolism is also related to the phallus and fertility.[200] Küster's chapter on the fruitfulness of the serpent is divided into sections, with the serpent symbolizing the fruitfulness of: (1) vegetables and (2) animals.[201] He grounded his thoughts, typically, on the central theme of the serpent's chthonic character; from this basic concept comes the most important symbolic meaning of ophidian symbolism: the serpent's fruitfulness. Along with the Earth-Mother goddesses, the serpent provides for the fruitfulness of trees and also for the fertility of animals (including humans). That symbology makes eminent sense in light of the conceptual link between the serpent and the tree with its fruit, not only in the Hesperides but also in Eden. The serpent is often depicted as part of the tree or wrapped closely around it. Both the tree and the serpent are chthonic; they are ones who can delve deep into the earth. The relation between serpent and tree is evident from earliest times and can be seen most likely on Late Bronze pottery from Betula.[202]

While the trees are stylized, they remain unmistakable. The serpents appear with large eyes, as in other examples from the second millennium BCE. The serpents seem to be depicted eating something (probably fruit

Figure 68. Ceramic Late Bronze Pot Probably with Tree and Serpents; from Betula, near Beth Shan. JHC Collection

that is not shown) at the base of the triangular upper part of the tree. If the one who painted the bowl or if those who used or saw it imagined this interpretation, then we have iconography and symbolism similar to and prior to the Yahwist who composed Genesis 3 from earlier cultures such as the one represented by this bowl. Note, especially, that the serpents are depicted upright and standing, but no feet are drawn.

Most likely the serpent goddesses or priestesses of ancient Crete also symbolized the link between the serpent and the fruitfulness of nature. The images of a man holding two serpents upright, in a fashion reminiscent of the Minoan goddesses or priestesses, also seems to symbolize fruitfulness.[203] The dove and serpents on the Canaanite cult stands found at Beth Shan probably, as indicated earlier, denoted the serpent's relation with fruitfulness. The spring harvest festivals often lift up the serpent as a symbol of the earth's return to rejuvenation (viz. with Agathadaimon and in the Demeter festivals in Athens in which Demeter and the serpent were intertwined). The power of the serpent to symbolize fruitfulness is linked with its presence and role in creation in so many of the world's myths (as, e.g., in Persephone and Zeus Meilichios).

Energy and Power

Although the snake is without legs (now), it is amazingly swift and energetic (cf. 2.1).[204] The serpent is strong and powerful (see Fig. 13). From the ancients we learn (of a myth) that there are snakes in India that can strangle and swallow a full-grown elephant. This mythic lore is grounded in the awesome power of snakes. They seem to be one big muscle (and, to some ancients, symbolic, as just said, of a fully erect phallus). It is clear why H. Egli in *Das Schlangensymbol* devoted a chapter to the serpent as the symbol of power.[205] Cassandra, Helenus, Melampus, and Iamos received power from serpents when they were sleeping.[206]

W. Foerster pointed to the "twofold character of the serpent." The animal represented the "primal power." He offered the opinion that this power resided in the ability of the snake to kill.[207] This interpretation is typically one-sided, as Foerster stressed only the negative features of ophidian symbolism. Snakes are characteristically docile. Hence, the Rabbis, observing that a poisonous snake will not bite if not aroused, advised that even if a snake is coiled around one's heel, one should still continue to recite the *Amidah* (*b. Ber.* 5:1) and, if one is about to be attacked, one may defend oneself while praying (*b. Ber.* 9a).[208]

When Foerster claimed that the power of the serpent resided only in its ability to kill, he apparently never felt awe before an upraised king cobra or held a part of a two-hundred-pound boa. If one studies the anguipede Giants on the Pergamum altar,[209] or the massive stone Giants with one anguipede in Agrippa's Odeion in the Agora of Athens,[210] or examines the ancient depictions of Laocoon, one feels the power of serpent iconography. One does think immediately about the lethal bite of a snake.

What is stressed iconographically is the awesome power of the muscular and speedy serpent. The artists bring out the power of serpent symbolism by revealing the way the anguipede Giants strangle the gods and highlighting the tensed and mighty muscles of Laocoon. Today one associates the power of a snake with its ability to administer swift death, but in ancient iconography more stress is placed on the serpent's awesomeness and mysteriousness, and its ability to avoid illness and regain the look of youth at least once each year.

In interpreting Job, the Rabbis offered an example of God's power. They tell a story. God prepared (אני מזמין) a dragon-snake (דרקון) for a female gazelle whose birth canal was too narrow for easy birth. The snake bites her in the birth canal. It subsequently becomes stretched, and the gazelle finally gives birth (*b. B. Bat.* 16b). The bite of the dragon-snake did not kill; it possessed the power to assist God in enabling the gazelle to give birth.

On the western wall in the Greek Orthodox Church at Capernaum, one may look up to see an attractive new mural. Christ sits enthroned in judgment. On his left and below him are two large figures. One is the earth (*gē*). How is Christ depicted? He sits on two lions and holds a serpent in his right hand. The other "being" judged is the sea *(thalassa)*. How is she portrayed? She is also with a serpent. What do these ophidian symbols represent? I directed this question to a young monk in the Greek Orthodox Church. Pondering Greek traditions, he instantaneously answered, "power."

Today fast and powerful sports cars are sometimes given the name "cobra." The Alfa Romeo's logo has the sign of the upright serpent on it. Lingering, sometimes unperceived, are examples of serpent symbolism that are positive. The serpent continues to symbolize power.

Beauty

The snake is simply one of the most beautifully decorated creatures (cf. 2.19; also see Figs. 10, 15, 18). If it were not for the fear of an asp, a cobra, a black mamba, and a Boomslang, the snake would be widely hailed as one of the most attractive creatures on earth. While traveling in the Sinai in 1877, A. F. Buxton saw a snake he described as "about 2 feet long, of a most gorgeous colouring." In his journals he described it as "lamé-coloured."[211] In December 2002, Natalie Angier, in "Venomous and Sublime: The Viper Tells Its Tale," wrote her subjective reflections on vipers: "Is there anything cooler than a snake or more evocative of such a rich sinusoidal range of sensations? Snakes are beckoning. Snakes are terrifying. Snakes are elegant, their skins like poured geometry." In the same publication, Dr. Jonathan A. Campbell of the University of Texas at Arlington added, "Even those who don't like snakes have to admit their beauty."[212]

Those who say they despise snakes are often found staring, somewhat mesmerized, at a captive snake. If the snake is so horrible, as most assume today, then why are there often four people in a zoo standing watching elephants, six observing lions or bears, but dozens investing their time within a serpentarium?

One reason we all watch snakes, in a place safe for us, is our fascination with the snake and its innate beauty. As I said at the beginning of this work, the large golden king cobra that rose and looked me in the eye when I had just become a teenager was, and remains, one of the most beautiful creatures I have ever confronted.

The Greek and Roman women who wore the gold bracelets and rings with serpents depicted in the most realistic manner most likely chose them—or were given the jewelry as a gift—because of the serpent's beauty. As we have seen, this serpentine jewelry is astonishingly beautiful and often realistic (see Figs. 34, 35; cf. Figs. 18, 37, 39). In fact, the usual Greek noun for "serpent," *ophis,* also signifies a bracelet in the form of a snake.[213]

Josephus apparently thought the serpent provided appropriate imagery for describing beauty. He mentions that the sumptuous linen garment of the high priest was loosely woven as if "were the skin of a serpent" (*Ant* 3.7.2).

Goodness

The snake does not aggressively attack, except for food. It protects humans from harmful animals (cf. 2.27) and helps cultivate the garden (cf. 2.26); hence, the serpent symbolizes goodness.

When I was in Galilee, in November 2002, while the present work was in its final stages, I encountered two snakes. One was on the Mount of Beatitudes. An Arab had cleared some brush and was burning it. A small gray snake emerged. It was frightened and sought every avenue for escape. The next day, while driving from Capernaum to Gamla, I sped past a long black object on the road. I stopped the car and slowly backed up. I found my camera and slid out of the car; soon I was about 6 meters in front of a large black snake. It raised its head, moved its body in contradictory directions, and then shot away to my right, to hide—thus, proving that, for snakes, as for most animals, the first line of defense is avoidance.[214] The farmers in the Golan protect these large harmless snakes because they rid their farms of mice and other harmful creatures. For the farmers, long ago and now, the snake was often a friend, and a symbol of goodness. The snake in the Golan is called "Bashan" by the Arabs (cf. Appendix I).

Perhaps the best example of the serpent as the symbol of goodness is the ubiquitous Agathadaimon, the good serpent that was so popular in many cities,[215] especially at Alexandria and Pompeii (see Figs. 34–36). In the Agora Museum in Athens one can see a bronze Agathadaimon with a human face and long hair. It is almost 8 centimeters high and dates from the Roman Period (Box 50). The goddess Isis, who is often shown with a serpentine lower torso, also represents goodness (see Figs. 50, 51). Athena symbolized wisdom and might in battle; the ancients often depicted her with serpents on her chest (Fig. 52). Sometimes Athena appears as Hygieia, as in the phrase "Athena Hygieia," and with realistic snakes on her breastplate.[216] In Palmyra, the statue of the goddess Allat is influenced by those of Athena; notably, she is depicted with curled snakes on her upper garment.[217]

Among Aphrodite's many attributes—beside might, beauty, and sex—is goodness; recall the serpent sometimes disclosed on her thigh (see Fig. 23). Rabbi Shimon ben-Menasya lamented that the serpent could have been "a great servant."[218] He also claimed: "[T]wo good serpents" (נחשים שני טובים) would have been given to each Israelite, to serve them and assist in their work.[219] In analyzing the votive feet and the statues of Asclepius and Hygieia found in Roman Caesarea Maritima, R. Gersht rightly stressed that the serpent "was perceived not only as the being that is able to heal, like a dog, with the licks of his tongue, but also as the embodiment of the mildness, goodness and the philanthropy of the god and his daughter."[220] Such insights bring to memory Plutarch's report that Demosthenes pronounced Asclepius' name so that the accent fell not on the final syllable, as is customary, but on the third syllable so that the god was perceived to be "mild" (epios).[221]

Guardian

Our ancestors perceived the snake as the one who kills animals harmful to humans, like rodents, mice, and rats (cf. 2.27); thus, it came to symbolize the Guardian. The snake has no eyelids, so it cannot close its eyes. This physiological characteristic has helped develop such symbols as the uraeus (the rearing cobra) that represents the Egyptian cobra *(Naja haje),* which can grow to about 3 meters.[222] The uraeus is not only the symbol of the Egyptian cobra goddess who represented "life, order, and legitimate kingship,"[223] it is also the quintessential symbol of the divine guardian (cf. 2.4). As W. A. Ward has demonstrated, a four-winged uraeus of the first millennium BCE on Hebrew seals is clearly the Egyptian uraeus-snake. The uraeus symbolizes the protection of gods and kings and destruction of all enemies. Ward concludes: "Within its Hebrew context, the flying serpent was both a protector and destroyer."[224] It is understandable, therefore, why Egli, in his *Das Schlangensymbol,* devoted a chapter to the serpent as guardian.[225]

In world folklore and myth, the serpent indeed symbolizes the guardian. Ladon guards the golden apples in the Hesperides. A snake watches Apollo's gold in Scythia. A snake is sentinel of the rowan tree of the Celts' Fraoch. A "hissing serpent" (in Syriac)[226] guards the priceless pearl of the *Hymn of the Pearl;* and a serpent was guardian of Athena's temple in Athens.[227] The Ishtar Gate was guarded by monsters with a dragon's tongue and a serpent tail.[228] Fearsome serpents, according to a text in Old Babylonian, were placed on a temple gate bolt for apotropaic purposes.[229] The Babylonian temple in Neriglissar's time boasted eight bronze serpents; two guarded each entrance.[230] Perhaps "the most accomplished piece of Middle Kingdom prose literature"[231] is the narrative about the Egyptian attendant to Sesostris, named Sinuhe. He is in danger before the pharaoh because he is a nomad and "roamed foreign lands." Notice how "the royal daughters" pleaded to the king for Sinuhe:

> While the Cobra decks your brow,
> You deliver the poor from harm.[232]

The reference is to the uraeus and it is a serpent that symbolizes the protector of the poor.

The use of the uraeus to represent the serpent extended far beyond the borders of Egypt. A four-winged uraeus from the seventh century BCE has been found on a red jasper seal containing in Hebrew: "Belonging to Delayahu, son of Gamliyahu."[233] The seal represents culture in ancient Palestine. One of the most remarkable works of art that heralded the beginning of the Classical Period in Amathus, on the southern coast of Cyprus, is a limestone polychrome Hathor capital with the image of two cobras above a small chapel. The two upraised snakes have prominent eyes and wings and face in opposite directions.[234] From Amathus, then, comes a uraeus with serpents facing in diametrically opposed ways. They are guardians.

We have examined and discussed the many serpents that appear on Canaanite pottery, especially during the second millennium BCE (Figs. 29–33). These serpents were placed on jars to protect the contents, especially wine, oil, and water. Long ago, in the seventh century CE, Topsell pointed out that serpents are the guardians of treasures.

Plutarch reports that Demosthenes became jaundiced about public service. He reputedly railed against Athena, the guardian of Athens who was symbolically related to serpents, as we have seen, and the owl, as illustrated on the many coins honoring her. Demosthenes, as he was leaving Athens, asked: "O potent Guardian of the City, Athena, how, pray, canst thou take delight in those three most intractable beasts, the owl, the serpent, and the people?"[235] Clearly, the guardian of Athens is not only Athena but also the serpents that are with her. Later, the Romans also put serpents on their coins to announce to the world the protection provided by Rome. For example, Nero put snakes on his coins.

A marble stele of about the third century BCE, now in the Thebes Museum, has the inscription:

ΔΙΟΣ   Zeus
ΚΤΗΣΙΟΥ   The Guardian[236]

Many in antiquity probably perceived in this stele an allusion to the guardian serpent, and few readers of the present work will miss a possible link with the serpent Zeus Meilichios (Fig. 11).

We have frequently observed that serpents occupy a distinctive place in the iconography of Athena, who played the greatest role in public and private life in Greece. According to L. Bodson, among the symbolic meanings of the different snakes depicted on the sculptures of Athena were the protection of Greeks (the snake called *Elaphe quatuorlineata*) and the destruction of their enemies (the *Vipera ammodytes*). Herodotus (*Hist.* 8.41.3–4) reported, with amazement, that Athenians continued to believe that a sacred snake dwelt in the Erecthium.[237]

Serpents were often painted on warriors' shields. Examples may be found in most archaeological museums that feature Roman and Greek antiquities, including the Vatican, the British Museum, the National Museum in Athens, the Hermitage, and the Museo Archeologico di Pithecusae on the Isle of Ischia at Lacco Ameno. In this museum are the earliest remains of Magna Graecia (the great expanse of Greek culture): ceramic cups and pitchers from about 700 BCE contain wavy lines, either water or serpents, perhaps both. A fifth-century BCE painted krater shows a coiled serpent on a soldier's shield.[238] No details highlight the snake; its head is raised and on a diagonal line with the head of the soldier. Most likely Greeks painted serpents on shields to symbolize the warrior's guardian.

A bronze serpent, without its head, was found beside a bust of Tiberius and Livia in a Roman ruin at Ephesus. It has markings for scales, seven curves, rises up, and is approximately 7 meters long. According to M. L. Robert, this bronze serpent is an example of the domestic cult in which the serpent symbolized protection and prosperity.[239]

The monstrous gorgons, especially Medusa, symbolized the protection offered by these deities (Figs. 17, 47, 48).[240] The Medusa is also found outside the Holy Land; a Medusa with serpent hair is chiseled on the basalt stone in the third-century synagogue at Chorazin. Many, including the famous Gian Lorenzo Bernini (1598–1680), crafted a marvelous statue or replica of Medusa; most prominent are the serpents in her hair.[241]

The serpent has been seen as the perfect symbol of the guardian (cf. esp. *Constitutions of the Holy Apostles* 4.4). He or she is placed on gates and fences. The Vikings carved a dragon-snake and put it on the prow of their ships to protect them from the dragon-serpent of the deep. Serpents and dragons interchange or are indistinguishable in iconography and symbology.

The Hebrew Bible seems to reflect the symbolism of the serpent as the quintessential guardian. The author of Ecclesiastes advises that one who "breaks through a wall" that protects another will "be bitten by a serpent (נחש)." Dan is heralded, as we have seen, according to Genesis 49:17, as the guardian of Israel; he is like the adder that causes one on a horse to fall. Recall the passage:

> Dan shall judge his people
> As one of the tribes of Israel.
> Dan shall be a serpent [נחש] on the way,
> An adder [שפיפן] on the path,
> The one who bites the hoofs of the horse
> So that its rider falls backward. [Gen 49:17]

Dan is here clearly portrayed as the serpent that guards the tribes of Israel.

Creation and Light

The snake goes into the earth from which new life was perceived to originate (cf. 2.18 and 2.24), and it disappears into the mysterious depths of the sea (cf. 2.16) that was frequently mythologized in creation accounts. Thus, the serpent became a symbol of creation in almost all the myths.[242] Many ancient thinkers and compilers of lore and myth imagined an earlier day in which primal floods and large serpents abounded (Leviathan especially). Winter's work removes any doubt about the abundant evidence from antiquity of the relation between creator gods (and goddesses) and the serpent.[243]

In southern Mesopotamia, millennia before the beginning of the Common Era, Akkadians used the serpent to signify birth, but our understanding of early Mesopotamian symbolism is far from clear since there is presently no comprehensive scientific study of serpent iconography and symbolism in Mesopotamia.[244] The emergence of a human or god from the mouth of a large serpent is depicted in an early Sumerian bowl now on display in the Staatliche Museen in Berlin. The birth of a god from a serpent is featured also in early Akkadian and Sumerian narratives.[245]

In many world cultures the serpent is seen as the source of creation. In some myths, it is often conquered and divided into the material world.[246] Thus, only after Marduk slays Tiâmat can he shape heaven and earth out of her remains. According to the sagas of India, Vasuki, the world serpent, is pulled in diverse directions by not only gods but also demons; the result is the creation of the world. In ancient Mexico, according to Nahuatl mythology, creation is dramatically described as occurring after the slaying of a female monster by Quetzalcoatl and Tezcatlipoca; the latter are gods who became serpents. In Melanesia, some natives believe that their islands were created by Wonajö, who was formed like a serpent. The Aborigines of northwestern Australia attribute creation to the eggs of Ungud, the serpent.[247] A legend associated with New Guinea and the Admiralty Islands indicates that the first humans came from a serpent.

Preserved on Coffin Texts of the Middle Kingdom in Egypt are the words of the creator; he has performed four good deeds, and he is with a serpent: "I repeat to you the good deeds which my own heart did for me in the midst of the serpent coil."[248] In "Conversation of Osiris with Atum," part of the Egyptian Book of the Dead, the creator god, Atum, discloses that he sometimes takes the form of the serpent: "I alone am a survivor—together with Osiris—when I have changed my form again into a serpent, which no man knows and which no god has seen."[249]

In the preceding chapter, we reviewed how serpent symbolism helped the Greeks, Romans, and their contemporaries imagine the creation of the world. The symbol looms large especially in the myth of the Giants with anguipedes etched in the Pergamum temple. Other myths of creation that shaped the Greeks and Romans come to mind. The serpent is associated with an egg and often is imagined impregnating a woman. Eurinome, one of the first Titans, the daughter of Ocean and Teti, was the celestial queen until she was banished to the sea. Her male counterpart is Ofione. He is the cosmic serpent who is imagined, and portrayed, as encircling her.[250]

Figure 69. Arch of Titus. Roman Forum. Note the menorah from the Temple. JHC

We have seen that the serpent can symbolize chaos and darkness. In antiquity it also could denote creation, just discussed, and light. I have selected only four examples of the serpent as a symbol of light. First, the image of the serpent representing light appears in the Melanesian, Finnic, and Aztec mythologies; in these myths the serpent symbolized lightning. Second, inside the Second Shrine of Tut-ank-amon,[251] who is the "bodily Son of the Sun," and on the ceiling, is a depiction of Nut, under the solar disk. On her right and left are five flying vultures; two of them have snake heads. On the left panel is a "large mummiform figure of the king, his head and feet encircled by two serpents biting their tails."[252] This figure may show one of the earliest representations of the Ouroboros. Third, perhaps our best insight into the serpent symbolizing light is a comment by the Egyptian scribe called Epeïs, whose work was translated into Greek by Areius of Heracleopolis. The scribe reported that the "first and most divine being is a serpent with the form of a hawk." When this serpent opened his eyes, he "filled all with light," but "if he shut his eyes, darkness came on."[253] Fourth, perhaps this early Egyptian serpent symbolism influenced the author of the *Pistis Sophia,* who thought of the sun's disk as a large serpent-dragon with its tail in its mouth (Ouroboros).

The Psalms constituted the hymnbook of the Second Temple. According to Psalm 27:1, God is "my light [יהוה אורי]." According to Psalm 18:28, Yahweh is "my lamp [נרי]." The concept of God as light appears in personal names: Neriah means "Yah[weh] is my lamp." The original form of "Abner" was "Abiner," as confirmed by the Greek translation in the

Septuagint (LXX), and it means "My [divine] Father is a lamp (or light) [for me]."[254] Perhaps more memorable are Psalm 119:105, "A lamp to my feet [is] your Word and a light to my path," and Psalm 36:10 [9]: "In your light we see light." Light was a prominent feature of the Jerusalem Temple. Most important, the flames from the Menorah filled the temple with light.[255] According to the depiction on the Arch of Titus, on the eastern end of the *via sacra* of the Roman Forum, two serpents, as Leviathan,[256] appear on shields of the octagonal base of the menorah (candelabrum), which was taken as a celebrated spoil of the Jewish War (66–70 CE).[257] God was perceived as light and lamp to Israelites and Jews, and in some way serpent symbolism was included.[258]

One may wonder to what extent the brilliant light reflected from the head of a cobra, especially a golden king cobra, may have aided in the development of the symbol of the serpent as light. While the king cobra is indigenous to India, one can imagine that some were brought to ancient Palestine. Such reflections about the relation of light and serpent symbolism are not restricted to the light seen stunningly reflected from one type of snake. Many types of snakes, with their glistening spotless skin, flash in the sun, especially cobras when upraised.

Cosmos

The limbless snake can form a circle. By holding its tail in its mouth (cf. 2.5), it becomes a symbol of the cosmos. In many cultures, the snake, or serpent, not only symbolizes but also shapes the concept of the cosmos. The Ouroboros often depicts the unity of the universe (cf. *AcThom* 31–33).

In India, Shiva is frequently depicted dancing within a circle,[259] which may represent a serpent that has formed its body into a circle. Shiva is also imagined as dancing with one pair of arms holding a large cobra overhead.[260] Kundalinî, the divine cosmic energy of our body, is called Bhujangî, the serpent.[261] This serpent imagery reflects the anatomy of a serpent, which is sometimes longer than a human and essentially one united tube of muscle. The serpent as a symbol of power and energy, from prehistory to the present, has helped humans not only articulate or imagine but also perceive the energy that shapes and defines the primordial essence of the universe, or cosmos, as revealed in such natural phenomena as "bradisismo,"[262] volcanic activity, and the seemingly infinite gravitational pull of black holes.[263] If our human bodies are primarily empty space, then it is the cosmic energy that unites the atoms of our bodies, which may be similar to the power that enables planets to revolve around a sun. After spiritual experiences, the human seeks to imagine or conceptualize the somatic indwelling of the supernatural and mystical (the feeling of the *soprannaturale e misterioso*). For the ancients and some today, the symbol of this cosmic energy is the serpent. We perceived it earlier when we focused on Zeus (Asclepius) Meilichios.

In western Europe, Thor is sometimes represented within a cosmos shaped by the serpent Miogarosormr. In the New Testament, "a great red dragon" defines the cosmos (Rev 12:1–6). M. Lurker summarizes the cosmic nature of the serpent in diverse world cultures:

> In Melanesian, Finnic, and Aztec mythologies, snakes represent the lightning; among the Babylonians, in India, and in ancient Mexico the Milky Way was associated with a serpent. The motif of the rainbow as a snake is found in Oceania and tropical Africa; the Dogon of West Africa, for example, think of the rainbow as the serpent of the water god Nommo. Australian tribes regard the rainbow snake, under the name of Yulunggul, as a creative divinity and bestower of culture.[264]

In the Egyptian Book of the Dead, the cosmos was defined by the serpent; the creator god, Atum, transforms himself into a serpent, and the primeval monster is the snake Apophis. The solar boat must transverse areas inhabited by snakes, change itself into a serpent, and, inter alia, pass through a long snake before it reappears each morning. According to Coffin Text 160, Re (the sun) tells the serpent god who tries to obstruct him: "O you who goes on his belly, your strength belongs to your mountain. But watch me as I go off with your strength in my hand!"[265] Also in Egypt the uraeus had solar significance, and in some Greek magical papyri Helios (the sun) was often portrayed as a serpent. In Egypt, the astral significance of the serpent was clearly recognized and celebrated.[266] In his "Conceptions of the Cosmos," Keel points out that in an Egyptian drawing of the heavens (Fig. 19) the "space between the two pillars and the sky is filled . . . with the king's name ('Serpent') inscribed on it."[267]

Thus, it is evident that R. S. Hendel was on target about the cosmic dimension of serpent symbolism when he wrote: "The semantic range of the snake in Egypt is well-illustrated by the contrast between two cosmic snakes: Apophis and Ouroboros." He argues, correctly, that in the contrast between the two cosmic snakes the serpent "appears as both exponent of and limit on the powers of chaos and nonexistence."[268] Again, we confront the striking double entendre of serpent symbology.[269]

In some legends and myths, rainbows are serpents touching the earth or drinking water.[270] The Aborigines developed a myth of the rainbow serpent, as mentioned earlier.[271] In Persian lore and elsewhere, the rainbow is explained as a great snake, and eclipses are understood as the attempts of dragon-serpents to swallow the sun or moon.[272] Apparently, the author of Job perceived the serpent in cosmic terms:

By his spirit he adorned the heavens,
His hand pierced the fleeing serpent [נחש; Job 26:13]

In Greek, Arabic, Syriac, and Latin the word for "snake," respectively *drakōn, ḥayya, ḥawwāyâ,* and *serpens,* also denotes the constellation Draco, which is between Ursa Major and Ursa Minor, as well as the constellation "Serpens," which is in the hand of Ophiuchos.[273] Servius reports that there are three serpents in the heavens.[274] The monument (c. 161 CE) celebrating the apotheosis of Antoninus Pius and Faustina features Mars holding a globe, the cosmos, around which is curled a large snake.[275] As we have seen, Zeus is often depicted as a serpent or partly serpentine, and it is no surprise that volume 1 of the magisterial work on Zeus by C. Cook is entitled *Zeus, God of the Bright Sky.*

In ancient times, the serpent is sometimes positioned entwined around a tree, with a piece of fruit on each side of its head and with the sun to the left and the moon to the right.[276] The author, or at least those who saw this symbol, thought about the ways the serpent helped the human conceive the cosmos.

Epiphanius mentions a gnostic system in which the archon of the lowest sphere is a dragon that swallows the souls without gnosis.[277] As Hans Jonas perceived, the serpent often symbolizes the cosmos and gnosis.[278] Serpents formed into a caduceus are featured on the Zodiacal Disk from Brindisi.[279] The heavens are sometimes imagined in the Hellenistic and Roman world as snakes. They appear either as stars or the stars are their symbols.[280]

These reflections disclose another meaning of the incense stands found at Beth Shan. The serpents and birds probably symbolized spring and the return of fertility. They also signified, at least to some of the Canaanites, something more. An informed imagination allows the human who participated in the serpent cult at Beth Shan often to perceive the serpent and dove as symbolizing the cosmos. Most likely for many in ancient Palestine, especially the Canaanites, the serpent symbolized the chthonic world, the human the earthly realm, and the dove the heavenly spheres.

The symbolism can be reversed. The snake could be depicted as threatening the dove, as in the Roman sculpture of a girl protecting a dove from a snake.[281] Then, the cosmic dimension of serpent iconography and symbology has been lost.

Shelley perspicaciously grasped the cosmic symbolic significance of the serpent. Note his words:

When priests and kings dissemble
In smiles or frowns their fierce disquietude;

Figure 70. China. Gold Cobra, about five
hundred years old. JHC Collection

When round pure hearts a host of hopes assemble;
    The *Snake* and Eagle meet—the world's foundations tremble! [282]

Jerusalem was built by Solomon and his descendants to replicate the
cosmic garden: Eden, or Paradise. The western side of the Kidron Valley
was sculptured into "a cascade of gardens and parks." As L. E. Stager
states: "The original Temple of Solomon was a mythopoeic realization of
heaven on earth, of Paradise, the Garden of Eden." [283] Would snakes have
not crept into this earthly paradise, and would that fact not have marred
the symbolism? Was not the snake banished from the Garden of Eden?
Surely, not only the author of Genesis 2:4b–3:24 (the Yahwist known as
"J"), but many Israelites knew that, according to the Genesis myth, the
serpent was never banished from Eden. Why would the Yahwist conclude
his story with the expulsion of only the humans: "So he drove out the man
[האדם]" (Gen 3:22–24)? If the Yahwist wrote at a time when Jerusalem
was richly endowed with flowering parks and gardens, undoubtedly an attractive habitat for crawling things like serpents, would he not have been
motivated to keep the snake in the edited story also? [284]

Chronos

The snake is elongated and limbless (cf. 2.5). When shaped into a line, it
can symbolize linear time. The ubiquitous and circuitous Ouroboros frequently, and perhaps fundamentally, symbolized time and eternity; it was
not only beginning but also end. Time was often perceived, as among the
Stoics, as circular.

    The shape of the serpent symbolized oneness, unity, and completion. It
could also symbolize time for the ancients.

In south-central Ohio there is a "Serpent Mound." It is a more than 400-meter-long image of a snake. The date now suggested, thanks to radiocarbon dating, is 900 to 1600 CE. Some experts believe that the Serpent Mound is aligned with the summer solstice sunset and perhaps with the winter solstice sunrise. The dating of wood charcoal found in situ points to circa 1070. Is it mere coincidence that Halley's comet appeared in 1066?[285]

Kingship

The snake shows no fear (cf. 2.15) and appears never to age and to be immortal (cf. 2.17). It (he, she) has a regal bearing (cf. 2.19 and 2.28), is physiologically unlike humans (and most creatures; cf. 2.23), and can administer death (cf. 2.20). These physical characteristics of the snake lie behind the perception of the serpent as denoting and connoting kingship. Analogous to the concept of the serpent symbolizing wisdom is the depiction of the "king" or ruler as protected or framed by serpents.

From Mesopotamia come mythological scenes in bas-relief on a steatite basin. These depict a man holding two serpents that are larger than he; they most likely date from the end of the fourth millennium BCE.[286] Likewise, from Mesopotamia (but from c. 2275 to 2260 BCE) comes a libation beaker that shows two serpents coiled around an upright staff. On both sides one can see a winged dragon with a serpent's head topped by a horned crown; it has front legs with lion paws and back legs with bird's claws.[287] Assyrian seals depict a serpent, thus representing godly and kingly powers and protection.

In various, sometimes antithetical, ways, the serpent represented "power." For Isaiah, the threatening powers were Leviathan and a dragon (Isa 27:1). For the Egyptians the uraeus, an aroused cobra or asp, was placed in royal palaces and on the heads of pharaohs to symbolize their godly and kingly powers (see Figs. 24 and 25). It is thus no surprise to see on Tutankhamen's throne winged serpents rising majestically from the back.

In the Greek world, the supreme God was Zeus and in the Latin world Jupiter (Fig. 57). He was sometimes challenged by the popularity of Asclepius, who promised health, healing, and immortality (e.g., Figs. 1 and 58). Both supreme gods appear with, and sometimes as, serpents and they sometimes conflate or merge (Fig. 11). Both were perceived to have kingly powers, especially Zeus, who is sometimes depicted as Zeus Meilichios.

In myths, especially in the Greek and Roman world, the divine kings were depicted as serpents or had serpent features.[288] Citing Pausanias (1.36.1), W. R. Halliday pointed out: "These snake kings were sometimes the slayer of snakes. Kychreus appeared in snake form at the battle of Salamis to help the patriot Greeks."[289]

Long ago, Wellhausen pointed out that the princely family of Taiji of the Arabian dynasty in Edessa and the kings of Abyssinia (Ethiopia) were supported by lore that claimed they were descended from serpents.[290] In Taiwan, the Paiwan chieftains during festivals are portrayed with a serpent. As is well known, the dragon (a mythically large serpent) signified the emperor in China.

Divinity

The apparent invisibility and elusiveness of the snake have evoked reflections on its divinity, since God has been experienced as not only invisible but also elusive (cf. 2.13). The same reflections apply to the snake's ability to symbolize the hidden one (cf. 2.14). The snake also appears to show no emotion (cf. 2.21); its expressionlessness suggests superiority, even divinity. The snake can only hiss and is without voice; its inability to make sounds like other animals might lead to reflections that it lives within the world of silence in which communication with God is possible (cf. 2.3). The snake's simulated smile might lead to reflections that it is at peace because it is one with the source of peace: God. The ability of the snake to forgo eating for months elicited reflections on its divinity (cf. 2.10). The fact that the snake is rare and unusual since it does not smell and is thus invisible and elusive (cf. 2.29) helped stimulate reflections on ways the serpent symbolized God.

In the preceding study, we saw ample evidence of ophiolatry, the worship of the snake.[291] Surely, many of the snakes made of gold and silver once belonged to an ophiolater (a worshipper of snakes). The second millennium BCE was a time of snake worshipping, and not only worshipping through snakes; the best examples are on Crete with the Minoan snake goddesses (or priestesses) and in the Canaanite snake cults at Beth Shan and Hazor. The Sinaitic Inscriptions contain a reference to a goddess of snakes, "the Serpent-Lady, my mistress."[292]

As H. Frankfort showed, the entwined serpents that form a caduceus on the steatite Gudea Vase from Lagash symbolized the god Ningizzida.[293] According to the author of the *Prayer of Jacob,* the Father of the Patriarchs, the Creator, sits upon "the s[er]pen[t] gods."[294]

According to Eusebius in his *Preparation for the Gospel,* Sanchuniathon, through Philo of Byblos' translation, explains how the serpent symbolizes divinity:

> The nature then of the dragon and of serpents Tauthus himself regarded as divine, and so again after him did the Phoenicians and Egyptians: for this animal was declared by him to be of all reptiles most full of breath, and fiery. . . . It is also most long-lived, and its nature is to put off its old skin, and so not only to grow young again, but

also to assume a larger growth; and after it has fulfilled its appointed measure of age, it is self-consumed.[295]

We are also dependent on Eusebius for the claim of the Egyptian scribe Epeïs, which was noted earlier, that the "first and most divine being is a serpent with the form of a hawk."[296]

In Greece, as we have demonstrated in Chapter 4, gods appear with serpents and as serpents. Earlier in Egypt the same was widespread; in hieroglyphics the snake is drawn to indicate ideograms, including "goddesses."[297] The hieroglyphic sign of a snake with horns, probably a horned viper *(f)*, combined with *t* dejotes a "viper," and as *f'g.t* (with a horned viper at the beginning and a cobra at the end) specifies the goddess Nechbet.[298] The "living god" Netjerankh is represented as an upright snake.[299] Josephus reports that the Egyptians believe that one who is bitten by an asp is "happy" and approved by the gods (*Against Apion* 2.7).

We need to add what has already been said about Zeus as a serpent. The Greeks believed that he transformed himself into a snake to woo his bride.[300] Herodotus (*Hist.* 2.74) reports that "sacred snakes" were "buried in the sanctuary of Zeus."

In the Agora Museum in Athens, one can see a ceramic plaque from the seventh century BCE (no. 21). It shows a goddess with both hands raised. On each side of her is a raised serpent.

In Persia, according to the historian Philo of Byblos, who wrote about the same time as the author of the Fourth Gospel, Zoroaster was sometimes celebrated and honored as a god who had the form of a serpent, but a hawk's head. According to this Philo, Zoroaster, in his teachings, held that the one

> who has the head of a hawk is god. He is the first, imperishable, everlasting, unbegotten, undivided, incomparable, the director of everything beautiful, the one who cannot be bribed, the best of the good, the wisest of the wise. He is also father of order and justice, self-taught, and without artifice and perfect and wise and he alone discovered the sacred nature.[301]

There is no reason to doubt that Philo of Byblos depicts Zoroaster as a serpent god. He includes this excerpt in his section on serpents, and prior to this excerpt refers to the "snake with the form of a hawk."[302] It is interesting to observe and ponder why centuries earlier the artisans who constructed the mask for Tutankhamen placed above his eyes the hawk and the serpent.

An Elamite seal impression of circa 1600 BCE depicts the Elamite serpent god seated on a snake and above a column of two entwined snakes.[303]

Figure 71. Byzantine Glass Appliquéd with Serpent with Prominent Head. Found in or near Jerusalem. JHC

This is reminiscent of the bronze column showing a serpent with three heads at Delphi. According to Herodotus (*Hist.* 9.81), the column commemorated the defeat of the Persians in 479 BCE. Constantine moved the snake column to Constantinople; it was unearthed in 1855 and what remains of the masterpiece can be seen today in Istanbul.[304]

Hezekiah destroyed the Nechushtan. Most likely this name represented a huge image of a serpent in the Jerusalem Temple (2 Kgs 18). Those who worshipped this serpent image could appeal to the tradition that Moses had created it, or one like it. And Moses had followed God's command, according to the ancient traditions (Num 21).[305] According to the *Acts of Philip,* Bartholomew and John suffer hardships because of much wickedness from those "who worship the viper, the mother of snakes" (8:94). The ways a snake may symbolize the divinity are thus not only varied and complex but also transcultural, even when we allow that in the Levant there was much shared symbolism.

Unity (Oneness)

No other animal is as streamlined as the snake. It is simple and sleek. The ancients perceived it as the quintessential symbol of unity or the symbol one. Thus, the limbless snake in its sheer simplicity represents unity and completeness. It can also, because of its lack of appendages, symbolize one (cf. 2.5). This aspect of serpent symbology is best represented by the Ouroboros that sometimes has inside it a Greek inscription that means "all (is) one."

The bronze, silver, and gold bracelets, earrings, and rings complete a circle (Figs. 34, 35, 38–40). Such serpent jewelry can represent more than apotropaic power.[306] They symbolize also unity or the symbol one.

Ancestor Worship

The snake often lives deep in the earth where the ancestors are buried (cf. 2.14, 2.18, 2.24); hence, the serpent came to symbolize ancestor worship. In Hastings' classic *Encyclopaedia of Religion and Ethics,* MacCulloch offered the opinion that ancestor worship was a dimension of the ancient serpent cult "in so far as certain snakes haunting houses or graves were associated with the dead." [307] Snakes are sometimes perceived as an embodiment of one who has died. Seeing snakes living near or in graves and tombs stimulated the imagination of the ancients. Perhaps such belief was enhanced if one, descending into a burial chamber, especially in or near Jerusalem in antiquity, notably during the Iron Age, approached a body that had lost its flesh and saw a snake slither away into the darkness.

In the Greek world, the snake could be a personification of the grave and bearer of the soul of the dead.[308] As W. Burkert states, the Greeks believed not only that "the deceased may appear in the form of a snake"; they also thought that "the spinal cord of the corpse" could be "transformed into a snake." [309] Plutarch, Ovid, and Pliny the Elder record the folk belief that the marrow of the dead could metamorphose into a snake.[310]

Earth-Lover

The snake must receive its warmth from the sun or the earth; hence, it is often associated with the earth and perceived as the Earth-Lover (cf. 2.12). In Babylon, the serpent is the offspring of Ka-di, the earth goddess. Küster devotes a full chapter to the serpent as the spirit of the earth *(Erdgeist).* This seems especially appropriate for legends and myths associated with Cybele, Cerberus, the Giants, Hydra,[311] Tryphon, and others.[312] Serpent symbolism is associated with the earth deities, like Demeter, Hecate, and Kore. In some myths, Asclepius was imagined to have originally been an earth god. According to the Hermetica, when Isis instructs Horus, we hear that "snakes (ὅι ὄφεις) and all creeping things love (φιλοῦσι) earth (γῆν)." [313]

Chthonic

The snake can disappear into the earth (cf. 2.18), lives in caves beneath the earth, frequents graves, and hibernates within the deep recesses of the earth for months (cf. 2.24).[314] Thus, the serpent is the primal symbol of the chthonic world.[315] Such iconography and symbology appear in neo-Assyrian and neo-Babylonian art and in the Egyptian Coffin Texts.[316] The numerous images of three chthonic gods standing on a serpent are a significant indication of the Egyptian perception of the serpent as a symbol of the underworld.[317] One can easily comprehend why Egli, in his book on serpent symbolism, emphasized that the serpent was the symbol of the underworld.[318]

In *Mythologies of the Ancient World*, S. N. Kramer points out that the serpent was customarily perceived as "the primary 'body' of any autochthonic deity in historical times."[319] Ancient Hittite mythology involved tales that served cultic needs. Perhaps the best known of these myths entails the fight between the Storm-god and the Dragon who is called *illuyanka*. This is both the proper name of the monster and the common noun for "dragon" or "serpent."[320]

Long before the Greeks and Romans, Assyrians and Egyptians, as well as others, observed the snake and accorded it mysterious chthonic knowledge. In *The Gods and Symbols of Ancient Egypt,* M. Lurker succinctly and accurately accesses this dimension of serpent symbolism:

> As a chthonic animal the snake was one of the life-creating powers, for example, the four female members of the Ogdoad bore snake heads and Amun appeared as a primeval deity in the form of he serpent Kematef. When the corn [= wheat][321] was brought in and wine was pressed, an offering was made to the harvest goddess, Thermuthis, who was serpentine in form or was depicted as a woman with a serpent's head. Furthermore, the demons of time and certain divisions of time were in the same form; the two-headed snake Nehebkau appears in the book of the netherworld, Amduat, and the attendant vignettes.[322]

Critical studies on hieroglyphics stress that Amun is symbolized in a serpent's body.[323]

When we discussed the Minoan serpent goddesses or priestesses we suggested that these images denoted chthonic power. Perhaps some Minoans saw in such images a way to control earthquakes and certainly to stimulate the fertility of the earth (Fig. 28). A. Evans offered his erudite opinion that the Minoan snake goddesses or priestesses signified "apparently the Underworld form of the great Minoan Goddesses."[324] As A. Golan states in *Myth and Symbol:* "The serpent was the preferred incarnation of the deified lord of the lower world."[325] Küster arrived at the conclusion that, for the Greeks, the major characteristic of the serpent is its chthonic character. Serpents were "chthonic gods" (χθόνοι θεοί).[326] We have seen funeral dedicatory reliefs that suggest that the serpent is chthonic. Asclepius and his companion snake were also considered to be chthonian. The dream of devotees of Asclepius, when they learned that an illness was fatal, could be comforted by the thought that Asclepius was chthonic. He controlled the next world; moreover, Asclepius had the power of resuscitation.

Magic

The snake is open-eyed (cf. 2.4) and elusive (cf. 2.6), can live for very long periods without food (cf. 2.10), can be almost imperceptible (cf. 2.13), and appears to have magical knowledge (cf. 2.16 and 2.17). These physiological characteristics and mysterious habits of the snake made it a symbol of magic. It appeared and disappeared without sound or warning. It can move through grass almost unperceived; the leaves do not even move.[327] In antiquity, the serpent's ability to move and climb became proverbial; for example, note the following imagery in twelfth-century BCE Assyria: "Like a viper on the rugged mountain ledges, I climbed dexterously" (*Annals of Tiglath-pileser I* 2.76–77).

The Ugaritic snakebite incantations use paronomasia (a play on words) to cause the desired magic.[328] MacCulloch surmises that the armlet or charm and other serpent iconography from the Paleolithic Period "might have been for some such magical rite as that of the Arunta." [329]

The hand of the god Sabazius is often shown holding a pinecone and animals, especially a snake. The depiction reflects some form of magic, since the pinecone, frog, lizard, and snake were imagined to possess magical powers.[330] In *Oneirokritica* 4.67, Artemidoros tells of a dream in which a woman sees herself giving birth to a snake who becomes a mantis.

Not only in the ancient world but also in modernity, snakes symbolize magic. The Australian shaman can claim that a snake is his *Budjan* (friend who supplies any necessary magic). Citing Hunt's *Drolls and Romances of the West of England*, Halliday reported that, within the past two hundred years, a Cornish magician was seen to appear as a large black snake.[331]

According to the authors and compilers of the Hebrew Bible (Old Testament), Moses' ability to change a staff into a snake is saluted as the presence and support of the only God. It is an example, however, of magic. Moses' use of the staff that he turned into a snake was a potent symbol because the snake was imagined to possess magical powers. This aspect of Moses' skills is highlighted in the Qur'an. Note the passage in "Poets": "So he (Moses) cast his staff down and imagine, it was clearly a snake! He pulled out his hand [from his shirtfront], and imagine, it was white to the spectators! He (Pharaoh) told the councilmen around him: 'This is some clever magician who wanted to drive you out of your land through his magic' " (26.32).[332]

In Hebrew, *nḥš* denotes not only snake (*nāḥāš* [with accent on the ultimate syllable]) but also "divination" or "magic curse" (*naḥaš* [with accent on the first syllable]). The latter provides the meaning of *nḥš* in Syriac; that is, ܢܚܫ means *augury*, or "divination." While it is conceivable that the two meanings are related etymologically in Hebrew, some, maybe many,

Figure 72. Aramaic Incantation Bowl with Serpent on the Handle. Circa 600 CE. JHC Collection

Hebrews, Israelites, and Jews imagined the "serpent" to be related to divination. Evidence of ophiomancy, divination through serpents, continued from the ancient world through to the medieval world, and is prevalent today in India and Africa.

Mystery, Wonder, and Awe

The unfathomable mechanisms of snakes, their ecological diversity and fascinating evolutionary process, their ability to retain feces (sometimes fecal matter can constitute 20 percent of a snake's weight), their skill in remaining inert 95 percent of their lives, and their ability to remain in or return to one home, cumulatively have elevated the snake so that it is mysterious, wondrous, and awesome to humans.[333] The quiet and swift movement of the snake and its elusiveness caused it to become a symbol of mystery, wonder, and awe (cf. 2.6). The snake's disturbing independence enabled it to symbolize mystery and wonder (cf. 2.11). The snake's grandeur and majestic beauty and size (cf. 2.28) helped to support the ability of the serpent to symbolize awe.[334]

In his *Histoires de serpents dans l'Égypte ancienne et moderne,* Keimer includes an insightful study of snake charmers. Most interesting is his study of serpents on ancient Egyptian monuments. According to some ancient authors (viz. Diadorus Siculus and Pliny the Elder) and ancient drawings, snakes were once imagined to be longer than full-grown elephants.[335] The uraeus, "the one who rises" according to hieroglyphics *(Iʿr·t),* appears today when a cobra rises before his charmer. The Arabic noun for cobra is *nâšir,* "the one which unfolds (or spreads out)." References to a snake charmer are ancient; they appear in Sumerian literature.[336]

In the distant past, before human recorded history, marvelous and mysterious creatures lived on this earth, according to ancient lore. Only two examples must now suffice to illustrate the wonder and mystery associated with snakes or serpents.

First, according to the Middle Kingdom Egyptian tale *The Shipwrecked Sailor*, an attendant to an official tells about a mysterious island that can disappear. The sailor relates how on this island he met a snake 30 cubits (about 16 m) long whose body is overlaid with gold and whose eyebrows are of "real lapis lazuli." This snake has awesome powers and can foresee the future. He is "the lord of Punt" and "the lord of the island." [337]

Second, a certain Babylonian named Berossus (βήρωσσος) sometime before the second century BCE, because Alexander Polyhistor cites him, composed a history of Babylonia. In his work, Berossus referred to the primordial time "in which there was nothing but darkness and an abyss of waters" (cf. Gen 1). Then, Berossus adds, "mysterious animals [ζῷα . . . θαυμαστα]" [338] like the snake appeared, mixing in their own forms the shapes of other animals. [339] The Dionysiac mysteries cherished a *cysta mystica*; that is, a box in which most likely a snake was kept. The snake was perceived, sometimes, to be Dionysus himself. As H. Leisegang pointed out, the serpent symbolized mystery to the Greeks. [340]

The author (or compiler) of Proverbs counts four things that are "too wonderful" for him so that he cannot understand them. The second listed is "the way of a serpent [נחש] on a rock" (Prov 30:19). As Halliday stated: "[The] snake has everywhere been an object of awe and reverence. The deadliness of the snake's bite and its uncanny appearance have marked it out for fearful adoration." [341] Thus, the serpent instills awe in many; he or she is the one filled with awe, and perhaps awful, whether one uses the category of the "Holy" with Otto, the "Powerful Awful" of Lang, or the "Zauberkraft" of Preuss. From ancient times until today the serpent symbolizes the awe-filled presence of "Le sacré."

Wisdom

The snake can descend into the bowels of the earth and learn the origins of plants and life (cf. 2.24); thus, the serpent can symbolize wisdom. The snake has no ears; its silence probably leads to speculations that it is attuned to the wisdom of the spiritual world (cf. 2.2). The snake also has no eyelids and cannot stop staring; this open-eyed quality of the snake gives grounds for reflections on how it represents wisdom, which is often associated with the eye. [342] W. Foerster rightly points to the "distinctive and often hypnotic stare" of the snake. [343] I recall this look in the eyes of the cobra that rose up before me when I was on my knees photographing it in Marrakech. As pointed out repeatedly, the eye is the one feature that appears most prominent in ancient ophidian iconography. The eye symbolized the wisdom of the serpent.[344] There is a proverb in Arabic: "He is more sharp-sighted than a serpent." [345]

In Utrecht, the Netherlands, an antiquarian bookseller has given the name "Cobra" to his store.[346] Why? It cannot be that he wants something devilish to be associated with his name; he is most likely thinking about the serpent as the symbol of wisdom. Beginning in the early second century CE, the Ophites imagined that the serpent embodied divine wisdom (see Appendix IV).[347]

Advanced research on serpents seeks to understand why and how so many different species of snakes can inhabit the same area. Is it because various snakes seek different prey? Is it because of the different times snakes devote to hunting: morning, noon, or night? Is it because the snake is one of the most inquisitive animals? Is that not related to the serpent as symbolizing wisdom?

The serpent denoted the ability to comprehend and obtain wisdom. Philo contended that the serpent symbolized "a bond of love and desire [ἔρωτος καὶ ἐπιθυμίας]. The serpent was under the rule and dominion of pleasure [ἡδονῆς]" so that the apprehension of objects is possible.[348] According to the author of the *Apocalypse of Moses,* the serpent is portrayed as the wisest of creatures. Thus, the Devil makes the serpent his vessel and speaks through him in order to deceive Adam.[349]

Another aspect of the serpent that is important for a perception of the intended meaning of John 3:14 is that the serpent represents Wisdom or the source of wisdom. Some ancient Greek myths, such as the story of Laocoon, suggest that one will understand the language of animals when the aspirant is touched on the ear by a serpent's tongue. By this means, the children of Hecuba, the Queen of Troy, were able to utter prophecies. In ancient Greece, Athena, the goddess of wisdom, was depicted as accompanied by serpents (see Fig. 52). In Aztec religion, the "feathered serpent," named Quetzalcoatl, was saluted as the source of wisdom, and the cultic priest was called "Prince of Serpents." As should be expected, the most famous connection between the serpent and wisdom is placed on the lips of Jesus by Matthew, as he sends out his disciples "among the wolves": "Be wise as serpents" (Mt 10:16).

God's Messenger (Judgment and Revelation)

The serpent represents God's messenger. Often biblical authors choose the serpent to symbolize the agent of God's judgment, usually punishment. According to Amos 9:3, God states that the end has come for "my people Israel": "I shall command the serpent (נחש), and he shall bite them." Thus, the serpent is God's messenger and the one who delivers divine judgment.[350]

Verses illustrative of the serpent as God's agent and the one who will bring justice and peace are found in Isaiah 14:29,

> Rejoice not, all you of Philistia,
> Because the rod that struck you is broken;
> For out of the serpent's root shall come forth a pit viper,
> And his offspring shall be a flying serpent.

Here we confront in one self-contained passage the use of the serpent and the pit viper to symbolize God's messenger.

In "Serpent Imagery in Ancient Israel," Le Grande Davies claimed that the God who sent " 'fiery flying serpents' was the God of Israel whose symbol of the bronze serpent stood before the people." [351] He suggested that the serpents were to administer justice. It seems more likely that "the serpent's root" of Isaiah 14:29 designates King Ahaz of Judah who has just died, as stated in Isaiah 15:28. The broader meaning seems to be that from the root of Judah, "the serpent's root, the deliverer shall come to save Israel." This one is symbolized as "a flying serpent." The importance of this point for an exegesis of John 3:14 will seem clear to most readers. God, of course, is identified in Isaiah and John with the final messenger from God, and both passages employ serpent imagery.

According to the author of Ecclesiastes, the one who breaks a hedge shall be bitten by a serpent (10:8; cf. Amos 5:19). Le Grande Davies claimed that the hedge and serpent are metaphors that denote the consequences of our actions; the serpent appears "as a symbol of the just judgments of God: whoever breaks down his law will be destroyed by the poisonous bite of the serpent." [352] This exegesis tends to paraphrase poetry—the symbol of the serpent is more multivalent than Davies realizes. The serpent, inter alia, symbolizes God's messenger who brings justice, judgment, and goodness. As L. H. Silberman pointed out: "The concept of a serpent as dispenser of divine justice was far more widespread than some commentators bothered to learn." [353]

Cassandra and her brother, Helenus, were left inadvertently in the temple of Apollo. Cassandra did not become pregnant as did the mothers of Alexander the Great and Augustus, but something prophetic happened. Their parents found them with two serpents. The serpents were licking their ears and eyes. Both Cassandra and Helenus, consequently, became messengers, or prophets, of the gods. Other Greek heroes and heroines, like Iamos and Melampus, had their ears purified by serpents and so obtained unusual, divine gifts. [354] As Chevalier and Gheerbrant state, in *The Penguin Dictionary of Symbols*, "the two facets of divination, both Apollonian and Dionysiac, derived from the serpent." [355] This means that the serpent sometimes symbolized God's messenger and brought God's voice to those who could hear.

Genesis Rabbah contains a story about a snake seen by Rabbi Jannai who was sitting and lecturing at the gate of a city. The Rabbi saw a snake (נחש) skimming along the ground, going from side to side. The Rabbi exclaimed, "This [snake] is going to carry out his mission [שליחותו]." [356] The snake had been sent on a mission. It accomplished its task. Soon the Rabbi heard a report that someone in the city had been bitten and died (10:7). [357] The snake was God's messenger (שליח); it delivered God's judgment.

In his masterpiece, Dante portrayed the snake as one who administers God's judgment. Note how Dante depicts the punishment of a thief:

> At once I liked the snakes; for one came sneaking
> About his [the thief's] throat, and wreathed itself around
> As though to say: "I will not have thee speaking";
> Another wrapped his arms, and once more bound
> All fast in front, knotting their coils till he
> Could give no jog, they were so tightly wound.
>
> [*Inferno,* Canto 25] [358]

Dante was inspired by reflections on other myths. Most likely he had been pondering the legend that snakes wreathed themselves around Laocoon. Dante "liked the snakes" because they caught, stopped, and punished thieves.

Beginning with the earliest examples of Christian art, Christ is shown defeating or trampling on a serpent or asp, and sometimes both, as we have seen. The depictions of Christ slaying a serpent were pictorial means of explaining to those who could not read that the Lord has defeated sin now and he will judge and condemn the serpent at the end of time.

The snake comes up from the earth (cf. 2.18) and ascends from the sea (cf. 2.16), thus symbolizing the one who has a message from the gods of the netherworld. The serpent becomes the consummate Revealer. In the *Encyclopaedia of Religion and Ethics,* MacCulloch opined: "The serpent is a revealer of the arts of civilization, this is probably because, where it was worshipped, it was often grafted on to a mythic culture-hero or eponymous founder." [359]

Hermes is the messenger of the gods. He reveals their will to humans. Hermes is usually identified with the caduceus. [360] Thus, the serpent is the symbol of the gods' messenger and the revealer of their will (Fig. 5). Infrequently, Hermes appears with a winged staff in his right hand and one snake curled around it; a rare example of this iconography is found in the

Capitoline Museum (just inside the front door of the Palazzo Nuovo and to the right).[361]

The Ophites rejected the "Great Church's" interpretation of the importance of the historical Jesus and the perception of the salvific importance of the Old Testament (see Appendix IV). They rejected the concept of a historical religion. They saw the serpent as symbolizing the heavenly realm of meaning, in a revived Platonic sense (with considerable Docetism).[362] The Ophites thus distorted the age-old symbol of the serpent as the one who revealed God's will.

Life

Since the snake is forced to swallow its food whole *and usually alive* (cf. 2.9), the serpent often symbolizes the embodiment of life. Whereas the lion kills and then eats sections of the kill periodically, the serpent often does not kill but swallows its prey alive and all at once. I have seen a snake with another snake, still alive and alert (with the mesmerizing unblinking eye), protruding from the victor's mouth. Thus, the snake does not always kill its prey; but, expanding its jaws perhaps five times the width of its neck, it absorbs life, swallowing it whole. Thus, the serpent becomes the symbol of life.[363] In *Das Schlangensymbol,* Egli devoted a chapter to the serpent as the symbol of life.[364]

In Arabic, *ḥayya* means "snake," *ḥayy* denotes "living," and *ḥayāh* indicates "life."[365] In Persian, *ḥayāt* denotes "life" and *ḥaiyāt* indicates "serpents (the plural of *ḥaiyat*)."[366] In Syriac, *hᵉwâ* is the verb "to be," but *ḥayyê* signifies "life," and *hewyâ* denotes "snake."[367] The sounds are similar, even if we might become lost searching for etymological links. Perhaps among some Semites "snake" and "life" were associated not only symbolically but also linguistically; in many Semitic languages and dialects, the sound of "snake" echoes the word "life."[368]

In Babylonian religion, Marduk struggles against and eventually slays the serpent-like (or dragon) Tiamât. Likewise in the Hebrew Scriptures (Old Testament) and the Old Testament Pseudepigrapha, the Creator is mythologically portrayed in a cosmic struggle with Leviathan, the sea serpent or dragon (see Appendix I). Also, in ancient Egyptian religion, Mehen, the serpent, was the god who protected Re on his journey through the sky. Likewise, in Indian mythology, the serpent Sesa is the companion of Vishnu, the god of preservation.[369] In ways conceptually odd for post-Enlightenment Western thinkers, the slaying of the dragon, or serpent, provides life.

Nourishment necessary for life is also often associated with the serpent. In many cultures, especially in Melanesia and South America, the serpent is the one who informs humans of the plants that are edible. In Egypt,

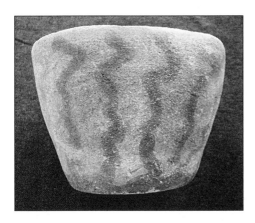

Figure 73. Ceramic Middle Bronze Pot with Serpents. Hebron, time of Abraham. JHC Collection

the goddess of agriculture was revered as a serpent. In Southwest Asia, in China, and among the Hopi Indians, the serpent is the deity who provides rain. The Aztec feathered serpent, Quetzalcoatl, becomes flesh, sacrifices itself for humans, and—according to the Dresden Codex—is the god that is "the cloud and his blood is the rain which will enable the maize to grow and mankind to live from the maize."[370] The serpent symbolizes life and sustenance.

The authors of the biblical and related literatures knew the snake's mysteriousness and chthonic nature. They thus chose it as an ideal creature for symbolism. The snake's ability to discard its old skin and grow more youthful evoked reflections by many humans on the fundamental relation between life and death.[371] According to the author of Numbers 21, and John 3 (as we shall see), the serpent represents life.

Water

The snake is amphibious (cf. 2.16); it can move over, through, and under water. Thus, it can symbolize water (both salt water and fresh water can be the snake's habitat). Numerous Greek names for a "snake" are associated with water (see Appendix II); for example, the *Columber natrix* is the "water snake" (ὕδρος [see Appendix II, no. 36]). Not only in Greek thought and myth but also in Etruscan, Roman, Egyptian, and Mesopotamian cultures, the serpent can symbolize water.[372] In discussing the serpent as a symbol of chaos and the cosmos, we confronted the many connections between this creature and water. The symbolism is grounded in reality. The snake can live in salt water and fresh water; it thrives in marshy land and in wetlands. It is clear why the serpent came to symbolize water, and why the hieroglyphic symbols for snake and water are so similar.

It is evident that the ancient symbol for water may be a double entendre: the serpent was included in the water symbol. The complex wavy line is prehistoric. Indeed, one of the oldest graphemes is a wavy line or zigzag. It appears in Paleolithic times and is prominent in the Levant and Asia Minor. In Sumerian cuneiform and Egyptian hieroglyphics, the ideograph for "water" is a zigzag or wavy line. Zigzags or waves decorate vessels on Crete, Asia Minor, ancient Palestine, and elsewhere. As A. Golan shows: "The zigzag as a graphic symbol had a specific meaning: it designated snake or water."[373]

The snake is often associated, from early times, with springs and gushing water.[374] The snake as a symbol of water is also evident when one observes that snakes and fish, so dissimilar, are ideologically associated and appear together iconographically and mythologically.[375] Of course, there is also the water snake that counters any suggestion that the serpent belongs on land and the fish in the water.[376] In Sumerian, *mūsh-ki* signified "snake-fish," and in Phoenician *nun* denoted "fish" as well as "water snake."[377] Apparently, the fascination with snake gods waned in Mesopotamia, beginning in the first half of the second millennium BCE.[378]

The Native Americans believed in a large serpent. He is often portrayed as a personification of water. According to the Ojibwa, he is connected with the primordial flood. According to the Hopi, the dance of their priests, holding rattlesnakes in their mouths, can produce rain. Although in China the snake is usually feared, the dragon is understood as one who can provide rain.[379]

MacCulloch suggested that the mythic association of the serpent with water and the waters is "either because some species lived in or near them or in marshy ground, or because the sinuous course and appearance of a serpent resembled those of a river."[380] Two Bactrian seal-stones, one in the Louvre and the other in the Kovacs Collection, were found in East Iran. The male figure on these seal-stones is similar to a man with serpents as arms known on other seals. According to G. Azarpay, this glyptic tradition suggests that the serpent symbolized longevity, immortality, fertility, and the fruitfulness of plants; moreover, the serpent also has phallic meaning and serves "as a reference to hidden sources of water."[381]

Adonijah, rivaling Solomon for David's throne, made sacrifices by a place called "the Serpent's Stone" (Heb.: *'eben hazzōḥelet* [1 Kgs 1:9]).[382] This stone is near En Rogel, which is usually identified with the spring at the southern end of the Kidron Valley where it meets the Hinnom Valley. Since "En" denotes a spring or well, in this ancient tradition we find an association of the concept of serpent with water.

Assyrians and Babylonians believed in the serpent god of the Euphrates or the deep. Leviathan and Rahab are monstrous dragon-serpents of the deep waters.[383] In the Ugaritic literature, for example, we find the statement that the Tanninim are "in the sea."[384] Psalm 74 contains a parallel thought to Babylonian and Assyrian myths. The Hebrew poet likewise identifies Leviathan with the flood and the mighty waters:

> You, you broke the heads of Leviathan in pieces,
> You gave him as food to the people inhabiting the wilderness.
> You, you broke open the fountain and the flood (or river);
> You, you dried up mighty rivers. [Ps 74:14]

Another important biblical passage that clarifies the link between water and serpent symbolism is Isaiah 27:1 (TANAKH):

> In that day the Lord will punish,
> With His great, cruel, mighty sword
> Leviathan, the Elusive Serpent—
> Leviathan, the Twisting Serpent;
> He will slay the Dragon of the sea.

In this passage it seems evident that the serpent personifies Assyria. Note the insightful comments by Le Grande Davies: "It is quite evident that Isa 27:1 used *Leviathan-naḥash* in a general historical context as the symbol of the once powerful Assyria, about to be destroyed. What appeared in the texts was a mythological symbolical personification of opposition and death to ancient Israel" (p. 43). Thus, the serpent as primordially a symbol of water has been shifted to a historical context.

In Arabia and Palmyra, the flow of wells or springs is imagined in lore to be controlled by serpents.[385] The concept of a serpent as present in such life-giving locales *(genius loci)* is well known in Greek and Roman times.[386] Clearly, not only in the Hellenistic and Roman periods but also in most world cultures, the sea, rivers, and springs were revered, even considered part of worship; the serpent is almost always present explicitly or implicitly in such contexts.[387]

In the previous chapters, we have studied the many pots or vessels with serpents depicted on them, usually with their heads near or on the rim.[388] The serpents may have been placed there to symbolize water and not only the protection of it, along with other liquids.

Soul (and Personal Names)

The snake was perceived to be chthonic,[389] immortal (or the creature that did not die),[390] and without distorting appendages;[391] hence, Greeks and Romans imagined the serpent as the animal that represented the soul. This perception derived primarily from its mysterious chthonic character. It could descend into the earth; it is there that the souls of the dead resided. Since snakes frequent tombs and graves,[392] the ancient Greeks, and others, associated the serpent with the soul of the departed.[393]

Evidence that the serpent was admired in antiquity is found in the names of different individuals. We find "dove" (Yona), "bee" (Deborah), "sheep" (Rachel), but also "adder" (Shepiphan) and "serpent" (Nachash), especially in 1 Samuel 11:1.[394]

Health and Healing

Since the snake is never perceived to be in pain or sick and rejuvenates itself through ecdysis or molting (cf. 2.17), it symbolized health and healing.[395] Maringer studied serpent images from the Paleolithic (at least 30,000 years before the present) to the Iron Ages. He perceived that, as early as the Iron Age, the serpent symbolized healing and medical properties. He surmised this meaning of serpent iconography because of the discovery of serpent images near thermal healing springs.[396]

Asclepius appears in dreams as a snake and is usually shown with a snake as a companion. His statues, with a staff around which a snake is entwined, permeated the ancient world. Today, Asclepius and his serpent can be seen as elegant sculptures in almost all the museums that feature ancient art, notably the British Museum, the Hermitage, the Greek National Museum in Athens, the museum at Epidaurus, the many museums in Rome, the archaeological museum in Naples, and elsewhere. For example, in the Capitoline Museum of Rome, a fourth-century dark bronze sculpture of Asclepius is on public display (no. 659). Asclepius is shown with a staff that is a small tree with broken branches and a serpent depicted realistically, with mouth, eyes, and scales. R. Jackson concluded that Asclepius' snake was the harmless *Elaphe longissima*.[397] Near the bronze statue of Asclepius is an image of Hygieia with a serpent in her right hand (no. 647).[398]

We need to recall that the son of Apollo, Asclepius, was not only associated with the serpent, but also often became the serpent. One example must now suffice. In *Metamorphoses*, Book 15, Ovid reports that Asclepius said: "Only look upon the serpent which twines about my staff [*hunc modo serpentem, baculum qui nexibus ambit*]." Then he announces his transmogrification: "I shall change myself to this [*vertar in hunc*]."[399]

By at least the first century CE, Asclepius seems to have reigned supreme as the god of healing. According to Porphyry's *Of the Philosophy Derived from Oracles*, as quoted by Eusebius in his *Preparation for the Gospel*, Asclepius spoke, revealing that he controlled wisdom and healing, and would answer requests. Note this excerpt:

> From sacred Tricca, lo! I come, the god
> Of mortal mother erst to Phoebus born,
> Of wisdom and the healing art a king,
> Asclepius nam'd. But say, what would'st thou ask?[400]

Not only Aslcepius but also Eshmun, a Phoenician god often identified with him, is placarded as the god of healing; and the two gods share the same symbols and become identified. Each is portrayed either as a serpent or accompanied by serpents, as we have seen numerous times in earlier chapters (see Figs. 1 and 53).

Hygieia, the daughter of Asclepius, is the goddess of healing; she is often depicted holding a bowl and tenderly feeding a large snake (see Fig. 60). On a bronze coin minted in 100 CE at Tiberias she is shown holding a ritual bowl (Greek: *phiale;* Latin: *patera*) in her right hand and a large snake in her left.[401] The snake is eating out of the bowl.[402] The date, 100 CE, is near to the final edition of the Gospel of John, about 95 CE. And a similar image appears on a bronze coin of 250 CE that was struck in Aelia Capitolina, the city that replaced Jerusalem, now utterly destroyed for a second time within one hundred years. It shows Hygieia holding a bowl in her lap and a large snake rearing up to eat from it.

In Aelia Capitolina (and perhaps earlier in pre-70 Jerusalem), an Asclepeian was erected in Bethzatha (in the northeast part of the city), as we have already indicated. Archaeologists have found ex-voto offerings; one depicts an impressive upraised serpent,[403] and the rustic Bethzatha Vase is loaded with serpents. At Roman Caesarea Maritima, experts have found evidence of an Asclepeian, with marble votive feet and statues of Asclepius and Hygieia.[404] Asclepius was associated with the hot springs at Hammat Tiberius; a coin struck at Tiberius in 99 CE shows on the obverse the bust of Trajan and on the reverse Hygieia holding the sacred snake.[405]

Before the time of the Fourth Evangelist and the culture in which his gospel took shape, Livy (died at Padua in 17 CE) explained why Asclepius was invited to come to Rome from Epidaurus. There had been a pestilence *(pestilentiae)* that had ravaged not only the city but also the countryside. Only Asclepius could heal this sickness. In Book 10.47.6–7, Livy preserved this report: "The Books [*libri*] were consulted to discover what end or what remedy the gods proposed for this misfortune [*eius mali*]. It was discovered in the Books that Aesculapius must be summoned to Rome from Epidaurus [*Aesculapium ab Epidauro Romam*]."[406] Eventually, a serpent was sent from Epidaurus to Rome; the Romans imagined the serpent was Asclepius.[407] It is remarkable that Livy recorded the tradition of how Greece and its gods helped the Romans and their gods, since he stressed in his *History of Rome,* which was written in the 20s BCE (when Herod the Great began the rebuilding of the Jerusalem Temple), that Rome had been blessed with a religious founding. He also emphasized the "necessity for the ancient cults to be located in Rome and the significance of Rome's sacred boundary, the pomerium (5.52)."[408]

A relief from circa 370 BCE shows the Greek hero healer named Amphiaraus. In the stone is carved a scene in which a serpent licks the wounds on a man's shoulder. The latter is sleeping in a sanctuary (incubation).[409] As R. Parker states: "There were healing gods and heroes throughout Greece, their shrines bedecked, like those of Catholic saints, with the votive offerings of grateful patients (often clay images of the affected organ)." [410] We discussed these ex-voto offerings to Asclepius and the Asklepieion at Corinth in an earlier chapter.

The image of the serpent as the symbol of salvation should be categorized under healing since healing and salvation are cognitively synonymous. The best example of the serpent as savior appears in a Jewish writing from the second century BCE. The author of the Wisdom of Solomon perceived Moses' raised serpent as a "symbol of salvation" (σύμβολον ἔχοντες σωτηρίας [15:6]). The serpent was a sign of salvation; God was the one who healed the Hebrews: "For he that turned himself toward it [the serpent] was not saved by the thing that he saw, but by you who are the Savior of all" (Wis 16:7).

Not only Native Americans, but also Arabs, Greeks, Jews, and Romans often believed that eating a snake's flesh, or placing its fat on one's skin, especially in the area bitten, would heal the person and protect him or her from dying.[411] In the ancient world, and not only in modernity, venom was extracted from a snake and used to heal humans. Thus, the connection with healing and the serpent is not only ancient but continues today.

Evident in most discussions of Numbers 21, and lacking in most interpretations of John 3:14–15, is the perception that the serpent is the symbol for healing in many cultures.[412] Those who trusted in God and looked up to the serpent were healed from the bite of a venomous snake. Thus, the lore reflected in Numbers 21 is paralleled by Phoenician culture, since Eshmun, the Phoenician god of healing, is symbolized by a serpent. About the same time in Egypt, amulets shaped like serpents were worn to protect not only the living but also the dead.[413] According to the Babylonian Talmud, portions from the snake were efficacious for healing skin diseases (Shabbat 133b).[414]

In Hinduism, Manasa, the snake goddess, is invoked from time immemorial to heal one who has been bitten by a cobra. The ancient Assyrians, Babylonians, and Egyptians revered the serpent as the creature that heals. In ancient Syria and Greece, Shadrapa and Asclepius, the gods of healing, were symbolically associated with the serpent. Today, the caduceus is the symbol of physicians and pharmacists; sometimes the staff of Asclepius with the snake symbolizes the medical profession. In the Hellenic, Hellenistic, and Roman worlds the caduceus was the staff of Asclepius with serpents curled around it.

Figure 74. Remains of Sculptured Boat, Asclepius Temple (*above*), and close-up of staff with serpent and bust of Asclepius (*left*). Tiber River, Rome. JHC

Purifying

The limbless and elongated snake symbolized not only unity and oneness, but also purity (cf. 2.5). The Hebrew noun *sārāph* (שרף), "burning-serpent," seems to have a connotation for purifying a human of sickness. In contrast to most other nouns for serpent or snake in biblical Hebrew, "burning-serpent" derives from and is etymologically grounded in the verb "to burn" (see Appendix I). Thus, the many passages in which שרף appears in the sense of burning to purify as in a sacrificial offering carry over to the noun, "burning-serpent."[415] It is possible that the "burning-serpents" sent by God to "punish" Israel were actually sent to purify it (Num 21). As stoning was a purifying act—to drive out the demon inside the possessed person[416]—so the bite of the "burning-serpent" may have been perceived as God's way of purifying those who had doubted and rejected the only true God.

In "Serpent Imagery in Ancient Israel," Le Grande Davies astutely suggests that an "examination of the contexts of *seraph* indicates its 'burning' aspects are related to cleansing, purifying or refining of objects, people, cities, etc." (p. 83). The clearest example of the relation between the Seraphim and purification is not grounded in the verb. Isaiah laments that he is impure: "A man of unclean lips I am; and in the midst of a people of unclean lips I dwell" (Isa 6:5). How is this great prophet cleansed? One of the Seraphim—winged serpents (see Appendix I)—takes a hot coal from the altar and touches his mouth. The divine burning-serpent declares:

> Behold, this has touched your lips;
> Your iniquity is taken away,
> And your sin purified. [Isa 6:7]

In Greek and Roman myth and folklore, the lick of the serpent is purifying and imparts unusual abilities. For example, snakes purified the ears of Melampus. On awakening, he could understand bird language and became a prophet.[417] Likewise, serpents licked the ears of Cassandra and Helenus, in the sanctuary of Apollo. So purified, they also were able to understand the language of birds.[418]

In our attempt to organize and categorize the symbolic meanings of the serpent, some reflections by Ambrose might be placed here. In his *Of the Christian Faith,* Ambrose urges his fellow Christians to be like serpents. Note his exhortation:

> For those are serpents, such as the Gospel intends, who put off old habits, in order to put on new manners: "Putting off the old man, together with his acts, and putting on the new man, made in the image of Him Who created him." Let us learn then, the ways of those whom the Gospel calls the serpents, throwing off the slough of the old man, that so, like serpents, we may know how to preserve our life and beware of fraud.[419]

Transcendence

The snake does not show emotion, fear, or pain (cf. 2.3, 2.15, 2.21), is fiercely independent (cf. 2.11), and can transcend the limitations of other creatures (cf. 2.17). These physiological and habitual characteristics of snakes helped stimulate the perception that the serpent symbolized transcendence.

In *Man and His Symbols,* C. G. Jung stressed the ability of the serpent to symbolize transcendence. Jung published the following conclusion: "Perhaps the commonest dream symbol of transcendence is the snake, as represented by the therapeutic symbol of the Roman god of medicine Aesculapius, which has survived to modern times as a sign of the medical profession."[420]

J. L. Henderson and M. Oakes point to the serpent as the symbol of transcendence. Especially noteworthy are the ways Hermes acquired wings and symbolized spiritual transcendence. The authors focused on the entwined serpents, the caduceus and the Indian Naga serpents; they explained this serpent iconography as an "important and widespread symbol of chthonic transcendence." [421]

It does seem clear that when Hermes becomes Mercury, he obtains wings. He became "the flying man" and possessed the winged hat, sandals, and even a dog as companion. Henderson and Oakes appear to be right in interpreting the iconography of Hermes: "Here we see his full power of transcendence, whereby the lower transcendence from underworld snake-consciousness, passing through the medium of earthly reality, finally attains transcendence to superhuman or transpersonal reality in its winged flight." [422]

Rejuvenation

Because the snake sheds its skin (ecdysis) and regains a youthful appearance (cf. 2.17), it came to symbolize rejuvenation. Without wrinkles and with no signs of old age, the serpent, through ecdysis, was imagined to symbolize youthfulness and rejuvenation. In the Asclepian cult, the serpent symbolized new life and health. Nicander preserves an old myth in which humans did receive the gift of youthfulness, but, being lazy, they let an ass carry the gift. The ass bucked and eventually sought a snake to quench his thirst. The serpent was pleased to bear the burden on the back of the ass because he then obtained eternal youthfulness or rejuvenation. [423] Once again, as in the Gilgamesh epic, the serpent wins the prize sought by humans. Of all creatures, the serpent symbolized the one who had the secret of rejuvenation.

Immortality, Reincarnation, and Resurrection

The Greeks and Romans knew that immortality without youthfulness would be a curse. [424] The lover of the goddess Dawn—who appears fresh and resplendent each morning—obtained immortality. There is an ironic twist; he continued living but he simply grew older each day (*Homeric Hymn* 5.218–38). Endymion receives eternal youth from Zeus, but he cannot sleep (Apollodorus 1.7.5). Juturna receives immortality from Zeus, but must witness the death of loved ones (*Aeneid* 12.869–86).

Because the snake sheds its skin and apparently obtains new life (cf. 2.17), it became the quintessential symbol of immortality and reincarnation. Among the Jews and Christians who held a belief in resurrection, sometimes the serpent represented that belief.

This point, at least for Sumerian culture, was clarified and emphasized by V. Lloyd-Russell in his 1938 PhD dissertation at the University of Southern California. It is entitled "The Serpent as the Prime Symbol of

Immortality Has Its Origin in the Semitic-Sumerian Culture." His dissertation, while interesting and informative, is undermined by the claim that the cradle of serpent symbolism must be in or near Sumer or Akkad and from "this homeland, the symbol followed the great migrations of people from the Old World to the New" (p. iii). While Küster sought to subsume all serpent symbology under the concept of the chthonic, Lloyd-Russell sought to prove that the primary and dynamic meaning of serpent symbolism is always immortality.[425] The result is the degeneration of an interrogative thesis into an attempted demonstration of an idea. We have seen that serpent symbolism does not suggest one originative locale; it is an aspect of the commonality of the human who lives in and near snakes and perceives something important for meaningful life. Without doubt, the human aspires to escape death and has often employed serpent symbolism to articulate this common, but elusive, dream.

The snake (like some other animals, especially the lizard) sheds its skin. When one walks in the wilderness or any place where snakes dwell, one often sees the sign of death: discarded snakeskin. But the reflective person readily knows that there is a live snake not far away. This rather "unique" habit of the snake influenced religious symbolism. In the world's religions, the serpent symbolized rebirth, reincarnation, and even (later) resurrection, because the snake leaves its old skin (it only apparently dies) and moves into what looks like a new body. The Phoenicians celebrated the rebirth, perhaps resurrection, of Adonis and chanted something analogous to *resurrexit dominus:* "The lord is resurrected."[426] Since the snake appears to die and live again, the waxing and waning moon is often depicted symbolically as a serpent.[427] This concept may help explain why in the Congo the Nagala believe that the moon was formerly a python on earth.

When the snake is depicted coiled, it may symbolize immortality.[428] The "Coiled One" *(mḥn)* game, with the serpent in a coil, in the Pyramid and Coffin texts was a means of transformation to rebirth and even ascension into heaven.[429] The serpent represented eternal life. As V. Lloyd-Russell stated: "It is not paradox that the reptile, whose venom caused the annihilation of the life of man, should be chosen to articulate eternal life. He might destroy but he contained life. If he were propitiated, if one could ingratiate oneself before him, the eternal Sa might even be communicated in the bite."[430]

In antiquity, the Gilgamesh epic, "the most famous literary relic of ancient Mesopotamia,"[431] which influenced some traditions in the Old Testament, solidified in writing the legend that the serpent alone possessed the plant of immortal life. W. F. Albright called the Gilgamesh epic "that remarkable work of early Babylonian genius . . . which attains its culmination in the hero's vain quest of eternal life."[432]

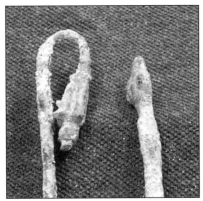

Figure 75. Bronze Stirrers. From Jerusalem (*left*) and Jericho (*right*); both are early Roman, probably Herodian Period. Note each serpent head. JHC Collection

In Egypt, the serpent is connected with some form of immortality or "resurrection." In the Pyramid Texts, the dead king is awakened and his odor is like that of a special serpent; he does not rot (*Utterance* 576). *Utterance* 683 has the following: "It is Horus, who comes forth from the Nile . . . it is the *ḏ.t*-serpent which comes from Rē'; it is the *'i'r·t*-serpent which comes from Set." [433]

In numerous Greek legends, especially concerning Glaucus and Tylon, serpents are depicted as those that can bring back the dead to life. Hercules leaves the snake in the tree in the Garden of the Hesperides and makes off with the golden apples of immortality (see Fig. 56). S. Reinach pointed out that at the heart of Orphism is the birth, death, and resurrection of Zagreus, who appears iconographically as a serpent with a small crown. [434]

The serpent can symbolize many ideas and concepts; some are negative and others positive. Among the latter are images of the serpent that reveal its symbolic power to represent rejuvenation, immortality, reincarnation, and resurrection.

Purely Decorative

On those occasions when human beings view the snake as attractive (cf. 2.19), they choose serpent images to exemplify that beauty. In this study, our focus has been on serpent symbolism. Hence, sometimes a drawing of a serpent or a golden serpent bracelet may merely be intended either for decoration or to enhance someone's attractiveness. Symbolism thus ceases and the symbol no longer has meaning; when the symbol is seen only as embellishment, symbolism ceases.

Images that had been richly symbolical can become merely decorative or aesthetic. In the *Dictionnaire d'archéologie chrétienne et de liturgie*,

H. Leclercq rightly stated that sometimes "the serpent appears simply to fulfill a decorative role."[435] While I disagree with him that a serpent on a sarcophagus is mere decoration (it probably signals a belief and hope in some new and better life after death), some lintels and jewelry may have been designed or intended only to appear attractive and decorative.

While I am persuaded that originally, at least, most of the serpent imagery had deep and complex symbolic meanings, many intellectuals, especially in the middle and later Roman periods, would have thought an anguine object was merely ornamental. The Roman bronze ladle for dipping wine mixed with water may have connoted for some guests many positive feelings, but other guests probably took them only as attractive decoration (see Fig. 63). Serpents on vases (Fig. 61), and the numerous bronze, silver, and gold serpent bracelets, rings, and earrings certainly connoted positive symbolic meanings, but for many they were mere jewelry (see Figs. 34, 35, 38, 39, 40, 41, 62). Elegantly made glass objects with serpent appliqué denote many symbols, but they were also ornamental (Fig. 71).[436]

The silver Viking serpent ring probably had mythological meanings, but it was also attractive, and the bearer may have worn it only for decoration (Fig. 9). The Minoan serpent goddesses or priestess (Fig. 28) and the Carmel Aphrodite with a serpent on her thigh (Fig. 23) symbolized many attributes, but some who viewed them may have had no symbolic imagination and took them as only artworks of magnetic attraction. The tattoos of snakes in ancient and modern Egypt, and elsewhere, may be merely for decorating the body, or they may have special meanings perhaps known only to those who wear them.[437]

No serpents appear on Jewish ossuaries (stone containers for the bones of the deceased); images on these ossuaries eventually lost the symbolic meaning given to them by Greeks and Romans.[438] The Medea sarcophagi—the depictions of Medea in a chariot pulled by winged snakes—originally symbolized that the serpents pulling her chariot knew the way to the abode of the deceased.[439] As stated many times before, we living today have lost the naïveté of the ancients and their feeling for symbolic language. How many of us still think about the symbolic meaning of the caduceus on our medical prescriptions?

Long ago, A. D. Nock made a comment about serpents, symbols, and decoration that deserves highlighting:

> A serpent can evoke a variety of associations—death, the renewal of life (as suggested by its sloughing its skin), the protective Hausschlange, the healing power of Asclepius, fecundity, a hostile power to be crushed etc. When however a Greek gem of the late sixth century B.C. shows a snake rising behind Nike, need it carry any meaning? Is

it not a fallacy to suppose that what an artist produces must involve or repeat something which could be put into words? The world of forms has a certain autonomy, smaller if you will than of the world of music, but undeniable.[440]

Riches and Wealth

The natural beauty of the snake (cf. 2.9) and its grandeur (cf. 2.28) helped stimulate thoughts about the serpent as a symbol of riches and wealth. The rich decorations in the tomb of Tutankhamen, for example, used the serpent to symbolize many things, including riches and wealth. The image of the serpent was used for games in ancient Egypt, and it sometimes lost its complex symbolism, degenerating into denoting the playful search for wealth.[441]

In West Africa, a heavenly serpent is worshipped. This rainbow serpent offers riches and wealth to its devotees. Sometimes it is perceived to be a python that promises the best weather, fertile crops, and abundant cattle. On the Bass River, a python is revered as the great warrior who promises, among other gifts, riches. Something similar is found in the Voodoo serpent cult in Haiti.[442]

These reflections clarify why ophiophilism, the love of snakes, has continued among humans for millennia. We humans once needed snakes for protection, even companionship. Those who fear them are usually those who are far removed from nature. I still marvel at the professor's wife in South Africa who told me, without emotion, how she had been forced to kill a mother cobra and her hatch when she cleaned up her backyard. I know Americans and Europeans who have not shared her experience feel that her actions are exceedingly foreign.

The snake has been erased from our perception. This costly reduction occurred by the fourth century CE. Prior to the first century CE, the snake was one of the animals most represented in mosaics,[443] but the relegation and pejorative treatment of the snake are reflected in later mosaics. The pagan mosaics of Orpheus include the snake, but the Christian mosaics of Orpheus delete it.[444] For example, in the extraordinarily decorated late third- or early fourth-century mosaic floor at Lod, Israel, the artist depicts numerous animals, notably a lion, rabbit, giraffe, elephant, and dolphins, bulls, birds, deer, and fish, but he does not celebrate the snake. If anguine symbolism is clear in the Lod mosaic, it is a snake biting a stag or a mythological dragon between two lions.[445] The appreciation of the serpent, as in the Asclepian cult, has not influenced the artist or the owner of the villa.

Figure 76. Bronze Serpent Bracelet, Lead Inkwell. Herodian Period. Jerusalem. JHC Collection

Summary

Why have snakes provided such various and diverse symbolic meanings? Clearly, the multivalence of serpent symbolism results from the fact that humans have experienced and expressed the most varied emotional reactions to this animal. From sometime about 40,000 BCE to the present we have amassed evidence that humans consistently fear and revere snakes. Why?

We fear snakes primarily because they can inflict death, spewing or injecting venom that attacks the blood and heart or the nervous system. The venom is lethal and has killed humans. We also fear these animals because it is impossible to control or communicate with them, let alone tame them. We abhor snakes because they can appear without warning in our homes. Finally, reflecting on past encounters with snakes and imagining future confrontations with them provide us no paradigm for avoiding being inadvertently controlled by them.

Having articulated what seems so obvious, even to those who have not and will not encounter snakes, can anything be said on why *Homo sapiens* have for forty-three millennia admired, even worshipped, snakes? Without striving to order the reasons why humans have found snakes symbolical of positive concepts (any such ordering would misrepresent the varieties of cultures and times to be covered), I can list no fewer than fifteen reasons why the snake was chosen as a positive symbol:

1. Snakes can rejuvenate themselves, appearing with new skin at least once a year, seemingly to live for ever.[446]
2. They never appear tired, sick, or old.
3. They are astonishingly beautiful.
4. Their bodies are smooth and glisten.

5. They never give off a smell.
6. They do not need washing or cleansing.
7. They (in contrast to humans) seldom defecate, never urinate, and relatively do not pollute the air (like dogs).[447]
8. They may have a rare tick or other parasite, but they are not bearers of pestilence or vermin (like mice).
9. They protect us from rats and other pests.
10. They can go deep into the earth or the sea but we cannot follow.
11. They aerate and enrich our gardens.
12. They provide venom for healings.
13. They are admirably independent of us.
14. They taste good.
15. They provide attractive skins for accessories and shoes.

At this point, some attentive readers might object, claiming that more should be added to the list of negative characteristics of snakes. They might contend that snakes are slimy and clammy and awful to touch. They would perhaps argue that snakes are aggressive, seeking by their nature to attack and kill humans. They probably would claim that snakes are filthy since they spend their lives in the filth of the earth.

What can we reply to these claims? Are they not patently accurate?

These claims do accurately reflect the fears of many, but they derive from mythology and not fact. Children who have not been taught to fear snakes find that when they hold a garden snake or a black indigo, they admit that the feeling is attractive and comfortable. Ophiologists have proved, from years of study and experimentation, that snakes are not aggressive; by nature they are defensive. Snakes do not seek to kill humans; in fact, when threatened they often release only a minor amount of venom (snakes can control the amount of venom excreted). If snakes come into the home from the sewer, they are filthy and dangerous as we would be if we had been in a sewer. The Ophites would never have imagined a serpent could consecrate the bread for the Eucharist if it were in any way perceived to be a bearer of pollution or filth.

Gifted symbologists and phenomenologists will now feel that the main issue has become distorted. They will point out that even though it has been proved that ophidian iconography and symbology derive from the physiological characteristics of snakes, a major point has been lost. They will stress—and rightly so—that it is not the physical characteristics of snakes that undergird ophidian symbolism, it is the human perception of these characteristics.

No one should deny that perception helps create symbols. Yet perception precedes symbolism. Our perception of snakes defines and allows for ophidian symbolism. We never see snakes sick or old; we see them rejuvenated periodically. That stimulates reflections on immortality (which eludes us as well as snakes). We sometimes cannot discern which end of a snake is a tail or a head, which is especially unclear in some earthworms or small snakes. Our perceptions of beginning and end—the continuum of philosophical reflections—are deepened when we see a snake's head protruding from another snake's mouth or a snake's tail close to or in its own mouth (Ouroboros). How did time begin and what is time and eternity? Ophidian iconography helps us broach and represent such perennial questions.

Around humans the heads of snakes are almost always raised and alert. The upraised snake is a fact of nature (Figs. 13 and 15) and of serpent iconography (e.g., Figs. 42 and 49). The upraised serpent provides the symbology we see in the uraeus, as well as in Numbers 21 and John 3. Thus, as we proceed, we should keep in mind the recognition that behind ophidian symbology lies the fascination of humans with snakes, the physiology of snakes, and most notably the perception of the phenomenology of snakes.

Now we may return, with deeper insight, to the fifteen reasons why humans have found snakes to be attractive and desirable. These reflections help us imagine the millennia when our ancestors lived in caves, with snakes, and the millennia others worked in the fields or sat in huts or houses in which a snake was welcome. The almost global penchant of frantically killing snakes, especially in Ireland and the United States, has changed the world that had been created. We also have become divorced from the earth and from nature. The words "Mother Earth" have disappeared from our lexicons. They no longer bring comfort to our lips.

CONCLUSION

Paul Tillich argued that a symbol obtains some of the meaning of what it points to, but a sign only points to something else. He influenced such luminaries as Reinhold Niebuhr, Paul Ricoeur, Langdon Gilkey, and David Tracy. We have seen that serpent images were not only signs; they were symbols that made present the ideas and concepts imagined. We have seen reasons to agree with C. G. Jung that serpent symbols appear in all human cultures, suggesting a shared archetypal collective unconscious in humans. I would agree with Ernst Cassirer that humans are distinct from other animals by their ability to create symbols.

Serpents symbolize neither something bad nor something good. They even provide more than just symbolically portraying both these opposites together (double entendre). Biblical scholars and experts in other fields of antiquity should grasp more fully a fact seldom perceived today but articu-

Figure 77. A Scarab Found in or Near Jerusalem. A man with a flute and an upraised cobra behind him. Circa eighth century BCE. JHC Collection

lated in 1850 by F. G. Welcker: of all animals, the serpent has provided the richest and most complex meanings to the human.[448] Because of the extraordinary physiological and habitual characteristics of these creatures, and their complex, contradictory relations with us humans over time and at the same time, they have become a symbol that reveals the vague, often contradictory, boundaries of the language of symbolism.[449]

We must be careful not to overinterpret symbols. As music cannot be said and poetry only misrepresented by prose, so symbols must not be equated with what are articulated concerning them. They have a language of their own. Their abilities to evoke thoughts and emotions cannot be reduced to words. Symbols do not display, not even when they are voluptuous serpent goddesses; they point to that which the human yearns for and needs for sustenance, survival, and—most of all—meaning in a phenomenologically chaotic world. It would not be in our own best interest to reduce the ophidian object in Fig. 77 to a limited number of meanings. The importance of this illustration may be in its power to evoke and instill wonder. Why is a man playing a flute with an upraised cobra *behind him*?

We humans named animals. We also gave animated onomatopoeic names to snakes—like *nachash, seraph, ephʿee, shephiphon,* and *ophis* (to bring out the hissing sound of these nouns; see Appendix I). Reading Numbers 21 aloud in Hebrew, as it was intended, brings to the attentive ear the sounds we have heard from snakes. With imaginative reflections on Genesis 3, we may hear from the animal world the remains of the serpents' speech in the hissing vibrations that accompany their names as we mention them in Hebrew and Greek (the languages of the texts we are about to explore). With their ability to spirantize, the ancient Hebrews read the Torah, customarily aloud, with a better intuitive feeling of the language that originates in another world.

The research discussed here is a summary of what I have learned over the past six years of focused explorations into serpent iconography and symbology. I began with the fear that images have no set denotation because the viewer supplies any meaning. Erwin Panofsky offered this warning: "There is admittedly some danger that iconology will behave, not like ethnology as opposed to ethnography, but like astrology as opposed to astrography." [450] We have seen that serpent symbology has a discernible denotation, even if it is multivalent. How, for example, can a uraeus be meaningful if it is a symbol of both evil and goodness?

We exegetes now have a guide to serpent iconology and symbology. Humans, virtually everywhere and from earliest times, have chosen a similar mass of limited images. It is now possible to reexamine the biblical texts in which serpent symbolism is prominent.

6

Serpent Symbolism in the Hebrew Bible (Old Testament)

Why was it necessary to emphasize the polyvalent symbolic meanings of the serpent in antiquity? It was necessary in order to stress the rich varieties of meanings in ancient serpent iconography and symbolism and to repeat them from different vantage points because biblical scholars are systematically trained in the biblical languages, but not sufficiently introduced to the worlds of iconography and symbology. Moreover, it is clear from my conversations with colleagues that they almost always are eager to confess an abhorrence of snakes. These colleagues do not seem to comprehend that they also, as did the ancients, almost always possess in tension a fear of and a fascination with enchanting snakes. In fact, my associates are sometimes misled by fallacious reports that are taken as factual. Such antipathy to serpents prohibits a sensitive exploration of the symbolic meaning of the serpent in ancient literature, especially the Hebrew Bible and the Gospel of John. The authors and editors of the Bible were surrounded by serpent cults and images that appeared at the beginnings of human drawing and art.[1]

One example only must now suffice. It is taken from the prestigious and influential *Theological Dictionary of the New Testament*. Three entries in *TDNT* are devoted to the serpent. These three are δράκων, which appears only in Revelation (12:3, 4, 7, 9, 13, 16, 17; 13:2, 4, 11; 16:13; 20:2),[2] ἔχιδνα, which is found only in Acts 28:3,[3] and ὄφις, which appears fourteen times in the New Testament.[4] W. Foerster contributed each of these three entries, and each is marred by his penchant to portray the serpent as a diabolical symbol. Note this excerpt:

> Of all beasts, the serpent was regarded as demonic in antiquity, thereby revealing the duality of the ancient conception of demons. It

269

plays a great part in Persian, Babylonian and Assyrian, Egyptian and Greek mythology and in essence this role is always the same; it is a power of chaos which opposed God either in the beginning or at the end of things, or both. [*TDNT* 3 (1964) 281]

The quotation represents Foerster's perspective. It does not accurately summarize the meaning of the serpent and serpent symbolism in biblical and parabiblical documents.

We have demonstrated that while the serpent can denote chaos (Neg. 3), the serpent does not "always" bear the same symbolic meaning. Foerster's report is not only one-sided; it is simply inaccurate. His work is typical of the lack of careful, disinterested research that grounds biblical exegesis in archaeology, iconography, and symbology. It seems evident why generations of biblical exegetes have been misled regarding symbology, especially serpent symbolism. The whole enterprise of exegesis and theology is undermined if biblical symbology is misperceived, since all Scripture is symbolical. And, moreover, symbols are often presented in dynamic, even contradictory, ways, since it is in the tension they arouse cognitively that reality is pointed at, not displayed.[5]

We must ever keep in mind what H. and H. A. Frankfort, and their colleagues, stressed long ago. Early humans did not distinguish between either the so-called objective and subjective or between the "real" and "appearance." For the early humans who created the world of symbology, "thoughts are not autonomous." We should try, as we proceed further, to comprehend "that our categories of intellectual judgment often do not apply to the complexes of cerebration and volition which constitute mythopoeic thought."[6]

Foerster, in discussing *ophis* (Greek for "serpent") claims: "[T]he snake is the sinister and peculiar animal *kat' exochen.*"[7] This judgment is not presented within a context, and it is not balanced by an equal stress on the positive symbolism of the serpent, even though Asclepius is mentioned (somewhat in passing and without perception).

BEING HONEST ABOUT HOW THE HEBREW BIBLE
(OR "OLD TESTAMENT") WAS "WRITTEN"

We now turn to the question, "How has ophidian iconography helped shape the formation of the Hebrew Bible?" That is, how has the image and symbol of the serpent affected narratives and stories, or been reflected (or refracted) in them?

When we pick up a bound book called the Hebrew Bible, we do not pick up one book.⁸ We hold a library, as it were. The library is a collection of writings that were composed from about 950 BCE to approximately 164 BCE. On the one hand, these writings absorb and inherit many ancient stories that have a history of developing in oral traditions long before they were written down by the Israelites. On the other hand, these books were often edited by later authors. In antiquity, learned persons did not imagine they were independent authors; they (like Plato) stood within a cherished tradition and sometimes school.

The twenty-four books in the Hebrew Bible⁹ originally circulated in separate scrolls. The earliest known copies are those found among the Dead Sea Scrolls. Thus, when we read the "Bible," we read a library of books that represent different centuries, contexts, and peoples (Hebrews, Israelites, and finally Judahites). The process of collecting these different works into one book, and arranging them into a canon, was preceded by oral traditions, writing, and expanding and editing the documents that were almost always separated into individual scrolls of varying lengths. Despite what is assumed far too often, no official body in Early Judaism (or Second Temple Judaism) ever promulgated what was to be in or out of a biblical canon. The myth of Jabneh (Jamnia) derives ultimately from Spinoza, was intimated by H. Graetz, and developed by H. E. Ryle and F. Buhl. No canon was defined by the Rabbis who met at Jabneh; this well-entrenched myth was exploded by D. E. Aune, and the latter's contention was supported and confirmed by S. Talmon, and many others, especially L. M. McDonald.¹⁰

In search of the influence of serpent iconography in the Hebrew Bible we need to remember how the writings took shape. Texts were shaped by "con-text"—the social and intellectual world of the writer. In that world, the serpent was a pervasive, and indeed a multivalent, symbol. Hebrews, Israelites, and Jews stand behind and within the books collected into the Hebrew Bible. They caused it to be written, to be expanded, and later to be edited and copied. Generations of Jews, long before the burning of Jerusalem and the Temple in 70 CE, also showed us how to read some of the sections, as the scribal notations in the Dead Sea Scrolls, especially the Isaiah Scroll, help us comprehend.

In studying biblical serpent symbolisms, we appreciate more fundamentally that the Bible is not only from a culture of "the People of the Book." It is also "the Book of the People." ¹¹ That is, the book—the Bible—reflects a long and intricate process by which the words of humans to God became the Word of God to humans. The books in the Bible were written by people like you and me, but they sometimes claimed to be inspired; that is, as Mozart contended he was not composing music but recording what he heard, so Isaiah, Jeremiah, Ezekiel, and many others professed they were saying to Israelites what they heard God say to them. For many Jews and Christians today, the Bible is thus an intricate mixture of divine timeless revelations and human timely conceptions.

Symbolism belongs to both worlds: the eternal Word and human time-bound expressions. Serpent symbolism deeply colored the garments of ancient biblical societies. While "the serpent" appears in numerous passages in the Hebrew Bible,[12] three are outstanding. First, Genesis 3 is important because of the prominence attributed by the author (the Yahwist)[13] to the serpent in the so-called "Fall" (Sündenfall)[14] of the human from grace and a blessed life in Paradise and the beginnings of sin, pain, suffering, and death. Second, Numbers 21 is also exceptional because of the narrative according to which Moses made a copper (or bronze) serpent and placed it on a pole so that the Hebrews, who looked up to it as God's sign, would not die. Third, 2 Kings 18 is chosen because its author reports that Israelites were worshipping a serpent (or through it),[15] Nechushtan,[16] in the Temple. All three texts are not only shaped by serpent symbology but are so singularly important that they have developed the understanding and explication of biblical theology or "Old Testament Theology" (i.e., the theologies preserved in the Hebrew Bible). Unfortunately, none of the three texts central for the present research has been found among the scrolls once preserved in the eleven Qumran caves.

After working through the commentaries on Genesis, Numbers, and 2 Kings, I was surprised by the lack of interest in the symbol of the serpent. Numerous scholars translated Genesis 3 so as to stress a negative image of the serpent; hence, the image of the serpent is presented from preconceived, and misleading, notions and not from interrogative investigations and research. This discovery was surprising to me because biblical scholars seek to be grounded in the world in which the scrolls and stories took shape. In that world, as is now clear to the reader, no symbol was so pervasive, so dynamic, and primarily so positive as the serpent.

As is well known to virtually all biblical exegetes, the serpent appears on the heads of the pharaohs, with Hermes (Mercury), on Asclepius' staff, on the walls of the Assyrian and Babylonian kings, and on gems, jewelry, seals, and scarabs. Moreover, when coins were invented for commerce, one of the prevalent symbols was the serpent. As the caduceus, the serpent was found on the coins of the early Herodian dynasty, as discussed earlier. We have reviewed the evidence of the symbol of the serpent in the previous chapters. Now, we can ask, "How have the various symbolic meanings of the serpent helped shape the words and worlds of the biblical authors?" By entering the world of the biblical authors, we obtain controls and insight for exegesis. We thus will be guided away from uninformed, indeed foolish, pronouncements, and avoid such claims as René Guénon's speculation

Figure 78. Babylonian Clay Table with a Serpent in the Center. Circa 2000 BCE. JHC Collection

that the tree of life[17] symbolized and in a way described the celestial Jerusalem.[18]

Before proceeding further, I may now introduce an example of ancient iconography that is challenging and enlightening. An artifact was found recently in the area of Hebron. It was made about 2000 BCE. It is a Babylonian clay tablet (9.2 centimers × 10.1 centimeters) with two male figures; the one on the left is fully garbed (8.6 centimeters high), and the one on the right is nude (8 centimeters high). The figure on the left seems to be a priest, which makes sense since he is taller and clothed in a long garment. His eyes, ear, and headdress (or braided hair) received the artist's attention. He holds an object in his right hand, and his left is lifted up toward something in the center. The man on the right has an object below his mouth and holds something upright before him with his left hand. His ear, eye, widely open mouth, and phallus are detailed.

What is in that something in the center? The central figure is either a tree or a serpent. The latter becomes more obvious after close examination. The upward curved circles on its body simulate the ribs of a reptile. The serpent's mouth is open, and a tongue protrudes. An eye is visible. The bottom of the serpent is turned upward and to the right. Most likely "a foot" is intended. The serpent is able to stand upright because of this foot and the help of the nude man.

What are the objects in the priest's right hand and below the nude man's mouth? The priest seems to be holding a harp under his right elbow, strumming it with a curved object in his right hand. The harp seems to have fourteen horizontal strings. His left hand rises upward and holds a rattle or a scepter. The nude man seems to be blowing into some object that hangs from his mouth, and a similar object, perhaps a rattle, is held in his right hand. His left hand holds the serpent. The viewer perhaps is to imagine a liturgical dance with music. The object of veneration by the priest and nude man is clearly the serpent, who is strong, mighty, and full of life. He is not only in the center but also clearly longer than either male (from tongue to tail is 10.1 centimeters). The scene is not erotic; it is cultic. We have been given a glimpse into the worship of and through the serpent at the beginning of the second millennium BCE.

DEVELOPMENT OF RESEARCH

From about the tenth century BCE until less than two hundred years ago, the Genesis account of creation was assumed to be factual and reliable by most in the West, but critics of the biblical story of creation began to appear with regularity in the seventeenth century. Many around the world today also assume it is a definitive account of creation. Most learned individuals know that the account is not about how the world began, but about who is behind the processes that continue until today. Two major events in the nineteenth century changed the presuppositions by which we now read Genesis. In 1853, the library of Ashurbanipal was unearthed, and it revealed a creation story prior to and strikingly similar to the famous stories in Genesis. The second event was even more mind-altering. In 1859, Charles Darwin published *On the Origin of Species,* which eventually made "evolution" a household word.[19]

The biblical text is not an "inanimate thing." It is alive. The ancient authors filled it with passion and dynamic meaning that is available to even those not professionally trained in biblical research.

Once Jerome was asked by a hunter what he did. Jerome replied that he studied a text until something moved, then he went after it. A similar thought was shared by Matthias Flaccius Illyricus. Illyricus, the father of biblical hermeneutics, was a Lutheran whom Melanchthon called "the Croatian snake." He wrote and published 263 publications in this field. Along with Luther, Melanchthon, and Calvin, Illyricus is one of the four geniuses of the Reformation. In 1555, he stressed that the Bible is alive like a living body, and that the three dimensions of hermeneutics are analytic, heuristic, and synthetic.

Biblical scholars today know the dangers of theological exegesis that is shaped by dogmatics. They do not make the mistake of assuming, as had M. J. Gruenthaner, that the "Serpent who plays such a sinister part in the fall of our first parents is the first principle of evil which we encounter in the Bible." Contextualizing the text, we know that the Yahwist is not one who was convinced that the "response of the Serpent" attempts "to dethrone God in the heart of His creatures, by inciting them to rebellion; at the same time it is an effort to destroy these creatures, body and soul."[20] Such interpretations arise out of Christian dogmatics; sound scholarship derives from a study of the historical context of the text, and—for us—the presence of serpent symbology in a text that the biblical author composed.

Two fundamental presuppositions shape the following search for a refined exegesis of the biblical passages in which serpent symbolism dominates. First, texts obtain meaning from contexts; these contexts are not only textual and narrative but also historical and sociological. Second, the biblical authors, editors, and compilers—and especially those who read and memorized the Scriptures—lived in cultures virtually teeming with serpent iconography and symbology.

The following work will proceed by focusing on the four main biblical passages in which serpent symbolism is focused: Genesis 3, Numbers 21, 2 Kings 18, and subsequently John 3. Each text will be studied according to the following paradigm:

1. Initial Observations
2. Text and Translation
3. Questions
4. Scholars' Reflections (which are not always scholarly)
5. Serpent Symbology and Exegesis
6. Summary

GENESIS 3

Initial Observations

Clearly, more than one reading of a story is permissible, indeed required. I shall offer an interpretation of Genesis 3, with a focus on the serpent, that significantly differs from the traditional one in which the serpent is simply the origin of evil. A penetrating study of serpent symbolism, evident in the preceding chapter, precludes assuming that the serpent of the Eden Story is a *kakodaimon,* an evil demon or snake, whose bite brought death to humans. This interpretation, found in M. Giebel's *Tiere in der Antike,* shows no exegetical examination of Genesis 3 and fails to observe that the Nachash has no venom and does not bite Adam and the woman.[21] Furthermore, I doubt that the Yahwist would agree that the serpent functions only to clarify the origin of evil.

I agree with D. Patte that it is illusory to imagine that a story or narrative presents us with only a monolithic meaning. Patte rightly points out that the search for the transparent literal meaning of a text leaves aside its traditional mysterious power, and that "the meaning of a story cannot be posited anymore than can the glitter of a jewel."[22]

In light of the previous excursions into serpent symbolism, I am convinced that what is about to be proposed now is not only in tension with the traditional exegesis but approximates the original meaning obtained in the paradigm from author, through text, to reader. We have demonstrated repeatedly that those who take a "mono-think" approach to serpent symbolism and those specialists who conclude that one meaning is always dominant simply have read their own presuppositions into the text or have not immersed themselves in the multiple, often intentionally conflicting, meanings of serpent symbolism.

Studying the story of the Garden of Eden in Genesis 3 involves examining a pictorial narrative that probably has had more impact on Jewish and Christian exegesis and theology—and art—than any other biblical story.[23] The explanations of human beginnings in Eden, the "Fall," and God's curse appear on center stage today during discussions of creation, evolution, and ecology. Humans in diverse sections of world culture have memorized the story, or portions of it, and understand it from divergent presuppositions, assuming the story is historical, mythical, folklore, or legendary. Put in central focus is the greatest human dream and dread: paradise and punishment. We will be entering the dramatic world of one of the earliest and best literary artworks in human culture.

The major theological libraries contain thousands of publications directly or indirectly devoted to a better understanding of this notoriously difficult narrative. Most of them are Christian and presuppose the story is about "the Fall of man" who was tempted by Satan in the form of a snake. Following the equation found in Revelation 12:9, St. Augustine identified Satan with the dragon (*Hom.* 36). In Albania, the devil is called *dreikj* (dragon); in Romania, he is *dracu*. Noting this and reading Genesis 3 in terms of the equation that the serpent equals Satan, A. de Gubernatis claimed: "A devil without a tail would not be a real devil; it is his tail which betrays him; and this tail is the serpent's tail." As will become clear, this presupposition is misleading and distorts the complex drama.[24]

The widespread assumption of biblical scholars and theologians, for millennia, has been that the serpent is and symbolizes evil. This presupposition has shaped the interpretation of Genesis. J. Morgenstern, for example, claimed: "The basis of the folk-tale in Gen 3 is, of course, the natural human horror of serpents." [25] We have seen that recent ophiological research proves that fear of snakes is learned, not experienced; it is an aspect of nurture, not nature.

One of the most insightful publications on the linguistic and theological subtleties of Genesis 2–3 is R. W. L. Moberly's article entitled "Did the Serpent Get It Right?" [26] Yet Moberly's skills are philological and theological; he has not devoted himself to archaeology, iconography, and symbology.

Thus, rather surprisingly, he can claim that "in the Old Testament, with the one notable exception of the brazen serpent made by Moses (Num. 21:4–9), the serpent consistently represents hostility and threat to man." [27] If the serpent tells the truth and what he predicts happens, as Moberly rightly perceives, how can the serpent be hostile and a threat? If Moses uses the magic of the serpent to win Israel's release from Egyptian bondage, how can the serpent be a threat? If Dan is like a serpent that protects Israel, how can the serpent be hostile and a threat? The preceding forays into serpent symbology should prove to assist, and ground, an exegesis and hermeneutical explication of Genesis 2–3.

The presupposition that the serpent symbolizes evil has also misled those psychologists and biblical scholars too influenced by Freudian psychoanalysis. In *Symbolism in the Bible,* Paul Diel, for example, examines the symbolical meaning of Genesis 3. He claims that the serpent "symbolizes a psychic function devoid of elevation, more or less impossible to grasp consciously, and whose bite is no longer lethal for the life of the body but for the life of the soul . . . . The serpent is therefore the symbol of guilty vanity, of exalted imagination with respect to oneself and one's desires." [28] Much earlier than Diel, E. Hampton-Cook presented a novel interpretation of Genesis 3 that was not based on philological analysis. He argued that the serpent in Genesis 3 "appears to be intended as a striking symbol of our lower, earthly nature, consisting of both mind and body, in rebellion against duty and conscience and the will of God." [29] The Freudian and Jungian psychologists should have known about the positive attributes of the serpent since they reputedly studied the dreams in which Asclepius appears as a serpent. [30]

It is startling how blind some biblical scholars can be to the images in the story of Eden. Despite the fact that the woman remains anonymous during the story, [31] or is only defined as "wife," exegetes habitually call her "Eve" and distort the narrative by discussing how the serpent lied to Eve. [32] An example is found in the "fully revised" *International Standard Bible Encyclopedia.* Note the double error: "In Gen 3 the serpent, characterized by his craftiness (*'ārûm,* v. 1), beguiles Eve." [33] Yet, in Genesis 3:1 the woman has no name until the narrative reaches its climax; [34] then, the anonymous woman is given a name: "And Adam called his wife's name 'Eve,' because she [35] was the mother of all life" (Gen 3:20). [36] Likewise, the unattractive features of God are either unperceived or sidestepped. Many to whom I point out the apparent correct interpretation (see the following "Questions") recoil with shock that conceivably God could say something misleading and the serpent speak the truth.

Even more misinterpretation is read eisegetically into the image of the serpent. Despite the ambiguous and sometimes positive image of the serpent in Genesis 3, some distinguished scholars presuppose that the serpent is an evil figure and slant both translation and exegesis so that a negative image of the serpent emerges.[37] The disparaging symbolic meaning of the serpent that begins to appear in the fifth century in some Christian regions is read back into the Genesis story, recasting and misrepresenting one of the main characters. This penchant not only fails to let the images be seen, it is also tantamount to refashioning them.

The eisegesis not only miscasts Genesis; it fails even to comprehend the symbolism of the serpent in subsequent Christian art. As L. Réau, in *Iconographie de l'art chrétien,* stated: "The serpent . . . is generally the symbol of a demon, but it may also, as we have seen, symbolize Christ, where it is the attribute of Prudence (wisdom)."[38] This quotation was not chosen to suggest that the serpent is a type of Christ in Genesis 3; the comment only suffices to show that the popular understanding of one of the most famous stories in the Bible fails to represent the complex nature of ophidian symbolism in Christianity. While in the eighteenth century it was still possible to claim that the serpent in Genesis 3 was the embodiment of evil and indeed both Satan (השטן) and the devil (ὁ διάβολος),[39] this interpretation is no longer possible in light of our insights obtained from studying serpent symbology. It cannot be said too forcefully or with too much necessary redundancy: the serpent must not be presupposed to symbolize Satan, or evil, in the Eden Story.[40]

What then is the popular understanding of the Temptation and Fall?[41] In sermons, popular publications, lore, and even books masquerading as scholarly, the following ten misinterpretations of Genesis 3 seem regnant in Christian lore and teaching, especially in Western culture. I have found the miscasting of the serpent especially fashionable in the sixteenth and seventeenth centuries, while the snake appears often with vigorious positive denotation in the second and third centuries CE. Here are ten misinterpretations regnant among Christians, and also frequently among Jews, as they interpret Genesis 3.

First, the serpent is simply the Devil, Satan. With all the power of evil, Satan is the serpent who tempts "Eve" (actually the woman).

Second, the serpent lies. Satan is the Liar. In Genesis 3, Satan appears for the first time in biblical literature and lore, and he is the grand antithesis to God. Satan lies. God speaks the truth.

Third, the serpent is the trickster. He beguiles "Eve." She is tricked into doing what she would never herself think of doing.

Fourth, the serpent—and the serpent alone—is responsible for all the evils in the world. The serpent, Satan, forced the woman to sin.

Fifth, the serpent cannot be one of God's creatures. He is not mentioned in Genesis 1–2, in which God's creation of the animals is described. The serpent is not one of God's creations because he is too evil.

Sixth, the serpent was ugly and a horrible-looking animal. He is imagined to be dark, black, and full of evil.

Seventh, the serpent is a male. He entices the woman, perhaps using some erotic powers to entrap her. When pushed on this point, people often resort to the unexamined and false assumption that the serpent is first and foremost a phallic symbol.

Eighth, the serpent is beastly. He has only male features and is an ugly beast. Here the image of Satan, especially in medieval Christianity, conflates with the image of the serpent in Genesis 3.

Ninth, before the serpent corrupted "Eve," all was peaceful in Eden. The male and female walked with God, together, in the cool of the evening. There was no tension. All was of one will and harmoniously unified: the human with all animals, all with the earth, and all with the Creator.

Tenth, the serpent alone is responsible for the entrance of sin into creation, the appearance of death. The serpent alone is the cause of punishment, suffering, and ultimately of banishment from Eden.

This understanding of the Story of Eden is so deeply entrenched in Christian (and often Jewish) culture, from the pulpit to the pew and from music to museum, that most would be aghast to hear that each of these ten so-called insightful readings are either false or a distortion of the original story in Genesis 3.

Text and Translation

Before we can reveal, and dismiss, these far too pervasive misinterpretations and misperceptions, we need first to revisit Genesis 2 and 3. Here is E. A. Speiser's translation from his *Genesis* in the Anchor Yale Bible Commentary (he was also the leading translator of the Torah published under the auspices of the Jewish Publication Society of America):

> God Yahweh planted a garden in Eden, in the east, and placed there the man whom he had formed. And out of the ground God Yahweh caused to grow various trees that were a delight to the eye and good for eating, with the tree of life in the middle of the garden and the Tree of Knowledge of good and bad. . . .
>
> God Yahweh took the man and settled him in the Garden of Eden, to till and tend it. And God Yahweh commanded the man, saying, "You are free to eat of any tree of the garden, except only the tree of knowledge of good and bad, of which you are not to eat. For the moment you eat of it, you shall be doomed to death."
>
> God Yahweh said, "It is not right that man should be alone. I will make him an aid fit for him." So God Yahweh formed out of the soil

various wild beasts and birds of the sky and brought them to the man to see what he called them; whatever the man would call a living creature, that was to be its name. . . . yet none proved to be the aid that would be fit for man.

Then God Yahweh cast a deep sleep upon the man and, when he was asleep, he took one of his ribs and closed up the flesh at that spot. And God Yahweh fashioned into a woman the rib that he had removed from the man, and he brought her to the man. Said the man,

> "This one at last is bone of my bones and flesh of my flesh.
> She shall be called Woman ['*Ishsha*], for she was taken from
>   Man ['*Ish*]." [42]

Thus it is that man leaves his father and mother and clings to his wife, and they become one flesh. The two of them were naked, the man and his wife, yet they felt no shame. Now the serpent was the sliest of all the wild creatures that God Yahweh had made. Said he to the woman, "Even though God told you not to eat of any tree in the garden . . ." The woman interrupted the serpent, "But we may eat of the trees in the garden! It is only about the fruit of the tree in the middle of the garden that God did say, 'Do not eat of it or so much as touch it, lest you die!' " But the serpent said to the woman, "You are not going to die. No, God well knows that the moment you eat of it your eyes will be opened and you will be the same as God in telling good from bad."

When the woman saw that the tree was good for eating and a delight to the eye, and that the tree was attractive as a means to wisdom, she took of its fruit and ate; and she gave some to her husband and he ate. Then the eyes of both were opened and they discovered that they were naked; so they sewed fig leaves together and made themselves loincloths.

They heard the sound of God Yahweh as he was walking in the garden at the breezy time of day; and man and his wife hid from God Yahweh among the trees of the garden.

God Yahweh called to the man and said to him, "Where are you?" He answered, "I heard the sound of you in the garden; but I was afraid because I was naked, so I hid." He asked, "Who told you that you were naked? Did you, then, taste of the tree from which I had forbidden you to eat?" The man replied, "The woman whom you put by my side—it was she who gave me of that tree, and I ate." God Yahweh said to the woman, "How could you do such a thing?" The woman replied, "The serpent tricked me, so I ate."

God Yahweh said to the serpent:

"Because you did this,
Banned shall you be from all cattle
And all wild creatures!
On your belly shall you crawl
And on dirt shall you feed
All the days of your life.
I will plant enmity between you and the woman,
And between your offspring and hers;
They shall strike at your head,
And you shall strike at their heel."

To the woman he said:

"I will make intense
Your pangs in childbearing,
In pain shall you bear children;
Yet your urge shall be for your husband,
And he shall be your master."

To the man he said: "Because you listened to your wife and ate of the tree from which I had forbidden you to eat,

Condemned be the soil on your account!
In anguish shall you eat of it
All the days of your life.
Thorns and thistles
Shall it bring forth for you,
As you feed on the grasses of the field.
By the sweat of your face
Shall you earn your bread,
Until you return to the ground,
For from it you were taken:
For dust you are
And to dust you shall return!"

The man named his wife Eve [ḥawwa], because she was the mother of all the living [ḥay]. And God Yahweh made shirts of skins for the man and his wife, and clothed them.

God Yahweh said, "Now that the man has become like one of us in discerning good from bad, what if he should put out his hand and taste also of the tree of life and eat, and live forever!" So God Yahweh banished him from the garden of Eden, to till the soil from which he was taken. Having expelled the man, he stationed east of the garden of Eden the cherubim and the fiery revolving sword, to guard the way to the tree of life. [Gen 2:8–9, 15–23; 3:1–23][43]

Questions

What a story! This is a folktale that must have had a long life in oral traditions before it was compiled from disparate sources by some unknown writer. During its oral stage, the story grew and was enriched by Canaanite culture that was shaped by Mesopotamia and Egypt.[44] The influences on the author of Genesis 3 from the creation myths of non-Israelite cultures are certain and not limited to oral traditions. These were often shaped by earlier accounts that reached a literary stage; paramount among these would be the Gilgamesh epic. The Yahwist's story is indebted to Akkadian, Canaanite, Egyptian, Hittite, North Arabian, and Ugaritic myths.[45]

The story is thus symbolical. The archetypal symbols are the story, not its embellishment.[46] Eliade rightly stressed an important insight: "Myth means a 'true story.' "[47] Myths are almost always about creation or origins, and these are always hidden from view. If one ignores the orality and metaphorical nature of the story and takes it rather literally, questions (even absurdities) pop out and begin to multiply. Here are some of them:

1. It is clear that "the tree of life" is in the middle of the garden (2:9), but where is "the tree of knowledge," and why is the relationship between them so ambiguous that some passages imply there is only one tree (2:9)?[48]
2. Why did God Yahweh think that man was alone when there was a deep relationship between the human and God, on the one hand, and the animals, on the other, and when the human had not complained of loneliness (2:18)?
3. In the whole history of salvation, recorded in the Bible, why are God's first words to the human a command and a prohibition?
4. What does that observation reveal about the relation between the divine and the human, according to the Yahwist?
5. Why does the author mention the tree of life only at the beginning and end of the story (Gen 2:9 and 3:22, 24)?
6. Why are trees so significant to the narrator, and are they symbolically related to the serpent that often appears in or with a tree (cf. the images of Hercules in the Hesperides)?
7. Why does the woman later describe the tree of life as being "in the middle of the garden" (3:3)?
8. Is there some confusion between the relations of the two significant trees? Do the words in Genesis 3 tend sometimes to imply that there is only one tree in Eden?[49] Did an original story behind Genesis 3 have two trees? Was one the tree of life and the other the tree of

death? Did the humans eat from the tree of death and the serpent from the tree of life, as J. G. Frazer suggested? [50]

9. From what place did God Yahweh take Adam when he "took the man and settled him in the Garden of Eden"? [51]

10. What kind of knowledge does the man have when God Yahweh commands him not to eat of the tree of knowledge?

11. Can the human know that the tree is "the tree of knowledge of good and evil," and if God has revealed what that means, then what does the serpent disclose (in Gen 3:5)? [52]

12. Why does the narrator not provide explanation for God's command and prohibition?

13. The serpent is a wild beast and appears already named, is he then not one of the "wild beasts" that God Yahweh had made (2:19) and the man named (2:20)?

14. Why was a rib taken from the man and not something else?

15. Is it because a rib could be taken and no difference would be noted?

16. Where on a man is the spot of the flesh that "was closed up"?

17. Why does the man refer to, or give two names to, the creature formed from him: "Woman" (2:23) and "Eve" (3:20)?

18. Are not two tales or myths being merged here?

19. Where does the serpent come from, who named him (or her), and why does the author claim that God Yahweh "made" it (him or her)?

20. What is the meaning of the description: "the sliest of all the wild creatures" (3:1), and does the serpent know good from evil, like God?

21. Is "sliest" representative of the Hebrew word and context, and since this characteristic defines not only the serpent but also the fox, why was the latter not chosen by the author? [53]

22. Are the serpent's first words a statement ("God has forbidden") or a question ("has God forbidden")?

23. Why has the Yahwist avoided his usual way of referring to God, "God Yahweh" (3:1), and placed merely "God" in the mouth of the serpent (3:1)?

24. Why are the serpent's first words inaccurate (3:1)?

25. Is the serpent the only creature, beside the human, who can talk?

26. Why does the woman speak to the serpent; is he attractive?

27. Is the serpent being presented as a male or female?

28. How does the woman know of the command God Yahweh gave to the man, and why is she responsible for a command given to another (2:16–17, 3:3)?

29. Why does the woman add to the commandment: "or so much as touch it" (3:3)?

30. What is meant by the words "Your eyes will be opened" (3:5), and

how are they related to the shamelessness of the man and his wife (2:25)?

31. What does the author mean by the words "knowing good and evil," and why does he place them in the serpent's speech (3:5)?

32. Is "knowing good and evil" mere discernment, or does it also involve moral perception?

33. Why did the author write the words "like God knowing good and evil" and not "knowing good and evil like God"?

34. If the tree of knowledge "was attractive as a means to wisdom" (3:6), then why would desiring it and taking from it be an act against God when wisdom was seen as a means to God, and in Judaism wisdom was equated with Torah, God's will (cf. viz. Sirach)?

35. What is meant by "the eyes of both were opened" (3:7), and how is that related to their physical awareness of being naked?

36. Is not their action of making garments from fig leaves (3:7) morally superior to God Yahweh's actions of making them out of "skins" (3:21)?

37. The humans hide "among the trees" (3:8), not behind them; is there some link here with the traditions, albeit later, that the righteous are like trees in the eternal planting or in Paradise? [54]

38. God told the man that he must not eat of the "tree of knowledge of good and evil" because "on the day [ביום] that you eat of it you shall surely die" (2:17); hence, since they do not die immediately, did God lie?

39. Why should one conclude that the serpent lied? Did he not tell the woman that if she eats of the tree she will not die but will have knowledge? And did she not obtain knowledge and does not die immediately on eating the forbidden fruit (3:7)?

40. Is not the veracity of the serpent underscored when God knows that the humans know because they ate of the forbidden fruit (3:11)?

41. The author portrays God Yahweh calling for the man, which is clearly rhetorical, but is God's ignorance here related to an apparent lie?

42. Who could have told the man he was naked (3:11)?

43. What is meant by the woman's excuse: "The serpent tricked (or deceived) me" (3:13)?

44. If the serpent told the truth, what portrayal of woman is being reflected?

45. What does the author mean by stating that the serpent is banned from "all cattle" and "all wild creatures" (3:14)?

46. If the serpent now must crawl, how did it move before?

47. Did the author imagine or presuppose that his readers knew that the

nachash originally had legs, as we know from ancient Near Eastern iconography (see Fig. 27)?

48. What kind of a God is being portrayed when God is the source of "enmity" (3:15)?

49. What kind of a God would be the one who is responsible for pains of childbirth and the man's laborious anguish all his life?

50. Is the woman's urge for her husband not sexual, and why is she to have a master, her husband? Is it because the reader is to assume now that she cannot be trusted (3:16)?

51. If God Yahweh made "skirts of skins" for the man and his wife (3:21), then has someone killed one or more animals, and, if so, who?

52. To whom does God Yahweh speak, and who is meant by God's words: "like one of us in discerning good from bad" (3:22)?

53. Why were the man and woman banished from the garden? Is it because of God Yahweh's fear that they would eat of the tree of life and "live forever" (3:22)?

54. Does the author or the source not comprehend God's omnipotence, or is there a residual of ancient myths (esp. regarding the anguipede giants) that God is vulnerable, even from humans, his creatures?

55. Why does an author (the same one?) state that only "the man" (3:24) was banished from Eden (3:22–24)?

56. Where is the Garden of Eden in the author's mind, and why does it seem Eden is protected only from the east (3:23)?

57. What would "the cherubim" look like to the author and what is the meaning of "the fiery revolving sword" (3:24)?

Even more questions could be listed, but at least one point has been made strikingly lucid. It is clear that a familiar story now seems strange. A once straightforward account now appears chaotic.

While there are answers to some of these questions, most lead beyond exegesis (which is focused on the probable meaning of the words) into unsupported speculation. Our focus will remain on that mysterious character in the story called simply Nachash; is "serpent" what the Yahwist had in mind for this noun from the beginning of Genesis 3?

Scholars' Reflections

These questions expose tensions and inconsistencies in the first biblical story, the Eden Story.[55] The Genesis story may be well written, but it is replete with problems. The story is not well constructed. Yet that is not the evaluation of Speiser, whose translation we quoted. He wrote: "There is action here and suspense, psychological insight and subtle irony, light and shadow—all achieved in two dozen verses. The characterization is swift

286 The Good and Evil Serpent

and sure, and all the more effective for its indirectness."[56] Where is there any description of or use of "light and shadow"? With so many contradictions, how can Speiser claim the narration is "swift" and "sure"?

Speiser's own pejorative opinion of the serpent apparently has brought more harmony to the Eden Story than is present in the Hebrew. Is not Speiser distorting the narrative when he reports that the serpent "is deliberately distorting a fact" in his first statement to the woman?[57]

Th. C. Vriezen summarized scholars' opinions regarding the form and function of the serpent in Genesis 3.[58] The serpent is interpreted to be a disguised Satan (the usual Christian interpretation), purely mythological (in the Talmudim; cf. N. P. Williams), a mythological being transformed into an animal (viz. H. Gunkel), or a very clever animal (Vriezen, Westermann).

It should be obvious why so many scholars, especially E. Williams-Forte, are convinced that in Genesis 3 the serpent symbolizes evil and cunning, not death, and that the serpent is primarily the Deceiver or Liar.[59] A careful analysis of serpent symbolism in Genesis 3, attention to details, and repeated attempts "to live in the story" reveals numerous meanings such as chaos, youthfulness, and wisdom, as Joines proved.[60] Among all of these, the serpent primarily symbolizes wisdom. The text vitiates the claim that the serpent is the Liar.

In the early centuries of this era, those interested in the Eden Story sometimes exaggerated the wisdom of the serpent. In *Adam, Eve, and the Serpent,* for example, E. Pagels points out that the author of the *Testimony of Truth* told "the story of Paradise from the serpent's point of view, and depicted the serpent as a teacher of divine wisdom who desperately tried to get Adam and Eve to open their eyes to their creator's true, and despicable, nature."[61]

Even in the past few centuries, far too much nonsense has been devoted to an explication of Genesis 3. In his book, *The Ophion or the Theology of the Serpent and the Unity of God,* J. Bellamy sought to rebuff the supposedly prevalent claim that it was a monkey rather than a serpent that "was the agent employed in the Fall of Man." He sought to lead readers so they will comprehend that "it was a *Serpent* instead of a *Monkey*" that "brought about this business."[62] Such misconceptions seem to reflect the fear of Darwinism in London in 1911. They are far from the world of scholarship in which questions, not answers, guide a study.

Many more examples could be selected of how scholars have failed to see the world of serpent symbology reflected in Genesis 3. Far too often scholars have read the Eden Story with presuppositions that were never examined and most likely unperceived. It seems best to keep the examples at a minimum now and to allude to them or present them as our exegesis proceeds.

Serpent Symbology and Exegesis

Before proceeding further, I must express, briefly, my deep indebtedness to the great minds that have helped us comprehend the oral and literary origin of the first books in the Hebrew Bible. In focusing on Genesis 1–3 and in particular the symbology of the Nachash in chapter 3, unfortunately I cannot now assume a consensus regarding the composition of the Pentateuch, the first five books of the Hebrew Bible (a better word than Hexateuch or Tetrateuch). The sequence of literary sources in the Pentateuch, J, E, D, and P, developed especially by Reuss, Graf, Kuenen, and particularly Wellhausen, is no longer a firm consensus, even if we add the possibility of a G document underlying J and E (Noth).[63] It also seems evident that Gunkel in 1895, in *Schöpfung und Chaos,* rightly perceived a long and ancient oral tradition behind the alleged Priestly document of Genesis 1. Yet, the existence of J, E, D, and P, their redactors, the exilic Dtr[2], and the editors and compilers of the prophetic and psalmic texts is a widely held consensus;[64] it seems strengthened, if not proved, by the study of the scribal activity evident in the biblical texts found in the eleven Qumran caves.[65]

Because there is no longer unanimous agreement on the existence of J, E, D, and P, there is no solid consensus regarding the date of Genesis 3. Some views now seem highly unlikely; for example, J. Morgenstern opined that the story originated "long before the time of Moses, when our ancestors still roamed the great Arabian Desert."[66] Young opts for the traditional view: Moses was the author of the Pentateuch, but there are some later editorial additions.[67] These views are not widely held today.

More representative of scholars' dating of Genesis 3 are the conclusions by Eissfeldt and Joines. While O. E. Eissfeldt argued for the composition of Genesis 3 sometime between 968 and 721 BCE,[68] K. Joines was convinced we should narrow the range. She suggests some time between 950 and 850 BCE.[69]

The earliest possible date for the composition of Genesis 3 is thus clearly uncertain. Perhaps Genesis 3 was composed, from older traditions, sometime in the tenth century BCE. Yet, even this prevalent view reflects our own individual training and perspective. As S. R. Driver pointed out, in making judgments regarding the date of Genesis 3, we are primarily reflecting our own particular view of a dark period in history.[70]

I shall base my reflections on the consensus that, during the reign of Solomon, in the middle of the tenth century BCE (perhaps 970–931) when Israel had established prosperous relations with the Philistines and Egyptians, a person, the Yahwist, composed the earliest document in the Pentateuch (the first five books in the Hebrew Bible). In contrast to the later Elohist, who was a moralist and nationalist, the Yahwist cast the history of

Israel with a universal perspective. The God of Israel is the Creator of the world, humans, and animals, including the serpent.[71]

Where does the Eden Story begin and end in Genesis? The story seems to begin in 2:4b and continues until 3:24. Genesis 2:4b shows a shift from calling the Creator Elohim to Adonai (YHWH) Elohim; 2:4b clearly represents another author and the beginning of another tradition. After the end of chapter 3, "the woman" is given a name. She is called "Eve," and then a new story begins; it is about the birth of sons to Adam and Eve and the tragic relation between Cain and Abel. This division is affirmed by many, including I. Engnell, who perceived in the Genesis story of the first man and woman divine beings, king and queen, and the remnants of a royal annual ritual. When God places skins on Adam and the woman, they receive royal investiture.[72] Genesis 3 no longer is a ritual, if it ever had been. For a study of serpent symbolism in Genesis 3, the division is crucial; in his masterful *Genesis*, Gunkel defined the "Paradiesesgeschichte" as covering Genesis 2:4b to 3:24 and attributed the composition to "J^e" and "J^i." [73]

In proceeding, it is essential to comprehend that the first four chapters of Genesis are not the work of only one author or source. The major criteria for discerning more than one source are the doublets, the two stories of the creation of the human, and the two different names for the Divine: Elohim and YHWH Elohim (and sometimes merely YHWH, esp. in chap. 4). Also important is the first use of the *toledot* (the generations of) formula in 2:4a that shapes Genesis. It appears in Genesis 2:4a, and these words seem to be P's introduction to the J source [*pace BHS* and RSV].

In what follows, I have come to agree with G. von Rad in seeing the author of Genesis 2:4b–4:26, the Yahwist, as the first genius in the long line of perspicacious Hebrew theologians.[74] In the following, it becomes clear, because of the theological integrity and linguistic skill throughout the source (2:4b–4:26), that the Yahwist who composed the second account of creation in Genesis was an individual (the narrative is not the product of a school [pace Gunkel]). It also seems likely that the Yahwist wrote because of some crisis (political or theological) in the tenth century BCE, as G. von Rad and W. Brueggemann concluded. It is conceivable also that P is a source or the result of redaction of J and E, as seems likely in Genesis 1–4, as F. Cross has argued.

Today the debate over the compositional character of Genesis rages, and the old form-critical consensus seems to be in shambles. While I cannot appeal to a consensus, it is only fair to admit that I find much insight from sociological sensitivities to the authors, P (broadly defined) and J (the Yahwist), and the fruitful insights from *religionsgeschichtliche* examinations (as with Gunkel). I tend to shy away from seeing tradition criticism in the rather narrow, traditional ways of critical orthodoxy. The author of Genesis 3, our focus, was deeply influenced by earlier myths found in Canaanite culture, and these (as I discovered and should now be evident) had not only originated locally in Palestine but had been inherited from Mesopotamia and Egypt,[75] as well as elsewhere (including Hittite culture). Now I focus on the work of the Yahwist. What has he given us, and what does he know about serpent symbology? Let us return to Speiser, since his translation has been chosen to represent a major position in advanced research.

Speiser offers misleading advice, based on his misperception of serpent symbolism, when he argues that the Hebrew in Genesis 3:1, *aph ki,* means "even though." That puts the serpent in a bad light. Martin Luther also took *aph ki* to denote something sinister about the Nachash. He offered this advice: "I cannot translate the Hebrew either in German or in Latin; the serpent uses the word *aph-ki* as though to turn up its nose and jeer and scoff at one." [76] Is this really what the Yahwist had in mind?

Far more likely than Speiser's exegesis and Luther's opinion is the well-accepted assumption that this expression opens a question. That is, the Nachash is not "distorting a fact"; he is asking a question. As G. von Rad pointed out, what the Yahwist has put into focus is not "what the snake is" but what the Nachash says. The Nachash "opens the conversation—a masterpiece of psychological shading!—in a cautious way, with an interested and quite general question (not mentioning the subtly introduced subject of the conversation, the tree of knowledge, which it leaves to the unsuspecting woman!)." [77]

In asking a question, the Yahwist thus portrays the serpent as being closer to the woman. This insight does not warrant, however, U. Cassuto's exegesis, which tends to remove the Nachash from the narrative. According to Cassuto, the only way to explain the conversation between the Nachash and the woman is to assume the "dialogue between the serpent and the woman is actually, in a manner of speaking, a dialogue that took place in the woman's mind, between her wiliness and her innocence, clothed in the garb of a parable." He continued, noting that this interpretation allows us "to understand why the serpent is said to think and speak; in reality it is not he that thinks and speaks but the woman does so in her heart." [78]

The serpent's cleverness is reflected in his first revealed characteristic: asking a question. To ask questions and draw close to others is a positive trait in Israelite and Jewish Wisdom, yet E. Wiesel imagines the serpent "meddles in affairs that do not concern him." [79]

Speiser thinks that *aph ki* cannot have an interrogative sense.[80] One should not be concerned that *aph ki* appears only in Genesis 3, in biblical Hebrew, as an introductory phrase. What should be in central focus are the vestiges of antique Hebrew in the language of the Yahwist,[81] his diverse and probably multilingual sources, the complexity of the Hebrew elsewhere in this story, and the clear meaning of the Greek, the other ancient Jewish source of this Eden Story:

καὶ εἶπεν ὁ ὄφις τῇ γυναικί Τί ὅτι εἶπεν ὁ θεός Οὐ μὴ φάγητε ἀπὸ παντὸς ξύλου τοῦ ἐν τῷ παραδείσῳ;[82]

> And the serpent said to (or questioned) the woman, "Why did God say, 'you may not eat from each tree in paradise?' "

The Greek is clearly an interrogative sentence: note the opening with the interrogative, "Why" (τί ὅτι) and the question mark at the end of the sentence (; [which is a question mark in Greek]).[83]

Speiser ignored a major obstacle to his understanding of the Hebrew: the witness of the Greek version. Once we scholars tended to mistrust the Greek version as a witness to a Hebrew version. We incorrectly assumed that such differences from the Hebrew were caused by the work of a translator. Now, we know from the Qumran Hebrew manuscripts that some (perhaps many) of the "variants" in the Septuagint are not the creation on the part of a translator; they often represent early Hebrew texts.[84] That observation indicates that we should keep in focus both the Hebrew and the ancient Greek.

It seems clear, therefore, that the serpent is not deceiving the woman. It is misleading to label the serpent "ill-omened."[85] He is addressing a question to the woman. That the serpent asks a question does not indicate that he is ignorant. Rather the interrogative aligns the serpent with God Yahweh, who asks the man, "Where are you?" Both interrogatives are rhetorical dimensions of the Eden Story. Both the serpent and God are related: God creates the serpent, and both God Yahweh and the serpent serve the Yahwist to move the narrative along by asking questions.

Thus, it is best to translate Genesis 3:1 as a question in Hebrew, as have most commentators and as is found in most popular translations; here are a few representative translations:

> Now the serpent was more cunning than any beast of the field which the Lord God had made. And he said to the woman, "Has God indeed said, 'You shall not eat of every tree of the garden'?" [NKJV]

> Nun war die Schlange listiger als alle Tiere des Feldes, die Jahve Gott geschaffen hatte; sie sprache zum Weibe: "sollte Gott euch denn wirklich verboten haben, von allem Bäumen des Gartens zu essen?"[86]

> Il dit à la femme: "Alors, Dieu a dit: Vous ne mangerez pas de tous les arbres du jardin?"[87]

Et le serpent dit à la femme: "Pourquoi Dieu a-t-il dit: 'Ne mangez pas de tout arbre dans le jardin'?"[88]

And he said to the woman, " 'Is it true that the Lord God said, 'You shall not eat of any tree of the garden'?"[89]

These reflections lead to an appreciation of the clever use of language in Genesis 3:1. The Yahwist has adeptly composed Genesis 3:1 so that it is possible to understand, in paradigmatically opposite ways, the first spoken words in the narrative: the serpents' words addressed to the woman (לא תאכלו מכל עץ הגן). How should one translate the Hebrew words in parentheses? Although the prohibition or command is in the emphatic form (לא and not אל), God's words may mean either "You may not eat from every tree of the garden" or "You may not eat from any tree of the garden." As Moberly reports, "The range of options given is as wide as it could be";[90] the Hebrew means either "every tree" or "any tree." The ambiguity underscores a little-known fact; the serpent points out the problem with the prohibition. We may assume that the humans lack knowledge, so they might have understood God's prohibition to mean that all the trees contain forbidden fruit ("que tous les arbes sont prohibés").[91]

Speiser's negative view of the serpent, which is presupposed and unexamined, led him to mistranslate the Hebrew that introduces the serpent: "Now the serpent was the sliest of all the wild creatures."[92] In fact, the Hebrew 'rwm, in Genesis 3:1, does not have a negative meaning, as too many exegetes, like Speiser, assume or claim. It is rather neutral, and obtains the meaning "sly" or "clever"—even "wise"—according to the context. The Hebrew noun ערום (from ערם) is used twice in Proverbs 12 to denote a wise or prudent man in contrast to a fool (vv. 16, 23). The translators of the Septuagint chose three words to translate this Hebrew noun:[93] πανοῦργος, which can have a positive sense but usually, especially as used by Aristotle, Philo, Josephus, and the New Testament authors, signifies one who is "clever," "crafty," or "sly"; συνετός, which in classics, the Septuagint, the Pseudepigrapha, Philo, Josephus, and the New Testament authors indicates one who is "intelligent," "wise," or "sagacious"; and φρόνιμος, which in all ancient Greek literature specifies one who is "wise," "prudent," and "thoughtful."

What is found in the Septuagint for 'rwm in Genesis 3:1? It is the superlative form of the Greek noun just discussed. The word is φρονιμώτατος and it means "most intelligent."[94] The Greek noun was chosen by Plato and Aristotle to describe the most sagacious of all animals.[95] Elsewhere in Septuagint Greek, phronimos is used to describe the knowledge and wisdom of Joseph. Indeed, the Greek noun φρόνιμος is used by Jesus, according to Matthew, to refer to the cleverness and wisdom of a serpent.

Later Jewish authors, working under the influence of the increasing perception of the negative meaning of the serpent, devalue the positive meaning of *phronimos*.[96] In fact, they replace this noun found, in the superlative, in the Septuagint, meaning "most intelligent." This is true of Philo (*QG* 1.32) and Theodoret (*Questions on Genesis* 31). It is typical of the Greek translations by Theodotion and Aquila, who chose to introduce the serpent with the Greek *panourgos,* "clever," "crafty," or "sly."

The Targumim also should be included, to see how one should translate Genesis 3:1, or to learn how later Jews understood 'rwm. As one might expect from studying the development of Jewish animosity to ophidian symbolism, the translator of *Targum Pseudo-Jonathan* stresses the serpent's evil knowledge: "Now the serpent was more skilled *in evil* than all the beasts of the field which *the Lord* God had made."[97] The Aramaic (חכים לביש) means "wiser for evil."[98] This understanding of serpent symbolism is typical of Palestinian traditions after the second century CE, and *Pseudo-Jonathan* represents Palestinian Targumic traditions. It is interesting that the older symbolic meaning of serpent has shaped this Targum; the noun *chkm*,[99] "wise one," is employed, signifying one of the meanings of 'rwm. The serpent is recognized to have skills and wisdom, even if it is perverse or evil.

Other Targumim do not, however, stress the pejorative sense of Genesis 3:1. The reading of *Targum Onkelos* is much more positive: "And the serpent was more crafty (or intelligent) than all the animals."[100] The Aramaic 'rym (ערים) simply represents the Hebrew 'rwm.[101] Thus, studying this Targum would be circuitous and add little to our understanding of the original Hebrew.

The positive meaning of Genesis 3:1 is preserved in *Targum Neofiti,* "The serpent was wiser (חכים מן) than all the beasts." A. Díez Macho's translation thus rightly brings out the positive sense: "Y la serpiente era más sabia [wiser] que todos los animales."[102] The Aramaic (חכים מן) means "wiser than" and not "shrewder than."[103] *Targum Neofiti,* therefore, preserves one of the earlier possible meanings of the Hebrew in Genesis 3:1, and, in light of the narrative and the preponderance of positive serpent symbolism before the second century CE, it probably represents accurately the original meaning of 'rwm in Genesis 3:1.

A study of *Targum Neofiti* brings into focus the linguistic art of the Yahwist. Why did he not simply use the noun *ḥkm* to reveal that the Nachash was "wise"? In doing so, he would not be able to bring out the unity between the Nachash ("the serpent") and the humans. He does this in many subtle ways, especially in moving from one line in which he described the man and wife as "naked," 'rwmym, to the next line in which he introduces the Nachash as "clever," 'rwm. The Yahwist is a gifted linguist; he knows how to use paronomasia with subtle force to unite his narrative.[104]

The Yahwist's attempt to show the unity between the Nachash and the humans is missed by modern commentators. Early Jews did not miss the point, however. Note, for example, the following excerpt from the Tosephta:[105]

> A. And so you find in the case of the snake (נחש) of olden times, who was smarter than all the cattle and wild beasts of the field, as it is said, *"Now the serpent was smarter than any other wild creature that the Lord God had made"* (Gen. 3:1).
>
> B. He wanted to slay Adam and to marry Eve.
>
> C. The Omnipresent (המקום) said to him, "I said that you should be king (מלך) over all beasts and wild animals. Now that you did not want things that way, *You are more cursed than all the beasts and wild animals of the field"* (Gen 3:14).
>
> D. "I said that you should walk straight-up like man (בקומה תילך זקופה). Now that you did not want things that way, *Upon your belly you shall go"* (Gen 3:14).
>
> E. "I said that you should eat human food and drink human drink. Now: *And dust you shall eat all the days of your life"* (Gen. 3:14). [*t. Sotah* 4:17][106]

According to this interpretation of Genesis, the Nachash was not originally a serpent. He (not she in *Sotah*) was smarter than all cattle and wild beasts (cf. the LXX), desired to kill Adam and marry Eve (cf. Oedipus), had been promised kingship, walked upright like humans, and ate human food and drank human drink. While the tradition shows attentiveness to Genesis 3, it is also expansionistic and midrashic. Yet the Rabbis knew more about the snake than biblical scholars today; they knew, for example, that the pupil in the eye of animals is oblong, but round in humans and snakes (see *b. Niddah* 23a).

In numerous ways, the Yahwist presents the serpent as "clever" and "intelligent." Speiser misses the point, mentioned by Gunkel earlier, that the serpent is more clever than the human. According to Genesis 3:5, the serpent has mysterious knowledge known only to gods.[107] He knows what God knows; the serpent says to the woman, "God knows [ידע] that in the day you eat of it your eyes will be opened, and you will be like God, knowing [ידעי] good and evil." Perhaps the verb "know" provides an *inclusio* for the thought in this verse. The humans are to experience good and evil; that is what "to know" entails in Hebrew. As G. von Rad stated in his commentary on Genesis, the verb "to know" in Hebrew "never signifies purely intellectual knowing, but rather an 'experiencing,' a 'becoming acquainted with' (cf. at Gen 3:5)."[108] The spotlight is cast again on the serpent as one who has godly knowledge. As J. F. A. Sawyer stresses, it is "thanks to the serpent that Adam and Eve [sic] came to resemble God, 'knowing good and evil' (3.22)." [109]

The supernatural knowledge of the serpent, reflected in Genesis 3, aligns it with the gods and reveals the world of mythology and lore focused on the serpent, which was central to worship and a grasp of the cosmos in ancient Palestine, especially at Beth Shan in the second millennium BCE and at Bethzatha in the Roman Period. In 1895 and in his influential *Schöpfung und Chaos in Urzeit und Endzeit*, H. Gunkel demonstrated the significance of the serpent motif in the history of religions and in Ancient Israel. [110]

Since the Yahwist announces from the outset that the Nachash is one of God's creatures, the Nachash cannot be a demonic being of chaos or represent a power or might opposed to God. [111] Even though *nachash* is used to denote Leviathan (Isa 27:1) and a monster in the sea (Amos 9:3), [112] the serpent in Genesis 3 is not one of the mythical monsters. In contrast to Moses' serpent staff, [113] the Genesis serpent has no magical powers. [114]

The Yahwist understood what scholars have failed to grasp; he knew about the mysterious power and knowledge of the serpent. He possesses supernatural knowledge and knows about life and death.

The Yahwist may have known and been influenced by the Gilgamesh epic, since fragments of this epic were found at Megiddo and it antedates the Yahwist. According to this influential and well-known tale in antiquity, the serpent possesses supernatural knowledge and has obtained the secret of "everlasting life." Only the crucial sections of the Gilgamesh saga of seventy-two poems may be excerpted now. The key passage for us is in Tablet 11, col. 6: [115]

> Utnapishtim said to him, to Gilgamesh:
> "Gilgamesh, you came here; you strained, you toiled.
> What can I give you as you return to your land?
> Let me uncover for you, Gilgamesh, a secret thing.
> A secret of the gods let me tell you.
> There is a plant. Its roots go deep, like the boxthorn;
> its spike will prick your hand like a bramble.
> If you get your hands on that plant, you'll have everlasting life."
>
> Gilgamesh . . . saw the plant.
> He seized the plant, though it cut into his hand;
> he cut the heavy stones from his feet;
> the sea cast him up onto its shore.
> "Urshanabi, this is the plant of Openings,
> by which a man can get life within.
> I will carry it to Uruk of the Sheepfold; I will give it to the

elders to eat; they will divide the plant among them.
Its name is The-Old-Will-Be-Made-Young.
I too will eat it, and I will return to what I was in my youth."

The words "return" to "my youth" are a foreshadowing of who will finally possess the secret of being made young again. Thus, a snake takes the secret knowledge, and can now be seen everywhere to have the power to regain its youth. Note how the saga continues:

Gilgamesh saw a pool of cool water.
He went down into it and bathed in the water.
A snake smelled the fragrance of the plant.
It came up through the water and carried the plant away.
As it turned it threw off its skin.

Few would deny the similarity between Genesis and the earlier myths to the East. As H. and H. A. Frankfort pointed out, in such ancient myths as Genesis 3 and Gilgamesh, "the assimilation of a concrete substance would have made the difference between death and immortality." [116] Most experts, thus, rightly conclude that the Yahwist was influenced by the Sumero-Babylonian literature,[117] perhaps via Canaanite culture.[118]

We find in Genesis 3 and the Gilgamesh saga the sacred plant or tree that brings eternal youth, a woman, and the special garden. The serpent also plays a prominent role in both stories, and he obtains what is offered by the tree of life in Genesis 3.[119] Note this passage regarding the huluppu-tree:

On that day a tree, a huluppu-tree, a tree—
On the bank of the pure Euphrates it had been planted . . .
A lady walking in fear at the word of Anu . . .
Seized the tree in her hand and brought it to Uruk . . .
The tree grew large, but she could not cut off its bark.
At its base the snake who knows no charm had set up for
   itself a nest;
In its crown the Zu-bird had placed his young.

A major part of the Eden Story is missing from the Babylonian myths. There is no Fall and the serpent does not mislead or cause the woman to eat from the forbidden tree. There is no myth of temptation and expulsion from a paradise in the East. There are no etiological concerns and cures as in Genesis 3. Thus, Cheyne turned to see an influence on Genesis 3 from elsewhere. He was convinced that the origin of the Eden Story is with the North Arabian kinsfolk of the Israelites; these had infiltrated Canaan, although most remained in Arabia. They had a "Paradise story on which the Israelitish tale is based"; indeed they "became to a large extent the religious tutors of the Israelites." [120] If ultimately a Babylonian origin is more attractive for the Yahwist, Cheyne drew attention to Ea, the lord of wisdom, who appears frequently as a serpent; he was especially interested in human affairs.

The issue is not if influences came from Gilgamesh to the Yahwist, but how, and through which media. Most likely the Yahwist knew the Gilgamesh saga and many other similar tales about serpents from Canaanite culture that was still present, though waning in influence, near Jerusalem. The purpose of the Gilgamesh saga for us is the ways in which it helps us understand serpent lore prior to the Yahwist and the link between serpent symbology and the concept of renewed life, a return to one's youthfulness. This perennial search for youth and immortal life is embodied by the serpent that does not seem to grow old and renews its skin or, as the Gilgamesh saga states, the snake "threw off its skin."

A ceramic tablet—perhaps from the first half of the first millennium BCE—seems to depict a scene reminiscent of the Eden Story, the Gilgamesh epic, and the description of the Hesperides. The tablet, now in Madrid and allegedly Phoenician, shows from left to right a winged upraised serpent with a white face (perhaps human), a tree full of fruit, a woman with "milk" flowing from her exposed breast, a fire at her feet, a man with a phallus out of which pours "semen" highlighted by what appears to be a scorpion (a symbol of fertility), a second tree, and a winged upraised serpent having a dark animal's head.[121] A fish (most likely part of the zodiac),[122] the sun, and three stars are depicted overhead. Something seems to be flowing between the mouths of the man and the woman—is it language? If the scene is primarily sexual, why are both humans clothed? [123] The scene with serpents and trees may have many meanings; one is fertility. The serpents are prominent and standing upright, as the position of their wings shows. The one on the left seems to have feet.[124]

The ongoing study has opened our eyes to the complexity of serpent imagery preserved in a refracted form in Genesis 3.[125] As we probe deeper, we observe that the genre of Genesis 3 helps one grasp this insight. Genesis 3 is an early example of Wisdom literature. In it the Yahwist explains how to live in a world sometimes filled with pain and death: the excruciating pangs of the woman while giving birth and the extended burdens of the man while working in the field. And there he confronts hostile snakes who threaten death.[126]

In "Serpent Imagery in Ancient Israel," Le Grande Davies offers these sane reflections:

> The serpent of the garden appeared—not as the malevolent, diabolical serpent, but the loving, kind, powerful, benevolent serpent.

He appeared as the serpent of glory, "one of the divine beings" who saved and imparted wisdom to the world. The serpent of the Garden appeared as one of the benevolent "anthropomorphical gods" who placed Adam and Eve in the Garden.[127]

For those who read this story and believed that the God of Israel was symbolized as a serpent, then we have a dualism. The first story recorded in the Bible seems to inherit the concept of two serpents: the obvious serpent who imparts wisdom but also initiates "the Fall" and the apparent serpent who is elusive, sometimes absent, but related to the wise Creator.[128]

In this context, one should observe how the Yahwist portrays the relation between the serpent and the woman. The woman seems to be confused. She knows supposedly only what the man had told her. She has no reason to doubt the sagacity of the serpent, who has the power of speech (the serpent is unlike Balaam's ass whose mouth was opened by God). Apparently, she thinks the serpent is attractive and knowledgeable because she talks with the Nachash. To her, the serpent appears to have secret knowledge that was seductive and would make one like God. This means that she knew God was greater than she was, or at least had something she desired. Thus, the serpent is an agent of wisdom and was most likely intended to appear wise and conferring wisdom, or at least knowledge of good and evil, on humans.[129] This claim may shock many scholars who are familiar with the usual approach found in commentaries on Genesis.

Yet this claim is not without some precedence in critical research. For example, C. Meyers indicates this "little-noticed feature" of Genesis 3. Meyers points out that the woman has a prominent role in this chapter. The woman, not the man, "perceives the desirability of procuring wisdom." She is the first human to represent language, the divine attribute in humanity, and she does not speak to Satan, despite later misinterpretations by Jewish and Christian scholars.[130]

The anonymous woman talks to God's creature who also can speak and who is wisely discerning.[131] She alone is the "articulate member of the first pair who engages in dialogue even before the benefits of the wisdom tree have been procured." As Meyers indicates: "The woman's dialogue with the prudent reptile should be considered not a blot on her character but rather a comment on her intellect." [132]

In Israelite and Jewish literature, including the document *Dame Wisdom and Lady Folly* found at Qumran, the woman is the spokesperson for Wisdom. In Proverbs and in the Wisdom of Solomon the portrayal of woman takes on a dominant role as the source of Wisdom; in the latter document Wisdom becomes a feminine personification (see esp. 6:1–7:30). The woman, like the serpent, has a close connection with Wisdom in the Bible.

It is now abundantly clear that the Eden Story became garbled and the serpent was misrepresented. As MacCulloch stated:

> The talking serpent of Gn 3 represents a primitive stage of thought. . . . It is doubtful whether the serpent was intended in the original story to be evil. More likely he was a divine being, with superior knowledge and a kindly desire to help man to knowledge denied him by other divinities. A later recension made his act have evil consequences, and therefore he himself had evil intentions. The story doubtless arose with a people to whom the serpent was sacred, and who were impressed with its wisdom.[133]

It is clear that the serpent was misrepresented by interpretation; it is less likely that the Yahwist's account was marred by a later redactor. The serpent as a symbol of Wisdom (Pos. 18)[134] appears, for over one thousand years, in biblical and parabiblical works. In the Christian Bible, the serpent's role in pointing the direction toward Wisdom, or in symbolizing it, begins with Genesis 3 and culminates in Jesus' injunction to his disciples to be wise as serpents.

The evidence from the ancient Hebrew and Greek texts of Genesis 3 indicates what we would expect from a careful analysis of ancient serpent symbology. The author of Genesis 3 is reporting that the serpent was created by God. The Nachash is associated with that other world. He was the wisest of all the beasts on the earth. With these newly acquired insights, let us return to ʿrwm of Genesis 3:1.

To what extent has the narrator intimated that the serpent was ערום, not in *sensu bono* but really a sinister character, and not only finally but also originally? Long ago, J. Skinner, a professor at Cambridge, overstressed the demonic features of the serpent, according to Genesis 3. For Skinner, the serpent was a beast with demonic wisdom. The Yahwist clarifies the serpent's connection with the beasts and concludes the story by cursing the serpent. The developing image of the serpent in Genesis 3 indicates that Nachash cannot be placarded as always good (Pos. 5). There are sinister features of the Nachash; it is the serpent who initiates the process that led to the banishment of Adam and all related and descended from him from Eden. The serpent as the symbol of the Death-Giver (Neg. 1),[135] Destroyer (Neg. 2), and Bearer of Corruptible Knowledge (Neg. 4) has left its mark on the Eden Story.

Once again we should recall the complicated multivalence of serpent symbolism and the fact that in the selfsame narrative—and at the same time—the serpent may represent good and evil (double entendre).[136] Skinner offers additional advice regarding serpent symbolism in Genesis 3, and this time his comments are more representative of the narrative. He suggested that probably "behind the sober description of the serpent as a mere creature of Yahweh, there was an earlier form of the legend in which he figured as a god or a demon." [137] Skinner meant that the serpent may represent a good demon. Reminiscent of our previous reflections on Agathadaimon are Skinner's words: "In the sphere of religion the serpent was usually worshipped as a *good* demon. Traces of this conception can be detected in the narrative before us." [138] These words, added to the previous reflections, help fill out the complex symbolic dimensions of the serpent in Genesis 3.

The serpent symbolism of Genesis 3 has evolved within the development of the story. The Yahwist inherited diverse and conflicted meanings of serpent symbolism, and he sought to answer issues not directly related to serpent symbology. He inherited over one thousand years of finely developed images of the serpent. As Moberly states, Genesis 3 "gives the impression of standing at the end point of a long and diverse history of reflection upon the issues and motifs that are central to it." [139] The long history reflected in Genesis 3 takes us back into Egyptian mythology and into Assyrian and Babylonian symbolism; we are also transported to ancient Canaan in which these, and other traditions, were inherited and formed to make the epitome of Canaanite mythology. When we look at Genesis 3, we might be reminded of the many images of serpents that have been found in controlled excavations in Israel today: the numerous pots with serpents crawling up and near the rim, the serpents on incense burners, the gold and silver serpents found in cultic settings, and the serpent jewelry. When we let these images speak, we are allowed to hear, in a purer form, the world of the Yahwist. It was a world in which symphonies were created around the symbology of the serpent. The Yahwist knew his readers would appreciate the mystery and complex symbolic world evoked by a serpent in a narrative about creation (cf. Pos. 7).

Again, we return to Speiser's commentary on Genesis because it represents some of the best work in the field. However, an immersion into serpent symbology reveals that Speiser has not always heard the images speak. There is no reason to assume, with Speiser, that the woman "interrupted the serpent" (3:2); that again suggests a negative view of the serpent. No one should think that the woman would interrupt God Yahweh, for example. The second address to the woman by the serpent in Genesis 3:4 may be translated more idiomatically: "You are certainly not going to die! No, the celestial beings well know that the moment you eat of it your eyes will be opened and you will be the same as the celestial beings in knowing good from bad." This translation might make it easier to see the serpent as one of "the celestial beings" since he knows "good from bad." The woman thus does not consider the serpent a lower being who could be interrupted.

The examination of Speiser's commentary on Genesis—a superb accomplishment that shows a master Semitist at work[140]—highlights how commentators simply assume that the serpent in Genesis must be totally a negative symbol, and that translations must be slanted, or skewed, to bring out only negative meanings regarding the serpent in the Eden Story. We have seen that both an attentive focus on the Hebrew and Greek primary texts and an appreciation of serpent symbology reveal many areas in which the standard commentaries on Genesis may be improved.

Yet one should not seek to portray the serpent only in a positive light. He does represent the primordial chaos (Neg. 3). The well-chosen words of Joines are now apposite: "The Yahwist has used the figure of the serpent to *objectify* chaos, *but not to personify it.*"[141] That is, the image of the primordial serpent as the beast of chaos that must be slain for order and creation—which we analyzed in Chapter 5—is present in the "serpent" of Genesis 3, but the serpent was not chosen by the Yahwist to personify or symbolize chaos.

The serpent serves the Yahwist to elucidate the danger in Eden and the problems with any commandment. The serpent begins the process that results in the humans' loss of innocence, happiness, and life (not necessarily immortality). The Nachash embodies the beginnings of pain, labor, danger, and death (see Ps 58:4–5, Prov 23:31–32, Amos 5:19, 9:3). Again, we see, as was demonstrated in the preceding chapter, that serpent symbolism is multivalent, and sometimes a good and evil meaning may be present at the same time in one symbol or word.

The Eden Story elicits many questions. The narrative seems surprisingly contradictory. For example, is Paradise situated in the East, as stated in Genesis 2:8, or in the North, as implied in the following verses (Gen 2:10–14)?[142]

Why does the story seem so crude and poorly composed? The most likely answer is that the author was a compiler of diverse and contradictory mythological traditions and different symbolic worlds; most of these developed outside Yahwism or Israelite religion, and certainly prior to and foreign from "Old Testament theology." Some of the influence on the Yahwist certainly came from Mesopotamian traditions[143] and from Egypt. But now we know that Mesopotamian and Egyptian influences had helped shape Palestinian culture before the arrival of the Israelites. For example, as previously intimated, a copy of Gilgamesh has been identified in the ruins at Megiddo, and an abundance of serpent imagery from Egypt and Mesopotamia has been found in the strata of ancient Palestine. In fundamental ways, the Yahwist's symbols, especially his serpent symbolism, came from waning Canaanite culture. No one should doubt that the Eden Story began as lore that was shaped by orality.[144]

Immersing oneself in the context of the Eden Story and the myths that shaped the cultures contiguous with that of the Yahwist, and certainly impacted his own, helps one distinguish between exegesis that is philologically, historically, and symbolically formed from a spiritualization of the story. One can avoid sweeping generalizations and myopic spiritualizations of Genesis 3 and protect the uninformed reader from such misleading claims as the following: the temptation induced by the bad appeared *sub specie boni,* and sin is "un rifiuto del bene." [145] Moralizing sermons are not to masquerade as critical scholarship.

The abundant questions generated by reading and and rereading of Genesis 2 and 3 should not lead to a failure to appreciate the artistry of the first biblical narrator: the Yahwist. There are many attractive features of the story. It is memorable and keeps one's interest. The Hebrew contains wonderful subtleties. For example, the Yahwist cleverly describes how Eve *(ḥawwāh)* is the mother of all the living *(ḥāi).* There is most likely much more than assonance here.[146] The laryngeals, when the Yahwist wrote, were emphasized and the first word echoed in memory and then was heard along with the second. Formerly, the woman *('iššāh)* was related to the man *('iš);* [147] now, she is related to the generations to come, which included those living in the time of the author. The Yahwist seems to underscore the fact that humans originate somewhat mysteriously, and probably more so to him than to us, even though we may need to be present at a birth to realize it is a grand miracle and mystery. All humans are born out of the woman, "the mother of all the living."

The Hebrew of Genesis 3 abounds with evidence that the Yahwist is a gifted author and has attentively crafted his narrative about the serpent and the humans in Eden. A. Wénin understands the serpent in Genesis 3 to symbolize limit, and he sees the concept reflected in the play on two Hebrew words (both have the same consonants: *'rm*): *'arôm,* "nude," and *'arûm,* "wise" or "clever":

> Le serpent est donc ce qui fait miroiter la limite. Le narrateur a d'ailleurs prévenu le lecteur, en l'avertissant à l'aide d'un superbe jeu de mots, que le serpent est "le plus nu" (en hébreu *'arôm*), "le plus rusé" (en hébreu *'arûm*) de tous les animaux. On a vu plus haut, à propos de 2,25, que la nudité représente entre autres choses l'exhibition, la mise en évidence de la limite.[148]

> The serpent is then that which mirrors limit. The narrator predisposes the reader to imagine, with the aide of a superb play on words, that the serpent is both the "most naked" (in Heb. *'arôm*), and the most crafty (in Heb. *'arûm*) of all animals. One sees earlier, in 2:25, that nudity represents more than exhibition, it implies the limit.[149]

P. Haupt points out the paronomasia in the cursing of the serpent: *šup* means first "to tread down" and then "to snap." Translating this verb as "will persecute," he suggests understanding verses 14–15 as two triplets:

Jhvh said to the Serpent,
Since thou hast done this   thou art accursed
Of all the beasts   all the days of thy life.
Thou shalt crawl on thy belly   biting the dust.

I'll put enmity   between thee and her,
Between thy progeny   and her progeny;
They will persecute thee [šup],   thou wilt persecute them
                                  [šup].150

The observations by Wénin and Haupt help emphasize the many uses of paronomasia in Genesis 3. Note the following examples of careful composition by the Yahwist:

1. The serpent is clever (ʿrwm) in Genesis 3:1, and the man and woman are nude (ʿrwmym) in Gen 2:25.151 The wisdom and cleverness of the serpent help the human couple to see their nudeness.
2. The serpent's cleverness (ʿrwm) echoes in the curse (ʿrwr).
3. The sound of the word tree (ʿṣ) is heard again in the pain (ʿṣb in Gen 3:16 and ʿṣbwn in Gen 3:16, 17) the humans will suffer.152
4. The double use of the verb "bruise" tends to unite the fate of the serpent and humans.
5. The woman eats (tʾkl) of the forbidden fruit so the serpent must forever eat (tʾkl) dust.
6. The serpent is condemned to eat dust (ʿpr) and the human to return to dust (ʿpr). Perhaps the Yahwist is intimating that when humans return to dust they will be eaten by the one who eats dust and—in terms of serpent symbology—never seems to die, or turn to dust.
7. Adam (ʾdm) "shall return to the ground [ʾdmh]," according to Genesis 3:19.

The careful use of words and repetitions sews the narrative together attractively (each of these words is a *Stichwort*). Notice that the author of Genesis 3 knew how to bring out the echoing memory of previous sounds by repeating words that begin with a laryngeal (ʿrwm), which is often followed by a re-echoing plosive consonant (ʿṣb and ʿṣbwn). The central idea of "tree" may have been highlighted for verbal and narrative effect, since it begins with both a laryngeal and a plosive (ʿṣ). In Preexilic Hebrew, the consonants had more distinct and distinguishing sounds than can be heard today, especially the sounds demanding effort, like the laryngeals and plosives (as can be still heard today among some Bedouins in the Arabah).

The linguistic "genius" of the Yahwist seems implied in more subtle ways. First, the serpent does not use the familiar name of God: Yahweh God (as the Hebrew order has it). He is permitted only to refer to "God." Thus, he is placed outside the framework in which a caring relation with Yahweh God is experienced. Second, since the serpent and the woman cannot quote Yahweh God accurately, they are thus portrayed as adding to or subtracting from God's word (cf. Deut 4:2 and Prov 30:6).[153]

The Eden Story elicits so many questions, was written so early, and absorbs so many earlier symbols and ideas. Yet the later writers did not rewrite or appreciably edit it, although the Priestly Writer added Genesis 1:1–2:4a and so framed the prefatory comments. That means the Eden Story had achieved an attractive status by the end of the tenth century BCE (most likely). The beauty of the Eden Story comes into focus again when we hear the words of Gunkel that are directed to the "stories in Genesis":

> We certainly . . . are of the opinion that whoever passes over these stories without attention to their artistic form is not only deprived of a great pleasure, but is also unable to carry out properly the scholarly duty of understanding Genesis. Indeed, scholarship is fully justified in asking the question; of what does the specific beauty of these stories consist? The answer penetrates deeply into their content and religion.[154]

We have seen how an attention to ancient Near Eastern serpent symbology has increased our appreciation of the artistic form achieved by the Yahwist in Genesis 3; he was a rare and gifted linguist. We have also skirted a misleading dichotomy; we did not ponder whether the Eden Story was the result of popular tradition or the creation of an individual poet. Genesis 3 is not only reflective of both, but it is also "ultimately a creation of the people in common," as Gunkel ascertained.[155] Using language shared with me by S. Talmon, we can perceive that the People of the Book have given us the Book of the People. That is, the Yahwist represented the emergence of Israel and the people united around a common story as Israelite religion took the shape we now find at the beginnings of the Hebrew Bible. Genesis 3 is not only at the beginning of the Hebrew Bible, it appeared at the beginning of Israelite narrative history.

More examples of the careful use of language by the Yahwist could be given. These would help us appreciate more deeply the beauty of the Eden Story, but that is not our chosen purpose. Our present task is to keep in focus the central question: What is the symbolic meaning of the serpent in Genesis 3? Let us now isolate the issues that pertain to the serpent.

First, the Nachash is one of the beasts of the field that "God Yahweh had made" (3:1; cf. 2:19). This information raises doubts whether the Nachash is adequately represented by "serpent" in Genesis 3:1. The author introduces the serpent the way it appears naturally; the serpent arrives unexpectedly and spontaneously. While the author does not clarify who named the serpent (2:20), he makes it clear that the serpent is one of God's creatures.

Second, we are not told from where the serpent has come. That is a part of the attractiveness of the narrative. The serpent simply appears. The author does clarify, in contrast to much of Near Eastern lore and symbolism, that the serpent is not a god and that he was "made" by God Yahweh. To what extent is the serpent in Genesis 3 presented as if he were a messenger from another world?

Third, we are not told where the serpent is located in the narrative. Most artists place him (her) on or around the tree. Far more likely, in light of serpent iconography, he is standing, on two or more feet.[156] Did the Yahwist imagine that the serpent stood face-to-face with the anonymous woman?

Fourth, is the "focal point of the narrative" the tree of knowledge?[157] That places the serpent in a minor position. The story does focus on knowledge and wisdom, but the serpent is as central as the tree. Genesis 3 opens with the Nachash, and he remains dominant either explicitly or implicitly from 3:1 until 3:15. At that point God curses him (her).

We asked what the serpent might reveal or disclose in Genesis 3:5. If there is a tree of the knowledge of good and evil, then it is either unknown to the humans or some knowledge about this tree is revealed to them by God Yahweh. G. von Rad points to the difficulty in the Hebrew behind "the tree of the knowledge of good and evil," and asks: "Does man already know it as such?" And if God here reveals the mystery, what sense has the snake's explanation (ch. 3.5)?" G. von Rad continues by pointing out that the suggested emendation (cf. *BHS*), "from the tree in the midst of the garden," agrees "with what the woman gives as the wording of the prohibition (ch. 3.7)." He then notes, correctly, that such knowledge entails more than the "law of psychological credibility." It involves "omniscience in the widest sense of the word."[158] Surely, knowing demands experiencing.

More in focus than any tree in these verses are the words between the woman and the serpent (3:1–5). No conversation with her husband is mentioned (3:6–7; cf. 3:12). After the conversation between God and Adam becomes central (3:9–12), God addresses the woman and she answers (3:13). God next addresses and curses the serpent and the land (3:14–15). God does not curse the woman (3:16) and the man (3:17–19).

Now, we may ask "Where is God in this story?" God does not appear to be the protector of Adam and the woman. Is he not an absent god (a *deus absconditus*)? Le Grande Davies offers some insight: "The serpent of Genesis 3 most certainly is portrayed as part of the Garden of Eden. He is the main character associating with Adam and Eve. As a matter of fact more is stated about his association with them than their association with their God, who seems for a time to have left their presence."[159]

The opening of Acts implies an absentee Christology: Christ has left the disciples and will return as he ascended into heaven. Likewise, the Eden Story God implies that Yahweh is absent in Genesis 3:1–7 so that the Yahwist must introduce him again: "walking in the garden in the cool of the day." Then, as the narrative develops, Adam and his wife can be shown to realize that they are now naked (not the עֲרוּמִּים of Gen 2:25 but עֵירֹם of Gen 3:10, 11) before the God who returns to walk with them.

Adam had been assigned tasks in the garden, so work antedates the punishment: Adam was to till the garden (Gen 2:15).[160] Paradise was no place of contemplation, rest, or sensual pleasure.

The narrative ends when God casts the man (and, by implication, the woman but not the serpent) out of the garden (3:24).[161] The dialogue moves from interrogatives to curses and rejection. If dialogue is central to this narrative, the serpent, the woman, and God are the dominant characters. This conclusion is strengthened by the recognition that in the patriarchal stories it is God's word that influences actions.[162]

Fifth, are the serpent's first words inaccurate (3:1)? According to Speiser, the serpent "is deliberately distorting a fact."[163] Speiser assumes the serpent is a male, since he uses the pronoun "he" in referring to the creature.[164] Speiser clearly believes the serpent is an evil creature. The serpent's words cannot be inaccurate if they are a question, which we have seen to be highly probable.

According to Genesis 2:16–17, God Yahweh gave only one command to Adam. Note the often-missed poetic form:

> From every tree of the garden you may freely eat;
> But from the tree of the knowledge of good and evil
>   you may not eat,
> For in the day that you eat from it you will surely die.

My translation represents the Hebrew words that are omitted in translating, and lays out God's first command in poetic parallel lines *(parallelismus membrorum)*, a form that signifies exceptionally important words[165] that are often intended to be memorized.

How are God's words reported by the serpent and the woman? The serpent does not report God's commandment to Adam; in 3:1, he asks the woman, "Did God really state, 'You may not eat from every tree of the garden'?"[166] If the Nachash asks a question, one cannot conclude that he is deliberately misquoting God. The woman summarizes God's commandment, repeating that she and her man, Adam, may eat of the fruit of the trees in the garden, but God had a proscription. Regarding "the tree in the middle of the garden," presumably the "tree of the knowledge of good and evil," God said, according to the woman, "You may not eat of it, and you must not touch it, lest you die." The woman is not quoting God verbatim; she is summarizing God's command and clarifying that the "tree of the knowledge of good and evil" is in the middle of the garden. Such repetition helps readers understand the lone commandment and helps them comprehend and imagine the scene: the place of the tree. The text does not suggest that the serpent has failed to represent God's commandment and thus has deceived the woman. The presupposition that the serpent in Genesis 3 is an evil symbol is not supported by the passage in focus.

Sixth, why does the serpent approach the woman and not the man? Is it perhaps, in the eyes of the Yahwist, because the woman is naïve and weaker than the man since she was taken from his body? Is she chosen because she really needs a "master" (3:16)? [167] Does she remain nameless, until 3:20, and subsumed under the category of "woman" and "wife" because of the dominance of men in the Yahwist's culture? Perhaps the correct answers partly lie along such lines that expose the Yahwist's patriarchalisms. This interpretation was inherited and emphasized by Philo, who in *Questions and Answers on Genesis* 1.33, explained that the serpent by trickery and artfulness deceives, and the woman "is more accustomed to being deceived than man." [168]

Genesis 3:20 ("And Adam called his wife's name Eve, because she was the mother of all living [humans]") seems out of context and perhaps inserted in its present place by a later editor (redactor). However, as A. J. Williams perceives, it actually provides "an important insight into the whole context of Gen 3." [169] The verse reveals an important relationship between Eve and the serpent, which was already present in the narrative.

H. Gressmann probably erred in thinking that Eve and the serpent were originally identical; [170] although there was probably far more kinship between "Eve" and the serpent in the mind of the Yahwist and his contemporaries than Genesis 3 now suggests to modern minds. [171] The ancient mother goddesses wreathed with serpents, or a serpent, does not seem significantly to shape the presentation of Eve in Genesis 3:20. Although too speculative to many biblical experts, W. F. Albright's claim that Eve had originally been a serpent goddess is stunningly astute and perceptive. [172]

There is some enigma in Genesis 3:20. It should, however, be seen against the context of Genesis 2–3. That is, "life" in Genesis 3:20 is intended to be seen in light of the "curse" of Genesis 3:16 and the "naming" in Genesis 2:20. Eve, the one who (along with the Nachash) brought death to humans, is to be the mother of all life.

What new perceptions are released when we recognize that the woman and the serpent may well both be feminine beings? If males are dominant in the society of the Yahwist, what do we learn when we comprehend that the serpent may well be feminine yet has a role more dominant and powerful than Adam (the man) in the narrative? [173] Again, with such penetrating questions the importance and positive attributes of the serpent begin to appear.

Seventh, what is meant by the woman's excuse, "the serpent tricked (or deceived) me" (3:13)? Has the Yahwist's source, or the Yahwist himself, included the concept of the serpent as the cosmic trickster, the Deceiver, or the Liar? The Hebrew verb translated as "tricked" (the Hiphil of נשא II) also means "cheat" or "deceive." Thus, it is misleading to assume that the Yahwist knew his reader would realize the serpent was a trickster. The words in Genesis 3:13 appear in the narrative to explain the woman's attempt to escape blame and punishment. The attempt of the woman to offer an excuse should not be assumed to be an accurate assessment of what the serpent has said and done.

Before proceeding further, we may learn from those who approach Genesis 2–3 from structuralism. R. Couffignal follows C. Lévi-Strauss' method for exploring the unknown realm *(terra incognita)* of the Garden of Eden. Cleverly seeing that the introduction of the first humans is "le commencement du commencement," he imagines the following structure in Genesis 2–3:

fruit not consumed	nudity without embarrassment	law accepted
fruit consumed	nudity with embarrassment	law violated

In this structure, Couffignal finds that the serpent is "the trickster par excellence, the Deceiver" ("le *trickster* par excellence, le Décepteur").

Is this "exegesis" a result of philological and textual analysis? Focusing on myths and not examining the text misleads Couffignal. For example, he imagines that "the serpent of Eden" ("le serpent de l'Eden") is "the Guardian of God's treasure" ("le gardien du trésor des dieux"). [174] In Genesis 2–3, the fruit and the tree are not defined by the Yahwist as God's treasure, and the Nachash is not described as a guardian, as in the Garden of the Hesperides.

Eighth, has the serpent or God lied? Moberly rightly points out the "fact that apparently the serpent and not God spoke the truth." He then suggests that this point may be "the central issue that the story raises." [175] How theologically sophisticated was the Yahwist? I shy away from concluding that he knew that God Yahweh was supercategorical and could not be subsumed under ethical norms, such as "truth." I can imagine, however, that the Yahwist grasped that God Yahweh could not be controlled or understood, and that the Creator remains far too elusive. He probably comprehended that God cannot be defined by consistency.

In such reasoning, we must avoid another misleading dichotomy. Far too often critical scholars distinguish too neatly between allegory and reality, concluding that the Paradise Story is simply allegory. The Yahwist did not fall into the trap of assuming that his stories were merely allegories and not a description of reality. For him, the narrative of Genesis 3 "really took place." [176] If we are to enter into his "real world," we need to imagine, on reading Genesis out loud, that the Nachash was attractive as well as someone with whom the woman could engage within a meaningful world of discourse. As von Rad stated, what distinguishes the Nachash "from the rest of the animals is exclusively its greater cleverness." [177] He was indeed the cleverest of all the beasts of the field created by God Yahweh.

If the serpent lied, then he is indeed the Deceiver or Liar (Neg. 5). If he had not lied, then he may symbolize a wise creature that knew and told the truth. God had said to Adam that if he ate from the forbidden tree, he would die on the same day. The serpent disagreed with God; he said if the woman ate from the forbidden fruit she would not die but obtain knowledge. Thus, the Nachash is portrayed as an authority on life and, as Joines stated, "This reptile was a respectable representative of life or recurring youthfulness." [178] These deep meanings of serpent symbology were clarified in the preceding chapter (cf. Pos. 20, 23, 26, and 27) and are evident when one sees a snake rise up before one, defining life and its limits.

In his *Slaying the Dragon: Mythmaking in the Biblical Tradition,* B. F. Batto perceptively writes: "In Christian tradition the serpent has been maligned as a figure of Satan, who duped an innocent couple through a blatant lie. But that is hardly the figure the Yahwist intended." Batto stressed: "The serpent spoke the truth." [179] Many scholars point out that the cleverness of the serpent is underscored in the narrative by his (or her) telling the truth; what he predicts is what happens. The couple gains knowledge. [180] And the acquisition of knowledge is a divine attribute, as becomes clarified in the Hebrew Bible and throughout Jewish and Christian literature.

The truthfulness of the serpent's prediction, and correction of God, is clarified twice in the narrative. First, God directly supports the serpent's wise perception, informing Adam that since he knows he is naked he must have eaten the forbidden fruit. The Yahwist does not inform us about the type of forbidden fruit on the tree. It is not the fig that appears later. It is not the apple, which arose in early Latin Christianity because *malum,* "apple," rhymed with *malus,* "bad." [181] The forbidden fruit, according to the Yahwist, would be some mysterious and attractive fruit known perhaps only in Eden (cf. Gen 3:6).

Second, upon eating the forbidden fruit, the woman lives to give some of it to her husband, and they both live to receive God's banishment. The narrator relates how the serpent's understanding and prediction are true. Adam must return to dust. Adam and presumably the woman are banished from Eden; later they die. The Yahwist would disagree with those exegetes who conclude that Adam and Eve die because they ate from the forbidden fruit. He concluded his narrative with God's condemnations. The cause of human death is God Yahweh's edict concerning Adam, which includes Eve, in Genesis 3:19: Adam *('dm)* will return to the ground *('dmh),* because he is from dust and shall return to dust.

The Yahwist's narrative does not imply, though it is prima facie conceivable, that the serpent has immortality. The Yahwist does suggest that God Yahweh announces that only the humans will die, but that scarcely implies that the serpent will not die. The serpent is cursed, and he is not banished from Eden, but that does not indicate he remains in the garden. He is not damned to mortality and death as is Adam, but that does not imply the serpent obtains immortality. Does the Yahwist know that the serpent symbolized immortality (Pos. 27), and does this understanding prohibit him from stating clearly that the serpent is condemned to death? The serpent symbolized immortality and eternal life in Canaanite culture and in all the cultures contiguous with ancient Palestine (Pos. 20). Has the ambient culture helped to shape the Yahwist's magnificent story regarding the serpent's only apparent immortality?

D. Jobling argues that the main problem in the Eden Story is the portrayal of God. Jobling even suggests that to "characterize him [God] as villain is not impossible, in view of 3:8 (the Garden is for his own enjoyment), and vs. 23 (where he feels 'threatened' by the man!). As villain, he is the *opponent* of the main program." [182]

Jobling frames the problem of God in the Eden Story. God is indeed the liar, in some ways, but he is primarily the Creator and has a right to make demands. Without any demand or prohibition there would be no possibility of human freedom, and God would not have created something "free" of him. The importance of Jobling's insight and exegesis for us should be clear. It frees us from the millennia of misguided exegesis of Genesis 3 and helps thinkers escape from the misperception that the serpent is the villain in the story.

Retrospectively, in the theology of the Pentateuch, the serpent receives the blame for sin. Death is associated with him (cf. Neg. 1). God proves to be benevolent and prescient; humans die as God predicted. One might even perceive that God's prediction of death was immediate—life was not defined quantitatively.[183] After the act of disobedience, the human, for the first time, and immediately, fears God. And, since the story concludes with etiological concerns, what was predicted by God must come true; that is, since the story is about the origins of such problems as childbirth,[184] hard physical labor, and death, any prediction about their future existence is proved by the retrospective explanation.

In Genesis 3, however, the serpent is at best indirectly related to the death of Adam and the woman. The threat of death antedates the appearance of the serpent. God had stated emphatically that, if Adam eats of the tree, he would certainly die (Gen 2:17). God's prohibition may have been comprehended as a prediction, since God foreknew that the command would be broken: "For on the day that you eat of it you shall surely die." The word "you eat" is a verb with a pronominal suffix; it literally means "your eating." Genesis 2:17 could be understood to mean that God Yahweh, whom the Yahwist knew was not limited by time, said: "And from the tree of the knowledge of good and evil you must not eat from it, for on the day of your eating from it you shall most certainly die." Perhaps there is foreshadowing here in the Yahwist's narrative, and conceivably he, and certainly subsequent readers, observed that God Yahweh knew that the prohibition would be broken. Indeed, in Genesis 3:11 God Yahweh does not seem shocked or surprised that Adam has broken the single commandment.

The serpent appears to tell the truth. The humans do not die "on the day";[185] that is, they do not die immediately.[186] One could argue that "on the day" eventually included the death of Adam and Eve because the length of days was presupposed.[187] One might claim that God does not allow Adam and the woman to die immediately because God is full of grace,[188] but that forces Christian theology on an ancient Israelite text. Such arguments reveal self-pleading and miss the philological fact that ביום (Gen 2:17, 3:5) denotes not only "on the (that) day," but also "concomitantly" (i.e., when you eat you die),[189] "when,"[190] and "immediately."[191] The serpent was correct; the woman and Adam ate and did not die immediately.[192] As Batto states:

> In Christian tradition the serpent has been maligned as a figure of Satan, who duped an innocent couple through a blatant lie. As D. O. Procksch, H. Seebass, and others have stated, the Nachash is the last figure in the drama to be introduced; he is one of God's creations, a beast of the field, and cannot be Satan, a demon, or any mythological creature.[193] But that is hardly the figure the Yahwist intended. In his telling, the serpent spoke the truth. The woman and her husband did not die, as Yahweh God had said, "on the day you eat of it" (2:17).[194]

Upon eating of the forbidden fruit, Adam and the woman instantaneously obtain knowledge. They also are now afraid of God Yahweh. Did not this "enlightenment" prove the veracity of the serpent?

According to the narrative, the serpent (to a minor extent), the woman, and the man (clearly and emphatically) are revealed as creatures who cannot accept responsibility for being disobedient to God Yahweh. We learn that it is the concept of disobedience, not falsehood, that defines "sin" in the Eden Story. G. von Rad accurately defined the Eden Story in light of ancient Near Eastern mythology: "How simple and sober is our narrative, compared to the sensual myths of the nations, in letting the meaning of life in Paradise consist completely in the question of obedience to God and not in pleasure and freedom from suffering, etc." [195]

Since God's command did not include the serpent and since he did not eat from the forbidden fruit, one should be cautious in concluding that the serpent was disobedient and sinful. Artists know what biblical scholars fail to discern. In painting the expulsion from Eden, one can depict the banishment of Adam and possibly Eve, but not the serpent. He was not banished from Eden. Why? Is it because he did not eat of the fruit and thus did not disobey God Yahweh's command—which was addressed only to Adam?

Ninth, what does the author mean by stating that the serpent is banned from, or cursed among (which is better), "all cattle" and "all wild creatures" (3:14)? The concept of banning seems inappropriate since the author might have been expected to have mentioned that the serpent was also banned from the birds (2:19–20), with which it is often connected phenomenologically, iconographically, and symbolically (as at Beth Shan). The Hebrew verb 'rr—translated as "banned" by Speiser—is the customary word for "cursed," especially when God is the subject, as in Genesis 3:14. The verb also seems to mean to "restrain (by magic)" or "bind (by a spell)." Perhaps the Yahwist has inherited words and concepts from Canaanite serpent cults in which the serpent's magic was honored or worshipped.[196] He certainly would not want to give the impression that the serpent was to be worshipped because it had magical powers. It is far from clear what serpent symbolisms the Yahwist inherited. It is certain, however, that he did not create the symbolism, but was deeply influenced by earlier serpent symbology, much of which was too contradictory for him, or anyone, to comprehend.

Tenth, if the serpent now must "walk [crawl] on its belly" (על־גחנך תלך) (Gen 3:14),[197] how did he move before? Did he originally have legs as we know from ancient Near Eastern iconography (see esp. Fig. 27)? If the author did not have this thought in mind, the author of his sources, and those who knew them, passed them on, or read his account of the Eden Story would have often made such an assumption. Possibly *Jubilees* 3:23, at least according to Glycas (c. 1150) and R. H. Charles, concluded with a mention of the serpent having his legs cut off.[198] Does this interpretation of Genesis 3:14 appear in Jewish documents?

According to Josephus, the serpent "maliciously induced the woman to taste of the plant of wisdom" and so lost the ability to talk, received "venom beneath his tongue," and was deprived of feet (*Ant* 1.42, 50).[199] Ephrem Syrus also seems to assume that the Nachash originally had feet.[200]

The serpent's transgression was not to use reason or to talk; these were gifts from God. The serpent's transgression was to use physical force; according to Midrashic exegesis, the serpent pushes the woman into the tree.

The *Targum Pseudo-Jonathan* adds to Genesis 3 the removal of the serpent's feet. Note the addition by the Meturgeman: The Lord God "said to the serpent [לחייא], 'Because you did this, cursed are you. . . . Upon your belly you shall go about, *and your feet shall be cut off* [וריגלך יתקצצון].' "[201] According to R. Simeon b. Lakish, in *Midrash Rabbah, Ecclesiastes*, when God had cursed the serpent (Gen 3:14), "the ministering angels descended and cut off its hands and legs [וקצצו ידיו ורגליו], and its cry went from one end of the world to the other."[202] The same interpretative expansion of Genesis 3:14 appears in *Midrash Rabbah Bereshith* (Genesis) 20.5.[203]

Are these Jews who report that the serpent originally had hands and feet (or legs) merely speculating, or are they perspicacious exegetes? They are assuredly the latter, and they saw what is in the text. They spent their lives debating the meaning of the text: focusing and digesting, and imagining the scene. They did not devote a large portion of their time to research reading and regurgitating the comments of others. Let us go back to Genesis 3 and see what should be before our eyes.

Biblical scholars have assumed the Nachash (נחש) is a reptile.[204] Everyone can defend such a translation by simply citing a lexicon. But the narrative is definitive in ascertaining the meaning of the Nachash. The author presents his composition with echoes; these clarify that the so-called serpent is not a reptile. Genesis 3 begins with the words that the Nachash (נחש) was the cleverest "beast of the field [חית השדה] that the Lord God had made." The Nachash is thus one of the beasts of the field, not one of the cattle or reptiles. The author cannot expect his reader to know that this verse echoes the subsequent chronologically, yet preceding literarily (P) account in Genesis 1:24. Yet, it is the Priestly Writer who makes it clear that the Nachash cannot be a reptile.

According to this passage (1:24), God created three types of living creatures on the earth: the cattle (בהמה), the creeping animals (or reptiles [רמש]), "and the beast of the earth" (וחיתו־ארץ). It should be obvious that the Nachash (נחש) is not like the cattle. Biblical exegetes may be astounded to discover that, in its final form, Genesis does not categorize the Nachash with reptiles.[205]

The categorization occurred even earlier. The Yahwist reports, according to Genesis 3:1, that the Nachash is one of the beasts of the field (or earth). The Yahwist seeks to stress that the Nachash was originally very much like the human: wise, able to speak, upright, and most likely with feet (at least, and maybe hands).[206] In Genesis 3:1–13, the Nachash (נחש) should be imagined as beautiful and attractive, as the great artists, like Mosolino (see the following), imagined and represented; after all, the woman associates and talks with him or her. The comment that the serpent must now crawl on its belly refers back to the beginning of the account. Is Genesis 3:14 (the Nachash is now clearly a crawling serpent) not an echo of 3:1 (the Nachash adumbrates a serpent who will have to crawl)?

It is clear that the Nachash has been altered. He formerly did not have to crawl on his belly; now, he must eat dust and crawl on his belly. This seems obvious now, but the perception has been missed by many scholars. For example, the esteemed Semitist P. Joüon argued: "[The] serpent, before the curse, was not able to move except creeping on his belly; after the curse, he continued to move on his belly: Nothing changed" ("[Le] serpent, avant la malédiction, ne pouvait marcher qu'en rampant sur le ventre; après la malédiction il continue à marcher sur le ventre: il n'y a rien de changé").[207] Being ignorant of the iconography and symbology that clarify the contexts of our biblical texts leads to such misperceptions. The Yahwist most likely knew the regnant serpent symbolism in the Levant by which the serpent had legs; he makes it clear that God Yahweh cursed the serpent and declared that "because you have done this" (3:14)—that is, deceive the woman—you are now cursed, and you shall henceforth crawl on your belly. Has not the Yahwist cleverly elevated the human above the beasts of the field by narrating that when Yahweh God again appears in the garden, he asks Adam, but condemns the serpent?[208]

Eleventh, to whom would the Yahwist imagine Yahweh God spoke when he said, "Now that the man has become like one of us in discerning good from bad"? To whom could Yahweh God be referring by "like one of us" (3:22)? The Yahwist does not inform us, but the text invites us to imagine who could be Yahweh God's interlocutor. Texts, no less than art, remain lifeless and meaningless without the reader's active imagination, which must be stimulated and guided by attention to the details in the narrative.[209] Thus, with erudition and imagination controlled by the details and innuendoes of the Yahwist, the Aramaic translators of the Targumim can surmise that God was talking to the administering angels. Yet angels are not mentioned in the Hebrew text. Another, probably divine, being is, however, present; and his role has been to be the talking creature.

In the narrative, beside Yahweh God, only the woman, the man, and the serpent speak. The first two are omitted as possibilities because God is speaking to someone about them (I assume "the man" in 3:22–24, because of its connection to the previous verses, is a collective for man and woman). The only option left open, in terms of the story, is the serpent. Could these words, somewhere in the past, have included the serpent? In the present narrative, one learns that only God and the serpent originally knew about good and evil. Perhaps the Yahwist, as editor and compiler, has left an echo of traditions that portrayed the serpent as a god among other gods, now dethroned by the Yahwist and the growing influence (or foreshadowing) of monotheism.

In the Yahwist narrative, the serpent seems to possess divine knowledge. He apparently has the knowledge of what will happen if, or when, the human eats of the fruit of the tree of knowledge. Thus, he has the knowledge that only God seems to possess. Does the serpent, then, also know what is in the future? How else could the serpent predict—correctly in contrast to God—what will happen when the woman and man eat of the forbidden fruit? The serpent also knows what only God Yahweh knows: he knows the difference between good and evil. Thus, the Nachash seems to have features of a god. Pondering these aspects of the story, one can imagine that perhaps Nachash had already eaten of the fruit of the tree of knowledge. That exegesis would explain why the Nachash is introduced as "clever," and speaks with assurance of what will happen when the human eats of the fruit. It then becomes remarkable that the Nachash would choose to share this knowledge with these humans, who otherwise would be left in a state of pitiful ignorance.[210]

The serpent has intimations of divinity in the biblical story of Eden, although the Yahwist most likely tried to remove them. The Yahwist attempts to tone down the possibility of many gods, including the serpent, by categorizing the serpent beneath God. He is among God's creatures. The Yahwist moves the story in the direction of portraying the serpent as an adversary of the Creator.[211] Hence, in speculating on pre-Yahwistic serpent symbolism, we are not seeking to discern the theology of the Yahwist.[212] We are exploring pre-monarchic serpent symbolism that may still be mirrored in Genesis 3 and causing the narration to be less than clear, evoking numerous questions. It is thus conceivable that the Yahwist has left a trace of an earlier myth in which a god speaks with a serpent god about knowledge (of good and evil)[213] and eternal life. According to H. Ringgren, the serpent of Genesis 3 is to be identified with either El, the supreme god in the Ugaritic pantheon, or Baal, the god of lightning and storms.[214]

The possibility that the one to whom Yahweh God is speaking may have been the serpent—in an earlier version of the story—arises because the Yahwist has left in his narrative traces from older myths and legends regarding the serpent. These make sense within Near Eastern serpent iconography and symbology in which the serpent is portrayed as divine and a god (Pos. 11). These traces suggest that, in traditions inherited by the Yahwist, the serpent may have been addressed by God. He discerns "good from bad" and was thought by some ancients to "live forever." By focusing on serpent iconography and symbolism, we come closer to perceiving the editorial work of the Yahwist and the possible contours of some of his more ancient sources. We approximate the goal of biblical exegesis in the historical-critical perspective: to grasp the formation of texts, the ancient traditions refracted in texts, and to strive for a hermeneutic that is informed by the original context of texts.

Summary

Serpent symbolism in Genesis 3 has now been studied philologically, exegetically, contextually, and symbolically. We may thus review the ten points of the Eden Story that, as stated earlier, are so popular in Christianity and Judaism (and also, in many ways, the culture of Islam).[215] Each of the ten points is now exposed as false.

First, *the serpent is not the Devil or Satan*.[216] Neither the Devil nor Satan is mentioned in the Eden Story; other names for "Satan" also do not appear in this first great story in the Bible. Yet Jews, especially in the first century, often intimate that either the serpent was really the Devil or the Devil used the form of the serpent; even Paul refers to the way the serpent cunningly deceived Eve (2 Cor 11:3). The early Syriac exegetes equated the serpent of Genesis 3 with Satan.[217]

Second, *the serpent does not lie*. The serpent is also not portrayed as the Liar. What he predicts if the woman eats of the forbidden fruit transpires: she does not die immediately, and she becomes like God in that she knows good and evil.

The snake does not lie, but he does not tell the whole truth. The humans do become like God in that they know good and evil. But, most important, they do not become God and have immortality.[218] The author of Genesis 2 and 3, the Yahwist, does not suggest that Adam was created with immortality. He may imply that the man and the woman had to eat daily, or at least periodically, from the tree of life, and that after the expulsion from Eden they could not do that.[219] Thus, the Jew who composed the Wisdom of Solomon erred, as do many modern exegetes, in ascribing immortality to Adam and death to the action of the serpent, who is the Devil (διαβόλου):

> For God created the human to be immortal,
> He made him as an image of his own nature;
> Death came into the cosmos only through the Devil's envy,
> As those who belong to him find to their cost. [Wis 2:23–24]

Finally, according to the narrator, the humans do not become like God. They die; there is no implication that God had made the humans either immortal or eternally youthful.[220]

It is clear that the Yahwist has not presented the serpent as the grand antithesis to God. Not only does the serpent *not* lie, God is depicted narratively as failing to speak the full truth. This insight clashes with the affirmation in the Bible that there is only one God and he is trustworthy and faithful; he is the God of truth (cf. e.g. Pss 19:10, 31:6, Deut 32:4; cf. also Jn 17:17, Tit 1:2, Heb 6:18).[221] Yet biblical theology does not ring with the affirmation that God is always truthful.

The Nachash, alone among the animals, is presented as able to speak. If the serpent alone speaks the truth in this Eden Story, and since in the mind of the Yahwist truth was associated with wisdom and unthinkable without it, then the serpent is associated not only with truth but also with wisdom. The stage is set for the later Jewish authors who see the serpent as a symbol of wisdom (Pos. 18). Not only is that evident in the *Apocalypse of Moses*, but it is also attributed to Jesus, who told his disciples, according to Matthew, to be wise like serpents.

The significant impediment to seeing the Nachash as the "truth-teller" is the fact that both Adam and Eve died. Their death became a major theme of the first-century writing called the *Vita Adae et Eva*. This author of this work portrays Seth and Eve going to Paradise in order to obtain "the oil of mercy" (40:1) so Adam, who is sick and appears dying, could be healed. On the way, Seth is attacked by "a serpent" (37:1–3), a "cursed beast" (37:3); eventually the angel Michael informs the two: "Truly I say to you that you are by no means able to take from it, except in the last days" (42:1).

Two points must be repeated and emphasized. First, God said that anyone who ate of the forbidden tree would die "on the (that) day"; but Eve lives to entice Adam, and both live until they are banished from the garden by God. Second, God tells Adam (and, by the concept of inclusion, also his wife) that since he heeded his wife and ate of the forbidden tree he will die. Why does death occur? It is not because God "curses" the humans and they subsequently die. It is because they are banished from the garden and cannot eat regularly from the tree of life, which alone provides continuous life. Thus, the author of Genesis 3 assumes that the key to living forever is to be in the garden and periodically to eat the fruit from the tree of life. Perhaps he assumed, as did all who lived in the early centuries of the first millennium BCE, that death was a natural part of living, and the end of it. Thus, God announces to Adam that he will "return to the ground." The point is repeated: "For dust you [are], and to dust you will return" (Gen 3:19). The first human, *Adam*, returns to the ground, *adamah*.[222]

Third, *the serpent is no trickster*. He does not beguile the woman. The narrator does not depict the woman being tricked into doing what she would never herself think of doing. It is the Rabbis, through midrashic expansion, who added that the serpent pushed Eve into the forbidden fruit. The woman was not tricked; the Yahwist suggests that she willingly participates in the act. Note that after the serpent's advice: "The woman saw that the tree [was] good for food, that it was pleasant to the eyes, and [that] the tree would make [her] wise." (3:6). The narrator does not suggest that the serpent caused her—or bewitched her so as—to see the tree in this manner. As Paul Tillich claimed, the serpent does not symbolize disintegration but integration (cf. Pos. 12, "Unity [Oneness]").[223]

Fourth, *the narrator does not depict the serpent—and the serpent alone—as fully responsible for all the evils in the world*. The serpent does not force the woman to appreciate the forbidden fruit, take it, and eat it. The author does not primarily intend to explain the origin of sin and evil.[224] Yet, long before 70 CE, Jews interpreted Genesis 3 as an explication of the origin of sin. The ancient people of the Book saw no problem with the two accounts of how evil and sin appeared on this earth: the serpent and woman in Eden (Gen 3) and the fall of the angels (Gen 6; cf. esp. *1 En*). Probably many Israelites and Jews imagined that the two accounts could be conflated. Most likely some early Jews imagined that the "serpent" was originally a fallen angel.

Fifth, *the narrator clearly states that the serpent was one of God's creatures*. As snakes often do in homes near the equator, on hiking outings, or in forests, the serpent appears suddenly and mysteriously. There is no introduction. In a moment, the serpent is present in the narrative. Once present, he acts or speaks. The narrative thus embodies the symbol of the serpent as being swift and elusive (cf. Pos. 3). The serpent does not come with the announcing roar of a lion. It does not arrive with the trumpeting of an elephant, or the pounding hoofs of a horse. It comes silently and unexpectedly. The serpent's ability to symbolize swiftness and elusiveness is reflected in the Eden Story. One thinks about the metal serpents, which are abundant now from ancient Palestine. They have numerous curves, and usually the head is shown upright.

Genesis 3:1 thus introduces the serpent abruptly; there is no transition from what precedes. The "serpent" had not been mentioned before; it is suddenly present in the narrative. It is one of God's creations, but the reader is not prepared for the appearance of the serpent and the resulting story. While there are echoes in Genesis 3 of previous verses, there is no foreshadowing of the serpent by the Priestly Writer in Genesis 1:1–2:4a, or by the Yahwist in 2:4b–3:1.

Sixth, *the Nachash was not depicted as ugly or as a horrible-looking animal*. The Nachash in fact appears without any description. We may assume he has legs because of God's curse on him, but we are not told how

Figure 79. Adam and Eve, According to Masolino in the Cappella Brancacci. JHC

the Nachash looks. He must have a mouth and a larynx since he talks with the woman. We are not told if he has eyes, as one might assume from the study of ancient Near Eastern serpent iconography (but there are also images of snakes without eyes). We do not know if the Nachash has a nose or scales. We do not know how tall the Nachash is or what he looks like. Perhaps this is intentional, since what is important are the serpent's wisdom or cunning and ability to talk with the woman. Most likely, not only did the Yahwist know that a full description would detract from the reader's ability to grasp his important point, but "serpents" were very familiar in life, image, and myth to his audience.

Seventh, *we may assume the serpent is probably a male, but he has no sexual approach to the woman.* There is no evidence that the serpent entices the woman, and the assumption that the serpent uses some erotic powers to entrap her comes out of the misguided imagination of the modern person. There is no evidence that the serpent is first and foremost a phallic symbol (Neg. 16 or Pos. 1).

A study of how gifted artists depict Adam,[225] the woman, and the serpent is revealing. Unlike exegetes, artists must decide if the serpent is male or female, in the tree or beside it, beautiful and appealing or ugly and disgusting.[226] To demonstrate the paradigmatic difference between artists and exegetes—one would hope that this ceases to be the rule—only a few select illustrations must suffice. The most riveting might be Masolino's painting in the Capella Brancacci in Florence. Note how feminine and appealing the serpent is depicted in the painting.[227] The serpent is inviting, clean, and intelligent looking. She and the woman are closely related to the tree and appear as virtual twins.

The depiction of the serpent as feminine and similar to the woman is exceptional, but not unique. In 1508, Raphael, when he was about twenty-five, painted on the walls of Pope Julius II's study in the Vatican a serpent that is angelic and cherubic. It is close to "the woman," and one is given a sense of tranquility as the friendly serpent winds its way up the tree. Adam's right hand and the woman's left hand are depicted moving up toward the serpent. Raphael seems to have influenced Michelangelo, who also presented the serpent with an appealing, even feminine, face.

Michelangelo thus depicted "the serpent" in Eden as a woman. The Nachash is similar to "the woman" except that her torso, as in Masolino's masterpiece, is a serpent, and it likewise winds around the tree. In Michelangelo's art, as in Raphael's masterpiece, both Adam and the woman are reaching up toward the serpent.[228]

Finally, in the Strasbourg Cathedral and in St. Catherine's Chapel, which was completed in 1349, there is a depiction of Adam and "Eve" (at that point in the narrative she is "a woman" and not yet Eve) with a serpent. The creature also has a feminine face. The crucifixion above them, based on the Fourth Gospel, is a depiction of Numbers 21.

These artists rightly perceived the attractiveness of the serpent. None of them, however, knew enough about ancient serpent iconography to depict the serpent upright, with hands and feet, and conversing animatedly with the woman. They did, nevertheless, bring out in their portraits of the Nachash the attractive features of the human in God's creation.

These later artistic renderings of the Genesis story must not influence our reading of Genesis 3. In the Hebrew text, the *nachash* is a masculine noun. The verbs associated with him are masculine. Though the wise creature is often depicted as a female, that should not be the guiding principle in studying the Nachash in Genesis 3. The creature seems to be male, both grammatically and conceptually in the Hebrew Bible. Moreover, images of serpents in ancient Palestine about the time of the Yahwist depict the serpent as a male (or at least devoid of feminine features).

Eighth, it should now be obvious that *the author of Genesis 3 does not depict the serpent as beastly.* The serpent does not have the features of an ugly beast. The imagined shape of Satan, especially in medieval Christianity, must not be imposed on the image of the serpent in Genesis 3. The woman speaks with the creature; that should indicate that she is not afraid of the animal nor finds it repulsive.

Ninth, *can one really be certain that,* before the serpent spoke with "Eve" (she is not named until 3:20), *all was peaceful in Eden?* It seems too imaginative and romantic to surmise that in Eden the male and female walked with God, together, in the cool of the evening. How much harmony was there, at the beginning, in creation? Did not the Creator's prohibition of Adam to eat from the fruit of the tree in the middle of the garden cause some tension? If Adam was human, was he not tempted by the Creator's prohibition? Since the human was bereft of knowledge and the forbidden fruit was not on a tree on the edges—but in the center—of Eden, did God not make it virtually impossible for the human to obey the commandment? Was Adam not like Paul who found that prohibitions became temptations (Rom 7–8)?

How peaceful and idyllic was Eden? What kind of an Eden can be bereft of knowledge? In apocalypticism, we might imagine that the Jewish author sought at the End-time a return to the First-time. This repeated cliché derives from Gunkel's claim that the *Endzeit wird Urzeit,* "the Endtime shall be (a return to) the Firstime." However, there are major differences: there is no commandment, and there is no foreboding future of disobedience with another disastrous distance between the human and others, nature, and the Creator. Moreover, if the first Eden depicts a human without any knowledge or experience of good and evil, the final Eden imagined by Jewish apocalyptic writers results from the human's experience of good and especially evil. There cannot be a return to a dialogue with a Nachash since God's curse on him was irreversible, as the Jewish sages knew and stressed.

Tenth, *no one should imagine that the serpent alone is responsible for the entrance of sin into creation,* the appearance of death, and the cause of punishment and ultimately of banishment. The one who compiled the story in Genesis 3 shared the blame with all—the woman, the man, and the serpent. That is why all three were punished by God. The narrator would have been surprised that he allowed for some blame to reside even with God, not only in the statement that the serpent was created by God, but also in God's prohibition to eat from the fruit of one tree. Thus, the Yahwist avoids an error that sometimes appears in apocalypticism: the infinite separation of the created from the Creator. God was also included in the drama; after all, if God had not provided a prohibition, there would have been no possibility of disobedience.

Thus, by focusing on the symbol of the serpent in Genesis 3, we become sensitive to contradictions in Christian theology and the age-old misinterpretations of the story of Eden. God is the creator of all, even the

Nachash—a beast of the field who becomes the serpent. If the definition of truth is what God states, then God spoke the truth in Eden. If, however, truth is defined by relationships, then what happened is not what God predicted: the humans do not drop dead immediately; they obtain knowledge of (and experience) good and evil. Perhaps the Yahwist attempted to bring God into the world of humans and to make God one with whom humans could have a covenant relationship. The Yahwist put human qualities on God. He portrayed God as apparently lying and not knowing what would happen when the woman, or anyone, ate from the forbidden fruit. According to the Eden Story, God also seems to have lost touch with the human, calling out to Adam: "Where [are] you?" (Gen 3:9).

It is not correct to claim that God did not make demands on the first humans (the protoplasts). The Yahwist pointed out that the Creator always comes to us as one who makes demands. According to the narrative, the Creator seems also responsible for the so-called Fall. The story binds the Creator to his creatures. The story is complex, somewhat inconsistent, but its main point comes home: sin (and evil) is disobeying God. According to the Yahwist's composition, God is not distant and categorically above human aspirations, like telling the truth and being consistent. Yet, in mysterious ways, God and the serpent represent another dimension of reality.

The Yahwist shows an inordinate amount of interest in and fascination with the serpent. The Nachash once spoke clearly and wisely, and he presumably walked. Now the snake has no eyelids to protect it from the sun or dirt. It no longer can speak or hear (it has no ears [the one who gave us Ps 58:5(4) seems to err and assume a snake can hear]). It now must crawl on its belly and be fearful of any relation with the human, who may crush it. According to the *Midrash on the Psalms (Midrash Tehillim),* which probably reached its present shape in the ninth century CE, there is a deep meaning in Psalms 58:5–6. Note this exegesis attributed to David, who composed the Psalms, according to ancient traditions: "David said further to them: Know ye not what the Holy One, blessed be He, did to the serpent [לנחש]? He destroyed his feet [רגליו] and his teeth so that the serpent now eats dust." [229] According to this same text, if the snake still had feet: "It could overtake a horse in full stride and kill him."

How does one explain the observations that God has cursed the serpent to eat dust forever and snakes do not eat dust? The Rabbis knew and observed that snakes drank milk and ate food left for them, but the power of Genesis 3:14 is significant. The compilers of the Babylonian Talmud preserved the tradition that although a snake (נחש) can eat "the delicacies of the world [מעדני עולם]," it will only have "the taste of dust [טעם עפר]" (b. Yoma 75a).

Ironically, the serpent—the quintessential and pervasive symbol of immortal life, especially in antiquity (Pos. 27)—becomes in the Bible the one who symbolizes the humans' loss of immortality. The author or compiler of the account in Genesis 3 knew some of the Near Eastern myths and legends, such as the Gilgamesh story.

The Yahwist seems obsessed with etiological issues when he compiled the Eden Story. He wanted to explain the following:

- Why a woman and a man are so similar, in contrast to the animals ("she was taken from a man" [2:23])
- Why a man leaves his parents and clings to his wife (2:24)[230]
- Why there was no shame about nakedness at the beginning (2:25, 3:7, 10)
- Why the serpent seems isolated and is often a loner (3:14)
- Why the serpent must crawl on its belly (3:24)
- Why there is enmity among serpents and humans (3:24)
- Why women have such pain in giving birth (3:15)
- Why women are passionate about their husbands (3:16)
- Why women must have their husbands as a master (3:16)
- Why men must till the soil sometimes fruitlessly (3:17)
- Why humans return to dust (3:19)
- Why the humans were banished from Eden and cannot return there (3:22–24)
- Why the paradisiacal life was once experienced but now lost (3:22–24)

The Eden Story is centered on etiological concerns, more so than any other biblical story. In so casting the story, the Yahwist miscasts not only the serpent but also God. For example, God is the cause of a woman's birth pangs and man's often-fruitless labor. God is responsible for the earth's lack of fruitfulness. God is responsible for the "enmity" on the earth. Yet God is not omnipotent; God fears his creations and expresses the fear that they might "become like one of us" (3:22). God does not want the human to live forever. As Gunkel saw: "The narrative [Erzählung] does not report that Yahweh knows all, sees all; but much more, that he likes to saunter in the garden, by chance to discover a violation. An (absolute) all-knowing Yahweh is thereby not presented."[231]

In the Eden Story, the Yahwist explains too much. He explains why men have to work so hard for sustenance and why women suffer so in childbirth. He also explains the origin of the fear that defines the human–snake relationship, and why the serpent crawls on its belly (a description that brings to mind the ways the serpent symbolizes the earth and the chthonic world [Pos. 15]).

What did the Nachash do to deserve such long-lasting punishment?[232] In some ways, the Yahwist leaves the impression, to those who indwell the story (i.e., those who so imagine the story that they become part of it), that the serpent comes off as more attractive than God Yahweh. In so doing, he reflects the pervasive depictions of the serpent as a good symbol in his time, but perhaps not in his theology in Jerusalem at that time. Some of the tension in his story of Eden derives from the tension between Israelite and Canaanite culture. Much of this tension may be caused by serpent symbology, a too multivalent symbolism. We have seen, inter alia, that it is misleading to conclude that, in Genesis 3, the "mention of the snake here is almost incidental."[233] This opinion of G. von Rad misled Westermann (p. 238), who then goes on and perceives that the "masterly dialogue holds the center of the scene." Who are the main actors? Westermann rightly answers: "The serpent and the woman are the sole actors."[234]

In the narrative of Genesis 3, the Nachash appears suddenly and mysteriously. He is defined as one of the beasts of the field created by God Yahweh, except he is distinguished by his cleverness or wise character (Gen 3:1). He is the first interlocutor to speak and asks a question (3:1). Then, he launches out with a declaration that discloses unusual knowledge of what will, and does, happen after the woman eats of the forbidden fruit (Gen 3:4–4). The Nachash reveals that he knows what "God knows" (Gen 3:5). The Nachash does not push, force, or even suggest that the woman eat of the forbidden fruit, but the Nachash does play a major role. He provides the stimulus that is essential for the initiative of the human. The Yahwist eventually discloses—through the woman's defense—that the serpent is one who "deceived" the woman (Gen 3:13). Then God Yahweh curses the serpent, condemns him to henceforth crawl on the earth and to eat dust; the serpent is not condemned to death (to dust), however, and is not expelled from the Garden of Eden.[235] The serpent is the source of enmity (Gen 3:15). In this narrative, we see refracted ancient myths and serpent symbology: the serpent represents knowledge, cleverness, and wisdom (Pos. 18), but also power (Pos. 3) and some divinity (Pos. 11), and seems to possess continuous or immortal life (Pos. 27). The symbolic meanings of the ancient Ouroboros, caduceus, and uraeus may be seen to cast shadows on the Eden Story. In summation, the Nachash remains in the shadows and is never clearly described; he remains, as it were, a mysterious character (Pos. 17). He is not so much presented incognito, as God's creature who elicits fascinating attention. Such is the nature of the snake in real life.

Most important, we have perceived the marvelous literary skills of the Yahwist. He is a master in developing the characters of his dramatis personae. The Nachash is a beast of the field, according to Genesis 3:1. He becomes a serpent who crawls, according to Genesis 3:14. The "woman" is presented in Genesis 3:1, but she becomes "Eve" only in Genesis 3:20. The Nachash does not tempt "Eve"; he asks her a question. Thus, there are three errors in the oft-repeated claim that "the serpent" talked to "Eve" and he "tempted" her.

THE UPRAISED SERPENT OF MOSES: NUMBERS 21:4–9

Initial Observations

It is necessary to study Numbers 21:4–9 and then 2 Kings 18:4 in conjunction with it. The first passage is a narrative about the serpent Moses made in the wilderness; the second one refers to the worship of a serpent called Nechushtan in the Temple and Hezekiah's banishment of this serpent cult from the Temple, Jerusalem, and the Land. Both passages refer to a similar phenomenon—the upraised serpent. Commentators on Numbers find it necessary to include 2 Kings 18:4 in their search for the meaning of Numbers 21:4–9, and commentators on 2 Kings 18:4 must include some evaluation of the meaning of Numbers 21:4–9.

One of the well-known features of the narrative of the Hebrews wandering in the wilderness, after the Exodus, is their grumbling about their present condition. Their final complaint occurs after the death of Aaron and before the blessing of Balaam. The people's complaint over the bread and water was egregious; it was not primarily a yearning for the comforts of Egypt, albeit in slavery. This lament was an open defiance of Yahweh and his chosen one, Moses (*contra Deum et Mosen* 21:5).[236] They had forgotten the wonders performed by God, sometimes through Moses, as when he was able to turn his staff into a serpent.[237]

Text and Translation

Here is the translation of Numbers 21:4–9 in J. Milgrom's masterful commentary on Numbers:

> They set out from Mount Hor by way of the Sea of Reeds to skirt the land of Edom. But the people grew restive on the journey, and the people spoke against God and against Moses, "Why did you make us leave Egypt to die in the wilderness? There is no bread and no water, and we have come to loathe this miserable food." The LORD sent *seraph* against the people. They bit the people and many of the Israelites died. The people came to Moses and said, "We sinned by speaking against the Lord and against you. Intercede with the LORD to take away the serpents from us!" And Moses interceded for the people. Then the LORD said to Moses, "Make a *seraph* figure and mount it on a standard. And if anyone who is bitten looks at it, he shall recover." Moses made a copper serpent and mounted it on a standard;

and when anyone was bitten by a serpent, he would look at the copper serpent and recover.[238]

In Hebrew, the "the *seraph*" (הנחשים השרפים) are literally "the fiery serpents." In Hebrew, "the serpents" is the collective meaning of the singular "the serpent" (הנחש). The Lord commanded Moses to make "a *seraph* figure," which is "burning serpent" (שרף; see Appendix I).

Questions

The questions regarding serpent imagery and symbolism that are raised by Numbers 21:4–9 and that we shall address are the following:

1. What is meant by *seraph*; that is, what kind of a snake does the author have in mind?
2. When the poisonous snakes bite the people, why do not all die?
3. Why does the Lord command Moses to make a *seraph* and place it on a standard?
4. What did the copper serpent look like or resemble?
5. What symbolic meaning would be conveyed by a metal serpent on a standard?
6. Does the Lord's command not break the commandment that the human must not make any image?
7. Why are those who look up to the copper serpent healed?
8. How does the study of ophidian iconography in Near Eastern culture, and especially in ancient Palestine, help us understand this passage in Numbers?
9. Our central question is "What does 'the serpent' symbolize in Numbers 21:4–9?"

In the endeavor to answer these questions, we should read not only the Hebrew text but also heed the Septuagint's translation of the Hebrew. For example, the word to denote the "standard" (נס) on which Moses placed the copper serpent has unusual symbolic power. The Greek means "upon a symbol-stake" (ἐπὶ σημείου [21:8, 9]) and the emphasis is on "sign."[239] The selfsame Greek noun, *sēmeion*, was chosen by the author of the Gospel of John to represent the "miracles" of Jesus as "miraculous signs." This observation seems important; we will conclude by exploring to what extent the Fourth Evangelist was influenced by Numbers 21.

Scholars' Reflections

Scholars' work on Numbers 21 is more informed by serpent iconography and symbology than we have seen in Genesis 3. Their attention to the serpent in Numbers 21 and 2 Kings 18 is not so distorted by misleading exegesis and interpretation. Most commentators know the importance of serpent imagery for the authors of these sections of the Hebrew Bible. Hence, our examination will not need to be so extensive or corrective.

While it is not certain whether Numbers 21:4–9 belongs to the Yahwist or the Elohist,[240] it seems likely that the narrative is the work of the Elohist who has inherited a considerable amount of diverse earlier traditions.[241] The narrative in Numbers 21:4–9 thus may well be a composite work by a northern Israelite writer (the Elohist) who was indebted to and incorporated (perhaps earlier) Judean sources (perhaps ultimately from the Yahwist). While the earliest source may go back to the ninth century (or even earlier), the present narrative reached its present form sometime about the seventh century BCE and in Judah.[242] More than one tradition in the account is evident, notably in the mixing of singular and plural verbs (cf. vv. 6 and 7), and the confusion of one (v. 9) or many serpents (vv. 6, 8).[243]

Both the author of Numbers 21:4–9 and the author of 2 Kings 18:4 attribute to Moses the making of a serpent of copper (or bronze).[244] Do these passages reflect some historical event or are they mere fabricated legend?[245] There seem to be three possible explanations to ponder.

1. The first possible explanation is that the account in Numbers 21:4–9 is legend without any historical reliability. There are problems with taking Numbers 21 as strictly historical. As G. B. Gray stated, the story of Moses' making a copper (or bronze) serpent contains neither an adequate explanation of the choice of this particular form of miracle, nor any clarification of how the Israelite nomads on the march were in a position to manufacture, with the speed which the circumstances demanded, so important a work in metal.[246]

The historicity of the Pentateuchal narrative depends on authors who wrote hundreds of years after the events they describe and relate. That is, Moses would have made a copper serpent sometime in the thirteenth century BCE, but the account would have not been written until the tenth century BCE and most likely much later. The transmission of oral traditions during these centuries was altered by nonhistorical interests, such as the movement from nomadic to urban settings and the continuing influence of myths and ideas that developed from Moses to David, and most likely later. The author (or editor) who gave us Numbers 21:4–9 was not seeking to be an objective historian; he was interested in reporting how the Lord heard the cries of the Israelites and provided a means so that those bitten could, through faith, look up to the copper serpent made by Moses, "and (continue) to live" (וחי; Num 21:8, 9). The motives for writing the account, therefore, were to provide comfort for Israelites who were suffering from snakes, and to celebrate Yahweh, who brings healing and life.

These comments are generally acknowledged by the experts, but such arguments leave open the possibility that there may be reliable historical traditions linking Hezekiah's time with Moses' time. One should observe that to choose between legend and history is to categorize ancient texts, such as Numbers 21, within false alternatives. History may be transmitted in myths, legends, and liturgies.

2. The second possibility is that the narrative in Numbers 21:4–9 is grounded in history. The story is not only about the upraised serpent; it depicts the plague of serpents *(die Schlangenplage)* and the upraised serpent. Moses made a copper serpent that was not regarded as an idol, but later in the Temple in Jerusalem it may have been treated in this fashion.

Some scholars conjecture that Moses most likely did make a serpent and placed it on a pole. They point out that, after all, as previously discussed, a copper serpent—with cultic significance—has been found at Timnaʿ, which was a copper-mining region in the Arabah just north of the Red Sea, and it is roughly contemporaneous with the action attributed to Moses (see Fig. 22). A study of this copper snake idol with gilded head, not a photograph, awakens in one the feeling that it is alive and moving. The seven curves may also be more than ornamental. The clear eyes, which are prominent as in almost all serpent images, awaken in the observer thoughts about intelligence and wisdom. Clearly, the metal serpent was crafted to signify many symbolic meanings; all would be positive since it is an idol and found in a cultic setting. One should not overlook the fact that the serpent is made with imperishable material; it has lasted in perfect condition since the twelfth century BCE. The material itself thus has symbolic power.[247]

According to some experts, this archaeological fact adds historical credence to the story in Numbers 21. There is much wisdom in Milgrom's comment that the copper snake found at Timnaʿ supplies iconographical and archaeological evidence that lends credence to the story in Numbers 21. He judges that since the copper snake of Timnaʿ dates approximately from "the same time and place that Moses fashioned a similar snake," this suggests "that the snake story was inserted into the itinerary precisely when Israel was in the vicinity of the Timnaʿ copper mines. This thesis is further supported by textual evidence of a break in the next stage of the itinerary."[248]

According to tradition, Aaron's rod (Num 17:25) and the receptacle of manna (Exod 16:34) survived from Moses' day. They may have been visible on occasion in Solomon's Temple. Some scholars contend that Moses' copper serpent was also on public display in the Temple. Note the insight shared by Milgrom, that while the meal offering

> was sacrificed on the altar, the officer would stare at the snake, hoping to repeat the Mosaic miracle of healing. Thus the sacrifice could

in effect have been offered to the snake rather than to Israel's God. Moreover, since the Canaanites regarded the snake as a cultic symbol of renewed life and fertility, it may have become over time a bridge to pagan worship within the Temple itself.[249]

Milgrom's judgment is undergirded by the vast amount of ophidian imagery we have from about 1300 to 700 BCE and not later, as we have presented selectively in the previous chapter. It is also likely that a serpent placed in the Temple could be a way to combat idolatry by absorbing its meanings and powers within the cult of Yahweh.

3. The third possible explanation is that, in the seventh century BCE, the author of Numbers 21:4–9 inherited and developed a story that had evolved to explain the origin and power of serpent symbolism and the worship of the serpent in the Temple during the time of Hezekiah.[250] As long ago as the beginning of the twentieth century, scholars saw major difficulties with Numbers 21:4–9. For example, H. Holzinger interpreted Numbers 21:4–9 to be a cult legend ("eine künstliche Legende") that provided legitimacy to the cult of the serpent in the Temple, but did not embody a "Jahwe-idol."[251] Thus, we are left with a possible explanation for the composition of Numbers 21: the story of Moses' making a metal serpent in the wilderness is an etiological legend that explains and gives legitimacy to the appearance of Nechushtan and its cult in the Temple.[252] In the words of Gray: "The responsibility of Moses for the making of the bronze serpent is probably merely traditional, this indicating the antiquity of this cult-symbol in Jerusalem. The story of its role as a prophylactic against serpents in Num. 21.6–9 (E) is an aetiological myth."[253]

Many scholars, like B. Baentsch, see the account in Numbers 21 to be linked with the worship of a serpent mentioned in 2 Kings. Thus, Numbers 21 is a cult legend (Kultussage) that was composed to add legitimacy to the Nechushtan in the Temple. The author sought to trace back to Moses the Nechushtan, and to legitimate the worship of a serpent in the Temple.[254] It is conceivable that the cult of Hezekiah's time originated prior to David within local lore and worship; perhaps the image had originally been Canaanite or Jebusite.[255]

Is it possible that Numbers 21:4–9 reflects an attempt to legitimize the worship of a serpent in the Temple? Yes, it is possible that some traditions in this section of Numbers antedate Hezekiah's reform. Before this king, Israelite worship was varied and not clearly centered only in Jerusalem. At the beginning of Hezekiah's reign, it apparently was not unusual or inconsistent to worship Yahweh as the only God and to acknowledge how he heals his people through the symbol of the serpent (Pos. 23). The raised serpent in the Temple—at least prior to Hezekiah's time—was not seen, by at least some Israelites, as inimical to Yahwism. M. Noth disagreed with the scholars who saw that Numbers 21:4–9 was an etiology, but he did point out that the story in Numbers was composed because there was a metal serpent in the Temple.[256]

It is clear, regardless of how one chooses among these previous three possibilities, that according to the author of Numbers 21:4–9, Moses' intention was not to establish a serpent cult, but to use the symbol of a serpent to heal those who had been bitten by a poisonous snake (Pos. 23). The Hebrews therefore were aware of the connection between the serpent and healing, which was well known in ancient Palestine from the serpent cult at Beth Shan in the middle of the second millennium BCE to the Asclepian cult in Jerusalem in the Roman Period. And we can continue such a rapid survey to the present, since the Bedouin believe that *jinn*, the desert demons, are like serpents and they congregate around healing waters.

Serpent Symbology and Exegesis

The author of Numbers 21:4–9 constructs a wordplay, *neḥaš neḥōšet*, "a serpent of bronze"; this symbol is represented by Nechushtan, which is another paronomasia on "serpent" and "copper."[257] As D. T. Olson states: "[The] serpent was a symbol of evil power and chaos from the underworld as well as a symbol of fertility, life, and healing."[258] In Numbers 21 and 2 Kings 18, the serpent symbolized, most likely, power (Pos. 3), life (Pos. 20), healing (Pos. 23), and even rejuvenation (Pos. 26). All of these human ideals were possible because of the intervention of Yahweh in the lives of the people, Israel. That is, serpent symbology was subsumed under Yahwistic theology.

The author of Numbers 21:4–9 may have sought to emphasize that the serpent cult in the Temple was within Yahwism, and that it absorbed all the competing serpent deities and cults, such as those at Hazor and especially at Beth Shan. If this is an accurate assessment, then the Elohist sought to legitimize the serpent cult in the Temple. He anchored the cult traditionally by making it part of God's saving action for his people during the time of Moses and in the wilderness, which was not the time or place of punishment but the time and place of preparation. We may now answer, seriatim, the questions raised by reading Numbers 21:4–9.

1. Our first question was "What is meant by *seraph;* that is, what kind of a snake did the author have in mind?" We can only guess.[259] As with the Yahwist in Genesis 3, the Elohist in Numbers 21:4–9 does not provide a detailed description of the snakes that bite the Israelites.

The Hebrew noun *seraph,* "a burning one [or fiery serpent]," is synonymous with *nachash,* "serpent," in Numbers 21. *Seraph* denotes a serpent that burns; the noun signifies that the serpent kills by burning poison.[260]

What kind of a snake could have been meant? The author uses this noun to signify a poisonous snake whose bite "burns." [261] The Greek of the Septuagint offers "deadly serpents" (τοὺς ὄφεις τοὺς θανατοῦντας); [262] and the Aramaic in *Targum Onkelos* signifies "burning or fiery serpents" (חיון קלן). [263] The Elohist clarifies only that the snakes are "fiery serpents" that are killing people; hence, they may have been any type of poisonous snake known in the lower Negev whose bite causes a fiery sensation. The *viper palestinensis* seems rather likely. Since the author depicts the Israelites leaving Egypt, he may have imagined that the "fiery serpents" were Egyptian asps.

Other possibilities are conceivable, including horned vipers, puff-adders, and cobras; [264] in fact, these snakes were mentioned by T. E. Lawrence when he described an abundance of snakes that plagued him in Wadi Sirhan east of the Dead Sea. [265] Numbers 21:5–7 may represent an imagined retelling of an actual event, since Esarhaddon, in his *Annals*, refers to serpents on the ground as numerous as grasshoppers, and Alexander the Great, according to Strabo (15.2.7), lost many soldiers from snakebites.

Whether the account is basically historical or imagined on the basis of known experiences, we might err in assuming only one type of deadly snake was represented by *seraph;* that may be the reason the Elohist added that *seraph* was synonymous with *nachash.*

2. Our second question was "When the poisonous snakes bite the people, why do not all die?" Again, the Elohist has not provided an answer. It was not something that concerned him. The narrator first makes it clear that some "people" had died because of the food, lack of water, and hardships of the journey from Egypt. The point the Elohist makes is that "many of the people of Israel died" (Num 21:6). The author does not say that every person was bitten. Those who lived after being bitten may have been considered people who had not, finally, been disobedient in murmuring against Moses and God. Perhaps some were thus assumed to have murmured only against Moses.

It is possible that one can be bitten by a poisonous snake and not die. As with Paul in Acts 28:4–6, sometimes it is assumed by those nearby that a person has been bitten when in fact the individual was not. We have pointed out that a poisonous snake can regulate the amount of poison administered, and that when a person is not threatening to an aroused snake, only a small portion of poison is injected. The snake saves venom to kill other animals, so that it can eat and survive.

3. Our third question was "Why does the Lord command Moses to make a *seraph* and place it on a standard?" God's instructions to Moses immediately follow Moses' prayer. He prayed to God on behalf of God's people (Num 21:7). The murmuring against God is the first significant un-

faithful action of the Israelites; now, they direct their complaints directly against God. Paul referred the Pharisee to Numbers 21:4–9 and stressed that this account revealed how people "tempted" God (1 Cor 10:9). This action is so exceptional and unthinkable that both the Targumists and the Greek translator change the meaning of the Hebrew to minimize the full force of the original text.

In the Hebrew, the preposition placed before "God" and Moses is the same: *b* (ב; see Num 21:5, 7), so the people "spoke against God and against Moses." The Greek translation, like some Targumim, has two different prepositions: "The people spoke to God and against Moses." This translation misrepresents the Hebrew, and the Greek may be an attempt to remove the theologically unattractive point that the people of Israel directed attacks against God. I do not think it is wise to conclude that the Greek states basically the same thing as the Hebrew, and the difference can be explained by pointing out that the Greek language has far more prepositions than Hebrew.[266]

The translators of the Targumim are most likely offended by Numbers 21:5. In a narrative about how Israel was saved from Egypt by God, it seems unacceptable that a narrator would report that God's people would turn on their only benefactor. How did the Aramaic translators avoid such unthinkable actions? The translator in *Targum Onkelos* employed the customary circumlocution: "The people grumbled against the Memra of the Lord (במימרא דייי [A K]),[267] and contended with Moses."[268] The translator of *Targum Neofiti* devised the following: "And the people spoke against the Memra of the Lord (ממרה דייי)[269] and murmured against Moses."[270] The expansive translator of *Targum Pseudo-Jonathan* imagined that the Hebrew meant: "Then the people complained in their hearts and talked against the Lord's Memra, and they quarreled with Moses."[271] In every case, the circumlocution seems an example of typical Targumic usage, yet it does appear that the Aramaic translators are trying to tone down the people's quarreling against Yahweh. This exegesis seems valid since, while the Hebrew text uses one verb ("the people spoke against God and Moses"), the Targumists use different verbs for talking against God and quarreling with Moses.

This is the first time in the history of salvation, according to the Bible, that God will not do everything for his chosen people. Now, God requires some participation in the process of salvation. The Lord demands more than that one who is bitten merely look up at the serpent. The Elohist does not say it explicitly, but he assumes something more than looking up at the copper serpent is required. Surely, looking up entails obedience; that is, by looking up, "the people of Israel" were obeying God. God demands some obedience; hence, there is a theological and ideological link between Genesis 3 and Numbers 21. According to Genesis, the humans disobeyed

God Yahweh and died; according to Numbers, those people who looked up obeyed God and obtained life (Num 21:9).

Thus, the individual Israelite must participate in his or her healing (or salvation); Moses must become involved in a unique way. He must make the copper serpent and place it on a standard. From henceforth, as the story of God and his people unfolds in the Bible, emphasis almost always will be placed on individual responsibility and on some personal response in the process of being helped or saved by God. As K. Sakenfeld states, God provides the means of healing: "Yet some level of personal human believing and initiative is required for its efficacy."[272]

4. Our fourth question was "What did the copper serpent look like or resemble?" The Elohist states only that Moses made some type of metal serpent; he does not tell us how Moses made it. G. Garbini argues that Moses' historicity is confirmed because his portrayal in the pre-Deuteronomic sources is different from the "canonical Moses." According to Garbini, these earlier sources portray Moses as from Egypt and as a craftsman who made a bronze snake.[273]

It is likely that Moses made not a bronze serpent, as in many translations of Numbers 21, but "a copper serpent." The Hebrew (נחש נחשת) denotes either a bronze or a copper serpent; the latter is more likely, since a gilded copper serpent was found in a cultic shrine at Timnaʿ, which dates from the second millennium BCE; that is, roughly, 1550–1200 BCE, which is near the time imagined by the Elohist when Moses made the copper serpent (see Fig. 22).

Our question entailed what this metal serpent looked like. The Elohist does not provide a clue that would help us imagine the copper serpent. One might suggest that it may have been like the uraeus, and it is conceivable that it had wings.[274] On Tutankhamen's throne were placed prominently winged serpents. The seraphim of Isaiah 6 most likely had not only wings but feet (see Appendix I). According to Isaiah 14:29 and 30:6, the *seraph* was a flying serpent (שרף מעופף);[275] throughout the Middle East we find images of flying and winged serpents. Often these are made of stone and are amulets worn around the neck to protect against snakebite (cf. the Ugaritic snake texts mentioned previously).

5. Our fifth question was "What symbolic meaning would be conveyed by a metal serpent on a standard?" For Philo, while the serpent who tempted Eve represented pleasure,[276] the copper serpent Moses raised in the wilderness symbolized endurance (καρτερία) since metal indicated firm stability (see *Leg.* 2.20 and *Agr.* 22; also see *m. Rosh Hash.* 3.8). Because metal signifies endurance, the symbolism of a copper serpent would make many think of the creature's power (Pos. 3) and divinity (Pos. 11). Most significant, it would be the symbolic power of the serpent to

represent youthfulness and rejuvenation (Pos. 26) and not to disintegrate through sickness, old age, and death.

Since weapons were made of metal, the copper serpent might elicit the serpent's ability to symbolize protection (Pos. 6). Clearly, the narrator specifies that the copper serpent primarily symbolized the healing of those who had been bitten, so the upraised copper serpent was fundamentally a symbol of healing (Pos. 23), health, and life (Pos. 20).

6. Our sixth question was "Does the Lord's command not break the commandment that the human must not make any image?" The Ten Commandments were for the human, not for God. The Creator is above any commandment, so God may instruct Moses to make an image and, in so doing, Moses would be obeying God, which supersedes all commandments. Neither God nor Moses should be imagined breaking the second commandment, which forbade the making of any image and worshipping it (Ex 20:1–17 and Deut 5:6–21): "You shall not make for yourself a carved image, or any likeness [of anything] that [is] in the heaven above, or that [is] on the earth beneath, or that [is] in the water under the earth. You shall not bow down to them, and you must not serve them" (Ex 20:4).[277] The Elohist never intimated that the Israelites were to worship the copper serpent lifted up on the pole.

One should not imagine that Moses disobeyed the Lord because the Lord told him to make a "burning serpent" and he constructed "a copper serpent." The different Hebrew nouns were most likely employed for literary variety, not conceptual distinction. When read aloud with dramatic intensity, this passage in Numbers is onomatopoeic; one can hear the hissing of serpents when the Hebrew is read with precision and elocution.

The ambivalence of religious symbols can be disconcerting. The context or the narrative is essential for careful and informed exegesis. For example, the golden calf and the copper serpent are both images of animals manufactured from metal, and both were revered in Israelite shrines, Bethel and Jerusalem, respectively, according to the ancient texts.[278] One brings condemnation and death; the other, acceptance and life.[279] Here texts and narrative force help to explain the meaning of the symbols as used by the respective authors. The difference in the two accounts is the one important aspect of any biblical narrative: the will of God. The golden calf was fashioned against God's will, the copper serpent by the command of God. Yet, later, Hosea polemicized against the golden calf and Hezekiah smashed the copper serpent.

7. Our seventh question was "Why are those who look up to the copper serpent healed?" Due to God's instructions to Moses, which were fully completed, those bitten could, through faith, look up to the copper serpent made by Moses, and continue to "live" (חי; Num 21:8, 9).[280]

We must avoid merely transferring what we know about serpent symbolism to Numbers 21. For example, in this passage we have people dying and a serpent used with great symbolic power. It would be methodologically imprecise, however, to suggest that because Cadmus and Harmonia were transformed into snakes and the departed kings and queens of Thebes were probably perceived to have transmigrated into serpents,[281] that the deceased were in any way identified with the copper serpent.

In the ancient Near East, as in many parts of the world today, the cause of the problem is at the same time its solution. Thus, homoeopathic, or sympathetic, magic is being employed. The *seraph* is confronted by the *seraph*. Thus, we have a type of the caduceus, which we have traced back into the centuries before the second millennium BCE. The caduceus is pervasive today on the walls of medical colleges (even in Amman and in Jerusalem), on the signia of the medical corps of some countries, and most conspicuously on prescriptions. In antiquity, as today, some medicines come directly from the venom of serpents.

The Elohist makes it clear, however, that the serpent is not the source of healing. One bitten is healed by his action of looking to the upraised serpent on the pole, and believing that God, the source of all healing, will make good on the promise to heal those who look up to the symbol of life (Pos. 20) and healing (Pos. 23). According to the compiler of *m. Rosh Hash.* 3:8, the copper serpent did not heal; it reminded the Israelites to serve God. This passage in the Mishnah, and the section of the Wisdom of Solomon (see the following), reveal an interpretation of Numbers 21 that is important as we continue to move toward a search for the symbolic meaning of John 3:14.

8. Our eighth question was "How does the study of ophidian iconography in Near Eastern culture, and especially in ancient Palestine, help us understand this passage in Numbers?" We can answer this question after we look again at the Targumim. The later, early medieval Aramaic translations and sermonic expansions of the Hebrew texts of Numbers 21:4–9 are revealing. On the one hand, the Targumim often reflect centuries of oral evolution of thought and also a concern with the contemporary conditions of Jews. On the other hand, especially with regard to the Targumic version of Numbers 21:4–9, they preserve oral traditions that often extend into the period before the first century CE. It would be foolish indeed to claim that the narrative expansion of Moses' upraised serpent in the Targumim appears for the first time in the Middle Ages. It does not reflect or serve the needs of the Jewish community, and it preserves serpent symbolism that antedates the first century CE by at least a millennium.

Note how the translator of *Targum Neofiti* emphasizes the difference between the two serpents of Numbers 21. One serpent "was cursed from the beginning"; the other serpent "will come and rule over the people which have murmured concerning their food." The expansive midrash in *Targum Neofiti* after verse five is indicative of the continuing importance of serpent symbolism:

> The Bath Qol came forth from the earth and its voice was heard on high: "Come, see, all you creatures; and come, give ear, all you sons of the flesh: the serpent was cursed from the beginning and I said to it: 'Dust shall be your food.' I brought my people up from the land of Egypt and I had manna come down from heaven, and I made a well come up for them from the abyss, and I carried quail from the sea for them; and my people has turned to murmur before me concerning the manna, that its nourishment is little. The serpent which does not murmur concerning its food will come and rule over the people which has murmured concerning their food." [282]

This is a remarkable sermonic expansion of Numbers 21.[283] The Targumist has taken the upraised serpent in the Hebrew text and elevated it so that it "will come and rule over the people." This interpretation, which may antedate the first century CE, brings out the symbolic meaning of the serpent, as previously interpreted. The serpent represents judgment, divinity (Pos. 11), power (Pos. 3), and divine kingship (or, at least the right to rule [Pos. 10]).

We need to pause and contemplate the positive meaning given to the serpent in this exceptional passage in *Targum Neofiti*. Like the Egyptian uraeus, the serpent here is a symbol of divine kingship (Pos. 10), eternal power (Pos. 3), and healing (Pos. 23). McNamara rightly sees the handiwork of the Targumist.[284] In *Neofiti,* the texts of Genesis 3 and Numbers 21 are combined. The people in Numbers 21 murmur against God, although he has blessed them: bringing them out of Egypt from slavery, creating a well of water for drink, and providing manna and quail for food. The serpent who was cursed by God in Genesis 3 does not complain about his food: dust. He obediently accepts God's condemnation; hence, God rewards and elevates the serpent so that he will rule over God's people.

The juxtaposition of two serpents is remarkable: "The serpent who was cursed from the beginning" (לטית חויה מן שרויה) and "the serpent who will come . . . and rule over the people" (ייתי חויה . . . וישלט בעמא). Of these two serpents, the more outstanding symbolically is the latter. The cursed serpent of Genesis 3 will be the ruler of God's people because he did not question or dare to dispute God's divine authority and curse. It is conceivable that for some Jews the serpent represented messianic power and rule (Pos. 10, 11, 19).

9. Our final and central question is "What does 'the serpent' symbolize

in Numbers 21:4–9?" The creativity of the Elohist should not be over-looked. He does not simply portray the upraised serpent as a symbol of healing. He does not appeal to serpents as guardians of houses, temples, springs, or people. He does not present the serpent as the source of life and rejuvenation. He also does not suggest that the serpent symbolizes Yahweh. While most of these symbolic meanings of the serpent are con-temporary with the author, and also with the time of Moses as depicted, and while such symbolic meaning lies in the background of the story,[285] the serpent is raised by Moses to fulfill the word of God.

The raised serpent was a sign of God's benevolence. In anger, God could have killed all the Israelites; they blamed him for the food and water that kept them alive in the desert. What did God do? God asked Moses to make a sign of his healing powers.

What sign was chosen? Was it a dove or a lion, both well-known iconogra-phies in the ancient Near East? Was it a scorpion that often appears on seals and images and signifies life? The image was none other than a serpent—the quintessential symbol of healing, health, and rejuvenation in the ancient Near East, including Palestine from circa 1850 BCE to at least 135 CE.

This interpretation is undergirded elsewhere in biblical Hebrew; for ex-ample, a *seraph* provides healing for Isaiah (Isa 6:5–7). Milgrom sees here in Isaiah "a link" between Isaiah's vision and Moses' serpent.[286] There should be no doubt that the author of Numbers 21 and his readers (hear-ers) would have known that the upraised serpent symbolized divine power (Pos. 3), healing (Pos. 23), purifying (Pos. 24), health (Pos. 23), rejuvena-tion (Pos. 26), and especially life (Pos. 20; חי; Num 21:8, 9).

Joines offers an assessment of the symbolic meaning of Moses' serpent in term of ancient Near East mythology:

> The most prominent element in the tradition of Moses and the bronze serpent seems to be that of sympathetic magic—the belief that the fate of an object or person can be governed by the manipulation of its exact image. Thereby a representation of a noxious creature could best drive off that creature, and an adversary could most effectively be controlled by the manipulation of his exact image.[287]

This paragraph is well stated and provides a good perception of ancient symbolism. There should be no doubt that some form of sympathetic magic is entailed in the act, or account, of Moses' making a likeness of the snakes that were killing the people. For the Yahwist, however, the empha-sis is to be placed elsewhere. This emphasis is on God's graciousness and willingness to remain with those who turn against him. As T. Fretheim so cogently explains, when interpreting Numbers 21:4–9:

> Yet even in the wilderness God is responsive to the needs of these his complaining people. . . . There is a gift of healing where the pain experienced is the sharpest. Deliverance comes, not in being removed from the wilderness, but in the very presence of the enemy. The movement from death to life occurs within the very experience of godforsakenness. The death-dealing forces of chaos are nailed to the pole. God transforms death into a source of life.[288]

The author of Numbers 21:4–9 seems to have acknowledged that serpents are important for healing, but he wanted to attribute this power to God, who told Moses to make a metal serpent as a means of healing those stricken. Even if we agree with Dillmann that there is no trace of the symbolic significance of healing in the narrative of Numbers 21:4–9, we should also agree with him that the evidence of the serpent as a symbol of healing was widespread in the ancient Near East.[289] Many centuries later, perhaps in the second century BCE, the author of the Wisdom of Solomon also stressed that the raised serpent was a "symbol of salvation" (σύμβολον ἔχοντες σωτηρίας [15:6]). As a sign of salvation, it was understood that God, not the serpent, was the source of healing (Pos. 23): "For he that turned himself toward it [the serpent] was not saved by the thing that he saw, but by you who are the Savior of all" (Wis 16:7). As D. Flusser clarified, the bronze serpent did not save; it was not efficacious in itself. The real purpose of the bronze serpent made by Moses "was to cause the people to turn their hearts towards their Father in heaven and to awake their faith in Him who commanded Moses to perform" this act.[290]

The serpent is a symbol to which those who are stricken can look up, so that God may heal them. Yahweh—and Yahweh alone, without any mediator or mediation—is the source of forgiveness, requested by "the people," and of healing, for those bitten by the poisonous snakes. At the center of the story is not the serpent,[291] and not even Moses; in central focus is Yahweh: he sends the vipers. God commands and Moses obeys. God tells those who are dying from snakebite to look up to the copper serpent on the pole. When they do so, God is the source of acceptance, healing, and life.

God's healing occurs within the context of the sickness, since the biting vipers are not removed by God and the Hebrews are not taken out of the wilderness. As T. Fretheim states: "Deliverance comes, not in being removed from the wilderness, but in the very presence of the enemy. The movement from death to life occurs within the very experience of godforsakenness."[292] In this context, in the wilderness with vipers, God offers to help all who have been bitten. God will not do everything for the Hebrews now, as he has in the past. Moses must make a copper serpent and place it on a staff. Those who are bitten must look up to it, believing God will heal them. God will do the rest. The serpent symbolizes the presence of God who wills to heal his chosen people.

The image and symbolism that shape the narrative in Numbers 21 are powerful and are reflected in Jewish thought long before the composition of the Fourth Gospel. The salubriousness alleged to come from placing a serpent on a stake was also a part of the Fourth Evangelist's culture. For example, Pliny informs us: "The head of a viper *(Viperae)*, placed on the bite, even though the same viper did not inflict it, is infinitely beneficial, as is the snake itself, held up on a stick in steam *(in vapore baculo sustineat)*—it is said to undo the harm done—or if the viper is burnt and the ash applied." [293]

The Brazen Serpent became a part of Western memory, and served not only theologians but also artists. For example, one of the worst plagues struck Venice in 1576. Not coincidentally, the Brazen Serpent was graphically depicted by Jacopo Tintoretto between 1575 and 1576. The painting may be overly dramatic, but serpents, in demonic forms, appear among the Hebrews in the lower part of the painting and the Brazen Serpent is prominent above and to the left of a burst of light shed on Moses. The Brazen Serpent twists around the stake that is in the form of a cross. The head of the serpent is a fish. Clearly, not only healing but also salvation are depicted on the ceiling of the upper hall in the Scuola Grande of San Rocco in Venice. [294]

Summary

The author of Numbers 21:4–9 was not creating a story out of nothing. His account may seem strange to modern readers, but to his intended audience such a tale was normal and expected. He did not have to describe the serpents in his narrative. Unlike us, his intended readers knew well what snakes were like. They were abundant in and around Jerusalem, and images of serpents were pervasive both in his culture and especially in all contiguous cultures. He lived in a world filled with serpent iconography and symbology. Images of serpents were pervasive in ancient Palestine. The images of serpents on jars, or serpents fashioned out of silver, gold, bronze, or copper, placed in cultic settings, or hung around the neck as amulets were well known to the author of Numbers 21:4–9, and we have abundant evidence today of these serpent images.

There were serpent cults in ancient Palestine, especially at Hazor, Beth Shan, and Jerusalem. Most of the evidence of a serpent cult in and around Jerusalem was destroyed by the reforms of Kings Hezekiah and Josiah. Hezekiah, it is clear according to the Hebrew text, smashed the copper serpent, so there is no possibility of discovering the Nechushtan. The Hebrew verb for "he smashed" (כתת) means to "crush to fine little pieces." Also,

Hezekiah "cut down the pole of Asherah"; that is, he also broke all the fig-urines of Asherah he could find. The evidence of this action is abundant in and around Jerusalem, as hundreds of images of Asherah have been found. Almost always their heads have been broken off or cut off with a sword. The date of these idols corresponds with the date assigned to the action by Hezekiah. These reflections, as intimated at the beginning of a study of Numbers 21, have led us into an exegesis of 2 Kings 18:4.

THE UPRAISED SERPENT IN THE TEMPLE (NECHUSHTAN): 2 KINGS 18:4

Initial Observations

One verse in 2 Kings is closely aligned with Numbers 21:4–9, as we have al-ready observed and discussed. If the author of Numbers 21:4–9 attempted to add legitimacy to the serpent cult in the Temple, the author of 2 Kings 18:4 had the opposite motive. The Elohist in Numbers 21 sought to salute God's graciousness in giving his people, the Israelites, a chance to regain life when they were bitten by poisonous snakes in the wilderness. The au-thor of 2 Kings 18:4 was vehemently opposed to any semblance of idolatry and included "Moses' copper serpent" in his equation.

Hezekiah was the thirteenth king of Judah. He reigned from 727 to 698 BCE. He witnessed the defeat and demise of Israel, to the north in circa 722, and fervently sought to deepen the allegiance to and worship of Yahweh in Judah, especially in the Temple. He thus initiated a massive program against any form of idolatry. Any explanation of Hezekiah must acknowl-edge that his motives were not purely religious; he wanted from his God political stability and protection. His actions are the result of religious conviction and political savvy.[295]

Text and Translation

Here is the context of the verse:

> It was in the third year of Hoshea son of Elah, King of Israel, that He-zekiah son of Ahaz, King of Judah, became king. He was twenty-five years old when he became king, and he reigned twenty-nine years in Jerusalem. His mother's name was Abi, [she was] Zechariah's daugh-ter. He did what was pleasing to YHWH, just as David, his ancestor, had done. It was he who abolished the high places, and broke the sacred pillars, and cut down the pole of Asherah and smashed the bronze ser-pent that Moses had made. For until those very days the Israelites were offering sacrifices to it. It was called Nechushtan. [2 Kgs 18:1–4][296]

After the usual formal introduction—the synchronistic accession formula and regal resumé[297]—comes the brief, but riveting, comment: Hezekiah "smashed [כתת] the bronze serpent [נחש הנחשת] that Moses had made; for until those very days the Israelites were offering sacrifices to it [מקטרים לו]."

Questions

Eleven key questions are raised by 2 Kings 18:4 as we seek to comprehend serpent symbolism in the Hebrew Bible. A reading of this one verse, focused on serpent symbolism, raises at least the following questions:

1. What is meant by "the high places" Hezekiah abolished?
2. What is the meaning of "the sacred pillars" Hezekiah broke?
3. What is meant by "the pole of Asherah" Hezekiah cut down?
4. What is meant by the statement that Hezekiah "smashed the bronze serpent"?
5. What is the relation among the high places, the sacred pillars, the pole of Asherah, and the copper (or bronze) serpent?
6. Why is the copper (or bronze) serpent placed last?
7. Was it really the copper (or bronze) serpent "Moses had made," and why would this connection be indicated at this point?
8. If there were Israelites devoted to the copper (or bronze) serpent, and if they "knew" it had been made by Moses, then would they not have been outraged at the smashing of a sacred and long-cherished artifact from Moses' own hand?
9. What is meant by "the Israelites were offering sacrifices to it," and is that the only, and accurate, translation of the Hebrew?
10. Why does the author add that the serpent "was called Nechushtan [נחשתן]"?
11. How does the study of serpent iconography and symbology help us comprehend this passage?

Before attempting to answer these questions, it is prima facie evident that such questions arise only after a detailed examination of serpent imagery and symbology in antiquity.

Scholars' Reflections

It seems probable that as the Yahwist wrote Genesis 3 and the Elohist Numbers 21, the Deuteronomist has given us 2 Kings 18. In the following discussion, thus, I shall assume that the Deuteronomistic Historian (Dtr) is responsible for 2 Kings 18:4.[298]

Did Moses make the serpent mentioned in 2 Kings 18:4? Some biblical experts claim that the answer is simply "yes." Other specialists ponder the question, but do not attempt to answer it. They sometimes simply assume the reference is not to Moses but to Moses' time; thus, Montgomery wrote that the serpent "was a surviving ancient fetich, coming down, as the annalist artlessly recorded from Moses' day and authority."[299] Many commentators do not perceive the question.

Cogan and Tadmor claim that the image of the serpent was within "Judahite tradition identified with the standard fashioned by Moses in healing those attacked by the fiery serpents; cf. Num 21:9)."[300] Perhaps the tradition was not Judahite, but the Deuteronomist sought to make it so. Their claim also may be misleading if it excludes the possibility that the Nechushtan was not related to Moses' copper serpent, but that it was a remnant of Canaanite or Jebusite serpent cults.

Some scholars claim that one should observe that, according to a late midrash, Yahweh becomes a large serpent and swallows Moses. They then assume that 2 Kings 18 reflects an ancient tradition "that Yahweh had at one time been identified with a Serpent-god."[301] Such speculation needs more foundation and attention to datable texts and archaeological artifacts.

Serpent Symbolism and Exegesis

Before discussing these eleven questions and attempting to answer them, we should first make some exegetical and historical observations. In the process, we shall be indebted, especially with 2 Kings 18:4, to the careful research of others. Comments, reflections, and a search for answers involve four related issues: (1) Hezekiah's reform; (2) Hezekiah's smashing a bronze serpent that was presumably in the Temple; (3) the evidence that Moses had made the bronze serpent; and (4) the offering of sacrifices by Israelites "to it." Our desire to answer our questions will be frustrated by the paucity of historical data in these verses and our ignorance of worship in the Temple, in all its diverse forms from Solomon to Hezekiah. These brief verses provide rare glimpses into the creative diversity in the Jerusalem cult. Apparently before and at the beginning of Hezekiah's reign, we must allow for the influence of non-Yahwistic worship (at least as presented by the Deuteronomist), and even possible remnants of Canaanite and Jebusite worship in the Temple cult.

1. Hezekiah's reform was not an innovation. It was not capricious or dominated by political exigencies or opportunities. It was a conservative religious move to *restore* the worship of Yahweh, according to the tradition of his ancestor, David (cf. also 20:5), and to *purify* the worship in the Temple. Although preceded by the reforms of Asa, Jehu, Joash, and Jehoiada, Hezekiah's effort at restoration was the first great reform of the cult within the history of Israel. It was followed by the even greater religious reform by Hezekiah's grandson, King Josiah.

Hezekiah's reform, doubtless undertaken by the pious king under the influence of the great prophets of the eighth century, should be understood as the preparation and prelude to the revolt against Assyrian domination of the whole area, and Hezekiah is rightly credited with being the leading figure in the coalition assembled and reorganized to overthrow the Assyrians. A major purpose of the reform was to unite the countries, Israel and Judah, around a common faith and a common practice, reflected in the Deuteronomic Code, preserved in the biblical text. In the end, both undertakings failed—the reform was terminated and reversed by the worst king in Judah's history: Manasseh. And the Assyrians overran the whole coalition, including Hezekiah, who barely survived his revolt. In other words, Hezekiah was smart enough to know that the country must be united to withstand the Assyrian invasion. His plan was to bring everyone under the banner of reform, and at the same time eliminate or suppress any dissent from the Deuteronomic Code.[302] In the beginning he was quite successful, as the Assyrian records show, but ultimately the greater power prevailed.[303]

Hezekiah had the backing of the leading Yahwistic prophets, in particular Isaiah, and there is reason to contend that his reform was developed along with a revival of the prophetic spirit in Judah. For the first time in the history of Israel, one of the great prophets, as J. A. Montgomery stated long ago, "[a]ppears in the active politics of the state."[304] There can be no doubt that the Deuteronomistic Historian wanted to portray Hezekiah as an exemplary reformer and one who marked a major turning point in the history of Israel. Hezekiah did what was "upright [הישר] in the eyes of Yahweh" (18:3).

2. There seems no reason to doubt that there was a metal serpent in the Temple, that sacrifices were being made to (or through) it by Israelites, and that King Hezekiah had it smashed. As many commentators point out, the same verb, "to smash," or "crush fine [כתת]," is used to denote both the smashing of the golden calf (Dt 9:21 [ואכת]) and the copper (or bronze) serpent (וכתת).[305] Thus, as Cogan and Tadmor comment, "Like Moses before him, Hezekiah is depicted as ridding Israel of an idolatrous relic."[306] As a Yahwist and in the mind of the Deuteronomistic Historian, Hezekiah's reasons for this action are understandable. Only Yahweh should be worshipped; in the mind of Dtr, Israelites had been offering sacrifices to the serpent. The action of smashing the serpent also would have entailed the proscription against such practices and the banishing of any priests or followers devoted to serpent worship not only from the Temple but also from Jerusalem and the Land. According to Dtr, the people—and all priests—had now only two options: either be banished or follow the edict, customs, and beliefs of Hezekiah and his royal group.

3. Most interesting is the claim that Moses is the one who made, or actu-

ally commissioned the making of, the serpent. Moses' making the serpent is the primary link with Numbers 21:4–9. The real question is whether the Nechushtan is the copper serpent Moses made, or whether Nechushtan represented a remnant of Canaanite or Jebusite serpent worship. According to the text of 2 Kings, it was accepted tradition in Judah that Moses had fashioned the copper serpent that was worshipped in the Temple. Hence, we dare not read Numbers 21:4–9 (the work of the Elohist) into 2 Kings 18:4 (the work of the Dtr). This issue cannot be fully discussed at this point.

4. Did the Israelites offer sacrifices to the Nechushtan? We must forgo a discussion of this question until later. Now, it is imperative to make clear that if the Israelites thought that the serpent was a symbol of healing, then the Deuteronomist has a different claim to set before them. According to him, the word of Yahweh came to Isaiah to announce to King Hezekiah: "I will heal you" (2 Kgs 20:5). Thus, Yahweh, and Yahweh alone, is the source of health and healing. If there were Israelites in the Temple worshipping the Nechushtan as the source of healing and health, as is possible in terms of serpent symbology of that period, then the oracle of Isaiah corrected such misinterpretations.

When did the author of 2 Kings 18:4 live? It is far from certain. A case may be made for him writing these verses during the time of Josiah,[307] but many commentators now think this introductory formula was composed during the exile and by the Deuteronomistic Historian.[308] Thus, under or after the influence of the reforms of the Judean Kings Hezekiah (727–698) and Josiah (640–609), the author of 2 Kings 18:4 reported why the serpent and those who were members of its cult had to be eliminated from the Temple and probably also banished from the Land.[309] The reason is that the symbol of the serpent was seen as an idol. It mattered little that the one intended might have been Yahweh. This option would be inappropriate to Dtr who believed in the commandment that forbids the making of any image. It also did not matter if the one intended was another god. This option was impossible within this author's monotheism (belief in the existence of only one God). Such an idea was inappropriate in the Temple, even for a henotheist (one who worshipped only one God, but acknowledged the existence of other gods). Thus, the Nechushtan had to be removed from the Temple. It had to be pulverized.

Most likely under the influence of Isaiah's attack on idolatry,[310] King Hezekiah banished from the Temple and Judah the worshippers of a copper (or bronze) serpent, called Nechushtan. Presumably, they had been offering sacrifices to it, and not only ostensibly through it to Yahweh. Now, we can examine the questions raised by 2 Kings 18:4.

First: What is meant by "the high places" Hezekiah abolished? In antiquity, the high places (*habbamot* in 2 Kgs 18:4) were sacred sites on which shrines were built. Thus, the Deuteronomistic Historian stresses that all the structures for the worship of any deity, including Yahweh, at the high places were demolished. Henceforth, worship was only to be to the one God, Yahweh, and this worship was to be celebrated only in Jerusalem. Worship was no longer permitted in such old traditional sites as Dan, Bethel, and Shiloh. Thus, "the high places" denoted elevated spots, on mountains or hills, in which worship of any deity had been organized. These high places ceased to be places for worship with Hezekiah's reform. It is conceivable, indeed likely, that serpent cults had continued not only in Jerusalem, with the Nechushtan, but also in these high places.

Second: What is the meaning of "the sacred pillars" Hezekiah broke? In Canaanite religion, notably in northern Galilee at Hazor and near Jerusalem especially at Gezer, there are massive stone monuments (*maṣṣēvôt* in 2 Kgs 18:4) erected for worship. These massevot were seen by Hezekiah and the Deuteronomistic Historian to rival the supremacy and exclusivity of Yahwism. Since stone pillars and a metal serpent would both symbolize permanency—and perhaps longevity or long life (if not immortality [perhaps too early in the evolution of human thinking]), there could be a relation between the worship through or to large raised stone pillars and the Nechushtan. Both pulled the eyes of the worshipper upward to what extended beyond the short life of humans.

Third: What is meant by "the pole of Asherah" Hezekiah cut down? We cannot be certain how to answer this question since a wooden pole would not survive 2,700 years, from Hezekiah's time to the present. Most likely the fertility goddess Asherah was worshipped in groves and was associated with a sacred tree. The tree and the serpent are related icongraphically and symbolically; both are chthonic symbols (Pos. 15) since the tree and serpent descend deep into the earth, the nether region and the source of life (Pos. 21). Hence, there could be a relation between the worship of the Canaanite Asherah and the Nechushtan, a serpent; both symbolized power (Pos. 3), divinity (Pos. 11), fertility (Pos. 1), and life (Pos. 20). Joines restricts the options for serpent symbology and opts only for the symbol of fertility: "Nehustan was borrowed from the Canaanites to affirm the agricultural powers of Yahweh."[311] While I am now persuaded that Nechushtan was inherited from Canaanite culture, I am even more convinced that it symbolized not only fertility but healing, divinity, and power.

Jerusalem had commercial and diplomatic links with the coastal cities, like Sidon to the north. Perhaps the worship of Nechushtan was influenced by worship in Sidon. Among the gods revered in Sidon was Eshmun, who was in Hellenistic times equated with Asclepius.[312] Both were "serpent gods." In Sidon, Eshmun was closely related to Astarte (who is identified with Aphrodite in the Greeek tradition) perhaps the most important deity in Sidon, and perhaps also in Ashlekon and Gaza.[313]

The veneration of Nechushtan, the copper serpent in the Temple, may be analogous to the worship of Asherah mentioned in 2 Kings 18:4. She is the goddess associated with the serpent cult in the ancient Near East. She often appears nude holding serpents in one hand or both hands. In the Ugaritic texts from Ras Shamra,[314] Asherah, in Ugaritic Athirat, is the consort of El, the supreme deity, and "the procreatrix" of all the lesser gods. In 2 Kings 23:7, Asherah is most likely linked with sacred prostitution. There can be no doubt that the snakes shown with her help indicate her symbolization of fertility (Pos. 1).

Fourth: What is meant by the statement that Hezekiah "smashed the copper (or bronze) serpent"? Note that Hezekiah did not merely destroy the copper serpent; he pulverized it. That means he forced out all its alleged power and positive symbolism. The object could no longer convey power, divinity, and life; it was obliterated by Yahweh's chosen ruler.

There is no reason to question the existence of a copper (or bronze) serpent in the Temple during the time of King Hezekiah. Copper and metal serpents or serpent images have been discovered throughout ancient Palestine, especially at Nahariyah, Hazor, Gezer, Megiddo, Tel Mevorakh, Timnaʿ, Tel El-ʿAjjul, Beth Shan, Kinneret, Ekron, and Shechem. Clearly, worshippers of God and God Yahweh knew about the serpent cults and, before Hezekiah's reform, allowed them to flourish within ancient Palestine, and also within the Yahweh cult.[315] Perhaps pre-Hezekiah devotees of Yahwism either saw no threat from such worshippers, or sought to bring them into line with the monotheism (or henotheism) of Yahwism. Hezekiah's reform is documented by controlled archaeological research; no metal serpents or serpent images that postdate the seventh century and antedate the Roman Period have been found in ancient Palestine. The many metal serpent images found in ancient Palestine all date from the Early Bronze Age (c. 2250 BCE) at Ein Samiya near Ramallah to Iron Age II (c. 586 BCE) at Ekron.[316] The metal serpents, serpent art, and other forms of serpent iconography peak in the Late Bronze Age in ancient Palestine, but they do not disappear until the end of the Iron Age.[317]

Fifth: What is the relation between the high places, the sacred pillars, the pole of Asherah, and the copper (or bronze) serpent? In his religious (and political) reform, Hezekiah had the Nechushtan smashed so that no one could continue to worship either the serpent or God through it. There is every reason to assume that this metal serpent had been revered in the Temple for centuries before the time of Hezekiah. There is no evidence that it had appeared recently; in fact, the text assumes that it antedates the dedication of the Temple by Solomon—that is, it dates back to the time of Moses.

We have seen that it would be absurd to assume that the copper serpent was the only serpent cult object in and around Jerusalem known to Hezekiah and the Deuteronomistic Historian. As should now be evident, serpent cult objects have been discovered in controlled archaeological excavations in sites near Jerusalem, and these serpent images or serpents always antedate Hezekiah's time or are roughly contemporaneous with it. The Nechushtan could have served as the main representative of a serpent cult in and around Jerusalem. With the action of Hezekiah, serpent cults ceased to exist in the Holy Land, and not only in and near the Holy City. Thus, as suggested earlier, there is most likely a connection between the abolishing of the holy places, the breaking of the sacred pillars, the cutting down of Asherah's tree, and the shattering of the Nechushtan. All may have been related—or some worshippers of the Nechushtan may have seen a connection among them. Hence, Hezekiah's actions are centered; he seems to be destroying the last vestiges of a serpent cult, and related cults, in and around Jerusalem. Hezekiah is not only centralizing the worship of Yahweh, he is making it possible to worship Yahweh, and Yahweh alone, in Jerusalem. The political implications can be discerned. Jerusalem becomes the undisputed capital as David had envisioned. Hezekiah proved to be a true son of David, his ancestor (2 Kgs 18:3).

Sixth: Why is the copper (or bronze) serpent placed last? The question is not easily answered by a scrutiny of the text. The Nechushtan is placed last probably because it was the most important and threatening place or object. The Nechushtan was not out of Jerusalem on some high place. It was in Jerusalem, and it was in the Temple. Most important, some Israelites felt they were good and faithful worshippers in the religion of Israel by worshipping at, or through it. What had been originally intended, according to the Elohist in Numbers 21, as a point of focusing the worshipper on being obedient to Yahweh had been reinvented. Now, the means became an end. Now, the benevolent Yahweh had been replaced by Nechushtan, a sacred serpent.

If we are correct in surmising that there is a relation among the high places, the sacred pillars, the tree of Asherah, and the Nechushtan, then the latter was mentioned last because it was not only in the Temple, but it was central to a serpent cult that surrounded Jerusalem.

Seventh: Was it really the copper (or bronze) serpent "Moses had made," and why would this connection be indicated at this point? As mentioned while studying Numbers 21:4–9, some scholars think the Nechushtan is indeed the serpent made by Moses. Others think that Moses never made such a serpent, and that the account in Numbers 21 is an etiological cult legend; that is, the passage in Numbers was composed to give legitimacy to the worship of a metal serpent in the Temple. In either case, the historicity of a metal serpent in the Temple and the adoration of it by Israelites are accepted as an historical fact. Certainly, both the Elohist and Deuteronomic Historian report that there was a metal serpent in the Temple.

The connection with Moses may represent what Moses made—that is, a copper serpent—but the connection can also denote only chronology and the esteem and reverence provided by a long-cherished item. In religion, asserting longevity provides, or enhances, sacredness. The reference to Moses may simply indicate a connection with the time of Moses. In that ancient time, before David and Solomon, the serpent had certainly been worshipped, or revered, in the place now called Jerusalem. If the text is primarily a connection with Moses' time and not with Moses, then the possibility of some connection with a Canaanite or Jebusite serpent deity or cult is at least conceivable.

Eighth: If there were Israelites devoted to the copper (or bronze) serpent, and if they "knew" that it had been made by Moses, would they not they have been outraged at the smashing of a sacred and long-cherished artifact from Moses' own hand? How could Hezekiah and those around him—especially the Yahwists of his time—remove from the Temple and its surroundings a cult object that was associated with Moses? Hezekiah and the Yahwists were attempting to revive the religion of Moses. The Elohist who composed Numbers 21:4–9 did not deny the connection with Moses; he clarified its emphasis. Denying what some in Israel must have thought—that is, Moses had established the serpent cult and the worship of Nechushtan—the Elohist sought to show that Moses had emphasized a means, a cult object, through which Yahweh could heal "the people."

It is dubious that Hezekiah and the Yahwists around him believed that Moses had made the copper serpent, the Nechushtan. Perhaps they knew that it derived from a Canaanite or Jebusite cult. It is possible, though speculative,[318] that, as H. H. Rowley maintained,[319] the worship of Nechushtan, which was banned by Hezekiah, may have originated within a Jebusite cult that had been conceivably administered by Zadok, who became David and Solomon's high priest.

The genealogies of Zadok seem manufactured to link him with Gibeon or even with Aaron, but he seems to be the Jebusite priest in Jerusalem when David conquered the city.[320] He then serves alongside David's own priest, Abiathar, until he becomes the sole "high priest" in the Temple, when Abiathar backs Adonijah against Solomon. The connection with a Canaanite or Jebusite cult seems much more likely than assuming the historicity of the connection between Nechushtan and Moses. There was clearly much borrowing in the tenth century. Joines thus, in my judgment, correctly concludes that the Nechushtan "was introduced into the Israelite cult apparently during either the time of David or Solomon."[321]

It is possible that the Nechushtan was a remnant of earlier non-Israelite beliefs and religious customs in ancient Palestine; after all, Hezekiah also "abolished the high places" and he "cut down the pole of Asherah." These latter two acts clearly denoted the removal of Canaanite, and perhaps Jebusite, religious cults or practices in and around Jerusalem. This account of Hezekiah and Nechushtan shows that serpent cults were not only present in ancient Palestine, they were connected with Moses by the Elohist, and had penetrated worship in the Jerusalem Temple.

Ninth: What is meant by: "The Israelites were offering sacrifices to it," and is that the only, and accurate, translation of the Hebrew? Is it clear that Israelites had been sacrificing *to* this serpent? The Deuteronomist states that "until those very days the Israelites were offering sacrifices to it (מקטרים לו)." The Deuteronomistic Historian certainly would approve of the interpretation that stresses that Israelites were worshipping the serpent, and not only worshipping Yahweh through it. Does the Hebrew mean that the Israelites were sacrificing to the image of a serpent, Nechushtan? One cannot be certain; the *lamad* may be a note of the accusative or a note of the dative. That is, the *lamad* can also denote that the Israelites were sacrificing through the image to God Yahweh.

The Hebrew words clearly indicate that the Israelites, and not others, were actively offering sacrifices to the image of a serpent in the Temple. That means that the Israelites were either offering sacrifices to God, Yahweh, through this symbol, or more likely that some Israelites were directly worshipping Nechushtan, a serpent. A serpent cult was well established throughout ancient Palestine, especially at Beth Shan and Hazor, and active during the time from Solomon to Hezekiah. Many Israelites did not think that the second commandment was binding or interpreted it differently than the Deuteronomistic Historian did.

Tenth: Why does the author add that the serpent "was called Nechushtan" (נחשתן)? Despite the usual hesitation by some scholars, I am convinced that the author of 2 Kings 18:1–4 carefully crafted his thought and produced paronomasia: *nechash hannechosheth . . . nechushtan.*[322] Montgomery and Milgrom[323] rightly draw attention to the "play on the two words": *nechash hannechosheth.*[324] The Hebrew phrase, *nechash han-nechosheth,* means "the copper (or bronze) serpent." The selection of words seems deliberate; the Deuteronomistic Historian chose his thought to bring out alliteration and paronomasia. He also succeeded in putting the serpent, nachash, in central focus. In English, the closest I can come to such a careful choice of words is "the copper cobra." Perhaps calling the serpent *nechushtan* accentuated this paronomasia. The sound *nechash han-nechosheth* may also be onomatopoeic; that is, it could recall the hissing sound made by a serpent. I doubt that Deuteronomy sought to appeal to the Moses tradition, since in Numbers the word for serpent is *seraph* (הנחשים השרפים in 21:6 and שרף in 21:8).

Eleventh: How does the study of serpent iconography and symbology help us comprehend this passage? Perceiving how widespread the worship and veneration of the serpent were in ancient Palestine and neighboring countries stimulates the imagination: perhaps ophidian symbolism was present and even a serpent worshipped in the Temple before the purifying reform of Hezekiah. Jerusalem was not cut off from the rest of the world.

I have found many serpents and serpent images in the antiquity shops of the Old City of Jerusalem, dating from the Middle Bronze Age to the Iron Age (and then beginning again in the Greek Period). Archaeologists have recovered serpent images in and near Jerusalem. Hence, merchants brought many serpent objects from Egypt, Babylonia, and Canaan into Jerusalem. They could have been personal belongings, accorded different levels of respect or attention, and they could have been brought to sell to those living in this metropolis.

It is unwise to think that before Hezekiah all Israelites or devotees of Yahweh had a fondness for Yahweh alone. Henotheism would have allowed for an amalgamation of non-Yahwistic religion. The religion of Israel was far more latitudinarian and complex than one would imagine from studying the religious beliefs recorded in the Hebrew Bible. In fact, the prohibitions in the Bible are sometimes, perhaps usually, an indication of the existence of a practice or belief deemed unattractive to the Deuteronomist or prophet.

Since Hezekiah is said to have removed the high places in which his father, Ahaz (16:4), had worshipped, and also to have cut down the pole of Asherah (ויכרת את־האשרה), we may continue our investigation that there was some relation between the Nechushtan and Asherah. This is an option affirmed by Long: "This cultic object [the copper serpent] was apparently a fertility symbol associated with the mother goddess Asherah at Ras Shamra and pre-Israelite Beth-shan, and thus a Canaanite legacy in the Israelite-Judahite religion."[325] It becomes more and more likely that the copper serpent, the Nechushtan, was a remnant from earlier religions competitive with Yahwism, but it is not obvious that the religion was Canaanite or that the serpent was associated with Asherah.[326] We have also seen that far more options are evident symbolically than "fertility" and that "life-giving" seems more representative of the serpent symbols that antedate and are contemporaneous with the time of Hezekiah. The Elohist in Numbers 21, as shown earlier, concluded his story of how Moses made a copper serpent, but stressed that it brought *life* to those who looked up to it.

The serpent cults near and within Jerusalem were perhaps "the widespread folk religion in Canaan." [327] The cult was deeply entrenched in ancient Palestine, and thinking about its power and popularity helps us understand those who were Israelites and sacrificing through, and even to, Nechushtan. Along with their other contemporaries, that would have found the serpent to be an ideal—indeed fascinating—symbol for some of their ideas and hopes. With the Egyptians, they would have found the serpent to be a good symbol for power (Pos. 3), deity (Pos. 11), eternity (Pos. 12, cf. Pos. 27), royalty (Pos. 10), healing (Pos. 23), and life (Pos. 20). With the Canaanites, and those who were attached in some fashion to the serpent cults elsewhere, perhaps at Beth Shan and Dan, they would have seen the serpent as a symbol of rejuvenation and of the new life of spring (Pos. 26). With many others they could have seen the serpent as the symbol of wisdom (Pos. 18) and adhere to the creature, made by God (Gen 3), who knew what was beneath the earth (Pos. 15).

Summary

What then was the symbolic power of the serpent, according to the words of the Elohist in Numbers 21 and the Deuteronomist Historian in 2 Kings 18? First and foremost, the serpent represented healing. Like the caduceus that can be traced back to 3100 BCE,[328] the upraised serpent that Moses is supposed to have made in the wilderness and that was worshiped later in the Temple was seen, at least in Numbers 21, to symbolize healing (Pos. 23) and life (Pos. 20). Those who were bitten by vipers could *look up* and be healed by God. The healing symbolic power of the serpent is deeply rooted in Near Eastern iconography, as we have abundantly demonstrated. The serpent as the symbol of life and healing extends in Western culture from at least the second millennium until the present. Perhaps the peak of interest in the serpent as the one who could heal and renew youth appeared in the Asclepian cult of the first and second centuries CE.

Second, for the citizens of Judah the serpent in 2 Kings 18, but not in Numbers 21, symbolized a god or divinity (Pos. 11). The Israelites in the Temple who revered Nechushtan most likely perceived the serpent as a celestial being either within God Yahweh's heavenly court or a god other than Yahweh. Analogous serpent symbolism appeared in Egypt in which the serpent was a god. The serpent also symbolized the deity of the pharaoh. One sees repeatedly the uraeus on the heads of pharaohs and one is impressed by the winged serpents on Tutankhamen's throne. Similar serpent iconography appeared in Mesopotamia and most likely in ancient Palestine. Henotheism never really ceased in Israel, not even with the clear proclamation of monotheism by Second Isaiah, and this author postdates Hezekiah's reform.

Third, it is conceivable and may be probable that the serpent in the Temple also represented fertility and fruitfulness. This theme or dimension of serpent symbolism in Palestine is well established. The Beth Shan serpent cult comes immediately to mind. The serpents and the doves on incense stands from Beth Shan most likely signified the rebirth of the earth and its vegetation at springtime. The serpent, which goes underground seemingly whenever it wishes and hibernates during the winter because it is cold-blooded, emerges with the coming of spring and warmth. The connection between serpent symbolism and Persephone, who also appears at spring from the underworld—the world of death—is evident in Greek and Roman symbolism. The connection in later Greek and Roman iconography and symbology helps us comprehend how the serpent earlier could indicate the rebirth of nature (Pos. 26). Most likely some who worshipped the serpent in the Temple may have thought about the serpent as a symbol of the fruitfulness of the earth (Pos. 2).

Fourth, the serpent Moses allegedly fashioned and the Nechushtan, if it is different from the one Moses made, most likely would have been seen by the Israelites who worshipped it, or through it, to embody power. It was upraised and perhaps denoted awesome divinity (Pos. 11 and 17). Thus, the serpent symbolized power (Pos. 3).

Fifth, other symbolic meanings could have been represented by the upraised serpent, both in the wilderness and in the Temple. It could symbolize God's creative powers (Pos. 7), mystery (Pos. 17), and beauty (Pos. 4). These characteristics are almost always present in serpent symbolism.

I have become persuaded that the origins of the story about the Nechushtan are not to be found within Yahwistic belief, but outside it. Perhaps the serpent symbol—the Nechushtan (נחשתן; 2 Kgs 18:4)—originated, and had its background, in Egyptian, Babylonian, Canaanite, or Jebusite religion. Since archaeological evidence of the Canaanites and Jebusites cannot be distinguished by archaeologists,[329] it is a moot point whether the Nechushtan was inherited by Israelites in Jerusalem from one or the other. The answer is probably that both helped to supply the image of and the worship of Nechushtan, or through it, in the Temple.

We have heard the words of three great authors. We have listened to the Yahwist who compiled from earlier myths the Eden Story in which the serpent has a voice. We have been attentive to the Elohist who described how Moses made a metal serpent in the wilderness that brought new life to those who were dying. We have learned from the Deuteronomistic Historian who explained how Hezekiah pulverized the Nechushtan. Cumulatively, we have seen how a study of serpent iconography and symbology in antiquity shines much light on previously dark passages.

7 The Symbolism of the Serpent in the Gospel of John

In the preceding chapters we examined the symbolic meaning of the serpent in many cultures and texts, especially in Greek and Latin literature and in the Hebrew Bible. We also noted the full spectrum of serpent symbolism, drawing attention to the symbol of the serpent in the so-called intertestamental writings. Now we come to the New Testament corpus. We may now conclude, as H. Gerhard surmised in 1847, that no animal symbol has such importance and such diverse, even contradictory, meanings as the serpent.[1]

There are forty-one nouns in ancient Greek to denote various types of snakes (see Appendix II). Only five of these nouns appear in the Greek New Testament.[2] This proportion, 5/41, should not seem surprising. The documents in the New Testament are theological works. They should not be imagined as quasi-zoological treatises (or a *De Natura Animalium*). Moreover, the Greek in the New Testament was used to convert the masses. Only on rare occasions (as in Luke's Prologue) was New Testament Greek directed to highly educated persons. This observation should be combined with the recognition that many New Testament authors knew and did occasionally use sophisticated Greek (see, e.g., Lk 1:1–4, Rom, and Heb; contrast Rev, whose author thought in Aramaic and Hebrew but wrote in Greek).

The five Greek nouns for snake or serpent that appear in the New Testament corpus are "asp" (ἀσπίς, Rom 3:13), "dragon" (δράκων, Rev 12:3, 4, 7 [*bis*], 9, 13, 16, 17; 13:2, 4, 11; 16:13; 20:2),[3] "snake" (ἑρπετόν, Acts 10:12; 11:6; Rom 1:23; James 3:7), "viper" (ἔχιδνα, Mt 3:7; 12:34; 23:33; Luke 3:7; Acts 28:3),[4] and "serpent" (and sometimes "snake"; ὄφις, fifteen times in the NT [including Mk 16:18]).[5]

Perhaps the most interesting insight regarding ophidian symbology in

352

the New Testament is the fact that the common word for serpent in Greek (ὄφις) is the usual word for serpent in the New Testament corpus. Surely this insight helps us grasp the desire of the New Testament authors to use common words, as had Jesus of Nazareth; that is, these authors chose simple language that was devoid of pretense or ostentation.

REVELATION

The "serpent" has positive and negative meanings in the New Testament, but only the negative meanings seem to have impressed the exegetes and commentators.[6] Our Western culture has too often featured sin as a serpent or as a human entwined by an evil serpent.[7] The key passages are in Revelation. The central text, as implied previously, is Revelation 12 in which the "serpent," the dragon, is equated with Satan and the Devil. The setting is a war in heaven; Michael and his angels fight against "the dragon" and his angels (cf. 1QM). After Michael and his angels win, there is no place for Satan and the Devil who is "the dragon." Thus, the author of Revelation offers this stunning equation: "And the great dragon was thrown down, that ancient serpent, who is called the Devil and Satan, the deceiver of the whole civilized world. He was thrown down to the earth, and his angels were thrown down with him" (Rev 12:9). The author of Revelation has inherited the concept of the serpent as a negative symbol, and emphasized it as the symbol of the Devil (Neg. 12), God's Antagonist (Neg. 11), and Liar or Deceiver (Neg. 5).

Why has this symbolic meaning of the serpent been embedded in the minds of so many scholars? Perhaps the answer lies in the recognition that the equation is so clear and so well known. Perhaps some have the impression that with Revelation we come to the conclusion of "the Book." While New Testament exegetes simply state that in the Bible the serpent is a symbol of evil, misreading Genesis 3 and exaggerating its importance, they do ultimately confess that the serpent, intermittently, has a positive meaning. In the preceding pages we saw that the serpent was predominantly a positive symbol in antiquity. In the following pages I shall attempt to show that the serpent is also fundamentally a positive symbol in the New Testament writings.

PAUL, ACTS, THE GOSPELS

The serpent has a quasi-positive or clearly positive meaning in some New Testament passages. While Paul is depicted as one who always uses the serpent as a negative symbol, a close examination of his works reveals not only negative ophidian symbolism but a remnant of positive symbolism. Obviously, as many Pauline scholars have emphasized (viz., C. H. Dodd, E. P. Sanders, and H. Räisänen), Paul did not strive to be consistent according to our post-Enlightenment criteria.[8] And as K. Ehrensperger shows, Paul must not be interpreted by a modern Western male-oriented agenda.[9]

A study of ophidian nomenclature in the New Testament discloses Paul's sophistication and learning, as well as his frequently erudite Greek audience. Both are reflected in his vocabulary. Paul employs more words for snake or serpent than any other New Testament author, including "asp" (ἀσπίς, Rom 3:13), "snake" (ἑρπετόν, Rom 1:23), and "serpent" (ὄφις, 1 Cor 10:9, 2 Cor 11:3).

Paul uses refined words for "snake" in Romans and the generic term in the Corinthian correspondence. This fact presents one with intriguing questions: Was Paul's intended audience more sophisticated in Rome than in Corinth? Or was he elevating his language so as to present himself authoritatively to the unknown Romans who belonged to the Jesus Movement?

In Romans 1:23, Paul's reference to "the snake" is generic and non-symbolic. In this verse he refers to humans who make idols that resemble snakes. In Romans 3:13 Paul argues that all people, Jews and Greeks, are "under the power of sin," and that no one does good; indeed: "[T]he venom of asps is under their lips." The ophidian symbolism is negative. Paul clarifies that such people "use their tongue to deceive." Uppermost in Paul's mind in Romans 3:13 seems to be the serpent as the symbol of the Liar or Deceiver (Neg. 5).

In 1 Corinthians 10:9, Paul warns against idolatry, pointing out that we must not test the Lord: "[A]s some did and were destroyed by serpents." The asps sent by God are apparently represented in Paul's next words: "[N]or grumble, as some of them did and were destroyed by the Destroyer." He assumes his readers know the story in Numbers 21:5. He is using the symbol of the serpent primarily to denote the one who is the Destroyer (Neg. 2) and the one who kills (Neg. 1). Also implicit is the symbolic meaning of the serpent as the one who carries out God's intentions (Pos. 19).

In 2 Corinthians 11:3, Paul reveals his exegesis of Genesis 3. He is convinced: "The serpent deceived Eve through his cunning." Paul rightly imagines that the serpent is masculine. But the serpent is not clever or wise, as indicated by the Hebrew text and clarified by the Septuagint. He is diabolically "cunning" (ἐν τῇ πανουργίᾳ αὐτοῦ). The serpent did not ask Eve a question and provide insight into what would happen if, or when, she ate of the forbidden fruit. He "deceived" Eve. The serpent is a knave or a rogue.[10] Paul seems also to miss the Yahwist's subtle use of language and careful development of the dramatis personae. At this point in the

Figure 80. Christ Enthroned on Lions. Note serpent in his left hand. Greek Orthodox Church. Capernaum. JHC

Eden Story, the serpent's interlocutor is an anonymous woman; she is not yet named "Eve." Paul misses the opportunity to point out the Yahwist's intention and insight: Humans are also partly responsible for evil. That position would have been helpful to Paul as he warns his readers of the false apostles, the theme of 2 Corinthians 11:1–15. In 2 Corinthians, Paul has inherited the concept of the serpent as the Liar or Deceiver (Neg. 5). While Paul knows the positive meanings of the serpent in his culture, he almost always emphasizes the negative meaning of the serpent—at least in his writings that have been preserved.

The author of Acts uses the word "viper" (ἔχιδνα) to describe an event that occurred on Malta. Paul, along with supposedly all on board a ship that was destroyed by a violent storm, made it to shore. The natives built a fire and Paul helped gather kindling. A viper shot out of a bunch of sticks and fastened on Paul's hand. The natives assume that the viper had been sent by a god to punish Paul, who must be a murderer. Paul shakes off the viper into the fire, suffering no harm. When Paul does not swell up and die, the natives conclude that Paul "was a god" (Acts 28:6). The narrator does not mention that the viper bit Paul. Perhaps the viper did not bite Paul, and that is likely in terms of ophiology, given the attempt of a viper to escape the fire and find safety in an "arm."

The author of Acts 28:1–6 inherits and uses many aspects of serpent symbolism. All are positive. Two are most important. The viper is initially perceived to be one who is a messenger of the gods; one who carries out a god's judgment (Pos. 19). Second, the appearance of the viper reveals Paul may be a god. Is that because the viper could not kill Paul? If so, the serpent may first symbolize the Death-Giver (Neg. 1) and then reveal Divinity (Pos. 11).

Numerous questions arise that are not discussed by the commentators. Is the relation between the viper and Paul a disclosure that Paul, like the gods, is symbolized by a serpent (Pos. 11)? To what extent is magic (Pos. 16) involved in this story? The author may have employed ophidian symbolism to bring out mystery, wonder, and awe (Pos. 17). To what extent is the author imagining the serpent to represent immortality (Pos. 27)? A study of ophidian symbolism has brought out dimensions of the story or history in Acts 28:1–6 that have been missed by exegetes, commentators, and even those who have mastered narrative exegesis.

The most stunning use of positive ophidian symbolism found in the Synoptics is attributed to Jesus. He sends his disciples out "as sheep in the midst of wolves" and instructs them to be "wise as serpents and innocent as doves" (Mt 10:16). This is a most intriguing passage that deserves study informed by ancient serpent symbolism. Now, only three points may be clarified. First, the symbolic association of serpents with doves antedates Jesus by at least fifteen hundred years.[11] For example, as we have already seen, serpents and doves appear on incense stands found at Beth Shan. The serpents seem to denote spring, life (Pos. 20), and the appearance of new life (Pos. 27). Second, since Jesus is depicted sending his disciples out as sheep among wolves, his injunction to be like serpents may mirror the serpent symbolizing the guardian (Pos. 6). Wolves eat sheep and the disciples need protection. Third, and clearly the prima facie meaning of Matthew 10:16, Jesus' saying brings out the predominantly Jewish symbolic meaning of the serpent: It represents wisdom. Jesus may be alluding, or the Evangelist may have him allude, to Proverbs 30:18–19. Jesus is not therefore mixing metaphors; he is not pointing to a deceptive serpent, but to the shrewdly alert serpent.[12] The serpent as a symbol of shrewdness and wisdom is found in the Jewish apocryphal works, as we have seen, and is clear in the Septuagint rendering of Genesis 3:1 (see that discussion). Most likely Matthew's choice of words—"be wise as serpents" (φρόνιμοι ὡς οἱ ὄφιεις)—was shaped in light of the Septuagint's version of Genesis 3:1: "And the serpent was the wisest" (ὁ δὲ ὄφις ἦν φρονιμώτατος).

According to Matthew 10, Jesus is speaking to men who know about daily life in Palestine. Jesus is sending out his disciples as sheep among wolves. The latter represent the ravenous ones who resist the disciples' good news and strive to devour them. Jesus tells his disciples in such circumstances to be as wise as serpents and innocent as doves. The serpents represent cunning, prudence, caution, and wisdom. The doves signify fidelity, revelation, simplicity, and innocence.[13] Thus, in Matthew 10:16, the serpent primarily symbolizes wisdom (Pos. 18).

Ignorant of the Jewish perception that the serpent can symbolize wisdom, Gregory of Nyssa in *On Virginity* quoted Jesus' words (probably from Matthew) but shifted Jesus' positive symbolical use of the serpent. Note how the Jesus tradition is rewritten:

> It is clearly contained in that passage where our Lord says to His disciples, that they are as sheep wandering amongst wolves, yet are not to be as doves only, but are to have something of the SERPENT too in their disposition; and that means that they should neither carry to excess the practice of that which seems praiseworthy in simplicity, as such a habit would come very near to downright madness, nor on the other hand should deem the cleverness which most admire to be a virtue, while unsoftened by any mixture with its opposite; they were in fact to form another disposition, by a compound of these two seeming opposites, cutting off its silliness from the one, its evil cunning from the other; so that one single beautiful character should be created from the two, a union of simplicity of purpose with shrewdness. "Be ye," He says, "wise as serpents, and harmless as doves." [14]

In *On Christian Doctrine*, Augustine cites Jesus' saying in Matthew 10, but he also is preoccupied with the serpent's negative symbolism. Note how far off from Jesus' positive use of the serpent is Augustine's teaching: "We were ensnared by the wisdom of the SERPENT: we are set free by the foolishness of God." [15] In his *Sermons on New-Testament Lessons*, Augustine repeats the misinformed exegesis: "The devil again is a serpent, 'that old serpent'; are we commanded then to imitate the devil, when our Shepherd told us, 'Be ye wise as serpents, and simple as doves'?" [16] Augustine seems lost for an answer because he misses the rich positive symbolism of the serpent. The answer is "yes"; the wise, intelligent, truth-speaking animal created by God (cf. our exegesis of Gen 3).

In the Gospel of Luke, Jesus is portrayed twice using serpent symbolism. In Luke 10, referring to the imagery in Psalm 91, Jesus gives the group of seventy followers authority "to tread upon serpents and scorpions" (Lk 10:19). In this verse, the serpent represents something negative, perhaps the Destroyer (Neg. 2), God's Antagonist (Neg. 11), and the Devil (Neg. 12).

According to Luke 11:11, Jesus asks: "What father among you if his son asks (for) a fish will give him a serpent instead of a fish?" What does "serpent" signify in this verse? When one fishes in the Sea of Galilee, a serpent may be caught in the net along with fish. The fisherman does not have to be very discerning to distinguish the serpent from the fish; he can easily cast the serpent back into the water and keep most of the fish. As the fish denote sustenance and renewed life, the serpent may symbolize death or the Death-Giver (Neg. 1).

MATTHEW 3:7 AND THE DEAD SEA SCROLLS

Three times Matthew uses a rare expression: "you brood (offspring) of vipers" (γεννήματα ἐχιδνῶν; 3:7, 12:34, and 23:33); the reference is clearly to a dangerous and poisonous snake.[17] This odd expression is first attributed to John the Baptizer, who according to John 3:7 calls the Pharisees and Sadducees a "brood of vipers." The expression is clearly negative, but its exact meaning is opaque. Perhaps it denoted that these Jewish leaders were Bearers of Corruptible Knowledge (Neg. 4). In Matthew 12:34 the selfsame expression is attributed to Jesus, perhaps mirroring the fact that Jesus had begun his public career as a disciple of John the Baptizer (cf. John 1:29–42, 3:22–30). According to Matthew 12, Jesus calls his opponents, most likely the Pharisees mentioned in verse 24, a "brood of vipers." That epithet is directed against Jesus' opponents because they do not speak the truth. They are evil (verse 34). In this passage, the serpent, the viper, symbolizes the Liar (Neg. 5) and Evil (Neg. 13).

In Matthew 23:33, Jesus again calls his opponents a "brood of vipers." The noun "serpent" appears before the formula found in Matthew. That is, Jesus addresses his opponents, now clearly the scribes and Pharisees (23:29), with ophidian symbolism: "you serpents, you brood of vipers." The meaning of the symbolism is clear. Matthew, through Jesus, portrays the scribes and Pharisees as "hypocrites," which is a Matthean theme. The Pharisees claim to honor the prophets, but are exposed to be the sons of those who murdered the prophets (23:30–31). Thus, the scribes and Pharisees are a brood of vipers. That expression may also imply that they are children of the Devil (Neg. 12). The expression "brood of vipers" in Matthew 23 symbolizes the Bearer of Corruptible Knowledge (Neg. 4) and the Liar (Neg. 5). They oppose Jesus, who is God's son. A study of ophidian symbology suggests that they are therefore God's Antagonist (Neg. 11).

This expression, "brood" or "offspring" of vipers, appears not only in Jewish texts; it is also found in Greek and Latin literature. For example, the expression appears in Ovid's *Metamorphoses*. When Pentheus sees a reveling mob rush out of a city to celebrate some new religious rites, he shouts against them these words: " 'You sons of the serpent, you offspring of Mars, what madness has dulled your reason?' Pentheus cries" (*"Quis furor, anguigenae, proles Mavortia, vestras attonuit mentes?" Pentheus ait*).[18] Thus, the expression—brood of vipers—known to be typical of John the Baptizer's language was an expression known elsewhere in the Hellenistic world. It may have been common coin in the Mediterranean world, thus signifying the prevalence of serpent imagery.

The same Greek noun that denotes "viper" in Acts 28:1–6 and in Matthew 12:34 and 23:33 appears also in Matthew 3:7 and Luke 3:7 (it is ἔχιδνα). In the 1950s, O. Betz argued that a phrase in the *Thanksgiving Hymns* reappears in the New Testament and links John the Baptizer with Qumran.[19] Betz argued that the Hebrew phrase meant "creatures of the viper" and that this same phrase appears on the lips of John the Baptizer, according to Matthew 3:7: "You brood of vipers [γεννήματα ἐχιδνῶν]! Who warned you to flee from the wrath to come?" During some discussions in Germany, the late Professor Betz reiterated to me this equation and interpretation. Earlier I thought it was stretching the point because the Hebrew phrase usually means "works of the asp," but some newly published Dead Sea Scroll fragments strengthen and tend to support Betz's interpretation.

In this hymnbook (1QH^a), in column 11 (= old 3) an author, surely not the Righteous Teacher, predicts the punishment to come to "the works of the sand viper" (literal rendering). What does "the works of the sand viper" (מעשי אפעה) mean in 1QH^a 11.17? Note the final lines of this section of the *Thanksgiving Hymns*:

> And they shall open the gates of [. . .] the works of the sand viper. (18)
>   And they shall close the doors of the pit
>   upon the one who is pregnant with perversity
>   and the bars of eternity upon all the spirits of the sand viper.

Although we do not now know what was on the torn leather before "the works of the sand viper," it must be parallel to "the doors of the pit" in the following line; hence the line may have read as: "shall open the gates of [Sheol before] the works of the sand viper." The "works" are clearly the products of the sand viper. They are to be punished, and that means "works" most likely means "creatures" or "children." The children of the sand viper are thus synonymous with the "Sons of Darkness"—that is, all those on the earth who are not "Sons of Light" (or Essenes).

This derived meaning of "works"—children or brood—is now found in a recently published Dead Sea Scroll. In *4QMysteries* (4Q299 Frg. 3a ii–b) we find the expression "every [or all] work," which in context idiomatically means "every creature" (כול מעשה).[20] The author intends to denote active beings. The full phrase appears in line 10, "the devices (or schemes) of every creature" and in line 15, "the destructions (or tribulations) of every creature." It makes no sense to translate the Hebrew as "the devices of every work." Hence, Betz's argument that the selfsame phrase appears in the Dead Sea Scrolls and in the New Testament is strengthened and should be sustained.

Clarification of what "vipers" might denote among the Qumran Scrolls may be provided by a passage in the *Damascus Document*. In the copies of the *Damascus Document* found at Qumran we find a reference to those who are like "[vip]ers" (צפע[ונים];[21] 4Q266 Frg. 3.2.2). The context refers to those who lack understanding and trespass God's commandments. The author of this passage chose "vipers" as a pejorative term to denote sinners.

Something further may be added. The author of the *Thanksgiving Hymns* probably was calling the Pharisees and Sadducees "creatures of the sand viper." It is thus significant that Matthew has John the Baptizer call Pharisees and Sadducees "creatures of vipers." Second, the final lines of the psalm in the *Thanksgiving Hymns* envision the punishment of these creatures at the end of time. The words attributed to John the Baptizer ring with this same accent: "You creatures of the viper! Who warned you to flee from the coming wrath?"

MARK 16:9–20

The appendix to Mark, 16:9–20, has a famous reference to serpents that has been taken literally by some fundamentalists in southern sections of the United States. In "the longer ending of Mark," the resurrected Jesus tells his eleven disciples that "the one who believes and is baptized" will be able to "pick up serpents" and not be harmed (16:18). It is interesting to observe that poisonous snakes are denoted by "serpent" (ὄφις) and not by "asp" (ἀσπίς as in Rom 3:13) or "viper" (ἔχιδνα as in Mt 3:7; 12:34; 23:33; Luke 3:7; Acts 28:3).

The compiler of this appendix to Mark was influenced by Greek mythology. Dionysus, who appears as a serpent, gave his devotees the power to handle serpents. Thus, like Athena, they, the Bacchantes, were possessed and could hold deadly snakes. Most likely in Mark 16:18 the serpent primarily symbolizes the Death-Giver (Neg. 1).

JOHN 3:14

Initial Observations

The Gospel of John was composed and edited over three or four decades, reaching its present form, without the story of the adulterous woman (7:53–8:11), which was inserted later, about 95 CE.[22] The work may have been first composed in Jerusalem in the mid-sixties and later edited and expanded elsewhere, perhaps in Antioch or Ephesus.[23] For almost two thousand years, Christians have assumed that the Fourth Evangelist, of all the Evangelists, was the one most influenced by Greek thought and was dependent on the Synoptics (Mt, Mk, Lk), and that the Beloved Disciple who appears only in the Fourth Gospel as the disciple "whom Jesus loved"

Figure 81. Bronze Symbol of Diana (Artemis). Deer with serpent around neck. From Ephesus [?]. Early Roman Period. JHC Collection

(Jn 13:23) is to be identified with the Fourth Evangelist. Since the discovery of the Dead Sea Scrolls, it has become obvious to many Johannine experts that the Fourth Gospel is the most Jewish of the Gospels.[24] Recently, P. Borgen, D. M. Smith, and other Johannine experts have rightly pointed out that the Fourth Evangelist may have known one or more of the Synoptics, but wrote "independently" of them.[25] In the past fifty years, Johannine experts have demonstrated why the Fourth Gospel is probably not apostolic or connected with the Apostle John but took its final form, perhaps, in Ephesus. Among the most important insights is the perception that this John and his brother—the sons of Zebedee—never appear in the Fourth Gospel, and it would be inexplicable why the Transfiguration, which was witnessed by John and would be so appropriate for the Fourth Evangelist's cosmic theology, would be omitted.[26]

M. L. Robert draws attention to an approximately 7-meter-long headless bronze serpent, rising up, with markings for scales and seven curves. Found with a bust of Tiberius and Livy in a Roman ruin at Ephesus, it is highly symbolical, representing a domestic cult. Most likely it symbolized protection (Pos. 6) and prosperity (Pos. 2).[27] Such images helped to clarify that only Rome was powerful and that the emperor was like a god, since the images of human heroes must be life-size but emperors and gods could be over 7 meters high.[28]

Text and Translation

There can be little doubt that the passage on which we are focusing was carefully composed by the Fourth Evangelist and reflects the culture of the first century. Here is the text and translation, with key symbolical words italicized in the translation:

Καὶ καθὼς Μωϋσῆς ὕψωσεν τὸν ὄφιν ἐν τῇ ἐρήμῳ,
οὕτως ὑψωθῆναι δεῖ τὸν υἱὸν τοῦ ἀνθρώπου,
ἵνα πᾶς ὁ πιστεύων ἐν αὐτῷ ἔχῃ ζωὴν αἰώνιον.[29]

And as *Moses lifted up the serpent in the wilderness,*
So *it is necessary* for *the Son of Man to be lifted up*
In order that *all who are believing* in him may have *eternal life.*
[Jn 3:14–15][30]

Arriving at this point in the study of ancient serpent symbolism, many readers might assume that the author of John 3:14 makes some connection between Jesus and the serpent. That is the understanding that slowly impressed me.

The possibility that the Fourth Evangelist is drawing some analogy between the serpent and Jesus is unthinkable if the serpent symbolizes evil.[31] However, the reader now knows that serpent symbolism was multivalent especially when the Gospel of John was being written and shaped.[32] Most readers will now comprehend why the Apocalypse of John and its portrayal of the serpent as Satan is not the proper perspective from which to understand chapter three of the Gospel of John.

Questions

As with Genesis 3 and Numbers 21 some questions arise, although they are not so numerous. Why does the Fourth Evangelist turn to an exegesis of Numbers 21 to make a point? Why does he attribute the teaching to Jesus? Was he imagining Moses' serpent as a "pre-Christian" symbol of Jesus? Was he imagining Moses' serpent as a type of Jesus? If so, what meaning was the author attempting to communicate and why?

Does the Fourth Evangelist in John 3:14–15 only make a comparison between the serpent and Jesus in terms of the verb "to lift up"? That is the usual advice of commentators,[33] but is it accurate, partially correct, or misleading? Does "to lift up" refer to the lifting up on a cross and, if so, why does the Greek verb never have that meaning? Does the verb denote Jesus' being lifted up into heaven and returning to the Father? What is the meaning of the "as" and "so" that begin the first and second stichoi? What is the precise meaning of the passive verb "be lifted up"? Who is the Son of Man? What is meant by "believing in him"? Is there any connection between "the serpent" and "eternal life"?

The well-known zodiac circle and its animal signs were employed symbolically by many Christians; they appear, for example, in Revelation. The palm and the crown were accorded Christian meaning. The vine and the tree of life from the Genesis story were used symbolically.[34] The ship was used to signify the early church buffeted by the seas of time. The plow and the axe symbolized the Christian interpretation of Isaiah 2:3–4 and the dream when people "will beat their swords into plowshares." Especially the fish, which is *ichthus* in Greek (an acronym: *ich* denotes *Iesus Christ*, *th* is Theou [= of God], *u* is *huios* [= Greek for " the Son," and *s* [= Savior]), and "living water" were employed to represent the Christian confession.[35] These symbols, some of which clearly originated in "pagan" cultures, were incorporated and redefined by Christians. Why was the serpent not a symbol widely used in Early Christianity as it was in the Asclepian cult—and was serpent symbolism employed in some communities? Why has virtually no Johannine scholar seen that Hellenistic and early Jewish serpent symbology may also clarify and enrich our understanding of the serpent in John 3:14–15?

One explanation is that the serpent is often always misperceived as a symbol of evil. Jews, Christians, and Muslims tell me repeatedly, before we discuss the traditions, that the serpent symbolizes Satan or the Devil. Another reason for the failure to perceive the richness of serpent symbology in antiquity is that the animal, concept, and symbolism are surprisingly absent in many reference works. For example, there is no entry for "serpent" or "snake" in G. Cornfeld et al., eds., the *Pictorial Biblical Encyclopedia* (1964).

Scholars' Reflections

Do Johannine experts not clearly see a connection between Jesus and the serpent in John 3? Fortunately, the specialists on the Fourth Gospel avoid the temptation to see Jesus as an evil or poisonous snake. The closest to this absurdity would be the suggestion that the Son of Man represented poison. In fact, J. G. Williams argued the "Son of Man who is lifted up was accused of being 'poison.' " He continued: "Unlike the serpent Moses held up, he [Jesus] is not poison."[36] Nowhere in early Jewish thought or in traditions that have shaped or appear in the New Testament can I find textual support for such a supposition. Fortunately, Johannine scholars are more informed and perceptive.

The German M. Claudius, by his own admission, loved to study the Bible, especially ("am liebsten") the Gospel of John. Using the exegetical method that was acceptable in his time, but is today recognized as conflationism (e.g., the mixing of Moses' ideas with those of the Fourth Evangelist), Claudius argued that Moses, in the upraised serpent of the wilderness period, perceived what would transpire centuries later and in Jerusalem: the crucifixion of the Son of Man.[37] Johannine scholars are more diachronically sophisticated than Claudius; they do not make the mistake of assuming Moses had foreknowledge of Jesus.

Yet we must ask again: Do they see a connection between the serpent and

Jesus? The answer is clearly "no"; they either miss the poetry that makes "the serpent" parallel to "the Son of Man" (see the following discussion) or they assume no comparison was intended by the Fourth Evangelist. This should not be revolutionary news, since we drew attention to commentators' failure to include ophidian symbology in an exegesis of John 3:13–16 in the opening pages of this book.

The commentators have unanimously opted for another comparison, observing that the grammar demands a comparison (note "as" followed by "so"; see the following discussion). Johannine experts conclude that the comparison in John 3:14–15 applies only to the verb "to lift up." Note again some pertinent comments:

> The phrase "to be lifted up" refers to Jesus' death on the cross. This is clear not only from the comparison with the serpent on the pole in vs. 14, but also from the explanation in xii 33. [Brown, 1966][38]

> . . . . the deepest point of connection between the bronze snake and Jesus was in the act of being "lifted up." [Carson, 1991][39]

> And, just as that snake was "lifted up" in the wilderness, so, Jesus says, "the Son of Man must be lifted up." This must refer to his being "lifted up" on the cross. [Morris, 1995][40]

> Und wie Gott in der Wüste seinen Zorn gegen das rebellische Volk durch die Rettungsgabe der erhöhten Schlange überwunden hat, so hat er Jesus . . . durch seine Hingabe und Erhöhung an das Kreuz—zu retten. [Wilckens, 2000][41]

> In dem Johannes den "erhöhten" Menschensohn . . . gibt er den gekreuzigten Jesus als Zeichen zu verstehen, das auf Gott weist. [Wengst, 2000][42]

In an erudite and insightful study on John 3:14–15, R. R. Marrs shows no interest in serpent iconography or symbology and misses the comparison between Jesus and the serpent.[43] For him, "the point of comparison" is clearly "not between Moses and Jesus, since Moses is the lifter of the serpent, while Jesus is the one lifted. The immediate point of comparison seems simply the lifting up that occurs in both scenes" (p. 146).

One of the most distinguished and gifted Johannine experts, and one who is probably the most informed specialist on what is a consensus in the study of John has served us well. In a book that appeared when the present work was nearing its completion, D. M. Smith summarizes the consensus on the meaning of John 3:14. Note his words:

> The biblical scene in view here is Num 21:8–9, where the Lord instructs Moses to make an image of a serpent and elevate it on a pole,

so that the rebellious Israelites, against whom the Lord had actually sent serpents in the first place, might, if snake bitten, look on it and live. The analogy with the work of the crucified Jesus, the Son of Man who is lifted up, is very striking indeed. It is a classic typology. The element that is new in John, and characteristically Christian, is the emphasis on belief, which is absent from the story in Numbers. (Of course, comparisons of Jesus with the serpent are misplaced; the analogy applies only to being lifted up.)[44]

Succinctly, and accurately, Smith reports what we surmised in the beginning of this book. There is a consensus among Johannine scholars: in commenting on John 3:14–16, either they fail to see the possibility of the parallel between the serpent and Jesus or they deny any "comparison" between Jesus and the serpent.

In Smith's clear assessment of the consensus several questions arise: (1) Does the Fourth Evangelist offer us a classic typology whereby Jesus, as the Son of Man lifted up, is portrayed as Moses' upraised serpent? If so, how can "comparisons of Jesus with the serpent" be "misplaced"? (2) While an element in the Fourth Gospel is clearly a reference to "believing," should it be categorized as a "new" element since the Hebrews who look up to the metal snake must trust in God's promise to heal them so they may live? (3) Would the Fourth Evangelist have agreed that "the emphasis on belief" is a "new" element and "absent from the story in Numbers 21"? (4) Does "the analogy" apply "only to being lifted up"? The research summarized in the following pages casts doubt on each of these claims.

Before proceeding further, I must record some concern, having checked over six hundred commentaries on the Fourth Gospel. It is astounding how focused some of the best exegetes are on philology; yet they show no interest in symbology. John 3:14–15 is not problematic philologically; it is complex symbolically. That has become pellucid. Virtually no commentary on the Fourth Gospel over the past hundred years shows interrogatives directed to the "serpent" in John 3:14. Contrast, however, the brilliant and focused attention of John Chrysostom (italics mine):

> "That whosoever believeth in Him should not perish, but have eternal life." Seest thou the cause of the Crucifixion, and the salvation which is by it? Seest thou the relationship of the type to the reality? There the Jews escaped death, but the temporal, here believers the eternal; there the hanging *serpent* healed the bites of *serpents,* here the Crucified Jesus cured the wounds inflicted by the spiritual *dragon;* there he who looked with his bodily eyes was healed, here he who beholds with the eyes of his understanding put off all his sins; there that which hung was brass fashioned into the likeness of a *serpent,* here it was

the Lord's Body, builded by the Spirit; there a *serpent* bit and a *serpent* healed, here death destroyed and a Death saved. But the *snake* which destroyed had venom, that which saved was free from venom; and so again was it here, for the death which slew us had sin with it, as the *serpent* had venom; but the Lord's Death was free from all sin, as the brazen *serpent* from venom. . . . For as some noble champion by lifting on high and dashing down his antagonist, renders his victory more glorious, so Christ, in the sight of all the world, cast down the adverse powers, and having healed those who were smitten in the wilderness, delivered them from all venomous beasts that vexed them, by being hung upon the Cross. Yet He did not say, "must hang," but, "must be lifted up" (Acts xxviii. 4); for He used this which seemed the milder term, on account of His hearer, and because it was proper to the type.[45]

It is impressive how many times John Chrysostom mentions the serpent, the dragon, and the snake.

Serpent Symbolism and Exegesis

Despite insights into the positive symbolism of the serpent by Ephrem Syrus and Cyril of Jerusalem, as well as Augustine and Calvin, the prevailing mood of New Testament exegetes who turn to John 3:14 is that snakes, or serpents, are vile animals who are simply pejorative symbols. This concept can be found in the New Testament, as we have just seen, but the turning point in exegesis of John 3:14–15 may well be seen in the writings of Eusebius (c. 260–c. 340 CE). In introducing Philo of Byblos' alleged excerpt from Sanchuniathon, which celebrates the mythological importance of the serpent, Eusebius cannot restrain himself. This genius, often celebrated as the father of Church history, prejudices the reader with these comments: snakes are "creeping and venomous beasts which certainly perform nothing beneficial for humans, but rather effect ruin and destruction for whomever they strike with deadly and cruel venom."[46] Under such denigration of the serpent, which became characteristic of the church, subsequent interpreters of John 3:14 will miss the rich symbolism provided by the culture in which the Fourth Gospel took shape. It was, as we have seen, filled with positive images of the serpent as the source of life, health, rejuvenation, new life, and resurrection. Recall again the epic of Gilgamesh, which was an ancient well-known legend a millennium and more before the Fourth Evangelist. According to Tablet XI, a snake, the "lion of the ground," steals from Gilgamesh the plant called "The Old Man Becomes a Young Man." Having obtained the plant, the snake "sloughed off its casing" and became eternally youthful.[47]

About the same time as Eusebius, the Christian apologist Arnobius (who died about 330 CE) ridiculed those who portrayed Asclepius as a serpent. He argues that "a serpent" crawls over the earth "as worms are wont to do, which spring from mud." The serpent "rubs the ground with his chin and breast, dragging himself in sinuous coils."[48] In this section of his seventh book, Arnobius reveals how powerful was the cult of Asclepius and what a threat it was for the success of Christianity. In such a setting, so different from the time in which the Fourth Gospel took shape, it will become more and more difficult to grasp the original intention of the symbolism in John 3:14–15. The backdrop for this stage of history was even set earlier by Tertullian. He was sidetracked from developing his own insights on the typology of the serpent for Christ because of the Ophites who exaggerated the literal meaning of 3:14–15.[49]

The time of the first Council of the Church—at Nicea in 325 CE—seems to be a barrier that separates a period when the serpent was predominantly a positive symbol from one in which it is almost always a negative symbol (cf., e.g., Fig. 7). It is abundantly clear, both from a study of Christian thought from the late second century CE to the fourth century CE and from conversations with learned colleagues in New Testament research, that the exegete is now prejudiced against the serpent symbolizing something positive. That attitude causes a misreading and a misinterpretation of New Testament passages.

The habit of assuming that the serpent symbolizes only evil has been a hallmark of Christian exegesis since about the fourth century. For example, even though Theodoret (c. 393–466), a bishop in Syria, grasps that the Fourth Evangelist drew a parallel between Jesus and the serpent, the serpent must symbolize something negative. Note the following excerpt from Theodoret's *Dialogues* (the characters are fictitious: "Eranistes" represents the opponent of "Orthodoxus," the one who argues on the basis of apostolic decrees):

> Eranistes.—Do you not think it irreverent to liken the Lord to goats?
>
> Orthodoxus.—Which do you think is a fitter object of avoidance and hate, a serpent or a goat?
>
> Eranistes.—A serpent is plainly hateful, for it injures those who come within its reach, and often hurts people who do it no harm. A goat on the other hand comes, according to the Law, in the list of animals that are clean and may be eaten.
>
> Orthodoxus.—Now hear the Lord likening the passion of salvation to the brazen serpent. He says: "As Moses lifted up the serpent in the wilderness even so must the Son of Man be lifted up: that whosoever believeth in Him should not perish, but have eternal life." If a brazen

serpent was a type of the crucified Saviour, of what impropriety are we guilty in comparing the passion of salvation with the sacrifice of the goats?

Eranistes.—Because John called the Lord "a lamb," and Isaiah called Him "lamb" and "sheep."

Orthodoxus.—But the blessed Paul calls Him "sin" and "curse." As curse therefore He satisfies the type of the accursed serpent; as sin He explains the figure of the sacrifice of the goats, for on behalf of sin, in the Law, a goat, and not a lamb, was offered. So the Lord in the Gospels likened the just to lambs, but sinners to kids; and since He was ordained to undergo the passion not only on behalf of just men, but also of sinners, He appropriately foreshadows His own offering through lambs and goats.[50]

Far too often biblical scholars tell me, over and over, that they hate snakes and are afraid of them. That viewpoint seems myopic—even unreflective. These scholars celebrate the power of the bull and with admiration hold a bronze bull artifact from the second millennium BCE; they exuberantly exclaim what a powerful and appropriate symbol the bull is for God's power. They never seem to grasp how dangerous and destructive the bull is. The same scholars write about the lion and admire it as the quintessential symbol of the king and the messiah.[51] They seem to forget that "the king of beasts" is far more ferocious and fearful than a snake. Such scholars' research is corrupted by unperceived presuppositions and nurturing (i.e., instruction that presupposes snakes are always to be feared, hated, and killed).

Indeed, the serpent is perceived to be feared not because of experience with nature but from nurturing. We do not obtain a fear of serpents only, or primarily, from experience or nature. The point I have been making, from the outset of the present book, was popularized in M. Ridley's "What Makes You Who You Are," in *Time* (June 2, 2003):[52]

Fear of snakes, for instance, is the most common human phobia, and it makes good evolutionary sense for it to be instinctive. Learning to fear snakes the hard way would be dangerous. Yet experiments with monkeys reveal that their fear of snakes (and probably ours) must still be acquired by watching another individual react with fear to a snake. It turns out that it is easy to teach monkeys to fear snakes but very difficult to teach them to fear flowers. What we inherit is not a fear of snakes but a predisposition to learn a fear of snakes—a nature for a certain kind of nurture.

We should avoid the error of positing a false dichotomy between nature and nurture. Is it not clear that we are taught to hate snakes? This is not a native disposition inherited. To appreciate ancient serpent symbolism we must be constantly aware to avoid the nurturing that brands snakes as dangerous, evil, and fearsome.

If we are to comprehend successfully the symbolism inherited by and developed by the Fourth Evangelist, we must immerse ourselves in his time. We must indwell the culture that shaped his thoughts and provided the symbolism and metaphors by which he could articulate his own thoughts. His context provided perceptions and symbolism by which he crafted his challenging Christology. G. Theissen, with erudition and sensitivity, illustrates how immersing oneself in the cultural and political context of a text creates new insights for reflection.[53] We have been attempting to demonstrate this point by focusing on serpent imagery and symbolism in the cultural and historical contexts of our texts, especially Genesis 3, Numbers 21, and John 3.

During the period when the Fourth Gospel was taking shape and for the next three centuries, the Asclepian cult and its bewitching serpent symbolism were a threat to Christian theologians and church leaders. In *A Plea for the Christians*, the second-century Athenagoras, the Athenian Christian apologist, reported that Hesiod said the following of Asclepius:

> The mighty father both of gods and men
> Was filled with wrath, and from Olympus' top
> With flaming thunderbolt cast down and slew
> Latona's well-lov'd son—such was his ire.[54]

Tertullian helps us understand Hesiod's cryptic verse. Citing the lyric poet Pindar, Tertullian comments that "Aesculapius," the god of medicine, was "deservedly stricken with lightning for his greed in practising wrongfully his art. A wicked deed it was of Jupiter—if he hurled the bolt—unnatural to his grandson, and exhibiting envious feeling to the Physician."[55]

Asclepius was thus killed by Zeus' thunderbolt, but Asclepius' story did not end with his death.[56] His devotees claimed to experience him alive again, as Origen reports in *Against Celsus* 3.24. Such beliefs and hopes challenged the kerygma (proclamation) in the Christian movement (cf. esp. Augustine, *The City of God* 7.23 and 10.16). Asclepius remained very popular, especially for all who were sick or injured.[57] In his *On the Incarnation of the Word*, Athanasius lists some of the connections between Asclepius and Christ and denies that there is any conceivable parallel. Note his reflections:

> You call Asclepius, Heracles, and Dionysus gods for their works. Contrast their works with His, and the wonders at His death.
>   For what man, that ever was born, formed a body for himself from a virgin alone? Or what man ever healed such diseases as the common

Lord of all? Or who has restored what was wanting to man's nature, and made one blind from his birth to see? Asclepius was deified among them, because he practised medicine and found out herbs for bodies that were sick; not forming them himself out of the earth, but discovering them by science drawn from nature. But what is this to what was done by the Saviour, in that, instead of healing a wound, He modified a man's original nature, and restored the body whole. Heracles is worshipped as a god among the Greeks because he fought against men, his peers, and destroyed wild beasts by guile. What is this to what was done by the Word, in driving away from man diseases and demons and death itself? Dionysus is worshipped among them because he has taught man drunkenness; but the true Saviour and Lord of all, for teaching temperance, is mocked by these people.[58]

Quite significantly, the noun "Savior" appears more than once in this passage; that is because both figures, Asclepius and Christ, were proclaimed to be the Savior. While it is possible that the prior use of "Savior" by the devotees of Asclepius influenced Christology, it is clear that the two "Roman cults" clashed. Both could not be the only Savior of the world.

Even Clement of Alexandria, who has some harsh things to report about Asclepius, recorded the claim that "the Phoenicians and the Syrians first invented letters; and that Apis, an aboriginal inhabitant of Egypt, invented the healing art before Io came into Egypt. But afterwards they say that Asclepius improved the art."[59] A vast number of Greeks and Romans agreed with Pindar that Asclepius was the "gentle craftsman who drove pain from the limbs that he healed,—that hero who gave aid in all manner of maladies."[60] Tertullian's comments mirror the threat of the Asclepiads to Christians; in his judgment they were all demons. Note his words:

Let that same Virgin Caelestis herself the rain-promiser, let Aesculapius discoverer of medicines, ready to prolong the life of Socordius, and Tenatius, and Asclepiodotus, now in the last extremity, if they would not confess, in their fear of lying to a Christian, that they were demons, then and there shed the blood of that most impudent follower of Christ.[61]

This confusing excerpt is chosen to make only one point. The words of Tertullian mirror the threat of Asclepius (Aesculapius) for Christ; the former seems merely to be an "impudent follower of Christ." In *The Chaplet,* Tertullian rejects the claim that Asclepius was "the first who sought and discovered cures." Tertullian claims that much earlier "Esaias [Isaiah] mentions that he ordered Hezekiah medicine when he was sick. Paul, too, knows that a little wine does the stomach good."[62]

Origen knew the claims that Jesus' death was similar to Asclepius' death. He rejects such claims and similarities between the two most famous miracle workers before the time of the Fourth Evangelist. Note Origen's words:

> But we, in proving the facts related of our Jesus from the prophetic Scriptures, and comparing afterwards His history with them, demonstrate that no dissoluteness on His part is recorded. For even they who conspired against Him, and who sought false witnesses to aid them, did not find even any plausible grounds for advancing a false charge against Him, so as to accuse Him of licentiousness; but His death was indeed the result of a conspiracy, and bore no resemblance to the death of Aesculapius by lightning.[63]

The threat to Jesus' followers from the devotees of Asclepius resulted not only from the popularity of the Asclepian cult but also because Asclepius' life was virtually a mirror of the story of Jesus. Asclepius was originally perceived as a human. In Homer and other early authors, Asclepius is a human. He is the great physician. He dies, and appears again in dreams, and, according to some of his devotees, he is alive again. He becomes a god equal to Zeus, an elevation that seems to have taken place during the time when the Fourth Gospel was being composed and edited.[64] Note these reflections by Justin Martyr: In what was it possible for Jesus Christ to make "whole the lame, the paralytic, and those born blind, we seem to say what is very similar to the deeds said to have been done by Aesculapius."[65] The similarities between the story of Asclepius and the gospel about Jesus are thus undeniable. The followers of Jesus were challenged not only by the Asclepiads and their devotion to Asclepius, but also by the story of Asclepius and his promise of health and everlasting life.[66]

Two of the most significant works on Christ and Asclepius were published in the 1980s. In 1980, E. Dinkler focused on the Christ typology reflected in a polychromatic scene of a meal and healings. This scene is found in high relief on a broken plaque in the Mesa National Romano.[67] He points out that the sculpture seems to depict Christ in light of Asclepius. The second is a 1986 Harvard University dissertation by R. J. Rüttimann: "The Form, Character and Status of the Asclepius Cult in the Second Century CE and Its Influence on Early Christianity."

Rüttiman has missed two of the major publications on Asclepius and Jesus. He seems not to know about Dinkler's publication, which appeared eight years earlier. He does know and benefit from a major study by K. H. Rengstorf that is devoted to the beginnings of the clash between Christians and devotees of Asclepius.[68] While Rengstorf dates the beginnings of this sociological and religious confrontation to the middle of the second century CE, there are reasons to assume it may already be present earlier.

We have obtained some insight into why the serpent was not a positive symbol for most early Christians. Those with whom Christians were struggling to survive and develop a normative self-understanding had appropriated the positive symbol of the serpent. It would have made an appropriate symbol, however, in light of Numbers 21 and John 3.

In the following pages we shall ask the questions allegedly already asked and answered if Johannine experts have concluded that Jesus cannot be parallel to the serpent in John 3:14. Are comparisons between Jesus and the serpent "misplaced"? Does the analogy in John 3 apply "only to being lifted up"?

What is the "classic typology" to which D. M. Smith refers? How can the typology be only to lifting up? Was it not important to the Fourth Evangelist that it was necessary *for Jesus* to be lifted up? Does not John 3:14–15 also include the full typology: Moses' serpent placed on a pole represents Jesus' "exaltation" on the cross? In John 12:32–33, the Fourth Evangelist makes it clear that to lift up refers to Jesus' crucifixion; is only crucifixion intended in John 3:14–15?

Is Smith correct to report that "comparisons of Jesus with the serpent are misplaced; the analogy applies only to being lifted up"?[69] How could the Evangelist think only about lifting up and never about the lifting up of Jesus? Are such comparisons misplaced, if Jesus is then portrayed to be the one who brings life abundantly, a key attribute of serpent symbology?

The interpretation of John 3:14 entails searching for the meaning of a symbol: the serpent. Four components are involved: the symbol maker (the Fourth Evangelist), the symbol, the meaning of the symbol, and the interpreter of the symbol (in antiquity and today). Clearly, the central concern for us is the third component part: the meaning of a symbol. Does it reveal or point toward meaning? We shall see that both are involved, especially the latter.

To establish the point that the Fourth Evangelist thinks about Jesus as Moses' serpent, and to forge against the stream of Johannine research, we need to demonstrate nine points:

1. The serpent was a powerful and positive symbol in the culture of the Fourth Evangelist.
2. The grammar of John 3:14 indicates some relation between Jesus and the serpent.
3. The syntax indicates that Jesus and the serpent are related.
4. The poetry of the passage draws a parallel between the serpent and Jesus.

5. The Son of Man traditions employed in this verse, John 3:14, are ancient and already rich with Christological overtones that would accommodate serpent imagery and symbolism.

6. The key symbols in Johannine theology support the insight that Jesus is seen in John 3 as a mirror reflection of Moses' serpent on the pole. Both demand commitment or belief and both promise "life." This is the dominant symbolic meaning of the serpent in the first century CE; for example, the Asclepiads claimed that Asclepius could heal and bring new life—and he was symbolized as the serpent in dreams and with shown with a serpent on his staff in paintings and sculptures.

7. Intertextuality.

8. The possible remnants of a synagogal sermon.

9. The evidence of an underlying anguine Christology in the Gospel of John.[70]

These explorations will help clarify to what extent the Fourth Evangelist imagined Jesus as a type of Moses' serpent as well as confirm that ophidian symbolism is found in John 3:14–15.

Cultural Symbolism. I have asked research assistants and colleagues what they think when they hear "Jesus, the serpent." They answer, "Jesus, the Devil." Their response is immediate and no reflection seemed required. If we were able to ask members of the Johannine community what they might think if they heard that a man was thought of as a serpent, they most likely would answer that he was divine. At the outset, we need to be aware of the vast difference between two cultures: that of the United States in the twenty-first century and that of the Fourth Evangelist in the first century.

A study of serpent symbolism in antiquity has proved to be revealing. The first emperor of Rome, Augustus (63 BCE–14 CE), was considered a god, even if he suffered occasionally from diarrhea. The Roman historian Suetonius (c. 69–c. 140 CE) in his only extant work, *The Twelve Caesars,* recorded the following startling account of the birth of Augustus Caesar:[71]

> Then there is a story which I found in a book called *Theologumena,* by Asclepiades of Mendes. Augustus' mother, Atia, with certain married women friends, once attended a solemn midnight service at the Temple of Apollo, where she had her litter set down, and presently fell asleep as the others also did. Suddenly a *serpent* glided up, entered her, and then glided away again. On awakening, she purified herself, as if after intimacy with her husband. An irremovable coloured mark in the shape of a *serpent,* which then appeared on her body, made her ashamed to visit the public baths any more; and the *birth of Augustus* nine months later suggested a *divine paternity.*[72]

Figure 82. The Resurrection. Christ holding a serpent. Mount Athos, Philopaedia Monastery. JHC

The spirit of the time when the Fourth Gospel was composed was imbued with the understanding and belief that serpents were positive symbols. The story of Augustus' birth from a serpent (although it was also acknowledged that he was the son of a *novus homo*) was well known and widely assumed to be accurate.[73] It shaped beliefs, myths, and reflections on other individuals deemed divine. Augustus was none other than the son of Apollo, the son of Jupiter and Latona.

In evaluating this story of Augustus' "divine paternity" by the great god, Apollo-Zeus, it is imperative to observe that Suetonius' account of the lives of the Caesars continues until the death of Domitian in 96 CE. That is about the time the Fourth Gospel reached its completion, or second edition.[74] During the time the Fourth Gospel was taking shape and moving through two editions,[75] the divinity of Augustus was widely expressed in terms of serpent imagery. It is thus prudent to ponder how and in what ways the Fourth Evangelist sought to stress Jesus' divinity by interpreting Numbers 21 so that Jesus is presented like Moses' upraised serpent.

The Fourth Evangelist completed his second edition of the Fourth Gospel about 95 CE, at which time he added the Logos Hymn (Jn 1:1–18), which was most likely chanted in the Johannine "school," and other sections of his Gospel, especially chapter 21. Also about 95 CE, Philo of Byblos was working on his compositions. As we have already seen, he discusses the divine nature of serpents. Philo of Byblos emphasizes that the serpent sheds its skin and so is immortal. Philo of Byblos refers to his own monograph, called *Ethothion*. In it he claims to "demonstrate" that the serpent is "immortal and that it dissolves into itself . . . for this sort of animal does not die an ordinary death unless it is violently struck. The Phoenicians call it 'Good Demon.' Similarly the Egyptians give it a name, Kneph, and they also give it the head of a hawk, because of the hawk's active character."[76] We can read portions of the *Ethothion,* which is lost, because Eusebius, the first Christian historian, cites it. According to Eusebius' citation, Philo of Byblos calls the serpent "exceedingly long-lived, and by nature not only does it slough off old age and become rejuvenated,[77] but it also attains greater growth. When it fulfills its determined limit, it is consumed into itself, as Taautos himself similarly narrates in his sacred writings. Therefore, this animal is included in the rites and mysteries."[78]

The excerpt from Philo of Byblos, regardless of his sources, is of paradigmatic importance for us. First, it informs us of the mythology and symbolic theology of the contemporaries of the Fourth Evangelist. Second, there can be no doubt that this perspective of the serpent was thought to belong not only to the Greeks, Syrians, Egyptians, but also to the Phoenicians. Third, and most important, the serpent was lauded for its ability to symbolize life without end (Pos. 27), new life (Pos. 20), rejuvenation (Pos. 26), and immortality (Pos. 27).

The Fourth Evangelist and those in his circle, community, or school, were reminded almost daily that the serpent symbolized immortality, reincarnation, and perhaps resurrection (Pos. 27). Since John 3:14–15 does portray Jesus as a type of the serpent raised up by Moses, it is imperative to explore the possibility of a remnant of ophidian Christology in the Fourth Gospel. Is it unlikely that the Fourth Evangelist and those in the Johannine circle might have been influenced by ophidian symbolism? Surely serpent symbology may have been intended or seen in such words as the following: "I am the way, the truth and the life" (14:6). And also "I am the *resurrection* and the *life;* he who believes in me, though he die, yet shall he live, and whoever lives and believes in me shall *never die*" (11:25). The Fourth Evangelist's favorite word for life is zōē (ζωή). While Mark uses the noun four times, Matthew seven, and Luke five, he uses it thirty-six times.[79] Since in the Evangelist's time the serpent was the quintessential symbol for "life" (Pos. 20), is one to be blind to possible ophidian symbolism in this noun?

A study of the serpent at Pompeii helps us grasp the culture of the Fourth Evangelist.[80] The serpent was extremely popular at Pompeii. It looms large in murals painted on the outside walls of houses. It appears within houses in small temples. It defines elegant gold rings, bracelets, and armlets. At

Pompeii there was a cult of the serpent (see Appendix III). The serpent almost always symbolized life (Pos. 20), beauty (Pos. 4), and protection (Pos. 6) at Pompeii. In 79 CE, Pompeii was destroyed; what remains helps us contemplate the world of serpent symbolism that shaped the Fourth Evangelist's symbolism.

In light of what we have learned already about the concept and symbolism of the serpent in the first century CE, and along with the Fourth Evangelist's accurate knowledge of the pools in and around Jerusalem, it is necessary to think about the possible meaning of "the Serpents' Pool" in Jerusalem. This statement needs unpacking.

The Fourth Evangelist alone of all the ancient authors knows about a pool in Jerusalem with five porticoes. Not too long ago Johannine experts concluded that the Fourth Evangelist could not have known about Jerusalem since he describes a pool that no ancient historian mentions and one that was apparently five-sided.[81] That is significant since there were no pentagons in antiquity. Now, archaeologists have unearthed a pool that is exactly where the Fourth Evangelist places this monumental structure. It is "by the Sheep Gate" (Jn 5:2). The pool dates from the early Roman Period, and it antedates Hadrian. Its construction is according to the Fourth Evangelist's description. It has four porticoes on each side of a rectangle and a portico between two pools; one of the pools is in the south and the other in the north. Thus, the area boasts five porticoes, but only four sides. The Fourth Evangelist knows about "the Pool of Bethzatha [Bethesda, or Bethsaida]" (Jn 5:2).

Did the Fourth Evangelist also know about "the Pool of the Serpents" that is mentioned by Josephus?[82] Where was this purification pool?[83] Why was it linked with "serpents"? What does the Pool of the Serpents inform us about serpents and cults in Jerusalem during the lifetime of Jesus and that of the Fourth Evangelist? These are questions that need deep examination; it is clear now that at Bethzatha there was a shrine to Asclepius. Was there a cult of the serpents near or in the Pool of the Serpents? How significant and influential was serpent symbolism in Jerusalem before 135/36, when it became a Roman city?

Before proceeding further to examine the theological symbolism of the key words in John 3:14–15—with our focus on the symbolism of the serpent—we should attend to the meaning poured into the grammar and the syntax by the Evangelist.

Grammar. Both in English and in Greek grammar "as" (καθώς) and "so" (οὕτως) indicate a comparison of a word (noun, adjective, or verb), phrase, or clause.[84]

If there is no discussion of the relation between Jesus and the serpent, it is irrelevant who or what was on the cross. That makes a travesty of the

Fourth Evangelist's theology. He is famous for the words: "The Word became flesh and tented among us" (1:14).

Docetic Christology may be reflected in the myopic focus only on the verb "to lift up." The Fourth Evangelist also was interested in the "who" and "why" of the One lifted up on the cross. The One on the cross was the Son of Man, Jesus, the Son of the Father, who is moving back to where he originated: above. The full drama of sending (a clear Johannine motif) is climaxed as Jesus ascends from the earth on the cross. And the full story is one of salvation for all humankind. The moment of death is the moment of life; those who know ophidian symbology will find an echo of it here.

The leading commentators, as we have just seen, assume that "as" denotes only the verb. Grammatically, it can describe the verb, but it can also define a verb with a noun, or a clause. One must argue which of these was probably intended by the implied author or comprehended by the reader.

It seems unlikely that the stress is placed only on "as" lifted up. The Fourth Evangelist did not put the adverb "as" before the verb both times; in the second clause he changed the verb from the active to the passive voice. He did not write "as lifted up . . . so lifted up." If he had, then the adverb would govern the verb. The Fourth Evangelists is a careful writer; he wrote: "And as Moses lifted up . . . so to be lifted up it is necessary."

The Fourth Evangelist three times mentions Jesus' being "lifted up" (3:14, 8:28, and 12:32–34). Too many commentators assume or even argue that the verb refers only to Jesus' being lifted up on the cross. The argument is very impressive.[85] In 8:28, Jesus tells "the Pharisees" that they "will lift up the Son of Man." That cannot refer to God's exaltation of Jesus as in Acts 2:33 and 5:31. In 12:32–34, Jesus states: "[W]hen I am lifted up from the earth, I will draw all to myself." The Evangelist adds: "He said this to show by what death he was about to die." The meaning of the verb "lifted up" in 8:28 and in 12:32–34 clearly refers to Jesus' death. Do they provide the only, or best, basis for understanding 3:14?

Should we read 8:28 and 12:32–34 back into 3:14? That method violates the integrity of chapter 3 and misses the double entendre: Jesus was lifted up on the cross and thereby exalted on his way to heaven and back to his Father. As T. Zahn explained in 1921 in his *Das Evangelium des Johannes:* "[T]he lifting up is to be understood as the elevation into heaven, the return of Jesus from the earthly world to the otherworldly realm of God."[86] It must be stressed again, against the tide of recent research, that "to lift up" in the Fourth Gospel does not denote only lifting up on the cross; it is a lifting up on the cross that symbolizes Jesus' exaltation and return to heaven. R. Schnackenburg stressed this point clearly: "The uplifted serpent in the wilderness appears typologically for the cross and throughout [for Jesus'] heavenly glory" ("[W]ie es die eherne Schlange in der Wüste typologisch anzeigt, am Kreuz, *und dann und dadurch auch in der himmlischen Herrlichkeit*").[87] A study of the ophidian symbolism in 3:14 helps protect the exegete from missing the full meaning of the verse.

Immediate context determines a text's meaning. The context of 3:14 thus is shaped by 3:13. That verse clarified that the Son of Man, as R. Bultmann observed, is "the one who has come down from heaven and who must again be exalted. That is stated explicitly in vv. 14f." Bultmann continued: "V. 14 mentions only the exaltation;[88] this is the fulfilment of the Son's mission, and by this alone is it made effective (cp. 13.31f.), for it is the exalted, glorified Lord who is the object of Christian faith. Yet the necessary condition of his exaltation is his humiliation, as v. 13 has already said.[89] The saving event embraces both these elements."[90] As M. Hengel points out, the Fourth Evangelist makes more references to Jesus' death as salvation than the other Gospels.[91] Beasley-Murray wisely discloses the "simple fact that the Evangelist views the death and resurrection of Christ as indissolubly one. The redemptive event is the crucifixion-resurrection of the Son."[92] H. Weder rightly saw that the "point de comparison" is not primarily to the "le *mode*" of this elevation; verse 15 indicates "le *sens*" of this elevation: the elevation of the Son of Man.[93] Likewise, F. Hahn, in his *Theologie des Neuen Testaments,* stresses correctly that the Son of Man in Johannine Christology is revealed to be shaped by "lifting up" and "glorification."[94] Thus, certainly not crucifixion alone is meant by verse 14; both crucifixion and resurrection collapse into one event for the Fourth Evangelist: the rising up of the Son of Man as an antitype of Moses' serpent.[95]

In *On the Spirit,* St. Basil "the Great" (c. 330–379) rightly perceived that the serpent in John 3 typified Christ. Note his reflections on typology: "The manna is a type of the living bread that came down from heaven; and the serpent on the standard of the passion of salvation accomplished by means of the cross, wherefore they who even looked thereon were preserved."[96] Though Augustine missed the positive symbolism of the serpent, he did see the typology: the serpent lifted up signifies Jesus' death on the cross. Augustine argues that as death came into the world through the serpent, its abolishment was fittingly symbolized by the image of a serpent on the cross (Augustine, *On the Gospel of St. John* 12.11–13; cf. Augustine, *On the Psalms* 74.4 and 119.122).

Some scholars have also seen the brilliant typology of the Fourth Evangelist; though it is missed by the mass of commentators who simply repeat the threefold claim that 3:14 denotes only Jesus' crucifixion, that only "lifting up" is implied, and that there is no connection between the serpent and the Son of Man (in fact, most commentators tend to ignore the serpent symbolism). Note, however, these exceptions to the rule: E. Haenchen wisely pointed out that the Fourth Evangelist avoids mentioning the crucifixion, except in the Passion narrative. He refers rather to "its divine meaning, the exaltation."[97] Long ago in his commentary on the Fourth Gospel, B. F. Westcott astutely perceived that the words of 3:14 "imply an exaltation in appearance far different from that of the triumphant king, and yet in its true issue leading to a divine glory. This passage through the elevation on the cross to the elevation on the right hand of God was a necessity . . . arising out of the laws of the divine nature."[98] As R. J. Burns states, in "Jesus and the Bronze Serpent," the Evangelist uses "lifting up" to refer "not only to Jesus' death by crucifixion but to his resurrection as well."[99] Beasley-Murray correctly claims: "To the lifting up of the snake on a pole that all may live corresponds the lifting up of the Son of Man on a cross that all may have eternal life."[100]

The narrator indicates what is lifted up (active verb for serpent and passive verb for Son of Man). One should not exclude what is lifted up: Moses' serpent and the Son of Man, Jesus. As Bernard stated: "Those who looked up in faith *upon the brazen serpent* uplifted before them were delivered from death by poison; those who look *upon the Crucified,* lifted up on the cross, shall be delivered from the death of sin."[101] Neither the author of Numbers 21 nor the Fourth Evangelist expected the reader to look only at the verb; such a possibility seems quite unlikely. Yet contemporary Johannine experts conclude, en masse, despite the brilliant insights of earlier commentators and the vast weight of serpent symbolism, that the emphasis is only on the verb "lifting up."

While the eyes of the Hebrews who trust God's promise look up at the copper serpent and the gaze of Johannine Jews is on Jesus, the Son of Man and Son of God, there is a difference. In the Septuagint of Numbers 21:8, the stake on which the copper serpent is raised is called a "sign" (probably of God's healing power).[102] The "signs" in the Fourth Gospel, Jesus' mighty works (Jn 5:31–47), correspond to the miracles of the Synoptics. These signs (τὰ σημεῖα [Jn 2:23]) witness to Jesus who is not a sign but the One to whom the signs point, according to God's plan (Jn 2:11, 23; 3:2; etc.). In light of this insight and recognizing the stress on Jesus' incarnation and physical nature (only in John does Jesus collapse from exhaustion and thirst and cry), it seems difficult to comprehend how Johannine experts can miss the narrative force of John 3:13–16; the Fourth Evangelist is not interested only in drawing attention to the verb "lifting up." He is focusing the readers' mind on things above (Jn 3:12) and proclaiming that Jesus' crucifixion was not a failure but his hour of triumph. While Luke trifurcates the crucifixion, resurrection, and ascension, the Fourth Evangelist stresses, against polemical Jewish groups (some of whom control the local synagogue), that Jesus' crucifixion was his exaltation (resurrection and ascension tend to be refocused on Jesus' lifting up on the cross; he will return to his Father finally, according to Jn 20).

As we intimated and is well known, the Fourth Evangelist stresses more than the Synoptics that Jesus is God's Son (cf. esp. Jn 3:13–16). More in the Fourth Gospel than elsewhere in the New Testament Jesus is portrayed as talking about God as Father (cf. esp. Jn 5:19–47). To comprehend that for the Fourth Evangelist Jesus is God's Son brings us back into first-century serpent symbolism. As we have seen, Caesar Augustus was portrayed as a god's son because a serpent impregnated his mother.

Theological aspects of the grammar. The simile includes a necessity: it is necessary (δεῖ) for the Son of Man to be lifted up. The implied author appeals to the divine plan of salvation and employs the word "necessary," which is used in apocalyptic literature to stress that certain events must take place before the End, when all normal time will cease. The reader already knows, or will learn from the narrative, that Jesus will die outside the walls of the Holy City, Jerusalem.

Again, commentators have assumed or argued that the very use of the word "necessary" (δεῖ) makes it obvious that 3:14 must refer only to Jesus' crucifixion. They point to the use of "necessary" in 3:13 and 12:34. The use of "necessary" (δεῖ) in the Fourth Gospel may prove them wrong. According to the Fourth Evangelist, the Scriptures prove that "it is necessary [δεῖ] for him [Jesus] to rise from the dead." (20:9)

J. Frey rightly points out that Jesus goes willingly to his death, according to the Fourth Evangelist. Jesus' death is unlike the concept of the hero who dies as an example, and it is not grounded in the evils of men. Jesus' crucifixion is a necessity; it is according to Scripture and according to God's will and love.[103]

What is parallel to "in the wilderness"? This dative phrase is followed by the dative phrase in the result clause: "in him." Hence, the theological thought develops out of the grammar: As the believers who looked up at the serpent lived in the wilderness, so all believers who look up to the exalted (upraised) Christ will live eternally "in him" (ἐν αὐτῷ). Grammar indicates a connection between serpent in the wilderness and the Son of Man, Jesus.

More may be learned by the implied author's use of "must" or "it is necessary" (δεῖ). The Fourth Evangelist did not write: "[A]s Moses lifted up, so the Son of Man is lifted up." The implied author draws attention to the connection between the serpent and the Son of Man. According to the author of Numbers 21, it is neither Moses' act of lifting up that saves the people nor the serpent on the pole. What saves the people in Numbers and the Fourth Gospel is God, and this saving power is available because of the commitment of the people who follow God's directive to look to the serpent.

The Fourth Evangelist does clarify the importance of believing (a fundamental word emphasized by him), but the concept is not entirely new in the typology; it seems implied in Numbers 21. What is crucial in Numbers is the commitment or belief of the people that God will save them when they look up to the serpent as a sign of God's power to save. In the Fourth Gospel, the Son of Man, Jesus, tends to take on the role of God. That is, it can be argued that Jesus is the one who saves through his incarnation and crucifixion. Note John 3:16, which follows 3:14–15: "For God so [οὕτως] loved the world that he gave his only son, that all who are believing in him may not perish but have eternal life." This verse (16) begins with "so"; thus, the parallel thought continues in Greek. Note the following constructions:

> And as Moses lifted up the serpent in the wilderness,
> So it is necessary for the Son of Man to be lifted up,
> In order that all who are believing in him may have eternal life;
> So did God love the world that he gave his unique son
> In order that all who are believing in him may not perish
>   but may have eternal life. [3:14–16}

By seeing the serpent as representing the Son of Man, one comprehends the intention of the Fourth Evangelist. No New Testament author, except perhaps Paul, puts Jesus in such a central focus. The Evangelist's theology is focused to serve his Christology.

It seems difficult to agree that the one who wrote "and the Word became flesh and tented among us" (Jn 1:14) would have intended to stress only the verb and not the verb and the noun; that is, only the lifting up and not the lifting up of the Son of Man. In the Fourth Evangelist's time and culture (whether he wrote in Jerusalem, Alexandria, or Ephesus), the serpent symbolized precisely what the Son symbolizes in the Fourth Gospel: life (Pos. 20) and eternal life (Pos. 27). Hence, perceiving this point, one begins to see that the intention of the Evangelist is most likely to draw a parallel between the serpent and the Son of Man, Jesus.

The "lifting up" is crucial and should not be minimized. The Fourth Evangelist's own Christology does become apparent when he stresses that the Son of Man must be lifted up (exalted) on the cross. The full meaning must not be lost by looking only at the verb and not the person. The Fourth Gospel is "good news" about a person. That means the image of Christ or Son of Man in Numbers, God's foreshadowing of Christ according to the Fourth Evangelist, is the serpent that symbolizes God's salvation.[104] As Saint Augustine (354–430) stated, in his homilies on the Fourth Gospel: "Just as those who looked on that serpent perished not by the serpent's bites, so they who *look in faith on Christ's death* are healed from the bites of sin." One cannot look at a verb; one looks up at the serpent or up at the Son of Man.[105]

Syntax. The syntax is attractive and impressive, as we have already seen. The simile is followed by a purpose clause, which signifies the necessary result of the comparison. The clause is a result clause: "in order that [ἵνα] all [πᾶς] who are believing [ὁ πιστεύων] in him may have eternal life [ζωὴν αἰώνιον]."

Attribution. John 3:14–15 is attributed to Jesus. As Johann Philipp Gabler stressed, we must "distinguish whether the Apostle [or Evangelist] is speaking his own words or those of others."[106] It is clear that the Evangelist wanted to stress that the interpretation of Numbers 21 was authoritative; it was not his own creation. It was divinely sanctioned. The Fourth Evangelist attributes the claim to the only One-from-above, Jesus. Jesus is informing "a ruler of the Jews" that the Son of Man must be lifted up as Moses lifted up the serpent.

Setting. Verses 14 and 15 are placed at a crucial point in the narrative. Jesus has been conversing with Nicodemus and the two verses contain the closure of that pivotally significant dialogue;[107] that is, it comes both as the climax of Jesus' words to this Pharisee and at the close of the first revelatory discourse of Jesus—a pattern of thought that characterizes and distinguishes the Fourth Gospel. And 3:14–15 immediately precedes one of the most stunning passages in the New Testament, which bears repeating since it concludes the thought: "For God so loved the world that he gave his only Begotten Son, that whosoever believeth in him would not perish but have eternal life" (3:16; KJV). It is in this narrative context that the Fourth Evangelist turned to Numbers 21 to explain that Jesus must be lifted up as Moses lifted up the serpent. A penetrating analysis of the Greek syntax helps clarify that serpent symbolism discloses the point that Jesus is the one who brings "eternal life" (3:14).

Poetry and *Parallelismus Membrorum*. As we have seen, the Greek (and the English) sentence employs the adverb as a conjunction to begin a sentence. "As" does not indicate only a comparison between the verb "lift up" or the noun "Son of Man." The full sentence needs to be observed. By looking at the full sentence, we should ask if the Evangelist has emphasized a major Christological point by using a simile that compares the Son of Man with the serpent. To reverse the order of the clauses makes the point perhaps more apparent to those who have memorized the verse:

The Son of Man must be lifted up
As Moses lifted up the serpent in the wilderness.

Often lost or unobserved by New Testament critics is the poetic structure of John 3:14–15. The thought is structured harmoniously in parallel lines of thought so that each word is then echoed by a following word *(parallelismus membrorum).*[108] Because repetition (or echoing) of thought or sound is the heart of all poetry, so parallelism is the hallmark of poetry in biblical Hebrew and was observed and given a technical name by R. Lowth in 1753 and 1778.[109] Only two psalms will be cited for clarification of the poetic attractiveness of *parallelismus membrorum*.

The first is from Psalm 145:13–14. Here is my translation:

> Your kingdom is a kingdom for all eternity,
> And your dominion is for all generations.
>
> The Lord upholds all who fall,
> And raises up all bowed down.

The thought in line *(stichos)* one reappears in the second line.[110] The four-fold repetition of "all," often not represented in translations, helps to clarify the parallel thoughts. That is, each is a universalistic statement; it is good for all places, times, and persons.

The second passage is from Psalm 8:

> What is man *('nwsh)*   that you are mindful of him,
> And the son of man *(bn-'dm)*   that you care for him?
>
> [Ps 8:5(4)]

The poetry is crafted so that lines of thought are in parallel lines; the poetic form is synonymous parallelism *(parallelismus membrorum)*. The first two beats in each line are synonymous: the "man" in the first line is synonymous with "the son of man" in the second line. The two beats at the end of each line are also synonymous: God is "mindful" of the human and does "care" for him.

The Fourth Evangelist, as M. Hengel demonstrated,[111] knew well the "Old Testament" and its literary forms. It is not a surprise, therefore, to find poetic forms appearing in the Fourth Gospel, especially in the words of Jesus. As D. N. Freedman has shown, poetry is central to the biblical message; prose and poetry can be, and must be, distinguished.[112] The Fourth Evangelist chose *parallelismus membrorum* to emphasize the divine words directed by Jesus to Nicodemus. The poetic form is synonymous. Note the poetic structure of John 3:14–15, following the Greek order:

> And as Moses lifted up   the serpent in the wilderness,
> So it is necessary to be lifted up   the Son of Man
> In order that all who are   may have life eternal.
>   believing in him

The parallelism is so clear as to need no discussion. It is also synonymous. "And as Moses lifted up" is synonymously parallel to "so it is necessary to be lifted up." Most important, "the serpent in the wilderness" is synonymously parallel to "the Son of Man." The poetic structure of the passage is carefully structured to clarify the virtual identity of "the serpent" to "the Son of Man."

The passage reflects careful thought and composition. Observe how the Evangelist has constructed his simile:

Numbers	Johannine Symbolism
As	So it is necessary
Moses	[God, according to the divine passive]
lifted up (active)	be lifted up (passive)
the serpent (objective case)	the Son of Man (objective case)
in the wilderness (dative)	[see "in him" in 3:15 (dative)]

The two parallel columns raise the question of the appropriate parallel to "Moses." The passive voice "be lifted up" in the Fourth Gospel needs no ruling noun to specify who is the one who has caused or allowed the lifting up, but the attentive reader is stimulated to ask: "Who is the actor?"

Could the passive verb "be lifted up" be a divine passive? When a passive voice is employed in the New Testament and the antecedent actor is not clear, the actor is often "God." Thus, in Mark 16:6, "he has been raised"[113] means that God raised Jesus from the dead. God is the actor. That meaning was most likely a common theme of the early Christian preachers and prophets; it makes excellent sense here in the Fourth Gospel, if we take "he was lifted up" (ὑψωθῆναι) to denote not only crucifixion but also, as its literal meaning indicates, "to be exalted."[114] God has exalted Jesus and raised him "above." This exegesis rings harmoniously with the opening play on the double meaning of anōthen (ἄνωθεν): "again" and "above," since Jesus has informed the ruler of the Judeans,[115] Nicodemus, that he must be born "from above." Nicodemus misunderstands; that is, one of the great teachers of the Judeans is one who is characterized by misunderstanding.[116] Nicodemus thinks Jesus means he must be born "again"; that is, to enter again into his mother's womb. The use of one adverb, which signifies not only "again" but also "above," makes sense within the context of John 3:12–15; note the structure of thought:[117]

| Earthly things | descended from heaven | Moses lifted up the serpent |
| Heavenly things | ascended into heaven | The Son of Man must be lifted up |

Again the "serpent" and "the Son of Man" are parallel. In this context, the lifting up on the cross is the Evangelist's method of presenting Jesus' highest hour on earth. The unbelievers see only a dying man; the Sons of Light see the exaltation of Jesus, who is from above and returning again to his Father.[118]

The issue, however, is more complex. The verb "be lifted up" may also have a literal meaning. But who would be those who literally lift Jesus up on the cross? That is the unique meaning given to this verb (ὑψόω) by the Fourth Evangelist. It means "lift up" or "raise." Only in the Fourth Gospel does the verb imply crucifixion. As we have seen, the verb is used twice in 3:14, first as an active verb and then as a passive verb.

Since the parallel is "Moses," the most likely suggestion would be that those who crucify Jesus are those who belong to Moses or the followers of Moses. Does that possible interpretation make sense for Johannine theology? The name "Moses" appears more often in the Fourth Gospel than any other Gospel (7/8/10/12).[119] It is clear from 5:46 that Jesus' antagonists are those who set their hope on Moses; quite significantly they are also those who refuse to come to Jesus that they "may have life" (5:40). It is easy to hear an echo from 3:15—specifically, all those who look to Jesus as the upraised one, like the serpent in the wilderness, "will have eternal life."

Our search for the ones who, according to the Fourth Evangelist, lift Jesus up on the cross is rewarded by the Judeans' declaration in 9:28: "We are disciples of Moses." [120] Here the Fourth Evangelist makes it unmistakably clear that Jesus' opponents are "the disciples of Moses." After this verse the name "Moses" never appears again in the Fourth Gospel. It is at least conceivable that this use of words is intentional by our gifted writer.

The antagonists in the Johannine drama are specified. The disciples of Jesus (9:27) are opposed by the disciples of Moses (9:28). Moreover, this clarification comes in the famous and pivotal passage in which the Judeans caustically interrogate the man born blind because Jesus healed him on the Sabbath. Observe that "the disciples of Moses" (9:28) claim: "We know that God has spoken to Moses, but as for this man, we do not know where he comes from" (9:29). The members of the Johannine circle or school and the one who comprehends the Fourth Gospel *know* where Jesus "comes from:" Jesus is "from above."

The irony of 9:29 is simply another example of the author's rhetorical skill. He has mastered the art of irony and misunderstanding.[121] These two aspects of the Fourth Evangelist's narrative art are first presented in the Fourth Gospel in the dialogue between Jesus and Nicodemus that ends in 3:15.[122] Jesus speaks not only about *anōthen*, he also speaks about the Son of Man being a type of the serpent raised up by Moses.

How do we locate irony in a document? As G. R. O'Day points out: "[S]ignals to irony are often difficult to detect, because the essence of irony is to be indirect. A straightforward ironic statement would be a contradiction in terms. The ironist's challenge is to be clear without being evident, to say something without really saying it." [123] Herein lies the problem:

the Fourth Gospel does contain narrative irony, but we cannot be certain where it is and where it is not.

How should we recognize irony in the Fourth Gospel? One of the best means is to feel the jar caused by a contradiction when the symbolic is taken literally. This happens in the narrative when one of the dramatis personae misses the symbolical meaning.[124] Examples help clarify this point; here are the clearest examples of irony revealed through the narrative of the Fourth Gospel:

> 2:21–22 Jesus tells the Judeans that the Temple if destroyed will be raised; they understand him to mean the Temple. (In this first appearance of irony, the narrator tends to clarify what he means by the use of irony.)
>
> 3:4 Jesus tells Nicodemus he must be born "anew," *anōthen*; Nicodemus thinks Jesus means to he must reenter the womb.
>
> 4:15 Jesus offers the Samaritan woman "living water"; she thinks she will not need to return to the well.
>
> 7:27 Some Jerusalemites claim Jesus may not be the Christ because they know his origins.
>
> 11:50 Caiaphas prophesies that it is expedient for one to die for the people *(laos)*.

Irony and misunderstanding help the Fourth Evangelist make several major theological points. Misunderstanding is an aspect of irony; it clarifies revelation.[125] Along with the Evangelist and Jesus, only the reader who knows the "end" of the story and has received the enlightening insights of the Holy Spirit can understand the drama of salvation. The representative disciple seems to be Thomas, who provides the final and perfect confession. The evangelist links 20:29 with 1:1. As Moody Smith states: "[W]hat is said in 1:1 about the word is based on post-resurrection knowledge and confession of Jesus."[126] For the Evangelist, irony and misunderstanding are not primarily rhetorical techniques. They are chosen to reveal that only one who is born from above can comprehend why it is necessary for the Son of Man to be lifted up like Moses' serpent.

Moses, who raised the serpent in the wilderness, cannot be contrasted with Jesus in the Fourth Gospel. Moses is the one through whom God gave the Torah (Law) according to 1:17 and 7:19. He is the one through whom God gave the manna (6:37).[127] This verse is a significant link with 3:14–15; both interpret the Torah so that Moses is seen foreshadowing the ministry of Jesus.[128] Most important, not only does Jesus refer to what Moses did, according to 3:14–15, but the Fourth Evangelist also stresses that Moses wrote the Pentateuch. Philip announces to Nathanael: "We have found him of whom Moses in the Torah . . . wrote" (1:45). This episode precedes and helps frame the theologoumenon of 3:14–15.

Who then raises Jesus up onto the cross in the Fourth Gospel? In Mark we come across the clause: "And they crucified him" (15:24). To whom does this refer? It seems to refer back to "the soldiers" (15:16) who are emphasized in the Markan narrative because they are associated with "the whole battalion" (15:16). In the Fourth Gospel we also find the possibly ambiguous verbal clause: "They crucified him" (19:18). To whom does the pronoun "They" refer? It is remarkable to discover that the antecedent is "the Judeans" in 19:14. John has interpolated into an earlier story of the Passion, somewhat represented by Mark, an account of the Judeans and the chief priests who are explicitly mentioned in 19:15.

The Johannine addition to the Passion occupies two significant sections: the Judaeans' altercation with Pilate in 19:12–16 and Jesus' crucifixion in 19:17–22. In neither of these sections are the Roman "soldiers" mentioned.

According to John 19:16, Pilate hands Jesus over "to them to be crucified." Who are these people? They are the "chief priests" mentioned in 19:15. According to 19:20, "They crucified him." According to John 19:23, it is "the soldiers" who "crucified Jesus." The "soldiers" are reintroduced in this verse. They had not been mentioned since 19:2. But who are "they" in John 19:18? The context of this verse gives the impression that it is the "chief priests" and "the Judeans." It is none other than "the chief priests and the officers" who, according to the Fourth Evangelist, cry out to Pilate: "Crucify him, crucify him!" (19:6).[129]

How do we explain this tension in the Johanine account? Who crucified Jesus? The Evangelist again mentions "the soldiers"; it is they who are said to have crucified Jesus (19:23). The Johannine narrative implies that the disciples of Moses, the Judeans, are those who crucified Jesus (unfortunately, the noun for "Judeans" is usually translated simply, and incorrectly, as "Jews"). The point is not lost on all who have already grasped that Nicodemus is none other than "a ruler of the Judeans" (3:1). Hence, we see the thought implicit in the carefully structured sentence in 3:14: "And as Moses lifted up the serpent in the wilderness, so it is necessary for the Son of Man to be lifted up." The Fourth Evangelist has clarified through his narrative those who have lifted up the serpent, Jesus, on the cross. It is the Judean leaders. And he has implied who has "exalted" Jesus. It is his Father, God.

In summation, it seems shocking to imagine that the passive verb "be lifted up"—which refers, according to most commentators, only to Jesus' crucifixion—can be a divine passive. In one sense, the verb "be lifted up" is a divine passive denoting the divine plan ("it is necessary") and the exaltation by God. In another sense, the passive verb reflects the reason for the crucifixion. It was due to the Judeans.

Most important for our present research, a study of the poetry of John 3:14–15 establishes the parallel between *"the serpent"* and *"the Son of Man."* Moreover, grammar also points out this fact. Both "serpent" and "the Son of Man" are clearly in the objective case (accusatives) and conclude the thought:

And as Moses lifted up	(τὸν) the serpent in the wilderness,
So it is necessary to be lifted up	(τὸν) the Son of Man.

Moreover, grammar, syntax, and poetic structure support the conclusion that the Fourth Evangelist has paralleled the serpent in thought and symbolism with the Son of Man.[130]

In his *Reply to Faustus the Manichaean,* Augustine perceived this insight: "Thus also, the serpent hung on the pole was intended to show that Christ did not feign death, but that the real death into which the serpent by his fatal counsel cast mankind was hung on the cross of Christ's passion."[131] What Augustine missed was the positive serpent symbolism: The uplifted serpent according to the authors of Numbers 21 and John 3 symbolized life.

According to the Fourth Evangelist, the Son of Man is Jesus. Recall John 9:35–37, in which Jesus tells the man born blind, who now not only sees, but perceives, that Jesus is the Son of Man. Thus, the serpent is a type of Jesus, the Christ according to the Fourth Evangelist. Ophidian symbolism helps ground the insight since the serpent symbolizes liberation from death and new life (Pos. 20),[132] as well as rejuvenation (Pos. 26) and immortality and even resurrection (Pos. 27).

John 3:14–15 is a significant passage. The unit is carefully composed, and most likely reflects long and in-depth discussions in the Johannine community of the meaning of Jesus' death and his relation to Moses. John 3:14–15 is shaped by a sociological context that has separated Johannine Jews from those who claim to be Moses' disciples. The latter introduce the Johannine narrative and are echoed repeatedly throughout the narrative theology that follows after 3:14–15.

What is the meaning of "in the wilderness" in John 3:14? A focus on 3:14 awakens something that the Jews in the Johannine community knew well. The phrase "in the wilderness," would, most likely, remind them of the heading of the fourth book of the Torah (= Pentateuch), which we call "The book of Numbers." The opening words of the Hebrew text are: "And Yahweh spoke to Moses." These are followed by: "In the wilderness."[133] This observation reveals another careful use of words by the Fourth Evangelist, and it would certainly have been noticed by at least some of the Jews who read the Fourth Gospel and the Book of Numbers as Scripture.

More than one typology from Numbers is evident in the Fourth Gospel.[134] The serpent was a type and Jesus the antitype; that seems indisputable.[135] This typology from Numbers is developed within a larger typology. The final editor of Numbers recounts, with a ritual celebration of God's mighty acts in history, how Israel journeyed through the wilderness successfully. They lived in tents. God's tabernacle was a tent. The people saw God's glory as a cloud by day and fire by night. Such imagery has shaped the Prologue of the Gospel of John, especially in the climactic verse 14: "And the Word flesh became, and pitched a tent among us. And we beheld his glory." The continuing presence of God, God's glory, and the imagery of God tenting among us were most likely derived by the Fourth Evangelist from the Book of Numbers. It is no wonder, then, that he was fond of this book of Scripture and obtained from it his typology of the serpent for Jesus' final day on earth: Jesus' crucifixion was also his exaltation.

The Book of Numbers apparently supplied two journeys for the Fourth Evangelist. First, it supplied the concept of Jesus' journey from above to the earth and his return above to the Father. Second, it provided a paradigm: the journey of Jesus' followers through the wilderness of life, and drinking "the living water" that provides eternal life. Thus, Jesus' followers were to perceive that Jesus' way led to the necessity of the cross on which Jesus was exalted like a serpent (the symbol of new life) and from which he was freed to return to his Father.

The Book of Numbers is not the only source of the Evangelist's thought in 3:14. The verb "to lift up" does not derive from Numbers 21. The Fourth Evangelist inherited it either from the kerygmata in the Palestinian Jesus Movement or from a study (perhaps his own) of Isaiah 52:13 (esp. in the LXX): "My Servant . . . shall be exalted" or "lifted up."[136] The fact that the passages in the Fourth Gospel in which the verb "to lift up" occurs (3:14–15, 8:28, 12:32–34) are linked traditionally with the Synoptic passion predictions (viz. Mk 831, 9:31, 10:32–33) should not suggest that the Fourth Gospel is dependent on the Synoptics. All four Gospels were preceded not only by the early proclamations *(kerygmata)* but also by the beginnings of teaching and research *(didache)* in the Palestinian Jesus Movement.

One final word on "as" (καθώς) and "so" (οὕτως) in John 3:14 seems prudent. We have seen that "as" most likely modifies a clause: "And as Moses lifted up the serpent in the wilderness, so it is necessary for the Son of Man to be lifted up."

This grammatical construction is used again by the Fourth Evangelist in 5:21 and 5:26. Each time it seems to echo the leading thought of 3:14–15;

that is, this unit of thought stresses that Jesus is the source of life. Note the
construction:

> For as (ὥσπερ) the Father raises the dead and gives life (ζῳοποιεῖ),
> So (οὕτως) also the Son gives life (ζῳοποιεῖ) to whom he will. [5:21]

> For *as* (ὥσπερ) the Father has life (ζωὴν) in himself,
> So (οὕτως) he has given to the Son also to have life (ζωὴν) in himself. [5:26]

These verses seem to echo the thought of 3:14–15; that is, they stress that
belief that resurrected life is possible now through Jesus (cf. Jn 5:21 and
25). He, Jesus, conveys to the Johannine Jews what the symbol of the serpent in the Asclepian and other cults conveyed to their devotees. The serpent symbolized life (Pos. 20), renewed life (Pos. 26), and immortality and
resurrection (Pos. 27) for the Johannine Jews. They shall have eternal life;
the conclusion of the result clause in John 3:15, "that all who are believing
in him may have eternal life."

Son of Man Traditions in John. The key Christological term in John
3:14–15 is "the Son of Man." As with the Synoptics (Mt, Mk, and Lk) so
with the Fourth Gospel, Jesus is portrayed as referring to himself as the
Son of Man. The Son of Man concept, not a title, appears for the first time
in Daniel 7:13. The seer Daniel has a dream in which he sees "one like a
Son of Man" who is "coming with the clouds of heaven." Scholars have
assumed this figure represents collective Israel, but Middle Aramaic and
the picture of one coming on clouds seem to indicate a cosmic person. This
mysterious vision or dream in Daniel influenced the author of the *Parables
of Enoch* (*1 En* 37–71). We now know that this text was composed by a
Jew and perhaps sometime in the late first century BCE.[137] The term, "Son
of Man," is attributed to Enoch, but only in the conclusion of chapter 71.

The Fourth Evangelist inherits this traditional designation, but only after it had become an established title within the Palestinian Jesus Movement. E. Ruckstuhl rightly perceives that the Son of Man title in the Fourth
Gospel does not originate in Gnostic circles; for him, it appeared within
early Jewish wisdom traditions.[138] O. Hofius correctly stresses that the
theme of John 3:14–15 is the way of the Son of Man (much more than the
crucifixion, as we have seen).[139]

More likely these wisdom traditions were shaped within Jewish apocalypticism, since *1 Enoch* is one of the most distinctive apocalypses. The
apocalyptic background of the Son of Man in the Fourth Gospel is shown
by the verses immediately preceding our central passage, 3:14–15. The
term "Son of Man" first appears in the Fourth Gospel in 1:51. The meaning is clearly apocalyptic; the reader is informed he will see "heaven opened
and the angels of God ascending and descending upon the Son of Man."

Just prior to 3:14, the reader is informed that no one has ascended into heaven; this is a rejection of the claims made in many Jewish apocalypses. The Fourth Evangelist then claims that the only one from above is the one "who descended from heaven: the Son of Man" (3:13).

The Fourth Evangelist is stressing that the Son of Man—assumed to be identical with the Word defined in 1:1–18—is the bearer of God's wisdom. The Son of Man brings God's wisdom to earth.[140] Since the serpent, especially in Judaism and in Jesus' teachings, is the symbol of wisdom (Pos. 18), the Evangelist may have held some ophidian image here. Most likely, many of his readers will know that the serpent symbolizes wisdom.

The cosmic dimension of the Son of Man in Daniel, *1 Enoch*, and the Fourth Gospel is clear and needs no elaboration. According to the Fourth Evangelist, the Son of Man, Jesus, is from "above" and is returning to his Father who is above. Perhaps the Fourth Evangelist did not intend in 3:14–15 to bring out the cosmic dimension of the serpent, but we should not deny that he portrayed the Son of Man, as the serpent, being "lifted up." If he did not initially intend to bring forward the cosmic dimension of ophidian symbolism, many of his readers would most likely understand that the Son of Man, as the serpent that is "lifted up," has cosmic power (Pos. 8).

What are the consequences of such reflection? Two are most important. First, the reflection is significant because it exposes the error of the biblical experts who refuse to see any relation between Jesus (the Son of Man) and the serpent reflected or explicit in John 3:14. Perhaps these scholars assumed that God was never symbolized as, or by, a serpent in the Hebrew Bible. The serpent was indeed a symbol of God. According to Numbers 21, the upraised copper serpent signifies not only the power of God to heal; it also symbolized the presence of God. Those who lifted up their eyes for God's help received it, because the upraised serpent symbolized the presence of God. As L. Ginzberg stated: "It was not, however, the sight of the serpent of brass that brought with it healing and life; but whenever those who had been bitten by the serpents raised their eyes upward and subordinated their hearts to the will of the Heavenly father, they were healed." [141] Likewise, the passage in 2 Kings 18 points back to Numbers 21; both use the serpent as a symbol of God. Those who worshipped God or Yahweh through Nechushtan (or even worshipped the image directly) most likely would have taken this image of a serpent as a symbol of the Creator (Pos. 7) and Protector (Pos. 6). As Augustine said, in *The City of God*, Moses' serpent, "a symbol of the crucifixion of death," was preserved in memory by the Hebrews and Israelites and later was "worshipped by the mistaken people as an idol, and was destroyed by the pious and God-fearing king Hezekiah, much to his credit." [142]

The TANAKH (Old Testament) records that Moses, through divine intervention, was able to turn his rod into a serpent. The serpent (נחש) clearly signals that "the God of Abraham, the God of Isaac, and the God of Jacob, has appeared to you" (Exod 4:5).

The farsighted vision of the Creator degenerated into the nearsighted worship of Nechushtan. Hezekiah wisely had the image of the serpent taken from the Temple. The Seventh Ecumenical Council seems rightly to have understood that those in Jerusalem (anachronistically called "Jews"), or at least some of them, began to worship the symbol of God's healing. They became idolaters. Note the wording of Quaestio LVI:

> Why was he praised in the Old Testament who broke down the brazen SERPENT (II. Kgs. xviii. 4) which long before Moses had set up on high? Answer: Because the Jews were beginning an apostasy from the veneration of the true God, venerating that SERPENT as the true God; and offering to it incense as the Scripture saith. Therefore wishing to cut off this evil, lest it might spread further, he broke up that SERPENT in order that the Israelites might have no longer that incentive to idolatry. But before they honoured the SERPENT with the veneration of adoration, no one was condemned in that respect nor was the SERPENT broken.[143]

Second, the reflection is significant because it reveals the error of scholars who assume or conclude that John 3:14–15 refers only to Jesus' crucifixion. For example, in *Herrenworte im Johannesevangelium,* M. Theobald contends that the focus of the Son of Man sayings in the Fourth Gospel, "without doubt" *(ohne Zweifel),* is on the death of Jesus.[144]

We have pointed out that crucifixion and exaltation (resurrection) are also intended in 3:14–15. These crucial verses are framed by the cosmic dimensions of Jesus, the Son of Man and God's unique son. In 3:13 the Fourth Evangelist stresses that only the Son of Man has been in heaven and descended to earth. In 3:16 he again emphasizes the cosmic dimension of 3:14–15: "For God so loved the cosmos that he gave his unique Son, that all who are believing in him may not perish but have eternal life."

Jesus is intending to teach Nicodemus "heavenly" insights (3:12). The Fourth Evangelist seeks to inculcate the poetic vision of the crucifixion, an earthly event, as a heavenly event. Some readers of the Fourth Gospel, and perhaps the author, might have imagined the cross of Jesus, symbolized by Moses' upraised serpent, as the pillar that once again united heaven and earth *(axis mundi)* and the way for Jesus to return to his Father. Perhaps, the Fourth Evangelist imagined that some believers would comprehend that the cross was Jacob's cosmic ladder on which angels ascended and descended upon the triumphant Son of Man (1:51).

Key Symbols in Johannine Theology. John 3:14–15 contains some of the Fourth Evangelist's technical terms *(termini technici)*. Highly charged with Johannine symbolism are the following: "Moses," "lifted up," "wilderness," "it is necessary," "Son of Man," "all who are believing," and "eternal life." These have already been discussed; perhaps it is necessary now only to point out the well-known fact that the Fourth Evangelist puts more stress on the verb "to believe" than any other New Testament author; it appears eleven times in Matthew, fourteen in Mark, nine in Luke, but ninety-eight times in the Fourth Gospel.[145]

The author of the *Epistle of Barnabas,* perhaps reading Numbers 21 through the lens of Johannine Christology, emphasizes that if one were to be healed by the serpent, he must have faith: "Moses said to them, 'Whenever one of you . . . is bitten, let him come to the serpent that is placed upon the tree, and let him hope, in faith that it though dead is able to give life, and he shall straightaway be saved.' "[146] It is likely that the author of the *Epistle of Barnabas* knew the Fourth Evangelist's interpretation of Numbers 21. He adds: "Moses makes a representation of Jesus" to show that Jesus must suffer, and thereby reveals how Jesus "shall himself give life."[147]

The Semitisms in 3:14–15 indicate that this saying of Jesus antedates the Greek of the Fourth Gospel. It may have originated in the preaching of Jesus' earliest Jewish followers. It is unlikely that it can be taken back to Jesus himself since all the evidence suggests that he imagined he might be stoned. Recall Jesus' words: "O Jerusalem, Jerusalem, killing the prophets and stoning those who are sent to you!" (Mt 23:37; Lk 13:34). Jesus thought he was a prophet. He also felt sent to Jerusalem, and that he would be stoned there. I agree with the numerous scholars who (perhaps disappointingly) have been forced to conclude that no authentic saying of Jesus indicates he contemplated that he would be crucified.

The double entendre of "to exalt" and "to lift up" on a cross is an Aramaism,[148] since the Aramaic *'ezd ᵉqeph*[149] denotes not only "to be erected" but also "to be crucified."[150] The paronomasia is not possible in Hebrew or Greek. In 1936, G. Kittel, in a major article unknown to many leading Johannine experts,[151] argued persuasively that the knowledge of this Aramaic verb indicates that the Fourth Gospel was composed in Palestine or Syria.[152]

Now we may explore the remaining three issues: (7) intertextuality, (8) the possible remnants of a synagogal sermon, and (9) the evidence of an underlying anguine Christology in the Gospel of John.

Intertextuality. John 3:14–15 is not a clear case of intertextuality, since no text appears within another text. Yet there is an echo of Numbers 21 in these verses. What text was in the mind of the Fourth Evangelist? That is impossible to discern, for two reasons. First, no text is quoted. Second, while he usually prefers the Greek translation of Israel's Scriptures (the

Septuagint), he is intermittently dependent on the Hebrew text (as in 19:35; perhaps in 12:41 he is influenced by a lost Targum).[153]

As Gabler long ago urged, we must ask if the Evangelist is supporting an argument "from the sayings of the books of the Old Testament, and even accommodating them to the sense of the first readers."[154] When we hear the echoes of Scripture, we perceive that the serpent symbolized not only wisdom (Pos. 18), but also life (Pos. 20), renewed life (Pos. 26), and eternal life (Pos. 27).

The importance of the allusion to Numbers 21 in the Fourth Gospel is brought into bold relief by the recognition that the Fourth Evangelist is unusually attracted by the vivid scenes from the Exodus narrative.[155] Especially influential on his thought are the theologically significant symbolism of the paschal lamb (1:29), the manna (6:16–21), and the elusive quotation from some Scripture in 7:38 that may well be, as R. E. Brown suggested, to the psalmic celebrations of the incident when, according to Numbers 21, Moses struck the rock and water flowed to quench the thirst of those dying from lack of water in the wilderness.[156] The pole on which Moses hung the metal serpent (נס) appears in the Septuagint as "sign" (σημεῖον); reflecting the Evangelist's tendency to stress that Jesus' miracles are "signs" suggests he may have been drawn to Numbers 21 because it was a "sign" that pointed to Jesus.

Thinking about how and why the Fourth Evangelist has interpreted Numbers 21 suggests that he imagines that Jesus is like the serpent. Both were raised up. Both provide healing and life.

What is the most important meaning of the serpent in the Fourth Gospel? The symbol of the serpent most often represents life (Pos. 20), but it also symbolized eternal life (Pos. 27). I am convinced that the Fourth Evangelist put the accent on the symbolism of eternal life; that is, Jesus is raised up symbolically like Moses' serpent. And while Moses' serpent gave life, Jesus guarantees eternal life for those who believe. The grammar proves the points; the conclusion to the two final purpose clauses is "eternal life":

> And as Moses lifted up the serpent in the wilderness,
> So it is necessary for the Son of Man to be lifted up;
> *In order that* all who are believing in him may have *eternal life;*
> So did God love the world that he gave his unique son
> *In order that* all who are believing in him may not perish
>   but may have *eternal life.* [3:14–16]

According to John 3:14, Jesus compares himself, as the Son of Man, to the serpent raised up by Moses. According to Matthew 10:16, Jesus told his twelve disciples: "Behold, I send you out as sheep in the midst of wolves, therefore be wise as serpents[157] and innocent as doves." The only parallel is in the Gospel of Luke, and it has only: "Go out, behold, I send you as lambs in the midst of wolves" (Lk 9:3). It seems to me that this saying belonged to Q, the putative lost source of Jesus' sayings, and that Luke, due to a disdain for the symbol of the serpent, removed the reference to the serpent. The two most clearly positive uses of the serpent in the New Testament are attributed to Jesus by the First and Fourth Evangelists, and—according to many New Testament experts—these are our most Jewish Gospels (and, ironically, sometimes the most anti-Jewish Gospels).[158] It seems to follow that Jesus' followers portrayed him as a prophet who used the serpent to symbolize wisdom (Mt 10:16) and eternal life (Jn 3:14).[159]

The Possible Remnants of a Synagogal Sermon. The preceding reflections indicate that in Greece, Italy, Syria, Egypt, India, Mesopotamia, indeed in all known cultures, the serpent was revered as a positive symbol. An objection might be raised; some might claim that while Jews in Palestine and Syria admired the serpent, they never would have depicted it anywhere near a synagogue. That is now proved to be another false presupposition.

The serpent is clearly shown iconographically in synagogues from southern to northern Roman Palestine. From the fifth-century synagogue at Gaza, once incorrectly identified as a church, comes a mosaic depicting David. An upraised serpent, along with a lion cub and a giraffe, is depicted listening to David, as Orpheus, playing a lyre.[160] Moving from the southwest to the northeast of Roman Palestine, we come to a serpent elegantly chiseled on a beam above a Hebrew inscription. It is not from a so-called pagan temple; it is from the Golan and the late fifth-century CE synagogue at 'En Neshut.[161] Moreover, the serpent is formed to represent a Hercules knot.[162] Also from the Golan, and this time from the village at Dabbura, and probably from a synagogue that dates from the early fifth century, is found a lintel with two eagles—each of them holding a serpent. Between the two eagles, and above the long serpent, is a Hebrew inscription: "This is the academy of the Rabbi Eliezar ha-Qappar."[163] Not only does this lintel take us back to the second century CE, but a serpent is depicted above the academy of a rabbi known to be famous according to the Mishnah and Talmudim (e.g., *t. Betzah* 1.7; *j. Ber.* 1.3).[164]

While the image of the serpent is now clearly shown to be part of the synagogue, and also of rabbinic academies, I would think it likely that some Jews depicted the serpent in light of mythological ideologies.[165] The serpent is associated not only with Orpheus but also with a Herculean knot; even still, the general absence of "pagan" iconography lifts the serpent out of mythology into the religious symbolic world of Judaism, both before and after 70 CE (when the Temple was burned and the nation destroyed).

Within this cultural setting for early rabbinic teaching and worship, I am persuaded that it is conceivable that the Fourth Evangelist had been influenced by a synagogal sermon he had heard—or even delivered—based on an exegesis of Numbers 21:8–9. He probably inherited the serpent symbolism from the Son of Man sayings, which he obtained from traditions known to the Johannine school or circle.[166]

The Fourth Evangelist is not dependent only on a so-called Christian exegetical and hermeneutical use of Numbers 21, as Bultmann claimed.[167] He may have known the Jewish traditions that shaped the Christological interpretation of Numbers 21 by the author of *Barnabas* (12) and Justin Martyr (*1 Apol.* 60 and *Dial.* 91, 94, and 112). These authors inherited traditions that are clearly Jewish.[168] The importance of Numbers 21, as we have seen, was developed by the author of the Wisdom of Solomon and later Jewish sources (esp. *m. Rosh Hash.* 3 and *Mekilta to Exod* 17:11).

Six observations have led me to the conclusion that the Fourth Evangelist was influenced by a synagogal sermon when he composed 3:14. These may now be mentioned only briefly:

1. The Fourth Gospel is very Jewish, and is shaped by the celebration of the Jewish festivals in synagogues after 70.

2. The members of the Johannine community desired to attend synagogal services.

3. Philo of Alexandria based two homilies on Numbers 21:8–9. He stresses, under the influence of the Septuagint, that "the serpent" is "the most subtle [φρονιμώτατος] of all the beasts" (*Leg.* 2.53). In *Legum allegoriae* 2.76–79, Philo claims that Moses' uplifted serpent symbolized "self-mastery" or "prudence" (σωφροσύνη) (cf. Pos. 6), which is a possession only of those beloved by God or God-lovers (τοῦ θεοφιλοῦς). In *De agricultura* 94–98, Philo centers again on serpent symbolism to assist his allegorical interpretations of Scripture. Philo perceives the serpent to be of "great intelligence," and able to defend itself "against wrongful aggression." Eve's serpent is an allegory of lust and pleasure (cf. Neg. 6), but Moses' serpent represented protection from death and self-control (cf. Pos. 6).[169] The serpent also symbolizes "steadfast endurance," and that is why Moses made the serpent from bronze. The serpent of Moses also symbolizes life; the one who looked on with "patient endurance," though bitten by "the wiles of pleasure, cannot but live" (98 [cf. Pos. 20, 26, 27]).[170]

4. The importance of Numbers 21:8–9 would be familiar to all early Jews who knew the Wisdom of Solomon 16:6–7, 13. Noteworthy are especially the interpretations that "the one who turned toward it [not the serpent but "the commandment of your Law"] was saved," and that God alone is "Savior of all." [171]

5. The Johannine emphasis of being from above—stressed in Jesus' con-

Figure 83. Gnostic Amulet. Roman Period. Jerusalem? JHC Collection

versation with Nicodemus—is the theme that leads to and frames 3:13–15. It is the same exegetical meaning brought out of Numbers 21:8–9 according to the Mishnah; that is, the Israelite must remain faithful, direct thoughts to heaven above, and remain in subjection to the Father. After quoting Numbers 21:8, *Rosh Hashanah* has this ethical advice *(halacha):* "But could the serpent slay or the serpent keep alive!—it is, rather, to teach thee that such time as the Israelites directed their thoughts *on high* and kept their hearts in subjection *to their Father in heaven,* they were healed; otherwise they pined away" (3:8 [italics mine]).[172] J. Neusner presents the following translation: "But: So long as the Israelites would set their eyes upward and submit to their Father in heaven, they would be healed." [173] Some readers might even be forgiven for imagining, before reflection, that *Rosh Hashanah* has a Johannine ring to it.

6. The Targum interprets Numbers 21 to denote that believers are to turn their heart toward the *Memra* of God (i.e., the divine Word of God).[174]

Do portions of John 3:13–15 derive from a synagogal sermon? For me, this question remains unanswered yet intriguing. It is likely, as many scholars have concluded (viz. M. É. Boismard and A. Lamouille), that John 3:14 develops from an old Jewish tradition that has been expanded by the Fourth Evangelist.[175]

I am now more interested in the possible evidence of ophidian symbolism and perhaps ophidian Christology (which was distorted by the Ophites) left elsewhere in the Fourth Gospel. It seems to me that serpent imagery is not a central concern of the Fourth Evangelist, but it may have been of keen interest to some in his circle (especially all the former devotees of Asclepius).

An Underlying Ophidian Christology in the Gospel of John? It is now virtually certain that the serpent served as a typology of Jesus for the Fourth Evangelist, and it is imperative to recall that, before the Fourth Evangelist, Moses' serpent was a symbol of salvation. According to the author of the Wisdom of Solomon 16:6, Moses' serpent was "a symbol of salvation" (σύμβολον σωτηρίας). As M.-J. Lagrange stated in 1927: "Jesus shall be reality" ("Jésus sera la réalité")—that is, Jesus is salvation.[176]

Now, we can ask to what extent the Evangelist left traces of an incipient ophidian Christology in the Fourth Gospel. While I am uneasy about clarifying what an ancient author might have meant by a symbol, I am convinced that the Fourth Evangelist thought things out along the lines already explained. The penchant of denying such thoughts to the Evangelist also seems unwise when one realizes that the Fourth Gospel reflects a living history. The Evangelist and others in the Johannine school reshaped and edited the gospel over forty years. The text was most likely discussed in the Johannine school, and concepts latent in the text might have become clearer to the Evangelist through his own study of the text or through discussions with others.

If the Evangelist did not think about some passages in the Fourth Gospel as mirroring serpent symbology, it would be rash to claim that none of his readers would be blind to what seems clear, after exploring the labyrinth of meanings attributed to the serpent by the ancient thinkers. Not only audience criticism and reader-response criticism but also narrative criticism allows us to ask to what extent the Evangelist or his readers might have seen the serpent, the symbol of life (Pos. 20) and immortality (Pos. 27), mirrored in chapters subsequent to John 3:14.

Eternal Life and Life Abundant. Since in the first century CE the serpent was the quintessential symbol for denoting abundant life and eternal life, to what extent did the Evangelist or his readers ever imagine that the "Gospel of Eternal Life" mirrored serpent symbolism?[177] Did he or they ever imagine a connection between the symbols of the serpent which were regnant around them, in the following selected passages:

3:15 in order that all who are believing in him may have eternal life.
3:16 in order that all who are believing in him may . . . have eternal life.
3:36 the one believing in the son has eternal life.
5:24 the one who is believing in him who sent me has eternal life.
6:40 so that all who are seeing the Son and are believing in him may have eternal life.
6:47 the one who is believing has eternal life.

10:10 I came that they may have life, and have it abundantly.

11:25 I am the resurrection and the life.

11:26 and all who are living and believing in me shall never die.

20:31 and that believing you may have life in his name.

Jesus' Legs Were Not Broken. The Fourth Evangelist distinguishes his presentation of Jesus on the cross by stressing, even redundantly, that Jesus' legs were not broken. What is the meaning of this aspect of Johannine theology? Is it because of the law recorded in Numbers 9:12? Recall the text: "They shall leave none of it until morning, nor break a bone of it; according to all the statute for the Passover they shall keep it" (NRSV). Or is the author thinking about Psalm 22? Numbers 9 seems without basis in the text and Psalm 22 has not been employed as in the other Gospels. What is the source of the Evangelist's inspiration and reason to include it in his narrative, and what images might come to the mind of a reader of the Fourth Gospel?

The answer may lie in the portrayal of Jesus. If he is a serpent on the upraised tree, then his legs cannot be broken. That is, when we study the serpentine feet of Yahweh—or, better, some depiction of his power—in images roughly contemporaneous with the composition of the Fourth Gospel, then we see legs that are bent. A bone can easily be broken. But the curved and flexible body of a serpent bends to a blow, such as that attributed to a Roman soldier's weapon. Similarly, the Fourth Evangelist knew the curse of the serpent, according to Genesis 3; since he loses his legs, no one can break them. Perhaps the Fourth Evangelist imagined such concepts. Or perhaps some in the Johannine school or circle might have developed such thoughts. Is it not absurd to imagine that we are the first to imagine such imagery and symbolism?

The Fourth Evangelist and most of his readers knew well the account of how Hezekiah broke the copper (or bronze) serpent in the Temple (which is an echo of Num 21). Did the Evangelist ever and some of his readers occasionally think that while the serpent was broken by Hezekiah, Jesus—the antitype of Moses' serpent—could not be broken?

Nicodemus Brings the Corpse Down from the Cross. Jesus' last words to Nicodemus are evident in John 3:14–15. Jesus tells this leading Jew that he, as the Son of Man, must be raised up on the cross like the serpent lifted up by Moses. Nicodemus appears on stage again briefly when he apparently defends Jesus by pointing to legal procedures (7:50–52). He is on center stage at the end, when Jesus has already died. He brings Jesus' corpse down from the cross.

Only the Fourth Evangelist mentions the so-called Beloved Disciple. He is at the foot of the cross and sees Jesus die. Why does the Evangelist have him leave the scene? Would not the Beloved Disciple be the ideal person to honor the corpse?

The Evangelist has a secret disciple of Jesus, Joseph of Arimathea, and Nicodemus obtain and honor Jesus' corpse. Then they laid Jesus' corpse in a garden. Why?

The passage is as full of emotion as it is of symbolism. What could be in the mind of the Evangelist or in the minds of some of his readers? Is it not possible that they understood the remains Nicodemus received in terms of a metaphor, that Jesus' corpse was seen as the abandoned skin of a serpent gone on to a better, even eternal life?

In the so-called *Epistle of Barnabas,* we find an exegesis of Numbers 21 and John 3. Note this excerpt:

> Moses makes a type of Jesus, [signifying] that it was necessary for Him to suffer, [and also] that He would be the author of life [to others], whom they believed to have destroyed on the cross when Israel was failing. For since transgression was committed by Eve through means of the *serpent,* [the Lord] brought it to pass that every [kind of] *serpents* bit them, and they died, that He might convince them, that on account of their transgression they were given over to the straits of death. Moreover Moses, when he commanded, "Ye shall not have any graven or molten [image] for your God," did so that he might reveal a type of Jesus. Moses then makes a brazen *serpent,* and places it upon a beam, and by proclamation assembles the people. When, therefore, they were come together, they besought Moses that he would offer sacrifice in their behalf, and pray for their recovery. And Moses spake unto them, saying, "When any one of you is bitten, let him come to the serpent placed on the pole; and let him hope and believe, that even though dead, it is able to give him life, and immediately he shall be restored." And they did so. Thou hast in this also [an indication of] the glory of Jesus; for in Him and to Him are all things. (*Barn.* 12:5–7) [178]

A later tradition attributed to Ignatius reflects on the meaning of John 3:14–15. An expansion to Ignatius' *Epistle to the Smyrnaeans* reads, "The Word, when His flesh was lifted up, after the manner of *the brazen serpent* in the wilderness, drew all men to Himself for their eternal salvation." [179] This reflection seems to suggest that the "flesh" denoted, or would have been understood by some readers to mean, the skin left by the serpent who had apparently died, but had actually gone on to a better and fuller life.

Does not the mention of a garden evoke the Eden Story, so that the end of salvation of history was mirrored in the beginning of history? What lies hidden behind John 19:38–42? Perhaps this passage was informed by discussions in the Johannine school of the serpent who brought death in the Garden of Eden and the antitype, Jesus, who brought eternal life from the final garden.

Appearance in a Garden. Only the Fourth Evangelist stages the first resurrection appearance of Jesus in a garden. If Jesus has been portrayed as an antitype of Moses' serpent, then it is symbolically significant that Jesus, as the life-giving serpent, appears in a garden. The garden is the mythical abode of the life-giving, perceptive, or guardian serpent, as we have seen from Gilgamesh, the Eden Story, and the Hesperides. The garden is also the natural habitat of the serpent. Did such myths and folklore help shape the Evangelist's creation or inform readers' imaginations?

The scene in John 20:11–18 is so reminiscent of the Eden Story that the Evangelist must have perceived the symbolic power of his account of Jesus' first resurrection appearance. His last story seems shaped by the first story in the Bible. Both stories highlight a garden, a man, and a woman. In both the man is portrayed as a gardener (Gen 2:15 and Jn 20:15). Both stress misperception and revealed knowledge. As the first story is shaped by the loss of life, the final story is defined by the proof of unending life.

A key link between the first biblical story and the last biblical story (Jesus' first resurrection appearance) has been missed by exegetes and commentators. Mary Magdalene hears Jesus call her by name,[180] and is told by him: "Do not touch me" (Jn 20:17); later she informs the disciples what Jesus had told her (Jn 20:18). The linguistic link between John 20 and Genesis 3 is interesting (μή μου ἅπτου in John 20:17 and μὴ ἅψησθε αὐτοῦ in Gen 3:3 [LXX]; MT = ולא תגעו בו). John 20:17 is an echo of what the first woman added to God's command when she tells the Nachash: "And you must not touch it" (Gen 3:3).[181] Would the Fourth Evangelist miss the link he had made when he created his own resurrection account? Should we imagine that he was deaf to the echoes from Genesis? Did he not imagine that the new creation (Jesus' resurrection) was parallel to Creation?

The echo has many sounds. The echo occurs when the woman in the garden is told by the one who has been lifted up as Moses' serpent that she must "not touch" him. The "original sound" was the woman's addition to God's command when she spoke to the serpent in the Garden of Eden: "And you [plural] shall not touch it." The serpent, as we have seen, was one of the major characters in the first story. Is the life-giving serpent missing in the final story, or have Johannine experts simply missed him among the trees in the garden?

Such reflections derive from contemplating, under the stimulus of John

3:13–16, that some readers of the Fourth Gospel imagined Jesus on the cross in light of Moses' upraised serpent. The brilliant interpreter John Chrysostom, in his *Homilies on Colossians,* obviously thinking about John 3:14–15, argued that Jesus was crucified in public as a serpent. Here are his words: "[W]hile the world was looking on, the serpent should be slain on high upon the Cross, herein is the marvel." [182]

DOUBTING THAT JESUS IS PARALLEL TO THE SERPENT IN JOHN 3

It is easy to doubt an exegesis that is directed against the tide in Johannine research. Here are some objections that may be raised against the exegesis that the Fourth Evangelist presents a typology of Jesus as Moses' upraised serpent and that Jesus is one who embodies the positive symbolic power attributed to the serpent.

1. The fact that the Ophites and others interpreted John 3:14–15 to signify that Jesus is like the serpent implies that the Fourth Evangelist did not intend that interpretation.

    Response: The Ophites' misleading interpretation cannot be a means of discerning the intention of the Fourth Evangelist. The only means of grasping the meaning in John 3:14–15 is to study the Greek within the immediate context of the Fourth Gospel and to comprehend the text within the social and historical context of the symbols that were known to and shaped the symbolic world of the Fourth Evangelist.

2. The Ophites are certainly heretical; their exegesis must be ignored in seeking to understand the Fourth Gospel.

    Response: Many mainline Christians in the second and third centuries CE thought the Fourth Gospel was heretical. The terms "orthodoxy" and "heresy" should not be labels that adequately define thinking within and on the borders of Christianity before the promulgation of orthodoxy in the fourth century.[183] In fact, some leading scholars today have judged the Fourth Gospel to be quasi-Docetic or to preserve a naïve Docetism (cf. Käsemann).

3. The portrayal of Asclepius with a serpent and as a serpent, which was dominant in the first century CE, would make it unlikely that the Fourth Evangelist would depict Jesus as a serpent, especially since there was tension between the devotees of Asclepius and the followers of Christ.

    Response: The tension between Asclepius and Christ does not appear before the late second century CE, at the earliest.

There are no innuendoes in the Johannine writings of any tension from those who worshipped Asclepius. In fact, one should contemplate that not only Samaritans and Essenes were probably in the Johannine circle or school; some Greeks in it (cf. 12:20) may have once been devoted to Asclepius. They would have joined the "new movement" because they found a far better "story" or convincing gospel. For them, and for many others, the serpent was sacred and a symbol of life and eternal life, not only among the Asclepiads but among the devotees of Athena, Apollo, Zeus, and others. Thus, the serpent was a most appropriate symbol for the Jesus who said, "I am the resurrection and the life. Those who believe in me, even though they die, will live, and everyone who lives and believes in me will never die" (Jn 11:25–26 [NRSV]).

4. The Greek of John 3:14–15 does not state that Jesus is a serpent. This insight is significant since the Fourth Evangelist habitually declares, especially through words attributed to Jesus, that he is the Lamb of God, Rabbi (and Rabboni), the prophet, Light, the Shepherd, the Way, the Truth, the Life, the Son; and he implies rather directly that Jesus is the Son of Man and the Messiah.[184]

Response: This insight is correct. The Fourth Evangelist does not declare that Jesus is a serpent or even "like Moses' serpent." An ophidian Christology is not proclaimed by the Fourth Evangelist. Yet, he attributes the words that reveal the Son of Man is parallel to Moses' serpent to Jesus.[185] He does not proclaim that Jesus is a serpent or should be symbolized as a serpent. He uses a simile; Jesus is like the serpent raised up by Moses, at God's command, in the wilderness. Jesus is not a serpent; he is like Moses' upraised serpent of copper.

Like Moses' serpent, Jesus brings life, even eternal life, to all who look up to and believe in him who is from above. The metaphor is clear: In the Book of Numbers, sin is associated with poisonous snakes, but salvation comes with commitment to God represented by the image of the upraised serpent. Intimations of idolatrous meaning are erased by the memory of Hezekiah's reform and smashing of the Nechushtan; the serpent is not to be worshipped. Trust is not put in Moses or in the image; trust is placed in God's promise that all who look up to the raised serpent on the stake may live and not die. The divine sanction is accomplished by the Evangelist's placing of the words in Jesus' mouth. Perhaps the Fourth Evangelist is appealing to those who in his community and region are imagining Jesus as

Moses' serpent; some of them could have been former devotees of Asclepius, Apollo, or Athena—to name only a few deities who were portrayed as serpent gods or gods with serpents. The Evangelist depends on Jewish exegesis of Numbers 21 because, as Jesus said, "The Scripture cannot be annulled" (10:35).

5. The exegesis presented in this study is weakened by the observation that the "serpent" appears in the Fourth Gospel only in John 3:14, and even in this passage the image is not developed.

Response: That is a caveat found in the preceding pages. The simile is introduced; Jesus is an antitype of Moses' upraised serpent. The Fourth Evangelist does not seem interested in developing the typology. He thus probably inherited this tradition. Does it derive ultimately from some teaching of Jesus not recorded elsewhere? [186] Is it a part of the early kerygmata in the Palestinian Jesus Movement? Does it provide a window into the kerygma and didache found in the Johannine school as Jewish scribes and sages searched the Scripture to prove that Jesus is the one who fulfills all prophecies and typologies? I am convinced that this latter possibility is more likely than the others.

Finally, we may return to the enigmatic report in Plato's *Phaedo* that Socrates, on his deathbed, ordered a student to offer a cock to Asclepius. Earlier we drew attention to this incongruous aspect of Socrates' life. What could it mean?

A rather scathing explanation was offered by Lactantius (c. 240–c. 320). He judged Socrates' actions to be not those of a wise man but of a deranged mind. Note his words in the famous *Divine Institutes:*

> For who can dare to find fault with the superstitions of the Egyptians, when Socrates confirmed them at Athens by his authority? But was it not a mark of consummate vanity, that before his death he asked his friends to sacrifice for him a cock which he had vowed to Aesculapius? . . . I should consider him most mad if he had died under the influence of disease. But since he did this in his sound mind, he who thinks that he was wise is himself of unsound mind.[187]

Such a critique reflects more the "Christianity" of Lactantius—the *Divine Institutes* were replies to attacks against Christianity by a philosopher—than the motives behind Socrates' apparently incongruous actions on his deathbed.

One of the best explanations of Socrates' instruction is provided by Tertullian.[188] In his *Apology*, Tertullian offered the explanation that Socrates customarily said: " 'If the demon grant permission.' Yet he, too, though in denying the existence of your divinities he had a glimpse of the truth, at his dying ordered a cock to be sacrificed to Aesculapius, I believe in honour of his father for Apollo pronounced Socrates the wisest of men." [189]

For approximately two thousand years, when the serpent is seen in the text, two categorically different interpretations of John 3:14–15 have been offered. One regards the serpent only as symbolic of evil. The other views the serpent as symbolic of life. Both frequently placard Moses' serpent as a typology of Christ. Four fourth-century authors who should help us understand the proper exegesis have been chosen to make this point: Ephrem Syrus (c. 306–373), Cyril of Jerusalem (c. 315–387), Gregory Nazianzus (329/30–389/90), and Ambrose (c. 339–397).

Ephrem Syrus, under the influence of the Fourth Gospel, perceived the parallel between Jesus' cross and the serpent.[190] In his *Hymns on the Nativity,* Ephrem offers this exegesis and hermeneutic: "His cross would eat the serpent up that had eaten Adam and Eve. Moses saw the uplifted serpent that had cured the bites of asps, and he looked to see Him who would heal the ancient serpent's wound." [191]

The link between Christ and the serpent is also stressed in the exegesis of John 3:14–15 by Cyril of Jerusalem. In his *Catechetical Lectures,* Cyril presents an interpretation of John 3:14–15 clarifying the comparison as focused not on the verb, "to lift up," but on the serpent as a typology of Christ: "This was the figure which Moses completed by fixing the serpent to a cross, that whoso had been bitten by the living serpent, and looked to the brazen serpent, might be saved by believing. Does then the brazen serpent save when crucified, and shall not the Son of God incarnate save when crucified also?" [192]

The paradigmatic opposite interpretation of Ephrem and Cyril is presented by Gregory of Nazianzus. In his *The Second Oration on Easter,* Gregory claims that the serpent is not a type of Christ because it was so evil it deserved to be destroyed. Note his apparent insensitivity to the wide range of serpent symbology:

> But that brazen serpent was hung up as a remedy for the biting serpent, not as a type of Him that suffered for us, but as a contrast; and it saved those that looked upon it, not because they believed it to live, but because it was killed, and killed with it the powers that were subject to it, being destroyed as it deserved. And what is the fitting epitaph for it from us? "O death, where is thy sting? O grave, where is thy victory?" Thou art overthrown by the Cross; thou art slain by Him who is the Giver of life; thou art without breath, dead, without motion, even though thou keepest the form of a serpent lifted up on high on a pole.[193]

A similar exegesis of John 3 was provided by Ambrose, who subsequently influenced Augustine. In his *Of the Holy Spirit*,[194] Ambrose offered the following interpretation that reflects a preoccupation with the negative image of the serpent:

> And well did the Lord ordain that by the lifting up of the brazen *serpent* the wounds of those who were bitten should be healed; for the brazen *serpent* is a type of the Cross; for although in His flesh Christ was lifted up, yet in Him was the Apostle crucified to the world and the world to him; for he says: "The world hath been crucified unto me, and I unto the world."(1) So the world was crucified in its allurements, and therefore not a real but a brazen *serpent* was hanged; because the Lord took on Him the likeness of a sinner, in the truth. Indeed, of His Body, but without the truth of sin, that imitating a *serpent* through the deceitful appearance of human weakness, having laid aside the slough of the flesh, He might destroy the cunning of the true *serpent*. And therefore in the Cross of the Lord, which came to man's help in avenging temptation, I, who accept the medicine of the Trinity, recognize in the wicked the offence against the Trinity.[195]

The verbosity should not camouflage the fact that the serpent symbolizes sin, weakness, and the Liar.[196]

Ephrem Syrus and Cyril of Jerusalem comprehended the typology I am convinced was intended by the Fourth Evangelist: the serpent is a type of the Son in the Fourth Gospel. Unfortunately, modern commentators either have been blind to the serpent symbolism that expresses the masterful insights in John 3:13–16 or have followed Gregory and Ambrose. Perhaps more now will see the wisdom and perceptions of the Fourth Evangelist as Cyril and Ephrem did.

SUMMARY

We began this study with questions that arose from focused reflections on John 3:14–15. Our central question may be rephrased: "How, why, and in what ways, if at all, is Jesus compared to Moses' upraised serpent?" We observed that the commentators on the Fourth Gospel failed to raise this question adequately and to explore the meaning of serpent symbolism in antiquity. Over one hundred years ago, commentators placed the Greek text of the Fourth Gospel on their desks and surrounded themselves with ancient sources. They asked: "What did the text mean in the first century?" In recent decades, the computer is placed on the desk. The Greek text is to the left and commentators are customarily surrounded by other commentaries. The question has changed; scholars ask: "What have others recently been saying about this text?" Commentaries now are too often "rush jobs" to meet publishers' deadlines. Far too often, regurgitation of others' thoughts replaces creative fresh reflection on what an author and his or her audience would have imagined a text to mean or suggest.

By focusing on one text and one central question and by exploring serpent symbolism, we obtained many surprising insights and were challenged by the creative mind of the Fourth Evangelist. We have seen how normal images of snakes were in antiquity and that the serpent symbolized, inter alia, life and eternal life. The serpent was a perfect image for portraying the theology of the Fourth Evangelist. In the Fourth Gospel we do not confront "one of the strangest images for Jesus Christ in Scripture." [197]

What are the significant discoveries of our exploration into John 3:13–16? Here is a summary of the major insights.

The intended thought is not only "to lift up." The Fourth Evangelist stresses the descent of the Son of Man (3:13) and his ascent again to his Father. In this narrative context, the lifting up of a serpent on a pole symbolizes Jesus on the cross.

The "as" and "so" construction of John 3:14 defines two clauses. The adverbs reveal the Evangelist's thought: "[A]s Moses lifted up the serpent . . . so it is necessary for the Son of Man to be lifted up."

The impersonal verb "it is necessary" does not refer only to the crucifixion. The Fourth Evangelist uses this construction to refer to the fulfillment of God's purpose revealed in Scripture. It thus refers to both crucifixion and resurrection (20:9; cf. also Mk 8:31).[198] Thus, serpent symbolism is apparent in 3:14; the serpent is the primary symbol for signifying new or renewed life (Pos. 26), and unending or eternal life (3:15 and 3:16; cf. Pos. 27).

The poetic structure of 3:14–15 is synonymous *parallelismus membrorum*. The serpent in stichos one is parallel to the Son of Man, Jesus, in stichos two.

The grammar of 3:14 points to the identity of the Son of Man as the serpent; only "serpent" and "Son of Man" are placed in the accusative case and aligned. John 3:15 has one noun in the accusative case: "eternal life." Thus, the thought moves from "serpent" to "Son of Man" and then to "eternal life." Looking up to the Son of Man and believing in him reveal the continuing influence of Numbers 21 and the life-giving serpent who symbolizes eternal life. The influence of ophidian symbology becomes clear: The serpent symbolizes life and immortality (Pos. 20 and 27).

A study of ophidian symbology in antiquity clarifies, sometimes for the first time, some major dimensions of the theology and Christology of the Fourth Gospel. To summarize:

1. Jesus is the Son of Man who is like the upraised serpent that gives life

to those who look up to him and believe. The Fourth Evangelist describes Jesus' crucifixion so that only his mother and the Beloved Disciple are narratively described looking up to Jesus on the cross (19:26–27, 35).

The serpent raised up by Moses is a typology of the Son of Man, Christ. The history of salvation does not begin at the baptism. As the Fourth Evangelist made clear in the Prologue to his Gospel, it began "in the beginning." That is, Jesus' life must be understood from the perspective of God's actions in history and foreshadowing in Scripture, especially Genesis 1:1, "In the beginning . . ."

2. As God gave life to those who looked up to the serpent and believed God's promise, so Jesus gives life to all who look up to him and believe in him. By looking up to Jesus, lifted up on the cross, one is looking not only at an antitype—the upraised serpent, the crucified Jesus. One is looking up to heaven—the world above. It is from there that the Johannine Jesus has come and is returning. He, the Son of Man, alone descended to earth (3:13) to prepare a place for those who follow him. In the words of conservative Old Testament scholar R. K. Harrison: "In the same way that the ancient Israelite was required to look in faith at the bronze serpent to be saved from death, so the modern sinner must also look in faith at the crucified Christ to receive the healing of the new birth (Jn 3:14–16)." [199]

3. Trust or believing is required so that God through the serpent and Jesus can provide life to all who look up to the means of healing and new life, including eternal life. No other New Testament author employs the verb "to believe" as frequently and deeply as the Fourth Evangelist. He chooses it, and accentuates it pervasively, and he indicates the dynamic quality of "believing" by avoiding the noun "faith."

4. The paradigmatic importance of "up" and "above," so significant for Johannine Christology, is heightened by a recognition that Jesus represents the serpent raised up above the earth. It helps us understand the double entendre Jesus is making while talking with Nicodemus. Jesus tells Nicodemus he must be born *anōthen,* which is a wordplay denoting both "again," and "above."

5. The serpent was chosen symbolically to indicate healing in the cult of Asclepius. The same symbol was used in Jewish groups contemporaneous with the Fourth Gospel. Later "Jews" and "Christians" created and employed amulets that depict the powers of Yahweh with serpent feet or other features taken from serpent iconography. Ophidian symbolism and iconography help us comprehend why the Fourth Evangelist indicates that Jesus, as the serpent, provides healing for all who turn to him.

6. We have seen ample evidence that the serpent is a symbol of immortality or resurrection in many segments of the culture in which the Fourth Gospel took shape. This dimension of serpent symbolism may be seen as

Figure 84. Jewish-Gnostic Amulet Showing Lion, Stork, Scorpion, Serpent, and Ram [?]. Greek inscription: IAW (= Yahweh, God's name in Hebrew), Sabaō (Sabaoth), Michael. Third–fifth centuries CE. Jerusalem? JHC Collection

undergirding the thought expressed by the Fourth Evangelist. Indeed, the Fourth Gospel appears to be a blurred mirror in which we see reflected discussions on this topic in the Johannine community, school, or circle.

7. Finally, Numbers 21:8–9 is a text used intertextually by the Fourth Evangelist. It helps shape his narrative and enables him to present the profundity of his Christology. We have also seen that Moses' upraised serpent was a subject of interest for many Jews (viz. in Wis 16, Philo's *Leg.* 2 and *Agr.* 94). A study of the Fourth Gospel needs to be informed by such Jewish exegesis of Genesis 3 and Numbers 21. In light of such traditions, it becomes clearer how and why the Fourth Evangelist perceived Jesus' crucifixion. The crucifixion was not a failure; it was a necessity and mirrors Jesus' exaltation and return to the world above.

8. The Fourth Evangelist shapes his thoughts and symbols by the use of the light–darkness paradigm. Johannine thought is enriched by the recognition that the serpent god is depicted as controlling light and darkness. According to an excerpt that Philo of Byblos derived from a "sacred scribe," when the serpent opened his eyes, "there was light" and when he shut his eyes "there was darkness." [200] For those in the Johannine community who were deeply influenced by the power of serpent symbolism, this allegorical imagery would help them understand a key passage: "I am the

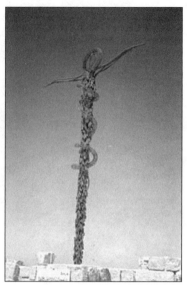

Figure 85. *Left.* Serpent on Cross. Picture, "St Virgil," in the Bildunghaus in Salzburg. Courtesy of Professor P. Hofrichter.

Figure 86. *Right.* Serpent on Cross. Mount Nebo. Modern. JHC

light of the world" (8:12; cf. 3:19, 12:35–36).[201] There should be no doubt that some who read the Fourth Gospel in antiquity would have seen Jesus in light of serpent symbolism. Both symbolized light (Pos. 3 and 7).

As we have already seen when studying Genesis 3, artists often serve as more perceptive biblical exegetes than biblical scholars. That is because they must live in the scene and story depicted, imagine all descriptions, and then transpose the prose and poetry into art.

Artists sometimes depict Jesus as a serpent on a cross. Two examples must suffice. One is in a painting in a church in Salzburg. The cross is clear, as is the serpent who symbolizes Jesus. On Mount Nebo today, Numbers 21 conflates with John 3. Not a stake but a cross is artistically depicted. The one on it is clearly a serpent who represents Jesus.

The Warburg Institute in London has collected many symbolic representations of the Son of Man (Jesus) as the serpent, according to John 3:14. Two examples may now be chosen to make the point that artists, under the influence of John 3:14, often see Jesus as a serpent on the cross. In his *S. Ioannes,* Jacques Callot (1592–1635) depicted a person kneeling and praying beside a small staff on which a serpent is entwined; a large tree is above both. Wolf Huber, also named Barthel Beham (1502–40), portrayed Jesus on the cross and to the left of him is the serpent on the pole.[202]

Other examples may be mentioned, but I shall limit my presentation to

Figure 87. *Mater Auxiliatrix.* Naples. JHC

just three.[203] First, a lead sarcophagus in Jerusalem, from the early Christian period, shows a cross with serpent feet. The imagery most likely derives from imaginative reflections on John 3:14. Second, the upper part of a gravestone, found perhaps in Luxor in 1906, contains a cross under which are two serpents with heads uplifted.[204] Third, a pottery figure from Drenthe in the Netherlands shows a large serpent coiling upward and around a cross or outstretched arms. As Leclercq concluded, most likely the figure represents the serpent of the wilderness as a symbol of Christ.[205] The ceramic figure thus was an interpretation of John 3:14 that equated "the Son of Man" with the serpent that Moses lifted up in the wilderness.

The painting in Fig. 87 focuses the viewer's attention on Jesus with Mary, a saint, and, most important, centered between them a cup with two upraised serpents. What does this picture symbolize? Is it possible that a gifted artist has created a scene that is based on an insightful interpretation of John 3:14–16? If so, this meaning has been lost for those who have studied it, as I learned talking with a priest who published a work devoted to it. The colorful painting seems to mystify those who focus on it. In order to perceive the in-depth meaning of this painting, I have divided the following presentation into facts, opinions, and my own explanation.

Facts. The painting has been moved many times. It was originally in the convent of Santa Maria di Casarlano, a village that is presently incorporated within Sorrento. The impressive painting is now in a chapel, Cappella del Noviziato, on an upper floor within Gesù Nuovo, the Jesuit residence in downtown Naples. The date of composition and the artist are unknown. Thus, any basis for interpretation cannot appeal to date or creator. What is the meaning of this picture? What do the two serpents symbolize?

Opinions. Some priests in Naples told me that the painting may have been composed to celebrate the founding of the convent, Santa Maria di Casarlano. If so, then the work would have been created about 1496. I asked a Jesuit who had studied the painting what the meaning of the two serpents was. He was drawn primarily to the dominant figure of the Virgin Mary, and admitted that, perhaps, the serpents represented some heresy. He confessed that he did not know.

My Interpretation. The painting has been moved because of embarrassment. Many consider the images of serpents in a cup to be heretical.

The painting is probably not connected with the founding of the convent.[206] It is later than the fifteenth century. It did exist in the sixteenth century because the Turks—who sought to desecrate a celebration of Christian symbols—shoved their swords and knives into it in 1558.[207] Its style seems to connect the painting with the school of Giotto. One may surmise that the painting dates from the middle of the sixteenth century.[208]

Why is the painting impressive? Most viewers have been drawn to it because of the beatific view of the Virgin Mary. She is the dominant figure, situated in the middle and elevated above the males on her right and left. She is feminine and attractive, especially as she leans her cheek adoringly on the head of the Christ child. One can appreciate why the "Madonna di Casarlano" is revered "come *Auxilium Christianorum*" or, more affectionately, *"Mater Auxiliatrix."*[209]

Our gaze is riveted by an unusual detail. A man, obviously a saint, holds a cup, but this is no ordinary depiction of the chalice. From it two small serpents ascend.[210] Prominence is given to the two bifid tongues. Who is the man holding the chalice? What is the meaning of the two serpents? Why are two depicted?

As one stands before the painting, one sees a man on the left (not shown). He is John the Baptizer, who is revealed by the animal skin around his chest. The man on the right is John, perceived to be the Beloved Disciple. He is the one who holds the cup with the two serpents.[211]

Two major questions arise: What is the meaning of the cup? What do the two serpents symbolize?

Alan Culpepper shared with me his impression that the cup with the serpents might signify the manner in which John the Evangelist died.[212] According to some texts and legends, John was forced to drink poison or was killed by a deadly snake.[213] This interpretation rightly grounds an interpretation with the Fourth Evangelist, but it focuses again only on the negative meaning of serpent symbolism.[214] If the serpents represented death, then why are Mary and John the Evangelist portrayed oblivious of any danger? If the cup is a chalice, then it represented Jesus' blood. It symbolized the source of eternal life, which—as we have seen—is first and foremost associated with the serpent in the first century CE.

The cup appears to represent the chalice in which the Eucharist contains the blood of Christ. The identification of John the Evangelist shows that the correct interpretation of the symbolism of this painting is to be found in the Fourth Gospel. And the only mention of the "serpent" in this Gospel is found at 3:14. While John the Baptizer points to the Virgin with his right hand, John the Evangelist lifts the chalice with two serpents in his right hand.[215]

The serpents do not seem to have negative meaning because they do not startle the baby, Virgin, or Evangelist. The serpent closest to the Virgin seems almost to touch her, but rather than threatening her with his deadly fangs, he seems to be communicating power and immortality through his tongue. The other serpent seems to be pointing the viewer' eye toward heaven. The most arresting aspect of the painting is also its spark of creativity: the serpents lift themselves up from the chalice.

Two serpents are depicted, perhaps, to remind the observer of the caduceus (cf. Fig. 5). The bifid tongue indicates the power of the serpents, which are clearly poisonous (as indicated by the triangular head). An exegesis of Genesis 3 or Numbers 21, whereby a serpent brings death, seems "checkmated" by the serpent, Christ, who restores life and promises "eternal life" (Jn 3:14–15). As indicated by the caduceus and pointed out in our exegesis of Numbers 21, the serpent who brings death is bested by the serpent who brings life. As Moses lifted up a serpent, and Jesus, the Son of Man, was lifted up on a cross, the two serpents are lifted up out of the chalice.

The unknown artist depicts a pensive John the Evangelist holding his Gospel in the left hand and lifting up the chalice with two serpents in his right hand. The artist seems to be stressing that the cup of Christ's blood brings immortality; the appropriate symbol for this thought is the serpent (Pos. 27). The artist knew the meaning of John 3:14–15: "the serpent" symbolizes that "the Son of Man" provides "eternal life" to all who look up to him and believe in him. The full symbolism breaks forth on observers when they realize what is on each side of the Virgin: John the Baptizer holds a wooden cross, John the Evangelist lifts up two serpents. Thus, she is framed by a cross and serpents. Our examination of serpent symbolism thus allows us to conclude that the symbolism in this painting is grounded in John 3:14–15.

We now turn to a painting in Hawaii; it is similar to the one in the Cappella del Noviziato. The painting shows a woman or man before a chalice with a serpent curled over it. The art is by Piero di Cosimo of the fifteenth century. It is now in the Samuel H. Kress Collection, Honolulu Academy of Arts, Honolulu, Hawaii.[216] This painting is also an interpretation of John 3:14–15. The chalice contains an inexhaustible supply of Christ's blood, the symbol of eternal life (Pos. 26, 27). The complexity of ophidian symbolism probably inspired Piero di Cosimo.

The serpents in the chalice that contains Christ's blood are indicative of the immortality symbolized by the "serpent" imagery in John 3:14. One is reminded of the teaching of Ignatius of Antioch: The Eucharist is "the medicine of immortality."[217] A fourth-century amulet with Samaritan writing, a cross, and a serpent may also indicate an interpretation of Christ's death as regeneration and eternal life.[218]

CONCLUSION

We have observed something remarkable and revealing. Modern scholars who work on the theology and Christology of the Fourth Gospel stress that 3:14 refers only to the "lifting up" of Jesus. Those who have focused on symbology and iconography perceive only that Jesus is symbolized as the serpent. In the present work, we have learned that each of these is only partially correct. The truth entails both: the typology entails both Jesus' being lifted up *and* his portrayal as the serpent on the pole or cross.

J. Asurmendi explains how the serpent symbolism of Numbers 21 was transformed into a spiritual symbol by the Fourth Evangelist. He argues that the typological analogy is between the serpent and the Son of Man ("El famoso texto opera una analogía entre la serpiente y el Hijo del hombre"). Asurmendi contends that "the serpent has been transformed by the Fourth Evangelist into the Son of Man" ("la serpiente se convierte en del Hombre").[219] This seems to be a perception of many early readers of the Fourth Gospel and perhaps many in the Johannine circle, but it is not clearly developed by the Fourth Evangelist.

In *Le Tohu-bohu, le Serpent et le bon Dieu,* A. Houziaux points out that no animal receives such an important place in the Hebrew Bible as the serpent. Indeed, we have seen that serpent symbolism appears at the beginning of Genesis, reappears in Exodus with Moses' magical staff, and explodes with symbolic significance in the wilderness with Moses uplifting a copper serpent on a pole. This famous and paradigmatic episode in the wilderness shapes the early centuries of worship in the Temple. Finally, Hezekiah destroys the copper serpent in the Jerusalem Temple. What about the Fourth Gospel? Houziaux, unlike other Johannine experts, contends that in John 3:14 the serpent became the symbol for Christ being lifted on a cross.[220] It seems clear from our research that as Moses' bronze serpent represented God's saving of those dying in the wilderness, so Jesus on the cross symbolized the saving of all humanity.[221] As H. Lesêtre stated: "Jesus was raised on his cross like the serpent on his pole" ("Notre-Seigneur sera donc dressé sur sa croix comme le serpent sur son poteau").[222]

In his thirty-seventh homily on the Fourth Gospel, John Chrysostom explained why Jesus did not simply declare: "I am about to be crucified." Jesus wanted his hearers to think about the analogy with the Old Testament, because "the old order was akin to the new." Note that Chrysostom sees more than merely a parallel between the *lifting up* of the serpent and the *lifting up of Jesus*. The parallel is also between the serpent and Jesus:

> In the former, the uplifted serpent healed the bites of serpents;
> in the latter, the crucified Jesus healed the wounds inflicted by
>   the spiritual dragon.
> In the former, he who looked with these eyes of earth was
>   healed;
> in the latter, he who gazes with the eyes of his mind lays aside all
>   his sins.

Chrysostom sees indeed a parallel between Jesus and the serpent: "In the former, there was the uplifted brass fashioned in the likeness of a serpent; in the latter, the Lord's body formed by the Spirit."[223]

It should not be surprising to see Jesus (the Son of Man) as a serpent. According to the Fourth Evangelist, Jesus was the One-who-was-to-come. One of his favorite Scriptures was the Book of Isaiah. This eighth-century prophet claimed that the One-who-was-to-come would be a serpent. Recall, Isaiah's prophecy:

> Rejoice not, all you of Philistia,
> Because the rod that struck you is broken;
> For out of the serpent's root shall come forth a pit viper,
> And his offspring shall be a flying serpent. [Isa 14:29]

Clearly, the serpent in the wilderness is a symbol of the Son of Man, Jesus, the Christ, according to the Fourth Evangelist.[224]

Conclusion

We have successfully fulfilled all six criteria established at the outset: (1) An abundance of evidence, iconographical and literary, has been amassed to prove that the serpent not only represented negative thoughts and concepts but also has often been a good symbol in world cultures. (2) The serpent was frequently admired in Old Testament times, not only in Near Eastern cultures but also within ancient Israel. The Yahwist in Genesis 3 portrays the Nachash as a beast of the field created by Yahweh God. He or she can talk and appears to represent the truth better than the Creator. The Brazen Serpent is created under God's orders so that those who look up toward it and trust in God's healing do not die but live. (3) The serpent was appreciated positively in the Greek and Roman periods. All the leading deities, especially Zeus, Apollo, Athena, Hermes, Asclepius, and Hygieia, were represented as serpents or are shown with serpents. (4) The serpent was sometimes a positive symbol in Judaism before and during the time of the Fourth Evangelist. (5) We found an exegesis of Numbers 21 by a Jew who lived in the same century as the Fourth Evangelist, and the Jewish expositor Philo stresses the positive symbolism of the Brazen Serpent (also see the *m. Rosh Hash.* and the *Mekilta* of Rabbi Yishmael).[1] (6) The Fourth Evangelist does not cavalierly treat the symbolism of the serpent he inherits directly from the text of Numbers 21, and he is indebted to Jewish reflections on the formative and well-known upraised serpent of Moses. The Evangelist is most likely also significantly influenced by ophidian symbology in his environment. He appreciates the power and positive dimensions of serpent symbolism, reflecting the prevalent viewpoint that the serpent symbolizes life and eternal life.

Finally, we may summarize the high points of my six years spent exploring ancient serpent iconography and symbolism. We started with one focused question, which arose from studying John 3:14–15: "What did the serpent symbolize in antiquity?" This focal question led to many others; in fact, over sixty questions ultimately appeared from examining Genesis 3.

We learned that the serpent is the most multivalent of all symbols. We recognized that serpent symbology should be categorized; indeed, the serpent symbolized sixteen negative and twenty-nine positive meanings, concepts, or ideas. This taxonomy was often grounded in serpent physiology (and ophiology). We observed that in the first century CE the dominant meaning of serpent symbology was positive. One reason was the serpent's association with the emperors (along with their quislings like Herod and Archelaus) and especially the healing god, Asclepius (see esp. Figs. 1, 58–60).

We comprehended that the serpent appears significantly in creation myths in all known cultures. These extended from Mesopotamia to Egypt, and from the Middle East and Africa to Mexico and Australia. A study of shared serpent symbols led us to appreciate the commonality of the human, even if in the Levant, Egyptian, Mesopotamian, and especially Canaanite symbolism influenced the great minds of ancient Israel, particularly the Yahwist, the author of Psalm 68 (David?), and Isaiah and his school.

We noted that Old Testament scholars often, and New Testament experts usually are insufficiently trained in iconography and symbology. The richest collection of books shaped by symbolism is clearly the Bible; yet Scripture is habitually read, even by the savants, without an informed perception of the world of symbols that stimulated the authors. Consistently, texts are studied without the requisite sensitivity to iconography and the meaning of symbols in the contexts that produced them. Most important, we saw that the biblical experts were often blind to the complex and rich serpent symbolism in Genesis 3, Numbers 21, and John 3.

We discovered that serpent symbolism in the Middle East absorbed many contradictory meanings—light and darkness, life and death, good and evil, Satan and God. The serpent ceased to be a dominantly positive symbol in our culture about the fourth century CE. Why? Perhaps serpent symbolism ceased (beginning with Eusebius) being widely perceived as multivalent because the image and symbol became so heavy with diverse meanings that it lacked clarity. Perhaps more so, the serpent became a predominantly negative symbol in Western culture (despite the serpents on medical notes and prescriptions) because of the leading minds in the triumphant Church. On the one hand, they were over-influenced by the negative serpent symbolism of "the final book of the Bible," Revelation 12. On the other hand, they sought to establish Christianity against some powerful and well-established religions; that is, they developed Christological symbols that would replace Hermes' caduceus and especially Asclepius' and Hygieia's serpent (see Fig. 60). Subsequently, in Judaism, Christianity, and Islam, the serpent ceased to be a multivalent symbol. In Western and Near Eastern cultures, the symbol of the serpent devolved until it became a synonym for Satan.

What was our most surprising discovery? There was more than one.

It was startling to discover the linguistic brilliance of the Yahwist, who lived about the same time as Homer. He was gifted with language. But he could not systematize all the previous and diverse folklore and myths into one coherent Eden Story. Was his creation marred by the clash of Canaanite and Israelite cultures (Kulturkampf)? Or was his story confused because the diverse mythologies, shaped by oral and literary history, simply could not be merged with the emerging new religion, Yahwism? The latter seems likely. Although Yahwism derives ultimately from Moses, it was shaped more definitively from 1100 to 800 BCE.

The Nachash appears suddenly in the Eden Story. Slowly it became apparent, through our research, that "Nachash" should not be translated as "serpent" in Genesis 3:1 because he is a "beast of the field" (3:1 = 3:14) and because he is transformed by God's curse (Gen 3:14). Jews who have given us documents in the Pseudepigrapha and in Rabbinics wisely imagined that the Nachash lost his legs when Yahweh God cursed him and was forevermore condemned "to walk" on his belly as a serpent.

Thus, it is surprising to hear, almost constantly, in many settings that "the serpent tempted Eve." As we have demonstrated, this one short sentence contains three misconceptions. The Nachash in Genesis 3:1 is a "beast of the field." The woman has not yet been named "Eve." The Nachash does not tempt; it asks the woman a question. These discoveries reveal that exegesis has been too focused on philology and lexicography; it needs to be enriched by symbology, narrative exegesis, and especially an immersion in the context of the text.

Why did the serpent lose most of its pellucid symbolic power in the work of the Yahwist? Was it because of the threatening power of serpent symbolism among the Canaanites (and Jebusites in and near Jerusalem)?

Yahweh God is portrayed as one who could not tell "the truth, the whole truth, and nothing but the truth." God is the one who receives the credit (really blame) for a woman's pains in childbirth and a man's fruitless toiling with a hardened earth (was not the earth also cursed?). Why is God so miscast?

Yet Yahweh God appears alive in the world created by the Yahwist. He knew that idolizing God and portraying God as perfect removes God from the human world. The Yahwist seems to have grasped a thought lost in recent theological works. He seems to have perceived that a deity can become a god only by entering the human realm. He also probably grasped that such a journey demands obtaining some human characteristics. Thus, anthropomorphism is a divine feature that weds the divine and human worlds.

We were astounded by the ancients' thoughtful attachment to a living being, the earth. They lived close to snakes, who knew the water, earth, and subterranean regions in ways unimagined by humans. The snake is not to be dreaded. The serpent is to be admired; it will not attack until threatened. Its venom is reserved for killing a prey that is necessary for survival.

Why is the serpent to be admired? Snakes have survived on this planet longer than humans—well over seventy million years longer. And the serpent is celebrated by Jews and Greeks as the animal who has wisdom. What an accomplishment! The snake was elevated above all beasts of the field, even though it could not close its eyes, cannot hear, and has to swallow its food whole, often by dislocating its jaw. It must slither on the earth without feet or arms.

The story of the serpent in our culture is a tale of how the most beautiful creature became seen as ugly, the admired became despised, the good was misrepresented as the bad, and a god was dethroned and recast as Satan. Why? Is it perhaps because we modern humans have moved farther and farther away from nature, cutting the umbilical cord with our mother: earth?

We came eventually to the Fourth Gospel. We saw that the Son of Man, Jesus, was a typos of Moses' upraised serpent. As God told Moses to make a metal serpent and lift him (or her) up on a pole so those bitten might live by looking up through him (or her) to God's power of healing revealed through him (or her), so God announces that it is necessary for Jesus to be lifted up on the cross so that all who believe in him may have eternal life through him. We observed in John 3:14–15 the poetic *parallelismus membrorum* that clarifies a parallel between "the serpent" and the Son of Man, Jesus. We perceived that the positive features of the serpent, regnant in the time and culture of the Fourth Evangelist, are harmonious with Johannine Christology: Jesus comes from above to bring life and eternal life to those on the earth. We speculated about possibilities in which an ophidian Christology may have existed behind the Fourth Gospel and within the Johannine community or school. We wondered to what extent serpent imagery and symbolism is mirrored, perhaps imperfectly, in the present, heavily edited, narrative of the Fourth Gospel.

We were amazed at the power in symbols. For reflecting minds, they create an exciting world of thought and imagination. The Yahwist gives us an Eden Story that is known throughout the world. We humans who know the Eden Story dream of a far-off day when God appears in the cool of the evening, takes our hand, and walks with us in Paradise. In such an environment are animals, especially a serpent that is attractive and converses with us, asking questions?

Epilogue

We have searched for the meaning of serpent symbolism over time and through all known cultures. We have perused ophiology, and exposed ophiophilism and ophiolatry.[1] We have pointed to the distorted exegesis of the Ophites who simplified the complex ophidian symbolism of John 3, in which Jesus is "like" Moses' upraised serpent. They erred in seeing Jesus as a snake.

Now we shall conclude by reflecting on one of the great masters of symbolism in our own time. He preserves the ancient richness of serpent symbology. His name is Marc Chagall. Again, our observations must be succinct and selective.

Through his genius with vivid and living colors, Chagall painted the scene envisioned by the author of Genesis 3:6: "And the woman saw the tree [was] good for food, and that it was pleasant to the eyes, and a tree desirable to make [one] wise. Then she took of its fruit and ate. And she gave [the fruit] also to her husband [who was] with her; and he ate." To the right of center of the painting, which is now on public display in the Musée National in Nice, are two nudes, in pale blue; they are holding each other. The woman lifts up her right hand and offers Adam a bright red apple. They are contented and peaceful. Behind them, in bright red, is the tree of life.

Around the tree curls a serpent whose colors blend with its surroundings. The serpent is thus green at the bottom and red at the top. Its face features a broad smile; it also seems happy. The serpent is certainly not dangerous or threatening.

Chagall returned to the image of the serpent again when he created the stained-glass windows for the Fraumünster in Zurich. The scene also is paradisiacal. The time, however, is the future. Chagall was trying to represent the time from the giving of the Torah to Moses to the end of time. The effect of his work is so significant in itself and as a fitting conclusion to a study on the meaning of serpent symbolism that it deserves more than a perfunctory presentation.

The Chagall windows are placed in the restored late-Romanesque chancel in the Fraumünster. They are featured within five vertically curvilinear windows. The chancel, dating from 1250 CE, is a simple yet austere feature of the Fraumünster, which contained colored windows as early as the ninth century. Chagall is reputed to have fallen in love with the chancel, stating that he felt it was there that he could best express his biblical images in a holy setting. In fact, he went to Rheims to paint the figures on the glass surfaces in grisaille.

It is surprising how Christian symbols are featured in the work of an artist who comes from a strict and Orthodox Jewish background in Eastern Europe. Russian icon paintings, with their interpretations of Christian symbols, seem to be what first instilled in Chagall a means for expressing ideas and feelings in art. And his chosen themes were usually derived from biblical stories. At the center of Chagall's work is frequently a portrayal of the obedience and suffering of God's chosen people; at the heart of the art is often Jesus' crucifixion.

This focal point comes into blazing view in the right window of the chancel in the Fraumünster in Zürich; that is, in the "Law" Window on the south side.[2] Here Chagall's oeuvre reaches a rare burst of perfection, and he chose to achieve it in a grand scale (9.77 meters high by 0.96 meters wide). This far right window is primarily dark blue with drippings of red, perhaps representing blood that increases in volume as it proceeds downward. At the top, suspended above the tortured world, is a depiction of an enthroned Moses receiving the Torah. The tables of the Law are in vivid white, stressing the purity and truthfulness inherent in them. Rays of light from Moses' head denote his exalted status. A space separates this scene with the depiction of disobedience and suffering, culminating in Jesus' crucifixion—a band of red streaks through Jesus' chest and heart. Such colorful details provide their own hermeneutic.

As our eye continues downward, we see a blue space that separates this scene from a depiction of the Kingdom of Peace and the appearance of the Messiah to come. The Messiah is depicted in living red. Beneath him is an imaginative reconstruction of Isaiah receiving the message of peace.

Only one item has not yet been mentioned. It is what is held in the left hand of the coming Messiah. What is it?

As one might have guessed by now, it is an upraised serpent. The serpent is larger than the Messiah. While Moses and Jesus occupy two panels, the serpent fills two and parts of two more. That is, the serpent occupies about twice as much space as the other dominant figures. Appropriately for our improved perception of serpent symbolism, the serpent is depicted in off-white.

Most important, the serpent is the dominant figure in the depiction of "The Kingdom of Peace of the Messiah to Come." Here Chagall seems to have captured the prophecy of Isaiah 11, which was so instrumental in shaping the concept of the Messiah, the Christ, by author of the *Psalms of Solomon*. Note now, Isaiah 11:8, the infant shall play over "the cobra's hole" and the child shall dance over "the viper's nest." The serpent, the feared one, is transformed back into the adored one through Chagall's brilliant exegesis of scripture. The restoration of creation is symbolized by the retransformation of the Nachash. Has not Marc Chagall urged us to return to the source of our expressive symbols and recover the positive force primordially inherent in ophidian symbolism?

Appendix I: Biblical Hebrew Terms for Various Types of Snakes

Prolegomena: Caveats

Perfunctory readers of the Hebrew Bible tend to think that there is only one word for "snake" or "serpent" (נחש).[1] More learned individuals might be able to suggest, in addition, נחש, אפעה, עכשוב, פתן, שרף, שרפים, שפיפן, and לויתן.[2] That would indicate that the erudite Semitist knew eight words for "serpent" in the Hebrew Bible. Over a century ago in one of the most informed publications on the serpent in the Bible, the learned scholar T. K. Cheyne reported that in the TANAKH (or Old Testament) "writers use eleven different words for serpents of one kind or another."[3] This number appears again in *The International Standard Bible Encyclopedia,* "Fully Revised" in 1988.[4]

Are there eleven different nouns for a "snake" or "serpent" in the Hebrew Bible? Many readers of the Bible will find that number exaggerated. In fact, I have discovered that there are eighteen different nouns for "snake" or "serpent" in the Hebrew Bible.[5] These nouns are sometimes interrelated Hebrew terms for various types of snakes. I have been surprised to discover that many of these nouns for a snake appear only once in the Hebrew Bible; these *hapax legomena* frequently occur in the Book of Isaiah.[6]

No one will be able to discern which type of snake each Hebrew noun designated, not only because different names were given to the same reptile in ancient Palestine (as in modern Israel and Palestine today),[7] but also because the ancient Hebrew-speaking sages were not interested in a taxonomy of ophiolatry. Yet it would be unwise and misrepresentative to translate so many different nouns with the one word "serpent." Thus, some order and a better relation between the Hebrew and the English will result if we agree to translate each Hebrew noun with only one English word. This method will establish consistency between the Hebrew and English nouns, and thus avoid the confusion found in translations produced by many different individuals, as in the Septuagint and modern publications of the Bible (notably such distinguished productions as the KJV, the NKJV, the RSV, and the NRSV).[8]

Any good translation strives for consistency and avoids indicating that all authors of books in the Hebrew Bible were simply thinking, unreflectively, about some nondescript snake or asp. Thus, I supply here not only the English supposed equivalent of a Hebrew word but also the various meanings of the ancient Hebrew word. That is, that while consistency in translating is an art and goal, the ancient Hebrews tended to think generically. It is prima facie obvious that נחש appears at times to be synonymous with other terms; for example, it is parallel to זחלי ארץ ("crawling things of the earth") in Micah 7:17, עכשוב ("asp") in Psalm 140:4[3], פתן ("cobra") in Psalm 58:5[4], and צפעונים ("vipers") in Jeremiah 8:17 and Proverbs 23:32. The noun also seems synonymous with לויתן ("Leviathan") and תנין ("dragon") in Isaiah 27:1, and with הנחשים השרפים ("fiery serpents") in Numbers 21:6–7. Obviously, all snakes belong to the reptile family.

Since Egyptian phenomena lie behind some Hebrew thoughts on and images of the snake, it might be helpful to state that reptile in hieroglyphics is *ḏdft,* which gives us the Coptic ϪΑΤϤⲈ. As we attempt to understand ancient herpetofauna, we should remember that the snake remains, even today in some ways, only a partially known reptile.[9]

It is imperative also to stress that biblical scholars and other experts have uncritically assumed, without studying ophidian iconography, that the serpent often, or always, denotes a negative symbol.[10] This tendency reads Paul (2 Cor 11:3) and Augustine back into Genesis 3,[11] and imagines unreflectively that Revelation 12:9 and 20:2 explain Numbers 21:6–9, John 3:14, and *Barnabas* 12:5–7. In light of the professed conviction that we biblical scholars usually strive to understand texts within contexts, it is disconcerting to observe the failure to see the links between the Hebrew Bible and the ancient Palestinian serpent cults (especially at Beth Shan and Hazor). The "religion of Israel" is allowed uncritically to define "the multifarious religions of Israel." Imaging the serpent as dominantly a negative symbol is myopic and uninformed; it fails to engage the complex symbology of the "serpent" in Genesis 3, the traditions concerning Moses' staff, the upraised serpent in the wilderness, as well as the tradition and cultic celebrations in the Jerusalem cult represented by Nechushtan. Moreover, ophidian iconography increased with deeper and wider positive symbolical meanings, especially from circa 1600 BCE to the first-century world, and especially in Minoan and Canaanite cultures, climaxing, in many ways, in the Asclepian cult at Epidaurus[12] and probably also in Jerusalem at Bethzatha.[13]

Only two examples seem necessary. First, to suggest, as too many established scholars have done in widely influential commentaries, that the Seraphim in Isaiah 6:2–7 cannot be examples of serpent symbolism because "serpents do not have feet"[14] misses the fact that they do, not only in ancient iconography,[15] but also in prehistory in the Middle East (the *Haasiophis* with "well-developed hindlimbs"),[16] and in large snakes (in atrophied forms).[17] Ancient iconography showed animals with human elements or creatures with a mixture of animal, reptile, and human elements.[18] The Brooklyn magical papyrus of the fourth or third century BCE depicts a serpent with two human hands and two human feet (Fig. 27).[19] The biblical exegetes who claim that the Seraphim cannot be serpents have not read the early Jewish sources and the evidence that suggests Israelites and even Jews sometimes adored serpents. Such modern scholars, for example, probably have missed the reference in the *Prayer of Jacob* that salutes "the Father of the Patriarchs," the Creator who sits upon "the s[er]pen[t] gods."[20]

Second, to claim that there cannot be any parallel between serpent symbolism and Jesus, the Son of Man, in John 3:14 is to fail to let the images be seen, as O. Keel showed some time ago.[21] Hence, we must avoid the simplistic assumption that the serpent symbolized destruction and powers opposed to God, a position found, for example, in W. Kramp's *Protest der Schlange: Signale zum Umdenken*.[22] It is now becoming obvious that in antiquity the serpent symbolized not only sixteen negative concepts but also twenty-nine positive meanings, including the complex ideas poured into the uraeus, Ouroboros, and caduceus. Moreover, it is now certain that these symbols often shown in works of art covered more than three millennia and were popular in many lands, including the Holy Land.

A List of Words for "Snake" in the Hebrew Bible

In the following chart, I list the major biblical passages, and whether the noun symbolically represents something Positive (P), Negative (N), or Both (B). For convenience, the Hebrew words are presented in alphabetical order.

Term	Translation	Major Biblical Passages	Symbol
1. אפעה	"sand viper"[23]	Isa 30:6, 59:5	N

This Hebrew noun can denote any poisonous snake,[24] yet A. Bahat and M. Mishor suggest אפעה is the *echis colorata*.[25] The noun אפעה is a figure of speech in Job 20:16, "He sucks the poison of cobras; The tongue of the sand viper kills him." The Hebrew *'eph'eh* may be onomatopoetic; that is, it may originate from an attempt to mimic the hissing of a snake.[26] The same may be said about all Hebrew names for a serpent in which *p* or *ph* appear. In Isaiah 30:6 the "sand viper," along with other creatures, especially the lion, are "the beasts of the South" who come from "the land of trouble and anguish," namely, Egypt. In the Hebrew Bible, the verb פעה appears only once, in Isaiah 42:14; it represents the groaning when one is in pain, as a woman in labor. The verb seems cognate to אפעה and the noun would then have arisen from thoughts on the pain when the "sand viper" bit a human.

The translators of the Septuagint rendered the Hebrew noun variously (ὄφις in Job 20:16, ἀσπίδες in Isaiah 30:6, βασιλίσκος [ἔχιδνα in Aquila] in Isa 59:5). The Hebrew אפעה can be equivalent to ἔχιδνα,[27] "viper," in Acts 28:3. This Greek noun in Matthew and Luke signifies "unbelievers," "hypocrites," and "evil people" (Mt 3:7, 12:34, 23:33; Lk 3:7).[28] The noun אפעה appears among the Qumran Scrolls, notably in the *Thanksgiving Hymns*.[29]

| 2. בשן | "dragon-snake" | Deut 33:22 | ? |

The meaning of the Hebrew noun בשן was once clear to scholars. It denoted only a proper name of a place, Bashan,[30] which was identified as the Kingdom of Og, the territory east of the Jordan, extending from the Jabbok River to Mount Hermon.[31]

Does this noun also have another meaning? The translator of the Septuagint in Psalm 68(67):23(22) seems to have been somewhat confused; he capitalized "from" and merely transliterated Bashan" ('Εκ Βασαν).[32] The translator of the passage in the Peshitta has rendered מבשן (and there is no reason to postulate a variant)[33] with the interesting ܕܒ ܣܢ ܕܓܫܐ, "which [is] from the house of teeth," or better idiomatically "from the edge of a steep rock."[34] The Peshiṭta text probably resulted from a Syriac scribe's guess concerning the meaning of the Greek. That translation presents a meaningful rendering of Psalm 68 [67 in the LXX, but 68 in the Peshiṭta]. A lucid translation, however, should not be misleading in regard to the sense of the original Hebrew.

We receive no help in understanding this Hebrew noun בשן from the hundreds of manuscripts found in the Qumran caves.[35] The word does not appear; a similar form is found, however, but the form is the noun "tooth" with a preformative *beth*. In the *Copper Scroll* we find "in a rock peak (or cliff)" (בשן הסלע, which is literally "in the tooth of a rock"). The form in the *Temple Scroll,* בשן, is again simply "tooth" plus the preposition (11QT 61.12 [an echo of the *lex talionis* following Deut 19:21]). Both passages in these scrolls parallel what we observed regarding the Peshiṭta of Psalm 68. Thus, while we have more data for ascertaining the meaning of the noun and root in antiquity, there is still no convincing evidence in extant Hebrew manuscripts that בשן denoted a snake.

The most help in comprehending בשן as having a second meaning, "dragon-snake," comes from cognate languages.[36] The Ugaritic triliteral root *b th n*[37] *(bṭn)* and the Akkadian *bašmu* are cognate to the Hebrew triliteral *b sh n* and the Aramaic *p t n*. These terms are equal to the Arabic *baṭan*.[38] All these nouns denote some type of "dragon" or "snake." Koehler and Baumgartner (et al.) indicate that the Hebrew בשן denotes a type of serpent similar to פתן, "cobra."[39] As already intimated, the key to the Hebrew may now be found in the Ugaritic *bṭn*, which is a type of serpent akin to תנין, "dragon."[40]

This research leads us to a well-known vexing problem in Psalm 68:23[22]. Here is the usual translation:

> The Lord said, "I will bring back from Bashan,
> I will bring [them] back from the depths of the sea."[41]

The translation is far from lucid and transparent.

Long ago, W. F. Albright contended that Psalm 68:23[22] is a passage with at least one word missing.[42] He restored the second colon as follows:

> מ>מחץ< בשן אשב

The bicolon thus means:

> YHWH said,
>　　From <smiting> the Serpent I return,
>　　　I return from destroying the Sea!

This meaning depends on the presupposition or perception:

- that Psalm 68 is a catalogue of the beginnings of poems
- that verse 23(22) is the *incipit* of a poem
- that one cannot appeal to a general context for this verse
- that a word has been lost

- that this word is מחץ
- that the Psalm is to be interpreted in light of south Canaanite, especially Ugaritic poems[43]
- and that the verb אשב is a Qal, "I will return," and not a Hiphil, "I will bring back" (this seems to demand an emendation from אשיב to אשב)[44]

Most drastic, as Albright admitted, is the emendation of ממצלות to מצמת. The change of the *lamed* to a *mem* is extreme. It is an emendation "for which no similarity of form or mechanical error of a copyist can be adduced."[45] This admission reveals that perhaps there may be a less drastic solution to this verse.[46] Moreover, Albright claimed that one should not appeal to context, in rendering this verse, since Psalm 68 is basically a catalogue containing *incipits* from early Canaanite or Hebrew poems.

What seems persuasive now, so many years after Albright's ingenious hypothesis? It appears obvious that the Ugaritic language and Canaanite myths are essential in understanding the Psalms, that the meter demands restoring a word in colon one, and that this restoration must be in line with the synonymous *parallelismus membrorum* of the bicolon so that this restoration is harmonious with "*from the depths of* the sea," or some similar understanding, as in Albright's restoration and rendering.

Albright argued that we "must almost certainly insert מחץ here in order to complete both sense and metric form." These three consonants were presumably lost "by a combination of vertical haplography and *homoioarkton*."[47] Most important, Albright rightly perceived that בשן denoted a serpent in verse 23(22). He was the first scholar to argue that this noun must mean a serpent, and he derived this meaning from an intimate understanding of Akkadian, Syrian Arabic, and especially Ugaritic.[48]

Does "Bashan" mean a type of serpent or snake? It is now certain that "Bashan" means "serpent" in Northwest Semitics (including Akkadian, Ugaritic, Hebrew, Aramaic, and related dialects)[49] because of a reading in the Ugaritic text RS 15.134. This mythological text presents a discussion between Baal and Anat after their victory over the dragon Tannin. In line six we find ḫr bšnm,[50] which means "the hole (or den) of snakes."[51] C. Virolleaud took ḫr bšnm to mean "trou de vipères" ("cave of vipers") and drew attention to the famous חר פתן in Isaiah 11:8, which denotes "the den of a cobra."

This Ugaritic text serves to guide us in restoring Psalm 68:23(22). It is possible, perhaps probable, that this section of Psalm 68 (now vv. 23–24[22–23]) once read:

> The Lord spoke:
> "From [the den of] the dragon-snake I will bring [them] back,
> I will bring [them] back from the depths of the sea,
> So that your foot might crush [them] in blood,
> And the tongues of your dogs [may have] their portion from [your]
>   enemies."

This rendering restores, within brackets, an original מחר בשן.[52] The original
3 + 3 meter is also restored; thus, the bicolon has a harmonious rhythm of 3 + 3
followed by 3 + 3.[53] Experts may have overlooked the missing beat in the first
colon since they may have not observed that אמר אדני that begins what we call
verse 23(22) is outside the meter of the first colon and was intended to introduce
the bicolon.

What is the date of Psalm 68? Many scholars date it early; that is, long before
the exilic period. A very early date for the traditions in Psalm 68 seems demanded
since God is associated with the mountains of Bashan.[54] Note S. Terrien's translation of 68:16,

> The mount of Bashan would be the mount of God,
> Mount of a thousand hills, the mount of Bashan.[55]

The text continues to stress that this "mount of Bashan" is where God desires to
dwell, and that he will "dwell [in it] forever" (לנצח; Ps 68:16–17[15–16]).[56] Such
an affirmation is impossible in Israel and Judea after the sixth century BCE. That
is the period either of the sixth-century BCE editor known as "the Deuteronomist"
(Dtr), advocated by M. Noth,[57] or of the slightly earlier Deuteronomistic school,
espoused by E. W. Nicholson and M. Weinfeld.[58] This school, among other tendencies, emphasized that Jerusalem, and only Jerusalem, was the abode of YHWH.
Thus, the celebration of Bashan as God's abode antedated by a considerable margin the Deuteronomic affirmation that became authoritative in Judaism.

The emphasis on Jerusalem as YHWH's home clearly antedates the sixth century
BCE. As recorded in 1 Kings 11:36 and 15:4 and 2 Kings 8:19, God gave David,
and his descendants, a lamp in Jerusalem.[59] The Zion tradition definitively shapes
Psalms 78:68 and 132:13, and as J. J. M. Roberts states: "[I]ts crystallization point
must still be sought in the Davidic–Solomonic era."[60] Perhaps Psalm 68 is as early
as Albright suggested: in the Solomonic period. Anderson offers a viable suggestion that the *Sitz im Leben* is the autumnal festival when YHWH's kingship was celebrated and his mighty deeds acclaimed.[61] Surely, the traditions we have isolated
in Psalm 68, especially verse 16, must antedate the Zion tradition that in the tenth
century BCE began to be dogma. Note Roberts' words: "The fundamental point
necessary for the formation of the Zion tradition was the belief that Yahweh had
chosen Jerusalem as his permanent abode. That dogma could not date much later
than David's decision to move the ark to Jerusalem, and certainly not later than
the decision to build the temple there."[62]

Verse 16(15), "the mountain of Elohim [is] the mountain of Bashan," clashes
with verse 30(29) ("your Temple at Jerusalem"), which refers to Solomon's Temple.[63] It seems prima facie evidence that verses 16(15) and 23(22) preserve traditions that both antedate the monarchy and reflect the popular Canaanite myth
about Baal and how he defeated Bashan.

Is not some restoration needed in Psalm 68:23(22)? Something in the first colon
needs to parallel "the depths of" in the second colon. On the basis of the poetic
meter and syntax, and in light of the Ugaritic phrase, which was perhaps a cliché,
the meaning of Psalm 68:23(22) may be restored. The context implies the word

"them," which is to be understood as a reference to "God's enemies" mentioned in the preceding verse (68:22[21]). The "God of our salvation" will bring back "his enemies" from far distant regions: "the [den of] the snake" and "the depths of the sea." It seems that the God of salvation, the one to whom belongs "escape from death," is bringing into judgment his enemies, those still alive (68:22[21]) and those who are in the den of the dragon-snake or in the depths of the sea; that is, all who have died, either on land or on sea. Thus, it is not necessary to emend the texts, which is always a precarious act, to obtain, as Gunkel did, a translation that is appealing: "From the furnace of fire I will bring them back."[64]

M. Dahood, who wisely employed Ugaritic to shine light on dark passages in the Psalms, has provided a different understanding of Psalm 68:23(22). What is important is that he perceives that Bashan in this verse refers to a dragon-snake or serpent:

> The Lord said:
>   "I stifled the Serpent,
>   muzzled the Deep Sea."[65]

In his notes, Dahood points out that *bāṭān* "is another name for Leviathan, as appears from UT 67.I.12."[66] The translators of the NEB also opted to bring out a reference to a snake in Psalm 68:23(22): "from the Dragon."

It now becomes clearer that in biblical Hebrew "Bashan" can denote a mythical snake: a dragon-snake. With this lexical insight and a restored text and meter, we can now appreciate the synonymous *parallelismus membrorum*. It is between "from the den of the dragon-snake" (מחר בשן) and "from the depths of the sea" (ממצלות ים).[67]

Is Psalm 68 fundamentally a catalogue of early Hebrew poems as Albright argued long ago? Most scholars have not been persuaded by his attempt to solve the seeming disjunctions that define this psalm. Many experts have followed Mowinckel, mutatis mutandis, in seeing Psalm 68 with some unity and as a processional psalm for the Jerusalem cult. Thus, it is helpful to quote Mowinckel's conclusion. He grouped Psalms 24, 68, 118, and 132 as festal procession psalms. Of them he wrote:

> They can only be understood in connexion with a vision of the procession itself and its different acts and scenes. The interpreter has to use both the descriptions of such cultic processions and the allusions to them in other Old Testament texts, and his own imagination, to recall a picture of the definite situation from which such a psalm cannot be separated. Only thus it is possible to find the inner connexion between the apparently incoherent stanzas of, e.g., Ps 68.[68]

This interpretation gives pride of place to verse 25 in Psalm 68; it follows the verse in focus now, verse 23(22). Note Mowinckel's translation (vol. 1, p. 11):

> We are seeing thy processions, O God,
> The procession of my God and my King in the sanctuary,

> Singers in front, musicians behind,
> Between them girls with tambourines. [Ps 68:25–26]

Mowinckel read Psalm 68 in its present (corrupt) form and with an eye on 68:25. There is far more discontinuity than he allows,[69] even when we try to imagine the procession toward the enthronement of YHWH. One should admit that there is nothing in verses 25–26 that suggests, let alone demands, that one think about Jerusalem and its Temple. It may originally reflect a procession at Bethel, Shiloh, Dan, or even a Canaanite sanctuary as at Megiddo or on Mount Bashan. Yet in their present setting, verses 25–26 are followed by verse 30(29), which refers to "your Temple in Jerusalem." Thus, Mowinckel's emphasis on unity in Psalm 68 lies behind the following reflections concerning echoes and connections within Psalm 68 (in the previous paragraphs, I was more influenced by Albright and the echoes from Canaanite cults and myths).

If Psalm 68 is not a catalogue of early Hebrew poems as Albright concluded,[70] or if it is a catalogue of *incipits* but there is in some passages a remnant of an original extremely early poem or extended selections from an early poem,[71] or a later compiler (the Elohistic editor) placed similar thoughts sometimes contiguously, or if the Psalm obtains its unity from the procession within the Temple cult (as I deem likely), then one should seek to understand 68:23(22) within its immediate context. With contextual insight is surely the way generations subsequent to its editing would have read Psalm 68.

Terrien indicates that Psalm 68 "reveals a rather spectacular structure of eleven strophes." One of them is our focal point: verses 23–26 that Terrien concludes reflect an editor's fascination with temple music.[72] As Roberts perceived, Albright's thesis of *incipits* is "unconvincing" and while parts of Psalm 68 lack clarity, "there are large blocks where there are more logical connections than one would expect in a random collection of incipits."[73] Roberts sees verses 22–24 as "connected"; they "may lead into the description of the processional in vv. 25–28."[74] Roberts, and many others, are influenced by Mowinckel's position. He saw Psalm 68 as devoid of meaning until we comprehend it within its edited context: a cultic processional psalm for the enthronement of YHWH in Jerusalem, perhaps during the new year festival and the festival of lights at Tabernacles.[75] We should not judge the ideas in Psalm 68 in terms of the logical progression of post-Enlightenment poems; there is hardly a logical progression in Ugaritic and Mesopotamian hymns (let alone in some sections of the *Hodayot* or *Odes of Solomon*).[76] Even today, those who live in the West tend to appreciate logic, while those in the East often find it annoying and misrepresentative of life.

Assuming that Psalm 68 reflects some unity, we may look for possible echoes of our restored text. First, the noun חר, "den," seems to echo הר, "mountain" in a preceding verse. In early square Hebrew scripts, the two forms, ח and ה, frequently appear identical. The text was intended to be read out loud. The two Hebrew nouns for "den" and "mountain" sound similar. They can be indistinguishable when the speaker does not bring out the force of the laryngeal (the ח).

By choosing his words carefully, a poet (or the compiler) may echo in 68:23(22) a passage in Psalm 68:16(15). Note the latter verse:

> A mountain of God [is] the mountain of Bashan;
> A mountain [of many] peaks (is) the mountain of Bashan.[77]

In this verse, הרבשן appears in colon one and in colon two. The poet then proceeds to develop his thought, so that a similar phrase evolves into the meaning "the den of the dragon-snake." Note how similar the two passages appear:

> *har-ʾelōhîm har-bāšān*
> *har gabhnunnîm har-bāšān* [Ps 68:16(15)]

This text seems to be echoed in the restored text:

> *miḥur bāšān ʾāšîbh*
> *ʾāšîbh mimmᵉṣulōth yām*

Because an echo of a sound bouncing off mountains does not identically reproduce the original sound, so the repetitive *har-bāšān (bis)* is echoed in memory when one hears *ḥur bāšān*. Even if Psalm 68 is fundamentally a compilation of *incipits,* some postexilic readers would likely have heard the echo. It is also conceivable that the two passages, now verses 16(15) and 22(23), were originally much closer than in the miscellany; both reflect early Canaanite myths ("Bashan" as the abode of God and "Bashan" as the enemy of Baal [the likely Urtext]) and the similar lexemes are not only harmonious but most likely created by the same poet.

Such a reader may have perceived an evolution of thought from the mount of Bashan as the place where God dwells forever (68:16–17[15–16]) to the extremities in which God's enemies now hide (68:20–24[19–23]). We have amassed additional data to demonstrate that בשן once also denoted a "dragon-snake." Surely, it is not wise now to follow the advice of H.-J. Kraus who has argued that in Psalm 68:23[22] Bashan is "certainly a designation for the 'highest height.' "[78]

Second, the context suggests that the thought of verse 23 flows from verses 20–22. In 68:23(22) the poet (through the paronomasia of double entendre) is drawing attention to the power of "the God of salvation" (68:21[20]). God will bring everything and everyone to judgment—that is, bring them back from a place poetically representing Sheol (the den of the dragon-snake and the depths of the sea).[79] The Warrior-God, YHWH, is bringing to judgment all his enemies.

My interpretation is not far from that of P. D. Miller. Note how he renders verses 22–24:

> How "Yahweh" has smitten
> The head of his enemies
> The head of the "wicked"(?)
> Roaming in his guilt.
> The Lord said:
> *I muzzled the Serpent,*
> *I muzzled the Deep Sea.*[80]

That you may wash
Your feet in blood,
The tongues of your dogs
From the enemies their portion. [?][81]

Miller was focused on the image of the "Divine Warrior in Early Israel." I am focusing on "Bashan" as denoting a serpent. Miller rightly found Albright's emendations "too extreme and actually unnecessary" (p. 111). He also is deeply influenced by Ugaritic, especially 'nt: III:37–38 (= CTA 3.III.37–38),[82] which he renders as follows:

I muzzled Tannin, I muzzled him.
I smote the twisting Serpent.[83]

In contrast to Miller, I prefer to see Psalm 68:23[22] in light of RS 15.134 instead of CTA 3.III.37–38. I take the verb אשיב in Psalm 68:23(22), in which it appears in colons one and two, as a Hiphil from the familiar שוב (with most scholars), and not as Miller, who follows Dahood,[84] from שבם, "muzzled," which is a verb known from Ugaritic and Arabic, but not extant in biblical Hebrew.[85]

My restoration does not appeal to any emendation, as many experts have concluded Psalm 68 must receive. It is not an unfounded speculation. It restores the meter and the *parallelismus membrorum*. That is, "*the den* of the dragon-snake" is parallel and synonymous to "*the depths* of the sea." The passage fits the early Canaanite origins of this psalm that reflects the Canaanite myth of how Baal defeated both *Yām* (the Sea) and Bashan (the Monster). This dating of the traditions behind Psalm 68 is in line with many experts who follow Albright in tracing the traditions to pre-Solomonic Canaanite culture.[86] As Miller contends, "when verse 23 is translated correctly, we see that Yahweh's enemies are also the monsters of the cosmos." Miller then salutes Albright for being "one of the first to call attention to this theme in the verse and particularly to the mention of the serpent Bašan."[87]

There is more that may be speculated. What is the etymological link between the two meanings of "Bashan"? The putative verbal source of this noun, בשן, may be *bāšān*, and analogous with the cognate Arabic; it would mean "to be smooth." The connection between the Bashan plain and the smooth skin of a snake becomes obvious. As a place, "Bashan" denotes the smooth fertile and stoneless plain east of the Jordan River with Hermon on the north and Gilead on the south, so as a dragon-snake "Bashan" denotes the unparalleled smoothness of a serpent's skin.[88] It is also possible that in the second millennium BCE the place called Bashan, which is ideal for snakes then and now, was noted for its vipers or "dragon-snakes."

What then evolves regarding the meaning of other passages with בשן in the Hebrew Bible? More challenging than the passage in Psalm 68, which most likely refers to a dragon-snake,[89] is the use of the noun in Deuteronomy 33:22. This verse contains the only other time בשן appears in the Hebrew Bible with the possible meaning of "dragon-snake." Little help is obtained from the Targumim in ascertaining the meaning of "Bashan" in Deuteronomy 33:22. The translator who gave us Targum Onkelos paraphrased the line, explaining of Dan that "his territory is watered by the wadis that flow from Matnan [Bashan]."[90] In contrast to the Targum, note the following translation of the Hebrew:

> And concerning Dan he [Moses] said:
> Dan [is] a lion's cub;
> He shall leap from the dragon-snake [or from Bashan (מן־הבשן)].[91]

This passage provides additional evidence that בשן in biblical Hebrew also meant "a dragon-snake." In the parallel tradition in Genesis 49:15, Dan is compared to a נחש and a שפיפן; hence, as in Deuteronomy 33:22, Dan is compared to a type of "snake." The *parallelismus membrorum,* which seems synonymous, indicates that "lion's cub" is followed in the second line by another powerful creature. Perhaps help comes from iconography, since an abundance of iconographical images shows lions and snakes appearing together. The translator of the Septuagint again chose to transliterate, or perhaps knew the name of the snake (ἐκ τοῦ Βασάν).[92]

As just translated, the Hebrew makes eminent sense; there is every reason to speculate that בשן denoted "dragon-snake" in biblical Hebrew. Perhaps the author is saying that Dan is like an agile lion's cub that jumps from a snake. Little sense is provided by the usual rendering that indicates Dan is "a lion's cub" that shall leap from Bashan (a place).

Albright offered a similar interpretation. He emphasized that מבשן denoted a serpent. He suggested the following translation of Deuteronomy 33:22,

> Dan is a young lion
> Which attacks [זנק = Akkad. *sanāqu*] a viper [*bāšān*].[93]

No doubt should remain that בשן denotes a snake in biblical Hebrew. Research published in the late 1940s by Frank Moore Cross, Jr., and David Noel Freedman should eliminate any conceivable hesitation.[94] They offered this insightful rendering of Deuteronomy 33:22,

> Dan is a lion's whelp
> Who shies away from a viper.[95]

Their note underscores much of what has just been argued; it deserves quoting in full:

> Contrary to the usual view, there is no natural association between Dan and Bashan. Professor Albright has suggested to the writers the rendering *bāšān* = serpent, viper; cp. Proto-Sinaitic and Ugaritic *btn*, "serpent," and Arabic *btn*, "viper." Hebrew *pétĕn* is possibly a very early Aramaic loanword, ultimately derived from the same root. We read *mibbāšān* for metrical reasons; in any case, the article is not expected in early Hebrew poetry. *bāšān* may have a similar meaning ("sea-dragon") in Ps 68 23; cf. also Ugaritic 67:I:1. It is interesting to note that in Gen 49 17 Dan is described as a viper.[96]

There is now available abundant evidence that בשן signifies a type of snake in early biblical Hebrew; it denoted a mythical snake-like monster: a "dragon-snake."

| 3. זחלי ארץ | "snakes of the earth"   Deut 32:24 | P for Israel[97] |
| זחלי עפר | "snakes of the dust"   Mic 7:17 | P for Israel |

The literal meanings of both Hebrew expressions just cited are "crawling things of the earth" and "crawling things of the dust." According to Micah, the nations that have persecuted Israel will "lick the dust like a serpent [כנחש]" and they will "crawl from their holes like snakes of the dust" (7:17). Compare the rendering of the LXX: "[A]s serpents crawling [on the] earth" (ὡς ὄφεις σύροντες γῆν). Since in antiquity a worm (in Hebrew תולע)[98] and a snake were classed together as a crawling thing, it is conceivable that "crawling things" sometimes meant a "worm."[99] According to the author of Deuteronomy 32:24, God will send against the idolaters "the poison of snakes [or crawling things] of the dust."

The phrase אבן הזחלת in 1 Kings 1:9 seems to denote a place near En Rogel at the southern end of the Hinnom Valley where it joins the Kidron Valley. It was called "the Stone of the Crawling Thing (or Snake)," "the Stone of Zoheleth," "the Gliding Stone," or simply "the Serpent's Stone."[100] It is clear that by the third century BCE אבן הזחלת was a recognized, perhaps well-known, place, since a translator of the Septuagint simply transliterated the Hebrew of 1 Kings 1:9 ("near the stone of Zoheleth"): παρὰ τὸν λίθον τοῦ Ζωελεθεί.

Most likely the "Zoheleth" on which Adonijah offered sacrifices was an altar associated with ophiolatry and perhaps it bore serpent iconography. Recall 1 Kings 1:9: "And Adonijah sacrificed sheep and oxen and fattened cattle upon (or by) the stone of Zoheleth, which is by En rogel."[101] Altars with horns have been found in many excavated sites in ancient Palestine, and an altar with an inscribed serpent was found at Beer-Sheba.[102] Most likely "the stone of Zoheleth" denoted (perhaps for the Canaanites) "the serpent's stone"; but, for Israel, these serpents were "snakes of the dust."[103]

4. לויתן	"Leviathan"[104]	Isa 27:1	N[105]
		Job 3:8; 40:25; 41:1	N
		Ps 74:14	B?

Leviathan, mentioned five times in the Hebrew Bible,[106] is the name of a mythical and legendary serpent that lives in the sea and is primordial (note the German: "Meeresurdrache").[107] Most likely, the name "Leviathan" was inherited by the Hebrews and Israelites from south Canaanite myths and traditions.[108] Ancient translators of the Hebrew Bible usually transliterated לויתן, as in the Peshitta (ܠܘܝܬܢ [Isa 27:1, bis]). In the Septuagint, the Greek translators choose not only "dragon" (τὸν δράκοντα [Isa 27:1 (bis)] and similarly in Psalm 74:14 and Job 40:20 LXX) but also "great sea-monster" (τὸ μέγα κῆτος [Job 3:8]). The fullest description of Leviathan in the Hebrew Bible appears in Job 40:25–41:26(41:1–34). According to Isaiah 27:1, a section of the so-called Isaiah Apocalypse, Leviathan is a large, terrifying dragon that is a "fleeing serpent" and a "twisted serpent";[109] it will be punished by the Lord when the beast exits his place.[110] According to some ancient texts and iconographical items, this serpentine monster has seven heads (OdesSol 22:5),[111] an indeterminable number of many heads (ראשי לויתן in Ps 74:14), or only one head (ראשו in Job 40:31[41:7]).[112]

Some positive symbolic meaning is also found in the noun.[113] After the Lord punishes Leviathan, he will become food for God's people in the future, latter days, or End-time (Ps 74:14). Thus, while לויתן was a symbol of evil for the Israelites and other Near Eastern cultures,[114] in one sense, Leviathan will have a positive meaning for God's people in the future. This positive meaning—the body of Leviathan will supply the meat course for the eschatological banquet—is usually paramount when Leviathan is mentioned in early Jewish texts, like *1 Enoch* 60:7,[115] *4 Ezra* 6:50–52, and *2 Baruch* 29:1–8.[116] The much later (probably post-seventh-century) *Targum Pseudo-Jonathan* renders Gen 1:21 as follows: "God created the great sea monsters, *Leviathan and his mate* [לויתן ובר זוגיה],[117] *that are designated for the day of consolation* [ליום נחמתא]."[118] According to the compilers of *Perek Shirah*, circa tenth century CE (but with older traditions),[119] Leviathan is depicted as saying: "Give thanks to God for God is good, for God's kindness endures forever" (Ps 136:1).[120] Likewise, if the Lord made Leviathan to play in the sea (Ps 104:24–26), he cannot be simply a negative symbol. "Leviathan" may have a neutral, ambiguous, or both positive and negative symbolic meaning in such passages.

The negative meaning for Leviathan continued. According to the author of the *Ladder of Jacob*, probably composed in the first or second century CE: "[W]hen the king arises" (*LadJac* 6:1), "the Lord will pour out his wrath against Leviathan the sea-dragon." (*LadJac* 6:13; cf. *Apocalypse of Abraham* 10:12, 21:4). Leviathan is mentioned in the Qumran Scrolls, but what remains of the manuscript is only a tiny fragment that yields no help in discerning the meaning of the noun (cf. *Qumran Pseudepigraphic Psalms;* 4Q380 Frg 3.1). The author of the *Ladder of Jacob* helps us comprehend that Leviathan is a snake-like monster; for him "the sea-dragon."

5. נחש	"serpent"	Gen 3:1	P?
		Gen 49:17, Ps 140:4[3]	N
		Exod 4:3, 7:15	P?
		Prov 23:31, Ps 58:5[4]	N
		Isa 14:29	P for Israel
נחשים	"serpents"	Jer 8:17, Amos 9:3	N for Israel

Appearing thirty-one times, נחש is the usual word for "serpent" or poisonous snake in the Hebrew Bible; the plural is the expected נחשים. The noun may be an example of onomatopoeia since *nachash* sounds like a human's approximation of a snake's "hissing."[121]

The noun נחש first appears in Genesis 3:1 in which it is portrayed as a "clever" (not negative "cunning"; cf. Prov 12:23) animal who can talk.[122] It is unlikely, despite the tendencies of translations and commentaries, that the "serpent" represents only evil in Genesis 3:1. For example, the translator of Genesis 3:1 in the Septuagint chose the rendering "a most sagacious" animal (φρονιμώτατος).[123] According to Exodus 4:3 and 7:15, God's legitimizing of Moses (Exod 4:1, 5) is placarded by the rod that is turned into a serpent (נחש).[124] When Isaiah, according to 14:29, states that the Philistines shall be plagued by a נחש, that symbolizes something good for Israel.[125] The "serpent" is thus parallel to a messenger from God; he aids and protects Israel. In contrast to Isaiah, Jeremiah reports that the Lord God will send serpents and vipers among those in and near Jerusalem because they have sinned against the Lord (Jer 8:17). Again, the "serpent" administers God's will.

Rather than denoting only a biological reptile called a snake, this Hebrew noun can denote a fantastic or mythological creature (cf. esp. Gen 2–3, Exod 4:3, 7:15, Amos 9:3). The translators of the Septuagint almost always chose to represent this Hebrew noun with the generic term for "serpent" in Greek, ὄφις;[126] however, in Job 26:13 and Amos 9:3 they preferred δράκοντι.[127] The translators of the Peshitta usually choose to translate נחש as "serpent" (ܚܘܝܐ).

The noun נחש (and ὄφις) is generic;[128] hence, in postbiblical Hebrew a qualifying term or adjective like ארסי, "venomous" or "poisonous," is added. Hence, נחש ארסי signifies "a poisonous snake."[129] The solution for specificity with this generic noun is only partly helpful, since one can think of numerous types of very different poisonous snakes in pre-70 Palestine.[130] Other constructs with נחש are known and they provide more helpful specificity, but do not inform us regarding the exegesis of biblical texts.[131]

In the ostraca, letters, and texts found in the Judean Desert and at Petra, נחש appears. In these nonbiblical writings the noun means only "copper" (viz. at Petra and dated to 28 CE and in the Nahal Hever and dated to 94 CE).[132]

The negative connotation of נחש increases in postbiblical or modern Hebrew, since "an evil man" (אדם רשע) is simply, as in English, called "a snake."[133] While the negative meaning of the noun is paramount in postbiblical Hebrew, the compiler of *Perek Shirah* has the נחש saying: "God supports all the fallen, and straightens all the bent" (Ps 145:14).[134]

Evidence of serpent cults in ancient Palestine, though not necessarily within the religion of Israel or represented in "Old Testament Theology,"[135] may be reflected in the meaning of the verb נחש. This verb appears only in the Piel in biblical Hebrew. It denotes "to seek and give omens."[136]

In the Qumran Scrolls, נחש appears in the *Pesharim*. In *Isaiah Pesher 3* we find the following collection of Hebrew words for serpent or snake:

[O Philistia, a]ny of you, that the rod [that smote you] is broken, [for from the root of the] snake will co[me] [a viper, and its off]spr[ing will be a] flying f[iery] s[erpent.][137]

These lines are taken from Isaiah 14, beginning with verse 28.

In Hebrew, the root *nḥš* denotes not only snake (*nāḥāš* [with accent on the second syllable]) but also "divination" or "magic curse" (*naḥaš* [with accent on the first syllable]). While it is conceivable, but unlikely, that the two meanings are related etymologically in Hebrew, some, maybe many, Hebrews, Israelites, and Jews imagined the "serpent" to be related to divination. Evidence of ophiomancy, divination through serpents, was well known in the ancient world and no doubt was practiced by many in Israel since passages in both the Law and the Prophets repeatedly condemn such practices.

6. נחש נחשת   "bronze serpent"   Num 21:4–9   P

Moses made a "bronze serpent" so that those who had been bitten by "fiery serpents" (הנחשים השרפים)[138] and looked up at the "bronze serpent" would be cured from the deadly bite (Num 21:4–9). Early worshippers in Jerusalem, up until the time of Hezekiah (who destroyed it), thought the bronze serpent in the Temple, apparently worshipped by some devotees of Yahweh, was the one Moses had made in the wilderness (2 Kgs 18:4). The נחשת seems to be a mixture of נחש, "serpent," and נחשת, "bronze." Clearly, the apotropaic function of the "bronze serpent" is salubrious and positive.

| 7. עכשוב | "asp" | Ps 140:3[4] | N |

The noun can denote any viper or an asp.[139] Evil and violent men sharpen their tongues "like a serpent [נחש]" and the "poison of an asp is under their lips" (Ps 140:3[4]). Since in the Hebrew Bible the noun for "asp" appears only in Psalm 140:3[4] and there it draws attention from the asp to evil men, it is far from clear what type of serpent or snake the author had in mind (and it is not to be presumed that he could distinguish among the various species [which had not yet received names]). The English "asp" seems the best choice for עכשוב, since the Greek translators of Psalm 140, who had access to a vocabulary more advanced than in Hebrew for snakes, chose "the poison of asps" (ἰὸς ἀσπίδων) in verse 4 (as also in the Peshiṭta: ܕܐܣܦܘܣ). The sound 'khshubb may have originated from the attempt to mimic the sound of an asp.[140]

| 8. פתן, | "cobra"[141] | Ps 91:13 | N |
| פתנים | "cobras" | Deut 32:33, Job 20:14, 16 N | |

The noun פתן appears only in Isaiah 11:8 and Psalm 58:5; פתנים is found in Deuteronomy 32:33 and Job 20:14, 16. The best choice, in light of a full study of all Hebrew nouns denoting a type of snake, seems to be "cobra." While the noun can denote any asp or viper (KB 3.990 chooses "horned viper"),[142] the *terminus technicus* seems to be *naja haje*. One cannot expect the translators of the KJV of 1611 to chose "cobra," since the noun "cobra" was not an English word until about 1668.

Those who make the Lord and the Most High their dwelling place "shall tread on the cobra" (Ps 91:13).[143] This passage in Psalm 91 is significant for a better understanding of ophidian vocabulary. Note the comparison of the Hebrew and Greek:

> You shall tread upon the lion [Gk "asp," ἀσπίδα] and the cobra
> [ופתן, Βασιλίσκον],
> The young lion and dragon [ותנין, δράκοντα] you shall trample
> underfoot.   [Ps 91:13]

The Greek translators apparently did not know what פתן denoted, choosing ἀσπίς in Psalm 58[7]:4, Βασιλίσκον in Psalm 91:13 as well as Deuteronomy 32:33, and δρακόντων in Job 20:16.[144]

While פתן gives us *ptn,* it is unlikely that it explains the Greek "Python" (Πύθων).[145] The Greek had a separate history; for example, Apollo defeated the Python at Delphi.

The present comparison discloses not only the broader vocabulary for snakes and serpents in Greek over Hebrew, but also the creativity of the translator and probably not a putative divergent Hebrew manuscript behind the Greek. The parallel to Hebrew *ptn* is the Ugaritic *bṭn*; it also denotes a certain type of poisonous snake.[146] Perhaps *ptn* originated and was pronounced *pthn* to approximate the hissing of a snake.

Iconographers focusing on this passage usually depict a cobra or perhaps a basilisk ("little king").[147] Not necessarily negative, and perhaps neutral and even positive, is Isaiah's prophecy of the child who will be safe with, or playing near, the cobra (Isa 11:8). According to Deuteronomy 32:33, perverse children are like cobras' venom. The term פתן probably represented the uraeus;[148] and scarabs with a uraeus have been discovered at Lachish, Beth-El, Beth Shan, Ashdod, Tel el-'Ajjul, and elsewhere in ancient Palestine, usually on the coast or in Egyptian garrison outposts.[149]

Only the plural form, פתנים, appears in the Qumran Scrolls. In the *Thanksgiving Hymns* it is chosen to represent the poison spewed out by the men of Belial (1QHᵃ 13.27 [Sukenik 5]). In 4Q381 Frg. 26.1, it appears with תנינים, "dragons," but the meaning is lost since the fragment provides no context. The plural noun appears three times in the *Damascus Document*. In CD MS A 8.10, the author quotes Deuteronomy 32:33: "The poison of serpents [is] their wine and the head of asps [is] cruel," then explains its meaning: "'The serpents' are the kings of the peoples and 'their wine' is their ways, and 'the head of the asps' is the head of the kings of Greece, who will come to do vengeance among them."[150] In CD MS B 19.22–23, Deuteronomy 32:33 receives a similar interpretation. In both passages, serpent imagery is used to bring out the negative aspects of the Greek invaders of the Land and in CD 19 the unfaithful in Judea (cf. "the princes of Judah" in CD 19.15).

| 9. צפע | "pit viper" | Isa 14:29 | P for Israel |

The noun צפע appears only in Isaiah 14:29 in which it is one of the serpents or vipers that plague the Philistines on behalf of Israel.[151] The noun may also denote the legendary cockatrice or basilisk.[152] No help in discerning the type of snake imagined by Isaiah is provided by the Greek translator who renders צפע ("pit viper") as "the young of asps" (ἔκγονα ἀσπίδων). Perhaps *ṣphʿ* is also onomatopoeic; it does sound like a hissing snake, especially when the plosive ṣ and laryngeal are accented.

| 10. צפעני, | "viper"[153] | Prov 23:31 | N |
| צפענים | "vipers" | Isa 59:5, Jer 8:17 | N |

Wine if not controlled will bite like a serpent (כנחש) and sting like a viper (Prov 23:31). The LXX renders the former noun with the familiar and generic "serpent" (ὄφεως) and the latter noun with "horned viper" (κεράστου) that is probably the *Cerastes cornutus*.[154] Again, according to Isaiah's prophecy in 11:8, the child will be safe playing near the cobra and viper (LXX: ἔκγονα ἀσπίδων). According to Isaiah 59:5, those whose iniquities have separated them from God have hatched viper's eggs from which a "sand viper" appears. This verse shows that צפעני, "viper," and אפעה, "sand viper," are closely related, at least in the mind of the author of Isaiah 59.[155] The onomatopoeic nature of this noun also seems apparent.

The form צפעונים , with the *mater lectionis,* appears in CD MS A 5.14: "[A]nd eggs of vipers [are] their eggs."[156] The author castigates those who profane the Torah in the Land.

11. קפוז	"arrow-snake"	Isa 34:15	N for Israel

This *hapax legomenon* in Isaiah 34:15 seems to describe a snake who shall "make her nest" in Zion. The relation with a hawk, in the same verse, may indicate some type of snake. The English "arrow-snake" is found in some lexicons[157] and translations;[158] the RSV and NRSV erroneously opted for "owl."[159] An analogy seems to be with Arabic *qafāzat,* which means "arrow-snake." Fabry thinks the קפוז denotes "the arrow snake," the most common reptile in Palestine, and identifies it with the *Coluber jugularis.*[160] The translator of the Septuagint has either reworked the passage or worked from a different text tradition; hence, the translator's choice of "hedgehog" (ἐχῖνος) is of little help in discerning the meaning of קפוז (which may not have been in his exemplar). The Peshiṭta also has "hedgehog" (ܩܘܦܕܐ), but the translator may be simply working from the Septuagint and cannot constitute a separate witness. Likewise, *Targum Jonathan* has: "There the hedgehog shall make a nest" (תמן תקנין קופדא).[161]

The Septuagint, Peshiṭta, and Targum (and there is most likely some interdependence here) cumulatively suggest that קפוד—"hedgehog," or "short-eared owl"[162]—was in the Hebrew text behind these translations.[163] On the one hand, we need to recall that often in Hasmonean scripts the *dalet* and *zayin* are indistinguishable; indeed in many manuscripts קפוז looks very similar to קפוד. On the other hand, it is evident that in the centuries before 70 CE the Hebrew texts were copied by Aramaic-speaking scribes who knew well the ז–ד substitution between Hebrew and Aramaic.

It is clear that 1QIsᵃ has קופד,[164] "hedgehog" (perhaps under the influence of Aramaic pronunciation the *wāw* was transposed).[165] The *dalat* is certain in this most ancient copy of Isaiah. Focusing myopically only on the ancient texts of Isaiah, we are left with the possibility that קפוז never existed in biblical Hebrew. One might be forgiven for thinking that the noun existed only in the minds of some biblical scholars.

At this point one might conclude that the scribe of 1QIsᵃ did not know about the existence of a word קפוז. That would reflect poor methodology and confuse two questions:

1. "What is the text of Isaiah 34:15?" is not equivalent to
2. "Is there evidence that 'arrow-snake' is a biblical noun?"

We need also to ask, "Does the scribe of 1QIsᵃ ever employ the name under scrutiny?" In fact, the scribe of 1QIsᵃ knew the noun under investigation. At Isaiah 14:23 he wrote:

ושמתי[166]	And I will make [it][167] [Babylon][168]
למורש קפז	a possession of the arrow-snake.

The zayin is unmistakable in the handwriting. No one should expect orthographically קפוז and be concerned about the lack of a *mater lectionis*; the noun is simply an example of the well-known, but poorly named, *scriptio defectiva*.[169] In fact, the Isaiah Scroll has a remnant of ancient orthography.[170]

In Isaiah 14:23 the MT has קפד, "hedgehog." This is a very interesting reading, especially when one knows that נחש, "serpent," צפע, "pit viper," and שרף מעופף, "flying-serpent" appear only a few lines later, in Isaiah 14:29. Surely, it is wise to follow the lead of Kutscher, who stated long ago that the scribe of 1QIsᵃ "[W] as aware of the existence of both words in Isa, but he wrote them in the wrong places."[171]

In terms of primary data presently available, it seems wise to imagine that קפוז in biblical Hebrew denotes "arrow-snake." There is evidence that proves this noun might well have been known to Isaiah and was certainly familiar to the gifted scribe who copied 1QIsᵃ. The preceding study of the Psalter raises the possibility that קפוז meant "arrow-snake" to a probability.[172]

12. רהב	"Rahab"	Ps 89:11, Isa 51:9–11	N
		Job 9:13–14, 26:12–13	N

It is unlikely that רהב is merely a personification of the chaos of the sea, even though the verb, with the same radicals, רהב, means "to behave stormily (boisterously, arrogantly)."[173] The Hebrew radicals רהב seem to denote "Rahab," the name of a mythical sea monster, probably a serpent or dragon,[174] slain by the Lord at creation.[175] Thus, the verb may reflect the stormy attributes of a mythical sea monster.

The conception of what God did at creation, calming the waters, was mixed with a celebration of the divine intervention that parted the sea and allowed the Israelites to escape the Egyptians.[176] Note especially Isaiah 51:9–10:

> Awake, awake, put on strength,
> O arm of Yahweh!
> Awake as in the ancient days,
> In the generations of old.
> Are you not the arm that cut Rahab (רהב) apart,
> And pierced the dragon (תנין)?
>
> Are you not the one who dried up the sea,
> The waters of the great deep;
> That made the depths of the sea a way
> For the redeemed to cross over?

Observe how "cut Rahab apart" is placed in synonymous parallelism with "pierced the dragon"; thus, Rahab is conceptually similar to "the dragon."[177] The same identity seems evident in Job 26:12–13;[178] there "Rahab" is equal to the "fleeing serpent (נחש)." The origin of the noun, and concept, seems to be Canaanite mythology.[179]

In Psalm 89:11 we are told that the Lord God has "crushed Rahab like a carcass." This verse certainly does not indicate that Rahab denotes the chaotic sea. It suggests that "Rahab" is a serpent-like creature that has been killed.[180]

13. שרף	"burning-serpent"	Isa 14:29	P for Israel
		Num 21:8	P for Israel

The Hebrew noun שרף seems etymologically linked with the verb with the same radicals that means "to burn"; hence, the snake imagined is one whose bite causes a burning sensation or a red (burning) color on the skin.[181] When one studies snakes and ophidian iconography, which stresses the eyes of serpents, one may also imagine that *saraph* denoted the red or fiery eye of the snake. According to Isaiah 14:29, the Philistines will be plagued by various serpents, including a "burning-serpent." According to Numbers 21:8, Yahweh told Moses to make a שרף and "set it on a pole" so that "everyone who is bitten (by the burning-serpents), when he looks at it, shall live."

The Greek translator chose for this noun an idiomatic rendering "flying serpents" (ὄφεις πετάμενοι), and that is the *terminus technicus* found in Isaiah 14:29 and 30:6. Most likely, as so many nouns in this list (and in contrast to Greek nouns for "snake"),[182] *śrph* sounds onomatopoeic.

The noun שרף appears in the Qumran Scrolls. In 4QpIsa[a] Frag. 8–10.13 it appears in a quotation from Isaiah 14:28–30 (see former comments). In 4Q159 Frag. 1.2.17 it is the verbal form "burned."

Under the basic root שרף are categorized two Hebrew expressions that denote various types of snakes. On the one hand, it is obvious that not all adjectives associated with a "serpent" designate another type of serpent; for example, in Isaiah 27:1 we hear about Leviathan as a "fleeing serpent" and a "twisted serpent." But, on the other hand, some compound forms do seem to indicate a type of snake; at least two with שרף are significant. The first is שרף combined with נחש:

14. נחש שרף	"fiery serpent"	Deut 8:15	N
הנחשים השרפים	"the fiery serpents"	Num 21:6	N

The author of Deuteronomy 8:15 states that the desert is defined by a "fiery serpent and scorpion" (ועקרב). According to Numbers 21:6, the Lord sent "fiery serpents" to bite the Hebrews who had murmured against God and Moses. Many of "the people of Israel" died from the bites.

15. שרף מעופף	"flying serpent"	Isa 14:29	P for Israel
		Isa 30:6	N for Israel

Though some translators and compilers of lexicons prefer "winged serpent,"[183] it is best to follow, in seeking to comprehend שרף מעופף, the Greek translators, who had an advanced vocabulary for speaking about snakes. See especially the Septuagint of Isaiah 14:29: ὄφεις πετάμενοι, which means "flying serpents." This rendering is also supported by the translators of the Peshitta. The translators of the Targumim prefer "biting serpent."

According to Isaiah 30:6, "flying serpents" and the "sand viper" came from the

South, which is "a land of trouble and anguish" (Isa 30:6). That seems to suggest that the creatures are negative for Israel.

The creature that swallowed Jonah, according to the Hebrew Bible (and the Peshiṭta) is a "large fish" (דג גדול [Jon 2:1 (1:17 in English); ܢܘܢܐ ܪܒܐ]). In the Septuagint, this creature becomes "a great sea-monster (or whale)":[184] κήτει μεγάλῳ. In the earliest iconography represented in the frescoes of the catacombs, beginning in the late second century CE, the great fish is perceived to be a sea monster like a dragon reminiscent of Leviathan.[185]

16. שרפים   "winged-serpents"   Isa 6:2–6   P

In the Hebrew Bible, the Seraphim are mentioned in Isaiah 6 (cf. Num 21:6, 8; Ezek 1; cf. Rev 4). They should not be equated with the Cherubim.[186]

The Book of Isaiah (esp. *First Isaiah*) has the most extensive vocabulary for serpents in the Bible. Thus, the author (editors and possible additional authors) shared an interest in serpents and serpent iconography that distinguished them among the authors and editors of the books in the Hebrew Bible. Since Isaiah is especially influenced by Egyptian lore, it is wise to see the שרפים as "winged-serpents."[187]

Informed experts are no longer influenced by Origen's suggestion that the two Seraphim in Isaiah 6 denoted the Logos and the Holy Spirit. Yet, some scholars still claim that the Seraphim cannot be serpents because they have feet and wings.[188] Note this sample of opinions:

> They [the Seraphim] have nothing in common with serpents except the name. (1941)[189]

> It may suffice to state that the שרפים are . . . not snake demons . . . they are preponderatingly of human type—though winged—as they have a face, feet, and evidently, hands, since one of them can handle a pair of thongs. (1949)[190]

> The word means "burning ones" in the transitive sense; the fact that it is used to describe the serpents in the wilderness (cf. Num. 21:6,8) has led some commentators here to the illogical conclusion that the seraphim of the vision were serpentine in form. . . . The seraphim . . . have the hands, faces, and voices of men, and stand upright; and they have three pairs of wings. (1956)[191]

> Seraphim (lit. "fiery ones"; the English simply transliterates the Hebrew) elsewhere are serpents (Num 21:6; Isa 14:29; 30:6; cf. 1 Kgs 6:23–28; 2 Kgs 18:4), but here they have six wings. (2001)[192]

The Seraphim have wings, faces, feet, and human features; these characteristics have confused some scholars who assume they thus cannot be serpents. Near Eastern iconography, as the present book illustrates, is replete with images of serpents with faces, feet, wings, and human features.[193] Thus, K. Joines and O. Keel rightly understand this noun, Seraphim, in light of the cobra and the Egyptian uraeus. Both were well known in Palestine during and before the time of the eighth-century prophet Isaiah.[194] It is interesting to note that the Greek translator chose to transliterate the Hebrew: "seraphim" (σεραφίμ).

The author of *1 Enoch* stated that the archangel Gabriel was in charge of paradise, the serpents (δράκοντες), and the cherubim. G. W. E. Nickelsburg suggests that these serpents "may be seraphim, identified with the fiery sword of Genesis 3:24."[195] The author of *Genesis Rabbah* 21:9, on the basis of Psalm 104:4 (God's ministers are like flaming fire), identified the Genesis sword with angels.[196]

| 17. שפיפן | "adder" | Gen 49:17 | P for Israel |

The Hebrew noun שפיפן, *shephîphōn*, can denote an "adder,"[197] as well as any type of viper including the horned viper.[198] According to Genesis 49:17, Dan shall guard Israel, being like the adder that causes one on a horse to fall. It is not easy to discern which type of poisonous snake this noun denoted, since the word is a *hapax legomenon* in Genesis 49:17 and there had not evolved a taxonomy for serpents when the author wrote these words.[199] That is, as we have seen, there are numerous words in biblical Hebrew to designate a snake, but they were used sometimes interchangeably.

The sound of the Hebrew, *shephîphōn*, seems to be onomatopoeic; thus, the one who originated this noun probably was trying to imitate a *hissing* serpent. The Greek translator probably did not know what type of snake the author had in mind, and rendered שפיפן with the generic ὄφις. The translator of the Peshitta chose "basilisk" or "cockatrice" (ܐܣܦܣ).[200] H. R. Cohen draws attention to the fact that שפיפן certainly denotes a snake, since it is cognate with Akkadian *šibbu/šippu* that are included in the lexical snake list.[201]

| 18. תנין, | "dragon"[202] | Ps 91:13, Job 3:8 | N |
| תנינים[203] | "dragons" | Ps 74:13, Deut 32:33 | N |

This noun denotes the mythical serpent that shall be trampled in the future (Ps 91:13).[204] While the etymological derivation of תנין is uncertain, it may be related to the Aramaic noun נון, "fish."[205] Perhaps, since the verbal root of תנין means "to wail" (cf. Jud 11:40), the noun may have originated with sailors who, at sea, heard from the deep the sounds of the whale.

Psalm 91:13, as we saw earlier, indicates that "dragon" is a good choice for תנין. The translators of the Septuagint chose, in Psalm 91:13, the noun δράκοντα.[206] The translators of the New King James Version (1982), which is part of *The Hebrew Scriptures: Hebrew and English,* offered this attractive rendering of Psalm 91:13:

> You shall tread upon the lion and the cobra,
> The young lion and the serpent (ותנין) you shall trample underfoot.[207]

The parallelism of the poetry, which is synonymous, indicates that תנין is similar to "the cobra."

While the "serpent" symbolically was multivalent—representing both positive and negative concepts—the "dragon" (which frequently meant "serpent") as a dragon represented the demonic (as in the Babylonian Tiâmat and Labbu, the Egyptian Apophis, the Persian Aži-Dahaka, and the Greek Python).

A background for the Hebrew *tnnîn* is the Ugaritic *tnn;* note this passage:

H   37   I muzzled Tannin [*tnn*][208] [the Sea Dragon], yea, I muzzled him,
     38   I smote the Crooked Serpent [*bṭn*],
     39   the monster of seven heads.[209]

Again, the synonymous *parallelismus membrorum* indicates a similarity between the "Tannin" and "the Crooked Serpent." The compilers of the *Perek Shirah* have the תנין saying: "Praise God from the land, the sea monsters and all the depths" (Ps 148:7).[210]

Summary

We have discovered that there are eighteen words, certainly not *termini technici*, for snake or serpent, in the Hebrew Bible. Here is the summary:

Term	Translation	Major Biblical Passage	Symbol
1. אפעה	"sand viper"	Isa 30:6, 59:5	N
2. בשן	"snake"	Deut 33:22	?
		Ps 68:23[22]	N
3. זחלי ארץ	"snakes of the earth"	Mic 7:17; cf. Deut 32:24	P for Israel
4. לויתן	"Leviathan"	Isa 27:1	N
		Job 3:8; 40:25 [41:1]	N
		Ps 74:14	B?
5. נחש	"serpent"	Gen 3:1	P
		Gen 49:17, Ps 140:4[3]	N
		Exod 4:3, 7:15; Num 21:7	P
		Prov 23:31, Ps 58:5[4]	N
		Isa 14:29	P for Israel
6. נחש נחשת	"bronze serpent"	Num 21:4–9	P
7. עכשוב	"asp"	Ps 140:3[4]	N
8. פתן	"cobra"	Ps 91:13	N
9. צפע	"pit viper"	Isa 14:29	P for Israel
10. צפעני	"viper"	Prov 23:32	N
11. קפוז	"arrow-snake"	Isa 34:15	N for Israel
12. רהב	"Rahab"	Ps 89:11, Isa 51:9–11	N
		Job 9:13–14, 26:12–13	N
13. שרף	"burning-serpent"	Isa 14:29	P for Israel
14. נחששרף	"fiery serpent"	Deut 8:15	N
15. שרף מעופף	"flying serpent"	Isa 14:29	P for Israel
		Isa 30:6	N for Israel
16. שרפים	"winged-serpents"	Isa 6:2–6	P
17. שפיפן	"adder"	Gen 49:17	P for Israel
18. תנין	"dragon"	Ps 91:13, Job 3:8	N

To discover eighteen different, but sometimes interrelated, expressions for snakes and serpents in the Hebrew Bible may be a surprise to biblical experts, especially when approximately thirteen nouns are known to denote a snake in Aramaic and Syriac, and these cognate languages have a vast vocabulary that covers more centuries than biblical Hebrew, and include the influence of Arabic.[211] It is not clear how many words for "snake" exist in Aramaic and Syriac because of the lack of a taxonomy of snakes and the vast corpus of texts (some not edited critically) that covers over two thousand years. Here is a list featuring the major words for snake in Aramaic and Syriac:

אים	= perhaps an indeterminate type of snake that causes fear[212]
ܐܦܥܐ or אפעה	= Hebrew loanword
ܒܣܘܡܬܐ	= פתן?, "cobra"? [see below]
אפר	= viper?[213]
ܐܟܣܐ[214]	= Hebrew צפע [cf. Peshiṭta of Isa 14:29]
דיפסדס or ܕܝܦܣܕܣ	= διψάδες[215]
חוי(א)ה, חוא[216]	= snake
ܣܟܝܢܐ	= Hebrew שפיפון and other Hebrew nouns for "snake"[217]
ܟܘܦܬܐ[218]	= a type of viper?[219]
ܠܘܝܬܢ	= Leviathan or "snake"
ܚܘܝܐ, ܡܪܢܝܬܐ	= some type of large snake[220]
עכשוב	= Hebrew loanword
ערוד	= perhaps a small snake[221]
פתן or ܦܬܢܐ	= Hebrew loanword (that explains βαθανηραθα)[222]
שרץ	= a "creeping thing," "reptile," or "snake"

To ophiologists, the number of words in Hebrew for "snake" will not be re-markable since there are at least forty-four types of snakes known in the Near East.[223] Moreover, eighteen is not a large number compared to the nouns in Greek for snake (see Appendix II). That is, thanks to the study of a large collection of Greek books on poisonous animals, Philumenus' book on poisonous animals, and especially an Egyptian Brooklyn papyrus on ophiology,[224] we can ascertain that the Greek language in antiquity developed at least forty-one names for snake.[225]

A study of words for snake and serpent in the Hebrew Bible is not complete, even with a study of the previous eighteen nouns or expressions. Other Hebrew nouns probably also indicated not "lizard" or "crawling animal," but some form of unclean reptile, including a snake. Only four possibilities must suffice for now.

First, Leviticus 11 is devoted to the dietary laws, and 11:29–38 focuses on the regulations regarding the creatures that swarm on the earth. In 11:30 the mean-ing of the *hapax legomenon* לטאה is uncertain. It may denote a gecko,[226] which is a type of small lizard that has obtained its name, onomatopoeically, from the sound of its cry.[227] If לטאה corresponds to καλαβώτης (= ἀσκαλαβώτης), as in the Septuagint of Leviticus 11:30,[228] then the Hebrew noun was understood by many Greeks as denoting a "spotted lizard" or "gecko." This rendering, however, is unattractive, since "gecko" is represented by אנקה, which appears first in the list in Leviticus 11.[229]

The noun לטאה may also denote "sand snake (or reptile)." In discerning the meaning of the Hebrew noun, we receive no help from cognate languages, such as Persian, Arabic, Aramaic, or Syriac. The translators of the Peshiṭta chose a word for "salamander." If לטאה denotes some type of lizard, then the author of Leviticus 11:30 lists five types of lizards without mentioning any type of snake: "[T]he gecko, the land crocodile, the lizard, the sand lizard, and the chameleon" (NRSV). Such a rendering is unattractively redundant. Far better is the NKJV, 1982: "[T]he gecko, the monitor lizard, *the sand reptile,* the sand lizard, and the chameleon" (my italics).[230] This translation seems preferable to those that opt merely for transliterations: "gecko, *koah, letaah,* chameleon and *tinshamet*" (New Jerusalem Bible). We should conclude that לטאה may denote a type of small snake.[231]

Second, also in Leviticus 11:30, חמט probably means "lizard," but it may also denote an impure reptile, like a snake. This speculation is stimulated by a study of languages cognate to Hebrew, since the root *ḥmt* appears in other Semitic languages. In Akkadian, the cognate form means "a lizard" or "a snake." In Syriac, ܚܘܡܛܐ denotes not only a chameleon but another reptile like a snake.[232]

Third, the noun רמש, "crawler," can generically denote a serpent because it crawls on the earth (cf. Gen 3:14). The noun רמש corresponds to ἑρπετός which means anything that moves on all fours; the Greek noun can also denote a snake.[233] According to the author of Genesis 7:21, the list of creatures that died in the Flood included "creeping" animals. Some of these included species of snake (see next paragraph).

Fourth, the generic noun שרץ seems to include snakes. The clause כל השרץ השרץ, which appears twice in Leviticus 11:41–42, means "all creeping (creatures) that creep." The clause includes snakes. A similar clause, כל שרץ העוף, which appears three times in Leviticus 11:20–23, denotes "all swarming (or flying) insects," like bees, flies, or edible locusts (recall Qumran and John the Baptizer); in this passage it does not include snakes. In Genesis 7:21, however, the clause השרץ השרץ על־הארץ, "the creeping [creature] that creeps on the earth,"[234] includes a snake (cf. Lev 11:29, 41–42 [compare Aramaic שרץ which also means a "creeping thing," "reptile," or "snake"]).[235] As we saw with Genesis 7:21, the verb שרץ *(šereṣ)* in the Qal means not only "to swarm" or "to fly," but also "to creep." In his commentary on Genesis,[236] Rashi insightfully opined that the *Sheratzim* could include a reptile.[237]

Biblical scholars have incorrectly presupposed that the נחש was originally a reptile and a serpent. The Yahwist, who compiled Genesis 3 from ancient lore and myths, presents his composition with echoes. Through his gifted ability to develop the characters in his story, he presents the Nachash with human characteristics; he does not yet crawl as a reptile. Genesis 3 begins with the words that the serpent was the cleverest "beast of the field [חית השדה] that the Lord God had made." The נחש is categorized among the beasts. The author expects his readers to know the concept later added to Genesis by the P-writer in 1:24. God created cattle (בהמה), creeping animals (or reptiles [רמש]), "and the beast of the earth" (וחיתו־ארץ). It should be obvious that "the snake" is not like the cattle. And he is not categorized with reptiles.[238] He is one of the beasts of the field or earth. After God curses "the serpent," the Nachash loses his earlier characteristics and is virtually indistinguishable from the "creeping animals," which includes, after God's curse, not only crocodiles and lizards, but also the snake.

Finally, more words for "snake" were probably known to the Israelites and Jews than those that we can now find in the Hebrew Bible.[239] First, the books collected into the Hebrew Bible are now heavily edited and reflect the needs of the exilic and postexilic Jewish community in Judea in which, as we have seen, an interest in snakes and serpent symbolism had already waned, especially from the period of the prophet Isaiah. Second, the lexicon of ancient Hebrew has been significantly increased due to the study of inscriptions and especially the Hebrew of the Dead Sea Scrolls.[240] Third, words known in public parlance do not always make their way into written records. For example, in the United States, Europe, and Israel, many people are familiar with the word "arachnophobia" (the fear of spiders), but this word is not found in the OED *(Oxford English Dictionary)* or in its supplement.[241] Thus, it is conceivable, but nondemonstrable, that חוה *(ḥawwāh)* meant "snake" in Old Canaanite (an ancestor of biblical Hebrew). This suggestion is not novel and has been offered by other scholars.[242] Perhaps this noun for snake, *ḥawwāh,* never made it into biblical Hebrew because it became established as the name of "Eve." The mother of life cannot be confused with the source of temptation or evil, according to biblical theology.

This scholarly speculation is supported by a study of cognate languages.[243] In Arabic, *ḥayya* means "snake."[244] In Persian the plural of *ḥaiyat, ḥaiyāt,* indicates "serpents."[245] In Aramaic, חוא, חויא (viz. in Onkelos), and חויה (viz. in Neophiti) denote snake,[246] and in Syriac *ḥewyâ* denotes "snake."[247]

J. Wellhausen surmised that the striking similarity of the first woman's name חוה *(ḥawwāh)* with the Arabic and Syriac noun for "snake" should be explained by the assumption that the author of Genesis 3 or his source knew this noun and imagined the woman (Eve) in a serpent form.[248] Wellhausen's insight is in line with Philo's contrast between a dragon that is cunning and a friendly serpent that is called Eve: "[T]hat friendly serpent, the counselor of life, which is wont to be called Eve" *(Agr. 95)*.[249]

In 1904, R. G. Murison asked: "Is the name given to the woman *(Ḥawwah,* Gen 3:20) connected with the name for serpent in Arabic *(ḥayyat)* and in Syriac *(ḥewyâ)*?"[250] Despite the vast increase in our knowledge of West Semitic philology since 1904, we cannot answer Murison's question with precise philological data. The name Eve, *ḥawwāh,* may well be related to "serpent," חוא, but this relationship is no longer clear in Genesis because the editor of the myths behind Genesis 3 often shows signs of not fully comprehending them.

Unobserved evidence of a possible relation between "Eve," the mother of all humans, and "Ḥeva," the name of a female snake in ancient nonbiblical Hebrew, is found in Clement of Alexandria's *Exhortation to the Heathens,* as recorded by Eusebius in his *Preparation for the Gospel.* Clement reports that the Bacchanals celebrate Dionysus with eating raw flesh and being crowned with "wreaths of serpents." Most significant for our present purposes, with these serpents representing a deity around their heads, they shout for help to "Eva, that Eva, through whom the deception crept in [and death followed in its train]." Clement adds the insight that "a consecrated serpent, too, is the symbol of the Bacchic orgies." Having reported this aspect of the Bacchic orgies, Clement adds this impressive information: "[A]ccording to the exact pronunciation of the Hebrews, the name Heva, with an aspirate, is at once interpreted as the female serpent."[251]

The eighteen nouns for snake in biblical Hebrew can be organized into three categories: specific terms, generic terms, and fundamentally mythological terms.[252] Here is a suggested categorization:

Specific Terms for Snake

1. אפעה	"sand viper"	Isa 30:6, 59:5	N
6. נחש נחשת	"bronze serpent"	Num 21:4–9	P
7. עכשוב	"asp"	Ps 140:3[4]	N
8. פתן	"cobra"	Ps 91:13	N
9. צפע	"pit viper"	Isa 14:29	P for Israel
10. צפעני	"viper"	Prov 23:31	N
11. קפוז	"arrow-snake"	Isa 34:15	N for Israel
13. שרף	"burning-serpent"	Isa 14:29	P for Israel
14. נחששרף	"fiery serpent"	Deut 8:15	N
15. שרף מעופף	"flying serpent"	Isa 14:29	P for Israel
		Isa 30:6	N for Israel
16. שרפים	"winged-serpents"	Isa 6:2–6	P
17. שפיפן	"adder"	Gen 49:17	P for Israel

Generic Terms for Snake

2. בשן	"snake"	Deut 33:22	?
		Ps 68:23[22]	N
3. זחלי ארץ	"crawling things"	Mic 7:17, Deut 32:24	P for Israel
5. נחש	"serpent"	Gen 3:1	P
		Gen 49:17, Ps 140:4[3]	N
		Exod 4:3, 7:15	P
		Prov 23:31, Ps 58:5[4]	N
		Isa 14:29	P for Israel

Fundamentally Mythological Terms for Snake or Serpent

4. לויתן	"Leviathan"	Isa 27:1	N
12. רהב	"Rahab"	Ps 89:11, Isa 51:9–11	N
		Job 9:13–14, 26:12–13	N
		Job 3:8; 40:25[41:1]	N
		Ps 74:14	B?
18. תנין	"dragon"	Ps 91:13, Job 3:8	N

The Ancient Hebrews and Snake Physiology

The snake was well known in ancient Israel. It seems obvious, from a close examination of the Hebrew Bible, that Israelites had carefully studied the snake and knew its physical characteristics. The zoological information regarding the snake or serpent in the Hebrew Bible often reflects careful observations.[253] Thus, the snake:

- lives, or hides, in the desert (Deut 8:15), under a rock (Prov 30:19), or in the sea (Amos 9:3)
- builds a nest in which it hatches its young (Isa 34:15)
- moves in an unusual way (Num 21:7,9)
- strikes suddenly (Gen 49:17)
- has a deadly bite (Gen 3:15, Amos 5:19, Ps 58:5[4], Job 20:14)
- has a forked tongue (Ps 140:4[3]), hisses (Jer 46:22)
- devours other snakes (Exod 7:12)
- eats dust with its prey (Mic 7:17, Isa 65:25)

Except in the Golan and Negev, in which the large black snake is appreciated for its protection of crops from mice and other harmful rodents, most Israelis today fear snakes and seldom see one. Perhaps only an Israeli ophiologist could match the ophidian knowledge of Isaiah and his school.

Conclusion

The symbol of the serpent is multidimensional in biblical Hebrew. In the Hebrew Bible, serpents are used to represent both a negative and a positive symbol. The upraised serpent made by Moses is a symbol that helps save people from deadly bites (Num 21), and the other positive uses of serpent symbolism reflected in the Hebrew Bible lead me to disagree with Fabry, who contends: "Nowhere in ancient Israel do we find any possibility of developing a positive attitude toward serpents."[254]

There certainly was no serpent cult in biblical theology, but there probably were at least innuendoes of such cults in the religions of ancient Israel. Hezekiah had to banish from the Temple precincts those who were devotees of and probably worshipped (perhaps through) Nechushtan. Overall, it is surprising how Isaiah and the School of Isaiah stand out in the Hebrew Bible in terms of an interest in serpents, as represented by Hebrew philology.

Finally, any attempt to be precise in terminology—except in English words to represent Hebrew nouns—fails to realize that the ancients did not develop a taxonomy for animals. Even Aristotle's *Historia Animalium* is a factual survey; he did not try to construct a system for classification.[255] As F. S. Bodenheimer stated in *Animal and Man in Bible Lands*: "[T]he large majority of animal names of the Old Testament are definitely *nomina nuda*: empty names which cannot be ascribed to any species, and often even not to a definite class of animals."[256]

Appendix II: A Lexicon of Words for "Serpent" in Ancient Greek

Though Latin has primarily only two words to denote "snake" (*serpens* and *serpula*), and Coptic scribes usually chose only one word to translate many Greek words for "snake,"[1] the ancient Greeks developed, by the first century CE, an extraordinarily rich vocabulary for snakes. While there are eighteen nouns that denote a snake or serpent in the Hebrew Bible (see Appendix I),[2] forty-one words probably denote a type of snake in ancient Greek texts.[3] In *Die Schlangennamen in den ägyptischen und griechischen Giftbüchern*, C. Leitz reported on Greek names for serpents in an ancient book on poison.[4] This list significantly increases our knowledge of ancient Greek words for the various types of snakes; however, it needs to be supplemented by the names for the mythical or legendary serpents that are found in E. Küster's *Die Schlange in der griechischen Kunst und Religion* (on p. 56), a noun in the Septuagint, one in the Greek Old Testament Pseudepigrapha, and studies of lexicons and ancient Greek texts. In order to be consistent, I have organized the Greek nouns in terms of the classical definition and English equivalent; as will be evident, some Greek terms represent the same English noun. I shall now present the Greek, Latin *termini technici,* and English words for snakes known to the ancients who knew or spoke Greek.

Greek	terminus technicus	English
1. ἀγαθοδαίμων	mythical serpent	good spirit serpent

This "good spirit serpent" or "good Genius serpent" produces good *(agathopoieō)* because it is benevolent *(agathothelēs)*. It was especially popular in Alexandria, but also appears throughout the Greek and Roman world; for example, a fresco featuring Agathadaimon was found in Pompeii. The noun Ἀγαθο-δίμονιασταί specifies devotees of the god Agathadaimon.[5]

2. αἱμορροίς		
αἱμόρρους	cerastes vipera	viper

This "viper" is probably so named because of the "discharge of blood" *(haimorroia)* when a person is bitten by it (cf. Epiphanius, *Pan.* 48.15).[6] This explanation is also supported by comments by the third-century CE physician named Philumenus (*De Venenatis Animalibus* 21) and the second-century BCE Epicurean named Nicander (*Theriaca* 282).[7]

3. ἀκοντίας   *vipera (daboia) xanthina* Asian viper

The "Asian viper" most likely derives its name because some Greeks thought of the quickness of the snake (Nicander, *Theriaca* 491, Philumenus, *De Venenatis Animalibus,* and Lucian, *Dipsades* 3)[8] or because of the "shooting forth" (ἀκοντίασις) of poison from (or the tongue of) the reptile (cf. Epiphanius, *Pan.* 61.8).[9]

4. ἀμμοβάτης   *pseudocerastes persicus* Persian viper

The etymology of "Persian viper" is not clear. Most likely the name of the snake is associated with the sandy soil in which it is found since ἀμμοδύτης means "sand-burrower" (see next entry).

5. ἀμμοδύτης   *cerastes cerastes*   Horn-viper

The fundamental meaning of "Horn-viper" in Greek is "sand-burrower"[10] since ἄμμος means "sand" or "sandy ground."

6. ἀμφίσβαινα   *blanus strauchi,*   unknown
                        typhlops vermicularis   worm serpent

While virtually every species of snake is amphibious, being equally at home in water or on land, the Greek noun ἀμφίσβαινα denotes a type of serpent that moves backward or forward.[11] Perhaps the noun denotes the small snake (and worm) that has a head virtually indistinguishable from its tail.

7. ἀργῆς   unknown   lightning serpent

The noun ἀργῆς also means "bright," as in bright and flashing lightning.[12] Perhaps the meaning originates from the lightning-fast movement of the snake or its shining skin, especially in bright sunlight.

8. ἀργόλας   uncertain   flashing snake

This name is the one the author of the *Lives of the Prophets (De Vitis prophetarum)* chose to indicate the species of snake that Jeremiah used to rid Egypt of poisonous snakes (Jer 2:6).[13] The name of this reptile is also probably etymologically derived from the Greek word meaning "bright" or "flashing."

9. ἀσπίς   *Coluber haié*   asp

The English word "asp" is a transliteration of the Greek name for the adder that is more threatening to humans than the cobra because it is more aggressive.[14] Most likely this Egyptian cobra provided the idea for the uraeus that signified royalty and kingship for the pharaohs.[15] This is the first word in our list that appears in the New Testament (see final comments). The word may be onomatopoeic since *asp* sounds like the hiss of an asp.

10. βασιλισκος   mythical serpent   Basilisk

Again, the English word is basically a transliteration of the Greek noun. Etymologically, the word relates to βασιλεύς, "king." The Basilisk is a mythical creature in Greek and Roman mythology. βασιλισκος is also a diminutive of βασιλευς, denoting "princelet" or "chieftain."[16]

11. διψάς   *pseudocerastes persicus*   Persian horn viper

Conceivably, the "Persian horn viper" derives its name from its association with water, since διψάω means "to thirst." Among many possible etymological meanings of the Persian horn viper is the concept of the one who causes intense thirst.[17] In antiquity, the serpent often symbolized "water" or was the guardian par excellence. In Palestine in the Middle Bronze Age, many ceramic water jugs were "decorated" with serpents whose heads were close to the top of the vessel. They most likely were added to the vessel to protect the contents, which could have been water, milk, wine, or other commodities.

12. δράκω   *python sebae*   python

This noun does not appear in LSJM,[18] Lampe, or Preisigke's *Wörterbuch der griechischen Papyrusurkunden*,[19] but the author of the Egyptian and Greek book on poison, highlighted by the work of Leitz, made a distinction between δράκω and δράκων.[20] The etymology of this Greek noun may be explained by the following entry.

13. δράκων   *draco*   dragon, snake, serpent

The "dragon" or "snake" was often conceived to be a god worthy of worship (cf. Aristides, *Apologia* 12).[21] This is the second word in our list that appears in the New Testament. The noun δράκων may develop from δέρκομαι, which means "to see clearly" and was used to denote the fire that can flash from one's eyes (as in the *Odyssey* 19.446);[22] the derivation is supported by a study of ophidian iconography, which often stresses the eye of the serpent. Often interchangeable with ὄφις,[23] as in Revelation 12:9, δράκων sometimes was synonymous with the mythical serpent-monster of chaos, Rahab. Some Christians identified the "dragon" with Satan (cf. Rev 12:7–9).[24] The dragon appears on shields and military banners since δρακωνάριος, a Latin loanword *(draconarius)*, denotes a "bearer of the serpent standard."[25] The word δράκων can also denote serpent jewelry, notably the silver and gold bracelets, rings, and earrings that were so popular in the Greek and Roman world. It also signified the constellation called Draco (cf. Aratus, 46).

14. δρυίνας   *vipera berus*   a viper

This Greek noun does not appear in Lampe or Preisigke, but it is listed in the Egyptian and Greek book on poison. The compilers of LSJM, p. 450, suggest the snake is one who lives in hollow oaks. This may be taking etymology too literally; it is true that δρῦς means "oak," but it also denotes various types of trees. Perhaps the ancient Greeks thought of this viper as one who would be found near or under a tree. While iconographically the snake is associated with a tree, as in the Hesperides and the Garden of Eden, it seems there is no textual evidence for seeing a mythological meaning for δρυίνας.

| 15. ἔλοψ | none | marshy snake |

The noun ἔλοψ or ἔλλοψ can mean a "fish" or "sea-fish," but it also denotes a snake.[26] Perhaps the name derives from the snake's association with "marshy ground" (ἔλος), but the rough breathing reduces the similar sound of the two Greek nouns.

| 16. ἑρπετόν | unknown | snake |

The noun ἑρπετόν denotes not only an animal that goes on all fours but also a snake. The basic meaning is an animal that crawls. The verb behind this noun is ἑρπύζω, which is found only in Homer (*Odyssey* 1.193, 13.220 and *Iliad* 23.225); it means "to creep" or "to crawl."[27] Thus, ἑρπετόν signifies a snake generically as a crawling creature. This is the third word in our list that appears in the New Testament (see final comments).

| 17. ἔχιδνα, ἔχις | *vipera ammodytes* | viper |

This is the fourth noun in our list that appears in Classical Greek, New Testament Greek (Mt 3:7, Acts 28:3),[28] and Patristic Greek (under the influence of Mt; viz. John Chrysostom, *Hom II.2 in Mt* [*7.150D*]).[29] The etymology of the noun is unclear. In Classics (viz. Aeschylus, *Choephori* 249 and Sophocles, *Antigone* 531) and the New Testament (viz. Mt 3:7; 12:34; 23:33; Lk 3:7),[30] the noun can connote or denote a negative meaning. The noun ἔχιδνα is also the proper name of a monster (Hesiod, *Theogony* 297). It would be misleading to assume that this noun always had a negative connotation. It can represent something positive; for example, it can denote the heavenly chariot drawn by vipers (Nonnus, *Dionysiaca* 13), which is elegantly shown on Medea sarcophagi (especially the one in Basel). In the *Sibylline Oracles* 5.169 we find the noun ἐχιδνοχαρής (not found in LSJM or Bauer [6th ed. of 1988]),[31] which means "delighting" or "rejoicing in vipers."[32] *Sibylline Oracle 5* was composed by a Jew, living in Egypt, between 70 and 132 CE; the author disparages those living in Rome and rejoicing in vipers. Those against whom he polemicizes revered snakes since they found "grace," "goodwill," and "beauty" (χάρις) in a "viper" (ἔχιδνα). Related to ἔχιδνα is the noun ἐχίδιον, which specifies a young viper (cf. Aristotle, *Hist. an.* 558ᵃ29).[33]

| 18. ἶρις | unknown | rainbow dragon |

The Greek that is listed in the lexicons as the messenger of the gods among themselves (cf. *Iliad* 8.398),[34] the Iris (as the iris of the eye), an iridescent garment, a brightly colored circle, especially the rainbow,[35] also denotes a "rainbow dragon."[36] The origin of the name resides most likely in the bright or iridescent color of this snake.

| 19. καύσων | *pseudocerastes presicus* | Persian viper |

This noun is previously known to denote the summer heat or heartburn;[37] hence, it seems that the name of the snake derives from the burning sensation in the skin when bitten.

20. κεγχρίας   *viper (daboia) xanthina*   Asian viper

The noun κεγχρίας also denotes numerous objects: eggs of a fish,[38] something reminiscent of grains of a metal (iron or gold), and eruptions on the skin. It thus seems likely that the Asian viper derives its name from the perception that it had protuberances that resembled small grains of iron.[39] Epiphanius refers to a serpent by κεγχρῖτις (*Pan.* 66.88); there is no reason to imagine that this noun is to be distinguished from κεγχρίας. Another name for perhaps the same snake is κεγχρίνες.[40]

21. κεντρίς   *pseudocerastes persicus*   Persian horn viper

The Persian horn viper apparently derives its name from the stinging sensation one feels when bit since the verb κεντρόω means "to furnish with a sting." The noun κεντρίς needs to be added to LSJM and perhaps to other lexicons of ancient Greek.[41]

22. κεράστης   *Cerastes cerastes*   Horn-viper

The Horn-viper is the proper name for this snake mentioned by Nicander (*Theriaca* 258) and used by the Greek translator of Proverbs 23:32, since κέρας means the "horn" of an animal and κεράστης means something "horned." The Horn-viper may also be associated with the *Cerastes cornutus*.[42]

23. κωφίας   *ophiosaurus apodus*   unknown

The compilers of LSJM suggest that the noun denotes a "burrowing snake" (see Aelian, *Nat. an.* 8.13 [of the second or third cent. CE]). Since κωφάω means "to be silent,"[43] most likely the name of the snake derived from observations of its silent movement, which is an astonishing feature of how snakes move effortlessly and silently without disturbing thin grass.[44]

24. μελάνουρος   *pseudocerastes persicus*   Persian viper (see no. 11)

The compilers of LSJM suggest that the noun meant "a kind of snake." They pointed our attention to Aelian's *Nat. an.* 6.51, and thought μελάνουρος may be equal to διψάς (= no. 11). We agree and suggest that μελάνουρος, like διψάς, is to be identified as *pseudocerastes persicus*. To preserve the distinction between the two Greek nouns, we suggest "Persian horn viper" for διψάς and "the Persian horn viper" for μελάνουρος.[45] Lampe did not find the latter word in Patristic Greek. The name may derive from its color since μέλαν denotes "black," and μελάνουρος can also denote a "black-tailed sea fish."[46]

25. μύαγρος   unknown   rat snake

This indeterminate snake probably was revered by Greeks,[47] who often kept pet snakes in the home. These snakes killed mice and rats; etymologically, the present noun derives from the appearance of μῦς, "mouse," or "rat" in its name.

26. ὄφις   *anguis*   snake, serpent

This noun is the generic name for "snake" or "serpent" in Greek. It is the fifth and final word in our list that appears in the New Testament, and it is the word for snake or serpent that is most frequently used by New Testament authors.[48] The word ὄφις can also denote serpent jewelry, notably the silver and gold bracelets, rings, and earrings that were so popular in the Greek and Roman world. The word also denotes the constellation "Serpent."[49] The noun may be onomatopoeic since *ophis* sounds like the hissing of a snake. Some Greeks may have associated ὄφις with ὀπή, as the animal from "a hole."

27. παρείας
   παρούας[50]   *elaphe quatuorlineata*   four-striped adder

The "four-striped adder" is the reddish-brown snake that was sacred to Asclepius.[51] The search for the etymology of this noun appears too speculative.

28. πάρωος   unknown   unknown

The noun that now appears in the Egyptian and Greek book on poison is not listed in LSJM and other similar lexicons. Is πάρωος the name of an unknown snake? We have not offered a name for the present snake since it may be another means of pronouncing παρούας, discussed in the previous entry.

28. πελιάς   *vipera ursinii*   reddening viper [?]

This noun also is not listed in the major lexicons. Perhaps the "new" word may have developed from perceiving the red coloring of the skin when one is bitten since πελιός denotes the discoloration of the body "by extravasated blood."[52] The new noun is not to be confused with the similar sounding πελειάς or "fruit-pigeon."[53]

30. πρηστήρ   *echis coloratus*   burning snake [?]

This noun denotes some genus of poisonous snake.[54] It derives its name probably from the burning caused when one is bitten, a pain somehow associated with lightning, since πρηστηριάζω means "to burn up as with lightning."

31. πτυάς   *naja mossambicca pallida*   Mossambic cobra

The πτυάς is a species of spitting cobra.[55] It etymologically derives its name from the habit of spitting since πτύω means "to spit."

32. σηπεδών   *echis pyramidum*   putrefying snake [?]

This is a kind of snake whose venomous bite causes putrefaction since σηπεδών means fundamentally "decay" and "putrefaction."[56]

33. σήψ   *echis pyramidum*   putrid snake [?]

This snake derives its name from two possible meanings. The name may have arisen because the snake, when it bites a human, causes a putrid sore (from σήπω [or σήπομαι (N.B. the Future: σήψω) which means "to be rotten" or "to be putrid"]).[57] It is less likely that the name was given to the snake because it arouses intense thirst (from δίψα, which means "thirst").[58]

34. σκυτάλη   *eryx jaculus*   boa

This noun signifies a serpent that is like a round stick,[59] since fundamentally σκυτάλη denotes a "baton," "staff," or "stick."[60]

35. τυφλώψ

τυφλίνης   *ophiosaurus apodus*   blind snake

Since τυφλώψ specifies someone who is "blind," the name was probably given to a snake that seemed blind (some small snakes are blind). The compilers of LSJM suggest that τυφλίνης denotes a "blind snake" and perhaps *Pseudopus pallasi*.[61]

36. ὕδρος   *Columber natrix*   water snake

The snake probably does not denote a "viper" or *vipera lebetina,* as suggested by C. Leitz in his *Die Schlangennamen in den ägyptischen und griechischen Gift-büchern.* The noun ὕδρος evolves from ὕδωρ, "water."[62] The noun appears frequently in Classical Greek, being used by Homer (*Iliad* 2.723), Herodotus (2.76), and Aristotle (*Hist. an.* 487ᵃ23 and 508ᵇ1). It may evolve further into ὕδρωψ, "an amphibious reptile," found in Patristic Greek (cf. Epiphanius, *Pan.* 25.7).[63]

37. φύσαλος   unknown   puff adder[64]

The compilers of LSJM reported that φύσαλος denoted "a kind of *toad said to puff itself up*" and "a poisonous *fish which puffs itself out.*"[65] Now we need to add the meaning "puff adder." The noun φύσαλος signifies a snake that "puffs"— obviously a "puff adder"—since φυσάω means "to puff." The Greek noun does not appear in Patristic Greek.[66]

38. χελιδονία   *walterinnesia aegyptica*   desert cobra

According to the compilers of LSJM, χελιδονία indicated only a "swallow's nest." This is the meaning in Aristotle's *Historia Animalium* (626ᵃ12), but we now know, thanks to the newly published papyrus on ancient poison, that the Greek noun also denotes a poisonous snake, perhaps a "desert cobra." Note that, according to the third-century CE physician Philumenus, χελιδόνιος ἀσπίς specified a kind of asp;[67] hence, in light of the new philological data, "desert cobra" seems a good choice. The etymology of the new noun seems uncertain. The noun χελιδόνια (note the shift in accent) has long been known to denote a certain type of fig.

39. χέλυδρος   *vipera berus*   water viper

The second-century BCE Epicurean Nicander in his *Theriaca* (411) used this noun to denote, perhaps, an "amphibious snake."[68] The base meaning, of course, is a snake associated with water (ὕδωρ); hence, "water viper" seems appropriate. The Greek noun does not appear in ancient Christian literature.[69]

40. χερσαία   *naja haje*   Egyptian cobra

The noun χερσαία is not known to the compilers of the Greek lexicons. It seems to derive from a poisonous snake that inhabits desert land (χερσαῖα denotes "arid land").[70] The Greek noun is not cited by Lampe, and thus it appears not to be used by the ancient scholars of the Church who wrote in Greek.

41. χέρσυδρος   *vipera lebetina*   amphibious viper

In his *Theriaca* (359), Nicander seems to use the Greek noun to indicate some generic amphibious snake.[71] Again, some type of poisonous water snake is indicated for χέρσυδρος since it bears the Greek word for "water."

I have erred in the direction of being conservative regarding the English equivalents. Thus, I have not sought to identify the Greek names with English nouns not found in the list, such as black mamba, Boomslang, garden snake, coral snake, copperhead, moccasin, rattlesnake, black indigo, and others. Most of these names did not appear in ancient Mediterranean culture. Translators of ancient Greek documents, including the Classics as well as the Septuagint and the Greek New Testament, have too often misrepresented the sophistication of the ancient Greeks simply by equating the forty-one Greek nouns with generic terms as "snake" or "serpent," and occasionally "viper" or "cobra."

Etymological research provides two insights. First, many nouns derive from the habits, effect on humans, or frequent location of a snake. Second, the ancients knew the phenomenal world of nature intimately. They lived in, among, and often with snakes; they frequently adored, even worshipped, serpents. We have lost not only the ancients' language of symbolism (symbology), but also their experience of the beauty and friendliness of nature. Translations and interpretations of such passages as John 3:14 have been marred and corrupted by the unexamined presupposition that serpents are snakes that are to be hated. Many biblical scholars tell me they despise snakes, yet this presupposition distorts the positive symbolism of a serpent found among many in antiquity; for example, Jesus, representing an aspect of Jewish Wisdom literature, advised the Twelve, when he commissioned and sent them into the world, to be "wise as serpents" (φρόνιμοι ὡς ὄφεις in Mt 10:16; see also *The Gospel of Thomas* 39 and the *Teaching of Silvanus*).

This initial list, especially the guesses as to proper English equivalents, will need to be improved by others, especially ophiologists and experts on ancient snakes, so that the uses of "unknown" or suggestions followed by a question mark may be replaced with a better guess. It is clearly amazing how many words the Greeks had for the serpent (the same applies to English). Studies based on the Egyptian book on poisons, the Brooklyn Egyptian Serpent Papyrus,[72] which informed Leitz when he wrote *Die Schlangennamen in den ägyptischen und griechischen Giftbüchern*, have greatly increased our knowledge of Greek and Egyptian ophiolatry.[73] On the basis of the information found in these publications and a minute study of lexicons and of ancient texts, it was possible to compile the first list of ancient Greek words for the various types of snakes or mythological dragon-serpents. Such research was fundamental for me as I wrote the previous chapters.

Although there may be forty-one nouns in ancient Greek to denote various types of snakes, only five appear in the Greek New Testament.[74] This figure, 5/41, should not seem surprising because the documents in the New Testament are theological works and should not to be confused with zoological treatises such as a *Historia Animalium* or a *De Natura Animalium*. Moreover, the Greek chosen as a vehicle by the New Testament authors was targeted for the masses; it was not intended to educate the intellectual in an academy. This perception is not diminished by the fact that many New Testament authors knew and did occasionally use sophisticated Greek (e.g. Lk 1:1–4, Rom, and Heb; contrast Rev, whose author thought in Aramaic and Hebrew but wrote in Greek).

The five Greek nouns for snake or serpent that appear in the New Testament corpus are ἀσπίς (Rom 3:13), δράκων (Rev 12:3, 4, 7 [*bis*], 9, 13, 16, 17; 13:2, 4, 11; 16:13; 20:2),[75] ἑρπετόν (Acts 10:12; 11:6; Rom 1:23; Jas 3:7), ἔχιδνα (Mt 3:7; 12:34; 23:33; Lk 3:7; Acts 28:3),[76] and ὄφις (fifteen times in the New Testament [including Mk 16:18]).[77] This lexicographical study reveals the richness of ancient Greek, and the interest of the Greeks in Egypt from which much of Greek ophidian iconography derives. It also discloses the penchant of the author of Revelation for δράκων.

Appendix III: Anguine Iconography and Symbolism at Pompeii

August 24, 79 CE, was a fateful day for the inhabitants of Pompeii and its environs. These Romans, as they headed toward their tasks while looking up to a blue sky and bright sun, would never again see a peaceful sky. Their frescoes, paintings, and gold jewelry remain. As we look at them, it becomes clear how much has changed, especially regarding anguine symbolism. Almost two thousand years later, we can pause and remember that horrific day, as we look at the outlines of their gray remains. Some Pompeians remind us how to die; for me especially poignant are the lovers who did not flee into the inferno, deciding to "go out" holding on to what was most dear.

About a decade earlier, in June 68 CE, the Qumranites also faced a tragic day. These Jews who gingerly placed over seventy scrolls in jars and on rocks inside what we call Cave I would never see the scrolls again. Many of these Jews scampered up the limestone cliffs, heading west to find safety behind the walls of Jerusalem. Some may have paused, and looking backward would have seen Vespasian astride a horse prancing before a massive tower behind which a community went up in flames. What the Qumranites hid in Cave I have become some of our greatest treasures from antiquity. These Dead Sea Scrolls contain ideas and perspectives we humans have not yet understood and practiced. They mirror minds who found secrets about the spiritual that still elude many of us.

Only eleven years separate these monumental events in our past. Both Pompeii before 79 and Qumran before 68 had been devastated previously by earthquakes. Pompeii was hit in 62 CE and Qumran in 31 BCE.[1] As N. Purcell states about Pompeii: "[T]he sudden destruction crystallized a problematic moment: the damage of the earthquake of 62 was still being patchily repaired and the opulence and modishness of some private and public projects of the last phase . . . contrast with chaos and squalor."[2] At Pompeii, and also at Qumran, there are vivid reminders of an earthquake that antedates the final destruction.

It is conceivable that one or more persons witnessed both horrors, the one in Judea in 68 and the other in Campania in 79. Perhaps one who had worked in the Qumran Library also slaved in the Herculanean Library known as "the Villa of Papyri." Why are these reflections not simply outlandish fantasies?

The Hebrew graffiti being found on the western slopes of Vesuvius, especially at Pompeii and Herculaneum, are often left by Jewish slaves. The inscriptions

Figure 88. The House of Criptoportico, Close-up. Pompeii. JHC

are "recent"—they were made shortly before 79. The Hebrew is common and unskilled, probably written by uneducated Palestinian Jews. Their vulgarity contrasts with the elegant and refined Hebrew in most Qumran scrolls.

Jewish slaves were certainly brought to Italy when Jerusalem fell in 70 CE. Hebrew scrolls are known to have been seen in Rome in the decades after 70 and they contain readings now being found in the Dead Sea Scrolls. Josephus tells us that he was allowed by Titus to take scrolls that were in the Temple (see his *Life*).[3]

One cannot refrain from wondering: "Were any of the Jewish slaves in Italy, especially at Pompeii, originally Qumranites?" Vespasian, who burned Qumran, enjoyed vacationing in the area highlighted by Cuma (and the Grotta della Sibilla),[4] Quarto, Puteoli, Baia, Capo Miseno, Neapolis [Naples], Herculaneum, and Pompeii. A temple to Vespasian was erected on the southern side of the famous forum in Pompeii. Did Vespasian in Campania ever recognize a face he had seen at Qumran or in Palestine? The answer is "probably no." But one cannot be certain, and good historicity requires such imaginative reflections.

Is it foolish to compare Roman Pompeii and Jewish Palestine? Again the answer is clear: "certainly not." Trade had long united the two areas, and the relation seems to have increased before 70 CE, when Titus took Jerusalem. Trade between Campania and first-century CE Palestine has become palpably evident. The so-called "Pompeian-red" ware has been found in Samaria and elsewhere in ancient Palestine. Excavators working in Jerusalem recently discovered Pompeian rim forms. Their date is singularly important for us. Why? The answer lies in the recognition that the wares date from the time of Augustine to the end of the first century CE.[5] That covers the period in present focus.

Many who have written on Pompeii stress the extreme distance between rich and poor. The houses of the wealthy in Pompeii are often more opulent than posh apartments in Manhattan; they were decorated with frescoes and elegant bronzes that make the modern usually pale into mediocrity. The average houses are frequently far better than the tenant apartments that multiply in and around New

Figure 89. House of the Hebrew. Pompeii. JHC

York City. Thus, contrasts must be understood in terms of contexts. Pompeii was a place for the wealthy; I know of no dwelling there that should be categorized as a dwelling for the abjectly poor.

A closer look at the remains of pre-79 Pompeii reveals something astounding. Serpent images are seen on private "chapels" in homes, in public thoroughfares, and especially on gold rings, bracelets, earrings, and armlets.

Larari with Serpents. In Pompeii and elsewhere in the Roman world, larari are featured in houses and homes. They are essentially little chapels and small shrines that remind me of a similar modern practice. Today, outside Pompeii in all directions I frequently see niches outside houses; these are for honoring the Virgin Mary. The human perpetuates the need for divine presence and protection.

The *larari* represent the domestic cult. They were destined to ensure the prosperity, health, and continuity of the household. Romans focused religion on household gods and ancestors.

In houses, the *larari* habitually feature elegant images of serpents.[6] Only a selection may be presented now.[7] In "the House of Criptoportico," in the *lararium* of the peristyle, are depicted three ophidian images: a large Agathadaimon,[8] a serpent encircling an altar (or fountain) then rising above it, and a depiction of Hermes with the caduceus (I-16-2).

The "House of Menandro," so called for the presence of a fresco of the poet Menandro, was restored recently by A. De Simone. The house has in the atrium, on the right, a *lararium* with an interesting representation of a snake, but it is not Agathadaimon. The monumental form of the *lararium* is an index of the wealth of the owners. This house belonged, in fact, to a *libertus* of the family of Poppea, the wife of Nero. There are undeniable signs of the inhabitant's wealth. For example, the house has expensive mosaics crafted from tiny tesserae,

Figure 90. House of the Pig; Shrine to Asclepius. Pompeii. JHC

and archaeologists found 130 pieces of an opulent silver service for sumptuous dining.

On the wall in front of the entrance to the House of Menandro, on the left, we may admire a scene of Laocoon with his sons, the snake *(dragon),* and the sacrifice of the bull. Not only Greek mythology but Jewish traditions left impressions on those who frequented the house. Near the garden, images represent biblical scenes (e.g., the Judgment of Solomon) with exotic characters as dwarves and pygmies. Moreover, one can examine the "images of the ancestors" *(immagines maiorum)* in wood.

The "Two Plans House," also called the "House of the Hebrew," was built during the Neronian Period. Particularly interesting is a fresco, in front of which is an altar. Featured in the fresco are two Agathadaimons, an egg, and fire.

A snake with an egg also is seen in Region I, insula 11, entry 10. The depiction of a serpent with an egg and before an altar clarifies that the serpent symbolizes something desirable and positive, perhaps fruitfulness (Pos. 2), creation (Pos. 7), the cosmos (Pos. 8), chronos (Pos. 9), divinity (Pos. 11), and rejuvenation (Pos. 26).

In Region I, insula 16, entry 4 (179), is a *lararium* featuring two snakes. Also, in Region I, insula 16, entry 3, one can see, in stucco, an embossed snake.

In Region I, insula 11, entry 8, one may see another impressive fresco. Most interesting for us is a depiction of Hermes (Mercury) with the caduceus, and a priest with the *praetexta* robe. He brings in his hands the horn of abundance, a *lares* with horn, and wine in a bucket. Below him are shown two snakes. In the

Figure 91. *Left.* Priapus. Pompeii. JHC

Figure 92. *Right.* Bacchus, Agathadaimon, and Vesuvius. Pompeii. JHC

"House of the Pig" is a painting of a snake and a pig. There is also a shrine to Asclepius.

In "the House of the Vettii," in the central panel of the *triclinium,* is a painting of Hercules, as a lad, strangling two serpents.[9] In the "House of the Criptoportico," already mentioned because of its *lararium,* is a painting of Hermes (Mercury) with the caduceus and the snake.

The "Brothel House" at Pompeii attracts a long line of visitors. Yet most of them do not see the picture of Priapus, inside the door, above and to the right.[10] He has two phalli, and he holds each in his hand. What could be the meaning of this symbol? Is it a male fantasy to double penetrate a prostitute? Is it a sign of double power and fertility?

Is it not more likely that the painting of Priapus mirrors the fascination of Pompeians with the serpent? Would it not be unperceptive of us to imagine that only we know that male serpents have two phalli? While there is no clear link between Priapus and ophidian symbolism at Pompeii, he does appear elsewhere (like Bes) with a phallus as a serpent. Perhaps specialists in symbology have not sufficiently studied the anatomy of snakes to see analogies in art that were put there, or seen there, by the Pompeians. The link between Priapus with two phalli and the serpent may be also indicated by the fact that he is standing near a tree; in ancient art, the serpent and tree are often associated (as clarified previously).

While working in the Hermitage in St. Petersburg, I was astounded by the attractive depictions of the serpent with Hygieia. In Pompeii and in the Naples Archaeological Museum, I was impressed by the many large serpents displayed in frescoes and paintings. For example, a serpent is featured in *Bacco e Vesuvio*

Figure 93. *Arrivo di Io a Canopo.* Painting No. 9558. Pompeii. JHC

(No. 11986). It is Agathadaimon. He fills the lower half of the painting, rising up beneath Mount Vesuvius, which appears tranquil and with its pre-79 top.

In *Arrivo di Io a Canopo,* found in the Temple of Isis, a woman sits serenely. In her right hand she holds an asp, who rises with hood spread and tongue projected (No. 9558).

Other serpents appear in paintings and frescoes for the visitor to the Naples Archaeological Museum (viz. *Oggetti del culto Dionisiaco*). Most of the artwork is from Pompeii. I have the impression that the serpent was the favorite animal for the Pompeians. For them, it clearly symbolized many positive concepts, ideas, and ideals. We also need to remember that living snakes were honored in homes for religious and practical reasons.

Streets. In "Vicolo Storto," one can still see a large painting of two snakes on the external wall of a house. The place is close to a room in which prostitutes worked. Surely Professor De Simone is right to point out that there is no connection between this representation and the exercise of such women.[11] There is no relation between the wall painting and the "Brothel House"; moreover, prostitutes could not afford such a fresco. The painting represented not the imaginations of sexually skilled women; it depicted the fascination of the average Pompeian with serpents.

In Region I, insula 8, one may see another painting of a snake on an external wall. The mural is badly destroyed, but the original size of the painted serpent is evident. It is at least 5 meters long (over 15 feet).[12] The undulating body of the depicted serpent most likely symbolized, inter alia, life (Pos. 20) as well as riches and wealth (Pos. 29).

Jewelry. Working in the Medagliere e Collezioni del Museo in the Naples Archaeological Museum, I learned that virtually all the attractive jewelry found in Pompeii and Herculaneum is gold with serpent images.[13] Again, my report must be selective (see also Chap. 3, esp. "Archaeological Evidence of the Influence of

Figure 94. Gold Serpent Ring. No. 25040. Pompeii. JHC

Greco-Roman Ophidian Iconography in Ancient Palestine: The Jewelry of Pompeii and Jerusalem").

No less than ten gold rings were examined in the Medagliere. Three of them are shaped so that at the ends of the open ring two serpents face each other, perhaps signifying the caduceus (11159, 25039, 25040). The most intricate and heaviest ring is No. 25040; it is 2.7 centimeters wide and 2.7 centimeters high. Tongues protrude from the serpents' mouths. Four holes indicate the eyes; no jewels remain in the holes and perhaps none were ever placed in them.

One gold ring is heavily worn (No. 113744). Probably this ring had been worn by other women, perhaps a mother and conceivably a grandmother. The ring is heavy and well made; it is 2.4 centimeters high. The serpent has four curves.

One gold ring (No. 80) features a serpent; it also has four curves. It is 0.8 centimeters high and 2 centimeters wide. When the ring lies on a table, it looks like a coiled, upraised cobra. Ring No. 25043 has the appearance of an Ouroboros.

The gold bracelets and armlets that are fashioned as serpents are too numerous to discuss. Examining the serpents' heads of some of these, I had the impression that jewels once had been in the holes that graphically represent the eyes of serpents. This assumption was proved by an examination of a gold bracelet (No. 126365). It is 8.4 centimeters high and 7.9 centimeters wide. The bracelet is very heavy and crafted from fine gold. It was intricately and artistically made. The serpent is realistic—its scales are represented by numerous indentations on the body.

This bracelet received minute attention from a skilled craftsman. The serpent's head obtained special focus. It is triangular; hence, a poisonous snake like an asp was imagined by the artisan. The head is 2.4 centimeters long and 1 centimeter high. The details of the head include the smooth area of a serpent's head and the customary prominent eyes. The circular depressions impressively indicate eyes in which jewels were set. As just intimated, one eye still retains a jewel; it is 0.3 centimeters in diameter and may be an emerald.

The serpent's mouth is open. Under the head, indentations in the gold denote scales. There are three curls. Studying the serpent bracelet, I considered the symbolic meanings intended by the creator, those added by the wearer, and those imagined by any who beheld it. The Pompeians would have seen symbolically represented at least the following: beauty, power, strength, and especially life.

Conclusion

In the first century CE, Pompeii was not a cult of serpents, but the Pompeians encouraged many cults that deified and worshipped the serpent—the evidence of Egyptian culture, with its many serpent gods and goddesses, is palpable.

The veneration of the serpent existed in this part of the world for centuries. A painted krater can be seen in the Museo Archeologico di Pithecusae; it features a serpent on a shield, and dates from the fifth century BCE. But the profusion of serpent images at Pompeii is uncommon. This city was wonderfully situated, and all segments of the populace were united by one image: the serpent.[14] This animal signified many aspirations and hope, notably, healing, long life, renewed life, and continued life (see, respectively, Positive Symbols 23, 20, 27). Many in Pompeii would have agreed that the serpent was a very positive symbol. An inscription celebrated love with the symbol of a bee, *amantes ut apes vitam mellitam exigent* ("lovers like bees make life [sweet as] honey"). I found no inscription that mentions a serpent. Yet the bee was celebrated at Luxor, not Pompeii. In the Roman city, the serpent was the dominant symbol.

Imagining the symbolic world of the Pompeians, I may more fully comprehend that a symbol is a synthetic reality. A symbol is obviously more than a word or a picture. It has many meanings, as we saw during our study of serpent symbolism in antiquity. Symbols embody magical meanings (Pos. 16 and 17). Perhaps words are the best medium for appealing to our intelligence. If so, symbols, pictures, and images are human creations designed to evoke feelings, past experiences, and future hopes. Perhaps at Pompeii the images of serpents helped the Pompeians to imagine not only new life (Pos. 20, 26, 27) but also the continuation of the family and the household. As the many notes in Mozart's *Don Giovanni* constitute a symphony of sound, so the many images at Pompeii create a world of symbology in which the serpent symbolizes all human dreams and aspirations.

Appendix IV: Notes on Serpent Symbolism in the Early Christian Centuries (Ophites, Justin, Irenaeus, Augustine, and the Rotas-Sator Square)

In the preceding pages, I frequently drew attention to the interest in the serpent that was shaped by an exegesis of John 3:14–15. Now, I shall organize some thoughts on the Ophites, add a select few comments by the so-called Fathers of the Church, and introduce a challenging, if speculative, meaning of the Rotas-Sator Square.

Ophites (Naasanes, Peritae)

The Ophites, a "sect" of Christians, appeared in the second century CE. They apparently vanished sometime in the fourth century, with the clarification of "orthodoxy" supported by the power of the "Holy Roman Empire."

Ophites. In the treatise *Against All Heresies,* dating perhaps from the third or fourth century CE, an unknown writer castigated Christians who were referred to as "Ophites." According to this writer, remembered as "Pseudo-Tertullian," this group was so named because of their interpretation of John 3:14–15 and the exaggerated and literal interpretation of Christ as the serpent. Pseudo-Tertullian claims that the Ophites "prefer" the serpent "even to Christ himself; for it was he, they say, who gave us the origin of the knowledge of good and of evil."[1] The writer continues to summarize the mythology of the Ophites, and contends that the Ophites believe that "Christ himself . . . in his gospel imitates Moses' serpent's sacred power, in saying: 'And as Moses raised the serpent in the wilderness, so it is necessary for the Son of man to be raised up.' "[2] It is singularly significant for our research to observe that John 3:14 is quoted. We should review critically, and with requisite suspicion, any polemical representation of another's views.

In his encyclopedic refutation of the so-called heretics, Epiphanius (c. 315–403) discusses the Ophite sect. He reports:

> [T]hey are called Ophites because of the serpent which they magnify. . . . and in their deception they glorify the serpent, as I said, as a new divinity. . . . But to those who recognize the truth, this doctrine is ridiculous, and so are its adherents who exalt the serpent as God. . . . these so-called Ophites too ascribe all knowledge to this serpent, and say that it was the beginning of knowledge for men.[3]

Epiphanius is not attempting to represent or be sympathetic to this sect; he unabashedly castigates it as "stupidities" (1.1), "foolishness" (5.1), and "silly opinion" (5.2). Yet he provides valuable information on this sect with its extreme exegesis of Numbers 21 and John 3, which they cite directly, per Epiphanius (7.1–8.1). According to Epiphanius, they hold a myth that the supreme god: "stared down at the dung of matter, and sired a power that looked like a snake, which they also call his son" (4.4). The Ophites apparently defended their mythology by claiming that "the entrails" of all humans are "shaped like a serpent" (5.1). Building their ideology on an exegesis of Genesis 3, they magnify the serpent because "he has been the cause of knowledge for the many" (5.2). They allegedly celebrate the Eucharist by allowing a snake, which they subsequently kiss, to encircle the bread placed on the table: "But they worship an animal like this, and call what has been consecrated by its coiling around it the eucharistic element. And they offer a hymn to the Father on high—again, as they say, through the snake—and so conclude their mysteries" (5.7).

In refuting the Ophites, Epiphanius reveals that he metaphorically interprets John 3:14 to mean that *Christ is like the serpent,* after the typos of Numbers 21. He rightly claims: "[The] thing [that is the serpent] Moses held up in those times effected healing by the sight of it—not because of the nature of the snake but by the consent of God, who used the snake to make a sort of antidote for those who were bitten then" (7.1). He denigrates the Ophites because they interpret the text of John 3:14 "literally" (7.6). His interpretation demands the recognition: "Jesus Christ our Lord . . . is no serpent" (8.1), and his portrayal of the serpent's symbolism is purely negative: "There is nothing wise about a snake" (8.1). Yet he perceives the metaphorical meaning of John 3:14: "And as healing came to the bitten by the lifting up of the serpent, so, because of the crucifixion of Christ, deliverance has come to our souls from the bites of sin that were left in us" (7.5). He notes that Jesus, according to Matthew, said that his followers must be "wise as serpents," and he struggles to interpret this saying. He attempts to find something wise about the serpent, but only reveals his ignorance of it. For example, he says that the serpent is wise because it "does not bring its poison" when it leaves its den for a drink of water (8.5).

Naassenes. The noun "Naassene" derives from the Hebrew *nāḥāš,* "snake" or "serpent." Hippolytus reported that this "sect" worshiped the snake. Note his words: "They worship nothing other than the *Naas,* whence they are called Naassenes. *Naas* is the snake, wherefore all the *naoi* [temples] under the heavens are so called after the *Naas*" (*Elenchos* 5.9, 12 [italics mine]). Hippolytus does not explain the relation between the Ophites, discussed by Pseudo-Tertullian and Epiphanius, and the Naassenes. He does mention another word *(Peratae)* for a sect similar to or perhaps identical with the Naassenes.

Peratae. In his *Refutation of All Heresies* (early third cent.), Hippolytus reported that the Peratae was an early Christian sect that understood John 3:14 in light of Numbers 21. This verse denoted the "perfect serpent" that delivered those who had been bitten. The Peratae held that the image of a serpent is in heaven and is constantly conspicuous in light. The beautiful image of the serpent becomes "an originating principle" of all life (Book 5, chap. 11).

Hippolytus continues to describe the doctrine of the Peratae, who clearly have focused their thoughts on an exegesis of John 3:14. Hippolytus claimed that "according to them, the universe is Father, *Son* (and) Matter. . . . Intermediate, then, between the Matter and the Father sits *the Son, the Word, the Serpent,* always being in motion towards the unmoved Father, and (towards) Matter itself in motion."[4] In his *Elenchos* (5.17, 8), Hippolytus stated that the Peratae held that

> The cosmos consists of Father, *Son,* and Matter. Each of these three principles contains infinitely many forces. Midway between the Father and Matter, *the Son, the Logos,* has his place, *the Serpent* that moves eternally toward the unmoved Father and moved Matter . . . no one can be saved and rise up again without *the Son, who is the Serpent.* For it was he who brought the paternal models down from above, and it is he who carries back up again those who have been awakened from sleep and have reassumed the features of the Father.[5]

The Peratae, clearly, were developing their doctrines out of an exegesis of John 3:14–15.

The Peratae were defined by their interpretation of the Fourth Gospel. They were also imagining the cosmos under the influence of Aristotle, who conceived of God as "the Unmoved Mover." Most important for our work is the recognition that the Peratae developed their theology by interpreting Jesus as the serpent, and their base text is John 3:14–15.

We must emphasize the basis for the Peratae's concept of the Son as the Serpent: it is an exegesis of John 3:14 in light of Numbers 21. Equally impressive as the preceding quotation is the following summary by Hippolytus of the Peratae's Christology: "No one, then, he says, can be saved or return [into heaven] without the Son, and *the Son is the Serpent.*"[6] Anatomically, the brain, because it is unmovable, symbolizes the Father, and the cerebellum, because of its motion and form of a serpent, represents the Son.[7]

Hippolytus' reference to the Peratae is so informative of serpent symbolism, especially in light of an exegesis of John 3:14–15, that it should be more fully quoted:

> No one, then, he says, can be saved or return [into heaven] without *the Son,* and *the Son is the serpent.* For as he brought down from above the paternal marks, so again he carries up from thence those marks roused from a dormant condition and rendered paternal characteristics, substantial ones from the unsubstantial Being, transferring them hither from thence. This, he says, is what is spoken: "I am the door." And he transfers [those marks], he says, to those who close the eyelid, as the naphtha drawing the fire in every direction towards itself; nay rather, as the magnet [attracting] the iron and not anything else, or just as the backbone of the sea falcon, the gold and nothing else, or as the chaff is led by the amber. In this manner, he says, is the portrayed, perfect, and con-substantial genus drawn again from the world by the serpent; nor does he [attract] anything else, as it has been sent down by him. For a proof of this, they adduce the anatomy of the brain, assimilating, from the fact of

its immobility, the brain itself to the Father, and the cerebellum to *the Son,* because of its being moved and being of the form of [the head of] *a serpent.* And they allege that this [cerebellum], by an ineffable and inscrutable process, attracts through the pineal gland the spiritual and life-giving substance emanating from the vaulted chamber [in which the brain is embedded]. And on receiving this, the cerebellum in an ineffable manner imparts the ideas, just as the Son does, to matter; or, in other words, the seeds and the genera of the things produced according to the flesh flow along into the spinal marrow. Employing this exemplar, [the heretics] seem to adroitly introduce their secret mysteries, which are delivered in silence. Now it would be impious for us to declare these; yet it is easy to form an idea of them, by reason of the many statements that have been made.[8]

Centuries later in his homilies on the Fourth Gospel, John Chrysostom (c. 347–407) compared Jesus to the serpent. Here are the four most important aspects of his homiletical interpretations for our study of serpent symbolism. First, the Fourth Evangelist has chosen to compare Jesus with the serpent described in Numbers 21 to emphasize that "the old order was akin to the new."[9]

Second, and far more important, Chrysostom argued: "[I]f the Jews escaped death by looking upon the brazen image of a serpent, with much greater reason would those who believe in the Crucified One enjoy an even greater benefit."[10]

Third, the clearest example of Chrysostom's comparison of Jesus and the serpent, following the lead of the Fourth Evangelist, follows: "[I]n the former, the uplifted serpent healed the bites of serpents; in the latter, the crucified Jesus healed the wounds inflicted by the spiritual dragon."[11]

Fourth, the comparison between the serpent and Jesus is without any doubt: "In the former, there was the uplifted brass fashioned in the likeness of a serpent; in the latter, the Lord's body formed by the Spirit."[12] Chrysostom can discuss how and in what ways the comparison between Jesus and the serpent is apt because of the rich positive symbolism given to the serpent in his time and culture.

Jesus and "the Serpent," According to Justin, Irenaeus, and Augustine

While modern commentators miss the symbolic meaning of the Fourth Evangelist, ancient exegetes frequently perceive the meaning intended by the Evangelist. Only three representative examples will suffice to clarify this point. They are Justin Martyr, Irenaeus, and St. Augustine.

Justin Martyr (c. 100–c. 165 CE), a Samaritan renowned for his apologies, was scourged and then beheaded because he refused to sacrifice to the emperor in Rome. After converting to Christianity, Justin taught in Ephesus, where he debated with a Jew named Trypho around the year 135. He then moved to Rome and published sometime after 155 his work titled *Dialogue with Trypho.* It is an anti-Jewish document; in it he argues that the Covenant God of the Old Testament is superseded, that the God of the Old Testament is the Logos, and that Gentiles replace Israel in the economy of salvation. In this work, Justin claims that Joshua and the Israelites were able to defeat the Amalekites because Moses stretched out his hands, and—most important for our understanding of John 3:14—Justin asserts that Moses had imitated the sign of the cross (*Dial.* 89). After this comment, Justin proceeds to discuss "the mystery of the cross." It is at this point that he reveals his exegesis of John 3:14 and, of course, Numbers 21 in light of it. The cross was "the type and sign" that God devised for "the salvation of those who believe that death was declared to come thereafter on the serpent through Him that would be crucified."[13]

Justin seems to perceive that Jesus, according to the Fourth Evangelist, is symbolically the upraised serpent, but he cannot make this exegetical move because of his interpretation of Genesis 3. He affirms that the serpent "was cursed by God from the beginning" (*Dial.* 91). Justin may be contemplating that Jesus on the cross became sin for the sinner; that is, he became the evil serpent so he could defeat him. That is, he may be using a double entendre, thinking that Jesus as the life-giving serpent was able to conquer the Devil, the serpent (see Rev 20:2).

It is far from clear what Justin means in this passage. Is it a "clumsy exposition of St. John, iii.14," as Coxe claimed?[14] I am persuaded that this judgment is possible only when one assumes that John 3:14 does not, and cannot, mean that Jesus is portrayed as Moses' serpent that has been raised up so that all who look up to it, or believe in it, will live.

Irenaeus (c. 130–c. 200), the Bishop of Lyons in southern France, is important in establishing the time when the Church, at least in the areas he represents, accepted only four gospels: Matthew, Mark, Luke, and John. In his major publication, *Adversus omnes Haereses,* which is a virulent attack against Gnosticism, he exhibits briefly his exegesis of John 3:14. He contends that humans "can be saved in no other way from the old wound of the serpent than by believing in Him who, in the likeness of sinful flesh, is lifted up from the earth upon the tree of martyrdom, and draws all things to Himself, and vivifies the dead."[15] Irenaeus is emphasizing the importance of Numbers 21 for understanding John 3:14. The serpent raised up is the source of hope and life. Thus, according to Irenaeus, the Law (the Torah) was the pedagogue and the means for exhorting all to believe. Taken to its logical consequences, which Irenaeus almost succeeds in doing, it seems obvious that Moses' serpent symbolizes Jesus. Thus, the old serpent's wound is healed by the upraised serpent, who is none other than Jesus. Again, Irenaeus, as Justin before him, seems to equate the serpent only with evil, since he refers to Jesus who "in the likeness of sinful flesh" was raised up above the earth. The distance from the time of the Fourth Evangelist becomes impressive. Yet, in so doing, Irenaeus brings out one of the characteristics of Asclepius, the serpent god—that is, Jesus and Asclepius raise the dead to life or vivify the dead.

Augustine (354–430), the Bishop of Hippo in North Africa, was a gifted rhetorician. His understanding of Christian theology was so profound that he became the dominant force in Christian thought until the thirteenth century when Aquinas (c. 1225–1274) became the recognized master of Christian philosophy and theology. Skilled in rhetoric, grammar, and syntax, Augustine might have grasped the meaning of John 3:14. In addition to the numerous references to Augustine's exegesis of Numbers 21 and John 3 noted in Chapter 7, we may now focus on his main perception of serpent symbolism.

Although Augustine's exegesis is frequently marred by inappropriate allegorizing, he rightly knew that Numbers 21, according to Jesus' words in the Fourth Gospel, was "a mysterious foreshadowing of what was to come."[16] Augustine does not simply state that the comparison is between the lifting up of the serpent and the lifting up of the Son of Man. He knows that the Evangelist, through words attributed to Jesus, is comparing Jesus with the serpent. Augustine contends that "snakes" represent human sins that lead to death. He also perceives that the serpent "up on the post" symbolizes Jesus. Note Augustine's exegesis of John 3:14: "What is meant by the snakes? They are the sins of men doomed to die. And the serpent lifted up on the post? The death of the master on the cross" (p. 75).

As the followers of Moses looked up to the serpent, so the followers of Jesus look up to the crucified one. The Hebrews "have to look at the snake in order to render the snake harmless." So also "we must look up at Christ crucified, in order that we may be healed from sin. That is what the Master meant" in 3:14–16 (p. 75). Augustine continues: "As none of those who looked up to the serpent died of the bites, so none who look with faith on the death of Christ shall fail to be healed of the poison of sin" (p. 76). In light of the pejorative meaning of snake, which he often equates with Satan,[17] Augustine refrains from stating that the serpent is a typos of (typology for) Jesus Christ. He perceives that the serpent adumbrates Christ's death on the cross, but he gives no impression that he knew the serpent could and did symbolize "life" and "resurrection."

Why has Augustine missed a major theological point? It may perhaps be because of the threatening power of the Asclepian cult and the "heretical" views of such groups as the Ophites, but the context gives me the impression that Augustine is focused not on life and resurrection. He was focused on the human's condemnation and sin.

The Rotas-Sator Square

A Latin cryptic word square of twenty-five letters has frustrated scholars' attempts to comprehend it. This cryptograph has been discovered in many parts of the Roman Empire, from the West in Britain to the East in Dura-Europos. It was also discovered in Pompeii; hence, it clearly antedates 79 CE when that Roman city was destroyed.[18] Here is the Latin cryptograph (note how TENET forms a cross pattern):

```
R   O   T   A   S
O   P   E   R   A
T   E   N   E   T
A   R   E   P   O
S   A   T   O   R
```

The Rotas-Sator Square should not be called a "rebus"[19] since that term refers to a series of words represented by pictures or symbols. A much better description would be to call it a cryptogram or better a cryptograph; that is, something composed in a code or in a mystical pattern.

The Square Is Not Christian

The square also hides a cruciform made from the word TENET (the palindrome). This form is certainly no evidence that the Latin square is Christian.[20] The cruciform should not be deemed Christian prima facie. It is ancient; for example, it can be seen in Mesopotamian art that antedates the first century CE by millennia. It is evident in the following works of art:

> a bowl from Ur (second half of the fifth millennium BCE)
> a bowl from Susa (beginning of the fourth millennium BCE)
> stamps and seals (fourth and third millennium BCE)
> proto-dynastic seals (end of fourth millennium BCE)
> cylinder seals (second millennium BCE)[21]

Jews also used a form of the cross to signify various ideas; none of them is to be confused with the meaning Christians give to the "cross." Many of these Jewish symbols that look like a cross date from near or in the first century CE, but we should not be confused into thinking about the development or even evolution of a cross symbol from Judaism to Christianity.[22]

The attempts to read the Latin cryptogram as a Christian inscription have proved unsuccessful. Christian scholars who imagined it as designating "Pater Noster" have not been persuasive.[23]

Numerous scholars, notably Moeller, Last, Fishwick, and Gunn,[24] were convinced that the Latin language makes it very difficult to arrange letters so that a five-lettered cryptograph that can be read both left to right and right to left is created. They were wrong. W. Baines draws attention to *eighty-eight possible squares* that can be created out of Latin, which he shows is "ideal for producing word-squares."[25]

I am persuaded that the Rotas-Sator Square cannot be a Christian composition because of the numerous presuppositions demanded by such a hypothesis. Yet, unfortunately, the Rotas-Sator Square is cited as a Christian creation in many handbooks and introductions to the origins of Christianity.

Here are my reasons why the square is probably not Christian: First, the cryptograph has been found in Pompeii. That means Christians must be living there before 79 CE, and probably even before 62, which is the most likely date for the graffiti in Pompeii.[26]

Second, while this assumption is not impossible, there are no supporting proofs for it,[27] and it also demands that Christians chose the cross to symbolize their religion by the early sixties, since TENET forms a cross. Yet we have no evidence that the cross was a Christian symbol in the first century; it most likely came into use after the first century, but before Constantine's vision in the fourth century (he saw a cross in the sky and believed that with "this sign" you will conquer), and is apparently to be discerned in the catacombs of Lucina and Priscilla. The symbol of the cross is perhaps mentioned in the second-century *Epistle of Barnabas*

(9:8), but all of these examples are too late to prove Christian use of the cross before 79.[28]

Third, the cryptogram is not fully understood by "Pater Noster" since "A" and "O" are left out of the meaning. To suggest that they represent Alpha and Omega smacks of special pleading.

Fourth, the Alpha and Omega symbolism associated with Christianity is clear only in the Revelation of John,[29] which is usually dated to the nineties. That date is thirty years too late to indicate Christian composition for the Rotas-Sator Square.

Attempts to Explain the Square

Why has the meaning of the Latin mystified scholars? Far too often, scholars come to a symbol or mystical sign with preconceptions; as O. Keel pointedly proved in *Das Recht der Bilder gesehen zu werden,* all symbols have the right to be seen before they are interpreted.

Past attempts to discern the meaning of this Latin cryptograph, which have been voluminous, allow the following possibilities:

Latin					*Possible English Meanings*
R	O	T	A	S	wheels (accus. pl.), or you (s.) cause to rotate
O	P	E	R	A	works (nom. or accus. pl.), or with effort (ablative)
T	E	N	E	T	he (she, it) holds, maintains, sustains
A	R	E	P	O	[not deciphered and assumed to be someone's name]
S	A	T	O	R	sower, creator, progenitor, father (nom. or voc.)

Sator. There is not only a square to the image, but a meaning that seems to run around it. *Sator* is written at the bottom left to right, then from the same starting point from bottom left to the top, and once again from top right in both directions, left and downward. The appropriate word with which to begin seems to be Sator. This crucial word means "sower," "progenitor," and especially "creator." What is the sequence for the words?

To discern the meaning of this Latin cryptic word square we should recognize that the square is magical or mystical and, thus, the author is not referring literally to a sower who works a field. The author is probably referring to "the Creator." Such a meaning would have been readily significant to the learned and average person in the Roman Empire. And we should assume that many, if not most, of them knew the meaning of the square.

Arepo, tenet, opera, and rotas. The sequence of words seems to provide a sentence as follows: SATOR AREPO TENET OPERA ROTAS. What would that mean? The Latin *Sator . . . tenet opera rotas,* prima facie, would mean "The Creator . . . holds with effort the wheels." The Latin word *tenet* means "to hold" or "to maintain" and it is the palindrome of the square; that is, it provides the same meaning when read right to left or left to right (as well as from top to bottom and bottom to top).[30]

Arepo. The suggested sentence, "The Creator . . . holds with effort the wheels," raises two questions and a problem. Why "with effort"? And also why the plural "wheels"? A suggestion for each of these problems must await the problematic word: *arepo*. As many have pointed out, this is a word that is unknown. Most lexicographers either speculate that it is the name of some unknown person or that it is merely a meaningless series of Latin letters demanded by the opposite of its mirror image in the cryptograph, *opera*.[31]

The hallmark of research is not to give up with easy solutions or be content with unattractive answers. Hence, what does *arepo* denote? It looks like a verb, which means that the scholarly attempts to assume it is the name of the "sower" is simply sufficient evidence that such a hypothesis has collapsed from the weight of its own assumptions.

The Latin *arepo* could be the first-person indicative of a verb. The most likely suggestion is that it is from *arrepo*, which is also *adrepo*,[32] or *arepo* and because of phonetics one "r" has elided; that is, to say "arrepo" eventually evolves into the easier-to-pronounce "arepo." Also, the six-letter *arrepo* would not fit into the five-lettered square, so it would be necessary to choose the truncated *arepo*. Thus, "to creep toward" is a possibility worth pursuing. A cognate verb is *r*p* (-ere, r*psi, r*ptum)*, which means "to creep" and "to crawl." Taking *arepo* as a verb, we thus derive the meaning: "The creator, I creep toward." The problem with this explanation is that "creator" is nominative and an accusative would be needed to clarify the object to which "I creep toward." Perhaps the sentence means, "The creator—[to whom] I creep—holds the wheels with effort." That is not attractive grammar, but it is possible and fits nicely with the needs of a magical square. We should not attempt to understand the Rotas-Sator Square primarily by means of refined grammar; not only does that move the common or "vulgar" cryptogram out of its sociological context, but it imposes false criteria for discerning the intent of the author.

Sator and arepo. Who is this "creator"? Could it be Asclepius?

The key to unlocking this long too mysterious Latin word square is the word immediately following "Sator"—that is, "Creator." The Latin word *arepo*, along with its cognate *repo*, provides us with "reptile" in English. The "Creator" to whom the devotee crawls, like a snake, may be Asclepius. This god is preeminently represented in the first century CE by the symbol of the serpent. Thus, "I creep toward" is to take on the symbolic meaning of the Creator, perhaps Asclepius.

It is good to select some ancient witnesses to the Asclepian cult to stress, again, the symbolic identity between serpents and Asclepius: "[S]erpents are just as much sacred to Trophonius as to Asclepius."[33] These are the words of Pausanias who wrote in Rome near the end of the second century CE. Earlier in the first century BCE, Ovid portrayed Asclepius saying: "Only look upon this serpent *(serpentem)* which twines about my staff."[34] Between Pausanias and Ovid, and a contemporary of the Fourth Evangelist, lived a man whose dedication to study and exploration led him to become "the martyr of nature" since his curiosity led him to Pompeii during the volcanic eruption of 79 CE. This scholar, Pliny the Elder, reported: "[T]he Asclepian snake [*Anguis Aesculapius*] . . . is commonly reared even in private houses [*vulgoque pascitur et in domibus*]."[35]

Asclepius was revered from the West to the East of the Roman Empire in the first century CE, thus explaining the widespread distribution of the Latin magical cryptograph. Xenophon (c. 430–c. 354 BCE) celebrated Asclepius and reported "he has everlasting fame among men."[36]

Significant for understanding the square, Asclepius is also called "savior." Note these random examples:

> Shall I go on to tell you how Helius took thought for the health and safety of all by begetting Asclepius to be the Savior of the whole world.[37] [Julianus, 332–63 CE]

> . . . Asclepius, the Savior and the adversary of diseases.[38] [Aelianus, c. 200 CE]

> . . . Savior . . . they called Asclepius that.[39] [Suidas, c. 950 CE]

Opera. Why "with effort"? Asclepius, as a demigod, is an excellent fit for the inscription. As Edelstein states, Asclepius "had endured so many hardships."[40] In fact, Porphyrius (232–304 CE), in his *Epistle to Marcellus,* states that Asclepius completed: "[T]he blessed road to the gods through toil and strength. For . . . the upward paths to god" are attained "by those who have learned nobly to endure the hardest circumstances."[41]

Rotas. Why does the inscription have the plural *rotas,* "wheels"? Would not the singular *rota,* "wheel," more adequately denote the wheel of the cosmos? Not necessarily, since the depictions of the zodiac often have it within two circles, or wheels.

What is the meaning of "The Creator—[to whom] I creep—holds the wheels with effort?" Aristides (129–189 CE) salutes Asclepius as the god who: "[H]as every power." Indeed, he is "the one who guides and rules the universe, the savior of the whole and the guardian of the immortals, or if you wish to put it in the words of a tragic poet, 'the steerer of government.' "[42] About the same time as the completion of the Fourth Gospel, Philo of Byblos mentioned the snake-like god who is named Ophioneus. Philo then mentions the Egyptians who portray the cosmos according to the same notion. Philo reports: "They draw an encompassing sphere, misty and fiery, and a hawk-shaped snake dividing the middle. . . . the circle is the cosmos, and they signify that the snake in the middle holding it together is Good Demon."[43]

While this latter information pertains to a god other than Asclepius, it is appropriate here as it helps us comprehend the relation between the snake and the circle of the cosmos, which is apparent also in the Asclepian cult. Asclepius, who is associated with Dionysus since both were lauded as the god of the sun, is not far from mind when Macrobius explains that Dionysus "moves in a circle round the infinite broad Olympus."[44] That means the god whirls around or rotates around the heavens.

To understand *rotas* as the second-person singular, indicative mood, of *roto,* "to cause to turn around like a wheel" or "revolve" would not improve the meaning of the group of words. We would have then only understood the words to mean, "The Creator I creep toward holds with effort, you rotate." The second person seems out of place and the sentence would then lack a direct object.

We might conceivably take *rotas* as a symbolic reference to the chariot wheels on which the Sun rides on its daily route around the earth—using the cosmology of the ancients. But is there any clear link between Asclepius and the sun? The answer is emphatically "yes." Note the following statement by Proclus who wrote shortly after the completion of the Fourth Gospel: "Porphyry declares it reasonable that even the art of healing comes from Athena, because also Asclepius is lunar intellect, just as Apollo is solar intellect. . . . In fact, one should place also Asclepius in the Sun."[45] Later, in the fourth century CE, Macrobius mentioned: "[T]he serpent is placed at the foot of the statues of Asclepius and Health, because these gods are traced back to the nature of the sun and moon. . . . the serpent is shown to be one of the special attributes of the sun [*ad solis naturam lunaeque referuntur*], because it derives its name from *derkein,* meaning 'to see.' "[46] In the fifth century CE, Proclus advised: "[O]ne should place also Asclepius in the sun letting him proceed from there to the world of becoming."[47] The previous quotations prove that Leisegang was correct when he reported: "[T]he Roman Janus and likewise Liber and Dionysus, Apollo, Asclepius, and Zeus are actually sun gods and are all connected with one another."[48]

Is Not *Sator* in the Nominative?

We turn now to a problem that seems to have hindered decipherment: the assumed nominative noun *Sator*. In a well-crafted sentence, we should expect precise grammar, and some experts seem to prefer the accusative *satorem*. But the square is not a narrative statement. Another word square found at Pompeii has the following:

R O M A
O   M
M   O
A M O R

The meaning is quite clear: "love of Rome." But notice that the square does not require the imposition of good grammar. *Roma* should have been in the genitive *Romae.*

Grammar is not a primary key for unlocking a cryptogram like the Rotas-Sator Square. On the one hand, such cryptograms are not to be confused with narrative, but, on the other, they are not the meaningless gibberish typical of the magical papyri.[49]

Sator, a third-declension noun, is most likely a vocative form. It probably means "O Creator."

Is *Sator* appropriate for Asclepius? It is used of Jupiter. Livy, Plautus, and Virgil would have agreed: *sator hominum atque deorum* ("Creator of men as well as of gods"). Asclepius is sometimes identified with Jupiter or Zeus, who is frequently known as sator. Note, for example, the following comment by Aristides: "Asclepius . . . has every power . . . the people here [i.e., at Pergamum] have built a temple [to honor] Zeus Asclepius."[50] Perhaps the one invoked is none other than Zeus, who is also depicted with serpents (as is clear in the previous chapters). The collapsing of any distinction between Zeus and Asclepius, and the depiction of Zeus plowing, is not far from the image of *Sator* as the "sower." *Sator* is appropriate equally for Zeus and Asclepius since it also means "Creator."

The clear mythological dimension of the Rotas-Sator Square is clarified by Philo of Byblos. His *Phoenician History* was composed in the late first or early second century CE, and that is close to the time for the completion of the Fourth Gospel (c. 95 CE). Philo reported: "Dagon, since he discovered grain and plough, was called Zeus Ploughman."[51] One of the Titanids who mated with Sydyk is called the " 'just one,' and bore Asclepius."[52]

The noun *sator* also means progenitor or father. That is important because we do have references to Asclepius as "father." Note, for example, the words attributed to Asclepius by Herondas in the third century BCE: "Father Paieon." Paieon is a nickname for Asclepius.[53]

In order to explain the Rotas-Sator Square, I prefer to stay with Asclepius. The Latin cryptic word square has been found in many parts of the Roman Empire. The square became popular exactly when Asclepius became the supreme god in many cities. An inscription from the third century BCE refers to Ascelpius as "the best of all the gods."[54] Asclepius is the one to beseech, "if any of the gods is to be invoked."[55] The author of a second-century CE papyrus from Oxyrhynchus salutes Asclepius as the "greatest of gods."[56] He is the god of healing, of resurrection, and of light.

Soldiers, particularly those wounded or fearing battle, would have been especially attracted to a mystical cryptogram honoring Asclepius. Note Philostratus' comment from the late second or early third century CE that Asclepius easily heals wounds from war, the chase, and all such chance occurrences.[57]

The Rotas-Sator Square thus does not seem to be Mithraic,[58] but devotees of Mithra most likely would have been attracted to it, since they also revered Asclepius. The cryptograph is also unlikely to be Orphic,[59] but again worshippers of Orpheus also invoked Asclepius. It is not Jewish.[60] I am also convinced that the weakest solution is to assume (or conclude) that the cryptograph is Christian.

My suggestion that the Latin cryptograph is a mystical invocation or celebration of the god of healing and life, Asclepius, meets the demands made on us by the archaeological settings in which it has been found. Any solution to the mystical cryptograph must obviously transcend all barriers and even cultures since the Latin square has been found inscribed on leather probably found in Saxony, in the Palaestra at Pompeii, on the wall of the Temple of Azzanathkona at Dura-Europos, and in the Palace of the Governor at Aquincum (in Budapest). As Julianus (332–363) commented, Asclepius "is present everywhere on land and sea."[61]

The cryptograph has been found in the parish church of Pieve Terzagni near Cremona, but it dates from a later period (the eleventh century).[62] The Christian reuse of the cryptograph should not influence our search for an understanding of its original meaning, and its importance in the first century CE.

My hypothesis also nicely fits the phenomena that accompanied the cult of Asclepius. In the first century CE, no other god was so well and widely worshipped in shrines and in the home as Asclepius. Apparently not only Romans but those living throughout the empire needed Asclepius for adoration, and prayed to him, as in the Hymn to Asclepius in the Orphic hymns: "Asklepios, Lord Paian, healer of all . . . come, O Blessed One, as Savior and bring life to a good end."[63]

Any interpretation of the cryptograph should explain the social needs of those who revered it. That would be the case since Asclepius was admired for good health and healing. That need transcends the normal influences of a cult.

An indication that my solution for the decipherment of the mystical cryptograph helps solve the mysterious Latin is the word that is composed of all the letters: *paterno*. This Latin form means "paternal" or "ancestor." It is found in Juvenal's *Satires*. He mentions a maiden "who lives on her paternal farm [*rure paterno*]."[64] The form also appears about the same time as the composition of the Fourth Gospel since Tacitus in his *Histories* uses it when he describes how Domitian was led to his "ancestral hearth" *(in paternos penatis deduxit)*.[65]

Is the arrangement of the letters in the cryptograph a subtle indication that Asclepius is meant to be invoked? He is called the ancestral god. For example, the famous Galen (129–199 CE) declared himself to be a worshipper of "the ancestral god Asclepius."[66]

Conclusion

The criteria for discerning the meaning of the Rotas-Sator Square have been met. Former attempts have failed to discern the meaning of this cryptograph. Some leave out letters, notably A and O. Others present a translation that would be meaningless in a cryptic square. That is, a nonmetaphorical meaning does not meet the requirements of a cryptograph; for example, the following prevalent suggestion is not cryptic: "Arepo the sower holds the wheels with labor." Many are content to give up with *arepo,* suggesting only that it is some unknown name. I have endeavored to show that it is not "simply the reverse of OPERA and that its form is determined entirely by the problems inherent in constructing a twenty-five letter square from the intersecting PATER NOSTER's with two A's and two O's."[67]

As Baines demonstrated, Latin offers itself easily for cryptic squares.[68] The key does not lie "with some unknown man called Arepo."[69] The key is provided by discerning that *arepo* denotes "to crawl toward." And this insight brings forward serpent imagery and symbolism; and that—in the historical context—suggests Asclepius. He is the god who comes to those needing healing in the form of a serpent.[70]

We have endeavored to establish that the cryptograph seems to mean "The creator—[to whom] I creep—holds the wheels with effort." Using this indicative sentence, soldiers and others could turn it into a prayer with invocatory power. They could say the word at the base of the square, *sator,* then the word at the top, *rotas,* which is its mirror image. Third, the two other mirror images would be chanted: opera arepo. Finally, the central—indeed structural importance—of *tenet,* the palindrome, would be an invocation. What would such a plea mean?

The first word, *sator,* would be a vocative that could be repeated: "O Creator, O Creator." Then Asclepius' desired attribute would be lauded in the second person: *rotas,* "you who cause (all) to rotate." The promise of the petitioner seems represented by *opera arepo,* "With effort I crawl toward [you]." Finally, the mantra would conclude with the request: *tenet, tenet, tenet, tenet,* which is written in the cryptograph, as it were, north to south, east to west, south to north, and west to east. That would mean: "Maintain [the rotations from the north, the east, the south, and the west]." Thus, the square would replicate the cosmology of four corners. The invocation is strikingly similar to others often connected with serpent mythology; note, for example, the following cited by Macrobius, admittedly rather late (c. fourth cent.) but recognized as containing ideas that originated much earlier:

> Hear, thou who [turns forever] the radiant sphere
> of distant motion [that runs round the celestial vortices].[71]

The *Prayer of Jacob* comes to mind when I think about the Rotas-Sator Square as an invocation. Recall the following from this Jewish magical prayer: "Creator of the angels . . . I invoke you. . . . Father of the [wh]ole [co]s[mos] [and of] all creation. . . . He[a]r me. . . . God of gods; amen, amen. . . . [S]ay [the p]r[a]y[e]r o[f] Jacob seven times to [the] Nor[th] and E[a]st."[72]

An alabaster bowl, dating from the beginnings of Christianity, depicts a very large serpent in the center. This artwork illustrates the universal god: "[The one] moving the whole cosmos in harmonious circles."[73] Invocations are found frequently in many genres; they shape apocalypses and appear on papyri. Perhaps one of the most important invocations for our present study is found on the Paris magic papyrus, which salutes and invokes the great serpent:

> Hail, beginning and end of immutable nature! Hail, *rotation* of the elements full of untiring service! Hail, *labor* of the sunbeams, *light* of the world! Hail glittering nocturnal *sphere* of the changing moon! . . . O great, *spherical,* unfathomable edifice of the world! . . . I praise thee God of gods . . . great art thou, lord, God, ruler of the universe.[74]

Words linked with our research on the serpent are in italics that I have added to this quotation.

All of the imagery of the cryptograph fits neatly within the mythology of the serpent in the first century CE. The serpent is depicted with his tail in his mouth, forming a complete circle (the Ouroboros). This pictorial image symbolizes the oneness of the universe. In Orphic etymology, we find these words: "Herakles" (Hercules) denotes the coiling, or encircling, serpent.[75]

In summation, in light of the perceptions obtained by studying serpent symbolism in antiquity, I offer for reflection the following suggestion.

The Rotas-Sator Square appears throughout the Roman Empire in this form:

```
R  O  T  A  S
O  P  E  R  A
T  E  N  E  T
A  R  E  P  O
S  A  T  O  R
```

The cryptogram seems to be an invocation to Asclepius, the serpent god (and conceivably thence to all gods considered to be symbolized as a serpent). It may mean: "O Creator, O Creator: You who cause [all] to rotate, with effort I crawl toward [you]." Then a mantra may appear, as words are repeated around the square: "Maintain [the rotations from the north, the east, the south, and the west]."

Glossary

This glossary focuses on terms for snake or serpent and related symbolism.

Agathadaimon a good god, spirit, or genius (Figs. 36, 92).

Anat (or Anath) a fierce warrior goddess, worshipped by the Amorites long before the Hebrews entered the "Land."

anguine the Latin loanword means "serpent-like."

anguine Christology reflections on Jesus Christ as a serpent.

anguipede serpent-footed; a figure with serpent legs or feet. The Giants and Sirenes often appear with anguipedes.

apotheosis the elevation or exaltation of a person to the status of a god.

apotropaism an object that averts evil (from Greek *apotrōpaion*), often by being the antidote for it; used in magic and ritual.

Asclepius, Asclepios (Greek), Aesculapias (Latin) Greek god of healing.

Asklepieion the name of a shrine to Asclepius.

basilisk a mythical serpent-like creature, often gallinaceous (Fig. 7).

Bes Egyptian god; a dwarf who symbolized music and dance.

bibil jars ceramic jars that tilt when placed on a table, perhaps named after the sound when a liquid pours from them (bibil).

bifid tongue the split tongue of a snake.

caduceus staff with two serpents facing each other; associated with Hermes (Mercury) (Fig. 5).

chryselephantine an object made of ivory and gold.

Coffin Texts inscriptions from the First Intermediate period of Egypt (7th through most of the 11th Dynasties: ca. 2150–2055 BCE). These spells and incantations were derived from the earlier Pyramid Texts but are now found in the tombs of those other than the pharaohs, for whom the Pyramid Texts were apparently reserved. Though often found on coffins, these inscriptions appear on tomb walls and objects associated with the burial. These texts, like the Pyramid Texts, were to aid the dead in their journey into the afterlife.

cyathus   an elegant ladle for serving wine (often mixed with water).

cysta mystica   a box or chest in which secret documents were deposited; in some, serpents were hidden, as shown on coin.

Eherne Schlange   German for "upraised serpent"; that is, a serpent on a cross. Sometimes the figure is iconographically a T-shaped cross. Usually the artist is influenced by Numbers 21 and John 3.

faience   a ceramic substance that looks like glass, but is glazed; faience was usually chosen to make small objects.

fibula   the clasp that held a garment (the toga) together.

gallinaceous   resembling a fowl.

gastrostege scales   serpentine-like markings on the belly of figures.

hemipenes   the two phalli of a serpent; neither is for urination.

Hygieia   daughter of Asclepius, goddess of good health; often shown with a serpent (see Fig. 60).

incubation   act of sleeping by a devotee, often in a temple, to obtain healing, usually through dreams, especially in the Asclepian cult.

Johannine community   the community whose traditions and sources gave rise to the Gospel of John and perhaps the Johannine letters.

kerygmata   related to the term "kerygma," the preaching of the Christian gospel message; kerygmata describes either the various communications of the gospel or the specific contents of the preaching itself.

leontocephaline   lion-headed figure, often in the cult of Mithra, frequently with serpent-entwined human figures.

mikva   Jewish bath for ritual purification.

ophidian   the Greek loanword denotes something having the features of a snake or serpent.

ophidian Christology   reflections on Jesus Christ as a serpent.

ophiolatry   the worship of snakes.

ophiology   the branch of zoology that studies snakes.

ophiophilism   a love of snakes.

Ouroboros   a figure of a serpent in a circle, swallowing its own tail. It can signify time being complete or repetitious and the male (tail) and female (mouth). It is important in Greek iconography and symbolism and in China (esp. the Yangshao culture of 4500 BCE).

Pharaonic snake-game   a pre-dynastic (4000–3200 BCE) game that uses a board that is circular with a serpent encircled within it.

Pyramid Texts   inscriptions from Old Kingdom Egypt found in the pyramids of Saqqarah on the sarcophagi of the pharaohs of the 5th and 6th Dynasties (c. 2498–

2183 BCE). These texts, which are largely spells and incantations, were to aid the pharaoh in the afterlife, reanimating his body and helping him in his ascent into the heavens. They were also to help protect his remains from corruption or disturbance.

simpulum   an elegant ladle for serving wine (often mixed with water).

uraeus   the raised cobra on the headdresses of pharaohs (Figs. 24, 25).

Notes

1. Introduction

1. The only noteworthy variant in these two verses is the different order of words at the end of verse 14. See the convenient layout of the important manuscript witnesses to these two verses by R. J. Swanson, *New Testament Manuscripts: Variant Readings Arranged in Horizontal Lines Against Codex Vaticanus; John* (Pasadena, Calif., 1995) pp. 29–30.

2. The Greek verb is ὑψόω. I decided to remove almost all the Greek and Hebrew scripts as well as other exotic scripts so that the discussion will be attractive to a large audience.

3. Epiphanius referred to "their kind of stupidity" in his *Panarion,* Section III, 37: "they are called Ophites because of the serpent which they magnify." See F. Williams, trans., *The Panarion of Epiphanius of Salamis,* 2 vols. (Leiden, 1987–1994) vol. 1, p. 241.

4. C. G. Jung, "Approaching the Unconscious," in *Man and His Symbols,* ed. C. G. Jung et al. (New York, 1968) pp. 1–94; the quotation is on p. 59.

5. J. Sandys-Wunsch and L. Eldredge, "J. P. Gabler and the Distinction Between Biblical and Dogmatic Theology: Translation, Commentary, and Discussion of His Originality," *SJT* 33 (1980) 138–39.

6. My colleagues here at Princeton Theological Seminary who are focusing their work on Systematic or Dogmatic Theology would wish to add, I am convinced, that their own disciplines must also be freed from the control of any dogmatic system or ecclesiastical sanction. They do not need to receive the approval of a biblical scholar before they complete and publish their own research.

7. W. Wrede, "The Task and Methods of 'New Testament Theology,' " in *The Nature of New Testament Theology,* ed. and trans. R. Morgan (London, 1973) p. 71.

8. A. Schlatter, "The Theology of the New Testament and Dogmatics," pp. 117–166 in *The Nature of New Testament Theology,* p. 118.

9. By anguine Christology I mean a Christology that in some ways portrays Jesus as a serpent or as having the powers culturally associated with a serpent at the time of the Fourth Evangelist and in his milieu. Those who do not read this book carefully and only wish to caricature and criticize it will err in assuming that I am thinking of Jesus as a snake. Obviously, I am not exploring this issue for those who are not willing to be challenged or venture out into uncharted waters.

10. See the reflections by E. Panofsky on the motif of Hercules as an image of Christ in *Studies in Iconology* (Oxford, 1939; Boulder, Colo., 1972) pp. 19–20.

11. See the color photograph in F. Mancinelli, *Catacombs and Basilicas: The Early Christians in Rome* (Florence, 1981) p. 37 (no. 72).

12. See Charlesworth, *The Beloved Disciple: Whose Witness Validates the Gospel of John?* (Valley Forge, Pa., 1995).

13. Charlesworth, *The New Discoveries in St. Catherine's Monastery: A Preliminary Report on the Manuscripts* (Winona Lake, Ind., 1981); see Plate 3. The copy of Mark is from the sixth century; over forty additional leaves have been recovered (it seems).

14. J. Ashton, *Understanding the Fourth Gospel* (Oxford, 1993) p. 365.

15. F. L. Godet, *Commentary on John's Gospel* (Grand Rapids, 1978 [1886]) pp. 391–92.

16. Translation mine. M.-J. Lagrange, *Évangile selon Saint Jean* (Paris, 1925 [2nd ed.]) p. 81.

17. C. H. Dodd, *The Interpretation of the Fourth Gospel* (Cambridge, 1960) p. 353.

18. R. Bultmann, *The Gospel of John: A Commentary,* trans. G. R. Beasley-Murray (Oxford, 1964) pp. 151–53. In a note on p. 152, Bultmann adds "John puts no emphasis on the identification of Jesus with the serpent." This is correct, but Bultmann perceived that John, without emphasis, did identify Jesus with the serpent.

19. R. Schnackenburg, *The Gospel According to St. John,* 3 vols., trans. K. Smyth (New York, 1965) vol. 1, pp. 395–96.

20. R. E. Brown, *The Gospel According to John,* 2 vols. (Anchor Yale Bible; Garden City, N.Y., London, 1966, 1971; reprint New Haven) vol. 1, pp. 145–46.

21. W. R. Cook, *The Theology of John* (Chicago, 1979) p. 75.

22. E. Haenchen, *John 1,* trans. R. W. Funk (Philadelphia, 1980) p. 204, see p. 207.

23. G. S. Sloyan, *John* (Atlanta, 1988) p. 46.

24. D. A. Carson, *The Gospel According to John* (Leicester, England, Grand Rapids, 1991) p. 201.

25. L. Morris, *The Gospel According to John* (Grand Rapids, 1995 [rev. ed.]) p. 199.

26. T. L. Brodie, *The Gospel According to John* (New York, Oxford, 1993) p. 199.

27. Schnackenburg, *The Gospel According to St. John,* vol. 1, p. 396.

28. Translation mine. E. Ruckstuhl, *Jesus im Horizont der Evangelien* (Stuttgart, 1988) p. 308.

29. P. W. Comfort and W. C. Hawley, *Opening the Gospel of John* (Wheaton, 1994) p. 50.

30. *Hellenistic Commentary to the New Testament,* ed. M. E. Boring, K. Berger, and C. Colpe (Nashville, 1995) pp. 260–61.

31. C. R. Koester, *Symbolism in the Fourth Gospel* (Minneapolis, 1995).

32. D. T. Olson, *Numbers* (Louisville, 1996) p. 137.

33. The Targum Onkelos to Numbers has the people grumble against "the Memra of the Lord." See I. Drazin, *Targum Onkelos to Numbers* (University of Denver, 1998) pp. 208–9.

34. Also see Num 21:8. The translators of the TANAKH chose "the Lord sent *seraph* serpents against the people," and added a footnote: "Others 'fiery'; exact meaning of Heb. *seraph* uncertain" (their use of italics). J. Milgrom also chooses not to translate *seraph.* He also points out that the LXX has "deadly" and Targum Onkelos "burning." J. Milgrom, *Numbers* (Philadelphia, 1990) p. 174.

35. Olson, *Numbers,* p. 136.

36. Note that Philo of Byblos refers to the sacred serpents or snakes that are "fiery" (*HE* 1.10.46).

37. Also see the discussion of 2 Kgs 18:4 later in this book.

38. See B. Rothenberg, *Timna: Valley of the Biblical Copper Mines* (London, 1972) pp. 129–32.

39. Milgrom, *Numbers,* p. 175.

40. S. R. Hirsch, *The Pentateuch: Numbers,* trans. I. Levy (Gateshead, 1989) vol. 4, p. 382.

41. P. J. Budd fails to do so in his *Numbers* (Waco, Tex., 1984) pp. 232–35.

42. T. R. Ashley and J. Scharbert do not clarify that the serpent was often viewed as a positive symbol in the ancient Near East. See Ashley, *The Book of Numbers* (Grand Rapids, 1993) pp. 402–6; J. Scharbert, *Numeri* (Würzburg, 1992) pp. 84–85.

43. M. Noth, *Numbers: A Commentary,* trans. James D. Martin (Philadelphia, 1968) p. 158.

44. B. Maarsingh, *Numbers,* trans. J. Vriend (Grand Rapids, 1985) p. 75.

45. Translation mine. H. Jagersma, *Numeri,* 3 vols. (Nijkerk, 1983–90) vol. 2, p. 89.

46. Milgrom, *Numbers,* p. 459.

47. R. K. Harrison, *Numbers* (Chicago, 1990) p. 278.

48. Olson, *Numbers,* p. 136.

49. Noth, *Numbers,* p. 157.

50. Maarsingh, *Numbers,* p. 76. Unfortunately, Maarsingh refers to the copper (bronze) serpent as an "objectified evil." The copper serpent is symbolic of the good; it is the sign that God is the source of healing.

51. Jagersma, *Numeri,* vol. 2, p. 90.

52. Milgrom, *Numbers,* p. 173.

53. Translation mine. Scharbert, *Numeri,* p. 84.

54. Harrison, *Numbers,* p. 277.

55. Ashley, *The Book of Numbers,* pp. 405–6.

56. Olson, *Numbers,* p. 137.

57. See esp J. G. Frazer, "The Story of the Cast Skin," *Folk-lore in the Old Testament: Studies in Comparative Religion, Legend and Law* (London, 1918) vol. 1, pp. 66–74.

58. K. R. Joines, *Serpent Symbolism in the Old Testament: A Linguistic, Archaeological, and Literary Study* (Haddonfield, N.J., 1974) p. vi.

59. *Barn.* 12.6; for the Greek see either K. Lake, *The Apostolic Fathers* (LCL 24; Cambridge, Mass., London, 1965) vol. 1, p. 384, or A. Lindemann and H. Paulsen, *Die Apostolischen Väter* (Tübingen, 1992) p. 56.

60. See the insightful comments and the abundance of iconographical symbols in M. Avi-Yonah, *Art in Ancient Palestine* (Jerusalem, 1981).

61. As W. B. Tatum proved, the LXX clarifies that some Jews after the Exile understood the Second Commandment to be polemically anti-idolic: "You shall not make for yourself an idol, whether in the form of anything that is in heaven above, or that is on the earth beneath, or that is in the water under the earth" (RSV; Exod 20:4 = Deut 5:8). Tatum rightly points out that in the Greek rendering the word for "idol," *eidōlon,* receives a unique new nuance in Hellenistic Judaism. It designates not something only partially real but "alien gods and their images." Tatum, "The LXX Version of the Second Commandment (Ex. 20, 3–6 = Deut. 5, 7–10): A Polemic Against Idols, Not Images," *JSJ* 17 (1986): 176–95; see esp. pp. 184–86.

62. D. Simpson, *Judas Iscariot: The Man of Mystery, History, and Prophecy* (Waterloo, Iowa, 1943).

63. M. Rudwin, *The Devil in Legend and Literature* (La Salle, Ill., 1931) p. 43.

64. J. B. Russell, *The Devil: Perceptions of Evil from Antiquity to Primitive Christianity* (Ithaca, London, 1977) p. 218. M. Eliade's insights, quoted on p. 68, are not formative.

65. J. B. Russell, *The Prince of Darkness* (Ithaca, London, 1988) p. 63.

66. A. K. Turner, *The History of Hell* (New York, London, 1993) p. 64. In so far as this statement is focused only on the *ApJn* it is somewhat accurate, but that is not clear in Turner's book.

67. P. Stanford, *The Devil* (New York, 1996) p. 2.

68. A better paradigm for studying the symbols of Satan and the various meanings of serpent symbolism is found in P. Carus, *The History of the Devil and the Idea of Evil* (Chicago, 1900; New York, 1996).

69. See the similar reflections by P. Stanford, when he is summarizing Jung's thought, in *The Devil*, p. 273.

70. We will see that the name "Eve" does not appear this early in the story; the quotation is from G. Messadié, *The History of the Devil,* trans. M. Romano (London, 1996) p. 228.

71. The first one to suggest that the serpent is the Devil may well be the author of the Wisdom of Solomon (cf. Wis 2:23–24). Also, see the judicious comments by S. H. T. Page, *Powers of Evil: A Biblical Study of Satan and Demons* (Grand Rapids, 1995) esp. pp. 14–15.

72. See esp. J. B. Russell, *Lucifer: The Devil in the Middle Ages* (Ithaca, London, 1984) p. 67.

73. E. Gardiner, ed., *Visions of Heaven and Hell Before Dante* (New York, 1989) esp. p. 177.

74. Lord Byron, "Cain: A Mystery," in *The Works of Lord Byron* (Ware, Hertfordshire, 1994) p. 511.

75. *The Works of Lord Byron,* p. 515 (italics not mine).

76. Calvin, *The Gospel According to St. John,* trans. T. H. L. Parker, ed. D. W. Torrance and T. F. Torrance (Grand Rapids, 1988) p. 73.

77. Most of the books that bear the noun "serpent" in the title have nothing to do with this creature. The fascination with snakes is simply employed to sell a book. N. Jones' *Power of Raven: Wisdom of Serpent* (1994) is, however, a penetrating examination of Celtic women's spirituality. For lore on the serpent, see pp. 106–7, 127, 130, 179. For research on the Yoga of Kundalini Sakti, see A. Avalon (Sir John Woodroffe), *The Serpent Power* (1919, 1964 [7th ed.]).

78. Far too many books also fail to include a discussion of the serpent. See, for example, K. Konig, *Bruder Tier: Mensch und Tier in Mythos und Evolution* (Stuttgart, 1967).

79. Some authors, whom one would expect to include a discussion of ophidian iconography, provide no help. The serpent does not fear the human when the latter is naked; *pace* O. Seel, *Der Physiologus: Tiere und ihre Symbolik* (Zürich, 1995 [7th ed.]) p. 20.

80. H. M. Westropp and C. S. Wake, *Ancient Symbol Worship* (1875; Whitefish, Mont., 1997) p. 39.

81. J. Wyly examines the Priapus myth, moving "freely between the realms of physiology and imagination," and avoids any connection between phallus and serpent, although he includes an image of Priapus with a snake (from the archaeological mu-

seum in Verona). Wyly, *The Phallic Quest: Priapus and Masculine Inflation* (Toronto, 1989). The quotation is on p. 12. The illustrations are frequently taken from the Greek and Roman periods, and many of them are from Pompeii or Herculaneum.

82. See the illustration on p. 39 in D. Leeming and J. Page, *Goddess: Myths of the Female Divine* (New York, Oxford, 1994).

83. For a drawing, see S. Schroer and T. Staubli, *Body Symbolism in the Bible,* trans. L. M. Maloney (Collegeville, Minn., 2001) p. 165.

84. The full bibliography for each work will be given in a note the first time the publication is cited. The reference data will also be found in the Selected "Serpent" Bibliography. I have cited only books at this point; that is to stress the abundant—basically unknown—research on serpent imagery.

85. K. Lapatin, *Mysteries of the Snake Goddess: Art, Desire, and the Forging of History* (Boston, New York, 2002). Lapatin amasses data that tend to discredit the authenticity of the statue of the snake goddess in the Boston Museum of Fine Arts. That figure and fifteen other so-called Minoan statuettes can no "longer be employed as evidence for Aegean Bronze Age art, religion, or culture" (p. 187).

86. Also, see R. W. Hood, "When the Spirit Maims and Kills: Social Psychological Considerations of the History of Serpent Handling Sects and the Narrative of Handlers," *IntJPsycholRelig* 8 (1998) 71–96. See the impressive bibliography on pp. 94–96.

87. Joines, *Serpent Symbolism in the Old Testament.*

88. See esp. regarding the serpent as the symbol of rejuvenation, Eliade, "Myths of the Origin of Death," in his *Essential Sacred Writings from Around the World* (San Francisco, 1967) pp. 139–44.

89. U. Winter, *Frau und Göttin* (OBO 53; Freiburg and Göttingen, 1983); H. Brunner, *Das Hörende Herz* (OBO 80; Freiburg and Göttingen, 1988); A. Berlejung, *Die Theologie der Bilder* (OBO 162; Freiburg and Göttingen, 1998).

90. J. Milgrom, *Handmade Midrash* (Philadelphia, 1992).

91. J. H. Charlesworth, "The Pictorial Apocrypha and Art History," in M. Bernabo, *Pseudepigraphical Images in Early Art* (North Richland Hills, Tex. 2001) p. ix.

92. See, e.g., C. Luz, *Das Exotische Tier in der Europäischen Kunst* (Stuttgart, 1987).

93. See S. Battaglia, *Grande dizionario della lingua Italiana,* 20 vols. (Turin, 1996).

94. Ibid., vol. 18, pp. 738–39. This noun appears in Dante's *Inferno* to denote the serpent that torments the wicked (*Inf.* 25–91).

95. Ibid., vol. 18, p. 739.

96. Ibid., vol. 18, pp. 740–41.

97. Ibid., vol. 18, pp. 741–42. For the meaning "to move elegantly and with agility," see *Verga* 2.308. For the meaning "to be astute," see *Fausto da Longiano* 4.43.

98. The Rainbow Spirit, the focus of all creation, is a serpent. See esp. J. Corowa and N. Habel, for "the Rainbow Spirit Elders," *The Rainbow Spirit in Creation* (Collegeville, Minn., 2000).

99. B. Johnson, *Lady of the Beasts: Ancient Images of the Goddess and Her Sacred Animals* (San Francisco, 1988) p. 124.

100. A. T. Mann and J. Lyle, *Sacred Sexuality* (Rockport, 1995) p. 16.

101. M. Gimbutas, *The Language of the Goddess* (San Francisco, 1989) p. 121.

102. See M. Girard, *Les symboles dans la Bible* (Paris, 1991) p. 827.

2. Physiology Undergirds Symbology

1. The sins of the institution called "the church" are many, of course. See the work by H.-J. Wolf, *Sünde der Kirche* (Hamburg, 1998). I celebrate the exposing of the sins of those who failed to lead the church and recall the depiction of the leaders of Israel as the wicked shepherds (*1 En* and Jn). Much of Wolf's presentation is jaded: the Christian belief is not a constructed picture of deception ("ein konstruiertes Trugbild," p. 443), and the Christian belief in the Devil is not a false interpretation of history and groundless (p. 484), but it is in need of demythologizing.

2. M. Martinek, *Wie die Schlange zum Teufel Wurde: Die Symbolik in der Paradiesgeschichte von der hebräischen Bibel bis zum Koran* (Wiesbaden, 1996).

3. J. J. Kambach, *Betrachtung des Geheimnisses Jesu Christi in dem Vorbilde der Ehernen Schlange* (Halle, 1728). Kambach explained "das alte Testament aus dem neuen zu erläutern" (p. 6). He was convinced that "es habe die erhöhete eherne Schlange nicht Christum, sondern den Satan abgebildet" (p. 6). The contrast is clear: "Es ist allzu klar, dass in der Auslgegung Jesu Christi die erhöhete Schlange und der erhöhete Menschen-Sohn einander entgegen gesetzet werden" (pp. 6–7).

4. "Die alte Schlange, Sünd und Tod, / die Höll, all Jammer, Angst und Not / hat überwunden Jesus Christ, / der heut vom Tod erstanden ist." Stuttgart, 1996, p. 242 (also see hymns 39, verse 5, 111, verse 9, 113, verse 2, 509, verse 1; all are negative images of the serpent).

5. A. Baeumler, ed., *Friedrich Nietzsche Werke* (Leipzig, 1930) vol. 4, p. 291.

6. See E. Fahmüller et al., *Das grosse Lexikon der Malerei* (Braunschweig, 1982) p. 601.

7. In Anonymous, *Meisterwerke der Kunst: Malerei von A–Z* (Chur, Switzerland, 1994) p. 694.

8. R. Briffault, *The Mothers: The Matriarchal Theory of Social Origins* (New York, 1931) p. 48. Briffault is intent on establishing his thesis that tender emotions and affection "have then their origins not in sexual attraction, but in maternal reactions" (p. 51). He does raise some valid points, and it is alarming to review the evidence that leads to the claim: "All carnivorous animals and rodents are cannibalistic" (p. 47), and that lions, tigers, leopards, and wolves have been observed eating their mates.

9. H. R. E. Davison, *God and Myths of Northern Europe* (London, New York, 1990) pp. 26–27, 138–39, 188, 202.

10. I have amassed so much data to illustrate ophidian iconography and symbology that it is difficult to be selective. One of my discoveries is the vast evidence of ophidian (anguine) artwork (esp. sculptures) and jewelry from antiquity. Much of it dates from or near the first century CE. For bibliographical data to publications on the items mentioned in the list, see the following pages and the Selected "Serpent" Bibliography.

11. He stands on the backs of two lions. Perhaps the mix of images (water, bulls, snakes, vegetation) was intended to support some ancient rain rite. See the discussion and photograph in S. Piggott, *The Dawn of Civilization* (New York, London, 1967) p. 69.

12. This ring was found at Vik in Sogn. It belonged to a woman and dates from about 300 CE. The woman was probably wealthy. The Vikings or Norsemen were gifted craftsmen, as we know not only from this ring but from the intricate woodwork on their ships. I am grateful to Professor P. Borgen for helping my study of Viking art. On Viking art and myth, see M. J. Roberts, *Mythologie der Wikinger* (Kettwig,

[1997?]). The god Jormungand is a serpent (see the image of the god swallowing his tail, as Orouboros, on p. 57).

13. See, notably, I. Clarus, *Keltische Mythen* (Augsburg, 1997) pp. 35–36; also see the snakes on pp. 302–3.

14. See the photograph and discussion in C. Meier-Seethaler, *Von der göttlichen Löwin zum Wahrzeichen männlicher Macht: Ursprung und Wandel grosser Symbole* (Zurich, 1993) esp. p. 214.

15. See E. J. Krige, *The Social System of the Zulus* (London, 1950 [2nd ed.]) p. 357.

16. The drum was found at Rio Grande de Nasca in southern Peru; see the color photograph and discussion in E. J. Milleker, ed., *The Year One: Art of the Ancient World—East and West* (New Haven and New York, 2000) pp. 202–3. Also see the serpent images displayed and discussed in K. Sälzle, *Tier und Mensch: Gottheit und Dämon: Das Tier in der Geistesgeschichte der Menschheit* (Munich, 1965) pp. 50–51.

17. See G. W. Locher, *The Serpent in Kwakiutl Religion* (Leiden, 1932); B. Mundkur, "The Cult of the Serpent in the Americas: Its Asian Background," *Current Anthropology* 17 (1976) 429–55. Mundkur points out that the serpent in American culture was venerated because of "the awe it generated," and because "man's reverential fear of this animal is extraordinarily primordial" (p. 429). A. M. Warburg, who founded the Warburg Institute in London, was fascinated by the Native Americans; note his publications on the serpent: *Schlangenritual: Ein Reisebericht* (Berlin, 1988), *Images from the Religion of the Pueblo Indians of North America* (Ithaca, London, 1955), and "A Lecture on Serpent Ritual," *Journal of the Warburg Institute* 2.277–92. Warburg pointed out parallels between the Native American snake ceremonies and the Dionysiac rituals in which "Maenads danced with live snakes entwining their hair like diadems," while holding a snake in one hand (p. 288). This thought should be kept and rekindled when we examine the Minoan snake goddesses (or priestesses). For the Hopi Indians, see G. A. Dorsey, *The Mishongnovi Ceremonies of the Snake and Antelope Fraternities* (Field Columbian Museum Publications 66; Chicago, 1902). For the Native American snake dance, see J. W. Fewkes, *Tusayan Snake Ceremonies* (Washington, 1897) and W. Hough, *The Moki Snake Dance* (Sante Fe Route, 1898). Hough published sixty-four photographs from the late nineteenth century; see esp. p. 13 for the entrance of the snake priests.

18. See H. Zimmer, *Myths and Symbols in Indian Art and Civilization* (New York, 1946, 1947). Also see A. Avalon, *The Serpent Power: Being the Shat-Chakra-Nirūpana and Pūdukū-Panchaka* (Madras, 1924).

19. See E. A. W. Budge, *Osiris and the Egyptian Resurrection*, 2 vols. (London, New York, n.d. [1911]) vol. 2, pp. 237–38.

20. L. N. Hayes reported that 70 percent of the Chinese in the 1920s believed in the existence of "real dragons." He pointed out that these dragons are not "horrible monsters" but "friendly creatures." See his *The Chinese Dragon* (Shanghai, China, 1922 [3rd ed.]). Also see J.-P. Diény, *Le symbolisme du dragon dans la Chine Antique* (Paris, 1994) and M. W. de Visser, *The Dragon in China and Japan* (Amsterdam, 1913). For a discussion of Chinese dragons and images from the fifth century BCE to the eighteenth century CE, see Sälzle, *Tier und Mensch*, pp. 233–76.

21. See H. Ritter, *Die Schlange in der Religions der Melanesier* (Basel, 1945).

22. See J. Verschueren, *Le culte du Vaudoux en Haïti: Ophiolâtre et Animisme* (Belgium, 1948).

23. See H. Cory, *Wall-Paintings by Snake Charmers in Tanganyika* (London, n.d.). H. Cory was the government anthropologist in Tanganyika.

24. F. C. Oldham, *The Sun and the Serpent* (London, 1905) p. 5.

25. Scholars are often asked to explain how they work and proceed with investigations. The published report cannot reflect the process. It is always a mixture of what had been asked previously and what has been discovered in the years of research. The previous statement, although it comes at the beginning of this work, could only have been written near the end of it.

26. R. C. Zaehner, *Hinduism* (London, New York, 1962) p. 191.

27. N. Smart, *The Religious Experience of Mankind* (New York, 1969) p. 120.

28. See I. Clarus' discussion in *Keltische Mythen*, p. 309. For the illustration of the three-headed god, see p. 39.

29. J. Boulnois, *Le caducée et la symbolique dravidienne indo-méditerranéenne, de l'arbre, de la pierre, du serpent et de la déesse-mère* (Paris, 1939).

30. J. B. Russell, *The Devil* (Ithaca, London, 1977) p. 69.

31. See B. D. Haage, "Das Ouroboros—Symbol in 'Parzival,' " *Würzburger Medizinhistorische Mitteilungen* 1 (1983) 5–22; S. Mahdihassan, "The Significance of Ouroboros in Alchemy and in Primitive Symbolism," *Iqbal* (1963) 18–47; and W. Deonna, "Ouroboros," *Artibus Asiae* 15 (1952) 163–70. Deonna rightly points out that in the Middle East, Iran, and Rome, there is abundant evidence "of the circular serpent, a symbol of the cosmos, and the notion of eternity which obtains diverse nuances" (p. 170).

32. For a good illustration, see B. Johnson, *Lady of the Beasts: Ancient Images of the Goddess and Her Sacred Animals* (San Francisco, 1990) illus. no. 174.

33. Johnson, ibid., pp. 158–59.

34. See P. Foucart in *Bull. Corr. Hell.* 7 (1883) 511ff.

35. See K. H. Hunger, *Der Äskulapstab* (Berlin, 1978) p. 112. See the other iconographical examples he presents, esp. on p. 113.

36. See the color photograph in Fahmüller et al., *Das grosse Lexikon der Malerei*, p. 614.

37. Copies of *Aurora consurgens* are housed in Glasgow (University Library; MS Ferguson 6), Zurich (Zentralbibliothek; MS Rhenoviensis 172), Leiden (MS Vossiani Chemici F. 29), Paris (the Bibliothèque Nationale; MS Parisinus Latinus 14006), Prague (Universitni Knihovna; MS VI. Fd. 26 and in Chapitre Métropolitain; MS 1663. O. LXXIX) and Berlin (Staatsbibliothek Preussischer Kulturbesitz; MS Germ. qu. 848).

38. D. Fontana, *The Secret Language of Symbols* (San Francisco, 1994) p. 8.

39. In western Europe, at the beginning of the twentieth century, women would go to a cave in Lanuvium in which there was a snake. If the snake ate what had been baked, their prayers would be answered. See E. Rein, "Die Schlangenhöhle von Lanuvium," *Annales Acad. Sc. Fennicae* B, XI, 3 (1919) 3–22.

40. See esp. E. Giancristofaro and I. Bellotta, *Il culto di San Domenico a Cocullo* (Corfinio, 1998); N. Chiocchio, *I serpari a Cocullo* (Tivoli, 2000). Also see P. D'Alberto et al., eds., *Popoli e riti: Aspetti di religiosità popolare nell'entroterra abruzzse* (Corfinio, 2000) esp. pp. 11–21. I am grateful to Maria Adelaide Ghinozzi, mother of G. Boccaccini, for helping me study this serpent cult now active in Italy. Also see L. C. Smith, "A Survival of an Ancient Cult in the Bruzzi," *Studi e Materiali di Storia delle Religioni* 4 (1928) 106–19; N. Lewis, "Snakes of San Domenico," *The Independent Magazine* (21 October 1989) 74–76.

41. H. Bayley, *The Lost Language of Symbolism*, 2 vols. (London, 1912; reprinted by The Book Tree of Escondido, Calif. in 2000) vol. 1, p. 11. It is frustrating to work

with Bayley's books; he illustrates his two volumes with 1,418 images but never clarifies their source.

42. See esp. E. Schmidt, *Le Grand Autel de Pergame* (Leipzig, 1962); see esp. Plate 710, and notably 16 and 28; also see A. Schober, *Die Kunst von Pergamon* (Vienna, 1951).

43. See esp. H. Busch and G. Edelmann, eds., *Etruskische Kunst* (Frankfurt am Main, 1969) p. 95. The Etruscans also depicted Persephone with snakes on her head, jewelry in the form of serpents, dancing girls with serpents in the background or at their feet, and lions with serpents as tails. See L. Banti, *Die Etrusker* (Essen, n.d. perhaps 1998).

44. J. A. Peters, "Serpents," *The New Encyclopeaedia Britannica; Micropaedia* (1968) vol. 16, p. 560.

45. J. Coborn, *The Atlas of Snakes of the World* (Neptune City, N.J., 1991) p. 11.

46. See esp. the reflections in G. R. Zug, L. J. Vitt, and J. P. Caldwell, *Herpetology* (San Diego, New York, London, 2001 [2nd ed.]) p. xi.

47. The snake appeared on the earth about 100 to 150 million years ago. See "Die Stammesgeschichte der Reptilien," in R. Bauchot, ed., *Schlangen,* trans. C. Ronsiek (Augsburg, 1994) p. 33. Also see C. Mattison, "Evolution," in *Snake* (New York, 1999) p. 8, and Mattison, *The Encyclopedia of Snakes* (New York, 1995) p. 11.

48. I am grateful to my numerous colleagues in South Africa with whom I discussed the snake. For eighteen years I lived in southern Florida and periodically near the Everglades. I frequented the Serpentarium in Miami. Yet I have learned the most, it seems, from reading ophiologists' publications. I have been especially influenced by the articles in R. Bauchot, ed., *Schlangen;* J. Coborn, *The Atlas of Snakes of the World;* G. Z. Zug, L. J. Vitt, and J. P. Caldwell, *Herpetology;* C. Mattison, *Snakes of the World* (London, 1992, 1998); H. W. Greene, *Snakes: The Evolution of Mystery in Nature* (Berkeley, London, 1997); C. Mattison, *The Encyclopedia of Snakes,* 1995); and C. Mattison, *Snake.* I have also studied snakes in many zoos, notably, the ones on Crete and in Berlin, Washington, London, Jerusalem, Johannesburg, and New York.

49. Mattison, *Snakes of the World,* p. 19.

50. D. Botting, *Humboldt and the Cosmos* (London, 1973) pp. 105, 122.

51. Mattison, *Snake,* p. 6.

52. Vestigial limbs are found on some snakes today. It seems evident that the snake evolved from lizards with legs. The legs were worn away and became useless, perhaps due to burrowing. See Mattison, *Snake,* pp. 8, 17 (photograph of vestigial limbs). Also see Mattison, *The Encyclopedia of Snakes,* p. 10 and p. 13 (the color photograph on the bottom right).

53. It is named *Haasiophis terrasanctus*; see "Fossil gets a leg up on snake family tree," *Science News,* April 1, 2000.

54. See J.-P. Gasc, "Fortbewegung," in Bauchot, ed., *Schlangen,* pp. 60–73.

55. *Encyclopaedia of Religion and Ethics* (New York, 1966) vol. 11, p. 407.

56. Coborn, *The Atlas of Snakes,* p. 38.

57. Coborn, *The Atlas of Snakes,* pp. 19–20.

58. See Greene, *Snakes,* pp. 143–53. The South African Blind Snake (Bibron's Blind Snake, *Typhlops bibronii*) is covered with scales and has minute eyes that "appear as black dots below the head shields." R. Patterson, *Snakes* (Cape Town, 1986) p. 4. R. Patterson is the director of the Transvaal Snake Park. B. Branch points out that snakes' eyes, "when present, lack eyelids and have an unblinking stare; many legless

lizards retain eyelids. However, burrowing snakes and lizards require neither eyes nor enlarged ventral scales, and many have lost both." B. Branch, *South African Snakes and Other Reptiles* (Cape Town, 1993) p. 6.

59. For pictures of a Boomslang, see the photographs in Mattison, *Snake,* pp. 110–11; for a photograph of a Yellow Blunt-headed Vinesnake, see the color photograph in Greene, *Snakes,* p. 29.

60. Lear has used the colloquial "sarpint" (which is not a word) to stress the vulgarity of the limerick. The German version is a free composition: "Es lockt' ein Flötist vom Trifels / eine Schlange ins Innre des Stiefels; / doch er spielte—o Graus!— / tagein und tagaus— / da verliess sie den Mann vom Trifels." See E. Lear, *Sämtliche Limericks: English/Deutsch,* ed. and trans. T. Stemmler (Stuttgart, 1988) p. 15.

61. For a color photograph see Bauchot, ed., *Schlangen,* p. 102; also see the diagram on p. 25. Also see Mattison, *Snake,* p. 30 (color photograph at top right of page). A picture of hemipenes removed from a rattlesnake is shown in J. Coborn, *The Atlas of Snakes,* on p. 95 (bottom right color photograph) and one removed from a cobra is presented on p. 96 (top color photograph).

62. See the arresting color photographs in Bauchot, ed., *Schlangen,* p. 53.

63. Sometimes the snake swallows its prey headfirst, sometimes tail-first; for the latter, see the picture of the Coral snake swallowing a Northern Cat-eyed Snake, whose mouth protrudes from the victor's mouth. See Greene, *Snakes,* p. 67.

64. Using the language of W. Rose in *Reptiles and Amphibians of Southern Africa,* according to Greene, *Snakes,* p. 143.

65. Greene reports that scientists discovered that a snake weighing 23 grams had eaten a 29-gram mouse. See Greene, *Snakes,* p. 51.

66. See the color photographs in Bauchot, ed., *Schlangen,* pp. 108–17.

67. I am indebted to Dr. Haast who along with his assistants shared similar thoughts with me in 1954.

68. Baltasar Gracián (1601–1658) thought that after "20 years the human is a peacock, after 30 a lion, after 40 a camel, after 50 a serpent, after 60 a dog, after 70 a monkey, after 80 nothing" (p. 275). See B. Gracián, *Handorakel und Kunst der Weltklugheit,* trans. A. Schopenhauer (Stuttgart, 1961). For the concept that the snake and pigeon evoke wonder, see p. 103.

69. Anonymous, *Meisterwerke der Kunst: Malerei von A-Z* (Chur, Switzerland, 1994) p. 403.

70. Note, e.g., how the green parrotsnake looks like depictions of aliens. See the color picture in Greene, *Snakes,* p. 3. Long after finishing this chapter, I came across J. Lewis' "The Reptilians: Humanity's Historical Link to the Serpent Race," *Fate* (June 1996). I read the work from the web, Reptilian Research Archives. I wish to disassociate myself from his claims. He seems not to know the difference between the caduceus and the Asclepian staff.

71. For color photographs of cobras, see J. Coborn, *The Atlas of Snakes,* esp. pp. 445–52.

72. See the color photograph in Bauchot, ed., *Schlangen,* front page, before title page, and p. 11.

73. See the color photograph in Bauchot, ed., *Schlangen,* p. 83.

74. The behavior of snakes when faced with apparent danger is difficult to access. In 2000, I was in a bass boat fishing with my son. We saw what we thought might be three cottonmouth moccasins swimming toward the boat. I watched as one swam by and

climbed up on the bank. It moved through the grass, without disturbing the grass and without giving any sign of moving. I have been told, while living near the Everglades, that moccasins are mean-tempered and have been known to chase someone up a path. The published reports tend to claim that "some cottonmouths are quick to retreat; others will coil, vibrate the tail, and open the mouth in a threatening pose." W. M. Palmer, *Poisonous Snakes of North Carolina* (Raleigh, 1978) p. 13.

75. Mattison is convinced that snakes "rely on passive strategies as a first line of defense." *Snake,* p. 26.

76. The python is the longest snake; it has been recorded to reach about 10 meters. There is reason to doubt the claim in 1907 that Sir Percy Fawcett killed an anaconda that measured 19 meters. See Mattison, *Snake,* p. 12.

77. See the magnificent color photographs and insightful reflection in M. Klum's "King Cobra: Feared, Revered," *National Geographic* (November 2001) 100–113, and p. 126 (not numbered).

78. C. Burland and W. Forman. *Gefiederte Schlange und Rauchender Spiegel,* trans. H. Schmidthüs (Freiburg, Basel, 1977).

79. See esp. the photographs in M. Schmidt, *Der Basler Medeasarkophag* (Tübignen, n.d. [c. 1998]) pp. 3, 28, 31, 32. The Medeasage Sarkophag in the Antikensammlung of the Pergamon Museum is arresting. It is Roman and dates from the second century CE. The marble is intricately carved. On the right are two large serpents with large eyes, scales, and wings. The serpents are curled around the wheels of Medea's chariot. She raises her right hand and directs the powerful creatures forward to her destiny.

80. See R. Bauchot and Y. Vasse, "Die Häuntung," in *Schlangen,* pp. 18–21. Mammals and birds shed skin continuously, but shedding "occurs from every four days for some amphibians to once or twice every year for old, large reptiles" ([No editor], *Reptiles and Amphibians* [Discovery Channel; New York, 2000] p. 34).

81. The serpent appears repeatedly in ancient fables, see esp. J. Irmscher, trans., *Antike Fabeln* (Berlin and Weimar, 1991). See the index, pp. 491–92.

82. T. Weber and R. Wenning, eds., *Petra: Antike Felsstadt zwischen Arabischer Tradition und Griechischer Norm* (Mainz am Rhein, 1997) illustrations 129a, 129b, 129c on p. 117.

83. R. Briffault, "The Serpent and Eternal Life," in *The Mothers: A Study of the Origins of Sentiments and Institutions,* 2 vols. (New York, 1927) vol. 2, pp. 641–51.

84. G. Balanchine and F. Mason, *Balanchine's Festival of Ballet* (London, 1978) pp. 204–5. See the color photographs on pp. 204–5. The gold serpent was found in Chiriquí, Panama.

85. Mattison, *Snake,* p. 120.

86. See the color photograph in A. B. Amaducci, *Die Brancacci-Kapelle und Masaccio* (Florence, 1978). Also see U. Baldini and O. Casazza, *The Brancacci Chapel,* trans. R. Sadleir (Florence, 1996 [rev. ed.]) esp. p. 16.

87. See the color photograph of the cigarette case in G. von Habsburg, *Fabergé: Hofjuwelier der Zaren* (Munich, 1986) p. 237. Also see the serpent on the sketches for an inkwell (p. 63). The sun umbrella is shown in color on p. 123 (no. 122). The pen, also in vivid color, is found on p. 169 (no. 237).

88. Greene points out the vast amount of unknown data regarding biochemistry, pharmacology, and the biological roles of venoms. See his *Snakes,* pp. 86–88.

89. See the color photographs in C. Laisné, *Kunst der Griechen* (Paris, 1995) pp. 172–73.

90. Fahmüller et al., *Das grosse Lexikon der Malerei*, p. 265 (in color).

91. See the color photographs in Bauchot, ed., *Schlangen*, p. 23.

92. Priapus appears in a wall-painting in the House of the Vettii in Pompeii. For a color photograph, see C. Jones, *Sex or Symbol? Erotic Images of Greece and Rome* (London, 1989) illus. 6.

93. See, e.g., H. Schmökel, *Ur, Assur und Babylon* (Stuttgart, 1955) esp. Plates 58 and 83.

94. *Farvardin Yasht* (*Yasht* 13, 131); see V. S. Curtis, *Persian Myths* (London, 1998) p. 26. Also see "Zahhak, the serpent-shouldered ruler" on pp. 33–34. Curtis is the editor of *Iran*, which is published by the British Institute of Persian Studies.

95. See W. W. Malandra, trans. and ed, *An Introduction to Ancient Iranian Religion* (Minneapolis, 1983) p. 91.

96. The mithraea at Ostia are late, dating from the second to third centuries CE.

97. In the second-century CE mural painting in Marino's Mithraeum, the serpent is depicted either drinking the blood of the injured bull or helping Mithra defeat the monster. In the mural painting in the Mithraeum in Via Morelli, S. Maria Capua Vetere, the serpent occupies the ground beneath Mithra. In all scenes the serpent is depicted as Mithra's assistant. See B. Andreae, *L'Art de l'ancienne Rome* (Paris, 1973) illustrations 105 and 106.

98. See the comments by E. M. Yamauchi, *Persia and the Bible* (Grand Rapids, 1996) pp. 502–14.

99. I have been able to discern a vast difference among examples of the Tauroctony in Cologne, Berlin, London, and elsewhere. In some, I am convinced, the serpent helps Mithra to slay the bull. The scorpion, which Cumont also thought was an evil creature, also helps Mithra; he is often depicted biting the testicles of the bull. The scorpion is frequently portrayed as a companion of the human as well as one who helps in copulation and creation, providing nourishment and prosperity. I am grateful to Professor O. Keel for discussion regarding the meaning of the scorpion. See Keel and C. Uehlinger, *Gods, Goddesses, and Images of God in Ancient Israel*, trans. T. H. Trapp (Minneapolis, 1998) esp. pp. 149–50.

100. R. Merkelbach, *Mithras: Ein persisch-römischer Mysterienkult* (Wiesbaden, 1998) p. 91; see the serpent apparently biting the bull in Plate 18 on p. 279. Also see p. 395.

101. See W. and B. Forman (illustrations) and N. Chotaš, H. Kreutz (text), et al., "Die Kunst der Luristanischen Hirten," in *Kunst ferner Länder* (Prague, [1969?]) pp. 28–33.

102. For a similar object, see H. Henning von der Osten, *Die Welt der Perser* (Stuttgart, 1956) Plate 31, and [R. Ghirshman, ed.?], *7000 Jahre Kunst in Iran* (Villa Hügel and Essen, 1962) Plate 139.

103. Dante Alighieri, *Die Göttliche Komödie: Italienisch und Deutsch,* ed. and trans. H. Gmelin, 2 vols. (Stuttgart, 1949 [reprinted in 1988 by Deutscher Taschenbuch Verlag in Munich]) vol. 1, p. 106. Also see Canto Decimosettimo for the depictions of monsters with long tails whose bodies are mostly serpents. In Canto Nono 76, Dante refers to the frogs, the damned, that are devoured by the evil serpent (vol. 1, p. 110; cf. vol. 2, p. 174 for a commentary). For the water serpent *(chelidri)*, see Canto Ventesimoquarto 86 (p. 286). For the serpent with six feet *(un serpente con sei piè si lancia),* see Canto Ventesimoquinto 50 (p. 296).

104. K. O. Conrady, ed., *Das grosse deutsche Gedichtbuch* (Königstein, 1978) p. 861.

105. See the color photograph in Bauchot, ed., *Schlangen*, p. 3.

106. This is true of the Uropeltidae family, in which there are two types, Cylinrophiinae and Uropeltinae. See Bauchot, ed., *Schlangen*, p. 36, also see the color photograph on that page.

107. See the color photographs in Bauchot, ed., *Schlangen*, pp. 106–7; also see G. Matz, "Teratologie," on the same pages.

108. Mattison reports that much of "the information" in his *Snake* is "quite new, since snakes, being secretive, are among the most difficult animals to study in their own habitat." *Snake*, p. 6. There are many unresolved controversies among herpetologists; see, e.g., Zug et al., *Herpetology*, pp. 3–10.

109. See the color photograph in Bauchot, ed., *Schlangen*, p. 107.

110. Translation mine; for text, see Coborn, *The Atlas of Snakes*, p. 14 (with accent restored).

111. I am grateful to J. A. Peters for this suggestion. See his "Serpentes," *Micropaedia*, vol. 16, p. 559.

112. M. Eliade, *Patterns in Comparative Religion* (New York, 1958) p. 164.

113. In *The Sacred and Profane: The Nature of Religion*, Eliade contended that the "dragon is the . . . symbol of the cosmic waters, of darkness, night, and death—in short, of the amorphous and virtual, of everything that has not yet acquired a 'form' " (trans. W. R. Trask; New York, 1959) p. 48.

114. See Mattison, *Snakes of the World*, p. 9. On the widespread legend of the combat myth between the serpent and the hero, see Eliade's comments in *Cosmos and History: The Myth of the Eternal Return* (trans. W. R. Trask; New York, 1959) pp. 37–48.

115. K. Sälzle, *Tier und Mensch*, p. 477.

116. See, e.g., M. L. Sancassano, *Il Serpente e le sue immagini: Il motivo del serpente nella poesia greca dall'Iliade all'Orestea* (Biblioteca di Atenaeum 36; Como, 1997).

3. Realia and Iconography

1. O. Keel, *Das Recht der Bilder gesehen zu werden* (OBO 122; Freiburg, Göttingen, 1992).

2. See the reflections on this thought by J. V. Taylor and E. Robinson in the latter's *The Language of Mystery* (London, Philadelphia, 1987, 1989). Robinson points out, correctly, that there "is indeed an almost complete separation between the world of religion and the world of the contemporary arts" (p. 1). This judgment does not apply to antiquity.

3. A. Margulies, *The Empathic Imagination* (New York, London, 1989) p. 107.

4. E. Panofsky, *Studies in Iconology* (Oxford, 1939; reprinted in 1972, Boulder, Colo.) p. 12.

5. See H. Müller-Karpe, *Geschichte der Steinzeit* (Augsburg, 1998) Tables 1–20; note the serpent images in Tables 14.4, 15.1, 21.3 and 18.

6. See M. Ruspoli, *Die Höhlenmalerei von Lascaux: Auf den Spuren des frühen Menschen*, trans. M. Ruck-Vinson (Augsburg, 1998). The French edition appeared in 1986.

7. See S. Giedion, *The Eternal Present: The Beginnings of Art* (New York, 1962) pp. 308–9.

8. B. Johnson, *Lady of the Beasts* (San Francisco, 1990) p. 122; see the drawing of the serpent on p. 123.

9. P. Graziosi, *Le pitture prehistoriche e della grotta di Porto Badisco* (Florence, 1980); see the drawing on p. 55. The drawings "costruzioni con spiraliformi e serpentiformi," p. 55.

10. See ibid., Tabella XVII; see esp. no. 22; there appear to be two serpents in T. XVIII.

11. See the following selection: W. R. Cooper, "Observations on the Serpent Myths of Ancient Egypt," *Journal of the Transactions of the Victoria Institute* (London) 6 (1873) 321–91; E. Amélineau, "Du rôle des serpents dans les croyances religieuses de l'Egypte," *Revue de l'histoire des religions* 51 (1905) 335–60; also see vol. 52 (1905) 1–32; L. Keimer, *Histoires de serpents dans l'Egypte ancienne et moderne* (Cairo, 1947); R. T. R. Clark, *Myth and Symbol in Ancient Egypt* (London, 1959). L. Störk, "Schlange," in *Lexikon der Ägyptologie* (ed. W. Helck and W. Westendorf. Wiesbaden, 1984) cols. 644–52. Also see Pritchard, *ANEP*, esp. Figs. 12–17, 265–69, 376–426.

12. See the following: A. Deimel, "Die Schlange bei den Babyloniern," *Orientalia* 14 (1924) 49–57; E. D. Van Buren, *Symbols of Gods in Mesopotamian Art* (Rome, 1945). The Gilgamesh epic is central to our search for the meaning of ophidian symbolism, but written sources are not necessarily a reliable guide to iconography; nevertheless, see N. K. Sanders, *The Epic of Gilgamesh: An English Version with an Introduction* (Baltimore, 1960). See also Pritchard, *ANEP*, esp. Figs. 18–24, 25–30, 427–54, 502–41. We shall examine the literary evidence of the symbolic meaning of serpents in later chapters.

13. See the numerous entries in *Lexicon Iconographicum Mythologiae Classicae* and the following: E. Küster, *Die Schlange in der griechischen Kunst und Religion* (Religionsgeschichtliche Versuche und Vorarbeiten 13.2; Giessen, 1913); L. Bodson, "Les grecs et leurs serpents: Premiers résultats de l'étude taxonomique des sources anciennes," *L'Antiquité Classique* 50 (1981) 57–78; Bodson, "Observations sur la vocabulaire de la zoologie antique: Les noms de serpents en grec et en latin," *Documents pour l'histoire du vocabulaire scientifique* 8 (1986) 65–119.

14. See the many entries in *Lexicon Iconographicum Mythologiae Classicae* and B. Andreae, *L'art de l'ancienne Rome* (Paris, 1973). For additional bibliographical works, see the Selected Serpent Bibliography.

15. See, however, the excellent work by O. Keel, "Polyvalenz der Schlange," *Das Recht der Bilder gesehen zu werden* (Freiburg, Göttingen, 1992) pp. 195–267.

16. J. B. Pritchard, *Palestinian Figurines in Relation to Certain Goddesses Known Through Literature* (New Haven, 1943) p. 27.

17. For a succinct description of many of the sites to be discussed and photographs, see Charlesworth, *The Millennium Guide for Pilgrims to the Holy Land* (North Richland Hills, Tex., 2000).

18. Abbreviations: PN (Pottery Neolithic Age), EB (Early Bronze), MB (Middle Bronze), LB (Late Bronze).

19. O. Bar-Yosef, "Munhata," *OEANE* 4.63–64.

20. See Y. Garfinkel, *The Pottery Assemblages of the Sha'ar Hagolan and Rabah Stages of Munhata (Israel)* (Paris, 1992) p. 84 (a description of each), Figs. 139:12 and 13 (a drawing of each).

21. For a photograph see ibid., Plate 13:5.

22. See the drawing ibid., p. 81 (No. 22).

23. See the photograph in *Highlights of Archaeology: The Israel Museum, Jerusalem*, p. 43. A drawing (p. 76) and photograph (p. 77) also appear in M. Avi-Yonah

and Y. Yadin, eds., *6000 Years of Art in the Holy Land* (Jerusalem, 1986). Also see J. P. O'Neill et al., eds., *The Treasures of the Holy Land: Ancient Art from the Israel Museum* (New York, 1986) pp. 100–102 (with a color photograph on p. 101).

24. Z. Yeivin, "A Silver Cup from Tomb 204a at 'Ain-Samiya," *Israel Exploration Journal* 21 (1971) 78–81. Also see the drawing on p. 79, Figs. 1 and 2.

25. Y. Yadin, "A Note on the Scenes Depicted on the 'Ain-Samiya Cup," *Israel Exploration Journal* 21 (1971) 82–85; the quotation is on p. 83.

26. Of special interest is the serpent-dragon on the Ishtar Gate; see E. Lutz-Ruoff, "Die Schlangendrachen am Ištartor zu Babylon: Eine motivgeschichtliche Untersuchung" (PhD diss., Tübingen, 1986). Also see B. Renz, *Der Orientalische Schlangen-drache* (Augsburg, 1930). For a color photograph, see Sälzle, *Tier und Mensch,* p. 43.

27. See the illustrations in J. Black and A. Green, *Gods, Demons and Symbols of Ancient Mesopotamia* (London, 1992) pp. 64–65, 96–97, 165, 166–68. The illustrations are by Tessa Rickards.

28. E. D. Van Buren, "The Dragon in Ancient Mesopotamia," *Orientalia* 15 (1946) 1–46 (with thirty-two illustrations); the quotations are from p. 45.

29. See K. M. Kenyon, "Jericho," *NEAEHL* 2.674–81; E. Netzer and G. Foerster, *NEAEHL* 2.681–92, R. Hachlili, *NEAEHL* 2.693–95.

30. J. Garstang and J. B. E. Garstang, *The Story of Jericho* (London, Edinburgh, 1948) Plate 3 (a rather poor photograph); see the discussion on p. 102.

31. Garstang and Garstang, *The Story of Jericho* p. 102 (see Plate 3).

32. K. M. Kenyon, *Excavations at Jericho: The Tombs Excavated in 1952–4* (Jerusalem, 1960) vol. 1, figure 162; also see the photography on Plate 18:3.

33. I am grateful to Ross Voss for this information, shared with me at the dig in Ashkelon.

34. I wish to express appreciation to Larry Steger and Ross Voss for the permission and opportunity to examine and photograph this ophidian iconography.

35. Note, e.g., an engraved mirror, from the third or second centuries BCE, that depicts the crowning of Hercules by Victory, behind whom are two serpents, with four curves, and three lines coming out of each mouth. See the photograph in *Encyclopédia Photographique de l'Art,* vol. 3, p. 112:B.

36. The lion in the third-century CE mosaic at Hammat Tiberias also has three horizontal lines coming out of the area of his nostrils and mouth; two others seem to be radiating from its chin.

37. See the photograph in E. Sellin, "Die Ausgrabung von Sichem," *Zeitschrift des Deutschen Palästina-Vereins* 50 (1927) 205–11; Plate 20:e. Also see Sellin's comments on p. 207, and G. E. Wright, *Shechem: The Biography of a Biblical City* (New York, 1965) p. 82.

38. F. M. Th. Böhl, "Die Sichem-Plakette: Protoalphabetische Schriftzeichen der Mittelbronzezeit vom *tell balata,*" *Zeitschrift des Deutschen Palästina-Vereins* 61 (1938) 1–25.

39. W. F. Albright, "The Bronze Age," *Annual of the ASOR* 17 (1936–1937) 43; and J. B. Pritchard, *Palestinian Figurines in Relation to Certain Goddesses Known Through Literature,* p. 27, no. 240. Pritchard also pointed to the similarity between the Shechem plaque and the Tell Beit Mirsim limestone relief.

40. W. F. Albright, *Annual of the ASOR* 17 (1936–1937) 43.

41. G. E. Wright, "The Second Campaign at Tell Balâtah (Shechem)," *BASOR* (1957) 11–28. The article by H. Thiersch ("Ein altmediterraner Tempeltyp," *ZAW* 50 [1932] 73–86, esp. 77) was severely criticized by E. Sellin ("Der gegenwärtige Stand der Ausgrabung von Sichem und ihre Zukunft," *ZAW* [50] 303–8).

42. See D. P. Cole, *Shechem I: The Middle Bronze IIB Pottery*, ed. J. F. Ross and E. F. Campbell (ASOR Excavation Reports; Winona Lake, Ind., 1984) Plate 29:h and i.

43. G. Loud, *Megiddo II: Seasons of 1935–39; Text* (Chicago, 1948) p. 5 ("Chronological Table"). Also, the more recent and precise dating is in line with Loud's stratigraphy; see the discussion in Y. Aharoni and Y. Shiloh, "Megiddo," *NEAEHL* 3.1003–23, and esp. "The Megiddo Stratification" on p. 1023. Stratum I now also runs from 600 to 350 BCE, but it is clarified that we have entered the Persian Period.

44. G. Loud, *Megiddo II: Seasons of 1935–39; Plates* (Chicago, 1948) Plate 240:1.

45. Loud, *Megiddo II*, Plates 22:11 and 26.

46. So also, Keel, *Das Recht der Bilder*, p. 198.

47. For a photograph of the tomb and the vessel in situ, see P. L. O. Guy, *Megiddo Tombs* (Chicago, 1938) Fig. 107. Note that "looting had evidently taken place in antiquity" (p. 88), and that the "bones in C had been badly disturbed" (p. 89).

48. H. G. May, *Material Remains of the Megiddo Cult* (Chicago, 1935) Plate 22: P4327.

49. May, *Material Remains of the Megiddo Cult*, Plate 22: P3060, 3083, 3061.

50. May opined that the "unplaced fragment (Pl. XIV 4) has near the pigeonhole a hatched mold or relief which may even be a snake motive." May, *Material Remains of the Megiddo Cult*, p. 14. This is possible, but far from certain. The fragment is small. The hole is rather rectangular. No remains of a serpent are visible, but an appliquéd piece of clay, perhaps a serpent, may have once lain near the hole. Also see May's comments on Rowe's discoveries at Beth Shan, and his interpretations and method of comparing Palestinian ophidian objects with much earlier ones in Egypt. May too closely follows Rowe (pp. 15, 21). Refreshing, however, are May's comments about the indigenous quality of ophidian artifacts found in ancient Palestine (p. 31).

51. R. S. Lamon, G. M. Shipton, *Megiddo I: Seasons of 1925–34; Strata I–IV* (Chicago, 1939) Plate 87:7, 8, 9.

52. The picture in Lamon, Shipton, *Megiddo I*, Plate 87, is too vague. It is not clear if the object is a serpent with eyes indicated.

53. These dates have been challenged. See Aharoni and Shiloh, "Megiddo." Note that IVA continues until the Assyrian conquest in 732 BCE (also see "The Megiddo Stratification" on p. 1023).

54. Lamon, Shipton, *Megiddo I*, Plates 69:24 (3 uraei with a fish), 69:47 (uraeus facing a Hyksos-figured man), 69:48 (uraeus), 69:52 (winged uraeus), 69:54 (four uraei, perhaps), 69:55 (a uraeus?), 69:59 (a lion before a uraeus), 69:69 (sphinx before a uraeus).

55. See, e.g., R. Giveon and T. Kertesz, *Egyptian Scarabs and Seals from Acco* (Freiburg, 1986).

56. See the massive work published by O. Keel, *Corpus der Stempelsiegel-Amulette aus Palästina/Israel*, 2 vols. (Freiburg and Göttingen, 1995 and 1997). See esp. the illustrations in vol. 1, p. 76, and vol. 2, pp. 13, 15, 41, 75, 97, 111, 119, 121, 127, 131, 149, 153, 155, 159, 171, 175, 189, 197, 199, 205, 207, 211, 213, 235, 237, 239, 243,

245, 543, 547, 549, 553, 597, 607, 611, 623, 627, 629, 633, 635, 665, 675, 687, 703, 709, 715, 717, 721, 725, 729, 735, 743, 749, 751, 767, 771, 780, 789, and 790.

57. Guy, *Megiddo Tombs,* Plate 161:20. Item no. 21 may also be the remains of a serpent-headed bracelet.

58. Guy, *Megiddo Tombs*, Plate 166:5.

59. J. G. Duncan, *Digging Up Biblical History* (London, 1931) vol. 2, p. 72.

60. See the drawing in R. A. S. Macalister, *The Excavation of Gezer* (London, 1912) vol. 2, p. 399, Fig. 488.

61. Macalister, ibid., p. 399.

62. Macalister, *The Excavation of Gezer* (London, 1912) vol. 1, p. 96.

63. Macalister, *The Excavation of Gezer,* vol. 1, p. 98. See the drawing in Macalister, *The Excavation of Gezer,* vol. 3 (London, 1912) Plate 26:13. For a photograph of Cave 15 IV see vol. 1, p. 97.

64. W. G. Dever et al., *Gezer IV: The 1969–71 Seasons in Field VI, the "Acropolis"* (Jerusalem, 1986) Part I, vol. 4, p. 43.

65. Dever et al., ibid., p. 45.

66. See the drawing in W. G. Dever et al., *Gezer IV: The 1969–71 Seasons in Field VI, the "Acropolis"* (Jerusalem, 1986) Part 2, vol. 4, Plate 51:2. Also, see the photograph on Plate 116B.

67. See J. D. Seger, *Gezer V: The Field I Caves,* ed. J. D. Seger and H. D. Lance (Jerusalem, 1988) vol. 5, Plate 69: A–E, H.

68. Seger, in *Gezer V,* vol. 5, pp. 77–78. For Cypriot ophidian iconography in the Cyprus Museum, see the early and dated report in J. L. Myres, *A Catalogue of the Cyprus Museum* (Oxford, 1899) pp. 43:91 (snake ornament, Bronze Age pottery [= Plate II:91]), 43:96–100 (snakes on Bronze Age pottery), 47:255 (snake ornament, Bronze Age pottery [= Plate II:255A]), p. 73:1114 (Greek-Phoenician Pottery with handles like serpents' heads), p. 86:1683 (a satyr attempts to catch a serpent), p. 110:3151 (Hercules and a serpent), p. 130:4259–64 (serpents' heads), p. 135:4566 (scarab showing a figure holding two serpents [= Plate 8:4566]), p. 176:100 (silver serpent-head bracelets), p. 182:76 (two silver spirals ending in serpent heads).

69. A. M. Roveri, "Qadesh," *EAA 5* (1965) 583–84; the photograph on p. 583 shows a nude Qadesh holding a serpent in her right hand and standing on a lion.

70. Macalister, *Excavation of Gezer,* Vol. 3, Plate 221:9.

71. See ibid., Plate 221:10. Pritchard (*Palestinian Figurines,* p. 7, No. 11) and Joines (*JBL* 87 [1968]) interpret the art work to denote serpents. This is conceivable, but far from probable (let alone certain).

72. See A. Ben-Tor, "Hazor," in *OEANE* 3:1–5.

73. For a photograph of the site, before and after excavation in 1957, see Yadin et al., eds., *Hazor III–IV: Plates* (Jerusalem, 1961) Plate 121.

74. Y. Yadin et al., *Hazor III–IV,* Plate 339:5–6. Joines (*JBL* 87 [1968] 245 n. 4) reports that "Yadin informed me of their provenance in a personal correspondence." The data given are taken from Yadin et al., ibid., Plate 339:5,6, but they are not exactly the ones she provides. Only the provenance of 139:5 is specified. The assumption is that both were found in the same locus.

75. See the drawings in Keel, *Das Recht der Bilder,* p. 233:178, 182. Also see the Babylonian black limestone deed of gift, also from c. 1200 BCE, and showing a serpent with a scorpion.

76. A. Ben-Tor, R. Bonfil, and A. Paris, *Hazor V* (Jerusalem, 1997) p. 42 (Photo II.20), p. 44 (Fig. II.14: L.628 no. 33 [drawing]).

77. Yadin et al., *Hazor III–IV*, Plate 313:13; also see Plate 196:13 and the description on the facing page.

78. Yadin et al., ibid., Plate 313:11 (photograph). Serpents seem to be applied to the MBII jug shown on Plate 239:20.

79. Yadin et al., *Hazor III–IV: Text* (Jerusalem, 1989) p. 223.

80. Yadin et al., *Hazor III–IV*, Plate 260:24 (drawing) and Plate 313:12 (photograph).

81. Yadin et al., *Hazor II* (Jerusalem, 1960) Plate 181. For another photograph, see [Y. Yadin, ed.], *Hazor: Excavation of a Biblical City* (London, 1958?) illus. 6. A photograph is also published in *NEAEHL* 2:596.

82. In Yadin et al., *Hazor II*, p. 117, it is reported that the "crescent is also found on the central stele (Vol. I, Pl. XXIX) among the elements of the deity symbols. The crescent on the bronze standard permits us to suppose that the latter's use was associated with the nearby Shrine, the subject of whose cult (as noted in Vol. I) was the Moongod." See the photograph in Pritchard, *ANEPTS* p. 352:834.

83. See the drawing by Tadmor and the discussion by Keel, *Das Recht der Bilder*, p. 202 (discussion) and p. 239:203 (drawing). Also see Keel and Uehlinger, *Gods, Goddesses, and Images of God*, pp. 66–67.

84. See the drawings in Keel, *Das Recht der Bilder*, pp. 239–45.

85. Yadin et al., *Hazor II*, p. 118.

86. Yadin, "Further Light on Biblical Hazor: Results of the Second Season, 1956," *Biblical Archaeologist*, 20 (1957) 43.

87. Yadin, "The Fourth Season of Excavation at Hazor," *Biblical Archaeologist*, 22 (1959) 5–6.

88. See Yadin, *Hazor III–IV*, Plate 282 (drawing and description), and 309 (photograph).

89. See C. F.-A. Schaeffer, *Ugaritica II* (Paris, 1949) Plate 30 (photograph).

90. See esp. A. Caquot and M. Sznycer, *Ugaritic Religion* (Leiden, 1980) Plate 14a (standing goddess with a serpent), Plate 15a (seated goddess with serpents), and Plate 19b (the Ugaritic pendant of a goddess with serpents). M. Pope is convinced that a limestone stela from Ugarit contains not only a uraeus but also a serpent held in the hand of El. See Pope, "The Scene on the Drinking Mug from Ugarit," in *Near Eastern Studies in Honor of William Foxwell Albright*, ed. H. Goedicke (Baltimore, London, 1971) pp. 393–405.

91. See Yadin, *Hazor III–IV*, Plate 282:1 for drawing and description and Plate 309 for a photograph. Also see Yadin, *Hazor II*, p. 109 for more details regarding the discovery of the vessel in 1957.

92. See Yadin, *Hazor II*, p. 109 (description), Plate 123:4 (drawing), and Plate 177:6 (photograph).

93. See B. Rothenberg, "Timnaʿ," *NEAEHL* 4.1475–86; W. G. Dever, "Timnaʿ," *OEANE* 5.217–18; D. W. Manor, "Timnaʿ (Place)," *AYBD* 6.553–56. Also see A. Negev, *The Archaeological Encyclopedia of the Holy Land* (New York, 1986 [rev. ed.]), pp. 507–8. the works of Benno Rothenberg are essential, such as *Timnaʿ: Valley of the Biblical Copper Mines* (London, 1972); with Paul Tylecote, *Chalcolithic Copper Smelting* (London, 1978); *The Egyptian Mining Temple at Timna* (London, 1988).

94. See the color photograph in Negev, *The Archaeological Encyclopedia of the Holy Land,* p. 49. A wonderful color photograph is found in J. M. Landay, *Silent Cities, Sacred Stones: Archaeology Discovery in the Land of the Bible* (London, Jerusalem, 1971) p. 88. Excellent color photographs are found in Rothenberg, *Timna,* Plate 19 (full view) and 20 (close-up of head).

95. Timnaʿ is not the site of copper mines belonging to King Solomon. See J. D. Muhly, "Timna and King Solomon," *Bibliotheca Orientalis* 41 (1984) 276–92.

96. B. Rothenberg, *Were These King Solomon's Mines? Excavations in the Timna Valley* (New York, 1972) p. 154. Also see Rothenberg, *The Egyptian Mining Temple.* The gilded copper serpent from Timnaʿ is shown in Plates 11 (full) and 12 (head close-up).

97. See Keel and Uehlinger, *Gods, Goddesses, and Images of God,* p. 68. Also, see F. M. Cross, *Canaanite Myth and Hebrew Epic* (Cambridge, Mass., 1997); for the relation between Hathor and "the serpent lady" inscription, see pp. 19, 32, 34.

98. See the large color photograph in R. Schulz and M. Seidel, eds., *Ägypten: Die Welt der Pharaonen* (Cologne, 1997) pp. 446–47.

99. For an aerial photograph of the tell, see *NEAEHL,* 1:214.

100. See the refined chronology intimated by A. Mazar in *OEANE* 1:305–09. Also see S. Geva, "A Reassessment of the Chronology of Beth Shean Strata V and IV," *Israel Exploration Journal* 29 (1979) 6–10.

101. Numbers in parentheses denote plates in A. Rowe, *The Four Canaanite Temples at Beth-shan* (Philadelphia, 1940).

102. The drawing in Rowe, ibid., on Plate 14:1 is misleading; see the photographs on Plate 58A:1–2, and the drawing on 58A:3.

103. The color photograph in A. Negev, *The Archaeological Encyclopedia of the Holy Land,* p. 249 is attractive, but it scarcely indicates how fragmented is the cult stand.

104. A decent photograph of the restored cylindrical cult stand is found in Pritchard, *ANEP* 585 (on p. 194).

105. The cylindrical stand is too fragmented to be certain; the drawing may be misleading. Too often the reality is confused with an artist's recreation.

106. The photograph in *OEANE* 1:222 can be misleading; the cult stand is very fragmented.

107. The placement of many fragments, especially numbers 16:5, 7, 8, 9, is unclear; that is, I cannot discern with which cylindrical cult stand they should be connected.

108. Rowe, *The Four Canaanite Temples of Beth-shan,* p. 43.

109. It is difficult to follow Rowe's publications and too easy to criticize him. We should, however, understand that he excavated after World War I, in the 1920s, and had difficulty working and publishing during the Depression, finally seeing his work published in 1930 and 1940. He also used Egyptian chronology to identify his finds; this is lamentable, but he worked before the agreement to use the ages of technology and before the refinement of pottery chronology by Albright and others. I am indebted to R. A. Mullins, the Albright Montgomery Fellow for 1998–99, for discussions about some of these insights.

110. H. Th. Bossert, *Altsyrien* (Tübingen, 1951) p. 196:646.

111. Rowe, *The Four Canaanite Temples of Beth-shan,* p. 36.

112. See the references and insights in Rowe, *The Four Canaanite Temples of Beth-shan,* pp. 50–51.

113. See also F. W. James, P. E. McGovern, and A. G. Bonn, *The Late Bronze Egyptian Garrison at Beth Shan,* 2 vols. (Philadelphia, 1993) vol. 2, Plates 83:1–84:1.

114. See the drawing in James, McGovern, and Bonn, *The Late Bronze Egyptian Garrison at Beth Shan,* vol. 2, 58:7 (see the descriptions on plate 57 where the item is misidentified as Rowe, Plate 33:11 [uraeus is also misspelled]).

115. Also see the drawing in James, McGovern, and Bonn, *The Late Bronze Egyptian Garrison at Beth Shan,* vol. 2, 60:1, 2. Each is called a pendant and a uraeus. The photograph is in vol. 2, Plate 26:d and e.

116. James and McGovern also suggest that this object is a cobra. See their "Zoomorphic Objects: Cobra Figurines (Figs. 83–85)," *The Late Bronze Egyptian Garrison at Beth Shan,* vol. 1, pp. 171–72. Also see "Cobra Figurines" on pp. 95–96 and "Cobra Figurines: Construction Methods" in vol. 2, Fig. 3. They proved that the cobra figures were hand formed, without a mold, with appliqués attached in two main ways.

117. See the drawing in James, McGovern, and Bonn, *The Late Bronze Egyptian Garrison at Beth Shan,* vol. 2, Plate 84:2, 85:2.

118. For photographs of this item and the following ones, which are cobra figurines, see James, McGovern, and Bonn, *The Late Bronze Egyptian Garrison at Beth Shan,* vol. 2, Plate 39.

119. Also see the photograph in A. Rowe, *The Topography and History of Beth-shan* (Philadelphia, 1930) vol. 1, Plate 35:4 (facing view) and 35:5 (side view). On this plate the pottery figurine is identified as "a serpent goddess in the form of a uraeus, with breasts and a cup below for the lacteal fluid." It is a pity that this insightful information was placed only here.

120. Rowe, ibid., p. 44, thought that the men were "gods(?)" and they were "in fighting attitudes(?)." This is too speculative. The other side of this cult stand seems to be shown in a photograph in Pritchard, *ANEP* 590 (p. 195).

121. See the drawing of one in E. D. Oren, *The Northern Cemetery of Beth Shan* (Leiden, 1973) Fig. 41:31.

122. Oren, ibid., Fig. 51:9; see the description on p. 97. For a photograph of Tomb 27, see Plate 2:3 (the plates are not numbered and no page numbers are provided).

123. Oren, ibid., Fig. 51:25; see the description on p. 127, no. 17. For a photograph of the tomb see Plate 3:1 (see preceding note).

124. Rowe wrote, "our excavations have shown that the site was the centre of a serpent cult in Palestine." Rowe, *Topography and History of Beth-shan,* p. 1, n.5.

125. N. H. Snaith, ed., *Leviticus and Numbers* (London and Edinburgh, 1967) p. 279.

126. See Rowe, *The Four Canaanite Temples at Beth-shan,* Part I, p. 45.

127. See the similar comments by G. M. Fitzgerald in D. W. Thomas, ed., *Archaeology and Old Testament Study* (Oxford, 1967) p. 196.

128. See the photograph in Charlesworth, *Millennium Guide,* p. 79.

129. A good popular synthesis, with color photographs, is found in J. C. H. Laughlin, "The Remarkable Discoveries at Tel Dan," *BAR* 7 (1981) 20–37.

130. A. Biran, *Biblical Dan* (Jerusalem, 1994) p. 165; see the photograph of the "snake" pithos *in situ* in Fig. 125, and assembled in Fig. 126, and the drawing in Fig. 128.

131. Biran, "Dan," *NEAEHL* 1.323–32; see esp. pp. 327–29.

132. Biran, *Biblical Dan,* p. 165.

133. Recall the Phoenician silver bowl from Palestrina in Italy. It shows a large serpent surrounding and on the circumference of a scene. The serpent is like Ouroboros. See the drawing in R. D. Barnett, "Ezekiel and Tyre," *Eretz-Israel [Albright Volume]* 9 (1969) 6–13; p. 12, Fig. 1.

134. See the photograph of one in Biran, *NEAEHL* 1.327, and the photographs of another in Biran, *Biblical Dan,* Fig. 126. For a drawing of two of them, see ibid., Fig. 128.

135. Biran, *Biblical Dan,* p. 153.

136. See the drawing in Fig. 79 and the photography on Plate 30 in C.F.-A. Schaeffer, *Ugaritica II.*

137. I have checked all of the following books: C. Warren, *The Recovery of Jerusalem* (London, 1871); F. J. Bliss and A. C. Dickie, *Excavations at Jerusalem, 1894–1897* (London, 1889); S. Merrill, *Ancient Jerusalem* (New York, London, 1908); G. Dalman, *Jerusalem und sein Gelände* (Gütersloh, 1930); J. Simons, *Jerusalem in the Old Testament* (Leiden, 1952); P. L.-H. Vincent and P. M.-A. Steve, *Jérusalem de l'Ancien Testament,* 2 vols. (Paris, 1954); K. M. Kenyon, *Digging Up Jerusalem* (London, 1974); B. Mazar, G. Cornfeld, and D. N. Freedman, *The Mountain of the Lord* (Garden City, N.Y., 1975); W. H. Mare, *The Archaeology of the Jerusalem Area* (Grand Rapids, 1987); H. Geva, ed., *Ancient Jerusalem Revealed* (Jerusalem, 1994); F. E. Peters, *Jerusalem* (Princeton, 1997).

138. Vincent's words, "serait pour le moment prématurée," concerned the Jebusite city and not serpent symbolism. See Vincent, *Jérusalem: Recherches de topographie, d'archéologie et d'histoire* (Paris, 1912) vol. 1, p. 161.

139. Mazar, Cornfeld, and Freedman, *The Mountain of the Lord,* p. 159.

140. In Hebrew, the Serpents' Pool was most likely ברכת הנחשים, but the Aramaic is not so clear. See G. Dalman, *Jerusalem und sein Gelände* (Gütersloh, 1930) p. 201.

141. C. Schick, "Recent Discoveries at the 'Nicophorieh,' " *Palestine Exploration Fund: Quarterly Statement* (1892) 115–19 (he announces the discovery of Herod's Monument); and Schick, "Birket es Sultan, Jerusalem," *PEFQS* (1898) 224–29 (Nehemiah's Dragon Well was at Birket es Sultan and the latter is Josephus' Pool of the Serpents). Also see Schick, "The Dragon Well," *PEFQS* (1898) 230–32 (the Dragon Pool of Nehemiah is not the Birket Mamilla but its lower pool, the Birket es Sultan).

142. D. Bahat, *The Illustrated Atlas of Jerusalem* (Jerusalem, 1996) pp. 35, 38, 39, and esp. p. 49.

143. E. Netzer and S. Ben Arieh, "Opus Reticulatum Building in Jerusalem," *IEJ* 33 (1983) 163–71; also see E. Netzer, "Herod's Family Tomb in Jerusalem," *BAR* 9 (1983) 52–59.

144. M. Broshi, "The Serpents' Pool and Herod's Monument—A Reconsideration," *MAARAV* 8 (1992) 213–22.

145. D. Bahat, "The Hasmonean Aqueduct Near the Temple Mount," *Ariel* 57–58 (1988) 132–42 (in Hebrew).

146. G. Bresc-Bautier, *Le Cartulaire du chapitre du Saint-Sépulcre de Jérusalem* (Documents relatifs à l'histoire des croisades 15; Paris, 1984) 314–15. I am grateful to Broshi for this reference.

147. For a drawing of the monument, in a reconstructed state, see Bahat, *The Illustrated Atlas of Jerusalem,* p. 50.

148. I am grateful to Broshi for discussing the Pool of the Serpents with me.

149. For succinct accounts, see T. Dothan and S. Gitin, "Miqne, Tel (Ekron)," *NEAEHL* 3.1051–59; T. Dothan and S. Gitin, "Miqne, Tel," *OEANE* 4.30–35.

150. I express appreciation to Noel Freedman for conversations on this point.

151. S. Gitin, T. Dothan, and J. Naveh, "A Royal Dedication Inscription from Tel Miqneh/Ekron," *Qadmoniot* 3 (1997) 38–43 (in Hebrew).

152. For a photograph of the altar, in its reconstructed stage but without the serpent image visible, see Z. Herzog, "Tel Beersheba," *NEAEHL* 1.167–73; see photograph on p. 171. No comment is made in this article about ophidian iconography.

153. Z. Herzog, "Beersheba," *OEANE* 1.287–91; Herzog discusses the horned altar at length but does not mention a serpent (p. 290).

154. Pritchard, *ANEP,* p. 107.

155. For photographs of the horned altar with the engraved ophidian iconography, see Y. Aharoni, "The Horned Altar of Beer-sheba," *Biblical Archaeologist* 37.1 (1974) 2–6, Fig. 2 (a good close-up) and H. Shanks, "Horned Altar for Sacrifice Unearthed at Beer-Sheva," *BAR* 1.1. (1975) 1, 8–9, 15; see p. 8 (a photograph of the altar reassembled). For a photograph of the altar in secondary use in a wall of a storehouse, see Aharoni, Fig. 3. It is clear that the serpent image is to be dated to the time of the construction of the altar and not to some decoration applied later in the storehouse. I cannot see the image of the serpent in the walls of the house; perhaps the image was turned inward from the eyes of those working in the storehouse.

156. Aharoni, "The Horned Altar of Beer-sheba," 4.

157. Keel, *Das Recht der Bilder,* p. 198.

158. Aharoni, "The Horned Altar of Beer-sheba," 6.

159. See A. Kloner, *Mareshah* (Jerusalem, 1996 [in Hebrew]); the centerfold has the photograph.

160. See the photograph in *EAA* 5 (1965) 674.

161. See O. Bar-Yosef, "Carmel Caves," *OEANE* 1.424–28. See E. C. M. Van den Brink, "An Index to Chalcolithic Mortuary Caves in Israel," *IEJ* 48 (1998) 164–73.

162. Tacitus, *Histories* 2.78. An inscription found on Mount Carmel proves that there was a cult of Zeus Heliopolitanus there.

163. See "Venere di Milo," *EDAA, Supplemento,* 1970, pp. 895–98.

164. Aphrodite appeared clothed in a clinging gown on the Parthenon; see L. Kreuz, *Begegnungen mit Aphrodite: Eine psychologische Studie zur Genetik des Schönen* (Stuttgart, 1966); see esp. the photographs of Aphrodite and Peitho (p. 259) and also of Aphrodite and Eros (p. 260) who were on the Parthenon. Aphrodite is shown in a clinging gown with right breast exposed on a statue in the Louvre (see p. 270).

165. See the photographs in L. Kreuz, *Begegnungen mit Aphrodite,* p. 275. In this statue Aphrodite has her weight on her right foot, and her right hand is shown above her privates. For other depictions of Aphrodite nude, see Aphrodite Crouching (p. 296), Aphrodite Bathing and in a Crouch (p. 297), Aphrodite of Kyrene (p. 301), and Aphrodite of Delos (p. 302). The depiction of Aphrodite with a garment only over her lower body, that is, Venus de Milo, is shown in the photograph on p. 299. Nike of Samothrace is shown in a full flowing garment (see p. 308).

166. Iliffe, "A Nude Terra-cotta Statuette of Aphrodite," *The Quarterly of the Department of Antiquities in Palestine* 3 (1934) 106.

167. We cannot be certain of the dates of Praxiteles' life. For a learned discussion, see R. Stupperich, "Praxiteles," in *Grosse Gestalten der Griechischen Antike* (Munich, 1999) pp. 287–95.

168. I. Pomerantz, ed., *Highlights of Archaeology: The Israel Museum, Jerusalem* (Jerusalem, 1984) p. 94; also see the color photograph on p. 95. A beautiful color photograph is also found in Avi-Yonah and Yadin, eds., *6000 Years of Art in the Holy Land,* p. 180. I am grateful to the Israel Museum for permission to publish the present photograph.

169. J. H. Iliffe, "A Nude Terra-cotta Statuette of Aphrodite," pp. 106–11, with Plates 32 and 33 (the photographs show the many joins of the fragments).

170. P. Diel, *Symbolism in Greek Mythology: Human Desire and Its Transformations* (Boulder, London, 1980); Diel, *Symbolism in the Bible: The Universality of Symbolic Language and Its Psychological Significance,* trans. N. Marans (San Francisco, 1986).

171. Long ago W. F. Albright rightly warned against such anachronistic interpretations. See his "The Bronze Age,' II of the Excavations of Tell Beit Mirsim," *Annual of the American Schools of Oriental Research* 17 (1936–37) 43.

172. See esp. E. Ghazal, *Schlangenkult und Tempelliebe: Sakrale Erotik in archaischen Gesellschaften* (Berlin, 1995). The illustrations are enlightening.

173. The Carmel Aphrodite is also similar to the Aphrodite with Eros found in Egypt and dated to the first century BCE or first century CE. See the color photograph in J. M. Eisenberg, *Art of the Ancient World* (New York, 1985) vol. 4, p. 100, no. 282 (cf. the Roman Aphrodite in no. 281—but neither of these bronze statuettes is accompanied by serpents).

174. See N. Asgari et al., *The Anatolian Civilisations II* (Istanbul, 1983) B187 (color photograph), p. 89 (photograph with description).

175. This Aphrodite belonged to Dr. Elie Borowski and was part of the Athos Moretti Collection. It was offered for sale in 2000. For a photograph, see *Christie's New York* (Tuesday 13 June 2000) pp. 58–59. She is also featured on the front and back covers.

176. See Kreuz, *Begegnungen mit Aphrodite.* The focus is on the depiction of Aphrodite in Greek art from circa 660 BCE to 335 BCE. The aesthetic and beautiful are contemplated. Kreuz's approach is via psychology.

177. See esp. A. Gardiner, *Egyptian Grammar* (Oxford, London, 1957 [3rd ed.], reprinted many times) p. 27.

178. See the beautiful color photographs in K. Michalowski, *L'Art de l'ancien Égypte* (Paris, 1968) esp. Illus. 14, 42, 106, 107, 385, 386, 391, 392, 504, and 581.

179. E. A. W. Budge, "Snake-worship," in *Osiris and the Egyptian Resurrection,* 2 vols. (London, New York, n.d. [1911]) vol. 2, pp. 236–38; the quotation is on p. 236. Budge points out that in the Book of the Dead, chap. 108, the serpent Ami-hemf was 30 cubits long and that the Papyrus Golénischeff refers to a serpent that was not only 30 feet long but had a beard 2 cubits long.

180. The two images are taken from a painting on papyrus by the Egyptian artist Monsef and an iron serpent.

181. See the Egyptian cobra (S. 408) with the "crown" (Vitrine 6, no. 6) and consult A. Schweitzer and C. Traunecher, *Strasbourg: Musée archéologique* (Paris, 1998) p. 27 (no. 6).

182. J. Y. Empereur, *Alexandria Rediscovered* (London, New York, 1998) p. 156. The work was translated from the French by M. Maehler.

183. See the close-up photograph in Empereur, *Alexandria Rediscovered,* p. 160.

184. Note esp. A. Rixens' "The Death of Cleopatra," which is in the Musée des Augustins in Toulouse; the seventeenth-century red chalk drawing of Cleopatra by Giovanni Francesco Barbieri in the British Museum (PD 1895-9-15-709); and the bronze statue of Cleopatra (c. 1636), with a serpent biting her breast, in the Royal Collection in Hampton Court Palace, London (no. 39714). See E. Law, *The History of Hampton Court Palace II* (London, 1888) p. 302. Note also the miniature in the

vellum manuscript of G. Boccaccio, *De casibus illustrium virorum et feminarum* (BM Royal MS 14 E.V., folio 348v); it depicts Cleopatra with her reddish gown pulled to the waist and holding two asps, one before each breast.

185. See G. Néret, *Michelangelo 1475–1564* (Cologne, London, New York, 1998) p. 81.

186. See S. Walker and P. Higgs, eds., *Cleopatra of Egypt: From History to Myth* (London, Princeton, 2001).

187. As quoted by E. Flamarion in her *Cleopatra: The Life and Death of a Pharaoh,* trans. A. Bonfante-Warren (New York, 1997) p. 3.

188. See the handy translation in Penguin Books: Suetonius, *The Twelve Caesars,* trans. R. Graves, rev. M. Grant (London, 1989) pp. 62–63.

189. A. Wallace-Hadrill in *The Cambridge Ancient History,* ed. A. K. Bowman, E. Champlin, and A. Lintott (Cambridge, 1996) vol. 10, p. 284.

190. The entirely nude Esquiline Venus in the Capitoline Museum in Rome (inv. 1141) has a serpent in relief beside her right leg.

191. H. B. Walters, *Catalogue of the Engraved Gems and Cameos, Greek, Etruscan and Roman, in the British Museum* (London, 1926) catalogue number 3085.

192. It is in the Charlesworth collection.

193. For literature and comments, see R. Stichel, *Die Namen Noes, seines Bruders und seiner Frau* (AAWG 112; Göttingen, 1979) p. 108, note 441.

194. See H. A. Kelly, "The Metamorphoses of the Eden Serpent During the Middle Ages and Renaissance," *Viator* 2 (1971) 301–28.

195. It is on public view in the Herakleion Museum; for a good picture, see C. P. Christ, *Odyssey with the Goddess: A Spiritual Quest in Crete* (New York, 1995) p. ii.

196. See S. Alexiou, *Minoische Kultur:* Sternstunden der Archäologie, translated by W. Liebich (Frankfurt, Göttingen, 1976) (also see the Greek original of 1964 or English translation of 1969); see esp. Fig. 12 (the snake goddess), p. 113 (gold amulet with serpent), and p. 119 (the serpents on a vessel). I studied the serpents on ancient vessels or of gold at Chania's Archaeological Museum. Some are very impressive, adding to the vast evidence for the appreciation of serpents on ancient Crete.

197. See J. Schäfer, "The Role of 'Gardens' in Minoan Civilization (Plates XIV–XVII)," in *The Civilizations of the Aegean and Their Diffusion in Cyprus and the Eastern Mediterranean Around 2000–1600 BC,* ed. V. Karageorghis (Larnaca, 1989) pp. 85–88.

198. The serpent goddesses were found in the Knossos palace. For illustrations of two of them (the third is fragmented), and for an insightful discussion, see L. Goodison and C. Morris, "Beyond the 'Great Mother,' " in *Ancient Goddesses,* pp. 112–32. Also see the snake goddess from Knossos holding two aroused cobras with tongues extended; the serpents are wound around each arm. See the photograph in R. D. Barnett, *Ancient Ivories in the Middle East* (Jerusalem, 1982) Plate 28:a and b.

199. At least fourteen alleged Minoan goddesses are claimed to be forgeries. See K. D. S. Lapatin, "Snake Goddesses, Fake Goddesses," *Archaeology* (January/February 2001) 33–36.

200. The chronology for Crete used by me is not that of Sir Arthur Evans. It is the revised one developed by N. Platon. See S. Alexiou, *Minoan Civilization,* trans. C. Ridley (Herakleion, n.d. but 6th rev. ed.) pp. 7–9. Stylianos Alexiou is a professor at the University of Crete.

201. See the color photograph in Higgins, *Minoan and Mycenaean Art* (London, 1997), Illustration no. 202. Another impressive color photograph appears in F. Durando, *Griechenland,* trans. D. Krumbach (Erlangen, [1997?]) p. 23.

202. The day I spent in Knossos a gentle rain fell on the ruins, but the setting was serene.

203. A. Kanta, *Phaistos, Hagia Triadha, Gortyn,* p. 28 (in full color).

204. See L. Nixon, "Changing Views of Minoan Society," in *Minoan Society: Proceedings of the Cambridge Colloquium, 1981,* ed. O. Krzyszkowska and L. Nixon (Bristol, 1983).

205. R. Castleden, *Minoans: Life in Bronze Age Crete* (London, New York, 1993) p. 161.

206. See the color photograph in A. Sp. Vassilakis, *Crete,* trans. W. W. Phelps (Athens, n.d. [1995?]) p. 169.

207. A. Kanta, *Phaistos, Hagia Triadha, Gortyn* (Athens, 1998) p. 115.

208. See esp. the gold ring from Mykenai; see the drawing in Schachermeyr, *Die minoische Kultur des alten Kreta* (Stuttgart, 1964) p. 147.

209. Castleden, *Minoans,* p. 161.

210. Alexiou, *Minoan Civilization,* p. 44.

211. See J. Hawkes, *Dawn of the Gods* (London, 1968).

212. Alexiou, *Minoan Civilization,* pp. 30–31.

213. See Alexiou, *Minoan Civilization,* pp. 30–31, 50, and Castleden, *Minoans,* p. 30.

214. See Alexiou, *Minoan Civilization,* p. 50.

215. The Bronze Age (c. 1400–1200 BCE) came to a surprising end around the twelfth century BCE. It is possible that earthquakes contributed to this disaster. For a popular and succinct study, see W. H. Stiebing, "When Civilization Collapsed: Death of the Bronze Age," *Archaeology Odyssey* (September/October 2001) 16–26, 62 (see the bibliographical information on this page). A. Nur and E. H. Cline are convinced that earthquakes did cause the end of the Bronze Age; see their "What Triggered the Collapse? Earthquake Storms," *Archaeology Odyssey* (September/October 2001) 30–36, 62–63 (a mine of bibliographical references to ancient earthquakes).

216. This scenario is well accepted; see, e.g., R. Higgins, *Minoan and Mycenaean Art* (London, 1997 [new rev. ed.]) pp. 17–18.

217. Schachermeyr writes, "Bei den Schlangen handelte es sich um das chthonische Begleittier der grossen Erdgöttin." *Die minoische Kultur des alten Kreta,* p. 154.

218. See B. Röder, J. Hummel, and B. Kunz, *Göttinnendämmerung: Das Matriarchat aus archäologischer Sicht* (Munich, 1996) esp. see pp. 299–345.

219. Tablet Gg 702; see Castleden, *Minoans,* p. 125.

220. See the color photograph in Vasilakis, *Herakleion Archaeological Museum* (Athens, n.d. [1998?]) p. 81.

221. See the ivory seal in the form of a dove with her two nestlings in Alexiou, *Minoan Civilization,* p. 222 (also the doves above the double axes, p. 104; see p. 109); also see Castleden, *Minoans,* p. 125.

222. See Higgins, *Minoan and Mycenaean Art,* p. 32.

223. As quoted by Christ in *Odyssey with the Goddess,* p. 73.

224. A. Michailidou, *Knossos,* trans. A. Doumas and T. Cullen (Athens, 1998) p. 124. Michailidou is the archaeologist who has recently excavated at Knossos.

225. See Vasilakis, *Herakleion Archaeological Museum;* for the gold ring with dancing bare-breasted women, see p. 117; the gold amulet is on p. 129.

226. There is a poisonous snake in the zoo at Herakleion, but it is a sand viper *(vipera ammodytes)* and comes from northern Greece. I am grateful to Mr. Liberakis, the herpetologist, for discussions on the snakes on Crete.

227. Both vessels were purchased by Charlesworth in 2002 from antiquities dealers in Jerusalem. They apparently come from Jerusalem, or more likely from Jericho or its environs.

228. I am grateful to the Cousins Family Foundation for permission to publish these Canaanite bowls.

229. F. R. Matson, "Potters and Pottery in the Ancient Near East," *Civilizations of the Ancient Near East,* ed. J. M. Sasson et al. (Peabody, Mass., 1995) p. 1553.

230. Sample 914A2. Date: 5/3/01. At Daybreak, Guilford, CT.

231. Sample 914A1. Date: 4/01. At Daybreak, Guilford, CT.

232. An excellent example has just been found in Ashkelon. I examined it, thanks to Ross Voss.

233. The cult standard is dated to the fourteenth–thirteenth cent. BCE; see the discussion and picture in Y. Yadin's "Hazor," *NEAEHL,* 2.593–603; esp. see p. 596. A color photograph of the cult stand appears in Yadin's popular *Hazor: The Rediscovery of a Great Citadel of the Bible* (London, New York, 1975) p. 54.

234. For a focused introduction to ancient pottery, see Matson, "Potters and Pottery in the Ancient Near East," pp. 1553–65.

235. See the helpful survey by W. G. Dever, "Ceramic Ethnoarchaeology," in *OEANE,* 1.448–65.

236. Mycenaean imports, including a highly sophisticated painted Mycenaean krater, have been found at Dan, from the Late Bronze Age (c. fourteenth–thirteenth cent.); see the color photographs in *Celebrating Avraham: Avraham Biran—The Excavator of Dan at 90* (Washington, D.C., 1999) esp. pp. 37, 49, 81. As with the two Canaanite vessels that seem to antedate the entry of Joshua and the Israelites into Palestine, so this Mycenaean krater antedates the conquest of Dan by the Israelites (Josh 19:47; Jud 18:29). They witness to the final heyday of Canaanite pottery.

237. While the two vessels now introduced generally contrast to the Cypro-Phoenician juglets, No. 2 is reminiscent of one of these types found at Horvat Rosh Zayit. See esp. the far-right jar shown in *NEAEHL,* 4.1291. It is necessary to point out, again, that while debate has continued over the time when Greek influence entered Palestine after the Exile, it is certain that such influence did not begin with Alexander the Great; as M. Hengel states, "Die Begegnung zwischen Hellas und dem alten Orient begann durchaus nicht erst mit dem Alexanderzug, sie hat eine sehr vielseitige Geschichte, die bis weit in das 2. Jahrtausend, in die mykenische Zeit, zurückreicht." Hengel, *Judaica et Hellenistica: Kleine Schriften I* (Tübingen, 1996) p. 153.

238. See esp. the photograph in B. Mazar, *Biblical Israel: State and People,* ed. S. Aḥituv (Jerusalem, 1992) pp. 29–30.

239. See T. Ornan, *A Man and His Land: Highlights from the Moshe Dayan Collection* (Jerusalem, 1986) pp. 86–87.

240. See K. M. Kenyon and T. A. Holland, *Excavations at Jericho: Volume Four—The Pottery Type Series and Other Finds* (London, 1982) Fig. 177, esp. no. 12.

241. Kenyon and Holland, ibid., Fig. 180.

242. K. M. Kenyon, *Excavations at Jericho: Volume Two—The Tombs Excavated in 1955–8* (London, 1965) p. 1.

243. See Yadin's suggestion, as reported by V. Goodside in "Why Is a Bilbil Called a Bilbil?," *BAR* 14 (1988) 60; and Queries and Comments in *BAR* 15 (1988) 10.

244. Goodside reports Seger's suggestion; *BAR* 14 (1988) 60.

245. See B. M. Gittlen, "The Cultural and Chronological Implications of the Cypro-Palestinian Trade During the Late Bronze Age," *BASOR* 241 (1981) 49–59 and C. J. Bergoffen, "Overland Trade in Northern Sinai: The Evidence of the Late Cypriot Pottery," *BASOR* 284 (1991) 59–76.

246. E.g., A. Biran, *Biblical Dan,* esp. see illustrations 76 (p. 110), 82 (esp. no 3, Cypriote Bibil and no. 4 "local imitation bilbil"). The two vessels in my "Announcing the Discovery of Canaanite Ophidian Vessels" have much thicker and rounded bodies. Thus, there is no juglet impressively similar to the ones now published.

247. See Dever in *OEANE,* 1.445.

248. See A. Mazar, "The 'Bull Site'—An Iron Age I Open Cult Place," *BASOR,* 247 (1982) 27–42. An attractive photograph appears in J. P. O'Neill et al., eds., *Treasures of the Holy Land: Ancient Art from the Israel Museum* (New York, 1986)) p. 153.

249. See the drawings of the bronze bull and the discussion in A. Mazar, "Bronze Bull Found in Israelite 'High Place from the Time of the Judges," in *Early Israel,* ed. H. Shanks and D. P. Cole (Washington, D.C., 1990) pp. 108–14. These reflections are preliminary; experts on early art and ceramics will certainly help refine my original speculations.

250. Here, among all the fights between the minimalists and maximalists, I follow B. Mazar; see esp. his succinct review of this history in "The Philistines," *Biblical Israel: State and People,* pp. 22–40.

251. I am grateful to the Israel Museum for permission to publish this work. See "Snake Jug," in *Highlights of Archaeology: The Israel Museum, Jerusalem,* p. 42.

252. Pliny the Younger, to Tacitus; Book 6.20. An authoritative and popular work on Pompeii is the following: R. Brilliant, *Pompeii—AD 79: The Treasure of Rediscovery* (New York, 1979). The work is an official publication of the American Museum of Natural History. For a gold anguine armband, see p. 72. I have quoted Pliny from this book; see p. 22.

253. Published by permission of the Museo Archeologico Nazionale di Napoli and with the assistance of Dr. Marcello Del Verme. See L. Breglia, *Catalogo delle oreficerie del Museo Nazionale di Napoli* (Rome, 1941) and R. Siviero, *Gli ori e le ambre del Museo Nazionale di Napoli* (Florence, 1954).

254. See J. J. Deiss, *Herculaneum: Italy's Buried Treasure* (Malibu, 1989 [rev. ed.]) p. 153.

255. A. S. Walker, *Animals in Ancient Art: From the Leo Mildenberg Collection: Part 2* (Mainz, 1996) pp. 18–19.

256. Also see G. Zahlhaas, *Aus Noahs Arche: Tierbilder des Sammlung Mildenberg aus fünf Jahrtausenden* (Mainz, 1996); see esp. pp. 33–35, "Die Schlange."

257. See the earlier discussion of the gold bracelets preserved in the State Hermitage Museum in St. Petersburg.

258. Charlesworth purchased them from antiquities dealers in the Old City of Jerusalem.

259. See the photograph in Deiss, *Herculaneum,* p. 89.

260. This object also belongs to the Charlesworth collection.

261. While not dating from 100 BCE to 100 CE, the Collection Stathatos in the Archaeological Museum in Athens houses some very attractive gold serpent jewelry. Of note are the following: two gold snake bracelets from the third cent. BCE or early second cent. BCE [they boast red semiprecious stones]; seven gold snake armbands of the same period; a gold serpent ring from the fourth cent BCE with two red semiprecious gems near the first curve and one near the tail. Stathatos was a private collector who gave her collection to the Athens museum.

262. The Hermitage and the BM, as well as other museums, feature earlier examples of ornate very advanced and expensive gold serpent jewelry; see *Greek Gold,* pp. 114, 210 (in Russian).

263. See the picture in the present book.

264. See the color photograph in A. M. Liberati and F. Bourbon, *Rom: Weltreich der Antike* (Erlangen, 1997) p. 91 (right).

265. Published and discussed earlier in this book.

266. See the color photograph in Liberati and Bourbon, *Rom: Weltreich der Antike,* p. 91 (left).

267. I know only about the photograph in A. Böhme-Schönberger, *Kleidung und Schmuck in Rom und den Provinzen* (Stuttgart, 1997) p. 58 (Abb. 46).

268. A gold piece of jewelry from an unknown site from the fifth or fourth cent. BCE depicts a wolf struggling with a large snake. See Busch, *Gold der Skythen,* p. 88.

269. See the discussion and photograph of a third-century CE example in *Highlights of Archaeology: The Israel Museum, Jerusalem,* pp. 116–17.

270. See the examples of "snake thread vessels" in Y. Israeli, *The Wonders of Ancient Glass at the Israel Museum, Jerusalem* (Jerusalem, 1998) p. 41.

271. The technique of decorating glass with snake-thread designs reached its apogee of sophistication at Cologne by the end of the second century CE; we know that glassmakers migrated from the eastern Mediterranean to Cologne in the second century CE. See C. W. Clairmont, "Snake-Thread," *The Glass Vessels* (The Excavations at Dura-Europos, Final Report, Part 5; New Haven, 1963) pp. 42–46; D. B. Harden, "Snake-thread Glasses Found in the East," *JRS* 24 (1934) 50–55; F. Fremersdorf, "Die Henkelkanne von Cortil-Noirmont im Brusseler Museum, eine Kolnische Arbeit," *L'Antiquité Classique* 7 (1938) 201–14. Also, see the publication cited by Clairmont, esp. on pp. xix–xx. For photographs of snake-thread glassware, see Clairmont, Plates 22:162, 163, 164, 165, 167, 168, 169, 170, 171, 172, 173, 174, 175, 176, 177.

272. See Clairmont, *The Glass Vessels,* pp. 44–46 (discussions) and Plates 22 and 23.

273. See the photography in *Highlights of Archaeology: The Israel Museum, Jerusalem,* p. 117.

274. The presentation by Clairmont needs to be updated and corrected.

275. This is a very old symbol that considerably antedates its use by the Greeks for Hermes and the Romans for Mercury; for example, see the two serpents facing each other and standing on the Gudea vase that dates from about 2100 BCE, in Pritchard *ANEP* 511. The caduceus in the eleventh-century BCE limestone Neo-Punic votive stele shows the serpents facing in opposite directions; see the photograph in *Encyclopédie Photographique de l'Art,* vol. 2, p. 134.

276. Jalame is also called Jalamet el-Asafna and Khirbet el Asafnh.

277. See G. D. Weinberg, *Excavations at Jalame: Site of a Glass Factory in Late Roman Palestine* (Columbia, 1988) pp. 81 (descriptions of 351 and 352), 330 (photographs of 351 and 352).

278. See Clairmont, "Pinched," *The Glass Vessels,* pp. 46–54; see Plates 5:180, 181, 185, 193, 194; 23:179, 186, 187, 188, 189, 190, 191, 195, 198.

279. See, e.g., the heroic votive bas-relief found at Piraeus and dating from the third century BCE (a serpent is shown below the hero). See M. Rostovtzeff, *The Social and Economic History of the Hellenistic World* (Oxford, 1941) vol. 1, Plate 21:1. Also, see the serpent bracelet in Plate 45:2.

280. I am indebted to the excellent reflections presented by P. de Montebello and E. J. Milleker in *The Year One: Art of the Ancient World—East and West* (New York, 2000) see esp. pp. vii, 62–67.

281. It is found in the Charlesworth collection and was purchased in Jerusalem.

282. For a convenient glossary and drawings of glass shapes and types, see N. Kunina, *Ancient Glass in the Hermitage Collection* (St. Petersburg, 1997) pp. 341–47.

283. An example of glass tableware is found in the Israel Museum. See the picture in Y. Israeli, *The Wonders of Ancient Glass at the Israel Museum*, p. 39. The example in the Israel Museum has only a thin snake-thread around the neck.

284. Note, e.g., how different it is from the examples shown in Kunina, *Ancient Glass,* pp. 221–24.

285. The example in the Israel Museum has only "trails applied in undulating, snake-like lines that are called 'snake thread vessels.' " No head, eye, or skin is depicted as in our example. See Israeli, *The Wonders of Ancient Glass at the Israel Museum,* p. 40 (discussion) and p. 41 (color photograph).

286. I am most grateful to Father Hermann Konings, curator of Saint Anne's Museum in Bethesda (Bethzatha), for allowing me to publish the ophidian objects found at Bethesda, and for discussing with me the evidence of an Asklepieion at Bethesda. We even obtained ladders and workmen to explore a significant cave or cistern in which a magnificent pillar and two arches were erected during the Hasmonean Period.

287. Since I did not excavate the site and no excavation reports were available to me, the present report is as precise as presently possible. I have profited from conversations with Dr. S. Gibson and Father Konings and am grateful to them for their suggestions and insights. I was able to examine the artifacts in the museum at Saint Anne's Church.

288. It seems that the two pools, especially the southern one, were shaped like trapezoids.

288. C. Clermont-Ganneau, "The Jerusalem Researches," *PEF* (1874) 261–80; see esp. pp. 264–69.

290. I am grateful to S. Gibson for drawing my attention to this anguine vase.

291. This was also the judgment of Clermont-Ganneau, *PEF* (1874) 268.

292. Clermont-Ganneau, *PEF* (1874) 264.

293. Can we be certain that Hermes and not also Asclepius were intended? Asclepius was sometimes shown holding the pine cone; see Pausanias, *Descriptio Graeciae* 2.10.3. The Greek and English are conveniently collected in E. J. Edelstein and L. Edelstein, *Asclepius: Collection and Interpretation of the Testimonies,* 2 vols. (Baltimore, 1998) p. 351. Also, see the comments in vol. 2, p. 226.

294. Clermont-Ganneau, *PEF* (1874) 265–66.

295. Clermont-Ganneau, ibid., p. 266.

296. Clermont-Ganneau, ibid., p. 267.

297. Clermont-Ganneau thought the vase was for water (p. 267). This is impossible, but I would think that it was designed for wine that was often mixed with water for drinking.

298. See the short description and photograph in S. Gibson, "Officers and Gentlemen," *Eretz* 52 (1997) 19–25; see esp. p. 24.

299. Wine mixed with water was served at banquets by means of an elegant ladle, called a *simpulum* or a *cyathus*.

300. Clermont-Ganneau, *PEF* (1874) 267.

301. For the Latin text and English translation, see Edelstein and Edelstein, *Asclepius,* pp. 361–62.

302. Artemidorus, *Onirocritica* 2.13; for the Greek and English, see Edelstein and Edelstein, *Asclepius*, p. 367.

303. Festus, *De Verborum Significatu* 67 M; for the Latin and English, see Edelstein and Edelstein, *Asclepius,* p. 366.

304. Edelstein and Edelstein, *Asclepius,* p. 229 (I added italics for clarity and emphasis).

305. Clermont-Ganneau, *PEF* (1874) 264. The photographs of the Bezatha Vase did not appear in this volume nor the next one of the *PEF, Quarterly Statement.* For further reflections by Clermont-Ganneau on ophidian iconography, see his "Les cerfs mangeurs de serpents," *Recueil d'archéologie orientale* (Paris, 1901) vol. 4, pp. 319–22; cf. p. 90.

306. See esp. Z. Amar, "The Metamorphosis of Holy Sites for Healing Purposes in Jerusalem," *Judea and Samaria Research Studies: Proceedings of the Seventh Annual Meeting 1997,* ed. Y. Eshel (Kedumim-Ariel, 1997) pp. 207–22 (Hebrew).

307. Asclepius appears with a chiton and wearing shoes, while the gods are depicted nude. See the draped Hygieia, e.g., in *LIMC,* vol. 5.2, pp. 380–95. Also see the discussions and illustrations in the present book, in the chapter on Greek and Latin texts.

308. See the painting in *LIMC,* vol. V.2, pp. 380, 382:18.

309. See the coin showing Hygieia in *LIMC,* vol. V.2, p. 382:19.

310. See the sculpture shown in *LIMC,* vol. V.2, p. 395:3.

311. See the female figure shown prominently in Gibson, *ErIsr* 52 (1997) 24.

312. Eusebius, *Praeparatio Evangelica,* 3.11.26: "A symbol is Asclepius to whom they attribute a staff, as a sign of support and relief for invalids." See the Greek text and English translation in Edelstein and Edelstein, *Asclepius,* p. 369.

313. See Cornutus, *Theologiae Graecae Compendium, Cp. 33* ("The serpent is a sign of attention . . . The staff also seems to be a symbol of some similar thing"); see the Greek text and English translation collected by Edelstein and Edelstein in *Asclepius,* p. 368.

314. *Metam.* 15.654–59 *(hunc modo serpentem, baculum qui nexibus ambit, perspice).* See the Latin text and English translation excerpted in Edelstein and Edelstein, *Asclepius,* p. 361.

315. Edelstein and Edelstein, *Asclepius,* p. 218.

316. Clermont-Ganneau, *PEF* (1874) 268–69.

317. The vase was given the number 11 for 1874. It is merely an insignificant item in a list published by Clermont-Ganneau in his thick *Archaeological Researches in Palestine During the Years 1873–1874* (London, 1896) vol. 2, p. 484. For Clermont-Ganneau's comments on Bethesda, see *Recueil* (Paris, 1906) vol. 7, pp. 369–70.

318. I am grateful to Dr. R. Chapman III and Dr. F. Cobbing for helping me examine this unique work. I am also appreciative to trustees of the Palestine Exploration Fund in London for permission to publish this anguine vessel. The object is reproduced by permission of the Palestine Exploration Fund.

319. It was purchased by Charlesworth in the early 1990s from an antiquities dealer in the Old City of Jerusalem.

320. I am grateful to the Studium Biblicum Franciscanum and in particular to Dr. M. Piccirillo for permission to publish their serpent realia. See Charlesworth, "Anguine Iconography in the Studium Biblicum Franciscanum Museum and Biblical Exegesis," *Liber Annus* 49 (1999) 431–42, Plates 5 and 6.

321. In D. F. Grose's *Early Ancient Glass,* all three examples of glass serpents are dated to the first century BCE or first century CE. See Grose, *Early Ancient Glass* (New York, 1989) p. 372, nos. 678, 679, 680.

322. Joines, *JBL* 87 (1968) 246.

323. Joines, *JBL* 87 (1968) 250.

324. When the serpent is shown with the eagle, however, battle and conflict are intended, as in the Nabatean sculpture found at Khirbet et-Tannur. It shows an eagle fighting a large serpent. See the photograph in *EAA* 5 (1963) 325:439.

325. See esp. the elegant ophidian iconography found on a vessel discovered at Dirmil near Bodrum in southwestern Anatolia. It is dated to 750–700 BCE and is far more advanced artistically than any object found in Palestine. See N. Asgari et al., *The Anatolian Civilisations,* p. 16 B19.

326. Joines, *JBL* 87 (1968) 250.

327. Macalister, *Gezer II,* p. 399, Fig. 488.

328. Yadin et al., eds., *Hazor II,* Plate 181.

329. See Rowe, *The Four Canaanite Temples of Beth-shan,* Plates 14:1,3,4,5; 16: 1–9; 17:1–3; 56A:1–4; 57A:1–4; 58A:1–3; 59A:3–4.

330. Rowe wrote, "The serpent on the cylinders certainly seems to be a benevolent and not a malevolent one." *The Four Canaanite Temples of Beth-shan,* p. 53.

331. See, e.g., the sophisticated and refined ware with ophidian iconography found at Tell Brak (741, 742, 747), at Byblos (744), and the silver vessel from Palestrina (816). For photographs, see Bossert, *Altsyrien,* pp. 219 (741, 742), 220 (744), 221 (747), and 230 (816).

332. For example, the cylindrical and rectangular incense stands found at Hazor (see Yadin et al., *Hazor III–IV,* Plate 309:3–6), Lachish (see Y. Aharoni, *Investigations at Lachish: The Sanctuary and the Residency* [Tel Aviv, 1975; Plate 26:3–6 (photograph) and 43:3–6 drawing]), Beth Shemesh (E. Grant, *Beth Shemesh,* p. 103 [photograph]), Dan (Biran, *Biblical Dan,* Figs. 133–34), and Ai (J. A. Callaway and W. W. Ellinger, *The Early Bronze Age Sanctuary at Ai Tell No. 1* [London, 1972] Fig. 73, 74) are devoid of ophidian iconography. The rectangular cult stands found at Taanach, under the direction of Sellin and later by Lapp, are quite different; the former includes lions and human faces, the latter lions with humanlike figures (see the photographs conveniently presented in A. E. Glock's "Taanach," *NEAEHL* 4.1428–33 (see the full-page color photography opposite p. 1476).

333. Rowe, *The Four Canaanite Temples of Beth-shan,* p. 52. Rowe also draws attention to a "Garden of Adonis" on a fresco in Pompeii. See Jeremias, *The Old Testament in the Light of the Ancient East,* vol. 1, p. 97 (Fig. 30).

334. Song 2:11–12 and Jer 8:7.

335. Rowe refers us to Evans (*The Palace of Minos,* vol. 1, p. 508) who suggested that the dove often symbolized inspiration that descends, and the serpent, the ascent of the spirit from the netherworld.

336. Ishtar (= Astarte) symbolized both the burst of life into the world at spring and its decay in fall and winter. Tammuz represented vegetation. Tammuz also was thought, during winter, to be in the netherworld, and according to Ezek 8:14 women wept for him at the northern gate of the House of the Lord.

337. The interpretation was advanced by Rowe, *The Four Canaanite Temples of Beth-shan,* p. 53.

338. This interpretation was first suggested by Rowe, *The Four Canaanite Temples of Beth-shan,* p. 54; also see "Additional Notes: Serpents," p. 57.

339. See Rowe, *The Four Canaanite Temples of Beth-shan,* Plate 35:11, 12, 14, 15, 16; 64A:2; 68A:1, 3, 4, 5, 6, 7. Also see the drawings in McGovern, *The Late Bronze Egyptian Garrison at Beth Shan,* vol. 2, Plates 76–77; and the photographs on Plate 37. Interpretations of these naked goddesses must be balanced by the recognition that women in Egypt often did not cover their breasts.

340. Isa 17:10.

341. See James, McGovern, and Bonn, *The Late Bronze Egyptian Garrison at Beth Shan,* vol. 1, p. 171, 241. They also suggest that this unique feature may "point to an amalgamation of Hathor, a principal Canaanite goddess, and a snake goddess" (vol. 1, p. 241). Hathor was an Egyptian goddess imported into the iconography of Canaan.

342. See May, *Material Remains of the Megiddo Cult,* Plates 14 and 15; also see the discussion on p. 14.

343. Albright, "The Goddess of Life and Wisdom," *AJSL* 36 (1919–1920) 227.

344. Joines, *JBL* 87 (1968) 250.

345. Joines, *JBL* 87 (1968) 249.

346. Koldewey, *The Excavations of Babylon,* p. 45 (italics mine). I am grateful to Joines for these references.

347. See S. Langdon, *Building Inscriptions of the Neo-Babylonian Empire. Part I: Nabopolassar and Nebuchadnezzar,* pp. 79, 85, 105, 131.

348. See the description and photographs in *Encyclopédie Photographique de l'Art,* vol. 1, pp. 266–67. Also see the limestone deed from the eleventh century BCE with the massive serpent at the top, ibid., p. 41.

349. Joines also interprets the ophidian symbolism this way; see her article in *JBL* 87 (1968) 247; also see Rowe, *The Four Canaanite Temples of Beth-Shan,* Plate 42A:5 and 45A:4.

350. Macalister, *Gezer III,* Plate 221:9.

351. Pritchard (*Palestinian Figurines,* p. 7 number 11) and Joines (*JBL* 87 [1968]) interpret the artwork to denote serpents.

352. Stern, *Excavations at Tel Mevorakh,* Part 2, p. 23.

353. The serpent on this vase from Susa is a work of art. The head is triangular and has two circles with black dots inside for eyes. Next to the curved body is a row of black dots on each side. The serpent curves upward in a S-shape until it runs perpendicular to the rim. See the photograph in *EAA* 7 (1966) 568.

354. This well-known fact can easily be seen in Pritchard, *ANEP* 413–17 (note the prominent uraeus).

355. See the photograph of the eleventh-century BCE decorated vessel with serpents on the shoulder in *Encyclopédie Photographique de l'Art,* vol. 2, p. 260.

356. See esp. the color photographs in Perrot and Chipiez, *History of Art in Phoenicia,* vol. 2, Plates 8, 9 (opposite p. 336 [unfortunately inadvertently unnumbered]).

357. See R. Boucharlat, "Archaeology and Artifacts of the Arabian Peninsula," *Civilizations of the Ancient Near East 2.* 1335–53; esp p. 1347.

358. Boucharlat, ibid., p. 1349.

359. Among numerous publications, many already cited, see E. Hornung, "Ancient Egyptian Religious Iconography," in *Civilizations of the Ancient Near East* 3.1711–30; esp. Figs. 1, 4, 12, 15, and 20.

360. A convenient chart with drawings is found in A. Green, "Ancient Mesopotamian Religious Iconography," in *Civilizations of the Ancient Near East* 3.1837–55; esp see pp. 1838–40, 1848–49. Also see the seven-headed dragon Mushmakkhu. In this regard, see the seven-headed enemy mentioned in Ps 74:13–14, Ps 89:10, Isa 51:9–11, Rev. 12:3, 13:1, 17:3, *OdesSol* 22:5, and *b. Qiddushin* 29b.

361. Stunning examples of gold and silver jewelry with serpents depicted, dating from the Greek and Roman periods, are housed in the leading museums. I have been impressed by the examples, often in areas for scholars alone to study, preserved in the Metropolitan, the British Museum, and the Hermitage, and express appreciation for the courtesy and support I always received from the knowledgeable staff. For superb photographs of the gold serpent jewelry in St. Petersburg, see [no editor], *Greek Gold* (London, 1955) pp. 114 and 210 (in Russian). A vast amount of gold was recovered from the tomb of Philip, the father of Alexander the Great. I studied it in Thessaloniki, but did not find serpent jewelry.

362. R. S. Bianchi, "The Ancient Mediterranean: Good and Evil Snakes," *Faces* (October 1995) 6–9.

4. The Perception That the Serpent Is a Positive Symbol in Greek and Roman Literature

1. A. Mazahéri, *Les Trésors de l'Iran* (Geneva, 1970) p. 119 (with photograph).

2. Persian Zarathustra is in Greek "Zoroaster." Some of the traditions in the *Avesta* are very old, in particular the *Yasht* and the myths of the gods, antedating Zarathustra who seems to have lived sometime between 900 and 500 BCE. See V. Sarkhosh Curtis, *Persian Myths* (London, 1993) pp. 9–10.

3. See Sarkhosh Curtis, *Persian Myths,* p. 44.

4. See, e.g., H. Henning von der Osten, *Die Welt der Perser* (Stuttgart, 1956) Plate 90.

5. See the photograph in Carus, *The History of the Devil and the Idea of Evil* (New York, 1996) p. 225.

6. See the illustration in Mazahéri, *Les Trésors de l'Iran,* p. 117.

7. See E. M. Yamauchi, *Persia and the Bible* (Grand Rapids, 1996) p. 498.

8. See the Greek vase in the British Museum numbered BM GR 1873.8–20.375 (Vase E140). For a published drawing, see L. Burn, *Greek Myths* (London, 1990) p. 9.

9. See Burn, in *Greek Myths,* p. 59.

10. J. Onians, *Classical Art and the Cultures of Greece and Rome* (New Haven and London, 1999) pp. 12–13.

11. R. P. Martin, ed., *Bulfinch's Mythology* (New York, 1991) p. 48.

12. I am grateful to Zanker for this insight; see his *The Power of Images in the Age of Augustus,* trans. A. Shapiro (Ann Arbor, 1990) p. 98.

13. See J. F. Gardner, *Roman Myths* (London, 1993) p. 15.

14. Zanker, *The Power of Images in the Age of Augustus,* p. v.

15. I am indebted to Zanker for these citations; see his *The Power of Images in the Age of Augustus,* pp. 102–3.

16. To make this work accessible to others besides specialists in Greek and Latin, I have added the dates to the names the first time they are given. Because it is often debated what dates are to be assigned to individuals, and because some of them are unknown, I have taken the dates (or approximate dates) from *The Oxford Classical Dictionary,* ed. N. G. L. Hammond and H. H. Scullard (Oxford, 1970 [2nd ed.]).

17. For photographs and illustrations, see *LIMC,* VI.2, pp. 94–95.

18. The Minoan culture influenced the Greek mind; see M. P. Nilsson, *The Minoan-Mycenaean Religion and Its Survival in Greek Religion* (New York, 1971 [2nd ed.]).

19. See the photograph of one of the goddesses in the preceding pages and also in *EAA* 5 (1963) 68 and of another Minoan goddess with serpents; it is from Iraklion; see p. 69.

20. I imagine that few of the millions who have seen the wall paintings in the Pentheus Room of the House of the Vettii at Pompeii will forget the depiction of Hercules as an infant struggling successfully with serpents. See the photograph in M. Grant and R. Kitzinger, eds., *Civilization of the Ancient Mediterranean* (New York, 1988) vol. 3, p. 1782, Figure 8.

21. See *LIMC,* IV.2, pp. 552–56.

22. See the succinct summary in P. Preston, *Metzler Lexikon: Antiker Bildmotive* (Stuttgart, 1997) pp. 165–69.

23. See the photograph of another gold serpent bracelet in *EAA* 2 (1959) 160. Also see the elegant ophidian bracelet pictured in *EAA* 5 (1963) 738.

24. See the photograph of the bronze fountain in the "palestra di Ercolano" in *EAA* 5 (1963) 512.

25. See LSJM 1278 and 1279.

26. L. Banti, "Serpenti, Pittore dei," *EAA* 7 (1966) 213–14.

27. See the photograph in *EAA* 7 (1966) 213.

28. BM EA 1539.

29. See the illustrations in *LIMC,* V.2, pp. 502–4.

30. See the illustrations in *LIMC,* V.2, p. 505. Also, see the photograph of the large vase showing two roosters with two large serpents in *EAA* 2 (1959) 265.

31. See F. J. M. de Waele, *The Magic Staff or Rod in Graeco-Italian Antiquity* (Gent, 1927).

32. See the illustrations in *LIMC,* V.2, p. 523.

33. See the illustrations in *LIMC,* V.2, pp. 524–26.

34. See the informed discussion by M. Malaise, *Les conditions de pénétration et de diffusion des cultes Égyptiens en Italie* (Leiden, 1972).

35. See the photograph in *EAA* 7 (1966) 853:961 (Typhon with anguipedes) and 962 (Typhon with a serpent's body). Also see the illustrations in *LIMC,* VIII.2, pp. 112–13.

36. See the illustrations in *LIMC,* VII.2, p. 511.

37. See the photograph in J. Leipoldt and W. Grundmann, eds., *Umwelt des Urchristentums,* 3 vols. (Berlin, 1971, 1972 [both 3rd ed.], 1967 [2nd ed.]) illustration no. 25, also see p. 16 for a good discussion.

38. See esp. the articles collected in *Les syncrétismes dans les religions de l'antiquité,* ed. F. Dunand and P. Lévêque (Leiden, 1975).

39. See the illustration in *LIMC,* VI.2, pp. 273–306.

40. See the illustrations in *LIMC,* V.2, pp. 217–83, and VIII.2, p. 382.

41. See the illustrations in *LIMC,* V.2, pp. 491–500, 518.

42. See the illustrations in *LIMC,* VII.2, pp. 379–82.

43. See the illustrations in *LIMC,* VII.2, pp. 373–76.

44. See the illustrations in *LIMC,* VII.2, pp. 422–27.

45. See the illustrations in *LIMC,* III.2, pp. 490–503.

46. See illustration no. 5 in Leipoldt and Grundmann, eds., *Umwelt des Urchristentums,* and the illustrations in *LIMC,* VI.2, pp. 107–26.

47. See the illustrations in *LIMC,* VI.2, pp. 110–12, 120–25.

48. See the illustrations in *LIMC,* V.2, pp. 376–79.

49. See the illustrations in *LIMC,* V.2, p. 606.

50. See the illustrations in *LIMC,* II.2, pp. 89–93.

51. See the illustrations in *LIMC,* IV.2, pp. 32–47.

52. See the illustrations in *LIMC,* VII.2, pp. 655–60.

53. See the illustrations in *LIMC,* VII.2, pp. 527–28.

54. See the illustrations in *LIMC,* VI.2, pp. 148–52.

55. Consult Cumont, *Recherches sur le symbolisme funéraire des Romains.*

56. A. D. Nock, "Sarcophagi and Symbolism," in *Essays on Religion and the Ancient World,* ed. Z. Stewart (Oxford, 1972) vol. 2, pp. 606–41; see esp. p. 606, n. 2 (the article originally appeared in 1946).

57. H. Merguet, *Lexicon zu den Reden des Cicero,* 4 vols. (Jena, 1877; reprinted in Hildesheim by Olms, 1962). Also see K. M. Abbott et al., eds., *Index Verborum in Ciceronis Rhetorica* (Urbana, Ill., 1964).

58. See the illustrations in *LIMC,* VII.2, pp. 594–98.

59. See the illustrations in *LIMC,* II.2, pp. 480, 484–85.

60. See the illustrations in *LIMC,* II.2, pp. 707, 716, 726–27, 747, 749–52, 754–55, 761.

61. See the illustrations in *LIMC,* II.2, pp. 717, 719, 757.

62. See the photograph in *Encyclopédie Photographique de l'Art,* vol. 3, p. 166. This is the best copy of the Athena that loomed so large in the Parthenon. Also see *EAA* 5 (1965) 1018.

63. See the illustrations in *LIMC,* II.2, p. 723.

64. See the illustrations in *LIMC,* II.2, p. 724.

65. See the illustrations in *LIMC,* II.2, p. 748.

66. See the illustrations in *LIMC,* II.2, pp. 748, 763.

67. See the illustrations in *LIMC,* II.2, pp. 728, 753, cf. 754.

68. See the illustrations in *LIMC,* II.2, pp. 729, 730.

69. I am grateful for the superb assistance I received from the staff at the National Archaeological Museum in Athens. Maria Zamanou of the museum is writing a PhD dissertation on the first appearance of the snake in Greek culture. The Varvakeion Athena is no. 129 in the museum.

70. See the illustration in *LIMC*, VII.2, p. 275.

71. See the illustrations in *LIMC*, III.2, pp. 364, 370. Note the reconstruction of the Erechtheum by L. Pallat; an upraised serpent is shown. See *EAA* 8 (1973) Plate 59. Also, two serpents are shown coming out of a circular object; see *EAA* 8 (1973) Plate 60. Note also the depiction of Hercules fighting a large serpent ("Tempio di Efesto" in Athens) Plate 65, (and the depiction of gods [?] fighting anguipede Titans [?] in the Theater of Dionysus; Plate 66:2). Also in Athens (in the "Monumento di Lisicrate"), a serpent is shown biting a man; Plate 69.

72. See the illustrations in *LIMC*, III.2, p. 430.

73. See the illustrations in *LIMC*, III.2, p. 477.

74. See the illustrations in *LIMC*, IV.2, p. 660.

75. See the illustrations in *LIMC*, V.2, p. 332.

76. See the photograph in *EAA* 6 (1965) 484.

77. See the photograph in *EAA* 6 (1965) 1087. Gina Salapata of the School of History, Philosophy and Politics in Massey University in Palmerston North, New Zealand, is writing an article on the image of the snake drinking out of a bowl. Her study scans the Greek world from prehistoric times to the Roman period.

78. See the illustrations in *LIMC*, VI.2, pp. 98–101.

79. See the illustrations in *LIMC*, II.2, p. 791.

80. See the illustrations in *LIMC*, II.2, p. 793.

81. See the illustrations in *LIMC*, II.2, p. 786.

82. See the illustrations in *LIMC*, II.2, pp. 794–806.

83. See the illustrations in *LIMC*, VII.2, p. 562.

84. See the photograph in *EAA* 6 (1965) 5, 11.

85. See the color photograph in *EAA* 6 (1965) opposite p. 30. Note the bust with a serpent on the left chest; *EAA* 6 (1965) 199.

86. It dates from the sixth century BCE and is from Samothrace. The scene was part of one side of a stone chair. See the photograph in *Encyclopédie Photographique de l'Art*, vol. 3, p. 135.

87. See the illustrations in *LIMC*, VIII.2, p. 19.

88. See the illustrations in *LIMC*, VIII.2, pp. 94–109.

89. See the illustrations in *LIMC*, VIII.2, p. 92.

90. See the illustrations in *LIMC*, VI.2, p. 455.

91. See the illustrations in *LIMC*, IV.2, p. 248.

92. See the illustrations in *LIMC*, VII.2, p. 577.

93. See the illustrations in *LIMC*, VI.2, pp. 673–719.

94. See the illustrations in *LIMC*, VII.2, p. 306.

95. See the illustrations in *LIMC*, VI.2, p. 51.

96. See the illustrations in *LIMC*, VI.2, p. 16.

97. See the illustrations in *LIMC*, VII.2, p. 186.

98. See the illustrations in *LIMC*, V.2, p. 418.

99. See the illustrations in *LIMC*, VII.2, pp. 159–70.

100. See A. M. Roveri, "Qadesh," *EAA* 5 (1965) 583–84; see the photograph of Qadesh standing on a lion and holding a serpent in her right hand (p. 583).

101. See M. J. Vermaseren, *Cybele and Attis: The Myth and the Cult* (London, 1977); see illustration nos. 38, 25, 26, and 53.

102. See Vermaseren, *Cybele and Attis*, illustration nos. 16, 53, and 77.

103. The silver patera is in Milan. See the photograph in G. M. A. Hanfmann, *Roman Art: A Modern Survey of the Art of Imperial Rome* (Greenwich, Conn., 1966) p. 222:144.

104. See the photograph in *EAA* 2 (1959) 250. The "Arca di Kypselos" shows a multiheaded hydra and also an anguipede and winged "god"; see *EAA* 8 (1973) Plate 186.

105. Aelian, *Nat. an.* 16.42. For the Greek and English translation, see Aelian, *On the Characteristics of Animals*, ed. A. F. Scholfield (LCL; London, Cambridge, Mass., 1972) vol. 3, pp. 318–19.

106. See the illustrations in *LIMC*, II.2, p. 432.

107. See the illustrations in *LIMC*, VII.2, pp. 540–41.

108. See the illustrations in *LIMC*, II.2, pp. 355–56.

109. See the illustrations in *LIMC*, V.2, pp. 559–61.

110. See the illustrations in *LIMC*, V.2, p. 428.

111. See the illustrations in *LIMC*, V.2, pp. 429–30.

112. See the illustrations in *LIMC*, V.2, p. 429.

113. Aelian, *Nat. an.* 10.25: serpents that have "beneath their chin" a beard (ὑπο τὴν ὑπήνην αὐτοῖς γένειον). For the Greek, see Aelian, *On the Characteristics of Animals*, vol. 2, p. 318.

114. For the Greek text and English translation, see Edelstein and Edelstein, *Asclepius*, vol. 1, pp. 364–65. A similar report that suggests a shared tradition is found in Nicander, *Theriaca*, 438–57; see Edelstein and Edelstein, *Asclepius*, vol. 1, pp. 363–64.

115. See the illustrations in *LIMC*, II.2, p. 134.

116. See the illustrations in *LIMC*, II.2, pp. 421–22.

114. See the illustrations in *LIMC*, VIII.2, pp. 527, 538. Also see the photograph in *EAA* 2 (1959) 170.

118. See the photograph in *Encyclopédie Photographique de l'Art,* vol. 3, p. 3:C. The serpent is upraised, rather proudly, and has five curls. His skin is marked by dots within circles.

119. See the illustrations in *LIMC*, VIII.2, pp. 531, 546.

120. See the illustrations in *LIMC*, VIII.2, pp. 784, 792.

121. See the illustrations in *LIMC*, III.2, pp. 206–08, 210, 212–13, 16–17.

122. See the illustrations in *LIMC*, VIII.2, pp. 22–23.

123. For the Greek and an English translation, see Cicero, *De Natura Deorum,* ed. H. Rackham (LCL; London, Cambridge, Mass., 1979) pp. 98–99.

124. *Nat. d.* 327.

125. Note, for example, how Virgil refers to the Chimera in Lycia that Aeneas must defeat (*Aeneid* 6.288, 7.785).

126. In the Schloessinger Collection of lamps one can see "a hybrid male with a club." The iconography looks to me more like a Giant with anguipedes; see R. Rosenthal and R. Sivan, *Ancient Lamps in the Schloessinger Collection* (Jerusalem, 1978) p. 29:92 (description and photography).

127. In Rome and on Trajan's Column one can see serpent-demons aligned with Roman soldiers (*EAA* 8 [1973] Plate 94:LXXVII).

128. Translation mine. For the Latin (and another English translation), see Lucretius, *De rerum natura,* ed. C. Bailey (Oxford, 1947) vol. 1, pp. 478–79.

129. James Elkins, *The Poetics of Perspective* (Ithaca and London, 1994).

130. Aelian, *Nat. an.* 11.17. For the Greek and English translation, see Aelian, *On the Characteristics of Animals,* vol. 2, pp. 382–83.

131. Translation mine; for the Greek, see Edelstein and Edelstein, *Asclepius,* p. 367.

132. See B. C. Farnoux, "Mercurio," *EAA* 4 (1961) 1031–35.

133. A. L. Frothingham argued that the caduceus can be traced back to the fourth millennium BCE; see Frothingham, "Babylonian Origin of Hermes the Snake-God, and of the Caduceus," *American Journal of Archaeology,* Second Series 20 (1916) 175–211; for more recent research, see J. T. Bunn, "Origin of the Caduceus Motif," *JAMA* 202.7 (1967) 163–67.

134. See the discussion and drawings in R. Ferwerda, "Le serpent, le noeud d'Hercule et le caducée d'Hermès, sur un passage orphique chez Athénagore," *Numeen* 20 (1973) 104–15; see esp. p. 113. Also see the drawing in Jung et al., *Man and His Symbols,* p. 154.

135. See the photograph in *EAA* 4 (1961) 1035:1227.

136. See the Roman art depicting a caduceus with serpents facing in different directions. It is associated with Hermes and is a piece of fabric. See the photograph in *EAA* 5 (1965) 1021.

137. See the references cited in LSJM, p. 1991.

138. Thus, Hermes dwells in the region often also associated with Hades, Pluto, Demeter, and Persephone. Demeter is depicted with the serpent known as the Python; the other chthonic gods are symbolized as snake-like or accompanied by a snake.

139. See the photograph in *EAA* 4 (1961) 8. In the illustration in *EAA* 4 (1961) 10, the caduceus has two entwined serpents who rise and face each other. This is the usual iconography for the caduceus.

140. J. L. Henderson, "Ancient Myths and Modern Man," in *Man and His Symbols,* p. 155.

141. I am thinking in particular of the Indian concept of the transmigration of the soul, which profoundly influenced Plato. Long before the writing of the Fourth Gospel, so-called Greek ideas also influenced Indian thought and culture: *dyaus pitar* derives from *deus pater,* which is Greek for "God, Father." Perhaps we should not think only about Greece or India influencing each other, but also about a common ancestor, the unknown and anonymous culture that poured into Greece through the Achaeans and into India through the Aryans of the second millennium BCE. See the fascinating discussion by H. Zimmer in *Philosophies of India,* ed. J. Campbell (New York, 1956); see esp. pp. 25–31, 311–12, 89 (notes by Campbell).

142. See the reflections by H. Leisegang in his *Das Mysterium der Schlange: Ein Beitrag zur Erforschung des griechischen Mysterienkultes und seines Fortlebens in der christlichen Welt* (Zürich, 1940) pp. 151–251. For English translation see H. Leisegang, *The Mystery of the Serpent,* trans. Apostolos Kontos (Athens, 1993).

143. I understand the references to "the waters under the earth" to be still part of the earth.

144. The first "E" was written backward.

145. The first "E" was again written backward.

146. The "H" is written defectively; it looks like an "F."

147. The first and second "E" are written backward.

148. See the discussion of "der gute Genius" in Leitz, *Die Schlangennamen,* pp. 31–33. Also see G. B. Montanari, "Agathadaimon," *EAA* 1 (1958) 134–35 (with a photograph on p. 135). Also see the photograph of the Agathadaimon in Pompeii in the previous chapter.

149. Also see the discussion later in this chapter of the annual festival in Alexandria that honored Aion. See notably, R. Ganszyniec, *De Agathodaemone* (Warsaw, 1919); O. Jakobsson, "Daimon och Agathos Daimon" (PhD diss., Lund, 1925); G. E. Visser, *Götter und Kulte im Ptolemaeischen Alexandrien* (Amsterdam, 1938); F. Dunand, *Les représentations de l'Agathodémon: À propos de quelques bas-reliefs du Musée d'Alexandrie* (*Bulletin de l'Institut français d'archéologie orientale* 167; [Paris?], 1967) pp. 7–48; and P. M. Fraser, *Ptolemaic Alexandria*, 3 vols. (Oxford, 1972) vol. 1, pp. 209–11; vol. 2, pp. 356–60 (= notes 164–79). See esp. the publications he cites in these notes.

150. See R. Ganshinietz, "Agathodämon," *Pauly-Wissowa* Suppl. 3 (1918) 37–59. See also O. Jakobsson, "Daimon och Agathos Daimon."

151. See F. Dunand, "Agathodaimon," *LIMC* I.1, pp. 277–82.

152. Fraser, *Ptolemaic Alexandria*, vol. 1, pp. 210–11.

153. See M. Pietrzykowski, "Sarapis—Agathos Daimon," in *Hommages à Maarten J. Vermaseren,* ed. M. B. de Boer and T. A. Edridge (Leiden, 1978) pp. 959–66.

154. Pompeii IX.7.21; for a photograph see *LIMC* I.2, p. 203 (no. 7).

155. See the illustration in *LIMC*, I.2, p. 207.

156. See the illustrations in *LIMC*, I.2, pp. 203–4. Dunand points out that on the marble, beneath the serpent, appear to be two humans who perhaps portray Agathadaimon and Agatha Tyche.

157. For the photographs, see *LIMC*, I.2, pp. 204–5.

158. See the photographs in *LIMC*, I.2, p. 206.

159. See the photograph in *LIMC*, I.2, p. 207.

160. Dunand, "Agathodaimon," p. 277.

161. Dunand, *Les représentations de l'Agathodémon,* pp. 7–48.

162. Fraser, *Ptolemaic Alexandria*, vol. 2, p. 357.

163. See Pietrzykowski in *Hommages à Maarten J. Vermaseren,* pp. 964–66.

164. The word "Gigantes" does not occur in the *Iliad.* It appears in the *Odyssey* three times (7.59, 7.201–6, 10.120) and seems to denote a tribe of monstrous men, not unlike demigods, who lived in the past and on the earth but in a far-off region. A reliable short introduction is by W. Scott, "Giants (Greek and Roman)," in *Encyclopedia of Religion and Ethics* (New York, 1966) vol. 6, pp. 193–97.

165. Prior to the fourth century BCE, Titanomachy was distinguished from Gigantomacy, but the two were meshed in the subsequent centuries.

166. See F. Vian with M. B. Moore, "Gigantes," *LIMC*, IV.1, pp. 191–270.

167. See *EAA* 8 (1973) Plates 218–25. Also see M. Grant and R. Kitzinger, eds., *Civilization of the Ancient Mediterranean* (New York, 1988) vol. 3, p. 1720, Fig. 15.

168. See E. Schmidt, *Le grand autel de Pergame* (Leipzig, 1962); see esp. p. 17, and illustrations 5, 10, 15, 16, 28, 29, 35, 36, 37, 38, and 39.

169. In biblical Hebrew there are numerous nouns that have been translated as "Giants": *Gibborim, Anakim, Emim, Zamzummim, Rephaim,* and *Nephilim.* Most of these are either hyperbolas for great fighters or mean "mighty warriors," as *Gibborim* surely does (*pace* the translators of the LXX, who took it to mean Giants). *Nephilim* denotes "Giants." No skeletons of persons 3 meters tall, or near that size, have been found in ancient Palestine.

170. See M. A. Harder in *Lexikon des früh griechischen Epos* (Thesaurus Linguae Graecae, 1991) vol. 2, col. 147. Also see M. Hofinger, *Lexicon Hesiodeum cum indice inverso,* 2 vols. (Leiden, 1978, 1985 [with D. Pinte]).

171. My translation is a revision of that by J. G. Frazer; for the Greek and his translation, see *Apollodorus: The Library* (LCL; London, Cambridge, Mass., 1967) vol. 1, pp. 42–43.

172. See the works cited by M. L. West—notably E. HF 853, Telecl. 1.15, *Epig. Gr.* Gr. 831.8, Epic. Alex. Adesp. 9.6.13–14, and Batr. 7—in Hesiod, *Theogony,* ed. M. L. West (Oxford, 1966) p. 173.

173. See L. Kjellberg, *"Die Giganten bei Homer,"* *Eranos* 12 (1912) 195–98; and F. Vian, *La guerre des Géants* (Paris, 1952).

174. See West, "The Titanomachy," in Hesiod, *Theogony,* pp. 336–59. He discusses the Titanomachy found in Hesiod, Epimenides, and Pherecydes, and ascribed to Eumelus or Arctinus.

175. Paris, Bibliothèque Nationale, Suppl. Gr. 247; see the illustration in *EAA* 4 (1961) 111.

176. See esp. the illustrations in *LIMC,* IV.2, nos. 24, 61h, 92, 93a, 93d, 400, 483, 501, 502, 511, 523, 571, 588, and 589c.

177. See the dracma of Telephos (70–68 BCE) that is shown in *EAA* 4 (1961) 155:4.

178. The Latin *anguipes,* "snake or serpent footed," is usually reserved for the Giants. See the *Oxford Latin Dictionary* (Oxford, 1968) ad loc. cit.

179. See esp. the ceramic depicting a Giant with massive anguipedes, now on display in the Staatliche Museen in Berlin V.I.3375; for a photograph, see *LIMC,* IV.2, Plate 149 (no. 389).

180. Aelian, *Nat. an.* 17.1.

181. For the Greek and English translation, see H. L. Jones, ed. and trans., *The Geography of Strabo* (LCL; London, Cambridge, Mass., 1966) vol. 7, pp. 336–37. Also see *Geography* 17.2.2 and 17.3.6.

182. Strabo, *Geography,* 2.1.9: ὄφεις τε καὶ βοῦς καὶ ἐλάφους σὺν κέρασι καταπίνοντας.

183. See Ovid, *Metam.* 1.184; for the Latin and English translation, see the edition of the *Metamorphoses,* 2 vols., ed. and trans. F. J. Miller (LCL; London, Cambridge, Mass., 1968, 1971), vol. 1, pp. 14–15.

184. My translation is essentially the same as that by Frazer; for the Greek and his translation, see Frazer, *Apollodorus,* vol. 1, pp. 44–49.

185. Frazer, *Apollodorus,* vol. 1, p. 49.

186. Herodotus, *Hist.* 4.9; see the edition by Godley, vol. 2, pp. 206–7.

187. For depictions of Hercules, see *LIMC,* IV.2, Plates 445–559.

188. See the photograph in *Encyclopédie Photographique de l'Art,* vol. 3, p. 82:C.

189. Apollodorus, *The Library* 2.4.8; see Frazer, *Apollodorus,* vol. 1, pp. 174–75.

190. The plates are in *LIMC,* IV.2.

191. See esp. T. Gants, *Early Greek Myth* (Baltimore, London, 1993) p. 410.

192. See the illustrations in *LIMC,* IV.2, pp. 552–56, V.2, pp. 9–30, 99, 103, 110–11.

193. Note the illustration in *EAA* 4 (1961) 90:117 and 697:841. Also, see the illustrations in *LIMC,* V.2, pp. 52–62.

194. See the photograph in *EAA* 7 (1966) 18.

195. See the photograph in *Encyclopédie Photographique de l'Art,* vol. 3, p. 2.

196. See the photograph in M. Avi Yonah and I. Shatzman, *Illustrated Encyclopaedia of the Classical World* (New York, London, 1975) p. 117.

197. For bibliography on Laocoon, see E. Simon, "Laokoon," in *LIMC,* VI.1, pp. 196–201, esp. p. 197.

198. See M. Wacht, *Concordantia Vergiliana*, 2 vols. (New York, 1996).

199. My translation is based on that by H. R. Fairclough; for the Latin and Fairclough's translation, see *Virgil* (LCL; London, Cambridge, Mass., 1967) vol. 1, pp. 296–97.

200. My translation is dependent, in most places, on the translation by Fairclough; for the Latin and English translation, see Fairclough, *Virgil*, vol. 1, pp. 308–9.

201. See the photographs in *EAA* 4 (1961) 467 and 469 (full page); also see the fragment of a vase showing Laocoon and the serpent on p. 466:546.

202. See the illustrations in *LIMC*, IV.2, pp. 94–95 and in the *Illustrated Encyclopaedia of the Classical World*, p. 260.

203. Simon calls them "Ein dämonisches Schlangenpaar." *LIMC*, VI.1, p. 196. I demur.

204. See the photograph of the elegant example of Glykon as a serpent with a friendly human face in *EAA* 9 (1973) p. 356:352. Also see G. Bordenacher, "Glykon," *EAA* 9 (1973) 356.

205. See the illustrations in *LIMC*, IV.2, Plate 161 and in *EAA* 9 (1973) 356:351.

206. See the drawing in *LIMC*, IV.1, p. 281 and F. Lenormant, "Un monument du culte de Glykon," *Gazette archéologique* 4 (1878) 179–83. Also see the bibliography and discussion by G. B. Battaglia in *LIMC*, IV.1, pp. 279–83.

207. See I. Krauskopf and S.-C. Dahlinger, "Gorgo, Gorgeous," in *LIMC* IV.1, pp. 285–330.

208. See *LIMC*, IV.2, Plates 178–88.

209. Ovid, *Metam.* 4.794–803; for the Latin and English translation, see Ovid, *Metamorphoses*, ed. and trans. Miller, vol. 1, pp. 234–35.

210. See R. J. Deferrari et al., *A Concordance of Lucan* (Washington, 1940; reprinted at Hildesheim and New York, 1965).

211. Lucan, *Pharsalia*, 9.629–55; for the Latin and English translation see J. D. Duff, *Lucan* (LCL; London, Cambridge, Mass., 1969) pp. 552–53.

212. Ovid, *Metam.* 4.492–502; for the Latin and English translation, see the *Metamorphoses*, ed. Miller, vol. 1, pp. 212–13.

213. Homer, *Iliad* 11.36–37: δ'ἐπὶ μὲν Γοργγὼ.

214. See the discussion by Krauskopf and Dahlinger in *LIMC* IV.1, p. 300. See the illustrations in *LIMC*, IV.2, Plates 165, 173, 174–76.

215. See the discussion by Krauskopf and Dahlinger in *LIMC*, IV.1, p. 309, and the illustration in *LIMC*, IV.2, Plate 181, no. 272.

216. See O. Paoletti, "Gorgones Romanae," in *LIMC*, IV.1, pp. 345–62.

217. See the photograph in *LIMC*, IV.1, Plate 195, no. 12. For a discussion, see K. M. D. Dunbabin in *Bulletin de l'Association Internationale pour l'Etude de la Mosaïque Antique* 7 (1978) 258. Also see Paoletti, *LIMC*, IV.1, p. 347.

218. Pherekydes of Athens FGrH 16b (according to Schol. Apoll. Rhod. IV 1396; Jacoby, *Fragmente*, p. 65).

219. The Latin adjective *insopitus* denotes "sleepless" and "wakeful." Lucan *Pharsalia*, 9.357; see Duff, *Lucan*, p. 530.

220. I. McPhee, "Ladon," *LIMC*, VI.1, pp. 176–80. For illustrations, see *LIMC*, VI.2, Plates 81–85.

221. Hyginus, *Poetica astronomica*, 2, 3–6; see McPhee, *LIMC*, VI.1, p. 177.

222. F. 16b. The Greek is not rendered correctly in F. Jacoby, *Die Fragmente der Griechischen Historiker* (Leiden, 1957) erster Teil, Neudruck A, p. 65.

223. Jacoby, *Fragmente*, F.16a, p. 65.

224. See E. E. Urbach on hypostatization; in *The Sages*, 2 vols., trans. I. Abrahams (Jerusalem, 1979). Also see C. G. Jung, *Gesammelte Werke* (Olten, 1976) vol. 9.2, p. 294.

225. See M. Zepf, "Der Gott Αἰών in der hellenistischen Theologie," *Archiv für Religionswissenschaft* 25 (1927) 225–44. Also see M. Le Glay, "Aion," *LIMC* I.1, pp. 399–411, and Nock, "A Vision of Mandulis Aiôn," in *Essays*, pp. 357–400.

226. My translation is idiomatic. I have avoided the temptation to produce a rhyme in English. I am convinced such efforts fail to represent the ancient flow of words.

227. For the Greek, see A. S. Way, *Euripides* (LCL; London, Cambridge, Mass., 1962) vol. 3, p. 324.

228. See the photograph in *EAA* 4 (1961) 1037.

229. εἰκόνα δ᾽ ἐπινοεῖ κινοεῖ κινητήν τινα αἰῶνος ποιῆσαι. See F. Astius (Ast), *Lexicon Platonicum sive vocum Platonicarum Index*, 2 vols. (Bonn, 1835–1838; reprinted: Darmstadt, 1956). For Plato there can be no eternity on earth; see H. Perls, "Zeit," *Lexikon der Platonischen Begriffe* (Bern, 1973) pp. 401–5.

230. See the similar thoughts expressed by A. E. Taylor, *A Commentary on Plato's Timaeus* (Oxford, 1928) p. 187.

231. See E. Norden, *Geburt des Kindes* (Leipzig, 1924) p. 28.

232. See *LIMC*, I.2, Plates 310–19.

233. One example is a mosaic from the Mithraeum of Sentinum in Italy from the third century BCE (illustration no. 13 on Plate 313 in *LIMC*, I.2). Another is in the relief at Modena that dates from the first half of the second century BCE (see illus. no. 17 on Plate 314 in *LIMC* I.2).

234. See illustration in *LIMC*, I.2, Plate 312, no. 12.

235. Horapollon, *Hieroglyphika* I.1 and Olympiodorus, *Alch.* 80.9–11; see Z. Kiss, "Ouroboros," *LIMC*, VII.1, pp. 136–37.

236. This is also the verdict of Kiss, *LIMC*, VII.1, p. 137. It is confirmed by a study of A. Piankoff, *The Shrines of Tut-Ankh-Amon* (Princeton, 1955) esp. Plate 48.

237. See the illustrations in *LIMC*, VII.2, Plate 93; see esp. no. 10.

238. See W. Deonna, "Ouroboros," *Artibus Asiae* 15 (1952) 163–70; K. Preisendanz, "Aus der Geschichte des Uroboros," *Brauch und Sinnbild* (Karlsruhe, 1940) pp. 194–209.

239. For the Greek, see K. Preisendanz, *Papyri Graecae Magicae* (Stuttgart, 1974 [2nd ed.]) vol. 2, pp. 71–72. For the English, see H. F. D. Betz, ed., *The Greek Magical Papyri in Translation* (Chicago, London, 1985) p. 161. Another extremely important PGM is 1.144–48.

240. *Metam.* 2.138. For the Greek and English translation, see Ovid, *Metamorphoses*, 2 vols., ed. Miller, vol. 1, pp. 68–69.

241. My idiomatic translation; *Metam.* 2.173–75; see *Metamorphoses*, ed. Miller, vol. 1, pp. 72–73.

242. Kiss in *LIMC*, VII.1, p. 137.

243. Contrast the comment by Z. Kiss in *LIMC*, VII.1, p. 137: Ouroboros "exprime que 'la fin est le commencement et le commencement la fin.' "

244. I saw the quotation while reading Taylor's *A Commentary on Plato's Timaeus;* see p. 187 on which this quotation appears from Vaughn's poem "The World," stanza 1.

245. See R. du Mesnil du Buisson, "Le grand serpent Babi Dieu Ṣid devenu le père des Sardes," *Nouvelles études sur les dieux et les mythes de Canaan* (Leiden, 1973) pp. 228–40.

246. None of these names appears in LSJM or in *OCD*. See A. Kossatz-Deissmann, "Chnoubis," *LIMC*, III.1, pp. 272–73.

247. For the Greek and English translation, see Jones, *The Geography of Strabo*, pp. 126–27.

248. As quoted by A. B. Cook, *Zeus: A Study in Ancient Religion*, 5 vols. (Cambridge, 1914–1940) vol. 1, p. xii.

249. See the photograph in Avi Yonah and Shatzman, *Illustrated Encyclopedia of the Classical World*, p. 261.

250. See the minor note in Cook, *Zeus*, vol. 3, part 2, p. 1182; also see p. 1041.

251. Aelian, *Nat. an.* 11.2. For the Greek and English translation, see Aelian, *On the Characteristics of Animals*, vol. 2, pp. 358–59.

252. See M. J. Vermaseren, *De Mithrasdienst in Rome* (Nijmegen, 1951); R. L. Gordon, "Mithraism and Roman Society," *Journal of Religion and Religions* (1973) 92–121; U. Bianchi, ed., *Mysteria Mihthrae* (Leiden, 1979); Vermaseren, *Mithriaca III: The Mithraeum at Marino* (Leiden, 1982); and the discussion of the Mithraeum excavated in 1922 at Capua by M. J. Vermaseren in *Mithriaca I: The Mithraeum at S. Maria Capua Vetere* (Leiden, 1971); also see the color photographs of the serpent on Plates III, IV, and V.

253. See illustration nos. 112 and 113 in Leipoldt and Grundmann, *Umwelt des Urchristentums*.

254. Note the second- or third-century depiction of Mithra, in S. Maria Capua Vetere, killing a bull with a knife and a large serpent attacking from below; see the color photographs in *EAA* 2 (1959) 335 and *EAA* 5 (1963) 117.

255. See L. A. Campbell, "Snake," in *Mithraic Iconography and Ideology* (Leiden, 1968) pp. 13–22. Also see *EAA* 5 (1963) 116.

256. See the illustrations and succint discussion by Vermaseren in *Mithriaca II: The Mithraeum at Ponza* (Leiden, 1974) pp. 20–21, and Plates 28–31.

257. See S. Insler, "A New Interpretation of the Bull-Slaying Motif," in *Hommages à Maarten J. Vermaseren,* ed. M. B. de Boer and T. A. Edridge (Leiden, 1978) pp. 519–38; the quotation is from p. 536. I think it is pertinent to clarify, as Insler knows, that his interpretation is not "new."

258. I think G. H. Halsberghe has tended to focus myopically on the cult of *Sol invictus;* Mithraism was not always inferior to this cult. See Halsberghe, *The Cult of Sol Invictus* (Leiden, 1972).

259. Vermaseren, "The Miraculous Birth of Mithras," in *Studia G. van Hoorn* (Leiden, 1951) pp. 285ff.

260. For a drawing and a brief discussion, see *Lexicon der Mythologie*, p. 12.

261. I shall use the popular English hybrid: Asclepius.

262. According to the *Iliad* 12, Hector, leader of the Trojans, rejects the idea that a serpent that has just bitten an eagle and thus escapes can be an omen. The event occurred in the presence of the Trojan army.

263. See A. Gehring, *Index Homericus* (Leipzig, 1891–1895; reprinted in Hildesheim and New York, 1970). Even better, see H. Dunbar, *A Complete Concordance to the Iliad of Homer* (London, 1975; reprinted by Olms in Hildesheim and New York,

1983). Also see H. Dunbar, *A Complete Concordance to the Odyssey of Homer* (Oxford, 1880; reprinted in Hildesheim and New York, 1971).

264. See J. R. Tebben, *Hesiod-Konkordanz* (New York, 1977). Also see W. M. Minton, *Concordance to the Hesiodic Corpus* (Leiden, 1976).

265. T. Schnalke with C. Selheim, *Asklepios: Heilgott und Heilkult* (Erlangen-Nürnberg, 1990) p. 7.

266. See ibid., p. 9: "Prinzipiell besass jeder griechische Gott Heilungskraft."

267. Pliny, *Nat.* 29.1; see the edition by W. H. S. Jones (LCL; London, Cambridge, Mass., 1963) vol. 8, pp. 182–83. Also see, P. Rosumek, *Concordantia in C. Plinii Secundi Naturalem Historiam,* 7 vols. (New York, 1996); for *anguis,* see vol. 1, p. 778.

268. See M. Hamilton, *Incubation* (Laurinburg, N.C., 1906). For bibliographical information on the study of incubation and a succinct summary, see T. A. Brady and J. E. Fontenrose, "Incubation," *OCD,* pp. 543–44.

269. S. G. Stauropoulos, *The Askleipeia of Peloponnesia* (Athens, 2000 [in Greek]).

270. Also note the beautiful green steatite amygdaloid of Epidaurus Limera that is an island gem by the "Serpent Master," which dates from the second half of the seventh century BCE. See the photograph in Grant and Kitzinger, eds., *Civilization of the Ancient Mediterranean,* vol. 3, p. 1724:a.

271. See A. Charitonidou, *Epidaurus* ([Athens], 1978) p. 7.

272. See Charitonidou, *Epidaurus* and the more scholarly T. Papadakis, *Epidauros: The Sanctuary of Asclepios* (Zürich, Athens, 1971 [7th ed.]).

273. See the reconstruction of the Asclepius temple at Epidaurus and at Cos in Schnalke and Selheim, *Asklepios: Heilgott und Heilkult,* pp. 14 and 19.

274. M. Lang, *Cure and Cult in Ancient Corinth* (Athens, Princeton, 1977) p. 24.

275. H. Avalos, *Illness and Health Care in the Ancient Near East: The Role of the Temple in Greece, Mesopotamia, and Israel* (Atlanta, 1995) p. 89.

276. For an examination of metamorphosis, see P. M. C. Forbes Irving, *Metamorphosis in Greek Myth* (Oxford, 1990). Note, in particular, the mention of coupling snakes in the Admetus' bedroom (Pseudo Apollodorus, *Library* 1.9.15), of two snakes signifying death (Cicero, *Div.* 1.6), of Cassandra, Helenus, and Melampus whose ears are cleaned out by snakes (Pindar, *Ol.* 6.45ff.; Porph. *VA* 1.20), and of Apollonius of Tyana who eats snakes (Philostr. *VA* 1.20). All citations are by Forbes Irving.

277. I am indebted to L. R. Farnell, "The Cult of Asklepios," in *Greek Hero Cults and Ideas of Immortality* (Oxford, 1921), pp. 234–79, esp. p. 236. Also see Farnell, *Reflections on Asclepius,* trans. E. Papadopoulos (Athens, 1997 [in Greek]).

278. See K. Kerényi, *Der Göttliche Arzt: Studien über Asklepios und seine Kultstätten* (Darmstadt, 1956) esp. p. 7. Also see the translation of this book: *Asklepios: Archetypal Image of the Physician's Existence,* trans. R. Manheim (New York, 1959).

279. CIA 31; as cited by Farnell, *Greek Hero Cults,* p. 277.

280. See H. Matthäus, *Der Arzt in römisher Zeit: Literarische Nachrichten—archäologische Denkmäler,* ed. Ph. Filtzinger (Stuttgart, 1987); see illustration no. 22, which depicts a Roman physician who was portrayed in sculpture as Asclepius.

281. *On Medicine* Prooemium 2–3. See Celsus, *De Medicina,* ed. and trans. W. G. Spencer (LCL; London, Cambridge, Mass., 1971) vol. 1, pp. 2–3.

282. Edelstein summarizes his study of Asclepius with the conclusion that "Asclepius was a 'special god,' created by men to be in charge of one task alone, that of healing." Edelstein and Edelstein, *Asclepius,* vol. 2, p. 91. Also see A. Esser, "Asklepios und die Schlange," *FF* 17/18 (1948) 196–198.

283. See the sixty-one photos that follow p. 214 in J. Schouten, *De slangestaf van Asklepios als symbool van de Geneeskunde* (Amsterdam, New York, 1963).

284. For the picture, see Schnalke and Selheim, *Asklepios: Heilgott und Heilkult,* p. 10.

285. R. J. Deferrari et al., *A Concordance of Ovid,* 2 vols. (Washington, 1939; reprinted in Hildesheim and New York, 1968).

286. Ovid, *Metam.* 15. 658–62. The text and translation is taken from Edelstein and Edelstein, *Asclepius,* vol. 1, pp. 435–41. Also see Ovid, *Metamorphoses,* trans. R. Humphries (Bloomington, 1957) p. 385. Also see Kerényi, *Asklepios,* vol. 3, p. 10.

287. Antoninus Pius circulated a medallion commemorating this event; see the photograph in *EAA* 4 (1961) 945:1126.

288. See the illustration in Kerényi, *Asklepios,* p. 4 (Fig. 2).

289. See the interesting speculation by Kerényi that depictions of mice can well denote that a meal for a serpent is symbolized. See his "On Snakes and Mice in the Cults of Apollo and Asklepios," in *Asklepios,* pp. 102–05.

290. See R. MacMullen, *Paganism in the Roman Empire* (New Haven, London, 1981) p. 12.

291. On the general phenomenon of healing in the Ancient Near East, see Avalos, *Illness and Health Care in the Ancient Near East,* esp. chapter 1, "Greece: The Temples of Asclepius."

292. R. Caton, *The Temples and Ritual of Asklepios at Epidauros and Athens* (London, 1900). See esp. the illustration on p. 46.

293. See esp. "Die Heilungen in Epidauros," in Kerényi, *Der Göttliche Arzt,* pp. 25–56 (with illustrations). Also see the map of Epidaurus and plan of the Asclepian Temple in illustrations 19 and 20 in Leipoldt and Grundmann, *Umwelt des Urchristentums.*

294. See "Die Asklepiossöhne auf Kos," in Kerényi, *Der Göttliche Arzt,* pp. 57–78 (with illustrations).

295. See the reconstruction by H. Schleif presented in Kerényi, *Der Göttliche Arzt,* p. 55 (with illustrations).

296. See "Asklepios in Rom," in Kerényi, *Der Göttliche Arzt,* pp. 9–24 (with illustrations).

297. Edelstein and Edelstein, *Asclepius,* vol. 2, p. 116.

298. See the same judgment expressed in Leipoldt and Grundmann, *Umwelt des Urchristentums,* vol. 1, p. 69.

299. See the serpent in illustration no. 2 in Leipoldt and Grundmann, *Umwelt des Christentums.*

300. See A. Bouché-Leclercq, *Histoire de la divination dans l'antiquité* (Paris, 1880; rep. in Darmstadt, 1978) vol. 3, p. 290.

301. See esp. the following publications: H. von Fritze, "Die Münze von Pergamon," *Abhandlungen der Königlich-Preussischen Akademie der Wissenschaften zu Berlin, Philosophisch-historische Klasse-Anhang* (Berlin, 1910); O. Bernhard, "Asklepios und sein Geschlecht auf griechischen und römischen Münzen," *Ciba-Zeitschr* (1936)

1014–20; P. R. Franke, "Asklepios—Aesculapius auf antiken Münzen," *Medizinischer Monatsspiegel* 3 (1969) 60–67; K. W. Harl, *Coinage in the Roman Economy: 300 B.C. to A.D. 700* (Baltimore, London, 1996); T. Kroha, *Grosses Lexikon der Numismatik* (Gütersloh, 1997); see esp. pp. 40, 95, 214, 242, and 466; and R. Plant, *Greek Coin Types and Their Identification* (London, 1979).

302. K.-H. Hunger seeks to comprehend what the Asclepian staff means in communication; see his *Der Äskulapstab* (Berlin, 1978).

303. See the drawing in Kerényi, *Der Göttliche Artz,* p. 18.

304. Ibid., p. 34.

305. Ibid., pp. 43 and 113.

306. I well remember how de Vaux so animatedly lectured at the Ecole Biblique in the 1960s. As when working on serpent symbolism we must forget the present negative connotations, so with canine symbolism we must forget the regnant positive assumptions and experiences (esp. in the West).

307. See esp. P. France et al., "Dog," in *An Encyclopedia of Bible Animals* (Tel Aviv, 1986) pp. 50–51.

308. An example of the dog as a negative symbol is found in Norse myths; it is the horrible Garm.

309. See H. Biedermann, "Dog," in *Dictionary of Symbolism,* trans. J. Hulbert (New York, 1994) pp. 97–99.

310. As cited by R. Jackson in *Doctors and Diseases in the Roman Empire* (London, 1988) p. 140.

311. Sometimes Hygieia is incorrectly reported to be the wife of Asclepius.

312. Aristides, *Oratio* 38, 22; see Edelstein and Edelstein, *Asclepius,* vol. 1, p. 133. For the text of Aristides, see C. A. Behr and F. W. Lenz, *P. Aelii Aristides Opera Quae Exstant Omnia,* 2 vols. (Leiden, 1976–1980). Also see P. Aelius Aristides, *The Complete Works,* 2 vols., ed. and trans. C. A. Behr (Leiden, 1981–86).

313. See notes 317 and 318 on ancient coins.

314. For bibliography and a succinct discussion of Hygieia, see Z. Gočeva, "Hygieia," *LIMC,* 5.1, pp. 554–73.

315. See esp. the photograph of the statue of Hygieia in Rhodes from about 140 CE in Kerényi, *Der Göttliche Arzt,* p. 68.

316. No mention of the snake is found in the Orphic Hymn to Hygieia (68).

317. Y. Meshorer, *The Coinage of Aelia Capitolina* (Jerusalem, 1989) pp. 114, 56–67. See esp. the anguine iconography on the reverse of coin no. 175 (p. 115).

318. K. Butcher, *Roman Provincial Coins* (London, 1988) see esp. pp. 67, 68, 78, 87.

319. See also the photograph in *LIMC,* V.2, Plate 381, no. 9.

320. See the photograph in *LIMC,* V.2, Plate 382, no. 22.

321. See the photograph in *LIMC,* V.2, Plate 390, no. 128.

322. According to a carving of c. 400 CE, the serpent is shown curled affectionately around her shoulder and nibbling from a fruit, or nut, held in her right hand. The mouth of the serpent is formed into a smile. See the photograph in *EAA* 3 (1960) 142.

323. For example, see *LIMC,* V.2, Plate 390, no. 124.

324. Consult A. N. Athanassakis, *The Orphic Hymns: Text, Translation and Notes* (Missoula, 1977) pp. 56–57.

325. On the image of "the father," see Y. Knibiehler, *Geschichte der Väter: Eine kultur- und socialhistorische Spurensuche* (Freiburg, Basel, 1996).

326. Pliny, *Nat.* 29.4 (22) 72; see the Latin and English translation in Edelstein and Edelstein, *Asclepius*, p. 362.

327. See the photographs of the game boards preserved in the Oriental Institute, Metropolitan Museum of Art, and Musée du Louvre published in A. Levey, "Bad Timing: Time to Get a New Theory," *BAR* 24.4 (1998) 18–23; the photographs are on p. 21. Also see "Jouer dans l'antiquité," *Musées de Marseille* (Paris, 1991) pp. 125–29; and see Catalogue Nos. 174–75; M.-N. Bellesort, "Le jeu de serpent: Jeux et jouets dans l'antiquité et le Moyen Age," *Dossiers d'archéologie* (1992) 8–9.

328. See M. Schmidt, *Der Basler Medeasarkophag: Ein Meisterwerk Spätantoninischer Kunst* (Tübingen, 1997); see the serpents depicted on illustration 1, 9, 19 (close-up of Medea and the curled and upright serpents), 21 (close-up of serpents and the man being crushed beneath them), 28 (from the Berlin Medea sarcophagus, showing two majestic serpents with wings drawing Medea in her chariot), p. 32 (the fleeing Medea on the backs of two winged serpents, from an ash urn from Ostia), photos of the Medea sarcophagi in Rome (Aula VI Thermen Museum) and in Mantua (Palazzo Ducale). Sometimes Medea is depicted feeding a serpent; see the illustration in *EAA* 4 (1961) 951:1135. Sometimes she is shown with two massive serpents; see the illustration in *EAA* 4 (1961) 956.

329. Inv. SK 843 b. See the photograph in Schmidt, *Der Basler Medeasarkophag,* illustration p. 28.

330. Inv. Nr. 10. See the photograph in Schmidt, *Der Basler Medeasarkophag,* illustration p. 31.

331. In Aula VI; Neg. Rom. Inst. 63. See the photograph in Schmidt, *Der Basler Medeasarkophag,* illustration on p. 32.

332. See Ch. Belting-Ihm, "Sarcofago," *EAA* 7 (1966) 2–40; esp. see the ophidian iconography shown on pp. 18 (Hercules), 21:31 (Eleusinian myth), 34:52 (S. Maria Antiqua). Also see p. 107 (caduceus in the hand of a male; Ny Carlsberg Glyptotek, Copenhagen). Note also the second-century CE shroud designed to be placed on a mummy that is now preserved in the Staatliche Museen in Berlin. It shows an upraised cobra. I have no doubt that in this instance rejuvenation and thoughts about the new life after death were intended. See the color photograph in *EAA* 7 (1966) opposite p. 546. Also see the picture of the anguiped Tritons and the Nereides depicted on the sarcophagus in the Musei Vaticani; it is found in *EAA* 7 (1966) 991. Also see the sarcophagi shown in *EAA* 9 (1973) 720 and 727.

333. See the photographs in *EAA* 4 (1961) 91:119 and 393:463 and 955:1139.

334. It is in the Museo Nazionale in Taranto; see *LIMC,* V.2, p. 433.

335. One is in the Hermitage Museum in St. Petersburg (no. 586; [St. 350]; see *LIMC,* II.2, p. 135), and another in Museo Nazionale in Policoro (see *LIMC,* II.2, p. 139).

336. It is in the Basel Antikenmuseum und Sammlung Ludwig. For a photograph see *LIMC,* VII.2, p. 610.

337. It is in the National Museum in Copenhagen (no. 731).

338. The sarcophagus is in the Museo degli Uffizi in Florence. See the illustration in *LIMC,* III.2, p. 679.

339. One is in the Palazzo Rospiglios, another in Amalfi Cathedral, and a third in the Villa Giustiniani Massimo; all are in Rome. See the illustrations in *LIMC,* IV.2, p. 233 and IV.2, p. 234.

340. See *LIMC,* VIII.2, pp. 645–46.

341. See *LIMC*, VIII.2, p. 652.

342. They are in the Aachen Cathedral, Walton House, the Louvre, and in the Cabinet des Médailles (he is depicted on a plate). See *LIMC*, IV.2, p. 605.

343. One is in Aachen (Dom G 3 [see the photograph in *LIMC*, V.2, p. 420]), and another in the Kunsthistorisches Museum in Vienna (I 1126 [see the photograph in *LIMC*, V.2, p. 420]).

344. See illustration no. 29 in Leipoldt and Grundmann, *Umwelt des Urchristentums*. See the discussion in G. D'Alviella, *The Mysteries of Eleusis* (Wellingborough, Northhamptonshire, 1981) esp. pp. 22–25 and in G. Siettos, *The Eleusinian Mysteries* (Athens, 1993 [in Greek]).

345. See G. Bauchhenss, *Jupitergigantensäulen*, ed. Ph. Filtzinger (Stuttgart, 1976); see the illustrations of Jupiter trampling with his horse on a Giant (Nos. 24, 26), or using the Giant with his massive serpentine feet to elevate his horses (Nos. 25, 27), and even sometimes his chariot. Sometimes the Giant uses his hands (Nos. 28, 29) or the serpent heads of his legs (not shown, but see RL 412 in the Württembergisches Landesmuseum Stuttgart, Altes Schloss).

346. In the third century CE, Alexander Severus issued a medallion that shows Asclepius riding on the back of a winged serpent that has a goatee. He also holds in his hand a staff with a serpent around it. See the drawing in Kerényi, *Der Göttliche Arzt*, p. 106.

347. For the Greek and English translation, see A. D. Godley, *Herodotus* (LCL; London, Cambridge, Mass., 1957) vol. 2, pp. 394–95. For the vocabulary of Herodotus, see J. E. Powell, *A Lexicon to Herodotus* (London, 1938 [2nd ed.]; reprinted in Hildesheim and New York in 1966).

348. See 2.75; for the Greek and English translation, see Godley, *Herodotus*, vol. 1, pp. 360–61.

349. See 3.109; for the Greek and English translation, see Godley, *Herodotus*, vol. 2, pp. 136–37.

350. Aelian, *Nat. an.* 2.38. For the Greek and English translation, see Aelian, *On the Characteristics of Animals*, vol. 1, pp. 134–35.

351. See F. Cumont, *Recherches sur le symbolisme funéraire des Romains* (Paris, 1842, repr. New York, 1995). See Nock's review of Cumont's work in *JRS* 38 (1948) 154–56; and Nock, "Sarcophagi and Symbolism."

352. I am indebted to the summary by F. R. Walton, "After-Life," in *OCD*, pp. 23–24.

353. See I. Rumpel, *Lexicon Pindaricum* (Stuttgart, 1883; reprinted in Hildesheim and New York in 1961).

354. For the Greek and English translation, see J. Sandys, *The Odes of Pindar* (LCL: London, Cambridge, Mass., 1961) pp. 22–25. Also see the references to the Island of the Blessed Ones in *The History of the Rechabites*, ed. and trans. Charlesworth (Chico, Calif., 1982).

355. Farnell, *Greek Hero Cults*, p. 379.

356. See G. Siettos, *The Pythagorean Mysteries* (Athens, 1993 [in Greek]).

357. See W. Burkert, *Ancient Mystery Cults* (Cambridge, Mass., London, 1987) p. 29. Contrast J. S. Jeffers, who thinks that "the mystery religion . . . promised Romans an afterlife." Jeffers, *The Greco-Roman World of the New Testament Era* (Downers Grove, Ill., 1999) p. 98.

358. See Numa Denis Fustel de Coulanges, *The Ancient City* (Baltimore, 1980 [a reprint of an earlier work, since the author died in 1889]) p. 7

359. See Vermaseren, *Cybele and Attis.*

360. See E. A. Wallis Budge, *Osiris and the Egyptian Resurrection* (New York, 1973).

361. W. W. G. Baudissin, *Adonis und Esmun: Eine Untersuchung zur Geschichte des Glaubens an Auferstehungsgötter und an Heilgötter* (Leipzig, 1911); see esp. pp. 325–39.

362. The Egyptians thought that their pharaohs were divine and would be "resurrected," and that does seem to be the proper word. See Wallis Budge, *Osiris and the Egyptian Resurrection.*

363. The Greek is taken from A. S. Way, ed. and trans. *Euripides* (LCL 330; London, Cambridge, Mass., 1958) vol. 4, pp. 386–87.

364. My translation is influenced by F. J. Miller's edition. For the Latin and English translation, see Ovid, *Metamorphoses,* vol. 1, pp. 358–59.

365. Varrus, 5.68; see R. G. Kent, ed., *Varro: On the Latin Language* (LCL; London, Cambridge, Mass., 1967) vol. 1, pp. 66–67. Also see S. Lunais, *Recherches sur la lune: Les auteurs latins* (Leiden, 1979).

366. Ovid, *Metam.* 7.219–23. My translation is based on the one by Miller.

367. Ovid, *Metam.* 5.642–44. My translation is essentially that by Miller.

368. See the photograph in *Encyclopédie Photographique de l'Art,* vol. 3, p. 252:B.

369. Ovid, *Metam.* 3. 41–45; according to the *Metamorphoses,* ed. Miller, vol. 1, pp. 126–27.

370. Ovid, *Metam.* 3. 77–80; according to the *Metamorphoses,* ed. Miller, vol. 1, pp. 128–31.

371. Ovid, *Metam.* 4.563–603. For the full story of how Cadmus was turned into a serpent see Ovid's *Metam.* 4. One of the most convenient editions is the one I have been using: Ovid, *Metamorphoses,* ed. Miller.

372. Translation mine; for the Latin, see Ovid, *Fasti,* edited and translated by J. G. Frazer (LCL; London, Cambridge, Mass., 1967) pp. 74–77.

373. The relief is now in the Berlin Museum; see the photograph in *EAA* 7 (1966) 432:532.

374. Hesiod, *Theogony,* p. 258.

375. For depictions of serpents at Pompeii, see the photographs in *EAA* 4 (1961) 480–81.

376. See *LIMC,* VIII.2, p. 691.

377. See *LIMC,* VIII.2, p. 766.

378. Notably, see P. Diel, *Le symbolisme dans la mythologie Grecque: Étude psychanalytique* (Paris, 1952). See his study of Asclepius on pp. 216–31. Also see C. A. Meier, *Antike Inkubation und Moderne Psychotherapie* (Zürich, 1949).

379. See Schnalke and Selheim, *Asklepios: Heilgott und Heilkult,* p. 11.

380. H. Busch and G. Edelmann, eds., *Etruskische Kunst,* introduction and discussion of pictures by W. Zschietzschmann (Frankfurt, 1969) p. 72.

381. Busch and Edelmann, *Etruskische Kunst,* p. xxxii.

382. On the pediment of the Acropolis in Athens two massive serpents are portrayed with two lions; see *EAA* 8 (1973) Plate 180:4.

383. Busch and Edelmann, *Etruskische Kunst,* pp. xxxii, 72.

384. Busch and Edelmann, *Etruskische Kunst,* pp. xxxvii, 95.

385. Clarus, *Keltische Mythen,* p. 310.

386. One was found in a Romano-British well at Emberton, Buckinghamshire, and another, for example, near Bonn. See the photographs in M. J. Green, *Dictionary of Celtic Myth and Legend* (London, 1992) p. 149.

387. It is no. 2356; the later Mercury with caduceus has no inventory number.

388. See Green, *Dictionary of Celtic Myth and Legend,* p. 150.

389. Ibid., p. 194.

390. See C. Squire, *Celtic Myths and Legends* (Bath, 2000) pp. 376–80. Five hundred years later, Merlin dug them up; thence the Red Dragon drove the White Dragon from Britain.

391. See the photograph in A. Krumm, *Der Keltische Armreif* (Tettnang, 1986) p. 26.

392. See J. Biel, *Der Keltenfürst von Hochdorf* (Stuttgart, 1981); K. Bittel, W. Kimmig, and S. Schiek, eds., *Die Kelten in Baden-Württemberg* (Stuttgart, 1981); and F. Unruh, *Aufbruch nach Europa: Hiemat der Kelten am Ursprung der Donau* (Stuttgart, 1994).

393. As far as I know, it is not yet published. It can be seen in the Württembergisches Landesmuseum in Stuttgart, Altes Schoss.

394. See Inv. R 130,4.12 in the Württembergisches Landesmuseum in Stuttgart, Altes Schoss.

395. See Br. Inv. R 73, 1706 in the Württembergisches Landesmuseum in Stuttgart, Altes Schoss.

396. These two bronze serpent clasps are on public display in the Württembergisches Landesmuseum in Stuttgart, Altes Schoss.

397. For photographs, see H. Gabelmann, *Römische Grabbauten der frühen Kaiserzeit,* ed. Ph. Filtzinger (Stuttgart, 1979) pp. 50–52, and especially Illustration no. 20 opposite p. 5.

398. Note, esp., A. Böhme-Schönbeger, *Kleidung und Schmuck in Rom und den Provinzen* (Stuttgart, 1997).

399. For a color photograph of the gold bracelets and a black-and-white photograph of the remains of the woman, see Böhme-Schönberger, *Kleidung und Schmuck,* p. 58.

400. See the photograph in Böhme-Schönberger, *Kleidung und Schmuck,* p. 59.

401. See the photographs in Böhme-Schönberger, *Kleidung und Schmuck,* pp. 62 and 64, respectively.

402. On the difficulty of understanding our sources on religion in Rome in the middle and late Republic, see esp. M. Beard, J. North, and S. Price, *Religions of Rome,* 2 vols. (Cambridge, 1998) vol. 1, p. 119.

403. See C. R. Long, *The Twelve Gods of Rome* (Leiden, 1987) p. 235.

404. The anguine figure is in the Charlesworth collection in Princeton.

405. Aelian, *Nat. an.* 1.51: "The corpse of a wicked man receives (so I think) the reward of his ways in becoming the progenitor of a snake [ὄφεως]." See Aelian, *On the Chracteristics of Animals,* vol. 1, pp. 70–71.

406. Farnell, *Greek Hero Cults and Ideas of Immortality,* p. 377.

407. Aelian thus celebrates the drug that comes from the Purple Snake (4.36). For the Greek and English, see Aelian, *On the Characteristics of Animals,* vol. 1, pp. 252–53.

408. *Vita Apollonii* 3.44. The Greek is translated idiomatically, and I am indebted to the translation of Edelstein and Edelstein in *Asclepius,* vol. 1, p. 189; for the Greek see vol. 1, p. 188.

409. O. Gruppe thought this Sanchuniathon never existed, but W. F. Albright claimed that he did exist, lived in Berytus, and was a refugee from Tyre. For us it is not relevant whether Sanchuniathon was a valuable source concerning Phoenician theology; it is more important that Philo of Byblos, about the time of the Fourth Gospel, published the ideas concerning a serpent.

410. Our only source for Philo of Byblos is Eusebius' *Praeparatio evangelica* (PE). Eusebius, as one might imagine, denigrates the idea that snakes can be beneficial. He thus marks one of the turning points in the appreciation of the serpent.

411. Actually, Eusebius is citing Philo of Byblos who claims to be translating Sanchuniathon, who in turn is quoting a certain Taautos at this point. This phenomenon often confronts one who is studying the first century; that is, we have only citations of otherwise lost works (see Charlesworth in *OTP,* vol. 2, pp. 775–76 and J. Strugnell, ibid., pp. 777–79.

412. For the Greek and translation see H. W. Attridge and R. A. Oden, *Philo of Byblos: The Phoenician History* (Washington, D.C., 1981), pp. 64–65. For another edition and translation, see A. I. Baumgarten, *The* Phoenician History *of Philo of Byblos* (Leiden, 1981).

413. For the Greek and English, see Baumgarten, *The* Phoenician History *of Philo of Byblos.*

414. Pliny, *Nat.* 29.22, *vulgoque pascitur et in domibus.* For the Latin and English translation, see Pliny, *Natural History,* ed. Jones, vol. 8, pp. 230–31.

415. I purchased them years ago in Cologne.

416. I acquired this in the 1980s or 1990s.

417. W. Burkert, *Structure and History in Greek Mythology and Ritual* (Berkeley and London, 1979) p. 20.

418. There is little information in Cicero's *De natura deorum* concerning serpents even though cats (1.82, 101; 3.47) and crocodiles (1.82, 101; 2.124, 129; 3.47) are discussed. I find this surprising. Is it because of the learned circles in which Cicero lived and worked?

419. Lucian, *Alex.* 4. The Greek and English translation of Lucian's "Alexander the False Prophet" is derived from A. M. Harmon, *Lucian* (LCL; London, Cambridge, Mass., 1969) vol. 4.

420. See esp. J. Wytzes, *Der Letzte Kampf des Heidentums in Rom* (Leiden, 1977).

421. See M. Smith, "How Magic Was Changed by the Triumph of Christianity," in *Studies in the Cult of Yahweh,* ed. S. J. D. Cohen (Leiden, 1996) vol. 2, pp. 208–16.

422. For a judicial assessment of the sociological ramifications of these edicts, see F. R. Trombley, *Hellenic Religion and Christianization c. 370–529,* 2 vols. (Leiden, 1993–1994).

423. See Porphyry, *De regressu animae* and *De philosophia ex oraculis hauriendis.* See esp. the discussion on demonology by A. D. Nock, *Essays on Religion and the Ancient World,* ed. Z. Stewart (Oxford, 1972) vol. 2, pp. 516–26.

424. Plato, *Apology of Socrates* 19. See the discussions by D. Tarrant and others in *Der historische Sokrates,* ed. A. Patzer (Darmstadt, 1987).

425. See K. Kleve, "The Daimonion of Socrates," in *The Many and the One,* ed. P. Borgen (Trondheim, 1985) pp. 183–201.

426. Tertullian, *An.* 1.5: *Socrates secundum Pythii quoque daemonis suffragium.* See A. Gerlo, ed., *Tertulliani Opera* (Corpus Christianorum, Series Latina II. Turnhout, 1954) part II, p. 782.

427. See illustration no. 74 in Leipoldt and Grundmann, *Umwelt des Urchristentums.*

428. See illustration no. 75 in Leipoldt and Grundmann, *Umwelt des Urchristentums.*

429. Goodenough, *Jewish Symbols,* vol. 2, p. 230; also see pp. 212–13.

430. This judgment is shared with M. P. Nilsson; see his *A History of Greek Religion* (New York, 1964 [2nd ed.]) pp. 292–93.

431. *Phaedo* 118; B. Jowett, *The Dialogues of Plato,* 2 vols. (New York, 1937) vol. 1, p. 501.

5. The Full Spectrum of the Meaning of Serpent Symbolism in the Fertile Crescent

1. See esp. J. Maringer, "Die Schlange in Kunst und Kult der vorgeschichtlichen Menschen," *Anthropos* 72 (1977) 881–920.

2. In the following presentation I am indebted especially to the following: *TDOT, TDNT,* J. Campbell, assisted by M. J. Abadie, "The Serpent Guide," *Mythic Image* (Princeton, 1974) pp. 281–301; and M. Lurker, "Snakes," in *The Encyclopedia of Religion,* ed. M. Eliade (New York, London, 1987) vol. 13, pp. 370–74.

3. See "Uphill Work," *Haaretz Online* 18 March 2003.

4. The speaker was described only as "a teenage girl." See N. Angier, "Venomous and Sublime: The Viper Tells Its Tale," *New York Times* 10 December 2002; see www.nytimes.com/2002/12/10/science/life/10VIPE.

5. See Appendix I and discussion of Seraphim.

6. Long ago, C. Fox drew attention to a Palestinian image of a snake with ears and a bird's beak. See Fox, "Circle and Serpent Antiquities," *PEF* (1894) 83–87.

7. See, notably, A. L. Frothingham, "Babylonian Origin of Hermes the Snake-God, and of the Caduceus," *AJA,* Second Series 20 (1916) 175–211. R. Ferwerda, "Le Serpent, le noeud d'Hercule et le Caducée d'Hermès: Sur un passage orphique chez Athénagore," *Numen* 20 (1973) 104–15.

8. I am grateful to Professor Yosef Garfinkel for showing me the site. See his *Sha'ar Hagolan: Neolithic Art in the Jordan Valley* (Jerusalem, 2002 [in Hebrew; this work is now being translated into English]). Also see Garfinkel, *The Yarmukians: Neolithic Art from Sha'ar Hagolan* (Jerusalem, 1999).

9. I am dependent on the following publications: K. Schmidt, "The 2002 Excavations at Göbekli Tepe (Southeastern Turkey)—Impressions from an Enigmatic Site," *Neo-Lithics* 2 (2002) 8–13; Schmidt, "Frühe Tier und Menschen Bilder vom Göbekli Tepe, Kampagne 1995–1998," *Istanbuler Mitteilungen* 49 (1999) 5–21.

10. I am grateful to Dan Cohen for drawing my attention to the snake reliefs at this Neolithic site.

11. Most experts have rightly followed R. Merhav's argument that Albright's suggestion (in *BASOR* 31 [1928]) that a stele found at Tell Beit Mirsim shows a serpent coming out of the ground is misleading. See Merhav, "The Stele of the 'Serpent Goddess' from Tell Beit Mirsim and the Plaque from Shechem Reconsidered," *IMJ* 4 (1985) 27–42.

12. For pictures, see Garfinkel, *Sha'ar Hagolan,* pp. 70 and 83.

13. For pictures, see Garfinkel, *Sha'ar Hagolan,* pp. 163–65.

14. G. Zuntz rightly argues: "Anyone drawing or carving a line—any line . . . therewith gives expression to some motive within himself; it may be superficial and momentary (especially if he is mechanically copying a model) or significantly expressive (especially if he is decorating a temple)." Zuntz, *Persephone: Three Essays on Religion and Thought in Magna Graecia* (Oxford, 1971) p. 26.

15. *The Penguin Dictionary of Symbols,* trans. J. Buchanan-Brown (London, New York, 1996) p. 844.

16. See the reflections on these categories and the search for a symbol's meaning (or the confusion of a decoration with a symbol) by R. W. Bagley in "Meaning and Explanation," in *The Problem of Meaning in Early Chinese Ritual Bronzes,* ed. R. Whitfield (London, 1993) pp. 34–55.

17. I can agree with Jung that the little girl had "very little religious background" (p. 61), but she lived in our culture in which snakes are dreaded both metaphorically and actually. Also his too literal interpretation of "four corners" leads him into the precarious thought that she must have had unconscious access to the quaternity myth that was once familiar in Hermetic philosophy but disappeared well over two hundred years ago. Jung, *Man and His Symbols,* p. 62.

18. "The images and ideas that dreams contain cannot possibly be explained solely in terms of memory." Jung, *Man and His Symbols,* p. 26.

19. Jung, *Man and His Symbols,* p. 25.

20. Jung, *Man and His Symbols,* pp. 56–57.

21. Jung, *Man and His Symbols,* p. 57.

22. Yet I am drawn, I hope not uncritically, to Jung's insight that the human does not come into this world with "a psyche that is empty," and that we should not "assume" that the human "is the only living being deprived of specific instincts, or that his psyche is devoid of all traces" of over three million years of evolution. Jung, *Man and His Symbols,* p. 64. My own experiences reveal hidden fears that cannot easily be attributed to what has occurred in my life during my sixty years. Of course, I am convinced that human experience is open to other dimensions, and that "God" (whatever that concept means in its full sense) is the Creator who actively interacts and breaks into my little world. If we all inherit DNA, then do we not inherit memories and thought patterns from our ancestors?

23. L. Boltin, D. Newton, et al., *Masterpieces of Primitive Art* (New York, 1978) p. 198. Also see the double-headed serpent shown in highly stylized form in embroidery that comes from Peru, and around the turn of the era (100 BCE to 200 CE), in color on p. 198.

24. J. Fergusson, *Tree and Serpent Worship; or, Illustrations of Mythology and Art in India in the First and Fourth Centuries After Christ* (London, 1868) p. 3.

25. G. E. Smith, *The Migrations of Early Culture* (Manchester, 1916); Smith, *The Influence of Ancient Egyptian Civilization in the East and in America* (London, 1916). Even MacCulloch, with whom I share many perspectives, was misled by Smith to think his analysis was "fruitful." *ERE* (1920) 11.399.

26. See D. Wildung and J. Liepe, *Die Pharaonen des Goldlandes: Antike Königreiche im Sudan* (Mannheim, 1998). Note, in particular, the following: p. 266 (see Illus. 43) the lion god Apelemuk has a body of a serpent; p. 349 (= no. 410) first or second century CE; a serpent on a pottery flask; no. 140, a serpent stele in black granite,

c. 1360 BCE; no. 168, Sphinx figure (670–660 BCE) with uraeus chiseled off; no. 368, a gold bracelet with serpents' heads on each end—the eyes are clear; in the mouth of each is a small hole, probably for a gold tongue; no. 32, Mercury with an ornate caduceus, one of the most detailed I have found. The caduceus has a serpent clearly depicted (the other one is off the frieze and worn away). Very interesting is no. 41. It shows a Mithra relief of about 250 CE, beneath and to the left of a bull being slain by two men brandishing weapons. The iconography is unique for Mithra shrines, and since the large serpent is drinking out of a large bowl, it is conceivable, even probable, that Mithra iconography has been influenced by Asclepius iconography. No. 21 is a gravestone in gray sandstone, from Mainz and the second century CE. It contains the figure of a male with two hands descending to his pelvic area. There a large hole, descending downward, has been chiseled. This person, Elima, the son of Solimutus, may have been commemorated with an upraised phallus and with two hands holding it. One is reminded of the mural to the right of the entrance to the House of the Vetti in Pompeii.

27. As indicated previously, the faience Minoan goddesses may be priestesses. The sensationalism of the Minoan excavations made goddesses more attractive. A. Evans opined that the "Snake Goddess" may be "an actual votary of priestess, whose 'possession' is thus indicated." Evans, *The Palace of Minos* (London, 1921) vol. 1.1, p. 233. The picture of the faience serpent goddesses shown earlier is of professionally prepared models, as was indicated. The smaller serpent goddess was found headless and everything from her left elbow outward is a restoration. See the object before restoration in Evans, *The Palace of Minos,* vol. 1, 3, Fig. 360, a and b on p. 502. The restoration of a serpent in her left hand is speculative; it is based on the serpent held in her right hand. Evans reported that the larger woman (34.2 cm. [13.5 in.] high) has three coiled and spotted snakes on her body. The snakes have greenish bodies that are spotted with purple-brown. Evans, *The Palace of Minos,* vol. 1,3, pp. 500–501. I am grateful to the American School of Classical Studies in Athens for permission to work on Evans' publications and notes in the Blegen Library.

28. On a visit to Hazor and the museum there in July 2002, I was impressed by the massive Canaanite palace discovered during the past eleven years by Professor A. Ben Tor and the serpent with dots for skin found in Locus 226.30 Area A, dating from MB2 that was found (Canaanite period; see photograph in Yadin's volumes, photograph CCCXIII[13]).

29. See the attractive drawings and photographs on pp. 146–50 in H.-G. Buchholz, "Furcht vor Schlangen und Umgang mit Schlangen in Altsyrien, Altkypros und dem Umfeld," *UF* 32 (2000) 37–168.

30. For a drawing, see L. Keimer, *Histoires de Serpents dans l'Égypte ancienne et moderne* (Cairo, 1947) p. 2.

31. Here I disagree with Plato and lean toward Aristotle; in fact, I am a phenomenologist influenced by Maurice Merleau-Ponty.

32. Eusebius, *PG* II.9 (101C); the translation is by E. H. Gifford in Eusebius, *Preparation for the Gospel* (Grand Rapids, 1981 [original is by Clarendon Press, 1903]) p. 110.

33. Hercules was celebrated throughout Magna Graecia and elsewhere in Italy; see the discussion of the serpent in the Hesperides in A. Pontrandolfo, *Le tombe dipinte di Paestum,* ed. M. Cipriani (Paestum [n.d.; 2003?]) esp. p. 27 (drawing).

34. See esp. M. Pagano, *Herculaneum,* trans. A. Pesce (Torre del Greco, 2000) pp. 76, 82–83.

35. Eusebius, *PG* III.11 (112b); Gifford in Eusebius, *Preparation for the Gospel,* p. 123. Also see Eusebius *PG* III.13 (119b–c); Gifford in Eusebius, *Preparation for the Gospel,* p. 131.

36. Eusebius, *PG* III.11 (112b); Gifford in Eusebius, *Preparation for the Gospel,* p. 123.

37. Porphyry's own views of the alleged powers of Asclepius and Jesus are clear in Fragment 80; see W. Den Boer, *Scriptorum paganorum I–IV saec. de christianis testimonia* (Leiden, 1965) p. 32.

38. For Latin and Greek texts see R. Hercher, ed., *Aeliani De Natura Animalium* (Paris, 1858); for the Greek and English translations cited, see A. F. Scholfield, trans. and ed., *Aelian: On Animals,* 3 vols. (LCL; London, Cambridge, Mass., 1958, 1959).

39. My translation. Pliny (x.c.66) had written, *"Anguem ex medulla hominis sinae gigni accepimus a multis."*

40. In Appendix II, I have named this snake "Asian viper."

41. Quite surprisingly, J. F. Nunn casually refers to the "dread with which the ancient Egyptians regarded snakes." See his *Ancient Egyptian Medicine* (London, 1996) p. 107.

42. See J. Mann, *Murder, Magic, and Medicine* (Oxford, 1992) p. 39.

43. M. Eliade, *Patterns in Comparative Religion* (New York, 1958) p. 164.

44. W. von Soden, "Verschlüsselte Kritik an Salomo in der Urgeschichte des Jahwisten?" *WO* 7 (1974) 228–40.

45. M. Görg, "Die 'Sünde' Salomos: Zeitkritische Aspekte der jahwistischen Sündenfallerzählung," *BN* 16 (1981) 42–59; Görg, "Weisheit als Provokation: Religionsgeschichtliche und theologische Aspekte der Sünderfallerzählung," in *Die Kraft der Hoffnung [Festschrift J. Schneider]* (Bamberg, 1982) pp. 19–34.

46. See K. Holter, "The Serpent in Eden as a Symbol of Israel's Political Enemies: A Yahwistic Criticism of the Solomonic Foreign Policy?" *SJOT* 1 (1990) 106–12.

47. Laubscher, "Der Schlangenwürgende Herakles: Seine Bedeutung in der Herrscherikonologie," *JdI* 112 (1997) 149–66.

48. Consult A. Barash and J. H. Hoofien, *Reptiles of Israel* (Tel Aviv, 1966 [Hebrew]). Also see the manual on the taxonomy and distribution of venomous snakes in the Near and Middle East published by U. Joger: *The Venomous Snakes of the Near and Middle East* (Wiesbaden, 1984). The attractiveness of snakes may be due to the fact that the mouths of many snakes form an alluring and inviting smile (see esp. the drawings on pp. 89–95).

49. F. S. Bodenheimer, *Animal Life in Palestine* (Jerusalem, 1935) p. 181. Also, see Bodenheimer, *Animal and Man in Bible Lands,* 2 vols. (Leiden, 1960, 1972). For images of the serpent, see esp. vol. 2, Figures 19, 37.

50. I cannot now present and discuss the many serpent images collected by Shlomo Moussaieff. I hope to publish his collection in the near future, and am most grateful to him for his kindness and generosity in showing me his many serpent images. Here is a preliminary selection: (1) a clay image with a serpent raised up facing a woman (Eve?). It is perhaps between 5,000 and 8,000 years old and was found near Lake Van; (2) a ceramic piece similar to no. 1 but the serpent is facing away from the woman; (3) a ceramic piece similar to nos. 1 and 2; it has two serpents raised up and facing a woman; (4) a clay image similar to nos. 1, 2, and 3 with three serpents that are upraised; (5) a

clay idol with two serpents on the head; it is perhaps between 5,000 and 8,000 years old; (6) a large bronze snake (84.4 cm long and about 10.5 cm wide) from Ptolemaic or Roman times. It was found in Israel. (7) a small iron snake (base is 1617 cm and height is 10.8 cm.). It dates from Iron II, probably, and was allegedly found in Wadi Masri in the southern Negev.

51. On discontinuity and continuity in ancient symbolism, with a stress on the fifth and fourth centuries BCE, see M. Torelli, *Il rango, il rito e l'immagine* (Milan, 1997) esp. pp. 8 and 194.

52. It is now unnecessary to demonstrate that iconography is essential for exegesis. See esp. the numerous publications by Keel already cited and B. A. Strawn, "Psalm 22:17b: More Guessing," *JBL* 119 (2000) 439–51.

53. Much later even Maimonides recognized the importance of art for relaxing and refreshing the mind. See Maimonides, *The Commandments,* 2 vols., trans. C. B. Chavel (London, New York, 1967) vol. 2, p. 4.

54. J. Maringer, "Die Schlange in Kunst und Kult der vorgeschichtlichen Menschen," *Anthropos* 72 (1977) 881–920; esp. p. 913.

55. I have transliterated the Ugaritic so nonspecialists might obtain some insight into how the words might sound. Consult Dillmann's *Lexicon;* for texts, see Whitaker, *A Concordance of the Ugaritic Literature,* pp. 159 and 446–47.

56. They are *KTU* 1.100 (= RS 1992.2014), *KTU* 1.107, RS 24.251 +, and RS 24.244. See B. A. Levine and J.-M. de Tarragon, " 'Shapshu Cries out in Heaven': Dealing with Snake-Bites at Ugarit (*KTU* 1.100, 1.107)," *RB* 94–95 (1988) 481–518; also consult D. Pardee in *Context* 1.295–98. The Ugaritic *nḥš ʿqšr* (e.g. in 1.100 4, line 7) seems to denote some type of snake; see Levine and Tarragon, op. cit., p. 495. For further discussion, see J. N. Ford "The Ugaritic Incantations Against Sorcery" (PhD diss., Jerusalem, 2002); see esp. p. 142. Much of this dissertation is to appear in *UF*.

57. See esp. the *Einblattdruck* by Hans Hauser (Ulm, 1495).

58. In Midrash Ecclesiastes this verse is interpreted to refer to anyone who "breaks down a fence erected by the Sages." Such a person will "eventually suffer penalties," either in this age or in the coming one. See H. Freedman and M. Simon, trans., *Midrash Rabbah* (London, 1939) p. 28.

59. See J. A. Fitzmyer in *Context* 2.213–17. Also see W. Beyerlin, *Near Eastern Religious Texts Relating to the Old Testament,* trans. J. Bowden (London, 1978) p. 259.

60. Diodorus Siculus, *Library of History* 4.9.1–10. The date of this work is sometime in the first century BCE.

61. See M. Albertoni et al., *The Capitoline Museums,* trans. D. A. Arya and S. Mari (Rome, 2000); the picture is on p. 52.

62. See the image in D. Stillwell, ed., *Antioch On-the-Orontes: III—The Excavations 1937–1939* (Princeton, London, The Hague, 1941) p. 182 (discussion and description), and Plate 56 (black-and-white photograph). Also see D. Levi, *Antioch Mosaic Pavements* (Princeton, London, The Hague, 1947) vol. 2, Plate IV.

63. See the depiction of Laocoon's wife on a fragment of a vase on p. 144 in Buchholz, "Furcht vor Schlangen und Umgang mit Schlangen in Altsyrien, Altkypros und dem Umfeld."

64. *LivPro* 2.3–4; translated by D. R. A. Hare in *OTP* 2.286–87.

65. Also see John Chrysostom, *Homily* 2.4: "For as the physicians taking serpents and cutting off their destructive members, prepare medicines for antidotes." Trans.

T. P. Brandram, "Homilies II and III: On the Power of Man to Resist the Devil," *NPNF1* 9, p. 189.

66. For the English translation and Latin text, see Celsus, *De Medicina,* trans. W. G. Spencer (LCL; London, Cambridge, Mass., 1971) vol. 2.

67. TAb 19, Recension A; translated by E. P. Sanders in *OTP* 1.895.

68. J. Preuss, *Biblical and Talmudic Medicine,* ed. and trans. F. Rosner (New York, 1978) chap. 5 and p. 569.

69. See G. M. Parássoglou, "A Christian Amulet Against Snakebite," *SPap* 13 (1974) 107–10. (P. Yale inv. 1792).

70. R. L'Estrange, *The Life and Fables of Æsop,* ed. S. Stern (New York, 1970) p. 156.

71. Scene 5; 1051–54; S. Wells and G. Taylor et al., eds., *William Shakespeare: The Complete Works—Original-Spelling Edition* (Oxford, 1986) p. 363.

72. For further discussion, see H. Egli, "Der Drachenkampf," *Das Schlangensymbol* (Freiburg im Breisgau, 1982) pp. 194–56.

73. Professor Dr. Shimeon Gitter informed me of this fact. He is one of the founders of the medical school at Tel Aviv University. He also informed me that decades ago he discovered that the venom of a cobra has more copper than zinc.

74. See, e.g., H. Brunner, "Seth und Apophis—Gegengötter im ägyptischen Pantheon?" in *Das Hörende Herz* (Freiburg Schweiz, 1988) pp. 121–29. Also see Sauneron, *Papyrus Brooklyn;* Esna III, 32 §15; Esna V, 265 §14 and D. Kurth, *"SUUM CUIQUE:* Zum Verhältnis von Dämon und Göttern im alten Ägypten," in *Die Dämonen,* ed. A. Lange, H. Lichtenberger, and K. F. D. Römheld (Tübingen, 2003) pp. 45–60; esp. p. 57.

75. See W. Robertson Smith, *The Religion of the Semites* (New York, 1956) pp. 118–33.

76. For the Hebrew text and translation, see N. Slifkin, *Nature's Song* (Southfield, Mich., 2001) p. 35.

77. *3 Bar* 5:3 (Greek and Slavonic); see *OTP* 1.668 and the trans. H. E. Gaylord.

78. *Beshallah,* Exodus 4. J. T. Townsend, trans., *Midrash Tanhuma (S. Buber Recension)* (Hoboken, N. J., 1997) vol. 2, p. 77.

79. E. A. Phillips points to the complexity of the "pre-texts" and "inter-texts" in which the serpent appears; see her "Serpent Intertexts: Tantalizing Twists in the Tales," *BBR 10* (2000) 233–45.

80. See the photographs and discussion in Y. Meshorer, *Ancient Means of Exchange: Weights and Coins* (Haifa, 1998) pp. 76, 79, 95. Also see L. Mildenberg, ed., *The Abraham Bromberg Collection of Jewish Coins,* 2 parts (Zürich, 1991–1992); see esp. vol. 1, pp. 12 (Herod the Great's bronze coin with winged caduceus), 14 (Herod Archelaus' bronze coin with caduceus); vol. 2, p. 9 (Herod the Great's bronze with winged caduceus [superb example]).

81. G. St. Clair, "The Subtle Serpent," *JTS* 7 (1960) 40–50; the quotation is from p. 40.

82. A. Luyster, "The *Femme-aux-Serpents* at Moissac: Luxuria (Lust) or Bad Mother," in *Between Magic and Religion,* ed. S. R. Asirvatham et al. (Lanham, Md., Oxford, 2001) pp. 165–91.

83. "Draconibus et igne et serpentibus atque viperis circa colla eorum." The Latin text and English translation presented are by Luyster, in *Between Magic and Religion,* pp. 176–77.

84. See the photographs and discussion in J. Charlesworth, ed., *Jews and Christians* (New York, 1990).

85. Mary Douglas, *Purity and Danger* (London, 1966).

86. G. Beckman in *Context* 1.150.

87. See J. W. van Henten, "Python," in *DDD*² 669–71.

88. See the brilliant reflections by J. Z. Smith in "Towards Interpreting Demonic Powers in Hellenistic and Roman Antiquity," *ANRW* II.16.1 (1978) 425–39.

89. Instrumenta Patristica 29; Turnhout, 1996.

90. Borsje, *From Chaos to Enemy;* for Apophis see pp. 118, 292, 297, for Behemoth pp. 30, 32, 117, 127, 191, 266, 304, for Cerberus pp. 151, 302, and for Leviathan pp. 12, 30–39 esp. (et passim).

91. Beyerlin, *Near Eastern Religious Texts Relating to the Old Testament,* p. 198.

92. C. M. Brown, "A Natural History of the Gloucester Sea Serpent: Knowledge, Power, and the Culture of Science in Antebellum America," *American Quarterly* (September 1990) 402–36; M. Meurger and C. Gagnon, *Lake Monster Traditions: A Cross-Cultural Analysis* (London, 1988).

93. J. P. O'Neill, *The Great New England Sea Serpent: An Account of Unknown Creatures Sighted by Many Respectable Persons Between 1638 and the Present Day* (Camden, Maine, 1999).

94. The snake is the lawless one, Satan. See *Vita* 33:3, *LivPro* 12:13, and *ApMos* 16:5.

95. J. Chevalier and A. Gheerbrant, *The Penguin Dictionary of Symbols* (London, New York, 1996) p. 846.

96. See Wittkower, *JWI* 2 (1938–1939) 296. He draws attention to S. Reinach, "Aetos Prometheus," *RAr* 2 (1907) 65ff.

97. Aristotle thought that the forked tongue of a snake doubled the pleasure of taste; cf. *Part. an.* 2.17 (660b); A. L. Peck, *Aristotle: Parts of Animals* (LCL; London, Cambridge, Mass., 1961) pp. 202–3.

98. See D. Pardee in *Context* 1.327–28.

99. As cited by Chevalier and Gheerbrant in *The Penguin Dictionary of Symbols,* p. 856.

100. Philo, *QG* 1.33.

101. E. Williams-Forte, "The Snake and the Tree in the Iconography and Texts of Syria During the Bronze Age," in *Ancient Seals and the Bible,* ed. L. Gorelick and E. Williams-Forte (Malibu, Calif., 1983) 18–43.

102. See S. Samek-Ludovici and H. Ravenna, *Dante Göttliche Komödie nach einer Handschrift aus dem 15. Jahrhundert,* trans. P. Aschner (Fribourg, Geneva, 1979) pp. 32–33.

103. Peter of Alexandria, *The Genuine Acts of Peter;* trans. J. B. H. Hawkins, "Peter of Alexandria: The Genuine Acts of Peter," *ANF* 6, p. 262.

104. Athanasius, *To the Bishops of Egypt* 1.19; trans. A. Robertson, "On the Incarnation of the Word," *NPNF2* 4, p. 233.

105. *ApEl* 5:33; trans. O. S. Wintermute in *OTP* 1.752.

106. The use of serpent imagery to illustrate base behavior is often used in poetry. For example, Friedrich Hölderlin denounces one who castigates his brother's failure with "the loose mockery of the serpent's tongue [*Schlangenzunge*]." F. Hölderlin, *Sämtliche Werke,* p. 304.

107. Lane, *An Arabic-English Lexicon,* Book I, Part 1 (1863) p. 681.

108. Paul Ricoeur, *Finitude et culpabilité* (Paris, 1960) esp. pp. 236–43. Also see A. Wénin, "Satan ou l'adversaire de l'alliance: Le serpent, père du mensonge," *Graphè* 9 (2000) 23–43.

109. Act 1, line 191. Also see Act 3, line 1234 for the reference to the poison of a viper. For the Greek, see A. S. Owen, ed., *Euripides Ion* (Oxford, 1939, 1957). I am grateful to Dr. Kevin Glowacki of Indiana University (who was at the American School of Classical Studies at Athens when I was working on ophidian iconography); he drew my attention to *Ion*.

110. See H. Goedicke, "The Snake in the Story of the Shipwrecked Sailor," *Göttinger Miszellen* 39 (1980) 27–31.

111. The eagle and serpent are sometimes used to complement each other, bringing together the tension between good and evil. See Ye. V. Antonova, "The 'Serpent' and the 'Eagle' in the Glyptics of the Oxus Civilization," *Journal of Ancient History* 2 (2000 [Moscow]) 46–52 (Russian).

112. In this passage, the "dragon" is most likely the river crocodile.

113. A use of language found in J. D. Ray, "Egyptian Wisdom Literature," in *Wisdom in Ancient Israel: Essays in Honour of J. A. Emerton,* ed. J. Day, R. P. Gordon, and H. G. M. Williamson (Cambridge, 1995) p. 17. Also see F. V. Greifenhagen, *Egypt on the Pentateuch's Ideological Map* (London, New York, 2002).

114. A. Perrot, "L'homme aux serpents," *Syria* 28 (1951) 57–61.

115. See E. Porada, "A Man with Serpents," in *Von Uruk nach Tuttul [Festschrift E. Strommenger],* ed. B. Hrouda et al. (Munich, Vienna, 1992) pp. 171–75 and Plates 72–78. Also see Porada, *Man and Images in the Ancient Near East* (Wakefield, R.I., London, 1995) esp. pp. 39–47.

116. L'Estrange, *The Life and Fables of Æsop,* p. 112 (with original italics, punctuations, and capitalizations).

117. See Foster in *Context* 1.390–402.

118. H. Leclercq, "Serpent," *DACL* 15 (1950) 1353.

119. See R. Schulz and K. Sabri Kolta, "Schlangen, Skorpione und feindliche Mächte: Ein koptisch-arabische Schutzspruch," *BN* 93 (1998) 89–104.

120. See ibid.

121. See the summary by R. S. J. Typwhitt, "Serpent," *DCA* vol. 2, 1889.

122. See Typwhitt, "Dragon," *DCA* vol. 1, pp. 579–80. In this publication and the one mentioned previously, Typwhitt errs in drawing a too rigid distinction between serpent and dragon; as we have seen, the two terms are interchangeable in texts and iconography (beginning in the second millennium BCE).

123. I. J. Gelb et al., eds., *The Assyrian Dictionary* (Chicago, 1962) pp. 148–50.

124. B. Meissner and W. von Soden, *Akkadisches Handwörterbuch* (Wiesbaden, 1981) vol. 3, p. 1093.

125. I am grateful to A. Biran for discussing the discoveries with me and clarifying that the three pithoi have now been found at Dan. See Biran, *Biblical Dan,* pp. 152–53, 165–77.

126. Act 1, line 191. For the Greek, see Owen, *Euripides Ion,* ad loc.

127. See J. G. Frazer, ed., *Apollodorus* (LCL; London, New York, 1921) pp. 84–85.

128. F. Hvidberg, "The Canaanite Background of Gen I-III," *VT* 10 (1960) 285–94.

129. See, inter alia, T. M. Probatake, *The Devil in Byzantine Culture* (Thessaloniki, 1980 [in modern Greek]).

130. *LivPro* 12:13; trans. D. R. A. Hare in *OTP* 2.394.

131. *Vita* 33:1–3; trans. M. D. Johnson in *OTP* 2.272.

132. *ApMos* 16:1–5; trans. M. D. Johnson in *OTP* 2.277.

133. For mature reflections on symbology and ontology and the language of symbols in terms of an intentionality that is intelligent, rational, and moral, see S. Muratore, "Simbolo, mistero e mito: Il quadro epistemologico," in *La conoscenza simbolica,* ed. C. Greco and S. Muratore (Milan, 1998) pp. 9–39.

134. Except for haplography, or removal of supposed redundancies, the scribes have offered us no verbal variants. They well knew what had been written.

135. See, notably, C. Sailer's *Der Feldzug der Schlange und das Wirken der Taube: Die Gottesprophetie der Zeitenwende* (Würzburg, 1998).

136. F. Majdalawi, ed., *The Noble Qur'an* (Brattleboro, Vt., 1999 [1412]) p. 153. Also see "Tā-Hā" XVI:20.120–21.

137. See Baudissin, "Die Symbolik der Schlange im Semitismus, insbesondere im Alten Testament," *Studien zur Semitischen Religionsgeschichte, Heft 1* (Leipzig, 1876) pp. 279–81.

138. See esp. K. van der Toorn, "The Theology of Demons," in *Die Dämonen,* pp. 65–66.

139. See F. Matchett, "The Taming of Kāliya: A Comparison of the Harivaṃśa, Viṣṇu-Purāṇa and Bhāgavata-Purāṇa Versions," *Religion* 16 (1986) 115–33.

140. The translation is by J. M. Baumgarten and D. Schwartz and published in *Damascus Document, War Scroll, and Related Documents* (Tübingen, 1995) vol. 2, p. 29.

141. In addition to the major works already cited, see E. Georgoula, gen. ed., *Greek Jewelry,* trans. T. Cullen et al. (Athens, 1999). See especially the following: a volute krater with a picture of a flute-playing Maenad wearing a snake bracelet on each arm (c. 410 BCE; Fig. 98); a pair of solid silver snake bracelets (fifth cent. BCE; Fig. 99); a solid silver bracelet ending with two snake heads with impressive details (fifth cent. BCE; Fig. 101); heavy silver bracelets with a pair of snakes (fifth cent. BCE; Fig. 102); a pair of solid silver earrings with loops in four snake heads (perhaps fifth cent. BCE; Fig. 103); pair of gold serpent bracelets—the serpents have marvelously detailed skins, head, mouth, and eyes (late Hellenistic Period; Fig. 174); gold bracelet with two ornate and sophisticated snake heads (second cent. BCE; Fig. 175); a gold snake ring with exceptional details of eyes, skin, and raised head (first cent. BCE or CE; Fig. 176); gold snake bracelet with amazing details of eyes, head, scales, and undulating tail section (first cent. CE; Fig. 177); Isis and Serapis Agathadaimon with snake bodies (Roman Period; Fig. 178); pair of gold bracelets with long serpent body and tail (first cent. BCE; Fig. 179); gold bracelet with two snake heads, exquisitely crafted with emerald in mouths and glass gems in eyes (first cent. CE; Fig. 184); and a gold Medusa medallion (second cent. CE; Fig. 188).

142. See D. Fotopoulos and A. Delivorrias, *Greece at the Benaki Museum* (Athens, 1997). Note especially the following: the gold bracelet with a serpent showing artistic and realistic details (first cent. BCE; no. 276); a gold ring in the form of a snake with detailed skin (first cent. BCE or CE; no. 284); gold chain necklace with the head of Medusa (second cent. CE; no. 279); and gold earrings, each with two serpents, boasting sapphires and pearls; from Antinoë, Egypt (fifth cent. CE; no. 366).

143. In addition to the ones already discussed, see the discussion and photographs in Maulucci, *The National Archaeological Museum of Naples,* pp. 66–67.

144. For the English translation, see A. C. Coxe *ANF* 2.269. For the Greek, see O. Stählin and U. Treu, *Clemens Alexandrinus* (Berlin, 1972) 1.231.

145. See N. I. Fredrikson, "La métaphore du sel et du serpent chez Aphraate, le Sage persan," *RHR* 219 (2002) 35–54.

146. *LivPro* 12:13; trans. D. R. A. Hare in *OTP* 2.394.

147. See the rabbinic sources collected by H. N. Bialik and Y. H. Ravnitzky and cited under "The Serpent and Sin," in *The Book of Legends: Sefer Ha-Aggadah,* trans. W. G. Braude (New York, 1922) pp. 20–21.

148. Archelaus, *The Acts of the Disputation with the Heresiarch Manes* 18; trans. S. D. F. Salmond, *ANF* 6, p. 191.

149. I am told it is unpublished. It is on public display on the second floor of the museum that is on the north side of the Acropolis in Athens.

150. See I. Tetzlaff, *Romanische Kapitelle in Frankreich: Löwe and Schlange, Sireene und Engel* (Cologne, 1979 [3rd ed.]), Illus. 67, Illus. 69, 70; see esp. pp. 99–100. The lion defeating the serpent is also featured in the sculpture by Antoine-Louis Barye (1833). See T. Flynn, *The Body of Scripture* (1998). In the Museo Arcivescovile in Ravenna is a depiction of Jesus Christ stepping on the heads of both a lion and a serpent. The Fourth Gospel is quoted *(ego sum via veritas et vita)*. See the illustration in G. Scaramuzza, G. Risegato, and C. Sterzi, *Ravenna Felix* (Ravenna, 1968) p. 23.

151. Aristotle incorrectly thought that large snakes close their eyes by using "the lower lid" (*Part. an.* 4.11 [691a]).

152. Etana, the first king mentioned in the Sumerian King list, is associated with a myth about an eagle and a serpent. The eagle defeats the serpent and carries Etana up into the heavens. See the discussion in G. S. Kirk, *Myth: Its Meaning and Functions in Ancient and Other Cultures* (Cambridge, 1970) pp. 125–26.

153. R. Wittkower, "Eagle and Serpent: A Study in the Migration of Symbols," *JWI* 2 (1938–1939) 293–325; esp. see the numerous photographs. I am grateful to the specialists at the Warburg Institute in London for helping me with my research into serpent symbolism. In his lengthy and erudite publication, Wittkower attempted to show that this symbol migrated. I am more persuaded that seeing an eagle swoop down and pick up a snake, especially a deadly one, was a common experience of humankind and, thus, the image does not have to be traced from the Mediterranean world to the Americas. There is no doubt that the iconography and culture of Babylon, Egypt, Greece, and Rome consecutively influenced symbolism in the land of Canaan and the Bible.

154. Ibid., photograph on p. 53.

155. MacCulloch, *ERE* 11.407.

156. In Rainer Maria Rilke's poem on "Schlangen-Beschwörung" we find again the fear of the serpent:
Dich feien keine Kräfte, / die Sonne gärt, das Fieber Fällt und trifft; / von böser Freude steilen sich die Schäfte, / und in den Schlangen glänzt das Gift. See R. M. Rilke, *Die Gedichte* (Himberg, Austria, 1986) p. 540.

157. See "Reptiles," in *The New Encyclopaedia Britannica: Micropaedia* (1992) vol. 26, p. 688.

158. Plutarch, *Alexander* 3.1–2(1); as cited by V. K. Robbins in *Ancient Quotes and Anecdotes* (Sonoma, Calif., 1989) p. 2.

159. The serpent dance by Nijinsky depicts the serpent as the tempter in a choreographically moving fashion. See the erotic and tempting movements of the serpent as pictured in A. Béjart, M. Béjart, and V. Markevitch, *Nijinsky: Clown de Dieu* (Paris, 1973); no pagination, but see the middle of the book. Paul Valéry's book *Die junge Parze* sometimes appears with a serpent wrapped around a column, and the 1922 edition of

Shakespeare's *Tragedy of Cymbeline* has as a title page a serpent stretched out under a picture of a woman. See the illustrations in U. Ott and F. Pfäfflin, eds., *"Fremde Nähe"*: *Celan als Übersetzer* (Marbach am Neckar, 1997) on pp. 281 and 418. The ballet based on Jean Cau, not John Milton, called *Paradise Lost,* depicts the first human's birth. With the appearance of the Serpent, "Eve" twists seductively so that Adam evidences sexual aggression, until he dances then jumps into a large mouth seen to belong to Eve. See G. Balanchine and F. Mason, *Balanchine's Festival of Ballet* (London, 1978) p. 410.

160. H. Breuil, *Quatre cents siècles d'art pariétal* (Montignac, 1952).

161. See H. Licht, *Sexual Life in Ancient Greece* (London, 1932) pp. 221–22.

162. Translated by H. Anderson in *OTP* 2.563.

163. This conceptual link between Paul and the author of 4 Mac was pointed out long ago by M. Dibelius in *Die Geisterwelt im Glauben des Paulus* (Göttingen, 1909) pp. 50–51.

164. R. H. Isaacs, *Animals in Jewish Thought and Tradition* (Northvale, N.J., 2000) p. 42. There is certainly much insightful information summarized, in a popular fashion, in Isaacs' book.

165. P. Haupt, "The Curse on the Serpent," *JBL* 35 (1916) 155–62; the quotation is on p. 162.

166. Buchholz, "Furcht vor Schlangen und Umgang mit Schlangen in Altsyrien, Altkypros und dem Umfeld"; "Im biblischen Volksglauben waren Schlangen unrein und umgenießbar" (p. 40).

167. See esp. Hunger, *Der Äskulapstab.*

168. See the excellent artwork displayed in the Archaeological Museum of Naples; it dates from the fourth century BCE.

169. See R. van den Broek, "Apollo," in *DDD*² 74–77.

170. See the marble statue of Apollo with his tripod, around which a snake is curled, in the Beirut National Museum; for a photograph, see N. Jidejian, *Lebanon: Its Gods, Legends and Myths* (a special printing of Banque Aud [Suisse], n.d.) p. 47.

171. For a discussion and images of goddesses with snakes, see L. Goodison and C. Morris, eds., *Ancient Goddesses* (London, 1998) see esp. pp. 86, 98, 123–32, 153.

172. See K. Koch, *Geschichte der ägyptischen Religion* (Stuttgart, Berlin, 1993) pp. 495–96.

173. Galen, *De simplicum medicamentorum temperamentis et facultatibus* 9; see P. Carus, *The History of the Devil and the Idea of Evil* (New York, 1996; originally published in 1900) pp. 227–28. Carus' work is severely dated.

174. The tripod of three entwined bronze serpents held a golden bowl. The object was taken to Constantinople by Constantine; parts of the bronze column can be seen in the Hippodrome Square before Hagia Sophia. As R. D. Barnett suggested, the Greek work was probably modeled on a Persian prototype, and a "connection of ideas between this group and the Greek votive tripod must surely be presumed." There seems to be some linkage, since the Elamite snake god does sit on a tripod with two entwined snakes (perhaps a third was hidden from view). Barnett, "The Serpent-Headed Tripod Base," *ErIsr* 19 (1987) 1. Also see B. S. Ridgway, "The Plataian Tripod and the Serpent Columns," *AJA* 81 (1977) 374–79. See the reconstruction of the tripod on p. 163 in Buchholz, "Furcht vor Schlangen und Umgang mit Schlangen in Altsyrien, Altkypros und dem Umfeld."

175. Inv. No. 9420. It is bronze, hollow cast, and a protome. It dates from the end of the Archaic Period or the first half of the fifth century BCE. It is 26 cm long. I am grateful to Dr. Elena C. Partida, archaeologist at Delphi, for pointing out this bronze ophidian

object. She is the author of *The Treasures at Delphi: An Architectural Study* (Jonsered, 2000). No ophidian objects were found at the area dedicated to Asclepius. No serpents should be expected to be found in or near the Temple of Apollo; he vanquished the python. Serpent realia found in situ at Delphi include the following: a snake ring-handle for a large cauldron (No. 2655), a bronze helmet showing an eagle with a serpent in its claws (no number available), three snakes on Athena's garment in the frieze of the treasury of Siphnos (525 BCE), a serpent handle for an oinoterion (no number), and another bronze handle with two snakes on the back (No. 4456). A gold Medusa holding two snakes was once part of a chryselephantine statue; see the color photograph in M. Carabatea, *The Archaeological Museum of Delphi*, trans. M. Carabatea (Athens, no date) p. 104, a.

176. The archaeologist at Delphi, Dr. Elena C. Partida, discussed serpent symbolism at Delphi with me. Virtually no evidence remains; in contrast to Epidaurus, the serpent was not worshipped at Delphi. Apollo slew the evil snake here. There is also no archaeological evidence for the Asclepian cult at Delphi mentioned by Plutarch.

177. See Herodotus, *Hist.* 8.41. Also see J. A. St. John, *The History of the Manners and Customs of Ancient Greece,* 3 vols. (London, 1842 [reprinted in 1971]) vol. 1 p. 83; cf. vol. 1, p. 363 and vol. 3, p. 209.

178. *HelSynPr* 12:31; trans. D. R. Darnell in *OTP* 2.691.

179. I define "the religion of Israel" to be broader than "the theology of the Old Testament (or TANAKH)."

180. See, e.g., the four silver-gilt Seraphim on the Book of Gospels (1645 CE) in the Monastery of Saint Stephen in Meteora. For color photographs (Monastery of St. Stephen), *The Treasures of the Monastery of Saint Stephen,* trans. D. Whitehouse (Meteora, 1999); see pp. 48–49.

181. See, e.g., T. M. Provatakis, *Meteora: History of the Monasteries and Monasticism* (Athens, 1991) pp. 7, 10.

182. Sister Theotekni, *Meteora: The Rocky Forest of Greece,* trans. Mrs. Despina (Meteora, 1986); see esp. pp. 9, 229; on p. 11 a "T," like a cross, with four flowers and wings, has a serpent curling up it (as if representing Num 21 and Jn 3).

183. See Aristotle, *Hist. an.* 4.4 (770a); A. L. Peck, *Aristotle: Generation of Animals* (LCL; London, Cambridge, Mass., 1943) pp. 422–423.

184. Notably, see D. Young, "With Snakes and Dates: A Sacred Marriage Drama at Ugarit," *UF* 9 (1977) 291–314, and R. Coote, "The Serpent and Sacred Marriage in Northwest Semitic Tradition," *HTR* 65 (1972) 594–95.

185. Eusebius, *PG* III.11 (114d); the translation is by Gifford in Eusebius, *Preparation for the Gospel*, p. 125.

186. See K. Kerényi, *Dioniso: Archetipo della vita indistruttibile,* ed. M. Kerényi (Milan, 1992); see esp. pp. 69–82. Dionysus symbolized for the Greeks wine, the bull, women, and the serpent (see p. 69).

187. See A. Dieterich, *Eine Mithrasliturgie* (Leipzig, 1903) pp. 125–26 and Küster, *Die Schlange in der griechischen Kunst und Religion,* p. 147.

188. See the coin with Antony and Octavian (obv) and the *cysta mystica* (rev) that is flanked by two large serpents (No. 608), and Antony (obv) and *cysta mystica* (rev) that is with two serpents (No. 607). For the photographs, see R. E. Levy and P. C. V. Bastien, *Roman Coins in the Princeton University Library* (Wetteren, Belgium, 1985).

189. Consult Küster, *Die Schlange in der griechischen Kunst und Religion,* p. 149. For a superb summary of the various meanings of ophidian symbols to which I am indebted, see J. A. MacCulloch, *ERE* (1920) 11.399–411.

190. Eusebius, *PG* II.3 (67a–b); see Gifford, trans., Eusebius, *Preparation for the Gospel,* p. 73.

191. Ibid.

192. Clement of Alexandria, *Exhortation to the Heathen* 2; trans. Coxe in *ANF* 2, p. 175. See G. W. Butterworth, *Clement of Alexandria* (LCL; Cambridge, Mass., 1919).

193. In Greece and Egypt, Bes and in Babylon Nergal are portrayed with a phallus that is a serpent.

194. See A. Esser, "Asklepios und Schlange," *FF* 24 (1948) 196–98.

195. I am influenced by the interpretation of Frazer; see J. G. Frazer, *The Golden Bough: A Study in Magic and Religion,* 12 vols. (London, 1911–1915 [3rd ed.]) vol. 5, p. 81.

196. On Artemis, see G. Mussies, "Artemis," in *DDD*² 91–97.

197. The image appears in many books; see, e.g., G. P. Carratelli, ed., *I Greci in Occidente* (Milan, 1996) p. 61.

198. See the Archeologico Regionale Cat. 362; Agrigento Museo. For a photograph, see Carratelli, *I Greci in Occidente,* p. 426.

199. A. M. Hocquenghem, "Les 'crocs' et les 'serpents': L'autorité absolue des ancêtres mythiques," in *Representations of Gods,* ed. H. G. Kippenberg (Leiden, 1983) pp. 58–74.

200. This is a point made by M. Hutter in "Schlange," in *LTK* (Freiburg, 2000) vol. 9, col. 153.

201. Küster, *Die Schlange in der griechischen Kunst und Religion,* pp. 137–53.

202. The ceramic pot is 21.5 cm wide (including handles), 12.5 cm high; the diameter, inside, of the opening is 14.4 cm.

203. See M.-L. and H. Erlenmeyer, "Über Schlangen-Darstellungen in der frühen Bildkunst des Alten Orients," *AfO* 23 (1970) 52–62.

204. Cf. Aristotle's use of "footless" (ἄπους); esp. see *Parts of Animals* 4.1 [676a], 4.11 [690b], and 4.13 [697a] and *Progression of Animals* 4 [705b], 8 [708a]; A. L. Peck, *Aristotle: Parts of Animals, Movements of Animals, Progression of Animals* (LCL; London, Cambridge, Mass., 1961) pp. 302–3, 392–93, 426–27, and 492–93, 504–7.

205. Egli, *Das Schlangensymbol,* pp. 31–58.

206. See esp. W. R. Halliday, *Greek Divination* (London, 1913) p. 90.

207. W. Foerster, "ὄφις," *TDNT* 5 (1967) 571. I shall later discuss Foerster's misrepresentation of snakes and serpent symbolism.

208. See J. Feliks, "Snake," in *EncJud* 15 (1971) cols. 14–15.

209. Also, one should not forget the serpent images on coins minted at Pergamon in the second and first centuries BCE. See, e.g., P. R. Franke, "Die Münzsammlung der Universität Erlangen-Nürnberg," *AA* 82 (1967) 67–92; esp. see the images on p. 83. For the Pergamon altar see esp. M. Kunze, *The Pergamon Altar* (Mainz, 1991) and E. Rohde, *Pergamon: Burgberg und Altar* (Berlin, 1976).

210. Agrippa was the son-in-law of Augustus; the Odeion was erected in about 15 BCE. Today one can see three of the original six huge Giants with anguipedes.

211. [Anonymous], "Fiery Serpents," *PEF* (January 1929) 58.

212. See Angier, "Venomous and Sublime," www.nytimes.com/2002/12/10/science/life/10VIPE.

213. See P. Chantraine, *Dictionnaire Étymologique de la Langue Grecque: Histoire des Mots* (Paris, 1968) p. 842.

214. See the comments in *The New Encyclopaedia Britannica: Macropaedia,* vol. 26, p. 692.

215. Another example appears to come from the beginning of third-century CE Ephesus; see H. Vetters, "Der Schlangengott," in *Studien zur Religion und Kultur Kleinasiens [Festschrift F. K. Dörner]* (Leiden, 1978) pp. 967–79.

216. The well-preserved Greek sculpture is on display in the Naples Archaeological Museum; see the photograph in F. P. Maulucci, *The National Archaeological Museum of Naples* (Naples, [2000?; no date]) p. 12. I am grateful to Professor Marcello del Verme for obtaining permission for me to work in the Naples Archaeological Museum.

217. G. Degeorge, *Palmyre* (Paris, 2001). See the color photograph on p. 195.

218. In *The Epitome of the Divine Institutes* 27, Lactantius calls the serpent "one of the servants of God."

219. I refer to a section of *b. Sanh.* 59b that is a Baraita.

220. R. Gersht in *Illness and Healing in Ancient Times,* trans. M. Rosovsky (Haifa, 1997 [2nd ed.]) p. 10.

221. Plutarch, *Demosthenes* 845; for the Greek and English translation, see H. N. Fowler, *Plutarch's Moralia* (LCL; Cambridge, Mass., London, 1936) pp. 418–19.

222. The noun οὐραῖος, "chieftain," is a loanword from Egypt; it is not related etymologically to οὐρά, "tail."

223. See esp. S. B. Johnson, *The Cobra Goddess of Ancient Egypt: Predynastic, Early Dynastic, and Old Kingdom Periods* (London, New York, 1990) pp. 3–33.

224. W. A. Ward, "The Four-winged Serpent on Hebrew Seals," *RSO* 42 (1968) 135–43; see esp. p. 143.

225. Egli, *Das Schlangensymbol,* pp. 119–43.

226. *aqys aywjd* in 13; cf. 58. The Greek recension has "the ravenous serpent" in 13 and "the fearful serpent" in 58. See J. Ferreira, *The Hymn of the Pearl* (Sydney, 2002).

227. I am influenced by T. H. Gaster's "The Serpent as Guardian," *Myth, Legend, and Custom in the Old Testament* (New York, 1969) p. 35.

228. See the color photograph in S. Shifra and J. Klein, *In Those Distant Days: Anthology of Mesopotamian Literature in Hebrew* (Tel Aviv, 1996 [in Hebrew]) in the color section following p. 504.

229. For text and translation, see D. R. Frayne's article in *JAOS* 102 (1982) 511–13.

230. See the sources cited by L. W. King in *A History of Babylon* (New York, 1914) p. 72.

231. M. Lichtheim in *Context* 1.77.

232. Lichtheim in *Context* 1.82.

233. See the photograph in R. Hachlili and Y. Meshorer, *Highlights from the Collection of the Reuben and Edith Hecht Museum* (Haifa, 1986, 1990) p. 55.

234. The limestone capital is on display in the Limassol Museum. For photographs, see P. Aupert, *Guide to Amathus,* trans. D. Buitron-Oliver and A. Oliver (Nicosia, 2000) p. 29 and back cover.

235. Plutarch, *Demosthenes* 26.6–7 (4–5); as cited by Robbins in *Ancient Quotes and Anecdotes,* p. 411.

236. See Cook, *Zeus,* vol. 2, part 2, pp. 1060–61 and Fig. 914 on p. 1061.

237. See L. Bodson, "Nature et fonctions des serpents d'Athéna," in *Mélanges Pierre Lévêque,* edited by M.-M. Mactoux and E. Geny (Paris, 1990) pp. 45–62.

238. Museo Archeologico di Pithecusae; Case 34, no. 1 (Inv. 166442).

239. See M. L. Robert, "Dans une maison d'Éphèse: Un serpent et un chiffre," *CRAI*, 126–32; esp. see p. 129.

240. I. Malkin devotes two of his four paragraphs on the "snake" to stress only the guardian aspect of ophidian symbolism in Greece, as if it were more important or dominant than others, such as healing in the Asclepian cult (which he mentions in one sentence). See "snakes," in *OCD*, pp. 1417–18.

241. See the photograph of Bernini's masterpiece in *The Capitoline Museums* (p. 112); it emphasizes the menacing snakes.

242. See, e.g., D. Leeming with M. Leeming, *A Dictionary of Creation Myths* (New York, Oxford, 1995); see esp. pp. 5, 7, 21, 39, et passim.

243. See Winter, *Frau und Göttin;* esp. see Illus. 37, 42, 123, 124, 355, 359, 379, and 469.

244. See B. L. Goff, *Symbols of Prehistoric Mesopotamia* (New Haven, London, 1963). Also, consult K. G. Stevens, *De iconografie van de slang in Mesopotamië vanaf het vijfde millennium voor Christus tot het einde van de Akkadische periode, Magisterarbeit,* 2 vols. [unpublished dissertation, 1984; see the following entry]; and Stevens, "Eine Ikonographische Untersuchung der Schlange im Vorgeschichtlichen Mesopotamien," in *Archaeologia Iranica et Orientalis: Miscellanea in Honorem Louis Vanden Berghe,* ed. L. De Meyer and E. Haerninck (Leuven, 1989) 1–32.

245. A. Falkenstein, W. von Soden, *Sumerische und akkadische Hymnen und Gebete* (Stuttgart, 1953).

246. See esp. C. Hentze, "Die Zerstückelte Schlange," *Antaios* 9 (1968) 253–61.

247. I have avoided the use of words like oviparity (egg laying) and ovoviviparity (egg hatching) because the terms seem onerous in the present work and because such distinctions prove to be misleading and arbitrary.

248. Beyerlin, *Near Eastern Religious Texts Relating to the Old Testament,* p. 7.

249. Beyerlin, ibid., p. 12.

250. See, e.g., G. Infusino, "La creazione del mondo," *Storia, miti e leggende dei Campi Flegrei* (Naples, 1995) pp. 70–77. See esp. the modern depiction of Eurinome embraced by the great serpent Ofione on p. 73.

251. Cairo Museum no. 1321.

252. See A. Piankoff, *The Shrines of Tut-ankh-amon,* ed. N. Rambova (New York, 1955) vol. 2, p. 120 (italics removed); for the exterior left panel, see Fig. 41. Also see the Ouroboros in the papyrus of Her-Uben A; see Fig. 3 in Piankoff, trans., *Mythological Papyri: Texts,* ed. N. Rambova (New York, 1957) vol. 1, p. 22.

253. Eusebius *PG* 40c; ibid.

254. See Keel, *The Symbolism of the Biblical World,* p. 188.

255. See the comments about the Menorah by C. Meyers, *The Tabernacle Menorah* (Missoula, Mont., 1976) and "Lampstand," *AYBD* 4.141–43.

256. For a discussion of the base and the controversial use of images, see M. Haran and H. Strauss, "Menorah," *EncJud* (1971) 11.1363–66. One cannot be certain that the base is original; conceivably, it was added by a Roman artist as it traveled to Rome or in Rome. Yet it is equally conceivable that Herod had the base added, perhaps to repair it.

257. See Haran and Strauss, "Menorah," *EncJud* (1971) 11.1355–70; esp. Fig. 1 beneath cols. 1355–56.

258. See the menorah with an apparent snake beneath and to the left of it on a stone from the catacomb Vigna Randanini. See E. R. Goodenough, "The Menorah Among Jews of the Roman World," *HUCA* 23 (1950–1951) vol. 2, pp. 449–92; esp. Fig. 7.

259. Shiva is also one of the gods who achieve life in dying. Serpent iconography and symbology help the devotee to symbolize Shiva. See D. Shulman, "The Serpent and the Sacrifice: An Anthill Myth from Tiruvārūr," *HR* 18 (1978) 107–37.

260. On the power of the serpent, see L. Silburn, "Il serpente del profondo," *La kuṇḍalinī o l'energia del profondo*, trans. F. Sferra (Milan, 1997) pp. 39–52, 401.

261. See the reflections by G. Krishna in *Kundalini: L'Energia evolutiva nell'uomo* (Rome, 1971 p. 57.

262. The word "bradisismo" (etymologically Greek) denotes the rise and fall of the land due to seismic and volcanic forces ("le oscillazioni alternanti della costa terrestre") in and near Pozzuoli, which is a northwestern suburb of Naples. See M. Sirpettino, *Il bradisismo di Pozzuoli* (Naples, 1983). The Italian is from this book, p. 19. The Greeks called the area Campi Flegrei, "burning fields." It was a special area for the early Romans, especially Nero and the Flavians. See G. Infusino, *Storia, miti e leggende dei Campi Flegrei* (Naples, 1995). The serpent symbol is grounded in myths and legends of this area, which is so charming that Horace could write, *nullus in orbis sinus Bais praelucit amoenis:* "Nowhere on earth is a gulf as lovely as the pleasant Baiae."

263. S. Muratore has been focusing on the modern advances in cosmology and their impact on theology. See his *L'Evoluzione cosmologica e il problema di Dio* (Rome, 1993).

264. M. Lurker in *ER* 13. 372.

265. Translated by R. K. Ritner in *Context* 1. 32.

266. See L. Kákosy, "The Astral Snakes of the Nile," *MDAI* 37 (1981) 255–60. I am grateful to Professor David Aune for this reference.

267. Keel, *The Symbolism of the Biblical World*, pp. 26–27.

268. R. S. Hendel, in *DDD*[2] 745.

269. See, e.g., E. Hornung, *Idea into Image: Essays on Ancient Egyptian Thought*, trans. E. Bredeck (Princeton, 1992) pp. 49–67.

270. A. H. Krappe, *La genèse des mythes* (Paris, 1952) p. 18.

271. See e.g., J. Bailey, K. McLeish, and D. Spearman, eds., "The Rainbow Snake," *Gods and Men: Myths and Legends from the World's Religions* (Oxford, New York, 1981) pp. 12–15.

272. For sources and discussions, see MacCulloch in *ERE* 11.408.

273. LSJM, p. 448; Lane, *An Arabic-English Lexicon* Book I, Part 1 (1863) p. 681; R. Payne Smith, *Thesaurus Syriacus* (Oxford, 1879) vol. 1, col. 1210; Glare, *Oxford Latin Dictionary* (1982, 1988) 1744–45.

274. *Commentary* on Virgil's *Georgics* 1.205. I am indebted to G. St. Clair for this citation. See his "The Subtle Serpent," *JTS* 7 (1906) 40–50.

275. Vatican Museum, Rome; for a color photograph, see J. Martin, *Das alte Rom* (Munich, 1994) pp. 390–91.

276. See U. Holmberg, *Der Baum des Lebens* (Bern, 1996) p. 82, Abb. 34.

277. Epiphanius, *Pan.* 26.40.

278. H. Jonas, *Gnosis und spätantiker Geist* (Göttingen, 1934) pp. 221–62. Also see Jonas, *The Gnostic Religion* (Boston, 1963 [rev. ed.]) pp. 91–97.

279. See the picture in Charlesworth, "Jewish Interest in Astrology During the Hellenistic and Roman Period," *ANRW* II 20.2 (1987) 926–50.

280. See Plutarch, *De Iside et Osiride* 74; also see A. Dieterich, *Eine Mithrasliturgie,* p. 71.

281. See the sculpture in the Capitoline museums; see the picture in *The Capitoline Museums,* p. 58.

282. My italics; as quoted by Wittkower, *JWI* 2 (1938–1939) p. 325.

283. For this and the preceding quotation respectively see L. E. Stager, "Jerusalem and the Garden of Eden," pp. 183 and 188–189.

284. About 1,500 figurines have been found in Jerusalem, dating from the eighth century BCE. Images of a hyena, gazelle, ibex, hippopotamus, sheep, and cow have been discovered. Most images are horses. No snake has been recovered from controlled excavations, according to my knowledge.

285. See the reflections by J. E. Saraceni and the report from the Archaeological Institute of America in http://www.archaeology.org/9611/newsbriefs/serpentmound .html.

286. British Museum 128887. See E. Strommenger, with photographs by M. Hirmer, *The Art of Mesopotamia* (London, 1964); for a photography see plate 38, and for the discussion p. 388.

287. Paris, Louvre AO 190. Strommenger and Hirmer, *The Art of Mesopotamia,* see the photograph in Plate 144, and discussion on p. 414.

288. See esp. Pseudo-Apollodorus, *Library* 3.177.

289. Halliday, *Greek Divination,* p. 87.

290. Wellhausen, *Prolegomena* (1905 [4th ed.]) p. 313.

291. J. Ph. Vogel pointed out that "genuine ophiolatry" is still preserved in southern India. See his "Serpent Worship in Ancient and Modern India," *AcOr* (1924) 279–312.

292. J. Coppens, "La dame-serpent du Sinaï," *ETL* 24 (1948) 409–12.

293. H. Frankfort, "Gods and Myths on Sargonid Seals," *Iraq* 1 (1934) 2–29.

294. PrJac 8; translated by Charlesworth in *OTP* 2.721.

295. Eusebius, *PG* I.10 (40a); the translation is by Gifford in *Preparation for the Gospel,* p. 46.

296. Eusebius *PG* 40c; ibid.

297. Consult A. Gardiner, "Sect. I. Amphibious Animals, Reptites, etc.," in *Egyptian Grammar* (London, 1927, 1964) pp. 475–76.

298. See A. Erman and H. Grapow, eds., *Wörterbuch der Aegyptischen Sprache* (Leipzig, 1926) vol. 1, p. 576. Also see esp. S. Schoske and D. Wildung, "112 Nechbet" in *Gott und Götter im alten Ägypten* (Mainz am Rhein, 1992) p. 165.

299. See, in addition to the many works already cited, P. F. Houlihan, "Serpents, Scorpions, and Scarabs," *The Animal World of the Pharaohs* (London, 1996) pp. 168–94; esp. the picture on p. 170.

300. See the large depictions of Zeus with the body of a serpent in Cook, *Zeus, God of the Bright Sky,* vol. 1, p. 359.

301. For the Greek and English see H. W. Attridge and R. A. Oden, *Philo of Byblos: The Phoenician History* (Washington, D.C., 1981) pp. 66–67.

302. Eusebius, *PG* 1.10.49.

303. E. Amiet, "Glyptique élamite à propos de documents nouveaux," *Arts Asiatiques* 26 (1973).

304. See Ridgway, "The Plataian Tripod and the Serpent Columns," and R. D. Barnett, "The Serpent-Headed Tripod Base," *ErIsr* 19 (1987).

305. See the similar insights of M.-L.Henry in "Schlange," *BHH* (1966) vol. 3, cols. 1699–1701; esp. see col. 1701.

306. See Buchhotz, *UF* 32 (2000) 81.

307. *ERE* 11.399.

308. See Küster's collection of ancient sources and reflections on "die Schlange als Seelentier" in his *Die Schlange in der griechischen Kunst und Religion,* p. 64.

309. W. Burkert, *Greek Religion: Archaic and Classical,* trans. J. Raffan (Oxford, 1985) p. 195.

310. Plutarch, *Cleomenes* 39; Ovid, *Metam.* 15.389; Pliny, *Nat.* 10.84 [64].

311. For a color photograph of Hydra from a Greek urn from the sixth century BCE, see J. Boardman et al., *Die Griechische Kunst* (Munich, 1992) Plate 13. The book is full of images of serpents. For an appreciably different understanding of Hydra's appearance, see the catacomb on the Via Latina, Rome; for a photograph, see J. Gray, *Near Eastern Mythology* (London, New York, 1969) p. 11.

312. Küster, *Die Schlange in der griechischen Kunst und Religion,* pp. 85–100.

313. For the Greek and English translation, see W. Scott, *Hermitica* (Oxford, 1924) vol. 1, pp. 504–7.

314. According to Sozomen, two serpents can be seen below ground in Palestine beside two coffins (*Ecclesiastical History* 9.17).

315. See also Halliday, *Greek Divination,* pp. 84–85.

316. See E. Porada, *Man and Images in the Ancient Near East* (Wakefield, R.I., London, 1995) pp. 39, 40, 42, 43, 45, 46, and 63. For the Coffin Texts, see Clark, *Myth and Symbol in Ancient Egypt,* p. 51.

317. A. Niwiński, "The 21st Dynasty Religious Iconography Project Exemplified by the Scene with Three Deities Standing on a Serpent," *Akten des Vierten Internationalen Ägyptologen Kongresses München 1985,* ed. S. Schoske (Hamburg, 1989) pp. 305–14.

318. Egli, *Das Schlangensymbol,* pp. 72–118.

319. S. N. Kramer, ed., *Mythologies of the Ancient World* (Garden City, N.Y., 1961) p. 30.

320. I am indebted here to many specialists, esp. Kramer, *Mythologies of the Ancient World,* p. 150.

321. Corn was not known to the Egyptians. It was introduced into Western culture by the Native Americans. In British English, "corn" means "wheat" or "grain."

322. M. Lurker, *The Gods and Symbols of Ancient Egypt* (London, 1980) p. 108.

323. See esp. K. Sethe, *Amun und die Acht Urgötter von Hermopolis* (Berlin, 1929) p. 26.

324. Evans, *The Palace of Minos,* vol. 1, 3, p. 500.

325. A. Golan, *Myth and Symbol,* p. 106.

326. Küster, *Die Schlange in der griechischen Kunst und Religion,* p. 62.

327. When fishing with my son on the Potomac River, I saw a large water snake swim past our boat and crawl up onto land. After sunning itself on a branch, it moved through the grass. The other fishermen nearby were excited because they assumed it was a moccasin.

328. Consult S. W. Greaves, "Wordplay and Associative Magic in the Ugaritic Snake-bite Incantation RS 24.244," *UF* 26 (1994) 165–67.

329. *ERE* 11.400.

330. See the picture in H. Koester, *History, Culture, and Religion of the Hellenistic Age* (New York, Berlin, 1982) p. 204.

331. Halliday, *Greek Divination,* p. 86.

332. F. Majdalawi, ed., *The Noble Qur'an,* p. 368.

333. See the new insights from herpetologists in Angier's "Venomous and Sublime: The Viper Tells Its Tale," *New York Times* 10 December 2002.

334. See especially Johnson, *Lady,* p. 122.

335. Keimer, *Histoires de serpents dans l'Égypte ancienne et moderne,* pp. 26–36.

336. See J. Cooper's brief note in *Revue d'Assyriologie et d'Archéologie Orientale* 4 (1898) 94.

337. Lichtheim in *Context* 1.83–84.

338. Fragment 1.25. For the Greek, see F. Jacoby, *Die Fragmente der Griechischen Historiker* (Leiden, 1958) third part, p. 371.

339. For the translation, see E. R. Hodges, *Cory's Ancient Fragments* (London, 1876) p. 58.

340. H. Leisegang, "Das Mysterium der Schlange," in *Eranos-Jahrbuch 1939,* pp. 151–252.

341. Halliday, *Greek Divination,* p. 84.

342. Note: the owl-eyed symbols for Athena, the goddess of wisdom, who is shown with snakes; cf. II.4.

343. *TDNT* 5 (1967) 567.

344. I wish to note that the serpent does not appear in the Song of Solomon and the eyes mentioned are "dove's eyes" (1:15, 4:1, 5:12). In 7:4 we find a comparison between the lover's eyes and "the pools in Heshbon."

345. See Lane, *Arabic-English Lexicon,* Book I, Part 1 (1863) p. 681.

346. See http://www.nvva.nl/swertz, though the name Cobra does not appear.

347. On the Ophites, see Appendix IV and Chapter 7.

348. See Philo, *Leg.* 2.71–74. For the Greek and English translation, see F. H. Colson and G. H. Whitaker, *Philo* (LCL; Cambridge, Mass., London, 1991) vol. 1, pp. 268–69. Also see P. Cazier, "Du serpent et de l'arbre de la connaissance: Lectures patristiques (Philon, Grégoire de Nysse, Jean Chrysostome, Augustin)," *Graphè* 4 (1995) 73–103; esp. pp. 84–87.

349. *ApMos* 16–17; trans. M. D. Johnson in *OTP* 2.277–78.

350. See J. Tabick, "The Snake in the Grass: The Problems of Interpreting a Symbol in the Hebrew Bible and Rabbinic Writings," *Religion* 16 (1986) 155–67.

351. Le Grande Davies, "Serpent Imagery in Ancient Israel: The Relationship Between the Literature and the Physical Remains" (PhD diss., Utah, 1986) p. 31.

352. Ibid. pp. 25–26.

353. L. H. Silberman, "Paul's Viper," *Foundations and Facets Forum* 8 (1992) 247–53; the quotation is on p. 252. Silberman was commenting on Acts 28:3–6.

354. See P. Grimal, *Dictionnaire de la mythologie grecque et romaine* (Paris, 1963 [3rd ed.]) p. 80.

355. *The Penguin Dictionary of Symbols* (London, New York, 1996) p. 851.

356. The Hebrew is from A. Z. Steinberg et al., eds., *Midrash Rabbah: Sepher Br'shyt* (Jerusalem, 1984) vol. 1, p. qmw.

357. H. Freedman, trans., *Midrash Rabbah* (London, 1951) p. 76. Also, see the collection of snake stories chosen to prove that even snakes are included in God's creation and carry out God's purpose.

358. I am grateful to Chevalier and Gheerbrant for this citation; see their *The Penguin Dictionary of Symbols,* p. 857.

359. *ERE* 11.399.

360. Also see M. Ullmann, ed., *Das Schlangenbuch des Hermes Trismegistos* (Wiesbaden, 1994).

361. There is no number on the piece of sculpture.

362. Doceticism denotes the heresy that claims Jesus only seemed to be human. On the Ophites' belief in a nonhistorical version of Christianity, see R. Liechtenhan, "Ophiten," in *RE* 14 (1904) 404–13; see esp. p. 410.

363. I am influenced by a comment by Lloyd-Russell in "The Serpent as the Prime Symbol of Immortality Has Its Origin in the Semitic-Sumerian Culture" (PhD diss., Los Angeles, 1938) p. 54.

364. Egli, *Das Schlangensymbol,* pp. 58–71.

365. See Lane, *Arabic-English Lexicon* Book I, Part 1 (1863) ad loc. cit.

366. F. Steingass, *A Comprehensive Persian-English Dictionary* (London, 1892, 1947) p. 434.

367. Payne Smith, *Thesaurus Syriacus,* vol. 1, col. 1254 and col. 1210; *LexSyr,* pp. 173, 220.

368. It is possible that *ḥawwāh* meant "snake" in Old Hebrew (not biblical Hebrew) as I argue in Appendix I; see, e.g., *LexSyr,* p. 220a.

369. See A. Sharma, "The Significance of Viṣṇu Reclining on the Serpent," *Religion* 16 (1986) 101–14.

370. R. Girard, *Le Popol-Vuh: Histoire culturelle des Maya-Quiché* (Paris, 1954) p. 269.

371. See the similar comments by M.-L. Henry in "Schlange," *BHH* (1966) vol. 3, cols. 1699–1701; the quotation is in col. 1700.

372. See esp. Buchholz, "Schlangen und Wasser," *UF* 32 (2000) 43–46.

373. A. Golan, "Snake-Water," in *Myth and Symbol: Symbolism in Prehistoric Religions* (Jerusalem, 1991) p. 101.

374. See esp. P. de Miroschedji, "Le dieu Élamite au serpent et aux eaux jaillissantes," *Iranica Antiqua* 16 (1981) 1–25, eleven plates.

375. It may seem surprising that not one serpent has been found on Jewish ossuaries, but these categorically come with floral designs. The appearance of the fish-like graffiti on them is challenging. See P. Figueras, *Decorated Jewish Ossuaries* (Leiden, 1983) esp. pp. 105–6.

376. See, e.g., G. Rondelet, *L'histoire entière des poisons* (Paris, 2002 [originally 1558]) vol. 1, pp. 316–17; vol. 2, pp. 168–69.

377. See Golan, *Myth and Symbol,* p. 104.

378. See F. A. M. Wiggerman, "Transtigridian Snake Gods," in *Sumerian Gods and Their Representations,* edited by I. L. Finkel and M. J. Geller (Groningen, 1997) pp. 33–55.

379. See MacCulloch's data in *ERE* 11.403.

380. *ERE* 11.399.

381. G. Azarpay, "The Snake-Man in the Art of Bronze Age Bactria," *Bulletin of the Asia Institute* NS 5 (1991) 1–10; the quotation is on p. 6.

382. See W. H. Mare, "Serpent's Stone," *AYBD* 5.116–17.

383. See Appendix I.

384. Text UT 62.50; see C. H. Gordon, *Ugaritic Literature* (Rome, 1949) p. 49.

385. At Palmyra there is a stone carving of two mounted heroes on either side of a dignitary, above whom is a long serpent. See the picture in E. Will, "Les aspects de l'intégration des divinités orientales dans la civilization Gréco-Romaine," *Mythologie Gréco-Romaine, Mythologies Périphériques: Études d'iconographie,* ed. L. Kahil and C. Augé (Paris, 1981) pp. 157–61; Plate I, bottom.

386. See Küster, "Die Schlange als Wasserdämon," *Die Schlange in der griechischen Kunst und Religion,* pp. 153–57.

387. See, e.g., F. Herrmann, *Symbolik in den Religionen der Naturvölker* (Stuttgart, 1961) esp. pp. 106–41.

388. I visited Cyprus after completing the previous chapters. In the Museum of Kykkos on Cyprus, I found a black-polished ceramic vessel with a serpent on it. It dates to approximately 2000–1850 BCE. The beak-shaped spout has the representation of a serpent. It has five curves. No physical features are indicated. The appliquéd serpent is inferior to the quality of the jug (Δ 113).

389. Cf. 2.18 and 2.24.

390. Cf. 2.17.

391. Cf. 2.5.

392. Emile Puech and Kevin McCaffrey killed a viper in the garden of the Ecole Biblique de Jérusalem; the garden is near and above the ancient and modern tombs.

393. Pliny, *Nat.* 7.172; also see Küster, *Die Schlange in der griechischen Kunst und Religion,* pp. 62–72.

394. See R. de Vaux, *Ancient Israel: Its Life and Institutions,* trans. J. McHugh (London, 1961) p. 44.

395. See the general reflections by W. A. Jayne in *The Healing Gods of Ancient Civilizations* (New Haven, 1925) pp. 222–85.

396. J. Maringer, "Die Schlange in Kunst und Kult der vorgeschichtlichen Menschen," *Anthropos* 72 (1977) 881–920.

397. R. Jackson, *Doctors and Diseases in the Roman Empire* (London, 1988).

398. Also see H. Sobel, *Hygieia: Die Göttin der Gesundheit* (Darmstadt, 1990); see esp. the forty illustrations (numbered per page); most important, see 3b (Hygieia, Asclepius, and a large serpent), 7a, 8b, 9a, 11b (Hygieia with a serpent), 18a (Hygieia, Asclepius, and the serpent).

399. Ovid, *Metamorphoses,* ed. F. J. Miller (LCL; London, New York, 1916) vol. 2, pp. 410–11.

400. Eusebius, *PG* III.14 (124a); Gifford, trans., Eusebius, *Preparation for the Gospel,* p. 135.

401. For a photograph, see E. Dvorjetski, "Properties of Therapeutic Baths in Eretz-Israel in Antiquity," in *Illness and Healing in Ancient Times,* p. 42.

402. For another (color) photograph, see Y. Meshorer, *TestiMoney* (Jerusalem, 2000) p. 50.

403. See H. Vincent and F.-M. Abel, *Jérusalem* (Paris, 1926) vol. 2, Plate LXVII, image V.

404. See the photographs in R. Gersht, "Gods of Medicine in the Greek and Roman World," in *Illness and Healing in Ancient Times,* pp. 8, 9, and 12.

405. See S. V. McCasland, "The Asklepios Cult in Palestine," *JBL* 58 (1939) 221–27; esp. p. 224.

406. B. O. Foster, *Livy* (LCL; London, New York, 1926) vol. 4, pp. 540–43.

407. See Livy, Book 11, summary.

408. S. R. F. Price in *The Augustan Empire, 43 B.C.–A.D. 69,* ed. A. K. Bowman et al. (Cambridge, [2nd ed.]) p. 812.

409. See M. Hamilton, *Incubation* (St. Andrews, London, 1906).

410. R. Parker in *The Oxford History of the Classical World,* ed. J. Boardman, J. Griffin, and O. Murray (Oxford, New York, 1986) 267.

411. Pliny, *Nat.* 29.71.

412. Far too often studies of sickness and health in the New Testament focus on how Jesus cast out demons and represented God's will in his actions and fail to see the importance of ophidian symbolism and the pervasive influence of the Asclepian cult and Asclepius in the first century. Such a blindness characterizes such works as F. Fenner's *Die Krankheit im Neuen Testament* (Leipzig, 1930).

413. I am grateful to Jacob Milgrom for this information.

414. Far more common in Rabbinics is the fear of the snake who poisons fruit and water. See the discussions in J. Preuss, *Biblical and Talmudic Medicine,* trans. F. Rosner (Northvale, N.J., London, 1978, 1993); see "Snake" in the Index. This classic is quite dated; Preuss lived from 1861 to 1913.

415. See P. D. Miller, "Fire in the Mythology of Canaan and Israel," *CBQ* 27 (1965) 256–61. The burning of Jerusalem was perceived to be purification of the city (viz. Jer 21:10, 32:29). See Exod 29:14; Lev 4:12, 4:21, 16:27; Ezek 43:21, and esp. Num 19:5 and Deut 21:1–9 (the burning of the red heifer). Note also the rules for burning and thus purifying the clothes that were contaminated or infected (Lev 13:52, 13:55). The burning of the Canaanite altars and gods and goddesses was a purifying of the land (Deut 7:5, 25; 12:3, Jer 43:12–13) that also demanded a burning of their cities (viz. Deut 13:16; Josh 11:6, 13 [*bis*]). I note that Le Grande Davies also suggests that "burning-serpents" in Num 21 had a cleansing connotation: "The serpents of the wilderness acted as 'servants' of YHWH to help cleanse Israel of its 'refuse.' " "Serpent Imagery in Ancient Israel," p. 104.

416. I am grateful to E. E. Urbach for conversations on the meaning of stoning among the Jews.

417. Pseudo-Apollodorus, *Library* 1.96.

418. Halliday, *Greek Divination,* pp. 82–83.

419. Ambrose, *Of the Christian Faith* 16.131e; trans. H. De Romestin, "Of the Christian Faith," *NPNF2* 10, p. 261.

420. Jung, *Man and His Symbols,* p. 153.

421. J. L. Henderson and M. Oakes. *The Wisdom of the Serpent: The Myths of Death, Rebirth, and Resurrection* (New York, 1963; repr. Princeton, 1990) p. 154.

422. Ibid., p. 156.

423. For the Greek text, translation, and commentary, see M. D. Reeve, "A Rejuvenated Snake," *Acta Antiqua: Academiae Scientiarum Hungaricae* 37 (1996/1997) 245–58.

424. For the following examples, I am indebted to Reeve, *Acta Antiqua: Academiae Scientiarum Hungaricae* 37 (1996/1997) 245.

425. See Lloyd-Russell, "The Serpent as the Prime Symbol of Immortality," esp. pp. iii, 9, 64, 66, 67, 77, 85, 90.

426. See C. Virolleaud, "Die Idee der Wiedergeburt bei den Phöniziern," *Uranos-Jahrbuch 1939,* ed. O. Fröbe-Kapteyn (Rhein, 1940) pp. 21–60.

427. See Eliade, *Patterns in Comparative Religion,* p. 165.

428. See Lloyd-Russell, "The Serpent as the Prime Symbol of Immortality," p. 79.

429. P. A. Piccione, "Mehen, Mysteries, and Resurrection from the Coiled Serpent," *Journal of the American Center in Egypt* 27 (1990) 43–52. Also see T. Kendall, *Passing Through the Netherworld: The Meaning and Play of Senet, an Ancient Egyptian Funerary Game* (Belmont, Mass., 1978). Kendall, "Schlangenspiel," *Lexicon der Ägyptologie* 5.1 (1983) 654–55.

430. Lloyd-Russell, "The Serpent as the Prime Symbol of Immortality," p. 90.

431. Foster in *Context* 1.458.

432. Albright, "The Goddess of Life and Wisdom," p. 258.

433. For the two quotations, respectively, see S. A. B. Mercer, *The Pyramid Texts in Translation and Commentary* (New York, London, 1952) vol. 3, pp. 237 and 302.

434. See S. Reinach, "Zagreus, le serpent cornu," *RAr* 3rd ser. 35 (1899) 210–17.

435. *DACL* 6 (1950) col. 1357.

436. An unrecognized serpent pin may be shown in M. Spaer, *Ancient Glass in the Israel Museum* (Jerusalem, 2001) p. 263. See the Adam, woman, and serpent pendant on p. 180 (no. 366) and Medusa disk on p. 254.

437. See L. Keimer, *Remarques sur le tatouage dans l'Égypte ancienne* (Cairo, 1948) esp. p. 32 and p. 86 (Fig. 67).

438. See esp. Figueras, "A Comprehensive Approach to the Question of Symbolism," in *Decorated Jewish Ossuaries,* pp. 83–86.

439. Also see the depiction of Triptolemus in a chariot pulled by winged serpents in the Vatican. For a photograph, see W. Zschietzschmann, *Hellas und Rom: Eine Kulturgeschichte des Altertums in Bildern* (Tübingen, 1959) p. 13.

440. A. D. Nock, *Essay on Religion and the Ancient World,* ed. Z. Stewart (Oxford, 1972) p. 906.

441. Consult P. Montet, "Le jeu du serpent," *ChrEg* 30 (1955) 189–97.

442. I am indebted to MacCulloch for this information. See *ERE* 11.400.

443. Among the animals most represented in mosaics is the snake; consult H. Lavagne et al., eds., *Mosaïque* (Paris, 2000) p. 45.

444. See the mosaics juxtaposed in J. Leipoldt, *Bilder zum neutestamentlichen Zeitalter* in J. Leipoldt and W. Grundmann, eds., *Umwelt des Urchristentums,* 3 vols. (Berlin, 1971) vol. 3, Plates 74 and 75. The book is replete with images of serpents.

445. See the photograph in *Depictions of Animals from the Leo Mildenberg Collection* (Haifa, 1999) p. 54 (Fig. 94).

446. Surely, no one should imagine that I am implying that snakes do not die. The facts are that we often see the skins of snakes in the forest, but we almost never find a dead snake.

447. The snake has no urinary bladder, but an anus. Snakes need to conserve the water they ingest, passing on waste as virtually a solid mass that had been stored in the cloaca. I am pointing to the contrasts between snakes and humans and other animals, like horses, cows, and dogs (who often seem to urinate almost constantly). Snakes usually are odorless, but some species, like the water snakes (*Natrix*) and garter snakes (*Thamnophis*), emit foul smells from anal glands as a defense mechanism. See *The New Encyclopedia Britannica: Macropaedia,* vol. 26, pp. 693 and 696.

448. *Antiken Denkm.* (1850) vol. 2, p. 264; as cited by Küster at the commencement of his *Die Schlange in der griechischen Kunst und Religion,* p. 1. Also see the similar insights provided by M. Provera in "Il tema e culto del serpente nella tradizione biblica e profana," *BeO* 166 (1990) 209–14.

449. In his encyclopedia on symbols, H. Biedermann rightly begins his entry on serpent symbolism by stressing its complex contradictory symbolic power. Biedermann, *Enciclopedia dei Simboli* (Milan, 2001) p. 483.

450. *Meaning in the Visual Arts*, p. 32. I am indebted to E. H. Gombrich who highlighted this caveat. See his "Introduction: Aims and Limits of Iconology," in *Symbolic Images: Studies in the Art of the Renaissance* (Oxford, 1972 [3rd ed.]) pp. 1–22. I am grateful to the director of the Warburg Institute, London, for discussions on iconology and for drawing my attention to Gombrich's work.

6. Serpent Symbolism in the Hebrew Bible

1. See, e.g., J. Maringer, "Die Schlange in Kunst und Kult der vorgeschichtlichen Menschen," *Anthropos* 72 (1977) 881–920.

2. See P. Joüon, "Le grand dragon, l'ancien serpent," *RSR* 17 (1927) 444–46; B. Renz, *Der orientalische Schlangendrache* (Augsburg, 1930); W. Foerster, "δράκων," *TDNT* 3 (1964) 281–83.

3. See W. Foerster, "ἔχιδνα," *TDNT* 2 (1964) 815–16.

4. See Appendix II and Foerster, "ὄφις," *TDNT* 5 (1967) 566–71.

5. See the reflections by many who study symbolism; notably, consult G. Busi in his *Mistica Ebraica*, ed. G. Busi and E. Loewenthal (Turin, 1995) p. xii.

6. H. and H. A. Frankfort, *Before Philosophy* (Baltimore, 1949) pp. 19–20.

7. *TDNT* 5 (1967) 567.

8. The following section is directed to those who have not been trained in the science of biblical research.

9. There are thirty-nine books in the Old Testament, since, for example, the Minor Prophets are counted as only one book in the HB but twelve in the OT.

10. D. E. Aune, "On the Origins of the 'Council of Javneh' Myth," *JBL* 110 (1991) 491–93. S. Talmon, "The Crystallization of the 'Canon of Hebrew Scriptures' in the Light of Biblical Scrolls from Qumran," in *The Bible as Book,* ed. E. D. Herbert and E. Tov (London, 2002) pp. 5–20. L. M. McDonald, *The Formation of the Christian Biblical Canon* (Peabody, Mass., 1995 [rev. and expanded ed.]).

11. I am grateful to S. Talmon for discussions on the "Book of the People."

12. Also see Appendix I.

13. Scholars have correctly concluded, for centuries, that two authors composed the beginning chapters of Genesis; the P writer is identified by his penchant for calling God "Elohim," and the Yahwist called God "Yahweh (or the Lord) God." See the following discussion of "JEDP" at the beginning of the exegesis of Gen 3.

14. This aspect of Gen 3 cannot be traced to other cultures, such as Babylonia. There is no good parallel to it, as many experts have pointed out. See esp. J. Ernst, *Die eschatologischen Gegenspieler in den Schriften des Neuen Testaments* (Regensberg, 1967) pp. 244–45.

15. During the time of writing this chapter, the standard for spelling "worshipers" changed to "worshippers." I have corrected all these spellings.

16. "Nechushtan" is the vocalization I have chosen to help the person who is not a biblical scholar.

17. I have chosen not to use capitalization for trees in Eden.

18. R. Guénon, *Simboli della Scienza sacra,* trans. F. Zambon (Milan, 1975 [French original was published in 1962]). See esp. the suggestion that the descriptions of the earthly Paradise symbolize the heavenly Jerusalem; p. 287: "C'è inoltre da notare che

di tutto il simbolismo vegetale del Paradiso terrestre solo l' Albero della Vita' sussiste con questo carattere nella descrizione della Gerusalemme celeste."

19. I am indebted to the reflections by B. W. Anderson in *Creation in the Old Testament* (Philadelphia, London, 1984) esp. pp. 1–2.

20. M. J. Gruenthaner, "The Demonology of the Old Testament," *CBQ* 6 (1944) 6–27; the quotations are from pp. 7 and 8, respectively.

21. See M. Giebel, *Tiere in der Antike* (Darmstadt, 2003) p. 166.

22. D. Patte, ed., *Genesis 2 and 3: Kaleidoscopic Structural Readings* (Chico, Calif., 1980) p. 4.

23. While the Jews who have given us the apocryphal books and the Haggadah and the early and later Christian scholars have been interested in the serpent in Gen 3, early rabbinic Jews did not seem fascinated or concerned with serpent imagery. Hillel and Shammai are reputed to have debated the meaning of Gen 2:4 and 3:4 but not 3:1; see N. Sed, *La Mystique cosmologique juive* (Paris, New York, 1981) esp. p. 31. As we shall demonstrate, and as Urbach indicated, "The story of the serpent in the Book of Genesis . . . which left no trace in the Biblical books, received extensive treatment in the apocryphal literature and in the Hagada [*sic*]." E. E. Urbach, *The Sages* 2 vols., trans. I. Abrahams (Jerusalem, 1979) vol. 1, p. 167.

24. A. de Gubernatis, *Zoological Mythology* (New York, 1972) vol. 2, p. 389.

25. *The Book of Genesis* (New York, 1965) p. 59.

26. Moberly, *JTS* NS 39 (1988) 1–27.

27. Ibid., p. 13.

28. P. Diel, *Symbolism in the Bible: The Universality of Symbolic Language and Its Psychological Significance,* trans. N. Marans (San Francisco, 1986) pp. 11–12.

29. E. Hampton-Cook, "The Serpent in Eden (Gen. iii)," *Expository Times* 18 (1906–1907) 287.

30. See esp. J. S. Hanson, "Dreams and Visions in the Greco-Roman World and Early Christianity," in *ANRW* II 23.2 (1980) 1395–1426; see esp. pp. 1397–98.

31. See J.-P. Picot, "Genèse et récits contemporains de contre-utopie: Eve et le serpent," in *La Bible: Images, Mythes et Traditions* (Paris, 1995) pp. 45–60. On p. 44, Picot rightly clarifies that Eve has not yet been named: "Et voilà Eve au côté d'Adam, Eve qui n'a pas encore de nom."

32. According to the Midrashim (rabbinic commentary on biblical texts), the serpent was jealous of the humans because the angels roasted the meat and poured the wine for the couple. This is attractive and imaginative hermeneutics, but it is not modern critical scholarship.

33. E. E. Day and G. D. Jordan, "Serpent," *ISBE* 4.417–18; the quotation is from p. 417.

34. This is pointed out by J.-P. Picot, "Genèse et récits contemporains de contre-utopie," 45–60.

35. The text has "he" (הוא); does that not suggest either that the snake was perceived to be male or that there is a paronomasia between הוא and חוה? Such would not be surprising since paronomasia shapes the flow of thought in Gen 3.

36. This verse seems intrusive because it attributes to the anonymous woman a very high role. See A. J. Williams, "The Relationship of Genesis 3:20 to the Serpent," *ZAW* 89 (1977) 357–74.

37. Cf. D. I. O. Smit, "Serpens aut Daemonium?" in *Miscellanea Biblica et Orientalia,* ed. A. Metzinger (Rome, 1951) pp. 94–97.

38. L. Réau, *Iconographie de l'art chrétien,* 6 vols. (Paris, 1955–1959); see vol. 1, pp. 98–99.

39. See C. F. Keil, *Biblischer Commentar über die Bücher Moses: Genesis und Exodus* (Leipzig, 1866 [2nd ed.]) vol. 1, p. 56. Keil explains his way out of the problem that the serpent has supernatural knowledge by the amazing subjective claim that this knowledge comes "not from the Serpent himself" ("nicht aus der Schlange selbst") but "only from a higher Spirit" ("nur von einem höheren Geist") p. 56. Now, why would the serpent, as Satan, receive such a higher spirit? It is best to allow an ancient author to say something shocking and to listen to him. It is evident that at this point the Yahwist has inherited the myth of the serpent itself being a higher spirit.

40. This fact was stressed long ago by H. Gunkel, one of the most insightful commentators on Genesis. See Gunkel, *Genesis* (Göttingen, 1977 [9th ed.]) p. 15, "Die spätere, jüdisch-christliche Erklärung (Sap Sal 2:24, Joh 8:44, ApJoh 12:9, 20:2), die Schlange sei der Teufel, ist unrichtig."

41. The story of the serpent with Adam and "Eve" in the Garden of Eden is so well known that the *New Yorker* has run cartoons featuring it. For example, the drawing by Whitney Darrow depicts in comic fashion an astronaut, who has landed on some far-off planet, running from his spacecraft toward a reclining Adam, a large upraised and benign serpent, and headed primarily for Eve, whose right hand reaches up to an apple, and to whom he shouts, "Miss! Oh, Miss! For God's sake, stop!" See *The New Yorker Album of Drawings 1925–1975* (New York, 1978) no pages, but about one-fifth into the book.

42. Transliterations added by me.

43. E. A. Speiser, *Genesis* (Garden City, N.Y., 1964) pp. 14–23. I have added transliterations of the Hebrew to draw attention to word plays (paronomasia) and to thoughts that unite the folktale like a special colored thread in a tapestry.

44. The Yahwist is far too early to imagine deep influences from Greece and Rome.

45. See, e.g., H.-P. Müller, *Mythos—Kerygma—Wahrheit* (Berllin, New York, 1991) esp. pp. 3–42.

46. See the similar thoughts expressed by Le Grande Davies, "Serpent Imagery in Ancient Israel," p. 42.

47. Eliade, *Myth and Reality,* trans. W. R. Trask (New York, 1968) p. 6. I am indebted to Le Grande Davies for this reference (p. 43).

48. E. Phillips rightly asks why the relation between the two trees is "stunningly ambiguous." Phillips, "Serpent Intertexts: Tantalizing Twists in the Tales," *BBR 10* (2000) 233–45; the quotation is on p. 236.

49. E. O. James rightly sees that the tree of life seems to be "introduced as if it were an after thought." James, *The Tree of Life: An Archeological Study* (Leiden, 1966) p. 75. James shows no interest in the serpent or snake. Contrast U. Holmberg's *Der Baum des Lebens.* She is primarily interested in the goddess, but she includes an interest in the serpent. See Holmberg, *Der Baum des Lebens: Göttinnen und Baumkult* (Bern, 1996); see Illus. No. 34 (serpent entwined on a tree), 37 (serpent goddess Ganga), 41 (the goddess Erde with a serpent), 53 (a serpent three times curled around the navel stone), 67 (two serpents, upraised, beneath a three-headed goddess).

50. J. G. Frazer, *Folk-Lore in the Old Testament* (London, 1918).

51. As J. Skinner pointed out long ago, the Yahwist implies that the Garden of Eden was planted after the creation of man. See Skinner, *Genesis* (Edinburgh, 1930 [2nd ed.]) p. 57.

52. A woodcutting of the sixteenth century shows Adam, the woman, and the serpent; what is remarkable is the depiction of the tree of knowledge as a human skeleton. See C. Baudelaire, *Sämtliche Werke/Briefe,* 6 vols., ed. F. Kemp et al. (Munich, 1975) vol. 4, Illus. No. 15.

53. As U. Cassuto asked: "If we answer that the cunning of the serpent was the determining factor, then why just this and not another wily creature, like the fox?" Cassuto, *A Commentary on the Book of Genesis,* trans. I. Abrahams (Jerusalem, 1961) vol. 1, p. 140.

54. Cf. esp. Ps 1, Isa 5, 1QH 16 (*olim* 8), *PssSol,* and *OdesSol* 11.

55. I am aware that Gunkel thought that the creation narrative in Genesis was not a "story," but he, as W. R. Scott points out, was not as precise as he imagined and often also referred to the creation narrative as a story. See Scott's reflections in H. Gunkel, *The Story of Genesis,* trans. J. J. Scullion and ed. W. R. Scott (Oakland, Calif., 1994) p. xi.

56. Speiser, *Genesis,* p. 25.

57. Speiser, *Genesis,* p. 23.

58. Th. C. Vriezen, *Onderzoek naar de Paradizsvoorstelling bij de oude Semietische Volken* (Wagenigen, 1937); see the succinct summary in English by C. Westermann in *Genesis 1–11,* trans. J. J. Scullion (Minneapolis, 1974) p. 237.

59. E. Williams-Forte, "The Snake and the Tree in the Iconography and Texts of Syria During the Bronze Age," in *Ancient Seals and the Bible,* ed. L. Gorelick and E. Williams-Forte (Malibu, Calif., 1983) pp. 18–43.

60. Joines, "The Serpent in Gen 3," *ZAW* 87 (1975) 1–11.

61. Pagels, *Adam, Eve, and the Serpent* (New York, 1988) p. 69. As reviewers of Pagels's book point out, there is in this work a "paucity of references to Adam, Eve, or the serpent." See esp. A. Jacobs, "Provocative and Tendentious," *The Reformed Journal* 39 (1989) p. 21.

62. J. Bellamy, *The Ophion or the Theology of the Serpent and the Unity of God* (London, 1911) pp. vi–vii.

63. For example, T. L. Brodie sees Genesis as a complex unity that has been influenced by Homer. See Brodie, *Genesis as Dialogue* (Oxford, New York, 2001); esp. see "Sources: Genesis's Use of Homer's *Odyssey,*" and "Sources: The Theory of Four Hypothetical Documents (J, E, D, and P)." Brodie does not discuss the image of the serpent in this book.

64. E.g., see G. von Rad, *Das Formgeschichtliche Problem des Hexateuch* (Stuttgart, 1938); W. Brueggemann, "David and His Theologian," *CBQ* 30 (1968) 156–81; P. Ellis, *The Yahwist: The Bible's First Theologian* (Collegeville, 1968) 21–50.

65. See esp. E. Ulrich, *The Dead Sea Scrolls and Origins of the Bible* (Grand Rapids, Leiden, 1999) p. 11.

66. *The Book of Genesis* (New York, 1965) pp. 47–48.

67. E. J. Young, *An Introduction to the Old Testament* (Grand Rapids, 1965) p. 33.

68. *The Old Testament: An Introduction,* trans. P. Ackroyd (New York, 1966) p. 198.

69. Joines, *Serpent Symbolism in the Old Testament,* p. 31.

70. S. R. Driver, *An Introduction to the Literature of the Old Testament* (New York, 1956) pp. 123–24. Le Grande Davies concurred with Driver: "All of the theories merely propound prejudices or feelings." "Serpent Imagery in Ancient Israel," p. 41.

There are limits; the story of Gen 3 took its present form by at least 800 BCE (according to most experts, viz. Kittel, Kuenen, and Wellhausen).

71. As A. Fanuli states, the originality of the Yahwist is the framing of Israel's history as "storia universale" as well as an attractive presentation: "é *un'unica storia di salvezza"* (his italics). A. Fanuli in *La spiritualità dell'Antico Testamento,* ed. A. Fanuli (Rome, 1988) p. 219.

72. I. Engnell, " 'Knowledge' and 'Life' in the Creation Story," *VTSupp* 3 (1955) pp. 112–16. Also see Engnell, *Studies in Divine Kingship in the Ancient Near East* (Oxford, 1967).

73. Gunkel, *Genesis,* p. 4.

74. For his textual work, see G. von Rad, *Das erste Buch Mose* (Göttingen, 1981 [11th ed.]) pp. 50–83.

75. Still valuable is W. R. Cooper, "Observations on the Serpent Myths of Ancient Egypt," *Journal of the Transactions of the Victoria Institute* 6 (1873) pp. 321–91; esp. note the 126 illustrations. Cooper was convinced: "The study of Egyptian mythology will throw more light upon the restrictive customs of the Jews, the allusions of the prophets . . . than that of any other country" (p. 391). We have seen that this view is now modified to account for the presence of Egyptian and other elements within Canaanite culture.

76. As cited by G. von Rad, *Genesis,* trans. J. H. Marks (Philadelphia, 1973 [rev. ed.]) p. 86.

77. Ibid., p. 88.

78. U. Cassuto, *A Commentary on the Book of Genesis,* trans. I. Abrahams (Jerusalem, 1961) vols. 1, pp. 142–43.

79. E. Wiesel, "The Serpent," *BRev* 13.6 (1997) 18–19; the quotation is on p. 19 (trans. A. Martin). Wiesel speaks of "Eve," but does recognize that there are two trees in Eden (p. 18).

80. Speiser, *Genesis,* p. 23.

81. Moberly is essentially right to point out that the language of Gen 2–3 is "the mature language of classical Hebew," but there are exceptions to this rule, and the earlier myths have shaped the story. See Moberly, *JTS* NS 39 (1988) 1.

82. Note how different this critical text is from the popular one found in handy editions of the LXX. See J. W. Wevers, ed., *Genesis* (Göttingen, 1974) p. 89.

83. The punctuation is less important; there is no punctuation in the Uncial Greek. The Greek text, however, does clarify that the Greeks, and not just the ones who added the punctuation marks, knew that the words formed an interrogative sentence.

84. For informed discussions and guides to publications, see E. Tov, *The Greek and Hebrew Bible* (Leiden, Boston, 1999).

85. Fanuli, *La spiritualità dell'Antico Testamento,* p. 229: "L'influenza 'astuta' (Gen 3, 1) e nefasta del serpente."

86. Gunkel, *Genesis,* pp. 15–16.

87. *La Bible de Jérusalem* (Paris, 1998 [new rev. and corrected ed.]) p. 41.

88. Translation from the LXX; see M. Harl, *La Genèse* (Paris, 1986) p. 106.

89. M. Maher, translator, *Targum Pseudo-Jonathan: Genesis* (Edinburgh, 1992) p. 25 (italics his).

90. Moberly, *JTS* NS 39 (1988) 4.

91. B. Gosse, "L'écriture de Gn 3, le serpent dualité de la femme et de l'homme," *BN* 98 (1999) 19–20; the quotation is from p. 19.

92. Contrast the far more insightful reflections on the wisdom of the serpent by B. Renz, "Die Kluge Schlange," *BZ* 24 (1938–1939) 241.

93. See T. Muraoka, *Hebrew/Aramaic Index to the Septuagint* (Grand Rapids, 1988) p. 115.

94. The Greek translator cannot preserve the paronomasia that links the nudity of the humans with the serpent as "the most clever (or wise) of all the beasts of the land"; the Greek word for nudity is *gumnoi*. See Wevers, ed., *Genesis,* p. 89.

95. Plato, *Politicus* 263d and Aristotle, *Historia Animalium* 488^{b}15.

96. See Harl, *Genèse,* p. 107.

97. Maher, trans., *Targum Pseudo-Jonathan: Genesis,* p. 25 (italics his).

98. For the text, see M. Ginsburger, ed., *Pseudo-Jonathan* (Berlin, 1903) p. 5.

99. In this book, which is designed for many who have no knowledge about transliteration techniques, I have decided not to use the scholarly norm, since *ḥkm* may remain meaningless to them. Readers may not know that *ḥ* denotes the sound "ch." Also, transliterations like *š* will be avoided since many readers will not grasp that "sh" is intended.

100. J. W. Etheridge, *The Targums of Onkelos and Jonathan ben Uzziel on the Pentateuch* (New York, 1968) p. 40 (Onkelos). Words within brackets are mine.

101. A. Sperber, ed., *The Bible in Aramaic: Volume 1, The Pentateuch According to Targum Onkelos* (Leiden, 1959) p. 4.

102. The Aramaic and Díez Macho's translation are from Díez Macho, ed., *Neophyti 1: Génesis* (Madrid/Barcelona, 1968) pp. 12–13.

103. This is the translation by M. McNamara in his *Targum Neofiti 1: Genesis* (Edinburgh, 1992) p. 59.

104. For more discussion, see P. Kübel, "Ein Wortspiel in Genesis 3 und sein Hintergrund: Die 'kluge' Schlange und die 'nackten' Menschen," *BN* 93 (1998) 11–22.

105. For the Hebrew text, see M. S. Zukermandel, *Tosephta* (Pasewalk, 1880) p. 300.

106. Neusner, trans., *The Tosefta* (New York, 1979) vol. Nashim, p. 165.

107. As Gunkel wrote, the serpent "is the cleverest of animals, he is also more clever than the childish human; he has, according to v. 5, mysterious knowledge, which beside him only God knows" ("ist das klügste der Tiere, sie ist auch klüger als der damals noch kindliche Mensch; sie hat nach v. 5 geheimes Wissen, das außer ihr nur noch Gott selber weiß"). Gunkel, *Genesis,* p. 15.

108. G. von Rad, *Genesis,* p. 81.

109. J. F. A. Sawyer, "The Image of God, the Wisdom of Serpents, and the Knowledge of Good and Evil," in *A Walk in the Garden: Biblical, Iconographical and Literary Images of Eden,* ed. P. Morris and D. Sawyer (Sheffield, 1992) pp. 64–73; the quotation is on p. 66.

110. For a translation of parts of Gunkel's well-known masterpiece, see C. A. Muenchow, "The Influence of Babylonian Mythology Upon the Biblical Creation Story," in *Creation in the Old Testament,* ed. B. W. Anderson (Philadelphia, 1984) pp. 25–52.

111. Jaroš perceives correctly that the serpent is "ein Gottesgeschöpf" and so "keine gottfeindliche Macht repräsentieren könne." K. Jaroš "Die Motive der Heiligen Bäume und der Schlange in Gen 2–3," *ZAW* 92 (1980) 214. Most commentators make the point that the Nachash cannot be Satan, and that he was created by God.

112. See B. W. Anderson, "The Slaying of the Fleeing, Twisting Serpent: Isaiah 27:1 in Context," in *Uncovering Ancient Sources: Essays in Memory of H. Neil Richardson,* ed. L. M. Hopfe (Winona Lake, Ind., 1994) pp. 3–15.

113. W. B. Kristensen, "De Slangenstaf en het Spraakvermogen van Mozes en Aäron," *Mededelingen der Koninklijke Nederlandse Akademie van Wetenschappen* NS 16.14 (1953) 591–610. Kristensen illustrates how Egyptian gods, and perhaps pharaohs, were depicted with serpents as staffs and serpents facing a staff.

114. Sawyer, "The Image of God, the Wisdom of Serpents, and the Knowledge of Good and Evil," p. 67.

115. The translation is from J. Gardner and J. Maier, *Gilgamesh* (New York, 1984) pp. 249–50.

116. *Before Philosophy,* p. 23.

117. See the classical study, published in 1895, by Gunkel, translated by C. A. Muenchow, "The Influence of Babylonian Mythology upon the Biblical Creation Story."

118. See J. Armstrong, "Themes in Sumerian and Greek Myth and Visual Imagery," in *The Paradise Myth* (London, New York, 1969) pp. 8–36.

119. To be as focused as possible on serpent symbolism, I cannot explore what is meant by the knowledge obtained by the man and his wife. I. Engnell makes a remarkable case that this knowledge means that they are, like God, capable of procreation. Engell, "Knowledge and 'Life' in the Creation Story," in *Wisdom in Israel and in the Ancient Near East* [H. H. Rowley Festschrift], ed. M. Noth and D. W. Thomas (Leiden, 1960) pp. 103–19; see esp. pp. 115–16.

120. Cheyne, *Encyclopedia Biblica,* 4.4396.

121. See C. Milani in *Studi e materiali di archeologia e numismatica* 1 (1899–1901) pp. 37ff; also see Buchholz, *Ugarit-Forschungen* 32 (2000) 126 and the drawing on p. 168.

122. The circular border and the fish within it suggest that the signs of the zodiac once encircled this fragment.

123. R. Seewald's *Orbis Pictus* contains an allegorical drawing of the human, with a large serpent, curled around a tree, "kissing" the right cheek of a nude "Eve." See R. Seewald, *Orbis Pictus: Siebzehn Allegorien und Texte über die sichtbare Welt* (Memmingen, 1965) Illus. No. 3 (cf. Illus. No. 4).

124. Another serpent may have been to the left of what remains since a wing protrudes into the scene. I am grateful to L. Guglielmo for discussing this piece with me.

125. See the further comments by Gunkel, *Genesis,* p. 15.

126. The paronomasia is cleverly developed by the Yahwist; see the following discussion.

127. Le Grande Davies, "Serpent Imagery in Ancient Israel," p. 57.

128. One of the brilliant aspects of Le Grande Davies' "Serpent Imagery in Ancient Israel," is the speculation that the "serpent in Genesis 3, [sic] is the 'earliest' recognizable challenge to the 'Serpent symbol' of YHWH." See p. 57.

129. For further discussion, see C. Meyers, *Discovering Eve* (New York, Oxford, 1988) p. 91.

130. G. von Rad rightly points out that the "Schlange" is one of God's creatures and certainly not some demonic power or Satan: "[S]ie ist also im Sinne des Erzählers nicht die Symbolisierung einer 'dämonischen' Macht und gewiß nicht des Satans." G. von Rad, *Das erste Buch Mose,* p. 61.

131. In African mythology, "the Snake" spoke in the language of mortals and died because he "should have used spirit language." G. Parrinder, *African Mythology* (New York, 1982) p. 61.

132. Meyers, *Discovering Eve*, p. 92.

133. MacCulloch, *ERE*, vol. 11, p. 403.

134. Perhaps at this point the reader has forgotten the meaning of Pos.; it refers to the Positive Meaning of a serpent explained in Chap. 5.

135. Perhaps at this point the reader has forgotten the meaning of Neg.; it refers to the Negative Meaning of a serpent explained in Chap. 5.

136. B. Gosse-Antony refers to the "duality represented by the serpent's role" ("dualité représentée par le rôle du serpent"). Gosse-Antony, "L'écriture de Gn 3, le serpent dualité de la femme et de l'homme," *BN* 98 (1999) 19–20; the quotation is on p. 19.

137. J. Skinner, *Genesis* (Edinburgh, 1910) pp. 71–72.

138. Ibid., p. 2.

139. Moberly, *JTS* NS 39 (1988) 2.

140. Since my work is focused on serpent iconography and Gen 3, I cannot engage in a dialogue with him and other scholars regarding many aspects of the text. I do agree with Speiser that the Yahwist has "transposed" everything "into human terms" (p. 25). I also am attracted to his insight that the Yahwist thereby "evoked" the "childhood" of humankind by portraying God Yahweh calling out to his creature with a meaning such as "And what have you been up to just now?"

141. Joines, *ZAW* 87 (1975) 8.

142. See, e.g., A. Van den Branden, "La création de l'homme et de la femme d'après le document Jahviste," *BeO* 166 (1990) 193–208.

143. See especially *Enuma Elish* I in *ANET*, pp., 63, 160–61 and the Gilgamesh epic Tablet I, col. 4, lines 16ff.in *ANET*, p. 75. Also see Speiser, *Genesis*, pp. 24–27.

144. It is now pertinent to report that S. Moussaieff has some unpublished ancient idols that may antedate 3000 BCE. They allegedly come from the Hurrian culture near Lake Van. One shows a seated creature; one end is uplifted to show a woman who faces a serpent with a mouth and distinct eyes. Another depicts a serpent facing one way and a woman another. The third has two serpents lifted up and facing a woman. A fourth has three serpents; beneath one may be a woman. For similar objects, see A. P. Kozloff, ed., *Animals in Ancient Art* (Cleveland, 1981) p. 16.

145. Fanuli, *La spiritualità dell'Antico Testamento*, p. 229.

146. Contrast Skinner: "Whether even in Heb. it is more than an assonance is doubtful." Skinner, *Genesis*, p. 70.

147. See esp. how carefully constructed is Gen 3:6: paronomasia, repetition, and an *inclusio* (from *ha'iššāh*, "the woman," to *'išāh*, "her husband").

148. A Wénin, *Actualité des mythes: Relire les récits mythiques de Genèse 1–11* (Sainte-Ode, 2001) p. 30.

149. My idiomatic translation.

150. P. Haupt, "The Curse on the Serpent," *JBL* 35 (1916) 155–62: the quotation is on p. 160 (transliterations mine).

151. See P. Kübel, "Ein Wortspiel in Genesis 3 und sein Hintergrund: Die 'kluge' Schlange und die 'nackten' Menschen." Moberly rightly points out that the Yahwist has avoided the usual way of spelling "naked," *'yrm* (cf. 3:7,10), and so brings out the paronomasia. Moberly, *JTS* NS 39 (1988) 24 n. 69.

152. See also G. J. Wenham, *Genesis* (Waco, Tex., 1987) p. 81.

153. Also see Moberly, *JTS* NS 39 (1988) 6–7.

154. Gunkel, *The Stories of Genesis,* p. 27.

155. Ibid., p. 29.

156. In addition to the other references to images of serpents with feet cited earlier, see the numerous images of serpents with feet in K. Michalowski, *L'Art de l'ancienne Égypte,* esp. nos. 386 (Tomb of Tutmosis III; Eighteenth Dynasty), 391 and 392 (both from the Tomb of Amenophis II; Eighteenth Dynasty).

157. I have placed in quotation marks the words of Speiser; see his *Genesis,* p. 26.

158. G. von Rad, *Genesis,* p. 81.

159. Le Grande Davies, "Serpent Imagery in Ancient Israel," p. 55.

160. See the philological work by Hamilton, *The Book of Genesis,* p. 171.

161. Gen 4 and following presuppose that the woman, now Eve, has been ejected with Adam. Perhaps the ancient Semitic concept of corporate solidarity applies in Gen 3: the man, Adam, alone is mentioned but the reader knows Adam includes "Eve." In ancient Semitic, the man often alone was mentioned, but he represented the whole family or clan (as in Lat. *paterfamilias*).

162. This is emphasized by Gunkel; see his *The Stories of Genesis,* p. 47.

163. Speiser, *Genesis,* p. 23.

164. It is difficult to discern to what extent the perception that the Nachash is female is to be found in German commentators since the serpent, "die Schlange," in German is feminine.

165. Note also the use of superlative verb forms, literally "eating, you may eat" and "dying, you will die"; I have used adverbs to convey the meaning in understandable English.

166. Long before Freud, Georg Christoph Lichtenberg (1742–1799) examined the meaning of dreams. He observed that often one reports having been spoken to by someone. Then, on reflection, it becomes clear that the person who had spoken is none other than the self. He then wonders what earlier generations meant when they said, like Eve: "The serpent spoke to me." Or "The Lord spoke to me. My spirit spoke to me." Then, we do not really know what we think. We seem to imagine that another had spoken to us, but in reality we have become a third person who speaks to us. In our dreams, the other person, or snake, is often a personification of our own selves. Cf. G. C. Lichtenberg, *Gedankenbücher,* ed. F. H. Mautner (Frankfurt, 1963) p. 170.

167. See the reflections by Gunkel, *Genesis,* p. 16.

168. For the original Greek and an English translation, see R. Marcus, *Philo* (LCL; Cambridge, Mass., London, 1979) supplement 1, pp. 20–21.

169. A. J. Williams, "The Relationship of Genesis 3:20 to the Serpent," *ZAW* 89 (1977) 357–74; the quotation is on p. 358.

170. H. Gressmann, "Mythische Reste in der Paradieserzählung," *Archiv für Religionswissenschaft* 10 (1907) 345–47.

171. Also see the linguistic study in Appendix I.

172. Albright, "The Goddess of Life and Wisdom," *AJSL* 36 (1919–20) 284ff.

173. An unpublished Ugaritic text contains data that may prove that YHWH was also, in some circles, considered feminine. I am indebted to Professor Marcel Sigrist.

174. R. Couffignal, *De 'L'arbre au serpent' au 'jeune homme en blanc'* (Toulouse Cedex, 1993) esp. p. 22.

175. Moberly, *JTS* NS 39 (1988) 9.

176. See Gunkel, *The Stories of Genesis*, p. 30.

177. Von Rad, *Genesis*, p. 87.

178. Joines, *ZAW* 87 (1975) 1.

179. B. F. Batto, *Slaying the Dragon: Mythmaking in the Biblical Tradition* (Louisville, 1992) p. 59. Batto rightly argues that the Yahwist probably "derived the character of the serpent in part from *Gilgamesh*" (p. 60).

180. See esp. Westermann, *Genesis*, vol. 1, p. 324, and O. H. Steck, *Die Paradieserzaehlung: Eine Auslegung von Genesis 2, 4b–3, 24* (Neukirchen-Vluyn, 1970) p. 101.

181. See von Rad, *Genesis*, p. 90.

182. D. Jobling, "The Myth Semantics of Genesis 2:4b–3:24," *Semeia* 18 (1980) 41–49; the quotation is from p. 42.

183. Moberly is convinced that the Yahwist is thinking that the human is often unaware of the processes that lead to decay and death; see Moberly, *JTS* NS 39 (1988) 17–18.

184. The curse that produces enmity between the serpent and women is not easy to understand. Long ago, Reinach argued that the miseries of menstruation and childbirth are to be traced to serpent symbolism. In Iran, menstruation is deemed to be caused by demons, esp. Angra Manyu, who is symbolized by the serpent. Reinach, "Le Serpent et la Femme," *L'Anthropologie* 16 (1905) 178–80.

185. The Hebrew words "You shall surely die!" perhaps indicate that the fruit is poisonous. For Hebraic forms for condemnation, see V. P. Hamilton, *The Book of Genesis 1–17* (Grand Rapids, 1990) pp. 172–73.

186. There may be some glosses in the present account. See K. Jaroš, "Die Motive der Heiligen Bäume und der Schlange in Gen 2–3."

187. One should not argue, as did biblical exegetes long ago, that the Yahwist is referring to a day of God as if it were a thousand years (cf. Ps 90:4).

188. See D. J. A. Clines, "Themes in Genesis 1–11," *CBQ* 38 (1976) 490.

189. E.g., cf. Gen 15:18.

190. See Moberly, *JTS* NS 39 (1988) 14.

191. E.g., cf. Prov 12:16.

192. There is the possibility that originally the story was much shorter and the disobedience was immediately followed by expulsion. See Westermann, *Genesis*, pp. 195 and 256–57; and Moberly, *JTS* NS 39 (1988) 19.

193. See D. O. Procksch, *Die Genesis* (Leipzig, Erlangen, 1924 [2nd and 3rd ed.]) p. 30 and H. Seebass, *Genesis I* (Neukirchener-Vluyn, 1996) p. 120.

194. Batto, *Slaying the Dragon: Mythmaking in the Biblical Tradition*, p. 59.

195. von Rad, *Genesis*, p. 81.

196. For a general discussion of serpent cults throughout the world and through time, see S. A. Cook, "Serpent Cults," *Encyclopedia Britannica* 20 (1949) 368–71.

197. The Hebrew noun behind "belly" comes from the verb to bend, which is better known in Aramaic. The noun "belly" appears elsewhere in the TANAKH only in Lev 11:41; there again it is used with the verb *hlk* and likewise pertains to reptiles or snakes.

198. R. H. Charles, *The Book of Jubilees* (Oxford, 1902) p. 26, note to *Jubilees* 3:23.

199. Josephus, *Judean Antiquities 1–4,* trans. and commented on by L. H. Feldman (*Flavius Josephus: Translation and Commentary,* ed. S. Mason (Leiden, Boston, 2000).

200. See Kronholm, *Motifs from Genesis 1–11 in the Genuine Hymns of Ephrem the Syrian,* p. 113.

201. For the Hebrew text, see E. G. Clarke et al., *Targum Pseudo-Jonathan of the Pentateuch* (Hoboken, N.J., 1984) p. 4. For the English translation, see M. Maher, trans. *Targum Pseudo-Jonathan: Genesis,* p. 27 (italics his).

202. Midrash Rabbah, Ecclesiastes X.11. For the Hebrew text, see קהלת רבה (Jerusalem, 1993) p. תקנז. For the English translation, see H. Freedman and M. Simon, *Midrash Rabbah* (London, 1951) p. 274.

203. For an English translation, see H. Freedman and M. Simon, *Midrash Rabbah* p. 162.

204. See Appendix I and especially the section on Gen 1:24.

205. I have enjoyed and benefited from conversations on this perspective with A. M. V. Capers.

206. Urbach saw that the serpent's punishment "implies a change in its original nature and qualities." Urbach, *The Sages,* vol. 1, p. 422.

207. P. Joüon, "Le grand dragon, l'ancien serpent," *RSR* 17 (1927) 444–46; the quotation is on p. 444.

208. See Ephrem Syrus, *Commentary on Genesis* 42.18–26; and T. Kronholm, *Motifs from Genesis 1–11 in the Genuine Hymns of Ephrem the Syrian* (Lund, 1978) p. 112.

209. See the reflections on imagination and art by P. Zanker, *Un 'arte per l'impero: Funzione e intenzione delle immagini nel mondo romano,* ed. E. Polito (Milan, 2002).

210. I am grateful to Noel Freedman for discussion on this issue.

211. It is clear that the serpent is in no way like God's adversary as "Satan" in the book of Job, in which Satan seems still to be among God's favored angels.

212. For pre-Yahwistic traditions, see L. Ruppert, "Die Sündenfallerzählung (Gn 3) in vorjahwistischer Tradition und Interpretation," *BZ* NF 15 (1971) 187.

213. The words "good and evil" may be an addition by the Yahwist. They look redactional.

214. H. Ringgren. *Israelite Religion,* trans. D. Green (London, 1966).

215. This point, always evident in my thought, jumped out as I discussed the symbol of the serpent with Muslims in the Old City of Jerusalem. They especially were fond of how Muhammed retold the story of Moses' use of serpent magic before Pharaoh.

216. See the comments by C. Westermann, *Am Anfang: 1. Mose* (Neukirchener-Vluyn, 1986) part 1, p. 38.

217. See A. Levene, *The Early Syrian Fathers on Genesis* (London, 1951) pp. 75–76.

218. See E. van Wolde, *Stories of the Beginning,* trans. J. Bowden (Harrisburg, 1996) esp. pp. 50–51.

219. Here I am grateful to Noel Freedman for conversations on the meaning of Gen 3.

220. Gen 1:26 and 2:7 were problematic for Jews because they implied that someone else, perhaps angels, made the human. According to the Samaritan Malef, the Angel of Yahweh made the human body and God created the soul or spirit of the human. See

E. C. Baguley, "A Critical Edition, with Translation, of the Hebrew Text of the Malef" (PhD diss., University of Leeds, 1962) p. 234. I am indebted to J. Fossum for this information; see his "Gen. 1,26 and 2,7 in Judaism, Samaritanism, and Gnosticism," *JSJ* 16 (1985) 202–39.

221. See J. J. M. Roberts, "Does God Lie?," *The Bible and the Ancient Near East: Collected Essays* (Winona Lake, Ind., 2002) pp. 123–31. Roberts points to the potential importance of understanding the serpent and Eve in Gen 3, but he does not broach the issue of God lying in this text.

222. Note other etymological connections: Latin provides *homo* (human) and *humus* (earth); Greek has *chthon* (earth), *chamai* (on the earth), and *epichthonios* (human). This observation is discussed by R. Graves and R. Patai in *Hebrew Myths: The Book of Genesis* (New York, 1966) p. 63.

223. P. Tillich, "The Meaning and Justification of Religious Symbols," in *Religious Experience and Truth,* ed. S. Hook (New York, 1968) pp. 3–11; the quotation is on p. 5.

224. As Westermann states, the author provides no explication for the origin of evil. Westermann, *Am Anfang,* part 1, p. 38.

225. For permission to publish this photograph, I am grateful to Dott. Silvia Gozzi and Dott. Chiara Silla, the Comune di Firenze, and the Musei comunali di Firenze.

226. L. Hansmann and L. Kriss-Rettenbeck, *Amulett und Talisman: Erscheinungsform und Geschichte* (Munich, 1966); see esp. Illus. No. 196 (anguipede demon), 46–65 (numerous serpent amulets), 474 (amulet against a serpent's bite), 608 (a hand with the finger closest to the little finger as a serpent), 639 (an amulet with a serpent biting a circle), 765 (a ring with a serpent [eighteenth/nineteenth cent. CE]), and especially 827 (Adam and the woman with a female serpent wound around a tree whose branches are depicted as antlers). See Illus. No. 99, a wood cutting of 1487 from the Netherlands; it shows Adam, the woman, and the serpent who is curled around the tree and looking only at Adam. This woodcut is remarkable because Eve is only beginning to eat the "apple," yet Adam has already covered his privates.

227. Contrast the work of Johann Heinrich Füssli dated to 1799–1800. This artist, who was fascinated by Milton's *Paradise Lost,* depicted "Eve" confronted by a much larger figure, the serpent, who seems to be masculine. Cf. C. Becker, *Johann Heinrich Füssli: Das Verlorene Paradies* (Stuttgart, 1997) p. 45.

228. See the color photograph in G. Néret, *Michelangelo 1475–1564* (Cologne, London, New York, 1998) pp. 34–35.

229. *Midrash Tehillim,* Comment Two. For the English, see W. G. Braude, trans., *The Midrash on Psalms* (New Haven, 1959) vol. 1, p. 506. The Hebrew is from S. Buber, ed., *Mdrsh Thlym* (New York, 1947 [reprinted]) p. 300.

230. This seems odd; why did the author not say that the woman left her parents? Is some form of *beema,* marriage, envisioned? If so, then the narrative is extremely old (as I have been intimating), but not all of it is old. See Skinner, *Genesis,* p. 70.

231. Gunkel, *Genesis,* p. 18.

232. The punishment of the serpent, according to the Midrashim, was to lose his pride and arrogance; henceforth he can no longer walk with an erect head—he must crawl in the dust. Jews and Christians knew that the serpent does not eat dust, so a purely literal interpretation was almost always avoided.

233. G. von Rad, *Genesis,* p. 87.

234. Westermann, *Genesis 1–11,* p. 239.

235. The serpent is sometimes incorrectly depicted slinking out of Paradise, ashamed and powerless. See the penciled sketch of 1851–52 by Julius Schnorr von Carolsfeld (1794–1872). See M. Bernhard, ed., *Deutsche Romantik Handzeichnungen* (Herrsching, n.d.) vol. 2, p. 1752.

236. The Latin is from *Biblia sacra iuxta latinam vulgatam versionem ad codicum fidem* (Rome, 1936).

237. Cf. Exod 4:3. L. Shalit relates how a poisonous snake became unconscious and stiff like a staff when it was twirled overhead and held by the tail. Shalit, "How Moses Turned a Staff into a Snake and Back Again," *BAR* 9 (1983) 72–73.

238. J. Milgrom, *Numbers* (Philadelphia, New York, 5750 or 1990) pp. 173–74.

239. See the reflections by J. Frey in "Wie Moses die Schlange in der Wüste erhöht hat" in *Schriftauslegung im antiken Judentum und im Urchristentum*, ed. M. Hengel and H. Löhr (Tübingen, 1994) pp. 153–205.

240. E. W. Davies attributes the account to the Yahwist. See Davies, *Numbers* (Grand Rapids, 1995) p. 215. I am persuaded that in Num 21 the Elohist has incorporated earlier traditions, some of which may be parallel to, or perhaps even from, the Yahwist.

241. Commentators once unanimously thought the story was primarily from the Elohist; but see the comments and observations by P. J. Budd, *Numbers* (Waco, Tex., 1984) pp. 232–33. M. Noth assigned Num 21:4–9 to the Elohist. See Noth, *Das vierte Buch Mose: Numeri* (Göttingen, 1966) p. 137. H. Jagersma thinks the narrative is primarily E with dependence on J. See Jagersma, *Numberi* (Nijkerk, 1988) vol. 2, p. 85. My position is that articulated by J. de Vaulx, published in his *Les Nombres* (Paris, 1972) p. 235.

242. In making these judgments, I am indebted to B. A. Levine, *Numbers 1–20* (Anchor Yale Bible; Garden City, N.Y., 1993; rpt. New Haven) pp. 48–49.

243. For example, see J. de Vaulx, *Les Nombres*, p. 235.

244. Copper is pure ore smelted in a furnace. Bronze is copper strengthened with tin. Brass, which appears much later in the Roman Period (perhaps in the late first century CE), is copper mixed with zinc.

245. See also Joines, *JBL* 87 (1968) 252–54.

246. G. B. Gray, *A Critical and Exegetical Commentary on Numbers* (Edinburgh, New York, 1903, reprinted in 1956) p. 275.

247. A snake idol is on display in the Nechustan Pavilion, Eretz Israel Museum, Tel Aviv (Display Case No. 40, item no. 4 and item identification 90302). After studying numerous pictures of this copper (gold-plated head) serpent (see Illus. No. 28), I was surprised that only studying this one directly awoke in me feelings that it was alive. It is easy then to imagine that it symbolized life and renewed life.

248. Milgrom, *Numbers*, p. 175.

249. Milgrom, *Numbers*, p. 460.

250. T. Staubli claims that Num 21:4–9 is to be understood as a projection back into the Wilderness Period to substantiate the Jerusalem cult until Hezkeiah's reform: "Die biblische Geschichte ist die in die Wüste zurückprojizierte Ätiologie eines Kultbildes, das bis zur Reform unter Hiskija in Jerusalem stand." T. Staubli, *Die Bücher Levitikus, Numeri* (Stuttgart, 1996) p. 286.

251. H. Holzinger, *Numeri* (Tübingen, Leipzig, 1903) p. 93.

252. M. Noth was convinced that Num 21:4–9 was not to be understood as an etiological legend ("eine Ätiologie des 'Nehusthan' von 2. Kön. 18,4"). See Noth's comments in his *Das vierte Buch Mose*, p. 137. Noth was convinced that Num 21:4–9 was

an occasion to explain the history of a plague of serpents in the wilderness, during the time of Moses. J. Sturdy, among other scholars, concludes that Num 21:4–9 is a "story" that was "developed to explain the origin of a bronze serpent that stood in the temple of Jerusalem down to the reign of Hezekiah." Sturdy, *Numbers* (Cambridge, New York, 1976) p. 147.

253. J. Gray, *I & II Kings* (London, 1970 [2nd ed.]) p. 670.

254. B. Baentsch, Professor of Theology in the University of Jena, was convinced that 2 Kgs 18:4 should be understood as a cult-saying that explained the presence of a serpent image in the Jerusalem Temple: "Wir haben es hier mit einer Kultussage zu tun, die beabsichtigt, die Entstehung des ehernen Schlangenbildes im Tempel zu Jerusalem (II Reg 18:4) zu erklären und dieses durch Zurückführung auf Moses als echtes Stück der unter Jahvereligion zu charakterisieren." Baentsch, *Exodus-Leviticus-Numeri* (Göttingen, 1903) p. 575.

255. This position is held also by J. de Vaulx in *Les Nombres,* p.236.

256. M. Noth, "Num. 21 als Glied der 'Hexateuch'-Erzahlung," *ZAW* 58 (1940–1941) 178–80.

257. J. A. Montgomery pointed out this double meaning and that the root of "brass" or "copper" is *lḥš* which means "to hiss." Montgomery, *The Books of Kings,* ed. H. S. Gehman (Edinburgh, 1951) p. 501. N. Freedman shared this information with me since Professor Gehman, his teacher at Princeton Theological Seminary, completed this commentary after Montgomery's death.

258. D. T. Olson, *Numbers* (Louisville, 1996) p. 136.

259. J. Preuss rightly points out that the type of snake in the wilderness with Moses, according to Num 21, is unknowable: "What type of snakes are here referred to can only be guessed at." J. Preuss, *Biblical and Talmudic Medicine,* ed. and trans. F. Rosner (New York, 1978) p. 197.

260. H. Cazelles contended that *seraph* should be conceived "as a winged dragon" ("comme des dragons ailés"). H. Cazelles, *Les Nombres* (Paris, 1958) p. 101.

261. The snakes were clearly poisonous. Most commentators make this point clear. As A. Dillmann stated over one hundred years ago, the story tells of poisonous snakes (Brandschlangen) through whose "bite many people die" ("Biss vielen Leuten den Tod brachten"). Dillmann, *Die Bücher Numeri, Deuteronomium und Josua* (Leipzig, 1886) p. 119. Dillmann draws attention to Strabo (15.2.7), according to whom Alexander the Great lost many soldiers to snakebites. And, as A. Drubbel opines, one should imagine poisoness snakes: "Men heeft te denken aan giftige slangen." Drubbel, *Numeri* (Roermond en Maaseik, 1963) p. 105.

262. J. W. Wevers, ed., *Numeri* (Göttingen, 1982) p. 254.

263. חיוי means "serpent," and קליא (Jastrow II.1376) "fiery" or "poisonous." For critical comments on the LXX in Num 21:4–9, see G. Dorival, *La bible d'Alexandrie: Les nombres* (Paris, 1994) pp. 399–401.

264. See O. Keel, M. Küchler, and C. Uehlinger, "Schlangen," *Orte und Landschaften der Bibel* (Zurich, Göttingen, 1984) vol. 1, pp. 163–66.

265. T. E. Lawrence, *Revolt in the Desert* (New York, 1927) p. 93; I am grateful to Milgrom, *Numbers,* p. 318, for this reference.

266. Yet the Greek seems odd. It is obvious that the Hebrew text has the same prepositions before God and Moses, but the Greek translator chose two different prepositions. I would expect the Greek πρός to represent either ל or לפני and κατά to translate ב or possibly נל.

267. See A. Sperber, *The Pentateuch According to Onkelos* (Leiden, 1959) p. 258 and note *ad loc.*

268. B. Grossfeld, trans., *The Targum Onqelos to Leviticus and the Targum Onqelos to Numbers* (Edinburgh, 1988) p. 125.

269. A. Díez Macho, *Neophyti 1: Tomo IV: Números* (Madrid, 1974) p. 193.

270. M. McNamara, trans., *Targum Neofiti 1: Numbers* (Edinburgh, 1995) p. 115.

271. E.g., Clarke, trans., *Targum Pseudo-Jonathan: Numbers* (Edinburgh, 1995) p. 247.

272. Sakenfeld, *Journeying with God: A Commentary on the Book of Numbers* (Grand Rapids, 1995) p. 118.

273. G. Garbini, "Le Serpent d'Airain et Moïse," *ZAW* 100 (1988) 264–67.

274. Milgrom opines that the *seraph* was a "winged snake similar to the winged Egyptian uraeus (cobra)." Milgrom, *Numbers,* p. 174. Also see Milgrom, "The Copper Snake," *Numbers,* pp. 459–60.

275. See, e.g., O. Keel, "Schwache altestamentliche Ansätze," in *Die Dämonen,* ed. A. Lange, H. Lichtenberger, and K. F. D. Römheld (Tübingen, 2003) p. 215.

276. ἡδονῆς ὢν σύμβολον; Philo, *Agr.* 108; F. H. Colson and G. H. Whitaker, *Philo* (LCL London, New York, 1930) p. 162.

277. The brackets indicate words only implied in the ancient, cryptic, Hebrew.

278. See K. Koenen, "Eherne Schlange und goldenes Kalb," *ZAW* 111 (1999) 353–72. Koenen rightly explains the attribution of Nechushtan to Moses as an etiological legend.

279. See the insights of A. Chouraqui in *Au Désert: Nombres* (Paris, 1993) p. 239.

280. Martin Luther used the copper serpent of Moses to make two points: the necessity of faith and the theological use of images. The uplifted serpent of Moses appeared frequently in the early Reformation, thanks to the artwork of Lucas Cranach the Elder. See D. L. Ehresmann, "The Brazen Serpent, a Reformation Motif in the Works of Lucas Cranach the Elder and his Workshop," *Marsyas* 13 (1966–1967) 32–47.

281. See Frazer, *The Dying God* (London, 1911) pp. 84–85.

282. McNamara, *Targum Neofiti 1: Numbers,* pp. 115–16.

283. The Samaritan Pentateuch is considerably expansionistic, especially in Numbers; but for Num 21:4–9 there are no significant additions. See K.-R. Kim, "Studies in the Relationship Between the Samaritan Pentateuch and the Septuagint" (PhD diss., Hebrew University, 1994) p. 205.

284. McNamara, *Targum Neofiti 1: Numbers,* p. 115, note 8.

285. It is no longer possible to assume with C. F. Keil that the serpent represents evil: "[H]eidnische Anschauung ist nicht nur dem Alten Testamente fremd . . . sondern steht auch mit der durch Gen. 3, 15 begründeten biblischen Anschauung von der Schlange, als Repräsentantin des Bösen, und ist aus der magischen Kunst der Schlangenbeschwörung geflossen, die das A. Testament als abgöttischen Greuel verabscheut." Keil, *Biblischer Commentar über die Bücher Mose's* (Leipzig, 1870) p. 297. Our knowledge of how indebted the authors of the biblical books were to surrounding and contemporary cults and myths no longer needs to be a source of embarrassment. Also, as we have seen, the Genesis account of the serpent cannot simply be interpreted as a symbol of evil.

286. Milgrom, *Numbers,* p. 460.

287. Joines, "The Bronze Serpent in the Israelite Cult," *JBL* 87 (1968) 251.

288. T. Fretheim, "Life in the Wilderness," *Di* 17 (1978) 266–72; the quotation is on p. 270.

289. Dillmann, *Numeri*, pp. 119–20.

290. D. Flusser, "It Is Not a Serpent That Kills," in *Judaism and the Origins of Christianity* (Jerusalem, 1988) pp. 543–51; the quotation is on p. 549.

291. J. Scharbert correctly perceived that the copper serpent was not intended to convey magic: "Die Kupferschlange soll kein magisches Zaubermittel sein, sondern die darauf Blickenden daran erinnern, dass Jahwe Auflehnung bestraft, aber bei Umkehr auch wider verzeiht." Scharbert, *Numeri* (Würzburg, 1992) p. 84.

292. T. Fretheim, "Life in the Wilderness"; the quotation is on p. 270.

293. Pliny, *Nat.* 29.21; For Latin text and English translation, see Pliny, *Natural History*, ed. and trans. W. H. S. Jones, vol. 8, pp. 228–29.

294. See F. Valcanover, *Jacopo Tintoretto and the Scuola Grande of San Rocco* (Venice, 2002) pp. 42–43.

295. On Deut 2:2–3, which is similar to 2 Kgs 18:4, see the reflections of B. M. Levinson, *Deuteronomy and the Hermeneutics of Legal Innovation* (New York, Oxford, 1997) p. 148.

296. My translation is based on the one offered by M. Cogan and H. Tadmor, *II Kings* (Anchor Yale Bible; Garden City, N.Y., 1988; rpt. New Haven) p. 215.

297. See B. O. Long, *2 Kings* (Grand Rapids, 1991) pp. 193–96. The introduction of Hezekiah follows the well-known Deuteronomistic sequence of summary, synchronism, and references to historical sources. See Gray, *I & II Kings,* p. 657.

298. Long contends that "the Dtr writer suggests that the reader imagine Hezekiah as a consummate reformer who forged a new epoch in Judah's history." Long, *2 Kings,* p. 195.

299. Montgomery, *The Books of Kings,* p. 481.

300. Cogan and Tadmor, *II Kings,* p. 217.

301. Graves and Patai, *Hebrew Myths* p. 32.

302. I am grateful for discussion on Hezekiah's reform with N. Freedman.

303. See M. Weinfeld, "Cult Centralization in Israel in the Light of a Neo-Babylonian Analogy," *JNES* 23 (1964) 202–12, and the insights by Cogan and Tadmor, *II Kings,* pp. 218–19.

304. Montgomery, *The Books of Kings,* p. 480.

305. See Long, *2 Kings,* pp. 194–95.

306. Cogan and Tadmor, *II Kings,* p. 217.

307. F. M. Cross argues that the themes in the Books of Kings "belong properly to a Josianic edition of the Deuteronomistic history" (p. 279). See F. M. Cross, *Canaanite Myth and Hebrew Epic* (Cambridge, Mass., 1973) pp. 278–89. Cross does not discuss 2 Kgs 18:4 specifically. For a critical review of attempts to date sources, see S. W. Holloway, "Kings, Book of 1–2," in *AYBD* 4.69–83.

308. See Long, *2 Kings,* pp. 194–96.

309. There is no evidence, but it is conceivable that Manasseh, Hezekiah's son and the King of Judah from c. 687 to 640 (or 642), in his attempt to revive the Canaanite religion in Jerusalem and the Temple, reintroduced a serpent cult. We are only told that Manasseh placed an image of Asherah in the Temple. It would be unwise to assume that Manasseh never reemployed serpent iconography. If he did, the ser-

pent images are not the pulverized Nechushtan and similar objects banished by his father.

310. See Isa 2:8, 17:8, 30:22, and 31:7.

311. Joines, *JBL* 87 (1968) 255.

312. See H. Niehr, *Religionen in Israels Umwelt* (Würzburg, 1998) pp. 123–24, 129–32.

313. Herodotus called Astarte "Aphrodite Ourania," and in the late Hellenistic and Roman periods Astarte is Atargatis. See Niehr, *Religionen in Israels Umwelt,* p. 201.

314. See the research and publications of the Ras Shamra Parallels Project. See, e.g., S. Rummel, ed., *Rash Shamra Parallels III* (Rome, 1981).

315. G. Hentschel imagines that the copper serpent was accepted into the Jerusalem cult: "In Israel hat man die kupferne Schlange zunächst auch akzeptiert und mit dem Jahwekult in Verbindung gebracht (Num 21:4–9)." G. Hentschel, *2 Könige* (Würzburg, 1985) p. 85, n. 7.

316. The gold cobra found in the palace at Ekron (Tel Miqne) dates from the seventh century BCE. For a study of serpent realia found in controlled excavations, see Charlesworth, *Serpent Iconography and the Archaeology of the Land from Dan to Bethsheba,* in press.

317. S. Koh, in 1994, could conclude that serpent iconography began to disappear "at the beginning of Iron Age I" in ancient Palestine. We now can extend the time down until the end of the Iron Age. See Koh, "An Archaeological Investigation of the Snake Cult in the Southern Levant: The Chalcolithic Period Through the Iron Age" (PhD diss., University of Chicago, 1994) p. 1 and Map 1.

318. Cogan and Tadmor, *II Kings,* p. 217, reject Rowley's suggetion as "highly speculative."

319. H. H. Rowley, "Zadok and Nehushtan," *JBL* 58 (1939) 113–41. Joines also claims a Canaanite origin for the serpent cult; Joines, *JBL* 87 (1968) 245–56.

320. This conclusion has been defended by leading experts of this period in the history of Israel, namely Bentzen, Rowley, Ringgren, Zimmerli, and Ramsey. For a recent succint discussion, see G. W. Ramsey, "Zadok," *AYBD* 6.1034–36.

321. Joines, *JBL* 87 (1968) 256.

322. In this work, my transliterations are without the diacritics and supralinears that confuse those who are not specialists in Semitics.

323. Milgrom insightfully suggests that "the paronomasia, or word play, adds to its homeopathic powers." Milgrom, *Numbers,* p. 174.

324. Montgomery, *The Books of Kings,* p. 481.

325. Long, *2 Kings,* p. 195.

326. I do not think it likely that Israelite religion was to a degree a continuation of Canaanite culture, as G. W. Ahlström and N. P. Lemche have concluded. See Ahlström, *Who Were the Israelites?* (Winona Lake, Ind., 1986) and Lemche, *The Development of the Israelite Religion in the Light of Recent Studies on the Early History of Israel* (Leiden, 1991).

327. This is developed attractively by Koh in "An Archaeological Investigation of the Snake Cult in the Southern Levant"; see esp. p. 140.

328. The precursor of the developed caduceus is found on an intricately carved flint knife found in northern Egypt. See the drawing and discussion in J. T. Burns, "Origin

and Date of the Caduceus Motif," *Journal of the American Medical Association* 202 (1967) 163–67.

329. I am indebted to R. Reich for this insight shared with me as we stood before the massive stone walls that he has recently uncovered beneath "David's City" in eastern Jerusalem.

7. The Symbolism of the Serpent in the Gospel of John

1. H. Gerhard, "Über Agathodämon und Bona Dea," *Akademie der Wissenschaften* (24 June 1847) 463–99.

2. See K. Aland, *Vollständige Konkordanz zum Griechischen Neuen Testament,* 3 vols. (Berlin, New York, 1978–1983).

3. See P. Joüon, "Le Grand Dragon," *RSR* 17 (1927) 444–46; B. Renz, *Der orientalische Schlangendrache* (Augsburg, 1930); W. Foerster, "δράκων," *TDNT* 2 (1964) 281–83. The nouns ἀσπίς and ἑρπετόν do not receive a separate entry in *TDNT*.

4. See Foerster, "ἔχιδνα," *TDNT* 2 (1964) 815–16.

5. See Foerster, "ὄφις," *TDNT* 5 (1967) 566–71.

6. In L. Réau's *Iconographie de l'art chrétienne* (1955), under animals as symbols of Christ we are told that the following animals symbolized Christ: the lamb, the dove, the fish, the hart (or stag), the peacock, the eagle, the ostrich, the weasel, "le Bélier," the scapegoat, "le Caladre," "la Carista," the cock, the dolphin, the griffin, the lobster, the water snake, the unicorn, the lion, the lynx, the pelican, the phoenix, "la Sauterelle," the serpent, the bull, and the calf. Lost in the forest may be the living sprout: "The serpent is almost always an image of a demon; however, it may, in certain passages, signify the Christ" (p. 98).

7. See the image of the personification of sin from the Chancel of Salerno (second half of the twelfth cent.) in W. Kemp, "Schlange, Schlangen," *Lexicon der christlichen Ikonographie* (1990), vol. 4, p. 79.

8. C. H. Dodd, *The Epistle to the Romans* (London, 1932), E. P. Sanders, *Paul and Palestinian Judaism* (Philadelphia, 1977), H. Räisänen, *Paul and the Law* (Tübingen, 1987 [2nd ed.]).

9. K. Ehrensperger, *That We May be Mutually Encouraged* (New York, London, 2004).

10. See LSJM 2.1299.

11. The image of the serpent often is seen with a bird. We earlier drew attention to the serpent together with the dove on ceramics found at Beth Shan. Also see W. Fauth, "Widder, Schlange und Vogel am heiligen Baum zur ikonographie einer Anatolisch-Mediterranen Symbolkonstellation," *Anatolica* 6 (1977–78) 129–57 with 12 Plates.

12. See the comments by A. Byatt in *New Testament Metaphors* (Edinburgh, 1995) p. 36.

13. Among many publications, see Byatt, *New Testament Metaphors,* esp. pp. 36 and 52.

14. Gregory of Nyssa, *On Virginity* 16; trans. W. Moore and H. A. Wilson, "Gregory of Nyssa: On Virginity," *NPNF2* 5, p. 362.

15. Augustine, *On Christian Doctrine* 1.14.13; trans. J. F. Shaw, "Augustine: On Christian Doctrine," *NPNF1* 2, p. 526.

16. Augustine, *Sermons on New-Testament Lessons* 23.3; trans. R. G. MacMullen, "The Works of St. Augustine: Sermons on New Testament Lessons," *NPNF1* 6, p. 334.

17. Long ago, E. Nestle rightly saw that John the Baptizer and Jesus use the expression "generation of vipers" to denote that the ones targeted "are not ordinary serpents, but venomous vipers." Nestle, "Generation of Vipers," *ExpTim* 23 (1911–12) 185. This comment is significant; it reveals a perception of good and evil ophidian symbolism.

18. Ovid, *Metam.* 3.531–32. Again in 7.212 Medea bewails her plight and refers to the "serpent-born band" *(vos serpentigenis)*. Translations mine. For the Latin see Miller (LCL 1971) vol. 1, pp. 160–61. The Latin *"anguigena"* denotes the offspring of a serpent; the word is typical of Ovid. See the *Oxford Latin Dictionary* (Oxford and London, 1968) vol. 1, p. 129.

19. O. Betz, "Die Proselytentaufe der Qumransekte und die Taufe im Neuen Testament," *RevQ* 2.1 (1958) 213–34.

20. See L. Schiffman in DJD 20 (1997) 41–42.

21. Brackets are used to denote restorations (the leather either has a hole in it or the ink has been abraded away).

22. R. E. Brown concluded (when he wrote his Commentary) that the Fourth Gospel reflects five stages of composition. See Brown, *The Gospel According to John* (Anchor Yale Bible; Garden City, N.Y., 1966; rpt. New Haven) vol. 1, pp. xxiv–xxxix.

23. See the contributions in P. L. Hofrichter, ed., *Für und wider die Priorität des Johannesevangeliums* (Zürich, New York, 2002); Charlesworth, "The Priority of John? Reflections on the Essenes and the First Edition of John," in *Für und wider die Priorität des Johannesevangeliums,* pp. 73–114. Although M. Slee focuses on the *Didache* and Matthew, she clarifies the importance of Antioch for Jesus' followers in the first century CE. See Slee, *The Church in Antioch in the First Century CE* (Sheffield, 2003).

24. See esp. the contributions in Charlesworth, ed., *John and the Dead Sea Scrolls* (New York, 1991); also see Charlesworth, "The Dead Sea Scrolls and the Gospel According to John," in *Exploring the Gospel of John: In Honor of D. Moody Smith,* ed. R. A. Culpepper and C. C. Black (Louisville, 1996) pp. 65–97; J. Ashton, *Understanding the Fourth Gospel* (Oxford, 1991) p. 237; and E. Ruckstuhl, *Jesus im Horizont der Evangelien* (Stuttgart, 1988) p. 393.

25. P. Gardner-Smith concluded that the Fourth Evangelist did not know any of the Synoptics; see his *Saint John and the Synoptic Gospels* (Cambridge, 1938). Now, see esp. D. M. Smith, *John Among the Gospels* (Minneapolis, 1992 [see the rev. ed., published by University of South Carolina Press in 2001]).

26. See Charlesworth, *The Beloved Disciple: Whose Witness Validates the Gospel of John?* (Valley Forge, Pa., 1995).

27. M. L. Robert, "Dans une maison d'Éphèse: Un serpent et un chiffre," *CRAI* (1982) 126–32.

28. I am indebted to insights shared by S. R. F. Price; see his *Rituals and Power: The Roman Imperial Cult in Asia Minor* (Cambridge, New York, 1987); see esp. "Images," pp. 170–206.

29. I am influenced by the division of texts provided by M. E. Boismard and A. Lamouille, *Synopsis Graeca Quattuor Evangeliorum* (Leuven, Paris, 1986) p. 29.

30. Translation and italics mine.

31. The serpent plays a significant role in many modern poems and it is usually a sinister creature. For example, Paul Valéry presents the serpent almost always as the intruding and dangerous presence in the garden of our lives. See Paul Valéry, *Gedichte: Französisch und Deutsch,* ed. R. M. Rilke (Frankfurt, 1988) see esp. pp. 48–49, 52–

53, 56–57, 72–73, 78–79, 90–91. I wish to express appreciation to Monica Merkle, executive secretary of the Institut für antikes Judentum und hellenistische Religionsgeschichte of the Universität Tübingen, for helping me find poems about serpents. For poems featuring serpents, in addition to those presented here, see Ernst Lehmann-Leander's "Der Sündenfall," in M. Hanke, ed., *Die schönsten Schüttelgedichte* (Stuttgart, 1967) pp. 41–42; and F. Hölderlin, *Sämtliche Werke* (Leipzig, no date) pp. 261, 304, 821.

32. X. Léon-Dufour has written an insightful study of symbolism in the Fourth Gospel, but he does not discuss the symbol of the serpent in John 3:14; see his "Spécificité symbolique du langage de Jean," in *La communauté Johannique et son histoire,* ed. J.-D. Kaestli et al. (Geneva, 1990) pp. 121–34.

33. W. Thüsing concluded that "lifting up" referred not to the resurrection of Jesus (cf. Bultmann); it denoted only Jesus' crucifixion. This exegetical error arises by his missing the symbolism and focusing myopically on only one theme. See his *Die Erhöhung und Verherrlichung Jesu im Johannesevangelium* (Münster, 1960; cf. the edition of 1970) pp. 7–8.

34. See esp. *PssSol* 14, *1 En* 91 and 93, *Jubilees* 16, 1QS 8, 1QH 16, *OdesSol* 11. For a helpful, but incomplete, study of the tree and plant in early Jewish thought, see S. Fujita, "The Metaphor of Plant in Jewish Literature of the Intertestamental Period," *JSJ* 7 (1976) 30–45.

35. For a succinct introduction, see J. Daniélou, *Primitive Christian Symbols,* trans. D. Attwater (Baltimore, 1964).

36. J. G. Williams, "Serpent and the Son of Man," *TBT* 39 (January 2001) 22–26; see esp. p. 26.

37. M. Claudius, *Der Wandsbecker Bote,* ed. W. Weber (Zürich, 1947) p. 259; for a discussion of the serpent in biblical theology see pp. 255 and 344.

38. Brown, *The Gospel According to John,* pp. 145–46.

39. Carson, *The Gospel According to John,* p. 201.

40. Morris, *The Gospel According to John,* p. 199.

41. U. Wilckens, *Das Evangelium nach Johannes* (Göttingen, 2000) p. 71.

42. K. Wengst, *Das Johannes-evangelium,* 2 vols. (Stuttgart, 2000) vol. 1, p. 134.

43. R. R. Marrs, "John 3:14–15: The Raised Serpent in the Wilderness: The Johannine Use of an Old Testament Account," in *Johannine Studies: Essays in Honor of Frank Pack,* ed. J. E. Priest (Malibu, 1989) pp. 132–47.

44. D. M. Smith, *John* (Nashville, 1999) p. 98.

45. John Chrysostom, *Homilies on St. John* 27; cf. (translator not specified), "John Chrysostom: Homilies on St. John," *NPNF1* 14, p. 94.

46. *PE* 1.10.45; for the Greek and English see H. W. Attridge and R. A. Oden, *Philo of Byblos: The Phoenician History* (Washington, D.C., 1981) pp. 62–63.

47. See M. G. Kovacs, *The Epic of Gilgamesh* (Stanford, 1989) pp. 106–7.

48. Arnobius, *Against the Heathen* Book 7, 44; *ANF* 6, p. 536. Since this work is directed toward those who are not specialists in early church history, I shall cite the early Christian texts according to the popular and easily available *ANF* and *NPNF.*

49. B. J. Brooten thinks rightly that the Naasenes (or Ophites) did not see the serpent as "the downfall of humanity," but rather "as a giver of wisdom and knowledge." Brooten, *Love Between Women: Early Christian Responses to Female Homoeroticism* (Chicago, London, 1996) p. 338, note 145. For a succinct introduction to the Ophites, see A. Schramm, "Ophiten," *Paulys Realencyclopädie* 35 (1939) cols. 654–

59, E. F. Scott, "Ophitism," *ERE* 9.499–501, and G. Quispel, "Ophiten," *Lexicon für Theologie und Kirche* 7 (Freiburg, 1962) cols. 1178–79. Also see Appendix IV.

50. Theodoret, *Dialogues* 3; trans. B. Jackson, "Dialogues," *NPNF2* 3, p. 226.

51. See the images and insightful research published in Charlesworth, ed., *The Messiah* (Minneapolis, 1992).

52. I am grateful to Professor Arthur Charlesworth for this citation.

53. See now esp. G. Theissen, *The Gospels in Context,* trans. L. Maloney (Minneapolis, 1991).

54. Athenagoras the Athenian, *A Plea for the Christians* 29:10; trans. B. P. Pratten, "A Plea for the Christians by Athenagoras the Athenian: Philosopher and Christian," *ANF* 2, p. 144.

55. Tertullian, *Apology* 14; see the translation by S. Thelwall, "Tertullian: Apology," *ANF* 3, pp. 29–30.

56. See also Tertullian, *Apology* 15; trans. S. Thelwall, "Tertullian: Apology," *ANF* 3, pp. 29–30.

57. On how Asclepius healed a youth who had been virtually mortally wounded, see Lactantius, *The Divine Institutes* 1.17.

58. Athanasius, *On the Incarnation of the Word,* 49; trans. A. Robertson, "On the Incarnation of the Word," *NPNF2* 4, p. 63.

59. Clement of Alexandria, *The Stromata* 16; trans. Coxe, "The Stromata, or Miscellanies," *ANF* 2, p. 317.

60. Pindar, *Pythian Odes* 1.6–7. For the Greek and English translation, see J. Sandys, *The Odes of Pindar* (LCL; Cambridge, Mass., London, 1968) pp. 184–85.

61. Tertullian, *Apology* 23; trans. Thelwall, "Tertullian: Apology," *ANF* 3, p. 37.

62. Tertullian, *The Chaplet* 8; trans. S. Thelwall, "Tertullian: The Chaplet, or De Corona," *ANF* 3, p. 97.

63. Origen, *Against Celsus* 3.23; trans. F. Crombie, "Origen Against Celsus," *ANF* 4, p. 472.

64. See the texts cited in Appendix IV on the Rotas-Sator Square.

65. Justin Martyr, *First Apology* 22; trans. Coxe, "First Apology," *ANF* 1, p. 170. Also see Justin Martyr, *First Apology* 14 and 60.

66. Angus, *The Mystery Religions and Christianity,* pp. 307–9.

67. E. Dinkler, *Christus und Asklepios* (Heidelberg, 1980); see Tafel II.

68. K. H. Rengstorf, *Die Anfänge der Auseinandersetzung zwischen Christusglaube und Asklepiosfrömigkeit* (Münster, 1953).

69. D. M. Smith, *John,* p. 98.

70. One of the major studies on typology is by L. Goppelt. He, however, does not discuss the serpent in Jn 3:14. See Goppelt, *Typos* (Darmstadt, 1969). Although G. W. Buchanan has focused only on the Synoptics, his work is helpful; see his *Typology and the Gospel* (New York, London, 1987).

71. Suetonius, *The Twelve Caesars,* trans. R. Graves, rev. with an intro. by M. Grant (London, New York, 1989) pp. 104–5.

72. Suetonius, "Augustus," 94.

73. It is possible that Suetonius' statement, "Everyone believes this story," refers not only to the astrologer's claim about Augustus, which immediately precedes it, but also to the story of the birth of Augustus from a snake. Suetonius, "Augustus," 94 (in Graves and Grant, *The Twelve Caesars,* p. 105).

74. Later, sometime in the second century CE, some words were altered and 7:53–8:11 was interpolated.

75. On the date of the first edition of the Fourth Gospel, see Charlesworth, "The Priority of John? Reflections on the Essenes and the First Edition of John," in *Für und wider die Priorität des Johannesevangeliums,* ed. P. L. Hofrichter (Zürich, New York, 2002) pp. 73–114.

76. For the Greek and English see Attridge and Oden, *Philo of Byblos,* pp. 64–65.

77. The Greek verb means "become young again."

78. For the Greek and English see Attridge and Oden, *Philo of Byblos,* pp. 64–65.

79. Paul (and his school) used it thirty-seven times. See R. Morgenthaler, *Statistik des Neutestamentlichen Wortschatzes* (Zürich, Frankfurt am Main, 1958) p. 103.

80. See Appendix III.

81. See Charlesworth, "Reinterpreting John: How the Dead Sea Scrolls Have Revolutionized Our Understanding of John," *BRev* 9 (1993) 18–25, 53.

82. Josephus, *War* 5.108; H. St. J. Thackeray, *Josephus* (LCL 210; Cambridge, London, 1968) vol. 3, p. 232.

83. The pool is not yet identified. It may be the Birket Mamilla, which is the Pool of Suleiman the Magnificent that is west and a little south of the western walls of Jerusalem. See J. J. Rousseau and R. Arav, *Jesus and His World: An Archaeological and Cultural Dictionary* (Minneapolis, 1995) p. 180. For the claim that the Serpent's Pool is not the "Dragon Well," see J. Simons, *Jerusalem in the Old Testament: Researches and Theories* (Leiden, 1952) pp. 162–63.

84. The use of *kathōs* and *houtōs* to clarify a comparison appears elsewhere in the New Testament; often in the first line Jonah or Noah appears and in the second the Son of Man Christology (see esp. Lk 11:30, 17:26).

85. The argument was presented by Bernard, *Gospel According to St. John* (Edinburgh, 1928) pp. 112–13.

86. T. Zahn, *Das Evangelium des Johannes* (Wuppertal, 1983 [reprint of 1921: 5th and 6th ed.]) p. 204.

87. My translation is intentionally idiomatic. R. Schnackenburg, "Die 'situationsgelösten' Redestücke in Joh 3," *ZNW* 49 (1958) 95 (italics mine).

88. The translation seems misleading. Bultmann wrote "Jn V. 14 ist allein die Erhöhung genannt." In light of other comments by him, Bultmann may be including both the crucifixion and the exaltation in the ambiguous German noun that means "raised" or "elevated." See Bultmann, *Das Evangelium des Johannes* (Göttingen, 1959 [16th printing; 10th ed.]) p. 110. In Bultmann's *Das Evangelium des Johannes: Ergänzungsheft* (Göttingen, 1959) he added, rightly against Dodd, that the "Erhöhte" of v. 14 "ist doch der καταβάς von v. 13" (p. 23).

89. I agree with Bultmann that there is a discernible flow of thought from 3:13 to 3:16. Other scholars see 3:14–15 either as originally a separate logion (Colpe, Schulz) or as a dialogue with a loose structure (Meeks). See the insightful discussion in H. Maneschg, *Die Erzählung von der ehernen Schlange,* p. 388.

90. Bultmann, *The Gospel of John,* trans. G. R. Beasley-Murray (Philadelphia, 1971); the quotations are from pp. 151–53.

91. M. Hengel, *The Johannine Question* (London, Philadelphia, 1989) p. 189 n. 69.

92. G. R. Beasley-Murray, *John* (Waco, Tex., 1987) p. 50.

93. H. Weder, "L'Asymétrie du salut: Réflexions sur Jean 3, 14–21 dans le cadre de la théologie Johannique," in *La communauté Johannique et son histoire,* ed. J.-D. Kaestli et al. (Geneva, 1990) 155–84; the quotation is on p. 161.

94. F. Hahn, *Theologies des Neuen Testaments* (Tübingen, 2002) vol. 1, p. 631. Hahn correctly claims that "lifting up" includes not only the crucifixion but the exaltation: "Hier ist mit dem 'Erhöhtwerden' nicht nur der äußere Akt der Befestigung am Kreuz gemeint, sondern das 'Erhöhtwerden von der Erde,' die Aufnahme in den Himmel, die mit Jesu Tod beginnt" (vol. 1, p. 650; also see vol. 2, pp. 246–47).

95. As L. Zani states, "l'evangelista Giovanni e i primi cristiani utilizzino l'Antico Testamento per riflettere sul mistero della vita, della morte e della risurrezione del Signore." Zani, "Il serpente di rame e Gesè," in *La storie de Jesu* (Milan, 1984) p. 1339.

96. Basil, *On the Spirit* 14.31; the translation is by B. Jackson, "Basil: The De Spiritu Sancto," *NPNF2* 28, p. 20. In *Letters* 260.8, Basil again takes up the *typos* of the serpent for Christ; each time he is clearly influenced by the LXX's *sēmeion* for "staff."

97. E. Haenchen, *John 1,* trans. R. W. Funk (Hermeneia; Philadelphia, 1984) p. 204.

98. Westcott, *The Gospel According to St. John* (London, 1919) p. 53.

99. R. J. Burns, "Jesus and the Bronze Serpent," *TBT* 28 (1990) 84. Perhaps Burns sees this connection because she is primarily an Old Testament specialist.

100. Beasley-Murray, *John,* p. 50.

101. Bernard, *Gospel According to St. John,* p. 113 (italics mine).

102. The Lord said to Moses: "Make yourself a serpent and put it on a staff" (Ποίησον σεαυτῷ ὄφιν καὶ θὲς αὐτὸν ἐπὶ σημείου). Most likely Justin Martyr is influenced by the LXX when he interprets Jn 3:14–15; cf. *Dialogue with Trypho* 92 and 94.

103. Frey, "Die *'theologia crucifixi'* des Johannesevangeliums," in *Kreuzestheologie im Neuen Testament,* ed. A. Dettwiler and J. Zumstein (Tübingen, 2002) pp. 169–238; see esp. pp. 223–24.

104. J. Asurmendi contends rightly: "[E]n el evangelio de Juan, la serpiente sirve de tipo para simbolizar la nueva y definitiva salvación." Asurmendi, "En Torno a la Serpiente de Bronce," *EstBib* 46 (1988) 283–94; the quotation is on p. 294.

105. Augustine, "On the Gospel of John," 12.11; the quotation is from *NPNF1* 7, p. 85. As P. Th. Calmes perceived, there is a clear "relationship between Jesus' crucifixion and the elevation of the serpent in the wilderness" ("rapprochement entre le crucifiement de Jésus et l'élévation du serpent d'airain"). Calmes, *L'Évangile selon Saint Jean* (Paris, 1904) p. 187.

106. J. P. Gabler, "An Oration," p. 141.

107. The symbols of an anchor, a shore, a harbor, a sunset, the completion of an *inclusion* in writing, a concluding summary by a chorus in a Greek tragedy—all portray or indicate closure. See D. H. Roberts, F. M. Dunn, and D. Fowler, eds., *Classical Closure* (Princeton, 1998).

108. *Parallelismus membrorum,* or *isocolon,* is thought, written or oral, that is focused on coordinated lines of similar length within an isolated linguistic group of words. See the reflections by W. G. E. Watson, "Hebrew Poetry," in *Text in Context* (Oxford, 2000) pp. 253–85; see esp. pp. 260–61.

109. See now the excellent study by K. Seybold, *Poetik der Psalmen* (Stuttgart, 2003); see esp. pp. 83–127 and the publications cited by him.

110. I shall not discuss meter since Freedman has convinced me that Hebrew poetry has quantity, but not meter (as in Greek and Latin and today in English and other

modern languages). See D. N. Freedman, "Another Look at Biblical Hebrew Poetry," in *Directions in Biblical Hebrew Poetry*, ed. E. R. Follis (Sheffield, 1987) pp. 11–27; esp. see p. 27.

111. M. Hengel, "Die Schriftauslegung des 4. Evangeliums auf dem Hintergrund der urchristlichen Exegese," in *"Gesetz" als Thema Biblischer Theologie* (Neukirchen-Vluyn, 1989) pp. 249–88.

112. D. N. Freedman, "Pottery, Poetry, and Prophecy: An Essay on Biblical Poetry," in *The Bible in Its Literary Milieu*, ed. V. L. Tollers and J. R. Maier (Grand Rapids, 1979) pp. 77–100. As Freedman states: "[P]rose and poetry are basically two different ways of using language. Each has its own rules of operation, and it is obligatory to understand each category according to its own pattern, even if the dividing line is not always certain" (pp. 78–79).

113. The translators of the RSV (2nd ed.) erred, "He has risen," but the NRSV has translated the verb correctly: "He has been raised."

114. See LSJM, p. 1910.

115. Often *ioudaioi* in the Fourth Gospel should be translated as "Judeans." See Charlesworth, "The Gospel of John: Exclusivism Caused by a Social Setting Different from That of Jesus (John 11:54 and 14:6)," in *Anti-Judaism and the Fourth Gospel*, ed. R. Bieringer et al. (Leuven, 2001) pp. 479–513.

116. See esp. H. Leroy, *Rätsel und Missverständnis: Ein Beitrag zur Formgeschichte des Johannesevangeliums* (Bonn, 1968). Also see T. Nicklas, *Ablösung und Verstrickung* (Frankfurt am Main, New York, 2001) pp. 232–37.

117. Also see the discussion by Y. Simoens in *Secondo Giovanni*, trans. M. A. Cozzi (Bologna, 2002) p. 255. Simoens sees a triple entendre in *anōthen*: "The new, the first (or beginning), and the above" ("di nuovo, dal principio, dall'alto," p. 251).

118. As Frey states, crucifixion and exaltation in John are not two events; they are one. Frey, "Die *'theologia crucifixi'* des Johannesevangeliums," in *Kreuzestheologie*; see esp. p. 259, "Die Erhöhung des Menschensohns wird hier in eine Analogie zur Erhöhung der Schlange durch Mose in der Wüste (Num 21,8f) gesetzt. Vergleichspunkt ist der Erhöhung, ihre Art und Weise . . . sowie ihre Ausrichtung auf die Menschen, vor denen sie geschieht." Since there is no "lifting up" in Num 21, it is clear that the link between the two texts, Num 21 and Jn 3, is the image of the upraised serpent.

119. That is, seven times in Mt, eight in Mark, ten in Lk, but twelve in John.

120. According to the *Acts of John* 94, "the lawless Jews," who are governed by "the lawless Serpent," are responsible for Jesus' death.

121. See esp. Jonsson, *Humor and Irony in the New Testament*, Leroy, *Rätsel und Missverständnis*, Culpepper, *Anatomy of the Fourth Gospel: A Study in Literary Design*, and Duke, *Irony in the Fourth Gospel*.

122. That Jesus' words end in 3:15 seems likely, though not certain. Schnackenburg opined that the monologue ended in 3:12 and that verses 13–21 are the theological reflections of the Fourth Evangelist. Schnackenburg, "Die 'situationsgelösten' Redestücke in Joh 3," 90.

123. G. R. O'Day, *Revelation in the Fourth Gospel: Narrative Mode and Theological Claim* (Philadelphia, 1986), p. 25.

124. See O'Day, ibid., pp. 25–27; Muecke, "Irony Markers," *Poetics* 7 (1978) 365; Booth, *The Rhetoric of Irony*; Duke, *Irony in the Fourth Gospel*, chap. 4.

125. Smith, *The Theology of the Gospel of John*, p. 114.

126. Smith, *The Theology of the Gospel of John*, p. 115.

127. See B. J. Malina, *The Palestinian Manna Tradition* (Leiden, 1968).

128. See esp. Borgen, *Bread from Heaven* (Leiden, 1965), W. A. Meeks, *The Prophet-King: Moses Traditions and the Johannine Christology* (Leiden, 1967), and S. Pancaro, *The Law in the Fourth Gospel* (Leiden, 1975).

129. According to the *Gospel of Nicodemus* 1:1–2, Pilate tells the Jews no one casts out demons, except by the name of Asclepius.

130. Commentators habitually miss the *parallelismus membrorum* of Jn 3:14–15. J. Mateos and J. Barreto rightly understand the poetic form and its importance for revealing the synonymity of the serpent and the Son of Man: "Tutttavia il parallelismo è chiaro: al serpente del primo membro corrisponde 'l'Uomo' del secondo." *Il Vangelo di Giovanni*, trans. T. Tosatti (Assisi, 2000 [4th ed.]) p. 184.

131. Augustine, *Reply to Faustus the Manichaean* 14.7; trans. R. Stothert, "The Works of St. Augustine: Reply to Faustus the Manichaean," *NPNF1* 4, p. 209. Also see Augustine, *On Forgiveness of Sins, and Baptism* 1.61.

132. As Mateos and J. Barreto state: "[T]he uplifted serpent" signifies "liberation from death." *Il Vangelo di Giovanni*, p. 184.

133. Not only the Fourth Evangelist but also many of his readers knew by heart, in Hebrew or Greek, the text and interpretations of Num 21. So also R. Marrs, *Johannine Studies*, ed. J. E. Priest (Malibu, Calif., 1989) p. 139.

134. As I. Nowell states, "Linking of a complex of traditions is illustrated by the relationship between the Gospel of John and the Book of Numbers." Nowell, "Typology: A Method of Interpretation," *TBT* 28 (1990) 73.

135. As J. Barr stated, typology when controlled and informed is "wholesome and viable." Allegory is not. Note Barr's insight: "[T]ypology is based on historical correspondences and thus related to the Bible's own historical emphasis; while, judged by that same emphasis, allegory is non-historical and anti-historical." Barr, "Typology and Allegory," *Old and New in Interpretation* (London, 1966); the quotation is from p. 104. In *Die Erzählung von der ehernen Schlange*, Maneschg sees the "Typus und Antitypus," but he fails to explore or show any interest in the serpent imagery and symbolism (p. 400).

136. P. Borgen shows how Isa 52:13 and Dan 7:13–14 shaped the thought of Jn 3:14; both were joined to indicate an "installation in a royal office." Borgen also brilliantly demonstrated how traditions later found in the Midrash to Ps 2 ("you are my son") were interpreted in light of Isa 52:13 and Dan 7:13–14 to reveal enthronement. See Borgen, "Some Jewish Exegetical Traditions," p. 252.

137. Charlesworth, "A Rare Consensus Among Enoch Specialists: The Date of the Earliest Enoch Books," *Hen* 24 (2002) 225–34.

138. E. Ruckstuhl, "Abstieg und Erhöhung des johanneischen Menschensohns," *Jesu im Horizont der Evangelien*, pp. 277–310.

139. O. Hofius, "Das Wunder der Wiedergeburt: Jesu Gespräch mit Nikodemus," in *Johannesstudien*, ed. Hofius and H.-C. Kammler (Tübingen, 1996) p. 59.

140. See M. Theobald, *Herrenworte im Johannesevangelium*, pp. 587–88 (New York, 2000).

141. Ginzberg, *Legends of the Jews*, vol. 3, p. 336. Le Grande Davies also points out that "the serpent as a symbol of YHWH does not appear after the time of Hezekiah in the literature of the kingdom of Judah in the Promised Land." He rightly stressed that the serpent was "a symbol or token of the saving powers of the God of Israel." See his "Serpent Imagery in Ancient Israel," pp. 33 and 34.

142. Augustine, *The City of God* 10.8; trans. M. Dods, "Augustine: The City of God," *NPNF2*, p. 185.

143. The Seventh Ecumenical Council, Quaestio LVI; trans. H. R. Percival, "The Seventh Ecumenical Council," *NPNF2* 14, p. 554.

144. Theobald, *Herrenworte im Johannesevangelium*, p. 588.

145. Consult Morgenthaler, *Statistik des Neutestamentlichen Wortschatzes*, p. 132.

146. *Barn.* 12.7; Lake, *Apostolic Fathers*, vol. 1, pp. 384–85.

147. *Barn.* 12.5; Lake, *Apostolic Fathers*, vol. 1, pp. 384–85.

148. See the discussion by M. Black, *An Aramaic Approach to the Gospels and Acts* (Oxford, 1967 [3rd ed.]) p. 141.

149. This verbal form is the Ethpe. of *zqp*. My transliterations are designed for those who do not know Semitics and the sophisticated way of transcribing the foreign words. I expect that they can comprehend how the word or words might sound.

150. See also the discussion by Frey in *Schriftauslegung im antiken Judentum und im Urchristentum*, pp. 186–87.

151. G. Kittel, "אזדקף = ὑψωθῆναι; Gekreuzigtwerden: Zur angeblichen antiochenischen Herkunft des vierten Evangeliums," *ZNW* 35 (1936) 282–85. This important article by a luminary in biblical studies is virtually unknown. It is not cited by those who justly are praised for knowing the work of other scholars, notably, R. E. Brown in his *The Gospel According to John*, W. Thüsing in *Die Erhöhung und Verherrlichung Jesu im Johannesevangelium* (Neutestamentliche Abhandlungen 21; 1.2) (Münster, 1959; 1970 [2nd ed.]), H. Maneschg in *Die Erzählung von der ehernen Schlange*, M. Hengel in his *Die johanneische Frage*, and J. Frey in his three-volume *Die johanneische Eschatologie*.

152. Many scholars today trace the beginnings of the Fourth Gospel to Palestine; as G. Theissen states: "[T]he prehistory of the Gospel of John leads to Palestine." Theissen, *Fortress Introduction to the New Testament*, trans. J. Bowden (Minneapolis, 2003) p. 146.

153. See Whiteley in *ANRW* II.25.3 and E. D. Freed, *Old Testament Quotations in the Gospel of John* (Leiden, 1965).

154. J. P. Gabler, "An Oration," p. 141.

155. He also knows the traditions preserved in Gen 26 according to which Isaac's servants find a well of freshwater (for the Evangelist "living water") in the Land and see it as a sign that "we shall be fruitful in the Land (26:22)." The Evangelist refers to this episode as "the gift of God" (4:10).

156. Brown, *John*, p. 322. See esp. Fabry's discussion in *Theologisches Wörterbuch zum Alten Testament;* vol. 5, pp. 468–73.

157. Sinaiticus (the first hand) and Epiphanius have "serpent."

158. In 1889, E. Schürer rightly pointed out that the Fourth Gospel should be seen within the world of Judaism; he, however, claimed that Philo's use of Logos was the probable origin of the Fourth Evangelist's thought. Note these words: "Der Evangelist sei ein Mann von alexandrinisch-philosophischer Bildung." See Schürer's publication in *Johannes und sein Evangelium*, ed. K. H. Rengstorf (Darmstadt, 1973) p. 21.

159. It is disappointing to observe that neither of these significant links between the Gospels and Greek and Latin literature is mentioned or noted in the *Hellenistic Commentary to the New Testament*.

160. See the photograph in L. I. Levine, ed., *Ancient Synagogues Revealed* (Jerusalem, 1981) p. 130. For a better photograph, see M. Avi-Yonah, *Art in Ancient Palestine: Selected Studies,* ed. H. Katzenstein and Y. Tsafrir (Jerusalem, 1981) Plate 41.

161. For a photograph see Levine, ed. *Ancient Synagogues,* p. 108.

162. For a discussion of this indissoluble knot see Avi-Yonah, *Art in Ancient Palestine,* pp. 76–77.

163. See Levine, *Ancient Synagogues,* pp. 110, 154–55; for a photograph of the lintel with the large snake see p. 156.

164. More than one Qappar is known, and the period is most likely from the second to the fourth centuries CE.

165. J. Ma'oz concludes his study of synagogal iconography in the Golan with the claim: "[W]e should emphasize the abundance of faunal reliefs and the complete absence of mythological wildlife scenes, so common in the synagogues at Capernaum and Chorazin." Ma'oz in Levine, *Ancient Synagogues,* p. 112.

166. See, e.g., Theobald, *Herrenworte im Johannesevangelium,* p. 201.

167. Bultmann concluded that the Evangelist derived the interpretation of Num 21 "wohl durch die christliche Tradition." *Das Evangelium des Johannes,* p. 109.

168. A work related to these early Christian compositions is the *Didache.* It is heavily influenced by early Jewish thought, as M. Del Verme has shown. See Del Verme's recent articles: "*DID*.16 e la considdetta 'Apocalittica Giudaica'," *Orpheus* N.S. 22 (2001) 39–76 and "*Didaché* e origini cristiane: Una bibliografia per lo studio della *Didaché* nel contesto del giudaismo cristiano," *Vetera Christianorum* 38 (2001) 5–39.

169. See Maneschg, *Die Erzählung von der ehernen Schlange,* pp. 175–82.

170. For Philo, see F. H. Colson and G. H. Whitaker, *Philo* (LCL; Cambridge, Mass., 1929, 1999) vol. 1 [*Allegorical Interpretation*] and Colson and Whitaker (LCL; Cambridge, Mass., 1930, 1988) vol. 3 (*On Husbandry*).

171. For reflections on Num 21 and the possible breaking of God's own commandment against making any images, see Tertullian, *On Idolatry 5*; see the translation by Thelwall, "On Idolatry," *ANF* 3, pp. 63–64.

172. Danby, *The Mishnah* (Oxford, 1933) p. 192.

173. J. Neusner, *The Mishnah: A New Translation* (New Haven, London, 1988) p. 305.

174. Brown, *John,* p. 133.

175. M.-É. Boismard and A. Lamouille, *L'Évangile de Jean* (Paris, 1977) vol. 2, p. 115.

176. M. J. Lagrange, *Évangile selon Saint Jean* (Paris, 1927) p. 81.

177. See esp. D. Crossan, *The Gospel of Eternal Life: Reflections on the Theology of St. John* (Milwaukee, 1967).

178. Ignatius, *The Martyrdom of Ignatius,* 12; trans. A. C. Coxe, "The Martyrdom of Ignatius," *ANF* 1, p. 145 (italics mine).

179. Trans. A. C. Coxe, "The Epistle of Ignatius to the Smyrnaeans," *ANF* 1, p. 87 (italics mine).

180. As M. M. Beirne states, Mary Magdalene and Thomas, through the narrative, prove the Johannine shepherd imagery; they respond to the shepherd's calling them by name. See Beirne, *Women and Men in the Fourth Gospel* (Sheffield, 2003) p. 210.

181. A gifted linguist might ask, "Since the Greek verb for 'to touch' also can mean 'to eat' (cf. *Odyssey* 4,60 and esp. Plutarch, *Antonius* 17[923]), is the Fourth Evan-

gelist creating a subtle paronomasia here with the forbidden fruit in the Garden of Eden?"

182. John Chrysostom, *Homilies on Colossians* 6; trans. G. Alexander, "John Chrysostom: Homilies on Colossians," *NPNF1* 13, pp. 286–87. I altered the translation by removing an archaism.

183. See esp. W. Bauer, *Orthodoxy and Heresy in Earliest Christianity,* ed. R. Kraft and G. Krodel (Philadelphia, 1971) and H. E. W. Turner, *The Pattern of Christian Truth: A Study of the Relations Between Orthodoxy and Heresy in the Early Church* (London, 1954).

184. For a list of titles of Jesus in the Fourth Gospel, see M.-É. Boismard and A. Lamouille, *L'Évangile de Jean,* vol. 2, p. 53.

185. The words are dominical and *ex ore Christi* (placed in Christ's mouth).

186. A good case may be made for some authentic Jesus traditions hidden behind Jn 3:14; see the arguments of C. L. Blomberg, *The Historical Reliability of John's Gospel* (Downers Grove, Ill., 2001) p. 183. Also see the general, often brilliant, reflections of P. N. Anderson in *The Christology of the Fourth Gospel: Its Unity and Disunity in the Light of John 6* (Tübingen, 1996).

187. Lactantius, *The Divine Institutes* 3.20; trans. W. Fletcher, "Lactantius: The Divine Institutes," *ANF* 7, p. 92.

188. Also see Origen, *Cels.* 6.4.

189. Tertullian, *Apology* 46; trans. Thelwall, "Tertullian: Apology," *ANF* 3, pp. 50–51. Also see Tertullian's *The Chaplet* 10, *Ad Nationes* 2.2 and *A Treatise on the Soul* 1, and *The Five Books Against Marcion* 3.28.

190. Ephrem had intensively and carefully studied Gen, esp. chap. 3; see the discussion by Kronholm, "The Cruse on the Serpent," *Motifs from Genesis 1–11 in the Genuine Hymns of Ephrem the Syrian,* pp. 112–18.

191. Ephraim Syrus, *Hymns on the Nativity* 1; trans. J. B. Morris, "Nineteen Hymns on the Nativity of Christ in the Flesh," *NPNF2* 13, p. 224.

192. Cyril of Jerusalem, *Catechetical Lectures* 13.20 (Cyril goes on to stress that the saving medium is "wood," and points back to Noah). The translation cited is by E. H. Gifford, "Cyril, Archbishop of Jerusalem: Catechetical Lectures," *NPNF2* 7, pp. 87–88.

193. Gregory Nazianzus, *The Second Oration on Easter* 22; trans. C. G. Browne and J. E. Swallow, "Gregory Nazianzen: The Second Oration on Easter," *NPNF2* 7, p. 431.

194. See the study of the concept of the Holy Spirit from Clement of Alexandria to Origen by H. Ziebritzki in *Heiliger Geist und Weltseele* (Tübingen, 1994).

195. Ambrose, *Of the Holy Spirit* 3.8.50; trans. H. De Romestin, "Of the Holy Spirit," *NPNF2* 10, p. 142. Italics are mine.

196. A similar exegesis is provided by Augustine, who then became carried away by typology: "[J]ust as by gazing on that serpent which was lifted up in the wilderness, they did not perish by the bites of the serpents. For 'our old man is crucified with Him, that the body of sin might be destroyed.' For by the serpent death is understood, which was wrought by the serpent in paradise, the mode of speech expressing the effect by the efficient. Therefore the rod passed into the serpent, Christ into death; and the serpent again into the rod, whole Christ with His body into the resurrection; which body is the Church; and this shall be in the end of time, signified by the tail, which Moses held, in order that it might return into a rod. But the serpents of the magicians, like those who

are dead in the world, unless by believing in Christ they shall have been as it were swallowed up by, and have entered into, His body, will not be able to rise again in Him." Augustine, *On the Trinity* 3.10.10; trans. A. W. Haddan, "Augustine: On the Trinity," *NPNF1* 3, p. 64. Also see Augustine, *Reply to Faustus the Manichaean* 12.30.

197. C. Lantinga, "Christ, the Snake," *Per* 6 (March 1991) 14.

198. See Theobald, *Herrenworte im Johannesevangelium*, pp. 209–18. He is convinced that Mk 8:31 is "den *Basistext*" for Jn 3:14.

199. Harrison, *Numbers*, p. 279.

200. See Attridge and Oden, *Philo of Byblos*, pp. 66–67.

201. Note also 11QPsᵃ 27.2–3: "And David, the son of Jesse, was wise, and a light like the light of the sun . . . and perfect in all his ways before God and men."

202. K. Gemälde-Galerie in Vienna; Klassischer Bilderschatz, Nr. 999.

203. P. E. Testa drew attention to images of the cross as or with a serpent; some of his interpretations are imaginative. See Testa, "La croce come serpente," *Il simbolismo dei Giudeo-Cristiani* (Jerusalem, 1962) pp. 278–82.

204. Berlin, SMB-PK, MSB, Inv.-Nr. 4730. For a photograph, see S. Schaten, "Oberteil einer Grabstele," in *Ägypten Schätze aus dem Wüstensand* (Wiesbaden, 1996) p. 122.

205. H. Leclercq, *DACL* 15 (1950) 1356 (see Illus. No. 10881).

206. G. Cioffari and M. Miele, *Storia dei Domenicani nell'Italia Meridionale* (Naples-Bari, 1993) vol. 1, p. 141.

207. The painting is now restored. On the destruction by the Turks, see G. Maldacea, *Storia di Sorrento* (Naples, 1843) vol. 2, p. 213; and F. J. [= Filippo Iapelli], "Mater Auxiliatrix," *Societas: Rivista dei Gesuiti dell'Italia Meridionale* 39 (1990) 53–54. I was assisted in studying the Madonna di Casarlano by la Dott.ssa Lara Guglielmo, and express my appreciation for her assistance during my tenure as Most Distinguished Foreign Professor of the University of Naples.

208. A. Caruso, *Mater Auxiliatrix* (Naples, 1946) pp. 9–10.

209. See F. Japelli [= Filippo Iapelli], "Mater Auxiliatrix," 53–54. I am grateful to Father Iapelli [he prefers "I"] for his insights and assistance as I studied the painting and worked in the Bibliotheca San Sebastiano, Casa Professa del Gesù Nuovo, Naples. I am also appreciative to him and his superiors for permission to publish my photograph of the painting.

210. Johann Friedrich Overbeck (1789–1869) also depicted John the Evangelist with a chalice from which a serpent ascends. See M. Bernhard, ed., *Deutsche Romantik Handzeichnungen* (Herrsching, n.d.) vol. 2, p. 1078.

211. "Giovanni il prediletto, con un calice di serpi." A. Caruso, *Ferite Aperte* (Bari, 1958) p. 7. Also see Caruso, *Mater Auxiliatrix* (the first edition of Caruso's booklet), p. 7.

212. According to the *Acts of John* and the *Acts of John by Prochorus*, John's death is peaceful; he lies down in a trench, with his disciples watching, and dies. According to the *Acts of John at Rome*, the apostle drinks a cup of poison before Emperor Domitian, but he does not die (as prophesied for apostles in Mk 16:18). According to the *Syriac History of John (= History of St. John at Ephesus)*, the apostle lived until he was 120 and died peacefully. According to the Gospels, John either seems to suffer a martyr's death (Mk 10:39) or did not suffer martyrdom (Jn 21:22–23).

213. According to *Liber Flavus Fergusiorum* (c. fifteenth cent.), John drank poison (but he did not die). See R. A. Culpepper, *John the Son of Zebedee: The Life of a Legend* (Columbia, S.C., 1994) pp. 241 and 236.

214. This negative meaning seems apparent in other paintings, especially the one by El Greco (1541–1614) in which John the Evangelist holds a cup out of which a dragon rises. See Culpepper, *John the Son of Zebedee*, p. 253. Perhaps some paintings of John the Apostle with a viper in a cup reflect the legend that Aristodemus, the high priest of Diana at Ephesus, forced John to drink poison (cf. also the legend that Domitian forced John to drink poison). In each legend, John drinks the poison but does not die.

215. The power of the serpent's blood continues to be paradigmatic. In Southeast Asia, men sometimes drink serpent's blood before entering a brothel. I am grateful to Magen Broshi for conversations focused on serpents and on the aphrodisiac use of their blood.

216. See J. Campbell, *The Mythic Image* (Princeton, N.J., 1974) Illus. No. 279.

217. Our present research adds to the probability that Ignatius may have known the Gospel of John.

218. P. E. Testa, "La mitica rigenerazione della vita in un amuleto Samaritano-Cristiano del iv secolo," *Liber Annuus* 23 (1973) 286–317.

219. Asurmendi, "En Torno a la Serpiente de Bronce," 292.

220. A. Houziaux, *Le Tohu-bohu, le serpent et le bon Dieu* (Paris, 1997) p. 7.

221. Under the influence of the Hebrew Bible or Septuagint, some scribe interpolated "bronze" into the text of Jn 3:14 in the Persian Harmony. See W. L. Petersen, *Tatian's Diatessaron* (Leiden, New York, 1994) p. 261. On Jesus' symbolism also see the brilliant insights of H. Ausloos, "Mozes' bronzen slang: Gods 'teken van redding.' " *Schrift* 195 (2001) 69–71.

222. H. Lesêtre in *Dictionnaire de la Bible* (Vigouroux, 1912) vol. 5, col. 1675.

223. See Saint John Chrysostom, *Commentary on Saint John*, trans. T. A. Goggin (New York, 1957) pp. 262–63.

224. In *L'univers fantastique des Mythes*, the reader is correctly informed that the serpent in the wilderness ("le serpent d'airain") is a symbol of Christ ("symbole du Christ"). See A. Eliot et al., *L'univers fantastique des Mythes* (Paris, 1976) p. 175.

Conclusion

1. See Charlesworth, "Bashan, Symbology, Haplography, and Theology in Psalm 68," in *David and Zion: Biblical Studies in Honor of J. J. M. Roberts,* ed. B. F. Batto and K. L. Roberts (Winona Lake, Ind., 2004) pp. 351–72.

Epilogue

1. Ophiology is the branch of zoology that studies snakes. Ophiophilism is a love of snakes. Ophiolatry is the worship of snakes. Other English words derive etymologically from "ophis," the Greek generic term for "snake" or "serpent." Among these are ophiomancy that denotes divination by means of serpents. This rich vocabulary witnesses to our fascination—even preoccupation—with snakes and serpents. The interest in snakes continues today, but the relation between the human and the snake has collapsed. The obsolescence of words like "ophiophilism" denotes the human attempt to make the snake extinct.

2. I am indebted to the reflections published by I. Vogelsanger-de Roche in *Marc Chagall's Windows in the Zürich Fraumünster: Origins, Content and Significance* (Zürich, 1997); see esp. the outline on p. 13.

Appendix I

1. This appendix presupposes the study of serpent symbolism in the preceding work. Notes will be kept to a minimum and will tend to highlight what is not available in the well-known and easily accessible publications, especially the lexicons. I am grateful to D. Talshir for conversations; see his "The Nomenclature of the Fauna in the Samaritan Targum" (PhD diss., Hebrew University, Jerusalem, 1981 [in Hebrew]). I understand he is preparing an English updated version for publication. For further study, see M. Zor, החי בימי המקרא (Tel Aviv, 1997) esp. pp. 157–63, Y. Pelikas, החי של התנ״ך (Tel Aviv, 1954), Pelikas, החי במשנה (Jerusalem, 1972), and [no author], *Fauna and Flora of the Bible* (London, New York, Stuttgart, 1980 [2nd ed.]) esp. pp. 72–74, "Serpent, Viper, Adder, Leviathan."

2. In this appendix, I recognize that the reader will probably be a scholar trained in Semitics, but I will attempt, when possible, to include the nonspecialist.

3. T. K. Cheyne, "Serpent," *Encyclopedia Biblica* (New York, London, 1902) 4.4391.

4. E. E. Day and G. D. Jordan, "Serpent," *ISBE* (fully revised) (Grand Rapids, 1988) 4.417–18; see p. 417, "The OT has eleven Hebrew terms for serpents."

5. In Rabbinic Hebrew there are additional nonbiblical Hebrew nouns that denote snakes or serpents: "dragon-snake" (דרקון) in the *b. B. Bat.* 16b and "dragon-snake" (דרקונא) in *b. Ber.* 62b.

6. A good, but not comprehensive, list is found in R. C. Stallman, "נחש," *Dictionary of Old Testament Theology and Exegesis,* ed. W. A. VanGemeren (Grand Rapids, 1997) 5.84–88. For studies of *hapax legomena,* see H. R. Cohen, *Biblical Hapax Legomena in the Light of Akkadian and Ugaritic* (Missoula, Mont., 1978) and F. E. Greenspahn, *Hapax Legomena in Biblical Hebrew* (Chico, Calif., 1984).

7. See, e.g., Stallman, "Reptiles," *Dictionary of Old Testament Theology and Exegesis,* 4.1129–32.

8. M.-L. Henry, professor in Hamburg, reports that "Luther übersetzt alle Arten mit Otter, *sepha*ʿ und *siphʿōnī* mit Basilisk, *qippōz* mit Natter." Henry, "Schlange," *BHH* (1966) vol. 3, cols. 1699–1701; the quotation is on col. 1700.

9. See the following rather popular work: K. Zimniok, *Die Schlange das unbekannte Wesen* (Hanover, 1984).

10. Many complex meanings of the serpent are found in O. Seel's *Der Physiologus: Tiere und ihre Symbolik Übertragen und erläutert* (Zürich, 1995 [7th ed.]), but they are not critically evaluated and are too impressionistic.

11. See the questions raised by C. Paul-Stengel in her *Schlangenspuren: Reptilien in der Kulturgeschichte* (Königstein/Taunus, 1996) pp. 156–68.

12. Of the numerous publications, see M. Lurker, *Symbol: Mythos und Legende in der Kunst* (Baden-Baden, 1984) esp. p. 60; E. J. Edelstein and L. Edelstein, *Asclepius: Collection and Interpretation of the Testimonies,* 2 vols. (Baltimore, London, 1945, 1998); K. Kerényi, *Der Göttliche Arzt: Studien über Asklepios und seine Kultstätten* (Darmstadt, 1956); and H. A. Cahn, "Asklepios," *LIMC* II.1.863–901 (text) and *LIMC* II.2.631–69.

13. I am preparing for publication an early Roman vase with numerous serpents depicted on it. It was discovered by Clermont-Ganneau near Bethzatha at the end of the nineteenth century. It is now housed in the Palestinian Exploration Fund archives in London. For a succinct and popular article on serpent symbolism, see R. S. Bianchi,

"The Ancient Mediterranean Good and Evil Snakes," *Faces: The Magazine About People* (October 1995) 6–9.

14. In his commentary on Gen 3, A. Clarke claimed that if it were a serpent that tempted the woman, then he went about on his tail before the Fall. See the rebuttal by J. Bellamy in his *The Ophion; or the Theology of the Serpent, and the Unity of God* (London, 1811) p. 7.

15. For example, see the four-footed seven-headed serpent-dragon according to an Old Akkadian seal from about 2200 BCE (*ANET* no. 691; also see no. 671). Also see the picture of a serpent with human arms and legs in Brooklyn Museum Papyrus 47.218.156 of the fourth or third century BCE. See especially S. Sauneron, *Le Papyrus magique illustré de Brooklyn [Brooklyn Museum 47.218.156]* (Oxford, New York, 1970). Consult A. Roitman, " 'Crawl upon your belly' (Gen 3.14): The Physical Aspect of the Serpent in Early Jewish Exegesis," *Tarbiz* 64 (1994) 157–82 (Hebrew); for serpents with legs, see illustrations. See the numerous drawings from Egypt of serpents with legs in K. Michalowski, *L'Art de l'ancienne Égypte,* esp. Illus. Nos. 386, 391, 392, 505. Also see Fig. 27 in this work.

16. See H. W. Greene and D. Cundall, "Limbless Tetrapods and Snakes with Legs," *Science* 287 (2000) 1939–41 and E. Tchernov et al., "A Fossil Snake with Limbs," *Science* 287 (2000) 2010–12.

17. See R. Bauchot, ed., *Schlangen,* trans. C. Ronsiek (Augsburg, 1994) p. 30 (photograph) and p. 60 (statement).

18. See the illustrations of "Demons, monsters and minor protective deities" in J. Black and A. Green, *Gods, Demons and Symbols of Ancient Mesopotamia: An Illustrated Dictionary* (London, 1992, 1998) Illus. No. 53.

19. See Sauneron, *Le Papyrus magique illustré de Brooklyn,* esp. pp. vii–29; also see Figs. 2 and 3.

20. PrJac 8 in OTP 2.721; trans. J. H. Charlesworth.

21. O. Keel, *Das Recht der Bilder gesehen zu werden.* (Freiburg, Göttingen, 1992). Also see O. Keel and C. Uehlinger, *Gods, Goddesses, and Images of God in Ancient Israel,* trans. T. H. Trapp (Minneapolis, 1998) and A. Berlejung, *Die Theologie der Bilder* (Freiburg, Göttingen, 1998).

22. W. Kramp, *Protest der Schlange: Signale zum Umdenken* (Berlin, 1981).

23. F. S. Bodenheimer, in החי בארצות המקרא (Jerusalem, 1949) p. 338, suggests that the noun represents the *echis carinatus* or *echis colorata.*

24. L. Alonso Schökel et al., in *Diccionario bíblico hebreo-español* (Madrid, 1994), gives the meaning of "asp," and "viper," p. 84.

25. A. Bahat and M. Mishor, *Dictionary of Contemporary Hebrew* (Jerusalem, 1995) p. 39 (Hebrew to Hebrew lexicon). Even if *echis colorata* is appropriate today, we have no means to discern what species of the snake was in the mind or eyes of an ancient author or writer.

26. So also H.-J. Fabry in *TDOT* 9.359.

27. Much valuable information and reflection appears in E. Küster, *Die Schlange in der griechischen Kunst und Religion* (Giessen, 1913).

28. This Greek noun is not found in the LXX, but Aquila used it to translate אפעה in Isa 59:5. See W. Foerster, "ἔχιδνα," *TDNT* 2.815–16. The LXX has βασιλίσκος.

29. See 1QHᵃ 10.28 [= Sukenik 2] (here the noun means "emptiness"); 11.12 [Sukenik 3], 17, 18). See Charlesworth et al., *GCDS* (Tübingen, Louisville, 1991).

30. In the Hellenistic and Roman periods, the region was called "Batanea." See J. C. Slayton, "Bashan," *AYBD* 1.623–24. With different vocalization the consonants can denote Beth Shan (Scythopolis); see N. Jechielis, *Aruch Completum sive Lexicon Vocabula et Res, quae in Libris Targumicis, Talmudicis et Midraschicis* (1970) vol. 1, p. 207.

31. See, e.g., F. Brown, S. R. Driver, and C. A. Briggs. *A Hebrew and English Lexicon of the Old Testament* (Oxford, 1907) 143.

32. Cf. the Vulgate: Dixit Dominus: "Ex Basan convertam, /convertam in profundum maris."

33. None is cited in BHS for this construct.

34. The Syriac is an idiomatic expression; John Mard., apud *Bibliotheca Orientalis Clementino-Vaticana* 2.227, uses the same phrase but with the Syriac word for lion, which qualifies and explains the whole phrase: "from the house of the teeth of a lion" (i.e., "from within a lion's mouth surrounded by teeth" or simply, idiomatically, "from a lion's teeth"). See R. Payne Smith, *Thesaurus Syriacus* 2.4231.

35. The word is not cited in M. Sokoloff, *A Dictionary of Jewish Palestinian Aramaic of the Byzantine Period* (Ramat-Gan, Israel, 1990), nor is it discussed in E. Qimron, *The Hebrew of the Dead Sea Scrolls,* (Atlanta, 1986).

36. In modern Hebrew, *bašan* denotes the large black snake in the Golan.

37. Ugaritic *btn* become *bšn* in Hebrew and is equal to *bšm* in Akkadian with the *n* to *m* shift. I am grateful to Professor J. J. M. Roberts for discussing this issue with me.

38. Spirantized *t* becomes unspirantized in Aramaic, and *b* shifts to *p*. See פתן, which means "snake," in Sokoloff, *A Dictionary of Jewish Palestinian Aramaic,* p. 456.

39. KBL 1.165.

40. F. C. Fensham, "Ps 68:23 in the Light of Recently Discovered Ugaritic Tablets," *JNES* 19 (1960) 292–93. Fensham restores and translates Ps 68:3 as follows: "From the hole of the snake (or Bashan) I will bring back" (p. 293).

41. A very similar translation is found in the NKJV and defended by M. E. Tate: "(He is) the Lord who says, / 'I will bring back from Bashan, / I will bring back from the depths of the sea, / so that you may shake the blood off your feet, / (and) the tongues of your dogs may have a portion from the enemy!' " See Tate, *Psalms 51–100* (Dallas, 1990) p. 161. A translation similar to that of Tate appears in H.-J. Kraus, *Psalms 60–150,* trans. H. C. Oswald (Minneapolis, 1989) p. 45. Note how this translation has become standard; see S. Terrien: "Adonai said, I'll bring back from Bashan; / I'll bring back from the abysses of the sea, / To let you bathe your feet in the blood of your foes, / And even your dogs' tongues will share in it!" (Terrien, *The Psalms* [Grand Rapids, 2003] p. 487).

42. W. F. Albright, "A Catalogue of Early Hebrew Lyric Poems (Psalm LXVII)," *HUCA* 23 (1950–1951) part 1, pp. 1–39.

43. Note Albright's words: "The bicolon is undoubtedly of Canaanite origin; the name *YHWH* has displaced original *Ba'al.*" Albright, *HUCA* 23 (1950–1951) part 1, p. 27.

44. A. Weiser also suggested this emendation. See his *The Psalms,* trans. H. Hartwell (Philadelphia, 1962) ad loc. cit.

45. Albright, *HUCA* 23 (1950–1951) part 1, p. 28.

46. M. E. Tate rightly states that Albright's rendering demands "obviously too much emendation," but that Bashan as "serpent" has been accepted by many experts. See Tate, *Psalms 51–100,* p. 167.

47. Albright, *HUCA* 23 (1950–1951) part 1, p. 27.

48. See Albright, *BASOR* 46 (1932) 19; and Albright, *HUCA* 23 (1950–1951) part 1, p. 27.

49. See D. J. A. Clines, *DCH* (Sheffield, 1995) vol. 2, p. 281, in which a second meaning is wisely given to בשן: "snake."

50. C. Virolleaud, *Le palais royal d'Ugarit II* (Paris, 1957) pp. 4–5 and Plate IV.

51. Also, see 15.134 rev. ʿl.bšnt.trtḥ[ṣ; Virolleaud, *Le palais royal d'Ugarit*, p. 6.

52. חר can denote a "hole" for people (1 Sam 14:11, Job 30:6) or a "den" for animals (Nah 3:13[12]). How can we explain the loss of a noun in Ps 68:23? On the one hand, copyists often miss a word in transcribing and one does not have to appeal for some homeoteleuton. The Qumran Scrolls, including the carefully copied biblical sacred texts, abound with supralinear corrections; that is, a word was missed by a copyist and he or a later scribe placed it above the line. These words, added above others, supply phrases or even clauses that were missed in transcribing. On the other hand, if the text had been read out loud and the laryngeal not carefully enunciated, then "ḥor" may have been lost in poor elocution or hearing (elderly scribes could have benefited by a hearing aid). We should assume that some of our texts are lacking words; thus, they may not be so extremely cryptic originally.

53. The poetic structure of verse 23[22] is a bicolon, 2 + 2, preceded by an introduction: (The Lord said) + 2 (I will bring back from the dragon-snake) +3 (I will bring back from the depths of the sea). For a seminal study of Canaanite rhythm, see F. M. Cross, "Notes on a Canaanite Psalm in the Old Testament," *BASOR* 117 (1950) 19–21.

54. Psalm 68 seems to presuppose a worship of some god, perhaps originally Baal (now edited to YHWH) on Mount Bashan. Mowinckel correctly perceived that Ps 68, in its present form, reflects the Jerusalem cult, but opined that it reflected "an old originally North Israelite psalm." See Mowinckel, *The Psalms in Israel's Worship,* 2 vols., trans. D. R. Ap-Thomas (Oxford, 1962) vol. 2, pp. 152–53.

55. Terrien, *Psalms,* p. 486.

56. Perhaps the editor of Ps 68 omitted an earlier "in it" or "on Bashan" in the last colon of verse 17.

57. M. Noth, *Überlieferungsgeschichtliche Studien* (Saale, 1943).

58. E. W. Nicholson, *Deuteronomy and Tradition* (Philadelphia, 1967); M. Weinfeld, *Deuteronomy and the Deuteronomic School* (Oxford, 1972); see especially "The Centralization of Worship—The Chosen Place and the 'Name' Theology," pp. 324–26.

59. See esp. F. M. Cross, *Canaanite Myth and Hebrew Epic* (Cambridge, Mass., 1973) pp. 274–89. Cross dates "the fundamental composition of the Deuteronomistic history in the eighteenth year of [King] Josiah," that is, "to the late Kingdom." He makes room for "only minor modification by a member of the Deuteronomistic school in the Exile" (p. 289).

60. J. J. M. Roberts, *The Bible and the Ancient Near East: Collected Essays* (Winona Lake, Ind., 2002) p. 343.

61. A. A. Anderson, *Psalms* (London, 1972) vol. 1, p. 482.

62. Roberts, *The Bible and the Ancient Near East,* p. 345.

63. Roberts argues that verse 30 must date "after Solomon's construction of that edifice" (i.e., the Temple). Roberts, *The Bible and the Ancient Near East,* p. 344.

64. H. Gunkel, *Die Psalmen* (Göttingen, 1929 [4th ed.], 1968 [5th ed.]) ad loc.

65. M. Dahood, *Psalms II: 51–100* (Anchor Yale Bible; Garden City, N.Y., 1968; rpt. New Haven) p. 131.

66. Dahood, *Psalms II,* p. 145.

67. The noun מצלות is the feminine plural of צולה, "abyss," "deep," or "depths." See Isa 44:27.

68. Mowinckel, *The Psalms in Israel's Worship*, vol. 1, p. 5.

69. See esp. H.-J. Kraus, *Psalms 60–150*, p. 48.

70. S. Mowinckel claimed that Ps 68 is essentially a unity. See Mowinckel's disagreement with Albright in *Der achtundsechzigste Psalm* (Oslo, 1953); esp. see pp. 1–78. In the early sixties, F. M. Cross followed his teacher, Albright: "Apparently each couplet is the *incipit* of a longer liturgical piece." See Cross, "The Divine Warrior in Israel's Early Cult," in *Biblical Motifs,* ed. A. Altmann (Cambridge, Mass., 1966) pp. 11–30; the quotation is from p. 25. Anderson finds Albright's atomistic approach "rather unlikely." He finds that Ps 68 does not fit the major psalm-types, although it is close to the *Gattung* of Hymns. He labels Ps 68 "A Song of Procession." Anderson, *Psalms,* vol. 1, p. 481.

71. See P. D. Miller: "The possibility of an older unified poem underlying this one cannot be completely denied, but the present state of the text points much more clearly to a piecing together of isolated bits of poetry or *incipits."* Miller leans toward Albright ("various parts of this psalm were not originally connected"), but judges that Albright has atomized this psalm too severely. See P. D. Miller, *The Divine Warrior in Early Israel* (Cambridge, Mass., 1973) p. 103.

72. Terrien, *Psalms,* p. 489. For the form and structure of Ps 68, according to Terrien, see the diagram on p. 490.

73. Roberts, *The Bible and the Ancient Near East,* p. 345.

74. Ibid.

75. Mowinckel, *The Psalms in Israel's Worship,* vol. 1, pp. 5, 11, 125, 170; vol. 2, pp. 152–53.

76. R. H. Charles misled scholars by emending, without manuscript support, the conclusion of *The Parables of Enoch,* as I have frequently pointed out. See *OTP* 1, ad loc.

77. S. A. Geller takes *"hr ʿlhm,"* to mean "O mighty mountains." See Geller, *Parallelism in Early Biblical Poetry* (Missoula, Mont., 1979) p. 213. Also see D. Winton Thomas, "A Consideration of Some Unusual Ways of Expressing the Superlative in Hebrew," *VT* 3 (1953) 209–24.

78. Kraus, *Psalms 60–150,* p. 55.

79. Although A. A. Anderson prefers the rendering "I will bring them back from Bashan," he understands that God's enemies are to be brought to punishment from any place in which they may have fled. See Anderson, *Psalms,* vol. 1, p. 494. One should note that Anderson was constrained to provide commentary on an established text, the RSV. In *Psalms 51–100,* Tate draws attention to a dissertation that contains the argument that God shall bring his enemies back from anywhere they may be; see J. P. LePeau, "Psalm 68: An Exegetical and Theological Study" (PhD diss., University of Iowa, 1981).

80. These lines represent a broken construct chain so that the meaning may be the following: "I muzzled the Serpent of the Deep Sea." This rendering explicates the meaning I consider intended by the author.

81. After completing my study of Psalm 68, I found Miller's arguments in his well-known monograph, *The Divine Warrior in Early Israel;* cf. p. 110 (italics mine).

82. For the text, see A. Herder, ed., *Corpus des Tablettes en cuneiform alphabétiques* (Paris, 1963) p. 17.

83. See Miller, "Two Critical Notes on Psalm 68 and Deuteronomy 33," *HTR* 57 (1964) 240; and Miller, *The Divine Warrior in Early Israel*, p. 111. Contrast Roberts' rendering (he attaches the *mem* in colon one to the end of אדני, as an enclitic, and takes the verb to be a hiphil): "The Lord said, "I will repulse the Serpent, / I will muzzle the depths of the Sea" (Roberts, *The Bible and the Ancient Near East*, p. 344).

84. Dahood, "Mišmār 'Muzzle' in Job 7:12," *JBL* 80 (1961) 270–71.

85. The probability that *šmr* meant "muzzle"—esp. in Job 8:12—should not lead to the far more speculative suggestion that *šbm* meant "muzzle" also, let alone in biblical Hebrew. In Job 8, the clause "set a guard over me" is distinct from the idea "place a muzzle on me." The verb *šbr* appears in a negative sense in Job 10:14.

86. See, e.g., Miller, *The Divine Warrior in Early Israel*, pp. 102–13; and Roberts, *The Bible and the Ancient Near East*, p. 344 (in which Roberts argues convincingly for archaic linguistic features and mythological elements that point to many contacts with the Baal myth).

87. Miller, *The Divine Warrior in Early Israel*, p. 111.

88. After I had completed this work, I discovered Albright's study. He opined, "It is likely that the place-name 'Bashan' had something to do with vipers originally." He did not offer further speculation. See Albright, *HUCA* 23 (1950–1951) part 1, p. 27.

89. KBL, 1. 165.

90. ארעיה שתיא מן נחליא דנגדין מן מתנן. See A. Sperber, *The Bible in Aramaic: The Pentateuch* (Leiden, New York, 1992) 1.351.

91. The Samaritan Pentateuch is similar to the BHS, except the word for "cub" (גר) is written without the medial vowel letter *(wāw)*, and the conjunction *(wāw)* is placed before the following verb ("and he shall leap"). When we come to the *maqqeph* after the מן, this is a Masoretic nuance that does not appear in pre-Masoretic manuscripts or Samaritan manuscripts. See A. Freiherrn von Gall, ed., *Der Hebräische Pentateuch der Samaritaner* (Giessen, 1918) vol. 5, p. 436.

92. It is unlikely that the translators of the LXX would preserve the name of the serpent, since they tend to omit the name of Leviathan or Rahab (see Job 9:13, Isa 51:9, Ps 74[73]:15 Codex Vaticanus). See Stallman in *Dictionary of Old Testament Theology and Exegesis* 3.87.

93. Albright, *HUCA* 23 (1950–1951) part 1, p. 27.

94. I would have been spared months of research if I had seen this article before the present work had been completed.

95. F. M. Cross and D. N. Freedman, "The Blessing of Moses," *JBL* 67 (September 1948) 191–210; the quotation is from p. 195.

96. Ibid., p. 208.

97. Recall the introductory comment that "P" denotes a positive symbolic meaning.

98. I know of no text in which תולע (see the plural in Ex 16:20) means "serpent," although it can also mean "scarlet stuff" (Isa 1:18; cf. Lam 4:5). See KBL, 4.1701–02; E. Klein, *A Comprehensive Etymological Dictionary of the Hebrew Language* (New York, 1987) p. 694; and Sokoloff, *A Dictionary of Jewish Palestinian Aramaic*, p. 577. The Syriac noun ܬܘܠܥܐ means "worm," "murex," "firefly," and "larva." In the Qumran Scrolls, תולע often means "scarlet" (4Q179 Frag. 1 2.12; 1Q19 10.10), but in 1QH 19.12 we find "the worms of the dead" (תולעת מתים) and in 11Q10, *Targum of Job,* we may have "wo[rm]" (תולע[תה]). For a discussion of the

symbolic relation of "serpent" and "worm," see Küster, *Die Schlange,* pp. 30–31, 63.

99. See S. Golowin, *Drache, Einhorn, Oster-Hase und anderes phantastisches Getier* (Basel, 1994) p. 33. During a study tour of Megiddo, numerous scholars came to me and said they had seen large worms, like snakes, crawling among the ruins. The worms were large, black, and had many tiny legs.

100. See H. Vincent, "La fontaine de Rogel, Gihon, Zoheleth," *Jérusalem Antique* (Paris, 1912) pp. 134–41. For a modern succinct summary on Zoheleth, see W. H. Mare, "Serpent's Stone," *IDB* 5.116–17.

101. See R. Kittel, "Der Schlangenstein im Kidrontal bei Jerusalem," in *Studien zur Hebräischen Archäologie und Religionsgeschichte* (Leipzig, 1908) pp. 159–88. Kittel offers his opinion about the location of the serpent's stone, and provides photographs of the area near Silwan, as well as the serpent rock of Petra.

102. See Y. Aharoni, "The Horned Altar of Beer-sheba," 3–5. Also see Le Grande Davies, "Serpent Imagery in Ancient Israel," Fig. 26 on p. 242.

103. It is possible that the altar was perceived by Adonijah to be the altar of Israel's God, but one should not forget that Adonijah is rebelling against Solomon and seeking David's throne. Le Grande Davies, too boldly, claims that Adonijah "probably sacrificed at a stone altar dedicated to 'the Serpent,' who should be identified as the God of Israel." "Serpent Imagery in Ancient Israel," p. 217.

104. M. J. Paul's suggestion that Leviathan might refer to a dinosaur is impossible, since they died out long before humans evolved. See Paul, "לויתן," *Dictionary of Old Testament Theology and Exegesis* 2.778–80.

105. At the outset, I indicated that "N" denoted negative symbolic meanings.

106. For citations of places where Leviathan appears in the Targumim, Midrashim, and Talmudim, see N. Jechielis, *Aruch Completum sive Lexicon,* ed. A. Kohut (New York, 1970 [original 1531]) 5.23–24.

107. While one must not conflate what is reflected in the Hebrew Bible about Leviathan with Rahab or Satan, it is informative to see this figure in light of creation motifs in other world cultures. See P. Bandini, *Drachenwelt von den Geistern der Schöpfung und Zerstörung,* trans. T. Prohn (Stuttgart, 1996). Alonso Schökel et al., in *Diccionario biblica hebreo-español,* provides accurate information: "*Leviatán,* serpiente o dragón mitológico; *crocodrilo,*" p. 388. He claims that Leviathan is not a good translation for Job 40:25 and that crocodile is better.

108. See E. Lipiński, *La royauté de Yahwé dans la poésie et le culte de l'ancien Israël* (Brussels, 1965) and Lipiński, "לויתן," *TDOT* 7.504–9. There is a striking link between the Ugaritic Ba'al myth and Isa 27:1; in both Leviathan is fleeing and twisting. See M. Dietrich et al., eds., *Die keilalphabetischen Texte aus Ugarit,* 1.5 I 1–3, 27–30, and Lipiński, *TDOT* 7.506. Also see J. A. Emerton, "Leviathan and LTN: The Vocalization of the Ugaritic Word for the Dragon," *VT* 32 (1982) 327–31. Quite unconvincingly, Stig I. A. Norin sought to derive both "Leviathan" and "Tanin" from the Egyptian monster called *apophis.* See Norin, *Er spaltete das Meer,* trans. C. B. Sjöberg (Lund, 1977) pp. 42–76. One line of development in Israelite poetry went from "dem ägyptischen Apep-Mythos aus und umfasst die eigentlichen Urgewässerungeheuer *liwjatan, tănnîn und răhăb (sic)*" (p. 76).

109. The words for "fleeing serpent" and "twisted serpent" are uncertain; see B. W. Anderson, "The Slaying of the Fleeing, Twisting Serpent: Isaiah 27:1 in Context," in *From Creation to New Creation* (Minneapolis, 1994) pp. 195–206.

110. As W. Rebiger reports, Leviathan has a "schlangenähnliches Wesen." See his contribution in *Religion in Geschichte und Gegenwart,* 3rd ed., ed. K. Galling, 7 vols. (Tübingen, 1957–65). 5.295–96. Koehler-Baumgartner, 1.498: "Meerdrache."

111. For the Ugaritic texts, see Lipiński, *TDOT* 7.506 (= KTU 1.5.I.1–3, 27–30; KTU 1.3.III.41–42).

112. For seven heads, see the very early clay depiction from the temple of Abu at Eshnunna (which is Tell Asmar). See H. Frankfort, *Stratified Cylinder Seals from the Diyala Region* (Chicago, 1955) no. 497 (also see no. 478). For more, see also the serpent-like reptiles collected in *ANEP* 670, 671, 691. For an excellent drawing of *ANEP* 671, see Black and Green, *Gods, Demons and Symbols of Ancient Mesopotamia,* illustration 135.

113. C. H. Gordon focused on Leviathan only as a symbol of evil. See Gordon, "Leviathan: Symbol of Evil," in *Biblical Motifs,* pp. 1–9.

114. See ibid.

115. See A. Caquot, "Leviathan et Behémoth dans la troisième 'parabole' d'Hénoch," *Semitic* 25 (1975) 111–22.

116. Also see, e.g., *b. B. Bat.* 74b–75a; *j. Sanh.* 10.29c; GenRab 7:4 (the Taninim are Behemoth and Leviathan); and Midrash Ps on Ps 23:7.

117. E. G. Clarke, with W. E. Aufrecht, J. C. Hurd, and F. Spitzer, *Targum Pseudo-Jonathan of the Pentateuch: Text and Concordance* (Hoboken, N. J., 1984) p. 2.

118. The italics are those of the translators; the italics highlight the differences between the Targum and the original Hebrew. The translation quoted is by M. Maher in *Targum Pseudo-Jonathan: Genesis* (Edinburgh, 1992) p. 19.

119. Consult M. Beit-Arié, "Perek Shirah," *EncJud* 13.273–75.

120. My translation; for the Hebrew text, see N. Slifkin, *Nature's Song* (Southfield, Mich., 2001) p. 32.

121. Again, let me clarify that I frequently do not use the means of representing Semitic sounds, since non-Semitists, for whom I am writing, would not find formal transliterations meaningful or helpful. Often my goal is to help readers who do not know Semitics get a feel of the language.

122. See also Fabry in *TDOT* 9.364.

123. This Greek term is used to signify the sagacity of animals; see Plato, *Politicus* 263d, Aristotle, *Historia Animalium* 488ᵇ15; also see LSJM, p. 1956.

124. This tradition is probably J and expanded by JE. According to P in Ex 7:9, the serpent is strikingly called a תנין, "dragon"; the redactor has also elevated the legitimization to a demonstration of power when the "dragon" devours the serpents of the Egyptian magicians (as Fabry states in *TDOT* 9.367).

125. The Hebrew term נחש does not appear in Isa 11:6–8, despite the impression given, unintentionally, by Fabry (*TDOT* 9.368).

126. For a general discussion, see W. Foerster, "ὄφις," *TDNT* 5.566–71.

127. Both these Greek nouns, as well as others, are translated by the Coptic ϩⲟϥ.

128. See also Z. Ben-Hayyim, *The Literary and Oral Tradition of Hebrew and Aramaic Amongst the Samaritans: Vol. IV, The Words of the Pentateuch* (Jerusalem, 1977) pp. 178–79.

129. See H. Dahan, *English-Hebrew Dictionary* (Jerusalem, 1997) pp. 36, 529.

130. The meaning of the Hittite noun *artaggaš* has not been clear. Now, in light of its appearance on a tablet found at Boghazkoy in 1933, it probably means an animal that molts; hence, it seems to signify some snake. The word—*artagga*—most likely

denotes a class of priests who are serpent-men. See H. G. Güterbock, "Le mot hittite—*artaggaš* 'serpent,' " *Revue Hittite et Asianique* 6 (1941) 102–9.

131. See Bodenheimer, בארצות המקרא, p. 344: נחש אסקולף (*Coluber aesculapi*), נחשי־ים (*Hydropinae*), נחש המים המזני (*Natrix tesselatus*), נחש עין החתנל (*Tarbophis martini*), נחש ענק (פיתנן) (*Python*), הנחש השחנר הגדנל (*Coluber jugularis [asianus]*), נחש שלשולי (*Typhlos vermicularis*).

132. See, respectively, C. Hammond, D. J. Johnson, and R. N. Jones, *BASOR* 263 (1986) 77–80 and Y. Yadin, J. C. Greenfield, A. Yardeni, and B. Levine, *The Documents from the Bar Kokhba Period in the Cave of Letters*, vol. 2, ad loc. See now A. Yardeni, *Textbook of Aramaic, Hebrew, and Nabataean Documentary Texts from the Judaean Desert and Related Material*, 2 vols. (Jerusalem, 2000) vol. 1, pp. 312 (partly but wisely restored), and 271 as well as vol. 2, pp. [103] and [87].

133. See Bahat and Mishor, *Dictionary of Contemporary Hebrew*, p. 464 (Hebrew-to-Hebrew lexicon).

134. For the text and translation, see N. Slifkin, *Nature's Song*, p. 35.

135. See Fabry in *TDOT* 9.358.

136. The verb *nḥš* cannot be a denominative form of *nāḥāš* because of its commonness in Syriac and Arabic. Boch claimed that the verb derives from the noun because the serpent in antiquity was thought to have powers of divination. R. Smith, however, pointed out the verb is well known in cognate Semitics, but the noun is peculiar to Hebrew. See the references and judicious comments by Cheyne in *Encyclopedia Biblica* (1902) 4.4392. There is another apparently unrelated noun that looks the same as *nḥš*; it means "divination." Other words not to be confused with *nāḥāš*, but spelled the same, denote a city or personal names. See Le Grande Davies, "Serpent Imagery in Ancient Israel," pp. 62–82.

137. For the text and translation, see M. P. Horgan in Charlesworth, ed., *Pesharim, Other Commentaries, and Related Documents* (Tübingen, Louisville, 2002) pp. 58–59.

138. The pestilent snakes are called הנחש in Num 21:7.

139. Alonso Schökel et al., in *Diccionario biblica hebreo-español*, prefers "*Vibora, serpiente*," p. 560.

140. I am not aware of any instance of the noun עכשנב in the Qumran Scrolls.

141. Bodenheimer, in החי בארצת המקרא, p. 347, suggests that the noun denotes the *naja haje*.

142. Alonso Schökel et al., in *Diccionario biblica hebreo-español*, provides only a generic meaning, making it very difficult to detect the Hebrew behind a translation: "*Serpiente, ofidio, áspid* (no especificado)" p. 629.

143. Cheyne rightly saw that this "word evidently denotes a highly poisonous snake, perhaps the cobra." Cheyne, *Encyclopedia Biblica* 4.4393.

144. This information helps clarify that different Greek scribes, probably independently, worked on translations of the Hebrew Bible.

145. Among those who hold the view that the word "python" derives from the Hebrew *ptn* are Fabry, *TDOT* 9.360, and Joines, *Serpent Sympolism in the Old Testament*. Joines suggests that the "Greek python may have come from this word"; p. 12 n.12. On python, see J. Fontenrose, *Python: A Study of Delphic Myth and Its Origins* (Berkeley, Los Angeles, 1959). The work, aimed at a wide audience of specialists, includes a study of the dragon in the ancient Near East.

146. See R. E. Whitaker, *CUL* (Cambridge, Mass., 1972) p. 159.

147. See S. Golowin, "Basilisk, König über sämtliche Gifte," *Drache, Einhorn, Oster-Hase,* pp. 50–52.

148. See the study by S. B. Johnson, "Meaning and Importance of the Uraeus," *The Cobra Goddess of Ancient Egypt: Predynastic, Early Dynastic, and Old Kingdom Periods* (London, New York, 1990) pp. 5–11.

149. See O. Keel, *Corpus der Stempelsiegel-Amulette aus Palästina/Israel: Von den Anfängen bis zur Perserzeit* (Freiburg, Göttingen, 1995) p. 76. See the drawings in Keel et al., *Corpus der Stempelsiegel-Amulette aus Pälistina/Israel* (Freiburg, Göttingen, 1997): Tel Abu Hawam nos. 21, 23, 24; Achsib nos. 59, 155; Afek no. 52; Tell el-ʿAǧul (7 km south-southwest of Gaza) nos. 16, 19, 28, 30, 44, 47, 48, 53, 54, 65, 66, 78, 128, 132, 140, 144, 146, 158, 159, 161, 162, 196, 209, 256, 263, 277, 278, 288, 299, 305, 309, 312, 322, 327, 389, 395, 396, 398, 401, 413, 420, etc.; Akko nos. 35, 36, 45, 50, 62, 68, 72, 190, 209, 212, 217, 230, 248 (as the left foot of an anthropoid), 260, 267, 275, 285, 290; Ashdod nos. 8, 32, 55, 64 (perhaps a cobra instead), 36, 48, 64 (three uraei together), 65, 68, 71, 84, 95, 108 (five uraei), 120; Askea no. 18; Asor (5 km southeast of Jaffa) nos. 5, 8, 14, 15; Atlit (14 km south of Haifa) no. 20, 33. Also, see p. 780 (Abb. 3–5 with the symbol of the sun god in a boat over a large undulating serpent, and p. 789 [Abb. 21], and p. 790 [Abb. 24–26]). On the relation of sun and serpent, especially in India, see C. F. Oldham, *The Sun and the Serpent: A Contribution to the History of Serpent-Worship* (London, 1905).

150. For text and translation, see J. M. Baumgarten and D. Schwartz in Charlesworth, ed., *Damascus Document, War Scroll, and Related Documents* (Tübingen, Louisville, 1995) p. 29.

151. D. J. Wiseman reads שרף מעונפף of Isa 14:29 in light of the Akkadian *appu,* which means "tip" or "spur." He thus prefers "deadly poisonous snakes" in place of the usual "fiery flying serpents." See Wiseman, "Flying Serpent," *TynBul* 23 (1972) 108–10. The connection between the Hebrew and Akkadian is tenuous and one does not have to presuppose Isaiah was thinking literally about a serpent that flies; as in Herodotus (iii, 107).

152. P. Lum contends that the cockatrice and basilisk "are almost indistinguishable; if there is a difference, the basilisk is more completely reptile while the cockatrice retains more features of the cock." P. Lum, *Fabulous Beasts* (New York, 1951) p. 38.

153. שפיפן, p. 348, suggest the noun specifies a *Vipera* and צפעוני ארץ ישראלי is the *Vipera palaestinae.*

154. Alonso Schökel et al., in *Diccionario biblica hebreo-español,* list the same meaning, "*Vibora,*" for both the צפע and the צפעני and thus fail to specify the distinctive nouns in the Hebrew (p. 643).

155. I assume that the Book of Isaiah is trifurcated: First Isaiah (chs. 1–39), Second Isaiah (chs. 40–55), and Third Isaiah (chs. 56–66).

156. Baumgarten and Schwartz, *Damascus Document,* p. 21.

157. KBL, 3.1118.

158. See esp.: *TANAKH, The Holy Scriptures* (Jerusalem, 1997); see also BDB 891, KB 3.1118; E. Klein in *A Comprehensive Etymological Dictionary of the Hebrew Language,* p. 587, seems confused, stating that this noun denotes "a kind of bird (prob. meaning 'arrow-snake')." Alonso Schökel et al., in *Diccionario biblica hebreo-español,* prefers "*Vibora, serpiente*" suggest only that the Hebrew noun, קפוז, may denote, perhaps, a "snake" *(¿Culebra?),* p. 665.

159. M. Sokoloff in *A Dictionary of Jewish Palestinian Aramaic* prefers "jumper," which is etymologically sound (p. 499).

160. Fabry, *TDOT* 9.361. I do not think we can link the Hebrew name for snakes or serpents with the *termini technici* in Latin developed by ophiologists.

161. See Sperber, *The Bible in Aramaic* (Leiden, 1992) 3.69.

162. See Klein, *A Comprehensive Etymological Dictionary of the Hebrew Language*, p. 587. Also see KBL, 3.117.

163. I have doubts that a "hedgehog" was known in biblical times. I have never seen one in Israel or Palestine, and it does not appear in P. France's *An Encyclopedia of Bible Animals* (Tel Aviv, 1986). France wrote for a popular audience.

164. See the color photograph in J. C. Trever, *Scrolls from Qumrân Cave I* (Jerusalem, 1972) Plate XXVIII.

165. For a discussion of Aramaic influence on 1QIs[a], see E. Y. Kutscher, *The Language and Linguistic Background of the Isaiah Scroll (1QIs[a])* (Leiden, 1974); see esp. chap. 4 and pp. 566–67. Note, e.g., that the scribe of this scroll in 24:7 inscribed for the Hebrew גפן the Aramaic form גופן. Invaluable, for working on Kutscher's masterpiece, is E. Qimron, *The Language and Linguistic Background of the Isaiah Scroll (IQIs[a])* (Leiden, 1979).

166. See Trever, *Scrolls from Qumrān Cave I*, Plate XII. Also see Kutscher, *The Language and Linguistic Background of the Isaiah Scroll*, pp. 281–82, 312.

167. The absence—not necessarily the omission—of the objective pronoun is noteworthy.

168. See Isa 14:3, 22.

169. See, e.g., E. Kautzsch, ed., *GKC*, trans. A. E. Cowley (Oxford, 1910); P. Joüon, *A Grammar of Biblical Hebrew*, trans. and revised T. Muraoka (Rome, 1991) pp. 48–50; B. K. Waltke and M. O'Connor, *An Introduction to Biblical Hebrew Syntax* (Winona Lake, Ind., 1990) see esp. pp. 24–25; and H. Bauer and P. Leander, *Historische Grammatik der habräischen Sprache des Alten Testamentes* (Tübingen, 1922 [2nd ed.]; reprinted as Olms Paperbacks 19; Hildesheim, Zürich, New York, 1991) p. 92.

170. As is well known, *scriptio defectiva* is earlier. Both so-called plene and defective spellings are found at Qumran and Masada. See the following publication: S. Talmon et al., *Hebrew Fragments from Masada* (Jerusalem, 1999) esp. pp. 134–34.

171. Kutscher, *The Language and Linguistic Background of the Isaiah Scroll*, p. 282.

172. I presently do not know of any Qumran text in which this noun appears.

173. So H. Gunkel, *Schöpfung und Chaos in Urzeit und Endzeit* (Göttingen, 1895) p. 32.

174. See Fabry in *TDOT* 9.358. Alonso Schökel et al., in *Diccionario biblica hebreo-español*, rightly report that this noun denotes *"Rahab, monstruo o fiera mitológica,"* p. 691.

175. So, BDB, p. 923; KBL 3.1193; Klein, *A Comprehensive Etymological Dictionary of the Hebrew Language*, p. 608.

176. Rahab is certainly "Egypt" in Ps 87:4 since it is associated with other nations, viz. "Babylon," Philistia," and "Ethiopia."

177. For more, see the excellent work by J. Day, *God's Conflict with the Dragon and the Sea: Echoes of a Canaanite Myth in the Old Testament* (Cambridge, New York, 1985) esp. pp. 91–92. Also see Day, "Rahab," *AYBD* V.610–11.

178. "The helpers of Rahab" in Job 9:13–14 are reminiscent of Tiamat's "helpers" (*Enuma Elish* 4.107). Perhaps one should think about Leviathan and Behemoth.

179. See Day, *God's Conflict with the Dragon and the Sea*, pp. 6–7.

180. Also see 4Q381 Frg. 15.5 and especially the critical notes to the Hebrew text in Charlesworth, ed., *Pseudepigraphic and Non-Masoretic Psalms and Prayers*, ed. E. M. Schuller (Tübingen, Louisville, 1997) p. 14.

181. S. A. Cook suggested that שרף, "burning-serpent," derived from "the Egyptian winged griffin *seref* or the Akkadian *sarrāpu*, 'the burner.'" *The Religion of Ancient Palestine in the Light of Archaeology* (London, 1930) p. 54.

182. See J. H. Charlesworth, "Phenomenology, Symbology, and Lexicography: The Amazingly Rich Vocabulary for 'Serpent' in Ancient Greek," *RB* 111 (2004) 499–515.

183. See, e.g., KBL 12.1360.

184. The noun τὸ τῆτς was used to describe the monster that confronted Andromeda (Euripides, *Fragmenta* 121). See LSJM 949.

185. See the mid-third-century fresco in the Catacomb of Saints Marcellinus and Peter. For a color photograph, see F. Mancinelli, *Catacombs and Basilicas: The Early Christians in Rome* (Florence, 1981) p. 41 (illus. 78).

186. In *Das Buch des Propheten Jesaja* (Göttingen, 1981 [5th ed.]) p. 127, O. Kaiser suggested this plural noun meant "geflügelte Schlangen" (flying serpents), but then this implies the appearance of noun no. 15.

187. Alonso Schökel et al., in *Diccionario biblica hebreo-español*, rightly report that שרפים means *"Serpiente, dragón, áspid,"* p. 739. I prefer choosing a word that distinguishes this Hebrew noun—namely "winged-serpents." Also possible would be "fiery winged-serpents" to bring out the etymological root "to burn." See the insights shared by G. B. Gray in *The Book of Isaiah* (Edinburgh, 1912) vol. 1, p. 105.

188. See the judicious response by J. N. Oswalt in *The Book of Isaiah* (Grand Rapids, 1986) p. 179. H. Wildberger opts for "a serpent-shaped demon" ("einen schlangengestaltigen Dämon"). *Jesaja* (Neukirchen-Vluyn, 1972) p. 247.

189. E. J. Kissane, *The Book of Isaiah, I* (Dublin, 1941) p. 74.

190. I. Engnell, *The Call of Isaiah* (Uppsala, 1949) p. 33.

191. R. B. Y. Scott, "The Book of Isaiah," *The Interpreter's Bible 5* (New York, 1956) p. 208.

192. G. M. Tucker, "The Book of Isaiah 1–39," in *The New Interpreter's Bible* (Nashville, 2001) vol. 6, p. 102. We have discussed serpent iconography that shows the serpent with wings; hence, the Seraphim can have wings and be serpents.

193. J. Blenkinsopp insightfully states that Seraphim "is elsewhere a poisonous snake," and that it "is tempting to associate this aspect of the vision scenario with the cult object in the Jerusalem Temple known as Nehushtan, a bronze serpent with healing powers of Mosaic origin to which incense was offered (2Kgs 18:4 cf. Num 21:6, 8 9)." *Isaiah 1–39* (New York, London, 2000) p. 225.

194. K. Joines, *JBL* 86 (967) 410–15; O. Keel and C. Uehlinger, *Gods, Goddesses, and Images of Gods*, p. 273. The contributor of שרפים to KBL 3.1360 seems so blinded by the traditional approach to Hebrew lexicography that he misses Keel's point. Apparently he never studied the lexicography of iconography in the ancient Near East. The contributor seems to think that ophidian iconography cannot have human form.

195. G. W. E. Nickelsburg, *1 Enoch 1*, ed. K. Baltzer (Minneapolis, 2001) p. 296.

196. See H. Freedman, trans., *Midrash Rabbah: Genesis* (London, 1951) vol. 1, p. 178.

197. I presently do not know of a passage in the Qumran Scrolls in which this noun appears. While Ethiopic has numerous loanwords from Hebrew, Aramaic, Syriac,

Greek, Coptic, and Arabic, it has tended to use only names for snake that are unique to it. For example, "adder" in Ethiopic is *'f' ot*. See W. Leslau, *Comprehensive Dictionary of Ge 'ez (Classical Ethiopic)* (Wiesbaden, 1991).

198. In the Peshiṭta this Hebrew noun is translated by *ḥarmānâ* which denotes some form of snake.

199. Bodenheimer, in החי בארצות המקרא, p. 349 suggests that שפיפון is the *Cerastes cerastes or Cerastes cornutus*.

200. For a drawing of a cockatrice, see France, *An Encyclopedia of Bible Animals,* p. 42.

201. Cohen, *Biblical Hapax Legomena in the Light of Akkadian and Ugaritic,* p. 109.

202. Today this noun often denotes the crocodile *(Crocodilus nilotica)*.

203. Both "dragon" and "dragons" appear in many passages in the Qumran Scrolls; cf. Charlesworth, *GCDS,* esp. pp. 522–23.

204. See Jechielis, *Aruch Completum sive Lexicon* 8.251–52.

205. See the citations collected by Sokoloff, *A Dictionary of Jewish Palestinian Aramaic,* pp. 344–45.

206. Theodotion translated תנין in Job 3:8 by δράκων. See Foerster, "δράκων," *TDNT* 2.283.

207. *The Hebrew Scriptures: Hebrew and English* (Jerusalem, 1996) p. 1095.

208. Words within brackets are mine.

209. U. Cassuto, *The Goddess Anath,* trans. I. Abrahams (Jerusalem, 1971) pp. 92–93.

210. For the Hebrew text and translation, see N. Slifkin, *Nature's Song,* p. 32.

211. Many Aramaic and Syriac nouns have erroneously been claimed to denote a "snake"; see I. Löw, "Aramäische Schlangennamen," *Fauna und Mineralien der Juden* (Hildesheim, 1969) pp. 35–40. He suggested eleven nouns probably denoted snake in "Aramaic" and Syriac. Other Syriac nouns for "snake" that he did not include are *dypsds* (vocalization uncertain) (this is a Greek loanword; see Appendix II), and *ḥewyâ* that is paralleled by Persian, Arabic, and possibly pre-biblical Hebrew. On *ḥewyâ* and Arabic, see Hassano Bar Bahlule's *Lexicon Syriacum,* ed. R. Duval; vol. 1, col. 724. Löw correctly rejected nouns that did not mean "snake."

212. See Löw, "Aramäische Schlangennamen," *Fauna und Mineralien der Juden,* p. 35. I do not find this noun in the lexicons; it is not, e.g., in Sokoloff's *A Dictionary of Jewish Palestinian Aramaic* and he often cites Löw's research.

213. See Löw, *Fauna und Mineralien der Juden,* p. 35. The noun is not listed in Sokoloff's *A Dictionary of Jewish Palestinian Aramaic.*

214. See Brockelmann, *LexSyr,* p. 134.

215. See Brockelmann, *LexSyr,* p. 162.

216. See חיוי in Jastrow's *A Dictionary of the Targumim,* p. 452 and חיווי in Sokoloff's *A Dictionary of Jewish Palestinian Aramaic,* p. 197.

217. See Löw, *Fauna und Mineralien der Juden,* p. 37.

218. See Brockelmann, *Lex Syr,* p. 451.

219. See Löw, *Fauna und Mineralien der Juden,* pp. 37–38.

220. See I. Löw, *Fauna und Mineralien der Juden,* p. 38.

221. See Löw, *Fauna und Mineralien der Juden,* p. 40. The noun is not listed in Sokoloff's *A Dictionary of Jewish Palestinian Aramaic.*

222. See Löw, *Fauna und Mineralien der Juden,* p. 35.

223. See L. Störk, "Schlange," *Lexikon der Ägyptologie* (1983) 4.1 645.

224. Pap. Brooklyn Mus. No. 47.218.48 and No. 47.218.85. See S. Sauneron, *Un traité Égyptien d'ophiologie* (Cairo, 1989). I am grateful to Diane Bergman (librarian of the Wilbour Library of Egyptology) and Edward Bleiberg (associate curator) for assistance and permission to study this papyrus.

225. See Appendix II; also see C. Leitz, *Die Schlangennamen in den ägyptischen und griechischen Giftbüchern* (Mainz, Stuttgart, 1997) pp. 16–17. The attempt to give the Latin names developed by biologists to each Greek name misses four points: such precision is anachronistic, the ancients usually did not know about the types of snakes, they often thought generically, and they were often inconsistent.

226. This is the only meaning supplied by KBL, 2.528.

227. See OED 1.92.

228. See also Muraoka, *Hebrew/Aramaic Index to the Septuagint*, p. 75.

229. See Lev 11:30, first word in the list of unclean reptiles; also note the meaning given in KBL 1.70. J. Milgrom also prefers gecko for *hā'ănāqâ*. See his masterful *Leviticus 1–16* (Anchor Yale Bible; Garden City, N.Y., 1991; rpt. New Haven) p. 671.

230. In his *Hexapla,* Origen gave an explanation for only the last word in the list; cf. F. Field, *Origenis Hexaplorum* (Oxford, 1875) 1.186.

231. B. A. Levine opted for "lizard"; see his *Leviticus* (Philadelphia, New York, 5749/1989) p. 69.

232. Consult I. J. Gleb et al., *The Assyrian Dictionary* 6.230 or R. Payne Smith, *Thesaurus Syriacus* 1.1284–85. The Aramaic noun חומטא is not listed in the most recent Aramaic lexicons; that is, it is in neither Sokoloff's *A Dictionary of Jewish Palestinian Aramaic* (1990) nor Koehler-Baumgartner's *The Hebrew and Aramaic Lexicon of the Old Testament: Aramaic,* vol. 5 (2000).

233. See the passages noted in LSJM 691.

234. Most exegetes, commentators, and translators have wisely not opted for "the swarming [flying] thing that swarms [flies] over the earth," which would exclude snakes. Nevertheless, some early Jewish thinkers were free to choose that rendering.

235. See the passages cited in Sokoloff's *A Dictionary of Jewish Palestinian Aramaic,* p. 568. Note also that the compilers of *Perek Shirah,* in chapter 6, have the "Creeping Creatures" and the "Prolific Creeping Creatures" praising God, quoting respectively Pss 104:31 and 128:3. For the Hebrew and English translation, see Slifkin, *Nature's Song,* p. 35.

236. The plural of *seret* appears in Rashi's commentary; the noun does not appear in the plural in the Hebrew Bible.

237. I am indebted to Slifkin for this reference; see his *Nature's Song,* p. 412.

238. I have enjoyed and benefited from conversations on this perspective with A. M. V. Capers.

239. The Hebrew noun רמש, cf. Akkadian *nammaštû(m),* is not to be confused with the Rabbinic רמש, "evening" (which also appears as a loanword in Syriac [ܪܡܫܐ]). The noun רמש means "crawling," but in extant texts it does not clearly denote a snake (cf. the verb in Ps 104:20: all the beasts of the forest "crawl" about in the darkness of night). It specifies a worm (cf. Sir 10:11 [the Greek is σκώληκας]) or an eel or sea monster (Ps 104:25). In Ps 148:10 רמש, "creeping things" is contrasted to "a flying fowl." It appears in CD 12.12 and denotes "swarming creatures," like locusts." Cf. also 4Q381 Frg. 1.10; perhaps restore רמ[ש]. It is odd to observe that in T. Muraoka's *Hebrew/*

Aramaic Index to the Septuagint (Grand Rapids, 1998) רמש is said to equal ἑρπετός, which denotes a "reptile" including a snake.

240. Among those experts who should be celebrated, few are as renowned as Elisha Qimron. He has demonstrated how the Qumran Scrolls have increased our knowledge of Hebrew vocabulary. See his numerous publications, especially his well-known grammar of Qumran Hebrew.

241. The supplement begins in the compact edition in vol. 2, pp. 3873 ff. The new entry would appear in vol. 2 on p. 3880.

242. See, e.g., Brockelmann, *LexSyr*, p. 220a.

243. In Ethiopic we find a word for "life" *(ḥiwat)* but no cognate, as in Arabic, Persian, Aramaic, and Syriac, to it for snake.

244. See Lane, *Arabic-English Lexicon* Book I, Part 1 (1863) ad loc. cit. Ch. Clermont-Ganneau reported that the Bedouins know a snake they call *haiyé taiyâra,* "flying serpent." See his "Les cerfs mangeurs de serpents," *Recueil d'Archéologie Orientale* (Paris, 1901) pp. 319–22.

245. F. Steingass, *A Comprehensive Persian-English Dictionary* (London, 1947) p. 434.

246. In Samaritan Aramaic נחשא denotes "snake." I am grateful to Professor D. Talshir for discussions on the Aramaic words for "snake."

247. See esp. *The Hymn of the Pearl,* 13 and 58; also see R. Payne Smith, *Thesaurus Syriacus* (1879) vol. 1, col. 1254 and col. 1210; Brockelmann, *LexSyr* (1928) pp. 173, 220.

248. Wellhausen, *Prolegomena zur Geschichte Israels* (Berlin, 1886 [3rd ed.]) p. 322; see the 4th ed., p. 313.

249. Trans. C. D. Yonge, *The Works of Philo* (Peabody, Mass., 1993) p. 182. Contrast the translation by F. H. Colson and G. H. Whitaker, *Philo* (Cambridge, Mass., London, 1988) vol. 3, pp. 156–57: "He did not liken the faculty to the serpent that played the friend and gave advice to 'Life'—to whom in our own language we call 'Eve.'" Philo's Greek is not clear, but I think he intends to suggest that Eve is the serpent and not the one to whom the serpent gave advice. Cf. *Midrash Rabbah* on Gen 3:20; Ḥawwāh "played the eavesdropper like the serpent . . . .Aḥa interpreted it: The serpent was thy [Eve's] serpent [i.e. seducer], and thou art Adam's serpent." See H. Freedman and M. Simon, trans., *Midrash Rabbah* (London, 1939) pp. 169–70. This exegesis may reflect some philological reflections similar to those of Philo.

250. R. G. Murison, "The Serpent in the Old Testament," *AJSL* 21 (1905) 115–30; the quotation is on p. 130.

251. Eusebius, *Preparation for the Gospel* II.3; the translation is by E. H. Gifford; see his edition of Eusebius, *Preparation for the Gospel* (Grand Rapids, 1981 [the original was published by the Clarendon Press in 1903]) p. 68.

252. Professor Haim Cohen of Ben-Gurion University suggested to me generic terms, specific terms, and terms of insufficient contextual evidence. In *Fauna und Mineralien der Juden* (pp. 25–35), Löw chose the following categories: "Die Schlange als Gefahr," "Die Schlange als Heilmittel," "Die Schlange im Sprichwort," and "Schlange allgemein."

253. H.-J. Fabry states that the "zoological information concerning the serpent in the OT is based entirely on observation: there are no flights of fancy." *TDOT* 9.359. If we include the mythological creatures noted in the Hebrew Bible, as I have and he tends to do, then this conclusion is misleading. Yet Fabry presents a helpful synthesis of the

knowledge of snakes in the Hebrew Bible. The list of physiological features of a snake, given earlier, is indebted to him.

254. Fabry, *TDOT* 9.359.

255. See the caution in this regard that was published by A. L. Peck in his edition of Aristotle's *Historia Animalium* (Cambridge, Mass., London, 1965) vol. i.

256. F. S. Bodenheimer, *Animal and Man in Bible Lands* (Leiden, 1960) p. 197. Also see S. Bodenheimer, החי בארצנת המקרא (Jerusalem, 1949).

Appendix II

1. Coptic ϩⲟϥ translates and corresponds to numerous Greek words for "snake"; see W. E. Crum, *A Coptic Dictionary* (Oxford, 1939) pp. 740–41.

2. See also Appendix I.

3. In *Der neue Pauly: Enzyklopädie der Antike,* only nine Greek nouns for snake are presented (and one appears twice), although two more appear in the opening paragraph (*chersudros* and *ophis*); see J. Bayet, "Schlange," *DNP* 2.178–84. Bayet errs in judging the symbol of the serpent to be ambivalent in Greek, Roman, Jewish, and Christian cultures. He also seems too impressed by the negative meaning of the serpent.

4. C. Leitz, *Die Schlangennamen in den ägyptischen und griechischen Giftbüchern* (Stuttgart, 1997) pp. 16–18.

5. Cf. Aristotle, *Ethica Eudemia* 3.6 and M. A. Bailly, *Dictionnaire Grec-Français* (Paris, 1919) p. 4.

6. See Lampe, *PGL* (Oxford, 1961) p. 50.

7. See LSJM, p. 39.

8. I am indebted to the compilers of LSJM, p. 52, for this information.

9. See Lampe, *PGL*, p. 63.

10. See LSJM, p. 84.

11. See Aeschylus, *Agamemnon* 11233; LSJM, p. 94.

12. See LSJM, p. 235.

13. See Lampe, *PGL*, p. 223. Also see *Lives of the Prophets,* trans. D. R. A. Hare in *OTP* 2.386–87.

14. Experts tend to concur that the Greek noun denotes the *Coluber haje.* See Leitz, *Die Schlangennamen* and LSJM, p. 259.

15. In his *Wörterbuch der griechischen Papyrusurkunden* (Berlin, 1925) vol. 1, col. 226, F. Preisigke reports that the Greek noun means "Uräusschlange" ("Uraeus Serpent").

16. See LSJM, p. 310.

17. See Nicander, *Theriaca* 334 and LSJM, pp. 439–40.

18. This noun is not listed in the *Greek-English Lexicon: Revised Supplement* (Oxford, 1996).

19. The noun is not found in the various supplements, not even *Supplement 2 (1967–1976),* which was published in 1991.

20. See Leitz, *Die Schlangennamen.*

21. See LSJM, p. 386.

22. I am indebted to the compilers of the LSJM for this citation.

23. See the corrections in LSJM, *Supplement,* p. 98.

24. See the references listed in Lampe, *PGL,* p. 386.

25. Not "bearer of the dragon standard"; see the correction in LSJM *Supplement*, p. 98.

26. LSJM, p. 537.

27. I am indebted to LSJM, p. 691, for this information.

28. The noun denotes a "Giftschlange" ("poisonous snake"). See W. Bauer, *Griechisch-deutsches Wörterbuch zu den Schriften des Neuen Testaments und der frühchristlichen Literatur,* ed. K. Aland and B. Aland (Berlin, New York, 1988 [6th ed.]) col. 670.

29. For other references, see Lampe, *PGL,* p. 589.

30. See W. Bauer, *A Greek-English Lexicon of the New Testament,* revised by W. F. Arndt and F. W. Gingrich (Chicago, London, 1958 [2nd ed.]) p. 331. Also see Bauer, *Griechisch-deutsches Wörterbuch,* p. 670.

31. For the Greek text, see J. Geffcken, *Die Oracula Sibyllina* (Leipzig, 1902) p. 112 [*Sibylline Oracles* 5.169].

32. See Lampe, *PGL,* p. 589 (but he incorrectly reports that the noun appears in *Sibylline Oracles* 2.169). In *Dictionnaire Grec-Français,* Bailly lists the noun, but also cites the text incorrectly as 5.168. For a good translation of the *Sibylline Oracles,* see J. J. Collins in *OTP* 1; for an updated introduction see "Les Oracles Sibyllins," in *Introduction à la Littérature Religieuse Judéo-Hellénistique,* ed. A.-M. Denis et al. (Turnhout, Belgium, 2000) vol. 2, pp. 947–992.

33. I am again indebted to LSJM, p. 748.

34. See P. Chantraine, *Dictionnaire Étymologique de la Langue Grecque: Histoire des Mots* (Paris, 1968) pp. 468–69. Also see LSJM, p. 836.

35. See LSJM, p. 836.

36. This meaning needs to be added to the lexicons. For example, the meaning is not found in the seemingly exhaustive LSJM.

37. See, e.g., LSJM, p. 932.

38. Chantraine, *Dictionnaire Étymologique de la Langue Grecque,* p. 508.

39. See the comments of Philumenus, the third-century CE physician, in *De Venenatis Animalibus* 22.1 and the comments in LSJM, p. 933.

40. Consult Chantraine, *Dictionnaire Étymologique de la Langue Grecque,* p. 508.

41. The noun is not listed in LSJM or the LSJM *Supplement* of 1996. It is not in Preisigke's *Wörterbuch der griechischen Papyrusurkunden* or the numerous supplements to 1991.

42. That was the decision of the compilers of LSJM; see p. 941.

43. In early Christian literature, the noun usually means "dumb" or "deaf" (cf. the fifth-century Isidorus Pelusiota, *Epistularum Libri Quinque* 1.54 (in J.-P. Migne, ed., *Patrologia Latina,* 217 vols. [Paris, 1844–64] 78.217A).

44. I remember observing a water snake climb out of the Potomac River; it moved though the grass without moving a blade and without making a sound. At times I had doubts the snake had been moving, but it proceeded gradually into the woods.

45. No correction or additional data is supplied in the *Supplement* of 1996.

46. See Aristotle, *Hist. an.* 591ª15.

47. The compilers of LSJM suggest the name of the snake could be "mouser." Cf. Nicander, *Theriaca* 490.

48. See W. Foerster, "ὄφις," *TDNT* 5 (1968) 566–82.

49. See Chantraine, *Dictionnaire Étymologique de la Langue Grecque,* p. 842.

50. See Aelian, *Nat. an.* 8.12, ὁ παρείας ἢ παρούας.

51. See Chantraine, *Dictionnaire Étymologique de la Langue Grecque,* p. 857. The compilers of LSJM cite the fifth-century BCE Cratinus 225, the fifth- and fourth-century Aristophanes, *Plutus* 690, and the fourth-century Demosthenes 18.260.

52. See LSJM, p. 1357.

53. See Chantraine, *Dictionnaire Étymologique de la Langue Grecque,* p. 874, and LSJM, p. 1357.

54. The compilers of LSJM cite the first-century CE physician Dioscorides 4.37, the third-century CE physician Philumenus, *De Venenatis Animalibus* 19, and the second- and third-century Aelian, *Nat. an.* 6.51.

55. Long ago the compilers of LSJM, p. 1549, suggested the Greek noun denoted a type of spitting asp. In *Dictionnaire Étymologique de la Langue Grecque,* p. 951, Chantraine reported that the noun denoted a serpent, without being specific.

56. Observe the second-century BCE Nicander's *Theriaca* 327 and the second- and third-century Aelian's *De natura Animalium* 15.18. I am indebted for these references to LSJM, p. 1594.

57. My analysis is supported by Chantraine in his *Dictionnaire Étymologique de la Langue Grecque,* pp. 998–99.

58. The compilers of LSJM, p. 1595, prefer the latter option: "a serpent, the bite of which causes intense thirst."

59. Consult especially Nicander, *Theriaca* 384. In *PGL,* Lampe does not list the noun, so it may not appear in Patristic Greek.

60. See Chantraine, *Dictionnaire Étymologique de la Langue Grecque,* p. 1024. The compilers of LSJM, p. 1617, offer the meaning "*a serpent,* of uniform roundness and thickness."

61. See LSJM, p. 1837 and Aristotle in his *Hist. an.* 567^b25.

62. So also LSJM, p. 1845.

63. We could update Lampe, *PGL,* p. 1423, and add to (or replace) "an amphibious reptile" with "water snake."

64. The Greek noun essentially signifies any animal that puffs itself up and is poisonous. It can also denote a wind instrument like a pipe or flute. See LSJM, p. 1963.

65. LSJM, p. 1963.

66. In his *Dictionnaire Étymologique de la Langue Grecque,* Chantraine could only report in 1968 that φύσРϋος denoted diverse animals (he did not reduce the options to a reptile).

67. See Philumenus, *De Venenatis Animalibus* 16.1.

68. See LSJM, p. 1987.

69. It is not cited by Lampe, *PGL.*

70. Consult LSJM, p. 1988.

71. For this and other locations of this noun, see LSJM, p. 1989.

72. S. Sauneron, *Un traité égyptien d'ophiologie* (Cairo, 1989).

73. Also see L. Bodson, "Observations sur la vocabulaire de la zoologie antique: Les noms de serpents en grec et en latin," *Documents pour l'histoire du vocabulaire scientifique* 8 (1986) 65–119.

74. See K. Aland, *Vollständige Konkordanz zum Griechischen Neuen Testament,* 3 vols. (Berlin, New York, 1978–1983).

75. See P. Joüon, "Le Grand Dragon," *RSR* 17 (1927) 444–46; B. Renz, *Der orientalische Schlangendrache* (Augsburg, 1930); W. Foerster, "δράκων," *TDNT* 3 (1964) 281–83. The nouns ἀσπίς and ἑρπετόν do not receive a separate entry in *TDNT*.

76. See Foerster, "ἔχιδνα," *TDNT* 3 (1964) 815–16.

77. See Foerster, "ὄφις," *TDNT* 5 (1967) 566–71.

Appendix III

I am indebted to Professor Antonio De Simone for taking me to Pompeii (my fifth trip there), showing me some serpent images, and allowing me to use much of his research on serpents in the present appendix. Professor De Simone also gave me a copy of G. F. De Simone's *Aristarchos*. L. Guglielmo helped me during my study of serpent images and symbols in Pompeii, Herculaneum, and the Archaeological Museum in Naples.

1. The last major earthquake in Israel or Palestine was in 1033. On 18 January 749 a massive earthquake shook Palestine. It probably would have been recorded as 7 or 7.5 on the Richter scale. Recent excavations in Tiberias have revealed a record in stone of that earthquake. Now we know that from Tiberias to Jericho the earth moved northward about 1.5 meters, and all at once. In Jerusalem thousands died. The devastation was so severe that a Syrian priest claimed a village near Mount Tabor moved 6 kilometers. The effect was felt elsewhere; for example, a Coptic priest in Alexandria reported that support beams in houses shifted. Many claimed that they saw tidal waves in the Mediterranean. The whole Jordan Rift Valley remains an active fault.

2. N. Purcell, "Pompeii," *OCD* (3rd ed. 1996) 1214–15; the quotation is on p. 1214.

3. This Appendix contains my own reflections after forty years of working on Qumran texts and realia and five trips to Pompeii, once leading a BAS seminar there. Hence, only a very few references will be provided. For bibliographical information, once can easily turn to the many entries in the leading encyclopedias.

4. See P. Caputo et al., *Cuma e il suo Parco Archeologico* (Rome, 1996).

5. See J. W. Hayes, " 'Pompeian-Red' Ware (Figs. 60.7–16)," in A. D. Tushingham, ed., *Excavations in Jerusalem 1961–1967* (Toronto, 1985) vol. 1, p. 185.

6. See G. K. Boyce, *Corpus of the Lararia of Pompeii* (Rome, 1937), and Boyce, "Significance of the Serpents on Pompeian House Shrines," *AJA* 46 (1942) 13–22. F. V. M. Cumont, "La *Bona Dei* et ses serpents," *MEFRA* 49 (1932) 1–5. D. G. Orr, "Learning from *Lararia*: Notes on the Household Shrines of Pompeii," *Studia in Honor of W. F. Jashemski* (New Rochelle, N.Y., 1988) pp. 293–99. Th. Frohlich, "Pompejanische Lararienbilder," *AntW* 26 (1995) 203–10. R. A. Tybout, "Domestic Shrines and 'Popular Painting': Style and Social Context," *JRA* 9 (1996) 358–74.

7. A. De Simone gave me the following list of *larari* with serpent images: I-16-2; I-7-11; I-7-11,18; I-8-8,1; I-8-10,1; I-8-17,3; I-9-1,8; I-10-7; I-10-18,9; I-11-1; I-11-10,1; I-11,10. 8; I-11-15,10; I-12-4,7; I-12-8,6; I-12-9,7; I-12-15,5; I-12-16,2; I-13-2,17; I-13-11. 5 and 6; I-16-3,7; I-16-4, 2; II-1-8,1; VI-16-15; V-2-D; VII-3-13.

8. Cf. Fig. 36 earlier in this book.

9. For a good color photograph, see E. De Carolis, *Gods and Heroes in Pompeii*, trans. L.-A. Touchette (Rome, 2001) p. 63. Also, compare Figs. 54 and 65 in this book.

10. Also see the ithyphallic Hermes (Mercury) depicted with a caduceus; it is a shop sign in Pompeii. See the color photograph in S. De Caro, ed., *The Secret Cabinet in the National Archaeological Museum of Naples* (Naples, 2000) p. 37.

11. I am grateful to De Simone for discussions on serpent symbolism at Pompeii.

12. The guard, Manzo Lanzaro, pointed out these large images of serpents to me, and helped me study some *larari*.

13. I am grateful to the Ministero per I Beni e le Attività Culturali del Museo Archeologico, Napoli, and in particular to the graciousness offered by Dott.ssa Mariarosaria Borriello.

14. For photographs of some of the serpent jewelry and frescoes, see A. d'Ambrosio et al., eds., *Storie da un'eruzione: Pompei Ercolano Oplontis* (Milan, 2003). See esp. the following: gold armbands or bracelets (pp. 50, 141, 147, 207 [*bis*], 254), silver bracelets (pp. 130, 457), silver rings (pp. 265, 270, 282, 314), gold rings (pp. 164, 166, 170, 171, 271, 272), frescoes (pp. 236, 392); Agathadaimon (p. 287), and Hermes (Mercury) with caduceus (282).

Appendix IV

1. Tertullian [text incorrectly attributed to him], *Against All Heresies* chap. 2; *The Ante Nicene Fathers ANF* 3, p. 650.

2. My translation; see Pseudo-Tertullian, *Against All Heresies*, chap. 2; *ANF* 3, p. 650.

3. Section 3. 37, 1,1–3,1. See F. Williams, trans., *The Panarion of Epiphanius of Salamis*, 2 vols. (Leiden, 1994) vol. 1, pp. 241–43.

4. Hippolytus, *Haer.* 5.12; *ANF* 5, p. 63 (italics mine).

5. Italics mine.

6. Hippolytus, *Haer.* 5.12 (italics mine).

7. Hippolytus, *Haer.* 5.12; *ANF* 5, p. 64.

8. Hippolytus, *Haer.* 5.12; trans. J. H. MacMahon, "Hippolytus: The Refutation of All Heresies," *ANF* 5, p. 64 (italics mine).

9. John Chrysostom, *Commentary on Saint John, the Apostle and Evangelist: Homilies 1–47*, trans. T. A. Goggin (New York, 1957) p. 262.

10. Chrysostom, *Commentary on Saint John: Homilies 1–47*, p. 262.

11. Chrysostom, *Commentary on Saint John*, pp. 262–63.

12. Chrysostom, *Commentary on Saint John*, p. 263.

13. Justin, *Dial.* 91; trans. A. C. Coxe in *ANF* 1, p. 245.

14. *ANF* 1, p. 245, note 4.

15. *Adv. Haer.* 4.2.7; trans. Coxe in *ANF* 1, p. 465.

16. A. P. Carleton, *John Shines Through Augustine* (New York, 1961) p. 75.

17. See his tractate on 1Jn, Tractate 3.2: "Was not his resurrection announced to the men by the women so that the serpent might be defeated by [his own] stratagem reversed?" Augustine, *Tractates on the Gospel of John 112–24; Tractates on the First Epistle of John*, trans. J. W. Rettig (Washington, 1995) p. 160.

18. For the plates of all these cryptograms see W. O. Moeller, *The Mithraic Origin and Meanings of the Rotas-Sator Square* (Leiden, 1973).

19. In his excellent article, D. Fishwick habitually refers to the Rotas-Sator Square as a rebus. See his "On the Origin of the Rotas-Sator Square," *HTR* 57 (1964) 39–53; see esp. pp. 40, 43, 45, 51, 53.

20. See also the crosses on the right margin of the Latin on the leather inscription found perhaps at Saxony. See the photograph that faces the title page of Moeller's *The Mithraic Origin*. D. Fishwick also points out how absurd the attempt is to explain the cryptograph as a Christian creation. He offers the suggestion that the cryptograph is

originally Jewish, but that raises many problems, not the least of which is the use of Latin to represent "Pater Noster," and the appearance of the cryptogram in Britain but not in Palestine. See Fishwick's article in the *HTR* 57 (1964) 39–53.

21. See E. Strommenger and M. Hirmer, *The Art of Mesopotamia* (London, 1964) Plates 7, 8, 34, 40, 157.

22. See the comments by E. Dinkler in *Signum Crucis* (Tübingen, 1967) esp. pp. 1–54.

23. See U. Ernst, "Satorformel," *Evangelisches Kirchenlexikon* (1996) vol. 5, cols. 58–60.

24. Moeller, *The Mithraic Origin,* pp. 35–36; H. Last, "The Rotas Sator Square: Present Position and Future Prospects," *JTS* N.S. 31 (1952) 92–97; Fishwick in *HTR* 57 (1964) 40–41; C. D. Gunn, "The Sator-Arepo Palindrome: A New Inquiry into the Composition of an Ancient Word Square" (Ph.D. diss., Yale University, 1969).

25. W. Baines, "The Rotas-Square: A New Investigation," *NTS* 33 (1987) 469–76.

26. See the study by A. Maiuri, "Sulla datazione de 'Quadrato magico' o criptogramma cristiano a Pompei," *Rendiconti della Accademia di Archeologia, Lettere ed Arti* [Naples] 28 (1953) 101–11.

27. There is an alleged "cross" image left on the wall of a house at Herculaneum. Is it merely the backing for something that once hung on the wall? An examination of the area reveals that the nails are at the top and bottom; a shelf or heavy object would have been anchored with nails on the ends of the horizontal bar. The plastered bench before "the cross" is identical to home shrines. Finally, the house is where non-Romans would have lived. Do these suggestions indicate that a cross was hung on a wall? If so, does that fact indicate the people who lived in the room were "Christians"? Without any doubt there were Christians in Rome in the sixties since Paul's letter to the Romans proves that conclusion, but proof of Christians in one city is not evidence of their existence in another.

28. The "cross" shape recently found at Bethsaida is interesting, and I await full publication for an assessment of it. It may, however, be only a cross shape. This cross appears on the cover of the first volume of the Bethsaida excavations. See R. Arav and R. A. Freund, *Bethsaida: A City by the North Shore of the Sea of Galilee* (Kirksville, Mo., 1995).

29. Rev 1:8, 21:6, 22:13. I am grateful to Fishwick for some of these insights. See Fishwick, *HTS* 57 (1964) 44–46.

30. A simple example of a palindrome in English is "Mom" and "Dad." The play with words is typical of many segments of society. Since our youth, most of us have heard that "evil" is "live" spelled backward.

31. Baines: "[T]he Rotas square contains one otherwise unknown word (AREPO)." *NTS* 33 (1987) 470. Fishwick: "AREPO is simply the reverse of OPERA" which is otherwise meaningless. *HTS* 57 (1964) 51.

32. See Lewis and Short, *Harpers' Latin Dictionary,* p. 164, and *TLL,* vol. 2, col. 634.

33. Pausanias, *Descr.* 39.3. For the text and translation see Edelstein, *Asclepius,* vol. 1, p. 361.

34. Ovid, *Metam.* 15.654–59. For text and translation, see Edelstein, *Asclepius,* vol. 1, p. 361.

35. Pliny, *Nat.* 29.4 (22) 72. For the text and translation, see Edelstein, *Asclepius,* vol. 1, p. 362.

36. Xenophon, *Cyn.* 1.6; for text and translation, see Edelstein, *Asclepius,* vol. 1, p. 112.

37. Julianus, *In Helium Regem* 155B; for the Greek and English translation, see Edelstein, *Asclepius,* vol. 1, pp. 151–52. Capitalization mine.

38. Aelian, *Nat. an.* 10.9. For the Greek and translation, see Edelstein, *Asclepius,* vol. 1, p. 265. Capitalization mine.

39. Suidas, *Lexicon,* ad loc. cit. For the Greek and English translation, see Edelstein, *Asclepius,* vol. 1, p. 265. Capitalization mine.

40. Edelstein, *Asclepius,* vol. 2, p. 77.

41. *Epistula ad Marcellam* 7. For the Greek text and translation, see Edelstein, *Asclepius,* vol. 1, pp. 111–12.

42. Aristides, *Oratio* 42, 1–15; Edelstein, *Aslepius,* vol. 1, pp. 156, 160.

43. For the Greek and English, see H. W. Attridge and R. A. Oden, *Philo of Byblos: The Phoenician History* (Washington, D.C., 1981) pp. 66–67.

44. See Macrobius, *Saturnalia;* I am indebted to Leisegang for this citation. See H. Leisegang, *The Mysteries: Papers of the Eranos Yearbooks,* vol. 2, ed. J. Campbell (New York, 1955) p. 200.

45. *In Platonis Timaeum* 1.49C. For the Greek and English translation, see Edelstein, *Asclepius,* vol. 1, p. 151.

46. Macrobius, *Saturnalia* 1.20, 1–4; Edelstein, *Asclepius,* vol. 1, pp. 148–49.

47. Proclus, *In Platonis Timaeum* 1, 49C; Edelstein, *Asclepius,* vol. 1, p. 151.

48. Leisegang, *The Mysteries,* p. 200.

49. In the Jewish magical papyri, the gibberish often seems to derive from phonetics related to the Tetragrammaton. See the *Prayer of Jacob:* "God Aba*th, Abrathia*th, [Sa]ba[oth, A]d*nai . . . Epa[g]a*l [El*]*l, Sou*l." Charlesworth in OTP 2.721–23.

50. Aristides, *Oratio* 42. 1–15; Edlestein, *Asclepius,* vol. 1, pp. 155–63. Translation mine.

51. The attempt to consider *arepo* as indicating a plow is without any basis in philology.

52. For the Greek and the translation, see Attridge and Oden, *Philo of Byblos,* pp. 52–53.

53. Herondas, *Mimiambi,* 4.11; Edelstein, *Asclepius,* vol. 1, p. 272.

54. Edelstein, *Asclepius,* vol. 1, pp. 143–44.

55. Aristides (128–189 CE), *Oratio* 48.4; Edelstein, *Asclepius,* vol. 1, p. 155.

56. Oxyrhynchus, Papyrus 11, 1381; Edelstein, *Asclepius,* vol. 1, p. 175.

57. Philostratus, *Epistulae* 18; cf. Edelstein, *Asclepius,* vol. 1, p. 200.

58. Moeller argues that the cryptograph originated in Italy among worshippers of Mithra. See Moeller, *The Mithraic Origin,* pp. 21–38. Before Moeller, others judged the cryptograph to be Mithraic; see A. Omodeo, "La croce d'Ercolano e il culto precostantiniano della roce," *La Critica* 38 (1940) 45–61.

59. J. Sundwall, "L'Enigmatica iscrizione ROTAS in Pompei," *Acta Academiae Aboensis, Humaniora* 15 (1945) 16–17.

60. See the hypothesis of Fishwick in *HTR* 57 (1964) 46–53.

61. Julianus, *Contra Galilaeos* 200 A–B; Edelstein, *Asclepius,* vol. 1, p. 152.

62. See the plates in Moeller, *The Mithraic Origin.*

63. Orphic Hymns 67; for the Greek and translation, see Apostolos N. Athanassakis, *The Orphic Hymns: Text, Translation, and Notes* (Missoula, Mont., 1977), pp. 88–89.

64. Juvenal, *Sat.* 6.55; see also line 57; *et agello cedo paterno.*

65. Tacitus, *Hist.,* book 3, 86.

66. Galen, *De libris propriis,* Cp. 2; Edelstein, *Asclepius,* vol. 1, p. 263. Also see Galen, *De sanitate tuenda,* 1.8, 20; ibid., vol. 1, p. 179.

67. Fishwick, *HTR* 57 (1964) 51.

68. Baines, *NTS* 33 (1987) 473.

69. Ibid., p. 473.

70. See H. Matthäus, *Der Arzt in römisher Zeit: Literarische Nachrichten—archäologische Denkmäler,* ed. Ph. Filtzinger (Stuttgart, 1987); see the forty-seven illustrations, many of which feature physicians and Asclepius with serpents.

71. My translation; brackets indicate restorations. See Leisegang, *The Mysteries,* p. 201.

72. Charlesworth in *OTP* 2.720–73.

73. Leisegang, *The Mysteries,* p. 218. For a photograph of the alabaster bowl, see p. 201.

74. K. Preisendanz, ed., *Papyri graecae magicae: Die griechischen Zauberpapyri* (Berlin, 1928) vol. 1, pp. 111ff. or vol. 4, pp. 1115–65.

75. See Leisegang, *The Mysteries,* p. 211.

Selected "Serpent" Bibliography

This bibliography on the serpent is focused first on antiquity (especially from 1000 BCE to c. fourth cent. CE), and second on the symbolic meaning of the serpent. The selection has also been guided by an emphasis on the Levant.

Not included are discussions in encyclopedias that are brief and usually anonymous. Numerals are given in Arabic numbers, unless Roman numerals are in the titles. The names of cities are translated into English. Authors' surnames that begin in van and von but are separated from the following noun, and other similar forms, are placed with the next letter in the alphabet in their names. Abbreviations are generally avoided to assist those in various disciplines; for abbreviations demanded to avoid excessive length, see the Abbrevations at the beginning of this book. Since works published outside the United States sometimes do not provide the city, publisher, or date, the following additional abbreviations have been used: n.c. (no city given), n.p. (no publisher indicated), n.d. (no date provided).

The bibliography is arranged alphabetically so as to serve the majority. For biblical historians and archaeologists who are interested in chronology, the list could have been arranged differently. They might want to organize it from the Nachash in the Eden Story, to Moses' bronze serpent (Num 21), Hezekiah's Nechushtan, through the Asclepian cult (which belongs to the pre and post-Christian eras), John 3:14 and other New Testament texts, the Ophites and Naassanes, and finally to the Gnostics and the early scholars of the Church. For those who are interested in the development of the symbolical meaning of the serpent, the list would have been arranged differently. It would lead from c. 40,000 BCE and the prehistoric era to Moses and then to the present with the worshipping of snakes in India and the handling of snakes in the southern parts of the United States (according to a literal reading of Mk 16:9–20). The bibliography could also have been arranged according to topics: Ophites and Naassanes, the Asclepian cult, Asian religions, Australian mythologies, an exegesis of New Testament and Old Testament passages, archaeology, the language of art, the commonality of the human from Paleolithic times to the present, psychology, and iconography and art. Usually the titles of articles and books clarify the focus of a publication. Sometimes I supply a brief notation to assist the reader and scholar. I annotate an entry especially when it contains illustrations that are a prerequisite for comprehending the variagated meanings of serpent symbolism.

This selected bibliography reflects an interest in iconography, mythology, and theology. The list shows only a little concern for zoology and herpetology; for such work, consult the publications in the *Zeitschrift der Societas Europaea Herpetologica* and the works published by the Herpetofauna-Verlag. Additional publications can be found in the periodicals, series, and publications cited here. For further works see the following collections: *American Anthropologist, L'Antiquité classique, Die Aquarien—und Terrarien Zeitschrift, Bonner Zoologische Monographien, British Herpetological Society Bulletin, Corpus medicorum graecorum, Fieldiana Zoology, Herpetofauna, Herpetological Review, Israel Journal of Zoology, Journal of Experimental Zoology, Journal of the Herpetological Association of Africa, Journal of Herpetology, Lexicon der christlichen Ikonographie, Lexicon Iconographicum Mythologiae Classicae, Pharmacy in History, Proceedings of the Zoological Society of London, Reallexikon für ägyptische Religionsgeschichte, Revue d'égyptologie, Salamandra: Zeitschrift für Herpetologie und Terrarienkunde,* and *Toxicon, Zoologische Abhandlungen Staatliches Museum für Tierkunde in Dresden.*

The selected serpent bibliography is also dedicated to the most recent and important publications. This bibliography was corrected and expanded by working in numerous major libraries in which I was always treated with professional respect and courtesy. I am especially indebted to the following libraries: Speer and Luce Libraries at Princeton Theological Seminary, the libraries in the University of Tübingen, the Ecole Biblique Library, the Israel National Library and Jewish Library, and the British Library. Additional bibliographical references will be found in the notes to the preceding discussions. Katherine A. Skrebutenas, the reference librarian in Speer and Luce Libraries, Princeton Theological Seminary, helped me discover some exotic abbreviations.

Adkins, L., and R. Adkins. "Aesculapius," *Dictionary of Roman Religions.* New York: Facts On File, 1996; p. 3.

Aharoni, Y. "Arad: Its Inscription and Temple," *Biblical Archaeologist* 31 (1968) 2–32.

———, ed. *Beer-Sheba I: Excavation at Tel Beer-Sheba, 1961–1971 Seasons.* Tel Aviv University Institute of Archaeology. Tel Aviv: Ramat Aviv, 1973.

———. "The Horned Altar of Beer-sheba," *Biblical Archaeologist* 37. (1974) 2–6.

Albright, W. F. "The Evolution of the West-Semitic Divinity 'An-'Anat-'Atta," *The American Journal of Semitic Languages and Literatures* 41 (1925) 73–101.

———. "Notes on the Goddess Anat," *The American Journal of Semitic Languages and Literatures* 43 (1927) 233–36.

———. "Anath and the Dragon," *Bulletin of the American Schools of Oriental Research* 84 (1941) 14–16.

———. " 'The Bronze Age,' II of the Excavation of Tell Beit Mirsim," *Annual of the American Schools of Oriental Research* 17 (1936–1937) esp. p. 43. [Albright rightly warned against interpreting the serpent as only or primarily a sexual symbol.]

————. "The Goddess of Life and Wisdom," *American Journal of Semitic Languages and Literatures* 36 (1919–1920) 258–94.

————. "The Excavation at Tell Beit Mirsim, Vol. II: The Bronze Age," *Bulletin of the American Schools of Oriental Research* 31 (1928) 1–11. [The image of a goddess was found in an MB II stratum. Albright assumed incorrectly she was bound around the legs by a large serpent.]

————. *Yahweh and the Gods of Canaan*. Garden City, N. Y.: Doubleday, 1968.

————, and G. Mendenhall. "The Creation of the Composite Bow in Canaanite Mythology," *The Journal of Near Eastern Studies* 1 (1942) 227–29.

Alexiou, S. *Minoan Civilization*, trans. C. Ridley. Heraklion, Crete: Spyros Alexiou Sons, 1969. N.V.

————. *Minoische Kultur. Sternstunden der Archäologie*, trans. W. Liebich. Frankfurt: Musterschmidt Göttingen, 1976 [also see the Greek original of 1964 or English translation of 1969]; see esp. Fig. 12 [the snake goddess], p. 113 [gold amulet with a serpent], and p. 119 [the serpents on a vessel].

Amaducci, A. B. *Die Brancacci-Kapelle und Masaccio*. Florence: Scala, 1978. [In the Triptychon in San Giovenale Church in Cascia, Masolino, the student of Masaccio, depicted the sepent in the Garden of Eden as a female, and she has an angelic face. See Fig. 2, opposite page 16. Also see Fig. 79 in the present book.]

Amélineau, E. "Du rôle des serpents dans les croyances religieuses de l'Egypte," *Revue de l'histoire des religions* 51 (1905) 335–60; also see vol. 52 (1905) 1–32.

Amiet, P. "Antiquités de Serpentine," *Iranica Antiqua* 15 (1980) 155–66, Plate 2.

————. *Elam*. Auvers-sur-Oise, France: Archée, 1966.

Amiet, P., et al., eds. *La grammaire des formes et des styles: Antiquité*. Fribourg: Production Office du Livre, 1981.

Amorai-Stark, S. *Wolfe Family Collection of Near Eastern Prehistoric Stamp Seals*. Orbis Biblicus et Orientalis 16. Series Archaeologica. Freiburg: University Press of Freiburg and Göttingen: Vandenhoeck & Ruprecht, 1997. See esp. Nos. 163 [5th millen.], 256 [4th millen.], 277 [4th millen.], 352 [4/3rd millen.], and 430 [3rd millen.]. It is impossible to discern the identity of some images; serpents are possibly found on Nos. 257, 277, 314, 339, 343, 395, 414, 461, 467, and 470.

Amsler, F. "The Apostle Philip, the Viper, the Leopard, and the Kid: The Masked Actors of a Religious Conflict in Hierapolis of Phrygia," *SBL Seminar Papers [1991]* Atlanta: Scholars Press, 1996; pp. 432–37.

Anderson, B. W. "The Slaying of the Fleeing, Twisting Serpent: Isaiah 27:1 in Context," *From Creation to New Creation*. Minneapolis: Fortress, 1994; pp. 195–206.

Andreae, B. *L'Art de l'ancienne Rome: L'Art et les grandes civilisations*. Paris: Mazenrod, 1973.

Andrews, C., ed. *The Ancient Egyptian Book of the Dead*, trans. R. O. Faulkner. Austin: University of Texas Press, 1990.

Anonymous. *Archaeology: Highlights from the Israel Museum.* Jerusalem: The Israel Museum, 1984.

Anonymous. *Ophiolatreia: An Account of the Rites and Mysteries Connected with the Origin, Rise, and Development of Serpent Worship.* 1889 [privately printed].

Anthes, R. "Der Gebrauch des Wortes 'Schlange,' 'Schlangenleib' in den Pyramidengtexten," *Drevnij Mir: Sbornik Statej. Akademiku Vasiliju Vasil'evicu Struve.* Moscow, 1962; pp. 32–49.

———. "König 'Schlange' . . . Schlange und Schlangengöttin Uto," *Zeitschrift für Ägyptische Sprache und Altertumskunde* 83 (1958) 79–82.

Antonova, Ye. V. "The 'Serpent' and the 'Eagle' in the Glyptics of the Oxus Civilization," *Journal of Ancient History* 2 (2000 [Moscow]) 46–52 [Russian]. [The images discussed are not clearly linked with Zoroastrianism, and the eagle and serpent complement each other, bringing together the tension between good and evil.]

Anzaldúa, G. "Entering into the Serpent," *Weaving the Visions: New Patterns in Feminist Spirituality,* ed. J. Plaskow and C. Christ. San Francisco: Harper & Row, 1989.

Apollodorus. *Apollodorus: The Library,* trans. Sir J. G. Frazier. Loeb Classical Library. London: William Heinemann and New York: G. P. Putnam's Sons, 1921; see esp. vol. 1, pp. 84–87.

Arbesmann, R. "The Concept of 'Christus medicus' in St. Augustine," *Traditio* 10 (1954) 1–28.

Armstrong, J. *The Paradise Myth.* London, New York, and Toronto: Oxford University Press, 1969; see esp. pp. 9–36.

Astour, M. C. "Two Ugaritic Serpent Charms," *Journal of Near Eastern Studies* 27 (1968) 13–36.

Asurmendi, J. "En Torno a la Serpiente de Bronce," *Estudios Bíblicos* 46 (1988) 283–94.

Athanassakis, A. N. *The Orphic Hymns: Text, Translation, and Notes.* Society of Biblical Literature Texts and Translations, 12. Society of Biblical Literature Graeco-Roman Series, 4. Missoula, Mont.: Scholars Press, 1977.

Attridge, H. W., and R. A. Oden, Jr., eds. *Philo of Byblos-The Phoenician History: Introduction, Critical Text, Translation, Notes.* The CBQ Monograph Series 9. Washington, D.C.: Association of America, 1981.

Augustine. *John Shines Through Augustine: Selections from the Sermons of Augustine on the Gospel According to Saint John,* trans. A. P. Carleton. World Christian Books, Second Series, 34. London: Lutterworth Press, 1959; reprinted in New York: Association Press (n.d.).

———. *The Literal Meaning of Genesis, Vol. 2: Books 7–12,* trans. J. H. Taylor, S. J. Ancient Christian Writers: The Works of the Fathers in Translation 42, ed. E. J. Quasten, W. J. Burghardt, and T. C. Lawler. New York, and Ramsey, N.J.: Newman Press, 1982; pp. 110–13, 133–40.

———. *Tractates on the Gospel of John 112–24; Tractates on the First Epistle of John,* trans. J. W. Rettig. The Fathers of the Church: A New Translation. Washington, D.C.: The Catholic University of America Press, 1995.

———. *De Trinate.* 2 Vols, ed. W. J. Mountain. Corpus Christianorum Series Latina L: Aurelii Augustini Opera, Pars XVI I/2. Turnholt: Typographi Brepolis Editores Pontificii, 1968.

———. *The Trinity,* trans. E. Hill, and J. E. Rotelle. The Works of Saint Augustine for the 21st Century, Part I, Vol. 5. Brooklyn, N.Y.: New City Press, 1991.

Ausloos, H. "Mozes' bronzen slang: Gods 'teken van redding,' " *Schrift* 195 (2001) 69–71.

Avalon, A. [John George Woodroffe]. *The Serpent Power.* Madras: Ganesh & Co., 1924.

Avalos, H. "Ancient Medicine: In Case of Emergency, Contact Your Local Prophet," *Bible Review* 11 (1995) 27–35; see esp. p. 31 for a color picture of the copper serpent with gilded head, dating to the twelfth cent. BCE, found at Timnaʿ.

Avi-Yonah, M. *Art in Ancient Palestine: Selected Studies,* ed. H. Katzenstein and Y. Tsafrir. Jesusalem: The Magnes Press, 1981.

Aymar, B. *Treasury of Snake Lore.* New York: Greenberg, 1956.

Azarpay, G. "The Snake-Man in the Art of Bronze Age Bactria," *Bulletin of the Asia Institute* N.S. 5 (1991) 1–10. [The unique male figures on two Bactrian sealstones, which are now in the Louvre and the Kovacs Collection, were found in East Iran. These are similar to other known seals that depict a man with serpents as arms.]

Bagatti, P. B., and J. T. Milik. *Gli Scavi del "Dominus Flevit," Parte I: La Necropoli del Periodo Romano.* Pubblicazioni Dello Studium Biblicum Franciscanum 13. Jerusalem: Tipografia dei PP. Francescani, 1958.

Bailey, J., K. McLeish, and D. Spearman. *Gods and Men: Myths and Legends from the World's Religions.* Oxford Myths and Legends. New York and Oxford: Oxford University Press, 1981.

Baines, W. "The Rotas-Sator Square: A New Investigation," *New Testament Studies* 33 (1987) 469–76.

Bakan, D. *Sigmund Freud and the Jewish Mystical Tradition: A Provocative Exploration of the Role Played by Jewish Mysticism in the Development of Psychoanalysis.* Boston: Beacon Press, 1958; paperback, Boston: Beacon Paperback, 1975.

Balz, H., and G. Schneider, eds. "ὄφις," *Exegetisches Wörterbuch zum Neuen Testament* Stuttgart: W. Kohlhammer, 1992 [2nd ed.]; vol. 2, p. 1354.

Bandini, P. *Drachenwelt: Von den Geistern der Schöpfung und Zerstörung,* trans. T. Prohn. Stuttgart: Weitbrecht, 1996. [The book is full of drawings; for ancient Near Eastern research, see esp. p. 37] [William Blake's depiction of Elohim creating Adam around which a serpent is coiled, helping God? (1796)], p. 75 [Zeus fighting the anguipede Typhon, from fifth cent. BCE], p. 81 [a serpent goddess from Crete, 1700-1600 BCE], p. 94 [two serpent gods and two dragon-bird gods, Sumeria, c. 2025 BCE], p. 95 [two gods in paradise with a large serpent, Sumerian, c. 250 BCE], and p. 175 [serpent and dragon gods, even Yahweh, second to first cent. BCE].

Barash, A., and J. H. Hoofien. *Reptiles of Israel*. Tel Aviv: Hakibuts Hamenchat, 1966 [Hebrew].

Barb, A. "Abrasax-Studien," *Hommages à W. Deonna*, 1957; pp. 67–86. N.V.

Bardtke, H. "Die Loblieder von Qumran," *Theologische Literatur Zeitung* 81 (1956) cols. 149–54, 589–604, 715–24; and also *TLZ* 82 (1957) cols. 339–48.

Barnett, R. D. "The Serpent-Headed Tripod Base," *Eretz-Israel* 19 [Michael Avi-Yonah Memorial Volume] (1987) 1.

Barrelet, M. Th. "Etudes de glyptique akkadienne: L'imagination figurative et le cycle d'Ea," *Orientalia* 39, N.S. 2 (1970) 213–51.

Battaglia, G. G. "Glykon," *Lexicon Iconographicum Mythologiae Classicae* 4.1, pp. 279–83 [see the bibliography]; see the photographs in *LIMC* 4.2, Plates 161–62.

Batto, B. F. *Slaying the Dragon: Mythmaking in the Biblical Tradition*. Louisville, Ky.: Westminster/John Knox Press, 1992; see esp. pp. 58–61, 206–7.

Bauchhenss, G. *Jupitergigantensäulen*, ed. Ph. Filtzinger. Kleine Schriften zur Kenntnis der römischen besetzungsgeschichte Südwestdeutschlands 14. Stuttgart: A. W. Genter Verlag, 1976. [See the illustrations of Jupiter trampling with his horse on a Giant (Nos. 24, 26) or using the Giant with his massive serpentine feet to elevate his horses (Nos. 25, 27) and even sometimes his chariot, either with his hands (Nos. 28, 29), or the serpent heads of his legs (not shown, but see RL 412 in the Württembergisches Landesmuseen Stuttgart, Altes Schloss)].

Bauchot, R., ed. *Schlangen*, trans. C. Ronsiek et al. Augsburg: Naturbuch Verlag, 1994 [French original is also 1994].

Baudissin, W. W. G. *Adonis und Esmun: Eine Untersuchung zur Geschichte des Glaubens an Auferstehungsgötter und an Heilgötter*. Leipzig: J. C. Hinrichs'sche Buchhandlung, 1911; see esp. pp. 325–39.

———. "Esmun—Asklepios," *Orientalische Studien: Theodor Nöldeke zum 70. Geburtstag*. Gieszen: A. Töpelmann, 1906; vol. 2, pp. 729–55.

———. "Eherne Schlange," *Realencycl. für protestant. Theol. und Kirche* 17 (1898) 580–86.

———. "Die Symbolik der Schlange im Semitismus, insbesondere im Alten Testament," *Studien zur Semitischen Religionsgeschichte, Heft 1*. Leipzig: W. Grunow, 1876; pp. 255–92.

Bauer, W., I. Dümotz, and S. Golowin. *Lexicon der Symbole*. Wiesbaden: Fourier Verlag, 1998; see esp. p. 46.

Baumann, H. *Schöpfung und Urzeit des Menschen im Mythus der afrikanischen Völker*. Berlin: Reimer, Andrews, and Steiner, 1936.

Baumgarten, A. K. "Child Sacrifice and Snakes," *The Phoenician History of Philo of Byblos: A Commentary*. EPRO 89. Leiden: Brill, 1981; pp. 244–60.

Bayley, H. *The Lost Language of Symbolism: An Inquiry into the Origin of Certain Letters, Words, Names, Fairy-Tales, Folklore, and Mythologies*, 2 vols. London: Williams and Norgate, 1912.

Bazala, W. *Asklepios, der göttliche Arzt.* Grünenthal Waage, n.p., 1961.

Beckman, G. "The Anatolian Myth of Illuyanka," *Journal of the Ancient Near Eastern Society of Columbia University* 14 (1982) 11–25.

Bell, R. "Serpent," *Dictionary of Classical Mythology Symbols, Attributes, and Associations.* Santa Barbara, Calif.: ABC-Clio, Inc., and Oxford: Clio Press Ltd., 1982; pp. 214–17.

Bellinger, G. J. *Lexicon der Mythologie.* Augsburg: Bechtermünz Verlag, 1997; see esp. pp. 11, 12, 18, 22, 34, 41, 52, 55, 72, 88, 95, 121, 136, 147, 157, 160, 163, 168, 181, 202, 205, 240, 242, 274, 277, 283, 317, 330, 331, 383, 399, 410, 416, 439, 464, 468, 485, 494, 498, 512, 520, and 539.

Berger, K. "Gnosis/Gnostizismus I," *Theologische Realenzyklopädie* 13. Berlin and New York: Walter de Gruyter, 1984; pp. 519–35 [for Ophites].

Bergman, E. *Medicinska Emblem och Symboler.* Eskilstuna: Svenska Läkartidningen, 1941.

Berlejung, A. *Die Theologie der Bilder.* Orbis Biblicus et Orientalis 162. Freiburg: Universitätsverlag and Göttingen: Vandenhoeck & Ruprecht, 1998.

Bernhard, O. "Asklepios und sein Geschlecht auf griechischen und römischen Münzen," *Ciba Zeitschrift* (1936) 1014–1020.

——. *Griechische und römische Münzbilder in ihren Beziehungen zur Geschichte der Miedizin.* Zurich, Berlin: n.p., 1926.

Betz, O. "Die Geburt der Gemeinde durch den Lehrer (Bemerkungen zum Qumranpsalm 1QH III, 1 ff.)," *New Testament Studies* 3 (1957) 314–26.

——. "Felsenmann und Felsengemeinde (Eine Parallele zu Mt 16, 17–19) in den Qumranpsalmen," *Zeitschrift fur die neutestamentliche Wissenschaft* 48 (1957) 49–77.

——. "Die Proselytentaufe der Qumransekte und die Taufe im Neuen Testament," *Revue de Qumran* 1.2 (1958) 213–34.

Beyerle, S. "Die 'Eherne Schlange'; Num 21, 4–9: Synchron und diachron gelesen," *Zeitschrift für die alttestamentliche Wissenschaft* 111 (1999) 23–44.

Biale, D. *Eros and the Jews: From Biblical Israel to Contemporary America.* New York: Basic Books, 1992.

Bianchi, R. S. "The Ancient Mediterranean: Good and Evil Snakes," *Faces* (October 1995) 6–9.

Biesantz, H. *Die kretisch-mykenische Kunst.* Ullstein Kunstgeschichte 4. West Berlin: Ullstein Bücher, 1964; see esp. Illus. 39 [gold ring with a gem showing goddesses with serpents], and Illus. 71 [a serpent and a boar? struggling in gold relief].

Boardman, J., J. Dörig, W. Fuchs, and M. Hirmer. *Die Griechische Kunst.* Munich: Hirmer Verlag, 1992; see esp. pp. 95, 97, 98, 219, Plate 12, and photographs 85, 126–27, 185, 278–80.

Boardman, J., O. Palagia, S. Woodford, "Herakles," in *Lexicon Iconographicum Mythologiae Classicae* 4.1, pp. 728–838 [bibliography]; see the photographs in *LIMC* 4.2, especially Plates 552–56.

Böcher, O. *Dämonenfurcht und Dämonenabwehr: Ein Beitrag zur Vorgeschichte der christlichen Taufe.* Stuttgart: W. Kohlhammer, 1970; pp. 92–95.

Bodenheimer, F. S. *Animal and Man in Bible Lands*. Collection de travaux de l'académie internationale d'histoire des sciences, No. 10 [in two vols.]. Leiden: Brill, 1960, 1972; see esp. 1960, pp. 64–68 and 1972, Figs. 19, 24, 31, and 38.

———. *Animal Life in Palestine: An Introduction to the Problems of Animal Ecology and Zoogeography*. Jerusalem: L. Mayer, 1935; see esp. pp. 181–91.

Bodenheimer, F. S., and W. S. McCullough, "Serpent," *Interpreter's Dictionary of the Bible* 4 (1962) 298–91.

Bodson, L. "Les grecs et leurs serpents: Premiers résultats de l'étude taxonomique des sources anciennes," *L'Antiquité Classique* 50 (1981) 57–78.

———. "Nature et fonctions des serpents d'Athéna," in *Mélanges Pierre Lévêque*, ed. M.-M. Mactoux and E. Geny. Centre de Recherches d'Histoire Ancienne 96. Paris: n.p., 1990; pp. 45–62.

———. "Observations sur la vocabulaire de la zoologie antique: Les noms de serpents en grec et en latin," *Documents pour l'histoire du vocabulaire scientifique* 8 (1986) 65–119.

Boelicke, U., et al. *Museum: Römisches Museum Köln,* ed. B. Schneider. Braunschweig: Georg Westermann Verlag, 1998; see esp. p. 110.

Boessneck, J. "Schlangen," *Die Tierwelt des Alten Ägypten*. Munich: C. H. Beck, 1988; pp. 114–16.

Böhl, M. Th. "Die Sichem-Plakette: Protoalphabetische Schriftzeichen der Mittelbronzezeit vom *Tell Balata*," *Zeitschrift des Deutschen Palästina-Vereins* 61 (1938) 1–25. [In an MB II stratum a large serpent was found. It is depicted moving from the earth to the prudenta of a goddess; see Plate I.]

Böhmer, R. M. "Stierkopf und Schlange: Die archaische Siegelabrollung W.22150," *Bagdader Mitteilungen* 12 (1981) 7–8.

Boismard, M. É., et al. *L'Évangile de Jean: Études et Problèmes*. Recherches Bibliques, 3. Louvain: Desclée de Brouwer, 1958.

Bon, C. "Schlangengifte und Heilmittel," in *Schlangen,* ed. R. Bauchot, trans. C. Ronsiek et al. Augsburg: Naturbuch Verlag, 1994 [French original is also 1994]; pp. 194–209, 47, 55, 76, and 509.

Bonnet, H. "Schlange," *Reallexicon der Ägyptischen Religionsgeschichte*. Berlin: Walter de Gruyter & Co., 1952; pp. 681–86.

Bonsirven, J. "Les aramaïsmes de S. Jean l'Évangeliste," *Biblica* 30 (1949) 405–32. [See esp. the grave monument of Lucius Poblicius and his family, which shows a serpent in a tree.]

Boraas, R. S. "Of Serpents and Gods," *Dialog* 17 (1978) 273–79.

Bordreuil, P. "Des Serpents et des Dieux: Magie et divinités syriennes dans le mythe ougartique de 'Horon et les serpents,' " *Annales Archéologiques Arabes Syriennes* 34 (1984) 183–88.

Borgen, P. "Some Jewish Exegetical Traditions as Background for Son of Man Sayings in John's Gospel [Jn 3, 13–14 and context]," *L'Évangile de Jean,* ed. M. de Jonge. Bibliotheca ephemeridum theologicarum lovaniensium 44. Gembloux and Leuven: J. Duculot, 1977; pp. 243–58.

Bornkamm, G. "Ophiten," *Pauly-Wissowa* 35 (1939) cols. 654–58.

Böttinger, ? "Über die vorgeblichen Schlangen am Merkuriusstabe," *Amalthea* 1 (1820) 104–16.

Boulnois, J. *La caducée et la symbolique dravidienne indo-méditeranéenne de l'arbre, de la pierre, du serpent et de la déesse mère.* Paris: Adrien Maisonneuve, 1989.

Bouquet, A. C. *Sacred Books of the World.* London: Cassell, 1962.

Bourke, J. G. *The Snake Dance of the Moquis of Arizona.* New York: Charles Scribner's Sons, 1884.

Bousset, W. *Hauptprobleme der Gnosis.* Forschungen zur Religion und Literatur des Alten und Neuen Testaments 10. Göttingen: Vandenhoeck & Ruprecht, 1907 [reprinted in 1973]; see esp. the section on Ophites.

Bowman, C. H., and R. B. Coote. "A Narrative Incantation for Snake Bite," *Ugarit-Forschungen* 12 (1980) 135–39.

Bradley, D. G. *A Guide to the World's Religions.* Englewood Cliffs, N. J.: Prentice-Hall, 1963.

Breasted, J. H. *Ancient Records of Egypt.* Chicago: n.p., 1927.

Brentjes, B. "Zur Rolle der Schlange in den alten Kulturen des ostmediteranen Raumes," *Wissenschaftliche Zeitschrift der Friedrich Schiller-Universität* 19 (1970) 731–46.

Briggs, C. A. *Messianic Prophecy: The Predictions of the Fulfillment of Redemption Through the Messiah.* New York: Charles Scribner's Sons, 1886; reprint, Peabody, Mass.: Hendrickson, 1988.

Bright, J. *History of Israel.* Philadelphia: Westminster Press, 1981 [3rd ed.]; see esp. p. 127.

Brilliant, R. *Pompeii—AD 79: The Treasury of Rediscovery.* New York: Clarkson N. Potter, Inc., 1979.

Brock-Utne, A. " 'Der Fiend': Die alttestamentliche Satangestalt im Lichte der sozialen Verhältnesse des Nahen Orients," *Klio* 28 (1935) 219–37.

Brommer, F. "Herakles und Hydra auf attischen Vasenbildern," in *Marburger Winckelmann-Programm*, 1949; see esp. p. 7.

Broshi, M. " 'The Serpents' Pool and Herod's Monument Reconsidered," *Cathedra* 55 (1990) 3–7 [Hebrew]. [Broshi argues that the serpents' pool was located northwest of the present Damascus Gate.]

———. " 'The Serpents' Pool and Herod's Monument—A Reconsideration," *Maarav* 8 (1992) 213–22. [This publication is a revision of the article that appeared in *Cathedra* 55.]

Buchanan, B. "A Snake Goddess and her Companions: A Problem in the Iconography of the Early Second Millennium B.C.," *Iraq* 32 (1970) 1–18. [The snake goddess examined is probably not related to the Cretan snake goddesses, and the role of the object is uncertain.]

Buchholz, H.-G. "Furcht vor Schlangen und Umgang mit Schlangen in Altsyrien, Altkypros und dem Umfeld," *Ugarit-Forschungen* 32 (2000) 37–168 [a major survey with twenty-five illustrations of serpent images].

Buchler, I. R., and K. Maddock, eds. *The Rainbow Serpent: A Chromatic Piece.* World Anthropology. Paris: Mouton Publishers, 1978; see esp. p. 77.

Budde, K. *Die biblische Paradiesesgeschichte.* Giessen: A. Topelmann, 1922.

Budge, E. A. W. *Egyptian Language: Easy Lessons in Egyptian Hieroglyphics.* New York: Dover, 1976; see p. 33 [the hieroglyphic for "goddess" is a cobra *naja haje*].

———. *The Gods of the Egyptians.* 2 vols. Chicago: Open Court Publishing Co., 1904. [The Egyptians thought the molting serpent represented eternal life.]

———. *Osiris and the Egyptian Resurrection,* 2 vols. London: Philip Lee Warner and New York: G. P. Putnam's Sons, 1911.

Buisson, R. du Mesnil du. "Le grand serpent Babi Dieu . . . le père des Sardes," *Nouvelles études sur les dieux et les mythes de Canaan.* EPRO 33; Leiden: Brill, 1973; pp. 228–40.

Bulfinch, T. *Myths of Greece and Rome.* [Originally published as *The Age of Fable* (n.c., n.p., n.d.).] New York: Penguin, 1981.

Bunn, J. T. "Origin of the Caduceus Motif," *Journal of the American Medical Association* 202.7 (1967) 163–67.

Buonaventura, W. *Die Schlange vom Nil: Frauen und Tanz im Orient,* trans. E. Pampuch and T. Pampuch. Hamburg: Rogner & Bernhard GmbH & Co., 1991 [2nd ed.]. [English original: London: Saqi Books, 1989].

Burkert, W. *Greek Religion,* trans. J. Raffan. Oxford: Blackwell, 1985.

———. *Ancient Mystery Cults.* Cambridge, Mass. and London: Harvard University Press, 1987.

Burkitt, F. C. "On 'Lifting up' and 'Exalting,' " *Journal of Theological Studies* 20 (1918/1919) 336–38.

Burland, C., and W. Forman. *Gefiederte Schlange und Rauchender Spiegel,* trans. H. Schmidthüs. Freiburg, Basel: Herder, 1977. [The English original was published in London: Orbis, 1975.]

Burns, R. "Jesus and the Bronze Serpent," *Bible Today* 28 (1990) 84–89.

Burrow, J. A. "The Serpent," *Methodist Quarterly Review* 70, no. 4 (October 1921) 720–27.

Burton, T. *Serpent-Handling Believers.* Knoxville: University of Tennessee Press, 1993.

Busch, H., and G. Edelmann, eds. *Etruskische Kunst,* introduction and discussion of pictures by W. Zschietzsmann. Frankfurt: Umschau Verlag, 1969.

Busch, P. *Der gefallene Drache: Mythenexegese am Beispiel von Apokalypse 12.* Texte und Arbeiten zum neutestamentlichen Zeitalter 19. Tübingen and Basel: A. Francke, 1996.

Buschan, G. "Tiere im Kult und im Aberglauben des nordischen Kulturkreises," *Ciba Zeitschrift* 8 (1942) 3016.

Busse, U. "Die Tempelmetaphorik als ein Beispiel von implizitem Rekurs auf die biblische Tradition im Johannesevangelium," *The Scriptures in the Gospels,* ed. C. M. Tuckett. Leuven: Leuven University Press and Peeters, 1997; pp. 395–428.

Butterworth, E. A. S. *The Tree at the Navel of the Earth*. Berlin: Walter de Gruyter, 1970.

Cahn, H. A. "Asklepios," *Lexicon Iconographicum Mythologiae Classicae*, 1.1, pp. 863–901 [and bibliography]; also see the photographs in *LIMC*, and 2.2, Plates 631–69.

Calvet, J., and M. Cruppi. *Les animaux dans la littérature sacrée*. Paris: Fernand Ianore, 1956; esp. pp. 17–19, 173–76.

Campbell, J. *Occidental Mythology*, 3 vols. New York: Viking Press, 1964. [Campbell demonstrates why the interpretation of the serpent as a phallic imagery is often inappropriate.]

———. *The Hero with a Thousand Faces*. Bollingen Series 17. Princeton, N.J.: Princeton University Press, 1949.

———. *The Mythic Image*. Bollingen Series 100. Princeton, N.J.: Princeton University Press, 1974.

———. *The Power of Myth*, ed. B. S. Flowers. New York, London, and Sydney: Doubleday, 1988.

Campbell, L. A. "Snake," in *Mithraic Iconography and Ideology*. Études Préliminaires aux religions orientales dans l'empire Romain 11. Leiden: Brill, 1968; pp. 13–22.

Cansdale, G. "The Serpent in the Wilderness and Other Reptiles," *Animals of Bible Lands*. Exeter: Paternoster Press, 1970; pp. 194–211.

Carnochan, F. G., and H. C. Adamson. *Das Kaiserreich der Schlangen*. Zürich and Leipzig, 1938.

Carrasco, D. *Quetzalcoatl and the Irony of Empire: Myths and Prophecies in the Aztec Tradition*. Chicago: University of Chicago Press, 1982.

Carson, D. A. "John and the Johannine Epistles," in *It Is Written: Scripture Citing Scripture: Essays in Honour of B. Lindars*, ed. H. G. M. Williamson. Cambridge: Cambridge University Press, 1988; pp. 245–64.

Carstensen, R. "Christus als Arzt, Christus als Apotheker," *Cesra-Säule* 11/12 (1963) 252–55.

Carus, P. *The History of the Devil and Idea of Evil*. New York and Avenel, N.J.: Gramercy Books, 1996.

Cassuto, U. *The Goddess Anath*, trans. I. Abrahams. Jerusalem: Magnes Press, 1971.

Castigliono, A. "The Serpent as Healing God in Antiquity," *Ciba Symposia* 3 (1942) 1164.

Catastini, A. "4Q Sam^a: II. Nahas il 'Serpente,'" *Henoch* 6 (1988) 17–49. [In contrast to the traditional version of 1 Sam 10:27b–11:2a, the readings in 4Q Sam^a show an interest in the Ammonite King named Nachash, "the serpent." The Qumran text has an addition between 1 Sam 10:27 and 11:1 that is not found in the BHS but is mirrored in Josephus (*Ant* 6.68–71).]

Caton, R. *The Temples and Ritual of Asklepios at Epidauros and Athens*. London: C. J. Clay and Sons, 1900 [2nd ed.].

Cauville, S. *Essai sur la théologie du temple d'Horus à Edfou*, 2 vols. Bibliothèque d'Étude 102. Cairo: Institut français d'archéologie orientale du Caire, 1987.

———. *La théologie du temple d'Horus à Edfou.* Bibliothèque d'Étude 91. Cairo: Institut français d'archéologie orientale du Caire, 1983.

Cazenave, M., ed. *Encyclopédie des symboles:* Encyclopédies d'aujourd'hui, trans. F. Périgaut, G. Marie, and A. Tondat. N.c: Le Livre de Poche, 1996 [originally published as: Biedermann, H. *Knaurs Lexikon der Symbole.* Munich: Knaur, 1989].

Cazier, P. "Du serpent et de l'arbre de la connaissance: Lectures patristiques (Philon, Grégoire de Nysse, Jean Chrysostome, Augustin)," *Grahè* 4 (1995) 73–103.

Chabas, F. J. "Horus sur les crocodiles," *Zeitschrift für Ägyptische Sprache und Altertumskunde* 6 (1868) 99–106.

Chamberlain, J. V. "Another Qumrân Thanksgiving Psalm," *Journal of Near Eastern Studies* 14 (1955) 32–41.

———. "Further Elucidation of a Messianic Thanksgiving Psalm from Qumrân," *Journal of Near Eastern Studies* 14 (1955) 181–82.

Champeaux, G. de, and D. S. Sterckx. *Einführung in die Welt der Symbole,* trans. C. Morano. Würzburg: Echter Verlag, 1990 [French original is of 1989]; see esp. "Der Baum" on pp. 307–35 and the serpent swallowing its tail in the middle of a zodiac on p. 54; also see pp. 63, 223, 281 and Illus. No. 110.

Charlesworth, J. H. "Anguine Iconography in the Studium Biblicum Franciscanum Museum and Biblical Exegesis," *Liber Annuus* 49 (1999) 431–42; Plates 5 and 6.

———. "Bashan, Symbology, Haplography, and Theology in Psalm 68," in *David and Zion: Biblical Studies in Honor of J. J. M. Roberts,* ed. B. F. Batto and K. L. Roberts. Winona Lake, Ind.: Eisenbrauns. Pp. 351–72.

———. "Phenomenology, Symbology, and Lexicography: The Amazingly Rich Vocabulary for 'Serpent' in Ancient Greek," *Revue biblique* 111 (2004) 499–515.

———. "Prolegomenous Reflections on Ophidian Iconography, Symbology, and New Testament Theology," in *The New Testament and Early Christian Literature in Greco-Roman Context [Studies in Honor of David E. Aune],* ed. J. Fotopoulos. Supplements to Novum Testamentum 122; Leiden, Boston: Brill, 2006; pp. 315–29.

———. "Serpents," in *Archaeological Encyclopedia of the Holy Land,* ed. A. Negev and S. Gibson. New York, London: Continuum, 2001; pp. 457–58.

———. "The Symbol of the Serpent in the Bible: Surprising and Challenging Archaeological Insights," in *Text Detectives: Discovery the Meaning of Ancient Symbols and Concepts,* Biblical Archaeology Lecture Series DVD; Bible and Archaeology Fest VIII Set 3. Washington, D.C.

Chassinat, E. *Le temple d'Edfou,* 14 vols. Cairo: Institut français d'archéologie orientale du Caire, 1928–34.

Cherry, J., ed. *Mythical Beasts.* London: British Museum Press, 1995.

Cheyne, T. K., and J. S. Black, eds. "Nehushtan," *Encyclopedia Biblica* 3. New York and London: Macmillan, 1902; pp. 3387–88.

————. "Serpent," *Encyclopedia Biblica* 4. New York and London: Macmillan, 1902; pp. 4391–97.

Christinger, R. *La mythologie de la suisse ancienne*. Geneva: Musée et Institut d'Ethnographie de Genève, 1965.

Chrysostom, John. *St. John Chrysostom: Commentary on Saint John the Apostle and Evangelist, Homilies 1–47*, trans. T. A. Goggin. The Fathers of the Church: A New Translation 33. New York: Fathers of the Church, Inc., 1957; see esp. pp. 261–67.

Cicero, M. Tullius. *De natura deorum*, ed. and trans. U. Blank-Sangmeister. Stuttgart: Philipp Reclam, 1995.

Cirlot, J. E. "Serpent," *A Dictionary of Symbols*, trans. J. Sage. London: Routledge & Kegan Paul, 1962; pp. 272–77.

————. "Tree," *A Dictionary of Symbols*, trans. J. Sage. London: Routledge & Kegan Paul, 1962; pp. 328–33.

Clark, R. T. R. *Myth and Symbol in Ancient Egypt*. London: Thames and Hudson, 1959; esp. pp. 50–53, 238–45.

Clarke, H., and C. S. Wake, *Serpent and Siva Worship* and *Mythology, in Central America, Africa, and Asia and the Origin of Serpent Worship. Two Treatises*. New York: J. W. Bouton, 1877.

Clarus, I. *Keltische Mythen: Zeugnisse aus anderen Welt*. Augsburg: Bechtermünz Verlag, 1997; see esp. the illus. with serpents on pp. 32–33, 36–37, and 302–3; also see the poem about the serpent on p. 310.

Clement of Alexandria. *Exhortation to the Heathen. Fathers of the Second Century*, ed. A. C. Coxe. The Ante-Nicene Fathers. The Writings of the Fathers Down to A.D. 325, ed. A. Roberts and J. Donaldson. Edinburgh: T & T Clark and Grand Rapids, Mich.: Eerdmans, 1986; pp. 174–75.

Clermont-Ganneau, Ch. "Les cerfs mangeurs de serpents," *Recueil d'Archéologie Orientale* (1901) 319–22. [Regarding Num 21:6–9, the Bedouins know a snake they call *haiyé taiyâra*, "flying serpent."]

Coats, G. *Rebellion in the Wilderness*. Nashville: Abingdon, 1968.

Cogan, M., and H. Tadmor. *II Kings: A New Translation with Introduction and Comment*. The Anchor Yale Bible. New York: Doubleday, 1988; rpt. New Haven. See esp. pp. 216–17.

Cohen, A. P. "Coercing the Rain Deities in Ancient China," *History of Religions* 17 (1978) 244–65.

Cole, H. M. *Mbari: Art and Life Among the Owerri Igbo*. Bloomington: Indiana University Press, 1982.

Collins, J. J. " 'The King Has Become a Jew': The Perspective on the Gentile World in Bel and the Snake," *Seers, Sybils and Sages in Hellenistic-Roman Judaism*. Supplements to the Journal for the Study of Judaism 54; Leiden, New York, 1997; pp. 167–77. [Daniel kills a live snake worshipped by the Babylonians; he feeds the snake a potion that causes it to burst.]

Condren, M. *The Serpent and the Goddess: Women, Religion, and Power in Celtic Ireland*. San Francisco: Harper and Row, 1989.

Contenau, G. *Everyday Life in Babylon and Assyria.* London: E. Arnold, 1954; see esp. Plate 23.

Cook, A. *Zeus: God of the Bright Sky.* Zeus: A Study in Ancient Religion 1. Cambridge: Cambridge University Press, 1914.

Cook, S. A. *The Religion of Ancient Palestine in the Second Millenium B.C. in the Light of Archaeology and the Inscriptions.* Religions: Ancient and Modern. London: Archibald, Constable & Co., Ltd., 1908; see esp. pp. 13–15, 47–49, 105–11.

———. "Serpent Cults," *Encyclopaedia Britannica* 20 (1949) 369–71.

Cooper, W. R. "Observations on the Serpent Myths of Ancient Egypt," *Journal of the Transactions of the Victoria Institute* [London] 6 (1873) 321–91; Plates 109, 111, 113, 115.

Coote, R. B. "Serpent and Sacred Marriage in Northwest Semitic Tradition," *Harvard Theological Review* 65 (1972) 594–95.

Copenhaven, B. P. *Hermetica: The Greek "Corpus Hermeticum" and the Latin "Asclepius" in a New English Translation, with Notes and Introduction.* Cambridge: Cambridge University Press, 1992.

Coppens, J. *La connaissance du bien et du mal et la péché du paradis.* Analecta Lovaniensia Biblica et Orientalia, Series II, Fasc. 3. Gembloux: J. Duculot; Bruges-Paris: Desclée de Brouwer; Louvain: É. Nauwelaerts, 1948; see esp. pp. 92–117.

———. "La dame-serpent du Sinaï," *Ephemerides Theologicae Lovanienses* 24 (1948) 409–12. [The text refers to "the Serpent-Lady, my mistress."]

Cosquin, E. "Un épisode d'un évangile syriaque et les contes de l'Inde: Le serpent ingrat.—l'Enfant roi et juge," *RB* NS 16 (1919) 136–57.

Cotterell, A. *The Macmillan Illustrated Encyclopedia of Myths and Legends.* New York: Macmillan, 1989.

Couffignal, R. "Adam et Eve, la pomme et le serpent," *Onomastique Biblique,* ed. Y. Le Boulicaut. Cahiers du Centre de Linguistique et de Littérature Religieuses 5. Angers: Institut de Perfectionnement en Langues Vivantes, 1990; pp. 27–36.

———. *De "L'arbre au serpent" au "Jeune homme en blanc": Etude littéraire de récits bibliques.* Etudes Littéraires: Bible et Littérature. Sud: Éditions Universitaires du Sud, 1993; see esp. pp. 11–27, "L'Arbre au serpent (Genèse II, 4-III)."

Couliano, I. P. *The Tree of Gnosis: Gnostic Mythology from Early Christianity to Modern Nihilism,* trans. H. S. Wiesner. San Francisco: Harper San Francisco, 1992 [originally published as *Les gnoses dualistes d'occident* and published by Editions Plon, 1990].

Cox, H. *On Not Leaving It to the Snake.* New York: Macmillan, 1967.

Crooke, W. "Serpent-Worship: Indian," *Encyclopaedia of Religion and Ethics,* ed. J. Hastings. Edinburgh: T. & T. Clark and New York: Charles Scribner's Sons, 1920 [1962]; vol. 11, pp. 411–19.

Cross, F. M. *Canaanite Myth and Hebrew Epic: Essays in the History of the Religion of Israel.* Cambridge: Harvard University Press, 1973.

———. "Yahweh and the Gods of the Patriarchs," *Harvard Theological Review* 55 (1962) 225–59.

Crown, A., ed. *The Samaritans.* Tübingen: Mohr (Siebeck), 1989; see esp. p. 356.

Cumont, F. *The Mysteries of Mithra.* New York: Dover, 1956 [original: *Die Mysterien des Mithra.* Leipzig: B. G. Teubner, 1903].

Curatola, G. "Serpenti e 'draghi' anatolici: Un'antica questione," *Studi su Harran* 6 (1979) 123–35.

Currid, J. D. "The Egyptian Setting of the 'Serpent': Confrontation in Exodus 7, 8–13," *Biblische Zeitschrift* N.F. 39 (1995) 203–24.

Dahan, G., ed. *Les juifs au regard de l'histoire: Mélanges en l'honneur de Berhard Blumenkranz.* Paris: Picard, 1985.

D'Alviella. *The Mysteries of Eleusis: The Secret Rites and Rituals of the Classical Greek Mystery Tradition.* Wellingborough, Northamptonshire: The Aquarian Press, 1918 [originally published as *Eleusinia: De mysteriën van Eleusis.* Amsterdam: W. N. Schors, 1981].

Dan, J. "Jewish Gnosticism?" *Jewish Studies Quarterly* 2 (1995) 309–28.

Daniélou, J. *The Development of Christian Doctrine Before the Council of Nicaea, vol. I: The Theology of Jewish Christianity,* trans. J. A. Baker. London: Darton, Longman, & Todd, 1964.

———. *Primitive Christian Symbols,* trans. D. Attwater. Baltimore, Md.: Helicon Press, 1964 [originally published by Paris: Éditions du Seuil, 1961].

Daugherty, M. L. "Serpent-handling as sacrament," *New and Intense Movements,* ed. M. Marty. New York: Saur, 1993.

Davidson, H. R. E. *Gods and Myths of Northern Europe.* New York: Pelican, 1964; reprinted in New York: Penguin, 1990.

Davies, L. G. "Serpent Imagery in Ancient Israel: The Relationship Between the Literature and the Physical Remains." PhD Dissertation, University of Utah, 1986.

Davies, N. M., and A. H. Gardiner. *Ancient Egyptian Paintings,* 2 vols. Chicago: University of Chicago Press, 1936.

Deane, J. B. *The Worship of the Serpent Traced Throughout the World.* London: J. G. & F. Rivington, 1833 [2d ed.].

Deimel, A. "Die Schlange bei den Babyloniern," *Orientalia* 14 (1924) 49–57.

Delcor, M. "Un psaume messianique de Qumran," in *Mélanges bibliques: Rédigés en l'honneur de André Robert.* Travaux de l'Institut Catholique de Paris 4. Paris: Bloud & Gay, 1957; see esp. pp. 334–40.

Delhalle, J. C., and A. Luykx. "Le Serpent à plumes des Olmèques à Teotihuacán," *Revue de l'histoire des religions* 199 (1982) 123–30.

Delumeau, J. *History of Paradise: The Garden of Eden in Myth and Tradition,* trans. Matthew O'Connell. New York: Continuum, 1995.

Deonna, W. "Emblèmes médicaux des temps modernes: Du bâton serpentaire d'Asklepos au caducée d'Hermès," *Revue intern. de la Croix-rouge,* 1933. pp. 128–51.

De Pury, A. *Homme et animal Dieu les créa: L'Ancien Testament et les animaux.* Geneva: Labor et Fides, 1993.

Dermoût, M. "The Good Serpent," trans. F. Franck. *Parabola* 4, no. 4. (1979) 54–57.

Derrett, J. D. M. "The Bronze Serpent," *Estudios Bíblicos* 49 (1991) 311–29.

———. *Symbolism in Greek Mythology: Human Desire and its Transformations.* Boulder, Colo., and London: Shambhala, 1980 [originally published as *Le symbolisme dans la mythologie grecque: Étude psychanalytique.* Paris: Payot, 1952].

———. *Symbolism in the Bible: The Universality of Symbolic Language and Its Psychological Significance,* trans. N. Marans. San Francisco: Harper & Row, 1986 [originally published as *Le symbolisme dans la bible.* Paris: Payot, 1975].

Diehl, U. "Die Darstellung der Ehernen Schlange von ihren Anfänge bis zum Ende des Mittelalters." PhD Dissertation, Munich, 1956.

Diel, P., and J. Solotareff. *Symbolism in the Gospel of John,* trans. N. Marans. San Francisco: Harper & Row, 1988 [originally published as *Le symbolisme dans l'Évangile de Jean.* Paris: Payot, 1983].

Dietrich, A. *Abraxas: Studien zur Religionsgeschichte des Spätern Altertums.* Festschrift Hermann Usener zur Feier seiner 25. Jährigen Lehrtätigkeit an der Bonner Universität, dargebracht vom Klassisch-Philologischen Verein zu Bonn. Leipzig: B. G. Teubner, 1891.

Diettrich, M., and O. Loretz. "Die Bannung von Schlangengift (KTU 1.100 und KTU 1.107:7b-13a. 19b–20)," *Ugarit-Forschungen* 12 (1980) 153–70.

Diettrich, M., O. Lorentz, and J. Sanmartín, "Bemerkungen zur Schlangenbeschwörung RS 24.244 = UG. 5, S. 564FF. NR. 7," *Ugarit-Forschungen* 7 (1975) 121–25.

Dillemann, G. "Le palmier, le serpent et les roches," *Produits et problèmes pharmaceutiques* 21.8 (1966). N.V.

Diller, H. "Edelstein, Asclepius," *Gnomon* (1950) 130–38.

Dillon, E. J. *The Sceptics of the Old Testament: Job, Koheleth, Agur.* London: Isbister and Co., Ltd., 1895.

Desroches-Noblecourt, C. "Poissons, tabours et transformations du mort," *Kemi* 13 (1954) 34–37.

Dinkler, E. *Christus und Asklepios: Zum Christustypus der polychromen Platten im Museo Nazionale Romano.* Sitzungsberichte der Heidelberger Akademie der Wissenschaften Ph.-his. Klasse 1980. 2. Abhandlung. Heidelberg: Carl Winter, 1980. [See the thirty illustrations, esp. the last one that shows Asclepius, perhaps, with a serpent.]

———. *Signum Crucis: Aufsätze zum Neuen Testament und zur Christlichen Archäologie.* Tübingen: Mohr (Siebeck), 1967.

Dioszégi, V. *Glaubenswelt und Folklore der sibirischen Völker.* Budapest: Akademiai Kiado, 1963.

Dombart, T. "Die Grabstele des Horus 'Schlange,' " in *Aus fünf Jahrtausenden morgenländischer Kultur* [*Festschrift M. Freiherrn von Oppenheim*].

Archiv für Orientforschung Beiheft 1. Berlin: Dr. Ernst F. Weidner, 1933; pp. 18–26.

D'Onofrio, C. "Serpente, nelle religioni antiche," *Enciclopedia Cattolica* 11 (1953) cols. 393–94.

Doresse, J. "Hermès et la gnose: A propos de l'Asclepius Copte," *Novum Testamentum* 1 (1956) 54–69.

Driver, G. R. *Canaanite Myths and Legends*. Old Testament Studies 111. Edinburgh: T & T Clark, 1956 [reprinted by Lewis Reprints Limited, Port Talbot, Glamorgan, 1971].

———. "Mythical Monsters in the Old Testament," *Studi orientalistici in onore di Giorgio Levi della Vida*. Vol. I. Istituto per l'Oriente (Italy) Pubblicazioni, no. 52. Rome: Istituto per l'Oriente, 1956; pp. 234–49.

Drumond, D. C. "Mouse Traps or Snake Houses," *Report of the Department of Antiquities; Cyprus, 1983*. Nicosia: Zavallis Press, 1983; pp. 199–200. [Drumond suggests that the erstwhile "snake houses" are traps to catch mice and other rodents.]

Duchaussoy, J. *Le bestiaire divin ou la symbolique des animaux*. Paris: La Colombe, Editions du Vieux Colombier, 1958; see esp. pp. 102–26.

Dukova, U. "Das Bild des Drachen im bulgarischen Märchen," *Fabula* 11 (1971) 227ff.

Dulaey, M. "Le bâton transformé en serpent: L'exégèse augustinienne d'Ex 4," *Collectanea Augustiniana: Mélanges T. J. van Bavel*, ed. B. Bruning et al. Louvain: Leuven University Press, 1990; vol. 2. N.V.

Dunand, F. "Agathodaimon," in *Lexicon Iconographicum Mythologiae Classicae* 1.1, pp. 277–82; see also the photographs in *LIMC*, 1.2, Illus. 203–206.

———. "Les représentations de l'Agathodémon: A propos de quelques bas-reliefs du Musée d'Alexandrie," *Bulletin de l'institut français d'archéologie orientale* 67 (1969) 9–48.

Dupont-Sommer, A. "La mère du messie et la mère de l'Aspic dans un hymne de Qumrân (DST iii, 6–18)," *Revue de l'Histoire des Religions* 147 (1955) 174–88.

———. *The Essene Writings from Qumran*, trans. G. Vermes. Gloucester, Mass.: Peter Smith, 1973; see esp. pp. 208–9 [originally published as *Les Écrits esseniens découverts près de la mer Morte*. Paris: Les Editions Payot, 1961].

Durando, F. *Griechenland: Wiege der westlichen Kultur*, trans. D. Krumbach. Erlangen: Karl Müller Verlag, 1997 [German translation of the English original].

Dvorák, K. "Zur Sage vom Schlangenbann," *Fabula* 18 (1977) 256–58.

Eberhard, W. "Von der Schlange, die für das Mädchen zeugte—Inselmärchen des Mittelmeeres," *MdW*. N.V.

Edelstein, E. J., and L. Edelstein. *Asclepius: A Collection and Interpretation of the Testimonies*, 2 vols. Publications of the Institute of the History of Medicine; Johns Hopkins University, Second Series: Texts and Documents 2. Baltimore, Md: Johns Hopkins Press, 1945.

Egli, H. *Das Schlangensymbol: Geschichte, Märchen, Mythos.* Freiburg im Breisgau: Walter-Verlag Olten, 1982. [*Il simbolo del serpente,* trans. M. Fragiacomo. Genova: Edizioni Culturali Internazionali Genova, 1993.]

Egmond, F. "The Cock, the Dog, the Serpent, and the Monkey: Reception and Transmission of a Roman Punishment, or Historiography as History," *International Journal of the Classical Tradition* 2 (1995) 159–92. [The *poena cullei* (punishment of parricide by throwing the guilty into water in a sack with cock, dog, monkey, and serpent) was popular in the fifteenth to seventeenth centuries, but may have evolved from early Roman times.]

Ehresmann, D. L. "The Brazen Serpent in the Works of Lucas Cranach the Elder and His Workshop: A Study in Lutheran Iconography." PhD. Dissertation, New York University, 1963.

———. "The Brazen Serpent, A Reformation Motif in the Works of Lucas Cranach the Elder and his Workshop," *Marsyas* 13 (1966/67) 32–47. [This important study shows how significant the Brazen Serpent was for Martin Luther and the Reformation.]

Ehrlich, E. L. *Die Kultsymbolik im Alten Testament und im nachbiblischen Judentum.* Symbolik der Religionen 3. Stuttgart: A. Hiersemann, 1959.

Eilberg-Schwartz, H. *God's Phallus and Other Problems for Men and Monotheism.* Boston: Beacon Press, 1994.

Eliade, M. *Birth and Rebirth: The Religious Meanings of Initiation in Human Culture,* trans. W. R. Trask. New York: Harper and Brothers, 1958.

———. *A History of Religious Ideas.* Chicago: University of Chicago Press, 1979.

———. *The Myth of the Eternal Return.* Bollingen Foundation Series 46. New York: Pantheon Books, 1954.

———. *Gods, Goddesses, and Myths of Creation.* New York: Harper & Row, 1974.

———. *Das Mysterium der Wiedergeburt: Initiationsriten, ihre kulturelle und religiöse Bedeutung.* Zürich: Rascher, 1961; see esp. pp. 67–68.

———. *Patterns in Comparative Religion,* trans. R. Sheed. New York: Mentor, 1958.

Eliot, A. *The Global Myths: Exploring Primitive, Pagan, Sacred, and Scientific Mythologies.* New York: Continuum, 1993.

Elkin, A. P. "The Rainbow-Serpent Myth in North-West Australia," *Oceania* 1 (1930) 349–51.

———. "Rockpaintings of North-East Australia," *Oceania* 1 (1930) 257–79.

Ellis, E. E. *The Old Testament in Early Christianity.* WUNT 54. Tübingen: Mohr (Siebeck), 1991; see esp. pp. 105–9.

Ellul, D., ed. "Un homme, une femme et un serpent," *Foi et Vie* 80 (1981) 1–81.

Engler, H. R. *Die Sonne als Symbol: Der Schlüssel zu den Mysterien.* Zürich and Künacht: Helianthus Verlag, 1962; see esp. pp. 135–59.

Engnell, I. " 'Knowledge' and 'Life' in the Creation Story," in *Wisdom in Israel and in the Ancient Near East.* Supplements to *Vetus Testamentum* 3. Leiden: Brill, 1960; see esp. pp. 103–19.

———. *Studies in Divine Kingship in the Ancient Near East.* Oxford: Blackwell, 1967.

Epiphanius of Salamis. *The Panarion of Ephiphanius of Salamis, Book I*, trans. F. Williams. Nag Hammadi and Manichaean Studies 35. Leiden and New York: Brill, 1987.

———. *The Panarion of Ephiphanius of Salamis, Books II and III*, trans. F. Williams. Nag Hammadi and Manichaean Studies 36. Leiden and New York: Brill, 1994.

Erdmann, J. E. *Der neue Mensch und die eherne Schlange.* N.c.: n.p., 1856.

Erlenmeyer, M. "Über Schlangendarstellungen in der frühen Bildkunst des Alten Osten," *Archiv für Orientforschung* 23 (1970) 52–62.

Erman, A. *A Handbook of Egyptian Religion*, trans. A. S. Griffith. London: Archibald, Constable, & Co., Ltd., 1907; see esp. pp. 20–21, 36–37, 224–27.

Ernst, J. "Die Schlange in der Schöpfungsgeschichte" (chapter from *Die eschatologischen Gegenspieler in den Schriften des Neuen Testaments*). Biblische Untersuchungen, Band 3. Regensburg, Germany: F. Pustet, 1967; pp. 241–50.

Erskine, T. *The Brazen Serpent; or, Life Coming Through Death.* Edinburgh: Waugh & Innes, 1831 (2nd ed.); see esp. pp. 112–22.

Esche, S. *Adam und Eva: Sündenfall und Erlösung.* Lukas-Bücherei zur christlichen Ikonographie. Düsseldorf: n.p, 1957.

Esser, A. "Asklepios und die Schlange," *Forschungen und Fortschritte* 17/18 (1948) 196–98.

Eusebius. *The Ecclesiastical History of Eusebius in Syriac,* ed. W. Wright and N. McLean. Cambridge: Cambridge University Press, 1898.

———. *Preparation for the Gospel, Part I: Books 1–9*, trans. E. H. Gifford. Oxford: Clarendon Press, 1903; reprinted in Grand Rapids, Mich.: Baker Book House, 1981; see esp. pp. 39a–41d.

Evans, A. "Mycenean Tree and Pillar Cult in its Mediterranean Relations," *Journal of Hellenic Studies* 21 (1901) 99–204.

———. "The Snake Goddess and Relics of Her Shrine," in *The Palace of Minos.* London: Macmillan, 1921; vol. 1.3, pp. 495–523.

———. "A 'Snake Room' of Domestic Cult; 'Snake Tube,' Their Origin and Survival," in *The Palace of Minos.* London: Macmillan, 1935; vol. 4.1; pp. 138–71.

Fabry, H.-J. "נחשׁ," *Theologisches Wörterbuch zum Alten Testament.* Stuttgart: W. Kohlhammer, 1986; vol. 5, cols. 384–97.

———. "נס," *Theologisches Wörterbuch zum Alten Testament.* Stuttgart: W. Kohlhammer, 1986; vol. 5, cols. 468–73.

Fader, E. *Die Bildersprache der Evangellien.* Berlin: n.p., 1937.

Farbridge, M. H. *Studies in Biblical and Semitic Symbolism.* New York: KTAV, 1970 [reprint of 1923 edition].

Farnell, L. R. *ΑΣΚΛΗΠΙΟΣ ΔΙΟΣΚΟΥΡΟΙ ΗΡΩΙΚΗ ΛΑΡΕΙΑ ΣΤΗΝ ΑΡΧΑΙΑ ΕΛΛΑΔΑ ΚΑΙ ΗΙΔΕΑ ΤΗΣ ΑΘΑΝΑΣΙΑΣ*, trans. E. Papadoúlou. Athens: ΙΑΜΒΛΙΧΟΣ, 1997.

Farrer, A. *A Rebirth of Image: The Making of St. John's Apocalypse.* Westminster: Dacre, 1949.

Faulkner, R. O. "A Statue of a Serpent-Worshipper," *Journal of Egyptian Archaeology* 20 (1934) 154–56, Plate XIX.

Faure, B. "Space and Place in Chinese Religious Traditions," *Harvard Theological Review* 26 (1987) 337–56.

Fauth, W. "Widder, Schlange und Vogel am Heiligen Baum: Zur Ikonographie einer Anatolisch-Mediterranean Symbolkonstellation," *Anatolica* 6 (1977–1978) 129–57, Plates 1–16.

Feliks, Y. *Nature and Man in the Bible: Chapters in Biblical Ecology.* London, Jerusalem, and New York: Soncino Press, 1981; see esp. pp. 94–100.

Fenton, T. "Baal au foudre: Of Snakes and Mountains, Myth and Message," in *Ugarit, Religion and Culture,* ed. N. Wyatt, W. G. E. Watson, and J. B. Lloyd. Münster, 1996; pp. 49–64. [In this Festscrift in honor of J. C. L. Gibson, Fenton demonstrates that the stela known as the "Baal of the Thunderbolt," unearthed near the Temple of Baal at Ugarit, contains not mountains, as supposed (e.g., as by C. Schaeffer), but a snake. Below Baal lies his foe: a serpent.]

Ferguson, E., ed. "Miracle," *Encyclopedia of Early Christianity.* New York and London: Garland, 1990; pp. 600–605.

Ferguson, G. *Signs and Symbols in Christian Art.* New York and London: Oxford University Press, 1954; paperback, New York and London: Oxford University Press, 1961.

Ferguson, J. *The Religions of the Roman Empire.* Aspects of Greek and Roman Life, ed. H. H. Scullard. Itaca, N. Y.: Cornell University Press, 1970.

———. *Tree and Serpent Worship, or Illustrations of Mythology and Art in India.* London: W. H. Allen (for India Museum), 1868.

Ferwerda, R. "Le serpent, le nœud d'Hercule et le caducée d'Hermès: Sur un passage Orphique chez Athénagore," *Numen* 20 (1973) 104–15.

Feyerick, A. *Genesis: World of Myths and Patriarchs.* New York and London: New York University Press, 1996.

Filée, J. "Polysémie de Sanguine Viperino dans l'Ode I,8 d'Horace?" *Les Études Classiques* 61 (1993) 139–41.

Finegan, J. *Light from the Ancient Past.* Princeton: Princeton University Press, 1946; see esp. pp. 139–46.

Finkielsztejn, G. "*Asklepios Leontoukhos* et le mythe de la coupe de Césarée Maritime," *RB* 93 (1986) 419–28.

Fischle, W. H. *Das Geheimnis der Schlange: Deutung eines Symbols.* Psychologisch Gesehen 46. Fellbach-Oeffingen: Verlag Adolf Bonz, 1983, 1989 [2nd ed.] [a valuable psychological study; see the Ouroboros on the cover; from the Schweizerisches Museum für Volkskunde in Basel].

Fishwick, D. "On the Origin of the Rotas-Sator Square," *Harvard Theological Review* 57 (1964) 39–53.

Flemming, J. "Die Ikonographie von Adam und Eva vom. 3. Bis zum 13. Jahrhundert." PhD. Dissertation, Jena, 1953.

Flusser, D. "It's Not a Serpent That Kills," *Judaism and the Origins of Christianity.* Jerusalem: Magnes Press, 1988; pp. 543–51.

Foerster, W. "δραχων," *Theological Dictionary of the New Testament,* ed. G. Kittel, trans. G. W. Bromiley. Grand Rapids, Mich.: Eerdmans, 1967; vol. 2, pp. 281–83.

———. "ὄφις," *Theological Dictionary of the New Testament,* ed. G. Friedrich, trans. G. W. Bromiley. Grand Rapids, Mich.: Eerdmans, 1967; vol. 5, pp. 566–82.

Fontenrose, J. *Python: A Study of Delphic Myth and Its Origins.* Los Angeles, Berkeley: University of California Press, 1959.

Ford, J. *The Story of Paradise.* Richmond, United Kingdom: H. & B. Publications, 1981.

Forrest, E. R. *The Snake Dance of the Hopi Indians.* Los Angeles: Westernlore Press, 1961.

Forsyth, N. *The Old Enemy: Satan and the Combat Myth.* Princeton, N.J.: Princeton University Press, 1987; see esp. pp. 232ff.

Fortune, R. F. "The Symbolism of the Serpent," *International Journal of Psychoanalysis* 3 (1926) 327ff. [tends to focus only on the symbol of the serpent as phallic].

Foster, B. "Gilgamesh: Sex, Love and the Ascent of Knowledge," in *Love and Death in the Ancient Near East: Essays in Honor of Marvin H. Pope,* ed. J. H. Marks and R. M. Good. Guilford, Conn.: Four Quarters Publishing Co., 1987; pp. 21–42.

Fourcade, P. "Mythen und Legenden," in *Schlangen,* ed. R. Bauchot, trans. C. Ronsiek et al. Augsburg: Naturbuch Verlag, 1994 [French original is also 1994]; pp. 184–93.

Fox, C. "Circle and Serpent Antiquities," *Palestine Exploration Fund* (1894) 83–87.

France, R. T., and D. Wenham. *Gospel Perspectives: Studies in Midrash and Historiography 3.* Sheffield: JSOT Press, 1983.

Franke, A. H. *Das Alte Testament bei Johannes: Ein Beitrag zur Eklärung und Beurtheilung der johanneischen Schriften.* Göttingen: Vandenhoeck & Ruprecht, 1885.

Franke, P. R. "Asklepios—Aesculapius auf antiken Münzen," *Mediz. Monatsspiegel* 3 (1969) 60–67.

———. "Die Münzsammlung der Universität Erlangen-Nürnberg," *Archäologischer Anzeiger* 82 (1967) 67–92. [On p. 83 are shown examples of the serpent images on coins minted at Pergamon in the second and first centuries BCE.]

Frankfort, H. "Gods and Myths on Sargonid Seals," *Iraq* 1 (1934) 2–29.

———. *Cylinder Seals: A Documentary Essay on the Art and Religion of the Ancient Near East.* London: Macmillan and Co., 1939, 1965 [2nd ed., Gregg Press].

———. *Kingship and the Gods.* Chicago: University of Chicago Press, 1948.

Frayne, D. R. "Naram-Suen and the *Mušuššu* Serpents," *JAOS* 102 (1982) 511–13. [Note how serpents are placed on a temple gate bolt for apotropaic purposes.]

Frazer, J. G. *The Belief in Immortality and the Worship of the Dead.* London: Macmillan, 1913; see esp. vol. 1, pp. 69–72. [Frazer argues that the molting serpent symbolized immortality.]

———. *Folk-lore in the Old Testament: Studies in Comparative Religion, Legend and Law.* London: Macmillan, 1919; see esp. vol. 1, pp. 66ff.

———. *The Golden Bough: A Study in Magic and Religion.* New York: Macmillan, 1911–1935.

———. "The Serpent and the Tree of Life," in *Essays and Studies Presented to William Ridgeway.* Cambridge: Cambridge University Press, 1913; pp. 413–26.

———. *Totemica: A Supplement to Totemism and Exogamy.* London: Macmillan, 1937.

———. *Totemism and Exogamy,* 4 vols. London: Macmillan, 1910.

Fredrikson, N. I. "La métaphore du sel et du serpent chez Aphraate, le Sage persan," *Revue de l'histoire des religions* 219 (2002) 35–54. [The serpent symbolizes evil.]

Freed, E. D. *Old Testament Quotations in the Gospel of John. Novum Testamentum* Supplements 11. Leiden: Brill, 1965.

Freedman, D. N. "Divine Names and Titles in Early Hebrew Poetry," in *Magnalia Dei, the Mighty Acts of God: Essays on the Bible and Archaeology in Memory of G. Ernest Wright,* ed. F. M. Cross. Garden City, N. Y.: Doubleday, 1976; pp. 55–107.

Frenschkowski, M. "Religion auf dem Markt," in *Hairesis [Festschrift K. Hoheisel].* Jahrbuch für Antike und Christentum Ergänzungsband 34; Münster: Aschendorff, 2002; pp. 140–58; see esp. pp. 150–53: "Der Schlangen-beschwörer." [Frenschkowski rightly points out that we often hear about serpents through exotic travelogues and from tourists.]

Frey, J. " 'Wie die Schlange in der Wüste erhöht hat . . .': Zur frühjüdischen Deutung der 'ehernen Schlange' und ihrer christologischen Rezeption in Johannes 3, 14f.," *Schriftauslegung im antiken Judentum und im Urchristentum,* ed. M. Hengel and H. Löhr. WUNT 73. Tübingen: Mohr (Siebeck), 1994; pp. 153–205.

Friedrich, J. "Der churritische Mythus vom Schlangendämon . . ." *Frederico Hrozný Dedicatae,* ed. V. Čihař et al. Archiv Orientální 17. Prague: Orientální, 1949; pp. 230–54.

Fritsche, H. *Die Erhöhung der Schlange: Mysterium, Menschenbild und Mirakel der Homöopathie.* Göttingen: Ulrich Burgdorf Verlag, 1994 [8th ed.]

Fritze, H. von, "Die Münze von Pergamon," *Abhandlungen der Königlich-Preussischen Akademie der Wissenschaften zu Berlin. Philosophisch-Historische Klasse-Anhang.* Berlin: Akademie der Wissenschaften, 1910.

Frothingham, A. L. "Babylonian Origin of Hermes the Snake-God, and of the Caduceus," *American Journal of Archaeology.* Second Series 20 (1916)

175–211. [The caduceus is foreshadowed or represented in cylinders from the fourth millennium.]

Frutiger, A. "Le serpent et la colombe," *La mémoire et le temps: Mélanges offerts à Pierre Bonnard,* ed. D. Marguerat et al. Geneva: Labor et Fides, 1991.

Fuchs, G. ed. *Lange Irrfahrt-grosse Heimkehr: Odysseus als Archetyp—zur Aktualität des Mythos.* Frankfurt am Main: Verlag Josef Knecht, 1994.

Fuldner, A. *De Ophitis.* 1834. N.V.

Gabler, J. P. "An Oration: On the Proper Distinction between Biblical and Dogmatic Theology and the Specific Objectives of Each," pp. 134–44 in John Sandys-Wunsch and Laurence Eldredge, "J. P. Gabler and the Distinction between Biblical and Dogmatic Theology: Translation, Commentary, and Discussion of His Originality," *Scottish Journal of Theology* 33 (1980): 133–58.

Gadd, C. J. "Some Contributions to the Gilgamesh Epic," *Iraq* 28 (1966) 105–21.

Galpaz-Feller, P. "Egyptological Motifs in the Sign of the Serpent (Exodus 4:2–5; 7:8–14)," *Beit Mikra* 171 (2002) [Hebrew]. [The biblical text is enlightened from Egyptian motifs.]

Ganszyniec, R. *De Agathodaemone.* Warsaw, 1919.

Garbini, G. "Le Serpent d'Airain et Moïse," *Zeitschrift für die alttestamentliche Wissenschaft* 100 (1988) 264–67.

Gardiner, A. "The Personal Name of King Serpent," *Journal of Egyptian Archaeology* 44 (1958) 38–39.

Gardiner, E., ed. *Visions of Heaven and Hell Before Dante.* New York: Italica Press, 1989.

Gardner, J., and J. Maier. *Gilgamesh: Translated from the Sî-leqi-unninni Version.* New York: Alfred A. Knopf, 1984.

Garstang, J., and J. B. E. Garstang, *The Story of Jericho.* London: Hodder and Stoughton (1940). [Plate 3 shows a serpent with its mouth open on a MBIIB chalice.]

Gaster, T. H. *Myth, Legend, and Custom in the Old Testament: A Comparative Study with Chapters From Sir James G. Frazier's "Folklore in the Old Testament."* New York: Harper & Row, 1969.

———. "Myth, Mythology," *Interpreter's Dictionary of the Bible,* ed. G. Buttrick et al. New York, Nashville: Abingdon, 1962; vol. 3, pp. 481–87.

———. "Mythic Thought in the Ancient Near East," *Journal of the History of Ideas* 16 (1955) 422–26.

———. "Sharper Than a Serpent's Tooth: A Canaanite Charm Against a Snakebite," *The Journal of the Ancient Near Eastern Society of Columbia University* 7 (1975) 33–51.

———. "The Ugaritic Charm Against Snakebite: An Additional Note," *The Journal of the Ancient Near Eastern Society of Columbia University* 2 (1980) 43–44.

Gauer, W. "Konstantin und die Geschichte zu den 'Spolien' am Konstantinsbogen und zur Schlangensäule," *Panchaia* [Festschrift K. Thraede], ed. M. Wacht.

Jahrbuch für Antike und Christentum Ergänzungsband 22. Münster: Aschendorffsche Verlagsbuchhandlung, 1995; pp. 131–40.

Gerber, Ch. "Die Schlange auf der Tonkugel," in *Beiträge zur Kulturgeschichte Vorderasiens* [*Festschrift M. Boehmer*], ed. U. Finkbeiner et al. Mainz: P. von Zabern, 1995; pp. 175–76. [This work is focused on the serpent relief in the Uruk-Sammlung in Heidelberg.]

Gerhard, H. "Über agathodämon und bona dea," *Akademie der Wissenschaften* (24 June 1847) 461–99.

Gerke, F. *Spätantike und Frühes Christentum.* Kunst der Welt. Baden-Baden: Holle Verlag, 1980 [original is 1967]; see esp. p. 30 [serpent with Adam and his wife, Chamber of the Good Sherperd, Coemeterium maius in Rome, early third cent. CE], p. 81 [Jonah expelled by a large serpent-dragon (not a fish), Aquileia, fourth cent. CE], and p. 235 [discussion of serpent symbolism].

Ghazal, E. *Schlangenkult und Tempelliebe: Sakrale Erotik in archaischen Gesellschaften.* Berlin: Simon and Leutner Verlag, 1995; see esp. the illustrations on p. 79 [the uraeus], p. 80 [serpents from various cultures], 81 [serpent image from Elam (c. 3500 BCE)], p. 83 [two serpent priestesses], p. 85 [Nagakal serpent stone], p. 124 [a serpent priestess from Crete, c. 1500 BCE], p. 148 [a nude "female dancer" with a serpent as a phallus].

Giedion, S. *The Eternal Present: The Beginnings of Art.* Bollingen Foundation Series 35.6.1. New York: Pantheon Books, 1962; see esp. pp. 308–309 [a line-drawing of a serpent from Le Baume-Latrone, France, c. 40,000 to 26,000 BCE, the earliest evidence of serpent iconography].

Gimbutas, M. *The Goddesses and Gods of Old Europe 6500–3500 B.C.* Berkeley, 1982 [rev. ed.].

———. *The Language of the Goddess.* New York: Harper & Row, 1989.

Ginzberg, H. L. "Did Anath Fight the Dragon?" *Bulletin of the American Schools of Oriental Research* 84 (1941) 12–14.

Ginzberg, L. *Die Haggada bei den Kirchenvätern und in der apokryphischen Litteratur.* Berlin: S. Calvary & Co., 1900; see esp. pp. 59–60.

———. *The Legends of the Jews,* 7 vols., trans. H. Szold. Philadephia: The Jewish Publication Society of America, 1909; see esp. vol. 5, pp. 40–42, 71–86.

Girardi, M. "Il cervo in lotta col serpente: Esegesi e simbolica antiariana nell'*Omelia sul Salmo 28* di Basilio di Cesarea," *Annali di Storia dell' Esegesi* 4 (1987) 67–85.

Gittin, S., T. Dotan, and J. Naveh, "A Royal Dedication Inscription from Tel Miqneh/Ekron," *Qadmoniot* 30 (1997) 38–43 [Hebrew]. [A cobra hammered out of fine gold, and in the Egyptian style, probably from the seventh century BCE, was discovered at Tel Miqneh/Ekron.]

Giversen, S., and B. A. Pearson, trans. "The Testimony of Truth," in *The Nag Hammadi Library,* ed. J. M. Robinson. San Francisco: Harper & Row, 1977; pp. 406–16.

Glasson, T. F. *Moses in the Fourth Gospel.* Naperville, Ill.: A. R. Allenson, 1963.

Glay, M. Le, "Abraxas," in *Lexicon Iconographicum Mythologiae Classicae* 1.1, pp. 2–7 [see the bibliography]; see the photographs in *LIMC* 1.2, Illus. 6–14.

———. "Aion," in *Lexicon Iconographicum Mythologiae Classicae* 1.1, pp. 399–411 [see the bibliography]; see the photographs in *LIMC* 1.2, pp. 315–19.

Gočeva, Z. "Hygieia," in *Lexicon Iconographicum Mythologiae Classicae* 5.1, pp. 554–73 [bibliography]; see the photographs in *LIMC* 5.2, Plates 380–95.

Goedicke, H. "The Snake in the Story of the Shipwrecked Sailor," *Göttinger Miszellen* 39 (1980) 27–31.

Goff, B. L. *Symbols of Prehistoric Mesopotamia*. New Haven, London: Yale University Press, 1963.

Golan, A. "Snake Water," *Myth and Symbol: Symbolism in Prehistoric Religions*, trans. R. Schneider-Teteruk. Jerusalem: n.p., 1991; see esp. pp. 101–14.

Goldberg, A. "Kain: Sohn des Menschen oder Sohn der Schlange," *Judaica* 25 (1969) 203–21; reprinted in Goldberg, *Gesammelte Studien I* Texte und Studien zum Antiken Judentum 61; Tübingen: Mohr (Siebeck), 1997; pp. 275–88.

Golowin, S. *Drache, Einhorn, Oster-Hase und anderes phantatisches Getier*. Basel: Sphinx Verlag, 1994.

Goodenough, E. R. *Jewish Symbols in the Greco-Roman Period*, 13 volumes. Bollingen Series, 37. New York: Pantheon Books, 1953.

Goodison, L., and C. Morris, eds. *Ancient Goddesses: The Myths and the Evidence*. London: British Museum Press, 1998; see esp. "Uncoiling Images: Minoan 'Snake Goddesses'?," pp. 123–25.

Goodspeed, E. J. *Die ältesten Apologeten: Texte mit kurzen Einleitungen*. Göttingen: Vandenhoeck & Ruprecht, 1914.

Goppelt, L. *Typos*. Gütersloh: Wissenschaftliche Buchgesellschaft, 1939. [reprinted Darmstadt, 1969]; see p. 220.

Gordon, C. H. "Leviathan: Symbol of Evil," in *Biblical Motifs, Origins and Transformation*, ed. A. Altman. Cambridge, Mass.: Harvard University Press, 1966; pp. 1–9.

———. *Ugaritic Literature*. Rome: Pontificum Institutum Biblicum, 1949.

Gorelick, L., and E. Williams-Forte, eds. *Ancient Seals and the Bible*. Malibu, Calif.: Undena, 1983.

Görg, M. *Aegyptiaca—Biblica*. Ägypten und Altes Testament 11. Wiesbaden: Otto Harrassowitz, 1991; see esp. pp. 252–71: "Das Wort zur Schlange (Gen 3, 14f): Gedanken zum sogenannten Protoevangelium." [See next entry.]

———. "Die 'Sünde' Salomos: Zeitkritische Aspekte der jahwistischen Sündenfallerzählung," *Biblische Notizen* 16 (1981) 42–59; Görg, "Weisheit als Provokation: Religionsgeschichtliche und theologische Aspekte der Sündenfallerzählung," in *Die Kraft der Hoffnung* [*Festschrift J. Schneider*] (Bamberg: St.-Otto-Verf., 1982); pp. 19–34.

————. "Das Wort zur Schlange (Gen 3, 14f): Gedanken zum sogenannten Proto-evangelium," *Biblische Notizen* 19 (1992) 121–40.

Gosse, B. "L'écriture de Gn 3, le serpent dualité de la femme et de l'homme," *Biblische Notizen* 98 (1999) 19–20.

Gossen, H., and Steier, A. "Schlange," *Pauly-Wissowa* Suppl. 2.3. Stuttgart: J. B. Metzlersche, 1921; cols. 494–557.

Gourbillon, J.-G. "La parabole du serpent d'airain et la 'lacune' du ch. III de l'Évangile selon S. Jean," *Vivre et Penser* 2 (1942) 213–26 [= *RB* N.S. 51–52 (1942)]

Graepler-Diehl, U. "Eherne Schlange," *Lexicon der christliche Iconographie* (1968) 583–86.

Grafman, R. "Bringing Tiamat to Earth," *Israel Exploration Journal* 22 (1972) 47–49.

Granshinietz, "Agathodämon," *Pauly-Wissowa* Suppl. 3 (1918) 37–59.

Grant, R. M. *Gnosticism: A Source Book of Heretical Writings from the Early Christian Period.* New York: Harper & Row, 1961; see esp. pp. 52–59, 89–92, 104–15 [for a translation of Ophite sources].

Graves, R., and R. Patai. *Hebrew Myths: The Book of Genesis.* New York: McGraw-Hill, 1966.

Gray, J. *I and II Kings: A Commentary.* The Old Testament Library. Philadelphia: Westminster Press, 1964 [2nd ed.]; see esp. pp. 669–71.

————. *Near Eastern Mythology.* London and New York: Hamlyn, 1969.

Greaves, S. W. "Wordplay and Associative Magic in the Ugaritic Snake-bite Incantation RS 24.244," *Ugarit-Forschungen* 26 (1994) 165–67.

Green, M. J. *Dictionary of Celtic Myth and Legend.* London: Thames and Hudson, 1992, reprinted 1997; see esp. p. 149 [Mercury], pp. 169–70 [phallus], pp. 194–95 [serpent], and pp. 195–96 [ram-horned snake].

Greenman, E. F. *Guide to Serpent Mounds.* Columbus: Ohio Historical Society, 1964.

Gressmann, H. "Der Zauberstab des Moses und die eherne Schlange," *Zeitschrift für Vereins für Volkskunde* 23 (1913) 18–35. [Gressmann claimed that Moses' staff became the raised copper serpent.]

Grether, O., and J. Fichtner, "Die Schlange im AT," *TWNT* 5 (1954) 571–75.

Grimm, J. *Teutonic Mythology,* 4 vols., trans. J. S. Stallybrass. London, 1888 [4th ed.].

Grimme, E. G. *Europäische Malerei im Mittelalter.* Ullstein Kunstgeschichte 12. West Berlin: Ullstein Bücher, 1963; see esp. Fig. 5 [the serpent in Eden] and Illus. 14 [serpent like a woman in Eden].

Gruber, J. R. *Die Ophiten.* Würzburg, 1864.

Gruenthaner, M. J. "The Demonology of the Old Testament," *Catholic Biblical Quarterly* 6 (1944) 6–27. [Gruenthaner thought that the "Serpent who plays such a sinister part in the fall of our first parents is the first principle of evil which we encounter in the Bible" (see p. 7)].

Grzimek, F. "Die Riesenschlangen," in *Grzimeks Tierleben.* Zürich, 1971; vol. 6, p. 371.

Gubernatis, A. de. *Zoological Mythology: The Legends of Animals,* 2 vols. New York: Macmillan, 1872 [reprinted by Singing Tree Press, 1968]; see esp. pp. 388–420: "The Serpent and the Aquatic Monster."

Guiley, R. E. *Harper's Encyclopedia of Mystical and Paranormal Experience.* San Francisco: HarperSanFrancisco, 1991.

Gunkel, H. *The Stories of Genesis: A Translation of the Third Edition of the Introduction to Hermann Gunkel's Commentary on the Book of Genesis,* ed. W. R. Scott, trans. J. J. Scullion. Vallejo, Calif.: BIBAL, 1994.

Güterbock, H. G. "Le mot hittite ḫartaggaš 'serpent'," *Revue Hittite et Asianique* 6 (1941) 102–09. [The meaning of ḫartaggaš has not been clear. Now, in light of its appearance on a tablet found at Bogazköy in 1933, the noun probably denotes a snake.]

Hall, H. R. *The Ancient History of the Near East.* London: Methuen and Co., Ltd., 1913; see esp. p. 485. [Hall also suggested that Moses' staff was also the upraised copper serpent.]

Halliday, W. R. *Greek Divination: A Study of Its Methods and Principles.* London: Macmillan, 1913; see esp. pp. 82–91.

Hallo, W. W., and J. J. van Dijk. *The Exaltation of Inanna.* New Haven and London: Yale University Press, 1968.

Hambly, W. D. *Serpent Worship in Africa.* Field Museum of Natural History Anthropological Series, Vol. XXI, no. 1. Chicago: Field Museum Press, 1931; note esp. pp. 56–67: "The Question of an External Origin of African Serpent Beliefs."

Hamilton, M. *Incubation or the Cure of Disease in Pagan Temples and Christian Churches.* London: Simpkin, Marshall, Hamilton, Kent & Co., 1906; see esp. pp. 1–79 [on the cult of Asclepius].

Hammond, P. C. "The Snake Monument at Petra," *American Journal of Arabic Studies* 1 (1973) 1–29.

Hampton-Cook, E. "The Serpent in Eden (Gen. iii)," *Expository Times* 18 (1906–1907) 287.

Hanauer, J. E. *Folklore of the Holy Land: Moslem, Christian, and Jewish.* London: Sheldon Press, 1907, 1935; see esp. pp. 211–13, 268.

Handy, L. K. "Serpent (Religious Symbol)," *The Anchor Yale Bible Dictionary.* New York: Doubleday, 1992; rpt. New Haven; vol. 5, pp. 1113–16.

Hankey, V. "A Snake Vase in Stone from a Late Bronze Age Temple at Amman," *Jahrbuch des Deutschen Archäologischen Instituts, Archäologischer Anzeiger* 82 (1967) 298–302. [The vase may have originated in Mesopotamia.]

———. "Imported Vessels of the Late Bronze Age at High Places," *Temples and High Places in Biblical Times,* ed. A. Biran. Jerusalem: Nelson Glueck School of Biblical Archaeology of Hebrew Union College—Jewish Institute of Religion, 1981; pp. 108–17.

Hanson, R. S. *The Serpent Was Wiser: A New Look at Genesis 1–11.* Minneapolis: Augsburg, 1972.

Haran, M. "The Ark and the Cherubim: Their Symbolic Significance in Biblical Ritual," *Israel Exploration Journal* 9 (1959) 30–38, 89–94.

Harl, K. W. *Coinage in the Roman Economy: 300 B.C. to A.D. 700.* Baltimore and London: The Johns Hopkins University Press, 1996.

Harnack, A. *The Mission and Expansion of Christianity in the First Three Centuries,* trans. J. Moffat. New York: Harper Torchbooks, 1962 [originally published in London: Williams and Norgate, 1908].

Hartlaub, G. F. "Mythos und Magie der Schlange," *Atlantis* 12 (1940) 570.

Haspecker, J., and N. Lohfink, "Gn 3,15: 'Weil du ihm Nach der Ferse Schnappst,' " *Scholastik* 36 (1961) 357–72.

Hastings, J., ed. "Serpent-worship," *Encyclopædia of Religion and Ethics.* Edinburgh: T. & T. Clark and New York: Charles Scribner's Sons, 1920, 1962; vol. 11, pp. 399–423.

Hauenstein, A. "Le serpent dans les rites, cultes et coutumes de certaines ethnies de Côtes d'Ivoire," *Anthropos* 73 (1978) 525–60.

Haupt, P. "The Curse on the Serpent," *Journal of Biblical Literature* 35 (1916) 155–62.

Hausenstein, W. *Das Bild Atlanten zur Kunst.* Munich: Piper, 1922; vol. 5–6, see esp. pp. 62 and 65. [Three squares in the bronze door of the Dom in Augsburg feature serpents; at least one seems to be a positive image of two serpents eating from a tree. Bowls depicting serpents eating from trees, antedating 1000 BCE, have been found in Israel.]

Havelock, C. M. *Hellenistic Art: The Art of the Classical World from the Death of Alexander the Great to the Battle of Actium.* New York and London: W.W. Norton & Co., 1981 [2nd ed.].

Hayes, L. N. *The Chinese Dragon.* Shanghai: n.p., 1922.

Hediger, H. "Die Schlangen," in *Grzimeks Tierleben.* Zürich, 1971; vol. 6, p. 352.

Hehn, J. "Zur Paradiesesschlange," *Festschrift Sebastian Merkle,* ed. W. Schellberg et al. Düsseldorf: L. Schwann, 1922; pp. 137–51.

Heidel, A. *The Gilgamesh Epic and Old Testament Parallels.* Chicago and London: University of Chicago Press, 1946 [2nd ed. 1949, 1963].

Heinz-Mohr, G. *Lexikon der Symbole: Bilder und Zeichen der christlichen Kunst.* Munich: Eugen Diederichs Verlag, 1971, reprinted 1998; see esp. "Schlange" on pp. 276–78.

Heizer, R. F. "The Hopi Snake Dance: Fact and Fancy," in *Readings in Anthropology,* ed. J. D. Jennings and E. A. Hoebel. New York: McGraw-Hill, 1955; pp. 243–45.

Hendel, R. S. "Nehushtan," *Dictionary of Deities and Demons in the Bible,* ed. K. van der Toorn, B. Becking, and P. W. van der Horst. Leiden and Boston: Brill and Grand Rapids: Eerdmans, 1999 [2nd ed.]; pp. 615–16.

———. "Serpent," *Dictionary of Deities and Demons in the Bible,* ed. K. van der Toorn, B. Becking, and P. W. van der Horst. Leiden and Boston: Brill and Grand Rapids: Eerdmans, 1999 [2nd ed.]; pp. 744–47.

Henderson, J. L. "Ancient Myth and Modern Man," in *Man and His Symbols,* ed. C. G. Jung et al. Garden City, N.Y.: Doubleday, 1964; pp. 89–141.

Henderson, J. L., and M. Oakes. *The Wisdom of the Serpent: The Myths of Death, Rebirth, and Resurrection.* New York: George Braziller, Inc., 1963; reprint, Princeton, N. J.: Princeton University Press, 1990.

Hengel, M. "Die Schriftauslegung des 4. Evangeliums auf dem Hintergrund der urchristlichen Exegese," *Journal of Bible and Theology* 4 (1989) 249–88.

Hennemann, A., ed. *Der Schlangenkönig: Märchen aus Nepal.* Kassel, 1980; pp. 19–33.

Henry, M.-L. "Schlange," *Biblisch-historisches Handwörterbuch,* ed. B. Reiche and L. Rost. Göttingen: Vandenhoeck & Ruprecht, 1966; vol. 3, cols. 1699–1701.

———. *Das Tier im religiösen Bewusstsein des alttestamentlichen Menschen.* Tübingen: Mohr (Siebeck), 1958.

Henton, J. W. van. "Dragon," *Dictionary of Deities and Demons in the Bible,* ed. K. van der Toorn, B. Becking, and P. W. van der Horst. Leiden and Boston: Brill and Grand Rapids: Eerdmans, 1999 [2nd ed.]; pp. 265–67.

———. "Python," *Dictionary of Deities and Demons in the Bible,* ed. K. van der Toorn, B. Becking, and P. W. van der Horst. Leiden and Boston: Brill and Grand Rapids: Eerdmans, 1999 (2nd ed.); pp. 669–71.

Hentze, C. "Le poisson comme symbole du fécundité dans la Chine ancienne," *Bulletin de Musée Royale.* N.V.

———. "Die Regenbogenschlange," *Anthropos* 61 (1966) 258–66.

———. "Die zerstückelte Schlange," *Antaios* 9 (1968) 253–61.

Herrmann, F. *Symbolik in den Religionen der Naturvölker.* Symbolik der Religion, IX, ed. F. Herrmann. Stuttgart: Anton Hiersemann, 1961; see esp. pp. 107–10, 138–141.

Herzog, R. "Asklepios," *Reallex. für Antike und Christentum* 1 (1950) 795–99.

Hieronymus. *Commentarium in Matheum: Libri IV.* Corpus Christianorum Series Latina 77. S. Hieronymi Presbyteri Opera: Pars 1, 7. Turnholt: Brepolis Editores Pontificii, 1969.

Hilgenfeld, A. "Der Gnosticismus und die Philosophumena," *Zeitschrift für wissenschaftliche Theologie* 5 (1862) 400ff. [This is a work on the Ophites.]

Hill, A. "The Temple of Asclepius: An Alternative Source for Paul's Body Theology?" *Journal of Biblical Literature* 99 (1980) 437–39.

Himmelfarb, M. *Tours of Hell: An Apocalyptic Form in Jewish and Christian Literature.* Philadelphia: Fortress Press, 1983.

Hjerl-Hansen, B. "Le rapprochement poisson-serpent dans le prédication de Jésus (Mt. VII, 10 et Luc. XI, 11)," *RB* N.S. 55 (1948) 195–98.

Hönig, A. *Die Ophiten.* Berlin, 1889. N.V.

Hobbs, T. R. *2 Kings.* Word Biblical Commentary 13. Waco, Tex.: Word, 1985; see esp. pp. 250–53.

Hocquenghem, A. M. "Les 'crocs' et les 'serpents': L'autorité absolue des ancêtres mythiques," *Representations of Gods,* ed. H. G. Kippenberg. Visible Religion 2; Leiden: Brill, 1983; pp. 58–74. [Hocquenghem discusses Peruvian figures with human and serpent features that date from approximately 200 BCE to 700 CE, and convey ideas preserved in sixteenth- and seventeenth-century Spanish lexicons. These images embody symbolically immortal power.]

Hofbauer, J. "Die Paradiesesschlange (Gn 3)," *Zeitschrift für katholische Theologie* 59 (1947) 228–31.

Hoffmann, I. "Die Schlange im Bett: Anlässe für Rituale bei den Hethithern," *Altorientalische Forschungen* 17 (1990) 186–88.

Holland, T. A. *Publications: The Oriental Institute 1906–1991: Exploring the History and Civilizations of the Near East.* Oriental Institute Communications 26. Chicago: University of Chicago Press, 1991.

Holmberg, U. *Der Baum des Lebens: Göttinnen und Baumkult.* Bern: Edition Amalia, 1996; originally published in 1922); see the following Illus.: 34 [serpent entwined on a tree], 37 [serpent goddess Ganga], 41 [the goddess Erde with a serpent], 53 [a serpent three times curled around the navel stone], 67 [two serpents, upraised, beneath a three-headed goddess].

Holter, K. "The Serpent in Eden as a Symbol of Israel's Political Enemies: A Yahwistic Criticism of the Solomonic Foreign Policy?" *Scandinavian Journal of the Old Testament* 1 (1990) 106–12. [With W. von Soden (see the entry) and M. Görg (see the entry), Holter sees a hidden polemic against Solomon's foreign policy, but rightly claims more than Egypt is in view, since *nachash* in the Old Testament symbolizes Egypt as well as other nations. Since the J writer perceived Israel as a blessing for all nations, Gen 12:3 ("and whoever curses you I will curse") has polemical political overtones directed against Solomon's foreign alliances.]

Holtom, D. C. *The Japanese Enthronement Ceremonies with an Account of the Imperial Regalia.* Tokyo: The Japan Advertiser Press, 1928.

Honecker, M. "Christus Medicus," *Kerygma und Dogma* 31 (1985) 307–23.

Hopfner, T. *Das Diagramm der Ophiten.* 1930; see esp. pp. 86ff. N.V.

———. "Der Tierkult der alten Ägypter," *Denkschriften der kaiserlichen Akademie der Wissenschaften in Wien,* Philosophisch-historische Klasse 57.2; Abhandlung 6 (1913) 136–49.

Hornung, E. "Die Bedeutung des Tieres im alten Ägypten," *Studium Generale* 20 (1967) 69–84.

———. *Idea Into Image: Essays on Ancient Egyptian Thought,* trans. E. Bredeck. n.c.: Timken Publishers, Inc., 1992; see esp. pp. 49–51, 62–67.

Houlihan, P. F. *The Animal World of the Pharaohs.* London and New York: Thames and Hudson, 1996.

Houziaux, A. *Le Tohu-bohu, le Serpent et le bon Dieu.* Paris: Presses de la Renaissance, 1997.

Howard-Brook, W. *Becoming Children of God: John's Gospel and Radical Discipleship.* The Bible and Liberation. Maryknoll, N. Y.: Orbis Books, 1994.

Howey, M. O. *The Encircled Serpent: A Study of Serpent Symbolism in All Countries and Ages.* New York: Arthur Richmond Company, 1955. [Originally published London, 1926; a valuable book, full of data, but not refined by scientific methodology.]

Hübner, J. "Christus Medicus: Ein Symbol des Erlösungsgeschehens und ein Modell ärztlichen Handelns," *Kerygma und Dogma* 31 (1985) 324–35.

Hultkranzt, A. *The Religions of the American Indians,* trans. M. Setterwall. Hermeneutics: Studies in the History of Religions 7. Berkeley: University of California Press, 1979.

Hunger, J. *Babylonische Tieromina nebst griechisch-römischen Parallelen.* Mitteilungen der Vorderasiatischen Gesellschaft 3. Rome: Peiser, 1909.

Hunger, K.-H. *Der Äskulapstab: Zur Funktion präsentativer Symbole in der Kommunikation.* Hochschul-Skripten: Medien 7. Berlin: Volker Spiess, 1978. [Seminal and important; the photographs are especially valuable, see esp. pp. 111–203.]

Hvidberg, F. "The Canaanite Background of Gen I–III," *Vetus Testamentum* 10 (1960) 285–94. [Recognizing that Canaan provided much of the iconography and symbology for ancient Israel, Hvidberg concluded that, according to Genesis 3, the serpent brought death and not life. He was the deceiver who is not synonymous with Satan but with Baal, Yahweh's old adversary.]

Ibuki, Y. "Gedankenaufbau und Hintergrund des 3. Kapitels des Johannesevangeliums," *Bulletin of Seikei University* 14 (1978) 9–33.

Inoltre, V. *The Dragon in China and Japan.* Wiesbaden, 1913.

Ions, V. *Indian Mythology.* New York: P. Bedrick Books, 1984 [rev. ed.].

Irenaeus. *The Refutation of All Heresies,* in *The Apostolic Fathers: Justin Martyr and Irenaeus.* The Ante-Nicene Fathers. Original publication facts not given; reprint in Grand Rapids, Mich.: Eerdmans, 1973; see esp. vol. 1, Book 4, chap. 2 and Book 5, chap. 9–14.

Irmscher, J., trans. *Antike Fabeln.* Bibliothek der Antike. Berlin: Aufbau-Verlag, 1991 [3rd ed.]. [a collection of Greek and Latin passages on the serpent].

Isser, S. J. *The Dositheans: A Samaritan Sect in Late Antiquity.* Leiden: Brill, 1976.

Jackson, H. M. "The Meaning and Function of the Leontocephaline in Roman Mithraism," *Numen* 32 (1985) 17–45.

Jackson, R. *Doctors and Diseases in the Roman Empire.* London: British Museum Press, 1988.

Jacobs, A. "Provacative and Tendentious," *The Reformed Journal* 39 (1989) 21–25 [a review of E. Pagels' *Adam, Eve, and the Serpent.* New York: Random House, 1988].

Jacobsen, T., and S. N. Kramer. "The Myth of Inanna and Bilulu," *Journal of Near Eastern Studies* 12 (1953) 160–88, with Plates.

Jakobsson, O. "Daimon och Agathos Daimon," PhD Dissertation, Lund, 1925.

James, E. O. *Myths and Rituals in the Ancient Near East.* New York: Frederick A. Praeger, 1958.

———. *The Tree of Life: An Archaeological Study.* Leiden: Brill, 1966.

Jaroš, K. "Die Motive der Heiligen Bäume und der Schlange in Gen 2–3," *Zeitschrift für die alttestamentliche Wissenschaft* 92 (1980) 204–15.

Jayne, W. A. *The Healing Gods of Ancient Civilizations.* New Haven: Yale University Press, and London: Oxford University Press, 1925; see esp. pp. 222–23, 230–31, 254–57, 282–85.

Jefremow, I. *Das Herz der Schlange,* trans. H. Angarowa et al. Moscow: Verlag für Fremdsprachige Literatur, n.d. [novelistic]

Jenson, R. W., ed. "Bronze serpent," *Dialog* 17 (1978) 251–86.

Jeremias, A. *Das Alte Testament im Lichte des Alten Orients.* Leipzig: J. C. Hinrichs, 1916 [3rd ed.].

Joger, U. *The Venomous Snakes of the Near and Middle East.* Beihefte zum Tübinger Atlas des Vorderen Orients Reihe A, Nr. 12; Wiesbaden: Ludwig Reichert Verlag, 1984 [a manual of the taxonomy and distribution of venomous snakes in the Near and Middle East; see esp. the drawings on pp. 89–95].

Johnson, B. *Lady of the Beasts: Ancient Images of the Goddess and Her Sacred Animals.* San Francisco: HarperSanFrancisco, 1988; see esp. "The Serpent" on pp. 121–91 [valuable, full of data, well organized, heavily influenced by Jung; at times lacks proper nuancing].

Johnson, S. B. *The Cobra Goddess of Ancient Egypt: Predynastic, Early Dynastic, and Old Kingdom Periods.* London, New York: Kegan Paul International, 1990; see the important discussion of the meaning of the uraeus on pp. 3–11 and the earliest known examples of it on pp. 19–33.

Joines, K. R. "The Serpent in Gen 3," *Zeitschrift für die alttestamentliche Wissenschaft* 87 (1975) 1–11.

———. "The Bronze Serpent in the Israelite Cult," *Journal of Biblical Literature* 87 (1968) 245–56.

———. "The Bronze Serpent in the OT." PhD Dissertation, Southern Baptist Theological Seminary, 1967.

———. "The Serpent in Gen 3," *Zeitschrift für die alttestamentliche Wissenschaft* 87 (1975) 1–11.

———. *Serpent Symbolism in the Old Testament: A Linguistic, Archaeological, and Literary Study.* Haddonfield, N.J.: Haddonfield House, 1974.

———. "Winged Serpents in Isaiah's Inaugural Vision," *Journal of Biblical Literature* 86 (1967) 410–15.

Jonas, H. *Gnosis und spätantiker Geist.* Vol. 1. Göttingen: Vandenhoeck & Ruprecht, 1934; see esp. pp. 221–23, 358–62 [for Ophites].

———. *The Gnostic Religion: The Message of the Alien God and the Beginnings of Christianity* [2nd. ed., rev.] Boston: Beacon Press, 1963; pp. 91–96.

Jones, G. H. *1 and 2 Kings, Vol. II: 1 Kings 17:1–2 Kings 25:30.* New Century Bible Commentary. Basingstoke, Hants. (United Kingdom): Marshall, Morgan & Scott, 1984; reprint, Grand Rapids, Mich.: Eerdmans (n.d); see esp. pp. 560–63.

Jordon-Smith, P. "The Serpent and the Eagle," *Parabola: The Magazine of Myth and Tradition* 14 (1989) 64–71.

Joüon, P. "Le grand dragon, l'ancien serpent," *Recherches de Science Religieuse* 17 (1927) 444–46.

Justin. *Justin: "Dialogue avec Tryphon,"* ed. G. Archambault. Textes et documents pour l'étude historique du Christianisme 11. Paris: Librairie Alphonse Picard et Fils, 1909.

—————. *Saint Justin: "Apologies,"* ed. A. Wartelle. Paris: Études Augustiniennes, 1987.

Kaestli, J. D. "L'interprétation du serpent de Genèse 3 dans quelques textes gnostiques et la question de la gnose 'Ophite,' " *Gnosticisme et monde Hellénistique,* ed. J. Ries et al. Publications de L'Institut Orientaliste de Louvain 27. Louvain-la-Neuve: Université Catholique de Louvain, Institut Orientaliste, 1982; pp. 116–30.

Kähler, H. *Rom und sein Imperium.* Kunst der Welt. Baden-Baden: Holle Verlag, 1979 [3rd ed.]; see esp. Illus. 11 [Apollo altar].

Kákosy, L. "The Astral Snakes of the Nile," *Mitteilungen des Deutschen Archäologischen Instituts Abteilung Kairo* 37 (1981) 255–60. [Festschrift for L. Habachi.]

Kambach, J. J. *Betrachtung des Geheimnisses Jesu Christi in dem Vorbilde der Ehernen Schlange.* Halle: Verlegung des Wausenhauses, 1728.

Karageorghis, V. "A 'Snake-house' from Enkomi," *Cyprus: Report of the Department of Antiquities* (1972) 109–12 [see the publication by Drummond].

Keel, O. *Jahwe-Visionen und Siegelkunst.* Stuttgarter Bibelstudien 84/85. Stuttgart: Verlag Katholisches Bibelwerk, 1977; see esp. pp. 71–74 and 83–92.

—————. *Das Recht der Bilder gesehen zu werden: Drei Fallstudien zur Methode der Interpretation altorientalischer Bilder.* Orbis Biblicus et Orientalis 122. Freiburg, Schweiz: Universitätsverlag and Göttingen: Vandenhoeck & Ruprecht, 1992; see esp. "Polyvalenz der Schlange," on pp. 195–267.

—————. *Die Welt der altorientalischen Bildsymbolik und das Alte Testament: Am Beispiel der Psalmen.* Zürich: Benziger Verlag, 1972. The focus preempts inclusion of Gen 3:1–23 and Num 21, perhaps; but see Illus. 19, 38, 41, 46–48 [the serpent as a symbol of chaos and evil to be conquered], 49–50 [the serpent as symbolizing creation, perhaps], 55 [the serpent as symbolic of time and chronology], 94 [the demonic serpent], 106 [the serpent as dangerous and bearer of death], 125–26.

Keel, O., and C. Uehlinger. *Gods, Goddesses, and Images of God in Ancient Israel,* trans. T. H. Trapp. Minneapolis: Fortress, 1998.

Kees, H. "Der angebliche Gauname 'Schlangenberg," *Mitteilungen des Deutschen Archäologischen Instituts Abteilung Kairo* 20 (1965) 102–9.

—————. *Der Götterglaube im Alten Ägypten.* Mitteilungen der Vorderasiastisch-Agyptischen Gesellschaft 45. Leipzig, 1941; Berlin, 1956 [2nd ed.].

—————. "Die Schlangensteine und ihre Beziehungen zu den Reichsheiligtümern," *Zeitschrift für ägyptische Sprache und Altertumskunde* 57 (1922) 120–36.

Keimer, L. *Histoires de serpents dans l'Égypte ancienne et moderne.* Mémoires de l'Institut d'Égypte 50. Cairo: Institut Français, 1947.

Keller, O. "Schlangen," *Die antike Tierwelt.* Hildesheim: Olms, 1963 [from original in Leipzig, 1913]; vol. 2, pp. 284–305.

Kemal, Y. *Töte die Schlange,* trans. C. Bischoff. Zürich: Unionsverlag, 1988 [the original Turkish is 1976]. [a novel]

Kendall, T. "Schlangenspiel," *Lexikon der Ägyptologie* 5.1 (1983) cols. 653–55 [plus see his bibliography on this game].

Kenyon, K. *Excavations at Jericho: The Tombs Excavated in 1952–1954.* Vol. 1. Jerusalem: British School of Archaeology, 1960. [See Fig. 162, which is a vase in the shape of a bird; the vase has images of two serpents.]

———. *Excavations at Jericho: The Tombs Excavated in 1955–1958.* Vol. 2. Jerusalem: British School of Archaeology, 1965.

Kerényi, C. *Asklepios: Archetypal Image of the Physician's Existence,* trans. R. Manheim. Bollingen Series 65. New York: Pantheon Books, 1959 [originally published as *Der Göttliche Arzt: Studien über Asklepios und seine Kultstätten.* Basel: Ciba Ltd., 1948 (republished in Darmstadt in 1964)].

———. *Dionysos: Archetypal Image of Indestructible Life.* Bollingen Foundation Series 65.2. Princeton, N.J.: Princeton University Press, 1976.

———. *Die Mysterien von Eleusis.* Zürich: Rhein-Verlag, 1962.

———. *The Gods of the Greeks,* trans. N. Cameron. New York: Thames and Hudson, 1951.

Kerschensteiner, "Die Schlange des Asklepios," *Knolls mitteil. für Ärzte," Jubil. Ausg.* (1866–1936) 250–55.

Kiernan, J. P. "The Fall: An Anthropological Answer to a Religious Riddle," *Religion in Southern Africa* 6, no. 1 (1985) 59–69.

Kimbrough, D. L. *Taking Up Serpents.* Chapel Hill and London: University of North Carolina Press, 1995. [Also see the book by W. La Barre.]

King, K. L. *Revelation of the Unknowable God.* California Classical Library. Santa Rosa, Calif.: Polebridge Press, 1995.

King, L. W. *A History of Babylon.* New York: F. A. Stokes, 18–?; p. 72 [6th cent. BCE bronze serpents are depicted beside the four doors of the temple of Esagila].

Kirk, G. S. *Myth: Its Meaning and Functions in Ancient and Other Cultures.* Sather Classical Lectures 40. Cambridge: Cambridge University Press, 1970, and Los Angeles and Berkeley: University of California Press, 1970.

Kiss, Z. "Ouroboros," in *Lexicon Iconographicum Mythologiae Classicae* 7.1, pp. 136–37; see the photographs in *LIMC* 7.2, Plate 93.

Kitagawa, J. M. "Ainu Myth," in *Myths and Symbols,* ed. Kitagawa and C. H. Long. Chicago: University of Chicago Press, 1969; pp. 309–23.

Kittel, G. "אזקרף = ὑψωθῆναι = gekreuzigt werden: Zur angeblichen antiochenischen Herkunft des Vierten Evangelisten," *Zeitschrift für die neutestamentliche Wissenschaft* 35 (1936) 282–85.

Kittel, R. "Der Schlangenstein im Kidrontal bei Jerusalem," in *Studien zur Hebräischen Archäologie und Religionsgeschichte.* Leipzig: Druck von A. Edelmann, 1908; pp. 159–88.

Kjeseth, P. "Nehushtan (Num 21, 4–9, 2Kgs 18,4) and Ernst Bloch," *Dialog* 17 (1978) 280–86.

Klímová, D. "Beitrag zur Problematik der Entwicklung der Folkloristischen Motive Schlafkraut und Lebenskraut der Schlangen," in *Symbolae Biblicae et*

Mesopotamicae [Dedicated to F. M. T. de Liagre Böhl], ed. M. A. Beek et al. Leiden: Brill, 1973; pp. 243–52.

Klinger, J. "Bethesda and the Universality of the Logos," *St. Vladimir's Theological Quarterly* 27 (1983) 169–85.

Klüsener, E., and F. Pfäfflin, eds. *Else Lasker-Schüler 1869–1945.* Marbacher Magazin 71. Marbach am Neckar: Deutsche Schillergesellschaft, 1995.

Koch, J. Chr. "De cultu serpentem apud antiquos," *Thesaurus Dissertationum,* ed. J. Chr. Martini. Leipzig, 1717; vol. 2, p. 1765.

Koehler, L., and W. Baumgartner. "נחשת," *The Hebrew and Aramaic Lexicon of the Old Testament,* rev. W. Baumgartner and J. J. Stamm, trans. and ed. M. E. J. Richardson. Leiden and New York: Brill, 1995; vol. 2, pp. 692–93.

Koenen, K. "Eherne Schlange und goldenes Kalb: Ein Vergleich der Überlieferungen," *Zeitschrift für die alttestamentliche Wissenschaft* 111 (1999) 353–72.

Koester, H. *History, Culture, and Religion of the Hellenistic Age: Introduction to the New Testament.* New York and Berlin: Walter De Gruyter, 1982; see esp. vol. 1, pp. 182–204.

Koh, S. "An Archaeological Investigation of the Snake Cult in the Southern Levant: The Chalcolithic Period Through the Iron Age." PhD Dissertation, University of Chicago, 1994.

Koldewey, R. *The Excavations at Babylon.* London: Macmillan, 1914; see esp. p. 45. [Nebuchadnezzar wrote that he placed "mighty figures of serpents" at the "thresholds" of the temple of Nana.]

Kong, W-y. *Zwischen Tiger und Schlange.* 1976. N.V.

König, K. *Bruder Tier: Mensch und Tier in Mythos und Evolution.* Stuttgart: Verlag Freies Geistesleben, 1967.

Koppens, W. *Geheimnisse des Dschungels.* Lucerne, 1947; see esp. p. 80.

Kossatz-Deissmann, A. "Chnoubis," in *Lexicon Iconographicum Mythologiae Graecae* 3.1, pp. 272–73 [see the bibliography]; see the photographs in *LIMC,* 3.2, Plates 218–19.

Kovacs, M. G., trans. *The Epic of Gilgamesh.* Stanford, Calif.: Stanford University Press, 1985; see esp. pp. 106–107.

Kramer, S. N. *Gilgamesh and the Huluppu-Tree: A Reconstructed Sumerian Text.* Assyriological Studies 10. Chicago: University of Chicago Press, 1938.

———. *Sumerian Mythology: A Study of Spiritual and Literary Achievement in the Third Millenium B.C.* Philadelphia: The American Philosophical Society, 1944; new and revised edition in 1961 by Harper & Row in New York.

Kramp, W. *Protest der Schlange: Signale zum Umdenken.* Berlin: Kreuz, 1970. [Kramp assumes that the symbol of the serpent embodies destruction and powers opposed to God.]

Krauskopf, I., and S.-C. Dahlinger, "Gorgo, Gorgones," in *Lexicon Iconographicum Mythologiae Classicae* 4.1, pp. 285–330 [bibliography]; see the photographs in *LIMC* 4.2, Plates 161–62.

Kraybill, J. N. "Cult and Commerce in Revelation 18." PhD Dissertation, Union Theological Seminary in Virginia, 1992.

Kretschmar, G. "Ophiten und Naassener," *Religion im Geschichte und Gegenwart* [Dritte] 4 (1960) cols. 1659–60.

Kristensen, W. B. "De Slangenstaf en het Spraakvermogen van Mozes en Aäron," *Mededelingen der Koninklijke Nederlandse Akademie van Wetenschappen* N.S. 16.14 (1953) 591–610.

Kroha, T. *Grosses Lexikon der Numismatik.* Gütersloh: Bertelsmann Lexikon Verlag, 1997; see esp. pp. 40, 95, 214, 242, and 466. [In the history of coins, the animals most often represented are serpents, bears, dolphins, lambs, owls, fish, scorpions, deer (esp. bucks), and especially eagles, lions, and horses.]

Kroll, W., and K. Witte, eds. "Schlange," *Paulys Real-Encyclopädie der classischen Altertumwissenschaft,* Zweite Reihe. Dritter Halbrand. Stuttgart: J. B. Metzlersche Verlagsbuchhandlung (1921) 494–557.

Kübel, P. "Ein Wortspiel in Genesis 3 und sein Hintergrund: Die 'kluge' Schlange und die 'nackten' Menschen," *Biblische Notizen* 93 (1998) 11–22.

Küster, E. *Die Schlange in der griechischen Kunst und Religion.* Religionsgeschichtliche Versuche und Vorarbeiten 13.2. Giessen: Töpelmann, 1913.

La Barre, W. *They Shall Take Up Serpents: Psychology of the Southern Snake-Handling Cult.* Minneapolis: University of Minnesota Press, 1962. [See the book by Kimbrough.]

Laeuchli, S. *The Serpent and the Dove: Five Essays on Early Christianity.* Nashville, and New York: Abingdon Press, 1966.

Laisné, C. *Kunst der Griechen,* trans. I. Hanneforth. Paris: Terrail, 1995; see esp. pp. 34, 83, 101, 125, 159–71, 172–73.

Langbrandtner, W. *Weltferner Gott oder Gott der Liebe: Der Ketzerstreit in der johanneischen Kirche. Eine exegetisch-religionsgeschichte Untersuchung mit Berücksichtigung der koptisch-gnostischen Texte aus Nag-Hammadi.* Beiträge zur Biblischen Exegese und Theologie 6. Frankfurt am Main, Bern and Las Vegas: Peter Lang, 1977.

Langdon, S. *Building Inscriptions of the Neo-Babylonian Empire. Part I: Nabopolassar and Nebuchadnezzar.* Paris: Ernest Leroux, 1905; pp. 79, 85, 105, 131 [Nebuchadnezzar records that he placed bulls and serpents in numerous cultic places.]

Lapatin, K. *Mysteries of the Snake Goddess: Art, Desire, and the Forging of History.* New York: Houghton Mifflin, 2002.

Laubscher, H. P. "Der Schlangenwürgende Herakles: Seine Bedeutung in der Herrscherikonologie," *Jahrbuch des Deutschen Archäologischen Instituts* 112 (1997) 149–66. [The depictions of Baby Hercules strangling the two snakes sent to him by the jealous Hera had political significance; it was used especially to legitimize the new power of the Ptolemies.]

Lavagne, H., et al., eds. *Mosaïque.* Ars Latina. Paris, 2000 [among the animals most often represented on mosaics is the snake; p. 45].

Lawrence, T. E. *The Seven Pillars of Wisdom: A Triumph.* Garden City, N.Y.: Doubleday, 1935; see esp. pp. 273–80.

Lawuyi, O. B., and J. K. Olupona. "Metaphoric Associations and the Conception of Death: Analysis of a Yoruba World View," *Journal of Religion in Africa* 18 (1988) 2–14.

Leclant, J., and G. Clerc, "Ammon," in *Lexicon Iconographicum Mythologiae Classicae* 1.1, pp. 666–89 [see the superb bibliography]; also see the photographs in *LIMC* 1.2, Plates 534–54.

Leclercq, H. "Abrasax," *Dictionnaire d'archéologie chrétienne et de liturgie* 1 (1924) 127–55 [see the excellent bibliography].

———. "Serpent," *Dictionnaire d'archéologie chrétienne et de liturgie* 15 (1950) cols. 1353–57. [Leclercq correctly points out that according to Jn 3:14 and a "poterie hollandaise" (Fig. 10881) "le serpent d'airain" is a "symbole du Christ."]

Lee, C. "Moses' Serpent as a Patristic 'Type,' " *Dialog* 17 (1978) 251–60.

Leeming, D. A. *The World of Myth: An Anthology.* New York and Oxford: Oxford University Press, 1990.

Leeming, D. A., and M. A. Leeming. *A Dictionary of Creation Myths.* New York, Oxford: Oxford University Press, 1995. [Leeming and Leeming argue that the serpent played a role, often major, in the creation myths of the Aztecs, Buriats, Hebrews, Lenapes, Mosetenes, and Yuchis (they missed many other cultures in which the serpent is crucial in creation myths, esp. the Aborigines of Australia and the Vedas).]

Leeuw, G. van der. *Phänomenologie der Religion.* Neue Theologische Grundrisse. Tübingen: J. C. B. Mohr (Paul Siebeck), 1956 [2nd ed.].

Legge, F. *Forerunners and Rivals of Christianity from 330 B.C. to 330 A.D.* New Hyde Park, N. Y.: University Books, 1964.

Legrain, L. *Seal Cylinders.* Ur Excavations 10. London: Oxford University Press, 1951.

Leipoldt, J., and W. Grundmann, eds. *Umwelt des Urchristentums,* 3 vols. Berlin: Evangelische Verlagsanstalt, 1971, 1972, 1967 [the first two volumes reached a third edition, the third only a second]; see esp. vol. 1, pp. 69–73, 112 [Asclepius]; vol. 2, pp. 68–72; vol. 3 [note these illustrations: from Greece: Nos. 2, 3, 18; from special places: Nos. 19, 20, 23; from Eleusis cult: No. 29; from Dionysus cult: nothing; from Orpheus cult: No. 74; from Asia Minor: No. 81; from Mithraism: Nos. 112, 113; from India: nothing [amazing]; from Syria: Nos. 135, 136; from Egypt: Nos. 212, 256, 266, 279, 292; from the Latin world: No. 320; from Etruria: nothing]. All notations pertain to the symbolism of the serpent.

Leisegang, H. *Η ΟΡΦΙΚΗ ΛΑΤΡΕΙΑ ΣΤΗ ΜΕΣΟΓΕΙΟ ΤΟ ΜΥΣΤΗΡΙΟ ΤΟΥ ΕΡΠΕΤΟΥ.* Athens: ΙΑΜΒΛΙΧΟΣ, 1993 [originally published as Leisegang, H. "Das Mysterium der Schlange: Ein Beitrag zur Erforschung des griechischen Mysterienkultes und seines Fortlebens in der christlichen Welt," *Eranos-Jahrbuch* (1939) 151–250]. [Fourteen illustrations.]

———. "The Mystery of the Serpent," *The Mysteries: Papers from the Eranos Yearbooks.* Vol. 2, ed. J. Campbell. Bollingen Series 30. New York: Pantheon Books, 1955.

Leitz, C. *Die Schlangennamen in den ägyptischen und griechischen Giftbü-chern.* Akademie der Wissenschaften und der Literatur Ab. Geites- und Sozialwissenschaftlichen Klasse 1997, no. 6. Stuttgart: Franz Steiner Verlag, 1997. [Scholarly; see esp. the bibliography on books concerning poisons.]

——. "Die Schlangensprüche in den Pyramidentexten," *Orientalia* N.S. 65 (1996) 381–427.

Lesêtre, H. "Serpent," *Dictionnaire de Bible* (1912) 1671–74.

Lesky, E. "Was ist über die ursprüngliche Bedeutung des Schlangenstabs bekannt?" *Deutsche Medizinische Wochenschrift* (1959) 2095. N.V.

Lessa, W. A., and E. Z. Vogt, eds. *Reader in Comparative Religion: An Anthropological Approach.* New York: Harper & Row, 1979 [4th ed.].

Levey, A. "Bad Timing: Time to Get a New Theory," *Biblical Archaeology Review* 24.4 (1998) 18–23. [See the three game boards in the form of a roundel for a game called *mehen;* they are formed to depict curled serpents, photos on p. 21.]

Levine, B. A., and J. M. de Tarragon. " 'Shapshu Cries out in Heaven': Dealing with Snake-bites at Ugarit (*KTU* 1.100, 1.107)," *RB* 95 (1988) 481–518.

Liberati, A. M., and F. Bourbon. *Rom: Weltreich der Antike,* trans. R. Kastenhuber. Erlangen: Karl Müller Verlag, 1997 [English original: *Ancient Rome*]; see esp. pp. 24 [Medusa], 91 [gold jewelry shaped like a serpent, from Pompeii], 109 [marble Laocoon].

Liechtenhan, R. "Ophiten," *Realencyklopädie für protestantische Theologie und Kirche* [*Dritte*] 14 (1904) 404–13.

Lienhardt, G. *Divinity and Experience: The Religion of the Dinka.* Oxford: Clarendon, 1961.

Lins, H. M. *Tiere in der Mythologie und ihre religiöse Symbolkraft.* Frankfurt: R. G. Fischer, 1994 [2nd ed.].

Lipiński, E. "La légende sacrée de la conjurion des morsures de serpents," *Ugarit-Forschungen* 6 (1974) 169–74 [concerns the bite of the serpent *(nḥš)* in Table RS 24.244].

Lippold, G. "Heilend Schlange," in *Studies Presented to D. M. Robinson.* Saint Louis, 1951; pp. 648–54. N.V.

Lipsius, R. A. "Über die ophitischen System," *Zeitschrift für wissenschaftliche Theologie* 6 (1863) 410–57.

Lloyd, S. *The Archaeology of Mesopotamia: From the Old Stone Age to the Persian Conquest.* London: Thames and Hudson, 1978 [rev. ed. in 1984, 1985].

Lloyd-Russell, V. "The Serpent as the Prime Symbol of Immortality Has Its Origin in the Semitic-Sumerian Culture." PhD Dissertation, University of Southern California, 1938.

Locher, G. W. *The Serpent in Kwakiutl Religion.* Leiden: Brill, 1932.

Loewenstamm, S. E. "The Muzzling of the Tannin in Ugaritic Myth," *Israel Exploration Journal* 19 (1959) 260–61.

Lonsdale, S. *Animals and the Origins of Dance*. London: Thames and Hudson, 1981.

López-Muñiz, R. B. "St. Phokas in a Spell for Snakes," *Zeitschrift für Papyrologie und Epigraphik* 95 (1993) 28. [Saint Phokas, who lived during the time of Trajan, is celebrated for curing those bitten by a poisonous snake.]

Lorein, G. W. "Het Thema van de Antichrist in de Intertestamentaire Periode." PhD Dissertation, Rijksuniversiteit Groningen, 1997.

Loth, H. *Vom Schlangenkult zur Christuskirche*. Frankfurt: Fischer Taschenbuch Verlag, 1987.

Loud, G., et al. eds. *Megiddo*, 2 vols. Chicago: Chicago Oriental Institute, 1939–1948. [See vol. 2, Plate 240 which shows two serpents from the second millenium BCE.]

Löwe, G., and H. A. Stoll. *Lexikon der Antike: Griechenland und das römische Weltreich*. Wiesbaden: VMA-Verlag, 1997; see esp. pp. 22, 49, 132–33, 233–34, 298, and 327.

Luckert, K. W. *Olmec Religion: A Key to Middle America and Beyond*. The Civilization of the American Indian Series. Norman: University of Oklahoma Press, 1976.

Lum, P. *Fabulous Beasts*. New York: Pantheon, 1951.

Lurker, M. "Adler und Schlange," *Antaios* 5 (1964) 344–52.

———. *Lexikon der Götter und Symbole der alten Ägypter*. Bern, Munich: Scherz Verlag, 1974, reprinted 1987; see esp. p. 15 [Uto, the serpent god], pp. 45–46 [Apophis], pp. 63–64 [demons], p. 118 [Harachte], and pp. 176–77 [serpent].

———. *Die Botschaft der Symbole: In Mythen, Kulturen und Religionen*. Munich: Kösel, 1990; see esp. pp. 179–91, "Adler und Schlange als Pole des Seins."

———, ed. *Wörterbuch der Symbolik*. Stuttgart: Alfred Kröner, 1991; see esp. p. 54 [the Asclepius' staff], p 122 [caduceus], and pp. 649–50 [the serpent].

———. *Adler und Schlange: Tiersymbolik im Glauben und Weltbild der Völker*. Tübingen: Rainer Wunderlich Verlag Hermann Leins, 1983.

———. *Götter und Symbole der alten Ägypter*. Bern, Munich, Vienna: Otto Wilhelm Barth, 1974.

———. *Lexikon der Götter und Dämonen: Namen, Funktionen, Symbole/Attribute*. Stuttgart: Kroner, 1984.

———. "Schlange," in *Lexikon der Götter und Symbole der alten Ägypter*. Bern, Munich: Scherz, 1987 [rev. ed]; pp. 176–77.

———. "Schlange," in *Wörterbuch biblischer Bilder und Symbole*. Munich: Kösel (1990) [4th ed.]; pp. 318–20.

———. *Symbol Mythos und Legende in der Kunst*. Studien zur Deutschen Kunstgeschichte 314. Baden-Baden: Valentin Koerner, 1984 [2nd ed.].

Macalister, R. A. S., and W. Dever. *Gezer II*. Jerusalem: Hebrew Union College/Nelson Glueck School of Biblical Archaeology, 1974. [A serpent was found at Gezer; it apparently belongs to the LB stratum; p. 399 and Fig. 488.]

MacCulloch, J. A. *The Celtic and Scandinavian Religions.* London: Constable, c. 1948.

———. "Serpent-Worship: Introduction," *Encyclopaedia of Religion and Ethics,* ed. J. Hastings. Edinburgh: T. & T. Clark and New York: Charles Scribner's Sons, 1920 [1962]; vol. 11, pp. 399–411.

MacKenzie, D. A. *Egyptian Myth and Legend.* New York: Bell, 1978.

Maggiani, A., ed. *Artigianato artistico.* Milan: Electa Editrice, 1985. [Illus. 68 depicted on a funeral urn is a god killing a serpent (second cent. BCE), Illus. 72 shows a demon with anguepedes on a funeral urn (late second cent. BCE).]

Mähly, J. *Die Schlange im Mythus und Cultus der classischen Völker.* Der Naturforsch. Gesellschaft von Basel zur Feier ihres 50j Bestehens gewidmet von der historischen Gesellschaft. Basel, 1867. N.V.

Malandra, W. W., ed. *An Introduction to Ancient Religion: Readings from the Avesta and the Achaemenid Inscriptions.* Minnesota Publications in the Humanities 2. Minneapolis: University of Minnesota Press, 1983.

Malinowski, B. *Myth in Primitive Psychology.* London: K. Paul, Trench, Trubner and Co., 1926.

Maneschg, H. *Die Erzählung von der ehernen Schlange (Num 21, 4–9) in der Auslegung der frühen jüdischen Literatur: Eine traditionsgeschichtliche Studie.* Europäische Hochschulschriften Reihe 23, Theologie 157. Frankfurt am Main: Peter D. Lang, 1981.

Mann, A. T., and J. Lyle. *Sacred Sexuality.* The Sacred Arts. Shaftesbury, Dorset and Rockport, Mass.: Element, 1995.

Mann, J. *Murder, Magic, and Medicine.* Oxford: Oxford University Press, 1992; see esp. p. 39.

Marchadour, A., ed. *Origine et postérité de l'évangile de Jean.* Association Catholique Française pour l'Étude de la Bible, Lectio Divina 143. Paris: Editions du Cerf, 1990.

Marcuzzi, L., and M. Zanette. *Aqvileia.* Aquileia: Società per la Conservazione della Basilica di Aquileia, 1993; see esp. p. 20 [a color photograph of the mosaic in which a large serpent-dragon swallows Jonah], p. 22 [the demon spits him out], p. 24 [a stork killing a snake above the depiction of Jesus as the Good Shepherd].

Maringer, J. "Die Schlange in Kunst und Kult der vorgeschichtlichen Menschen," *Anthropos* 72 (1977) 881–913. [This is a study of serpent images from the Paleolithic (at least 30,000 years before the present) to the Iron ages.]

Markschies, C. *Zwischen den Welten Wandern: Strukturen des antiken Christentums.* Frankfurt: Fischer Taschenbuch, 1997.

Marrs, R. "John 3.14–15: The Raised Serpent in the Wilderness: The Johannine Use of an Old Testament Account." *Johannine Studies,* ed. J. E. Priest. Malibu, Calif.: Pepperdine University Press, 1989; pp. 132–47.

Marshack, A. *The Roots of Civilization: The Cognitive Beginnings of Man's First Art, Symbol and Notation.* London: Weidenfeld and Nicolson, 1972;

see esp. Fig. 97 [a serpent from the Upper Magdalenian], 100 [a serpent, also Upper Magdalenian], 109 [a forked-tongued viper], 118 [a symbolic snake].

Martinek, M. *Wie die Schlange zum Teufel Wurde: Die Symbolik in der Paradies-geschichte von der hebräischen Bibel bis zum Koran.* Studies in Oriental Religions 37. Wiesbaden: Harrassowitz Verlag, 1996.

Martínez, F. G. *The Dead Sea Scrolls Translated: The Qumran Texts in English,* trans. W. G. E. Watson. Leiden and New York: Brill, and Grand Rapids, Mich.: Eerdmans, 1996 [2nd ed.]; see esp. pp. 330–31.

Martyn, J. L. *History and Theology in the Fourth Gospel.* Nashville: Abingdon, 1968 [2nd ed.].

Mathers, S. L. M. *The Kabbalah Unveiled.* London: Routledge and Kegan Paul, 1926; reprint, London and New York: Arkana, 1991.

Matthäus, H. *Der Arzt in römisher Zeit: Literarische Nachrichten—archäologische Denkmäler,* ed. by Ph. Filtzinger. Stuttgart: Württemberg-ischen Landesmuseums Stuttgart, 1987; see the 47 illustrations, of which many feature physicians and Asclepius with serpents.

May, H. G. *Material Remains of the Megiddo Cult.* Chicago: University of Chicago Press, 1935. [A serpent was found on a vase from a tomb dating from MB or LB; see Plate 22 (P4327).]

———. "The Sacred Tree on Palestine Painted Pottery," *Journal of the American Oriental Society* 59 (1939) 251–59.

Mazar, B. "The Middle Bronze Age in Palestine," *Israel Exploration Journal* 18 (1968) 65–97.

Mazis, G. A. *The Trickster, Magician and Grieving Man: Reconnecting Men with Earth.* Santa Fe, N.M.: Bear & Company, 1993.

Mbiti, J. *African Religions and Philosophy.* New York: Praeger, 1969.

McCasland, S. V. "The Asklepios Cult in Palestine," *Journal of Biblical Literature* 57 (1939) 221–27.

McConnel, U. "The Rainbow-Serpent in North Queensland," *Oceania* 1 (1930) 347–48.

McCown, C. C. "The Goddess of Gerasa," *Annual of the American Schools of Oriental Research* 13 (1933) 129–66.

McCullough, W. S. "Serpent," *Interpreter's Dictionary of the Bible* 4. Nashville: Abingdon, 1962; pp. 298–91.

McEwan, G. J. "ᵈMuš and Related Matters," *Orientalia* 52 (1983) 215–29.

McGinn, B. *The Foundations of Mysticism: Origins to the Fifth Century.* The Presence of God: A History of Western Christian Mysticism, vol. 1. New York: Crossroad, 1994.

McNally, S. "The Maenad in Early Greek Art," in *Women in the Ancient World: The Arethusa Papers,* ed. J. Peradotto and J. P. Sullivan. Albany: State University of New York Press, 1984; pp. 107–41. [Although not focused on the serpent, the study does present images of maenads with serpents (see esp. Figs. 3, 8, and 10).]

McPhee, I, "Ladon," in *Lexicon Iconographicum Mythologiae Classicae* 6.1, pp. 176–80 [with bibliography]; see the photographs in *LIMC* 6.2, Plates 81–85.

Mead, G. R. S. *Thrice-Greatest Hermes: Studies in Hellenistic Theosophy and Gnosis*, 3 vols. [This book was originally published in 1904; a reset third impression appeared in London: J. M. Watkins, 1964.]

Mecquenem, R. de "Inventaire de cachets et de cylindres," *Revue d'Assyriologie et d'Archéologie Orientale* 22 (1925) 1–13.

Medhi, B. K. "Snake Goddess Marai of the Pati Rabhas of Assam," *Eastern Anthropologist* 37 (1984) 159–64.

Meeks, W. A. *The Prophet-King: Moses-Traditions and the Johannine Christology*. *Novum Testamentum* Supplements 14. Leiden: Brill, 1967.

Meier, C. A. *Antike Inkubation und moderne Psychotherapie*. Zürich: Rascher Verlag, 1949.

———. "Asklepios," *The Encyclopedia of Religion*. New York: Macmillan and London: Collier/Macmillan, 1987; vol. 1, pp. 463–66.

Meier, J. "A kaga oder der Schlangenaberglaube bei den Eingeborenen der Blanchebucht (Neupommern)," *Anthropos* 3 (1908) 1005–29.

Meier-Seethaler, C. *Von der göttlichen Löwin zum Wahrzeichen männlichere Macht: Ursprung und Wandel grosser Symbole*. Zürich: Kreuz, 1993.

Mercer, S. A. B. *Horus: Royal God of Egypt*. Grafton, Massachuttes: Society of Oriental Research, 1942.

———. *The Pyramid Texts in Translation and Commentary*. New York, London, and Toronto: Longmans, Green and Co., 1952; see esp. vol. 1, pp. 188–89, 230–33, 235–39, 302–5, 318–19. [the symbol of the serpent frequently conflates with a bull].

———. *The Pyramid Texts in Translation and Commentary*. New York, London, and Toronto: Longmans, Green and Co., 1952; see esp. vol. 2, pp. 712–13, 730–31, 950–53.

Merhav, R. "The Stele of the 'Serpent Goddess' from Tell Beit Mirsim and the Plaque from Shechem Reconsidered," *Israel Museum Journal* 4 (1985) 27–42. [Merhav correctly points out that Albright's suggestion (in *BASOR* 31 [1928]) that a stele found at Tell Beit Mirsim shows a serpent coming out of the ground is misleading.]

Merkelbach, R. "Drache," in *Reallex. für Antike und Christentum* 4 (1959) 226–50.

———. *Mithras: Ein persisch-römischer Mysterienkult*. Wiesbaden: Albus, 1998; see esp. p. 91, and Plates 18, 20, 22, 23, 24, 25, 37, 39, 40, 41, 42, 44, 45, 47, 50, 51, 52, 54, 65, 66, 70, 71, 73, 74, 77, 90, 91, 95, 116, 117, 143, 144, 146, 149, 152, 153, 157, 160, 161, 162, 164, and 169.

Merloni, G. *Saggi di Filologia* Semitica. Rome, 1913; see esp. pp. 234–36, "Una serpe azdita."

Mertz, B. A. *Dein archetypisches Tier*. Munich: Ariston Verlag, 1997.

Meshel, Z. "Did Yahweh Have a Consort?" *Biblical Archaeology Review* 5 (1979) 24–35.

Meshorer, Y. *Ancient Jewish Coinage, Volume I: Persian Period Through Hasmonaeans.* Dix Hills, N.Y.: Amphora Books, 1982.

———. *Ancient Jewish Coinage, Volume II: Herod the Great Through Bar Cochba.* Dix Hills, N.Y.: Amphora Books, 1982.

Messadié, G. *The History of the Devil,* trans. M. Romano. London: Newleaf, 1996. [The work was originally published in France in slightly different form in 1993 as *Histoire générale du Diable* by Editions Robert Laffront.]

Mettinger, T. N. D. "Seraphim," *Dictionary of Deities and Demons in the Bible,* ed. by K. van der Toorn, B. Becking, and P. W. van der Horst. Leiden and Boston: Brill and Grand Rapids: Eerdmans, 1999 [2nd ed.]; pp. 742–44.

Meyer, M. W. *The Ancient Mysteries: A Sourcebook.* San Francisco: Harper & Row, 1987.

Meyer, W. with H. and R. Bukor. *100x Archäologie.* Vienna, Zürich: Bibliographisches Institut Mannheim, 1983; see esp. pp. 5–6 [Laocoon], pp. 86–87 [Artemis temple in Ephesus], pp. 90–91 [Pergamon friese in East Berlin], p. 136 [Faience statute of a "goddess" holding two serpents, from Knossos], pp. 142–43 [Asclepius and Hygieia], pp. 158–59 [Apollo with a serpent].

Meyers, C. *Discovering Eve: Ancient Israelite Women in Context.* New York and London: Oxford University Press, 1988; see esp. pp. 90–93.

Michalowski, K. *L'Art de l'ancienne Égypte.* L'Art et les grandes civilisations. Paris: Mazenrod, 1968.

Milburn, R. L. P. *Early Christian Art and Architecture.* Berkeley and Los Angeles: University of California Press, 1988; reprinted in Aldershot, England: Wildwood House, 1989.

Mildenberg, L., ed. *The Abraham Bromberg Collection of Jewish Coins,* 2 parts. Zürich: Bank Leu Numistics, 1991–199; see esp. vol. 1, pp. 12 [Herod the Great's bronze coin with winged caduceus], p 14 [Herod Archelaus' bronze coin with caduceus]; vol. 2, p. 9 [Herod the Great's bronze with winded caduceus (superb example)].

Miles, M. R. "Adam and Eve and Augustine," *Christianity and Crisis* 48 (1988) 347–49.

Milgrom, J. *Numbers.* The JPS Torah Commentary. Philadelphia and New York: The Jewish Publication Society, 1990.

Miroschedji, P. de. "Le dieu Élamite au serpent et aux eaux jaillissantes," *Iranica Antiqua* 16 (1981) 1–25, 11 Plates.

Moberly, W. "Did the Serpent Get it Right?" *Journal of Theological Studies,* N.S. 39 (1988) 1–27.

Moeller, W. O. *The Mithraic Origin and Meanings of the Rotas-Sator Square.* Études préliminaires aux religions orientales dans l'Empire Romain 38. Leiden: Brill, 1973.

Mohr, G. H. "Schlange," *Lexikon der Symbole.* Düsseldorf and Cologne: Eugen Diedrichs, 1971; pp. 255–57 [also the introduction on pp. 9–16].

Moloney, F. J. *The Johannine Son of Man*. Rome: LAS, 1976.

Montet, P. "Le jeu du serpent," *Chronique d'Égypte* 30 (1955) 189–97. [An image of a serpent, when formed into a circle by winding it from its head in the center to its tail on the circumference and often with three lions and three lionesses, represents a game played by Egyptians in antiquity.]

Montford, C.P. "The Rainbow-Serpent Myths of Australia," in *The Rainbow Serpent,* ed. I. R. Buchler and K. Maddock. Paris: Mouton, 1978; pp. 23–97.

Montgomery, J.A. *Aramaic Incantation Texts from Nippur*. Philadelphia: University Museum, 1913.

———. *A Critical and Exegetical Commentary on the Books of Kings*. The International Critical Commentary. Edinburgh: T & T Clark, 1951; see esp. pp. 500–01.

———. "A Magical Bowl Text and the Original Script of the Manicheans," *Journal of the American Oriental Society* 32 (1912) 43–48.

———. "Some Early Amulets from Palestine," *Journal of the American Oriental Society* 31 (1911) 272–81.

Moor, J. C. de. "East of Eden," *Zeitschrift für die alttestamentliche Wissenschaft* 100 (1988) 105–11.

Mosheim, J. *Geschichte der Schlangenbrüder*. 1746. N.V.

Muehly, J. *Die Schlange im Mythus und Cultus der klassischen Völker*. 1867. N.V.

Müller, U. B. *Die Geschichte der Christologie in der johanneischen Gemeinde*. Stuttgarter Bibelstudien 77. Stuttgart: KBW Verlag, 1975.

Müller-Karpe, H. *Geschichte der Steinzeit*. Augsburg: Bechtermünz Verlag, 1998. [The author claims that the serpent image appears in Egypt around 3000 BCE (Plate 14). We have seen that serpent iconography is present in the Neolithic Age or from 8000 to 3000 BCE (Plates 20 and 21). B. Mundkur shows cobras that date from about 13,000 BCE. One should also see B. Johnson, who, in *Lady of the Beasts,* argues for a serpent image from La Baume-Latrone that is 40,000–26,000 BCE, and esp. Gedion, who supplies the scientific data for the serpent art.]

Mundkur, B. *The Cult of the Serpent: An Interdisciplinary Survey of Its Manifestations and Origins*. Albany: State University of New York Press, 1983; see esp. p. 17 [three undulating "cobras" etched on a Mammoth tooth, c. 13,000 BCE].

———. "The Cult of the Serpent in the Americas: Its Asian Background," *Current Anthropology* 17 (1987) 429–55.

Murison, R. G. "The Serpent in the Old Testament," *American Journal of Semitic Languages and Literatures* 21 (1905) 115–30.

Murray, A. S. *Who's Who in Mythology: A Classic Guide to the Ancient World*. New York and Avenel, N.J.: Wings Books, 1989 [2nd ed.; originally published as *Manual of Mythology* (n.c.: n.p., 1874)].

Nebehay, C. M. *Wien: Speziell, Architektur und Malerei um 1900*. Vienna: Verlag Christian Brandstätter, 1983. [See esp. p. I/11 which presents a painting by Gustav Klimt (1899) entitled *Nuda veritas*. It depicts a nude woman with red hair and with a serpent around her feet. Also see p. 1/12, which is a depiction by Gustav Klimt (1931) of Hygieia with a large serpent curled around her right arm and drinking out of a bowl in her left hand.]

Nelson, J. B., and S. P. Longfellow, eds. *Sexuality and the Sacred: Sources for Theological Reflection*. Louisville: Westminster/John Knox Press, 1994.

Nestle, E. "Generation of Vipers," *Expository Times* 23 (1911–1912) 185. [John the Baptizer and Jesus use the expression "generation of vipers" to denote that the ones targeted "are not ordinary serpents, but venomous vipers."]

———. "Otterngezüchte," *Zeitschrift für die neutestamentliche Wissenschaft* 14 (1913) 267–68. [The Greek noun, *echidnön*, used by John the Baptizer and Jesus echoes the LXX of Isa 11:8; it denotes *semen serpentis inimicum* or *semini muleris,* and evil vipers; see the publication by U. Treu.]

Nettleship, A. "The Problem of Symbolism in Medicine, Primitive and Greek Era Symbols in Relationship to Modern Scientific Medicine," *Bull. Sign. Hist. Sci. Tech.* 17 (1963) 513–15.

Neumann, E. *The Great Mother: An Analysis of the Archetype*. Bollinger Foundation Series 47. New York: Pantheon Books, 1955.

Neusner, J. *The Ecology of Religion: From Writing to Religion in the Study of Judaism*. Nashville: Abingdon, 1989.

Newberry, P. E. "A Statue and a Scarab," *Journal of Egyptian Archaeology* 19 (1933) 53–54, Plate X.

Ninck, M. *Die Bedeutung des Wassers in Kult und Leben der Alten: Eine symbolgeschichtliche Untersuchung*. Philologus, Supplementband XIV, Heft 11. Leipzig: Dietrich, 1921.

Nissenson, M., and S. Jonas. *Snake Charm*. New York: Harry N. Abrams, 1995. [This book is full of illustrations of the snake and the discussion is focused.]

Niwiński, A. "The 21st Dynasty Religious Iconography Project Exemplified by the Scene with Three Deities Standing on a Serpent," *Akten des Vierten Internationalen Ägyptologen Kongresses München 1985,* ed. S. Schoske. Studien zur Altägyptischen Kultur Beihefte 3; Hamburg, 1989; pp. 305–14.

Nock, A. D. "Religious Symbols and Symbolism II," *Arthur Darby Nock: Essays on Religion and the Ancient World*, ed. Z. Stewart. Oxford: Clarendon Press, 1972; pp. 895–907.

———. "Two Notes," *Vigilae Christianae* 3 (1949) 48–56.

Noth, M. *Die Welt des Alten Testaments*. Berlin: A. Topelmann, 1962.

Nougayrol, J. *Cylindres-Sceaux et empreintes de cylindres trouvés en Palestine au cours de fouilles regulières*. Bibliothèque Archéologique et Historique 33. Paris: P. Geuthner, 1939.

Nowak, V., trans. *Der Schlangenknabe: Georgische Volksmärchen*. Moscow, 1977.

Nunn, J. F. *Ancient Egyptian Medicine*. London: British Museum Press, 1996.

Ogdon, J. R. "Studies in Ancient Egyptian Magical Thought IV: An Analysis of the 'Technical' Language in the Anti-Snake Magical Spells of the Pyramid Texts," *Discussions in Egyptology* 13 (1989) 59–71.

Oldham, C. F. *Ophiolatreia*. Privately printed, 1889.

———. *The Sun and Serpent: A Contribution to the History of Serpent-Worship*. London: Archibald Constable & Co., Ltd., 1905.

Oliver, J. A. *Snakes in Fact and Fiction*. New York: Macmillan, 1958.

Olson, D. T. *Numbers*. Interpretation: A Bible Commentary for Teaching and Preaching. Louisville, Ky.: John Knox Press, 1996; see esp. pp. 135–38.

Osing, J. "Sprüche gegen die . . . Schlange," *Mitteilungen des Deutschen Archäologischen Instituts Abteilung Kairo* 43 (1987) 205–10.

Osten, H. Henning von der. *Die Welt der Perser*. Grosse Kulturen der Frühzeit. Stuttgart: Gustav Kilpper Verlag, 1956. [See Plate 29, which shows a bronze idol, like the one in the JHC Collection (Fig. 16 in the present book), but here the demon holds the two serpents by the throat; from Luristan (p. 276).]

Otto, W. F. *Die Götter Griechlands: Das Bild des Göttlichen im Spiegel des griechischen Geistes*. Frankfort: G. Schulte-Bulmke, 1929.

Page, S. H. T. *Powers of Evil: A Biblical Study of Satan and Demons*. Grand Rapids, Mich.: Baker, 1995.

Pagels, E. *Adam, Eve, and the Serpent*. New York: Random House, 1988; paperback New York: Vintage Books (1989).

———. "Adam and Eve and the Serpent in Genesis 1–3," *Images of the Feminine in Gnosticism*, ed. K. L. King. Philadelphia: Fortress Press, 1988; pp. 412–23.

———. *Satan in the New Testament Gospels*. The Loy H. Witherspoon Lectures in Religious Studies at the University of North Carolina, Charlotte. Charlotte: University of North Carolina, Charlotte, 1994.

Pailler, J. M. "La vierge et le serpent," *Mélanges de l'École Française de Rome: Antiquité* 109 (1997) 513–75.

Pancaro, S. *The Law in the Fourth Gospel. Novum Testament* Supplements 42. Leiden: Brill, 1975; see esp. p. 333.

Paper, J. "The Meaning of the 'T'ao-T'ieh," *History of Religion* 18 (1978) 18–37.

Parássoglou, G. M. "A Christian Amulet Against Snakebite," *Studia Papyrologica* 13 (1974) 107–10 [P. Yale Inv. 1792].

Pardee, D. "Philological and Prosodic Analysis of the Ugaritic Serpent Incantation UT 607," *Journal of the Ancient Near Eastern Society of Columbia University* 10 (1978) 73–108.

Paribeni, E. "Harmonia," in *Lexicon Iconographicum Mythologiae Classicae* 4.1, pp. 412–14 [bibliography]; see the photographs in *LIMC* 4.2, Plates 238–40.

———. "Harmatidas," in *Lexicon Iconographicum Mythologiae Classicae* 4.1, pp. 412–14 [bibliography]; see the photographs in *LIMC* 4.2, Plates 163–87.

Parrinder, G. *African Mythology*. New York: P. Bedrick Books, 1986 [rev. ed.]; see esp. pp. 56–65.

———. *The Hebrew Goddess*. New York: KTAV, 1967.

Patai, R. "The Goddess Asherah," *Journal of Near Eastern Studies* 24 (1965) 37–52.

Patte, D. *Early Jewish Hermeneutic in Palestine.* Society of Biblical Literature Dissertation Series 22. Missoula, Montana: Scholars Press, 1975; see esp. pp. 218ff.

Paul-Stengel, C. *Schlangenspuren: Reptilen und ihre Bedeutung in der Kulturgeschichte.* Königstein/Taunus: Ulrike Helmer Verlag, 1996; see the following Illus.: p. 21 [a serpent on a cross], p. 22 [Hermes], p. 48 [Moses with the upraised serpent], p. 132 [Aborigine serpent], p. 157 [expulsion from Eden], p. 177 [a woman's face and breasts, with a serpent's body].

Pederson, J. "Wisdom and Immortality," *Wisdom in Israel and in the Ancient Near East,* ed. M. Noth and D. W. Thomas. Supplements to *Vetus Testamentum* 3. Leiden: Brill, 1960; pp. 238–46.

Pelton, R. W., and K. W. Carden. *Snake Handlers: God-Fearers or Fanatics?* New York and Nashville: Thomas Nelson, 1974. [See the book by W. La Barre.]

Perrot, A. "L'homme aux serpents," *Syria* 28 (1951) 57–61.

Perrot, N. *La représentation de l'arbre sacré sur les monuments de Mésopotamie et d'Elam.* Paris: P. Geuthner, 1937.

Peters, H. von Stokar, "Zur Herkunft des Äskulapstabes," *Therapeutische Berichte* 16 (1939) 57–60.

Petrie, F. *Ancient Gaza I.* Jerusalem: British School of Archeology, 1931. [More than two vessels with serpents were discovered from the MB stratum; see Plate 35 and pp. 9–10, 112–13.]

Philastrius. *Diversarum Herseon Liber.* Corpus Christianorum Series Latina 9. Turnholt: Typographi Brepolis Editores Pontificii, 1957.

Phillips, E. A. "Serpent Intertexts: Tantalizing Twists in the Tales," *Bulletin for Biblical Research* 10 (2000) 233–45.

Philo. *De Agricultura,* in *Philo 3,* trans. F. H. Colson and G. H. Whitaker. Loeb Classical Library. London: William Heinemann and New York: G. P. Putnam's Sons, 1930; see esp. pp. 156–65.

Philpott, J. H. *The Sacred Tree, or the Tree in Religion and Myth.* New York: Macmillan, 1897; see esp. pp. 15–23. [The perennial tree, like the serpent, renews itself each year, thus symbolizing rebirth.]

Piankoff, A., trans. *Mythological Papyri.* 2 vols., ed. N. Rambova. Bollingen Series 15, 3, Parts 1/2. New York: Pantheon Books, 1957.

Piccione, P. A. "Mehen, Mysteries, and Resurrection from the Coiled Serpent," *Journal of the American Center in Egypt* 27 (1990) 43–52. [The *mḥn* game was a means of transformation to rebirth.]

Picot, J.-P. "Genèse et récits contemporains de contre-utopie: Eve et le serpent," in *La Bible: Images, Mythes et Traditions.* Cahiers de l'Hermétisme. Paris: Albin Michel, 1995; pp. 45–60.

Piddington, R. "The Water-Serpent in Karadjeri Mythology," *Oceania* 1 (1930) 352–76.

Pietschmann, R. "Asklepios," *Pauly-Wissowa* 4 (Stuttgart: J. B. Metzlersche, 1896) cols. 1642–69.

Piggot, J. *Japanese Mythology*. London, 1969.

Pinney, R. *The Animals in the Bible*. Philadelphia, New York: Chilton Books, 1964; see esp. pp. 17–18, 173–76.

Piperov, P. "Die Symbolik der Schlange bei den biblischen Schriftstellern," *Jb. der geistlichen Akademie* 32 (Sofia, 1957) 369–90.

Plantinga, C. Jr. "Christ, the Snake," *Perspectives* 6 (1991) 14–15.

Pleyte, C. M. "Die Schlange im Volksglauben der Indonesier," *Globus* 65 (1894) 95–100.

Poignant, R. *Oceanic Mythology: The Myths of Polynesia, Micronesia, Melanesia, Australia*. London: Hamlyn, 1967.

Pope, M. "The Scene on the Drinking Mug from Ugarit," in *Near Eastern Studies in Honor of William Foxwell Albright,* ed. H. Goedicke. Baltimore and London: Johns Hopkins Press, 1971; pp. 393–405.

Popham, M. R. " 'Snakes and Ladders' at Knossos: The Shifting Late Minoan Stratigraphy," *Kadmos* 13 (1974) 11–23.

Porada, E. *Corpus of Ancient Near Eastern Seals in North American Collections*. Vol. 1. The Collection of the Pierpont Morgan Library. New York: Pantheon Books, 1948.

———. "A Man with Serpents," in *Von Uruk nach Tuttul* [*Festschrift E. Strommenger*], ed. B. Hrouda et al. Munich and Vienna, 1992; pp. 171–75 and Plates 72–78. [In the Cincinnati Art Museum is a figure of a nude man with two fish hanging from a neck ring that fits below his beard. His arms are bound by four snakes that come from behind him; two snakes curl to face his beard and the heads of two more appear above his waist.]

Potter, E. S. *Serpents in Symbolism, Art and Medicine*. Santa Barbara, Calif., 1937.

Pottier, E. *L'art Hittite,* 2 vols. Paris: P. Geuthner, 1926–1931.

———. "Draco," *Dictionnaire des antiquités grecques et romaines d'après les textes et les monuments*. Paris: Librairie Hachette et CIE, 1892; vol. 2.1, pp. 403–14.

———. *Man and Images in the Ancient Near East*. The Frick Collection: Anshen Transdisciplinary Lectureships in Art, Science, and the Philosophy of Culture, Monograph 4. Wakefield, R.I., and London: Moyer Bell, 1995; see esp. pp. 39–46, 63.

Preston, P. *Metzler Lexikon Antiker Bildmotive,* trans. S. Bogutovac and K. Brodersen. Stuttgart: Weimer, 1997 [English original appeared in 1983]; see esp. pp. 165–69.

Price, I. M. *The Great Cylinder Inscriptions A and B of Gudea*. Leipzig: J. C. Hinrichs, 1899 [King Gudea of Lagash linked the bull with the serpent and represented them at the portal of a temple; see Cylinder A, col. 26, lines 24–25.]

Prigent, P. *L'image dans le Judaisme du IIe au VIe Siècles*. Le monde de la bible 24. Geneva: Labors et Fides, 1991.

Pritchard, J. B. *Ancient Near Eastern Texts Relating to the Old Testament.* Princeton, N. J.: Princeton University Press, 1950. [For an image of a serpent related to worshipping Nabu, see p. 331.]

———. *The Ancient Near East in Pictures Relating to the Old Testament.* Princeton, N. J.: Princeton University Press, 1954. [For LB and Iron I depictions of a goddess holding serpents; see nos. 470–74.]

———. *The Bronze Age Cemetery at Gibeon.* Philadelphia: University of Pennsylvania, 1963. [Jugs with serpents were found in the Hyksos stratum.]

———. *Palestinian Figurines in Relation to Certain Goddesses Known Through Literature.* New Haven: American Oriental Society, 1943.

Probatake, Th. M. *Ο ΔΙΑΒΟΛΟΣ ΕΙΣ ΤΗΝ ΒΥΖΑΝΤΙΝΗΝ ΤΕΧΝΗΝ.* Thessaloníki: n.p., 1980; see esp. pp. 131–67, 306–25 [original English = *The Devil in Byzantine Imagination.* Thessalonika, 1980; see esp. pp. 131–67].

Provera, M. "Il tema e culto del serpente nella tradizione biblica e profana," *Bibbia e Oriente* 166 (1990) 209–214. [In Jn 3:14 the serpent symbolism is positive (p. 213). Ophiolatria is the most ancient, widespread, and important of human traditions (p. 214).]

Prury, A. de. *Homme et animal dieu les créa: Les animaux et l'ancien testament.* Genéve: Labors et Fides, 1993.

Quinones, R. J. *The Changes of Cain: Violence and the Lost Brother in Cain and Abel Literature.* Princeton, N.J.: Princeton University Press, 1991.

Radbill, S. X. "The Symbolism of the Staff of Aesculapius as Illustrated by Medical Bookplates," *Journal of the Albert Einstein Medical Center* 10 (1962) 108–19.

Radcliffe-Brown, A. R. "The Rainbow Serpent Myth in South-East Australia," *Oceania* 1 (1930) 342–46.

Rawlinson, A. "Nāgas and the Magical Cosmology of Buddhism," *Religion* 16 (1986) 135–53.

Réau, L. *Iconographie de l'art chrétien.* Paris: Presses Universitaires de France, 1958.

Reeve, M. D. "A Rejuvenated Snake," *Acta Antiqua: Academiae Scientiarum Hungaricae* 37 (1996/1997) 245–58.

Reichel-Dolmatoff, G. *Amazonian Cosmos: The Sexual and Religious Symbolism of the Tukano Indians,* trans. G. Reichel-Dolmatoff. Chicago: University of Chicago Press, 1971.

Reifenberg, A. *Ancient Hebrew Seals.* London: East and West Library, 1950.

Reinach, S. "Divinités Gauloises au Serpent," *Revue Archéologique* 65 (1911) 221–56.

———. "Le Serpent et la Femme," *L'Anthropologie* 16 (1905) 178–80. [Reinach's "new" exegesis of Genesis 3 is to perceive the miseries of menstruation and childbirth on the daughters of Eve by pointing out that in Iran menstruation is deemed to be caused by demons, esp. Angra Manyu, who is symbolized by the serpent.]

———. "Zagreus, le serpent cornu," *Revue Archéologique* 3rd Ser. 35 (1899) 210–17. [At the heart of Orphism is the birth, death, and resurrection of Zagreus who appears inconographically as a serpent with a small crown.]

Reitzenstein, R. *Poimandres.* Leipzig: B. G. Teubner, 1904; see esp. pp. 81–101 [for Ophites].

Rengstorf, K. H. *Die Anfänge der Auseinandersetzung zwischen Christusglaube und Asklepiosfrömigkeit.* Münster: Verlag Aschendorff, 1953.

Renker, G. *Verkanntes Schlangenvolk.* Hameln and Hannover: Sponholz Verlag, 1966.

Renz, B. "Die kluge Schlange," *Biblische Zeitschrift* 24 (1938/39) 236–41.

———. *Der orientalische Schlangendrache: Ein Beitrag zum Verständnis der Schlange im biblischen Paradies.* Augsburg, 1930.

———. "Schlange und Baum als Sexualsymbole in der Völkerkunde," *Archiv für Sexualforschung* 1 (1915–1916) 341ff. [Renz interprets the serpent as a phallic symbol.]

Richards, L. O. *The Revell Concise Bible Dictionary.* Tarrytown, N.Y.: Fleming R. Revell Co., 1990.

Richardson, P. "Religion, Architecture, and Ethics: Some First Century Case Studies," *Horizons in Biblical Theology* 10 (1988) 19–49; see esp. pp. 27–29 on the Asclepian cult.

Richter, W. "Schlange," *Der Kleine Pauly* 5 (1975) 12–17.

Ridgway, B. S. "The Plataian Tripod and the Serpent Columns," *American Journal of Archaeology* 81 (1977) 374–79.

Riley, G. J. "Demon," *Dictionary of Deities and Demons in the Bible,* ed. K. van der Toorn, B. Becking, and P. W. van der Horst. Leiden and Boston: Brill and Grand Rapids: Eerdmans, 1999 [2nd ed.]; pp. 235–40.

Rinaldi, G. "Serpente di Bronzo," *Enciclopedia Cattolica.* Vatican: Libro Cattolico, 1953; vol. 11, cols. 394–95.

Ringgren, H. "Handskrifterna från Qumran," *Symbolae Biblicae Upsalienses* 15 (1956) 41ff.

———. *Israelite Religion,* trans. D. Green. Philadelphia: Fortress, 1966. [Ringgren argues that the serpent of Genesis 3 is to be identified with either El, the supreme god in the Ugaritic pantheon, or Baal, the god of lightning and storms.]

Ritter, H. *Die Schlange in der Religion der Melanesier.* Acta Tropica Suppl. 3. Basel, 1945; see esp. pp. 26–27, 65–68, 73–74.

Rivett-Carnac, J. R. "The Snake Symbol in India, Especially in Connection with the Worship of Śiva," *Journal of the Anthropological Society of Bombay* 1 (1879) 17ff.

Rivinus, T. A. *Sive serpens iste antiquus seductor è Gen. III.1. seqq. ad mentem doctorum Judaeorum & Christianorum dissertatione inaugurali exhibitus.* Leipzig, 1686.

Robert, M. L. "Dans une maison d'Éphèse: Un serpent et un chiffre," *Académie des Inscriptions & Belles-Lettres: Comptes Rendus* (1982) 126–32.

————. "Le serpent Glycon d'Abônouteichos à Athènes et Artémis d'Éphèse à Rome," *Académie des Inscriptions & Belles-Lettres: Comptes Rendus* (1981) 513–35.

Roberts, M. J. *Mythologie der Wikinger.* Kettweg: Athenaion Verlag, 1997; for the serpent, see pp. 24, 45, 51, 56–57 [Jormungand, the serpent, swallowing his tail like Aion], 95, 99, 100, 104 [Jormungand again].

Robinson, E. *The Language of Mystery.* London: SCM Press, 1987 and Philadelphia: Trinity Press International, 1987.

Robinson, H. W. "Council of Yahweh," *Journal of Theological Studies* 45 (1944) 151–57.

Rock, J. F. *The Na-khi Nâga Cult and Related Ceremonies.* Series Orientale Roma 4/1.2. Rome: Is. M. E. O., 1952.

Roe, P. G. "Of Rainbow Dragons and the Origin of Designs: The Waiwal and Shipibo Ronin Ehua," *Latin American Indian Literatures Journal* 5 (1989) 1–67.

Röhrich, L. *"Die Sagen vom Schlangenbaum,"* Sage und Märchen. Freiburg: Herder, 1976; pp. 195–209.

————. *"Die Sagen vom Schlangenbaum" Festschrift für Kurt Ranke.* Göttingen, 1968; pp. 327–44.

————. "Schlange," *Lexikon der sprichwörtlichen Redensarten.* Freiburg, Vienna: Herder, 1973; vol. 3, pp. *849–50.*

Roitman, A. "Crawl upon your belly' (Gen 3.14): The Physical Aspect of the Serpent in Early Jewish Exegesis," *Tarbiz* 64 (1994) 157–82 [Hebrew; serpents with legs; see the many illustrations].

Römer, W. H. Ph., "Miscellanea Sumerologica IIIa: Eine Beschwörung in sumerischer Sprache gegen die Folgen von Schlangend Hundebiß, sowie Skorpionenstich," *Vom Alten Orient zum Alten Testament [Festschrift W. F. von Soden]*, ed. M. Dietrich and O. Loretz. Alter Orient und Altes Testament 240. Neukirchen-Vluyn: Butzon & Bercker Kevelaer, 1995; pp. 413–23.

Ronecker, J. P. *Le symbolisme animal: Mythes, croyances, légendes, archétypes, folklore, imaginaire . . .* St-Jean-de-Braye: Editions Dangles, 1994.

Roquefeuil, S. De. "Le serpent d'Asclépios-Esculape," *Le bestiaire,* ed. P. Dehaye et al. Paris, 1974.

Ross, A. *Pagan Celtic Britain.* London: Routledge & Kegan Paul, Ltd., 1967.

Rothenberg, B. *Timna.* London: Thames and Hudson, 1972.

Rouse, W. H. D. *Gods, Heroes, and Men of Ancient Greece: Mythology's Great Tales of Valor and Romance.* New York and Scarborough, Ontario: Mentor, 1957.

Rousselle, E. "Drachen und Stute-Gestalten der mythischen Welt," *Eranos-Jahrbuch 1934.* Zürich: Rhein-Verlag, 1935; pp. 11–33.

Rowe, A. *A Catalogue of Egyptian Scarabs, Scaraboids, Seals and Amulets in the Palestine Archaeological Museum.* Cairo, 1936.

————. *The Four Canaanite Temples of Beth-shan. Part I: The Temples and Cult Objects.* Philadelphia: University of Pennsylvania Press, 1940. [A serpent with breasts was found in an LB stratum; see Plate 42A:2.]

————. "Note on Serpent-cult at Palestine," *Palestine Exploration Fund Quarterly Statement* 61 (1928) 110. [Rowe argued that what has been seen as "two small rude bird figures" on a vessel from the "High Place" at Tell eṣ-Ṣâfi are "figures of serpents in *uraeus*-form." He offered the opinion that the two serpents may represent Nekhebit and Wadjet.]

Rowley, H. H. "Zadok and Nehushtan," *Journal of Biblical Literature* 58 (1939) 113–42.

Ruckstuhl, E. "Abstieg und Erhöhung des johanneischen Menschensohns," in *Jesus im Horizont der Evangelien,* ed. E. Ruckstuhl. SBAB 3. Stuttgart: Katholisches Bibelwerk, 1933; pp. 277–310.

Rudolf, W. "Um die historische Existenz Aeskulaps," *Mediz. Klin.* 11 (1960) 442ff.

Rudwin, M. *The Devil in Legend and Literature.* La Salle, Ill.: The Open Court Publishing Company, 1931.

Ruppert, L. "Die Sündenfallerzählung (Gn 3) in vorjahwistischer Tradition und Interpretation," *Biblische Zeitschrift* (1971) 185–202.

Russell, J. B. *The Devil: Perceptions of Evil from Antiquity to Primitive Christianity.* Ithaca, N.Y. and London: Cornell University Press, 1977.

————. *Lucifer: The Devil in the Middle Ages.* Ithaca, N.Y., and London: Cornell University Press, 1984.

————. *The Prince of Darkness: Radical Evil and the Power of Good in History.* Ithaca, N.Y. and London: Cornell University Press, 1988.

————. *Satan: The Early Christian Tradition.* Ithaca, N.Y., and London: Cornell University Press, 1981.

Rüttimann, R. J. *Asclepius and Jesus: The Form, Character and Status of the Asclepius Cult in the Second Century CE and its Influence on Early Christianity.* Harvard Divinity School, ThD, 1986.

Saladino, V. *Belser Kunstbibliothek: Die Meisterwerke aus den Uffizien in Florenz, Antike Skulpturen,* trans. C. Galliani. Florence: Arte e Pensiero, 1983; see esp. "Persephone-Sarkphag" on pp. 38–39, "Asklepius" on pp. 52–53, and "Herakles als Schlangentöter" on pp. 76–77. [See the photograph (p. 39) of a sarcophagus of Persephone showing, in high relief, two raised serpents (without wings) pulling a chariot. Hades (Pluto) holds the dead Persephone (Proserpina). The marble work dates from the second century CE. It is in the Collection of Michelozzi. Also see the photograph (p. 53) of Asclepius holding in his right arm a staff with an entwined serpent. The white marble stature is a Roman copy that is based on a Greek original of c. 370 BCE. It is in the Villa Medici in Rome. Finally, note the depiction of Hercules, as a child, fighting a serpent (p. 77). The art work, now in the Tribuna of Uffizien, is an Italian marble based on a Greek original of the third century BCE.]

Sälzle, K. *Tier und Mensch, Gottheit und Dämon: Das Tier in der Geistesgeschichte der Menschheit.* Munich: Bayerischer Landwirtschaftsverlag, 1965. [This massive book is full of important data and insight; see esp. pp. 258–68.]

Samonà, G. A. *Il sole, la terra, il serpente: Antichi miti di morte, interpretazioni moderne e problemi di comparazione storico-religiosa.* Chi Siamo 21. Rome: Bulzoni Editore, 1991.

Sandars, N. K. *The Epic of Gilgamesh: An English Version with an Introduction.* Baltimore, Md.: Penguin, 1960.

Sander, F. *Hoch und Heilig: Kosmische Symbole und ihre Deutung.* Königsburg-Stein: Verlag Hans Schöner, 1993; see pp. 88–89, 100, 181, 190–91, 204, 211, and 239.

Sarna, N. "The Chirotonic Motif on the Lachish Altar," in *Investigations at Lachish: The Sanctuary and the Residency (Lachish V),* ed. Y. Aharoni. Tel Aviv: Gateway Publishing, Inc., 1975.

————. *Understanding Genesis: The Heritage of Biblical Israel.* New York: The Melton Research Center of the Jewish Theological Seminary of America, 1966 [paperback, New York: Schocken Books, 1970].

Sas-Zaloziecky, W. *Die altchristliche Kunst.* Ullstein Kunstgeschichte 7. West-Berlin: Ullstein Bücher, 1963; see esp. the depictions of the serpent in Eden on sarcophagi (Illus. 10, 11) and on the ceiling of a catacomb (Illus. 16).

Sauer, G. *Traumbild Schlange: Von der Vereinigung der Gegensätze . . . Träume als Wegweiser.* Freiburg: Walter Verlag, 1992 [3rd ed.]; see esp. the Illus. on p. 10 [a diptych with Asklepios and Hygieia, God creating Adam with the serpent encircled around Adam (by Blake)], and p. 77 [Pesttaler showing the crucifixion on one side and Moses' raised serpent on the other].

Sauerländer, W. *Die Skulptur des Mittelalters.* Ullstein Kunstgeschichte 11. West Berlin: Ullstein Bucher, 1963; see esp. color photograph No. 4 [bishop's miter in the form of a serpent) and Illus. 5 (the dragon-like serpent, with arms, in Eden].

Sauneron, S. *Un traité Égyptien d'ophiologie.* Bibliothèque générale 11. Cairo: Publication de l'Institut Français d'Archéologie Orientale, 1989 [a study of Pap. Brooklyn Museum, Nos. 47.218.48 and 47.218.85].

————. *Le Papyrus magique illustré de Brooklyn [Brooklyn Museum 47.218.156].* Wilbour Monographs 3. Oxford, New York: Brooklyn Museum, 1970.

Sauren, H. *Der Genius der Sonne und der Stab des Asklepios.* Leuven: Peeters, 1979.

Sawyer, J. F. A. "The Image of God, the Wisdom of Serpents, and the Knowledge of Good and Evil," in *A Walk in the Garden: Biblical, Iconographical and Literary Images of Eden,* ed. P. Morris and D. Sawyer. JSOTS 136; Sheffield: Sheffield Academic Press, 1992; pp. 64–73.

Sayce, A. H. "The Serpent in Genesis," *Expository Times* 20 (1909) 562 [Sayce claims "that the serpent in Genesis is a symbol of the Babylonian god Ea." More recently, the tendency is to look to Canaan for the source of the symbolism in Genesis.]

————. "Serpent Worship in Ancient and Modern Egypt." *Contemporary Review* (October 1893). N.V.

Schadewaldt, H. "Asklepios und Christus," *Medizinische Welt* (1967) 1755–61.

———. "Symbole in Medizin und Pharmazie," *Deutsche Apotheker-Zeitung* (1961) 1161–68.

———. "Was hat die Schlange Asklepios mit ihm und seiner Funktion als Heilgott zu tun?" *Asklepios* 3 (1955) 86.

Schaefer, E. H. *The Divine Woman: Dragon Ladies and Rain Maidens*. San Francisco: North Point Press, 1980.

———. "Les fouilles de Ras-Shamra-Ugarit, quinzième campagne (printemps 1937)," *Syria* 19 (1938) 193–255. [A serpent allegedly seeking water was found in a tomb in the MB stratum (was the serpent shown guarding water and the area?).]

Schaeffer, C. F. A. *Beschwörungsformel, gegen Schlangenbisse: Neue Entdeckungen in Ugarit*. Archiv für Orientforschung 20. (1963). N.V.

Schechter, H. *The Bosom Serpent: Folklore and Popular Art*. Iowa City: University of Iowa Press, 1988.

Schimmel, A. "Schlange," *Religion in Geschichte und Gegenwart [Dritte]*, ed. H. F. v. Campenhausen et al. Tübingen: Mohr (Siebeck), 1961; vol. 5, col. 1419–20.

Schirmann, J. "The Battle Between Behemoth and Leviathan According to an Ancient Hebrew *Piyyut*," *Proceedings of the Israel Academy of Sciences and Humanities* 4.13 (1970) 327–69.

Schlatter, D. A. *Der Evangelist Johannes: Wie er Spricht, Denkt und Glaubt*. Stuttgart: Calwer, 1930; see esp. pp. 95–97.

Schlüter, M. *Derāgōn und Götzendienst: Studien zur antiken judischen Religionsgeschichte*. Frankfurt am Main: Peter Lang, 1982.

Schmerber, H. *Die Schlange des Paradieses. Religionsgeschichtlich-kunsthistorische Studie*. Strassburg: Heitz, 1905.

Schmidt, K. P., and R. F. Inger. *Knaurs Tierreich in Farben: Reptilien*. Munich, Zürich, 1970.

Schmidt, M. *Der Basler Medeasarkophag*. Monumenta Artis Antiquae 3. Tübingen: Verlag Ernst Wasmuth, 1997. [Plate 58 depicts a cult vase from Lakisch with the symbol of the god Ningischzida, holding an upraised staff before which is an upraised and elegant serpent (p. 64). Plate 83 shows a stele of Tukultininurtas II from Terqa with the god holding up a serpent.]

Schmökel, H. *Ur, Assur und Babylon: Drei Jahrtausende im Zweistromland*. Grosse Kulturen der Frühzeit. Stuttgart: Gustav Kilpper Verlag, 1955.

Schnackenburg, R. "Die 'situationsgelösten' Redestücke in Joh 3," *Zeitschrift für die neutestamentliche Wissenschaft* 49 (1958) 88–99.

Schnalke, T. with C. Selheim. *Asklepios: Heilgott und Heilkult*. Erlangen-Nürnberg: Instituts für Geschichte der Medizin der Friedrich-Alexander-Universität, 1990.

Schneemann, G., and J. Heller, "Feuerschlangen in Num 21, 4–9," *Communio Viatorum* 20 (1977) 251–58.

Schneemelcher, W.-P., "Zur Gestalt der Eva in der Gnosis, in *Hairesis [Festschrift K. Hoheisel]*. Jahrbuch für Antike und Christentum Ergänzungsband 34. Münster: Aschendorff, 2002; pp. 48–63.

Schoebel, G. *Le mythe de la femme et du serpent.* Paris, 1876. N.V.

Schouten, J. *The Rod and Serpent of Asklepios, Symbol of Medicine.* Amsterdam, New York, 1967.

———. *De Slangestaf van Asklepios als Symbool van de Geneeskunde.* Utrecht: Schotnus & Jens, 1963.

Schouten van der Velden, A. "Palästina Viper," *Tierwelt der Bibel.* Stuttgart: Deutsche Bibelgesellschaft, 1992; pp. 150–51, with a color photograph.

Schramm, A. "Ophites," in *Paulys Realencyclopädie der classischen Altertumswissenschaft,* 35. Stuttgart: J. C. Mezlersche, 1939; cols. 658–59.

Schuchhardt, W.-H. *Griechische Kunst.* Ullstein Kunstgeschichte 5. West-Berlin: Ullstein Bücher, 1964; see esp. Fig. 3 [Hercules with hydra], colored photograph 3 [raised cobras], Illus. 13 [gorgon with two serpents entwined as a belt], Illus. 64–66 [Pergamon friese], and Illus. 76 [Laocoon].

Schulmann, D. "The Serpent and the Sacrifice: An Anthill Myth from Tiruvārūr," *History of Religion* 18 (1978) 107–37.

Schulz, R., and K. Sabri Kolta, "Schlangen, Skorpione und feindliche Mächte: Ein koptisch-arabische Schutzspruch," *Biblische Notizen* 93 (1998) 89–104.

Schulz, R., and M. Seidel, eds. *Ägypten: Die Welt der Pharaonen.* Cologne: Könemann Verlagsgesellschaft, 1997; see esp. p. 221 [the sun god in a bark pulled by two groups of men and following a serpent]; p. 437 [Horus holding two serpents in each hand], pp. 446–47 [the sun god pulled by four jackals and four cobra-kings, and riding in a bark supported by a large serpent].

Schulz, S. *Untersuchungen zur Menschensohn-Christologie im Johannesevangelium.* Göttingen: Vandenhoeck & Ruprecht, 1957; see esp. pp. 104–9.

Schütz, J. *Serpens Antiquus: Die alte Schlange. Das ist: Der Sacraments Teuffel.* Eisleben: Andream Petri, 1580. [This work illustrates the denigration of serpent symbolism.]

Schwartz, F. L. W. *Die altgriech. Schlangengottheiten.* Berlin: Nauck, 1858.

Scott, E. F. "Ophitism," *Encyclopaedia of Religion and Ethics,* ed. by J. Hastings. Edinburgh: T. & T. Clark and New York: Charles Scribner's Sons, 1917 [1961]; vol. 9, pp. 499–501.

Seebass, H. "Biblisch-theologischer Versuch zu Num 20, 1–13 und 21, 4–9," "Altes Testament—Forschung und Wirkung: Festschrift für Henning Graf Reventlow,* ed. by P. Mommer and W. Thiel. Frankfurt and New York: Peter Lang, 1994; pp. 219–29.

Seel, O. *Der Physiologus: Tiere und ihre Symbolik.* Zürich: Artemis & Winkler Verlag, 1995 [7th ed.]; see esp. pp. 18–21 [concerning the asp and serpent], p. 77 [stork with a serpent]. [This work is primarily a Christian meditation.]

Seele, K. C. "Horus on the Crocodiles," *Journal of Near Eastern Studies* 6 (1947) 43–52. [Note the two thirteenth cent. BCE depictions of Horus controlling snakes.]

Seethaler, P. A. "Kleiner Diskussionsbeitrag zu Gen 3, 1–5," *Biblische Zeitschrift* N.F. 23 (1979) 85–86.

Servier, J. "Le miroir du serpent," *Spiegelung in Mensch und Kosmos,* ed. R. Rit-sema. Frankfurt am Main: Insel Verlag, 1988.

Sethe, K. *Amun und die acht Urgötter von Hermopolis: Eine Untersuchung über Ursprung und Wesen des Ägyptischen Götterkönigs.* Berlin: Verlag der Akademie der Wissenschaften and Walter De Groyter and Co., 1929; see esp. pp. 26–27, 55, 124.

―――. *Imhotep, der Asklepios der Ägypter.* Leipzig: J. C. Hinrichs, 1902.

Shalit, L. "How Moses Turned a Staff into a Snake and Back Again," *Biblical Archaeology Review* 9, No. 3 (1983) 72–73.

Shuker, K. *Drachen: Mythologie—Symbolik—Geschichte.* Augsburg: Bechter-münz Verlag, 1997 [English original of 1995 by Marshall Editions, Ltd., London]; see esp. "Schlangendrachen" on pp. 11–38, "Fliegende Drachen [oder Schlange]" on pp. 77–94, and also p. 55 [Old Babylonian cylinder seal with a serpent], pp. 70–71 [Ishtar gate], and p. 107 [Hercules and the serpents].

Siegel, R. H. "The Serpent and the Dove: Christabel and the Problem of Evil," *Imagination and the Spirit,* ed. C. A. Huttar. Grand Rapids, Mich.: Eerd-mans, 1971.

Sietto, G. B. *Ta Eleus . . . niva Musthvria.* Musthri . . . ake "Paradosei" 23. Athens: Purino "Kosmo," 1993.

―――. *Ta Puqagovreia Musthvria.* Musthri . . . ake" Paradosei" 19. Athens: Purino "Kosmo," 1993.

Silberman, L. H. "Paul's Viper," *Foundations and Facets Forum* 8 (1992) 247–53. [While focusing on Acts 28:3–6, Silberman demonstrates from Greek and Hebrew sources that the concept of a snake as the dispenser of divine judgment "was far more widespread than some commentators bothered to learn."]

Simon, E. "Hesperides," in *Lexicon Iconographicum Mythologiae Classicae* 5.1, pp. 394–407 [bibliography]; see the photographs in *LIMC* 5.2, Plates 287–91.

―――. "Laokoon," in *Lexicon Iconographicum Mythologiae Classicae* 6.1, pp. 196–201 [bibliography]; see the photographs in *LIMC* 6.2, Plates 94–95.

Sist, L. "Stele magica con figurazione di dea serpente da aninoe," *Vicino Oriente* 1 (1978) 93–97.

Smelik, K. A., and E. A. Hemelrijk, " 'Who Knows Not What Monsters Demented Egypt Worships?': Opinions on Egyptian Animal Worship in Antiquity as Part of the Ancient Conception of Egypt," *ANRW* II.17.4 (1984) 1852–2000.

Smit, D. I. O. "Serpens aut Daemonium?" in *Miscellanea Biblica et Orientalia,* ed. A. Metzinger. Studia Anselmiana 27–28; Rome: Herder, 1951; pp. 94–97 [a study of Gen 4:7].

Smith, J. Z. "Towards Interpreting Demonic Powers in Hellenistic and Roman Antiquity," *ANRW* II.16.1 (1978) 425–39.

Smith, R. *Lectures on Religions of the Semites*. London: A. C. Black, 1894; see esp. pp. 120, 133, 168.

Smith, S. "What Were the Teraphim?" *Journal of Theological Studies* 33 (1932) 33–36.

Smith, W., and S. Cheetham, eds. "Serpent," *A Dictionary of Christian Antiquities* 2 London: John Murray, 1880, 1889–91.

Smith, W. R. *The Religion of the Semites: The Fundamental Institutions*. New York: Meridian Books, 1956; see esp. pp. 118–35, 166–73, 441–43.

Smith, W. S. *The Art and Architecture of Ancient Egypt*. Pelican History of Art. Harmondsworth, 1965.

Smyth-Florentin, F. *Les mythes illégitimes*. Entrée Libre 30. Geneva: Labor et Fides, 1994.

Sobel, H. *Hygieia: Die Göttin der Gesundheit*. Darmstadt: Wissenschaftliche Buchgesellschaft, 1990; see esp. the forty illustrations (numbered per page); most important, see Illus. 3b [Hygieia, Asclepius, and a large serpent], Illus. 7a, 8b, 9a, 11b [Hygieia with a serpent], 18a [Hygieia, Asclepius, and the serpent].

Soden, W. von. *Grundriss der Akkadischen Grammatik*. Rome: Pontificium Institutum Biblicum, 1952; see esp. §56r.

———. "Verschlüsselte Kritik an Salomo in der Urgeschichte des Jahwisten?" *Die Welt des Orients* 7 (1974) 228–40.

Soggin, J. A. "La caduta dell'unomo nel terzo capitolo della Genesi," *Studi e Materiali di Storia delle Religioni* 33 (1962) 227–56.

Speiser, E. A. *Excavations at Tepe Gawra I: Levels I–VIII*. Philadelphia: University of Pennsylvania Press, 1935; see esp. pp. 111–12 [at least seventeen bronze serpents were found in EB strata].

———. "Preliminary Excavations at Tepe Gawra," *Annual of the American Schools of Oriental Research* 9 (1929) 17–94 [see preceding].

Speiser, W. *Ostasiatische Kunst*. Ullstein Kunstgeschichte 17. West Berlin: Ullstein Bücher, 1964; see esp. Illus. 3 [dragons on a vase from four-three cent. BCE], and 35 [dragons on a chest from 1585].

Stallman, R. C. "נחש," *New International Dictionary of Old Testament Theology and Exegesis,* ed. W. A. Van Gemeren. Grand Rapids, Mich.: Zondervan, 1997; vol. 3, pp. 84–88.

Stanford, P. *The Devil: A Biography*. New York: Henry Holt and Company, 1996.

Stauch, L. "Drache," in *Realex. d. dt. Kunstgesch.* 4 (1958) 342–66.

Stauropoulos, S. G. *ΤΑ ΑΣΚΛΗΠΙΕΙΑ ΤΗΣ ΠΕΛΟΠΟΝΝΗΣΟΥ*. Athens: Aiolos, 2000.

St. Clair, G. "The Subtle Serpent," *The Journal of Theological Studies* 7 (1906) 40–50.

Steel, Otto, *Der Physiologus, Tiere und ihre Symbolik*. Zürich, Artemis and Winkler, 1995.

Stemmler-Morath, C. *Schlangen*. Basel, 1968; see esp. pp. 78ff.

Stephanus, H., et al., eds. "ὄφις" *Thesaurus Graecae Linguae*. Paris: Didot, n.d.; cols. 2454–55.

Stevens, K. G. *De iconografie van de slang in Mesopotamië vanaf het vijfde millennium voor Christus tot het einde van de Akkadische periode, Magisterarbeit*, 2 vols. [unpublished dissertation, 1984; see the following entry]
———. "Eine Ikonographische Untersuchung der Schlange im Vorgeschichtlichen Mesopotamien," in *Archaeologia Iranica et Orientalis: Miscellanea in Honorem Louis Vanden Berghe*, ed. L. De Meyer and E. Haerninck. Leuven: Gent, 1989; pp. 1–32. [Stevens laments the lack of a comprehensive study of serpent iconography in Mesopotamia and attempts to offer a succinct presentation.]
Stichel, R. "Die Verführung der Stammeltern durch Satanael nach der Kurzfassung der slavischen Baruch-Apokalypse," in *Kulturelle Traditionen in Bulgarien*, ed. R. Lauer and P. Schreiner. Abhandlungen der Akademie der Wissenschaften in Göttingen; Phil.-Hist. Klasse, Third Series, no. 177. Göttingen: Vandenhoeck & Ruprecht, 1989; pp. 116–28.
Störk, L. "Schlange," *Lexikon der Ägyptologie*, ed. W. Helck and W. Westendorf., 5.1 (1983) cols. 644–52.
Strackmann, R. "Asklepios in Epidaurus," in *Materia Medica Nordmark* 30 (November, December 1978). N.V.
Strauss, S. "Zur Symbolik der Schlange," *Psyche* (1948) 340–57.
Sullivan, L. E. *Icanchu's Drum: An Orientation to Meaning in South American Religions*. New York: Macmillan and London: Collier/Macmillan, 1988.
Tabick, J. "The Snake in the Grass: The Problem of Interpreting a Symbol in the Hebrew Bible and Rabbinic Writings," *Religion* 16, no. 2 (April 1986) 155–67.
Tatum, W. B. "The LXX Version of the Second Commandment (Ex. 20,3–6 = Deut. 5,7–10): A Polemic Against Idols, Not Images," *Journal for the Study of Judaism*, 17 (1986) 177–95.
Taylor, L. "The Rainbow Serpent as Visual Metaphor in Western Arnhem Land," *Oceania* 60 (June 1990) 329–44.
Tertullian. *Opera Montanistica*. Corpus Christianorum Series Latina, II: Tertullian Opera, Pars II. Turnholt: Typographi Brepolis Editores Pontificii, 1954.
———. *Tertulian—"De Idolatria": Critical Text, Translation, and Commentary*, ed. J. H. Waszink and J. C. M. Van Winden. Supplements to Vigiliae Christianae: Texts and Studies of Early Christian Life and Language 1. Leiden and New York: Brill, 1987.
Teselle, E. "Serpent, Adam, and Eve: Augustine and the Allegorical Tradition," *Augustine: Presbyter Factus Sum*, ed. J. Lienhard et al. New York: Peter Lang, 1993.
Testa, P. E. *Il Simbolismo dei Giudeo-Cristiani*. Studium Biblicum Franciscanum 14. Jerusalem: Tipografia dei PP. Francescani, 1962; see esp. pp. 278–82.
———. "La mitica rigenerazione della vita in un amuleto Samaritano-Cristiano del IV Secolo," *Studii Biblici Franciscani, Liber Annus* 22 (1973) 286–317.
Tetzlaff, I. *Romanische Kapitelle in Frankreich: Löwe und Schlange, Sirene und Engel*. Cologne: DuMont Buchverlag, 1979 [3rd ed.].

Thielicke, H. *How the World Began: Man in the First Chapters of the Bible.* Philadelphia: Fortress Press, 1961.

Thiersch, H. "Ein altmediterraner Tempeltyp," *Zeitschrift für die alttestamentlichen Wissenschaft* 50 (1932) 73–85 [a serpent image applied to a pot was found near an MB altar at Shechem].

Thomas, D. W., ed. *Archaeology and Old Testament Study: Jubilee Volume of the Society for Old Testament Study 1917–67.* Oxford: Clarendon, 1967.

Thomas, H. "Beispiele der Wandlung: Adler und Schlange als Natursymbole," *Antaios* 12 (1971) 48–57.

Thompson, S. *Motif-Index of Folk-Literature.* 6 vols. Rev. Bloomington: Indiana University Press, 1955–58 [rev. and enlarged edition].

Thureau-Dangin, "Le serpent d'airain," *Revue d'histoire et de littérature religieuses* 1 (1896) 151–58.

Thüsing, W. *Die Erhöhung und Verherrlichung Jesu im Johannesevangelium.* Neutestamentliche Abhandlungen 21. Münster, 1979 [3rd ed.].

Ting, N.-T. "The Holy Man and the Snake-Woman: A Study of a Lamia Story in Asian and European Literature," *Fabula* 8 (1966) 145–91.

Tintelnot, H. *Vom Klassizismus zur Moderne.* Ullstein Kunstgeschichte 16. West Berlin: Ullstein Bücher, 1964; see esp. Fig. 14 [Ernst Barlach's Pan playing the flute before an upraised serpent], and Illus. 73 [Henri Rousseau's "Die Schlangenbeschwörerin"].

Tischendorf, C., ed. *Acta Pilati A,* in *Evangelia Apocrypha,* Editio Altera. Leipzig: Hermann Mendelssohn, 1876.

Tobler, A. J. *Excavations at Tepe Gawra II: Levels IX-XX.* Philadelphia: University of Pennsylvania Press, 1950. [See the depiction of a serpent rising beneath a couple who are copulating; Plate 163: 87.]

Torn, K. van der. "Viper," *Dictionary of Deities and Demons in the Bible,* ed. K. van der Toorn, B. Becking, and P. W. van der Horst. Leiden and Boston: Brill and Grand Rapids: Eerdmans, 1999 [2nd ed.]; p. 890.

Torrey, C. C. "Jeremiah and the Reptiles of Egypt," *The Lives of the Prophets: Greek Text and Translation.* Philadelphia: Society of Biblical Literature, 1946; pp. 49–52.

———. " 'When I Am Lifted Up from the Earth' John 12,32," *Journal of Biblical Literature* 51 (1932) 320–22.

Toscanne, P. "Etudes sur le serpent, figure et symbole dans l'antiquité Elamite," *Mémoires de la Délégation en Perse, Tome XII: Recherches Archéologiques.* Quatrième Série. Paris: Ernest Leroux, 1911; pp. 153–228.

Tottoli, R. "Il bastone di Mosè mutato in serpente nell'esegesi e nelle tradizioni islamiche," *Annali* 51 (1991 [Naples]) 225–43; see esp. pp. 383–94 [on Moses' staff].

Trendall, A. D. "Alkmene," in *Lexicon Iconographicum Mythologiae Classicae* 1.1, pp. 552–56 [see the bibliography]; also see the photographs in *LIMC* 1.2, Plates 414–15.

Treu, U. " 'Otterngezücht': Ein patristischer Beitrag zur Quellenkunde des Physiologus," *Zeitschrift für die alttestamentlichen Wissenschaft* 50 (1959) 113–22.

Tristan, F. *Les premières images chrétiennes: Du symbole à l'icône: IIe–VIe siècle.* n.c.: Fayard, 1996.

Trokay, M. "Les origines du dieu élamite au serpent," *Mesopatamie et Elam,* ed. by M.J. Steve, et al. Ghent, Belgium: University of Ghent, 1991.

Tsevet, M. "God and the Gods in Assembly," *Hebrew University College Annual* 40/41 (1969/1970) 123–37.

———. "Der Schlangentext von Ugarit," *Ugarit-Forschungen* 11 (1979) 759–78.

Turner, A. K. *The History of Hell.* New York and London: Harcourt Brace & Co., 1993.

Turner, C. W. "Wie die Schlange zum Symbol der Medizin wurde," *Ciba Zeitschrift* (1934) 535–43.

Uehlinger, C. "Leviathan," *Dictionary of Deities and Demons in the Bible,* ed. K. van der Toorn, B. Becking, and P. W. van der Horst. Leiden and Boston: Brill and Grand Rapids: Eerdmans, 1999 [2nd ed.]; pp. 511–15.

Ullmann, M. *Das Schlangenbuch des Hermes Trismegistos.* Wiesbaden: Harrossowitz, 1994.

Van Buren, E. D. "Entwined Serpents," *Archiv für Orientforschung* 10 (1935–1936) 54–65.

———. "The God Ningizzida," *Iraq* 1 (1934) 60–89.

———. "The Guardians of the Gate in the Akkadian Period," *Orientalia* N.S. 16 (1947) 312–32.

———. *Symbols of Gods in Mesopotamian Art.* Rome: Pontificium Institutum Biblicum, 1945; see esp. p. 40.

Van den Branden, A. "La création de l'homme et de la femme d'après le document Jahviste," *Bibbia e Oriente* 166 (1990) 193–208.

Vassilakis, A. *Knossos: Mythology-History-Guide to the Archaeological Site,* trans. D. Kapsambelis. Athens: Adam Editions, n.d.

Vázquez, J. A. "The Cosmic Serpent in the Codex Baranda," *Journal of Latin American Lore* 9 (1983) 3–15.

Veith, I. "Symbol of Medicine: Caduceus of Hermes or the Knotted Staff of Aesculapius," *Modern Med.* 15 (July 1958) 138–48.

Veldhuis, N. "An Ur III Incantation Against the Bite of a Snake, a Scorpion, or a Dog," *Zeitschrift für Assyriologie und Vorderasiatische Archäologie* 82 (1992) 161–69.

Vergote, J. "Le nom du roi 'Serpent,' " *Orientalia* 30 (1961) 355–65.

Vermaseren, M. J. "A Magical Time God," *Mithraic Studies* 2; 446–56 [an important study of a male figure entwined by a snake].

Vermes, G. *The Complete Dead Sea Scrolls in English.* New York: Penguin, 1997; see esp. p. 260.

Vermes, M. "Le serpent d'airain fabriqué par Moïse et les serpents guérisseurs d'Esculape," *Revue Archéologique* Series 5, vol. 6 (1918) 36–49.

Vetters, H. "Der Schlangengott," in *Studien zur Religion und Kultur Kleinasiens* [*Festschrift F. K. Dörner*]. Etudes Préliminaires aux Religions Orientales dans l'Empire Romain 66.2. Leiden: Brill, 1978; pp. 967–79.

Vian, F., and M. B. Moore, "Gigantes," in *Lexicon Iconographicum Mytholo-giae Classicae* 4.1, pp. 191–270 [bibliography]; see also the photographs in *LIMC* 4.2, esp. Plates 112–17, 149–58.

Vieyra, M. *Hittite Art*. London: A. Tiranti, 1955. [See esp. the LB bronze statue of a god holding a serpent.]

Vincomb, J. *Fictitious and Symbolic Creatures in Art with Special Reference to Their Use in British Heraldry*. London, 1906.

Virolleaud, M. "La mort de Baal: Poème de Ras-Shamra (I* AB)," *Syria* 15 (1934) 305–36.

Visser, M. W. de. *The Dragon in China and Japan*. Wiesbaden, 1913.

Vlastos, G. "Religion and Medicine in the Cult of Asclepius," *The Review of Religion* 13 (1948) 269–90.

Vogel, J. P. *Indian Serpent-Lore, or the Nagas in Hindu Legend and Art*. London: Arthur Probsthain, 1926.

———. "Serpent Worship in Ancient and Modern India," *Acta Orientalia* 2 (1924) 279–312.

Voth, H. R. *The Oraibi Summer Snake Ceremony*. Field Columbian Museum Publication 83: Anthropological Series 3/4. Chicago, 1903.

Wackernagel, M. *Renaissance, Barock und Rokoko I*. Ullstein Kunstgeschichte 13. West Berlin: Ullstein Bücher, 1964; see esp. Illus. 31 [Simonetta Vespucci as Cleopatra (with a live serpent around her neck)], 38 [Benvenuto Cellini's Perseus with the head of Medusa], and 39 [Giambologna's Mercury with the caduceus].

Waele, F. J. M. de. *The Magic Staff or Rod in Graeco-Italian Antiquity*. Ghent: Drukkerij Erasmus, 1927.

———. "Zauberstab," *Roschers Lexicon* 6 (1924–1937) 542–59.

Walker, A., ed. *Animals in Ancient Art: From the Leo Mildenberg Collection, part 3*. Mainz: Verlag Philipp von Zabern, 1996; see esp. III, 24 (bronze snake from Egypt, c. 1320–1200 BCE), III, 25 (serpent in cornelian, Egypt, Ptolemaic Period), III, 26 (granite cobra head from Egypt, Greco-Roman Period), III, 27 (bronze serpent, first or second cent. CE).

Walker, J. R. *Lakota Belief and Ritual*, ed. R. J. DeMallie and E. A. Jahner. Lincoln: University of Nebraska Press, 1980.

Wallace, H. N. *The Eden Narrative*. Harvard Semitic Monographs 32. Atlanta, Ga.: Scholars Press, 1985.

Warburg, A. M. *Schlangenritual: Ein Reisebericht, with an Afterword by U. Raulff*. Berlin: Verlag Klaus Wagenbach, 1988. [This work is devoted to the Pueblo Indians in North America; see esp. p. 17 (Ttzitz Chu'i, the serpent), p. 45 (dancing woman with serpents), p 46 (Laocoon), p. 47 (Asclepios), p. 52 (serpents and selling medicine against snake bites), p. 53 (raised serpent and the crucifixion according to Add. MS. 31303), p. 80 (serpents collected for the New Year's ceremony), and p. 81 (Pueblos dancing with snakes in their mouths)].

Ward, W. A. "The Four-winged Serpent on Hebrew Seals," *Rivista degli studi orientali* 43 (1968) 135–43.

―――. "The *Hiw*-Ass, the *Hiw*-Serpent, and the God Seth," *Journal of Near Eastern Studies* 37 (1978) 23–34.

Ward, W. H. *The Seal Cylinders of Western Asia.* Carnegie Institute of Washington Publication no. 100. Washington, D.C.: Carnegie Institute, n.d. [See the bulls next to a serpent entwined around the staff of a god (No. 905).]

―――. *Cylinders and Other Ancient Oriental Seals in the Library of J. Pierpont Morgan.* New Haven: Yale University Press, 1920.

Waters, F. *Book of the Hopi.* New York: Viking Press, 1963.

Watzinger, C. *Denkmäler Palästinas: Eine Einführung in die Archäologie des Heiligen Landes,* 2 vols. Leipzig: J.C. Hinrichs, 1933, 1935.

Weber, O. *Die Dämonenbeschwörung bei den Babyloniern und Assyrern:* Der Alte Orient 7.4. Leipzig: J.C. Hinrichs, 1906.

Weder, H. "L'asymétrie du salut. Réflexions sur Jean 3, 14–21 dans le cadre de la théologie Johannique," in *La communauté Johannique et son histoire: La trajectoire de l'évangile de Jean aux deux premiers siècles,* ed. by J.-D. Kaestli, J.-M. Poffet, and J. Zumstein. Geneva: Labor et Fides, 1990; pp. 156–84.

Wellman, M. "Basilisk," *Paulys Realencyclopädie der classischen Altertumswissenschaft,* 3.7 (1987) cols. 10–101.

Welsford, E. "Serpent-Worship: Teutonic and Balto-Slavic," *Encyclopaedia of Religion and Ethics,* ed. J. Hastings. Edinburgh: T. & T. Clark and New York: Charles Scribner's Sons, 1920 [1962]; vol. 11, pp. 419–23.

Welten, P. "Schlange," *Biblische Reallexikon* (1977) 280–82.

Wénin, A. "Adam et Ève: La jalousie de Caïn, 'semence' du serpent," *Revue des sciences religieuses* 73 (1999) 3–16.

―――. "Satan ou l'adversaire de l'alliance: Le serpent, père du mensonge," *Graphè* 9 (2000) 23–43.

Werner, E. T. C. *A Dictionary of Chinese Mythology.* New York: Shangai, Kelly and Welsh, 1961; see esp. p. 448.

―――. *Myths and Legends of China.* London: G. G. Harrap & Co., 1922; see esp. pp. 227–30.

West, J. A. *Serpent in the Sky: The High Wisdom of Ancient Egypt.* Wheaton, Ill: The Theosophical Publishing House, 1993 [to be read with a critical eye].

Westermann, C. *Genesis 1–11: A Commentary,* trans. J. J. Scullion. Minneapolis: Augsburg, 1974; see esp. pp. 237–242.

Westheim, P. *Die Kunst Alt-Mexikos.* Ullstein Kunstgeschichte 18. West Berlin: Ullstein Bücher, 1964; see esp. Illus. 25 [a black granite serpent made by the Aztecs].

―――. *The Gospel of John: In Light of the Old Testament,* trans. S. S. Schatzmann. Peabody, Mass.: Hendrickson, 1998.

Westropp, Hodder M., and C. Staniland Wake, *Ancient Symbol Worship.* Whitefish, Mont.: Kessinger, 1997.

Whitehead, N. L. "The Snake Warriors—Sons of the Tiger's Teeth: A Descriptive Analysis of Carib Warfare, ca. 1500–1820," *Acta Antiqua* 37 (1996–1997)

146–70. [The Caribs originate, according to a widely held myth, from a giant snake's rotting body.]

Whitekettle, R. "Rats Are Like Snakes, and Hares Are Like Goats: A Study in Israelite Land Animal Taxonomy," *Biblica* 82 (2001) 345–62.

Whiting, R. M. "Six snake omens in New Babylonian Script," *Journal of Cuneiform Studies* 36, no. 2. (1984) 206–10.

Whittaker, M. *Jews and Christians*. Cambridge Commentaries on Writings of the Jewish and Christian World 200 B.C. to A.D. 200; No. 6. Cambridge: Cambridge University Press, 1984; see esp. pp. 188–89, 195–97, 212–13.

Widengren, G. *The King and the Tree of Life in Ancient Near Eastern Religion: King and Savior*. Wiesbaden: Otto Harrassowitz, 1951.

Wiedemann, A. *Der Tierkult der alten Ägypter*. Leipzig: J. C. Hinrichs, 1912.

Wiesel, E. "The Serpent," *Bible Review* 13.6 (1997) 18–19 [trans. A. Martin].

Wiggerman, F. A. M. "Transtigridian Snake Gods," in *Sumerian Gods and Their Representations*, ed. I. L. Finkel and M. J. Geller. Cuneiform Monographs 7; Groningen: STYX Publications, 1997; pp. 33–55.

Wiggins, S. A. "The Myth of Asherah: Lion Lady and Serpent Goddess," *Ugarit-Forschungen* 23 (1991) 383–94. [Wiggins clarifies that as the Serpent Goddess, Asherah has connections with Qedeshet, Eve, and Tanit.]

Wilbert, J. "Eschatology in a Participatory Universe: Destinies of the Soul Among the Warao Indians of Venezuela," in *Death and the Afterlife in Pre-Columbian America*, ed. E. P. Benson. Cambridge, Mass.: Harvard University Press, 1975; pp. 163–89.

Will, E. "Le tour de straton: Mythes et réalités," *Syria* 64 (1987) 245–51.

Williams, A. J. "The Relationship of Genesis 3:20 to the Serpent," *Zeitschrift für die alttestamentliche Wissenschaft* 89 (1977) 357–74.

Williams, C. A. S. *Outlines of Chinese Symbolism and Art Motives*. Tokyo: Charles E. Tuttle, 1974.

Williams, J. G. "Serpent and the Son of Man," *The Bible Today* 39 (2001) 22–26.

Williams, W. G. "Serpent, Bronze," *Interpreter's Dictionary of the Bible*, vol. 4. Nashville: Abingdon, 1962; p. 291.

Williams-Forte, E. "The Snake and the Tree in the Iconography and Texts of Syria During the Bronze Age," in *Ancient Seals and the Bible*, ed. L. Gorelick and E. Williams-Forte. Malibu, Calif.: Undena Publications, 1983; 18–43. [The author claims that in Genesis 3, the serpent symbolizes evil and cunning, not death. The serpent is the deceiver.]

Wilpert, C. B. *Kosmogonische Mythen der australischen Eingeborenen*. Munich, 1970.

Wilson, K. V. K. *The Legend of Etana*. Warminster: Aris and Phillips, 1985.

Wilson, Leslie S., *The Serpent Symbol in the Ancient Near East*. New York: University Press of America, 2001.

Wilson, P. J. "Snake on a Stick," *Christian Century* 111 (1994) 223.

Wilson, R. McL. "Gnosis/Gnostizismus II," *Theologische Realenzyklopädie*. Berlin: Walter de Gruyter, 1984; vol. 13, pp. 535–50 [for Ophites].

Windisch, H. "Angelophanien um den Menschensohn auf Erden," *Zeitschrift für die alttestamentliche Wissenschaft* 30 (1931) 215–35.

Winston, D. *The Wisdom of Solomon: A New Translation with Introduction and Commentary.* The Anchor Bible. New York: Doubleday, 1979; see esp. pp. 294–97.

Winter, U. *Frau und Göttin.* Orbis Biblicus et Orientalis 53. Freiburg: Universitätsverlag and Göttingen: Vanderhoeck & Ruprecht, 1983, 1987.

Winternitz, M. "Der Sarpabali, ein altindischer Schlangencult,' in *Mitteilungen der anthropologischen Gesellschaft* 18 (1888). N.V.

Wiseman, D. J. "Flying Serpent," *Tyndale Bulletin* 23 (1972) 108–10.

Wohlstein, H. "Zur Tier-Dämonologie der Bibel," *Zeitschrift der deutschen morgenländischen Gesellschaft* 113 (1963) 483–92.

Wolde, E. van. "A Reader-Oriented Exegesis Illustrated by a Study of the Serpent," *Pentateuchal and Deuteronomistic Studies,* ed. C. Brekelmans and J. Lust. Louvain: Leuven University Press, 1990.

Wolkstein, D., and S. N. Kramer. "The *Huluppu—*Tree," *Inanna, Queen of Heaven and Earth: Her Stories and Hymns from Sumer.* New York: Harper & Row, 1983.

Woloschin, M. *Die Grüne Schlange.* Stuttgart: Verlag Freies Geistesleben, 1982 [6th printing; the original is 1954; a novel].

Woude, A. S. van der. *Die messianischen Vorstellungen der Gemeinde von Qumrân.* Studia Semitica Neerlandica 3. Assen: Van Gorcum & Co., 1957; see esp. pp. 144–56.

Wright, G. E. "Archaeological Observation on the Period of the Judges and the Early Monarchy," *Journal of Biblical Literature* 60 (1941) 27–42.

Wrigley, C. "The River-God and the Historians: Myth in the Shire Valley and Elsewhere," *Journal of African History* 29 (1988) 367–83.

Wyatt, N. "Attar and the Devil," *Glasgow University Oriental Society Transactions* 25 (1973/1974) 85–97. [Wyatt contends that the serpent is to be seen as the Ugaritic god Athtar.]

———. "Interpreting the Creation and Fall Story in Genesis 2–3," *Zeitschrift für die alttestamentliche Wissenschaft* 93 (1981) 10–21.

Wyly, J. *The Phallic Quest: Priapus and Masculine Inflation.* Studies in Jungian Psychology by Jungian Analysts 38. Toronto: Inner City Books, 1989.

Yadin, Y. "The Fourth Season of Excavations at Hazor," *Biblical Archaeologist* 22 (1959) 2–20. [The Canaaanite temple had bronze serpents.]

———. "Further Light on Biblical Hazor: Results of the Second Season, 1956" *Biblical Archaeologist* 20 (1957) 34–47. [Yadin interpreted (rightly) some figures as serpents on a cult standard.]

———. *Hazor.* London: Oxford University Press, 1972.

———. "A Note on the Scenes Depicted on the 'Ain-Samiya Cup," *Israel Exploration Journal* 21 (1971) 82–85.

———. "Symbols of Deities at Zinjirli, Carthage and Hazor," in *Near Eastern Archaeology in the 20th Century,* ed. J. A. Sanders. Garden City, N.Y.: Doubleday, 1970; pp. 199–232.

Yadin, Y., et al., eds. *Hatzor III-IV: Plates*. Jerusalem: Magnes Press, 1961. [Two bronze serpents, perhaps from LB II, were found near the temple in Area H.]

Yahuda, A. S. "The Symbolism and Worship of the Serpent," *Religions* 26 (1939) 16–29.

Yamauchi, E. M. *Persia and the Bible*. Grand Rapids, Mich.: Baker Books, 1996; see esp. pp. 495–96 [the tauroctony and the serpent], and Illus. 497–98 [the lion-headed image entwined with a snake.]

Yeivin, S. "The Brazen Serpent," *Bet Mikra* 72 (1977) 10–11.

———. "A Silver Cup from Tomb 204a at 'Ain-Samiya," *Israel Exploration Journal* 21 (1971) 78–81.

Yen, Y.-S. "Biography of the White Serpent: A Keatsian Interpretation," *Fabula* 1 (1957) 227–43.

Young, B. *The Snake of God: A Story of Memory and Imagination*. Montgomery, Al.: Black Belt Press, 1996.

Young, D. W. "With Snakes and Dates: A Sacred Marriage Drama at Ugarit," *Ugarit-Forschungen* 9 (1977) 291–314.

Zahlhaas, G. *Aus Noahs Arche: Tierbilder des Sammlung Mildenberg aus fünf Jahrtausenden*. Mainz: Verlag Philipp von Zabern, 1996; see esp. pp. 33–35, "Die Schlange."

Zani, di Lorenzo. "Il serpente di rame e Gesù," *La Storie de Jesu*. Milan: Rizzoli, 1984; see esp. pp. 1338ff.

Zauzich, K.-Th, "Ein neuer Schlangengott," *Göttinger Miszellen* 87 (1985) 89.

Zeegers-VanderVorst, N. "Satan, Ève et le serpent chez Théophilie d'Antioche," *Vigiliae Christianae* 35 (1981) 152–69.

Zimmer, H. *Philosophies of India*, ed. J. Campbell. New York: Bollingen, 1961; reprinted in New York: Meridian Books, 1956.

Zimmerli, W. "Das Bilderverbot in der Geschichte des Alten Israel (Goldenes Kalb, Eherne Schlange, Mazzeben und Lade)" *Schalom: Studien zu Glaube und Geschichte Israels,* ed. K.-H. Bernhardt. Stuttgart: Calwer Verlag, 1971; pp. 86–96 [republished in *ThB* 51 (1974) 247–60].

Zimmermann, F. *Der ägyptische Tierkult nach der Darstellung der Kirchenschriftsteller und die ägyptischen Denkmäler*. Dissertation, Bonn, 1912.

Zimniok, K. *Die Schlange das unbekannte Wese: In der Kulturgeschichte, freien Natur und im Terrarium*. Hanover: Landbuch, 1984; see esp. "Die Schlange in der Antike und im Christentum" on pp. 58–71.

Zschietzschmann, W. *Kunst der Etrusker, Römische Kunst*. Ullstein Kunstgeschichte 6. West Berlin: Ullstein Bücher, 1963; see esp. Illus. 3 [7th cent. BCE urn with serpents], 11 and 12 [gorgo], and 36 [lions with tails like serpents].

Zuntz, G. *Persephone: Three Essays on Religion and Thought in Magna Graecia*. Oxford: Clarendon Press, 1971.

General Index

Index of Modern Authors

Gunkel, H., 286, 287, 288, 293,
   294, 303, 320, 322, 431, 563n40,
   564n55, 565nn73,86, 566nn107,110,
   567nn117,125, 569nn154,162,167,
   570n176, 572n231, 594n64, 601n173
Gunn, C. D., 475, 611n24
Güterbock, H. G., 599n130
Guy, P. L. O., 502n47, 503nn57–58

Haage, B. D., 494n31
Haast, W. E., xi, 496n67
Habel, N., 491n98
Habsburg, G. von, 497n87
Hachlili, R., 27, 501n29, 551n233
Haddan, A. W., 589n196
Haenchen, E., 12, 378, 488n22, 583n97
Haerninck, E., 552n244
Hahn, F., 378, 583n94
Halliday, W. R., 238, 244, 246, 550n206,
   554n289, 555n315, 556nn331,341,
   559n418
Halsberghe, G. H., 529n258
Hamilton, M., 530n268, 559n409
Hamilton, V. P., 569n160, 570n185
Hammond, C., 599n132
Hammond, N. G. L., 28, 520n16
Hampton-Cook, E., 277, 562n29
Hanfmann, G. M. A., 523n103
Hanke, M., 580n31
Hansmann, L., 572n226
Hanson, J. S., 562n30
Haran, M., 552nn256–57
Harden, D. B., 514n271
Harder, M. A., 525n170
Hare, D. R. A., 542n64, 545n130, 547n146,
   606n13
Harl, K. W., 532n301
Harl, M., 565n88, 566n96
Harmon, A. M., 537n419
Harrison, R. K., 17, 18, 408, 489nn47,54,
   589n199
Hastings, J., 242
Haupt, P., 217, 301, 302, 548n165, 568n150
Hawkes, J., 511n211
Hawkins, J. B. H., 544n103
Hawley, W. C., 14, 488n29
Hayes, J. W., 609n5
Hayes, L. N., 493n20
Heinz-Mohr, G., 28
Helck, W., 500n11
Hendel, R. S., 235, 553n268
Henderson, J. L., 26, 140, 258, 259,
   524n140, 559n421
Hengel, M., 378, 383, 512n237, 573n239,
   582n91, 584n111, 586n151
Henry, M.-L., 555n305, 557n371, 591n8
Hentschel, G., 577n315

Hentze, C., 552n246
Herbert, E. D., 561n10
Hercher, R., 541n38
Herder, A., 595n82
Herrmann, F., 558n387
Herzog, Z., 508nn152–53
Higgins, R., 511nn201,216,222
Higgs, P., 510n186
Hirmer, M., 554nn286–87, 611n21
Hirsch, S. R., 17, 489n40
Hirschen, J., 27
Hocquenghem, A. M., 224, 550n199
Hodges, E. R., 556n339
Hofinger, M., 525n170
Hofius, O., 390, 585n139
Hofrichter, P. L., 410, 579n23, 582n75
Holland, T. A., 512nn240,241
Holloway, S. W., 576n307
Holly, M. A., 29
Holmberg, U., 553n276, 563n49
Holter, K., 196, 541n46
Holzinger, H., 328, 573n251
Hood, R. W., 491n86
Hoofien, J. H., 541n48
Hoorn, G. van, 529n259
Hopfe, L. M., 567n112
Horgan, M. P., 599n137
Hornung, E., 519n359, 553n269
Hough, W., 493n17
Houlihan, P. F., 554n299
Houziaux, A., 414, 590n219
Howey, M. O., 26
Hrouda, B., 545n115
Hummel, J., 511n218
Humphreys, D., 204
Humphries, R., 531n286
Hunger, K. H., 40, 494n35, 532n302, 548n167
Hunt, R., 244
Hurd, J. C., 598n117
Hutter, M., 550n200
Huxley, F., 26
Hvidberg, F., 210, 545n128

Iliffe, J. H., 508n166, 509n169
Illyricus, M. F., 274
Infusino, G., 552n250, 553n262
Insler, S., 126, 159, 529n257
Irmscher, J., 497n81
Isaacs, R. H., 217, 548n164
Israeli, Y., 514n270, 515nn283,285

Jackson, B., 581n50, 583n96
Jackson, R., 254, 532n310, 558n397
Jacobs, A., 564n61
Jacoby, F., 527nn218,223, 556n338
Jagersma, H., 17, 18, 489nn45,51, 573n241
Jakobsson, O., 525nn149–50

Index of Ancient Sources

New Testament

New Testament Apocrypha

Hypothetical Sources of Jesus Tradition(s)

Assyrian Sources

Persian Sources

Ancient Greek Sources

Aeschylus, *Agamemnon*
 11233, 606

Aeschylus, *Choephori*
 249, 455

Alexander, *Voyage Round the Red Sea,* 144

Alexander Romance, 141

Aristides, *Apologia*
 12, 454

Aristides, *Oratio*
 22, 532
 38, 532
 42, 612
 42.1–15, 612
 48.4, 612

Aristophanes, *Plutus*
 690, 608

Aristotle, *Ethica Eudemia*
 3.6, 606

Aristotle, *Historia Animalium,* 451, 460,
  544, 547
 487ª23, 458
 488ᵇ15, 566, 598
 508ᵇ1, 458
 558ª29, 455
 591ª15, 607
 626ª12, 458
 770a, 549

Aristotle, *Parts of Animals*
 2.17, 544
 4.1, 550
 4.11, 550
 4.13, 550

Aristotle, *Progression of Animals*
 4, 550
 8, 550

Artemidorus, *Onirocritica,* 139
 4.67, 244

Diodorus Siculus, *Library of History*
 4.9.1–10, 542

Epiphanius, *Panarion,* 469
 1.205, 553
 3.37, 487
 4.4, 470
 5.1, 470
 5.2, 470
 5.7, 470
 7.1, 470
 7.1–8.1, 470
 7.5, 470

 7.6, 470
 8.1, 470
 8.5, 470
 25.7, 458
 48.15, 452
 61.8, 453
 66.88, 456

Euripides, "The Children of Hercules"
 898–99, 154

Euripides, *Fragmenta*
 121, 601

Euripides, *Ion,* 207

Euripides, *Medea*
 1317–22, 172
 1379–84, 173

Herodotus, *Histories*
 2.74, 240
 2.75, 534
 2.76, 170, 458
 3.107, 169
 3.109, 170, 534
 4.9, 526
 4.191, 169
 8.41, 230, 549
 9.81, 241

Hesiod, *Theogony*
 297, 455
 333–35, 147
 334, 175

Herondas, *Mimiambi*
 4.11, 480, 612

Homer, *Iliad,* 128, 525
 2.723, 458
 2.729, 160
 8.398, 455
 11.36–37, 527
 12, 529
 23.225, 455

Homer, *Odyssey,* 128, 171
 1.193, 455
 4.60, 587
 7.59, 525
 7.201–6, 525
 10.120, 525
 13.220, 455
 19.446, 454

Homeric Hymns
 5.218–38, 259

Horapollon, *Hierogrlyphika*
 1.1, 528

Josephus, *Against Apion*
 2.7, 240

Early Christian Sources (Greek, Latin, Syriac, Coptic)